BRISTOL ROVERS
FOOTBALL CLUB

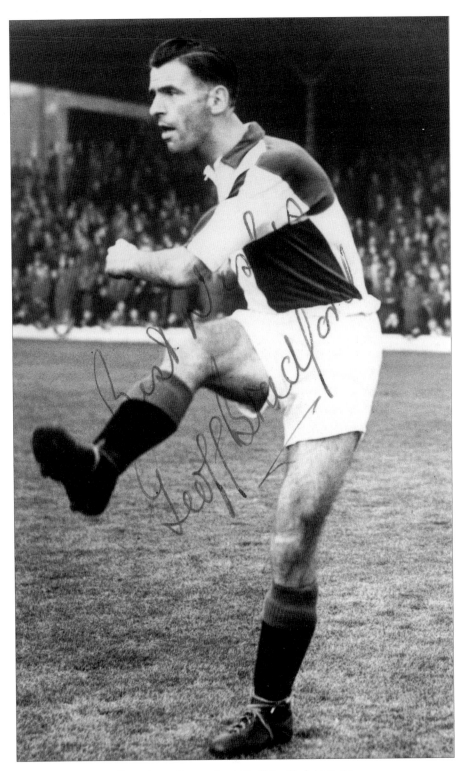

Rovers' most famous player, Geoff Bradford, 1949-64.

BRISTOL ROVERS
FOOTBALL CLUB

The Definitive History 1883-2003

STEPHEN BYRNE & MIKE JAY

TEMPUS

Stephen Byrne was born in Wimbledon in December 1966 and was brought up in Bristol from the age of two. He graduated in French and German from Durham University and teaches Modern Languages at Clayesmore School in Iwerne Minster, Dorset, where he is also housemaster to sixty pupils. He and his wife Stitch have three children – Toseland, Ophelia and Horatio. Stephen watched his first Rovers game in November 1974 at the age of seven, was co-author of *Pirates in Profile*, the definitive who's who of Rovers players, and is a regular contributor to the Rovers match-day programme.

Mike Jay was born in Eastville, Bristol during Rovers' halcyon days of the mid 1950s. A longstanding civil servant, he is an office manager with the DTI. Mike watched his first Rovers match at Eastville in 1967 and was immediately hooked. He has missed just a handful of home matches in the past 36 years and has travelled to watch the club in over a hundred different league grounds throughout England and Wales. His wife Sue and teenage children, Kelly and Ian are also ardent fans. Mike, a former programme editor of the club and contributor for over twenty-five years, completed his first book on the history of the club in 1987, *Bristol Rovers: The Complete Record 1883-1987*. He was co-author with Stephen Byrne for *Pirates in Profile: Who's Who of Rovers Players 1920-94*, and also compiled a photographic history of the club entitled *Images of Sport, Bristol Rovers Football Club*, published in 1999 by Tempus.

Front cover: Eastville Stadium 1973; *(inset from left)* Jesse Whatley 1919-30; Ray Warren 1936-56; Geoff Bradford 1949-64; Alfie Biggs 1953-68; Bruce Bannister 1971-76 & Alan Warboys 1972-77

Back cover: Rovers' Championship Teams *(from left)*: Southern League 1904/05; Division 3 (South) 1952/53; Third Division 1989/90

First published 2003

Tempus Publishing Limited
The Mill, Brimscombe Port,
Stroud, Gloucestershire, GL5 2QG
www.tempus-publishing.com

© Stephen Byrne & Mike Jay, 2003

The right of Stephen Byrne & Mike Jay to be identified as the Authors of this work has been asserted by them in accordance with the Copyrights, Designs and Patents Act 1988.

British Library Cataloguing in Publication Data.
A catalogue record for this book is available from the British Library.

ISBN 0 7524 2717 2

Typesetting and origination by Tempus Publishing Limited
Printed in Great Britain by Midway Colour Print, Wiltshire

CONTENTS

ACKNOWLEDGEMENTS

The greatest thanks of all are of course due to the authors' wives, Stitch Byrne and Sue Jay, without whose love, care and support this book would never have been possible. Our growing families are also due our grateful thanks. Kelly and Ian Jay are knowledgeable regulars at the Memorial Stadium, Toseland Byrne a youthful sporadic visitor and Ophelia and Horatio Byrne are vociferous supporters of the imminent future. We would also like to acknowledge the hard work of Kevin Byrne.

No book containing this degree of information could be a feasible proposition without recourse to considerable help from a number of sources. Mervyn Baker, a historian of Bristol football, has given tirelessly and unstintingly of his time and has unearthed thousands of snippets of invaluable information during his long hours in the newspaper vaults at Bristol Central Library. We are as indebted to him as we are to Jim Creasy and Mike Davage for their definitive research into the birth, death and career details of many thousands of footballers from years gone by and for their willingness to share otherwise inaccessible information on countless inter-war players. Keith Brookman kindly allowed access to certain of the sadly minimal documents the club has been able to save in the wake of decades of fires and floods. Alan Lacock is always an excellent source for obscure details relating to Rovers' history and club photographer Alan Marshall has allowed unhindered access to his wealth of pictures covering generations of Rovers players. David Woods, the Bristol City historian, has shared freely his extensive records on late-Victorian football around the Bristol area.

Of many people whose help has contributed to the production of this volume, we are most indebted, in no particular order but with very grateful thanks in every case, to Ray Spiller, the former secretary of the Association of Football Statisticians; the freelance journalist David Foot; genealogical researcher Julie 'Mole' Osman; Lynn Case of Shaftesbury for her unstinting hours of typing and saintly patience in waiting for payment; David Eveleigh, the curator of Social History at Blaise Castle House Museum; Iain McColl at Greenock Morton; Jim McNeill as the chair of Living Easton; John Penny who is treasurer of the Fishponds Historical Society; Peter Fleming at the University of the West of England for his knowledge regarding the Black Death; Alex Young for his Kedens genealogy; Ivor Cornish at Ambra Books; Pam Bishop at the Bristol and Avon Family History Society, who kindly permitted the publication of my article on Stapleton in its September 2000 journal; Margaret McGregor as archivist at the Bristol Record Office; Colin Timbrell historian of the Gloucestershire Football Association; and John Jurica of the Bristol and Gloucestershire Archaeological Society. There is also Kevin Byrne, the most assiduous and vigilant of proofreaders in the south-west of England. Many excellent club historians and statisticians, among them prolific writers such as Garth Dykes, Tony Matthews, Mike Jones, Trefor Jones, Richard Harnwell, Michael Braham, David Downs, Paul Taylor and Tony Brown, were listed in the acknowledgements for our Who's Who of Bristol Rovers, *Pirates in Profile*, which appeared on the shelves in February 1995. Their information continues to be a source of much football-related material. Thank you to you all for your time and energy.

PHOTOGRAPHS
A wide variety of sources but primarily Alan Marshall, Rovers Official Photographer since 1973. Alan has been very generous in providing a great number of the pictures in this book. Other sources include *Bristol Evening Post*, *Western Daily Press*, *Bristol Times* and *Mirror*, Empics and a wealth of photographs from other individuals to whom we are particularly appreciative.

While every effort has, of course, been made to ensure that the details included in this book are as accurate as possible, typographical errors are inevitable in a work of this magnitude and the authors apologize for these in advance. We are also keen to point out that any opinions stated are the views of the authors, reflecting on the statistics to hand, and not necessarily those of Bristol Rovers Football Club.

BIBLIOGRAPHY

Research for this book has necessitated a thorough investigation of local newspapers, primarily the *Bristol Evening News, Bristol Times and Herald, Western Daily Press* and, in comparatively recent years, the *Bristol Evening Post*. Details relating to other clubs has taken the authors to a wide range of libraries to consult all manner of newspapers and journals and our thanks is due to the staff at each of these. It has also involved comparing facts and figures against numerous excellent histories of other clubs, far too many to mention here, *Rothmans Football Yearbooks* as well as similar if less detailed equivalents in years gone by and various editions of *Burke's Peerage, Burke's Landed Gentry, Kelly's Directory* and *Crockford's Clerical Directory*. Other books, which have provided valuable information and may be of further interest to the reader include, in alphabetical order by author:

Football Hooligans: Knowing the Score, Gary Armstrong, Berg, 1998.
Not just on Christmas Day: an Overview of Association Football in the First World War, John Bailey, 3-2 Books, 1999.
Who's Who of Cricketers, Philip Bailey, Philip Thorne and Peter Wynne-Thomas, Hamlyn, 1993.
Sport and the Making of Britain, Derek Birley, Manchester University Press, 1993.
Inspection of Bristol Rovers Football Club Limited, Board of Trade, HMSO, 1951.
The History of Kingswood Forest, A Braine (1891), Kingsmead, 1961.
Gloucestershire Population Figures, 1801-1921, Census returns.
Greater Bristol by 'Lesser Columbus', Leonard Cohen, Pelham, 1893.
Stapleton, Past and Present, Louis Harald Dahl, 1934.
Concise Oxford Dictionary of English Place-Names, Eilert Ekwall, Clarendon, 1936 and 1960.
Bristol, 1850-1919, David J Eveleigh, Britain in Old Photographs series, Budding Books, 1996.
England Football Fact Book, Cris Freddi, Guinness, 1991.
The Diocese of Clifton, 1850-2000, J A Harding, Clifton Catholic Diocesan Trustees, 1999.
Follies: a Guide to Rogue Architecture in England, Scotland and Wales, Gwyn Headley and

Wim Meulenkamp, Jonathan Cape, 1986.

The Great Book of Trains, Brian Hollinsworth and Arthur Cook, Salamander, 1996.

Sport and the British: a Modern History, Richard Holt, Oxford University Press, 1989.

The Mid-Victorian Generation, 1846-1886, K Theodore Hoppen, Clarendon Press, 1998.

Football League Players' Records, ed. Barry J Hugman, Tony Williams, 1992.

The Football Grounds of Great Britain, Simon Inglis, Collins Willow, 1985.

History of Bristol's Suburbs, Frederick Creech Jones and William Gordon Chown, Reece Winstone, 1977.

An Away Game Every Week: Memories of Bristol Rovers, Ray Kendall, Breedon, 2001.

The Church Goer, Rural Rides or Calls at Country Churches, Joseph Leach, Ridler, 1847.

Easton in the Twentieth Century, Living Easton, 2001.

Walk the Historic River Frome, Living Easton, 2000.

Sport in Society, Peter McIntosh, West London Press, 1987.

Minute Book of the Kingswood Enclosure Commissioners, 1779-1784.

The Matter of Wales, Jan Morris, Penguin, 1984.

Bristol Past and Present, J F Nicholls and John Taylor, 1881.

Rites and Religions of the Anglo-Saxons, Gale R Owen, Barnes and Noble, 1996.

The Trade in Lunacy, William Parry-Jones, Routledge and Kegan Paul, 1972.

George Müller of Bristol, Arthur T Pierson, James Nisbet, 1899.

Soccer at War, 1939-45, Jack Rollin, Collins Willow, 1985.

A History of Britain: at the Edge of the World?, Simon Schama, BBC, 2000.

The Breedon Book of Football League Records, Gordon Smailes, Breedon, 1991.

The Street Names of Bristol, Veronica Smith, Broadcast Books, 2001.

Through the Turnstiles, Brian Tabner, Yore Publications, 1992.

Things not Generally Known, John Timbs, Lockwood, 1861.

The Bristol Region, Frank Walker, Nelson, 1972.

A View from the Terraces: One Hundred Years of Western League Football, Sandie and Doug Webb, Addkey Print Limited, 1992.

Willelmi Malmesbiriensis monachi de gestis Regum Anglorum, Rolls Series I, ed. W Stubbs, 1885-86.

Bristol and Clifton Directory, J Wright & Co., 1890.

FOREWORD

It is a privilege to be asked to write the foreword for this wonderful book detailing the history of Bristol Rovers Football Club. We are very fortunate to have such dedicated historians and statisticians as Mike Jay and Stephen Byrne. This book is the result of six years' work, tracking down information and statistics that otherwise may have been lost in time. The resulting volume, which includes over 300 pictures, many from private collections, paints an overview of times past and the characters involved to give the reader a feel of 'being there'. Indeed, some of the match reports and descriptions of the players read as though the games were played yesterday.

Documenting the club history from the formation of The Black Arabs in 1883 to Eastville Rovers in 1884 and the birth of Bristol Rovers in 1899, from the nicknames of 'The Purdown Poachers' to 'The Pirates' and the fans' adopted name of 'The Gas', the club's turbulent history is recorded here in detail for future generations to enjoy.

It is often said that one can choose their friends but cannot choose their relatives. Well, the same can be said for supporting a football club. The choice is usually made for us by our parents or through family tradition. My grandparents and parents have all been avid supporters of the club. I, therefore, had very little choice but to continue the family involvement and my sons Peter and Matthew have also been 'educated' as to why the colours blue and white exist, and how they represent all that is good in the world. All I can say is that if you are reading this publication as a supporter of 'The Pirates' then you are a lifelong member of Bristol Rovers' family!

My first game watching Rovers was in the South Enclosure at Eastville in 1964, where a certain young man by the name of Gordon Bennett persisted in blowing a trumpet adjacent to the players' tunnel. I stood at the front by the greyhound lights and I saw my heroes run out in their blue and white kit, to a tremendous roar from a 17,698-strong crowd (according to Mike and Stephen's statistics!). The smell of embrocation and tobacco, mixed with gas fumes from the works next to Eastville filled the air, and a 3-1 victory over QPR sealed my allegiance, thanks to a brace of goals from Ian Hamilton and one from John (Farmer) Brown.

In recent times, football has been in crisis. The changes due to 'Bosman' and EEC employment law have affected the transfer market to the extent that only very few gifted players with lower division clubs have any long term value. This has come as a big blow

to most clubs, who have used transfer fees to subsidise operating losses. With the recent loss of television and internet revenue, the immediate financial future looks bleak. However, for Bristol Rovers, a club which sold its Eastville birthright, endured two major fires (and floods), played 'home' matches at six different venues in the last two decades, moved to another *city* for ten years, and purchased a stadium on returning to Bristol, the present troubles are but a drop in the ocean!

Thanks for the memories, Mike and Stephen.

Geoff Dunford
Chairman
Bristol Rovers Football Club

INTRODUCTION

The chill autumnal air, a sullen greying sky hinting at cold, wet evenings and the imposing darkness of the late afternoon were descending in equal measure all around. Above us, the eerie light from the floodlights enabled bizarrely configured shadows to play uneasily on the grass before us, while the waiting crowd jumped individually from foot to foot to keep collective circulation flowing adequately. Out on the hallowed turf, the distinctive figure of Lindsay Parsons played a confident ball across the heart of the defence to his full-back partner Trevor Jacobs, who set off up the right wing as if he were acting the part of Sir Stanley Matthews in an amateur-dramatic production. The night closed in all around, the Rovers held on for another well-fought home draw and the eternal support of one young spectator. Of such mediocre performances are life-long interests born and, though the pedant will no doubt point out

George Muller, the great local benefactor died on 10 March 1898. Eastville Stadium's Muller Road Terrace was named after him

Chairman George Humphreys ensured Rovers' survival in the early days of professionalism

that the two named defenders did not appear together when I, as a wide-eyed seven-year-old, watched Rovers scramble to a goalless draw with Orient, their partnership remains an enduring image of my footballing infancy. So too will the crude challenge on David Pritchard that earned Oxford United's Steve Anthrobus a red card be an abiding memory for my eldest child Toseland only eight days after his fourth birthday, to liven up a game noteworthy only for Jason Roberts' winning goal on the hour mark. From such insignificant openings can lives appreciative of sport develop.

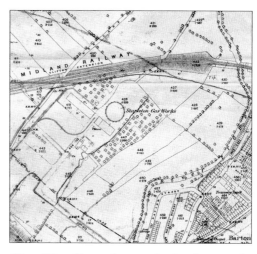

Map of Eastville area in 1882, showing the gas works

Every football club deserves a definitive history and Bristol Rovers Football Club is no exception. The first and longest surviving professional club in Bristol can boast Football League status since 1920 and remained, until 2001, the only club never to have appeared in either the top or bottom division. Rovers were Southern League champions in 1905, twice FA Cup quarter-finalists and Division Three champions in 1953 and 1990, in which year they made the first of two appearances under the celebrated Twin Towers at Wembley Stadium. Yet this history serves to record as full a story as space permits. Within these pages lie the tales of missed penalties and red cards, of seven-goal home defeats and a 20-0 home victory, the Conservative Member of Parliament who played for Rovers, the Lithuanian-born Irishman in the opposition, the unidentifiable spectator who fell in the river and the sad demise of baker's boy Fred Foot. Of such snippets of gilded cloth is the entire club history woven and I make no excuses for allowing the cultural and demographic backdrop of east Bristol to impinge so readily and frequently into the narrative. Indeed, the opening chapter of this book is, in my opinion, an essential element in the Bristol Rovers story. It attempts to explain and put into context why and how a sporting club, and a footballing one in particular, would have grown up amid the industry and poverty of the 1880s in this neck of the woods; the role of the gentry; the undeniably influential increase in rail transport; the late-Victorian surge in population growth as illustrated by the building of churches throughout the area; the subsequent emergence of leisure time as a concept; and the remarkable success story that enabled this club, from among the multitude springing up during this era, to survive into the 21st century.

The Bristol Rovers story is written for all those who understand why I would have rung up from a public telephone box in Spennymoor to reserve my ticket for a Rovers game or walk the three miles from Godramstein to Landau-in-der-Pfalz railway station on Tuesday mornings because that was when the one copy of a daily English newspaper would arrive carrying the score from Rovers' weekend escapades. Such a story has a past, a present and a future. I trust this book satisfies the reader's curiosity about the past, maintains our enthusiasm about the present club and all that is good in the 'beautiful game' and inspires Bristol Rovers to unprecedented glory in the future.

PREFACE

On 26 May 946, while keeping the feast of St Augustine at Pucklechurch in the forest of Kingswood in south Gloucestershire, King Edmund I of the West Saxons, a grandson of Alfred the Great, was assassinated. An assailant named Leofa, previously banished by Edmund, burst into the banquet-hall and was restrained by a cup-bearer acting on the King's orders. However, the robber resisted and Edmund, perhaps recklessly going to his guard's aid, seized him by the hair and flung him to the ground but was stabbed with a dagger in the ensuing struggle[1]. At this time, the forest of Kingswood covered an expanse of 18 square miles, including the future homeland of Bristol Rovers to the east of the growing settlement at Brycgstow. The Saxon hamlet of Stapelton, as it is recorded in 1208, stood at the edge of the forest, to the north of the river Frome.

Yet, still earlier settlements on the site remain a highly plausible proposition. In February 1934, George Lovell of Mayfield Park South, Fishponds found, in a neighbour's garden, a Roman coin dating from the time of Vespasian, Roman Emperor between AD 69 and 79. Around AD 45, as Titus Flavius Vespasianus, he had led Emperor Claudius' Second Legion Augusta across the south-west of England, raiding hill-forts on their way to modern-day Devon. The Roman roadway Via Julia, which ran from Sea Mills to Bath across Dobunni territory, is believed to have crossed the Frome at Baptist Mills, just yards from where Eastville Stadium was to stand. Two monoliths that stood in Armoury Square, Stapleton Road, now long disappeared beneath the relentless construction of buildings, were believed by many to be Druidical remains, but Nicholls and Taylor claim they were probably Roman landmarks erected by agrimensores, or land surveyors[2]. The suffix 'dun' in Purdun and Stapeltun, as these places were recorded, indicates Celtic heritage, the latter covering an area of some 2,554 acres in 1086. According to the Domesday Book of that year, this Bristol Rovers territory formed part of the six-square-mile Manor of Bertune in the Swineshead Hundred, Gloucestershire. Future Rovers homelands Twertone, near Bade, which by 1225 was known as Twyuertone, and Horefelle, or 'dirty, muddy field', were also noted in 1086[3].

There must have been significant devastation caused by the regular arrivals of the plague, as this area stood in such close proximity to the prosperous port of Bristol. The 1348 Black Death, for instance, will have caused numerous fatalities for, even though figures for such rural areas are unrecorded, 25 million people were killed by this disease across Europe between 1347 and 1352. The population of England, which stood at 4.75 million in 1348, had dropped to a mere 2 million by the time of Richard II's abdication on 29 September 1399. Fifteen out of 52 members of Bristol Town Council died in 1349 and, with society at a standstill, grass grew several inches high in Broad Street and High Street. 'Virtually the whole town was annihilated,' reported the historian Henry Knighton. 'It was as if sudden death had marked them down beforehand for few lay sick for more than two or three days.'[4] Likewise, as the population of England fell by 6 per cent between 1556 and 1560, the Eastville district would certainly have been affected. Jones and Chown claim that 100 Bristolians per day died of the plague during 1645, when the Eastville air would have been full of the noise of gunpowder[5]. Oliver Cromwell was said to have hidden in a cave near the current position of Colston School, as infantry and cavalry headed for nearby Wickham Court and some of the eroded escarpment of local hills clearly dates from this war-stricken epoch.

An early 19th-century discovery of human bodies buried to the east of Bristol with their faces turned to the earth in boggy ground, rather than with their feet facing east to enable them to walk to Jerusalem at the Day of Judgement, prompted an eager discussion of views in the *Notes and Queries* weekly. Were these grisly findings evidence of writhing in the later stages of death, following premature interment, as gravediggers acted with understandable but undue haste in the face of fears of the plague spreading?[6] One correspondent later reacted by quoting Juliet's soliloquy:

> How, if when I am laid into the tomb,
> I wake... there's a fearful point![7]

The eventual birthplace of Bristol Rovers was, by 1793, '... a fine verdant hill – the surrounding woods ... well deserve the traveller's attention.'[8] Purdown was essentially a series of dark horse chestnut woods on Silurian limestone, reachable from Eastville down a narrow lane to the left of Bell Hill and just below Stapleton Court. Barn Wood was nearest to Stoke House, next to Long Wood, while Hermitage Wood and Splatts Abbey Wood both indicated the proximity at some time of religious buildings. One long-established apocryphal tale speaks of King Charles II hiding as a fugitive in Stoke House on the Stapleton Park estate, while some reports suggest that fossils found on Purdown indicate it was submerged in prehistoric times.

By 1883, with urban development stretching through Eastville and incorporating ancient villages, Purdown had become a series of hillside fields on the edge of the city of

Bristol. It was here that the Black Arabs, as they were then known, played their first home matches during 1883 on a field flanked by rugby pitches. Yet here, the Duke of Beaufort's family, which recurs through the club's history, appears in the form of the ghost of a long-lost Duchess, possibly the Dowager Duchess Elizabeth who, killed when struck by lightning while out riding near Staple Hill on 7 May 1760, apparently haunts Purdown on horseback. Seriously underused throughout the 20th century, the hill today overlooks the M32 motorway, which acts as the vital link with the city centre just one mile away, and boasts a communications tower. There is also Purdown Hospital, which was established in 1916 in the 18th-century Dower House and designed on a 14-hectare site beside Duchess Pond by Thomas Wright of Durham, and the remains of a World War Two anti-aircraft gun site.

The neighbouring hamlet of Stapleton was donated to Tewkesbury Abbey in 1174 by William, Earl of Gloucester. By the late 16th century the landlord was Richard Berkeley of Stoke Gifford, through whose landed family the village was passed down to the Duke of Beaufort. Although the largest landowners in the mid-19th century, the Beauforts were forced to sell the Elizabethan manor of Stoke Gifford in December 1917. Roger de Gossington, a forester of Kingswood and the owner of considerable tracts of land, also lived at Stapleton. One short-lived law of 1272 forbade the burning of coal. However, the area had gradually been developed for coal mining, with some 73 pits working in the Kingswood Forest in 1669 and, by the middle of the 18th century, this industry employed a vast number of local men. The Reverend George Whitefield (1714-70), the celebrated Methodist preacher who co-wrote 'Hark! The herald angels sing', recorded meeting 2,000 colliers at Fishponds on 5 March 1739. The shallow mines of the Kingswood and Parkfield Colliery Company, which included those at Easton and on the Pennant Sandstone of the Beaufort estate at Stapleton, produced a thousand tons of coal per day by the 1890s. Pennywell Road colliery, the nearest geographically to Eastville Stadium, was closed by 1908. Deep Pit, next to Rovers' one-time home at Ridgeway, was more than 2,000 ft in depth, while nearby Speedwell Pit employed 690 men by 1923. A parliamentary move of 1779 that authorized the enclosure of parishes including Fishponds led to many of the ubiquitous mud huts being replaced by sturdier, more comfortable stone dwellings and to century-old common land belonging to the people being auctioned off to wealthy landowners. Jacob Sturge was commissioned to survey the area in order to draw up the Stapleton Enclosure Act – 19GeoIIIc65, which was to come into force in 1781. As a result, nine lots of Stapleton Common, comprising some 57 acres, were sold for £1,600 in October 1779. The Duke of Beaufort, the largest purchaser, bought 34½ acres, though his claim to the rights of 41 coal pits in the parish was dismissed at a meeting in the Bell Inn, Stapleton, four days prior to Christmas Day 1779. Five years of wrangling over ownership ensued but these actions sounded the death knell for the era of English yeomanry.

One local collier was Victor Purdy, who had worked the mines through the enclosure period. A prominent evangelist, who had known Charles Wesley and composed an astonishing 1,853 hymns in his 75 years, Purdy worked in the Duke of Beaufort's colliery at Stapleton and, on his greatly mourned death in July 1822, was buried in Stapleton. He had apparently read the Old and New Testaments 40 times each, preached 2,882 sermons and travelled 22,896 miles, mostly on foot. Frances Milton, the mother of the novelist Anthony Trollope, was born in the village in 1780, while Sarah Young, another Stapleton-born girl, was the mother of the poet Thomas Chatterton. The religious writer Hannah More was born in Stapleton on 2 February 1745, at which time her father Jacob was the schoolmaster at the Free School in the local village of Fishponds.

By 1883 many local men worked the Easton mine, which could boast a surface area of five acres, and whose 'outlook was black, gaunt and smoky against the skyline'[9]. Easton had been the subject of a government enquiry in 1841, led by Elijah Waring, into the working conditions of 10- and 11-year-old boys. This enquiry discovered that the youngest worker in the mine was seven-and-a-half years old and had already been working there for a year. Tragedies were frequent occurrences in the mines, one such incident at this time being the death of 12-year-old John Sampson on 2 August 1889, who was struck by a rock fall while riding a horse-drawn tram. On 19 February 1886, eight miners had been killed in a massive gas explosion in Easton mine and a further 13 seriously injured. Among the dead were Isaac Rawlings of Stapleton Road and Samuel Long of Bloy Street, as well as a father and son in George and Henry Bennett. Moreover, the manager, William Boult Monks, never fully recovered from the shock of this tragedy and threw himself down the pit shaft to his death in March 1892. Easton mine was abandoned in 1911. East Bristol Colliery Company closed its last pit in 1936, when just 180 men were employed. In the Bristol area, only Coalpit Heath was working as late as 1949, although a new mine at Harry Stoke was open between 1955 and 1963.

Other local employers included the Baptist Mills Brass Works, set up in 1702 on the site of an old grist mill, with the Stapleton merchant Nehemiah Champion II cited as one of the partners. The site of the Brass Works was abandoned in 1814, though traces could be seen until the late 1960s, when it disappeared beneath Junction 3 of the new M32 'Portway' motorway. There was also a flourmill at the foot of Blackberry Hill, known for many years as John Watts' Mill. Brothers Joseph and James White had bought up Baptist Mills Pottery from the Harford Brass Battery Company in 1840, and until 1891 it served as an additional employer for much of the local population. The celebrated Quaker merchant, Abraham Darby I, was manager of the Bristol Wire Company at Baptist Mills which, from its foundation in 1702, was at the forefront of the development of industrial techniques and thus in the vanguard of the Industrial Revolution. This company produced, as a by-product, slag building-blocks, which can be seen to this day topping perimeter walls of the Greek Orthodox Church of Saints Peter and Paul, formerly the parish church of St Simon the Apostle at Lower Ashley Road, Baptist Mills, though the last traces of the Wire Company and the Pottery disappeared forever in the construction of the M32 motorway.

By 1898, a total of 11,096 Bristolians lived under the care of guardians at asylums, orphanages or workhouses and an understanding of the development of such places is essential in any study of the socio-economic conditions prevalent in east Bristol in the late Victorian era. Fishponds Workhouse was home to 774 Spaniards and 15 Dutch naval prisoners in 1782 and to some 2,000 Frenchmen in 1797. Eveleigh states that, in 1898, there were 2,357 inmates in workhouses around the Bristol area, while 22 almshouses housed a further 377 people and the Ashley Down orphanage provided housing for at least 2,000 children by the 1880s[10]. Increasing emphasis was being placed, alongside greater education, improved housing, sewers and lighting, on care for the destitute and ill. As early as 1746, the Town Clerk of Bristol, William Cann, certified mad in the same week as two of his deputies, was lodged in the Fishponds Lunatic Asylum. On 1 October 1774 Joseph Mason was granted a licence to keep an asylum at Stapleton, for which privilege he paid £15. Within five years he was dead and the affairs of the asylum were continued by his two daughters, Elizabeth and Sarah. Between 1817 – when the establishment housed 57 patients – and 1837 the owner was Joel Lean, who simultaneously kept the school at Beechwood. A Cornishman, born at Gwennap in 1774, he was to return to Penzance in 1837, though his death on 2 February 1856 was at Briton Ferry, Glamorgan. Dr George Gwinnett Bompas bought the property in 1839, but his attempts to run the school and the asylum led to complaints and an enquiry. He resided there until 1855 but, from 1849, the new superintendent of the asylum was his cousin, Dr Joseph Mason Cox (1763-1818), a great-grandson of Mason and undeniably the most distinguished of several generations of asylum keepers. In 1851, of a total population in Stapleton of 4,840, almost a third lived within its two major workhouses. A total of 658 people lived in the Clifton Union Workhouse, established in 1841, and 729 in the Asylum for the Poor of Bristol[11]. By 1859 the Stapleton establishment was abandoned, though Dr Joseph Carpenter Bompas, a son of the earlier surgeon, opened an asylum at Fishponds in February 1861 with provision for 200 patients, accommodation for a further 849 patients being added between 1868 and 1923. Elsie Marie Kingdom, mother of the Bristol-born Hollywood actor Cary Grant, was admitted to this home in 1913. Equally, the Clifton Union had, in 1847, opened the Eastville Institution in Fishponds Road, which was assimilated in 1898 into the Bristol Union and Bristol Borough Asylum opened in 1861. Dr William Henry Brown, one of Rovers' directors at the adoption of professionalism in 1897, was Medical Adviser to the Bristol Magistrates in lunacy cases and a member of the Medical Psychological Association.

The history of Fishponds, or 'New Pooles', as one reference in 1610 names it, is inextricably linked to these developments. Two of its many quarry pits were filled with water, from which derived the area's name. One of these ponds was drained in or around 1800 on the orders of Elizabeth Somerset, wife of Henry, the fifth Duke of Beaufort, after a small girl had slipped off the weir and drowned. The second was filled in by Joel Lean and Bompas senior, on purchasing the land in 1839, promptly turned it into an orchard. The threat of drowning did not disappear, however, as one sad tale from 1844 relates. Twenty-eight-year-old Hester Tilly, whose father William ran an 11-acre farm at Ashley Down between Horfield and Stapleton, was banned from the house after her father heard of her secret affair with a farm-hand named Williams. Distraught, on 16 October 1844 she threw herself into a pond in her parents' orchard, where she floated temporarily until 'her garments, heavy with their drink, pulled the poor wretch to muddy death'[12]. Found guilty of suicide, her body was buried by torchlight just before midnight that evening, as bystanders struggled to prevent Williams throwing himself into the grave. Commentators have likened her plight to that of Hamlet's Ophelia:

> Hold off the earth awhile
> Till I have caught her once more in my arms[13]

From one mill on the river Frome at the time of the Domesday survey, there were five by 1297. Witherly's later gave its name to Snuff Mills Park while, 600 yards downstream, Whitwood (sic) Corn Mill – as it became known after John Whitewood, who ran the mill in 1609 – was owned and run between 1846 and 1899, including the formative period of Rovers' early growth, by Josiah Bell of Stapleton. The fifteenth-century historian William Wycestre refers to Bagpath's Mills, apparently named after a French cloth called 'baptiste', which was woven at the mill. The mill weir is said to have stood adjacent to the current position of the 'Old Fox' public house.

Besides the Beaufort family, another moneyed landowner had been the Bristol merchant and alderman John Smyth, twice mayor of the city, who bought Estune or Ashton Court from Sir Thomas Arundel in 1545 and set about acquiring other large estates in and around Bristol. By the end of the 16th century, the Smyth family of Long Ashton owned Eastville Park; not the 70-acre Victorian site purchased by the City Council from the Breddy family of market gardeners in 1887 that now bears this name, but a more extensive parkland. They also owned Ridgeway or Rudgeway Manor, a country house of 14th- or 15th-century origin, mentioned in the Survey of the Boundaries of Kingswood Chase, dated 26 May 1652. On the north-eastern boundary lay the grassland that was to be Rovers' home between 1894 and 1897. The Breddy family came into possession of much land in 1767 around the current site of St Werburgh's. Sir Jarritt Smyth of Ashton Court, who died aged 91 in 1783, was hence the father of Thomas Smyth of Stapleton, whose great-grandson, the Reverend John Hugh Way, Honorary Canon of Bristol Cathedral from 1897, was Rural Dean for Stapleton between 1889 and 1905, through Rovers' formative years. Humphry Repton, who designed the 850-acre Ashton Court Estate, also designed Oldbury Court by the Frome in what became Rovers territory. Its long-demolished 16th-century mansion was, home, until December 1938 to the prosperous Vassall family, and prior to that to Oliver Bigg.

The Beaufort family itself can claim descent from Charles Somerset, the first Duke of Worcester, appointed captain of the Yeomen of the Guard in 1486, who was in turn an illegitimate son of Henry Beaufort, Duke of Somerset. This Henry Beaufort could trace his genealogy back to William St Maur, who helped Gilbert Marshal, Earl of Pembroke defend border territory at Woundy from Welsh marauders in 1240. The line passes through Edward Beaufort, who died in 1667, variously credited with the first descriptions of a theoretical steam engine, to the 10th Duke, Henry Hugh Arthur Fitzroy Beaufort, High Steward of Bristol since 1925 and latterly President of Bristol Rovers up to his death at the age of 83 on 5 February 1984. He, in turn, was succeeded as 11th Duke by a cousin, David Robert Somerset, the Earl of Worcester. Numerous roads and landmarks in Bristol and across the West Country bear the names of the land-owning Beaufort and Berkeley families. Beaufort Road, Horfield runs within yards of the northern end of the Memorial Stadium, to which Rovers moved in 1996, while Stapleton's Beaufort House still bears carved pineapples on its gateposts, a pertinent reminder of the slave trade through which countless Bristol merchants made their fortune.

From a village of 700 people in 160 inhabited dwellings in 1734, Stapleton, which included Eastville within its boundaries, grew steadily in size through the early 19th century. The largest changes in development are indicated by the census returns

W G Grace was a famous English cricketer, but he was also a football referee who officiated at Rovers matches

showing 6,960 inhabitants in 938 dwellings in 1871, rising to 10,833 in 1,554 homes 10 years later and 14,589 living in 2,391 inhabited homes in 1891. The census return for 1901 reveals that, in 3,755 houses in Stapleton, the settlement was now home to some 21,236 residents. Next door lay the civil parish of St George, where the population more than doubled in 20 years from 16,209 in 3,230 inhabited houses in 1871 to 36,718 in 6,763 dwellings in 1891. Similarly Horfield, later to be Rovers' home, where only 125 had lived in 1778, grew from an 1871 population of 2,985 to house 14,757 by the time of the 1901 census, the majority living in homes constructed out of the distinctive blue-grey sandstone that characterizes Horfield houses. Within a quarter of a mile of where the embryonic Memorial Stadium would first appear in 1921 stood the peaceful church of the Holy Trinity. This is a building with medieval origins rebuilt (all but the 15th-century West Tower) to William Butterfield's designs in 1847. This was a time of great expansion, for the population of Bristol as a whole rose from 154,093 in 1861 to 206,874 in 1881 and, though including some boundary changes with the inclusion in 1897 of Horfield and Stapleton, following considerable work from councillors George Pearson and F Gilmore Barnett, an astonishing 329,366 in 1901.

These were indeed times of great change. Huge population growth coincided with the new concept of leisure time among the working classes. In 1866, a cricket club was formed at Stapleton that could boast the following year four members of the celebrated Grace family, including a 19-year-old club captain in the future Gloucestershire and England batsman, Dr William Gilbert Grace. He lived at 61 Stapleton Road and, from 11 May 1881 until March 1895, leased from one Joseph Hennessey the property at 57 Stapleton Road as his surgery. The car park of Easton Leisure Centre now covers this site and a colourful plaque commemorating the celebrated cricketer was unveiled on 29 September 2000 by Tony Brown, the Chair of Cricket at Gloucestershire County Cricket Club. The rise in popularity in the north of England of the relatively new sport of Association Football was sweeping inexorably across the entire country. In Bristol, as in numerous other industrial cities in Britain, many football clubs were formed during the 1880s, with workers spilling out of factories every Saturday lunchtime to watch or play for a local team.

Several local sides were established in north-east Bristol, notably Eastville Athletic, Eastville Rovers, Eastville United and Eastville Wanderers. The Wanderers side, who played in black and white stripes, took over in 1895 the tenancy of 'Mr Lait's Field', next to Eastville Park, from Barton Hill FC and, with their headquarters at the White Lion, replaced Rovers at Ridgeway during 1896/97. Their captain in 1898/99 was Richard Osborne, a former Rovers inside-right. United were East Bristol and District League Challenge Vase finalists in 1895/96, while blue-shirted Athletic, Challenge Vase winners for the Bristol and District League for 1901/02, shared changing rooms at Bicknell's Restaurant with Glendale, who themselves took over Ridgeway for the 1898/99 season, alongside the Brixton House club and Stapleton-based Rudgway. To add to this complex local scene, St Vincent's was a flourishing club playing in Eastville Park, while the black-and-blue-striped shirts of Avonside played at an unidentified location in Eastville. By 1898, there were at least three clubs operating in Fishponds, too. Fishponds themselves were captained by William Nolan who, in 1892, had scored the first Western League goal Rovers conceded, while Fishponds Rovers and Fishponds United were both well-known locally. Meanwhile, nearer to the present site of the Memorial Stadium, Horfield appeared as early as 1898/99 in black-and-white-striped shirts in the North Bristol and District League, playing home fixtures on Horfield Common and changing at the Wellington Hotel. Rovers retained close links with the club's roots, appearing in July 1984 in the first fixture on the new ground of Stapleton, a club formed as comparatively recently as 1932.

In addition, the introduction of a large-scale, efficient public transport system revolutionized the daily lives of many people. The Bristol to Gloucester railway, which was authorized on 19 June 1828 and opened throughout on 6 August 1835, included the 515-yard-long Staple Hill Tunnel, while the 10 trains that ran on 31 August 1840, the day the Bristol to Bath line was opened, carried 6,000 passengers and brought in £476 in revenue. An initial nine-and-a-half-hour rail link with London had been established on 30 June 1841 and connections with the metropolis increased rapidly in comfort, frequency and speed. When Daniel Gooch, later a Member of Parliament, drove the Bristol-London train on the fine, sunny evening of 19 June 1843, carrying the Queen's husband HRH Albert, the Prince Consort, after he had launched the steamer SS *Great Britain*, the journey took just two hours and four minutes. Two Great Western Railway branch lines adjoined Eastville Stadium, Rovers' home from 1897, offering fast links to London and other cities, while Stapleton Road station was opened to passenger and freight traffic on 8 September 1863. The Thirteen Arches viaduct was constructed in 1872 and carried its first trains in 1874. The Bristol electric tramway, set up in 1875, promoted extensive urban development along its routes. Despite its evident reputation for tardiness, as cumbersome cars drawn by four horses struggled with the numerous hills, an estimated five to six million passengers per year travelled on Bristol trams in the 1890s. The tram service reached Fishponds in 1897, the year of Rovers' move to Eastville. The Bristol company Fox and Walker was building six steam tram engines to export to Rouen and, on 4 December 1877 in the early hours, to avoid frightening the horses, gave a trial run to 40 selected guests in a horse car pulled by a steam engine from Eastville depot.

During this era, urban development had yet to take hold. Where Bloy Street has stood since late-Victorian times was once a cherry orchard owned by the Harding family, while William Bird (1815-1896) was well-known locally for his extensive fields in Lower Easton and his market-gardening trade. As late as 1874, it was possible to wander across the open countryside of Horfield, as illustrated by the tragic story of six-year-old Archie John Hamilton Walters. Young Archie and a younger boy, Ernest Price (three years and two months), had gone missing on 23 October 1874 after walking from St Paul's as far as Horfield and spent a bleak night outdoors. As the cold set in, Archie had apparently covered his friend with his own clothes as they sheltered in a field belonging to Berry Lane Farm and, succumbing to the elements, died overnight. Dr William Eney stated, at the inquest held on 28 October 1874 at the Royal Oak public house in Horfield, that death was due to acute congestion to the lungs and brain following exposure to the cold. Within a generation, however, the urban face of eastern Bristol had changed beyond all recognition.

Urban growth may also be measured in terms of the abundance of late-Victorian churches in the area. The Christian faith had been a prominent factor within society in the area for well over 1000 years and Oswald, the Anglo-Danish Archbishop of York from 972, had established a monastery at Westbury-on-Trym. The growth of Christianity was such that there were 83 churches of all denominations in Bristol in 1850 and 260 in 1919. The church in Fishponds, constructed on a one-acre site purchased in 1806, had been dedicated as Trinity Chapel on 31 August 1821, but did little to enhance the appearance of the mining village if Joseph Leach, proprietor of the *Bristol Times*, is to be believed. 'Fishponds,' he wrote, 'is a most miserable-looking place, so cold and cheerless, indeed, that a man instinctively buttons his coat and quickens his pace as he passes through it.'[14] It was renamed the Parish Church of St Mary the Virgin and designated a separate parish on 14 December 1869, at the time that the Reverend William Henry Bromley Way, later a vicar in north Gloucestershire and Huntingdonshire, a younger brother of the aforementioned John Way and a brother-in-law of Sir John Henry Greville Smyth of Ashton Court, was Rector of Stapleton. The Reverend Arthur Benjamin Day was vicar of St Mary's from 1869 to 1889.

Holy Trinity Church in Bell Hill, Stapleton, a Norman edifice initially dedicated to St Giles, the patron saint of forests and hunters, with baptismal records dating back to 1720, was rebuilt by John Norton and reconsecrated in 1857, creating a prominent local landmark as its spire measures some 170 ft. This was achieved with the financial support of James Henry Monk, Bishop of Gloucester and Bristol, who lived in Stapleton for many years from 1840. St Thomas the Apostle in Fishponds Road, Eastville was consecrated in 1889, though H C M Hirst's design was not completed for a further 15 years. This church was built in 1888 at a cost of £6,000 in a cruciform Early English style, with seating for 530 parishioners. It remained in constant use until 1975 and is now a New Testament Church of God Pentecostal Hall. In Easton, St Gabriel's church in Bouverie Street was erected between 1868 and 1870 at a cost of £4,400 and was consecrated on 14 March 1870. The parish was formed on 20 May 1870 from Sts Philip and Jacob, as was the parish of St Lawrence on 24 August 1883. St Gabriel's was demolished in 1975 while St Lawrence, consecrated in 1885, lasted until 1984. St Simon's in Hampton Place, Baptist Mills, a further offshoot of Sts Philip and Jacob, was consecrated on 22 December 1847. Methodist churches were built in Fishponds Road in 1872, Easton Road in 1879 and Stapleton Road in 1883, the year of Rovers' formation. By 1919, there were more than 60 Methodist churches within the city of Bristol. A Baptist place of worship, the Kensington Chapel on Stapleton Road, was opened in 1888

Hat-trick hero Giuliano Grazioli being congratulated by his team-mate Paul Tait during the 5-2 win at Shrewbury in 2002 – these points would prove vital in the battle against relegation.

with seating for a thousand people, while the future Foreign Secretary Ernest Bevin was a prominent early member of St Mark's Baptist Church. The Catholic population in the diocese of Clifton rose from 5,471 in 1880 to 8,210 in 1890[15]. As the size of the local population increased at an unprecedented rate, the civil parishes of Stapleton, Fishponds and Eastville were placed in 1897 inside the bounds of the City and County of Bristol. This alteration was ratified by an Order of the Local Government Board, dated 9 September 1898. From a settlement 'easily recognized by the narrowness of its streets and a plethora of aldermen,'[16] Bristol approached the 20th century as a revolutionized city prepared to support a number of professional football clubs.

[1] William of Malmesbury, *Gesta Regum*, Rolls Series, I, p159.
Bizarrely, this tale echoes the Icelandic Hrolfs Saga Kraka, in which Bodvarr, later a hero in the saga, arrives at the court of King Hrolfr and kills a retainer.

[2] J F Nicholls and John Taylor, *Bristol Past and Present*, 1881, p14.

[3] Eilert Ekwall, *The Concise Dictionary of English Place-Names*, Clarendon, 1936, Pp 250, 483.

[4] Simon Schama, *A History of Britain: At the edge of the World?*, BBC, 2000 p230.

[5] Frederick Creech Jones and William Gordon Chown, *History of Bristol Suburbs*, Reece Winstone, 1977, p48.

[6] *Notes and Queries*, 1st Series vol.8, no. 192, 2 July 1853, p6.

[7] William Shakespeare, *Romeo and Juliet*, IV.iii.

[8] *Matthew's Guide and Bristol Directory 1793*, quoted in Frederick Creech Jones and William Gordon Chown, *History of Bristol's Suburbs*, Reece Winstone, 1977, p42.

[9] Ben Tillett, *Memories and Reflections*, p23, quoted on www.fishponds.freeuk.com.

[10] David J Eveleigh, *Bristol 1850-1919, Britain in Old Photographs* series, Budding Books, 1996, p101.

[11] *Census Returns: Gloucestershire Population Figures, 1801-1921*, p17.

[12] Joseph Leach, *The Church Goer, Rural Rides or Calls at Country Churches*, Ridler, 1847, vol.3, p125.

[13] William Shakespeare, *Hamlet*, V.i.

[14] Joseph Leach, *The Church Goer, Rural Rides or Calls at Country Churches*, Ridler, 1847, vol.3, p116.

[15] J.A. Harding, *The Diocese of Clifton*, 1850-2000, Clifton Catholic Diocesan Trustees, 1999.

[16] Leonard Cohen, *Greater Bristol by 'Lesser Columbus'*, Pelham, 1893, p3.

BRISTOL ROVERS
THE OFFICIAL CLUB HISTORY

We blossom and flourish as leaves on a tree.

Walter Chalmers Smith

1883-92

It was a brave move in a rugby-playing environment, but a meeting of five young schoolmasters in September 1883 in the Eastville Restaurant in Queen's Parade, Stapleton Road in Bristol led to the founding of a football club. This restaurant, run by J Collins, stood between J J Bond the grocer and George West, a furniture broker. This was the birth of an organization that grew into the first professional team in the city and developed in turn into Bristol Rovers. Yet the circumstances surrounding the club's foundation were by no means unique. A group of young schoolteachers led by James Allan had formed Sunderland FC in 1879, while many other clubs, notably Bolton Wanderers, Everton, Leicester City and Northampton Town, had their roots in the education system. That first meeting in Eastville was organized by Bill Somerton, a 19-year-old teacher born in Summertown, Oxfordshire, who had moved to the area from Grove Street, Oxford just a few months earlier. They established a side that swiftly became known as Black Arabs FC, since they were to wear black shirts with a golden sash and play on a pitch flanked by those of several rugby teams, one of whom went under the name of The Arabs. Rugby flourished at this time in this corner of the world and The Arabs were able to attract a crowd of 2,000 when they entertained a strong Newport side on The Downs on 7 March 1885.

The following month, eight young men met at the home of Charles Davis, at 33 Clifton Place, Stapleton Road, near the locally famous Thirteen Arches railway bridge in Eastville. One was R C Conyers, a former pupil of and now teacher at St Mark's School, Easton, who was to follow Rovers beyond his retirement in 1934 to Hayle in Cornwall until his death there in August 1938. Reynard Conyers, born in Rodmarton, Gloucestershire in 1863, lived at that time at 16 Frenchay Villas, St George. Also present were Henry Martin of 20 Bellevue Road, Easton, Harry Phillips of Glendale House, Upper Easton, William Braund, an 18-year-old from 10 Frenchay Terrace, St George, F L Evans, F Hall and E Edgell. They began to establish a team, recruiting a number of local players. Herbie Hand, for instance, had played for Bristol St George and he and his son Bill were both to play for Clevedon Town. Frank Laurie, whose brothers Archie and Tony also played for the side, was a stalwart figure, elected to the Rovers' selection committee in 1893 and a supporter of the club up to his death from pneumonia in April 1925, at the age of 59. One member of the original team was Harry Horsey, a carpenter of 16 Wood Street, Eastville, born in 1867, and later managing director of Horfield match makers Octavius Hunt Ltd. His allegiance to the club continued from the Black Arab days until his death in July 1938. He had served as player, committeeman, secretary, treasurer, financial secretary, director, vice-chairman and chairman. Fifty-six years with his only club indicates a level of dedication and commitment few can equal and the history of Bristol Rovers would undoubtedly be all the poorer but for the contributions made by Henry James Horsey and fellow founder members.

A pitch was found among those of local rugby sides, at Purdown, a mile north of the future Eastville stadium. This first ground could well have been on the site of the current playing fields at the junction of Sir John's Lane and Lindsay Road. Ironically,

SEASON 1883/84			
01/12/1883	Wotton-under-Edge	(a)	0-6
22/12/1883	Warmley	(a)	1-3
12/01/1884	Bristol Wagon Works	(a)	
19/01/1884	Bristol Wagon Works	(h)	
26/01/1884	Warmley	(h)	0-4
16/02/1884	Wotton-under-Edge	(h)	0-2
01/03/1884	Bristol Wagon Works	(a)	postponed
08/03/1884	Bristol Wagon Works	(h)	3-0
15/03/1884	Right & Might (Jones & Co)	(h)	
22/03/1884	Right & Might (Jones & Co)	(a)	

SEASON 1884/85			
	Bristol Wagon Works		
	Cardiff *		
13/12/1884	Clifton Wanderers	(h)	0-2
	Clifton Association 2nd X1		
	Gloucester		
	Melksham		
	Right & Might (Jones & Co)		
	St George		
29/11/1884	Warmley 2nd X1	(h)	0-0
	Wotton-under-Edge		

*Fixture arranged but Rovers team refused to travel.

St John's Lane, a near-namesake across the city, was where Bristol South End, the club that grew into Bristol City, played its first game on 1 September 1894. Opposition proved harder to find, as few clubs yet existed. Two early rivals were Clifton and Warmley, and they were among the first recognized football teams in Bristol, a city where boxing, cricket and rugby continued to command greater mass interest. Clifton Association were, like Rovers, formed in 1883, a year after Bristol St George and, most notably, Warmley who were acclaimed as the oldest football team in Bristol. Not far away, though, Paulton Rovers had first appeared in their distinctive dark maroon shirts as early as 1881.

Black Arabs soon found a wealthy patron in Henry Haughton Reynolds, Lord Moreton. Holt demonstrates how, of 740 directors of football clubs between 1888 and 1915, all but 78 were businessmen who saw the potential in this lucrative, up-and-coming leisure pursuit[1]. Moreton's undisputed business acumen is however, shaded by his background, for he was also a Justice of the Peace and was Member of Parliament for West Gloucestershire between 1880 and 1885. Lord Moreton, who was born on 4 March 1857, died on 8 February 1920, shortly before Rovers' accession to the Football League. Further patrons were found in Colonel Kingscote; Rev. Thomas Henry Barnett, vicar of St Mark's, Easton and formerly of St Stephen's, Guernsey; Robert Brison of Gloucester Villa, Hill View, Bishopston; George T Howe, proprietor of the Queen's Head, Fishponds Road, Eastville; and a Miss Osborne. Colonel Sir Robert Nigel Fitzhardinge Kingscote was, like Moreton, a West Gloucestershire Member of Parliament, serving his constituency between 1852 and 1885. He was also a Justice of the Peace, had been Groom-in-Waiting to Queen Victoria between 1859 and 1866 and was to serve as Extra Equerry, when well past his 70th birthday, to Edward VII. A Crimean War veteran, Kingscote was born on 28 February 1830, descended through a female line from the wealthy Berkeley family and lived in Gloucestershire until his death on 22 September 1908. His was indeed from a distinguished family. In 1788 his great-aunt Catharine had married Edward Jenner, who introduced the smallpox vaccine, while a great-niece Flavia married a nephew of the poet Siegfried Sassoon. The initial set of rules stated that 'jerseys, which members are expected to wear in all matches, shall be the club colours, viz black. That for all engagements, players shall be chosen by Captain and Secretary, any gentleman wishing to join shall be proposed by a member and selected by a majority of the committee and pay the entrance fee of two shillings and sixpence. Also that no player shall leave the ground during a match without permission of the Captain, there shall be practice on Saturday afternoons and any other time when not less than six members are present.' The first president, Rev. John Gage Norman, was the curate under Rev. Barnett at St Mark's, Easton, between 1881 and 1885. He worked in Oxfordshire, Leicestershire and Nottinghamshire and was a vicar at the Bay of Islands in Newfoundland, Canada between 1886 and 1887. After later work in London and Suffolk, he was a curate in Shepton Mallet in 1898. It was no coincidence that church leaders were involved in the early years of the club, for they had been also at the foundation of several top sides. A new 'muscular Christianity' was encouraging physical exercise as a means to keep workers' bodies fit and minds distracted from the lure of heavy drinking and the associated potential social unrest. Aston Villa's foundation in 1874 owed much to the church, as did that of Wolverhampton Wanderers (1877), Everton (1878), Queen's Park Rangers and Southampton (both 1885) and Barnsley(1887). The historian John Latimer (1824–1904), writing in 1887, recorded that Bristol could boast 650 inns, taverns and beer shops in 1840 and as many as 1,250 by 1870[2]. Beer consumption in the United Kingdom as a whole rose from 19.4 gallons per annum per adult in the years between 1845 and 1849 to 33.2 gallons between 1875 and 1879, while one survey carried out in Bristol in 1882 showed that, on a random weekend, some 104,557 people visited the city's pubs on the Saturday evening and 116,148 attended church or chapel the following morning[3]. L B Pearce and C E Marsh were vice-presidents of the Black Arabs, Henry Martin the first captain, Bill Somerton vice-captain, F L Evans was treasurer, William Braund was honorary secretary and George Coopey of 2 Spring Mount Villas, Stapleton Road was a committee member alongside Reynard Conyers, Harry Phillips and F Hall.

On 1 December 1883, the Black Arabs played their first game, losing convincingly. The *Dursley Gazette* of 3 December reported: 'Football: Wotton-under-Edge v Black Arabs (Bristol). A match under Association rules has been played at Wotton-under-Edge between these clubs, resulting in the defeat of the visiting team. The home team were in every point superior to their antagonists and after a one-sided game Wotton were declared victors by six goals to nil.' The 'Purdown Poachers', as the Black Arabs became affectionately known, played in 10 games in this inaugural season, their opponents being Wotton, Warmley, Bristol Wagonworks and Right and Might. To their initial all-black strip, they added a golden diagonal sash to the shirt.

A number of significant changes were made prior to the start of the 1884/85 season. Now known from November 1884 as Eastville Rovers, a name that was to endure until 1898/99, the club played home matches at Three Acres at Ashley Hill and Bill Somerton was appointed

SEASON 1885/86

	Bristol Wagon Works		
	Cardiff		
	Chippenham		
	Clifton Association		
	Clifton Association 2nd X1		
02/01/1886	Gloucester	(h)	1-0
	Melksham		
	Right & Might (Jones & Co)	(h)	1-0*
	St George		
11/10/1885	Warmley		
	Warmley Reserves		
	Wotton-under-Edge		

* Only 40 mins play possible due to late arrival of opponents

SEASON 1886/87

23/10/1886	Warmley	(h)
30/10/1886	Clifton Association	(h)
13/11/1886	Warmley Reserves	(a)
20/11/1886	Warmley Reserves	(h)
27/11/1886	St Mathias	(h)
04/12/1886	Bridgwater	(h)
11/12/1886	St George	(a)

SEASON 1887/88			
08/10/1887	St George	(a)	3-2
15/10/1887	Warmley	(h)	1-0
12/11/1887	Warmley Reserves	(a)	
19/11/1887	St George	(a)	
26/11/1887	Weston-Super-Mare	(a)	1-2
19/12/1887	Warmley	(a)	1-2
07/01/1888	St George	(a)	2-0
14/01/1888	Clifton (Glos C)	(a)	1-4
28/01/1888	Wotton Under Edge	(h)	1-0
30/03/1888	Warmley	(a)	4-4
31/03/1888	Warmley	(a)	3-0

captain. The change of name certainly had the desired effect of broadening the base of the club and encouraging players and interest from a much wider local area. The new pitch would have been an open field with no changing facilities. In fact, since newspaper interest in such a contemporarily unorthodox sport was scant, the precise location of this pitch remains a mystery. Three Acres was quite possibly an area off Muller Road and next to the Narrowby Hill footpath, where St Thomas More RC School now stands. A larger area, though, of some 80 acres, beside the County Cricket Ground, later developed into housing, was also noted around this time as a 'Football Ground', although this terminology will mean little more than open fields.

Rovers played at Three Acres for one season and, from 1885 to 1891 and 1892 to 1894, at an unidentified location on the limestone plateau of Durdham Downs, where numerous pitches house regular football to this day. However, the first game for which a Rovers line-up is given in the press, a 2-0 defeat at home to Clifton Association by a goal in each half, was played on 13 December 1884 at Purdown. The Rovers side on that day was: E Tucker, W Pepperall, F Channing, W E Braund, R C Conyers, J Miller, R H Horsey, F Andrew, L W Davies, F Laurie, W J Somerton.

Fred Channing, at left-back, was a Bristol-born defender who had played football in Nottingham and London prior to joining the Black Arabs in 1883. He was appointed Rovers' captain in 1886 and later served the club off the field. On 7 April 1885 he was Rovers' sole representative in the first competitive fixture involving Gloucestershire, a 1-0 win thanks to centre-half G T Pocock's goal two minutes before half-time against Somerset at the Bedminster Cricket Ground. Channing was later a stalwart member of the board of directors until resigning through ill health in September 1919.

The first match on The Downs, in which Rovers sported their new strip of blue-and-white-hooped shirts and white shorts, was against Right and Might, a works team from Jones and Company, in October 1885. The Purdown Poachers, captained by Bill Somerton, won through a single goal, although the identity of the scorer is unknown. The opposition was late in arriving and, after a 5.10 p.m. kick-off, only 40 minutes' play was possible.

The teams lined up:
EASTVILLE ROVERS: W E Braund, W J Somerton, W Pepperall, F Andrew, W S Perrin, C Forster, H J Horsey, F Churchill, F Laurie, Walter Perrin, S Darlington.
RIGHT AND MIGHT: H G Iles, L Davies, W Wiseman, W Anderson, H O Ashton (capt), G Barnes, J Picton, L W Harvey, R Wells, W Wiles, T K Jarvis.

While Rovers' players apparently shuffled their positions on the field, the club played an ever-increasing range of opponents. In 1885/86, Rovers having refused to travel to Cardiff on the Aust-Beachley ferry the previous season, a journey through the Severn

Tunnel, opened in 1886, enabled the first game against Welsh opposition. Matches against sides from Swindon, Trowbridge and Bath were regular features even before Rovers entered a recognized league in 1892. In 1886, as interest in the club increased, Rovers formed a reserve side and now played in shirts of Oxford and Cambridge blue. Between 1887 and 1895, however, the club's colours were a tasty combination of claret and cream.

Rovers continued to play friendlies against an increasingly wide circle of clubs. In October 1887, despite being reduced to ten men in the second half, with goalkeeper Edward Tucker stretchered off, Rovers secured a 3-2 win at St George. At the close of the 1887/88 season, a combined Clifton and Rovers side, supplemented by the contemporary England full-back pairing of the brothers Arthur and Percy Walters, drew 4-4 at Warmley. The largest win of the 1888/89 season was by eight clear goals at Kingswood, where Claude Hodgson and Harry Cade both registered hat-tricks; this was the last occasion before the victory at Brighton in December 1973 that two Rovers players both completed hat-tricks in an away match. In the autumn of 1889, Rovers led 2-0 at Warmley after only thirty-five minutes after two opponents had conceded own goals and Frank Laurie's hat-trick paved the way to a comprehensive victory over St Simon's. The most extraordinary result, though, was the 8-4 defeat at St George in October 1890, where Rovers had trailed 3-1 at the interval.

In addition to friendlies, Eastville Rovers competed in the Gloucestershire Cup from its inception in 1887/88. The Gloucestershire Cup was the brainchild of Clifton Association's Charles Lacy-Sweet and grew from a meeting in September 1887 attended by Clifton and Rovers, along with Globe, a team made up of former pupils of Queen Elizabeth's Hospital, three church sides in St Agnes, St George and St Simon's and Southville, one of the components of the future Bristol City. Details as to the format of the tournament were finalized at a further meeting, held on 5 October 1887 at the Montpelier Hotel. This competition was to run to 99 finals before grinding to a halt in the 1990s. The first taste of cup action, on 14 January 1888, resulted in a 4-1 defeat at the hands of Clifton, who wore their distinctive 'chocolate and cardinal' shirts. In a match played at Bell Hill, St George. Rovers lost Horsey with a strained leg muscle after only two minutes and were forced to play the remainder of the game with only ten men.

SEASON 1888/89

				GOALSCORERS
24/09/1888	Right v Might (Jones & Co)			
06/10/1888	Warmley	(h)	3-1	
13/10/1888	St George	(a)	2-0	
0310/1888	Clifton	(a)	0-3	
01/12/1888	Clifton	(a)	3-3	
29/12/1888	Queen Elizabeth's Hospital Old Boys	(h)		
05/01/1889	Warmley	(a)	1-3	
19/01/1889	Southville	(h)	1-0	

GLOUCESTERSHIRE CUP

26/01/1889	St Agnes	(a)	3-1	
6/04/1889	Warmley *Final at St George	(n)*	1-0	Perrin

SEASON 1889/90

				GOALSCORERS
21/09/1889	KINGSWOOD	(a)	0-2	
12/10/1889	WARMLEY	(a)	3-3	
26/10/1889	BATH ASSOCIATION	(h)	1-0	
09/11/1889	CLIFTON ASSOCIATION	(a)	0-1	
16/11/1889	TROWBRIDGE TOWN	(a)	2-4	
23/11/1889	ST GEORGE	(a)		
07/12/1889	CLIFTON ASSOCIATION	(a)	0-3	
14/12/1889	CLEVEDON	(h)	2-0	
21/12/1889	WARMLEY	(h)	0-0	
28/12/1889	QUEEN ELIZABETH HOSPITAL OLD BOYS	(a)	2-1	
11/01/1890	TROWBRIDGE TOWN	(h)	1-2	
08/02/1890	KINGSWOOD	(a)	2-1	
15/03/1890	ST GEORGE	(a)	0-2	

GLOUCESTERSHIRE CUP

18/01/90	WARMLEY	(a)	1-0	
15/02/90	CLIFTON ASSOCIATION	(a)	2-7	PERRIN (2)

Against the odds, however, outside-left Bill Bush put Rovers ahead five minutes before half-time. A B Colthurst equalised moments before the break and scored again after 55 minutes, Clifton's third of the game. Charles Wreford-Brown, the first Bristolian to play football for England and the man who, as vice-chairman of the Football Association, was allegedly the first to coin the term 'soccer', had put his side 2-1 ahead on 50 minutes, and Harry Francis completed the scoring two minutes from time. It is believed that this final goalscorer was none other than 19-year-old Howard Henry Francis, a Bristol-born sportsman who later emigrated to South Africa, played in two cricket Test matches for his adopted country in 1898/99 and died in Cape Town in January 1936.

The Rovers line-up was:
 E Tucker, W Somerton, W Berry, F Channing (capt), H Horsey, A Attwell, H Cade, C Hodgson, F Laurie, W Perrin, W Bush.

However, the following season, after a 3-1 victory at St Agnes, Rovers defeated Warmley by a single goal to win their first final. The all-important goal was scored by Walter Perrin 20 minutes from time following a smart interchange of passes with Attwell. This brought the first tangible reward to the Eastville club.

The only Rovers side to win the Gloucestershire Cup in the 19th century was:
 E Tucker, C Hodgson, W Somerton, A Attwell, W Howe, C H Lawrence, W Taylor, F Laurie, W Higgins, F Channing (capt), W Perrin.

The aforementioned Lacy-Sweet and Francis were the two linesmen. Rovers also reached the final in 1893/94, when George Gerrish, R Lane, and Bruton had all scored for a strong St George side before Horsey's late low shot brought a consolation goal in Rovers' 3-1 defeat in front of a crowd of 4,000 at The Chequers, Lodge Road, Kingswood. In 1889/90, despite Perrin's two goals, Rovers lost 7-2 to Clifton Association, for whom R Innes-Pocock and Barlow scored twice each, with Attwell putting through his own goal for the fifth. This game was refereed by the famous

Gloucestershire and England cricketer W G Grace, who had been approached by the Rovers club committee to take charge of a number of matches. He and Bill Somerton had been the linesmen for the replay of the inaugural Gloucestershire Cup final in March 1888. Rovers were to win the trophy next in April 1903 yet, from a tournament involving a large number of local sides, the competition evolved into a straightforward two-club play-off from 1908 between Bristol's two major sides.

For the 1890/91 season, when Rovers defeated Craigmore College 5-1, with five different members of the team getting on the scoresheet, but lost by the same score at both Warmley and Trowbridge Town, Rovers could boast a 14-man squad. Led by captain Bill Somerton, several old hands remained, among them Walter Perrin, Harry Horsey, Fred Lovett and both Frank and Archie Laurie. Other squad members included A Attwell, J Batchelor, Brown, T Hardwick, Claude Hodgson, George Howe, E Tucker and F Yates. A 3-2 home defeat to Bedminster saw Rovers eliminated early from the Gloucestershire Cup, with H J Batchelor and W G Griffiths, who both scored against Rovers, contributing the goals with which the South Bristol side beat Warmley 2-0 in the final.

In May 1891, Eastville Rovers negotiated a seasonal rental of £8 to use the Schoolmasters Cricket Ground in Downend Lane, Horfield. The pitch would have been at the present site of the crossroads between Downend Road and Dovercourt Road. A surviving Cricket Club minute book reveals that the hire agreement stipulated that Rovers would provide a groundsman and maintain fencing at the ground, but would take all the proceeds from the gate.

The summer of 1891 saw the introduction of the penalty kick into British football but, of greater concern to Eastville Rovers, was the side's alarming capacity to ship goals. Rovers conceded seven twice and six in games played at Warmley and also conceded five on three occasions, twice against Trowbridge Town and once at Swindon Town. Yet they also beat Craigmore College 10-0, after being seven goals up by half-time. In addition, Rovers won 3-1 at Kingswood in November, despite fielding only nine players. Indeed, the Gloucestershire Cup campaign of 1891/92 featured two 7-1 scorelines. In

SEASON 1890/91

				GOALSCORERS
20/09/1890	WARMLEY	(a)	0-1	
04/10/1890	ST GEORGE	(a)	4-8	A LAURIE (2), PERRIN, TAYLOR
11/10/1890	BEDMINSTER	(a)	2-4	PERRIN (2)
25/10/1890	TROWBRIDGE TOWN	(a)	1-5	YATES
08/11/1890	CRAIGMORE COLLEGE	(h)	5-1	YATES, W TAYLOR, A LAURIE, PERRIN, HODGSON
15/11/1890	CLIFTON ASSOCIATION	(a)	3-0	YATES (3)
22/11/1890	BATH	(h)	3-3	YATES (2), A LAURIE
13/12/1890	BEDMINSTER	(a)	1-4	YATES
26/12/1890	BRADFORD ON AVON	(h)	3-2	
19/02/1891	CLIFTON	(h)	1-1	
21/02/1891	CLIFTON	(h)	1-1	
26/02/1891	CLIFTON	(h)	1-1	PERRIN
28/03/1891	TROWBRIDGE TOWN	(a)	1-3	
11/04/1891	WARMLEY	(a)	1-5	A LAURIE

GLOUCESTERSHIRE CUP

15/02/91	CLIFTON	(a)	2-7	

SEASON 1891/92

FRIENDLIES

				ATT	GOALSCORERS
26/09/1891	WARMLEY	A	0-7		
10/10/1891	MANGOTSFIELD	H	1-1		YATES
17/10/1891	BEDMINSTER	H	1-2		untraced
24/10/1891	SWINDON TN	A	2-5		2 untraced
31/10/1891	ST GEORGE	H	1-2		untraced
07/11/1891	CRAIGMORE COLLEGE	H	10-0		10 untraced
21/11/1891	CLIFTON	H	1-0		YATES
28/11/1891	KINGSWOOD*	A	3-1		A LAURIE, THOMAS, YATES
05/12/1891	ST GEORGE	A	2-8		A LAURIE, LUKE
12/12/1891	SWINDON TOWN	H	2-2		YATES, A LAURIE
19/12/1891	TROWBRIDGE TOWN	H	1-1		YATES
26/12/1891	ST.SIMONS	H	3-0		3 untraced
02/01/1892	TROWBRIDGE TOWN	A	2-5		ROGERS 2
16/01/1892	WARMLEY	H	1-6		A LAURIE
23/01/1892	CLIFTON	A	3-1		YATES (2), ROGERS
06/02/1892	WARMLEY	A	1-6	300	A LAURIE
13/02/1892	MANGOTSFIELD	A	2-1		2 untraced
05/03/1892	TROWBRIDGE TOWN	A	1-1		untraced
17/03/1892	CRAIGMORE COLLEGE	A	7-1		7 untraced
26/03/1892	ST.SIMONS	A	2-0		2 untraced
09/04/1892	TROWBRIDGE TOWN	A	1-5		ROGERS

* Rovers only fielded 9 players

GLOUCESTERSHIRE CUP

				ATT	GOALSCORERS
30/01/1892	CRAIGMORE COLLEGE	A	7-1		A LAURIE (2), THOMAS (2), TAYLOR, PURSER, YATES
27/02/1892	WARMLEY * *Semi-Final	A	1-7	700	YATES

driving rain and gale-force winds, Rovers raced to a 5-0 half-time lead over Craigmore College in January, Thomas scoring his second goal right on the interval to add to a brace from Archie Laurie. Rovers conceded a consolation goal only in the last minute of the match. Four weeks later, in a semi-final initially postponed due to frost, T Nelmes, J King and J MacKay scored twice each for Warmley, who defeated Rovers convincingly before a crowd of 700. That Rovers stalwart William Braund was linesman for both games.

The Rovers side that lost at Warmley was:

A Attwell, Claude Hodgson, Bill Somerton, W Wallace, F Purser, Fred Lovett, Archie Laurie, W Thomas, F W Yates, Bill Rogers, Billy Taylor

Warmley was also the venue for the worst result of the season. In September, with Fred Channing running the line on this occasion, Rovers had held the home side to a goalless first half but, with the strong wind in their favour after half-time, Warmley ran in seven second-half goals without reply. King, going one better than in the Gloucestershire Cup, scored a hat-trick.

Apparently unable to extend their hire agreement at the Schoolmasters Cricket Ground, Eastville Rovers reverted to the Durdham Downs for the 1892/93 season. In what must have appeared a different world, Alf Jasper Geddes, later a Rovers player, scored in the FA Cup final in March 1892, as West Bromwich Albion beat Aston Villa 3-0. His was the opening goal after only four minutes, firing home a first-time shot, following a cross from the England outside-right Billy Bassett.

The growing trend to formalize football fixtures reached Bristol in 1892. When the Football League was founded in 1888, the majority of the 12 inaugural sides had hailed from the industrial heartlands of Lancashire and the Birmingham area. However, football developed throughout the country through the late 19th century as the popular pastime in working-class society and gradually replaced boxing as the major crowd-pulling sport in east Bristol. Bristol, as its motto suggests, was a city of great industry and 'Lesser Columbus' reported in 1893 that 'there is scarcely anything that is not made in Bristol.'[4] Yet, social conditions were altering and the previously unheard-of commodity of leisure time slowly emerged, the introduction of half-day Saturdays into the workplace encouraging many workers to go to football matches in the afternoon. These matches were, in turn, reported in newspapers for an increasingly literate population, with the first Special Saturday Football Edition of the *Bristol Evening News* appearing on 14 October 1893. In the aftermath of the Reform Act of 1884, prominent politicians took a keen interest in football as a means of wooing voters and the embryonic game was allowed to flourish.

The sport was also seen as a vehicle for boosting the general level of health within the working classes, especially in Bristol, where a cholera epidemic as recently as 1849 had killed 444 people. Following a previous epidemic of cholera in October 1831, when 584 of 1,521 afflicted were to die, 600 people were apparently living in St Peter's Hospital in Easton, and a second epidemic in 1866 accounted for 29 deaths. Moreover, scarlet fever, typhoid and smallpox were rife in the city in 1865, when severe gales followed the previous year's drought. There were epidemics of measles in 1885, 1898 and 1905 and of scarlet fever in 1896 and 1900, in addition to a further outbreak of smallpox in 1880. A Parliamentary Report on the Sanitary Condition of Bristol in 1845 had investigated the appalling squalor of the city and yet, in 1869, *The Times* reported Bristol to be one of the healthiest towns in Great Britain[5]. In chapter 38 of Charles Dickens' *Pickwick Papers*, Mr Winkle visits Bristol. It 'struck him as being a shade more dirty than any place he had ever seen', while Virginia Woolf, in 1935, described Bristol as 'the most hideous of all towns.'[6] Moreover, Thomas Chatterton's *Last Verses* refer to 'Bristolia's dingy piles of brick'.

While the Southern League did not come into existence until 1894, a recommendation from Percy Wyfold Stout of Gloucester led to the idea of establishing a regional league in the Bristol area. Bedminster, Clifton Association, Eastville Rovers, Mangotsfield, St George and Warmley sent representatives to the Earl Russell Hotel, Without a game on the opening day, Rovers kicked off their first match in this competition at 3.30 p.m. on 1 October 1892 and lost 3-1 to Mangotsfield. Although officially a 'home' game, Rovers were forced to play at their opponents' ground and, a goal down to William Nolan's fifteenth-minute opener, conceded two second-half goals to 21-year-old Courtney Punter, the first a penalty and the second just moments after Walter Perrin had briefly brought the side back into contention. Rovers' two ever-presents this season were goalkeeper A Long and centre-half Len John, who was to

SEASON 1892/93

BRISTOL & DISTRICT LEAGUE

				ATT	GOALSCORERS
01/10/1892	MANGOTSFIELD*	H	1-3		PERRIN
08/10/1892	TROWBRIDGE TOWN	A	2-6	200	ROGERS (2)
22/10/1892	ST GEORGE	A	0-2		
12/11/1892	WARMLEY	H	2-2*		THOMPSON, BRITTON og
19/11/1892	WELLS	H	2-2		LOVETT, YATES
26/11/1892	CLEVEDON	H	1-2		TAYLOR
03/12/1892	BEDMINSTER	A	0-5	1000	
24/12/1892	CLIFTON ASSOCIATION	H	3-1		
26/12/1892	ST GEORGE	A	1-3		F LAURIE
21/01/1893	TROWBRIDGE TOWN	H	2-2		ROGERS, JOHN
11/02/1893	ST GEORGE	H	2-1		ROGERS, BEVERLEY
18/02/1893	WARMLEY	A	2-8		TAYLOR, A LAURIE
04/03/1893	CLEVEDON	A	0-1		
11/03/1893	WELLS	H	5-1		A LAURIE (2), TAYLOR (2), HORSEY
18/03/1893	CLIFTON ASSOCIATION	A	3-1		JOHN (2)
25/03/1893	BEDMINSTER	H	5-2		ROGERS (2), THOMPSON, HODGSON, W LAURIE
31/03/1893	MANGOTSFIELD	A	5-0		ROGERS (3), PERRIN, HORSEY

* Home match but played at Mangotsfield

FRIENDLIES

10/09/1892	WARMLEY	A	3-2		
17/09/1892	ST GEORGE	A	1-4	300	
04/02/1893	BEDMINSTER	A	0-0	600	
15/04/1893	SWINDON ATHLETIC	A	1-0		

GLOUCESTERSHIRE CUP

untraced	MANGOTSFIELD	H	Drew	
untraced	MANGOTSFIELD	A	Lost	

appear regularly in goal himself in the 1895/96 season. Bob Horsey, who made his debut in January, when Rovers started against Trowbridge Town with only ten men, as Frank Laurie arrived late, had played at St Gabriel's alongside future team-mates in George Hockin, Archie Laurie, A Furse and T Jeffs. Eastville Rovers won 6 out of 16 games in this inaugural season, finishing sixth out of nine clubs. They put five goals past Wells, who fielded only ten men, Archie Laurie and Bill Taylor scoring twice each, Bedminster and Mangotsfield, Bill Rogers scoring a hat-trick, but also conceded five at Bedminster and six, despite being level 2-2 at half-time, at Trowbridge Town. The 5-2 victory at home to Bedminster was an ill-tempered affair, with the visitors' second goalscorer Scottie Milne being sent off after a dreadful foul on Claude Hodgson. Twice behind, Rovers were indebted to Bill Rogers for two equalisers, while the aforementioned Hodgson added the home side's fourth goal. The worst defeat, however, was at Warmley on 18 February, where Rovers trailed 3-1 in a strong wind by half-time and, with 'Nipper' Britton completing his hat-trick in the second half, lost 8-2. Rovers were also involved in a game with the same opposition in November which was abandoned at 2-2 in failing light twelve minutes from time. Warmley were champions by a point and, in a show of electioneering, were presented with the 19in trophy on an ebony plinth at the league dinner on 9 September 1893 by Charles Edward Hungerford Atholl Colston, the newly-elected Member of Parliament for South Gloucestershire.

In 1893/94 Rovers finished second from bottom, above Mangotsfield whom Rovers defeated 3-0 and 5-2, Archie Laurie and Bill Thompson scoring in both games. A further home victory, this time against Swindon Wanderers, was played in a temperature of

90°F, while the game at home to Warmley, in which left-back Fred Lovett scored twice in defeat, was decreed a friendly and had to be replayed, as the pitch was saturated, having been underwater on the Friday evening. Rovers kicked off with only six men on the field when they entertained Clifton Association on a foggy December afternoon. Defeat at Gloucester in November featured a first appearance for the club by Hugh McBain, an inspirational captain in years to come. The following season, an enlarged division was won by newcomers Hereford Thistle, who, in their chocolate and sky blue shirts, twice put four goals past Rovers. All four of their goals at the Ridgeway Ground in November 1894 came after half time. Ten wins and eight defeats left Rovers in sixth place out of twelve clubs. Clevedon, bottom of the table with three points and 136 goals conceded in 22 games, were defeated 7-2 in October, six players scoring for Rovers, all five forwards plus left-half Claude Hodgson, with the captain and outside-right Hugh McBain opening the goalscoring after only two minutes. For this game, Rovers lined up as follows: W Stone, J Hodgkins, F Lovett, A Furse, L Johns, C Hodgson, H McBain, W Thompson, R Horsey, W Rogers, A Laurie.

Rovers also took part in a six-a-side tournament at Kingswood in April 1894, beating Gloucester and Bedminster, the latter by an astonishing 21-0 margin, before losing their semi-final to Clifton, runners-up to Warmley.

The 1894/95 season was Rovers' first away from Durdham Downs, as the club played home matches a mile to the east of Eastville on a ground variously known as Rudgeway,

SEASON 1893/94

BRISTOL & DISTRICT LEAGUE

				ATT	GOALSCORERS
23/09/1893	WARMLEY	A	2-4		
07/10/1893	BEDMINSTER	A	0-2	GOOD	
14/10/1893	GLOUCESTER	H	5-2		ROGERS (2), LAURIE, HORSEY (2)
21/10/1893	WARMLEY	A	0-1	700	
27/10/1893	ST PAULS	H	4-1		
04/11/1893	MANGOTSFIELD	A	3-0	FAIR	LAURIE, THOMPSON, ROGERS
11/11/1893	GLOUCESTER	A	0-3	600	
25/11/1893	TROWBRIDGE TOWN	H	4-2	600	HORSEY (2), ROGERS, TAYLOR
02/12/1893	ST GEORGE	A	1-3	GOOD	THOMPSON
16/12/1893	SWINDON ATHLETIC	H	1-2		
26/12/1893	ST GEORGE	H	0-2		
30/12/1893	CLIFTON	H	1-3	POOR	ROGERS
13/01/1894	ST GEORGE	A	1-2	1,500	HORSEY
20/01/1894	WARMLEY	H	2-4	POOR	LOVETT (2)
10/02/1894	TROWBRIDGE TOWN	A	0-3	1,000	TAYLOR
03/03/1894	BEDMINSTER	H	3-3	V GOOD	ROGERS, HORSEY, LAURIE
10/03/1894	CLEVEDON	H	1-2		
17/03/1894	STAPLE HILL	H	3-1		LAURIE, ATTWELL, McBAIN
23/03/1894	MANGOTSFIELD	H	5-2		LAURIE (2), HORSEY, THOMPSON, McBAIN
24/03/1894	WARMLEY	H	1-1	4,000	BRITTON (og)
07/04/1894	CLEVEDON	A	1-3	GOOD	ROGERS
14/04/1894	CLIFTON	A	0-4	FAIR	

FRIENDLIES

07/12/1893	ST GEORGE	A	4-0	GOOD	HORSEY (2), ROGERS, TAYLOR
23/12/1893	SWINDON ATHLETIC	H	1-0		
03/02/1894	WARMLEY	H	5-1		

GLOUCESTERSHIRE CUP

27/01/1894	MANGOTSFIELD	A	1-0	GOOD	TAYLOR
24/02/1894	GLOUCESTER	A	1-0	800	HORSEY
31/03/1894	ST GEORGE (Final)	N	1-3	V. GOOD	R HORSEY

SEASON 1894/95

BRISTOL & DISTRICT LEAGUE

				ATT	GOALSCORERS
15/09/1894	HEREFORD THISTLE	A	2-4		
29/09/1894	SWINDON WANDERERS	A	2-1		
06/10/1894	STAPLE HILL	H	2-2		
13/10/1894	CLEVEDON	H	7-2		McBAIN (2), ROGERS, R HORSEY, HODGSON (2), LAURIE
20/10/1894	GLOUCESTER	A	2-1		
27/10/1894	MANGOTSFIELD	H	3-0		
03/11/1894	TROWBRIDGE TOWN	A	2-2		
17/11/1894	HEREFORD THISTLE	H	0-4		
01/12/1894	ST GEORGE	H	0-1		
08/12/1894	CLIFTON ASSOCIATION	H	2-3		
15/12/1894	BEDMINSTER	H	4-2	600	
22/12/1894	MANGOTSFIELD	A	0-1		
29/12/1894	TROWBRIDGE TOWN	H	3-3		
05/01/1895	CLEVEDON	A	2-1	200	
09/03/1895	CLIFTON ASSOCIATION	A	1-0		
16/03/1895	GLOUCESTER	H	3-5		
23/03/1895	ST GEORGE	A	2-0	800	
01/04/1895	WARMLEY	A	0-1	800	
06/04/1895	SWINDON WANDERERS	H	4-2		
13/04/1895	WARMLEY	H	0-0		
18/04/1895	STAPLE HILL	A	1-4		
20/04/1895	BEDMINSTER	A	4-1		

FRIENDLIES

08/09/1894	WARMLEY	A	4-0	600	
22/09/1894	BRISTOL SOUTH END	A	1-2		
02/03/1895	BRISTOL SOUTH END	A	5-2	600	
27/04/1895	BRISTOL SOUTH END	A	3-1		
02/05/1895	BRISTOL SOUTH END	A	2-5	600	

GLOUCESTERSHIRE CUP

26/01/1895	MANGOTSFIELD	H	3-5		

Rudgway or Ridgeway. It appears likely that the Ridgeway ground, home from 1894 to 1897, was one of two fields lying between Crooked Lane, later Ridgeway Road, and Fishponds Road. Indeed, the club played on one pitch before moving to another just yards across the road which dried more satisfactorily and the first match there was a 2-2 draw with Staple Hill on 6 October 1894. Bill Rogers was credited with the club's first goal on the new ground, with Bob Horsey also scoring in this inaugural game. Staple Hill, frequent and regular visitors in late Victorian football, were to achieve their Warholian fifteen minutes of fame in January 1906, when they briefly held a 1-0 lead in an FA Cup-tie away to Manchester United. Rovers' headquarters at this time was the Star Inn, which still stands at 539 Fishponds Road, opposite Star Lane. Three consecutive games were won at the end of October, and Trowbridge Town missed a penalty before Rovers grabbed a last-minute equaliser in the subsequent match, but it has to be admitted that the club's form as the season wore on was patchy. Bill Porter scored a hat-trick against Bedminster in December and twice more a fortnight later as Rovers, despite losing left-back Hodgkins through injury, fought back from 3-0 down to claim a draw. In the Gloucestershire Cup, Hugh McBain converted the first recorded penalty awarded in Rovers' favour, but Brain scored twice for Mangotsfield before leaving the field early with a broken collar-bone. One star of this Rovers side was a youthful Tot Farnall, who left Rovers in the summer of 1895 to join First Division Small

Eastville Rovers in 1894. W Stone, C Hodgson, F Lovett, H McBain, L John, A Furze, W Taylor, A Laurie, R Horsey, W Rogers, A Attwell

Heath and was to represent Rovers in four different spells during his long career. On 26 November 1894, Fred Lovett was Rovers' sole representative in a Bristol and District XI which lost 5-0 to First Division Stoke in front of a 2,000 crowd at Greenway Bush Lane.

The first meeting between the clubs which were to become Bristol Rovers and Bristol City took place on 22 September 1894. Eastville Rovers lost 2-1 to Bristol South End in a friendly at St John's Lane, Bedminster, having trailed by two clear goals at half-time. Bob Horsey scored for Rovers in a match which kicked off at the delayed time of 4.40 p.m. after a demonstration to raise money for a lifeboat charity. South End, who were compelled to play solely in friendlies this season, were grateful to their two star names of the time, Hamlet Horatio Clements and Frank Ernest Mayger, two twenty-year-olds destined for highly successful roles with the embryonic Bristol City, who scored a goal each. The Rovers line-up for this first local derby was: W Stone, C Llewellyn, F Lovett, C Hodgson, L E John, A Furze, H McBain, W Rogers, R Horsey, G Hockin, F Laurie.

When the sides next met, once again at St John's Lane, a March crowd of 600 saw Rovers lead 3-0 at half-time before running up a 5-2 inaugural victory over their rivals, Bob Horsey scoring a hat-trick.

Bill Somerton, one of Rovers' founders, refereed a rough Western League game on 23 February 1895, where he reported ten Mangotsfield players and an official for insulting him. Nine players were suspended for three weeks and one until September 1895. The following season, Somerton refereed a cup game between Warmley and Clifton, which was held up for a quarter of an hour after a pitch invasion when elements in the crowd had attempted to attack the referee.

In the face of competition, the Bristol and District League chose to upgrade its image and, on 8 May 1895, changed its name to the Western League. The competition it faced came from the South Bristol League, which had begun operations in 1893, as well as the East Bristol League and the prestigious Southern League, which had both been started up in 1894. Rovers were allocated two places in the Western League, one in Division One for the first team and one in Division Two for the reserves. A later meeting, also attended by Rovers officials, again held at the Earl Russell Hotel, took place on 12 June 1895. The Western League set out its plans for the season ahead and invited further applications from any club playing within a fifty-mile radius of Bristol. Eastville Rovers were amongst a group of ambitious local clubs heading inexorably towards the world of professional football. Some apparently successful clubs, most notably Clifton Association in December 1897 and Warmley in January 1899, despite their continued on-field success, were to fold. Rovers would keep moving along the slow road to the Southern League and ultimately the Football League.

1895-99

Participation in the newly renamed Western League from 1895 was an indication of the high aspirations the club entertained. Rovers were quick to adopt profess-ionalism as a means of gaining access to the higher levels of football available in the Southern League. When the board of directors agreed to the club joining this prestig-ious league in 1899, Rovers changed their kit, appointed a full-time manager and altered their name to Bristol Rovers. This was, however, merely the end-product of a series of key changes which had taken place over a period of a few years from 1895.

By the summer of 1895, Eastville Rovers were based at the Star Inn on Fishponds Road and played all their home matches at the Ridgeway Ground in a kit of buff and green. Prior to the first season in Division One of what was now the Western League, the club appointed George Pay as their first trainer. Pay, though born in Bristol, was the Welsh champion over 150 yards, had raced under the pseudonym C Lewis in important meetings at Sheffield and Manchester and had allegedly never been beaten in a professional race. His considerable awareness of stamina training was an essential feature of Rovers' drive in the early professional years and the players' fitness was rarely called into question. He remained with the club until 1923.

The first Western League game of the 1895/96 season, at Mangotsfield on 14 September, resulted in a 4-0 victory, with C Leese playing his first game following a summer move from Clifton Association. A fortnight later, in their first home game, Tony Laurie and Bill Thompson scored to give Rovers a 2-0 half-time lead over Trowbridge en route to a 7-3 victory. Rovers were to beat Swindon Wanderers 9-0 at the Ridgeway Ground in April 1896 in addition to inflicting 5-0 defeats on St Paul's. Edward Brown scored a hat-trick against St Paul's, while two December games were played on snowbound pitches. An ultimate tally of 14 wins and 54 goals in 20 Western League games gave Rovers a final league position of equal second, six points behind champions

SEASON 1895/96

WESTERN LEAGUE DIVISION ONE

Date	Opponent		Score	ATT	GOALSCORERS
14/09/1895	MANGOTSFIELD	A	4-0		GALLIER (2), THOMPSON, BROWN
28/09/1895	TROWBRIDGE TOWN	H	7-3		THOMPSON (2), BROWN (2), HOCKIN, GALLIER, LAURIE T
26/10/1895	BEDMINSTER	A	3-1	900	THOMPSON (2), GALLIER
09/11/1895	SWINDON WANDERERS	A	2-1		LEESE, ROSS
16/11/1895	GLOUCESTER	H	1-2		LAURIE A
23/11/1895	CLIFTON ASSOCIATION	H	3-2		OSBORNE, McBAIN, LEESE
30/11/1895	ST PAULS	H	5-0		BROWN (3), OSBORNE, GALLIER
07/12/1895	CARDIFF *	A	3-2		ROSS(2), OSBORNE
14/12/1895	STAPLE HILL	H	2-1		BROWN, GALLIER
21/12/1895	WARMLEY	H	1-2		BROWN
28/12/1895	CLIFTON ASSOCIATION	A	1-1		GALLIER
11/01/1896	ST GEORGE	H	2-1		ROSS, GALLIER
01/02/1896	GLOUCESTER	A	3-2		GALLIER (2), BROWN
08/02/1896	BEDMINSTER	H	1-2		GALLIER pen
15/02/1896	ST PAULS	A	5-0		THOMPSON, GALLIER, BROWN, ROSS, OSBORNE
22/02/1896	WARMLEY	A	0-2	3000	
07/03/1896	ST GEORGE	A	1-2		LEESE
21/03/1896	STAPLE HILL	A	1-0		GALLIER
04/04/1896	TROWBRIDGE TOWN	A	1-0		
25/04/1896	SWINDON WANDERERS	H	9-0		OSBORNE (2), GALLIER (2), BROWN (2), LEESE, THOMPSON, McBAIN
01/05/1896	STAPLE HILL**	N	2-2		untraced
untraced	MANGOTSFIELD	H	5-0		

* Cardiff expelled from league
** Test match for runners-up spot played at St George

GLOUCESTERSHIRE CUP

Date	Opponent		Score	ATT	GOALSCORERS
25/01/1896	BRISTOL SOUTH END	H	4-0	2000	OSBORNE (2), LEESE, BROWN
29/02/1896	ST GEORGE	A	1-1	4000	ROSS
14/03/1896	ST GEORGE	H	4-0	3000	THOMPSON, GALLIER, BROWN, OSBORNE
28/03/1896	BEDMINSTER	A	1-0	4000	OSBORNE
06/04/1896	WARMLEY*	N	0-2	5651	

*Final: Played at St George

FA CUP

Date	Opponent		Score
05/10/1895	WARMLEY	H	0-2

FRIENDLIES

Date	Opponent		Score	ATT	GOALSCORERS
21/09/1895	WARMLEY	H	2-1	600	THOMPSON, GRIFFITHS
12/10/1895	RADSTOCK	H	4-0		GALLIER (2), LEESE, BROWN
19/10/1895	BRISTOL SOUTH END	A	1-1	2000	GALLIER
02/11/1895	HEREFORD THISTLE	H	2-4	2000	LEESE (2)
12/11/1895	SWINDON WANDERERS	H	2-1		ROSS, LEESE
26/12/1895	ST GEORGE	A	1-2		LAURIE A
04/01/1896	BRISTOL SOUTH END	H	3-0	2000	BROWN, THOMPSON, GALLIER
18/01/1896	WYCOMBE WANDERERS	H	2-2	1000	OSBORNE (2)
11/04/1896	BEDMINSTER	A	1-2		GALLIER
18/04/1896	BRISTOL SOUTH END	A	0-1		
30/04/1896	EASTLEIGH	H	3-1		untraced

WESTERN LEAGUE TOURNAMENT

Date	Opponent		Score	ATT
27/04/1896	STAPLE HILL***	N	3-1	500

***Final: Played at St George, Rovers won by 3 goals and 2 corners (14 points) to 1 goal, 3 corners (7 points)

Warmley. A 3-2 victory over Cardiff in December was chalked off on the Welsh club's expulsion from the league for non-payment of fines. In a play-off match for runners-up medals, Rovers drew 2-2 at Staple Hill and the clubs were declared joint second. Rovers defeated the same opposition 14-7 in the final of a Western League six-a-side tournament at St George in April.

In October 1895, a first foray into the FA Cup led to disappointment, as Rovers lost 2-0 at home to Warmley, 'Nipper' Britton, always a thorn in Rovers' collective side, and

Bill Bowler, from a classic header, scoring in the space of two first-half minutes on a rain-soaked pitch. The same opposition, this time by a single first-half Bowler goal, defeated Rovers in the 1896 Gloucestershire Cup Final, which produced takings of £161 10s 5d. Bill Demmery, a future Rovers goalkeeper, played for this Warmley team, while 'Nipper' Britton was appearing in one of his five Gloucestershire Cup finals. Rovers' side in the final was: W Stone, R Horsey (capt), F Lovett, H McBain, J Ross, G Hockin, W Thompson, R Osborne, H Gallier, G Brown, C Leese.

Rovers had beaten Bristol South End, the first meeting in this tournament with the future Bristol City, as well as St George and Bedminster to reach the final, but the 1-0 semi-final win at Greenway Bush Lane was overshadowed by tragedy. Bedminster's 27-year-old forward Herbert Edward Smith challenged Fred Lovett for the ball and received a head injury. Although he twice returned to the field, his injuries were such that he did not complete the match. Nonetheless, the serious nature of his condition went unnoticed and Smith returned home where he collapsed in the evening. Unconscious overnight, the young man never recovered and died at about six o'clock the following morning.

Eastville Rovers also defeated a Walkers Combination side 2-0 in April 1896, in a match played at Ridgeway for the benefit of Eastville cricket club, while the friendly at Bedminster that month was the last fixture played at the opposition's Greenway Bush Lane. A friendly against Swindon Wanderers in November 1895 had seen Rovers trail for an hour, yet recover to win through a goal from Lewis three minutes from time.

It had been a good season, but 1896/97 proved a tougher proposition as, despite winning a pre-season friendly 8-1 at Barton Hill who, in their chocolate and red shirts, had missed a first-half penalty before Richard Osborne scored a hat-trick, Rovers struggled in the Western League Division One. Prior to the start of the new season, Rovers played Singers, the forerunners of Coventry City and, 3-1 up by half-time, ran out 5-1 winners. One of their four goalscorers was Tommy McCairns, who was to enjoy several successful seasons with the club. He had scored six times when Grimsby Town defeated Leicester Fosse in a Second Division game the previous April. Until Easter 1897, home fixtures were still played at Ridgeway, including the first competitive game against the soon-to-be Bristol City, when a crowd of 3,000 saw Bristol South End win 2-0 through a first-half goal from H Porter and one after the interval from J S Ross.

This season, Rovers finished fifth out of nine clubs in Division One of the Western League, their biggest victory being 5-1 at home to Staple Hill in December. John McLean scored three times in that game, though F Gallier was the club's top scorer and captain Hugh McBain the only ever-present. Rovers lost to a very late penalty from 'Nipper' Britton at Warmley in February and, after what the *Western Daily Press* described as a 'wretched performance', lost 2-0 in April to a Clifton Association side which fielded only nine men. Rovers and Barton Hill also played out a 2-2 draw over Christmas in the first-ever Bristol Charity Cup fixture. This competition ran from 1896/97 to 1941/42, with clubs competing for a bowl donated by the jeweller C H. Flooks of Bristol and Merthyr Tydfil. Rovers were finalists in 1899/1900 before the tournament developed into a league format, after which the club's reserve and 'A' sides were winners on eleven occasions and shared the trophy in two further seasons. Rovers also beat Newbury, in a replay, and St George in the FA Cup but, drawn away to Royal

Eastville Rovers 1897/98. Back row: Pay (Trainer), Horsey, Farnall, Turley, Kinsey, Bunch, Roach, Shenton, Draycott. Front row: Cotterell, Jones, Green, Clithero, McLean

Artillery Portsmouth, decided they had no chance of avoiding a humiliating defeat and, saving the relatively steep travel expenses, withdrew from the competition. In the Gloucestershire Cup, victory over St Paul's was followed by defeat at Clifton Association, whilst Rovers went on to beat Clifton but lose to Bedminster in the Bristol Charity Cup.

Rovers arrived forty minutes late for an extraordinary New Year's Day Western League encounter at Bedminster. John McLean scored after twenty-five minutes and Bill Stone's goal put Rovers 2-0 ahead a minute before half-time. However, Rovers were by then reduced to nine men for, in the aftermath of a mass brawl, despite the paucity of sendings off in Victorian football, Shenton and Leese had been ordered off the field, along with the home side's Baugh. Rovers took to the field after half-time with one full-back and two half-backs, but were further hampered when goalkeeper John, injured earlier in the game, received a kick in the eye and was carried off. Stone reverted to his more customary goalkeeping position and, though McAuliffe pulled a goal back from Harris' pass, eight-man Rovers held out for a 2-1 victory.

Breaking even was an ongoing struggle which affected all local sides. For one Western League game with Fishponds, Rovers even charged their opponents and the referee admission to the ground. This was ruled excessive and the league ordered Rovers to refund those concerned. On another occasion, spectators supporting Rovers attempted to attack the referee and the club was instructed to supply suitable changing quarters for match officials. The fact that Rovers survived this era to grow into a major

SEASON 1896/97

WESTERN LEAGUE DIVISION ONE

Date	Opponent	H/A	Score	ATT	GOALSCORERS
19/09/1896	BEDMINSTER	H	0-1		
26/09/1896	BRISTOL SOUTH END	H	0-2	3000	
03/10/1896	TROWBRIDGE TOWN	A	0-3		
24/10/1896	STAPLE HILL	A	4-1		BROWN (2), McEWAN, BRACEY og
07/11/1896	ST PAULS	H	2-0		GALLIER, McBAIN
21/11/1896	WARMLEY	H	0-2		
05/12/1896	BRISTOL ST GEORGE	H	2-3		OSBORNE (2)
12/12/1896	STAPLE HILL	H	5-1		McLEAN(3), LEESE(2)
02/01/1897	BEDMINSTER	A	2-1		McLEAN, STONE
09/01/1897	BRISTOL SOUTH END	A	3-1		GALLIER(2), OSBORNE
16/01/1897	TROWBRIDGE TOWN	H	0-0		
06/02/1897	ST PAULS	A	1-1		McBAIN
20/02/1897	WARMLEY	A	1-2		OSBORNE
06/03/1897	CLIFTON	A	3-2		GALLIER(2), HORSEY
13/03/1897	BRISTOL ST GEORGE	A	2-1		GALLIER, HORSEY
21/04/1897	CLIFTON	H	0-2		

GLOUCESTERSHIRE CUP

Date	Opponent	H/A	Score	GOALSCORERS
30/01/1897	ST PAULS	H	1-0	McBAIN
27/02/1897	CLIFTON	H	0-1	

FA CUP

Date	Opponent	H/A	Score	ATT	GOALSCORERS
03/10/1896	NEWBURY	A	1-1		LEESE
14/10/1896	NEWBURY	H	2-1		OSBORNE, GALLIER
31/10/1896	BRISTOL ST GEORGE	H	1-0	3500	LEESE
21/11/1896	R A PORTSMOUTH*	A			

*Rovers scratched as they thought they had no chance of winning

BRISTOL CHARITY CUP

Date	Opponent	H/A	Score	GOALSCORERS
untraced	STAPLE HILL	H	2-2	
23/01/1897	CLIFTON	H	2-1	GALLIER, BUBB
10/04/1897	BEDMINSTER	H	0-2	

FRIENDLIES

Date	Opponent	H/A	Score	ATT	GOALSCORERS
05/09/1896	BARTON HILL	A	8-1		OSBORNE (3), THOMPSON (2), HARVEY (2), BROWN
12/09/1897	BRISTOL ST GEORGE	H	0-2		
17/10/1896	HEREFORD THISTLE	H	1-0		HOCKIN
14/11/1896	STAPLE HILL	A	1-1		LEESE
28/11/1896	HEREFORD THISTLE	H	1-1		GALLIER
19/12/1896	BRISTOL ST GEORGE	A	1-2		O'GRADY
26/12/1896	BRADFORD-ON-AVON	H	3-2		TURNER, BROWN, McLEAN
20/03/1897	BEDMINSTER	H	2-0		HORSEY, LEWIS og
27/03/1897	EBBW VALE	H	3-1		GALLIER, BROWN, HORSEY
03/04/1897	ASTON VILLA*	H	0-5	5000	
16/04/1897	SWINDON TOWN	H	1-6		OSBORNE
17/04/1897	BEDMINSTER	A	6-1		GALLIER(2), BROWN(2), OSBORNE, MCBain

* Match commemorated official opening of Eastville Stadium

force in football in the Bristol area is due partly to good management and partly to sheer chance. At this juncture even the league itself was, on occasions, out of pocket and Rovers donated £10 during 1896/97 to help stave off the Western League's large £120 debt.

During the course of the 1896/97 season, Rovers purchased a sixteen-acre site on heavy red clay soil, which stretched from the watercress meadows of Eastville along the river Frome to the Stapleton Gasworks and as far as the 'Thirteen Arches' on one of two nearby Great Western Railway branch lines. The stench from the gasworks behind what was later the Tote End was a familiar experience to hardened regulars in Rovers' years at Eastville and gave rise to the popular sobriquets 'The Gas' and 'Gasheads', by which the club and its supporters have been called ever since Rovers' departure from the ground in 1986. Eastville Stadium, formerly home to the Bristol Harlequins Rugby Football Club, was purchased for £150 from Sir Henry Greville Smyth of Ashton Court, an extensive landowner in late Victorian Bristol. It was 'a ground surrounded with a gasworks, a railway viaduct and a river that always threatened to swamp the ground' (C B Fry, 30 August 1919). The Frome, or 'Danny' as it was fondly termed locally, was highly susceptible to flooding and there had been terrible damage caused by rising waters in 1607 and 1703. In October 1882, just months before Rovers' formation, the Baptist Mills and Eastville areas were reported to be badly affected by flooding. Frederick Hunt, landlord of the 'Black Swan' on Stapleton Road, where Rovers were to be based until 1910, had stated he was ruined, as all his stock was under 5 feet of water. There was a fatality, too, as nineteen-year-old Frederick Foot, attempting to deliver bread from Williams' bakery of Lower Easton, was swept away by floodwater, along with his pony, from beside the railway bridge in Mina Road on 25 October 1882. Despite rescue attempts made by three locals and a policeman, both deliveryman and pony were drowned.

More recently, an area of some 200 acres had been flooded in March 1889 as snow thawed and Sevier Street was reported as impassable by 9 March. On 8 April 1889 it was reported that a Floods Relief Fund had raised £11,700. There were to be further problems of this nature in 1936, 1937, 1947 and 1968. In addition, there was water seven feet deep on Rovers' pitch on 21 November 1950. The Bristol Flood Prevention Acts of 1885 and 1890 promised a series of schemes but it was to be the Northern Stormwater Interceptor, incepted in 1962 and completed shortly after the floods six years later, which finally solved the problem. Much of the Frome is now intercepted at Eastville and taken underground to join the Avon at the Portway below Clifton Downs. Rovers thus inherited the 'Stapleton Road Enclosure', or 'Black Swan Ground' in 1897, a ground smelling of gas and sometimes underwater but which included a wooden stand capable of seating 501 spectators, a press box and a small directors' box with cloth-covered seats. A prompt investment of a further £1,255 ensured cover for the north side with the stated aim of creating a stadium capable of holding 20,000. Entry to the ground was from Stapleton Road for, parallel to the pitch and the river, was a rugby pitch occupied by the North Bristol Rugby Union Football Club.

On 26 March 1897 the club was registered as a Public Limited Liability Company under the name of Eastville Rovers. Just days later, on 3 April, a crowd of 5,000 watched the Football League and FA Cup double winners Aston Villa take on Rovers in the official opening game at Eastville Stadium. Villa, whose own ground at Villa Park was opened fourteen days later, won 5-0 and Swindon Town also won 6-1 there, before Rovers restored their self belief by winning a friendly 6-1 at Bedminster. Warmley defeated Bristol South End 2-1 before 2,000 spectators at Eastville in the Bristol Charity Cup final at the end of April. Rovers were, however, compelled to play one final game at Ridgeway, Clifton Association, who fielded only nine men, nonetheless winning through two second-half goals on 24 April, while Eastville was being used for an athletics meeting. It is no coincidence that the electric tramway reached Fishponds in 1897. Since the construction of the first line in Bristol from Perry Road to Redland in 1875, this means of rapid transport and communication had moved progressively closer, with the Horfield section opening in 1880. The growth of Rovers as a club mirrored the

SEASON 1897/98

BIRMINGHAM & DISTRICT LEAGUE

				ATT	GOALSCORERS
01/09/1897	WEST BROM ALBION RES	H	6-0	1200	McLEAN (2), GREEN, JONES, FARNALL
04/09/1897	SINGERS	A	2-1	2000	JONES, GREEN
11/09/1897	SHREWSBURY TOWN	H	1-0	2000	JONES
18/09/1897	SMALL HEATH RESERVES	A	4-2	7000	GREEN (2), JONES, McLEAN
02/10/1897	ASTON VILLA RESERVES	H	1-1	4531	CLITHEROE
09/10/1897	BRISTOL ST GEORGE	A	1-2	3000	COTTERELL
23/10/1897	BERWICK RANGERS	A	0-1	2000	
06/11/1897	WORCESTER ROVERS	H	4-0	3500	GREEN, McLEAN, JONES, TURLEY
13/11/1897	HALESOWEN	H	7-1	2000	GREEN (2), JONES (2), TURLEY, FARNALL, McLEAN
27/11/1897	WEST BROM ALBION RES	A	3-4		SEALEY (3)
29/11/1897	HALESOWEN	A	4-3		JONES (2), GREEN (2)
04/12/1897	SINGERS	H	11-3	3000	GREEN (4), JONES (2), COTTERELL, McLEAN, TURLEY, KINSEY, FARNALL
18/12/1897	STOURBRIDGE	H	2-1		COTTERELL, McLEAN
28/12/1897	SMALL HEATH RESERVES	H	1-3	4000	McLEAN
08/01/1898	BRIERLEY HILL ALLIANCE	H	4-0	2000	SAWERS, GREEN, McLEAN, JONES
15/01/1898	HEREFORD TOWN	A	1-0	3000	SAWERS
22/01/1898	WOLVES RESERVES	A	0-3		
05/02/1899	SHREWSBURY TOWN	A	2-1	2500	SAWERS, HORSEY
12/02/1898	HEREFORD THISTLE	H	3-0		HORSEY (2), McLEAN
19/02/1898	STOURBRIDGE	A	1-2	2000	JONES
05/03/1898	BERWICK RANGERS	H	2-0		KINSEY, McLEAN
12/03/1898	BRISTOL ST GEORGE	H	1-0		SMELLIE
19/03/1898	WORCESTER ROVERS	A	4-1		TURLEY (2-1pen), McWHINNIE (2)
23/03/1898	KIDDERMINSTER HARRIERS	H	5-0		SMELLIE (3), BUNCH, JONES
31/03/1898	HEREFORD THISTLE	A	2-2		JONES, SMELLIE
09/04/1898	BRIERLEY HILL ALLIANCE	A	3-0		McWHINNIE, JONES, McLEAN
11/04/1898	KIDDERMINSTER HARRIERS	A	3-2		JONES (2), SMELLIE
12/04/1898	WOLVES RESERVES	H	1-1		JONES
16/04/1898	HEREFORD TOWN	H	5-1	2000	SMELLIE (3), FARNALL, TURLEY
23/04/1898	ASTON VILLA RESERVES	A	0-0		

WESTERN LEAGUE PROFESSIONAL SECTION

15/09/1897	SWINDON TOWN	H	0-1	2000	
13/10/1897	BRISTOL CITY	A	0-4	3000	
25/12/1897	TROWBRIDGE TOWN	A	3-1	1500	
27/12/1897	BRISTOL ST GEORGE	A	1-1	3000	
01/01/1898	EASTLEIGH	A	3-1		
02/03/1898	READING	H	1-3	1000	
16/03/1898	BRISTOL CITY	H	2-3	4000	SMELLIE, McLEAN
30/03/1898	SWINDON TOWN	A	0-3		
02/04/1898	TROWBRIDGE TOWN	H	9-1	1200	SMELLIE (3), 6 untraced
08/04/1898	BRISTOL ST GEORGE	H	2-1	4000	
13/04/1898	WARMLEY	H	5-0	2000	
27/04/1898	READING	A	3-2	200	
30/04/1898	EASTLEIGH	H	8-1		SMELLIE (2), McLEAN (3), 3 untraced

FA CUP

25/09/1897	WARMLEY	A	0-0	5500	
29/09/1897	WARMLEY	H	6-2	1000	JONES (3), FIELD, McLEAN, GREEN
16/10/1897	BEDMINSTER	H	4-2	1000	COTTERELL (2), 2 untraced
30/10/1897	EASTLEIGH	H	2-0	2000	2 untraced
20/11/1897	COWES	H	6-2	3000	GREEN (3), KINSEY, COTTERELL, JONES
11/12/1897	SOUTHAMPTON	A	1-8	8000	

GLOUCESTERSHIRE CUP

29/01/1898	STAPLE HILL	H	5-0		COTTERELL (2), McLEAN, SAWYER, JONES
26/02/1898	BRISTOL CITY	A	0-2	6400	

BRISTOL CHARITY CUP

19/01/1898	READING	A	0-1	1000	

EASTVILLE ROVERS FOOTBALL CLUB, LIMITED.

INCOME ACCOUNT

From 5th April, 1897, to 31st May, 1898

	£	s	d		£	s	d
To Players Wages	1051	1	3	By Season Tickets &c	88	7	1
" Commission and Bonus	127	10					
" Match Expenses				" Gate Money and Sundry Receipts	1914	15	9
Tea Money, Hotel Expenses, Railway Fares — 170 6 9							
Players' Outfit — 45 5 9				" Sundries	40	.	2
Referees — 11 19 2							
Gatemen & Checkers — 1 12 9				" Balance to Balance Sheet	1237	14	..
Entrance Fees — 45 7 6	274	11	1				
" Gate Money paid away	499	1	6				
" Printing, Advertising, postage & Sundries	144	11	7				
" Formation of Ground including Wages, hauling, Horse Hire, Materials, Stands, Hoarding &c.	955	14	..				
" Law Expenses	37	14	6				
" Rent & Taxes	114	17	9				
" Players Insurance	25	5	..				
" Balance taken over from Old Club	47	1	4				
" Bankers Charges	3	8	2				
	£ 3280	17	..		£ 3280	17	..

Eastville Rovers' first Income Account for season 1897/98, which shows players' wages of £1,051

development of east Bristol so that, by the turn of the century, Eastville could boast a thriving society, well-established links with the centre of Bristol and a professional football club competing in the Southern League.

In registering themselves as a limited company and acquiring a permanent home, Rovers were pressing their claim for a place in the newly-flourishing professional Southern League, which had been formed in 1894. The Black Swan Hotel at 438 Stapleton Road, built around 1640, was adopted as the club's headquarters and was to remain as such until 1920. The new company was to have seven directors:

Samuel Sinclair Rinder (Ostrich Feather Manufacturer of 79 Stapleton Road)
Samuel Joy (Licensed Victualler of 'The Waggon and Horses', 83 Stapleton Road)
William Henry Brown (Gentleman of Chester Park Road, Fishponds)
Frederick W Hunt (Licensed Victualler, 'The Black Swan Hotel', 438 Stapleton Road)
Albert Beaven (Building Contractor of Gotley Lodge, Brislington)
Henry James Horsey (Commercial Clerk of Dove Steet, St George)
Imlah Hewys (Coal Merchant of Old Market)

The company was to sell 1,500 shares at £1 each to raise capital and its aims, as stated in its 'Memorandum of Association', were:

Black Swan Hotel, Stapleton Road, Eastville. This was Rovers secretary Alf Homer's home and office from late 1897 to about 1920

to promote the practice and play of football, cricket, lacrosse, lawn tennis, hockey, golf, bowls, bicycle and tricycle riding, running, jumping, skating, physical training and development of the physical frame and other athletic sports, games and exercise of every description and any other games, pastimes, sports recreations, amusements or entertainments.

The ever-improving standard of Western League football, coupled with the introduction of the electrified tram system around the city, led to a significant increase in support for football from the Bristol public. Around this time, the five major clubs in the area, Eastville Rovers, Warmley, Bristol St George, Bedminster and Bristol South End, began to pay their players. One of the first professionals at Eastville Rovers was John McLean, a Stoke-born player who earned his keep working through the summer as the club's groundsman. McLean's former professional contract at Port Vale led South End at first to query Rovers' payment to the player of 15s per week. Even though it was proved that South End had offered the same player 25s per week, the complaint was upheld and Rovers received a £1 fine and were deducted two Western League points, leaving the club with fourteen points from the sixteen Western League games played in 1896/97. Another early professional was George Kinsey, a 30-year-old half-back who had won four England caps and an FA Cup winners' medal in 1893 with Wolverhampton Wanderers. He had also represented Aston Villa and Derby County before arriving at Eastville as captain from Notts County. A Western League committee meeting on

SEASON 1898/99

BIRMINGHAM & DISTRICT LEAGUE

				ATT	GOALSCORERS
03/09/1898	WORCESTER ROVERS	H	8-1	3000	JONES (4), FISHER (2), PAUL (2)
10/09/1898	ASTON VILLA RESERVES	A	1-3	5000	McCAIRNS
17/09/1898	COVENTRY CITY	H	5-1	8000	BROWN (2), JONES, McCAIRNS, SMELLIE
24/09/1898	STOURBRIDGE	A	0-3	7000	
27/09/1898	BRIERLEY HILL ALLIANCE	A	3-0	6000	JONES (2), FISHER
01/10/1898	DUDLEY	H	8-0	2000	McCAIRNS (6), JONES (2)
08/10/1898	HALESOWEN	A	1-1		JONES
15/10/1898	HEREFORD TOWN	H	5-0	3000	JONES (2), FISHER, PAUL, FARNALL
22/10/1898	SHREWSBURY TOWN	A	4-2		TURLEY, BROWN, JONES, FISHER
05/11/1898	WORCESTER ROVERS	A	6-0		JONES (3), SMELLIE (2), BROWN
12/11/1898	SMALL HEATH RESERVES	H	6-3	3000	JONES (2), McCAIRNS (2), FISHER (2)
26/11/1898	KIDDERMINSTER HARRIERS	H	9-1		SMELLIE (3), JONES (2), FISHER (3), BROWN
03/12/1898	WOLVES RESERVES	A	1-1	3000	FARNALL
10/12/1898	HEREFORD THISTLE	H	10-2	1200	PAUL (3), SMELLIE (3), KINSEY, McCAIRNS, FISHER, BROWN
17/12/1898	WELLINGTON	A	6-1		McCAIRNS (2), FISHER, JONES, BROWN
27/12/1898	KIDDERMINSTER HARRIERS	A	0-0		
07/01/1899	ASTON VILLA RESERVES	H	2-3		BURTON, FISHER
14/01/1899	COVENTRY CITY	A	3-1		McCAIRNS (2), PAUL
04/02/1899	BRISTOL ST GEORGE	H	3-2	5500	FISHER, KINSEY, BROWN
11/02/1899	HEREFORD TOWN	A	1-2		SMELLIE
14/02/1899	WEST BROM ALBION RES	A	1-2		McCAIRNS
18/02/1899	SHREWSBURY TOWN	H	9-1	3500	McCAIRNS (5), JONES (2), BROWN, PAUL
25/02/1899	BRISTOL ST GEORGE	A	2-2	5000	McCAIRNS, FISHER
27/02/1899	HALESOWEN	H	5-4		McCAIRNS (2), FISHER, PAUL, FARNALL
04/03/1899	WEST BROM ALBION RES	H	10-0		McCAIRNS (3), PAUL (2), TURLEY (2), KINSEY, SMELLIE, BROWN
11/03/1899	SMALL HEATH RESERVES	A	1-2	3000	McCAIRNS
18/03/1899	BRIERLEY HILL ALLIANCE	H	6-0		McCAIRNS (2), JONES (2), FISHER, PAUL
01/04/1899	WOLVES RESERVES	H	1-2	5000	FISHER
04/04/1899	STOURBRIDGE	H	1-2		BROWN
08/04/1899	ASTON VILLA RESERVES	H	4-4	4000	JONES (2), McCAIRNS, FARNALL
09/04/1899	HEREFORD THISTLE	A	6-0		SMELLIE (2), UNDERWOOD, PEARCE, ALLEN, BUBB
15/04/1899	WELLINGTON	H	3-1		McCAIRNS (2), FISHER
17/04/1899	BERWICK RANGERS	H	3-3		JONES (2), FISHER
22/04/1899	BERWICK RANGERS	A	3-1		JONES, SMELLIE, FISHER
29/04/1899	DUDLEY	A	0-2	2000	

WESTERN LEAGUE PROFESSIONAL SECTION

07/09/1898	SWINDON TOWN	A	3-1		
14/09/1898	WARMLEY	H	5-0	2000	
21/09/1898	SOUTHAMPTON	H	3-1	3000	
05/10/1898	SWINDON TOWN	H	1-2	2000	
24/12/1898	BEDMINSTER	A	0-1	6000	
26/12/1898	BRISTOL ST GEORGE	H	2-3	14897	
28/01/1899	BEDMINSTER	H	2-2	2000	
01/03/1899	SOUTHAMPTON	A	1-7		
31/03/1899	BRISTOL ST GEORGE	A	2-2	4000	

FA CUP

29/10/1898	READING	H	0-1	8000	

GLOUCESTERSHIRE CUP

25/03/1899	BEDMINSTER	H	1-0	3000	JONES
03/04/1899	BRISTOL CITY*	N	1-2	11433	

* Final played at St George

BRISTOL CHARITY CUP

12/04/1899	READING	A	1-3	1000	

26 May 1897 voted unanimously to adopt professionalism from the start of the following season. In 1900, South End and Bedminster amalgamated to form Bristol City and, as quickly as professionalism had taken root, there were soon just two professional clubs in the Bristol area.

For the 1897/98 season, Rovers sported the Duke of Beaufort's racing colours of light blue and white hoops and were able to play league football in two leagues at their new stadium. The Western League established a Professional Division of eight clubs, four from Bristol plus Eastleigh, Reading, Swindon Town and Trowbridge Town, while Bedminster, who won all but their last game, won an Amateur Division which included Eastville Wanderers. Rovers never fully recovered from losing their first two games and Bristol City, as South End had begun to be known, were crowned champions. David Smellie, who scored nine times in only nine league games, had given Rovers a third-minute lead when the two sides met before a 4,000 crowd at Eastville in March, but McLean's goal five minutes from time served merely as a consolation as Rovers lost 3-2. Frank Seeley scored a hat-trick and yet ended up on the losing side, when Rovers lost 4-3 at Stoney Lane in November 1897. His two equalisers and a late consolation goal proved in vain and he next reappeared in the Rovers story as a member of the New Brompton side that played at Eastville in a Southern League fixture in October 1899. Rovers were able to record two large home victories in April. Trowbridge Town found themselves 3-0 down after only eleven minutes as Rovers, 5-0 up by half-time, won 9-1 thanks to a hat-trick from Smellie. He scored twice more, opening the scoring after only ten minutes as Rovers, with six second-half goals, beat Eastleigh 8-1 in the final match of the season, McLean scoring three times. Bristol City, by means of contrast, had scored fourteen times in their home fixture against the Hampshire side.

The shrewd aspirations of the board were, however, best illustrated by the club's participation in the Birmingham and District League. The three seasons spent in this league, between 1897 and 1900, proved tough but essential experience as Rovers prepared for the challenge the Southern League would offer. Despite some good victories, the strength of the reserve sides of Wolverhampton Wanderers, Aston Villa and West Bromwich Albion was too much for a young Rovers side at this stage. However, Rovers were able to attract a crowd of 4,500 to Eastville in October 1897 for the visit of Aston Villa reserves, while 4,000 paid £108 gate receipts to witness Rovers' 3-1 Christmas defeat at the hands of the reserve side of Small Heath, later Birmingham City. The biggest victory, 11-3 at home to Singers, the future Coventry City, saw Rovers compile a 6-2 half-time lead, despite trailing 2-1 early on, and score five more times while attacking the Railway End in the second half. This was the only occasion that all three of Rovers' half-backs scored in the same competitive fixture. George Green scored the eleventh to complete his hat-trick, while Tot Farnall, who scored the eighth, was a 26-year-old forward newly returned to Rovers after gaining Football League experience with Small Heath and Bradford City. Rovers also ran up five goals before half-time in defeating Halesowen 7-1 in November.

After two Cotterell goals had helped defeat Staple Hill 5-0, Rovers lost 2-0 to the eventual winners, Bristol City, in the Gloucestershire Cup. Billy Jones and Jock Russell scored the first-half goals in front of a crowd of 6,400, which produced gate receipts of £170. City's victory over the holders Warmley in the final took place on Rovers'

Sketch of Eastville Stadium published in The Magpie *newspaper on 27 April 1899*

Eastville pitch. The most unlikely of opponents, Reading, knocked Rovers out of the Bristol Charity Cup, a tournament won by Bedminster. The South Bristol side was, however, one of four clubs Rovers eliminated from the FA Cup to earn a place in the fifth qualifying round. Twenty-three-year-old Jack Jones, a summer signing from Small Heath with 35 Football League games to his name, had struck an early hat-trick against Warmley, while a second 6-2 victory, achieved over Cowes despite an own goal from goalkeeper Bill Stone, was secured through a George Green hat-trick after a visiting forward, Bill Baker, had been sent off in the first half. The fifth qualifying round tie at Southampton attracted a crowd of 8,000, but the Southern League champions overwhelmed Rovers and recorded an 8-1 win, with forwards Jimmy Yates, Bob Buchanan, Watty Keay and Joe Turner all scoring twice each. The Saints were to reach the FA Cup semi-finals before losing in a replay to First Division Nottingham Forest.

On 10 March 1898 the great local benefactor George Müller died in Bristol. His death had a profound effect on the community, for he had founded and established the Ashley Down orphanage and the main road to the west of Eastville Stadium was to bear his name. Born in Kroppenstedt in Prussia, some twenty-five miles south-west of Magdeburg on 27 September 1805, he had become very much an adopted son of Bristol, especially in this corner of the city, where the public had taken warmly to his pioneering work. By May 1886, some 7,294 children had been entrusted to his orphanages and the 'New Road' constructed in 1922 and 1923 was later renamed in his honour, so that the earth banking behind one goal at Eastville became known in the 1920s as the Muller Road End.

The 1898/99 season saw Rovers win just two out of eight Western League games and suffer early elimination from both the FA Cup and the Bristol Charity Cup. In the Gloucestershire Cup, a first-half Jack Jones goal defeated Bedminster, for whom the former Scottish international Bob Kelso appeared as captain at left-back, but Rovers lost the final to Bristol City 2-1 after a goal-less first forty-five minutes, Robert Brown scoring for Rovers. This final, played at Bell Hill, the home ground of Bristol St George, attracted an astonishingly high crowd of 11,433, easily the largest at any game involving Eastville Rovers, and took £356 in takings. City had finished in second place in both their opening Southern League seasons and their rivals' ongoing on-field success proved a spur to Rovers' directors in getting their club accepted into the competition. In the final, Rovers lined up: J Cook, W Bunch, A Griffiths, T Farnall, Burton, G Kinsey (captain), J McLean, R Brown, J Jones, D Smellie, J Paul.

It was, however, the strength of Rovers' performance in the Birmingham and District League which was their greatest asset. After finishing third in this league in 1897-98, Rovers were fourth in 1898-99, scoring 132 goals in only 34 matches. Twenty matches were won and only nine lost, just three of these at home. The squad was strengthened hugely by the signing in May 1898 of goalkeeper Richard Gray from Grimsby Town and forwards John Paul from Derby County and Bill Fisher from Burton Swifts. All three had played in the Football League the previous season, as had the returning Tommy McCairns, who now made a permanent move to Eastville. After Fisher's first-half goal had given Rovers a morale-boosting victory in a pre-season friendly against Bristol City, the team entered the 1898/99 campaign with high hopes.

In the opening fixture, Rovers scored six second-half goals in defeating Worcester City 8-1, with Jones scoring four times, twice in each half, and Fisher contributing the final two goals. Against Dudley, McCairns scored a hat-trick in the opening fifteen minutes and a fourth on the half-hour mark. Rovers ran up an 8-0 win, McCairns eventually claiming six of the goals. After finding themselves a goal down with only five minutes on the clock, Rovers beat Kidderminster 9-1, with Smellie scoring three times and Jones, Brown and Fisher twice each. Five goals in each half helped Rovers defeat Hereford Thistle 10-2, Paul scoring the opening three and Smellie claiming a second-half hat-trick. Jones scored a hat-trick in the game against Cowes which was later expunged when the opposition resigned from the league. A similar fate befell Brighton United, a side Rovers had defeated comfortably in January, despite a spurned second-half penalty from James Lamont and an injury to Tom Lee which left Rovers a man short. McCairns scored five times, including a hat-trick in the opening 26 minutes, as Rovers, playing for the first time under the name Bristol Rovers, defeated Shrewsbury 9-1 and three times in a 10-0 victory over West Bromwich Albion reserves. This final result, coupled with a compelling 4-4 draw with Aston Villa reserves, where second-half goals from McCairns, Farnall and Jones, his second of the game, hauled Rovers back from a 4-1 half-time deficit, showed just how far the side had progressed. Indeed, on 8 April the club put out two separate sides in league encounters.

Eastville Rovers had gradually become known as Bristol Eastville Rovers, especially as their reputation spread before them into the Midlands and South Wales and, on 7 February 1899, the club formally became Bristol Rovers, the name being approved by the Gloucestershire Football Association. It was under this new title that the directors applied for membership to join the prestigious Southern League. It was Rovers' good fortune that the May 1899 Annual General Meeting of this league was presided over by Samuel Rinder, a Rovers stalwart who had joined the club's board in 1897 and was to continue to support the side until his death, at the age of 64, on the Tuesday leading up to Easter 1919. Bristol Rovers, without further ado, were admitted to the First Division of the Southern League and a place in the Second Division for the reserve side was also secured.

Rovers did continue, however, to play in the Birmingham and District League for one final season and there was one astonishing result in 1899/1900. On 2 December 1899, Coventry City, as Singers FC were gradually becoming known, were defeated 7-6 at Eastville. Rovers took a fifth-minute lead through Bill Thompson and George Webster doubled the lead three minutes later. However, three Coventry goals, including two in a minute from M. Rideout, put the visitors ahead after just 21 minutes. Twice before half-time Rovers required equalisers to make the interval score 4-4. Thereafter seventeen-year-old Jack Lewis, who had not scored previously, grabbed a quick-fire hat-trick to give the home side a 7-4 lead which not even two late Coventry goals could overcome. The match had been refereed by Rovers' Bill Somerton until the delayed arrival of the appointed referee, Mr T Green of Redditch, but this extraordinary score-line was allowed to stand. Rovers also reached the Bristol Charity Cup final in 1899/1900, losing 4-1 to Bedminster before a 6,000 crowd at St John's Lane.

Rovers also continued to participate in the Western League well into the twentieth century. With the disappearance of Bedminster, who announced at the Annual General Meeting on 10 April 1900 that they would merge with Bristol City, Rovers became the only surviving side from the nine founder members eight years earlier. Rovers' first team and reserves appeared in the league until the end of the 1908/09 season and the reserves until 1920/21 and from 1925/26 to 1947/48, winning the title on five occasions. Rovers were represented by a Colts side in Western League football from 1948/49 until 1962/63.

[1] Richard Holt, 'Sport and British: A Modern History', Oxford University Press, 1989, p283.

[2] David J. Eveleigh, 'Bristol 1850-1919; Britain in Old Photographs series, Budding Books, 1996, p50.

[3] K. Theodore Hoppen, 'The Mid-Victorian Generation, 1846-1886', Clarendon Press, 1998, pp 353-4.

[4] Leonard Cohen, 'Greater Bristol by Lesser Columbus', Pelham, 1893, p1.

[5] David J. Eveleigh, 'Bristol 1850-1919', Britain in Old Photographs series, Budding Books, 1996, p11.

[6] Peter Sager, 'The West Country', Pallas Guides, 1996, p113.

1899/1900

Elevation to the Southern League in 1899 brought with it a number of changes at Eastville. The club changed its name to Bristol Rovers, the new title being given its consent by the Board of Trade on 13 October 1899. Alf Homer was appointed as Rovers' first full-time manager-secretary and the distinctive strip of black-and-white-striped shirts was adopted. These shirts, worn by Rovers throughout their years in Southern League football, were also the Gloucestershire FA colours and favoured the Duke of Beaufort's 'Badminton hoops'. Like the majority of fellow Southern League clubs, Rovers continued to put out a side in the Western League for many years. This situation allowed clubs to offer trial games to potential players and field reserve sides in competitive fixtures.

Homer, formerly assistant secretary at Villa Park, where he worked for the well-known administrator George Ramsey, brought a number of high-profile signings to Eastville. Tommy Tait, Jimmy Howie and James Young, all of whom were to win Scottish caps later in their careers, joined Rovers in the early Southern League years. For the 1899/1900 season Rovers relied on continuity, playing their opening game at Reading with George Kinsey still at centre-half and Jack Jones maintaining his position in the forward line. James Lamont, a steady right-half with Bedminster in two Western League games against Rovers in 1898/99, signed for the club and was to miss only one game all season. Arthur Rowley, who also played in that game at Reading, was a former Stoke full-back and laid claim to being the first Football League player to have scored from a direct free-kick. His goal for Port Vale in a 3-2 defeat against Bolton Wanderers in 1903 was fired past goalkeeper Dai Davies, a Welsh rugby International. Twenty-six-year-old Bill Robertson was signed from Small Heath, while the former Derby County and Notts County forward John Leonard arrived from Bedminster. The first Southern League game ended in a 3-0 defeat at Reading. Twenty-two-year-old former Bury outside-left Michael Kelly opened the scoring after 15 minutes, Richard 'Jammer' Evans added a second 20 minutes later and Richard Davies bagged the third half an hour from the end.

Two players who made their first appearances in the third game were Jack Lewis and Archie Ritchie. Inside-forward Lewis was a 17-year-old September signing from Kidderminster Harriers, who was to win a full Welsh cap during his second spell with Rovers in 1906. Ritchie, a right-back, had played for Nottingham Forest in the 1898 FA Cup final and was to give Rovers a reliable season's work. However, in only their second game, Rovers trailed 3-0 by half-time at Fratton Park to lose 8-2 to Portsmouth. Pompey had beaten Ryde 10-0 in an FA Cup tie only seven days earlier and four of their goals against Rovers came from Danny Cunliffe. It was to be April 1922 before Rovers next conceded eight goals in a competitive fixture.

Rovers were soon establishing themselves as a competent Southern League side. A 7-2 victory over Swindon Town, where Rovers led 4-2 at half-time, featured a Jack Jones hat-trick, while Tom McInnes scored three times against Gravesend United. Jones's hat-trick against Cowes and Boucher's three goals in a 6-0 victory over Chatham were

Bristol Rovers 1899/1900. Back row: Pay (Trainer), Farnall, Bunch, Cook, Griffiths, Turley, Kinsey. Middle row: McLean, Jones, McCairns, Smellie, Fisher. Front row: Brown, Paul

expunged from the records when the respective opponents resigned mid-season. The last game of 1899 saw Rovers fall a goal behind at home to Reading, before McInnes equalised from Brown's cross. Jones took advantage of defensive hesitancy to score the winner. Rovers beat Bedminster 5-2 in January, the only away win of the season, with Jones and John Paul scoring twice each, Ritchie contributing an own goal for Bedminster's second. Jones and Lewis both scored as Rovers drew with a strong Tottenham Hotspur side, after the initial fixture had been abandoned in the Eastville fog with Rovers a goal down after 55 minutes. The first 10,000 crowd at Eastville saw a solitary Bill Fisher goal, from a McInnes through ball 10 minutes before half-time, defeat Bristol City on Good Friday.

One notable opponent in this inaugural season was Herbert Chapman, later a highly influential manager at Huddersfield Town and Arsenal. His sole Southern League appearance against Rovers was for the Sheppey United side beaten 2-1 at Eastville in September, on the day Rovers recorded their first win in this league. In Western League football, an early-season game saw opponents Bedminster field three future Rovers players in Bill Davies, Bill Draycott and the former Notts County forward Tom Boucher, while Alf Geddes played for them against Rovers in a different fixture. The Minsters also fielded the former Northern Ireland International Robert Crone and former England goalkeeper George Toone at Eastville, while Francis Becton, winner of two England caps, appeared in their maroon and gold shirts in the Western League draw with Rovers in September.

After an early run of four defeats, Rovers performed sufficiently well to finish 11th in the Southern League, despite losing their final five away games. Jones finished as top

OGDEN'S CIGARETTES.

A. GRIFFITHS.

Arthur Griffiths. A consistent left full-back who played more than 100 Southern League matches

scorer with 11 Southern League goals, while Lamont, Lewis, Paul, Alf Griffiths, Robert Brown and goalkeeper Richard Gray all just missed the occasional game. In the FA Cup, Lewis scored three times in an easy five-goal victory over Eastleigh, with George Kinsey recording his final goal for the club, before Rovers were comprehensively beaten in a replay at Portsmouth. Two locally based representative sides met at St John's Lane on 9 October 1899 in aid of Western League Funds, when two first-half Jack Jones goals gave English Players, who also included Lewis, a 2-1 victory over Scottish Players – featuring four Rovers players in Ritchie, Lamont, Brown and Paul – before a 1,911 crowd. In addition, Rovers were finalists in the Bristol Charity Cup for the only time in the club's history, losing 4-1 to Bedminster for whom future Rovers players Tom Boucher and Alf Jasper Geddes scored. Rovers' third Annual Report revealed that players' wages from 1 June 1899 to 30 April 1900 were £2,196, while gate money had brought in £2,496.

SEASON 1899/1900

SOUTHERN LEAGUE DIVISION ONE

Date	Opponents		Score	ATT	G	2	3	4	5	6	7	8	9	10	11	Goalscorers
02/09/1899	READING	A	0-3	5500	GRAY	ROWLEY	GRIFFITHS A	LAMONT	KINSEY	ROBERTSON	LEONARD	JONES	VAIL	FISHER	PAUL	
09/09/1899	SHEPPEY UNITED	H	2-1	SMALL	GRAY	LEE	GRIFFITHS A	LAMONT	BROWN G	ROBERTSON	LEONARD	JONES	VAIL	FISHER	PAUL	LAMONT, PAUL
23/09/1899	BEDMINSTER	H	0-3	8000	STONE	RITCHIE	GRIFFITHS A	LAMONT	LEE	ROBERTSON	LEONARD	JONES	FISHER	LEWIS	PAUL	
07/10/1899	PORTSMOUTH	A	2-8	7000	STONE	RITCHIE	WELSH	LAMONT	LEE	KINSEY	BROWN R	JONES	LEONARD	FISHER	PAUL	LEONARD (2)
14/10/1899	NEW BROMPTON	H	0-1	6000	GRAY	RITCHIE	ROWLEY	LEE	LAMONT	KINSEY	LEONARD	JONES	PAUL	LEWIS	McINNES	
04/11/1899	GRAVESEND UNITED	A	3-5	3000	GRAY	RITCHIE	GRIFFITHS A	LAMONT	ROBERTSON	KINSEY	BROWN R	LEWIS	JONES	FISHER	McINNES	JONES, FISHER, McINNES
11/11/1899	SWINDON TOWN	H	7-2	15000	GRAY	RITCHIE	GRIFFITHS A	LAMONT	ROBERTSON	LEE	BROWN R	LEWIS	JONES	FISHER	PAUL	JONES (3), BROWN R, FISHER, PAUL, 1 untraced
02/12/1899	SOUTHAMPTON	A	0-4	LARGE	GRAY	RITCHIE	GRIFFITHS A	LAMONT	ROBERTSON	LEE	BROWN R	LEWIS	McINNES	FISHER	PAUL	
09/12/1899	SHEPPEY UNITED	A	3-1	5000	GRAY	RITCHIE	GRIFFITHS A	LAMONT	ROBERTSON	LEE	BROWN R	LEWIS	JONES	FISHER	PAUL	FISHER 2, BROWN R
16/12/1899	QUEENS PARK RANGERS	A	0-3	5000	GRAY	RITCHIE	GRIFFITHS A	LAMONT	BROWN G	LEE	BROWN R	LEWIS	JONES	FISHER	PAUL	
23/12/1899	CHATHAM	H	4-1	4000	GRAY	RITCHIE	GRIFFITHS A	LAMONT	ROBERTSON	LEE	BROWN R	LEWIS	JONES	FISHER	PAUL	LEWIS (2), JONES, LAMONT (pen)
26/12/1899	BRISTOL CITY	A	0-1	3000	GRAY	LEE	GRIFFITHS A	LAMONT	BROWN G	ROBERTSON	BROWN R	LEWIS	JONES	FISHER	PAUL	
30/12/1899	READING	H	1-5	FAIR	GRAY	LEE	GRIFFITHS A	LAMONT	BROWN G	ROBERTSON	BROWN R	LEWIS	JONES	McINNES	PAUL	McINNES, JONES
15/01/00	THAMES IRONWORKS	H	1-1	2000	GRAY	RITCHIE	GRIFFITHS A	LAMONT	BROWN G	KINSEY	BROWN R	LEWIS	ROBERTSON	McINNES	PAUL	PAUL
20/01/00	BEDMINSTER	A	5-2	1000	GRAY	RITCHIE	GRIFFITHS A	LAMONT	BROWN G	ROBERTSON	BROWN R	LEWIS	JONES	McINNES	PAUL	PAUL (2), JONES (2), LEWIS
10/02/00	PORTSMOUTH	H	4-0	6000	GRAY	RITCHIE	GRIFFITHS A	LAMONT	ROBERTSON	LEE	BROWN R	LEWIS	JONES	McINNES	PAUL	JONES, BROWN R, McINNES (2)
17/02/00	THAMES IRONWORKS	A	0-0	5000	GRAY	RITCHIE	GRIFFITHS A	LAMONT	BROWN G	ROBERTSON	BROWN R	LEWIS	JONES	McINNES	PAUL	
24/02/00	TOTTENHAM HOTSPUR	H	2-2	6000	GRAY	RITCHIE	GRIFFITHS A	LAMONT	BROWN G	ROBERTSON	BROWN R	LEWIS	JONES	McINNES	PAUL	JONES, LEWIS
03/03/00	NEW BROMPTON	A	0-2	6000	GRAY	RITCHIE	GRIFFITHS A	LAMONT	ROBERTSON	LEE	BROWN R	LEWIS	JONES	McINNES	PAUL	
14/03/00	MILLWALL	A	3-0	4000	GRAY	RITCHIE	GRIFFITHS A	LAMONT	ROBERTSON	LEE	BROWN R	LEWIS	JONES	McINNES	PAUL	McINNES, PAUL, JONES
17/03/00	SWINDON TOWN	A	0-1	2000	GRAY	RITCHIE	GRIFFITHS A	LAMONT	ROBERTSON	LEE	BROWN R	LEWIS	JONES	McINNES	PAUL	
19/03/00	TOTTENHAM HOTSPUR	A	1-5	3000	GRAY	HORSEY	GRIFFITHS A	LAMONT	BROWN G	LEE	BROWN R	LEWIS	JONES	McINNES	PAUL	LEWIS
07/04/00	SOUTHAMPTON	H	1-3	5000	GRAY	LEE	RITCHIE	LAMONT	ROBERTSON	BROWN G	BROWN R	LEWIS	JONES	McINNES	PAUL	JONES
13/04/00	BRISTOL CITY	H	1-0	10000	GRAY	RITCHIE	GRIFFITHS A	LAMONT	ROBERTSON	BROWN G	BROWN R	LEWIS	FISHER	McINNES	PAUL	FISHER
14/04/00	MILLWALL	H	0-2	5000	GRAY	RITCHIE	GRIFFITHS A	LAMONT	ROBERTSON	BROWN G	BROWN R	LEWIS	FISHER	McINNES	PAUL	
18/04/00	GRAVESEND UNITED	H	3-1	LARGE	GRAY	RITCHIE	GRIFFITHS A	LAMONT	ROBERTSON	LEE	BROWN R	LEWIS	HARRIS	McINNES	PAUL	McINNES 3
21/04/00	QUEENS PARK RANGERS	H	1-0	2000	GRAY	RITCHIE	GRIFFITHS A	LAMONT	ROBERTSON	LEE	BROWN R	LEWIS	HARRIS	McINNES	PAUL	HARRIS
28/04/00	CHATHAM	A	1-2	1000	GRAY	RITCHIE	GRIFFITHS A	LAMONT	ROBERTSON	LEE	BROWN R	LEWIS	JONES	McINNES	PAUL	McINNES

FA CUP

Date	Opponents		Score	ATT	G	2	3	4	5	6	7	8	9	10	11	Goalscorers
28/10/1899	EASTLEIGH	H	5-0	3000	GRAY	RITCHIE	GRIFFITHS A	LAMONT	ROBERTSON	KINSEY	BROWN R	LEWIS	JONES	FISHER	PAUL	JONES, LEWIS (3), KINSEY
18/11/1899	PORTSMOUTH	H	1-1	4000	GRAY	RITCHIE	GRIFFITHS A	LAMONT	ROBERTSON	LEE	BROWN R	LEWIS	JONES	FISHER	PAUL	FISHER
22/11/1899	PORTSMOUTH	A	0-4	6000	GRAY	RITCHIE	GRIFFITHS A	LAMONT	ROBERTSON	LEE	BROWN R	LEWIS	JONES	FISHER	PAUL	

GLOUCESTERSHIRE CUP

Date	Opponents		Score	ATT	G	2	3	4	5	6	7	8	9	10	11	Goalscorers
02/04/00	BRISTOL CITY *	H	1-1	3000	GRAY	RITCHIE	GRIFFITHS A	LAMONT	ROBERTSON	BROWN G	BROWN R	LEWIS	JONES	McINNES	PAUL	JONES
09/04/00	BRISTOL CITY *	A	1-0	2000	GRAY	RITCHIE	GRIFFITHS A	LAMONT	ROBERTSON	BROWN G	BROWN R	LEWIS	JONES	McINNES	PAUL	PAUL

*Semi Final

Players	Apps	Gls
BROWN G	13	
BROWN R	24	3
FISHER W	12	5
GRAY R	26	
GRIFFITHS A	25	
HARRIS G	2	1
HORSEY H	1	
JONES J	23	12
KINSEY G	5	
LAMONT J	27	2
LEE T	20	
LEONARD J	5	2
LEWIS J	25	5
McINNES T	19	9
PAUL J	27	6
RITCHIE A	22	
ROBERTSON W	25	
ROWLEY A	2	
STONE W	2	
VAIL T	2	
WELSH C	1	
untraced		1

Rovers opened the new season with a confidence-boosting run of four wins and a draw in their opening five games. Yet the team that started the season against Queen's Park Rangers included eight new faces. Bill Draycott, the former Boltonian Bill Davies and Tom Boucher, who scored the club's first goal of the new season, had all joined from Bedminster. Inside-left Hillary Griffiths had played for Wolverhampton Wanderers in their 2-1 defeat against Sheffield Wednesday in the 1896 FA Cup final. Jack Kifford, a July signing from Derby County, was ever-present in his sole season with Rovers, while Billy Clarke, later the winner of a Division Two Championship medal in 1907/08 with Bradford City, arrived from East Stirlingshire.

This was a highly satisfying season for Alf Homer's side. Rovers never lost more than two consecutive games and recorded some convincing wins. Boucher scored twice in a 4-0 win at Gravesend United. Jack Jones grabbed a hat-trick in February against a Watford side that included Tot Farnall. Jones, though, went one better when Gravesend played their return game at Eastville just after Christmas. Rovers' 10-0 win that day was to be the side's largest victory in 17 Southern League seasons. It took Rovers 25 minutes to open the scoring before Jackie Neilson scored two of five Rovers goals in 15 minutes. Jones, who had scored the third, also added a 19-minute second-half hat-trick, with Gravesend reduced by injury to only ten men.

An advert, which appeared in the Athletic News *on 29 April 1901, asking for players*

SEASON 1900/1901

SOUTHERN LEAGUE DIVISION ONE

Date	Opponent		Result	Att	G	2	3	4	5	6	7	8	9	10	11	Goalscorers
01/09/00	QUEENS PARK RANGERS	H	2-1	7000	GRAY	KIFFORD	GRIFFITHS A	DRAYCOTT	ROBERTSON	NEILSON	WILLIAMS	CLARKE	BOUCHER	GRIFFITHS H	PAUL	BOUCHER, WILLIAMS
08/09/00	READING	A	1-1	3000	GRAY	KIFFORD	GRIFFITHS A	DRAYCOTT	ROBERTSON	NEILSON	WILLIAMS	JONES	BOUCHER	GRIFFITHS H	PAUL	PAUL
15/09/00	KETTERING TOWN	H	3-1	4000	GRAY	KIFFORD	GRIFFITHS A	DRAYCOTT	ROBERTSON	NEILSON	WILLIAMS	JONES	BOUCHER	GRIFFITHS H	PAUL	NEILSON, BOUCHER, GRIFFITHS H
22/09/00	GRAVESEND UNITED	A	4-0	1200	GRAY	KIFFORD	GRIFFITHS A	DRAYCOTT	ROBERTSON	NEILSON	CLARKE	JONES	BOUCHER	GRIFFITHS H	PAUL	BOUCHER (2), PAUL, JONES
29/09/00	MILLWALL	H	2-1	7000	GRAY	KIFFORD	GRIFFITHS A	DRAYCOTT	ROBERTSON	NEILSON	CLARKE	JONES	BOUCHER	GRIFFITHS H	PAUL	BOUCHER, PAUL
06/10/00	SOUTHAMPTON	A	3-5	5000	GRAY	KIFFORD	GRIFFITHS A	DRAYCOTT	ROBERTSON	NEILSON	WILLIAMS	JONES	BOUCHER	GRIFFITHS H	PAUL	JONES, GRIFFITHS H, 1 untraced
20/10/00	BRISTOL CITY	A	0-1	15500	GRAY	KIFFORD	GRIFFITHS A	DRAYCOTT	ROBERTSON	NEILSON	CLARKE	JONES	BOUCHER	GRIFFITHS H	PAUL	
27/10/00	SWINDON TOWN	H	1-0	LARGE	GRAY	KIFFORD	GRIFFITHS A	DAVIES	ROBERTSON	NEILSON	CLARKE	JONES	BOUCHER	GRIFFITHS H	PAUL	BOUCHER
10/11/00	LUTON TOWN	H	1-0	5000	GRAY	KIFFORD	GRIFFITHS A	DRAYCOTT	ROBERTSON	NEILSON	CLARKE	JONES	BOUCHER	GRIFFITHS H	PAUL	GRIFFITHS H
24/11/00	WEST HAM UNITED	H	2-0	5000	BOYCE	KIFFORD	GRIFFITHS A	DRAYCOTT	ROBERTSON	NEILSON	CLARKE	JONES	BOUCHER	GRIFFITHS H	PAUL	JONES, GRIFFITHS H
01/12/00	PORTSMOUTH	A	0-1	4000	GRAY	KIFFORD	GRIFFITHS A	DRAYCOTT	ROBERTSON	NEILSON	CLARKE	JONES	BOUCHER	GRIFFITHS H	PAUL	
15/12/00	QUEENS PARK RANGERS	A	3-4	3000	GRAY	KIFFORD	GRIFFITHS A	DAVIES	ROBERTSON	NEILSON	CLARKE	JONES	BOUCHER	GRIFFITHS H	PAUL	CLARKE, BOUCHER, PAUL
22/12/00	READING	H	0-0	FAIR	GRAY	KIFFORD	GRIFFITHS A	NICHOLLS	ROBERTSON	NEILSON	CLARKE	JONES	BOUCHER	GRIFFITHS H	WILLIAMS	
27/12/00	GRAVESEND UNITED	H	10-0	2000	GRAY	KIFFORD	GRIFFITHS A	NICHOLLS	ROBERTSON	NEILSON	CLARKE	JONES	BOUCHER	GRIFFITHS H	WILLIAMS	JONES (4), CLARKE, BOUCHER, NEILSON (2), GRIFFITHS (2)
29/12/00	KETTERING TOWN	A	0-1	1000	GRAY	KIFFORD	GRIFFITHS A	DAVIES	ROBERTSON	NEILSON	CLARKE	JONES	BOUCHER	GRIFFITHS H	PAUL	
12/01/01	MILLWALL	A	0-4	6000	GRAY	KIFFORD	GRIFFITHS A	DAVIES	ROBERTSON	NEILSON	CLARKE	JONES	BOUCHER	GRIFFITHS H	PAUL	
19/01/01	SOUTHAMPTON	H	0-0	5000	GRAY	KIFFORD	GRIFFITHS A	DRAYCOTT	ROBERTSON	NEILSON	CLARKE	JONES	BOUCHER	GRIFFITHS H	PAUL	
26/01/01	TOTTENHAM HOTSPUR	A	0-4	6000	GRAY	KIFFORD	GRIFFITHS A	DAVIES	ROBERTSON	NEILSON	CLARKE	JONES	BOUCHER	GRIFFITHS H	PAUL	
16/02/01	SWINDON TOWN	A	1-0	6000	GRAY	KIFFORD	GRIFFITHS A	DAVIES	ROBERTSON	NEILSON	CLARKE	WILLIAMS	BOUCHER	GRIFFITHS H	PAUL	BOUCHER
23/02/01	WATFORD	H	4-1	4000	GRAY	KIFFORD	GRIFFITHS A	DAVIES	ROBERTSON	NEILSON	CLARKE	JONES	WILLIAMS	GRIFFITHS H	PAUL	JONES 3, PAUL
02/03/01	LUTON TOWN	H	1-0	2000	GRAY	KIFFORD	GRIFFITHS A	DAVIES	ROBERTSON	LEE	CLARKE	JONES	WILLIAMS	GRIFFITHS H	PAUL	WILLIAMS
09/03/01	TOTTENHAM HOTSPUR	H	1-0	5000	GRAY	KIFFORD	GRIFFITHS A	DAVIES	ROBERTSON	NEILSON	WILLIAMS	JONES	BOUCHER	GRIFFITHS H	PAUL	ROBERTSON
16/03/01	WEST HAM UNITED	A	0-2	4000	GRAY	KIFFORD	GRIFFITHS A	DAVIES	ROBERTSON	NEILSON	WILLIAMS	JONES	BOUCHER	GRIFFITHS H	PAUL	
23/03/01	WATFORD	A	1-2	600	GRAY	KIFFORD	LEE	DAVIES	ROBERTSON	NEILSON	WILLIAMS	JONES	BOUCHER	GRIFFITHS H	PAUL	PAUL
23/03/01	PORTSMOUTH	H	2-1	4000	GRAY	KIFFORD	GRIFFITHS A	DAVIES	ROBERTSON	NEILSON	CLARKE	JONES	BOUCHER	GRIFFITHS H	PAUL	PAUL, ROBERTSON
08/04/01	BRISTOL CITY	H	1-1	10000	GRAY	KIFFORD	GRIFFITHS A	DAVIES	ROBERTSON	NEILSON	CLARKE	JONES	BOUCHER	GRIFFITHS H	WILLIAMS	WILLIAMS
10/04/01	NEW BROMPTON	H	3-2	6000	GRAY	KIFFORD	GRIFFITHS A	DRAYCOTT	ROBERTSON	NEILSON	CLARKE	JONES	BOUCHER	GRIFFITHS H	WILLIAMS	JONES, BOUCHER, CLARKE
17/04/01	NEW BROMPTON	A	0-2	1500	GRAY	KIFFORD	GRIFFITHS A	DAVIES	ROBERTSON	NEILSON	CLARKE	WILLIAMS	BOUCHER	GRIFFITHS H	PAUL	

FA CUP

Date	Opponent		Result	Att	G	2	3	4	5	6	7	8	9	10	11	Goalscorers
17/11/00	WEYMOUTH	H	15-1	SMALL	GRAY	KIFFORD	GRIFFITHS A	DRAYCOTT	DAVIES	NEILSON	CLARKE	JONES	WILLIAMS	GRIFFITHS H	PAUL	JONES (6), CLARKE (3), WILLIAMS (3), GRIFFITHS H (2), PAUL
08/12/00	SWINDON TOWN	H	5-1	5000	GRAY	KIFFORD	GRIFFITHS A	DRAYCOTT	ROBERTSON	NEILSON	CLARKE	JONES	BOUCHER	GRIFFITHS H	DAVIES	JONES(2), CLARKE, NEILSON, GRIFFITHS H
05/01/01	LUTON TOWN	A	2-1	4000	GRAY	KIFFORD	GRIFFITHS A	DRAYCOTT	ROBERTSON	NEILSON	DAVIES	JONES	BOUCHER	GRIFFITHS H	PAUL	JONES, BOUCHER
09/02/01	READING	A	0-2	SMALL	GRAY	KIFFORD	GRIFFITHS A	DRAYCOTT	ROBERTSON	NEILSON	DAVIES	JONES	BOUCHER	GRIFFITHS H	PAUL	

GLOUCESTERSHIRE CUP FINAL

Date	Opponent		Result	Att	G	2	3	4	5	6	7	8	9	10	11	Goalscorers
29/04/01	BRISTOL CITY	A	0-4	2800	GRAY	KIFFORD	GRIFFITHS A	DRAYCOTT	ROBERTSON	LEE	CLARKE	JONES	BOUCHER	GRIFFITHS H	PAUL	

PLAYERS	APPS	GLS
BOUCHER T	27	10
BOYCE A	1	
CLARKE W	21	3
DAVIES W	12	
DRAYCOTT W	14	
GRAY R	27	
GRIFFITHS A	27	
GRIFFITHS H	28	6
JONES J	25	11
KIFFORD J	28	
LEE T	2	
NEILSON J	27	3
NICHOLLS	2	
PAUL J	24	7
ROBERTSON W	28	2
WILLIAMS W	16	2
untraced		1

A crowd of 10,000 at Eastville for the local derby in April saw Rovers draw 1-1 with Bristol City, thanks to a goal after 35 minutes from Bill Williams. However, a new ground record at Ashton Gate of 15,500, bringing gate receipts of £380, saw Rovers lose 1-0 to a second-half Bill Michael goal in October. When the sides drew 1-1 in the Western League on Boxing Day, City's scorer was John McLean, who was to join Rovers in 1902. Fred Corbett, a Rovers player only months later, scored the opening goal in West Ham's 2-0 win in March, while John Lewis, sold to Portsmouth, fired in the only goal of the game with a low shot 10 minutes after half-time when Rovers visited Fratton Park in December.

Over New Year, immediately following the ten goals against Gravesend, Rovers hit a goal drought. It was five games before the side next scored, Boucher's headed winner five minutes

Jack Jones netted a record six goals against Weymouth in an FA Cup tie on 17 November 1900

from time at Swindon Town sparking a run of four straight victories. The goalless run had included 4-0 defeats at both Millwall and Tottenham Hotspur. At White Hart Lane, both sides wore armbands in respect for Queen Victoria, who had died four days earlier. Rovers conceded three first-half goals and a last-minute Cameron free-kick. Fred Bevan followed up his two goals in that game against Millwall with two more when the London side won 4-1 in a Western League match at Eastville five weeks later. Millwall also inflicted a 5-0 defeat on Rovers in the Western League in December, with George Henderson and Bert Banks, later a Bristol City player, scoring twice each.

Rovers were expected to defeat Weymouth in the FA Cup but the poor attendance reflects the fact that few would have predicted the glut of goals. Hill Griffiths put Rovers ahead with a tap-in after only three minutes, while Jack Jones, with two long-range shots, and Billy Williams had scored twice each before the visitors' centre-forward Murphy pulled a goal back on the stroke of half-time. Rovers then scored ten second-half goals to record a 15-1 victory, the club's record score in any competitive first-team match. Billy Clarke scored a second-half hat-trick, his second goal being a spectacular long-distance strike, while Williams ended up with three goals and Jones six. Hill Griffiths scored his second of the game, Rovers' 13th and John Paul scored the 15th. This was the only occasion a Rovers player has scored six goals in one game, though Jones almost repeated the feat 12 months later against the same opposition. It was also the only time three Rovers players have scored hat-tricks in the same game.

Jones scored twice more in the next round, as Rovers beat Swindon Town, and once in the victory at Luton Town, before Rovers lost at Reading in the first round proper. The FA Cup run had seen Rovers score 22 goals and concede only five. Jones' nine FA Cup goals remain a club seasonal record, though his own tally in 1901/02 and that of Jason Roberts in 1998/99 were not far behind. Clarke and Williams both scored more

Cup than League goals. The Gloucestershire Cup final was lost 4-0 to Bristol City, who gained Football League status over the following summer. City had boldly and over-ambitiously sought membership of the Football League at the Annual General Meeting of that organization on 20 May 1898, at the end of their first season of professionalism. Now, despite a financial deficit of £2,000 incurred during the 1900/01 season, the Ashton Gate club tried again, displaying a degree of ambition that Rovers' directors were not prepared to follow, and were duly elected to Division Two in place of Walsall.

1901/02

It was a largely new-look Rovers side that lost its opening six Southern League games before consolidation brought a final placing of ninth. Tom Boucher had joined Bristol City, while Bill Clarke had moved to Aston Villa, after which he later appeared for Bradford City and Lincoln City. Right-back Jack Kifford joined West Bromwich Albion in June and played for Millwall, Carlisle United and Coventry City before joining Fred Karno's circus troupe in 1909.

Young goalkeeper Arthur Cartlidge, a key figure through the decade, arrived from Stoke. He was Rovers' only ever-present in the Southern League in 1901/02. The signing of full-back Hugh Dunn from Preston North End was inspired, since he had previously spent three successful years at West Bromwich Albion, culminating in an FA Cup semi-final. Further experience was added through the re-signing of 30-year-old right-half Tot Farnall from Watford for his third spell at the club. Younger talent was also allowed to emerge, most notably in the shape of Fred Wilcox, a 21-year-old August signing from Glendale. Wilcox was to score four times in Rovers' largest win of the season, a midweek 8-1 victory over Wellingborough at the end of February.

The alarm bells began to ring after six straight defeats. The worst result had been a four-goal loss at Watford who featured Billy Wragg, who later appeared on stage alongside Stan Laurel and Charlie Chaplin. Homer's response was to sign two new forwards. Fred Corbett had scored West Ham United's second goal in their opening day victory at Eastville, while Alf Jasper Geddes, a former Bristol City player standing just five feet four inches tall, could boast an impressive pedigree, having scored for West Bromwich Albion in the 1892 FA Cup final when they had beaten Aston Villa 3-0.

With Corbett, Wilcox and Jack Jones in the forward line, Rovers' fortunes revived. All three were to score Southern League hat-tricks. Corbett scored all the goals in a 3-0 victory over Kettering Town in February and ended the season with 11 goals, three behind Jones. Wilcox's eight goals came in only three games, as he and Corbett both scored twice each against Brentford on Good Friday, with Rovers three goals ahead before half-time, and against Luton Town eight days later. Going into the final game of the season, Jones and Corbett had, in fact, scored 11 Southern League goals each. But the former marked what was to be his final appearance for the club with a finely-taken hat-trick, as Rovers defeated Queen's Park Rangers 4-1, to complete a third consecutive season as the club's top scorer. In so doing, he also set Rovers' Southern League goalscoring record at 36 goals.

SOUTHERN LEAGUE DIVISION ONE

SEASON 1901/02

Date	Opponent	H/A	Score	ATT	G	2	3	4	5	6	7	8	9	10	11	GOALSCORERS
07/09/01	WEST HAM UNITED	H	0-2	5000	CARTLIDGE	DUNN	GRIFFITHS	FARNALL	ROBERTSON	NEILSON	LYON	JONES	HULME	PIERCE	BECTON	
14/09/01	NEW BROMPTON	A	0-3	3000	CARTLIDGE	DUNN	GRIFFITHS	FARNALL	ROBERTSON	NEILSON	LYON	JONES	McINTYRE	PIERCE	BECTON	
21/09/01	NORTHAMPTON TOWN	H	1-2	4000	CARTLIDGE	DUNN	GRIFFITHS	FARNALL	ROBERTSON	LYON	MUIR	JONES	McINTYRE	PIERCE	BECTON	NEILSON
28/09/01	WATFORD	A	0-4	3000	CARTLIDGE	BOULTON	DAVIES	FARNALL	ROBERTSON	NEILSON	MUIR	JONES	JONES	PIERCE	BECTON	
05/10/01	TOTTENHAM HOTSPUR	H	1-2	7000	CARTLIDGE	DUNN	GRIFFITHS	FARNALL	ROBERTSON	NEILSON	MUIR	JONES	JONES	LYON	JONES	JONES
12/10/01	WELLINGBOROUGH	A	1-2	2000	CARTLIDGE	DUNN	BOULTON	FARNALL	ROBERTSON	NEILSON	MUIR	PIERCE	JONES	PIERCE	JONES	DUNN
19/10/01	PORTSMOUTH	H	1-1	LARGE	CARTLIDGE	DUNN	GRIFFITHS	FARNALL	DAVIES	LYON	MUIR	JONES	GEDDES	BECTON	BECTON	FARNALL T
26/10/01	SWINDON TOWN	A	1-0	2000	CARTLIDGE	DUNN	GRIFFITHS	FARNALL	DAVIES	LYON	MUIR	JONES	GEDDES	BECTON	JONES	GEDDES J
09/11/01	KETTERING TOWN	H	0-0	1000	BOULTON	DUNN	DAVIES	FARNALL	NEILSON	LYON	MUIR	WILCOX	JONES	GEDDES	BECTON	GEDDES J
07/12/01	READING	A	1-2	3000	CARTLIDGE	DUNN	GRIFFITHS	NEILSON	DAVIES	LYON	MUIR	JONES	CORBETT	JONES	BECTON	JONES
21/12/01	WEST HAM UNITED	A	0-2	2000	CARTLIDGE	DUNN	GRIFFITHS	FARNALL	DAVIES	LYON	MUIR	JONES	CORBETT	WILCOX	BECTON	
04/01/02	NEW BROMPTON	H	2-1	4000	CARTLIDGE	DUNN	GRIFFITHS	FARNALL	NEILSON	LYON	MUIR	JONES	CORBETT	WILCOX	BECTON	CORBETT, NEILSON
11/01/02	NORTHAMPTON TOWN	A	3-0	5000	CARTLIDGE	DUNN	GRIFFITHS	FARNALL	NEILSON	LYON	MUIR	JONES	CORBETT	WILCOX	BECTON	CORBETT 2, JONES
18/01/02	WATFORD	H	2-2	2000	CARTLIDGE	DUNN	GRIFFITHS	FARNALL	DAVIES	NEILSON	MUIR	JONES	CORBETT	WILCOX	JONES	NEILSON MUIR
01/02/02	TOTTENHAM HOTSPUR	A	0-1	6000	CARTLIDGE	DUNN	HULME	FARNALL	DAVIES	LYON	MUIR	JONES	CORBETT	WILCOX	BECTON	
15/02/02	PORTSMOUTH	A	0-3	4000	CARTLIDGE	DUNN	GRIFFITHS	FARNALL	DAVIES	LYON	MUIR	WILCOX	CORBETT	LAMB	BECTON	
22/02/02	BRENTFORD	H	0-2	1000	CARTLIDGE	DUNN	GRIFFITHS	DAVIES	NEILSON	LYON	MUIR	WILCOX	McINTYRE	CORBETT	BECTON	
26/02/02	KETTERING TOWN	A	3-0	3000	CARTLIDGE	DUNN	GRIFFITHS	DAVIES	NEILSON	LYON	MUIR	WILCOX	CORBETT	JONES	BECTON	CORBETT 3
??	WELLINGBOROUGH	H	8-1	2000	CARTLIDGE	DUNN	GRIFFITHS	DAVIES	NEILSON	LYON	MUIR	WILCOX	LAMB	JONES	BECTON	WILCOX 4, JONES 2, CORBETT, MUIR
01/03/02	LUTON TOWN	A	1-1	2000	CARTLIDGE	DUNN	GRIFFITHS	DAVIES	NEILSON	LYON	MUIR	JONES	LAMB	WILCOX	BECTON	JONES
05/03/02	SOUTHAMPTON	H	1-0	6000	CARTLIDGE	DUNN	GRIFFITHS	DAVIES	NEILSON	LYON	MUIR	JONES	CORBETT	WILCOX	BECTON	CORBETT, NEILSON
08/03/02	SOUTHAMPTON	A	2-0	4000	CARTLIDGE	DUNN	GRIFFITHS	DAVIES	NEILSON	LYON	MUIR	JONES	CORBETT	WILCOX	BECTON	CORBETT 2, JONES
15/03/02	QUEENS PARK RANGERS	H	0-0	3000	CARTLIDGE	DUNN	GRIFFITHS	DAVIES	NEILSON	LYON	MUIR	JONES	CORBETT	WILCOX	BECTON	
22/03/02	READING	H	1-0	4000	CARTLIDGE	DUNN	GRIFFITHS	DAVIES	NEILSON	LYON	MUIR	JONES	WILCOX	CORBETT	BECTON	NEILSON MUIR
28/03/02	BRENTFORD	H	5-0	1500	CARTLIDGE	DUNN	GRIFFITHS	DAVIES	NEILSON	LYON	MUIR	JONES	CORBETT	WILCOX	BECTON	CORBETT 2, WILCOX 2, JONES
29/03/02	SOUTHAMPTON	A	0-6	3000	CARTLIDGE	DUNN	HULME	DAVIES	NEILSON	LYON	MUIR	JONES	LAMB	WILCOX	BECTON	
01/04/02	SWINDON TOWN	H	1-0	3000	CARTLIDGE	DUNN	GRIFFITHS	DAVIES	NEILSON	HULME	PIERCE	JONES	CORBETT	WILCOX	BECTON	CORBETT
05/04/02	LUTON TOWN	H	4-0	3000	CARTLIDGE	DUNN	GRIFFITHS	FARNALL	DAVIES	LYON	MUIR	JONES	CORBETT	WILCOX	BECTON	CORBETT, WILCOX 2, JONES 2, JONES
28/04/02	MILLWALL	A	0-1	4000	CARTLIDGE	DUNN	GRIFFITHS	FARNALL	DAVIES	NEILSON	MUIR	JONES	CORBETT	WILCOX	PIERCE	
30/04/02	QUEENS PARK RANGERS	H	4-1	3000	CARTLIDGE	DUNN	GRIFFITHS	FARNALL	DAVIES	NEILSON	PIERCE	JONES	LAMB	WILCOX	PIERCE	JONES 3, PIERCE

FA CUP

Date	Opponent	H/A	Score	ATT	G	2	3	4	5	6	7	8	9	10	11	GOALSCORERS
02/11/01	WEYMOUTH	H	5-0	SMALL	FRANKHAM	DUNN	HULME	DAVIES	DAVIES	LYON	MUIR	JONES	LAMB	WILCOX	BECTON	JONES 5
27/11/01	BRISTOL CITY	A	3-2	5000	CARTLIDGE	DUNN	GRIFFITHS	FARNALL	NEILSON	LYON	MUIR	WILCOX	LAMB	WILCOX	BECTON	JONES, LAMB, BECTON
30/11/01	SWINDON TOWN	A	1-0	LARGE	CARTLIDGE	DUNN	GRIFFITHS	FARNALL	NEILSON	LYON	MUIR	JONES	LAMB	JONES	BECTON	BECTON
14/12/01	MILLWALL	A	1-1	3000	CARTLIDGE	DUNN	GRIFFITHS	FARNALL	DAVIES	LYON	MUIR	JONES	LAMB	JONES	BECTON	JONES
18/12/01	MILLWALL	H	1-0	4000	CARTLIDGE	DUNN	GRIFFITHS	FARNALL	DAVIES	LYON	MUIR	WILCOX	CORBETT	JONES	BECTON	WILCOX
25/01/02	MILLWALL	H	1-1	12000	CARTLIDGE	DUNN	GRIFFITHS	FARNALL	DAVIES	LYON	MUIR	JONES	CORBETT	WILCOX	BECTON	JONES
29/01/02	MIDDLESBROUGH	A	1-0	7586	CARTLIDGE	DUNN	GRIFFITHS	FARNALL	DAVIES	LYON	MUIR	JONES	CORBETT	WILCOX	BECTON	JONES
28/02/02	STOKE CITY	H	0-1	19860	CARTLIDGE	DUNN	GRIFFITHS	FARNALL	DAVIES	LYON	MUIR	JONES	CORBETT	WILCOX	BECTON	

GLOUCESTERSHIRE CUP FINAL

Date	Opponent	H/A	Score	ATT	G	2	3	4	5	6	7	8	9	10	11	GOALSCORERS
31/03/02	BRISTOL CITY	H	0-0	14000	CARTLIDGE	DUNN	GRIFFITHS	DAVIES	NEILSON	LYON	MUIR	JONES	CORBETT	WILCOX	BECTON	
23/04/02	BRISTOL CITY	A	0-0	4223	CARTLIDGE	DUNN	GRIFFITHS	DAVIES	NEILSON	LYON	MUIR	JONES	CORBETT	WILCOX	BECTON	

PLAYERS	APPS	GLS
BECTON T	25	
BOULTON W	3	
CARTLIDGE A	30	
CORBETT F	16	11
DAVIES W	20	
DUNN H	29	
FARNALL T	20	
GEDDES J	7	
GRIFFITHS A	25	
HARVEY	1	
HULME A	4	
JONES J	28	14
LAMB J	6	
LYON W	26	
McINTYRE R	3	
MUIR R	25	
NEILSON J	22	3
PIERCE J	12	1
ROBERTSON W	5	
WILCOX F	23	8

Reliable at centre-half was Jackie Neilson, who contrived to score in both fixtures against Northampton Town. The 2-2 draw in January came only seven days after the Cobblers had lost 11-0 at Southampton. Albert Brown, who scored seven goals that day, scored three more for the Saints when Rovers were crushed 6-0 at The Dell on Easter Saturday. This defeat was all the more galling since, in the middle of an injury crisis, the Saints had fielded the veteran former England inside-forward Harry Wood in goal. Rovers also relied on the strong full-back pairing of Hugh Dunn and Arthur Griffiths; when the former missed his only game of the season Rovers lost 4-0 at Watford, while heavy defeats at Southampton and Portsmouth coincided with the latter's rare absences. At Fratton Park, Rovers trailed 3-0 by half-time to a Pompey side including, at left-half, player-manager Bob Blyth, an uncle of the future Liverpool manager Bill Shankly.

Rovers drew both Gloucestershire Cup matches, but enjoyed a hugely successful FA Cup run, knocking out Football League sides Bristol City and Middlesbrough. It all started with Jack Jones' five goals, shades of November 1900, beating Weymouth at Eastville. Rovers then led Bristol City 2-0 with only 10 minutes remaining, when fog descended and the match was abandoned. When the game was restaged, it was again abandoned, this time in extra time. Rovers won a momentous replay at St John's Lane, their first competitive victory over Football League opposition, with Tom Becton scoring the winning goal. After victories over Swindon Town and Millwall, Rovers were drawn away to Middlesbrough who were on course for promotion from Division Two that season. Rovers caused a huge shock by drawing 1-1 and proceeding to beat Boro in a midweek replay at Eastville. Before the rematch, Middlesbrough discovered the distance between the underside of the crossbar and the ground was 7ft 11in, not the regulation 8ft, but the Football Association was to reject their protests. Three minutes from the end of the match, Cartlidge and Dunn collided, leaving Boro's inside-left Bill Wardrope with an open goal. He missed and, within moments, Tommy Becton had scored a crucial goal to give Rovers a famous 1-0 victory. The visit of Division One Stoke brought an Eastville crowd of 19,860 and receipts of £547 – both records that stood for many years. Rovers lost 1-0 after an inspired performance by Stoke's Welsh International goalkeeper Leigh Richmond Roose, later an Everton and Sunderland player. Bizarrely, an anonymous letter falsely claimed Roose had played for London Welsh in the Preliminary Round against Crouch End Vampires and was thus cup-tied, but the Rovers management was quick to distance itself from such rumours. Rovers played a Western League Crocks XI at Eastville on 29 March 1902 and raised 30 shillings for the Western League Fund.

1902/03

As if to prove that Rovers' late-season form in 1901/02 had been no fluke, a run of four straight wins opened up a season in which the club finished fifth, its highest placing to date in the Southern League. There were, of course, numerous changes of personnel. The most significant departure was the free-scoring Jack Jones, whose July move to Tottenham Hotspur preceded his early death from typhoid in London in September 1903. Alf Jasper Geddes joined Bristol City and the former England

Bristol Rovers 1902/03. Back row: G Pay (Trainer), Dunn, Young, Frankham, Cartlidge, Pudan, A Griffiths, Homer (Secretary) Middle row: Muir, McCall, Howie, Graham, Corbett, Wilcox, Marriott. Front row: Lyon, McLean, Davies

International George Kinsey signed for Burton Early Closing. Goalkeeper Richard Gray moved to Burton United for six successful seasons.

A direct and immediate replacement for Jones was the inspirational Jimmy Howie, who was on the verge of a great career. A May signing from Kettering Town, he was to finish as the club's joint top scorer, with Fred Wilcox, registering ten Southern League goals. The experienced full-back Dick Pudan joined from West Ham United. In the half-back line Rovers signed James Young from Barrow who contributed an own goal at Queen's Park Rangers in March. Former Grimsby Town and Liverpool centre-half Jock McLean joined from Bristol City.

The season began with a gymkhana and sports event, including archery tournaments and a 100-yard dribbling contest won by Fred Corbett. An opening day victory at Northampton Town, Rovers' first victory against the Cobblers was down to two goals from Wilcox, with Wilson, who joined Rovers at the end of the season, scoring for the home side. Seven days later Wilcox went one better, registering his second hat-trick for Rovers, while Corbett added two goals as Rovers put five past Watford. Brentford lost their opening nine Southern League matches and were easy prey, Howie contributing his first Rovers goal, before a crowd of 11,000 saw Rovers defeat a strong Tottenham Hotspur side at Eastville. It took a tap-in by Billy Grassam from Bill Linward's cross 15 minutes from time to shatter the run of wins and give West Ham United a 1-0 win.

Consistently convincing wins maintained Rovers' challenge through the winter. Jimmy Howie and John Graham were on target in big wins over Luton Town, Queen's

SEASON 1902/03

SOUTHERN LEAGUE DIVISION ONE

Date	Opponent			ATT	G	2	3	4	5	6	7	8	9	10	11	GOALSCORERS
06/09/02	NORTHAMPTON TOWN	A	2-1	2500	CARTLIDGE	PUDAN	GRIFFITHS	YOUNG	McLEAN	LYON	MUIR	HOWIE	CORBETT	WILCOX	MARRIOTT	WILCOX (2)
13/09/02	WATFORD	H	5-1	6000	CARTLIDGE	DUNN	GRIFFITHS	YOUNG	McLEAN	LYON	MUIR	HOWIE	CORBETT	WILCOX	MARRIOTT	WILCOX (3), CORBETT (2)
20/09/02	BRENTFORD	H	2-0	2000	CARTLIDGE	DUNN	GRIFFITHS	YOUNG	McLEAN	LYON	MUIR	HOWIE	CORBETT	WILCOX	McCALL	HOWIE, CORBETT
27/09/02	TOTTENHAM HOTSPUR	H	3-2	11000	CARTLIDGE	DUNN	GRIFFITHS	YOUNG	McLEAN	LYON	MUIR	HOWIE	CORBETT	WILCOX	McCALL	CORBETT, WILCOX, McCALL
04/10/02	WEST HAM UNITED	A	0-1	6500	CARTLIDGE	DUNN	GRIFFITHS	YOUNG	McLEAN	LYON	MUIR	HOWIE	CORBETT	WILCOX	MARRIOTT	
11/10/02	PORTSMOUTH	H	1-1	5000	CARTLIDGE	DUNN	GRIFFITHS	DAVIES	McLEAN	LYON	MUIR	HOWIE	CORBETT	WILCOX	MARRIOTT	CORBETT
18/10/02	NEW BROMPTON	A	0-0	3000	CARTLIDGE	DUNN	GRIFFITHS	DAVIES	McLEAN	LYON	MUIR	HOWIE	GRAHAM	WILCOX	MARRIOTT	
25/10/02	SWINDON TOWN	A	2-3	6000	CARTLIDGE	DUNN	GRIFFITHS	DAVIES	McLEAN	LYON	MUIR	WILCOX	CORBETT	HOWIE	MARRIOTT	WILCOX, HOWIE
01/11/02	MILLWALL	A	2-0	6000	CARTLIDGE	DUNN	GRIFFITHS	DAVIES	McLEAN	PUDAN	MUIR	WILCOX	GRAHAM	HOWIE	MARRIOTT	MUIR, GRAHAM
08/11/02	LUTON TOWN	H	4-1	5000	CARTLIDGE	DUNN	GRIFFITHS	YOUNG	McLEAN	LYON	MUIR	WILCOX	GRAHAM	HOWIE	MARRIOTT	DUNN, GRAHAM, HOWIE, MARRIOTT
15/11/02	READING	A	0-2	5000	WILLIAMS	DUNN	GRIFFITHS	YOUNG	McLEAN	LYON	MUIR	WILCOX	GRAHAM	HOWIE	CORBETT	
22/11/02	QUEENS PARK RANGERS	H	4-0	5000	CARTLIDGE	DUNN	GRIFFITHS	DAVIES	McLEAN	LYON	MUIR	CORBETT	GRAHAM	HOWIE	McCALL	CORBETT, GRAHAM, HOWIE, LYON
29/11/02	SOUTHAMPTON	A	1-3	3000	CARTLIDGE	DUNN	GRIFFITHS	DAVIES	McLEAN	LYON	WILCOX	CORBETT	GRAHAM	HOWIE	McCALL	HOWIE
06/12/02	WELLINGBOROUGH	H	2-0	3000	CARTLIDGE	DUNN	GRIFFITHS	YOUNG	McLEAN	LYON	WILCOX	CORBETT	GRAHAM	HOWIE	McCALL	HOWIE (2)
20/12/02	NORTHAMPTON TOWN	H	1-1	4000	CARTLIDGE	PUDAN	GRIFFITHS	YOUNG	McLEAN	DAVIES	VEYSEY	CORBETT	GRAHAM	McCALL	ROWLANDS	ROWLANDS
27/12/02	WATFORD	A	2-1	2500	CARTLIDGE	PUDAN	GRIFFITHS	YOUNG	McLEAN	DAVIES	WILCOX	CORBETT	GRAHAM	ROWLANDS	McCALL	WILCOX, ROWLANDS
03/01/03	BRENTFORD	A	2-0	2000	CARTLIDGE	DUNN	GRIFFITHS	YOUNG	McLEAN	LYON	GRAHAM	CORBETT	ROWLANDS	WILCOX	MARRIOTT	ROWLANDS, MARRIOTT
10/01/03	TOTTENHAM HOTSPUR	A	0-3	12000	CARTLIDGE	DUNN	GRIFFITHS	YOUNG	McLEAN	LYON	MUIR	CORBETT	ROWLANDS	WILCOX	MARRIOTT	
17/01/03	WEST HAM UNITED	H	1-1	3000	CARTLIDGE	DUNN	GRIFFITHS	YOUNG	McLEAN	LYON	HOWIE	CORBETT	ROWLANDS	WILCOX	MARRIOTT	LYON (pen)
24/01/03	PORTSMOUTH	A	0-3	8000	CARTLIDGE	DUNN	GRIFFITHS	PUDAN	McLEAN	LYON	GRAHAM	HOWIE	CORBETT	WILCOX	MARRIOTT	
31/01/03	NEW BROMPTON	H	2-0	LARGE	CARTLIDGE	DUNN	GRIFFITHS	DAVIES	McLEAN	LYON	GRAHAM	HOWIE	CORBETT	WILCOX	MARRIOTT	CORBETT, HOWIE
07/02/03	SWINDON TOWN	A	1-2	FAIR	CARTLIDGE	DUNN	GRIFFITHS	DAVIES	McLEAN	LYON	GRAHAM	HOWIE	CORBETT	WILCOX	MARRIOTT	HOWIE
14/02/03	KETTERING TOWN	H	3-0	SMALL	CARTLIDGE	DUNN	GRIFFITHS	DAVIES	McLEAN	LYON	MUIR	HOWIE	CORBETT	GRAHAM	MARRIOTT	MARRIOTT, GRAHAM, HOWIE
21/02/03	LUTON TOWN	A	1-1	2000	CARTLIDGE	DUNN	GRIFFITHS	DAVIES	McLEAN	LYON	MUIR	HOWIE	CORBETT	WILCOX	MARRIOTT	WILCOX
28/02/03	READING	H	1-1	6000	CARTLIDGE	DUNN	GRIFFITHS	DAVIES	McLEAN	YOUNG	MUIR	HOWIE	CORBETT	WILCOX	MARRIOTT	GRIFFITHS (pen)
07/03/03	QUEENS PARK RANGERS	A	0-2	4000	CARTLIDGE	DUNN	GRIFFITHS	DAVIES	McLEAN	YOUNG	MUIR	HOWIE	CORBETT	WILCOX	MARRIOTT	
14/03/03	SOUTHAMPTON	H	1-1	8000	CARTLIDGE	DUNN	GRIFFITHS	DAVIES	McLEAN	YOUNG	MUIR	HOWIE	CORBETT	WILCOX	MARRIOTT	HOWIE
21/03/03	WELLINGBOROUGH	A	0-1	2000	CARTLIDGE	DUNN	GRIFFITHS	DAVIES	McLEAN	YOUNG	MUIR	HOWIE	CORBETT	GRAHAM	MARRIOTT	
28/03/03	MILLWALL	H	1-0	4000	CARTLIDGE	DUNN	PUDAN	DAVIES	YOUNG	LYON	MUIR	HOWIE	CORBETT	GRAHAM	MARRIOTT	MUIR
04/04/03	KETTERING TOWN	A	2-2	2000	CARTLIDGE	DUNN	PUDAN	YOUNG	McLEAN	LYON	MUIR	HOWIE	CORBETT	GRAHAM	MARRIOTT	MUIR McLEAN

FA CUP

Date	Opponent			ATT	G	2	3	4	5	6	7	8	9	10	11	GOALSCORERS
13/12/02	MILLWALL	H	0-0	11790	CARTLIDGE	DUNN	PUDAN	YOUNG	McLEAN	LYON	MUIR	McCALL	CORBETT	GRAHAM	MARRIOTT	
18/12/02	MILLWALL	A	0-0	4044	CARTLIDGE	DUNN	PUDAN	YOUNG	McLEAN	LYON	VEYSEY	McCALL	CORBETT	WILCOX	MARRIOTT	
22/12/02	MILLWALL *	N	0-2	4985	CARTLIDGE	DUNN	PUDAN	YOUNG	McLEAN	LYON	McCALL	CORBETT	GRAHAM	WILCOX	MARRIOTT	

* Played at Villa Park

GLOUCESTERSHIRE CUP FINAL

Date	Opponent				G	2	3	4	5	6	7	8	9	10	11	GOALSCORERS
13/04/03	BRISTOL CITY	H	0-0		CARTLIDGE	DUNN	PUDAN	YOUNG	McLEAN	LYON	MUIR	HOWIE	CORBETT	GRAHAM	MARRIOTT	
20/04/03	BRISTOL CITY	A	1-1		CARTLIDGE	DUNN	PUDAN	YOUNG	McLEAN	LYON	MUIR	HOWIE	CORBETT	GRAHAM	MARRIOTT	CORBETT
29/04/03	BRISTOL CITY	A	4-2		CARTLIDGE	DUNN	PUDAN	DAVIES	YOUNG	LYON	MUIR	HOWIE	CORBETT	GRAHAM	MARRIOTT	CORBETT (2), MARRIOTT, DUNN (pen)

Appearances and Goals

PLAYERS	APPS	GLS
CARTLIDGE A	29	
CORBETT F	26	7
DAVIES W	17	1
DUNN H	27	4
GRAHAM J	17	1
GRIFFITHS A	28	1
HOWIE J	26	11
LYON W	23	2
MARRIOTT W	22	3
McCALL J	7	1
McLEAN J	29	
MUIR J	21	3
MUIR R	7	
PUDAN D	5	
ROWLANDS H	5	3
VEYSEY A	1	
WILCOX F	25	9
WILLIAMS A	1	
YOUNG J		

Rare action photo of Bristol City against Rovers on 1 September 1902 in a pre-season friendly

Park Rangers and Kettering Town, when Graham's goal, Rovers' second, came directly from a corner just before half-time. Rovers also won 2-0 at Millwall and Brentford and in home games with Wellingborough and New Brompton. The away game at Brentford mirrored the Eastville game in September. The Bees, now in the middle of seven consecutive Southern League defeats, made five changes to their side but lost to goals from Harold Rowlands and Bill Marriott. They were to gain only five points from their 30 Southern League fixtures.

January saw two 3-0 defeats, at Tottenham Hotspur and at Portsmouth. In the latter, the great C B Fry played against Rovers. A double International for England at cricket and football, he had recently played for Southampton in the 1902 FA Cup final. Among numerous claims to fame, he had also held the world long-jump record, stood unsuccessfully for parliament and famously declined the kingship of Albania. Rovers managed to draw 1-1 with a strong Southampton side in March, with Howie scrambling the ball across the line to give Rovers the lead after half an hour and Fred Harrison, who had scored all the goals when Saints had beaten Wellingborough 5-0 seven days earlier, contributing the visitors' 75th minute equaliser, after Howie's twice-taken penalty had been saved.

There were no ever-presents in 1902/03. Cartlidge and McLean missed only one game each, while Arthur Griffiths played in all but the final two matches. The 3-0 win against Kettering Town on Valentine's Day was the 100th Southern League game of Griffiths' Rovers career. He was the first player at the club to achieve this feat and was to play in a total of 105. The only goal of his career was a first-half penalty in the 1-1 draw with Reading at the end of February, in a match where, to avoid a colour clash, Rovers played in all white.

Four meetings with Millwall in December saw Rovers lose in an FA Cup second replay at Villa Park. However, Rovers gained revenge with four second-half goals after a scoreless opening half of a Western League fixture at Eastville. Tom Lee, on Rovers' books until nine months earlier, made a rare appearance for Millwall at left-back in this final game. Graham and Wilcox had scored in the initial FA Cup tie and, after the replay was abandoned goalless in extra time due to bad light, the decider took place on a neutral ground. The Gloucestershire Cup was won for the first time since 1889, Bristol City being defeated 4-2 in a second replay, through two Fred Corbett goals, one for Bill Marriott and a Hugh Dunn penalty.

Rovers in FA Cup action at Millwall in December 1902. Top: *Rovers kick off.* Centre: *Rovers defend a corner.*
Bottom: *Rovers goalkeeper Cartlidge watches a shot go by*

As the season closed, Andrew Smith was signed from West Bromwich Albion to replace Wilcox, whose late move to Small Heath, later Birmingham City, was in time for him to score four goals in a 12-0 Division Two victory against Doncaster Rovers. A crowd of 3,000 at Eastville on 11 April saw a game of American Pushball, won 10-4 by a Stapleton Road XV using a 40lb ball, 5ft 6in high and costing £35.

1903/04

Rovers were challengers for the Southern League championship and, though they faded at the season's end, the potential was clear to see. Alf Homer's side, now playing with far greater consistency, was to claim the Championship in 1904/05.

Several changes were made to the side that had finished fifth in the Southern League in 1902/03. Tot Farnall joined Bradford City, John McCall went to Notts County, Jimmy Lyon moved to Manchester City and James Young returned north of the border to join Celtic. John McLean joined Millwall in April and spent three years at The Den before moving to Queen's Park Rangers; McLean was in the Millwall side that drew a six-goal thriller at Eastville in March, after Rovers had trailed 3-2 at the interval. The biggest name to depart was Jimmy Howie, who was to win three Scottish caps at Newcastle United, where he played his part in three League Championships and appeared in four FA Cup finals.

Homer signed two relatively inexperienced players from West Bromwich Albion. Although George Elmore had only three League games to his name and centre-half Ben Appleby just one, a Division Two match against Glossop North End, these players were

Bristol Rovers 1903/04. Back row: Tait, Dunn, Marriott, Cartlidge, Robertson, Pudan, Pay (Trainer). Middle row: Wilson, Gray, Appleby, Beats. Front row: Elmore, Smith

SEASON 1903/04

SOUTHERN LEAGUE DIVISION ONE

Date	Opponent	H/A	Score	ATT	G	2	3	4	5	6	7	8	9	10	11	GOALSCORERS
05/09/03	SWINDON TOWN	H	2-0	7000	CARTLIDGE	DUNN	PUDAN	TAIT	APPLEBY	GRAY	ROBSON	ELMORE	BEATS	SMITH	MARRIOTT	BEATS, MARRIOTT
12/09/03	BRIGHTON & H ALBION	A	2-2	4500	CARTLIDGE	DUNN	PUDAN	TAIT	DAVIS	GRAY	WILSON	ELMORE	BEATS	SMITH	MARRIOTT	GRAY, BEATS
19/09/03	PORTSMOUTH	H	1-2	5000	CARTLIDGE	DUNN	PUDAN	TAIT	ROBERTSON	APPLEBY	TOUT	ELMORE	SMITH	WILSON	MARRIOTT	SMITH
26/09/03	NORTHAMPTON TOWN	A	1-2	2000	CARTLIDGE	DUNN	PUDAN	TAIT	ROBERTSON	APPLEBY	TOUT	GRAY	BEATS	SMITH	MARRIOTT	GRAY
03/10/03	BRENTFORD	H	5-1	2000	CARTLIDGE	DUNN	PUDAN	TAIT	ROBERTSON	GRAY	WILSON	ELMORE	BEATS	SMITH	MARRIOTT	BEATS 2, SMITH 2, WILSON
10/10/03	WEST HAM UNITED	A	4-1	5000	CARTLIDGE	DUNN	PUDAN	TAIT	APPLEBY	GRAY	WILSON	ELMORE	BEATS	SMITH	MARRIOTT	ELMORE (2), APPLEBY, WILSON
17/10/03	TOTTENHAM HOTSPUR *	H	1-0	8000	CARTLIDGE	DUNN	PUDAN	TAIT	APPLEBY	GRAY	WILSON	ELMORE	BEATS	SMITH	MARRIOTT	BEATS
24/10/03	LUTON TOWN	A	0-1	4000	CARTLIDGE	DUNN	PUDAN	TAIT	APPLEBY	GRAY	WILSON	ELMORE	BEATS	SMITH	MARRIOTT	
31/10/03	NEW BROMPTON	H	2-0	6000	CARTLIDGE	DUNN	PUDAN	TAIT	APPLEBY	GRAY	WILSON	ELMORE	BEATS	SMITH	MARRIOTT	ELMORE, SMITH pen
14/11/03	SOUTHAMPTON	H	1-1	5000	CARTLIDGE	DUNN	PUDAN	TAIT	APPLEBY	GRAY	WILSON	ELMORE	BEATS	SMITH	MARRIOTT	BEATS
21/11/03	FULHAM	A	1-0	6000	CARTLIDGE	DUNN	PUDAN	TAIT	APPLEBY	GRAY	JACK	WILSON	BEATS	SMITH	MARRIOTT	SMITH
28/11/03	MILLWALL	H	3-1	5000	CARTLIDGE	DUNN	PUDAN	TAIT	APPLEBY	GRAY	JACK	WILSON	BEATS	SMITH	MARRIOTT	WILSON, SMITH, APPLEBY
05/12/03	QUEENS PARK RANGERS	A	1-2	2000	CARTLIDGE	DUNN	PUDAN	TAIT	APPLEBY	GRAY	WILSON	ELMORE	BEATS	SMITH	MARRIOTT	BEATS
19/12/03	READING	A	0-3	3000	CARTLIDGE	DUNN	PUDAN	TAIT	APPLEBY	ROBERTSON	WILSON	DARKE	BEATS	SMITH	MARRIOTT	
26/12/03	PLYMOUTH ARGYLE	H	1-2	12000	CARTLIDGE	DUNN	PUDAN	TAIT	APPLEBY	GRAY	WILSON	ELMORE	BEATS	SMITH	MARRIOTT	SMITH
28/12/03	WELLINGBOROUGH	H	7-1	4000	CARTLIDGE	DUNN	PUDAN	TAIT	ROBERTSON	GRAY	WILSON	ELMORE	BEATS	SMITH	MARRIOTT	WILSON 2, BEATS 2, GRAY, ROBERTSON, MARRIOTT
02/01/04	SWINDON TOWN	A	2-0	8000	CARTLIDGE	DUNN	PUDAN	TAIT	ROBERTSON	GRAY	WILSON	ELMORE	BEATS	SMITH	MARRIOTT	BEATS, SMITH
09/01/04	BRIGHTON & H ALBION	H	2-0	4000	CARTLIDGE	DUNN	PUDAN	TAIT	ROBERTSON	GRAY	WILSON	ELMORE	BEATS	SMITH	MARRIOTT	WILSON 2
16/01/04	PORTSMOUTH	A	1-2	8000	CARTLIDGE	DUNN	PUDAN	TAIT	APPLEBY	GRAY	WILSON	ELMORE	BEATS	SMITH	MARRIOTT	APPLEBY
18/01/04	KETTERING TOWN	A	3-2	1000	CARTLIDGE	DUNN	PUDAN	TAIT	APPLEBY	GRAY	WILSON	ELMORE	BEATS	SMITH	MARRIOTT	ELMORE, MARRIOTT, SMITH
23/01/04	NORTHAMPTON TOWN	H	1-1	3000	CARTLIDGE	DUNN	PUDAN	TAIT	APPLEBY	GRAY	WILSON	ELMORE	BEATS	SMITH	MARRIOTT	SMITH
30/01/04	BRENTFORD	A	2-1	3000	CARTLIDGE	DUNN	PUDAN	TAIT	APPLEBY	GRAY	WILSON	DARKE	BEATS	SMITH	MARRIOTT	BEATS, TAIT
06/02/04	WEST HAM UNITED	H	4-0	2000	CARTLIDGE	DUNN	PUDAN	TAIT	APPLEBY	GRAY	WILSON	JACK	BEATS	SMITH	MARRIOTT	BEATS, JACK, SMITH, WILSON
13/02/04	TOTTENHAM HOTSPUR	A	1-5	10000	CARTLIDGE	DUNN	PUDAN	TAIT	APPLEBY	GRAY	WILSON	ELMORE	BEATS	SMITH	MARRIOTT	APPLEBY
20/02/04	LUTON TOWN	H	3-1	3000	CARTLIDGE	DUNN	PUDAN	TAIT	APPLEBY	GRAY	WILSON	JACK	BEATS	SMITH	MARRIOTT	WILSON, ELMORE, SMITH
27/02/04	NEW BROMPTON	A	1-1	4000	CARTLIDGE	DUNN	HARGETT	TAIT	APPLEBY	GRAY	WILSON	JACK	BEATS	SMITH	MARRIOTT	JACK
05/03/04	KETTERING TOWN	A	5-1	3000	CARTLIDGE	DUNN	HARGETT	TAIT	APPLEBY	GRAY	WILSON	JACK	BEATS	SMITH	MARRIOTT	BEATS, JACK 2, WILSON, SMITH
12/03/04	SOUTHAMPTON	A	1-6	3000	CARTLIDGE	DUNN	PUDAN	TAIT	APPLEBY	GRAY	WILSON	JACK	BEATS	SMITH	MARRIOTT	JACK
19/03/04	FULHAM	H	1-0	3000	CARTLIDGE	DUNN	PUDAN	TAIT	APPLEBY	GRAY	WILSON	JACK	BEATS	SMITH	MARRIOTT	BEATS pen
26/03/04	MILLWALL	A	3-3	7000	CARTLIDGE	DUNN	PUDAN	TAIT	APPLEBY	GRAY	WILSON	JACK	BEATS	SMITH	MARRIOTT	BEATS 2, JACK
01/04/04	PLYMOUTH ARGYLE	A	0-0	12000	CARTLIDGE	DUNN	PUDAN	TAIT	ROBERTSON	GRAY	WILSON	JACK	BEATS	SMITH	MARRIOTT	
02/04/04	QUEENS PARK RANGERS	H	1-1	6000	CARTLIDGE	DUNN	PUDAN	TAIT	ROBERTSON	GRAY	WILSON	JACK	BEATS	SMITH	MARRIOTT	JACK
16/04/04	READING	H	0-0	5000	CARTLIDGE	DUNN	PUDAN	TAIT	APPLEBY	GRAY	WILSON	ELMORE	BEATS	JACK	MARRIOTT	
23/04/04	WELLINGBOROUGH	A	3-1	1500	CARTLIDGE	DUNN	PUDAN	TAIT	APPLEBY	GRAY	WILSON	ELMORE	BEATS	SMITH	MARRIOTT	BEATS 2, APPLEBY

* played at St Johns Lane, Bedminster

FA CUP

Date	Opponent	H/A	Score	ATT	G	2	3	4	5	6	7	8	9	10	11	GOALSCORERS
12/12/03	WOOLWICH ARSENAL	H	1-1	14000	CARTLIDGE	DUNN	PUDAN	TAIT	APPLEBY	GRAY	WILSON	ELMORE	BEATS	SMITH	MARRIOTT	WILSON
16/12/03	WOOLWICH ARSENAL	A	1-1	12000	CARTLIDGE	DUNN	PUDAN	TAIT	APPLEBY	GRAY	WILSON	ELMORE	BEATS	SMITH	MARRIOTT	BEATS
21/12/03	WOOLWICH ARSENAL **	N	0-1	10000	CARTLIDGE	DUNN	PUDAN	TAIT	APPLEBY	GRAY	WILSON	ELMORE	BEATS	SMITH	MARRIOTT	

** played at White Hart Lane, Tottenham"

GLOUCESTERSHIRE CUP FINAL

Date	Opponent	H/A	Score	ATT	G	2	3	4	5	6	7	8	9	10	11	GOALSCORERS
04/04/04	BRISTOL CITY	A	1-2	10537	CARTLIDGE	DUNN	PUDAN	TAIT	ROBERTSON	GRAY	WILSON	JACK	BEATS	SMITH	MARRIOTT	BEATS

PLAYERS	APPS	GLS
APPLEBY B	28	5
BEATS W	32	18
CARTLIDGE A	34	
DARKE W	3	
DAVIS	2	
DUNN H	34	
ELMORE G	21	5
GRAY J	32	3
HARGETT G	2	
JACK W	11	6
MARRIOTT W	34	3
PUDAN D	32	
ROBERTSON W	7	1
ROBSON D	1	
SMITH A	33	13
TAIT T	34	1
TOUT W	2	
WILSON D	32	11

Postcard c.1903 showing Rovers' South Stand at Eastville

to become regulars in a successful Rovers side. They were joined by high-profile centre-forward Billy Beats, who had played for Wolves in the 1896 FA Cup final and who quickly established a powerful partnership with Andrew Smith. Beats had played for England against Scotland in the 1902 Ibrox game that had ended in tragedy, when a 50ft bank of terracing behind the west goal had collapsed. 26 spectators fell to their deaths, and 500 more were injured. Beats was to be the club's captain and top scorer with 18 Southern League goals, five more than Smith. Homer also signed Scottish International Tommy Tait in 1911, who was, with established players Cartlidge, Dunn and Marriott, one of four ever-presents.

A poor September was compounded by news from London of the premature death of former Eastville favourite Jack Jones. A testimonial game in December between Spurs and an International XI featured the Millwall full-back and concert hall singer, George Robeson. October began with five first-half goals against Brentford and Rovers barely looked back. Beats and Smith scored a couple each as the Bees were overrun, Rovers scoring three times in five minutes immediately prior to half-time. George Parsonage scored for Brentford and added a consolation penalty in the return game with Rovers already two goals to the good. Rovers scored four times in both fixtures against West Ham United, a Tommy Allison penalty being the only consolation goal. Walter Jack scored twice in a 5-1 win against Kettering Town and there were five different scorers when

Rovers defeated Wellingborough 7-1 at the end of December. Wilson gave Rovers a 10th-minute lead before a goal flurry put the side 5-0 ahead after just 25 minutes. Wellingborough lost two players through illness and were forced to change goalkeeper twice during a largely goal-free second-half.

Success on the field was reflected off it. There were 12,000 spectators at both matches with Plymouth Argyle and 8,000 for the 'home' tie with Tottenham Hotspur, even though it was staged at St John's Lane. Rovers completed League doubles over six different sides and gradually eased their way up the table. The crunch game came on 12 March, when Rovers, by now the main challengers, played the leaders Southampton at The Dell. It was a year to the weekend since Fred Harrison's goal had earned a draw against Rovers. This time, the Saints forward scored a hat-trick, two of these coming

Billy Beats. The former England International was leading goalscorer with 18 goals in 1903/04

from Harry Turner crosses, as the home side ran up a 4-1 lead by half-time, in a 6-1 win that virtually secured the Championship. Rovers, with four straight draws before final day success at Wellingborough, had to settle for third place. One young Bristolian given a brief run-out was Billy Tout, who was to spend 15 years with Swindon Town, winning two Southern League Championship medals and twice appearing in FA Cup semi-finals, before becoming player-manager at Bath City during the 1920/21 season.

In the FA Cup Rovers drew twice with Woolwich Arsenal before succumbing to Tom Briercliffe's 16th-minute goal in the second replay at neutral White Hart Lane, after Tommy Tait had conceded an own goal at the Manor Ground. The Gloucestershire Cup final was lost 2-1 to Bristol City, the large crowd of 10,537 producing gate receipts of £296. A postscript to the Freddie Wilcox transfer was a meeting between Rovers and Small Heath at Eastville on a sunny September afternoon as part of the transfer deal. Rovers held the Division One side 1-1 at half-time and ran out 3-2 winners. George Elmore scored twice and Billy Beats once for Rovers, with Jimmy Robertson and Bob McRoberts replying for the visitors.

1904/05

Prior to the 1952/53 Division Three (South) Championship, the one outstanding achievement in Rovers' history had been being crowned champions of the Southern League in 1904/05. This was achieved by fielding a highly experienced squad of professionals. Cartlidge in goal and his full-backs Dunn and Pudan were retained. In the half-back line, Tait and the dependable Appleby were joined by Gavin Jarvie, while

Bristol Rovers 1904/05. Back row: Appleby, Tait, Dunn, Cartlidge, Pudan, Jarvie. Middle row: Pay (Trainer) Clark, Lewis, Beats, Smith, Dunkley, Homer (Secretary). Front row: Directors

Smith and Beats, with nineteen and sixteen Southern League goals respectively, continued to lead the line.

With Hill Griffiths appearing only sporadically, Homer wisely strengthened his forward line with three astute signings. Billy 'Darkie' Clark was signed in May from Port Glasgow Athletic to play at outside-right. Inside him was Jack Lewis, who returned to the club on the eve of the new season, having spent 1903/04 on the books of Division Two Burton Albion. Lewis' subsequent selection for Wales made him the first player to appear in International football while on Rovers' books. Albert Dunkley, at outside-left, who signed from Blackburn Rovers, had enjoyed considerable football experience with Northampton Town, Leicester Fosse and New Brompton. Homer also signed wing-half Bill Hales, who had played in one League game for Bristol City in 1904, and left-back Harold Wassell from Small Heath, the future Birmingham City, a team-mate of Fred Wilcox in the Blues' famous 12-0 victory against Doncaster Rovers in 1903.

Of four players released, two joined Division Two Bristol City, Tom Darke and Andrew Hargett having appeared in only five Southern League games between them. Hargett was a Boer War veteran who had served at Spion Kop and at the Relief of Ladysmith. Reliable outside-right George Elmore joined Glossop North End, from where he later moved to Partick Thistle and St Mirren, while Walter Jack was to spend a year with West Bromwich Albion before he too moved north of the border, joining Clyde in the summer of 1905.

On the field, after an opening day hiccough at Northampton Town, Rovers' experienced and settled side found defeat to be a rare experience. Portsmouth were beaten 5-0 at Eastville, with Jack Lewis scoring twice, and Rovers completed the double

SEASON 1904/05

SOUTHERN LEAGUE DIVISION ONE

Date	Opponent		Score	ATT	G	2	3	4	5	6	7	8	9	10	11	GOALSCORERS
03/09/04	NORTHAMPTON TOWN	A	0-2	4000	CARTLIDGE	DUNN	PUDAN	TAIT	APPLEBY	JARVIE	CLARK	LEWIS	BEATS	GRIFFITHS	DUNKLEY	
10/09/04	PORTSMOUTH	H	5-0	8000	CARTLIDGE	DUNN	WASSELL	TAIT	APPLEBY	HALES	CLARK	LEWIS	BEATS	GRIFFITHS	SMITH	LEWIS 2, BEATS, CLARK, GRIFFITHS
17/09/04	BRENTFORD	A	1-0	6000	CARTLIDGE	DUNN	WASSELL	TAIT	APPLEBY	HALES	CLARK	LEWIS	SMITH	GRIFFITHS	DUNKLEY	LEWIS
24/09/04	QUEENS PARK RANGERS	H	0-0	7000	CARTLIDGE	DUNN	WASSELL	TAIT	APPLEBY	JARVIE	CLARK	LEWIS	BEATS	GRIFFITHS	SMITH	
01/10/04	MILLWALL	A	0-0	5000	CARTLIDGE	DUNN	WASSELL	TAIT	APPLEBY	JARVIE	CLARK	LEWIS	BEATS	SMITH	DUNKLEY	
08/10/04	TOTTENHAM HOTSPUR	H	3-1	6000	CARTLIDGE	DUNN	WASSELL	TAIT	APPLEBY	JARVIE	CLARK	LEWIS	BEATS	SMITH	DUNKLEY	BEATS, CLARK, LEWIS
15/10/04	LUTON TOWN	A	2-1	3000	CARTLIDGE	DUNN	WASSELL	TAIT	APPLEBY	JARVIE	LEWIS	BEATS	SMITH	CLARK	DUNKLEY	LEWIS 2
22/10/04	SWINDON TOWN	H	3-0	7000	CARTLIDGE	DUNN	WASSELL	TAIT	APPLEBY	JARVIE	CLARK	LEWIS	BEATS	SMITH	DUNKLEY	LEWIS 2, BEATS
29/10/04	NEW BROMPTON	A	1-1	1500	CARTLIDGE	DUNN	WASSELL	TAIT	APPLEBY	JARVIE	CLARK	LEWIS	BEATS	SMITH	DUNKLEY	CLARK
05/11/04	WELLINGBOROUGH	H	4-1	4500	CARTLIDGE	DUNN	WASSELL	TAIT	APPLEBY	JARVIE	CLARK	LEWIS	BEATS	GRIFFITHS	DUNKLEY	GRIFFITHS 2, BEATS, DUNKLEY
12/11/04	SOUTHAMPTON	A	2-4	9000	CARTLIDGE	DUNN	WASSELL	TAIT	APPLEBY	JARVIE	CLARK	SMITH	BEATS	GRIFFITHS	DUNKLEY	DUNKLEY, SMITH
19/11/04	FULHAM	H	4-1	7000	CARTLIDGE	DUNN	PUDAN	TAIT	APPLEBY	JARVIE	CLARK	GRIFFITHS	BEATS	SMITH	DUNKLEY	GRIFFITHS 2, BEATS, CLARK
26/11/04	WEST HAM UNITED	A	2-0	7000	CARTLIDGE	DUNN	PUDAN	TAIT	APPLEBY	JARVIE	CLARK	GRIFFITHS	BEATS	SMITH	DUNKLEY	CLARK, BEATS
03/12/04	PLYMOUTH ARGYLE	H	4-0	6000	CARTLIDGE	DUNN	PUDAN	TAIT	APPLEBY	JARVIE	CLARK	GRIFFITHS	BEATS	SMITH	DUNKLEY	SMITH pen, CLARKE og
17/12/04	READING	H	0-0	10000	CARTLIDGE	DUNN	PUDAN	TAIT	APPLEBY	JARVIE	CLARK	GRIFFITHS	BEATS	SMITH	DUNKLEY	
24/12/04	BRIGHTON & H ALBION	A	2-1	4000	CARTLIDGE	DUNN	PUDAN	TAIT	APPLEBY	JARVIE	CLARK	LEWIS	BEATS	SMITH	DUNKLEY	LEWIS, MELLORS og
31/12/04	NORTHAMPTON TOWN	H	3-0	8000	CARTLIDGE	DUNN	PUDAN	TAIT	APPLEBY	JARVIE	CLARK	GRIFFITHS	BEATS	SMITH	DUNKLEY	SMITH 2, BEATS
07/01/05	PORTSMOUTH	A	2-1	10000	CARTLIDGE	DUNN	PUDAN	TAIT	APPLEBY	HALES	CLARK	LEWIS	BEATS	SMITH	DUNKLEY	BEATS 2
21/01/05	QUEENS PARK RANGERS	A	0-5	11000	CARTLIDGE	DUNN	PUDAN	WASSELL	APPLEBY	JARVIE	WILSON	LEWIS	BEATS	SMITH	DUNKLEY	
28/01/05	MILLWALL	H	4-1	8000	CARTLIDGE	DUNN	PUDAN	HALES	APPLEBY	JARVIE	WILSON	LEWIS	BEATS	SMITH	DUNKLEY	BEATS 2, LEWIS, SMITH
11/02/05	LUTON TOWN	H	3-2	8000	CARTLIDGE	DUNN	PUDAN	TAIT	APPLEBY	JARVIE	WILSON	LEWIS	BEATS	SMITH	DUNKLEY	SMITH 2-1pen, WILSON
18/02/05	SWINDON TOWN	A	1-2	3000	CARTLIDGE	DUNN	PUDAN	TAIT	APPLEBY	JARVIE	CLARK	LEWIS	BEATS	SMITH	DUNKLEY	DUNKLEY
25/02/05	NEW BROMPTON	H	0-0	5000	CARTLIDGE	DUNN	PUDAN	TAIT	APPLEBY	HALES	CLARK	LEWIS	BEATS	SMITH	DUNKLEY	
04/03/05	WELLINGBOROUGH	A	4-2	2000	CARTLIDGE	DUNN	PUDAN	TAIT	APPLEBY	JARVIE	CLARK	LEWIS	BEATS	SMITH	DUNKLEY	SMITH 3, BEATS
11/03/05	SOUTHAMPTON	H	6-1	10000	CARTLIDGE	DUNN	PUDAN	TAIT	APPLEBY	HALES	CLARK	LEWIS	BEATS	GRIFFITHS	DUNKLEY	BEATS 2, CLARK, GRIFFITHS, LEWIS, HALES
18/03/05	FULHAM	A	0-0	8000	CARTLIDGE	DUNN	PUDAN	TAIT	APPLEBY	HALES	CLARK	LEWIS	BEATS	SMITH	DUNKLEY	
25/03/05	WATFORD	H	3-1	6000	CARTLIDGE	DUNN	WASSELL	TAIT	APPLEBY	JARVIE	CLARK	LEWIS	SMITH	GRIFFITHS	DUNKLEY	SMITH 2, CLARK
29/03/05	WATFORD	A	4-1	2000	CARTLIDGE	DUNN	WASSELL	TAIT	APPLEBY	JARVIE	CLARK	LEWIS	SMITH	GRIFFITHS	DUNKLEY	SMITH 3, CLARK
01/04/05	PLYMOUTH ARGYLE	A	1-3	12000	CARTLIDGE	DUNN	PUDAN	TAIT	APPLEBY	JARVIE	CLARK	LEWIS	SMITH	GRIFFITHS	DUNKLEY	GRIFFITHS
08/04/05	WEST HAM UNITED	H	2-2	7000	CARTLIDGE	DUNN	PUDAN	TAIT	APPLEBY	JARVIE	CLARK	LEWIS	BEATS	GRIFFITHS	DUNKLEY	DUNKLEY, LEWIS
15/04/05	READING	A	1-1	10000	CARTLIDGE	DUNN	PUDAN	TAIT	APPLEBY	JARVIE	CLARK	LEWIS	BEATS	SMITH	DUNKLEY	SMITH
22/04/05	BRIGHTON & H ALBION	H	4-0	10000	CARTLIDGE	DUNN	PUDAN	TAIT	APPLEBY	JARVIE	CLARK	LEWIS	BEATS	SMITH	DUNKLEY	APPLEBY, BEATS, SMITH, ROBINSON og
25/04/05	BRENTFORD	H	3-0	5000	CARTLIDGE	DUNN	PUDAN	TAIT	APPLEBY	JARVIE	CLARK	LEWIS	BEATS	SMITH	DUNKLEY	SMITH 2-1pen, LEWIS
29/04/05	TOTTENHAM HOTSPUR	A	0-1	8000	CARTLIDGE	DUNN	PUDAN	HALES	APPLEBY	JARVIE	WILSON	LEWIS	BEATS	CORBETT	GRIFFITHS	

FA CUP

Date	Opponent		Score	ATT	G	2	3	4	5	6	7	8	9	10	11	GOALSCORERS
14/01/05	BRIGHTON & H ALBION	A	2-1	8000	CARTLIDGE	DUNN	PUDAN	TAIT	APPLEBY	JARVIE	CLARK	LEWIS	BEATS	SMITH	DUNKLEY	SMITH, DUNKLEY
04/02/05	BOLTON WANDERERS	H	1-1	15000	CARTLIDGE	DUNN	PUDAN	TAIT	APPLEBY	JARVIE	CLARK	LEWIS	BEATS	SMITH	DUNKLEY	DUNN
08/02/05	BOLTON WANDERERS	A	0-3	5000	CARTLIDGE	DUNN	PUDAN	HALES	APPLEBY	JARVIE	CLARK	LEWIS	OVENS	SMITH	DUNKLEY	

GLOUCESTERSHIRE CUP FINAL

Date	Opponent		Score	ATT	G	2	3	4	5	6	7	8	9	10	11	GOALSCORERS
24/04/05	BRISTOL CITY	H	2-2	10510	CARTLIDGE	DUNN	PUDAN	TAIT	APPLEBY	JARVIE	CLARK	LEWIS	BEATS	SMITH	DUNKLEY	BEATS, SMITH
28/04/05	BRISTOL CITY	A	3-1	3916	CARTLIDGE	DUNN	PUDAN	TAIT	APPLEBY	JARVIE	CLARK	LEWIS	BEATS	SMITH	DUNKLEY	BEATS, LEWIS, DUNKLEY

PLAYERS	APPS	GLS
APPLEBY B	34	1
BEATS W	29	16
CARTLIDGE A	34	
CLARK W	31	9
CORBETT F	1	
DUNKLEY A	30	4
DUNN H	34	
GRIFFITHS H	19	8
HALES W	8	1
JARVIE G	27	
LEWIS J	27	12
OVENS G	1	
PUDAN D	22	
SMITH A	29	19
TAIT T	32	
WASSELL H	13	
WILSON D	3	1
OWN GOALS		3

Rovers full-back Dick Pudan made 116 Southern League appearances between 1902 and 1905

Goalkeeper Arthur Cartlidge, Rovers' record Southern League appearance maker with 258 games

with a 2-1 win at Fratton Park after Pompey's full-back Roderick Walker had been sent off. Smith scored hat-tricks at Watford and Wellingborough, the latter conceding four goals in each meeting with Rovers and becoming the first club in Southern League history to give away 100 goals in a season. Rovers scored four goals or more on nine occasions. It was the 4-1 win against Fulham in November, with Griffiths scoring twice, which put Rovers top of the table for the first time and they stayed there for two months. A crushing 5-0 defeat at Queen's Park Rangers in January saw them lose the top spot, but it was regained when Southampton came to Eastville in March for what became effectively a Championship decider. It was bizarre that, for the second consecutive season, a crunch fixture between Rovers and the Saints ended 6-1 to the home side. Fred Harrison gave the Saints a 20th-minute advantage, but two goals in a minute gave Rovers a half-time lead, after which Beats burst through for a solo goal and then headed another. As Rovers piled on the agony for their visitors, two goals in the final 20 minutes left the home side clear favourites for the Championship.

After victory over Southampton, there was still time for a Tommy Tait own goal to contribute to a 3-1 defeat at Plymouth. However, a second draw with eventual closest rivals Reading and a second victory over Brighton thanks to an own goal left Rovers to secure the Championship with a 3-0 victory at home to Brentford. Rovers were still able to lose the final match, with Fred Corbett playing for the first time in two years. Cartlidge, Dunn and Appleby were ever-presents while, of only 17 players used, three had played in just five games between them.

Charity football match at Eastville, 8 March 1905

In the Western League, life was not so simple. Danny Cunliffe, scorer of four goals in a game against Rovers in October 1899, scored a first-half hat-trick at Fratton Park. George Hilsdon scored four goals for West Ham United against Rovers. He also managed a Southern League goal in April against Rovers, one in each fixture in 1905/06 and a Football-League record five on his debut for Chelsea against Glossop North End in September 1906. Bob Dalrymple and Jack Picken both scored in each game as Plymouth Argyle completed the double over Rovers. Fred Latham and a young Walter Gerrish scored six goals each in November as Rovers reserves, 11-2 ahead by half-time, ran up an astonishing 18-2 victory over HMS *Antelope*. The FA Cup brought an unlikely draw at Burnden Park, before Bolton Wanderers swept Rovers aside in a replay, Pudan putting a through ball from Sam Marsh into his own net after only eight minutes. Dunkley's winning goal secured the Gloucestershire Cup in an end-of-season replay at Ashton Gate. The former Aston Villa outside-left Albert Fisher scored Bristol City's goal.

If defending championships was supposed to be difficult, Rovers began as if they had not read the script. A 6-0 opening day victory, nine goals without reply in two games and four wins and a draw with which to open the season: were Rovers about to retain the Southern League championship? A 7-1 defeat at Luton Town indicated they were not and precipitated a run of four straight defeats. By the season's end, eighth-placed Rovers had suffered a crushing seven-goal loss at the hands of Queen's Park Rangers. The club reported an annual loss of £595.

Yet, Rovers were able to afford the luxury of opening the season with the side which had cruised through much of the previous season. New signing Archie Taylor, who was to play for Barnsley in the 1912 FA Cup final, did not appear in the opening seven games. Davie Walker, who had two Division One matches with Wolverhampton Wanderers to his name, made the side sooner and eclipsed even the illustrious Beats. His 12 goals for the season made him runner-up behind the club's top scorer, 13-goal Jack Lewis. Harold Wassell had been sold to Queen's Park Rangers and Fred Corbett, at the end of his second spell with the club, to Brentford.

The champions put six goals past Northampton Town, three in each half, on the opening day of the new season. Albert Dunkley scored twice, after 12 and 85 minutes, and the previous year's three top scorers, Smith, Lewis and Beats grabbed one each. There was also a rare goal, after 65 minutes, for the imperious Ben Appleby. Lewis was to score in five of the first six games. Four days after the Northampton game, Rovers played Bristol City in a friendly at Eastville and crashed to a 6-0 defeat, the former Scottish International William Maxwell scoring a hat-trick. This was the first of several demoralizing results through the season. Rovers were, however, to record large wins of their own. Clark and Walker scored three goals between them in large victories in November, Southampton being defeated 5-1 and Watford, with defender Jack Richardson contributing an own goal, losing 6-1. Four goals at Northampton saw Rovers complete ten without reply against the Cobblers.

Andrew Smith scored an impressive 35 goals in 70 appearances in his Rovers career

On the other hand, Rovers suffered too many defeats. Two 1-0 defeats against the eventual champions Fulham came courtesy of Bill Wardrope – who should have knocked Rovers out of the FA Cup three years earlier – at Craven Cottage and Walter Freeman in the Cottagers' first-ever victory at Eastville. Peter Turner scored for Watford in both fixtures against Rovers. Sam Graham scored the only goal of the game, a long-range strike a minute before half-time, in the first-ever meeting with Norwich City. The return

SEASON 1905/06

SOUTHERN LEAGUE DIVISION ONE

Date	Opponent	H/A	Score	ATT	G	2	3	4	5	6	7	8	9	10	11	GOALSCORERS
02/09/05	NORTHAMPTON TOWN	H	6-0	9000	CARTLIDGE	DUNN	PUDAN	TAIT	APPLEBY	JARVIE	CLARK W	LEWIS	BEATS	SMITH	DUNKLEY	DUNKLEY 2, BEATS, LEWIS, SMITH, APPLEBY
09/09/05	NEW BROMPTON	A	3-0	4000	CARTLIDGE	DUNN	PUDAN	TAIT	APPLEBY	JARVIE	CLARK W	LEWIS	BEATS	WALKER	DUNKLEY	BEATS, LEWIS, DUNKLEY
16/09/05	PORTSMOUTH	H	1-1	8000	CARTLIDGE	DUNN	PUDAN	TAIT	APPLEBY	JARVIE	CLARK W	LEWIS	BEATS	SMITH	DUNKLEY	SMITH
23/09/05	SWINDON TOWN	A	2-1	5000	CARTLIDGE	DUNN	PUDAN	TAIT	JARVIE	HALES	CLARK W	LEWIS	BEATS	WALKER	DUNKLEY	BEATS, LEWIS
30/09/05	MILLWALL	H	2-1	10000	CARTLIDGE	DUNN	PUDAN	TAIT	JARVIE	HALES	CLARK W	LEWIS	BEATS	WALKER	HAXTON	CLARK W, LEWIS
07/10/05	LUTON TOWN	A	1-7	8000	CARTLIDGE	DUNN	PUDAN	HALES	APPLEBY	JARVIE	CLARK W	LEWIS	BEATS	SMITH	DUNKLEY	LEWIS
14/10/05	TOTTENHAM HOTSPUR	H	0-2	8000	CARTLIDGE	DUNN	PUDAN	TAIT	APPLEBY	JARVIE	CLARK W	LEWIS	BEATS	WALKER	DUNKLEY	
21/10/05	BRENTFORD	A	0-1	10000	CARTLIDGE	TAYLOR	PUDAN	TAIT	JARVIE	HALES	CLARK W	LEWIS	BEATS	WALKER	DUNKLEY	
28/10/05	NORWICH CITY	H	0-1	6000	CARTLIDGE	DUNN	PUDAN	TAIT	JARVIE	HALES	CLARK W	LEWIS	BEATS	SMITH	DUNKLEY	
04/11/05	PLYMOUTH ARGYLE	A	2-1	4500	CARTLIDGE	DUNN	PUDAN	TAIT	TAYLOR	JARVIE	CLARK W	WALKER	BEATS	SMITH	HAXTON	WALKER, HAXTON
11/11/05	SOUTHAMPTON	H	5-1	6000	CARTLIDGE	DUNN	PUDAN	TAIT	APPLEBY	JARVIE	CLARK W	WALKER	BEATS	SMITH	DUNKLEY	WALKER 2, CLARK W, DUNKLEY, SMITH,
18/11/05	READING	A	1-1	5000	CARTLIDGE	DUNN	PUDAN	TAIT	APPLEBY	JARVIE	CLARK W	WALKER	BEATS	SMITH	DUNKLEY	WALKER
25/11/05	WATFORD	H	6-1	7000	CARTLIDGE	DUNN	PUDAN	TAIT	APPLEBY	JARVIE	CLARK W	WALKER	BEATS	LEWIS	DUNKLEY	CLARK W 2, BEATS, LEWIS, WALKER, RICHARDSON og
02/12/05	BRIGHTON & H ALBION	A	1-2	5000	CARTLIDGE	DUNN	PUDAN	TAIT	APPLEBY	JARVIE	CLARK W	WALKER	BEATS	LEWIS	DUNKLEY	APPLEBY
09/12/05	WEST HAM UNITED	H	2-1	5000	CARTLIDGE	DUNN	PUDAN	TAIT	APPLEBY	HALES	CLARK W	WALKER	BEATS	SMITH	HAXTON	HALES, HAXTON
16/12/05	FULHAM	A	0-1	12000	CARTLIDGE	DUNN	PUDAN	TAIT	APPLEBY	JARVIE	CLARK W	WALKER	BEATS	WALKER	HAXTON	
23/12/05	QUEENS PARK RANGERS	H	2-1	7000	CARTLIDGE	DUNN	PUDAN	TAIT	APPLEBY	JARVIE	CLARK W	WALKER	BEATS	WALKER	DUNKLEY	LEWIS 2
30/12/05	NORTHAMPTON TOWN	A	4-0	5000	CARTLIDGE	DUNN	PUDAN	TAIT	APPLEBY	JARVIE	HAXTON	WALKER	BEATS	WALKER	DUNKLEY	WALKER 2, BEATS, DUNKLEY
06/01/06	NEW BROMPTON	H	1-2	4000	CARTLIDGE	DUNN	PUDAN	HALES	APPLEBY	JARVIE	CLARK W	WALKER	BEATS	ORR	DUNKLEY	WALKER
20/01/06	PORTSMOUTH	A	1-2	5000	D CLARK	DUNN	PUDAN	HALES	APPLEBY	JARVIE	CLARK W	WALKER	BEATS	WALKER	DUNKLEY	WALKER
27/01/06	SWINDON TOWN	H	2-1	8000	D CLARK	HALES	TAYLOR	HALES	APPLEBY	JARVIE	CLARK W	LEWIS	BEATS	WALKER	DUNKLEY	LEWIS 2
10/02/06	LUTON TOWN	H	3-2	5000	D CLARK	HALES	PUDAN	TAIT	APPLEBY	JARVIE	TAIT	LEWIS	BEATS	WALKER	DUNKLEY	BEATS 2, WALKER
17/02/06	TOTTENHAM HOTSPUR	A	2-2	4000	D CLARK	DUNN	PUDAN	TAIT	APPLEBY	JARVIE	CLARK W	LEWIS	BEATS	WALKER	DUNKLEY	CLARK W, BEATS
03/03/06	NORWICH CITY	A	0-0	5000	D CLARK	HALES	PUDAN	TAIT	APPLEBY	JARVIE	CLARK W	LEWIS	BEATS	WALKER	DUNKLEY	
10/03/06	PLYMOUTH ARGYLE	H	1-5	5000	HALL	DUNN	PUDAN	TAIT	APPLEBY	TAYLOR	CLARK W	LEWIS	BEATS	JARVIE	DUNKLEY	WALKER
12/03/06	MILLWALL	A	1-2	5000	D CLARK	DUNN	PUDAN	CLARK W	APPLEBY	JARVIE	CLARK W	LEWIS	BEATS	DUNKLEY	HAXTON	CLARK W
17/03/06	SOUTHAMPTON	A	0-3	4000	D CLARK	DUNN	TAYLOR	TAIT	APPLEBY	JARVIE	TAIT	LEWIS	BEATS	LEWIS	DUNKLEY	
24/03/06	READING	H	1-1	4000	D CLARK	DUNN	TAYLOR	TAIT	APPLEBY	HALES	CLARK W	WALKER	BEATS	WALKER	HAXTON	WALKER
31/03/06	WATFORD	A	1-1	5000	CARTLIDGE	DUNN	PUDAN	HALES	APPLEBY	HALES	CLARK W	LEWIS	HUXTABLE	HAXTON	HAXTON	HAXTON, LEWIS
07/04/06	BRIGHTON & H ALBION	H	2-1	5000	CARTLIDGE	DUNN	PUDAN	TAIT	APPLEBY	TAYLOR	HUXTABLE	LEWIS	BEATS	SMART	JARVIE	BEATS, LEWIS
14/04/06	WEST HAM UNITED	A	0-2	9000	CARTLIDGE	DUNN	PUDAN	TAIT	APPLEBY	HALES	CLARK W	LEWIS	BEATS	GERRISH	BENNETT	
21/04/06	FULHAM	A	0-1	4000	CARTLIDGE	DUNN	PUDAN	TAIT	APPLEBY	HALES	CLARK W	LEWIS	BEATS	JARVIE	JARVIE	
28/04/06	QUEENS PARK RANGERS	A	0-7	3000	CARTLIDGE	DUNN	PUDAN	TAIT	STONE	HALES	CLARK W	LEWIS	BEATS	WALKER	HUXTABLE	
30/04/06	BRENTFORD	H	2-1	2000	CARTLIDGE	DUNN	PUDAN	TAIT	STONE	TAYLOR	CLARK W	LEWIS	BEATS	WALKER	OLLIS	BEATS, LEWIS

FA CUP

Date	Opponent	H/A	Score	ATT	G	2	3	4	5	6	7	8	9	10	11	GOALSCORERS
13/01/06	SHEFFIELD WEDNESDAY	A	0-1	15661	CARTLIDGE	DUNN	PUDAN	TAIT	APPLEBY	JARVIE	HAXTON	LEWIS	BEATS	WALKER	DUNKLEY	

GLOUCESTERSHIRE CUP FINAL

Date	Opponent	H/A	Score	ATT	G	2	3	4	5	6	7	8	9	10	11	GOALSCORERS
16/04/06	BRISTOL CITY	A	0-4	8836	CARTLIDGE	HALES	PUDAN	TAIT	APPLEBY	TAYLOR	CLARK W	LEWIS	BEATS	WALKER	BENNETT	

PLAYERS	APPS	GLS
APPLEBY B	27	2
BEATS W	33	10
BENNETT H	1	
CARTLIDGE A	25	
CLARK D	8	
CLARK W	31	6
DUNKLEY A	24	5
DUNN H	31	
GERRISH W	1	
HALES W	16	1
HALL J	1	
HAXTON J	8	3
HUXTABLE T	3	
JARVIE G	28	
LEWIS J	29	13
OLLIS H	1	
ORR R	1	
PUDAN D	31	
SMART J	1	
SMITH A	8	3
STONE R	2	
TAIT T	30	
TAYLOR A	9	
WALKER D	25	12
OWN GOALS		1

Jack Lewis became Rovers' first ever International when he won a Welsh cap in 1906 against England

fixture was the third of four consecutive goalless draws for the Canaries. Fred Wilcox returned to Eastville in the Plymouth side in March and scored twice as Argyle recorded a 5-1 victory. For the second consecutive season, the future Rovers forward Isaac Owens scored for Plymouth against Rovers, this time in the Western League on Boxing Day. Queen's Park Rangers scored seven times without reply in April, with George Ryder contributing two goals in a minute early on and completing his hat-trick shortly after half-time.

In February, Rovers conceded four first-half goals in a Western League game at Portsmouth, losing 5-1 with 'Sunny Jim' Kirby scoring a hat-trick. In March, on the back of the sale of Andrew Smith to Millwall, where he gained Southern League experience before moving on to Swindon Town and Orient, Rovers crashed 4-1 in a Western League match at North Greenwich. At half-time Rovers held a strong Millwall side, which included former Rovers players John McLean and Smith, but three second-half goals brought a heavy defeat. Smith got his name on the scoresheet and Alf Twigg, who was to score two more at Eastville in April 1908, scored a hat-trick.

There were no ever-presents in the Rovers side. Beats, Dunn, Pudan, Tait and Clark all played, however, in at least 30 Southern League games. Beats scored the opening goal at Swindon in September to register his 37th Southern League goal, beating Jack Jones' club record. His 44th goal, in the final game of the season, set a figure only surpassed by Fred Corbett on Christmas Day 1909. The 1904 League Champions Sheffield Wednesday scraped past Rovers in the FA Cup at Hillsborough, George Simpson scoring the only goal with a 40th-minute snap shot, while Bristol City scored four times without reply in a one-sided Gloucestershire Cup final. On 19 March 1906, Jack Lewis became the first player to appear for his country while on Rovers' books. He won his only cap for Wales in the 1-0 defeat against England in Cardiff.

1906/07

The summer of 1906 marked the break-up of Rovers' 1904/05 Southern League Championship-winning side. In May, Billy Beats returned to the Football League with Port Vale, where he was joined by full-back Hugh Dunn. Jack Lewis moved to fellow Southern League side Brighton and was to play for Southampton and Croydon Common in the same League. On the eve of the new season, outside-left Albert Dunkley signed for Division Two Blackpool.

Bristol Rovers 1906/07. Back row: Owens, Appleby, Stewart, Hales, Cartlidge, Pudan, Jarvie, Hutchinson. Front row: Pay (Trainer), Clark, Young, Latham, Walker, Gould

Of Rovers' new signings, outside-left Bill Gould and wing-half Harold Hutchinson were regulars for the new season. Isaac Owens, who had played in five Southern and Western League games for Plymouth Argyle against Rovers, arrived at Eastville for what was to be a one-season stay. Arthur Cartlidge missed just one game in goal, while Gould was the side's only ever-present. Jock Young missed only five games and was the top scorer with 14 league goals. For the third consecutive season, three Rovers players took their individual goal tally into double figures. Defeats against Tottenham Hotspur and Fulham attracted 10,000 crowds, while the highest crowd to date at any Southern League game featuring Rovers – 16,000 – saw the 2-0 defeat at the hands of Portsmouth at Fratton Park on Boxing Day.

Rovers won at New Brompton on the opening day in temperatures approaching 90°F. However, inconsistency dogged Rovers early in the season and after New Year the side won only three Southern League fixtures. When they did win, though, they often did so in style. Bill Clark, Davie Walker and Jock Young all scored when West Ham United were defeated 3-0 at Eastville. Clark scored twice in a convincing 4-0 victory over New Brompton. Young scored three goals and Walker two as Southampton were thumped 5-0 three days before Christmas. Walker's hat-trick helped Rovers to a 6-1 victory against Northampton Town, with Isaac Owens adding two and Bill Gould scoring the only goal of his Rovers career.

Conversely, Rovers lost 4-0 at home to Brighton and conceded four goals at Tottenham Hotspur and Leyton Orient. However, a seasonal tally of five 1-0 defeats tells its own tale. Luton Town, in fact, beat Rovers by a single goal both home and away. Norwich City beat Rovers 1-0 at Newmarket Road in March, thanks to an 85th-minute penalty following John Smart's foul on outside-right George Lamberton. It was converted by right-back

David Walker had two spells at Rovers scoring 28 goals

Arthur Archer, and was his eighth successful penalty in the Southern League inside 15 months. Goals from Clark and young Walter Gerrish gave Rovers a 2-0 half-time lead at home to Portsmouth on Good Friday, only for Pompey to score three second-half goals, through Jack Bainbridge, 'Sunny Jim' Kirby and Bill Smith, to snatch victory. Bainbridge was later to score for Southampton against Rovers, the opening goal in the FA Cup tie in February 1908 and a Southern League goal 13 months later.

The accomplished violinist Bert Badger was an opponent at Eastville. He was in the Watford side that drew 1-1 in March and was to spend two years with the Hertfordshire club prior to season 1908/09 at Brentford.

The FA Cup brought some excitement, with Woolwich Arsenal playing at Eastville in the third round. Queen's Park Rangers had drawn with Rovers, but Clark's goal had earned the Bristol side victory in London. Then Millwall were comfortably beaten 3-0 before 15,070 spectators who produced gate receipts of £413. For the third round at Highbury, where Bristol City had lost in the previous round, a large crowd saw a strong Arsenal side defeat Rovers through a solitary David Neave goal 20 minutes after half-time. Rovers were down to 10 men at the time of the goal, captain Pudan receiving treatment after a collision with Tim Coleman, who had played for England against Ireland just seven days earlier. 22,000 spectators brought Rovers match takings of £772. After returning from a brief club tour of East Anglia, Rovers lost the Gloucestershire Cup final 2-0 at home to Bristol City, as Sammy Gilligan scored twice. It was also a highly successful season for the future Rovers manager Andrew Wilson, who played centre-forward in the Sheffield Wednesday side that won the FA Cup final and who won the first of his 6 full caps for Scotland.

The Southern League had twice supplied an FA Cup final team, with Tottenham Hotspur famously winning the trophy in 1901. There were proposals made in 1907, as there had been in 1898, for the division to be merged into the Football League. Indeed, relative performances of clubs suggest this would have been a viable proposition. However, working on plans first mooted in 1909, it was as Division Three that the clubs finally attained Football League status in 1920.

SEASON 1906/07

SOUTHERN LEAGUE DIVISION ONE

Date	Opposition		Score	Att	G	2	3	4	5	6	7	8	9	10	11	Goalscorers
01/09/06	NEW BROMPTON	A	1-0	4000	CARTLIDGE	PUDAN	HALES	JARVIE	APPLEBY	HUTCHINSON	CLARK	WALKER	OWENS	YOUNG	GOULD	OWENS
08/09/06	TOTTENHAM HOTSPUR	H	2-3	10000	CARTLIDGE	PUDAN	HALES	JARVIE	APPLEBY	HUTCHINSON	CLARK	WALKER	OWENS	YOUNG	GOULD	WALKER, YOUNG
15/09/06	PLYMOUTH ARGYLE	A	0-3	8500	CARTLIDGE	PUDAN	HALES	HUTCHINSON	APPLEBY	JARVIE	CLARK	YOUNG	LATHAM	WALKER	GOULD	
22/09/06	SWINDON TOWN	H	2-0	7000	CARTLIDGE	PUDAN	HALES	HUTCHINSON	OWENS	JARVIE	CLARK	YOUNG	LATHAM	WALKER	GOULD	LATHAM, YOUNG
24/09/06	WEST HAM UNITED	A	3-0	3000	CARTLIDGE	PUDAN	HALES	HUTCHINSON	OWENS	JARVIE	SAVAGE	YOUNG	CLARK	WALKER	GOULD	CLARK, WALKER, YOUNG
29/09/06	BRIGHTON & H ALBION	A	1-1	7370	CARTLIDGE	PUDAN	HALES	HUTCHINSON	OWENS	JARVIE	CLARK	YOUNG	LATHAM	WALKER	GOULD	MACDONALD og.
06/10/06	NORWICH CITY	H	3-1	7000	CARTLIDGE	HALES	PUDAN	HUTCHINSON	OWENS	JARVIE	CLARK	YOUNG	LATHAM	WALKER	GOULD	LATHAM, WALKER, YOUNG
13/10/06	READING	A	0-1	5000	CARTLIDGE	HALES	PUDAN	HUTCHINSON	OWENS	JARVIE	CLARK	YOUNG	LATHAM	WALKER	GOULD	
15/10/06	WEST HAM UNITED	H	1-0	4000	CARTLIDGE	HALES	APPLEBY	HUTCHINSON	JARVIE	SMART	SAVAGE	YOUNG	CLARK	WALKER	GOULD	SMART
20/10/06	LUTON TOWN	H	0-1	5000	CARTLIDGE	HALES	APPLEBY	HUTCHINSON	OWENS	JARVIE	SAVAGE	YOUNG	CLARK	WALKER	GOULD	
27/10/06	WATFORD	H	0-0	5000	CARTLIDGE	HALES	PUDAN	HUTCHINSON	OWENS	JARVIE	CLARK	YOUNG	LATHAM	WALKER	GOULD	
03/11/06	CRYSTAL PALACE	H	1-1	5000	CARTLIDGE	HALES	PUDAN	HUTCHINSON	APPLEBY	JARVIE	CLARK	YOUNG	LATHAM	WALKER	GOULD	YOUNG
10/11/06	NORTHAMPTON TOWN	A	2-2	2000	CARTLIDGE	HALES	PUDAN	SMART	APPLEBY	JARVIE	SAVAGE	WALKER	OWENS	YOUNG	GOULD	YOUNG 2
17/11/06	BRENTFORD	H	3-1	4000	CARTLIDGE	HALES	PUDAN	SMART	OWENS	JARVIE	SAVAGE	YOUNG	CLARK	WALKER	GOULD	SAVAGE, WALKER, YOUNG
24/11/06	QUEENS PARK RANGERS	A	2-0	6000	CARTLIDGE	APPLEBY	PUDAN	SMART	OWENS	JARVIE	SAVAGE	YOUNG	CLARK	WALKER	GOULD	CLARK
01/12/06	MILLWALL	A	1-0	3000	CARTLIDGE	HALES	PUDAN	SMART	OWENS	JARVIE	SAVAGE	YOUNG	CLARK	WALKER	GOULD	CLARK, WALKER
08/12/06	FULHAM	A	0-3	10000	SWEET	APPLEBY	PUDAN	HUTCHINSON	OWENS	JARVIE	SAVAGE	YOUNG	CLARK	WALKER	GOULD	
15/12/06	LEYTON ORIENT	A	2-4	4000	CARTLIDGE	APPLEBY	PUDAN	HALES	OWENS	JARVIE	SAVAGE	YOUNG	CLARK	WALKER	GOULD	CLARK, YOUNG
22/12/06	SOUTHAMPTON	H	5-0	4000	CARTLIDGE	HALES	PUDAN	HUTCHINSON	APPLEBY	SMART	SAVAGE	YOUNG	CLARK	WALKER	GOULD	YOUNG 3, WALKER 2
26/12/06	PORTSMOUTH	A	0-2	16000	CARTLIDGE	HALES	PUDAN	HUTCHINSON	APPLEBY	JARVIE	SAVAGE	YOUNG	CLARK	WALKER	GOULD	
29/12/06	NEW BROMPTON	H	4-0	5000	CARTLIDGE	HALES	PUDAN	SMART	APPLEBY	JARVIE	SAVAGE	YOUNG	CLARK	WALKER	GOULD	CLARK 2, SMART, YOUNG
05/01/07	TOTTENHAM HOTSPUR	A	0-4	5000	CARTLIDGE	HALES	PUDAN	SMART	APPLEBY	JARVIE	SAVAGE	YOUNG	OWENS	WALKER	GOULD	
19/01/07	PLYMOUTH ARGYLE	H	2-0	6000	CARTLIDGE	HALES	PUDAN	SMART	HUTCHINSON	JARVIE	SAVAGE	YOUNG	OWENS	WALKER	GOULD	OWENS, WALKER
26/01/07	SWINDON TOWN	A	0-1	9000	CARTLIDGE	HALES	PUDAN	SMART	HUTCHINSON	JARVIE	SAVAGE	YOUNG	CLARK	WALKER	GOULD	
16/02/07	READING	H	2-2	5000	CARTLIDGE	HALES	PUDAN	HUTCHINSON	APPLEBY	JARVIE	CLARK	YOUNG	OWENS	WALKER	GOULD	OWENS 2
02/03/07	WATFORD	A	1-1	4000	CARTLIDGE	HALES	APPLEBY	HUTCHINSON	JARVIE	SMART	CLARK	YOUNG	OWENS	WALKER	GOULD	SAVAGE
07/03/07	NORWICH CITY	A	0-1	5000	CARTLIDGE	HALES	APPLEBY	HUTCHINSON	JARVIE	SMART	CLARK	YOUNG	OWENS	WALKER	GOULD	
11/03/07	LUTON TOWN	A	6-1	3500	CARTLIDGE	HALES	APPLEBY	HUTCHINSON	JARVIE	SMART	CLARK	YOUNG	OWENS	WALKER	GOULD	WALKER 3, OWENS 2, GOULD
16/03/07	NORTHAMPTON TOWN	H	1-2	2000	CARTLIDGE	APPLEBY	HALES	HUTCHINSON	JARVIE	SMART	CLARK	YOUNG	OWENS	GERRISH	GOULD	CLARK
23/03/07	BRENTFORD	H	2-3	2000	CARTLIDGE	HALES	APPLEBY	HUTCHINSON	JARVIE	SMART	CLARK	YOUNG	OWENS	GERRISH	GOULD	CLARK, GERRISH
29/03/07	PORTSMOUTH	H	3-1	5000	CARTLIDGE	HALES	HALES	HUTCHINSON	JARVIE	SMART	CLARK	YOUNG	OWENS	WALKER	GOULD	CLARK 2, YOUNG
30/03/07	QUEENS PARK RANGERS	H	0-4	9000	CARTLIDGE	APPLEBY	HALES	HUTCHINSON	GERRISH	SMART	CLARK	YOUNG	OWENS	WALKER	GOULD	
03/04/07	BRIGHTON & H ALBION	A	1-2	3000	CARTLIDGE	OWENS	HALES	HUTCHINSON	GERRISH	SMART	CLARK	YOUNG	SHERDLEY	WALKER	GOULD	GERRISH
06/04/07	MILLWALL	H	0-2	4000	CARTLIDGE	OWENS	HALES	HUTCHINSON	OWENS	SMART	YOUNG	SAVAGE	OWENS	WALKER	GOULD	
13/04/07	FULHAM	A	3-3	8000	CARTLIDGE	APPLEBY	SHAPCOTT	SMART	JARVIE	APPLEBY	CLARK	YOUNG	CLARK	GERRISH	GOULD	HUTCHINSON, JARVIE, WALKER
17/04/07	CRYSTAL PALACE	H	0-0	8000	CARTLIDGE	HALES	PUDAN	SMART	JARVIE	HUTCHINSON	CLARK	YOUNG	OWENS	GERRISH	GOULD	
20/04/07	LEYTON ORIENT	A	1-2	2000	CARTLIDGE	HALES	APPLEBY	SMART	JARVIE	HUTCHINSON	CLARK	YOUNG	OWENS	WALKER	GOULD	WALKER
27/04/07	SOUTHAMPTON	A	1-2	2000	CARTLIDGE	HALES	APPLEBY	HUTCHINSON	OWENS	HUTCHINSON	SAVAGE	YOUNG	CLARK	WALKER	GOULD	

FA CUP

Date	Opposition		Score	Att	G	2	3	4	5	6	7	8	9	10	11	Goalscorers
12/01/07	QUEENS PARK RANGERS	H	0-0	6000	CARTLIDGE	HALES	PUDAN	HUTCHINSON	APPLEBY	JARVIE	CLARK	YOUNG	OWENS	WALKER	GOULD	
14/01/07	QUEENS PARK RANGERS	A	0-1	8000	CARTLIDGE	HALES	PUDAN	HUTCHINSON	APPLEBY	JARVIE	CLARK	YOUNG	OWENS	WALKER	GOULD	CLARK
02/02/07	MILLWALL	H	3-0	15070	CARTLIDGE	HALES	PUDAN	HUTCHINSON	APPLEBY	JARVIE	CLARK	YOUNG	OWENS	WALKER	GOULD	JARVIE, CLARK, HUTCHINSON
23/02/07	WOOLWICH ARSENAL	A	0-1	22000	CARTLIDGE	HALES	APPLEBY	HUTCHINSON	OWENS	SAVAGE	CLARK	YOUNG	OWENS	WALKER	GOULD	

GLOUCESTERSHIRE CUP FINAL

Date	Opposition		Score	Att	G	2	3	4	5	6	7	8	9	10	11	Goalscorers
01/04/07	BRISTOL CITY	H	0-2	12629	CARTLIDGE	HALES	OWENS	HUTCHINSON	JARVIE	SMART	CLARK	YOUNG	WALKER	GERRISH	GOULD	WALKER

PLAYERS	APPS	GLS
APPLEBY B	30	
CARTLIDGE A	37	
CLARK W	35	10
GERRISH W	5	2
GOULD W	38	1
HALES W	35	
HUTCHINSON H	30	1
JARVIE G	34	1
LATHAM F	6	2
OWENS G	15	
OWENS I	17	6
PUDAN D	24	
SAVAGE A	18	2
SHAPCOTT J	1	
SHERDLEY	1	
SMART I	22	2
SWEET A	1	
WALKER D	36	13
YOUNG J	33	14
OWN GOALS		1

1907/08

Several experienced players were allowed to leave Eastville in 1907, as Rovers strove to improve on a disappointing season. Dick Pudan, after five seasons at left-back, joined Newcastle United, for whom he earned an FA Cup final appearance in his first season. Although the former Rovers forward Jimmy Howie scored for the Magpies, the final score was 3-1 to Wolverhampton Wanderers. Davie Walker joined West Bromwich Albion, but was to return to Rovers in June 1911. Isaac Owens joined Crystal Palace, while stand-in forward Fred Latham went on to play one Division One game for Bristol City.

Tom Strang, an experienced centre-half who replaced Ben Appleby at centre-half, the latter moving to full-back, was a close season recruit from Aberdeen. He had been a founder member of the Dons in 1903 and played in 71 Scottish League games, scoring once and captaining the side between 1905 and 1907. Rovers started the season with four new forwards. John Smith, from Birmingham, had spent four years at Wolverhampton Wanderers, while outside-left Harry Buckle from Portsmouth had represented Northern Ireland when on the books of Sunderland and played against Wales on 11 April 1908 while a Rovers player. Astonishingly, Smith, Buckle, inside-right Isiah Turner and inside-left John Roberts (only three minutes into his first game) all scored on their Southern League debuts.

Indeed, Rovers opened the season in style. 1906/07 had begun with a single-goal victory over New Brompton, but now they recording their highest-ever opening-day win. Smith missed a penalty before contributing four goals, including a hat-trick inside twenty second-half minutes on a memorable first appearance for the club as Rovers recorded a 9-1 win. A 4,000 crowd became 11,000 for the visit of Brentford three days later and Smith scored twice more in a 3-0 victory. Then the bubble burst. Rovers crashed 10-0 at Tottenham Hotspur in a Western League match where centre-forward Jimmy Pass scored eight times, and lost two consecutive Southern League games. Smith was never to score more than once in a match during the remainder of his Rovers career.

With their feet back on the ground, Rovers began to put together some good runs and, by Christmas, were just three points behind joint leaders Plymouth Argyle and Queen's Park Rangers. At this point Rovers, unbeaten at home, had won five consecutive games, even if all were by close margins. Shortly after Christmas, three first-half goals gave Rovers a second 3-0 victory over Brentford, with Fred Corbett, due to rejoin Rovers in the summer, playing for the Bees. Following this result, however, Rovers won just four more league games, and lost three in succession while Harry Buckle was away on International duty with Northern Ireland. Despite a 3-0 victory over Portsmouth on the final day, Rovers finished the season in sixth place.

Rovers were unable to achieve the results they required against the top sides. Queen's Park Rangers beat Rovers 5-3 in October, with Rovers a goal down in three minutes and 2-1 up after 10. This was on the day that goalkeeper Arthur Cartlidge played his 200th Southern League game for Rovers, a club record subsequently equalled only by David Harvie and Billy Peplow. Rangers also inflicted Rovers' first home defeat of the season,

Bristol Rovers 1907/08. Back row: Cox, Hales, Sweet, Appleby, Cartlidge, Phillips, Gerrish, Murphy. Middle row: Pay (Trainer), Clark, Shapcott, Smart, Strang, Handley, Boyle, Buckle. Front row: Savage, Turner, Smith, Roberts

as Easter approached. Reading and Portsmouth also scored five times in a game, while Rovers conceded four goals on a further four occasions. Bradford Park Avenue, who through a geographical quirk were playing in a sole Southern League season, beat Rovers 4-1, thanks to a George Reid hat-trick. Millwall won 4-0 at Eastville; Danny Cunliffe, who had scored four goals against Rovers in October 1899 and a total of 15 Western and Southern League goals for Portsmouth against Rovers between 1899 and 1906, scored the opening goal after only four minutes, before Alf Twigg scored twice and Harry Shand once in 12 second-half minutes.

Norwich City's James Bauchop was sent off during the goalless draw at Newmarket Road in February and was banned for one game. When Norwich played at Eastville, Peter Roney, a Rovers goalkeeper in 1909, and James Young, a wing-half from 1902/03 with Rovers, were in their side. Jack Lewis, a veteran of two spells with Rovers, scored for Southampton at Eastville in October. In the Western League, two second-half goals in October brought Rovers a 2-0 victory over Millwall, inflicting on the champions their only defeat of the season.

Remarkably, four Rovers players scored 10 or more Southern League goals, while Turner, who was latterly out of the side, contributed nine. Roberts was top scorer with 14. The highlight of the FA Cup run was a 2-0 victory over Division Two Chesterfield, with Billy Clark scoring twice before an Eastville crowd of 15,000, which brought gate receipts of £380. Rovers were eliminated from the FA Cup at Southampton and the Gloucestershire Cup at Bristol City by two-goal margins.

SOUTHERN LEAGUE DIVISION ONE

SEASON 1907/08

Date	Opponent	H/A	Score	ATT	G	2	3	4	5	6	7	8	9	10	11	GOALSCORERS
04/09/07	NEW BROMPTON	H	9-1	4000	CARTLIDGE	HALES	BOYLE	SMART	STRANG	HANDLEY	CLARK	TURNER	SMITH	ROBERTS	BUCKLE	SMITH 4, BUCKLE 2, CLARK, ROBERTS, BOYLE
07/09/07	BRENTFORD	H	3-0	11000	CARTLIDGE	HALES	BOYLE	SMART	STRANG	HANDLEY	CLARK	TURNER	SMITH	ROBERTS	BUCKLE	ROBERTS, TURNER, SMITH
14/09/07	NEW BROMPTON	A	0-1	6000	CARTLIDGE	HALES	BOYLE	SMART	STRANG	HANDLEY	CLARK	TURNER	SMITH	ROBERTS	BUCKLE	
21/09/07	LEYTON ORIENT	A	0-2	4000	CARTLIDGE	HALES	BOYLE	SMART	APPLEBY	HANDLEY	CLARK	TURNER	SMITH	ROBERTS	BUCKLE	
28/09/07	READING	H	2-1	8000	CARTLIDGE	HALES	BOYLE	SMART	APPLEBY	HANDLEY	CLARK	TURNER	SMITH	ROBERTS	BUCKLE	SMITH 2, BUCKLE
05/10/07	WATFORD	A	2-1	4000	CARTLIDGE	HALES	BOYLE	SMART	APPLEBY	HANDLEY	CLARK	TURNER	SMITH	ROBERTS	BUCKLE	BOYLE, BUCKLE
12/10/07	NORWICH CITY	H	2-2	7000	CARTLIDGE	HALES	BOYLE	SMART	APPLEBY	HANDLEY	CLARK	MURPHY	ROBERTS	SMITH	BUCKLE	MURPHY, ROBERTS
19/10/07	NORTHAMPTON T	A	2-2	8000	CARTLIDGE	HALES	BOYLE	SMART	APPLEBY	HANDLEY	CLARK	MURPHY	ROBERTS	SMITH	BUCKLE	MURPHY, ROBERTS
26/10/07	NORTHAMPTON T	H	4-2	8000	CARTLIDGE	HALES	BOYLE	SMART	APPLEBY	HANDLEY	CLARK	TURNER	ROBERTS	SMITH	BUCKLE	CLARK 2, ROBERTS, SMITH
02/11/07	PLYMOUTH ARGYLE	A	2-4	11000	CARTLIDGE	HALES	BOYLE	SMART	APPLEBY	HANDLEY	CLARK	TURNER	SMITH	ROBERTS	BUCKLE	ROBERTS 2
09/11/07	WEST HAM UNITED	H	1-0	10000	CARTLIDGE	HALES	BOYLE	SMART	APPLEBY	HANDLEY	CLARK	TURNER	SMITH	ROBERTS	BUCKLE	SMITH
16/11/07	QPR	A	3-5	10000	CARTLIDGE	HALES	BOYLE	SMART	APPLEBY	HANDLEY	SAVAGE	TURNER	SMITH	ROBERTS	BUCKLE	CLARK 2, ROBERTS, SMITH
23/11/07	TOTTENHAM HOTSPUR	H	0-0	15000	CARTLIDGE	HALES	BOYLE	SMART	APPLEBY	HANDLEY	CLARK	TURNER	SMITH	ROBERTS	BUCKLE	
30/11/07	SWINDON TOWN	A	1-4	6000	CARTLIDGE	HALES	APPLEBY	SMART	STRANG	HANDLEY	CLARK	TURNER	SMITH	ROBERTS	BUCKLE	SMITH
07/12/07	CRYSTAL PALACE	H	2-1	6000	CARTLIDGE	HALES	BOYLE	SMART	STRANG	SMART	SAVAGE	TURNER	SMITH	ROBERTS	BUCKLE	BUCKLE, CLARK
14/12/07	LUTON TOWN	A	2-0	3000	CARTLIDGE	HALES	BOYLE	SMART	STRANG	HANDLEY	CLARK	TURNER	SMITH	ROBERTS	BUCKLE	BUCKLE, TURNER
21/12/07	BRIGHTON & H ALBION	H	2-1	6000	CARTLIDGE	HALES	BOYLE	SMART	STRANG	HANDLEY	CLARK	TURNER	SMITH	ROBERTS	BUCKLE	ROBERTS, GERRISH
25/12/07	BRADFORD	H	2-1	10000	CARTLIDGE	HALES	BOYLE	SMART	STRANG	HANDLEY	CLARK	TURNER	SMITH	ROBERTS	BUCKLE	BUCKLE, TURNER
26/12/07	MILLWALL	A	1-0	7000	CARTLIDGE	HALES	APPLEBY	SMART	STRANG	HANDLEY	CLARK	TURNER	SMITH	ROBERTS	BUCKLE	SMITH
28/12/07	PORTSMOUTH	H	2-5	10000	CARTLIDGE	HALES	APPLEBY	SMART	STRANG	HANDLEY	CLARK	TURNER	SMITH	ROBERTS	BUCKLE	APPLEBY, BUCKLE, ROBERTS
04/01/08	BRENTFORD	A	3-0	2000	CARTLIDGE	HALES	APPLEBY	SMART	STRANG	HANDLEY	CLARK	SMITH	ROBERTS	GERRISH	BUCKLE	CLARK, BUCKLE, TURNER
25/01/08	READING	A	0-0	3000	CARTLIDGE	HALES	APPLEBY	SMART	STRANG	HANDLEY	CLARK	SMITH	ROBERTS	GERRISH	BUCKLE	
08/02/08	NORWICH CITY	A	0-0	5000	CARTLIDGE	SCOTHERN	BOYLE	SMART	ROBERTS	HANDLEY	SAVAGE	SMITH	SAVAGE	ROBERTS	BUCKLE	
15/02/08	PLYMOUTH	A	0-5	3000	CARTLIDGE	HALES	BOYLE	SMART	ROBERTS	HANDLEY	SAVAGE	SMITH	SAVAGE	ROBERTS	BUCKLE	
29/02/08	WEST HAM UNITED	A	0-1	5000	CARTLIDGE	HALES	BOYLE	SMART	STRANG	HANDLEY	SAVAGE	TURNER	SMITH	ROBERTS	BUCKLE	
07/03/08	PLYMOUTH ARGYLE	H	1-0	8000	CARTLIDGE	HALES	APPLEBY	SMART	STRANG	HANDLEY	SAVAGE	TURNER	SMITH	ROBERTS	BUCKLE	SMART
14/03/08	QUEENS PARK RANGERS	H	0-0	10000	CARTLIDGE	SCOTHERN	APPLEBY	SMART	STRANG	HANDLEY	SAVAGE	CLARK	GERRISH	ROBERTS	GERRISH	
21/03/08	TOTTENHAM HOTSPUR	H	2-1	12000	CARTLIDGE	HALES	BOYLE	SMART	STRANG	HANDLEY	CLARK	TURNER	SMITH	ROBERTS	BUCKLE	SMITH 2, BUCKLE
28/03/08	SWINDON TOWN	A	1-1	9000	CARTLIDGE	HALES	BOYLE	ROBERTS	STRANG	HANDLEY	CLARK	TURNER	SMITH	SAVAGE	BUCKLE	BUCKLE, ROBERTS
30/03/08	WATFORD	H	1-1	8000	CARTLIDGE	HALES	BOYLE	SMART	STRANG	HANDLEY	CLARK	TURNER	SMITH	ROBERTS	BUCKLE	BUCKLE, TURNER
04/04/08	CRYSTAL PALACE	A	1-1	10000	CARTLIDGE	HALES	BOYLE	SMART	STRANG	HANDLEY	CLARK	TURNER	SMITH	SAVAGE	BUCKLE	SAVAGE
06/04/08	SOUTHAMPTON	A	0-1	9000	CARTLIDGE	HALES	OVENS	SMART	STRANG	HANDLEY	CLARK	GERRISH	TURNER	SAVAGE	BUCKLE	BADDELEY og
11/04/08	LUTON TOWN	H	1-4	9000	CARTLIDGE	HALES	OVENS	SMART	STRANG	HANDLEY	SAVAGE	GERRISH	TURNER	ROBERTS	CLARK	ROBERTS
17/04/08	BRADFORD	A	1-4	5000	CARTLIDGE	HALES	OVENS	SMART	STRANG	HANDLEY	SAVAGE	GERRISH	SMITH	CLARK	ROBERTS	SAVAGE
18/04/08	BRIGHTON & H ALBION	A	2-2	4000	CARTLIDGE	HALES	OVENS	SMART	STRANG	HANDLEY	SAVAGE	GERRISH	TURNER	CLARK	BUCKLE	CLARK, ROBERTS
20/04/08	LEYTON ORIENT	H	1-4	9000	CARTLIDGE	HALES	OVENS	SMART	STRANG	HANDLEY	CLARK	GERRISH	SMITH	CLARK	BUCKLE	CLARK
21/04/08	MILLWALL	A	0-4	5000	CARTLIDGE	HALES	OVENS	SMART	APPLEBY	HANDLEY	CLARK	GERRISH	GERRISH	SAVAGE	BUCKLE	
25/04/08	PORTSMOUTH	A	3-0	4000	CARTLIDGE	SCOTHERN	OVENS	SMART	STRANG	HANDLEY	SAVAGE	GERRISH	SMITH	ROBERTS	BUCKLE	ROBERTS 2, BUCKLE

FA CUP

Date	Opponent	H/A	Score	ATT	G	2	3	4	5	6	7	8	9	10	11	GOALSCORERS
11/01/08	NORTHAMPTON TOWN	H	1-4	13000	CARTLIDGE	HALES	BOYLE	SMART	STRANG	HANDLEY	CLARK	TURNER	SMITH	ROBERTS	BUCKLE	SMITH
03/02/08	CHESTERFIELD	H	2-0	15000	CARTLIDGE	HALES	BOYLE	SMART	STRANG	HANDLEY	CLARK	TURNER	SMITH	ROBERTS	BUCKLE	CLARK 2
22/02/08	SOUTHAMPTON	H	0-2	13000	CARTLIDGE	HALES	BOYLE	SMART	STRANG	HANDLEY	CLARK	TURNER	SMITH	ROBERTS	BUCKLE	

GLOUCESTERSHIRE CUP FINAL*

Date	Opponent	H/A	Score	ATT	G	2	3	4	5	6	7	8	9	10	11	GOALSCORERS
29/04/08	BRISTOL CITY		0-2	8186	CARTLIDGE	APPLEBY	OVENS	SMART	STRANG	HANDLEY	CLARK	TURNER	SMITH	ROBERTS	BUCKLE	

* From this season Glos Cup was competed for by Rovers & City only

PLAYERS	APPS	GLS
APPLEBY B	34	1
BOYLE P	29	1
BUCKLE H	33	30
CARTLIDGE A	38	
CLARK W	36	10
GERRISH W	14	1
HALES W	18	
HANDLEY F	33	1
MURPHY E	2	
OVENS G	10	
ROBERTS J	29	14
SAVAGE A	17	1
SCOTHERN A	3	
SMART J	37	
SMITH I	31	10
STRANG T	24	9
TURNER I	9	1
OWN GOAL		1

The prominent politician Ernest Bevin, whose early years had been spent in St Werburgh's and who had been a pioneer at St Mark's Baptist Church, proposed in 1908 a series of potential work schemes to the Bristol City Council. Within the immediate area, he planned a lake within Eastville Park that naturally acquired, on its construction in 1910, the nickname Bevin's Lake.

1908/09

The success of 1907/08 was repeated as a more consistent Rovers side completed the season in fifth place in the Southern League. Ben Appleby had retired to senior non-league football in Gloucester and, despite the additional loss of reliable outside-right Billy Clark to Sunderland and Harry Buckle and Isaiah Turner to Coventry City, manager Alf Homer strengthened Rovers' side with a number of shrewd purchases. Clark's replacement was Billy Peplow, a Derbyshire lad signed from Birmingham, who was to be a fixture in the Rovers side until World War One. Young reserve Walter Gerrish, who had first played for Rovers in April 1906, became Turner's permanent successor. The former Bishop Auckland wing-half Martin Higgins arrived after a successful career with Grimsby Town. Reserve goalkeeper Bill Demmery signed from Bristol City with whom he had played in Division One and Fred Corbett, rejoining from Brentford, began a third spell at Eastville.

Consistent form, especially at home, was the key to Rovers' success. After all, they were never again going to finish in the top 12 of the Southern League. Five times 10,000 or more spectators watched Southern League fixtures at Eastville. When the champions-elect Northampton Town, under player-manager Herbert Chapman, came to visit in a temperature of 90°F, a crowd of 12,000 saw the prodigal hero Fred Corbett's 22nd-minute goal earn Rovers a 1-0 victory. Corbett was the club's top scorer. His 19 goals, which equalled Andrew Smith's achievement in 1904/05, was never to beaten during Rovers' Southern League years. He scored a hat-trick early in January in the largest win of the season, 5-1 at home to Exeter City.

Rovers also scored four goals in the home matches against Millwall and Southampton, Roberts scoring twice in the former and Gerrish twice in the latter. Peplow also scored in both and these three forwards supported Corbett ably as Rovers ran up 60 Southern League goals, the most since the Championship season. Half-backs Strang and Higgins scored two goals each during the season and, in each case, these were in consecutive fixtures. In the case of Martin Higgins, his penalties against Luton Town on Christmas Day and at Swindon Town on Boxing Day, brought successive 1-0 victories. The return fixture at Luton Town on Easter Monday marked goalkeeper Arthur Cartlidge's final appearance for Rovers, his 258 Southern League matches for the club remaining an unbeaten record.

Isaiah Turner, sold to Coventry City, played for his new club in both fixtures against Rovers, while his team-mate Harry Buckle scored Coventry's opening goal after ten minutes at Eastville in October. Both sides then scored penalties, Peplow only doing so when his initial kick, which had hit the post, had to be retaken. Norwich City, with Peter

Bristol Rovers 1908/09. Back row: Higgins, Appleby, A Sweet, Cartlidge, Strang, Handley, Ovens. Middle row: Bates (Trainer), Peplow, Corbett, Savage, J Sweet, Chalmers, Roberts, Gerrish, Dargue, Pay (Trainer). Front row: Floyd, Phillips, McCubbin, Fear, Nichols

Roney in goal, defeated Rovers 4-1 in March, having made seven changes to their side after defeat at Coventry. The Canaries scored twice in each half, with full-back Charles Craig registering his only ever goal for the club. When the sides met at Eastville, Norwich's Walter Rayner was sent off for head-butting Billy Peplow, who was also sent off for retaliation. Rovers held on for a late single-goal victory over New Brompton in November with Frank Handley in goal, after Cartlidge, just moments after half-time, had been taken to hospital with a head injury. Irishman Frank Kelly scored for Watford in both games against Rovers while Scotsman David McKinley contributed two goals in the Vicarage Road game. There were five different scorers when Millwall beat Rovers 6-0 in a Western League game in October. Portsmouth fielded Arthur Knight in their side against Rovers, an Olympic gold medal winner for football in 1912, who appeared regularly for Pompey at Eastville between 1908 and 1922.

An exciting FA Cup draw brought Division Two Burnley to Eastville, but Rovers were outclassed. Although Billy Peplow scored for the home club, Rovers were not able to produce the result the crowd of 7,000 desired. Burnley's inside-right Arthur Ogden scored a hat-trick as the visitors won 4-1. While Rovers were out, Bristol City reached the FA Cup final, where they lost to Manchester United. Sandy Turnbull scored the only goal of the game after 22 minutes. With the Gloucestershire Cup final held over until 1909/10, Rovers set off for Paris in March to play in an exhibition match under floodlights against Southampton. The game finished 5-5, after Rovers had held a 2-1

SOUTHERN LEAGUE DIVISION ONE

SEASON 1908/09

Date	Opposition		Score	ATT	G	2	3	4	5	6	7	8	9	10	11	GOALSCORERS
05/09/08	EXETER CITY	A	3-3	8000	CARTLIDGE	APPLEBY	OVENS	HIGGINS	STRANG	HANDLEY	PEPLOW	GERRISH	CORBETT	ROBERTS	DARGUE	ROBERTS 2, PEPLOW
07/09/08	PORTSMOUTH	H	3-2	5000	CARTLIDGE	APPLEBY	FLOYD	SMART	HIGGINS	HANDLEY	PEPLOW	GERRISH	CORBETT	ROBERTS	DARGUE	CORBETT 2, GERRISH
12/09/08	NORTHAMPTON TOWN	H	1-0	12000	CARTLIDGE	APPLEBY	OVENS	HIGGINS	STRANG	HANDLEY	SAVAGE	GERRISH	CORBETT	ROBERTS	DARGUE	CORBETT
19/09/08	NEW BROMPTON	A	0-2	6000	CARTLIDGE	APPLEBY	FLOYD	SMART	STRANG	HANDLEY	PEPLOW	GERRISH	CORBETT	ROBERTS	DARGUE	
26/09/08	MILLWALL	H	4-2	5000	CARTLIDGE	APPLEBY	FLOYD	SMART	STRANG	HANDLEY	PEPLOW	GERRISH	CORBETT	ROBERTS	DARGUE	ROBERTS 2, DARGUE, PEPLOW pen
07/10/08	PORTSMOUTH	A	0-2	3000	CARTLIDGE	APPLEBY	FLOYD	HIGGINS	STRANG	HANDLEY	PEPLOW	GERRISH	CORBETT	ROBERTS	DARGUE	
10/10/08	COVENTRY CITY	H	1-3	10000	CARTLIDGE	SCOTHERN	FLOYD	HIGGINS	STRANG	HANDLEY	PEPLOW	McCUBBIN	CORBETT	ROBERTS	DARGUE	PEPLOW pen
17/10/08	PLYMOUTH ARGYLE	H	2-0	5000	CARTLIDGE	APPLEBY	FLOYD	SMART	STRANG	HIGGINS	PEPLOW	GERRISH	CORBETT	ROBERTS	DARGUE	CORBETT, GERRISH
24/10/08	WATFORD	A	1-4	3000	CARTLIDGE	APPLEBY	FLOYD	HIGGINS	STRANG	HANDLEY	PEPLOW	GERRISH	CHALMERS	CORBETT	DARGUE	CHALMERS
31/10/08	NORWICH CITY	H	2-0	10000	CARTLIDGE	APPLEBY	FLOYD	SMART	STRANG	HANDLEY	PEPLOW	GERRISH	CORBETT	ROBERTS	DARGUE	PEPLOW, ROBERTS
07/11/08	READING	A	2-2	4000	CARTLIDGE	APPLEBY	FLOYD	SMART	STRANG	HIGGINS	PEPLOW	GERRISH	CORBETT	ROBERTS	DARGUE	GERRISH, PEPLOW
14/11/08	SOUTHAMPTON	H	4-1	10000	CARTLIDGE	APPLEBY	FLOYD	SMART	STRANG	HIGGINS	PEPLOW	GERRISH	CORBETT	ROBERTS	DARGUE	GERRISH 2, DARGUE, PEPLOW
21/11/08	CLAPTON ORIENT RES.	A	1-0	6000	CARTLIDGE	APPLEBY	FLOYD	SMART	STRANG	HIGGINS	PEPLOW	GERRISH	CORBETT	ROBERTS	DARGUE	ROBERTS
28/11/08	WEST HAM UNITED	H	1-0	5000	CARTLIDGE	APPLEBY	FLOYD	SMART	STRANG	HIGGINS	SAVAGE	GERRISH	CORBETT	ROBERTS	DARGUE	GERRISH
05/12/08	BRIGHTON & H ALBION	A	0-5	4000	CARTLIDGE	NICHOLS	FLOYD	McCUBBIN	STRANG	HANDLEY	PEPLOW	PHILLIPS	CORBETT	ROBERTS	DARGUE	
12/12/08	CRYSTAL PALACE	H	2-2	10000	CARTLIDGE	APPLEBY	FLOYD	SMART	STRANG	HANDLEY	PEPLOW	PHILLIPS	CORBETT	ROBERTS	DARGUE	CORBETT, DARGUE
19/12/08	BRENTFORD	A	2-2	4000	CARTLIDGE	APPLEBY	FLOYD	SMART	STRANG	HIGGINS	PEPLOW	GERRISH	CORBETT	ROBERTS	DARGUE	CORBETT, GERRISH
25/12/08	LUTON TOWN	H	1-0	7000	CARTLIDGE	APPLEBY	FLOYD	SMART	STRANG	HIGGINS	PEPLOW	GERRISH	CORBETT	ROBERTS	DARGUE	HIGGINS pen
26/12/08	SWINDON TOWN	A	1-0	10000	CARTLIDGE	APPLEBY	FLOYD	SMART	STRANG	HANDLEY	PEPLOW	McCUBBIN	HIGGINS	ROBERTS	DARGUE	HIGGINS pen
02/01/09	EXETER CITY	H	5-1	10000	CARTLIDGE	APPLEBY	FLOYD	SMART	STRANG	HIGGINS	PEPLOW	McCUBBIN	CORBETT	ROBERTS	DARGUE	CORBETT 3, McCUBBIN, ROBERTS
09/01/09	NORTHAMPTON TOWN	A	0-3	7000	CARTLIDGE	APPLEBY	FLOYD	SMART	STRANG	HIGGINS	PEPLOW	McCUBBIN	CORBETT	ROBERTS	DARGUE	
23/01/09	NEW BROMPTON	H	1-0	5000	CARTLIDGE	OVENS	FLOYD	SMART	STRANG	HANDLEY	SAVAGE	GERRISH	CORBETT	ROBERTS	DARGUE	CORBETT
25/01/09	QUEENS PARK RANGERS	A	2-4	5000	DEMMERY	OVENS	FLOYD	SMART	STRANG	HANDLEY	SAVAGE	GERRISH	CORBETT	ROBERTS	DARGUE	CORBETT 2
30/01/09	MILLWALL	A	1-2	5000	DEMMERY	OVENS	FLOYD	SMART	STRANG	HANDLEY	PEPLOW	McCUBBIN	CORBETT	ROBERTS	DARGUE	ROBERTS
06/02/09	SOUTHEND UNITED	A	1-2	5000	DEMMERY	OVENS	FLOYD	SMART	STRANG	HANDLEY	PEPLOW	GERRISH	CORBETT	ROBERTS	DARGUE	GERRISH
13/02/09	COVENTRY CITY	H	2-2	6000	DEMMERY	OVENS	FLOYD	SMART	STRANG	HIGGINS	PEPLOW	GERRISH	CORBETT	ROBERTS	DARGUE	CORBETT, PEPLOW
27/02/09	WATFORD	H	1-1	4000	DEMMERY	OVENS	FLOYD	HIGGINS	STRANG	HANDLEY	PEPLOW	PHILLIPS	CORBETT	ROBERTS	DARGUE	PHILLIPS
06/03/09	NORWICH CITY	A	1-4	4000	CARTLIDGE	APPLEBY	FLOYD	SMART	STRANG	HIGGINS	PEPLOW	GERRISH	CORBETT	ROBERTS	DARGUE	CORBETT
13/03/09	READING	H	2-2	6000	CARTLIDGE	OVENS	FLOYD	SMART	STRANG	HIGGINS	PEPLOW	GERRISH	CORBETT	ROBERTS	ROBERTS	CORBETT, STRANG
17/03/09	PLYMOUTH ARGYLE	A	1-0	2000	CARTLIDGE	APPLEBY	FLOYD	SMART	STRANG	HIGGINS	PEPLOW	PHILLIPS	CORBETT	ROBERTS	DARGUE	CORBETT
20/03/09	SOUTHAMPTON	A	0-1	4000	CARTLIDGE	OVENS	FLOYD	SMART	STRANG	HIGGINS	PEPLOW	PHILLIPS	CORBETT	GERRISH	DARGUE	
27/03/09	CLAPTON ORIENT RES.	H	1-1	4000	CARTLIDGE	APPLEBY	FLOYD	SMART	STRANG	HIGGINS	PEPLOW	GERRISH	CORBETT	ROBERTS	DARGUE	STRANG
29/03/09	QUEENS PARK RANGERS	H	0-0	2000	CARTLIDGE	APPLEBY	OVENS	SMART	STRANG	HIGGINS	PEPLOW	GERRISH	CORBETT	ROBERTS	DARGUE	
03/04/09	WEST HAM UNITED	A	2-0	7000	CARTLIDGE	APPLEBY	OVENS	SMART	STRANG	HANDLEY	PEPLOW	ROBERTS	CORBETT	McCUBBIN	DARGUE	CORBETT, ROBERTS
05/04/09	SOUTHEND UNITED	H	1-0	2000	CARTLIDGE	APPLEBY	FLOYD	SMART	STRANG	HANDLEY	PEPLOW	GERRISH	CORBETT	McCUBBIN	DARGUE	GERRISH
09/04/09	SWINDON TOWN	H	1-3	8000	CARTLIDGE	OVENS	FLOYD	HIGGINS	STRANG	HANDLEY	PEPLOW	ROBERTS	CORBETT	GERRISH	DARGUE	PEPLOW
10/04/09	BRIGHTON & H ALBION	H	3-0	4000	CARTLIDGE	OVENS	FLOYD	HIGGINS	STRANG	HANDLEY	PEPLOW	ROBERTS	CORBETT	GERRISH	DARGUE	CORBETT, PEPLOW, ROBERTS
12/04/09	LUTON TOWN	A	0-1	6000	DEMMERY	OVENS	FLOYD	APPLEBY	STRANG	HANDLEY	PEPLOW	GERRISH	CORBETT	ROBERTS	DARGUE	
17/04/09	CRYSTAL PALACE	A	1-4	4000	DEMMERY	OVENS	FLOYD	HIGGINS	STRANG	HANDLEY	PEPLOW	ROBERTS	CORBETT	McCUBBIN	DARGUE	ROBERTS
24/04/09	BRENTFORD	H	3-2	3000	DEMMERY	OVENS	FLOYD	SMART	STRANG	HANDLEY	PEPLOW	ROBERTS	CORBETT	McCUBBIN	JONES	CORBETT 2, McCUBBIN

FA CUP

Date	Opposition		Score	ATT	G	2	3	4	5	6	7	8	9	10	11	GOALSCORERS
16/01/09	BURNLEY	H	1-4	7000	CARTLIDGE	APPLEBY	FLOYD	STRANG	SMART	HIGGINS	PEPLOW	McCUBBIN	PHILLIPS	ROBERTS	DARGUE	STRANG

PLAYERS	APPS	GLS
APPLEBY B	29	
CARTLIDGE A	32	
CHALMERS J	1	1
CORBETT F	38	19
DARGUE J	37	3
DEMMERY W	8	
FLOYD B	36	
GERRISH W	31	9
HANDLEY F	24	
HIGGINS M	28	2
JONES C	1	
McCUBBIN A	9	2
NICHOLS W	1	
OVENS G	16	
PEPLOW W	35	9
PHILLIPS G	5	1
ROBERTS J	35	11
SAVAGE A	5	
SMART J	31	
STRANG T	37	2
SCOTHERN A	1	

lead at half-time. Corbett scored a hat-trick, with Gerrish and Gilbert Ovens claiming a goal apiece.

On the afternoon of Saturday 26 June 1909, the future – if temporary – Rovers home at Twerton Park, then known as Innox Park, was officially opened on land donated by Thomas Carr of Poolemeade, West Twerton. The ceremony began at 3 p.m. and featured a procession of scholars, the singing of hymns and a speech given by Robert Hope, a pattern maker of Maybrick Road, South Twerton, who was Chairman of the Parish Council.

1909/10

Despite retaining several key players, most notably a trio of goalscorers in Corbett, Peplow and Roberts, Rovers found season 1909/10 more of a struggle. Ultimately, finishing in 13th place in the Southern League was something of a success. Martin Higgins had joined New Brompton, for whom he played twice this season against Rovers, while the inspirational Walter Gerrish and experienced Arthur Cartlidge, the latter after an impressive 258 Southern League appearances for Rovers, had both moved to Aston Villa, where they were to help their new side to the Football League Championship in their first season. Bill Nichols, after just one game, moved to Merthyr Town. Peter Roney, a goalkeeper with a very good reputation, joined Rovers from Norwich City. He and John Laurie were to be Rovers' two ever-presents. Two other players viewed as major signings, Fred Riddell, a former Derby County player, and

Goalkeeper Peter Roney scored penalty goal in the last match of 1909/10

Charles Jones, who had played for Birmingham in Division Two, managed just 5 Southern League appearances between them.

Corbett set his stall out for the season with a goal in the drawn Gloucestershire Cup final and two in a remarkably one-sided opening-day victory over Portsmouth. Bristol City's success in reaching the 1909 FA Cup final had led to the regional cup competition being held over, with the result that, after two draws, Rovers had the dubious pleasure of losing two Gloucestershire Cup finals in ten weeks in the spring. Left-half Frank Handley may not have scored in 93 Southern League matches for Rovers, but his 35th-minute equaliser at Ashton Gate in October ensured a second replay to the initial tie.

Bristol Rovers 1909/10. Back row: Smart, Ovens, Shaw, L Williams, Roney, Demmery, McKenzie, Handley, Gange, Phillips. Middle row: Osborne, Peplow, Glendenning, Jones, Mason, Corbett, Roberts, Laurie, Bennett, Riddell, Westwood. Front row: O Williams, Lucas

Free-scoring Northampton Town found Rovers' defensive line of goalkeeper Roney and full-backs Bill Westwood and Gilbert Ovens impenetrable. Rovers recorded 1-0 victories on both grounds to score a memorable double over the Cobblers, Corbett scoring on both occasions. On Christmas Day, the centre-forward's 80th-minute consolation goal in defeat at Luton Town set a new Southern League goalscoring record for the club. It was Corbett's 45th goal, surpassing Billy Beats' record set in 1906. One further milestone for Rovers' top scorer was that, in scoring the opening goal in the final home game of the season, Corbett became the only Rovers player during the Southern League era to record 50 goals in this competition for the club.

For the most part though, it was a fairly demoralizing season. In one eight-match run in early spring for instance, the only goals Rovers scored were two Bill Shaw penalties. Watford put four goals past Rovers and Clapton Orient bagged six. West Ham United had not scored in their previous six Southern League meetings with Rovers, but recorded a comfortable 5-0 victory early in October. The good news was that Danny Shea, scorer of 10 goals in the opening eight games of the season was, like George Webb, restricted to one goal. The bad news for Rovers was a Tommy Caldwell hat-trick, his first goals of the season for the Hammers. Harry Buckle returned to haunt his former club by scoring in both fixtures against Rovers for Coventry City, who fielded Patsy Hendren for the February game at Eastville, the first of many appearances at the ground for the famous England cricket International. Even Portsmouth avenged their heavy defeat, their second goal in January being scored from the penalty spot 15 minutes from time by the former Trowbridge Town outside-left Teddy Long, who signed for Rovers in 1911.

SOUTHERN LEAGUE DIVISION ONE

Date	Opponent	H/A	Score	ATT	G	2	3	4	5	6	7	8	9	10	11	GOALSCORERS
04/09/09	PORTSMOUTH	A	4-0	6000	RONEY	McKENZIE	WESTWOOD	SMART	WILLIAMS	HANDLEY	PEPLOW	MASON	CORBETT	ROBERTS	LAURIE	CORBETT 2, MASON, SMART
08/09/09	CRYSTAL PALACE	A	1-3	4000	RONEY	McKENZIE	WESTWOOD	SMART	GLENDENNING	SHAW	PEPLOW	CORBETT	MASON	ROBERTS	LAURIE	GLENDENNING
11/09/09	EXETER CITY	A	1-1	5000	RONEY	McKENZIE	WESTWOOD	SMART	WILLIAMS	SHAW	PEPLOW	MASON	CORBETT	ROBERTS	LAURIE	
18/09/09	NORWICH CITY	A	3-0	6000	RONEY	McKENZIE	WESTWOOD	SMART	WILLIAMS	HANDLEY	PEPLOW	MASON	CORBETT	ROBERTS	LAURIE	
25/09/09	BRENTFORD	H	3-1	8000	RONEY	McKENZIE	WESTWOOD	SMART	WILLIAMS	SHAW	PEPLOW	MASON	CORBETT	ROBERTS	LAURIE	CORBETT, LAURIE, ROBERTS,
02/10/09	COVENTRY CITY	A	0-5	3000	RONEY	McKENZIE	WESTWOOD	SMART	WILLIAMS	SHAW	PEPLOW	MASON	CORBETT	MASON	LAURIE	
04/10/09	WEST HAM UNITED	H	0-5	3000	RONEY	McKENZIE	WESTWOOD	SMART	WILLIAMS	SHAW	PEPLOW	MASON	CORBETT	McCOLL	LAURIE	
09/10/09	WATFORD	H	1-3	6000	RONEY	McKENZIE	WESTWOOD	SMART	WILLIAMS	HANDLEY	PEPLOW	CORBETT	MASON	McCOLL	LAURIE	MASON
16/10/09	READING	A	1-0	2500	RONEY	McKENZIE	WESTWOOD	SMART	WILLIAMS	HANDLEY	PEPLOW	MASON	CORBETT	McCOLL	LAURIE	PEPLOW pen
23/10/09	SOUTHEND UNITED	H	2-0	5000	RONEY	McKENZIE	WESTWOOD	SMART	WILLIAMS	HANDLEY	PEPLOW	WALLACE	CORBETT	McCOLL	LAURIE	PEPLOW, LAURIE
25/10/09	WEST HAM UNITED	A	1-0	4000	RONEY	McKENZIE	WESTWOOD	SMART	WILLIAMS	HANDLEY	LAURIE	RIDDELL	CORBETT	McCOLL	JONES	PEPLOW
30/10/09	SOUTHAMPTON	H	0-6	5000	RONEY	McKENZIE	WESTWOOD	SMART	WILLIAMS	HANDLEY	PEPLOW	WALLACE	CORBETT	McCOLL	LAURIE	
06/11/09	PLYMOUTH ARGYLE	A	0-0	8000	RONEY	McKENZIE	WESTWOOD	SMART	WILLIAMS	HANDLEY	PEPLOW	RODGERS	CORBETT	ROBERTS	JONES	
13/11/09	SOUTHAMPTON	H	0-3	7000	RONEY	McKENZIE	WESTWOOD	SMART	WILLIAMS	HANDLEY	LAURIE	RODGERS	CORBETT	McCOLL	LAURIE	
27/11/09	MILLWALL	A	1-1	4000	RONEY	McKENZIE	WESTWOOD	SMART	WILLIAMS	HANDLEY	PEPLOW	RODGERS	CORBETT	McCOLL	LAURIE	CORBETT
11/12/09	NORTHAMPTON T	A	1-0	7000	RONEY	McKENZIE	WESTWOOD	SMART	WILLIAMS	HANDLEY	PEPLOW	RODGERS	CORBETT	McCOLL	LAURIE	MASON
25/12/09	LUTON TOWN	H	1-2	8000	RONEY	McKENZIE	WESTWOOD	SMART	WILLIAMS	HANDLEY	PEPLOW	RODGERS	CORBETT	McCOLL	LAURIE	CORBETT
27/12/09	LUTON TOWN	A	2-1	9000	RONEY	McKENZIE	WESTWOOD	SMART	WILLIAMS	HANDLEY	PEPLOW	MASON	CORBETT	MASON	LAURIE	MASON, PEPLOW
28/12/09	BRIGHTON & H ALBION	A	0-1	6000	RONEY	McKENZIE	WESTWOOD	SMART	WILLIAMS	HANDLEY	PEPLOW	RODGERS	CORBETT	McCOLL	LAURIE	CORBETT
01/01/10	CRYSTAL PALACE	H	1-1	7000	RONEY	McKENZIE	WESTWOOD	SMART	WILLIAMS	HANDLEY	PEPLOW	TAYLOR	CORBETT	McCOLL	LAURIE	CORBETT
08/01/10	PORTSMOUTH	A	0-2	7000	RONEY	McKENZIE	WESTWOOD	SMART	WILLIAMS	HANDLEY	PEPLOW	RODGERS	CORBETT	McCOLL	LAURIE	PEPLOW pen
22/01/10	EXETER CITY	H	1-1	8000	RONEY	OVENS	WESTWOOD	WILLIAMS	SHAW	HANDLEY	PEPLOW	RODGERS	McCOLL	McCOLL	LAURIE	SHAW pen
29/01/10	NORWICH CITY	A	1-0	3000	RONEY	McKENZIE	OVENS	WILLIAMS	SHAW	HANDLEY	PEPLOW	RODGERS	McCOLL	ROBERTS	LAURIE	ROBERTS
12/02/10	COVENTRY CITY	H	0-2	4000	RONEY	McKENZIE	WESTWOOD	WILLIAMS	SHAW	HANDLEY	LAURIE	RODGERS	CORBETT	McCOLL	JONES	
14/02/10	BRENTFORD	A	1-0	3000	RONEY	McKENZIE	WESTWOOD	WILLIAMS	SHAW	HANDLEY	PEPLOW	ROBERTS	WILLIAMS	McCOLL	LAURIE	McCOLL, SHAW
19/02/10	WATFORD	A	0-0	3000	RONEY	McKENZIE	WESTWOOD	WILLIAMS	SHAW	HANDLEY	PEPLOW	PHILLIPS	McCOLL	McCOLL	LAURIE	
26/02/10	READING	H	0-0	3000	RONEY	McKENZIE	WESTWOOD	WILLIAMS	SHAW	HANDLEY	PEPLOW	TAYLOR	CORBETT	McCOLL	LAURIE	
05/03/10	SOUTHEND UNITED	A	0-4	3000	RONEY	McKENZIE	WESTWOOD	WILLIAMS	SHAW	HANDLEY	PEPLOW	RODGERS	CORBETT	McCOLL	LAURIE	SHAW pen
07/03/10	CROYDON COMMON	A	1-0	1500	RONEY	McKENZIE	WESTWOOD	WILLIAMS	SHAW	HANDLEY	PEPLOW	ROBERTS	WILLIAMS	McCOLL	LAURIE	ROBERTS
12/03/10	CLAPTON ORIENT	A	0-0	3000	RONEY	McKENZIE	WESTWOOD	WILLIAMS	SHAW	HANDLEY	PEPLOW	RODGERS	CORBETT	McCOLL	LAURIE	
14/03/10	QUEENS PARK RANGERS	H	2-0	1000	RONEY	McKENZIE	WESTWOOD	WILLIAMS	SHAW	HANDLEY	LAURIE	RODGERS	McCOLL	JONES	LAURIE	McCOLL, SHAW
19/03/10	PLYMOUTH ARGYLE	H	0-2	4500	RONEY	McKENZIE	WESTWOOD	WILLIAMS	SHAW	HANDLEY	PEPLOW	RODGERS	CORBETT	McCOLL	LAURIE	
25/03/10	SWINDON TOWN	A	0-0	8000	RONEY	McKENZIE	WESTWOOD	WILLIAMS	SHAW	HANDLEY	PEPLOW	RODGERS	CORBETT	McCOLL	LAURIE	CORBETT
26/03/10	SOUTHAMPTON	H	1-0	4000	RONEY	McKENZIE	WESTWOOD	WILLIAMS	SHAW	HANDLEY	PEPLOW	RODGERS	CORBETT	McCOLL	LAURIE	
28/03/10	SWINDON TOWN	H	0-2	7000	RONEY	McKENZIE	WESTWOOD	WILLIAMS	SHAW	HANDLEY	PEPLOW	RODGERS	CORBETT	McCOLL	LAURIE	
29/03/10	BRIGHTON & H ALBION	H	0-0	7000	RONEY	McKENZIE	WESTWOOD	WILLIAMS	SHAW	HANDLEY	PEPLOW	RODGERS	CORBETT	McCOLL	LAURIE	
02/04/10	CROYDON COMMON	H	0-0	1500	RONEY	McKENZIE	WESTWOOD	WILLIAMS	SHAW	HANDLEY	PEPLOW	RODGERS	WILLIAMS	McCOLL	LAURIE	
09/04/10	MILLWALL	H	0-2	5000	RONEY	McKENZIE	WESTWOOD	SMART	SHAW	HANDLEY	PEPLOW	SHERVEY	CORBETT	McCOLL	LAURIE	
16/04/10	NEW BROMPTON	H	0-2	1000	RONEY	McKENZIE	WESTWOOD	SMART	WILLIAMS	HANDLEY	PEPLOW	RODGERS	CORBETT	McCOLL	LAURIE	
23/04/10	NORTHAMPTON TOWN	H	3-1	2000	RONEY	McKENZIE	WESTWOOD	SMART	SHAW	HANDLEY	PEPLOW	SAUNDERS	CORBETT	McCOLL	LAURIE	CORBETT, SAUNDERS, PEPLOW
27/04/10	NEW BROMPTON	A	1-0	4500	RONEY	McKENZIE	WESTWOOD	SMART	SHAW	SMART	PEPLOW	ROBERTS	CORBETT	McCOLL	LAURIE	RONEY pen
30/04/10	QUEENS PARK RANGERS	A	1-2	6000	RONEY	McKENZIE	OVENS	WILLIAMS	SHAW	SMART	PEPLOW	ROBERTS	CORBETT	McCOLL	LAURIE	

FA CUP

Date	Opponent	H/A	Score	ATT	G	2	3	4	5	6	7	8	9	10	11	GOALSCORERS
15/01/10	GRIMSBY TOWN	A	2-0	6000	RONEY	McKENZIE	WESTWOOD	WILLIAMS	SHAW	HANDLEY	PEPLOW	RODGERS	MASON	McCOLL	LAURIE	PEPLOW, RODGERS
05/02/10	BARNSLEY *	A	0-4	10285	RONEY	OVENS	McKENZIE	WILLIAMS	SHAW	HANDLEY	PEPLOW	McCOLL	MASON	ROBERTS	LAURIE	

* Rovers drawn at home but Barnsley offered £500 to switch tie

GLOUCESTERSHIRE CUP FINAL

Date	Opponent	H/A	Score	ATT	G	2	3	4	5	6	7	8	9	10	11	GOALSCORERS
01/09/09	BRISTOL CITY *	H	1-1	9521	RONEY	McKENZIE	WESTWOOD	SMART	WILLIAMS	HANDLEY	PEPLOW	MASON	CORBETT	ROBERTS	LAURIE	CORBETT
13/10/09	BRISTOL CITY *	A	1-1	1175	RONEY	McKENZIE	WESTWOOD	WILLIAMS	SHAW	HANDLEY	PEPLOW	MASON	CORBETT	ROBERTS	LAURIE	HANDLEY
26/01/10	BRISTOL CITY *	H	1-2	1175	RONEY	OVENS	WESTWOOD	SMART	SHAW	HANDLEY	PEPLOW	ROBERTS	CORBETT	McCOLL	LAURIE	ROBERTS
06/04/10	BRISTOL CITY	A	0-2	1000	RONEY	OVENS	WESTWOOD	WILLIAMS	SHAW	HANDLEY	PEPLOW	RODGERS	CORBETT	McCOLL	ROBERTS	

* 1908/09 Held over

PLAYERS	APPS	GLS
CORBETT F	37	13
GLENDENNING J	1	
HANDLEY F	37	
JONES C	4	
LAURIE J	42	3
MASON J	14	5
McCOLL A	22	1
McKENZIE J	20	
OVENS G	24	
PEPLOW W	37	6
PHILLIPS G	1	
RIDDELL F	1	
ROBERTS F	20	3
RODGERS A	24	
RONEY P	42	
SAUNDERS J	1	1
SHAW W	38	1
SHERVEY J	3	
SMART J	16	1
TAYLOR R	2	
WALLACE F	2	
WESTWOOD W	40	
WILLIAMS L	36	

Rovers scored fewer goals – 37 – than in any other Southern League season. Even Croydon Common, relegated at the end of their first season, conceded just one goal against Rovers and drew both fixtures. The final goal in a meaningless end-of-season encounter at Queen's Park Rangers, was a dubious penalty awarded 10 minutes from time for a trip on McColl. It was successfully converted by Roney, who became the only goalkeeper to score for Rovers. In the FA Cup, Rovers earned an unlikely 2-0 victory at Division Two Grimsby Town, with Billy Peplow and Rodgers, who never scored in the league, both shooting past the celebrated goalkeeper Wally Scott. Rovers were subsequently drawn at home to Barnsley but accepted a £500 offer to play the tie at Oakwell. The perhaps inevitable 4-0 defeat came through goals from Ernie Gadsby, a Bristol City player by the following summer, Wilf Bartrop, Tom Forman and George Utley.

1910/11

If 13th place had summed up a poor season, Rovers slumped in 1910/11 to their lowest position so far in the Southern League. Yet 16th was to be the highest the club could manage in the final seasons prior to elevation to the Football League. Goals continued to be hard to come by, Corbett scoring only twice. Billy Peplow was the club's top scorer but no individual player reached double figures and only large end-of-season wins against Southampton and New Brompton could bring an air of respectability to the season. In addition, the club's balance sheet on the annual report for 1910/11 showed a £381 loss.

Prior to the start of this season, inside-forward James Mason signed for Wrexham, from whom he moved to Llandudno Town in 1913. F Boyle, a former Darlington wing-half, joined from Gainsborough Trinity, George Dodsley from Denaby United and Ben Hurley from Avonmouth. One major signing, in June, was that of the Scottish Junior International inside-left George Hastie from Kilmarnock. He did not play in Rovers' opening seven league games but his presence in the side as the season progressed enabled him to influence the side's performance greatly. Another key figure was tough-tackling David Harvie from Stevenson Thistle, who arrived on the recommendation of the former Rovers defender James Young and was to play in more than 200 Southern League games for Rovers prior to 1920. 'Hit-him' Harvie and his full-back partner Bill Westwood were the club's two ever-presents. Peter Roney. Louis Williams, Harry Phillips and the reliable Peplow missed just one game each.

Bill Ingham's second-half goal gave Norwich City victory at Eastville on the opening day, the Canaries giving a debut to Fred Wilkinson, who was to score an own goal in Watford's first Football League visit to Eastville in March 1921. Rovers lost their opening six games in the Southern League. The only goal in Adam McColl's first-class career was all Rovers had to show as their run included four 1-0 defeats. The side had interrupted this run with a 1-0 victory over Exeter City in the Southern Charity Cup, but even the Grecians were to record a league double over Rovers, with the future Rovers inside-forward Archie Hughes scoring in both games. It was the seventh game

Bristol Rovers 1910/11. Back row: Gange, Williams, Westwood, Silvester, Shaw, Roney, Phillips, Harvie. Front row: Boyle, Hindle, Spelvins, Corbett, McCall, Dodsley, Peplow

before Rovers gained their first points, with amateur centre-forward Frank Woodhall, later a highly successful coach in New Zealand, scoring the winner at Plymouth, his only goal for the club.

Most bizarrely, Rovers conceded not one but two goals scored by opposition goalkeepers. On 17 September Brentford won 1-0 at Eastville through a penalty from goalkeeper Archie Ling, a professional cricketer with Cambridgeshire. The penalty, conceded after 20 minutes when Westwood pushed Bert Hollinrake, was driven in off the underside of the bar. Rovers themselves had not scored all season while Ling had scored both Brentford's goals as he had converted a penalty against Swindon Town seven days earlier. Then, a week before Christmas, after the amateur Ben Hurley and Harry Phillips had scored for Rovers and Fred Whittaker and Fred McDiarmid had replied for Northampton Town, another goalkeeper scored the winning goal. Tommy Thorpe, who scored past Rovers' reserve custodian Edward Silvester, was also scoring his second goal of the year, both penalties, following one against Watford on the opening day of the season.

While Rovers took three points off champions-elect Swindon Town, who fielded the former Rovers wing-half Billy Tout, own goals lost the club points against Watford (Harvie, five minutes after half-time) and Coventry City (Phillips after 18 minutes). Victory at home to the Robins on Good Friday was marred by a series of nasty fouls. Both captains, Shaw and Bannister, were sent off by referee Pellowe two minutes from time and the Swindon left-back Walker received a police escort from the pitch. Corbett's 52nd and final Southern League goal for Rovers, in an exciting 3-3 draw with Crystal Palace, was tempered by news of the death of former Rovers stalwart George Kinsey in his early 40s. A run of 10 games without victory ended abruptly with an unexpected

SEASON 1910/11

SOUTHERN LEAGUE DIVISION ONE

Date	Opponent		Score	ATT	G	2	3	4	5	6	7	8	9	10	11	Goalscorers
03/09/10	NORWICH CITY	H	0-1	6000	RONEY	HARVIE	WESTWOOD	WILLIAMS L	SHAW	PHILLIPS	PEPLOW	SPELVINS	CORBETT	McCOLL	DODSLEY	
10/09/10	CRYSTAL PALACE	A	0-1	8000	RONEY	HARVIE	WESTWOOD	WILLIAMS L	SHAW	PHILLIPS	WILLIAMS S	CORBETT	SPELVINS	McCOLL	DODSLEY	
17/09/10	BRENTFORD	H	0-1	8000	RONEY	HARVIE	WESTWOOD	WILLIAMS L	SHAW	PHILLIPS	PEPLOW	RODGERS	CORBETT	McCOLL	DODSLEY	
21/09/10	LUTON TOWN	A	0-4	3000	RONEY	HARVIE	WESTWOOD	WILLIAMS L	SHAW	BOYLE	PEPLOW	RODGERS	SPELVINS	PHILLIPS	DODSLEY	
24/09/10	CLAPTON ORIENT RES.	A	1-4	3000	RONEY	HARVIE	WESTWOOD	WILLIAMS L	GLENDENNING	PHILLIPS	PEPLOW	RODGERS	McCOLL	GLENDENNING	DODSLEY	McCOLL
01/10/10	WATFORD	H	0-1	6000	RONEY	HARVIE	WESTWOOD	WILLIAMS L	SHAW	PHILLIPS	PEPLOW	McCOLL	WOODHALL	SCOTT	RANKIN	
08/10/10	PLYMOUTH ARGYLE	A	2-1	5000	RONEY	HARVIE	WESTWOOD	WILLIAMS L	SHAW	PHILLIPS	PEPLOW	CORBETT	WOODHALL	McCOLL	RANKIN	PEPLOW, WOODHALL
15/10/10	SOUTHAMPTON	H	0-0	6000	RONEY	HARVIE	WESTWOOD	WILLIAMS L	SHAW	PHILLIPS	PEPLOW	CORBETT	WOODHALL	McCOLL	RANKIN	
22/10/10	SOUTHEND UNITED	A	1-1	3000	RONEY	HARVIE	WESTWOOD	WILLIAMS L	SHAW	PHILLIPS	PEPLOW	CORBETT	McCOLL	HASTIE	RANKIN	SHAW
29/10/10	COVENTRY CITY	H	1-1	5000	RONEY	HARVIE	WESTWOOD	WILLIAMS L	SHAW	PHILLIPS	PEPLOW	CORBETT	HURLEY	HASTIE	RANKIN	PEPLOW
05/11/10	NEW BROMPTON	A	0-1	5000	RONEY	HARVIE	WESTWOOD	WILLIAMS L	SHAW	PHILLIPS	PEPLOW	CORBETT	HURLEY	HASTIE	RANKIN	
12/11/10	MILLWALL	H	1-0	11000	RONEY	HARVIE	WESTWOOD	WILLIAMS L	SHAW	PHILLIPS	PEPLOW	CORBETT	HURLEY	HASTIE	RANKIN	HURLEY
19/11/10	QPR	A	2-1	5000	RONEY	HARVIE	WESTWOOD	WILLIAMS L	SHAW	PHILLIPS	PEPLOW	CORBETT	HURLEY	HASTIE	RANKIN	HURLEY 2
26/11/10	WEST HAM UNITED	H	1-1	6000	SILVESTER	HARVIE	WESTWOOD	WILLIAMS L	SHAW	PHILLIPS	PEPLOW	CORBETT	HURLEY	HASTIE	RANKIN	HASTIE
10/12/10	PORTSMOUTH	H	3-2	12000	SILVESTER	HARVIE	WESTWOOD	WILLIAMS L	SHAW	PHILLIPS	PEPLOW	CORBETT	HURLEY	HASTIE	RANKIN	HASTIE 2, CORBETT
17/12/10	NORTHAMPTON TOWN	A	2-3	3000	SILVESTER	HARVIE	WESTWOOD	WILLIAMS L	SHAW	PHILLIPS	PEPLOW	CORBETT	HURLEY	HASTIE	RANKIN	HURLEY, PHILLIPS
24/12/10	BRIGHTON & H ALBION	H	1-2	5000	SILVESTER	HARVIE	WESTWOOD	WILLIAMS L	SHAW	PHILLIPS	PEPLOW	CORBETT	HURLEY	HASTIE	RANKIN	HURLEY
26/12/10	EXETER CITY	A	1-2	6000	SILVESTER	HARVIE	WESTWOOD	WILLIAMS L	SHAW	PHILLIPS	PEPLOW	CORBETT	HURLEY	HASTIE	RANKIN	PEPLOW
27/12/10	EXETER CITY	H	1-3	5000	SILVESTER	HARVIE	WESTWOOD	WILLIAMS L	SHAW	PHILLIPS	PEPLOW	CORBETT	HURLEY	HASTIE	RANKIN	PEPLOW
31/12/10	NORWICH CITY	A	0-1	4000	SILVESTER	HARVIE	WESTWOOD	WILLIAMS L	CHANNING	PHILLIPS	PEPLOW	CORBETT	HURLEY	HASTIE	RANKIN	
07/01/11	CRYSTAL PALACE	H	3-3	5000	SILVESTER	HARVIE	WESTWOOD	WILLIAMS L	CHANNING	PHILLIPS	PEPLOW	CORBETT	HURLEY	HASTIE	RANKIN	HASTIE 2, CORBETT
21/01/11	BRENTFORD	A	0-3	4000	RONEY	HARVIE	WESTWOOD	WILLIAMS L	SHAW	PHILLIPS	PEPLOW	RODGERS	CORBETT	McCOLL	DODSLEY	
28/01/11	CLAPTON ORIENT RES.	H	0-0	5000	RONEY	HARVIE	WESTWOOD	WILLIAMS L	SHAW	PHILLIPS	PEPLOW	McCOLL	HURLEY	HASTIE	RANKIN	
04/02/11	WATFORD	A	0-1	6000	RONEY	HARVIE	WESTWOOD	WILLIAMS L	SHAW	PHILLIPS	PEPLOW	CORBETT	HURLEY	HASTIE	RANKIN	
11/02/11	PLYMOUTH ARGYLE	H	1-3	5000	RONEY	HARVIE	WESTWOOD	WILLIAMS L	SHAW	PHILLIPS	PEPLOW	CORBETT	HURLEY	HASTIE	RANKIN	HASTIE
18/02/11	SOUTHAMPTON	A	5-1	3000	RONEY	HARVIE	WESTWOOD	WILLIAMS L	SHAW	PHILLIPS	PEPLOW	HURLEY	JONES	HUGHES	RANKIN	PEPLOW, JONES, HUGHES, RANKIN, SHAW
25/02/11	SOUTHEND UNITED	H	1-0	5000	RONEY	HARVIE	WESTWOOD	WILLIAMS L	SHAW	PHILLIPS	PEPLOW	HURLEY	JONES	HUGHES	RANKIN	JONES
04/03/11	COVENTRY CITY	A	0-4	3000	RONEY	HARVIE	WESTWOOD	WILLIAMS L	SHAW	PHILLIPS	PEPLOW	HURLEY	JONES	HUGHES	RANKIN	
11/03/11	NEW BROMPTON	H	6-2	5000	RONEY	HARVIE	WESTWOOD	WILLIAMS L	SHAW	PHILLIPS	PEPLOW	HASTIE	JONES	HUGHES	RANKIN	JONES 2, 1pen, HUGHES, RANKIN, PEPLOW, SHAW
18/03/11	MILLWALL	A	0-1	10000	RONEY	HARVIE	WESTWOOD	WILLIAMS L	SHAW	PHILLIPS	PEPLOW	HASTIE	JONES	HUGHES	RANKIN	
25/03/11	QUEENS PARK RANGERS	H	0-0	6000	RONEY	HARVIE	WESTWOOD	ALDIN	SHAW	PHILLIPS	PEPLOW	HASTIE	JONES	HUGHES	RANKIN	
01/04/11	WEST HAM UNITED	A	2-2	5000	RONEY	HARVIE	WESTWOOD	WILLIAMS L	SHAW	PHILLIPS	PEPLOW	SHERVEY	JONES	HUGHES	RANKIN	PEPLOW pen, SHERVEY
08/04/11	LUTON TOWN	H	4-2	9000	RONEY	HARVIE	WESTWOOD	WILLIAMS L	SHAW	PHILLIPS	PEPLOW	SHERVEY	JONES	HUGHES	RANKIN	PEPLOW 2,1 pen, SHERVEY, JONES
14/04/11	SWINDON TOWN	A	1-0	10000	RONEY	HARVIE	WESTWOOD	WILLIAMS L	SHAW	PHILLIPS	PEPLOW	SHERVEY	JONES	HUGHES	RANKIN	RANKIN
15/04/11	PORTSMOUTH	A	2-1	10000	RONEY	HARVIE	WESTWOOD	WILLIAMS L	SHAW	PHILLIPS	PEPLOW	SHERVEY	JONES	HUGHES	RANKIN	JONES, YATES og
17/04/11	SWINDON TOWN	H	0-0	10000	RONEY	HARVIE	WESTWOOD	WILLIAMS L	SHAW	PHILLIPS	PEPLOW	CORBETT	JONES	HUGHES	RANKIN	
22/04/11	NORTHAMPTON TOWN	H	0-1	6000	RONEY	HARVIE	WESTWOOD	WILLIAMS L	GANGE	PHILLIPS	PEPLOW	HUGHES	JONES	HASTIE	RANKIN	
29/04/11	BRIGHTON & H ALBION	A	0-0	5000	RONEY	HARVIE	WESTWOOD	WILLIAMS L	SHAW	BROGAN	PEPLOW	HUGHES	JONES	HASTIE	RANKIN	

FA CUP

Date	Opponent		Score	ATT	G	2	3	4	5	6	7	8	9	10	11	Goalscorers
11/01/11	HULL CITY	H	0-0	9666	RONEY	HARVIE	WESTWOOD	WILLIAMS L	SHAW	PHILLIPS	PEPLOW	McCOLL	CORBETT	HASTIE	RANKIN	
19/01/11	HULL CITY	A	0-1	15000	RONEY	HARVIE	WESTWOOD	WILLIAMS L	SHAW	PHILLIPS	PEPLOW	McCOLL	CORBETT	HASTIE	RANKIN	

GLOUCESTERSHIRE CUP FINAL

Date	Opponent		Score	ATT	G	2	3	4	5	6	7	8	9	10	11	Goalscorers
19/04/11	BRISTOL CITY	H	0-1	4466	RONEY	HARVIE	GANGE	ALDIN	SHAW	PHILLIPS	PEPLOW	SHERVEY	JONES	HUGHES	RANKIN	

PLAYERS	APPS	GLS
ALDIN C	1	
BOYLE F	1	
BROGAN J	1	
CHANNING P	2	
CORBETT F	23	2
DODSLEY G	6	
GANGE J	1	
GLENDENNING J	1	
HARVIE D	38	
HASTIE G	20	6
HUGHES A	13	2
HURLEY W	16	5
JONES J	14	6
McCOLL A	10	1
PEPLOW W	37	9
PHILLIPS H	37	1
RANKIN J *	32	3
RODGERS A	4	
RONEY P	29	
SCOTT J	1	
SHAW W	34	3
SHERVEY J	5	2
SILVESTER E	9	
SPELVINS E	3	
WESTWOOD W	38	
WILLIAMS L	37	
WILLIAMS S	1	
WOODHALL F	3	1
OWN GOALS		1

Bristol Rovers

OFFICIAL · PROGRAMME

SEASON · · 1910·1911· · ·

No. 31.   April 22nd, 1911.   ONE PENNY

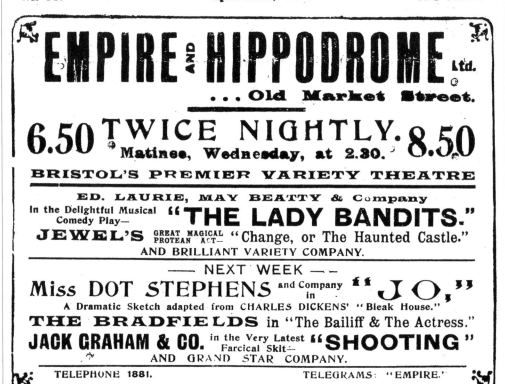

EMPIRE AND HIPPODROME Ltd.

... Old Market Street.

6.50 TWICE NIGHTLY. 8.50
Matinee, Wednesday, at 2.30.

BRISTOL'S PREMIER VARIETY THEATRE

ED. LAURIE, MAY BEATTY & Company

In the Delightful Musical Comedy Play— **"THE LADY BANDITS."**

JEWEL'S GREAT MAGICAL PROTEAN ACT— "Change, or The Haunted Castle."

AND BRILLIANT VARIETY COMPANY.

—— NEXT WEEK ——

Miss DOT STEPHENS and Company in **"JO,"**

A Dramatic Sketch adapted from CHARLES DICKENS' "Bleak House."

THE BRADFIELDS in "The Bailiff & The Actress."

JACK GRAHAM & CO. in the Very Latest Farcical Skit— **"SHOOTING"**

AND GRAND STAR COMPANY.

TELEPHONE 1881.   TELEGRAMS: "EMPIRE."

BURLEIGH LTD., Photo Engravers & Printers. LEWIN'S MEAD, BRISTOL.

The official programme for Rovers' game against Northampton Town on 22 April 1911

5-1 victory at The Dell, with five Rovers players appearing on the scoresheet. For Southampton, normally such tough opponents, George Kimpton's goal could not prevent a second consecutive 5-1 defeat. Archie Hughes, signed from Exeter City in early February, and Jimmy Jones, from Aston Villa in part-exchange for goalkeeper Bredel Anstey, both scored their first Rovers goals that day and followed this up with three of Rovers' six at home to New Brompton. A new Eastville favourite, Jimmy Shervey, was given a few games as the season drew to a close.

A 1-0 defeat in the Gloucestershire Cup Final was matched by the same score in an FA Cup replay. After two goalless games, Rovers took Hull City into extra time at Anlaby Road before being beaten by a freak goal. The home side's left-back Jack McQuillan had been injured and was hobbling at outside-left. When Tommy Nevins' through ball reached Wally Smith, his shot was only parried by Roney and McQuillan's first goal for more than four years with the Tigers sent Rovers out of the cup.

1911/12

The late-season form of Archie Hughes and Jimmy Jones allowed Rovers a basis upon which to build a forward line. Davie Walker returned in June from Leicester Fosse, four years after he had first left Eastville. Ted Long, a former Swindon Town outside-left, arrived just days before the new season started. The former Grimsby Town inside-forward Martin Bradley, whose brother James had won a League Championship medal with Liverpool in 1906, arrived from Sheffield Wednesday, where he had made 2 League appearances as a stand-in for Herbert Chapman's brother Harry. Two major absences from Rovers' side were George Hastie, who had joined Bath City and Arthur Griffiths, sold to Notts County.

Rovers' main strength lay in defence, where goalkeeper Peter Roney was, with Billy Peplow (joint top scorer with George Richards), an ever-present. In front of him, David Harvie missed only one game, forging a strong full-back partnership with Bill Westwood and later Bert Bennett, while Louis Williams and Sam Morris played regularly at half-back. Until mid-December, Rovers did not concede more than two goals in any Southern League game. However, they also never scored more than two in this spell. Indeed, while four of the first five matches were drawn, it was an own goal by Southampton's goalkeeper Arthur Brown that brought Rovers' first goal of the season in the third game.

Despite a paucity of goals, Rovers entered November having suffered just one defeat. The visit of Queen's Park Rangers to Eastville attracted a 16,000 crowd, the highest ever for a Rovers home match in the Southern League years. But Rovers crashed to a 2-0 defeat, only their second home defeat in the league since January. Thereafter, the season was more of a struggle, a run of eight defeats in ten matches in the spring leaving Rovers happy to settle for a final league placing of 17th. The highlight was a 4-1 victory over Norwich City, with Peplow scoring twice. Rovers also completed doubles over Southampton and Coventry City. The Sky Blues were beaten on Christmas Day and Boxing Day; and on 27th December they defeated Brentford 9-0.

Bristol Rovers 1911/12 Goalkeeper Peter Roney (back row, third from left) and winger Billy Peplow (front row, first left) were the only two ever presents in the team

Rovers conceded four or more goals in five Southern League games, the heaviest defeat being 6-2 at West Ham United in March. Danny Shea and Fred Harrison, both prolific goalscorers against Rovers, scored twice each. For the second consecutive season, Shea scored in both fixtures against Rovers. He also scored a hat-trick, as did Bill Kennedy, in a 7-4 victory over Brentford just before the Bees met Rovers. However, despite the Bees' leaky defence, Rovers contrived to lose a two-goal half-time lead and Brentford, with Patsy Hendren inspirational, drew 2-2 with goals from Billy Brawn and the former Bristol City forward, Willis Rippon, who scored twice more in the return game. When Rovers crashed to a 5-0 defeat at Northampton Town just after Easter, Walter Tull, one of the first black players in British football, scored four times and Albert Lewis once. Forty-eight hours later, the world was shocked by news that the Titanic had sunk. Rovers met Bristol City in May before a 1,500 crowd at Ashton Gate in a charity game for the Titanic Disaster Fund and, despite taking the lead through Ben Hurley five minutes before half-time, lost 3-1 to goals from Charles Gould, Ebenezer Owens and Billy Wedlock.

On the day Rovers conceded six at West Ham, two future Rovers managers were playing for Scotland against England. Centre-forward David McLean, who was winning his only cap, was to become manager of Rovers in 1929. At inside-left was Andrew Wilson, Scotland's goalscorer in a 1-1 draw. The holder of six caps, he managed Rovers between 1921 and 1926. Both forwards, at this stage, were on the books of Sheffield Wednesday.

Rovers lost the Gloucestershire Cup final by a single goal at Ashton Gate and were eliminated from the FA Cup by Portsmouth in front of an Eastville crowd of 15,000. Although Hughes got on the scoresheet for Rovers, Pompey scored twice through the

SEASON 1911/12

SOUTHERN LEAGUE DIVISION ONE

Date	Opponent		Score	ATT	G	2	3	4	5	6	7	8	9	10	11	Goalscorers
02/09/11	NORWICH CITY	A	0-0	8000	RONEY	HARVIE	WESTWOOD	WILLIAMS	MORRIS	PHILLIPS	PEPLOW	HUGHES J	JONES	WALKER	LONG	
09/09/11	CRYSTAL PALACE	H	0-0	10000	RONEY	HARVIE	WESTWOOD	WILLIAMS	MORRIS	BROGAN	PEPLOW	BRADLEY	JONES	HUGHES A	LONG	
16/09/11	SOUTHAMPTON	A	1-0	7000	RONEY	HARVIE	WESTWOOD	WILLIAMS	SHAW	BROGAN	PEPLOW	BRADLEY	JONES	HUGHES A	LONG	BROWN og
23/09/11	PLYMOUTH ARGYLE	H	1-1	8000	RONEY	HARVIE	WESTWOOD	WILLIAMS	SHAW	PHILLIPS	PEPLOW	WALKER	JONES	HUGHES A	LONG	HUGHES A
30/09/11	READING	A	1-1	4500	RONEY	HARVIE	WESTWOOD	WILLIAMS	SHAW	BROGAN	PEPLOW	WALKER	JONES	BRADLEY	LONG	BRADLEY
07/10/11	WATFORD	H	0-2	8000	RONEY	HARVIE	GANGE	WILLIAMS	SHAW	BROGAN	PEPLOW	WALKER	JONES	BRADLEY	LONG	
14/10/11	NEW BROMPTON	A	0-0	5000	RONEY	HARVIE	WESTWOOD	WILLIAMS	MORRIS	SHAW	PEPLOW	WALKER	HUGHES A	BROGAN	RANKIN	
21/10/11	EXETER CITY	H	2-1	6000	RONEY	HARVIE	WESTWOOD	WILLIAMS	MORRIS	SHAW	PEPLOW	WALKER	RICHARDS	BROGAN	RANKIN	RICHARDS, WILLIAMS
28/10/11	BRENTFORD	A	2-2	4500	RONEY	HARVIE	WESTWOOD	WILLIAMS	MORRIS	SHAW	PEPLOW	WALKER	RICHARDS	BROGAN	LONG	RICHARDS, WALKER
04/11/11	QUEENS PARK RANGERS	H	0-2	16000	RONEY	HARVIE	WESTWOOD	WILLIAMS	MORRIS	SHAW	PEPLOW	WALKER	RICHARDS	BROGAN	LONG	
11/11/11	MILLWALL	A	1-2	15000	RONEY	HARVIE	WESTWOOD	WILLIAMS	MORRIS	BROGAN	PEPLOW	BRADLEY	JONES	RICHARDS	LONG	JONES
18/11/11	WEST HAM UNITED	H	1-1	5000	RONEY	HARVIE	WESTWOOD	WILLIAMS	MORRIS	BROGAN	PEPLOW	HUGHES J	JONES	RICHARDS	LONG	PEPLOW
25/11/11	LUTON TOWN	A	2-1	6000	RONEY	HARVIE	WESTWOOD	WILLIAMS	MORRIS	BROGAN	PEPLOW	HUGHES A	RICHARDS	WALKER	HUGHES J	PEPLOW, J HUGHES
02/12/11	SWINDON TOWN	A	0-2	3000	RONEY	HARVIE	SHAW	WILLIAMS	MORRIS	BROGAN	PEPLOW	HUGHES A	RICHARDS	WALKER	RANKIN	
09/12/11	NORTHAMPTON TOWN	H	0-0	3000	RONEY	HARVIE	SHAW	WILLIAMS	MORRIS	BROGAN	PEPLOW	HUGHES A	JONES	WALKER	RANKIN	
16/12/11	BRIGHTON & H ALBION	A	1-5	4000	RONEY	HARVIE	SHAW	WILLIAMS	MORRIS	BROGAN	PEPLOW	WALKER	RICHARDS	BROGAN	RICHARDS	PEPLOW
25/12/11	COVENTRY CITY	H	2-1	10000	RONEY	HARVIE	WESTWOOD	WILLIAMS	MORRIS	SHAW	PEPLOW	WALKER	RICHARDS	BROGAN	RANKIN	RANKIN 2
26/12/11	COVENTRY CITY	A	1-0	10000	RONEY	HARVIE	WESTWOOD	WILLIAMS	MORRIS	SHAW	PEPLOW	WALKER	RICHARDS	BROGAN	RANKIN	RICHARDS
30/12/11	NORWICH CITY	H	4-1	6000	RONEY	HARVIE	SHAW	WILLIAMS	MORRIS	HUGHES A	PEPLOW	WALKER	RICHARDS	BROGAN	RANKIN	PEPLOW 2, RANKIN, RICHARDS
06/01/12	CRYSTAL PALACE	A	1-4	4000	RONEY	HARVIE	SHAW	WILLIAMS	HUGHES A	PHILLIPS	PEPLOW	WALKER	RICHARDS	BROGAN	RANKIN	WALKER
20/01/12	SOUTHAMPTON	H	2-0	7000	RONEY	HARVIE	SHAW	HUGHES A	MORRIS	BROGAN	PEPLOW	SHERVEY	JONES	RICHARDS	RANKIN	RICHARDS, SHERVEY
27/01/12	PLYMOUTH ARGYLE	A	0-2	8000	RONEY	HARVIE	SHAW	HUGHES A	MORRIS	BROGAN	PEPLOW	BRADLEY	JONES	RICHARDS	RANKIN	
10/02/12	WATFORD	A	1-2	3000	RONEY	HARVIE	BENNETT	WILLIAMS	MORRIS	SHAW	PEPLOW	HUGHES A	RICHARDS	WALKER	RANKIN	WALKER
17/02/12	NEW BROMPTON	A	0-1	4000	RONEY	HARVIE	BENNETT	WILLIAMS	MORRIS	SHAW	PEPLOW	HUGHES A	HUGHES A	BROGAN	RANKIN	
24/02/12	EXETER CITY	A	1-2	5000	RONEY	HARVIE	BENNETT	WILLIAMS	MORRIS	SHAW	PEPLOW	BRADLEY	RICHARDS	RANKIN	LONG	HUGHES A
28/02/12	STOKE CITY	H	2-2	2000	RONEY	HARVIE	BENNETT	WILLIAMS	MORRIS	SHAW	PEPLOW	SHERVEY	RICHARDS	WALKER	LONG	RICHARDS 2
02/03/12	BRENTFORD	A	1-3	4000	RONEY	HARVIE	BENNETT	BROGAN	MORRIS	HUGHES A	PEPLOW	HUGHES A	JONES	BROGAN	RANKIN	PEPLOW
09/03/12	QUEENS PARK RANGERS	A	2-4	4000	RONEY	HARVIE	BENNETT	WILLIAMS	MORRIS	SHAW	PEPLOW	SHERVEY	JONES	WALKER	RANKIN	BROGAN, PEPLOW
16/03/12	MILLWALL	H	3-1	5000	RONEY	HARVIE	BENNETT	MORRIS	SHAW	WILLIAMS	PEPLOW	PHILLIPS	JONES	BROGAN	LONG	JONES 2, BROGAN
23/03/12	WEST HAM UNITED	A	1-3	4000	RONEY	HARVIE	BENNETT	MORRIS	SHAW	WILLIAMS	PEPLOW	PHILLIPS	JONES	BROGAN	LONG	BROGAN, JONES
30/03/12	LUTON TOWN	H	2-6	4000	RONEY	HARVIE	BENNETT	MORRIS	SHAW	WILLIAMS	PEPLOW	HURLEY	JONES	BROGAN	LONG	BROGAN
05/04/12	LEYTON ORIENT	A	0-0	6000	RONEY	HARVIE	BENNETT	MORRIS	SHAW	WILLIAMS	PEPLOW	HAGGARD	JONES	BROGAN	LONG	
06/04/12	SWINDON TOWN	H	3-0	11000	RONEY	HARVIE	BENNETT	WILLIAMS	SHAW	MORRIS	PEPLOW	HAGGARD	JONES	BROGAN	HUGHES A	BROGAN, HAGGARD, JONES
08/04/12	LEYTON ORIENT	H	0-0	2000	RONEY	HARVIE	BENNETT	WILLIAMS	SHAW	MORRIS	PEPLOW	HAGGARD	JONES	BROGAN	HUGHES A	HUGHES A
09/04/12	READING	H	1-1	4000	RONEY	HARVIE	BENNETT	WILLIAMS	SHAW	MORRIS	PEPLOW	HAGGARD	JONES	BROGAN	HUGHES A	HUGHES A
13/04/12	NORTHAMPTON TOWN	A	0-5	6000	RONEY	HARVIE	BENNETT	WILLIAMS	SHAW	MORRIS	PEPLOW	HAGGARD	JONES	BROGAN	HUGHES A	
20/04/12	BRIGHTON & H ALBION	H	1-1	3000	RONEY	HARVIE	BENNETT	WILLIAMS	SHAW	MORRIS	PEPLOW	SHERVEY	JONES	BROGAN	LONG	HARVIE pen
27/04/12	STOKE CITY	A	1-3	5000	RONEY	SHAW	BENNETT	WILLIAMS	BRADLEY	MORRIS	PEPLOW	SHERVEY	JONES	RANKIN	BROMAGE	JONES

FA CUP

Date	Opponent		Score	ATT	G	2	3	4	5	6	7	8	9	10	11	Goalscorers
13/01/12	PORTSMOUTH	H	1-2	15000	RONEY	HARVIE	SHAW	WILLIAMS	MORRIS	HUGHES A	PEPLOW	WALKER	RICHARDS	BROGAN	RANKIN	HUGHES A

GLOUCESTERSHIRE CUP FINAL

Date	Opponent		Score	ATT	G	2	3	4	5	6	7	8	9	10	11	Goalscorers
03/02/12	BRISTOL CITY	A	0-1	8966	RONEY	HARVIE	BENNETT	WILLIAMS	MORRIS	SHAW	PEPLOW	HUGHES J	JONES	BROGAN	RANKIN	

PLAYERS	APPS	GLS
BENNETT H	16	
BRADLEY M	8	1
BROGAN J	32	5
BROMAGE G	1	
GANGE J	1	
HAGGARD W	5	1
HARVIE D	37	1
HUGHES A	21	3
HUGHES J	3	1
HURLEY W	2	
JONES J	25	6
LONG E	18	
MORRIS S	33	
PEPLOW W	38	7
PHILLIPS H	6	
RANKIN J	15	3
RICHARDS G	18	7
RONEY P	38	
SHAW W	31	
SHERVEY J	6	
WALKER D	17	3
WESTWOOD W	14	
WILLIAMS L	33	1
OWN GOALS		1

Stewards and helpers for a carnival at Eastville in 1911

delightfully named Love Jones and Lionel Louth. Fred Hunt, a Rovers director since 1897, tendered his resignation in mid-season, to be replaced the following December by a former Aston Villa shareholder, Mr Allen of His Majesty's Picture Palace, the local cinema later renamed Concorde before being closed down in the 1980s.

1912/13

In recognition of its strength, Rovers' defence remained largely unchanged for the new season. Peter Roney in goal was to miss just the final game of the season, while David Harvie and Harry Bennett formed a reliable full-back partnership. Jack Nevin, a 25-year-old with League experience at West Bromwich Albion, joined Sam Morris and Harry Phillips at half-back. Harry Harris was signed as cover, the former Kidderminster Harriers player breaking into Southern League football at the age of 30. His Kidderminster team-mate Harry Boxley also signed for Rovers. James Brogan and George Walker, who were to give Rovers loyal service, joined Peplow in a forward line that also boasted Billy Palmer, while David Walker joined Willenhall Swifts. Palmer's opening day debut meant the former Rotherham County and Nottingham Forest player became the first of Rovers' future Football League players to make the first team.

One rule change for the new season was that goalkeepers could only handle the ball inside the penalty area, not anywhere in their half of the field. This alteration did little to

Bristol Rovers 1912/13. This Rovers team managed, on 11 January 1913, to defeat Division One Notts County in a giant-killing 2-0 FA Cup victory at Eastville

help Rovers, who needed to wait until their ninth Southern League match to record their first win. When at last they did, Brogan, Shervey and Phillips scored in a 3-0 victory over Queen's Park Rangers. Rovers were to record just two Southern League doubles. Coventry were beaten home and away, with Harry Stansfield carried off injured in his debut as goalkeeper at Highfield Road and Bert Bennett appearing as a stand-in on goal. Merthyr Town were beaten twice over Christmas. Brogan, Rovers' top scorer with 11 Southern League goals, scored four times as Rovers won 7-1 at Eastville on Boxing Day. Goalscoring though, was not Rovers' forté and a 4-0 victory over Stoke in March, when George Richards scored his only three goals of the season, was the next largest win.

Harold Roe's first goal for Rovers, from Palmer's cross 20 minutes from time, brought a 1-0 win at Griffin Park in October and inflicted on Brentford a seventh consecutive Southern League defeat. Three days earlier, Rovers had crashed 4-0 at Exeter City, for whom Ellis Crompton, latterly a highly successful Rovers player, and Arthur Rutter both scored twice. Several players were perennial scorers against the Rovers side of the immediate pre-war period. Charlie White scored for Watford on four consecutive visits by Rovers to Colney Butts Meadow. George Hilsdon, who had scored against Rovers in 1904/05 and 1905/06, scored West Ham United's third goal in the April fixture. Bill Voisey, the scorer in 1920 of the first goal Rovers conceded in the Football League, was in the Millwall side defeated by two Jimmy Shervey goals at Eastville in November. Rovers let slip a 2-0 half-time lead that month, to draw with Portsmouth, whose goals came from Frank Stringfellow and Fred Rollinson. This was the first of Stringfellow's eight Southern League goals against Rovers – he also scored in both the 1920/21 Division Three (South) fixtures.

SOUTHERN LEAGUE DIVISION ONE

SEASON 1912/13

Date	Opposition	H/A	Res	ATT	G (1)	2	3	4	5	6	7	8	9	10	11	GOALSCORERS
07/09/12	PLYMOUTH ARGYLE	H	1-4	8000	RONEY	HARVIE	BENNETT	MORRIS	NEVIN	PHILLIPS	PEPLOW	ROE	BLUNT	BROGAN	PALMER	BENNETT
11/09/12	WATFORD	A	1-2	3000	RONEY	HARVIE	BENNETT	MORRIS	HARRIS	PHILLIPS	PEPLOW	ROE	HURLEY	BROGAN	PALMER	HURLEY
14/09/12	SOUTHAMPTON	A	2-2	5000	RONEY	BOXLEY	BENNETT	MORRIS	NEVIN	PHILLIPS	PEPLOW	ROE	HURLEY	BROGAN	PALMER	BLUNT, BOXLEY
21/09/12	READING	H	1-2	5000	RONEY	BOXLEY	BENNETT	MORRIS	HARRIS	PHILLIPS	PEPLOW	WALKER	HURLEY	BROGAN	PALMER	WALKER
28/09/12	NORWICH CITY	A	1-1	5000	RONEY	HARVIE	BENNETT	MORRIS	NEVIN	PHILLIPS	PEPLOW	WALKER	WALKER	BROGAN	PALMER	WALKER
02/10/12	WATFORD	H	2-2	2000	RONEY	HARVIE	BENNETT	MORRIS	NEVIN	PHILLIPS	PEPLOW	SHERVEY	RICHARDS	BROGAN	PALMER	BROWN, PALMER
05/10/12	GILLINGHAM	H	0-2	6000	RONEY	HARVIE	BENNETT	MORRIS	NEVIN	PHILLIPS	PEPLOW	RICHARDS	RICHARDS	BROGAN	PALMER	
12/10/12	NORTHAMPTON TOWN	A	1-2	6000	RONEY	HARVIE	BENNETT	MORRIS	NEVIN	PHILLIPS	PEPLOW	HAGGARD	RICHARDS	WALKER	HAGGARD	DIXON
19/10/12	QUEENS PARK RANGERS	H	3-0	5000	RONEY	HARVIE	BENNETT	MORRIS	NEVIN	PHILLIPS	PEPLOW	SHERVEY	WALKER	WALKER	PHILLIPS	HAGGARD, SHERVEY, PHILLIPS
23/10/12	EXETER CITY	A	0-4	3000	RONEY	HARVIE	BENNETT	MORRIS	WALKER	PHILLIPS	HAGGARD	HAGGARD	WALKER	BROGAN	GRIFFITHS	
26/10/12	BRENTFORD	A	1-0	2000	RONEY	HARVIE	BENNETT	MORRIS	NEVIN	NEVIN	PEPLOW	HAGGARD	ROE	BROGAN	GRIFFITHS	ROE
02/11/12	MILLWALL	A	2-1	8000	RONEY	HARVIE	BENNETT	MORRIS	WALKER	PHILLIPS	PEPLOW	SHERVEY	ROE	BROGAN	GRIFFITHS	SHERVEY 2
09/11/12	STOKE CITY	H	1-2	6000	RONEY	HARVIE	BENNETT	MORRIS	WALKER	NEVIN	PALMER	HAGGARD	ROE	BROGAN	GRIFFITHS	PALMER
16/11/12	SWINDON TOWN	A	2-2	6000	RONEY	BOXLEY	BENNETT	MORRIS	WALKER	NEVIN	PEPLOW	SMITH	ROE	BROGAN	GRIFFITHS	ROE, PEPLOW
23/11/12	PORTSMOUTH	H	2-2	8000	RONEY	HARVIE	BENNETT	MORRIS	WALKER	PHILLIPS	PEPLOW	HAGGARD	ROE	BROGAN	GRIFFITHS	HAGGARD, PEPLOW
07/12/12	WEST HAM UNITED	A	2-1	3000	RONEY	HARVIE	BENNETT	MORRIS	WALKER	PHILLIPS	PALMER	RICHARDS	BLUNT	BROGAN	GRIFFITHS	RICHARDS, BLUNT
14/12/12	BRIGHTON & H ALBION	H	1-3	3000	RONEY	HARVIE	BENNETT	MORRIS	WALKER	PHILLIPS	PEPLOW	SHERVEY	ROE	BROGAN	GRIFFITHS	ROE
21/12/12	COVENTRY CITY	A	2-0	6000	RONEY	HARVIE	BENNETT	MORRIS	WALKER	PHILLIPS	PEPLOW	SHERVEY	ROE, BROGAN	BROGAN	GRIFFITHS	ROE, BROGAN
25/12/12	MERTHYR TOWN	A	1-0	6000	RONEY	HARVIE	BOXLEY	MORRIS	WALKER	BROGAN	PEPLOW	SHERVEY	ROE	BROGAN	GRIFFITHS	WALKER
26/12/12	MERTHYR TOWN	H	7-1	8000	RONEY	HARVIE	BENNETT	MORRIS	NEVIN	BROGAN	PEPLOW	ROE	WALKER	BROGAN	GRIFFITHS	BROGAN 4, PEPLOW 2, ROE
28/12/12	PLYMOUTH ARGYLE	A	1-3	8000	RONEY	HARVIE	BENNETT	MORRIS	NEVIN	PHILLIPS	PEPLOW	ROE	WALKER	BROGAN	PALMER	WALKER
04/01/13	SOUTHAMPTON	H	2-0	3000	RONEY	HARVIE	BENNETT	MORRIS	NEVIN	PHILLIPS	PEPLOW	SHERVEY	WALKER	BROGAN	GRIFFITHS	SHERVEY, WALKER
18/01/13	READING	A	1-3	4000	RONEY	HARVIE	BENNETT	MORRIS	WALKER	NEVIN	PEPLOW	RICHARDS	ROE	BROGAN	PALMER	ROE
25/01/13	NORWICH CITY	H	2-1	5000	RONEY	HARVIE	BENNETT	MORRIS	WALKER	NEVIN	PEPLOW	RICHARDS	ROE	BROGAN	GRIFFITHS	RICHARDS, PALMER
08/02/13	GILLINGHAM	H	0-1	4000	RONEY	HARVIE	BENNETT	MORRIS	WALKER	PHILLIPS	GRIFFITHS	SMITH	ROE	BROGAN	PALMER	
15/02/13	NORTHAMPTON TOWN	H	2-0	7000	RONEY	HARVIE	BENNETT	MORRIS	NEVIN	PHILLIPS	PEPLOW	SHERVEY	WALKER	BROGAN	PALMER	SHERVEY, WALKER
01/03/13	BRENTFORD	H	1-1	4000	RONEY	BROWN	BENNETT	MORRIS	NEVIN	PHILLIPS	GRIFFITHS	SMITH	WALKER	RICHARDS	PALMER	WALKER
08/03/13	MILLWALL	H	0-4	7000	RONEY	HARVIE	BENNETT	MORRIS	WALKER	MORRIS	PEPLOW	SHERVEY	ROE	BROGAN	PALMER	
15/03/13	STOKE CITY	H	4-0	3000	RONEY	BROWN	BENNETT	HARRIS	WALKER	MORRIS	PEPLOW	RICHARDS	RICHARDS	BROGAN	PALMER	RICHARDS 3, HARRIS
21/03/13	CRYSTAL PALACE	A	2-2	9000	RONEY	HARVIE	BENNETT	HARRIS	WALKER	MORRIS	PEPLOW	ROE	ROE	BROGAN	PALMER	ROE, PEPLOW
22/03/13	SWINDON TOWN	H	1-4	10000	RONEY	BROWN	BENNETT	HARRIS	WALKER	MORRIS	PEPLOW	ROE	BLUNT	BROGAN	PALMER	BLUNT
24/03/13	CRYSTAL PALACE	H	0-3	20000	RONEY	BROWN	BENNETT	HARRIS	WALKER	MORRIS	PEPLOW	ROE	ROE	BROGAN	PALMER	
29/03/13	PORTSMOUTH	A	1-2	8000	RONEY	HARVIE	BENNETT	HARRIS	WALKER	MORRIS	PEPLOW	ROE	ROE	BROGAN	PALMER	PALMER
05/04/13	EXETER CITY	H	1-1	5000	RONEY	BROWN	BENNETT	HARRIS	WALKER	MORRIS	PEPLOW	RICHARDS	ROE	BROGAN	PALMER	WALKER
10/04/13	QUEENS PARK RANGERS	A	0-2	3000	RONEY	BROWN	BENNETT	HARRIS	NEVIN	PHILLIPS	PEPLOW	ROE	ROE	BROGAN	PALMER	
12/04/13	WEST HAM UNITED	A	1-3	8000	RONEY	BROWN	BENNETT	HARRIS	MORRIS	NEVIN	PEPLOW	POWELL	BROGAN	RICHARDS	PALMER	BROGAN
19/04/13	BRIGHTON & H ALBION	A	0-0	4000	STANSFIELD	ROE	BROWN	MORRIS	WALKER	NEVIN	PEPLOW	SHERVEY	DIXON	BROGAN	PALMER	
26/04/13	COVENTRY CITY	A	3-2	3000	RONEY	BROWN	BENNETT	MORRIS	WALKER	NEVIN	PEPLOW	POWELL	DIXON	BROGAN	PALMER	DIXON 2, POWELL

FA CUP

Date	Opposition	H/A	Res	ATT	G (1)	2	3	4	5	6	7	8	9	10	11	GOALSCORERS
11/01/13	NOTTS COUNTY	H	2-0	15000	RONEY	HARVIE	BENNETT	MORRIS	MORRIS	HARRIS	PEPLOW	SHERVEY	ROE	BROGAN	PALMER	SHERVEY, ROE
03/02/13	NORWICH CITY	H	1-1	14614	RONEY	HARVIE	BENNETT	MASON	NEVIN	HARRIS	PEPLOW	SHERVEY	ROE	BROGAN	PALMER	BROGAN
06/02/13	NORWICH CITY	A	2-2	13173	RONEY	HARVIE	BENNETT	HARRIS	NEVIN	HARRIS	PEPLOW	SHERVEY	ROE	BROGAN	PALMER	PEPLOW, ROE
10/02/13	NORWICH CITY *	N	1-0	16706	RONEY	HARVIE	BENNETT	MORRIS	NEVIN	HARRIS	PEPLOW	SHERVEY	ROE	BROGAN	PALMER	SHERVEY
22/02/13	EVERTON	H	0-4	15719	RONEY	HARVIE	BENNETT	MORRIS	NEVIN	NEVIN	PEPLOW	SHERVEY	ROE	BROGAN	PALMER	

GLOUCESTERSHIRE CUP FINAL

Date	Opposition	H/A	Res	ATT	G (1)	2	3	4	5	6	7	8	9	10	11	GOALSCORERS
25/03/13	BRISTOL CITY	H	1-0	9590	RONEY	BROWN	BENNETT	MORRIS	NEVIN	HARRIS	PEPLOW	SHERVEY	ROE	BROGAN	PALMER	BROGAN

* Played at Stamford Bridge, Chelsea

PLAYERS	APPS	GLS
BENNETT H	35	
BLUNT W	3	1
BOXLEY H	6	
BROGAN J	36	11
BROWN T	7	
DIXON T	2	2
GRIFFITHS J	20	
HAGGARD W	8	2
HARRIS H	13	1
HARVIE D	29	
HURLEY W	3	1
MORRIS S	36	
NEVIN J	23	
PALMER W	33	7
PEPLOW W	20	1
PHILLIPS C	1	
POWELL A	1	
RICHARDS G	10	3
ROE H	21	8
RONEY P	37	
SHERVEY J	17	2
SMITH H	2	
STANSFIELD H	1	1
WALKER G	37	8

The FA Cup brought great excitement and success to Eastville. On 11 January, having unusually won four out of five Southern League matches, Rovers recorded a 2-0 victory over Notts County. Prior to World War One, this was the club's only victory over a Division One club. County's record appearance maker, Albert Iremonger, was in goal, at 6ft 5½ins being the tallest opponent to face Rovers until Stockport County's Kevin Francis in 1993. Despite eight hours of heavy rain, the match went ahead and Harry Roe's low drive gave the home side the lead after 25 minutes. Seven minutes from time, Peplow's cross was turned in by Shervey with the aid of a deflection off County's right-back Herbert Morley. A crowd of 15,000 – all five FA Cup crowds surpassed the highest league attendance – made Rovers' day complete.

It took three games to defeat Norwich City. Rovers led 1-0 at half-time in all three matches, Harry Woods scored for Norwich in both drawn games and Jimmy Shervey snatched Rovers' winner in the second replay at Stamford Bridge. Prior to this game, Rovers had made six changes to the side to play Gillingham in the Southern League and were fined for fielding a weakened side. However, as if to prove the quality of these replacements, all six players were to appear again later in the season. The deciding game with Norwich was unsavoury and the Canaries' goalkeeper William Mellor was suspended for two weeks following an incident during the match. Four Everton goals at Eastville without reply ended the cup run, the second of four scorers being the England International, Frank Jefferis. In February 1913, the Empire Theatre, which stood where the Old Market-Temple Way underpass is found today, showed a sketch in which Rovers, uncharacteristically in red, led an Everton side by a goal to nil. After seven straight losses, the Gloucestershire Cup was won through Brogan's close-range goal five minutes after half-time. One representative honour was given to the former Rovers player Bill Tout. He was in the Southern League side that beat the Scottish League 1-0 at Millwall in October.

1913/14

Hopes of finishing higher than 16th, ultimately dashed as Rovers completed the season one place lower, had been boosted by the summer signing of the inspirational Ellis Crompton. The former Blackburn Rovers and Tottenham Hotspur inside-forward cost £400 from Exeter City. Murray and Arthur Squires were also new names in the attack, while Rovers relied on the sturdy defensive line that had proved so successful in the past. Full-backs David Harvie and Bert Bennett were the only two ever-presents. Harry Phillips was a notable absentee when Rovers lined up for the new season, while Billy Palmer had joined Division One Everton for £800, a sizeable fee that boosted the club's finances and led to a £437 net profit for the year.

Crompton scored against Cardiff City on his debut. He also scored in the next home game, against West Ham United, for whom Tom Brandon, a Rovers player in 1919/20, was making his Southern League debut. However, Rovers picked up just one point in the opening seven fixtures and the perennial struggle was underway. Rovers recorded a meagre nine Southern League wins, beat no individual opponents home and away and,

101

Bristol Rovers 1913/14. Back row: Brown, Harvie, Roney, Stansfield, Bennett. Middle row: Roe, Nevin, Walker, Westwood, Morris, Brogan. Front row: Peplow, Dixon, Crompton, Murray, Kay, Squires, Griffiths

were it not for Crompton's 13 goals, might have been in real trouble. It was noticeable that he was absent for the Gloucestershire Cup final when Rovers, fielding Bill Westwood at left-back for his first game in more than two years, lost 2-0 to Bristol City.

One particularly poor run of results for Alf Homer's side came in January. During this month, Rovers lost all four Southern League games, an FA Cup-tie and a friendly 1-0 at home to Bristol City, the scorer being Tom Howarth, who played for Rovers in 1922/23. These defeats were not even by small margins. The Plymouth Argyle defeat was 4-1 at Eastville, with Fred Burch scoring a hat-trick. Preston North End scored five goals at Deepdale in the FA Cup and West Ham United defeated Rovers 6-1. Syd Puddefoot scored a hat-trick for the Hammers, towards the start of an illustrious career that was to see him score for Blackburn Rovers against Rovers in an FA Cup game in January 1931. All five Swindon Town forwards had scored against Rovers on Boxing Day.

There were, of course a number of positive aspects to 1913/14. The game at Millwall in December attracted a crowd of 18,000 to The Den, the largest attendance at any Southern League game between 1899 and 1920 featuring Rovers. 15,000 saw the 2-1 home win over Merthyr Town – with Crompton and Shervey scoring – and three other home games attracted a five-figure crowd. On Christmas Day, 12,000 spectators saw Rovers defeat Swindon Town 5-2 to record the largest win since the previous Boxing Day. Stand-in centre-forward Gallacher scored the only two goals of his brief Rovers career, Crompton and Shervey again grabbed one each and the Robins' Matthew Lochhead

SEASON 1913/14

SOUTHERN LEAGUE DIVISION ONE

Date	Opponent		Score	ATT	G	2	3	4	5	6	7	8	9	10	11	GOALSCORERS
01/09/13	CARDIFF CITY	H	1-3	10000	RONEY	HARVIE	BENNETT	MORRIS	WALKER	NEVIN	PEPLOW	DIXON	MURRAY	CROMPTON	SQUIRES	CROMPTON
06/09/13	MERTHYR TOWN	H	0-1	8000	RONEY	HARVIE	BENNETT	MORRIS	WALKER	NEVIN	PEPLOW	DIXON	MURRAY	BROGAN	SQUIRES	
13/09/13	WEST HAM UNITED	H	1-2	8000	RONEY	HARVIE	BENNETT	MORRIS	WALKER	WESTWOOD J	PEPLOW	DIXON	CROMPTON	BROGAN	SQUIRES	CROMPTON
20/09/13	PLYMOUTH ARGYLE	A	1-1	10000	RONEY	HARVIE	BENNETT	MORRIS	WALKER	MAINDS	PEPLOW	DIXON	CROMPTON	BROGAN	GRIFFITHS	BROGAN
27/09/13	SOUTHAMPTON	H	1-3	9000	RONEY	HARVIE	BENNETT	MORRIS	WALKER	MAINDS	PEPLOW	CROMPTON	MURRAY	CROMPTON	SQUIRES	WALKER
04/10/13	READING	A	1-2	4000	RONEY	HARVIE	BENNETT	MORRIS	NEVIN	MAINDS	PEPLOW	DIXON	MURRAY	CROMPTON	SQUIRES	MURRAY
11/10/13	CRYSTAL PALACE	H	1-2	8000	RONEY	HARVIE	BENNETT	ROE	WALKER	MAINDS	PEPLOW	DIXON	MURRAY	CROMPTON	SQUIRES	
18/10/13	COVENTRY CITY	A	2-2	4000	RONEY	HARVIE	BENNETT	MORRIS	NEVIN	WESTWOOD J	PEPLOW	DIXON	MURRAY	CROMPTON	GRIFFITHS	MURRAY, CROMPTON
25/10/13	WATFORD	H	2-1	7000	RONEY	HARVIE	BENNETT	MORRIS	WALKER	BROGAN	DIXON	MURRAY	CROMPTON	SQUIRES	ROE	DIXON, MURRAY
01/11/13	NORWICH CITY	A	1-1	6000	RONEY	HARVIE	BENNETT	MAINDS	WALKER	WESTWOOD J	PEPLOW	DIXON	MURRAY	CROMPTON	GRIFFITHS	CROMPTON
08/11/13	GILLINGHAM	H	3-1	8000	RONEY	HARVIE	BENNETT	MAINDS	WALKER	WESTWOOD J	PEPLOW	CROMPTON	DIXON	BROGAN	GRIFFITHS	BROGAN, CROMPTON, PEPLOW
15/11/13	NORTHAMPTON TOWN	A	0-2	4000	RONEY	HARVIE	BENNETT	MAINDS	WALKER	WESTWOOD J	PEPLOW	CROMPTON	DIXON	BROGAN	GRIFFITHS	
22/11/13	SOUTHEND UNITED	H	0-0	8000	RONEY	HARVIE	BENNETT	MAINDS	WALKER	MAINDS	GRIFFITHS	CROMPTON	DIXON	BROGAN	SQUIRES	
29/11/13	BRIGHTON & H ALBION	A	1-2	5500	RONEY	HARVIE	BENNETT	MAINDS	WALKER	WESTWOOD J	DIXON	CROMPTON	MURRAY	BROGAN	GRIFFITHS	CROMPTON
06/12/13	PORTSMOUTH	H	3-1	5000	RONEY	HARVIE	BENNETT	MAINDS	WALKER	WESTWOOD J	PEPLOW	SHERVEY	MURRAY	CROMPTON	GRIFFITHS	CROMPTON 2, PEPLOW
13/12/13	MILLWALL	A	0-2	18000	RONEY	HARVIE	BENNETT	MAINDS	WALKER	WESTWOOD J	PEPLOW	SHERVEY	MURRAY	CROMPTON	GRIFFITHS	
20/12/13	EXETER CITY	H	1-1	5000	RONEY	HARVIE	BENNETT	MAINDS	WALKER	WESTWOOD J	PEPLOW	SHERVEY	GALLAGHER	CROMPTON	GRIFFITHS	CROMPTON
25/12/13	SWINDON TOWN	H	5-2	12000	RONEY	HARVIE	BENNETT	MAINDS	WALKER	WESTWOOD J	PEPLOW	SHERVEY	GALLAGHER	CROMPTON	GRIFFITHS	GALLAGHER 2, CROMPTON, SHERVEY, LOCHEAD og
26/12/13	SWINDON TOWN	A	0-5	10000	RONEY	HARVIE	BENNETT	MAINDS	WALKER	WESTWOOD J	PEPLOW	SHERVEY	GALLAGHER	CROMPTON	SQUIRES	
27/12/13	MERTHYR TOWN	H	2-1	15000	RONEY	HARVIE	BENNETT	MAINDS	WALKER	WESTWOOD J	PEPLOW	SHERVEY	GALLAGHER	CROMPTON	SQUIRES	CROMPTON, SHERVEY
01/01/14	CARDIFF CITY	A	0-2	10000	RONEY	HARVIE	BENNETT	MAINDS	WALKER	WESTWOOD J	PEPLOW	CROMPTON	GALLAGHER	CROMPTON	SQUIRES	
03/01/14	WEST HAM UNITED	A	1-6	8000	RONEY	HARVIE	BENNETT	MORRIS	WALKER	WESTWOOD J	PEPLOW	DIXON	WALKER	BROGAN	SQUIRES	SQUIRES
17/01/14	PLYMOUTH ARGYLE	H	1-4	8000	STANSFIELD	HARVIE	BENNETT	MORRIS	NEVIN	WESTWOOD J	PEPLOW	SHERVEY	THOMPSON	BROGAN	SQUIRES	CROMPTON
24/01/14	SOUTHAMPTON	A	0-2	6000	STANSFIELD	HARVIE	BENNETT	MORRIS	WALKER	MAINDS	PEPLOW	SHERVEY	THOMPSON	BROGAN	SQUIRES	
07/02/14	READING	H	2-2	6000	STANSFIELD	HARVIE	BENNETT	MORRIS	WALKER	MAINDS	PEPLOW	CROMPTON	THOMPSON	BROGAN	GRIFFITHS	BROGAN, PEPLOW
14/02/14	CRYSTAL PALACE	A	3-5	6000	McDONALD	HARVIE	BENNETT	MORRIS	WALKER	ROE	PEPLOW	SHERVEY	THOMPSON	CROMPTON	SQUIRES	SQUIRES 2, SHERVEY
21/02/14	COVENTRY CITY	H	3-2	7000	STANSFIELD	HARVIE	BENNETT	MAINDS	WALKER	ROE	PEPLOW	SHERVEY	THOMPSON	CROMPTON	SQUIRES	SHERVEY 2, THOMPSON
28/02/14	WATFORD	A	1-1	4000	STANSFIELD	HARVIE	BENNETT	MAINDS	WALKER	ROE	PEPLOW	SHERVEY	THOMPSON	CROMPTON	SQUIRES	WALKER
07/03/14	NORWICH CITY	A	1-1	9000	STANSFIELD	HARVIE	BENNETT	MORRIS	WALKER	ROE	PEPLOW	SHERVEY	THOMPSON	CROMPTON	SQUIRES	CROMPTON, PEPLOW
14/03/14	GILLINGHAM	H	0-3	5000	STANSFIELD	HARVIE	BENNETT	MORRIS	WALKER	MAINDS	PEPLOW	SHERVEY	THOMPSON	CROMPTON	SQUIRES	
21/03/14	NORTHAMPTON TOWN	H	1-1	7000	STANSFIELD	HARVIE	BENNETT	MORRIS	WALKER	BROGAN	PEPLOW	SHERVEY	ROE	CROMPTON	SQUIRES	SHERVEY
28/03/14	SOUTHEND UNITED	A	2-2	6000	STANSFIELD	HARVIE	BENNETT	MORRIS	WALKER	BROGAN	PEPLOW	SHERVEY	ROE	CROMPTON	SQUIRES	ROE, PROBERT og
04/04/14	BRIGHTON & H ALBION	H	1-0	8000	STANSFIELD	HARVIE	BENNETT	MORRIS	WALKER	BROGAN	PEPLOW	SHERVEY	THOMPSON	CROMPTON	SQUIRES	WALKER
10/04/14	QUEENS PARK RANGERS	A	0-1	8000	STANSFIELD	HARVIE	BENNETT	MORRIS	WALKER	BROGAN	PEPLOW	SHERVEY	ROE	CROMPTON	SQUIRES	
11/04/14	PORTSMOUTH	A	0-1	4000	STANSFIELD	HARVIE	BENNETT	MORRIS	WALKER	BROGAN	PEPLOW	SHERVEY	ROE	CROMPTON	SQUIRES	
13/04/14	QUEENS PARK RANGERS	H	2-1	12000	STANSFIELD	HARVIE	BENNETT	MORRIS	WALKER	BROGAN	PEPLOW	SHERVEY	ROE	CROMPTON	SQUIRES	ROE, SQUIRES
18/04/14	MILLWALL	H	1-0	5000	STANSFIELD	HARVIE	BENNETT	MORRIS	WALKER	BROGAN	PEPLOW	SHERVEY	ROE	CROMPTON	SQUIRES	ROE
25/04/14	EXETER CITY	A	1-1	4000	STANSFIELD	HARVIE	BENNETT	MORRIS	WALKER	WESTWOOD J	PEPLOW	ROE	THOMPSON	KAY	SQUIRES	THOMPSON

FA CUP

Date	Opponent		Score	ATT	G	2	3	4	5	6	7	8	9	10	11	GOALSCORERS
10/01/14	PRESTON NE	A	2-5	14000	RONEY	HARVIE	BENNETT	MAINDS	WALKER	WESTWOOD J	PEPLOW	SHERVEY	ROE	CROMPTON	SQUIRES	SHERVEY 2

GLOUCESTERSHIRE CUP FINAL

Date	Opponent		Score	ATT	G	2	3	4	5	6	7	8	9	10	11	GOALSCORERS
14/04/14	BRISTOL CITY	A	0-2	8501	STANSFIELD	HARVIE	WESTWOOD W		NEVIN	GALLACHER	WESTWOOD J	KAYE	DIXON	ROE	MURRAY	GRIFFITHS

PLAYERS

PLAYERS	APPS	GLS
BENNETT H	38	
BROGAN J	16	3
CROMPTON E	36	13
DIXON T	15	1
GALLACHER H	6	
GRIFFITHS J	14	2
HARVIE D	38	
KAY H	1	
MAINDS C	23	
McDONALD H	2	
MORRIS S	20	
MURRAY W	10	3
NEVIN J	5	
PEPLOW W	36	4
ROE H	12	2
RONEY P	22	
SHERVEY J	21	6
SQUIRES A	25	4
STANSFIELD H	14	
THOMPSON R	10	2
WALKER G	36	3
WESTWOOD J	18	
OWN GOALS		2

conceded an own goal. The ever-consistent Billy Peplow scored with a first-time shot after only five minutes at home to Reading on his 200th Southern League appearance for the club. After Arthur Cartlidge, he was only the second player to reach this milestone.

It was no surprise when Rovers signed Henry McCann from Exeter City in the summer of 1914. On the final day of the season he had scored the Grecians' goal as Rovers drew at St James' Park. In fact, both games against Exeter City finished 1-1 and, in both cases, McCann was the goalscorer. Len Andrews achieved a similar feat as Southampton became one of four clubs to complete a league double over Rovers. He was to play for the Saints against Rovers as late as Good Friday 1922 and for Watford against Rovers in 1924/25.

The Gloucestershire Cup was not retained, as Bristol City won 2-0 at Ashton Gate. In the FA Cup, a tough away fixture at Preston North End was made all the more difficult when goalkeeper Peter Roney left the field with an injury which ruled him out for the rest of the season. Bert Bennett took over in goal and, although Jimmy Shervey scored twice, the home side ran up five goals. North End scored three goals in eight minutes early in the game and Fred Osborne, who had collided accidentally with Roney after 15 minutes, scored a hat-trick, including two penalties. Roney's injury prompted the signing from Fulham of Hugh McDonald, who had saved a penalty on his Grimsby Town debut against Bradford Park Avenue in Division Two in December 1911.

On 29 April, a crowd of 4,000 saw a Bristol XI lose 3-0 to FA Cup holders Aston Villa at Ashton Gate in a testimonial following the death of the Bristol City secretary E J Locke. Bert Bennett, one of five Rovers players present, opened the scoring with an own goal after 20 minutes. A combined Rovers and City reserve team beat a Gloucestershire XI 4-1 at Eastville that month in a benefit game for the E J Clarke Testimonial Fund.

1914/15

There were four new faces in the Rovers side that drew with Crystal Palace on the opening day of the season. George Davison, at centre-forward, scored Rovers' goal and ended up top scorer with 15 Southern League goals, six more than Henry McCann, signed from Exeter City. Joe Caddick, at inside-right, added seven goals and David Taylor, shaking off the challenge of Bert Bennett, soon made the left-back position his own. Bill Westwood returned to the side for his first Southern League appearance in almost three years. Tom Dixon returned to the North-East. Jack Nevin had joined Ayr United, while Sam Morris, Joe Griffiths and Jimmy Shervey were conspicuous by their absence, but the world was more engrossed in events elsewhere.

Despite the outbreak of war on 4 August 1914, professional football, though much affected, was allowed to continue. It would, with hindsight, have been logical for football to take a back seat. Lessons were learned by the time World War Two was declared. But in 1914 Field-Marshal John Denton Pinkstone French, Commander-in-Chief of the Forces, assured Britain that the war would be over by Christmas. On the strength of this unfounded but generally-held myth, the Football League and Southern League

SEASON 1914/15

SOUTHERN LEAGUE DIVISION ONE

Date	Opponent		Score	ATT	G	2	3	4	5	6	7	8	9	10	11	GOALSCORERS
05/09/14	CRYSTAL PALACE	H	1-1	6500	RONEY	HARVIE	TAYLOR	WESTWOOD	GALLACHER	BROGAN	PEPLOW	CADDICK	DAVISON	McCANN	SQUIRES	DAVISON
09/09/14	SOUTHEND UNITED	H	0-2	4000	RONEY	HARVIE	TAYLOR	WESTWOOD	WALKER	BROGAN	PAYNE	CADDICK	DAVISON	McCANN	SQUIRES	
12/09/14	CROYDON COMMON	A	3-0	3000	RONEY	HARVIE	BENNETT	ROE	WALKER	WESTWOOD	PAYNE	CADDICK	DAVISON	McCANN	SQUIRES	DAVISON 2, PAYNE
16/09/14	SWINDON TOWN	A	1-4	3000	RONEY	HARVIE	TAYLOR	WESTWOOD	WALKER	BROGAN	PAYNE	CADDICK	DAVISON	McCANN	SQUIRES	CADDICK
19/09/14	READING	H	3-3	7000	RONEY	HARVIE	BENNETT	WESTWOOD	WALKER	BROGAN	PAYNE	CADDICK	DAVISON	McCANN	SQUIRES	DAVISON, McCANN, PAYNE
26/09/14	SOUTHAMPTON	A	1-3	4000	RONEY	HARVIE	BENNETT	CROMPTON	WALKER	BROGAN	PAYNE	CADDICK	DAVISON	McCANN	FORTUNE	McCANN
03/10/14	NORTHAMPTON TOWN	H	2-3	7000	RONEY	HARVIE	BENNETT	CROMPTON	GALLACHER	WESTWOOD	PAYNE	CADDICK	DAVISON	McCANN	FORTUNE	DAVISON 2
10/10/14	WATFORD	A	0-2	4000	RONEY	HARVIE	BENNETT	CROMPTON	WALKER	ROE	PAYNE	CADDICK	DAVISON	McCANN	FORTUNE	
14/10/14	LUTON TOWN	A	1-3	3000	RONEY	HARVIE	BENNETT	CROMPTON	WALKER	ROE	PAYNE	CADDICK	DAVISON	McCANN	FORTUNE	McCANN
17/10/14	PLYMOUTH ARGYLE	H	3-2	7000	RONEY	HARVIE	BENNETT	CROMPTON	WALKER	ROE	PAYNE	CADDICK	DAVISON	McCANN	SQUIRES	CADDICK, McCANN, SQUIRES
24/10/14	WEST HAM UNITED	A	1-4	6000	STANSFIELD	HARVIE	BENNETT	CROMPTON	WALKER	ROE	PAYNE	CADDICK	DAVISON	McCANN	SQUIRES	CADDICK
31/10/14	NORWICH CITY	H	4-2	7000	STANSFIELD	HARVIE	BENNETT	CROMPTON	WALKER	HARDMAN	PAYNE	CADDICK	DAVISON	McCANN	SQUIRES	CADDICK 2, McCANN, WOODLANDS og
07/11/14	GILLINGHAM	A	1-0	7000	STANSFIELD	HARVIE	BENNETT	CROMPTON	WALKER	HARDMAN	PAYNE	CADDICK	DAVISON	McCANN	SQUIRES	McCANN
14/11/14	BRIGHTON & H ALBION	H	4-0	7000	STANSFIELD	HARVIE	BENNETT	CROMPTON	WALKER	HARDMAN	PAYNE	CADDICK	DAVISON	McCANN	SQUIRES	McCANN 2, CADDICK, DAVISON
21/11/14	CARDIFF CITY	A	0-7	6000	STANSFIELD	HARVIE	BENNETT	CROMPTON	WALKER	HARDMAN	PAYNE	CADDICK	DAVISON	McCANN	SQUIRES	
28/11/14	EXETER CITY	H	2-1	5000	STANSFIELD	HARVIE	TAYLOR	CROMPTON	WALKER	HARDMAN	PAYNE	CADDICK	DAVISON	McCANN	SQUIRES	DAVISON, SQUIRES
12/12/14	PORTSMOUTH	H	2-3	5000	STANSFIELD	HARVIE	TAYLOR	BROGAN	WALKER	HARDMAN	PAYNE	CADDICK	DAVISON	McCANN	SQUIRES	CADDICK, DAVISON
25/12/14	QUEENS PARK RANGERS	H	1-3	8000	STANSFIELD	HARVIE	TAYLOR	CROMPTON	WALKER	HARDMAN	PAYNE	CADDICK	DAVISON	McCANN	SQUIRES	DAVISON pen
26/12/14	QUEENS PARK RANGERS	A	1-2	3000	STANSFIELD	HARVIE	TAYLOR	CROMPTON	WALKER	ROE	PAYNE	CADDICK	DAVISON	McCANN	SQUIRES	SQUIRES
28/12/14	SOUTHEND UNITED	H	4-1	5000	STANSFIELD	HARVIE	TAYLOR	CROMPTON	WALKER	ROE	PAYNE	CADDICK	DAVISON	McCANN	SQUIRES	DAVISON 2, McCANN, PAYNE
01/01/15	CRYSTAL PALACE	A	0-1	3000	STANSFIELD	HARVIE	TAYLOR	CROMPTON	WALKER	ROE	PAYNE	CADDICK	DAVISON	McCANN	SQUIRES	
06/02/15	NORTHAMPTON TOWN	A	0-2	9500	STANSFIELD	HARVIE	TAYLOR	MAGGS	WALKER	HARDMAN	PAYNE	CROMPTON	DAVISON	EDWARDS	SQUIRES	
13/02/15	WATFORD	H	2-3	1500	STANSFIELD	HARVIE	TAYLOR	MASON	WALKER	HARDMAN	PAYNE	ROE	DAVISON	BROGAN	SQUIRES	DAVISON, ROE
20/02/15	PLYMOUTH ARGYLE	A	1-0	3000	STANSFIELD	HARVIE	TAYLOR	CROMPTON	WALKER	ROE	SQUIRES	CADDICK	DAVISON	BROGAN	FORTUNE	DAVISON
27/02/15	WEST HAM UNITED	H	1-3	2000	STANSFIELD	HARVIE	TAYLOR	ROE	WALKER	HARDMAN	CROMPTON	CADDICK	DAVISON	BROGAN	SQUIRES	BROGAN
03/03/15	READING	A	1-5	2000	STANSFIELD	HARVIE	TAYLOR	ROE	WALKER	HARDMAN	CROMPTON	CADDICK	DAVISON	BROGAN	SQUIRES	CROMPTON
06/03/15	NORWICH CITY	A	2-1	2000	STANSFIELD	HARVIE	TAYLOR	CROMPTON	HARDMAN	ROE	PAYNE	CROMPTON	DAVISON	BROGAN	SQUIRES	BROGAN, DAVISON
13/03/15	GILLINGHAM	H	3-1	1000	STANSFIELD	HARVIE	TAYLOR	CROMPTON	HARDMAN	ROE	PAYNE	CADDICK	DAVISON	BROGAN	SQUIRES	CROMPTON pen, ROE, SQUIRES
17/03/15	SOUTHAMPTON	H	0-0	2000	STANSFIELD	HARVIE	TAYLOR	ROE	HARDMAN	WALKER	PAYNE	CROMPTON	DAVISON	CROMPTON	SQUIRES	
20/03/15	BRIGHTON & H ALBION	A	1-2	4000	STANSFIELD	HARVIE	TAYLOR	ROE	WALKER	HARDMAN	PAYNE	CADDICK	DAVISON	BROGAN	SQUIRES	SQUIRES
27/03/15	CARDIFF CITY	H	3-2	4000	STANSFIELD	HARVIE	TAYLOR	HARDMAN	WALKER	HARDMAN	PAYNE	CADDICK	DAVISON	BROGAN	SQUIRES	CROMPTON 2, BROGAN
02/04/15	MILLWALL	H	0-1	3000	STANSFIELD	HARVIE	TAYLOR	HARDMAN	WALKER	MASON	PAYNE	CROMPTON	DAVISON	BROGAN	SQUIRES	
03/04/15	EXETER CITY	A	0-2	6000	STANSFIELD	HARVIE	TAYLOR	HARDMAN	WALKER	MASON	PAYNE	CROMPTON	ROE	BROGAN	SQUIRES	
05/04/15	MILLWALL	A	3-1	3000	STANSFIELD	HARVIE	TAYLOR	HARDMAN	WALKER	MASON	PEPLOW	CROMPTON	ROE	BROGAN	HURLEY	WALKER, CROMPTON pen, HURLEY
06/04/15	CROYDON COMMON	H	1-0	3000	STANSFIELD	HARVIE	TAYLOR	HARDMAN	WALKER	MASON	CROMPTON	CROMPTON	ROE	BROGAN	HURLEY	BROGAN
10/04/15	LUTON TOWN	H	0-3	4121	STANSFIELD	HARVIE	TAYLOR	ROE	WALKER	HARDMAN	ROE	ROE	DAVISON	BROGAN	HURLEY	
17/04/15	PORTSMOUTH	A	1-0	4000	STANSFIELD	HARVIE	TAYLOR	HARDMAN	WALKER	HARDMAN	PAYNE	CROMPTON	DAVISON	McCANN	SQUIRES	BROGAN
24/04/15	SWINDON TOWN	H	0-1	4000	STANSFIELD	HARVIE	TAYLOR	ROE	WALKER	HARDMAN	PAYNE	CROMPTON	DAVISON	McCANN	SQUIRES	

FA CUP

Date	Opponent		Score	ATT	G	2	3	4	5	6	7	8	9	10	11	GOALSCORERS
19/12/14	BOURNEMOUTH	H	3-0	2000	STANSFIELD	HARVIE	TAYLOR	ROE	WALKER	HARDMAN	PAYNE	CROMPTON	DAVISON	McCANN	SQUIRES	CROMPTON, DAVISON, SQUIRES
16/01/15	SOUTHEND UNITED	H	0-0	8060	STANSFIELD	HARVIE	TAYLOR	ROE	WALKER	HARDMAN	PAYNE	CROMPTON	DAVISON	McCANN	SQUIRES	
20/01/15	SOUTHEND UNITED	A	0-3	3000	STANSFIELD	HARVIE	TAYLOR	ROE	WALKER	HARDMAN	PAYNE	CROMPTON	DAVISON	McCANN	SQUIRES	

PLAYERS	APPS	GLS
BENNETT H	12	
BROGAN J	21	5
CADDICK J	27	7
CROMPTON E	31	5
DAVISON G	35	15
EDWARDS T	1	
FORTUNE J	5	
GALLACHER H	2	
HARDMAN J	23	
HARVIE D	38	
HURLEY W	2	1
MAGGS W	1	
MASON H	6	
McCANN H	21	9
PAYNE C	31	3
PEPLOW W	2	
ROE H	24	2
RONEY P	10	
SQUIRES A	32	4
STANSFIELD H	28	
TAYLOR D	26	
WALKER G	34	1
WESTWOOD W	6	
OWN GOALS		1

continued as normal. Manager Homer, so certain of imminent peace, agreed a £2 contract for the duration of the war, a commitment he faithfully honoured. Of course, some players were conscripted and Rovers relied on a number of local players to make up the numbers. Ben Hurley, who 'if (he) had chosen to turn professional…would have been famous like Stanley Matthews' (Ron Best, Gillingham School magazine, July 1960), played his first game for two-and-a-half years when Croydon Common visited Eastville on Easter Tuesday. After George Walker and Ellis Crompton (penalty) had scored, Hurley added Rovers' third past the future England goalkeeper Ernie Williamson, with left-back Arthur Hutchings replying for the Cock Robins from the penalty spot. Victory marked a final Rovers game for Billy Peplow, who had been rewarded with the proceeds of a benefit match against Coventry City on 21 February 1915. This result also effectively meant that Rovers had avoided relegation.

Despite the early-season form of Davison, who scored six times in his opening seven games, Rovers were to conform to their pattern of recent years and win just one of their first nine Southern League matches. Through autumn, though, came a run of good results, shattered ultimately by a 7-0 defeat at Cardiff City. Prior to that, Rovers had won back-to-back games for the first time since Christmas 1912. One of these, a 4-2 victory over Norwich City when Rovers gave a debut to former Derby County and Oldham Athletic wing-half John Hardman, saw Caddick score twice for Rovers and Harry Woods twice for the visitors. McCann who, along with an Arthur Woodlands own goal, also scored in that game, added the winner at Gillingham and two more as Brighton were defeated 4-0.

Rovers were to suffer two runs of four consecutive Southern League defeats. The second of these ended dramatically at Eastville in February, when a well-struck 25th minute Davison goal, following a fine three-man move, gave Rovers victory over West Ham United, who had previously not lost for nine games. The next time the two sides would meet was a 2-2 draw at Eastville in September 1953.

However, Rovers conceded 75 Southern League goals in 1914/15, more than in any other season spent in that league. Only bottom-placed Gillingham conceded more. Arthur Dominy, scorer of 30 goals in the season for Southampton, scored the Saints' opening goal as Rovers lost 3-1 at The Dell. The return game at Eastville was watched by a crowd of only 1,000, a sure sign of the times as the equivalent fixture in 1913/14 had attracted 9,000. Once Harry Stansfield had replaced the veteran Roney in goal, Rovers conceded seven at Cardiff City and five at Norwich City, where Danny Wilson scored twice and the Canaries ran up four second-half goals. The Welsh International Wally Davies, on Good Friday and Easter Monday, scored for Millwall in both fixtures against Rovers. Albert Green had scored only once in 13 months prior to his brace of goals in Watford's 3-2 win at Eastville in February.

Despite the ravages of war, some Rovers players continued to find success. Billy Palmer, for instance won a League Championship medal with Everton in 1914/15, having appeared in 17 Division One matches. In the FA Cup, Rovers recorded a 3-0 victory over Bournemouth in December, with Crompton, Davison and Squires all scoring. The predicted victory over Southend United, whom Rovers had recently defeated 4-1, failed to materialise, though. Taken to a replay, Rovers conceded three goals at The Kursaal and were eliminated. The Gloucestershire Cup final was cancelled and was next played in September 1919.

The massive trail of grief and destruction caused by World War One touched every corner of the world and at least 4,000 Bristolians died in the conflict. John Hardman, who had played for Rovers during 1914/15, was killed in action in France in February 1917. Walter Gerrish, an inside-forward with Rovers between 1905 and 1909 and subsequently the winner of a League championship medal with Aston Villa in 1909/10, was also killed during World War One, as was Harry Phillips, who had left the club in 1913. Joseph Caddick, a Rovers player in 1914/15, served with the 13th Worcestershire Regiment and lost a leg. Several players who had played against Rovers also lost their life in the war. Bristol City's goalkeeper Tommy Ware, killed in June 1915, had played in the Gloucestershire Cup finals of 1913 and 1914. Arthur Evans, who played at left-back for Exeter City in three games immediately prior to the war, Steve Jackson, Coventry City's right-back in October 1913 and Norman Wood, who had played inside-right for Plymouth Argyle against Rovers in October 1910, were among the fatalities. John Hesham, who died on active service in France on 17 November 1915, had scored Croydon Common's second-half goal against Rovers at The Nest in April 1910. Leigh Richmond Roose, whose goalkeeping had done so much to eliminate Rovers from the 1901/02 FA Cup, and who was once a medical trainee and pupil of H G Wells, was killed on the Somme on 7 October 1916, while Walter Tull, whose four goals had helped Northampton Town defeat Rovers at Easter 1912, was killed on the battlefield on 15 March 1918. Some clubs were seriously depleted through war injuries. For instance, three Exeter City players who had appeared against Rovers, Fred Marshall,

Bristol Rovers 1915/16. Ellis Crompton (back row, third from left) was Rovers' leading goalscorer with 17 goals

SEASON 1915/16

FRIENDLIES

Date	Opponent		Score	ATT	GOALSCORERS	PLAYERS	GLS
						BENN	3
04/09/15	CARDIFF CITY	A	1-4	3000	FUGE	BOWEN	1
11/09/15	NEWPORT CNY	H	3-1	1000	HURLEY 3, 1 pen	BRIGHT	1
18/09/15	SOUTHAMPTON	A	3-4		BENN 3	BROWN	2
25/09/15	READING	H	1-4		FUGE	CHAPPLE	3
09/10/15	CARDIFF CITY	H	3-2		CHAPPLE, WESTON, BROWN	COOK	3
						CROMPTON	17
16/10/15	NEWPORT COUNTY	A	2-1		BROWN pen, CHAPPLE	DANDO	4
23/10/15	SOUTHAMPTON	H	4-2		CROMPTON 3, PHILLIPS	FUGE	2
30/10/15	SWINDON TOWN	A	2-5		ROE 2	GREEN	11
06/11/15	HIGHLAND LIGHT INFANTRY	H	4-0		CHAPPLE, POWELL, CROMPTON, COOK	HURLEY	7
						HYAM	2
13/11/15	BRISTOL SUBURBAN LGE	H	4-1		CROMPTON 2, ROE 2	PHILLIPS	2
20/11/15	NEWPORT COUNTY	H	7-2		WESTON 3, SWEET 2, ROE, CROMPTON	POTTER	1
						POWELL	2
27/11/15	ROYAL SCOTS BRIGADE	H	1-4		POWELL	ROE	6
04/12/15	SWINDON TOWN	H	0-1			SMITH	1
11/12/15	R.A.M.C	H	9-2		HURLEY 2, GREEN 2, BRIGHT, SWEET 2, CROMPTON, COOK	SWEET	6
						WESTON	6
18/12/15	TYNESIDE SCOTTISH	H	5-0		DANDO 2, CROMPTON, GREEN, COOK		
27/12/15	BRISTOL CITY	A	0-0	3000			
08/01/16	A.S.C WELLS	H	4-0		HURLEY, DANDO, SWEET, CROMPTON		
15/01/16	NEWPORT CNY*	A	3-0		CROMPTON, GREEN , POTTER		
22/01/16	BARRY DISTRICT	H	2-2		GREEN 2, 1pen		
29/01/16	CARDIFF CITY *	A	2-1		GREEN 2		
05/02/16	BRISTOL CITY	H	0-0	3000			
12/02/16	PORTSMOUTH	A	0-3	3000			
19/02/16	SOUTHAMPTON	H	2-4		DANDO, CROMPTON		
04/03/16	SWINDON TOWN	H	0-0				
11/03/16	BARRY DISTRICT	A	0-3				
18/03/16	PORTSMOUTH *	H	2-1		GREEN , CROMPTON		
25/03/16	DOUGLAS BROS.	H	2-0		CROMPTON, ROE		
01/04/16	CARDIFF CITY *	H	0-2				
08/04/16	A.S.C SHIREHAMPTON	H	3-2		BOWEN, WESTON. GREEN		
15/04/16	NEWPORT COUNTY *	H	3-0		WESTON, HYAM, CROMPTON		
21/04/16	BRISTOL CITY *	H	1-1	4000	GREEN		
22/04/16	SWINDON TOWN *	A	2-2		CROMPTON, SMITH		
24/04/16	BRISTOL CITY *	A	2-0	4000	HYAM pen, HURLEY		
29/04/16	SOUTHAMPTON *	A	0-6				
05/05/16	A.S.C SHIREHAMPTON	H	3-0		CROMPTON, SWEET pen, PHILLIPS		

* South West Combination matches
Note: Line-up details during World War One are very difficult to establish.

Herbert Tierney and Bill Smith, suffered such serious war wounds that they never played again. In Smith's case, one of his legs had to be amputated in 1919. Other clubs were even more unfortunate; Croydon Common folded on 15 March 1917 on the approval of His Honour Judge Edward Harington.

The story of Blakey Martin, a former Derby County player, is a more positive one. He could claim a more distinguished war record that culminated in the receipt of the Military Medal and bar. Martin was to play at left-half for Southend United in both League fixtures against Rovers in 1920/21 and 1921/22. John Hughes, a Rovers player in 1911/12 and a former Welsh amateur international, received a Military Cross in April 1916 for his actions on the battlefield.

In July 1915, following a meeting of football authorities in Blackpool, all first-class football was suspended for the duration of the war. Rovers did, however, compete in the

SEASON 1916/17

FRIENDLIES

Date	Opponent		Score	ATT	GOALSCORERS
09/09/16	BRISTOL CITY	H	2-0		HURLEY, CROMPTON
16/09/16	PORTSMOUTH	A	2-2		ROWLEY, HURLEY
23/09/16	SWINDON TOWN	H	5-0		CROMPTON, HYAM 4, 1 pen
30/09/16	BRISTOL CITY	A	1-3	1500	HYAM pen
07/10/16	AVONMOUTH MT	H	10-2	1000	CROMPTON 4, STONE 2, PEARS 4
14/10/16	3RD OFFICERS CADETS	H	1-0		ROE
21/10/16	SWINDON TOWN	H	0-1		BUTLER
28/10/16	ROYAL WARWICKS	H	3-2		SMITH 2, HOBBS
04/11/16	BRISTOL CITY	H	1-5	2000	GREEN pen
11/11/16	BARRY DISTRICT	A	0-1		
18/11/16	ARMY ORDNANCE	H	5-2		GREEN 2, JAMES, STONE, CROMPTON
25/11/16	BRISTOL CITY	A	1-3		GREEN
02/12/16	BARRY DISTRICT	H	2-2		GREEN 2
09/12/16	CENTRAL FYING SCHOOL	H	3-2		GREEN, CROMPTON, BRYANT
16/12/16	ROYAL NAVAL DEPOT	H	2-8		GREEN, HYAM
23/12/16	SOMERSET LIGHT INFANTRY	H	7-0		GREEN 2, CROMPTON 2, SMITH 2, HYAM
25/12/16	BRISTOL CITY	H	3-0	2000	GREEN 2-1pen, ROE
26/12/16	BRISTOL CITY	A	1-0	2000	HYAM
06/01/17	3RD OFFICERS CADETS	H	10-0		STONE 4, HYAM 2, ROE 2, COOK, HURLEY
13/01/17	ASC REMOUNTS	H	6-1		GREEN 2, STONE 2, HURLEY, BROOKS,
20/01/17	MT ASC AVONMOUTH	H	2-0		STONE, GREEN
27/01/17	ROYAL FLYING CORPS	H	1-1		FOWLER
03/02/17	BRISTOL CITY	A	0-1	1000	
17/02/17	RFA BULFORD	H	7-2		GREEN 2, HYAM 3, CROMPTON 2
24/02/17	BRISTOL CITY	H	0-2		
03/03/17	BRISTOL DOCKERS	A	7-0		HYAM 3, GREEN 2, BROOKE, CROMPTON
10/03/17	BRISTOL YMCA	H	10-1		LUCAS 6, GREEN 2, HYAM, BROOKS
17/03/17	BRISTOL CITY	H	2-1		WESTON 2
24/03/17	MT ASC AVONMOUTH	H	3-1		WESTON 3
31/03/17	"BRAZIL, STRAKER & CO"	H	3-2		LEWIS, STEVENS, OSBORNE
06/04/17	BRISTOL CITY	H	1-1	2000	STEVENS
07/04/17	3RD OFFICERS CADETS	H	6-0		CROMPTON 2, WESTON 2, HURLEY 2
09/04/17	BRISTOL CITY	A	0-1	2000	
14/04/17	RENOWN	H	5-0		GRUBB 3, HURLEY, ROE
21/04/17	BRISTOL DOCKERS	H	0-0		
28/04/17	BRISTOL CITY	H	0-0		
05/05/17	3RD OFFICERS CADETS	H	2-1		CROMPTON, HURLEY

PLAYERS	GLS
BENN	3
BAKER	
BISHOP	
BROOKE	1
BROOKS	2
BROWN	
BRYANT	
BUSH	
COOK	
COX	
CROMPTON	16
FOWLER	1
GANGE	
GOODMAN	
GORDON	
GREEN	21
GRUBB	3
GYLES	
HOBBS	1
HOLT	
HOWES	
HURLEY	8
HYAM	17
ILES	
JAMES	1
LEWIS	1
LUCAS	6
NORRIS	
NYLAND	
OSBORNE	1
PANES	
PAYNE	
PEARS	4
ROE	5
ROWLEY	1
RUBERY	
SMITH	4
STEVENS	2
STONE	10
TOOSE	
TUCKER	
WARE	
WEAR	
WEBB	
WESTON	7
WILLIAMS	

South-Western Combination of 1915/16, winning five of 12 games and finishing two points above Bristol City. Three players scored twice each in a 9-2 victory over RAMC in December and separate players scored hat-tricks in each of two fixtures with both Newport County and Southampton.

Rovers, along with a number of provincial sides, were refused admission, for reasons of restricted wartime travel, to the London Combination for 1916/17 and, between 1916 and 1919, played solely in games around the Bristol area. The Bristol County Combination of 1917/18 saw Rovers win 28 out of 37 matches, scoring 137 goals in the process, but still miss out on the Championship to Bristol City. The following season,

SEASON 1917/18

FRIENDLIES

Date	Opponent	H/A	Score	ATT	GOALSCORERS
01/09/17	BRISTOL DOCKERS	H	5-0		RAWLINS 3, WESTON 2
08/09/17	BRISTOL CITY	H	1-2		CROMPTON
15/09/17	TRACTOR DEPOT	H	4-1		CROMPTON, BUSH, SHAW, RAWLINS
22/09/17	ASC REMOUNTS	H	12-0		RAWLINS 4, CROMPTON 2, KELSTON 2, WESTON 2, BAKER, BUSH,
29/09/17	BRISTOL CITY	A	0-2		
06/10/17	BRISTOL DOCKERS	H	8-0		WESTON 2, KELSTON 2, BENNETT og, SKUSE, GILES, RAWLINS
13/10/17	SWINDON TOWN	H	4-2		CROMPTON, RAWLINS, WESTON 2
20/10/17	BRISTOL Y.M.C.A	H	7-0		RAWLINS 3, KELSTON, WESTON, SKUSE, BRACE
27/10/17	BRISTOL CITY	H	3-1		RAWLINS 2, WESTON
03/11/17	MILITARY X1	H	11-0		CROMPTON 4, RAWLINS 4, KELSTON 2, ROE
10/11/17	R.E (WHITE CITY)	H	4-2		WESTON 3, RAWLINS
17/11/17	BRISTOL CITY	A	0-0		
24/11/17	R.F.C CIRENCESTER	H	4-0		SKUSE 2, GYLES, RAWLINS
01/12/17	H.M FACTORY	H	3-1		WESTON 2, SKUSE
08/12/17	G.W R CARRIAGE X1	H	13-0		WESTON 9, CROMPTON 2, SKUSE, GYLES
15/12/17	R.E (HENBURY)	H	1-0		SKUSE
22/12/17	R.F.C (FILTON)	H	4-1		WESTON 4
25/12/17	BRISTOL CITY	H	1-2	2000	WESTON
26/12/17	BRISTOL CITY	A	3-0	1000	WESTON, WEDLOCK og, SKUSE
29/12/17	R.E (WHITE CITY)	H	2-3		SKUSE, BUSH
29/03/18	BRISTOL CITY	A	0-2	2000	
01/04/18	BRISTOL CITY	H	0-1	2500	

PLAYERS	GLS
BAKER	1
BRACE	1
BRIGHT	
BUSH	3
CHAPPELL	
CROMPTON	11
EMSLEY	
FORBES	
FORBES	
FORD	
FOSTER	
GILES	1
GOODMAN	
GYLES	2
HALL	
HENDERSON	
HOPES	
HOWES	
ILES	
KELSTON	7
KIRK	
PANES	
PENDRICK	
RAWLINS	21
ROE	1
SHAW	1
SKUSE	9
WESTON	30
WOOLEY	
OWN GOALS	2

BRISTOL COUNTY COMBINATION

Date	Opponent	H/A	Score
02/02/18	H.M FACTORY*	H	5-0
09/02/18	BRISTOL CITY	H	2-0
16/02/18	R.E (PORTBURY)	H	6-1
23/02/18	BRISTOL DOCKERS	H	2-1
02/03/18	H.M FACTORY*	H	5-0
09/03/18	BRISTOL CITY	A	0-1
23/03/18	R.E (PORTBURY)	H	3-1
30/03/18	R.F.C (FILTON)	H	3-1
13/04/18	BRISTOL DOCKERS	H	3-1
27/04/18	R.E (WHITE CITY)	H	1-2
29/04/18	RAF (FILTON)	H	2-1
29/04/18	R.E (WHITE CITY)	A	1-0

* Note: Line-up details during World War One are very difficult to establish.

only four sides participated in this tournament, with Rovers (11 points) above Bristol city (nine), Bristol Docks (four) and RAVC (no points). Rovers also played a series of friendly matches through the war, many against local cadet corps. There were several large wins, Rovers reaching double figures on nine occasions. The highest victory was 20-0 against Great Western Railway on 15 February 1919. Edward Rawlings scored four goals, Ellis Crompton, Bill Panes, Len Gyles and goalkeeper Harry Grubb, who played outfield after half-time, bagged three each, Harry Roe scored twice and Bert Bennett and Percy Whitton once each. Bill Weston scored nine goals in a 12-0 win over the same opponents on 8 December 1917 and Lucas netted six when Rovers defeated

SEASON 1918/19

FRIENDLIES

Date	Opponent		Score	ATT	GOALSCORERS	PLAYERS	GLS
07/09/18	BRISTOL & COL CO	H	3-2		SKUSE 2, GYLES	BAKER A	3
14/09/18	BRISTOL CITY	H	5-2		WESTON 3, BAKER,	BENNETT	2
					PENDRICK	BUCKLE H	4
05/10/18	BRISTOL CITY	A	2-4		BUSH, WESTON	BUSH	1
26/10/18	BRISTOL CITY	H	1-0	2000	WESTON	COOKE	1
02/11/18	ROYAL ENGINEERS (PORTBURY)	H	3-1		BENNETT, STONE,	CROMPTON E	14
					FARQUHARSON og	GRIFFITHS J	6
16/11/18	YMCA	H	5-0		SKUSE 3, WESTON, HARDING	GRUBB H	3
30/11/18	BRISTOL CITY	A	0-0			GYLES L	6
07/12/18	R.A.F YATE	H	5-1		WESTON 3, CROMPTON 2	HARDING	1
14/12/18	DISCHARGED NAVY X1	H	5-0		WESTON 3, GYLES, PENDRICK	PANES W	3
21/12/18	BRISTOL & COL CO	H	3-2		RAWLINGS 2, PENDRICK	PENDRICK	6
25/12/18	BRISTOL CITY	H	2-2	3000	WALKER, WESTON	RAWLINGS E	24
28/12/18	BRISTOL DOCKERS	H	10-1		SKUSE 4, RAWLINS 2,	ROE H	4
					CROMPTON, WALKER,	SKUSE E	24
					WESTON, BAKER pen	SLEIGH	2
11/01/19	REPAT SOLDIERS & SAILORS	H	6-0		SLEIGH 2, CROMPTON,	STONE	6
					WESTON, WALKER, SKUSE	WALKER J	4
25/01/19	R.F.A LARKHILL	H	5-1		SKUSE 2, STONE, WALKER, ROE	WESTON W	37
01/02/19	BRISTOL CITY	A	2-2		SKUSE 2	WHITTON P	1
08/02/19	NEWPORT COUNTY	H	3-0		CROMPTON, STONE 2	OWN GOALS	1
15/02/19	GREAT W. RAILWAY CARTAGE	H	20-0		CROMPTON 3, 1 pen,	UNTRACED	9
					RAWLINGS 4, GRUBB 3,		
					PANES 3-1pen, ROE 2, GYLES 3,		
					WHITTON, BENNETT		
01/03/19	ARMY X1	H	5-2		WESTON 2, SKUSE 2, CROMPTON		
08/03/19	BRISTOL CITY	A	0-1	4000			
22/03/19	SWINDON TOWN	H	3-2		SKUSE, WESTON, ROE		
29/03/19	CARDIFF CITY	H	3-0		WESTON, RAWLINGS, BUCKLE		
05/04/19	BRISTOL CITY	H	2-0	6431	SKUSE, RAWLINGS		
18/04/19	BRISTOL CITY	A	5-1	7321	SKUSE 3, RAWLINGS 2		
19/04/19	SWINDON TOWN	H	5-2		BUCKLE, SKUSE 2, WESTON, RAWLINGS		
22/04/19	NEWPORT COUNTY	A	2-1		RAWLINGS 2		
26/04/19	CARDIFF CITY	A	0-1				
28/04/19	DOUGLAS FC	H	1-0		COOKE		
30/04/19	SWANSEA TOWN	A	0-4				
03/05/19	GLOUCESTER COUNTY X1	H	1-1		BUCKLE		
10/05/19	BRISTOL CITY	H	4-1	7450	WESTON 2, RAWLINGS 2		
24/05/19	BRISTOL CITY	H	1-2	4044	RAWLINGS		
	(Crompton X1 v Wedlock X1)						

BRISTOL COUNTY COMBINATION

Date	Opponent		Score	ATT	GOALSCORERS
21/09/18	DISCHARGED SOLDIERS & SAILORS	H	14-1		PENDRICK, STONE, SKUSE, CROMPTON, GYLES, 9 untraced
28/09/18	R.A.F (FILTON)	H	3-0		WESTON 2, BAKER
12/10/18	ROYAL ENGINEERS (PORTBURY)	H	0-0	2000	
19/10/18	BRISTOL DOCKERS	H	4-1		WESTON 2, PENDRICK, STONE
23/11/18	RAF (FILTON)	H	3-0		PENDRICK, CROMPTON,
26/12/18	BRISTOL CITY	A	3-2	3000	WESTON 3
18/01/19	BRISTOL DOCKERS	H	4-0		GRIFFITHS J 3, WESTON
15/03/19	R.A.V.C	H	7-0		WESTON 4, RAWLINGS 2, BUCKLE
12/04/19	R.A.V.C	H	8-0		RAWLINGS 4, CROMPTON 2, SKUSE, WESTON
21/04/19	BRISTOL CITY	H	1-1	11053	CROMPTON pen

Note: Line-up details during World War One are very difficult to establish.
* Goals scored in friendlies and Bristol Combination matches

Bristol YMCA 10-1 on 10 March 1917. The apparently free-scoring goalkeeper Grubb had earlier scored another hat-trick when Rovers beat Renown 5-0 in April 1917. On the other hand, the former England International Wally Hardinge scored a hat-trick when the Royal Naval Depot won 8-2 at Eastville in December 1916.

Jonah Wilcox, who scored for Bristol City in six different matches against Rovers during the war, was to be Rovers's top scorer in 1925/26. He scored a hat-trick in Bristol City's 5-1 win at Eastville in November 1916. The game against the Robins in September 1916 featured three penalties, scored by Green for Rovers and Chapman and Smith for City, who won 3-1. The second goal in Rovers' comfortable win at Ashton Gate on Boxing Day 1917 was put through his own net by City's 26-times-capped England International centre-half Billy Wedlock. Edward Skuse scored a hat-trick in the convincing victory at Ashton Gate on Good Friday 1919. Three days later, on Easter Monday, Rovers and City drew 1-1 through a penalty each, Jones putting the visitors ahead after 50 minutes from the spot and Ellis Crompton, playing at centre-half, similarly equalised five minutes later. Crompton also scored from 40 yards in April, Rovers' fourth in an emphatic 8-0 victory over RAVC.

Rovers' penultimate fixture of the 1918/19 season was held at Eastville on 3 May. Following the contemporary fashion of such representative games across the country, Rovers played Gloucestershire, in a match that finished 1-1.

1919/20

Twenty years after first accepting the job of manager of Bristol Rovers, it fell to Alf Homer to reconstruct a team in the aftermath of four years of war. For the first full season after the war, Rovers were in the newly reformed Southern League devoid of West Ham United and the now defunct Croydon Common. Brentford returned to this division and three South Wales sides – Merthyr Town, Newport County and Swansea Town – brought the number of clubs up from 20 to 22.

Harry Grubb, a regular wartime goalkeeper with Rovers, opened the new season as first choice, although Harry Stansfield and Jesse Whatley, a signing from Trowbridge Town, were also to appear as the season progressed. David Harvie and Bill Panes, signed from Bath City in 1916, were reliable full-backs, with Percy Whitton, later an experienced Football League player at Newport County alongside Harry Roe at half-back. The new centre-half was Steve Sims from Leicester Fosse, who was joined in November by David Steele, signed from Douglas Water Thistle, who won domestic honours and Scottish International caps while at Huddersfield Town. Ellis Crompton, who missed only one game all season, and George Davison were joined in the forward line by wartime goalscorer Edward Rawlings. Billy Palmer, or 'Lady Palmer' in reference to his perceived reluctance to get muddy, returned from a highly successful stint with Everton, while Joe Walter, Rovers' only ever-present and Wally Bullock were signed from Horfield United. Two more experienced signings were West Ham United's left-back Tom Brandon and the Bristol City inside-forward Leslie Hughes, who was to return to Ashton Gate in 1920.

Just as in the five final pre-war seasons, Rovers got off to a very poor start. An opening home defeat against Queen's Park Rangers and an exciting 4-4 draw with Cardiff City set the season underway, but it was seven games before Rovers' first victory.

SOUTHERN LEAGUE

Date	Opponent	H/A	Score	ATT	G	2	3	4	5	6	7	8	9	10	11	Goalscorers
30/08/19	QPR	H	0-2	7000	GRUBB	HARVIE	PANES	WHITTON	SIMS	ROE	WALTER	RAWLINGS	DAVISON	CROMPTON	PALMER	CROMPTON pen
01/09/19	CARDIFF CITY	H	4-4	6000	GRUBB	HARVIE	PANES	WHITTON	SIMS	ROE	WALTER	RAWLINGS	DAVISON	CROMPTON	THOMAS	DAVISON, THOMAS, WALTER
06/09/19	SWINDON TOWN	A	1-4	7000	GRUBB	HARVIE	BRANDON	WHITTON	SIMS	ROE	WALTER	RAWLINGS	DAVISON	CROMPTON	THOMAS	DAVISON
08/09/19	CARDIFF CITY	A	0-0	8000	GRUBB	HARVIE	BRANDON	CROMPTON	SIMS	ROE	WALTER	RAWLINGS	WHITTON	THOMAS	GRIFFITHS	
13/09/19	MILLWALL	H	1-1	8500	GRUBB	HARVIE	BRANDON	CROMPTON	SIMS	WHITTON	WALTER	RAWLINGS	DAVISON	THOMAS	GRIFFITHS	CROMPTON
20/09/19	BRIGHTON & H ALBION	H	1-3	8000	GRUBB	HARVIE	BRANDON	CROMPTON	SIMS	WHITTON	WALTER	RAWLINGS	SKUSE	THOMAS	GRIFFITHS	RAWLINGS
27/09/19	NEWPORT COUNTY	H	2-1	10000	GRUBB	HARVIE	BRANDON	CROMPTON	SIMS	HUGHES	WALTER	RAWLINGS	DAVISON	HENDERSON	GRIFFITHS	DAVISON 2
04/10/19	PORTSMOUTH	A	0-0	16000	GRUBB	HARVIE	BRANDON	CROMPTON	SIMS	WHITTON	WALTER	RAWLINGS	DAVISON	GRIFFITHS	THOMAS	
11/10/19	NORTHAMPTON TOWN	H	3-0	9000	GRUBB	HARVIE	BRANDON	CROMPTON	SIMS	WHITTON	WALTER	RAWLINGS	HUGHES	GRIFFITHS	THOMAS	HUGHES 2, THOMAS
18/10/19	CRYSTAL PALACE	H	1-5	7000	GRUBB	HARVIE	BRANDON	CROMPTON	SIMS	GRIFFITHS	WALTER	RAWLINGS	BULLOCK	THOMAS	PALMER	BULLOCK
25/10/19	SOUTHEND UNITED	A	4-1	8000	GRUBB	HARVIE	BRANDON	CROMPTON	SIMS	HUGHES	WALTER	RAWLINGS	BULLOCK	GRIFFITHS	PALMER	RAWLINGS 3, GRIFFITHS
01/11/19	NORWICH CITY	H	1-5	7000	WHATLEY	HARVIE	BRANDON	WHITTON	SIMS	CROMPTON	WALTER	BULLOCK	DAVISON	WESTON	PALMER	SIMS
08/11/19	BRENTFORD	H	3-1	10000	WHATLEY	HARVIE	PANES	CROMPTON	SIMS	HUGHES	WALTER	RAWLINGS	DAVISON	WESTON	PALMER	CROMPTON, PALMER, RAWLINGS
15/11/19	MERTHYR TOWN	A	1-2	5000	WHATLEY	HARVIE	PANES	CROMPTON	SIMS	CROSSLEY	WALTER	RAWLINGS	DAVISON	WESTON	PALMER	CROMPTON pen
22/11/19	PLYMOUTH ARGYLE	A	2-0	12000	STANSFIELD	HARVIE	PANES	CROMPTON	SIMS	HUGHES	WALTER	RAWLINGS	CROSSLEY	WESTON	PALMER	RAWLINGS, WALTER
29/11/19	WATFORD	A	0-1	10000	STANSFIELD	HARVIE	PANES	CROMPTON	SIMS	STEELE	WALTER	RAWLINGS	HYAM	WESTON	PALMER	
06/12/19	READING	A	2-2	8000	STANSFIELD	HARVIE	PANES	CROMPTON	SIMS	STEELE	WALTER	RAWLINGS	THOMAS	WESTON	PALMER	SIMS, WALTER
13/12/19	SOUTHAMPTON	A	1-1	12000	STANSFIELD	HARVIE	PANES	CROMPTON	SIMS	STEELE	WALTER	RAWLINGS	HYAM	WESTON	PALMER	HYAM
25/12/19	SWANSEA TOWN	A	1-2	10000	WHATLEY	HARVIE	PANES	HOWES	CROMPTON	STEELE	WALTER	RAWLINGS	ROE	WESTON	PALMER	ROE
26/12/19	SWANSEA TOWN	H	3-3	6000	WHATLEY	HARVIE	PANES	WHITTON	SIMS	CROMPTON	WALTER	RAWLINGS	HYAM	WESTON	PALMER	RAWLINGS, WALTER, WESTON
27/12/19	GILLINGHAM	H	1-1	11000	WHATLEY	HARVIE	PANES	WHITTON	SIMS	CROMPTON	WALTER	RAWLINGS	HYAM	WESTON	PALMER	HYAM
03/01/20	QUEENS PARK RANGERS	A	1-7	10000	WHATLEY	HARVIE	BRANDON	WHITTON	SIMS	HOWES	WALTER	RAWLINGS	HYAM	BULLOCK	PALMER	HYAM
17/01/20	SWINDON TOWN	H	2-1	10000	GRUBB	HARVIE	PANES	WHITTON	CROMPTON	STEELE	WALTER	RAWLINGS	HYAM	THOMSON	PALMER	HYAM, CROMPTON
24/01/20	MILLWALL	A	1-2	8000	STANSFIELD	HARVIE	PANES	WHITTON	CROMPTON	STEELE	WALTER	RAWLINGS	HYAM	THOMSON	PALMER	THOMSON
31/01/20	BRIGHTON & H ALBION	A	2-3	3000	WHATLEY	HARVIE	PANES	WHITTON	SIMS	STEELE	WALTER	RAWLINGS	HYAM	THOMSON	PALMER	HYAM 2
07/02/20	NEWPORT COUNTY	A	2-0	7000	STANSFIELD	HARVIE	PANES	WHITTON	SIMS	STEELE	WALTER	CROMPTON	HYAM	THOMSON	PALMER	CROMPTON, HYAM
14/02/20	PORTSMOUTH	H	0-3	14000	STANSFIELD	HARVIE	BRANDON	WHITTON	SIMS	STEELE	WALTER	CROMPTON	HYAM	THOMSON	PALMER	
21/02/20	NORTHAMPTON TOWN	H	2-3	3000	STANSFIELD	HARVIE	BRANDON	WHITTON	CROMPTON	STEELE	WALTER	HYAM	SIMS	THOMSON	PALMER	THOMSON, PALMER
28/02/20	CRYSTAL PALACE	H	1-0	15000	STANSFIELD	HARVIE	BRANDON	WHITTON	CROMPTON	STEELE	PALMER	WALTER	SIMS	THOMSON	THOMAS	WALTER
06/03/20	SOUTHEND UNITED	H	1-1	3000	STANSFIELD	HARVIE	BRANDON	WHITTON	CROMPTON	STEELE	WALTER	DAVISON	SIMS	THOMSON	PALMER	WALTER
13/03/20	NORWICH CITY	H	5-3	5000	STANSFIELD	HARVIE	BRANDON	WHITTON	CROMPTON	STEELE	WALTER	DAVISON	SIMS	THOMSON	PALMER	SIMS 2, CROMPTON, WALTER, DEXTER og
20/03/20	BRENTFORD	A	0-3	8000	STANSFIELD	HARVIE	BRANDON	WHITTON	CROMPTON	STEELE	WALTER	DAVISON	SIMS	THOMSON	PALMER	
27/03/20	MERTHYR TOWN	H	0-0	12000	STANSFIELD	HARVIE	BRANDON	WHITTON	CROMPTON	STEELE	WALTER	THOMSON	SIMS	THOMSON	PALMER	
02/04/20	EXETER CITY	A	4-2	14000	STANSFIELD	HARVIE	BRANDON	WHITTON	CROMPTON	STEELE	WALTER	DAVISON	SIMS	WESTON	PALMER	DAVISON, SIMS, WALTER, WESTON
03/04/20	PLYMOUTH ARGYLE	H	0-2	11440	STANSFIELD	HARVIE	BRANDON	WHITTON	CROMPTON	STEELE	WALTER	DAVISON	SIMS	WESTON	PALMER	
05/04/20	EXETER CITY	A	1-2	12000	WHATLEY	HARVIE	BRANDON	HOWES	CROMPTON	HOWES	WALTER	DAVISON	SIMS	WESTON	PALMER	SIMS
06/04/20	LUTON TOWN	H	5-0	10000	WHATLEY	HARVIE	BRANDON	HOWES	CROMPTON	HOWES	WALTER	DAVISON	SIMS	WESTON	PALMER	SIMS 3, CROMPTON, STEELE
17/04/20	READING	H	0-0	5000	WHATLEY	HARVIE	BRANDON	HOWES	CROMPTON	HOWES	WALTER	DAVISON	HYAM	WESTON	PALMER	
19/04/20	SOUTHAMPTON	H	0-2	5000	WHATLEY	HARVIE	BRANDON	HOWES	CROMPTON	HOWES	WALTER	DAVISON	HYAM	WESTON	PALMER	
24/04/20	WATFORD	A	0-2	12000	WHATLEY	BRANDON	PANES	HOWES	CROMPTON	WHITTON	WALTER	DAVISON	HYAM	VAUGHAN	PALMER	
26/04/20	LUTON TOWN	A	1-1	3000	WHATLEY	BRANDON	PANES	WHITTON	CROMPTON	STEELE	WALTER	DAVISON	HYAM	VAUGHAN	PALMER	WHITTON
01/05/20	GILLINGHAM	A	2-2	6000	CHANNON	BRANDON	WEAR	WHITTON	CROMPTON	STEELE	WALTER	THOMSON	THOMSON	MORGAN	PALMER	THOMSON 2

FA CUP

Date	Opponent	H/A	Score	ATT	G	2	3	4	5	6	7	8	9	10	11	Goalscorers
20/12/19	NORTHAMPTON TOWN	A	2-2	9000	GRUBB	HARVIE	PANES	ROE	SIMS	STEELE	WALTER	RAWLINGS	HYAM	CROMPTON	PALMER	HYAM, RAWLINGS
24/12/19	NORTHAMPTON TOWN	H	3-2	14000	GRUBB	HARVIE	PANES	ROE	SIMS	STEELE	WALTER	RAWLINGS	HYAM	CROMPTON	PALMER	RAWLINGS, HYAM, CROMPTON
10/01/20	TOTTENHAM HOTSPUR	H	1-4	17260	GRUBB	HARVIE	PANES	ROE	SIMS	STEELE	WALTER	RAWLINGS	HYAM	CROMPTON	PALMER	CROMPTON

GLOUCESTERSHIRE CUP FINAL

Date	Opponent	H/A	Score	ATT	G	2	3	4	5	6	7	8	9	10	11	Goalscorers
24/09/19	BRISTOL CITY	H	0-4	7000	GRUBB	HARVIE	PANES	CROMPTON	SIMS	WHITTON	WALTER	RAWLINGS	HUGHES	SKUSE	GRIFFITHS	

Players	APPS	GLS
BRANDON T	26	
BULLOCK W	5	1
CHANNON F	1	
CROMPTON E	41	8
CROSSLEY F	2	
DAVISON G	22	5
GRIFFITHS J	10	1
GRUBB H	13	
HARVIE D	39	
HENDERSON J	1	
HOWES D	7	
HUGHES L	5	2
HYAM J	14	7
MORGAN J	1	
PALMER W	34	2
PANES W	18	
RAWLINGS E	24	7
ROE H	5	
SIMS S	32	9
SKUSE E	1	
STANSFIELD H	14	
STEELE D	22	1
THOMAS A	12	2
THOMSON J	12	4
VAUGHAN W	3	
WALTER J	42	8
WEAR A	1	
WESTON W	12	2
WHATLEY J	14	
WHITTON P	29	1
OWN GOALS		1

Rovers were to struggle all year and finished in 17th place. Steve Sims was top scorer with nine goals, including a hat-trick in a 5-0 victory over Luton Town on Easter Tuesday, in which game Jesse Whatley saved John Elvey's penalty. Crompton and Walter scored eight each, Rawlings and Jim Hyam one fewer that season. Rawlings' total included three in a 4-1 victory over Southend United in October.

An exciting game at home to Norwich City saw the visitors give three players a debut. Rovers led 3-2 by half-time and won 5-3. Sims scored twice and the Canaries' George Dexter, in his only first-class appearance for Norwich, scored an own goal as did Rovers' Brandon in the second-half. Five minutes from time, trying to stop the ball as it flew out of play, an unfortunate spectator fell headlong into the river Frome. As the season drew to a close, benefit games for manager Alf Homer were played against Gillingham and Aston Villa.

The season's heaviest defeat came in January. Queen's Park Rangers, managed by Jimmy Howie, Rovers' joint top scorer in 1902/03, defeated Rovers 7-1 at Loftus Road, John Smith scoring four times while Rawlings had his 65th minute penalty easily saved by Joe Merrick. A 5-1 defeat at Norwich City featured a John Doran hat-trick. A 3-0 defeat at Brentford was precipitated by Patsy Hendren's opening goal shortly after half-time. Jimmy Broad scored for Millwall in both Southern League fixtures against Rovers and four against Northampton Town just 48 hours after the Eastville game. The defeat at Plymouth Argyle on Easter Saturday featured an opening goal from David Jack, a future England International who was to play in two FA Cup finals with Bolton Wanderers and two more with Arsenal.

Jim Hyam marked his home debut in December with a goal after only 12 seconds against Southampton. Unfortunately for Rovers, goalkeeper Harry Stansfield was injured, Billy Weston went in goal and 10-man Rovers held on for a 1-1 draw. Arthur Dominy scored the equaliser for the Saints. Two games later, Harvie clocked up his 200th Southern League appearance, becoming the third Rovers player, after Arthur Cartlidge and Billy Peplow to achieve this feat. The rugged and uncompromising full-back was to leave the club within months under a cloud, however, having allegedly sold his landlady's piano without her permission.

No fewer than 11 Southern League and two FA Cup-ties at Eastville were watched by five-figure crowds. Rovers progressed in the Cup after two high-scoring games with Northampton Town. Rawlings and Hyam scored in both games, as did Billy Pease for the Cobblers. Rovers then crashed 4-1 at home to Tottenham Hotspur, before a crowd of 17,260, paying 1/6d a head on the terraces and 7/6d in the stands. The Division Two side knocked Rovers out of the cup for the first of two consecutive seasons, 37-year-old centre-forward Jimmy Cantrell scoring a hat-trick. Tom Howarth, later a Rovers player, scored twice as Bristol City won the Gloucestershire Cup final 4-0. At the season's end, Football League and Southern League representatives met in Sheffield on 18 May 1920 and voted 19-1, with one abstention, to elevate the Southern League *en bloc* to form Division Three, a recommendation first proposed as early as 1909. It was a momentous decision, ratified at the Football League's Annual General Meeting 11 days later, opening up a new chapter in the history of Bristol Rovers.

Presented with the opportunity of participation in the Football League, Bristol Rovers set about on the journey that was to see League status preserved into the 21st century. It was certainly a fresh start for the club and required careful preparation. Sixty-year-old club chairman George Humphreys made the first move by appointing Ben Hall in July 1920 as Rovers' first full-time manager. Alf Homer, stepping down from managerial duties, became the club secretary, a post he was to hold for a further eight years. Hall had enjoyed a successful playing career as a centre-half with Grimsby Town, Derby County, Leicester Fosse and South Shields and a post-war spell as trainer at Huddersfield Town preceded his move to Eastville. His was the task of creating a side to represent Rovers in League action and building a team spirit worthy of the club.

Four regular players from 1919/20 – club captain Steve Sims, Joe Walter, Ellis Crompton and Bill Palmer – as well as emerging goalkeeper Jesse Whatley became the backbone of the side. In all, 11 Southern League players reappeared for Rovers in the Football League. Bill Panes, who had broken into the side at left-back, formed a full-back partnership with Jock Bethune, a Glaswegian who had gained considerable experience in Division Two with Barnsley and was to represent England at indoor bowls between 1936 and 1938. At half-back, David Steele was joined at the end of 1919/20 by Scotsman David Kenny and, on the eve of the new season, by Derby County's Harry Boxley. Homer's last signings, inside-forwards Bill Bird and Joe Norton, a former Manchester United player, were joined shortly before the new season by inside-right Harold Bell. Another former Barnsley player, Bell, was to play in the inaugural League game and on only one further occasion in his sole season at Eastville.

Before the season started, Humphreys held a special meeting to introduce Hall. At this occasion, he also informed the gathering that the club was now out of debt. He had paid for the Eastville ground in full and the club now owned 19 acres of land, including property right up to the famous Thirteen Arches railway bridge, which overlooked the ground until its demolition in May 1968. The club was also planning to dispose of striped shirts and play in white tops with navy blue shorts, a kit to which Rovers were to adhere for the opening decade in the Football League.

Hall made one additional signing during the season, that of wing-half George Gane. A Bristolian by birth, Gane had played League football north and south of the border, once commanding an alleged transfer fee of £750, a world record at the time. He had moved into non-League football and, though now aged 34, was able to make one final League appearance in the 2-2 draw at home to Norwich City in October. This game also marked the end of Billy Vaughan's Rovers career. Vaughan was to enjoy a further decade in high-quality football and was in the Exeter City side which defeated Rovers through four Fred Dent goals in November 1927. In one final twist, Vaughan claimed Rovers' second goal in the Norwich game, his only one in Division Three for the club, even if, as the *Western Daily Press* reported, Joe Walter applied the finishing touch.

The opening game, on a sunny August afternoon, ended in a 2-0 defeat at the hands of Millwall. A crowd of 25,000 at The Den saw a goalless first-half. Then, after 52

Bristol Rovers 1920/21. Back row: George Endicott (Trainer), Denis Howes, Walter Bird, Jesse Whatley, Sam Furniss, Harry Boxley. Front row: Bill Panes, George Chance, Jerry Morgan, Joe Hall, Joe Norton, Harold Bell

minutes, Bill Voisey's powerful shot from the edge of the penalty area put Millwall ahead. Only seven minutes later, goalkeeper Harry Stansfield, playing as ever in glasses, lost the flight of outside-left Jack Dempsey's cross in the late afternoon sun and Jimmy Broad's header put the result out of Rovers' reach.

Four days later, in the first League match played at Eastville, Rovers gained their first victory. Ellis Crompton had missed the opening match, but returned to the side at inside-left to score the first goal as Rovers defeated Newport County 3-2. It is, of course, in the nature of such a season that a number of club firsts were set. Bill Bird claimed a hat-trick in a bad-tempered 3-1 win against Brighton in September. In this match, Kenny dislocated his collar-bone and the visitors' centre-half Jack Rutherford, who was to join Rovers in 1922, was sent off.

Rovers won 15 out of 21 home League fixtures during 1920/21. Victory over Crystal Palace in October was partly due to a last-minute penalty save by Whatley from Bert Menlove, while Merthyr Town earned a point at Eastville in April when Rees Williams equalised with a shot so hard it broke the net. Two goals in the final five minutes earned Rovers a 2-1 victory over Southend United in March. Away from home, Rovers won only at Newport, Luton and Northampton. A typical story was the game at Swindon Town in January, when Harry Boxley gave Rovers a first-minute lead only for two Albert Denyer goals to give the Robins victory. The heaviest defeat was against the divisional champions Southampton at The Dell, when four goals in 20 minutes during the second-half gave the Saints a 4-0 victory. Joe Barratt, who was to join Rovers from

Fixture card for Rovers' first Football League season

Official programme for fourth home match, a 3-1 victory over Brighton

Lincoln City in 1926, scored one of them. Defeat at Watford in February came courtesy of outside-left Tommy Waterall's goal scored direct from a corner. Crystal Palace scored three times in eight second-half minutes to beat Rovers in October.

On New Year's Day, Luton Town full-back Alf Tirrell became the first player to score for both sides in a League fixture involving Rovers. Sid Leigh's early goal had given Rovers a lead that Tirrell's well-taken free-kick cancelled out. As half-time approached, Leigh's shot was deflected by Tirrell off the greasy turf past his own goalkeeper to give Rovers a 2-1 victory. Luton were awarded a penalty kick in both League fixtures against Rovers and on both occasions Jesse Whatley saved from the future England International Ernie Simms. The return game at Eastville on Easter Tuesday, however, was a more one-sided affair. Boxley scored twice and Crompton, Leigh and Palmer bagged one each in a straightforward 5-0 victory. Luton fielded, at outside-right, the unlikely figure of Louis Bookman, born Louis Buckhalter in 1890 in the Lithuanian town of Zagaren. Bookman was a naturalised Briton who had represented Ireland at cricket and Northern Ireland at football. Robert Faulkner, Queen's Park Rangers' outside-right in both League fixtures against Rovers, later emigrated to Canada, for whom he played three Internationals during 1925 and 1926.

Rovers won seven of their final eight home League games, two of them by five-goal margins. The home game with Southend United was won after Rovers trailed 1-0 five minutes from time. In the final match at Eastville, Rovers defeated Exeter City 5-0. This Exeter game was a personal triumph for Sid Leigh, who completed a first-half hat-trick

FOOTBALL LEAGUE DIVISION THREE

Date	Opponent		Score	Att	G	2	3	4	5	6	7	8	9	10	11	Goalscorers
28/08/20	MILLWALL	A	0-2	25000	STANSFIELD	BETHUNE	PANES	BOXLEY	KENNY	STEELE	CHANCE	BIRD	SIMS	BELL	PALMER	
01/09/20	NEWPORT COUNTY	H	3-2	10000	STANSFIELD	BETHUNE	PANES	BOXLEY	KENNY	STEELE	CHANCE	NORTON	SIMS	CROMPTON	PALMER	CROMPTON, NORTON, SIMS
04/09/20	MILLWALL	H	1-2	20000	STANSFIELD	BETHUNE	PANES	BOXLEY	NORTON	STEELE	CHANCE	BIRD	CROMPTON	VAUGHAN	PALMER	CHANCE
09/09/20	NEWPORT COUNTY	A	0-2	5000	WHATLEY	STANSFIELD	PANES	BOXLEY	KENNY	STEELE	CHANCE	BIRD	SIMS	VAUGHAN	NORTON	
11/09/20	GRIMSBY TOWN	H	2-0	20000	WHATLEY	BETHUNE	PANES	CROMPTON	KENNY	STEELE	CHANCE	WALTER	SIMS	LEIGH	PALMER	WALTER 2
18/09/20	GRIMSBY TOWN	A	1-3	10000	WHATLEY	BETHUNE	PANES	CROMPTON	KENNY	STEELE	CHANCE	WALTER	SIMS	LEIGH	PALMER	LEIGH
25/09/20	BRIGHTON & H ALBION	H	3-1	10000	WHATLEY	BETHUNE	PANES	CROMPTON	KENNY	STEELE	CHANCE	WALTER	BIRD	LEIGH	PALMER	BIRD 3
02/10/20	BRIGHTON & H ALBION	A	0-2	7000	WHATLEY	BETHUNE	PANES	CROMPTON	KENNY	STEELE	CHANCE	WALTER	BIRD	LEIGH	PALMER	
09/10/20	CRYSTAL PALACE	H	2-1	20000	WHATLEY	BETHUNE	PANES	CROMPTON	STEELE	CROMPTON	CHANCE	WALTER	BIRD	LEIGH	NORTON	LEIGH 2
16/10/20	CRYSTAL PALACE	A	0-3	16000	WHATLEY	BETHUNE	PANES	CROMPTON	SIMS	STEELE	CHANCE	WALTER	GANE	VAUGHAN	WALTER	
23/10/20	NORWICH CITY	H	2-2	12000	WHATLEY	HALL	PANES	HOWES	CROMPTON	STEELE	CHANCE	BIRD	SIMS	LEIGH	WALTER	LEIGH, VAUGHAN
30/10/20	NORWICH CITY	A	1-1	10000	WHATLEY	HALL	PANES	HOWES	CROMPTON	GANE	BOXLEY	BIRD	SIMS	MORGAN	LEIGH	BIRD, PALMER
06/11/20	BRENTFORD	H	2-1	8500	WHATLEY	HALL	PANES	HOWES	CROMPTON	STEELE	CHANCE	BIRD	SIMS	MORGAN	LEIGH	BIRD, PALMER
13/11/20	BRENTFORD	A	0-0	9000	WHATLEY	HALL	PANES	HOWES	CROMPTON	STEELE	BOXLEY	BIRD	SIMS	MORGAN	LEIGH	
20/11/20	SOUTHAMPTON	H	0-4	17000	WHATLEY	HALL	PANES	HOWES	CROMPTON	STEELE	CHANCE	BIRD	SIMS	MORGAN	LEIGH	
27/11/20	SOUTHAMPTON	A	1-2	17000	WHATLEY	BETHUNE	PANES	HOWES	CROMPTON	PANES	BOXLEY	BIRD	SIMS	MORGAN	LEIGH	MORGAN
04/12/20	READING	H	1-2	3000	WHATLEY	BETHUNE	HALL	HOWES	SIMS	STEELE	WALTER	BIRD	MORGAN	LEIGH	PALMER	SMITH og
11/12/20	READING	A	3-2	12000	WHATLEY	BETHUNE	HALL	HOWES	SIMS	STEELE	WALTER	BIRD	MORGAN	LEIGH	PALMER	BOXLEY, WILKINSON og
25/12/20	SWANSEA TOWN	H	1-2	12000	WHATLEY	BETHUNE	PANES	CROMPTON	SIMS	STEELE	WALTER	BIRD	MORGAN	LEIGH	PALMER	LEIGH, PALMER
27/12/20	SWANSEA TOWN	A	2-2	12000	WHATLEY	BETHUNE	PANES	CROMPTON	SIMS	STEELE	WALTER	BIRD	BOXLEY	LEIGH	PALMER	CROMPTON 2, BOXLEY, PALMER
01/01/21	LUTON TOWN	A	2-1	6000	WHATLEY	HALL	PANES	CROMPTON	SIMS	STEELE	WALTER	BIRD	BOXLEY	LEIGH	PALMER	CROMPTON 2, BOXLEY
15/01/21	SWINDON TOWN	H	1-2	9000	WHATLEY	HALL	PANES	MORGAN	SIMS	CROMPTON	WALTER	BIRD	BOXLEY	LEIGH	NORTON	PALMER, SIMS
22/01/21	SWINDON TOWN	A	3-1	12000	WHATLEY	HALL	PANES	CROMPTON	SIMS	STEELE	WALTER	BIRD	BOXLEY	LEIGH	NORTON	CROMPTON 2, BOXLEY
29/01/21	GILLINGHAM	H	0-1	8000	WHATLEY	HALL	PANES	CROMPTON	SIMS	STEELE	WALTER	BOXLEY	MORGAN	LEIGH	NORTON	SIMS
05/02/21	GILLINGHAM	A	2-0	10000	WHATLEY	BETHUNE	PANES	CROMPTON	SIMS	STEELE	WALTER	BOXLEY	LEIGH	MORGAN	NORTON	BOXLEY 2, CROMPTON, LEIGH pen, PALMER
12/02/21	PORTSMOUTH	H	0-1	14000	WHATLEY	BETHUNE	PANES	CROMPTON	SIMS	STEELE	WALTER	BIRD	BOXLEY	LEIGH	NORTON	LEIGH, TIRRELL og
19/02/21	PORTSMOUTH	A	2-2	13996	WHATLEY	BETHUNE	PANES	CROMPTON	SIMS	STEELE	WALTER	BOXLEY	LEIGH	MORGAN	NORTON	SIMS, WALTER
26/02/21	WATFORD	H	1-2	6000	WHATLEY	BETHUNE	PANES	CROMPTON	SIMS	STEELE	WALTER	BIRD	BOXLEY	LEIGH	NORTON	WALTER 2
05/03/21	WATFORD	A	2-0	11000	WHATLEY	BETHUNE	PANES	CROMPTON	SIMS	STEELE	WALTER	BIRD	LEIGH	MORGAN	NORTON	LEIGH 2
12/03/21	NORTHAMPTON TOWN	A	2-1	5000	WHATLEY	BETHUNE	PANES	CROMPTON	SIMS	STEELE	WALTER	BIRD	LEIGH	MORGAN	NORTON	BIRD, LEIGH
19/03/21	NORTHAMPTON TOWN	H	4-2	6000	WHATLEY	BETHUNE	PANES	CROMPTON	SIMS	STEELE	WALTER	CROMPTON	LEIGH	MORGAN	PALMER	LEIGH pen
25/03/21	QUEENS PARK RANGERS	H	3-0	20000	WHATLEY	BETHUNE	PANES	CROMPTON	SIMS	STEELE	WALTER	CROMPTON	BOXLEY	MORGAN	PALMER	LEIGH 2
26/03/21	SOUTHEND UNITED	A	2-1	14000	WHATLEY	BETHUNE	HALL	CROMPTON	SIMS	STEELE	WALTER	CROMPTON	BOXLEY	LEIGH	PALMER	
28/03/21	QUEENS PARK RANGERS	A	1-2	10000	WHATLEY	BETHUNE	HALL	CROMPTON	SIMS	STEELE	WALTER	BOXLEY	BOXLEY	LEIGH	PALMER	
29/03/21	LUTON TOWN	H	5-0	6000	WHATLEY	BETHUNE	PANES	HOWES	CROMPTON	STEELE	WALTER	CROMPTON	BOXLEY	LEIGH	PALMER	BOXLEY 2, CROMPTON, LEIGH pen, PALMER
02/04/21	SOUTHEND UNITED	H	0-1	7000	WHATLEY	BETHUNE	PANES	HOWES	CROMPTON	STEELE	MORGAN	BOXLEY	LEIGH	MORGAN	PALMER	
09/04/21	MERTHYR TOWN	H	1-1	7000	WHATLEY	BETHUNE	PANES	HOWES	CROMPTON	STEELE	NORTON	MORGAN	BOXLEY	LEIGH	MORGAN	LEIGH
16/04/21	MERTHYR TOWN	A	2-2	6420	WHATLEY	BETHUNE	PANES	HOWES	CROMPTON	CROMPTON	NORTON	MORGAN	LEIGH	MORGAN	PALMER	LEIGH, MORGAN
23/04/21	PLYMOUTH ARGYLE	H	2-0	14000	WHATLEY	BETHUNE	PANES	HOWES	LEIGH	STEELE	WALTER	LEIGH	CROMPTON	MORGAN	PALMER	CROMPTON, PALMER
30/04/21	PLYMOUTH ARGYLE	A	1-2	12500	WHATLEY	BETHUNE	PANES	HOWES	LEIGH	STEELE	WALTER	LEIGH	CROMPTON	PALMER	CROMPTON	CROMPTON
02/05/21	EXETER CITY	H	5-0	7000	WHATLEY	HALL	PANES	HOWES	SIMS	STEELE	CHANCE	WALTER	CROMPTON	CROMPTON	PALMER	LEIGH 4, CROMPTON
07/05/21	EXETER CITY	A	0-1	8000	WHATLEY	HALL	PANES	HOWES	SIMS	STEELE	CHANCE	WALTER	MORGAN	CROMPTON	PALMER	

FA CUP

Date	Opponent		Score	Att	G	2	3	4	5	6	7	8	9	10	11	Goalscorers
18/12/21	WORKSOP TOWN	H	9-0	14000	WHATLEY	BETHUNE HALL		HOWES	SIMS	CROMPTON	WALTER	MORGAN	LEIGH	MORGAN	PALMER	MORGAN 3, LEIGH 2, PALMER, BIRD, KENNY, SIMS
08/01/21	TOTTENHAM HOTSPUR	A	2-6	35000	WHATLEY	BETHUNE HALL		HOWES	SIMS	CROMPTON	WALTER	BIRD	LEIGH	LEIGH	NORTON	LEIGH, MORGAN

GLOUCESTERSHIRE CUP FINAL

Date	Opponent		Score	Att	G	2	3	4	5	6	7	8	9	10	11	Goalscorers
29/09/20	BRISTOL CITY	A	0-1	11994	WHATLEY	BETHUNE	PANES	CROMPTON	HOWES	STEELE	CHANCE	BIRD	VAUGHAN	LEIGH	PALMER	

PLAYERS

PLAYERS	APPS	GLS
BELL H	2	
BETHUNE J	30	
BIRD W	21	8
BOXLEY H	23	5
CHANCE G	14	2
CROMPTON E	41	10
GANE C	1	
HALL J	19	
HOWES D	18	
KENNY D	11	1
LEIGH S	36	21
MORGAN J	20	3
NORTON J	12	1
PALMER W	30	6
PANES S	37	
SIMS S	34	4
STANSFIELD H	3	
STEELE E	29	
VAUGHAN W	6	1
WALTER J	36	4
WHATLEY J	39	
OWN GOALS		3

and went on to score four goals in all. No Rovers player has yet scored more than four times in a League match. Leigh was Rovers' top scorer of the season, contributing 21 goals in 36 League appearances and even affording the luxury of a missed penalty in the home win over Watford. Rovers finished the season in tenth place.

One feature of Rovers' 2-1 victory at Northampton in March was the appearance for the Cobblers of 39-year-old goalkeeper Tommy Thorpe. As he was born in Kilnhurst on 19 May 1881, Thorpe is chronologically the first-born of all footballers who have played in a Football League game involving Bristol Rovers.

The Gloucestershire Cup final was lost to a first-time volley, after an hour, from Bristol City left-back Laurie Banfield who, injured earlier in the game, was playing as a passenger at outside-left. The real excitement, however, came in the FA Cup. Non-League Worksop Town proved no obstacle at Eastville, where six Rovers players got on the scoresheet, although it took 30 minutes for the deadlock to be broken. Jerry Morgan, one of a handful of players to appear for Rovers in both the Southern League and the Football League, contributed a hat-trick. Rovers were rewarded for this win with a game for the second season in succession against Division One Tottenham Hotspur at White Hart Lane. It was the perfect stage for Rovers to prove their worth before a crowd of 35,000. Sadly, though, Dennis Howes had to leave the field injured and, later, so too did Jock Bethune. In the days before substitutes were allowed, such misfortunes were too great to overcome. Although Walter and Norton both scored, nine-man Rovers lost 6-2. Spurs went on to win the FA Cup that season, defeating Wolverhampton Wanderers by a solitary goal in the final. Wolves featured in their side, at outside-left, Tancy Lea, who was to become a Rovers player 12 months later.

In January, Rovers hosted a first-class rugby game at Eastville. In a bizarre twist to later developments at the Memorial Ground, Bristol entertained Cardiff, losing by 11 points to 5. Panes, Sims, Crompton and Walter, meanwhile, played for the Bristol XI that beat an International XI 3-2 before an Ashton Gate crowd of 8,000, in a benefit game for Billy Wedlock.

1921/22

Despite the relative success of Rovers' first League season, manager Ben Hall did not stay at the club. He left in May to take up a scouting post with Southend United, later worked for the Leicestershire FA and died, aged 82, in 1963. The new manager was Andrew Wilson, a highly successful centre-forward with Sheffield Wednesday and Scotland, who was to spend five years at Eastville, with George Endicott at first assuming the mantle of club coach.

Summer signings were largely defensive. George Stockley, Sam Furniss and Tom Winsper all added to Rovers' full-back and half-back lines. With George Chance effectively ruled out of the season through injury, James Liddell, the scorer of a sensational goal just seconds into a reserve game in October, played in the forward line but was to contribute only 4 League goals. Jack Ball, an inside-forward who was to win an England cap in 1927, proved a propitious signing from Sheffield United. Wally

119

Bristol Rovers 1921/22. Joe Walter, Jerry Morgan, Bill Panes, Steve Sims, Joe Kissock, Jesse Whatley, Sid Leigh, Jack Ball, Billy Palmer, Tom Winsper, David Steele

Hammond, a speedy inside-right, played in 6 League games in the first of two seasons with Rovers before pursuing a cricket career of legendary proportions. Hammond's debut at Brighton over Christmas saw him become the first player born in the 20th century to play first-team football for Rovers.

The season began with four straight defeats in the League. Captain Steve Sims, successfully converted to centre-half, scored the club's only goal in this poor start, as well as the goal that earned the first point of the season from a 1-1 draw with Portsmouth before the season's best Eastville crowd of 20,000. During the opening game, in a series of events oddly predictive of Graeme Power's injury in 1997, full-back George Stockley broke his leg. The crack was loud enough to be heard all around Eastville. With Stockley sidelined until Easter, Rovers needed extra cover at left-back. This was found in the form of Jock Kissock, who later played for New Zealand after his emigration there in 1922, and latterly in Jimmy Haydon, a young local defender who gave loyal service to Rovers for a decade.

On the opening day, Plymouth's Frank Richardson, making his Argyle debut, scored the first hat-trick Rovers had conceded in League football. It was quickly followed by others. Bill Keen remains the only Millwall player to have scored three goals in a League game against Rovers. Then there were three hat-tricks conceded in the calendar month of April, one at Reading and two at Swansea. Rovers had been leading 3-1 at Elm Park in November when the game was abandoned after 52 minutes due to fog. Once replayed, the story was quite different. Reading – featuring centre-half Ted Hanney, the winner of a gold medal for football at the 1912 Olympics – stormed to a comfortable 4-0 victory. Sam Jennings scored three times. Then just ten days later came the debacle at the Vetch Field.

Rovers' game at Swansea on Easter Saturday should have posed few problems. Only seven days later Rovers were to draw with the same opposition. Going virtually full-strength into the game, though Jack Thomson had a rare game in goal, there was no hint of the goal glut to follow. However, Steve Sims left the field injured after 15 minutes, Joe Walter soon followed and Bill Panes was merely a passenger. Swansea were 5-0 up by half-time and their 8-1 win constituted Rovers' heaviest League defeat at that time, a score kept down by Thomson's heroics in goal. Two forwards, Bill Brown and Jimmy Collins, helped themselves to hat-tricks, this being the first of three occasions when two opponents have scored three each against Rovers in the same League match. Collins, ended up with four goals, the first opponent to score this many against Rovers in the League.

The fact that Rovers finished the season in 14th place was largely due to two successful mid-season runs. There were six consecutive wins in late autumn and a spell of five victories in seven games into the New Year. These wins included a 2-0 victory at Merthyr in October, where the home side played for 70 minutes with only ten men after an early injury to their full-back Hugh Brown and a 1-0 victory at Norwich thanks to Billy Palmer's last-minute goal after Whatley had saved a Gordon Addy penalty. Another 1-0 away victory, this time at Swindon, was secured only after goalkeeper Kossuth Barnes, named after a 19th-century Hungarian revolutionary leader, had saved a penalty from Town's Albert Weston. Rovers also won by a single goal at Newport, with Jerry Morgan scoring the only goal. Again, Rovers conceded a penalty at Somerton Park. Jimmy Haydon, thinking Barnes was injured, picked the ball up in the penalty area, the referee awarded a penalty and County's left-half Andrew Walker missed it.

Two defeats at the hands of Brighton over Christmas also featured a first League appearance for inside-right Wally Hammond. Hammond's significant contribution to sporting history was to be made in cricket, where he captained England in 20 Test matches and headed the first-class batting averages in seven separate summers. He scored 336 not out against New Zealand in the Auckland test of 1932 and made a first-class double century on 36 occasions.

Rovers' trainer Bert Williams maintained that he was the fastest runner in the 50 years that the veteran coach was attached to the Eastville club. In both Christmas fixtures, Brighton fielded Zechariah March at outside-left who, by the time of his death in September 1994 at the age of 101, was to be the oldest ex-professional footballer.

The 4-2 home victory over Charlton Athletic in September featured players called Steele scoring for both sides. In this game, right-back Jack Hall spent 25 minutes in goal after Jesse Whatley had been injured. However, Whatley recovered to return for the final minutes and saved a penalty from Arthur Whalley in the return fixture seven days later. Rovers lost 1-0 at Watford, with Ernie Wallington scoring, after being reduced to nine men once Sid Leigh and Jimmy Haydon had left the field injured. Perhaps Rovers were

Jack Ball: after leaving Rovers he went on to play for England in 1927

FOOTBALL LEAGUE DIVISION THREE (SOUTH)

Date	Opponent	H/A	Score	ATT	1 (G)	2	3	4	5	6	7	8	9	10	11	Goalscorers
27/08/21	PLYMOUTH ARGYLE	H	1-3	12000	WHATLEY	PANES	STOCKLEY	HOWES	SIMS	STEELE	WALTER	LIDDELL	LEIGH	MORGAN	PALMER	SIMS
31/08/21	PORTSMOUTH	H	0-1	15050	WHATLEY	HALL	PANES	WINSPER	FURNISS	STEELE	WALTER	MORGAN	SIMS	LEIGH	PALMER	
03/09/21	PLYMOUTH ARGYLE	A	0-1	17000	WHATLEY	HALL	PANES	WINSPER	FURNISS	STEELE	WALTER	MORGAN	SIMS	LEIGH	PALMER	
07/09/21	PORTSMOUTH	A	1-1	20000	WHATLEY	HALL	PANES	WINSPER	FURNISS	STEELE	WALTER	MORGAN	BOXLEY	LEIGH	NORTON	BOXLEY
10/09/21	CHARLTON ATHLETIC	H	2-4	12000	WHATLEY	PANES	KISSOCK	WINSPER	FURNISS	BOXLEY	WALTER	MORGAN	BALL	LIDDELL	NORTON	LIDDELL, MORGAN
14/09/21	BRENTFORD	H	0-0	12000	WHATLEY	HALL	PANES	WINSPER	FURNISS	STEELE	WALTER	MORGAN	SIMS	LEIGH	NORTON	
17/09/21	CHARLTON ATHLETIC	A	0-2	11000	WHATLEY	HALL	PANES	WINSPER	HOWES	STEELE	CHANCE	MORGAN	SIMS	LEIGH	NORTON	
24/09/21	NORTHAMPTON TOWN	H	2-0	10000	WHATLEY	PANES	KISSOCK	WINSPER	FURNISS	STEELE	WALTER	HAMMOND	LEIGH	BALL	NORTON	LEIGH, WALTER
01/10/21	NORTHAMPTON TOWN	A	2-2	10000	WHATLEY	PANES	KISSOCK	WINSPER	FURNISS	STEELE	WALTER	LEIGH	BOXLEY	BALL	HARVEY	BALL, WALTER
08/10/21	QUEENS PARK RANGERS	H	1-1	10000	WHATLEY	PANES	KISSOCK	WINSPER	FURNISS	STEELE	NORTON	WALTER	SIMS	BALL	HARVEY	BALL
15/10/21	QUEENS PARK RANGERS	A	2-1	15000	WHATLEY	PANES	KISSOCK	WINSPER	FURNISS	STEELE	WALTER	MORGAN	LEIGH	BALL	HARVEY	LEIGH, PALMER
22/10/21	MERTHYR TOWN	H	2-0	10000	WHATLEY	PANES	KISSOCK	WINSPER	SIMS	STEELE	WALTER	MORGAN	LEIGH	BALL	NORTON	KISSOCK
29/10/21	MERTHYR TOWN	A	2-0	7000	WHATLEY	PANES	KISSOCK	WINSPER	SIMS	STEELE	WALTER	MORGAN	LEIGH	BALL	NORTON	HOWES D
05/11/21	NORWICH CITY	H	1-0	8000	WHATLEY	PANES	KISSOCK	WINSPER	SIMS	STEELE	WALTER	MORGAN	LEIGH	BALL	HARVEY	LIDDELL, MORGAN
12/11/21	NORWICH CITY	A	4-2	16000	WHATLEY	PANES	KISSOCK	WINSPER	SIMS	STEELE	WALTER	MORGAN	LEIGH	BALL	NORTON	MORGAN 2, LEIGH, SIMS
19/11/21	READING	H	2-0	15000	WHATLEY	PANES	KISSOCK	WINSPER	SIMS	STEELE	WALTER	MORGAN	LEIGH	BALL	PALMER	LEIGH pen, PALMER
10/12/21	SOUTHAMPTON	H	0-1	14000	WHATLEY	PANES	KISSOCK	WINSPER	SIMS	STEELE	WALTER	MORGAN	LEIGH	BALL	NORTON	
17/12/21	BRENTFORD	A	2-4	10000	WHATLEY	PANES	KISSOCK	BOXLEY	SIMS	STEELE	WALTER	MORGAN	LEIGH	BALL	NORTON	LEIGH, PALMER
24/12/21	BRIGHTON & H ALBION	H	1-2	20000	WHATLEY	HALL	KISSOCK	BOXLEY	SIMS	STEELE	WALTER	WALTER	LEIGH	BALL	NORTON	BALL, LEIGH
26/12/21	BRENTFORD	H	1-2	12000	BARNES	PANES	KISSOCK	BOXLEY	SIMS	STEELE	WALTER	MORGAN	BALL	LIDDELL	NORTON	BALL
27/12/21	BRIGHTON & H ALBION	A	1-3	12000	BARNES	PANES	KISSOCK	BOXLEY	SIMS	STEELE	WALTER	MORGAN	BALL	LIDDELL	NORTON	SIMS
31/12/21	ABERDARE ATHLETIC	H	0-2	7000	BARNES	PANES	PANES	BOXLEY	SIMS	STEELE	WALTER	MORGAN	BALL	LIDDELL	NORTON	
14/01/22	ABERDARE ATHLETIC	A	5-1	10000	BARNES	PANES	KISSOCK	BOXLEY	SIMS	STEELE	WALTER	MORGAN	LEIGH	LIDDELL	NORTON	LEIGH 3 -1 pen, MORGAN 2
21/01/22	NEWPORT COUNTY	H	3-4	10000	BARNES	PANES	STOCKLEY/BOXLEY	HAYDON	FURNISS	BOXLEY	WALTER	MORGAN	LEIGH	LIDDELL	NORTON	WALTER, STEELE, LIDDELL
28/01/22	NEWPORT COUNTY	A	1-0	6000	BARNES	PANES	KISSOCK	HAYDON	SIMS	STEELE	WALTER	CHANCE	LEIGH	LIDDELL	NORTON	CHANCE
04/02/22	LUTON TOWN	H	2-0	6000	BARNES	PANES	HAYDON	HAYDON	SIMS	STEELE	WALTER	MORGAN	LEIGH	LIDDELL	NORTON	CHANCE 2
11/02/22	LUTON TOWN	A	2-1	8000	BARNES	PANES	HAYDON	HAYDON	SIMS	STEELE	WALTER	WALTER	CHANCE	LIDDELL	NORTON	WALTER
18/02/22	SWINDON TOWN	H	1-1	16000	BARNES	PANES	HAYDON	HAYDON	SIMS	STEELE	WALTER	MORGAN	BALL	LIDDELL	NORTON	MORGAN
25/02/22	SWINDON TOWN	A	1-0	10000	BARNES	PANES	HAYDON	HAYDON	SIMS	STEELE	WALTER	MORGAN	BALL	LIDDELL	NORTON	LEIGH 2
11/03/22	GILLINGHAM	A	2-3	8000	BARNES	PANES	HAYDON	HAYDON	SIMS	STEELE	WALTER	MORGAN	BALL	LIDDELL	NORTON	LEIGH
18/03/22	GILLINGHAM	H	1-4	18000	BARNES	HALL	HAYDON	HAYDON	SIMS	STEELE	WALTER	MORGAN	BALL	LIDDELL	NORTON	LEIGH
25/03/22	MILLWALL	H	0-0	10000	BARNES	PANES	HAYDON	HAYDON	SIMS	STEELE	WALTER	MORGAN	BALL	LIDDELL	NORTON	
01/04/22	MILLWALL	A	2-2	4000	BARNES	PANES	HAYDON	HAYDON	SIMS	STEELE	WALTER	MORGAN	BALL	LIDDELL	WALTER	LEIGH, MORGAN
05/04/22	EXETER CITY	A	0-4	6000	THOMSON	PANES	HAYDON	HAYDON	SIMS	STEELE	WALTER	MORGAN	BALL	LIDDELL	WALTER	
08/04/22	READING	A	1-3	10000	THOMSON	PANES	HAYDON	HAYDON	SIMS	STEELE	WALTER	MORGAN	LEIGH	BALL	NORTON	NORTON
10/04/22	EXETER CITY	H	0-3	4000	THOMSON	PANES	HAYDON	HAYDON	SIMS	STEELE	WALTER	MORGAN	LEIGH	BALL	NORTON	
12/04/22	GILLINGHAM	H	0-0	6000	THOMSON	STOCKLEY	HAYDON	HAYDON	FURNISS	SIMS	STEELE	WALTER	LEIGH	BALL	NORTON	
15/04/22	SOUTHAMPTON	A	0-0	6000	THOMSON	PANES	HAYDON	WINSPER	SIMS	STEELE	WALTER	HAMMOND	LEIGH	BALL	NORTON	
17/04/22	WATFORD	A	0-1	8000	THOMSON	PANES	HAYDON	FURNISS	SIMS	STEELE	WALTER	LEIGH	LIDDELL	BALL	NORTON	
18/04/22	WATFORD	H	1-8	3000	THOMSON	PANES	HAYDON	FURNISS	SIMS	STEELE	WALTER	LEIGH	PALMER	LIDDELL	PALMER	HAYDON
22/04/22	SWANSEA TOWN	A	0-1	3000	THOMSON	PANES	KISSOCK	WINSPER	SIMS	STEELE	WALTER	MORGAN	PALMER	LIDDELL	NORTON	
29/04/22	SWANSEA TOWN	H	0-0	9000	THOMSON	PANES	HAYDON	STOCKLEY	SIMS	STEELE	WALTER	MORGAN	BOXLEY	LIDDELL	NORTON	
06/05/22	SOUTHEND UNITED	A	0-3	5000	THOMSON	PANES	HAYDON	FURNISS	SIMS	STEELE	WALTER	MORGAN	LEIGH	LIDDELL	STOCKLEY	
	SOUTHEND UNITED	H	1-0	3000	THOMSON	KISSOCK	HAYDON	STOCKLEY	SIMS	STEELE	WALTER	MORGAN	BALL	LIDDELL	HAYDON	SIMS pen

FA CUP

Date	Opponent	H/A	Score	ATT	1 (G)	2	3	4	5	6	7	8	9	10	11	Goalscorers
03/12/21	EXETER CITY	H	0-0	4000	THOMSON	PANES	HAYDON	WINSPER	SIMS	STEELE	WALTER	WALTER	LEIGH	BALL	NORTON	
07/12/21	EXETER CITY	A	2-0	5000	WHATLEY	PANES	KISSOCK	WINSPER	SIMS	STEELE	WALTER	MORGAN	LEIGH	BALL	PALMER	BALL, STEELE
17/12/21	SWANSEA TOWN	A	0-2	15000	WHATLEY	PANES	KISSOCK	WINSPER	SIMS	STEELE	WALTER	MORGAN	LEIGH	BALL	PALMER	

GLOUCESTERSHIRE CUP FINAL

Date	Opponent	H/A	Score	ATT	1 (G)	2	3	4	5	6	7	8	9	10	11	Goalscorers
01/05/22	BRISTOL CITY	H	0-0	4991	THOMSON	PANES	HAYDON	FURNISS	SIMS	STEELE	WALTER	MORGAN	BALL	LIDDELL	NORTON	

PLAYERS	APPS	GLS
BALL J	23	4
BARNES K	17	
BOXLEY H	17	
CHANCE G	2	2
FURNISS S	17	
HALL J	8	
HAMMOND W	5	
HARVEY E	5	1
HAYDON J	19	1
HOWES D	2	
KISSOCK J	32	
LEIGH S	32	15
LIDDELL J	28	4
MORGAN J	32	8
NORTON J	25	1
PALMER W	14	4
PANES W	37	
SIMS S	32	4
STEELE D	38	
STOCKLEY G	5	
THOMSON J	6	
WALTER J	39	7
WHATLEY J	19	
WINSPER T	22	

fortunate for, in the concurrent reserve game, the Hertfordshire club lost both Frank Pankhurst and James Short with broken collar-bones.

Bill Panes, generally a highly dependable left-back, and 'a usually inoffensive man' (*Western Daily Press*) became the first Rovers player to be sent off in a League game. Ten minutes after half-time during the 2-0 home victory over Luton Town in February, he over-reacted to provocation by the visitors' Australian-born inside-right Harry Higginbotham, struck him in the face and was sent from the field by referee Mr Tolfree of Southampton. This was the first time that a Rovers player had been sent off at Eastville since 1897.

Rovers were involved in two high-scoring games against Welsh opposition at Eastville in January. First, Rovers were three goals ahead after only 10 minutes against Aberdare Athletic and ended up winning 5-1, with top scorer Sid Leigh scoring a hat-trick. The following week, Rovers led 2-0 inside the first 10 minutes against Newport County. Although Jimmy Liddell scored on his comeback game after a three-month absence, Newport staged a brave recovery to lead 3-2 at the interval and win 4-3, with Charlie Britton scoring twice, to record only their second away victory in the League that season. Earlier in the season, Rovers had scored twice in the first seven minutes *en route* to a 4-2 victory over Norwich City. A collection was taken at this game for the former Rovers and Norwich goalkeeper, Peter Roney, who was seriously ill in Ashington. The Rovers directors sent him 10 guineas.

An unsuccessful season was capped by an FA Cup defeat at Swansea Town and a Gloucestershire Cup defeat at Bristol City. Rovers were also under investigation following crowd trouble at successive reserve-team matches against Portsmouth and Luton Town. In January, Walter's 5th-minute goal gave Rovers an early lead in a friendly with Coventry City which, after Leigh had left the field injured, was lost 6-1, Alick Mercer scoring a hat-trick. However, success lay just around the corner for two players. David Steele and Joe Walter, who had missed just seven games between them all season, joined Huddersfield Town who then, under the management of Herbert Chapman and his assistant, the former Rovers trainer Jack Chaplin, won three consecutive League Championships. Steele also won three Scottish caps and later managed Sheffield United, Huddersfield Town and both Bradford clubs. On 11 January, George Osborne died in Bristol. A founder member of the Rovers Supporters' Club, he had served as treasurer during the dark years of World War One. In early February, Nipper Britton, a key figure in the formative years of Bristolian football, died of pneumonia.

On 24 September 1921, Rovers' future home, newly developed from wartime allotments on the evocatively-named Buffalo Bill's Field, was opened and named the Memorial Ground by G B Britton, Lord Mayor of Bristol, prior to Bristol Rugby Club's 19-3 victory over Cardiff. The land was purchased for £26,000 and equipped as a memory to the 300 rugby players from the city who had been killed in World War One. The president of the rugby club at that time was one Harry Willoughby Beloe, whose name is remembered in two street names in the vicinity. Bristol Rugby Club had been formed in 1888, when Carlton and Redland Park amalgamated. Sanger's Circus, meanwhile, put on two shows on the pitch at Eastville on 3 June 1922.

1922/23

Andrew Wilson's side played out an extraordinarily unsuccessful season in 1922/23. The defence conceded only 36 goals in 42 League games, a club record until the 1973/74 promotion season. In attack, Rovers scored just 35 League goals, a club record for even longer, broken only in the relegation year of 1980/81. As it was, mid-table Rovers won and lost matches in equal measure. The side also played out a club seasonal record of ten goalless draws, including three in succession around New Year.

Whereas the forwards scored three goals in only four League matches and it took until April for an individual player to score twice in a game, the defence performed admirably all season. Goalkeeper Jesse Whatley and half-backs Sam Furniss and Walter Currie were ever-presents, while left-back Jimmy Haydon missed only one game. Whatley kept 21 clean sheets. Rovers lost 4-1 at Newport County and conceded three goals in a game on only four other occasions. It was a consistent defensive display not to be bettered by a Rovers side for half a century, but also one that highlighted a general trend towards lower goalscoring, which was to lead to a change in the offside rule in 1925.

During the summer of 1922 changes had been made to the pitch at Eastville. 400lbs of grass seed were sown and the pitch itself, so susceptible as it was to flooding from the river Frome, was raised by 18 inches. The price of the matchday programme was to remain 2d. The make-up of the Rovers side on the field was also largely unchanged, though Rovers bought a number of fringe players. Meanwhile, Billy Palmer had moved to Gillingham, from where he joined Doncaster Rovers, Tom Winsper had moved to Shrewsbury Town, Denis Howes had joined Bath City and other players had moved locally. Two players were to gain International recognition; Jack Ball was to play for England in 1927 when on Bury's books, and Joe Kissock, who moved first to Scotland and then the United States, won six caps for New Zealand in 1923.

Wilson returned to Sheffield Wednesday for a number of his summer signings. In defence, the fearless and tough-tackling Harold Armitage and north-easterner Harold O'Neill were two such cases, while Ernie Sambidge was a naval architect who hailed from the Newcastle area. At wing-half, Walter Currie came from Scotland while Harry Rose had been on the books of Reading. In the forward line, Fred Lunn – whose goals as the club's top scorer were, as was the case with David Mehew in 1989/90, all scored in separate games – was a former Wednesday player, while Arthur Wainwright, a fellow Yorkshireman, had played for the now-defunct Leeds City. Jack Taylor and Tosh Parker were from non-League football, while Ken Boyes was the brother of a famous Hampshire cricketer. Tancy Lea, a new outside-left, was a veteran forward who had played for Wolverhampton Wanderers in the 1921 FA Cup final.

The first of many local League derbies was played at Ashton Gate in September. Whatley saved a 65th-minute penalty from Laurie Banfield, who had apparently not missed a spot-kick in the previous four seasons and Tosh Parker's 30th-minute goal gave Rovers victory. The attendance at this game, some 30,000, contrasts starkly with the 2,000 who watched Rovers' final home game of the season, a 1-1 draw with Brentford. To typify the season, Rovers were beaten by Bristol City at Eastville only seven days

Bristol Rovers 1922/23. Back row: Taylor, Liddell, Boxley, Leigh, Woodward, Whatley, O'Neill, Boyes, Armitage, Parker. Middle row: Furniss, Currie, Sambidge, Smith, Lunn, Haydon, Hammond. Front row: Chance, Morgan, Rose, Wainwright, Lea

after the first derby match, despite a goal from back-in-favour outside-right George Chance. The crowd at this game, again 30,000, was a new ground record, easily surpassing the estimated 20,000 at the match against Crystal Palace two years earlier. Incredible though it may sound, as many as 7,000 spectators saw Rovers reserves lose 1-0 at Ashton Gate in a Southern League game in April 1923.

Parker – joint second top scorer with Jerry Morgan on six League goals behind Lunn's 10 – scored some vital goals. Four of his six, plus one at Reading in the FA Cup, earned 1-0 victories. Indeed, there was an identical story for Rovers' Cup and League visits to Elm Park. When Reading returned for a League fixture at Eastville, Rovers had a wonderful opportunity to secure a League double over the Berkshire side. Wally Hammond's second-minute goal set Rovers on the way, but inside-left Sam Jennings equalised for the visitors before half-time. Rovers' visit to Griffin Park in December, Lunn scoring the only goal of the game, was notable for the fact that both sides fielded an England International cricketer. Patsy Hendren was in the Brentford side while Hammond was to retire at the end of the season, after 19 League games and two goals to concentrate on his blossoming career in cricket. He was to play 85 times for England – 20 as captain – and set an unequalled record by heading the first-class batting averages for eight consecutive seasons.

Quite clearly, goalscoring was a major failing of the club. In all four divisions, only Southport, with 32 League goals, scored fewer. Rovers failed to score in six consecutive games in the autumn and in a run of five games in the New Year. In an attempt to counter this problem, Rovers signed a new centre-forward in November. Tom Howarth, 32, a £500 buy from Leeds United, had also represented Bristol City either side of World War One. He had scored a 71st-minute goal in the FA Cup semi-final of 1920 which the Robins lost 2-1 to Huddersfield Town but had later served a 12-month ban imposed by the Football Association after re-signing for Bristol City while still on

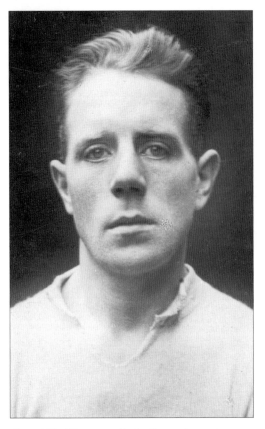

Rovers' Fred Lunn was the leading goalscorer in 1922/23 with 10 League goals from Rovers' total of just 35 for the entire season

military service. However, this goal-scoring scheme backfired, for the veteran Howarth scored just 4 times in 21 League appearances and joined Western League Lovells Athletic as player-manager at the end of the season.

In February, Luton Town held out for a 1-1 draw at Eastville despite losing goalkeeper Tom Gibbon with an injury after only 30 minutes. Outside-right Sid Hoar went in goal and conceded nothing, thanks in particular to Rovers' centre-half Jock Rutherford who shot wide from a penalty. In April, a refereeing mistake meant that the game at Aberdare finished five minutes early. However, persuaded by a linesman, referee E A Hore resumed the match after a short break. Another error led to referee H C Curtis of London not arriving for the match at Swansea on the final day of the season. Linesman U Jones of Ton Pentre took over with D Sambrooke of Swansea running the line and Rovers won 1-0 when Tosh Parker scored direct from a corner.

Just when goals appeared at a premium, inside-left Jerry Morgan doubled his tally for the season with an opportunist hat-trick at home to Norwich City. Morgan had a new left-wing partner in Durham-born Jack Pattison and took full advantage of a hesitant Canaries defence to score three goals, one from the penalty spot. Joe Hannah, who had also scored at Eastville in 1921/22, scored once in each half for the visitors, his only two goals of the season.

An FA Cup run ended abruptly when Third Division (North) Stalybridge Celtic won in a replay at Eastville. Howarth scored for Rovers, but first the former Stockport County forward Joe O' Kane and later Edward Wordley were Celtic's goalscorers. The Gloucestershire Cup final was abandoned in bad light with Bristol City leading 3-1 only 10 minutes from time. When the match was replayed, Rovers lost 1-0 to an extra-time goal from John Smith, who had scored City's opening goal in the original game. Smith was to reappear in the Rovers story in his later career with Plymouth Argyle and Aberdare Athletic, missing a penalty against Rovers in December 1925. A Rovers side also drew 2-2 with the North Somerset XI in November in a match that raised £35 for Paulton Hospital. The *Western Daily Press* of 11 July 1923 reports a proposed 350-yard New Road linking Eastville and Stapleton which would cost an estimated £11,260. Work was created for 80 unemployed people for 26 weeks and the road was named in honour of the great local benefactor George Müller.

SEASON 1922/23

FOOTBALL LEAGUE DIVISION THREE (SOUTH)

Date	Opponent	A	G	ATT	1	2	3	4	5	6	7	8	9	10	11	GOALSCORERS
26/08/22	PORTSMOUTH	A	0-0	18455	WHATLEY	ARMITAGE	HAYDON	BOXLEY	FURNISS	CURRIE	WAINWRIGHT	PARKER	LUNN	MORGAN	LEA	
28/08/22	NEWPORT COUNTY	H	3-1	12000	WHATLEY	ARMITAGE	HAYDON	BOXLEY	FURNISS	CURRIE	WAINWRIGHT	PARKER	LUNN	MORGAN	LEA	PARKER, LUNN, MORGAN
02/09/22	PORTSMOUTH	H	0-1	18000	WHATLEY	ARMITAGE	HAYDON	BOXLEY	FURNISS	CURRIE	WAINWRIGHT	PARKER	LUNN	MORGAN	LEA	
07/09/22	NEWPORT COUNTY	A	1-4	3000	WHATLEY	ARMITAGE	SAMBIDGE	FURNISS	O'NEILL	CURRIE	WAINWRIGHT	PARKER	LUNN	MORGAN	LEA	LUNN
09/09/22	READING	A	1-0	9000	WHATLEY	ARMITAGE	HAYDON	FURNISS	O'NEILL	CURRIE	WAINWRIGHT	PARKER	LUNN	LIDDELL	LEA	PARKER
13/09/22	WATFORD	H	1-2	7000	WHATLEY	ARMITAGE	HAYDON	FURNISS	O'NEILL	CURRIE	WAINWRIGHT	PARKER	LUNN	LIDDELL	LEA	LUNN
16/09/22	READING	H	1-1	12000	WHATLEY	ARMITAGE	HAYDON	FURNISS	O'NEILL	CURRIE	LEA	HAMMOND	PARKER	MORGAN	BOYES	HAMMOND
23/09/22	BRISTOL CITY	H	1-2	30000	WHATLEY	ARMITAGE	HAYDON	BOXLEY	FURNISS	CURRIE	CHANCE	PARKER	LUNN	MORGAN	LEA	PARKER
30/09/22	BRISTOL CITY	A	1-2	30000	WHATLEY	ARMITAGE	HAYDON	BOXLEY	FURNISS	CURRIE	CHANCE	PARKER	LUNN	MORGAN	LEA	CHANCE
07/10/22	SOUTHEND UNITED	H	2-0	9000	WHATLEY	ARMITAGE	HAYDON	FURNISS	RUTHERFORD	CURRIE	CHANCE	PARKER	LUNN	MORGAN	LEA	LUNN, FURNISS
14/10/22	SOUTHEND UNITED	A	0-1	9000	WHATLEY	ARMITAGE	HAYDON	FURNISS	RUTHERFORD	CURRIE	CHANCE	PARKER	LUNN	MORGAN	LEA	
21/10/22	MILLWALL	H	0-0	15000	WHATLEY	ARMITAGE	HAYDON	FURNISS	RUTHERFORD	CURRIE	CHANCE	PARKER	LUNN	MORGAN	LEA	
28/10/22	MILLWALL	A	0-0	10000	WHATLEY	ARMITAGE	HAYDON	FURNISS	RUTHERFORD	CURRIE	CHANCE	PARKER	LUNN	MORGAN	LEA	
04/11/22	PLYMOUTH ARGYLE	A	0-3	12000	WHATLEY	ARMITAGE	HAYDON	FURNISS	RUTHERFORD	CURRIE	CHANCE	HAMMOND	LUNN	PARKER	LEA	
11/11/22	PLYMOUTH ARGYLE	H	0-1	20000	WHATLEY	ARMITAGE	HAYDON	FURNISS	RUTHERFORD	CURRIE	CHANCE	HAMMOND	HOWARTH	PARKER	LEA	
18/11/22	CHARLTON ATHLETIC	A	1-1	6000	WHATLEY	ARMITAGE	HAYDON	FURNISS	RUTHERFORD	CURRIE	WAINWRIGHT	HAMMOND	HOWARTH	BOXLEY	LEA	HOWARTH
25/11/22	CHARLTON ATHLETIC	H	1-0	8000	WHATLEY	ARMITAGE	HAYDON	FURNISS	RUTHERFORD	CURRIE	WAINWRIGHT	HAMMOND	HOWARTH	BOXLEY	LEA	LUNN
09/12/22	WATFORD	A	1-0	7000	WHATLEY	O'NEILL	HAYDON	FURNISS	RUTHERFORD	CURRIE	CHANCE	PARKER	HOWARTH	LUNN	LEA	HOWARTH
23/12/22	BRENTFORD	H	1-0	10000	WHATLEY	ARMITAGE	HAYDON	FURNISS	RUTHERFORD	CURRIE	WAINWRIGHT	MORGAN	LUNN	HAMMOND	LEA	PARKER
25/12/22	EXETER CITY	H	1-0	10000	WHATLEY	ARMITAGE	HAYDON	FURNISS	RUTHERFORD	CURRIE	WAINWRIGHT	MORGAN	LUNN	HAMMOND	LEA	LUNN
26/12/22	EXETER CITY	A	3-3	11000	WHATLEY	ARMITAGE	HAYDON	FURNISS	RUTHERFORD	CURRIE	PATTISON	MORGAN	LUNN	PARKER	LEA	LUNN, HAMMOND, RUTHERFORD
06/01/23	NORWICH CITY	A	0-0	8000	WHATLEY	ARMITAGE	HAYDON	FURNISS	RUTHERFORD	CURRIE	WAINWRIGHT	MORGAN	LUNN	HAMMOND	LEA	
20/01/23	NORTHAMPTON TOWN	H	0-0	8000	WHATLEY	ARMITAGE	HAYDON	FURNISS	RUTHERFORD	CURRIE	WAINWRIGHT	MORGAN	LUNN	PARKER	LEA	
27/01/23	NORTHAMPTON TOWN	A	0-1	10000	WHATLEY	ARMITAGE	HAYDON	FURNISS	ROSE	CURRIE	CHANCE	HAMMOND	PARKER	MORGAN	LEA	
03/02/23	LUTON TOWN	A	0-1	8000	WHATLEY	ARMITAGE	HAYDON	FURNISS	RUTHERFORD	CURRIE	HAMMOND	MORGAN	HOWARTH	LUNN	LEA	
10/02/23	LUTON TOWN	H	1-3	9000	WHATLEY	ARMITAGE	HAYDON	FURNISS	RUTHERFORD	CURRIE	CHANCE	MORGAN	HOWARTH	LUNN	LEA	LEA
17/02/23	QPR	A	1-0	9000	WHATLEY	ARMITAGE	HAYDON	FURNISS	RUTHERFORD	CURRIE	CHANCE	MORGAN	HOWARTH	LUNN	LEA	MORGAN
03/03/23	GILLINGHAM	A	1-0	6000	WHATLEY	ARMITAGE	HAYDON	FURNISS	RUTHERFORD	CURRIE	CHANCE	MORGAN	HOWARTH	LUNN	LEA	CHANCE
10/03/23	GILLINGHAM	H	1-0	9000	WHATLEY	ARMITAGE	HAYDON	FURNISS	RUTHERFORD	CURRIE	CHANCE	MORGAN	HOWARTH	LUNN	LEA	LUNN
17/03/23	BRIGHTON & H ALBION	H	0-0	8000	WHATLEY	ARMITAGE	HAYDON	FURNISS	RUTHERFORD	CURRIE	CHANCE	MORGAN	HOWARTH	LUNN	LEA	
24/03/23	BRIGHTON & H ALBION	A	1-2	7500	WHATLEY	ARMITAGE	HAYDON	FURNISS	RUTHERFORD	CURRIE	CHANCE	MORGAN	HOWARTH	LUNN	LEA	LUNN
26/03/23	QUEENS PARK RANGERS	H	1-3	18000	WHATLEY	O'NEILL	HAYDON	FURNISS	WEBB	CURRIE	CHANCE	MORGAN	LUNN	BOYES	LEA	FURNISS
31/03/23	SWINDON TOWN	H	2-0	10000	WHATLEY	O'NEILL	HAYDON	FURNISS	WEBB	CURRIE	CHANCE	MORGAN	HOWARTH	LUNN	LEA	LUNN, HOWARTH
02/04/23	MERTHYR TOWN	H	3-0	8000	WHATLEY	O'NEILL	HAYDON	FURNISS	RUTHERFORD	CURRIE	CHANCE	MORGAN	HOWARTH	LUNN	LEA	HOWARTH 2, CHANCE
03/04/23	MERTHYR TOWN	A	1-1	5000	WHATLEY	O'NEILL	HAYDON	FURNISS	RUTHERFORD	CURRIE	CHANCE	MORGAN	HOWARTH	LUNN	LEA	MORGAN
07/04/23	SWINDON TOWN	A	1-0	6000	WHATLEY	O'NEILL	HAYDON	FURNISS	RUTHERFORD	CURRIE	CHANCE	MORGAN	HOWARTH	LUNN	LEA	MORGAN
14/04/23	ABERDARE ATHLETIC	H	1-0	8000	WHATLEY	O'NEILL	HAYDON	FURNISS	RUTHERFORD	CURRIE	CHANCE	PARKER	HOWARTH	MORGAN	LEA	LEA
21/04/23	ABERDARE ATHLETIC	A	0-0	5000	WHATLEY	O'NEILL	HAYDON	FURNISS	RUTHERFORD	CURRIE	CHANCE	PARKER	HOWARTH	MORGAN	PATTISON	
23/04/23	NORWICH CITY	H	3-2	4000	WHATLEY	O'NEILL	HAYDON	FURNISS	RUTHERFORD	CURRIE	CHANCE	PARKER	HOWARTH	MORGAN	PATTISON	MORGAN 3-1 pen
28/04/23	SWANSEA TOWN	H	0-0	10000	WHATLEY	O'NEILL	HAYDON	FURNISS	RUTHERFORD	CURRIE	CHANCE	PARKER	HOWARTH	MORGAN	LEA	
30/04/23	BRENTFORD	A	1-1	2000	WHATLEY	O'NEILL	HAYDON	FURNISS	RUTHERFORD	CURRIE	WAINWRIGHT	PARKER	HOWARTH	MORGAN	LEA	PARKER
05/05/23	SWANSEA TOWN	A	1-0	10200	WHATLEY	O'NEILL	HAYDON	FURNISS	RUTHERFORD	CURRIE	WAINWRIGHT	PARKER	HOWARTH	LIDDELL	LEA	PARKER

FA CUP

Date	Opponent	A	G	ATT	1	2	3	4	5	6	7	8	9	10	11	GOALSCORERS
02/12/22	READING	A	1-0	10713	WHATLEY	ARMITAGE	HAYDON	FURNISS	RUTHERFORD	CURRIE	WAINWRIGHT	PARKER	HOWARTH	MORGAN	LEA	PARKER
16/12/22	STALYBRIDGE CELTIC	H	0-0	8800	WHATLEY	ARMITAGE	HAYDON	FURNISS	RUTHERFORD	CURRIE	WAINWRIGHT	PARKER	HOWARTH	MORGAN	LEA	
20/12/22	STALYBRIDGE CELTIC	A	1-2	6600	WHATLEY	ARMITAGE	HAYDON	FURNISS	RUTHERFORD	CURRIE	WAINWRIGHT	PARKER	HOWARTH	MORGAN	LEA	HOWARTH

GLOUCESTERSHIRE CUP FINAL

Date	Opponent	A	G	ATT	1	2	3	4	5	6	7	8	9	10	11	GOALSCORERS
07/05/23	BRISTOL CITY	A	0-1	4991	WHATLEY	PATTISON	HAYDON	SMITH	FURNISS	CURRIE	CHANCE	WAINWRIGHT	PARKER	HOWARTH	MORGAN LEA	

PLAYERS	APPS	GLS
ARMITAGE H	30	
BOXLEY H	7	
BOYES K	2	
CHANCE G	25	
CURRIE W	42	3
FURNISS S	42	2
HAMMOND W	10	2
HAYDON J	41	
HOWARTH T	21	4
LEA T	39	1
LIDDELL J	3	
LUNN F	31	10
MORGAN J	34	6
O'NEILL H	17	
PARKER J	25	6
PATTISON J	4	
ROSE H	1	
RUTHERFORD J	29	1
SAMBIDGE E	1	
WAINWRIGHT A	14	
WEBB G	2	
WHATLEY J	42	

In September 1922 Rovers gave a trial in a reserve team game against Reading to an Egyptian student of engineering at Bristol University, Mahmoud Mokhtar. His stated date of birth was 23 December 1907 in Cairo, though this appears unlikely as he represented his country in the 1920 Antwerp Olympics. 'Titch' Mokhtar also spent a fruitless trial with Tranmere Rovers, but enjoyed huge success in Egypt and played in two further Olympics and the 1934 World Cup in Italy. Six times Egyptian player of the year, he spent 17 seasons with National SC Cairo, seven times being the league's top scorer, and winning six league Championship medals and seven Egyptian Cup winner's medals. Despite his lack of success at Eastville, Mokhtar's legendary billing in his native country was such that, following his death in Cairo on 21 December 1965, the national stadium was renamed the 'Titch' Mahmoud Mokhtar Stadium.

1923/24

In scoring more than 50 League goals, Andrew Wilson's Rovers side finished the season in the club's highest position to date, ninth in Division Three (South). Only 46 goals were conceded in the League, where goalkeeper Jesse Whatley, outstanding as ever, played in every match for a second consecutive season. It was to be 1950/51 before so few goals were again conceded in a season. Besides Whatley, Rovers' other ever-present was Wilkie Phillips, a robust centre-forward signed in the close season after several years in non-League football in the Midlands. He was the club's top scorer with 23 goals, a figure that could have been higher had he not missed a penalty in a goalless draw at Swindon and another at Exeter, where two penalties were awarded in the opening 12 minutes.

Phillips was ably supported in the forward line by Bill Woodhall, Ernie Whatmore and, once Tancy Lea had lost his place, Jimmy Lofthouse. A former Rotherham County outside-left, Lofthouse added stability to Rovers' left side. He was to be an ever-present in the side in 1924/25. Lofthouse scored twice in a week in December, continued Rovers' ill luck from spot-kicks when his penalty struck the crossbar during a 3-1 victory over Norwich City at Eastville in March – Phillips scored from a second penalty – and found his season prematurely ended by a broken elbow. Six players appeared at inside-left, Alec Smeaton and Jerry Morgan performing well. But Whatmore, again an influential figure the following season, was Lofthouse's most reliable partner. Woodhall, despite injury, was the second highest scorer with 11 League goals. The side was coached by Ted Jones, appointed on 21 July 1923, who was also to work for Bristol City and, from July 1938, Torquay United.

Rovers relied on a number of familiar names. Whatley was ably supported by Haydon and Armitage at full-back, with Furniss at right-half, Ernie Sambidge. Harry Rose had also appeared in the side before, while George Chance was back in favour at outside-right. One new face at half-back was the former Leeds United player Jimmy Walton, who missed just 2 League matches all season and scored in the game at Exeter. As the season progressed, he was joined at half-back by several former non-League players,

Bristol Rovers 1923/24. Back row: E Jones (Trainer), Taylor, Price, Sambidge, Wainwright, Pattison. Second row: Rose, Smith, Whatley, Walton, Murphy, Wragge, Haydon, B Williams (Asst. Trainer). Third row: Furniss, Smeaton, Whatmore, Parker, Chance, Lea. Front row: Cuff, Armitage, Woodhall, Phillips

notably Syd Smith, Frank Wragge and the inappropriately named Bob Scorer, who remained goalless in his 37 League matches in two seasons at Eastville.

An otherwise consistent side was disrupted by injury and Rovers were unable to mount a serious Championship challenge. Wragge missed several weeks with a broken arm, Woodhall broke his collar-bone in the home draw with Plymouth Argyle in January and was out for 11 games, while Lofthouse's broken elbow sustained against Luton Town on Easter Monday effectively ruled him out for the rest of the season. On the other hand, Swansea Town played most of the second-half of their game at Eastville in April with only nine men. Robert Booth and Jimmy Collins, the latter having scored four goals against Rovers at the Vetch Field in 1922, both left the field injured and Rovers won 2-0. Harry O' Neill, a former Rovers full-back, broke his arm after only 15 minutes on his return to Eastville, but his Swindon Town side beat Rovers through a second-half goal from centre-forward Arthur Ruddlesdin.

Twice during the season Rovers faced a side with a makeshift goalkeeper following injury crises. Bournemouth's regular right-back Edgar Saxton played in goal during Rovers' 1-0 victory at Dean Court in December and was beaten only by Lofthouse's oblique shot after 12 minutes. Griff James, the reserve left-half at Aberdare Athletic, was an emergency goalkeeper against Rovers in March. Rovers contrived to leave the stand-in largely untroubled and Athletic were comfortable winners 2-0. At Norwich in March, Rovers' opponents fielded the veteran former England International Albert Sturgess

Former Sheffield Wednesday full-back Harold Armitage
made 122 League appearances in four seasons with Rovers

who, at 41 years and five months, was to be the oldest player to appear in any inter-war League fixture involving Bristol Rovers and who remains the fifth oldest opponent the club has faced in the Football League.

Despite an opening day defeat at Gillingham, Rovers were able to post their intentions with a run of four straight victories. New signing Phillips scored in all these matches, grabbing six of the side's eight goals. Further runs of results hinted at the club's potential, particularly three consecutive wins early in March when Phillips again scored in every game. However, this was instantly followed by three defeats in succession, in each case in matches Rovers could have won with ease. Such a series of results necessarily undermines any Championship challenge, yet so too does a proliferation of drawn matches. Rovers' early-1920s instinct for drawing games – another 13 in the League this season and one in each cup competition – was again the side's undoing. One particular run of five draws in six matches in the New Year starved the club of the points required for success.

A convincing 4–1 win over Millwall just before Christmas was the first time in almost two years that Rovers had scored four goals in a League game. It was enough to persuade Rovers' highest crowd of the season, 16,000, to visit Eastville four days later, only for the match against Reading to finish goalless. Rovers also scored four goals in the match with Watford a week before Easter. It was, of course, no surprise that Phillips and Woodhall scored three of the four goals between them on both occasions. Phillips scored three times – though never in one game – against each of Swansea Town, Queen's Park Rangers and Charlton Athletic, scoring in the first minute of the home game with Athletic, while Woodhall and Whatmore scored for Rovers in both victories over Brentford.

The home game against Bournemouth in January brought great concern to Eastville. At half-time, with Rovers trailing 3–2 in an exciting match, a drunken spectator assaulted referee R R Crump and knocked him to the ground. Although the assailant was promptly ejected from the ground, Rovers were faced with further disciplinary problems following crowd trouble at reserve games against Portsmouth and Luton Town early in 1922. On the pitch, despite a goal in each half from Woodhall, Rovers lost

SEASON 1923/24

FOOTBALL LEAGUE DIVISION THREE (SOUTH)

Date	Opponent	A/H	Score	ATT	G	2	3	4	5	6	7	8	9	10	11	GOALSCORERS
25/08/23	GILLINGHAM	A	0-1	8000	WHATLEY	ARMITAGE	HAYDON	FURNISS	ROSE	WALTON	CHANCE	PHILLIPS	WOODHALL	PARKER	LEA	
27/08/23	QPR	H	2-1	8000	WHATLEY	ARMITAGE	HAYDON	FURNISS	ROSE	WALTON	CHANCE	PHILLIPS	WOODHALL	WHATMORE	LEA	PHILLIPS 2
01/09/23	GILLINGHAM	H	2-0	12000	WHATLEY	ARMITAGE	HAYDON	FURNISS	ROSE	WALTON	CHANCE	PHILLIPS	WOODHALL	WHATMORE	LEA	PHILLIPS, FOX og
05/09/23	QPR	A	2-1	8000	WHATLEY	PRICE	HAYDON	FURNISS	ROSE	WALTON	CHANCE	PHILLIPS	WOODHALL	WHATMORE	LEA	PHILLIPS, WOODHALL
08/09/23	BRIGHTON & H ALBION	H	2-0	14000	WHATLEY	ARMITAGE	HAYDON	FURNISS	ROSE	WALTON	CHANCE	PHILLIPS	WOODHALL	WHATMORE	LEA	PHILLIPS 2
10/09/23	NORTHAMPTON TOWN	H	0-0	10000	WHATLEY	ARMITAGE	HAYDON	FURNISS	ROSE	WALTON	CHANCE	PHILLIPS	WOODHALL	WHATMORE	LEA	
15/09/23	BRIGHTON & H ALBION	A	1-2	6500	WHATLEY	ARMITAGE	HAYDON	FURNISS	ROSE	WALTON	CHANCE	PHILLIPS	WOODHALL	WHATMORE	LEA	CHANCE
22/09/23	SOUTHEND UNITED	H	3-1	9000	WHATLEY	ARMITAGE	HAYDON	FURNISS	ROSE	WALTON	CHANCE	PHILLIPS	WOODHALL	PARKER	LEA	PHILLIPS 2, CHANCE
29/09/23	SOUTHEND UNITED	A	0-1	9000	WHATLEY	ARMITAGE	HAYDON	CUFF	FURNISS	WALTON	CHANCE	PHILLIPS	WOODHALL	WHATMORE	LEA	
06/10/23	BRENTFORD	H	2-0	10000	WHATLEY	ARMITAGE	HAYDON	CUFF	ROSE	WALTON	CHANCE	PHILLIPS	WOODHALL	WHATMORE	LEA	WHATMORE, WOODHALL
13/10/23	BRENTFORD	A	2-2	9000	WHATLEY	ARMITAGE	HAYDON	FURNISS	ROSE	WALTON	CHANCE	PHILLIPS	WOODHALL	WHATMORE	LEA	WHATMORE, WOODHALL
20/10/23	PORTSMOUTH	A	1-1	11500	WHATLEY	ARMITAGE	HAYDON	FURNISS	ROSE	WALTON	CHANCE	PHILLIPS	WOODHALL	WHATMORE	PATTISON	PATTISON
27/10/23	PORTSMOUTH	H	0-1	15000	WHATLEY	ARMITAGE	HAYDON	FURNISS	ROSE	WALTON	CHANCE	PHILLIPS	WOODHALL	WHATMORE	PATTISON	
03/11/23	EXETER CITY	H	0-0	9000	WHATLEY	ARMITAGE	HAYDON	FURNISS	ROSE	WALTON	CHANCE	PHILLIPS	WOODHALL	WHATMORE	PATTISON	
10/11/23	EXETER CITY	A	1-3	5000	WHATLEY	ARMITAGE	HAYDON	FURNISS	WRAGGE	WALTON	CHANCE	PHILLIPS	WOODHALL	WHATMORE	PATTISON	WALTON
24/11/23	ABERDARE ATHLETIC	H	2-0	7000	WHATLEY	ARMITAGE	HAYDON	FURNISS	WRAGGE	WALTON	CHANCE	PHILLIPS	WOODHALL	WHATMORE	PATTISON	PHILLIPS, WOODHALL
08/12/23	NORTHAMPTON TOWN	A	1-1	8000	WHATLEY	ARMITAGE	HAYDON	WAINWRIGHT	SCORER	SMITH	CHANCE	PHILLIPS	WOODHALL	WHATMORE	LOFTHOUSE	WOODHALL
15/12/23	MILLWALL	H	0-1	12000	WHATLEY	ARMITAGE	SAMBIDGE	FURNISS	SCORER	SMITH	CHANCE	PHILLIPS	WOODHALL	WHATMORE	LOFTHOUSE	
22/12/23	MILLWALL	A	4-1	7000	WHATLEY	ARMITAGE	SAMBIDGE	FURNISS	SCORER	SMITH	CHANCE	PHILLIPS	WOODHALL	WALTON	LOFTHOUSE	WOODHALL 2, LOFTHOUSE, PHILLIPS
25/12/23	READING	A	2-3	8000	WHATLEY	ARMITAGE	SAMBIDGE	FURNISS	SCORER	SMITH	CHANCE	PHILLIPS	WOODHALL	WALTON	LOFTHOUSE	CHANCE, PHILLIPS
26/12/23	READING	H	1-0	16000	WHATLEY	ARMITAGE	SAMBIDGE	FURNISS	SCORER	SMITH	CHANCE	PHILLIPS	WOODHALL	WALTON	LOFTHOUSE	LOFTHOUSE
29/12/23	BOURNEMOUTH	A	1-0	4000	WHATLEY	ARMITAGE	HAYDON	FURNISS	SCORER	SMITH	CHANCE	PHILLIPS	WOODHALL	WALTON	LOFTHOUSE	LOFTHOUSE
05/01/24	BOURNEMOUTH	H	3-4	8000	WHATLEY	ARMITAGE	HAYDON	FURNISS	SCORER	SMITH	CHANCE	PHILLIPS	WOODHALL	WHATMORE	LOFTHOUSE	WOODHALL 2, PHILLIPS
19/01/24	PLYMOUTH ARGYLE	A	2-2	10000	WHATLEY	ARMITAGE	HAYDON	FURNISS	SCORER	WALTON	CHANCE	PHILLIPS	WOODHALL	WHATMORE	LOFTHOUSE	PHILLIPS 2
26/01/24	PLYMOUTH ARGYLE	H	1-1	12000	WHATLEY	ARMITAGE	HAYDON	FURNISS	SCORER	WALTON	CHANCE	PHILLIPS	HAMMOND	WHATMORE	LOFTHOUSE	WHATMORE
02/02/24	NEWPORT COUNTY	A	0-1	7000	WHATLEY	ARMITAGE	HAYDON	FURNISS	WRAGGE	WALTON	CHANCE	PHILLIPS	HAMMOND	WHATMORE	LOFTHOUSE	
09/02/24	NEWPORT COUNTY	H	0-0	8000	WHATLEY	ARMITAGE	SAMBIDGE	SCORER	WRAGGE	WALTON	CHANCE	PHILLIPS	HAMMOND	WAINWRIGHT	LOFTHOUSE	
16/02/24	MERTHYR TOWN	A	1-1	5000	WHATLEY	ARMITAGE	SAMBIDGE	FURNISS	SCORER	WALTON	CHANCE	PHILLIPS	TAYLOR	SMEATON	LOFTHOUSE	SMEATON
23/02/24	MERTHYR TOWN	H	4-2	5000	WHATLEY	ARMITAGE	SAMBIDGE	FURNISS	SCORER	WALTON	HAMMOND	PHILLIPS	TAYLOR	SMEATON	LOFTHOUSE	PHILLIPS, TAYLOR, STEELE og
01/03/24	CHARLTON ATHLETIC	A	3-1	4000	WHATLEY	ARMITAGE	HAYDON	FURNISS	SCORER	WALTON	CHANCE	PHILLIPS	TAYLOR	MORGAN	LOFTHOUSE	PHILLIPS 2
08/03/24	CHARLTON ATHLETIC	H	3-0	7000	WHATLEY	ARMITAGE	HAYDON	FURNISS	SCORER	WALTON	PATTISON	PHILLIPS	TAYLOR	MORGAN	LOFTHOUSE	MORGAN 2, PHILLIPS pen
15/03/24	NORWICH CITY	H	3-1	7000	WHATLEY	ARMITAGE	HAYDON	FURNISS	SCORER	WALTON	CHANCE	PHILLIPS	WHATMORE	MORGAN	LOFTHOUSE	PHILLIPS 2
22/03/24	NORWICH CITY	A	1-3	6000	WHATLEY	ARMITAGE	HAYDON	FURNISS	SCORER	WALTON	CHANCE	PHILLIPS	WHATMORE	MORGAN	LOFTHOUSE	CHANCE
29/03/24	SWINDON TOWN	H	0-1	10000	WHATLEY	ARMITAGE	HAYDON	FURNISS	SCORER	WALTON	CHANCE	PHILLIPS	WHATMORE	SMEATON	LOFTHOUSE	
31/03/24	ABERDARE ATHLETIC	A	0-2	3000	WHATLEY	ARMITAGE	SAMBIDGE	SCORER	WRAGGE	WALTON	CHANCE	PHILLIPS	WHATMORE	SMEATON	LOFTHOUSE	
05/04/24	SWINDON TOWN	A	1-1	5000	WHATLEY	ARMITAGE	SAMBIDGE	WALTON	WRAGGE	SMITH	TAYLOR	PHILLIPS	WHATMORE	SMEATON	LOFTHOUSE	
12/04/24	WATFORD	H	4-2	5000	WHATLEY	ARMITAGE	SAMBIDGE	WALTON	SMITH	WRAGGE	CHANCE	PHILLIPS	WOODHALL	WHATMORE	LOFTHOUSE	PHILLIPS 2, WHATMORE, WOODHALL
18/04/24	LUTON TOWN	A	0-0	8000	WHATLEY	ARMITAGE	SAMBIDGE	WALTON	WRAGGE	SMITH	CHANCE	PHILLIPS	WOODHALL	WHATMORE	LOFTHOUSE	
19/04/24	WATFORD	A	0-4	4933	WHATLEY	PRICE	SAMBIDGE	WALTON	WRAGGE	SMITH	CHANCE	PHILLIPS	WOODHALL	WHATMORE	LOFTHOUSE	
21/04/24	LUTON TOWN	H	1-1	6000	WHATLEY	PRICE	SAMBIDGE	WALTON	WRAGGE	SMITH	HAMMOND	PHILLIPS	WOODHALL	WHATMORE	LOFTHOUSE	WOODHALL
26/04/24	SWANSEA TOWN	H	2-0	10000	WHATLEY	PRICE	SAMBIDGE	WALTON	WRAGGE	SMITH	CHANCE	PHILLIPS	WOODHALL	WHATMORE	PATTISON	PHILLIPS 2
03/05/24	SWANSEA TOWN	A	1-3	14000	WHATLEY	PRICE	SAMBIDGE	WALTON	WRAGGE	SMITH	CHANCE	PHILLIPS	WOODHALL	WHATMORE	SMEATON	PHILLIPS

FA CUP

Date	Opponent	A/H	Score	ATT	G	2	3	4	5	6	7	8	9	10	11	GOALSCORERS
01/12/23	EXETER CITY	A	2-2	9260	WHATLEY	ARMITAGE	HAYDON	FURNISS	SCORER	SMITH	CHANCE	PHILLIPS	WOODHALL	WHATMORE	PATTISON	WHATMORE 2
05/12/23	EXETER CITY	A	0-1	7000	WHATLEY	ARMITAGE	HAYDON	ROSE	FURNISS	WALTON	CHANCE	PHILLIPS	WOODHALL	WHATMORE	PATTISON	

GLOUCESTERSHIRE CUP FINAL

Date	Opponent	A/H	Score	ATT	G	2	3	4	5	6	7	8	9	10	11	GOALSCORERS
30/04/24	BRISTOL CITY	H	1-1	7396	WHATLEY	PRICE	SAMBIDGE	WALTON	WRAGGE	SMITH	CHANCE	PHILLIPS	WOODHALL	WHATMORE	PATTISON	
05/05/24	BRISTOL CITY	A	0-2	6091	WHATLEY	ARMITAGE	HAYDON	GOUGH	WRAGGE	SMITH	HAMMOND	PHILLIPS	WOODHALL	SMEATON	SCORER	

PLAYERS

PLAYERS	APP	GLS
ARMITAGE H	37	
CHANCE G	39	4
CUFF W	2	
FURNISS S	31	
HAMMOND W	4	
HAYDON J	24	
LEA T	10	
LOFTHOUSE J	24	2
MORGAN J	7	2
PARKER J	2	
PATTISON J	8	1
PHILLIPS W	42	23
PRICE J	5	
ROSE H	13	
SAMBIDGE E	18	
SCORER R	19	
SMEATON A	5	1
SMITH S	15	
TAYLOR J	5	1
WAINWRIGHT A	2	
WALTON J	40	1
WHATLEY J	42	
WHATMORE E	27	4
WOODHALL W	31	11
WRAGGE F	10	
OWN GOALS		2

4-3, having been behind at 2-0 and 4-2. Foster Robinson, a former Coventry City outside-left, was tormentor-in-chief and fully deserved to claim Bournemouth's fourth goal 15 minutes from time. It was the first time in more than a year that Rovers had conceded four goals in a League game, a fate repeated in more devastating fashion at Watford on Easter Saturday.

Jesse Whatley, a dominant and influential figure in goal, saved a penalty from Jock Henderson of Gillingham, who had apparently scored all ten spot-kicks his side had been awarded during 1922/23. The defence again conceded relatively few goals, but Rovers lacked goals from all but Phillips and Woodhall. Once the latter was sidelined in January, it was clearly the lack of goals that proved to be the club's downfall. Nor was there any respite in the FA Cup, where Rovers made a swift exit. Whatmore's brace at Exeter City had earned a draw, but the Grecians won the replay at Eastville through a solitary goal from their centre-forward John Davis. The Gloucestershire Cup was also lost, Bristol City winning in a replay and Tot Walsh scoring in both games.

A Departmental Committee on Crowds issued a report on 13 March 1924 (Command Paper 2088) to Home Secretary, Arthur Henderson. It was recommended that terracing be subdivided into smaller enclosures, in view of safety following the perilous overcrowding at the first Wembley FA Cup Final in 1923 and the death of a spectator in a crush at the Burnley v. Huddersfield Town FA Cup tie in February 1924. At Eastville, in line with the official recommendations, crowd barriers were staggered so as to prevent the existence of vertical gangways, the absence of which was ironically to contribute greatly to the 33 deaths at Bolton Wanderers' Burnden Park in March 1946.

1924/25

The mid-1920s was an era of growth in British football and one that looked at means of improving the game. By 1924 talks were underway regarding changes to the offside law, a proposal that made common sense viewed in conjunction with Rovers' miserly goals for and against columns for the two previous seasons. From the summer of 1924, players could now score direct from a corner, although several opponents claimed to have already scored against Rovers in this way. The new South Stand had been constructed over the summer at Eastville, a 2,000-seater including a paddock, dressing-rooms and club offices. Rovers responded with four straight home victories from the start of the season, with no goals conceded.

Sid Holcroft, a summer signing from Stourbridge, scored the winning goal against Merthyr Town in the first game and, in fact, scored in each of the first five matches. The fifth of these was a 4-0 victory over Charlton Athletic at Eastville. Rovers scored three goals in a four-minute spell in the second-half, with Ernie Whatmore completing his first hat-trick for the club. He and Wilkie Phillips, once Holcroft's goals had dried up, were Rovers' joint top goalscorers with nine league goals each.

Jesse Whatley played his hundredth consecutive League match in goal when Rovers beat Brentford 2-0 in November. He and outside-left Jimmy Lofthouse were the club's

Bristol Rovers 1924/25. Back row: Gough, Daws, Whatmore, Haydon, Wragge, Armitage, Smith, Gibbs, Scorer, Sambidge. Second row: E Jones (Trainer), Phillips, Woodhall, Whatley, Densley, Lofthouse, Roberts, Williams (Asst Trainer). Front row: Edwards, Holcroft, Ramsey, Smeaton, Pither

two ever-presents. Holcroft and outside-right Sam Edwards established themselves as regulars in a largely unaltered side. Billy Woodhall was sidelined, allowing Whatmore to lead the attack, while Frank Wragge's stabilizing influence at centre-half was now more consistent. The mid-season arrival of Arthur Gibbs from Brierley Hill Athletic and Leicester City's William Thomson added defensive options, while the late-season return to form of Jerry Morgan offered greater scope in attack.

Rovers enjoyed early success over that season's champions Swansea Town. A 2-2 draw in Wales was followed by a three-goal victory at Eastville, the triumvirate of Holcroft, Phillips and Whatmore all scoring in the opening 15 minutes before Town's Lachlan McPherson missed a penalty. Several opponents were to miss penalties against Rovers before the season was out, while Jimmy Lofthouse's erratic record led to Jerry Morgan taking and scoring the final spot-kick of the season in the match at Reading. This fixture marked the sole appearance in a Rovers shirt of Hubert Ashton, elder brother of the erstwhile England football captain Claude Ashton. Hubert Ashton was to enjoy 34 years as a Conservative MP and was President of the MCC at the time of the South Africa crisis in 1960. At Elm Park, however, he was given the run-around by Belfast-born Hugh Davey, who scored a hat-trick in Reading's 4-1 victory, his only three goals of the season.

A crowd of 30,000 at Eastville in October, equalling the ground record, saw Rovers fight out a goalless draw with freshly relegated Bristol City. At the end of February,

Bill Woodhall in action against Bristol City on 28 February 1925

Rovers were to lose an ill-tempered return fixture at Ashton Gate. William Thomson was sent off for a foul, only the second Rovers player to suffer this fate in the League, and City scored through the ever-reliable Tot Walsh and Johnny Paul. City were to finish third in Division Three (South). Illegal play was also suspected at Eastville on Christmas Day. During the 2-1 defeat against Brighton, Wilkie Phillips appeared to score for Rovers with his hand. As with the infamous opening goal that Diego Maradona scored for Argentina against England in the 1986 World Cup, the goal was allowed to stand.

Matches against Southend United were marked by dramatic starts. At The Kursaal in October, Rovers were a goal down in only two minutes, conceding a penalty that was converted by Jim McClelland. Rovers lost 2-1, despite Whatmore's goal. Only a fortnight later, Lofthouse scored a second-minute penalty awarded in Rovers' favour at Plymouth. When Southend visited Eastville in February, Ernie Edwards turned Lofthouse's cross into his own net off his knee to give Rovers a first-minute lead, before the visitors recovered to win 3-1. One of their goalscorers was Sammy Brooks, who stood just 5ft 2½in. Only three players shorter than him have appeared against Rovers in League action. Defeat at home to Southend prompted manager Wilson to make six changes to the side that was to travel to Gillingham.

In addition to the large win over Charlton Athletic, Rovers also won 3-0 on three occasions. Two of these came in the space of four days in March, with recalled inside-forward Jerry Morgan scoring twice in both matches. Yet, Rovers also lost 3-0 at Swindon Town, conceded four at Newport County and Reading and were beaten 5-0 by Northampton Town, where the Cobblers scored three times in 10 minutes. Louis Page, one of four brothers who represented England at baseball, scored two of these goals. It was Rovers' heaviest League defeat since the debacle at Swansea Town on Easter Saturday 1922. After centre-half Edmund Wood had opened the scoring with a rare goal, courtesy of a wicked deflection off Harry Armitage, the Cobblers' strike-force of Colin Myers and Louis Page grabbed two goals apiece. The return game with Northampton was a 2-0 defeat in January, almost lost in the Eastville fog. Newspaper reporters disagree over whether the figure emerging from the shadows to score the opening goal was Ernie Cockle or Bill Poyntz. It was a precursor to the meeting between the sides in December 1928 that was decided, in dense fog, by a farcical own goal from the unfortunate Mick Cosgrove.

Rovers used only 21 players in the season, including three who made 5 League appearances between them. Not since 1907/08 had the club required the services of so

SEASON 1924/25

FOOTBALL LEAGUE DIVISION THREE (SOUTH)

Date	Opponent	H/A	Score	ATT	G	2	3	4	5	6	7	8	9	10	11	GOALSCORERS
30/08/24	MERTHYR TOWN	H	1-0	8000	WHATLEY	ARMITAGE	SAMBIDGE	ROBERTS	DAWS	SMITH	EDWARDS	PHILLIPS	WOODHALL	HOLCROFT	LOFTHOUSE	HOLCROFT
01/09/24	SWANSEA TOWN	A	2-2	15000	WHATLEY	ARMITAGE	HAYDON	DAWS	WRAGGE	SMITH	EDWARDS	PHILLIPS	WHATMORE	HOLCROFT	LOFTHOUSE	HOLCROFT, PHILLIPS
06/09/24	QUEENS PARK RANGERS	A	2-1	12000	WHATLEY	ARMITAGE	HAYDON	DAWS	WRAGGE	SMITH	EDWARDS	PHILLIPS	WHATMORE	HOLCROFT	LOFTHOUSE	HOLCROFT, WHATMORE
08/09/24	SWANSEA TOWN	H	3-0	15000	WHATLEY	ARMITAGE	HAYDON	DAWS	WRAGGE	SMITH	EDWARDS	PHILLIPS	WHATMORE	HOLCROFT	LOFTHOUSE	HOLCROFT, PHILLIPS,
13/09/24	CHARLTON ATHLETIC	H	4-0	10000	WHATLEY	ARMITAGE	HAYDON	DAWS	WRAGGE	SMITH	EDWARDS	PHILLIPS	WHATMORE	HOLCROFT	LOFTHOUSE	WHATMORE 3, HOLCROFT
15/09/24	MILLWALL	A	0-0	8000	WHATLEY	ARMITAGE	HAYDON	DAWS	WRAGGE	SMITH	EDWARDS	PHILLIPS	WHATMORE	HOLCROFT	LOFTHOUSE	
20/09/24	NORTHAMPTON TOWN	H	0-5	8000	WHATLEY	ARMITAGE	HAYDON	SCORER	WRAGGE	SMITH	EDWARDS	PHILLIPS	WHATMORE	HOLCROFT	LOFTHOUSE	
27/09/24	WATFORD	H	2-0	12000	WHATLEY	ARMITAGE	HAYDON	SCORER	WRAGGE	SMITH	EDWARDS	PHILLIPS	WHATMORE	HOLCROFT	LOFTHOUSE	EDWARDS, PHILLIPS
04/10/24	SOUTHEND UNITED	A	1-2	8000	WHATLEY	ARMITAGE	HAYDON	SCORER	DAWS	SMITH	CHARLESWORTH	PHILLIPS	WHATMORE	HOLCROFT	LOFTHOUSE	WHATMORE
11/10/24	NEWPORT COUNTY	H	0-1	10000	WHATLEY	ARMITAGE	HAYDON	SCORER	DAWS	SMITH	CHARLESWORTH	PHILLIPS	WHATMORE	HOLCROFT	LOFTHOUSE	
18/10/24	PLYMOUTH ARGYLE	H	2-3	18000	WHATLEY	GIBBS	HAYDON	THOMSON	WRAGGE	SMITH	EDWARDS	PHILLIPS	WHATMORE	HOLCROFT	LOFTHOUSE	EDWARDS, LOFTHOUSE pen
25/10/24	BRISTOL CITY	H	0-0	30000	WHATLEY	GIBBS	HAYDON	THOMSON	WRAGGE	SMITH	EDWARDS	PHILLIPS	WHATMORE	HOLCROFT	LOFTHOUSE	
01/11/24	SWINDON TOWN	A	0-3	7000	WHATLEY	GIBBS	HAYDON	THOMSON	DAWS	SMITH	EDWARDS	PHILLIPS	WHATMORE	HOLCROFT	LOFTHOUSE	
08/11/24	ABERDARE ATHLETIC	H	1-0	10000	WHATLEY	ARMITAGE	GIBBS	THOMSON	WRAGGE	SMITH	EDWARDS	PHILLIPS	WHATMORE	HOLCROFT	LOFTHOUSE	EDWARDS
15/11/24	NORWICH CITY	H	1-1	7000	WHATLEY	ARMITAGE	GIBBS	THOMSON	WRAGGE	SMITH	EDWARDS	PHILLIPS	WHATMORE	HOLCROFT	LOFTHOUSE	EDWARDS
22/11/24	BRENTFORD	H	2-0	10000	WHATLEY	ARMITAGE	GIBBS	THOMSON	DAWS	SMITH	EDWARDS	PHILLIPS	WHATMORE	HOLCROFT	LOFTHOUSE	PHILLIPS 2
06/12/24	LUTON TOWN	H	1-1	8000	WHATLEY	HAYDON	WRAGGE	SCORER	DAWS	THOMSON	EDWARDS	PHILLIPS	WHATMORE	HOLCROFT	LOFTHOUSE	WHATMORE
20/12/24	BOURNEMOUTH	H	1-0	8000	WHATLEY	GIBBS	HAYDON	THOMSON	DAWS	SMITH	EDWARDS	PHILLIPS	MORGAN	HOLCROFT	LOFTHOUSE	MORGAN
25/12/24	BRIGHTON & HOVE ALBION	H	1-2	19000	WHATLEY	GIBBS	HAYDON	THOMSON	DAWS	SMITH	EDWARDS	PHILLIPS	WOODHALL	HOLCROFT	LOFTHOUSE	PHILLIPS
26/12/24	BRIGHTON & HOVE ALBION	A	0-1	15732	WHATLEY	GIBBS	HAYDON	THOMSON	DAWS	SMITH	EDWARDS	PHILLIPS	WHATMORE	PITHER	LOFTHOUSE	EDWARDS og
17/01/25	CHARLTON ATHLETIC	A	1-1	6000	WHATLEY	ARMITAGE	GIBBS	DAWS	WRAGGE	SCORER	EDWARDS	PHILLIPS	WOODHALL	PITHER	LOFTHOUSE	WOODHALL
24/01/25	NORTHAMPTON TOWN	A	0-2	6000	WHATLEY	ARMITAGE	HAYDON	THOMSON	DAWS	SMITH	EDWARDS	ROBERTS	WOODHALL	MORGAN	LOFTHOUSE	WOODHALL
30/01/25	WATFORD	A	0-1	5000	WHATLEY	GIBBS	SAMBIDGE	THOMSON	WRAGGE	SMITH	EDWARDS	PHILLIPS	WHATMORE	MORGAN	LOFTHOUSE	
07/02/25	SOUTHEND UNITED	H	1-3	7000	WHATLEY	GIBBS	SAMBIDGE	THOMSON	WRAGGE	SMITH	EDWARDS	PHILLIPS	WHATMORE	MORGAN	LOFTHOUSE	
11/02/25	GILLINGHAM	H	0-0	4000	WHATLEY	ARMITAGE	HAYDON	THOMSON	WRAGGE	SCORER	EDWARDS	PHILLIPS	WHATMORE	MORGAN	LOFTHOUSE	LOFTHOUSE
14/02/25	NEWPORT COUNTY	A	1-4	14000	WHATLEY	ARMITAGE	HAYDON	THOMSON	WRAGGE	SCORER	EDWARDS	PHILLIPS	WHATMORE	MORGAN	LOFTHOUSE	MORGAN 2, WHATMORE
21/02/25	PLYMOUTH ARGYLE	H	1-1	8000	WHATLEY	ARMITAGE	HAYDON	THOMSON	WRAGGE	SCORER	EDWARDS	PHILLIPS	WHATMORE	MORGAN	LOFTHOUSE	MORGAN 2, EDWARDS
28/02/25	BRISTOL CITY	A	0-2	15000	WHATLEY	SAMBIDGE	HAYDON	THOMSON	WRAGGE	SCORER	EDWARDS	PHILLIPS	WHATMORE	MORGAN	LOFTHOUSE	LOFTHOUSE
07/03/25	SWINDON TOWN	H	0-1	10000	WHATLEY	ARMITAGE	HAYDON	THOMSON	WRAGGE	SMITH	EDWARDS	PHILLIPS	WHATMORE	MORGAN	LOFTHOUSE	PHILLIPS
14/03/25	ABERDARE ATHLETIC	H	1-2	4000	WHATLEY	ARMITAGE	HAYDON	DAWS	WRAGGE	SCORER	EDWARDS	PHILLIPS	WHATMORE	MORGAN	LOFTHOUSE	
18/03/25	QUEENS PARK RANGERS	H	3-0	3000	WHATLEY	ARMITAGE	HAYDON	DAWS	WRAGGE	SCORER	EDWARDS	PHILLIPS	WHATMORE	MORGAN	LOFTHOUSE	WHATMORE
21/03/25	NORWICH CITY	H	1-1	7000	WHATLEY	ARMITAGE	HAYDON	DAWS	WRAGGE	SMITH	CHARLESWORTH	PHILLIPS	WHATMORE	MORGAN	LOFTHOUSE	CHARLESWORTH
28/03/25	BRENTFORD	H	1-1	2500	WHATLEY	ARMITAGE	HAYDON	DAWS	WRAGGE	SMITH	CHARLESWORTH	PHILLIPS	WHATMORE	MORGAN	LOFTHOUSE	PHILLIPS
30/03/25	MERTHYR TOWN	H	1-1	7000	WHATLEY	ARMITAGE	HAYDON	DAWS	WRAGGE	SMITH	CHARLESWORTH	PHILLIPS	WHATMORE	MORGAN	LOFTHOUSE	LOFTHOUSE
04/04/25	MILLWALL	H	0-1	7000	WHATLEY	ARMITAGE	HAYDON	DAWS	WRAGGE	SMITH	CHARLESWORTH	PHILLIPS	WHATMORE	MORGAN	LOFTHOUSE	
10/04/25	EXETER CITY	H	0-1	12000	WHATLEY	GIBBS	HAYDON	DAWS	WRAGGE	THOMSON	CHARLESWORTH	PHILLIPS	WHATMORE	MORGAN	LOFTHOUSE	
11/04/25	LUTON TOWN	H	1-1	6000	WHATLEY	GIBBS	HAYDON	DAWS	WRAGGE	THOMSON	CHARLESWORTH	PHILLIPS	WHATMORE	MORGAN	LOFTHOUSE	PHILLIPS
13/04/25	EXETER CITY	A	1-1	12000	WHATLEY	GIBBS	SAMBIDGE	DAWS	WRAGGE	THOMSON	CHARLESWORTH	PHILLIPS	WHATMORE	MORGAN	LOFTHOUSE	WHATMORE
14/04/25	READING	H	1-0	4000	WHATLEY	SAMBIDGE	HAYDON	DAWS	WRAGGE	SCORER	CHARLESWORTH	PHILLIPS	WHATMORE	MORGAN	LOFTHOUSE	PHILLIPS
18/04/25	GILLINGHAM	H	0-0	6000	WHATLEY	ARMITAGE	HAYDON	THOMSON	DAWS	SCORER	EDWARDS	PHILLIPS	WHATMORE	MORGAN	LOFTHOUSE	
25/04/25	BOURNEMOUTH	A	1-0	4000	WHATLEY	GIBBS	HAYDON	THOMSON	DAWS	SCORER	EDWARDS	PHILLIPS	WHATMORE	MORGAN	LOFTHOUSE	
02/05/25	READING	A	1-4	7000	WHATLEY	GIBBS	HAYDON	DAWS	WRAGGE	SCORER	EDWARDS	PHILLIPS	WHATMORE	MORGAN	LOFTHOUSE	MORGAN pen

F A CUP

Date	Opponent	H/A	Score	ATT	G	2	3	4	5	6	7	8	9	10	11	GOALSCORERS
29/11/24	YEOVIL & PETTERS UTD	A	4-2	6528	WHATLEY	WHATLEY	ARMITAGE	HAYDON	DAWS	WRAGGE	THOMSON	EDWARDS	PHILLIPS	WHATMORE	MORGAN	WHATMORE, PHILLIPS, MORGAN 2
13/12/24	YEOVIL & PETTERS UTD	H	2-0	6000	WHATLEY	WHATLEY	ARMITAGE	HAYDON	THOMSON	DAWS	SMITH	EDWARDS	PHILLIPS	WHATMORE	HOLCROFT	HOLCROFT, PHILLIPS
17/12/24	WEYMOUTH	A	2-0	7000	WHATLEY	WHATLEY	ARMITAGE	HAYDON	THOMSON	DAWS	SMITH	EDWARDS	PHILLIPS	WHATMORE	HOLCROFT	
10/01/25	BRISTOL CITY	H	0-1	31500	WHATLEY	WHATLEY	ARMITAGE	HAYDON	THOMSON	DAWS	SMITH	EDWARDS	PHILLIPS	WHATMORE	ARMITAGE	

GLOUCESTERSHIRE CUP FINAL

Date	Opponent	H/A	Score	ATT	G	2	3	4	5	6	7	8	9	10	11	GOALSCORERS
27/04/25	BRISTOL CITY	A	1-1	5102	WHATLEY	WHATLEY	DAWS	ARMITAGE	HAYDON	DAWS	SCORER	CHARLESWORTH	PHILLIPS	WHATMORE	MORGAN	WHATMORE
29/04/25	BRISTOL CITY	H	2-0	4500	WHATLEY	WHATLEY	WRAGGE	ARMITAGE	HAYDON	DAWS	SCORER	CHARLESWORTH	PHILLIPS	WHATMORE	MORGAN	PHILLIPS, MORGAN

Appearances & Goals

PLAYERS	APP	GLS
ARMITAGE H	32	
ASHTON H	1	
CHARLESWORTH G	9	1
DAWS J	30	
EDWARDS S	33	5
GIBBS A	19	
HAYDON J	29	
HOLCROFT S	19	5
LOFTHOUSE J	41	4
MORGAN J	22	6
PHILLIPS W	36	9
PITHER G	2	
ROBERTS F	2	
SAMBIDGE E	4	
SCORER R	18	
SMITH S	24	
THOMSON W	21	
WHATLEY J	42	
WHATMORE E	37	9
WOODHALL W	7	2
WRAGGE F	34	

few players. Despite promising early form, a dreadful run through the winter of three draws and nine defeats in 12 games, added to by a run of six games without a win in the run up to Easter, left Rovers in 17th place, their worst final Division Three (South) position to date. Several players were released, including Ernie Sambidge who had scored an own goal at Exeter on Easter Monday in his final game, with George Charlesworth scoring his first goal for Rovers in a 1-1 draw.

Jesse Whatley was rewarded for his consistency by being given a place in the prestigious South side, which beat the North 3-1 at Stamford Bridge in January. The future Rovers player Tommy Cook scored one of the goals and Jack Townrow, who was to arrive at Eastville in 1932, also played in this game. Whatley's commitment to the Bristol Rovers cause was rewarded with a benefit game at Eastville in April 1925, in which Portsmouth were defeated 2-1. Simply playing in a trial match of this nature represented a major achievement for a Division Three player, although Whatley was not to win any full International honours.

Two future Rovers managers were also in the news. David McLean played for Dundee in the Scottish Cup final, while Albert Prince-Cox refereed the Gloucestershire Cup final and replay, which saw Rovers lift the trophy for the first time since 1913. In the FA Cup, where the future Rovers outside-left Jack Evans played for Cardiff City in the final, non-League Yeovil and Petters United were beaten 4-2 and Weymouth were seen off after a replay. Victory at Yeovil was secured despite an outstanding performance from the home side's outside-right Jimmy Gardner. Rovers were so impressed that he was signed by the Eastville club at the end of the season. A goalless draw at home to Weymouth, who were captained by Steve Sims, a former Rovers centre-half, was not an ideal result, especially as the Dorset side had already beaten Division Three (South) Merthyr Town in the FA Cup, and Rovers relied on Whatley's penalty save from Walker before defeating the Southern League side in a replay. This set up a Bristol derby in January and the ground attendance record, equalled earlier in the season, was shattered. An Eastville crowd of 31,500, the highest there between the wars, watched Bristol City defeat Rovers with a goal from centre-forward Tot Walsh after 55 minutes.

1925/26

A fundamental rule change regarding offside meant that, from the start of the 1925/26 season, a forward now needed just two instead of three defenders between him and the goal. This adjustment brought the anticipated goal glut around the country. In the Football League, 4,700 goals had been scored in 1924/25, but 6,373 were scored in 1925/26. Several individuals were able to benefit greatly in the late 1920s, most notably Middlesbrough's George Camsell, who hit 59 goals in only 37 League matches in 1926/27. So it was that Rovers scored 66 times in the League in 1925/26, almost twice the figure for three seasons earlier, and yet finished the season in 19th place in Division Three (South), the club's lowest final placing since entering the Football League.

With Wilkie Phillips contributing only 3 League goals, the goalscoring burden fell on new signing Jonah Wilcox, from New Brighton. Wilcox responded with 19 goals, including four against Bournemouth on Boxing Day, to finish the season as the club's top scorer. Jimmy Gardner from Yeovil and Petters United and Worcester City's Bill Wilson were new faces in the side. A number of other signings enjoyed only brief spells in an ever-changing team. Alex Crichton, Albert Rotherham, Andrew Dick and Alf Bowers all featured in the half-back line, while Stafford Rangers' Charles Heinemann, the son of an England rugby International, started the season at inside-right.

Wilcox scored on his debut at Charlton Athletic where, with the club's train held up in holiday traffic, Rovers had been forced to hire a fleet of taxis to reach the ground in time. When Ernie Whatmore appeared for the third game, he and Wilcox both scored and the season was up and running. Gillingham's goalkeeper in this match was Alex Ferguson, whose final League appearance against Rovers was to be more than 21 years later in the Bristol City side that won 3-0 at Eastville in September 1946. Whatmore was second-highest scorer with 11 League goals,

Jimmy Lofthouse, a tricky left-winger who made 105 appearances, scoring 15 times, in his three seasons at Eastville

Lofthouse scored 9 and both Holcroft and mid-season signing Bill Culley, a highly experienced leader of the attack who had won a Scottish Cup winner's medal with Kilmarnock, scored hat-tricks. Holcroft's three in a 5-0 thrashing of Queen's Park Rangers in October were his first for over a year. Culley joined from Weymouth and his hat-trick led Rovers to a 4-2 victory on Good Friday over Reading, who were divisional champions that season.

The home encounter with Bournemouth on Boxing Day was the first time Rovers had scored seven in a League fixture. Two strikes in the first five minutes from Albert Burnell, who only scored three times in his Rovers career, sparked a flood of goals. Rovers, 4-1 up by half-time, won 7-2, with Jonah Wilcox equalling Sid Leigh's club record of four goals in a League game. Two of Wilcox's goals were penalties, both scored in the final ten minutes. He became the first Rovers player to score two penalties in a league match, a record first equalled by Jackie Pitt in 1948. Both Bournemouth's goals were scored by Ron Eyre, his first against Rovers. He was to score a total of 15 League

Bristol Rovers 1925/26. Back row: Haydon, Jones, Crichton, Dick, Densley, Wilson, Bowers, Whatley, Wragge, Rotherham, Lennon, Ashton, Armitage, Williams (Asst Trainer). Second row: Charlesworth, Phillips, Wilcox, Heinemann, Whatmore, Lofthouse, Holcroft, Foster. On Ground: Gardner, Roberts, Duckers

goals against the club in his long career, plus another in an abandoned game in December 1929, more than any other opponent in Rovers' history.

Rovers lost 21 League games this season, the heaviest being a 6-3 defeat at Gillingham, for whom Fred Brown scored a hat-trick. From the penalty spot, former Rovers full-back Harry O'Neill scored the only League goal of his career to give Swindon Town a 2-1 victory at Eastville. In the away fixture, Swindon Town had led 4-0 with only ten minutes remaining, before late Lofthouse and Whatmore goals lent the final scoreline a touch of respectability. Rovers, reduced to ten men by half-time at Newport, with full-back Harry Armitage off the field injured in this his final League game, lost 3-1 to a strong County side. In fact, Rovers had scraped a draw at home to the same opposition after Whatley, with Newport were already 2-0 ahead, had saved a penalty which would have given John Davis his hat-trick.

In September, Rovers played at Luton in Mission Week and Rt Rev. Michael Furse, the Bishop of St Albans gave an address to the crowd before the match. In the return game at Eastville, Luton lost two men through injury while David Richards played on for 30 minutes with a broken right leg; Rovers again fought back from two goals down, a late goal from Tom Williams earning a 2-2 draw. Aberdare Athletic's goalkeeper Brown was injured five minutes after half-time in the game in December, with Rovers a goal ahead through Whatmore after 20 minutes. Tom Brophy, a full-back, went in goal, and Rovers clung on for victory, after Athletic's John Smith and David James had both missed penalties. It was Rovers' only ever League victory at the Athletic Ground and, in May's return game, Jesse Whatley's own goal contributed to a 3-0 win for Aberdare.

SEASON 1925/26

FOOTBALL LEAGUE DIVISION THREE (SOUTH)

Date	Opposition		Score	ATT	G	2	3	4	5	6	7	8	9	10	11	GOALSCORERS
29/08/25	CHARLTON ATHLETIC	A	1-0	5600	WHATLEY	ARMITAGE	HAYDON	DICK	WILSON	CRICHTON	GARDNER	HEINEMANN	WILCOX	HOLCROFT	LOFTHOUSE	WILCOX
31/08/25	EXETER CITY	H	0-1	10000	WHATLEY	ARMITAGE	HAYDON	BOWERS	WILSON	CRICHTON	GARDNER	HEINEMANN	WILCOX	HOLCROFT	LOFTHOUSE	
05/09/25	GILLINGHAM	H	2-0	6000	WHATLEY	ARMITAGE	HAYDON	BOWERS	WILSON	CRICHTON	GARDNER	HEINEMANN	WILCOX	WHATMORE	LOFTHOUSE	WHATMORE, WILCOX
09/09/25	EXETER CITY	A	0-3	6000	WHATLEY	ARMITAGE	HAYDON	BOWERS	WILSON	CRICHTON	GARDNER	PHILLIPS	WILCOX	WHATMORE	LOFTHOUSE	
12/09/25	MERTHYR TOWN	A	3-2	7000	WHATLEY	ARMITAGE	HAYDON	CRICHTON	WRAGGE	JONES	CHARLESWORTH	PHILLIPS	WHATMORE	WILCOX	LOFTHOUSE	WILCOX 2, LOFTHOUSE
16/09/25	SWINDON TOWN	A	2-4	6500	WHATLEY	ARMITAGE	HAYDON	CRICHTON	WRAGGE	JONES	CHARLESWORTH	PHILLIPS	WHATMORE	WILCOX	LOFTHOUSE	LOFTHOUSE, WRAGGE
19/09/25	NEWPORT COUNTY	H	2-2	6000	WHATLEY	ARMITAGE	HAYDON	CRICHTON	WILSON	JONES	CHARLESWORTH	PHILLIPS	WHATMORE	WILCOX	LOFTHOUSE	CHARLESWORTH, PHILLIPS
26/09/25	LUTON TOWN	A	0-1	7000	WHATLEY	ARMITAGE	HAYDON	ROBERTS	WILSON	JONES	CHARLESWORTH	PHILLIPS	WILCOX	WHATMORE	LOFTHOUSE	
03/10/25	QUEENS PARK RANGERS	H	5-0	9000	WHATLEY	ARMITAGE	HAYDON	ROBERTS	WILSON	JONES	CHARLESWORTH	PHILLIPS	WILCOX	HOLCROFT	LOFTHOUSE	HOLCROFT 3, WILCOX, LOFTHOUSE
10/10/25	CRYSTAL PALACE	A	2-0	14272	WHATLEY	ARMITAGE	HAYDON	ROBERTS	WILSON	JONES	CHARLESWORTH	PHILLIPS	WILCOX	HOLCROFT	LOFTHOUSE	LOFTHOUSE, PHILLIPS
17/10/25	BRENTFORD	H	1-2	10000	WHATLEY	ARMITAGE	HAYDON	ROBERTS	WILSON	JONES	CHARLESWORTH	PHILLIPS	WILCOX	HOLCROFT	LOFTHOUSE	WILCOX pen
24/10/25	WATFORD	H	1-2	6242	WHATLEY	ARMITAGE	HAYDON	ROTHERHAM	WILSON	JONES	CHARLESWORTH	WHATMORE	WILCOX	ROBERTS	LOFTHOUSE	WHATMORE
31/10/25	PLYMOUTH ARGYLE	H	2-3	25000	WHATLEY	ARMITAGE	HAYDON	ROTHERHAM	WILSON	ROBERTS	GARDNER	WHATMORE	WILCOX	BURNELL	LOFTHOUSE	GARDNER 2
07/11/25	BRISTOL CITY	A	0-0	18816	WHATLEY	ARMITAGE	HAYDON	ROTHERHAM	WILSON	ROBERTS	GARDNER	PHILLIPS	WILCOX	HOLCROFT	LOFTHOUSE	
14/11/25	NORTHAMPTON TOWN	A	1-2	8000	WHATLEY	ARMITAGE	HAYDON	ROTHERHAM	WILSON	ROBERTS	GARDNER	PHILLIPS	WILCOX	HOLCROFT	LOFTHOUSE	PHILLIPS
21/11/25	MILLWALL	A	0-0	12000	WHATLEY	ARMITAGE	HAYDON	ROTHERHAM	WILSON	ROBERTS	GARDNER	WHATMORE	WHATMORE	WILCOX	LOFTHOUSE	
05/12/25	SOUTHEND UNITED	A	1-3	5661	WHATLEY	ARMITAGE	HAYDON	DICK	WILSON	ROBERTS	GARDNER	WILCOX	WILCOX	HOLCROFT	LOFTHOUSE	EDWARDS og
12/12/25	BRIGHTON & HOVE ALBION	H	4-0	5008	WHATLEY	ARMITAGE	HAYDON	DICK	WILSON	ROBERTS	GARDNER	WILCOX	WILCOX	HOLCROFT	LOFTHOUSE	WHATMORE 2, WILCOX 2-1pen
19/12/25	ABERDARE ATHLETIC	A	1-0	4000	WHATLEY	ARMITAGE	HAYDON	DICK	WILSON	ROBERTS	GARDNER	WILCOX	WILCOX	WHATMORE	LOFTHOUSE	WHATMORE
25/12/25	BOURNEMOUTH	A	0-2	5000	WHATLEY	ARMITAGE	HAYDON	DICK	WILSON	ROBERTS	GARDNER	HOLCROFT	WILCOX	BURNELL	LOFTHOUSE	
26/12/25	BOURNEMOUTH	H	7-2	12000	WHATLEY	ARMITAGE	HAYDON	DICK	WILSON	ROBERTS	GARDNER	HOLCROFT	WILCOX	BURNELL	LOFTHOUSE	WILCOX 4-2pens, BURNELL 2, HOLCROFT
28/12/25	SWINDON TOWN	H	1-2	6396	WHATLEY	LENNON	HAYDON	DICK	WILSON	ROBERTS	GARDNER	PHILLIPS	WILCOX	BURNELL	LOFTHOUSE	WILCOX
09/01/26	NORWICH CITY	A	2-2	6000	WHATLEY	ARMITAGE	HAYDON	DICK	WILSON	ROBERTS	GARDNER	PHILLIPS	WILCOX	BURNELL	LOFTHOUSE	WILCOX 2
16/01/26	GILLINGHAM	A	3-6	3000	WHATLEY	LENNON	HAYDON	DICK	WILSON	ROBERTS	GARDNER	WHATMORE	WILCOX	BURNELL	LOFTHOUSE	LOFTHOUSE, WHATMORE, WILCOX
23/01/26	MERTHYR TOWN	H	0-0	5000	WHATLEY	WRAGGE	HAYDON	DICK	STALLARD	ROBERTS	GARDNER	WILLIAMS	WHATMORE	CULLEY	LOFTHOUSE	
30/01/26	NEWPORT COUNTY	H	1-3	5000	WHATLEY	WRAGGE	HAYDON	DICK	STALLARD	ROBERTS	GARDNER	WILLIAMS	WHATMORE	CULLEY	LOFTHOUSE	GARDNER
06/02/26	LUTON TOWN	H	2-2	7000	WHATLEY	GRIFFITHS	HAYDON	DICK	WILSON	ROBERTS	CHARLESWORTH	WILLIAMS	CULLEY	WHATMORE	LOFTHOUSE	WILCOX, WILLIAMS
13/02/26	QUEENS PARK RANGERS	A	1-2	10000	WHATLEY	WRAGGE	HAYDON	DICK	WILSON	ROBERTS	GARDNER	WILLIAMS	WILCOX	CULLEY	LOFTHOUSE	WILCOX
27/02/26	BRENTFORD	A	1-4	10000	WHATLEY	BENNETT	HAYDON	DICK	WRAGGE	ROBERTS	CHARLESWORTH	WILLIAMS	WHATMORE	CULLEY	LOFTHOUSE	WHATMORE
06/03/26	WATFORD	H	2-1	6000	WHATLEY	BENNETT	HAYDON	DICK	WRAGGE	ROBERTS	GARDNER	WILLIAMS	CULLEY	WHATMORE	LOFTHOUSE	LOFTHOUSE, WILLIAMS
13/03/26	PLYMOUTH ARGYLE	A	2-1	17000	WHATLEY	BENNETT	HAYDON	DICK	WRAGGE	ROBERTS	CHARLESWORTH	WILLIAMS	CULLEY	WHATMORE	LOFTHOUSE	CULLEY 2
20/03/26	BRISTOL CITY	H	0-1	28500	WHATLEY	BENNETT	HAYDON	DICK	WRAGGE	ROBERTS	GARDNER	WILLIAMS	WILCOX	WHATMORE	LOFTHOUSE	
27/03/26	CRYSTAL PALACE	H	3-1	2417	WHATLEY	BENNETT	LENNON	DICK	WRAGGE	ROBERTS	GARDNER	WILLIAMS	CULLEY	WHATMORE	LOFTHOUSE	WHATMORE 2, WILLIAMS
27/03/26	NORTHAMPTON TOWN	A	0-2	7000	WHATLEY	BENNETT	LENNON	DICK	WRAGGE	ROBERTS	GARDNER	WILLIAMS	WILCOX	WHATMORE	LOFTHOUSE	
02/04/26	READING	H	4-2	24000	WHATLEY	BENNETT	HAYDON	ROTHERHAM	WRAGGE	ROBERTS	GARDNER	WILLIAMS	CULLEY	BURNELL	LOFTHOUSE	CULLEY 3-1pen, LOFTHOUSE
03/04/26	MILLWALL	H	0-1	20000	WHATLEY	BENNETT	HAYDON	ROTHERHAM	WRAGGE	ROBERTS	GARDNER	WILLIAMS	CULLEY	BURNELL	LOFTHOUSE	
05/04/26	READING	A	0-3	20000	WHATLEY	BENNETT	HAYDON	ROTHERHAM	WRAGGE	ROBERTS	GARDNER	WILLIAMS	WHATMORE	BURNELL	FOSTER	
06/04/26	CHARLTON ATHLETIC	H	4-1	5000	WHATLEY	BENNETT	HAYDON	ROTHERHAM	WRAGGE	ROBERTS	GARDNER	WILLIAMS	WHATMORE	BURNELL	FOSTER	BURNELL, FOSTER, WHATMORE, WILLIAMS
10/04/26	NORWICH CITY	A	0-1	7000	WHATLEY	BENNETT	HAYDON	ROTHERHAM	WRAGGE	ROBERTS	GARDNER	WILLIAMS	WILCOX	WHATMORE	FOSTER	
17/04/26	SOUTHEND UNITED	H	2-0	5000	WHATLEY	BENNETT	HAYDON	ROTHERHAM	WRAGGE	ROBERTS	GARDNER	WILLIAMS	WILCOX	BURNELL	LOFTHOUSE	LOFTHOUSE, WILLIAMS
24/04/26	BRIGHTON & HOVE ALBION	A	3-2	6059	WHATLEY	BENNETT	HAYDON	ROTHERHAM	WRAGGE	ROBERTS	GARDNER	WILLIAMS	WILCOX	WHATMORE	LOFTHOUSE	GARDNER, WHATMORE, WILCOX
01/05/26	ABERDARE ATHLETIC	H	0-3	5000	WHATLEY	BENNETT	HAYDON	ROTHERHAM	WRAGGE	ROBERTS	GARDNER	WILLIAMS	WILCOX	WHATMORE	LOFTHOUSE	

F A CUP

Date	Opposition		Score	ATT	G	2	3	4	5	6	7	8	9	10	11	GOALSCORERS
28/11/25	ABERDARE ATHLETIC	A	1-4	4000	WHATLEY	ARMITAGE	HAYDON	ROTHERHAM	WILSON	ROBERTS	GARDNER	PHILLIPS	WHATMORE	DUCKERS	LOFTHOUSE	PHILLIPS

GLOUCESTERSHIRE CUP FINAL

Date	Opposition		Score	ATT	G	2	3	4	5	6	7	8	9	10	11	GOALSCORERS
19/04/26	BRISTOL CITY	H	1-4	4123	WHATLEY	BENNETT	HAYDON	ROTHERHAM	WRAGGE	ROBERTS	GARDNER	WILLIAMS	WHATMORE	HOLCROFT	LOFTHOUSE	HOLCROFT

PLAYERS

PLAYERS	APPS	GLS
ARMITAGE H	23	
BENNETT F	14	
BOWERS A	3	
BURNELL A	9	3
CHARLESWORTH G	11	1
CRICHTON A	7	
CULLEY W	8	5
DICK A	19	
DUCKERS S	1	
FOSTER J	3	1
GARDNER J	32	4
GRIFFITHS L	1	
HAYDON J	40	
HEINEMANN C	3	
HOLCROFT S	13	4
JONES R	8	
LENNON G	4	
LOFTHOUSE J	39	9
PHILLIPS W	12	3
ROBERTS T	35	
ROTHERHAM A	13	
STALLARD Ivor	2	
WHATLEY J	42	
WHATMORE E	28	11
WILCOX J	32	19
WILLIAMS T	18	5
WILSON W	24	
WRAGGE F	18	1

One game that typified Rovers' goalscoring potential was the 4-0 home victory over Brighton, where Wilcox and Whatmore scored twice each. Whatmore and Wilcox both scored again when Rovers won the return fixture 3-2, with Brighton's Bill Little scoring twice from the penalty spot. However, there were still sufficient off-days to cause concern. Successive away goalless draws at Bristol City and Millwall in November, on top of one run of eight matches and one of seven without a win, showed work needed to be done. The draw at The Den was played in somewhat sombre circumstances, both sides wearing black armbands as a mark of respect for Alexandra, the Queen Mother and widow of Edward VII, who had died 24 hours earlier.

A series of late-season purchases improved Rovers' lot and seven wins in the final 13 League matches certainly staved off the ignominy of seeking re-election. Two of Culley's former Weymouth team-mates broke into the side. Scotsman George Lennon, an £80 signing from the Southern League side, had previous League experience with Luton Town and Stoke City, while Welsh centre-half Ivor Stallard offered cover for Bill Wilson. Full-back Lew Griffiths was signed for £60 from Mid Rhondda United but it was local 19-year-old Fred Bennett who succeeded Armitage at right-back. Griffiths joined with the highly experienced Tom Williams, whose long career included a dependable two-and-a-half-year stay at Eastville.

As Rovers hovered above the re-election position, Andrew Wilson attempted to rescue his inconsistent side. Inexperienced outside-left Jabez Foster, for instance, was given three games and his goal against Charlton Athletic was greeted with genuinely warm enthusiasm. Yet only 5,000 watched this game at Eastville, poor in comparison with the 28,500 that had seen Tot Walsh's 82nd-minute penalty, awarded after Wragge had brought down Charlie Sutherland, earn Bristol City victory only two weeks earlier. When the season finished with Rovers safe by a point, Wilson resigned. He subsequently became manager at Oldham Athletic and Stockport County.

Rovers took little time in appointing Bradford Park Avenue's trainer Joe Palmer on 21 April 1926 as the new manager. Although a Yorkshireman, Palmer was the first man to manage both Bristol's professional clubs. He was a strong disciplinarian and placed great emphasis on physical fitness. During his three years with Bristol City, the Robins had reached the semi-finals of the FA Cup in 1920 and he had been immensely popular with the Ashton Gate crowd. The close season of 1926 saw the release of 15 players who had appeared in League action for Rovers – 10 to League clubs north or south of the border and five to senior non-League sides. Queen's Park Rangers, for instance, signed Bowers, Charlesworth, Lofthouse and Wilcox free of charge. The new season was to see a fresh start.

Once again, cup competitions had brought little cheer to Eastville. Rovers crashed 4-1 to Bristol City in the Gloucestershire Cup final and by the same score to Aberdare Athletic in the FA Cup. This heavy defeat at the Athletic Ground was brought about by two former Portsmouth players, the veteran Jack Harwood scoring the first goal before Harry Burnham compiled a well-taken 15-minute hat-trick in the second half.

It was a busy summer for Joe Palmer, as he constructed a new-look Bristol Rovers side. Four new half-backs and five forwards were signed in the close season, leaving just the defensive line retaining its familiar look. The key element in Rovers' ongoing progress, ever-reliable goalkeeper Jesse Whatley, was once again the club's only ever-present. In front of him, Fred Bennett and Jimmy Haydon formed a consistent full-back pairing. Of the old guard elsewhere on the pitch, however, only Tom Roberts, Tom Williams and Ernie Whatmore made any sizeable impact.

One familiar face in the side was Steve Sims, Rovers' captain in their first League season. His return from Bristol City was a popular one and his winning goal at Bournemouth in

October was his first for the club in more than four years. Left-half Len Smith had experienced League action with Leeds United, while a combined total of £750 bought Coventry City's Joe Rowley and 30-year-old Jimmy Forbes from Bolton Wanderers. Age was certainly no barrier, for Palmer signed two 37-year-old forwards in Stoke's Joe Clennell and the former Welsh International Jack Evans from Cardiff City. Thirty-three-year-old George Douglas from Oldham Athletic cost £100 as did Clennell. Halifax Town's Tommy Duncan, Merthyr Town's Jack Rumney and outside-left Joe Barrett, who joined from Lincoln City in an exchange deal involving Harry Armitage, could all boast considerable League experience. By the end of the season, Rovers' regular forward line of Clennell and Evans (both 38), Bill Culley (34), Douglas (33) and Duncan, a mere youth at 29, could boast a combined age of 172.

Recent changes in the offside law were slowly leading to a far higher rate of goals. Rovers scored and conceded more goals, in finishing the season mid-table, than in any previous season in the Football League. While scoring at least once in 16 out of 21 away League fixtures, Rovers also scored reliably at home. The 2-0 home defeat against Watford in December was the last time Rovers failed to score in a match at

Rovers appointed Joe Palmer as manager in 1926 to replace Andrew Wilson, after his five years at the club

141

Bristol Rovers 1926/27. Back row: Bennett, McGloughlin, Whatley, Densley, Haydon, Ashford. Second row: Douglas, Milsom, Rowley, Jordan, Dick, Sims, Smith, Duncan, Evans. Front row: J Palmer (Manager), Barratt, Holcroft, Culley, Whatmore, Rumney, Williams, B Williams (Asst Trainer). On Ground: Rotherham, Roberts

Eastville in any competition until February 1928. Culley's 26 goals in only 31 League appearances included three hat-tricks, while Williams and Whatmore each scored three times in a game.

Culley scored his first hat-trick of the season in a 5-2 home victory over Northampton Town in February, Joe Clennell claiming the other two. In Rovers' next home fixture, the Scottish forward went one better, scoring all the club's goals in a convincing 4-1 win against Queen's Park Rangers. In doing so, Culley equalled the Rovers individual goalscoring record, held by Sid Leigh and Jonah Wilcox, of four goals in a League fixture. On Good Friday, with the aid of a penalty, his third hat-trick of the season helped Rovers to a 5-3 win at Swindon Town, for whom 16-year-old forward Charlie Jeffries scored twice in a four-minute spell before half-time. A brace of goals in the return game three days later meant Culley became the first of six Rovers players to score five League goals against any particular club in a season.

Ably supporting Culley were 14-goal Williams and 11-goal Whatmore. Williams' greatest game for Rovers was the visit to Millwall in October when, recalled to the side, he scored his first three goals of the season to give the Lilywhites a 3-2 win. This was the first time a Rovers player had scored a hat-trick in an away League game and one of only four such cases prior to 1953. Whatmore narrowly missed out on a hat-trick at Plymouth Argyle in March, before scoring one in the final home game of the season. At Home Park, having scored twice, he ended up in goal with Jesse Whatley off injured. Rovers lost 3-2. A first-half hat-trick against Crystal Palace, the first one deflecting in off Henry Hopkins, helped the side to score four goals before half-time in both League fixtures against the London side. Rovers scored three times in a six-minute spell in the home fixture.

Yet, there were also heavy defeats. Rovers lost 5-0 at Eastville against Bristol City, a devastating result from a psychological point of view. City were to be Third Division (South) champions that season. Conceding two penalties at Brighton for a second consecutive season, Rovers lost 7-0 at the Goldstone Ground. On his sole League appearance, James Kedens, a miner's son from the Ayrshire pit village of Glenburn, almost put Rovers ahead in the opening seconds, but Paul Mooney scored from one of the penalties, after Bill Little had missed the first, James Hopkins compiled a hat-trick and there was a goal for the future Rovers forward Tommy Cook.

The 3-0 defeat at Northampton Town in September saw the Cobblers field the 38-year-old former Spurs outside-right 'Fanny' Walden. At 5ft 2½in, Frederick Ingram Walden remains the fourth shortest opponent to face Rovers in League football. He played football for England and, after 20 summers of cricket with Northamptonshire, was umpire in 11 Test Matches between 1934 and 1939. Rovers also crashed 2-0 at Gillingham in March. In severe wind and rain, both sides agreed to forfeit their half-time break and play on. The Gills, who recalled Jabez Foster, briefly a member of Rovers' League side at the tail end of the previous season, won with two Bill Arblaster goals, the second deflecting in off the luckless Jimmy Haydon.

The season's most bizarre result was from the visit to Crystal Palace in March. Rovers had rushed into a 3-0 lead inside 17 minutes, with Culley scoring after only six minutes and Rowley four minutes later before Williams had given the visitors an apparently unassailable lead. However, Palace retaliated with two quick goals, the future Bristol City striker Cyril Blakemore making the score 3-2 with still only 25 minutes played. Culley's second goal of the game gave Rovers a 4-2 half-time lead, before Palace responded with five goals to win an extraordinary game 7-4. The scores were level within seven minutes of the restart and Percy Cherrett scored a second-half hat-trick, completing the scoring in the final minute to give the home side an emphatic victory.

Rovers missed two penalties – taken by Barratt, who always played with a straw in his mouth, and Douglas in the home games with Watford and Northampton Town respectively. On the other hand, four penalties conceded by Rovers were taken by players called Brown. The first, in August, was saved from Henry Brown by Whatley at Penydarren Park, but Rovers, 2-0 ahead at one stage, slipped to a 3-2 defeat, with George Pither scoring Merthyr's second against his former club. Both Rovers' goals were scored by Jack Rumney, making his club debut against his former side. Then there were three penalties in four days over the Easter period. Alfred Brown of Swindon Town scored one on Good Friday but missed one on Easter Monday, while the penalty converted by Gillingham's Fred Brown on Easter Saturday following his hat-trick the previous season served merely as a consolation goal, as Rovers won 2-1.

The 78 League goals Rovers scored featured five on three occasions and four on five others. 4-0 home victories were recorded over two Welsh opponents. Aberdare Athletic were comfortably defeated in November, Whatmore scoring twice. Newport County were also victims of a heavy defeat, with Tom Williams scoring two of the four goals, one within seconds of the re-start after half-time. Culley's kick-off reached Douglas, also a goalscorer, whose through pass was smashed into the goal by Williams. Culley scored a brilliant winner, 10 minutes from time as Rovers clawed back a two-goal deficit to defeat FA Cup holders Sheffield United 3-2 in an Eastville friendly in February.

FOOTBALL LEAGUE DIVISION THREE (SOUTH)

SEASON 1926/27

Date	Opponent	H/A	Score	ATT	G	2	3	4	5	6	7	8	9	10	11	GOALSCORERS
28/08/26	LUTON TOWN	H	1-2	14000	WHATLEY	BENNETT	HAYDON	ROWLEY	FORBES	SMITH	BARRATT	WILLIAMS	WHATMORE	CLENNELL	EVANS	WHATMORE
30/08/26	MERTHYR TOWN	A	2-3	5000	WHATLEY	BENNETT	HAYDON	ROWLEY	FORBES	SMITH	BARRATT	RUMNEY	WHATMORE	CLENNELL	EVANS	RUMNEY 2
04/09/26	NORWICH CITY	A	0-2	8000	WHATLEY	BENNETT	HAYDON	ROWLEY	SIMS	SMITH	DOUGLAS	RUMNEY	CULLEY	CLENNELL	EVANS	
06/09/26	MERTHYR TOWN	H	2-1	6000	WHATLEY	BENNETT	HAYDON	ROWLEY	SIMS	SMITH	DOUGLAS	DUNCAN	CULLEY	CLENNELL	EVANS	DUNCAN, EVANS pen
11/09/26	BRIGHTON & HOVE ALBION	H	0-0	9390	WHATLEY	BENNETT	HAYDON	ROWLEY	SIMS	SMITH	DOUGLAS	DUNCAN	CULLEY	CLENNELL	EVANS	
15/09/26	EXETER CITY	A	1-1	6000	WHATLEY	BENNETT	HAYDON	ROWLEY	SMITH	ROBERTS	DOUGLAS	DUNCAN	CULLEY	CLENNELL	EVANS	CULLEY W
18/09/26	NORTHAMPTON TOWN	H	0-3	6318	WHATLEY	BENNETT	HAYDON	ROWLEY	SIMS	SMITH	DOUGLAS	DUNCAN	CULLEY	CLENNELL	EVANS	
25/09/26	BRENTFORD	A	1-3	8000	WHATLEY	BENNETT	HAYDON	ROWLEY	SIMS	SMITH	DOUGLAS	DUNCAN	CULLEY	CLENNELL	EVANS	DOUGLAS G
02/10/26	MILLWALL	H	3-2	20000	WHATLEY	BENNETT	HAYDON	ROWLEY	SIMS	SMITH	BARRATT	DOUGLAS	CULLEY	CLENNELL	EVANS	BARRATT 2 -1 pen, SIMS
09/10/26	BRISTOL CITY	A	0-5	28731	WHATLEY	BENNETT	HAYDON	ROWLEY	SIMS	SMITH	BARRATT	DOUGLAS	CULLEY	CLENNELL	EVANS	
16/10/26	QUEENS PARK RANGERS	H	2-2	7000	WHATLEY	BENNETT	HAYDON	ROWLEY	SIMS	SMITH	DOUGLAS	RUMNEY	CULLEY	CLENNELL	EVANS	BARRATT, EVANS, FORBES
23/10/26	CHARLTON ATHLETIC	A	1-1	6000	WHATLEY	BENNETT	HAYDON	ROWLEY	SIMS	SMITH	DOUGLAS	RUMNEY	CULLEY	CLENNELL	EVANS	FORBES
30/10/26	BOURNEMOUTH	H	1-0	7000	WHATLEY	BENNETT	HAYDON	ROWLEY	SIMS	SMITH	DOUGLAS	WILLIAMS	CULLEY	WHATMORE	EVANS	ROBERTS T
06/11/26	PLYMOUTH ARGYLE	A	2-2	9000	WHATLEY	BENNETT	HAYDON	ROWLEY	SIMS	SMITH	DOUGLAS	WILLIAMS	CULLEY	WHATMORE	EVANS	CULLEY, CLENNELL
13/11/26	NEWPORT COUNTY	H	0-1	6000	WHATLEY	ASHFORD	HAYDON	ROWLEY	SIMS	SMITH	DOUGLAS	WILLIAMS	CULLEY	WHATMORE	EVANS	
20/11/26	ABERDARE ATHLETIC	A	4-0	5000	WHATLEY	ASHFORD	HAYDON	ROWLEY	SIMS	SMITH	BARRATT	WILLIAMS	CULLEY	WHATMORE	EVANS	CULLEY 4
04/12/26	WATFORD	H	0-2	6000	WHATLEY	ASHFORD	HAYDON	ROWLEY	FORBES	SMITH	BARRATT	WILLIAMS	CULLEY	WHATMORE	EVANS	
18/12/26	COVENTRY CITY	A	1-2	6000	WHATLEY	ASHFORD	HAYDON	ROWLEY	FORBES	SMITH	BARRATT	WILLIAMS	CULLEY	WHATMORE	EVANS	CULLEY
25/12/26	SOUTHEND UNITED	H	5-1	4000	WHATLEY	ASHFORD	HAYDON	ROWLEY	FORBES	SMITH	BARRATT	WILLIAMS	CULLEY	WHATMORE	EVANS	CULLEY 2, BARRATT, EVANS, FORBES
27/12/26	SOUTHEND UNITED	A	1-2	11991	WHATLEY	ASHFORD	ROTHERHAM	ROWLEY	FORBES	SMITH	BARRATT	WILLIAMS	CULLEY	WHATMORE	EVANS	DUNCAN
28/12/26	EXETER CITY	H	3-1	10000	WHATLEY	ASHFORD	HAYDON	ROWLEY	FORBES	SMITH	BARRATT	WILLIAMS	CULLEY	WHATMORE	EVANS	CULLEY 2, EVANS
15/01/27	NORWICH CITY	H	1-1	5000	WHATLEY	ASHFORD	HAYDON	ROWLEY	FORBES	SMITH	DOUGLAS	WILLIAMS	CULLEY	CLENNELL	EVANS	CULLEY
22/01/27	BRIGHTON & HOVE ALBION	A	1-0	5000	WHATLEY	ASHFORD	HAYDON	ROWLEY	FORBES	ROBERTS	DOUGLAS	WILLIAMS	CULLEY	CLENNELL	EVANS	CLENNELL
29/01/27	NORTHAMPTON TOWN	H	7-2	7472	WHATLEY	BENNETT	HAYDON	ROWLEY	FORBES	ROBERTS	DOUGLAS	WILLIAMS	CULLEY	CLENNELL	EVANS	CULLEY 3, CLENNELL 2
05/02/27	BRENTFORD	H	5-2	4000	WHATLEY	BENNETT	HAYDON	ROWLEY	FORBES	ROBERTS	DOUGLAS	WILLIAMS	CULLEY	CLENNELL	KEDENS	CULLEY 2, BARRATT, EVANS
12/02/27	BRISTOL CITY	A	2-0	10000	WHATLEY	BENNETT	HAYDON	ROWLEY	FORBES	ROBERTS	DOUGLAS	WILLIAMS	CULLEY	WHATMORE	EVANS	WHATMORE 2
26/02/27	QUEENS PARK RANGERS	A	1-3	28696	WHATLEY	BENNETT	HAYDON	ROWLEY	FORBES	ROBERTS	DOUGLAS	WILLIAMS	CULLEY	WHATMORE	EVANS	CULLEY
05/03/27	CHARLTON ATHLETIC	H	4-1	5000	WHATLEY	BENNETT	HAYDON	ROWLEY	FORBES	ROBERTS	DOUGLAS	WILLIAMS	CULLEY	CLENNELL	EVANS	CULLEY 3-1 pen, EVANS
12/03/27	CRYSTAL PALACE	A	0-7	5347	WHATLEY	ASHFORD	HAYDON	ROWLEY	FORBES	ROBERTS	DOUGLAS	WILLIAMS	CULLEY	CLENNELL	EVANS	
16/03/27	NORTHAMPTON TOWN	A	4-7	5000	WHATLEY	ASHFORD	HAYDON	ROWLEY	FORBES	ROBERTS	DOUGLAS	WILLIAMS	CULLEY	CLENNELL	EVANS	CULLEY 2, WILLIAMS
19/03/27	BOURNEMOUTH	H	2-1	2500	WHATLEY	BENNETT	HAYDON	ROWLEY	FORBES	ROBERTS	DOUGLAS	WILLIAMS	CULLEY	WHATMORE	EVANS	CULLEY 2, ROWLEY, WILLIAMS
23/03/27	GILLINGHAM	A	0-2	5000	WHATLEY	BENNETT	HAYDON	ROWLEY	FORBES	ROBERTS	DOUGLAS	WILLIAMS	CULLEY	WHATMORE	EVANS	
26/03/27	PLYMOUTH ARGYLE	A	7-0	7000	WHATLEY	BENNETT	HAYDON	ROWLEY	FORBES	ROBERTS	DOUGLAS	WILLIAMS	CULLEY	WHATMORE	EVANS	DOUGLAS 2, WILLIAMS
02/04/27	NEWPORT COUNTY	H	6-0	6000	WHATLEY	BENNETT	HAYDON	ROWLEY	FORBES	ROBERTS	DOUGLAS	WILLIAMS	CULLEY	WHATMORE	EVANS	WILLIAMS 2, DOUGLAS, EVANS
09/04/27	ABERDARE ATHLETIC	H	1-2	2000	WHATLEY	BENNETT	HAYDON	ROWLEY	FORBES	ROBERTS	DOUGLAS	WILLIAMS	WHATMORE	CLENNELL	EVANS	WHATMORE 2
15/04/27	SWINDON TOWN	A	5-3	10000	WHATLEY	BENNETT	HAYDON	ROWLEY	FORBES	ROBERTS	DOUGLAS	WILLIAMS	CULLEY	WHATMORE	EVANS	CULLEY 2, DOUGLAS, EVANS
16/04/27	GILLINGHAM	H	2-1	9000	WHATLEY	BENNETT	HAYDON	ROWLEY	SIMS	ROBERTS	DOUGLAS	WILLIAMS	CULLEY	WHATMORE	EVANS	CULLEY 2
18/04/27	SWINDON TOWN	H	3-1	12000	WHATLEY	BENNETT	HAYDON	ROWLEY	FORBES	ROBERTS	DOUGLAS	WILLIAMS	CULLEY	WHATMORE	EVANS	CULLEY 2, WILLIAMS
19/04/27	MILLWALL	H	2-1	10000	WHATLEY	BENNETT	HAYDON	ROWLEY	FORBES	ROBERTS	DOUGLAS	WILLIAMS	CULLEY	WHATMORE	WILLIAMS	CULLEY, WHATMORE
23/04/27	WATFORD	H	3-3	4447	WHATLEY	BENNETT	HAYDON	ROWLEY	FORBES	ROBERTS	DOUGLAS	WILLIAMS	CULLEY	WHATMORE	WILLIAMS	WHATMORE 3, CULLEY
30/04/27	CRYSTAL PALACE	H	4-1	5905	WHATLEY	BENNETT	HAYDON	ROWLEY	FORBES	ROBERTS	DOUGLAS	WILLIAMS	CULLEY	WHATMORE	WILLIAMS	CULLEY, WHATMORE, WILLIAMS
07/05/27	COVENTRY CITY	A	2-2	10000	WHATLEY	BENNETT	HAYDON	ROWLEY	SIMS	ROBERTS	DOUGLAS	WILLIAMS	CULLEY	WHATMORE	WILLIAMS	WHATMORE, WILLIAMS

FA CUP

Date	Opponent	H/A	Score	ATT	G	2	3	4	5	6	7	8	9	10	11	GOALSCORERS
27/11/26	TORQUAY UNITED	A	1-1	4218	WHATLEY	ASHFORD	HAYDON	ROWLEY	FORBES	SMITH	BARRATT	WILLIAMS	CULLEY	WHATMORE	EVANS	BARRATT
01/12/26	TORQUAY UNITED	H	1-0	5000	WHATLEY	ASHFORD	HAYDON	ROWLEY	FORBES	SMITH	BARRATT	WILLIAMS	CULLEY	WHATMORE	EVANS	WILLIAMS
11/12/26	CHARLTON ATHLETIC	A	4-1	8000	WHATLEY	ASHFORD	HAYDON	ROWLEY	FORBES	SMITH	DUNCAN	WILLIAMS	CULLEY	WHATMORE	EVANS	CULLEY 2, BARRATT, EVANS
08/01/27	PORTSMOUTH	H	3-3	25000	WHATLEY	ASHFORD	HAYDON	ROWLEY	FORBES	SMITH	DOUGLAS	WILLIAMS	CULLEY	WHATMORE	EVANS	CULLEY 3-1 pen, EVANS, WILLIAMS
12/01/27	PORTSMOUTH	A	0-4	20693	WHATLEY	ASHFORD	HAYDON	ROWLEY	FORBES	SMITH	DOUGLAS	WILLIAMS	CULLEY	WHATMORE	EVANS	

GLOUCESTERSHIRE CUP FINAL

Date	Opponent	H/A	Score	ATT	G	2	3	4	5	6	7	8	9	10	11	GOALSCORERS
01/01/27	BRISTOL CITY	A	0-4	9601	WHATLEY	ROTHERHAM	HAYDON	ROWLEY	FORBES	SMITH	DOUGLAS	BARRATT	CULLEY	CLENNELL	EVANS	

APPEARANCES

PLAYERS	APP	GLS
ASHFORD J	12	
BARRATT I	21	4
BENNETT F	32	
CLENNELL J	19	5
CULLEY W	31	26
DOUGLAS G	25	3
DUNCAN T	13	2
EVANS J	39	6
FORBES J	28	1
HAYDON J	37	
HOLCROFT S	1	
KEDENS J	1	
ROBERTS T	24	1
ROTHERHAM A	3	
ROWLEY J	42	
RUMNEY J	4	2
SIMS S	13	1
SMITH L	21	1
WHATLEY	42	
WHATMORE E	11	11
WILLIAMS T	27	14

The Gloucestershire Cup final was lost 4-0, Tot Walsh scoring twice, once from a penalty, exactly as he had done for Bristol City in the League meeting at Eastville. The FA Cup saw Rovers grab a draw at Plainmoor when Barratt equalised three minutes from time. They finally defeated non-League Torquay United, unbeaten in their previous 12 home games, in an untidy first-round replay, thanks to Williams' goal a minute before half-time. Torquay, who fielded the former Rovers outside-left Jack Pattison and future Rovers centre-half Ivor Perry, missed a penalty, given against Ashford for handball. Whatley saved Harry Hughes' spot-kick. A 5,000 crowd, which brought in takings of £308, saw the Gulls' Harold Andrews sent off 15 minutes from time. Culley scored twice past the future Rovers goalkeeper Charles Preedy in a 4-1 win over Charlton Athletic and twice more as Rovers led Division One Portsmouth 3-1 with minutes to go. The 25,000 Eastville crowd was denied a momentous victory, however, as Pompey recovered to draw 3-3 and win the replay, with Billy Haines and David Watson scoring in both matches. The future Rovers wing-half Sam Irving was a member of the Cardiff City side that beat Arsenal in an historic 1927 FA Cup final.

Rovers were also successful in the Allan Palmer Cup, an invitation competition first staged in 1924. It was set up by Brigadier-General George Llewellen Palmer, formerly MP for Westbury, Wiltshire, and his wife Louie Madeleine Gouldsmith, in memory of their son, a Captain in the 14th Hussars, who was killed at Amiens on 15 November 1916. Joe Clennell's goal brought victory over holders Bristol City and the right to defend the trophy 12 months later.

1927/28

Palmer's second season as Bristol Rovers manager saw the side plummet to 19th in Division Three (South). Successful runs over Christmas and Easter were enough to keep the club above water, but it was nonetheless a poor season. Rovers conceded a then-club-record 93 League goals, a figure only ever surpassed in the 1935/36 season. It was only in the relegation season of 1980/81 that Rovers equalled the 24 league defeats suffered this year. While the small tally of only four draws in 1927/28 remains a seasonal lowest for Rovers, 14 League victories was a commendable total.

The side that defeated Walsall 5-2 on an encouraging opening day at Eastville, with Bill Culley contributing a cameo hat-trick, contained no new faces to Rovers fans. However, a couple of defeats prompted the introduction of several summer signings. Outside right Syd Homer was

On 3 March 1928 Ronnie Dix, the 15-year-old England schoolboy International, became the youngest ever League goalscorer when he scored for Rovers against Norwich City

Bristol Rovers 1927/28. Back row: McKenna, Bennett, Whatley, Densley, Haydon, Rotherham. Second row: Dix, Rowley, Mason, Perry, Forbes, Smith, Roberts, B Williams (Asst Trainer), J Palmer (Manager). Front row: Douglas, Homer, Thom, Williams, Culley, Ormston, Whatmore, Russell, Davies, Evans

to serve Rovers well until November 1929 and Bristol City better thereafter. Full-back Jack Russell had represented Birmingham City in League football and had recently recovered from almost a year out of the game with a fractured leg. Jack Thom, who cost £175 from Leeds United, Ivor Perry, Reg Trotman and Roy Davies all had roles to play. Of the previous season's side, Joe Clennell joined Rochdale, Steve Sims moved to Newport County and Joe Barratt dropped out of League football to sign for Nuneaton Town. Inside-forward Syd Holcroft, who also moved into non-League football, was to die in the spring of 1934 at the age of 32. Club chairman George Humphreys retired in August 1927 and was elected President, a post he held until his death in 1939.

Perhaps it was an omen that, in the pre-season trial match on 13 August, the innovative concept of playing with a white football backfired as the paint gradually peeled off. Rovers went on to concede four or more League goals in a game on 10 occasions. Four different opponents scored at Brentford, who won 5-1, and at Brighton, where a 5-0 scoreline included two goals for the future Rovers centre-forward Tommy Cook. Frank Sloan scored a hat-trick in a 4-1 defeat at Plymouth Argyle, the first of three opponents to do so in ten weeks. The *Western Daily Press* reporter at the home defeat at the hands of Brentford in September recorded that 'it was Bristol Rovers weather last evening – that is, it was raining'. The worst defeat, however, was 6-1 on Christmas Eve at home to Millwall who, in registering what remains their record away victory in the League, were on their way to 127 Third Division (South) goals for the season. Wilkie Phillips returned to his old club to score twice, while Perry conceded an own goal.

March 1928. Construction of the Greyhound Track started

At St James' Park on Guy Fawkes' Day, Fred Dent equalled the achievement of Swansea Town's Jimmy Collins by scoring all Exeter City's goals in Rovers' 4-1 defeat. Dent scored after six and 12 minutes and, although Tom Williams pulled a goal back eight minutes later, the former Bristol City forward completed a first-half hat-trick 10 minutes before the break. Just nine minutes from time he completed the Grecians' scoring. On the same day, Rovers reserves had led their Exeter counterparts at half-time through a Roy Davies goal, only to lose 5-1. Culley missed a penalty, before he and Albert Rotherham both conceded own goals. The following Saturday, Rovers recovered to draw 2-2 with Northampton Town, who had beaten Walsall 10-0 seven days earlier. Gillingham, with a quick three-goal burst, and Queen's Park Rangers, with Jonah Wilcox scoring from a Jimmy Lofthouse cross (shades of 1925/26) both scored four at Eastville.

In October, the month that pre-war club favourite Alf Jasper Geddes died, Rovers conceded four goals at both Queen's Park Rangers and Norwich City. The Canaries had led 3-2 by half-time. The Rangers game, in which George Goddard scored a hat-trick, marked the debut of new £350 signing Arthur Ormston. This much-travelled centre-forward had attained almost legendary status at Boundary Park after scoring 8 goals in his first 2 appearances for Oldham Athletic. He was to finish the season as Rovers' top scorer with 15 League goals. Ormston scored twice in a tempestuous home debut, where Rovers had built up a seemingly unassailable 4-1 lead, with Williams and Russell scoring for the home side and inside-right Maurice Wellock replying for Torquay United. However, the final 20 minutes were chaotic, with several bookings and an official admonishment for the crowd. One particularly bad tackle earned Rovers a penalty,

FOOTBALL LEAGUE DIVISION THREE (SOUTH)

SEASON 1927/28

Date	Opposition	V		ATT	G	2	3	4	5	6	7	8	9	10	11	GOALSCORERS
27/08/27	WALSALL	H	5-2	11899	WHATLEY	BENNETT	BENNETT	FORBES	PERRY	SMITH	DOUGLAS	WILLIAMS	CULLEY	WHATMORE	EVANS	CULLEY 3, DOUGLAS,
31/08/27	PLYMOUTH ARGYLE	A	1-4	10084	WHATLEY	BENNETT	HAYDON	ROWLEY	FORBES	SMITH	DOUGLAS	WILLIAMS	CULLEY	WHATMORE	EVANS	WHATMORE
03/09/27	GILLINGHAM	A	1-3	8000	WHATLEY	BENNETT	HAYDON	ROWLEY	FORBES	SMITH	DOUGLAS	WILLIAMS	CULLEY	WHATMORE	EVANS	DAVIES R
07/09/27	PLYMOUTH ARGYLE	H	3-1	9013	WHATLEY	BENNETT	HAYDON	ROWLEY	FORBES	SMITH	HOMER	WILLIAMS	CULLEY	WHATMORE	DENSLEY H	HOMER, FORBES, RUSSELL
10/09/27	COVENTRY CITY	H	1-1	10000	WHATLEY	BENNETT	HAYDON	ROWLEY	FORBES	SMITH	HOMER	WHATMORE	CULLEY	WILLIAMS	DIX R	DIX R
14/09/27	BRENTFORD	A	1-3	3000	WHATLEY	BENNETT	HAYDON	ROWLEY	FORBES	SMITH	HOMER	WHATMORE	CULLEY	HOMER	DIX R	DOUGLAS G
17/09/27	NEWPORT COUNTY	H	1-3	8000	WHATLEY	BENNETT	HAYDON	ROWLEY	FORBES	SMITH	HOMER	WHATMORE	CULLEY	WHATMORE	EVANS	EVANS J
01/10/27	QUEENS PARK RANGERS	A	2-4	8000	WHATLEY	BENNETT	HAYDON	ROWLEY	FORBES	ROBERTS	HOMER	WHATMORE	CULLEY	WHATMORE	EVANS	WHATMORE
08/10/27	WATFORD	H	3-1	2000	WHATLEY	BENNETT	HAYDON	ROWLEY	FORBES	ROBERTS	HOMER	WHATMORE	CULLEY	WHATMORE	EVANS	CULLEY 2, ORMSTON
15/10/27	CHARLTON ATHLETIC	A	1-2	12000	WHATLEY	BENNETT	HAYDON	ROWLEY	FORBES	ROBERTS	HOMER	WILLIAMS	CULLEY	RUSSELL	EVANS	RUSSELL, pen
22/10/27	NORWICH CITY	A	2-4	8000	WHATLEY	BENNETT	HAYDON	ROWLEY	PERRY	ROBERTS	HOMER	WILLIAMS	ORMSTON	RUSSELL	EVANS	FORBES, ORMSTON
29/10/27	TORQUAY UNITED	H	5-1	6824	McKENNA	BENNETT	BENNETT	ROWLEY	FORBES	ROBERTS	DOUGLAS	WILLIAMS	ORMSTON	RUSSELL	EVANS	RUSSELL 2, 1 pen,
05/11/27	EXETER CITY	A	1-4	6000	WHATLEY	BENNETT	HAYDON	WILLIAMS	FORBES	SMITH	HOMER	WILLIAMS	ORMSTON	THOM	RUSSELL	ORMSTON A
12/11/27	NORTHAMPTON TOWN	H	2-2	8000	WHATLEY	BENNETT	HAYDON	WILLIAMS	FORBES	SMITH	HOMER	TROTMAN	ORMSTON	WHATMORE	RUSSELL	WILLIAMS
19/11/27	SOUTHEND UNITED	A	1-2	4421	WHATLEY	McKENNA	HAYDON	ROWLEY	PERRY	SMITH	DOUGLAS	PATERSON	CULLEY	RUSSELL	RUSSELL	ROBERTS T
03/12/27	BOURNEMOUTH	A	3-4	6000	WHATLEY	McKENNA	HAYDON	ROWLEY	FORBES	SMITH	HOMER	PATERSON	CULLEY	RUSSELL	RUSSELL	ROTHERHAM A
17/12/27	LUTON TOWN	H	0-2	6000	WHATLEY	McKENNA	HAYDON	ROTHERHAM	PERRY	SMITH	HOMER	PATERSON	CULLEY	WHATMORE	EVANS	ROWLEY J
24/12/27	MILLWALL	H	1-6	8000	WHATLEY	BENNETT	HAYDON	ROTHERHAM	PERRY	ROBERTS	HOMER	WILLIAMS	CULLEY	WHATMORE	EVANS	CULLEY 2, EVANS
26/12/27	MERTHYR TOWN	A	3-2	1000	WHATLEY	BENNETT	HAYDON	ROTHERHAM	PERRY	ROBERTS	DOUGLAS	WILLIAMS	CULLEY	WHATMORE	EVANS	SMITH L
27/12/27	MERTHYR TOWN	H	2-1	4000	WHATLEY	BENNETT	HAYDON	ROTHERHAM	FORBES	SMITH	DOUGLAS	THOM	CULLEY	RUSSELL	EVANS	CULLEY
31/12/27	WALSALL	A	2-1	4000	WHATLEY	BENNETT	HAYDON	WILLIAMS	FORBES	SMITH	DOUGLAS	THOM	ORMSTON	RUSSELL	EVANS	FORBES, RUSSELL, THOM
07/01/28	GILLINGHAM	H	2-4	5000	WHATLEY	BENNETT	HAYDON	WILLIAMS	FORBES	ROBERTS	DOUGLAS	THOM	ORMSTON	RUSSELL	EVANS	ORMSTON, RUSSELL
21/01/28	COVENTRY CITY	A	3-2	10000	WHATLEY	BENNETT	HAYDON	WILLIAMS	FORBES	ROBERTS	HOMER	THOM	ORMSTON	RUSSELL	WILLIAMS	THOM, WILLIAMS,
28/01/28	NEWPORT COUNTY	A	2-1	5000	WHATLEY	BENNETT	HAYDON	WILLIAMS	FORBES	ROBERTS	HOMER	ORMSTON	THOM	WHATMORE	RUSSELL	FORBES, ORMSTON
04/02/28	SWINDON TOWN	H	1-2	5500	WHATLEY	BENNETT	HAYDON	WILLIAMS	FORBES	ROBERTS	HOMER	ORMSTON	ORMSTON	WHATMORE	RUSSELL	ORMSTON
11/02/28	QUEENS PARK RANGERS	H	0-4	7000	WHATLEY	BENNETT	HAYDON	WILLIAMS	FORBES	SMITH	HOMER	PATERSON	ORMSTON	RUSSELL	RUSSELL	
18/02/28	WATFORD	A	1-2	7246	WHATLEY	BENNETT	HAYDON	ROTHERHAM	FORBES	SMITH	HOMER	PATERSON	ORMSTON	WHATMORE	RUSSELL	ORMSTON
25/02/28	CHARLTON ATHLETIC	H	2-1	8000	WHATLEY	BENNETT	HAYDON	ROTHERHAM	FORBES	SMITH	HOMER	WILLIAMS	ORMSTON	WHATMORE	EVANS	ORMSTON 2
03/03/28	NORWICH CITY	A	3-0	7000	WHATLEY	BENNETT	HAYDON	ROTHERHAM	PERRY	SMITH	HOMER	WILLIAMS	ORMSTON	WHATMORE	EVANS	ORMSTON 2,
10/03/28	TORQUAY UNITED	A	0-0	4018	WHATLEY	BENNETT	HAYDON	ROTHERHAM	PERRY	SMITH	HOMER	WILLIAMS	ORMSTON	DIX	DOUGLAS	
17/03/28	EXETER CITY	H	1-2	8000	WHATLEY	BENNETT	HAYDON	ROTHERHAM	PERRY	ROBERTS	HOMER	WILLIAMS	ORMSTON	DIX	EVANS	DIX, ORMSTON, WILLIAMS
24/03/28	NORTHAMPTON TOWN	A	0-2	9770	WHATLEY	BENNETT	HAYDON	ROWLEY	FORBES	ROBERTS	HOMER	WILLIAMS	ORMSTON	WHATMORE	RUSSELL	
31/03/28	SOUTHEND UNITED	H	1-3	8000	WHATLEY	BENNETT	HAYDON	WILLIAMS	FORBES	ROBERTS	HOMER	WILLIAMS	ORMSTON	WHATMORE	KING	WILLIAMS pen
06/04/28	CRYSTAL PALACE	A	2-3	16126	WHATLEY	BENNETT	HAYDON	McKENNA	FORBES	ROWLEY	HOMER	WILLIAMS	ORMSTON	THOM	RUSSELL	WHATMORE
07/04/28	BRENTFORD	H	1-5	12000	WHATLEY	BENNETT	HAYDON	McKENNA	FORBES	McKENNA	HOMER	WILLIAMS	CULLEY	WHATMORE	KING	CULLEY/PATERSON
09/04/28	CRYSTAL PALACE	H	1-1	6275	WHATLEY	BENNETT	ROTHERHAM	WILLIAMS	FALCONER	ROBERTS	DOUGLAS	PATERSON	CULLEY	WHATMORE	EVANS,	THOM
14/04/28	BOURNEMOUTH	H	3-0	6000	WHATLEY	BENNETT	ROTHERHAM	DENSLEY	FORBES	FALCONER	HOMER	PATERSON	CULLEY	THOM	WHATMORE	WHATMORE
18/04/28	SWINDON TOWN	A	1-0	5445	WHATLEY	BENNETT	BENNETT	DENSLEY	FORBES	FALCONER	HOMER	PATERSON	CULLEY	WHATMORE	KING	HOMER 2, ROBERTS
21/04/28	BRIGHTON & HOVE ALBION	A	0-5	4118	WHATLEY	BENNETT	HAYDON	DENSLEY	PERRY	FALCONER	HOMER	PATERSON	CULLEY	WHATMORE	DAVIES	ROBERTS
23/04/28	BRIGHTON & HOVE ALBION	H	1-0	4155	WHATLEY	BENNETT	HAYDON	FORBES	PERRY	FALCONER	HOMER	PATERSON	ORMSTON	ROBERTS	KING	ORMSTON
28/04/28	LUTON TOWN	A	1-2	5000	WHATLEY	LUTON TOWN	HAYDON	FORBES	PERRY	FALCONER	HOMER	PATERSON	ORMSTON	ROBERTS	KING	ORMSTON
05/05/28	MILLWALL	H	0-1	20000	WHATLEY	BENNETT	ROTHERHAM	FORBES	PERRY	FALCONER	HOMER	PATERSON	ORMSTON	ROBERTS	DOUGLAS	

FA CUP

Date	Opposition	V		ATT	G	2	3	4	5	6	7	8	9	10	11	GOALSCORERS
26/11/27	WALSALL	H	4-2	6000	WHATLEY	McKENNA	HAYDON	ROWLEY	FORBES	SMITH	DOUGLAS	WILLIAMS	CULLEY	WHATMORE	EVANS	WILLIAMS 2, DOUGLAS, CULLEY
10/12/27	BOURNEMOUTH	A	1-6	9000	WHATLEY	WHATLEY	HAYDON	ROWLEY	FORBES	SMITH	DOUGLAS	WILLIAMS	CULLEY	RUSSELL	EVANS	EVANS

GLOUCESTERSHIRE CUP FINAL

Date	Opposition	V		ATT	G	2	3	4	5	6	7	8	9	10	11	GOALSCORERS
10/04/28	BRISTOL CITY	H	1-0	7600	DENSLEY	BENNETT	BENNETT	FORBES	PERRY	FALCONER	HOMER	PATERSON	ORMSTON	ROBERTS	DAVIES	ORMSTON

PLAYERS	APPS	GLS
BENNETT F	33	
CULLEY W	18	14
DAVIES R	2	
DENSLEY H	6	
DIX R	4	1
DOUGLAS G	20	2
EVANS J	24	1
FALCONER F	9	
FORBES J	31	4
HAYDON J	33	
HOMER S	24	4
KING A	8	
McKENNA J	10	
ORMSTON A	24	15
PATERSON J	11	
PERRY I	17	1
ROBERTS T	22	2
ROTHERHAM A	16	
ROWLEY J	19	2
RUSSELL J	22	6
SMITH L	16	
THOM J	6	4
TROTMAN R	3	1
WHATLEY J	36	
WHATMORE E	18	4
WILLIAMS T	30	8

Ormston eschewing the opportunity of a hat-trick and leaving the kick to Russell, whose second goal earned Rovers a 5-1 victory.

Goals were plentiful, with Rovers scoring in all but one home game and not keeping a clean sheet until March. Even Jimmy Haydon's well-earned testimonial, played against Bristol City at Eastville in October, finished 3-3. Over Christmas, Rovers completed a League double over Merthyr Town. Russell, who scored inside the first minute in the home game, and the Welsh forward Albert Mays, both contributed goals in both fixtures. The meeting at Penydarren Park on Boxing Day was watched by only 1,000 spectators, the lowest crowd to see a League match involving Rovers.

An astonishing flurry of goals highlighted the game at Bournemouth earlier in December. There were six goals in a remarkable 15-minute spell before halftime. Three times Bournemouth had taken the lead, only for Rovers to peg them back. Ron Eyre scored twice for Bournemouth,

Bill Culley managed a remarkable 14 goals in just 18 appearances in 1927/28

although Rovers claimed his second had not crossed the line. When Patrick Clifford put the home side in front for a third time, 37-year-old Bill Culley responded almost instantly with his own second goal. Theophilus Pike played against Rovers on a number of occasions for Southend United, Norwich City and Bournemouth, but his second-half winning goal for the Cherries was the only time he scored against Rovers. Seven days later, Rovers returned to Dean Court only to concede four first-half goals and crash 6-1 in an FA Cup tie, the indomitable Eyre scoring again.

By March, Palmer was working to maintain Rovers' position in Division Three (South). Three Scottish players, Alf King, Fleming Falconer and John Paterson, were encouraged to move south of the border. The game against Charlton Athletic saw Rovers plunge Bristol-born 15-year-old inside-forward Ronnie Dix into the starting line-up. He remains the only player to have appeared for Rovers in League football before his sixteenth birthday. Although not the youngest player with any League club, he became the youngest to score a Football League goal, a record for all clubs that stands to this day, when he scored Rovers' second goal with a rasping drive 20 minutes from the end of a convincing 3-0 home victory over Norwich City seven days later. He was 15 years 180 days. Dix, who had also set up Ormston for the 40th-minute opening goal, later hit the bar. The Norwich City game also represented Rovers' first clean sheet in the League for 13 months.

On Easter Monday, Jesse Whatley made the last of his club record 246 consecutive League appearances in goal. After the 1-1 draw with Crystal Palace, he stepped aside to allow Bert Densley to appear in the final six League matches of the season. A measure of Rovers' problems is that, Whatley apart, only Fred Bennett, Jimmy Haydon and Jim Forbes appeared in more than 30 League games. Rovers fielded an experienced but ageing side. At 37 years of age, Culley was the side's second highest scorer. Jack Evans' goal in the first-half goal rush at Dean Court meant he, at 38 years 306 days, became the oldest scorer of a League goal for Bristol Rovers.

Lack of success in the FA Cup was mirrored in the Allan Palmer Cup where Rovers, as holders, played Exeter City at Trowbridge. Billy Vaughan, once an inside-forward for Rovers, played for the Grecians and his team-mate Billy McDevitt scored the only goal after 20 minutes. Defeated, Rovers were nonetheless to regain this trophy on three further occasions in the 1920s. On the success side, the former Rovers half-back David Steele was in the Huddersfield Town side that reached the FA Cup final. Arthur Ormston's goal was enough for Rovers to recapture the Gloucestershire Cup, defeating Bristol City at Eastville.

At the end of the season, some Rovers players were involved in a Bristol football representative side playing cricket. At Rovers' future home, The Memorial Ground, in June, Bristol Rugby Club scored 122-6, their footballing counterparts responding with 104-8.

1928/29

During the summer of 1928, Alf Homer stepped down as secretary, ending an association with Rovers that dated back to 1899. His days as manager had seen the club achieve some success, so it is a disappointing parallel that what was to be Joe Palmer's final season in this role could not live up to expectations. There was a large element of inconsistency about Rovers. Only goalkeeper Jesse Whatley, who missed just 1 game, Fred Bennett and Mick Cosgrove appeared in more than 30 League games, while 28 players were used in all. Reserve goalkeeper Bert Densley suffered the misfortune of scoring an own goal against Newport County in his only appearance of the season and Rovers conceded six at Fulham and Bournemouth as well as five on Boxing Day at Crystal Palace.

Jack Evans retired as a player in 1928 and a number of his team-mates moved to other League clubs. Ernie Whatmore joined Queen's Park Rangers, Reg Trotman moved to Rochdale and Bill Culley signed up for Swindon Town, while Tom Williams made the short journey to Ashton Gate. Many more players moved into non-League football. Jim Forbes became player-coach at Workington, taking with him Jack Thom and John McKenna. Joe Rowley spent the 1928/29 season at Oswestry Town, George Douglas at Tunbridge Wells Rangers, Jack Russell at Worcester City and Roy Davies at Ebbw Vale.

Palmer turned north of the border to buy players. Three Raith Rovers players, including George Barton, a rare example of a full-back who scored on his League debut, were joined by three former Aberdeen team-mates. One of these, Mick Cosgrove, was a veteran of English, Scottish and American football, while Tom Pirie had been Cardiff City's 12th man for the 1927 FA Cup final. Billy Compton joined from Exeter City, Wattie White from Reading, Bert Turner from Torquay United and Maurice Dando from Bath City. The returning hero, however, was Joe Walter, who had left Eastville in 1922 to win a League Championship medal with Huddersfield Town. His comeback game, on Christmas Day 1928 against Crystal Palace, attracted a crowd of 12,106, easily the club's highest home attendance of the season.

For the second consecutive season, Rovers finished 19th in Division Three (South). Yet, surprisingly, Rovers did the double over champions Charlton Athletic. Although Wilson Lennox scored a first-minute goal at The Valley in March, two Athletic defenders, Norman Smith and Albert Langford, scored own goals to give Rovers a 2-1 victory. Five weeks later, goals from Homer, Dando and King earned Rovers a 3-0 win at Eastville. King certainly scored some timely goals. One came in the 5-3 victory over Fulham, the only time all season that Rovers scored five goals in a game. He also scored the best goal of the season, finishing off a sweeping five-man move during the 4-1 victory at home to Southend United in March.

George Barton may have scored five goals from full-back, all of them penalties, but Rovers' top scorer was Jack Phillips. At the end of September, after a crushing defeat at Fulham, Rovers paid Brentford £450 for their centre-forward and his 13 League goals were almost double the total of any other player. Rovers had lost 6-1 at Craven Cottage to a mediocre Fulham side just hitting an uncharacteristic glut of goals, 24 in 5 games. Fred Avey, the Essex 2nd XI cricketer who was to score a hat-trick against Rovers in November 1930, scored twice.

Conceding goals was no longer a burning issue, but Rovers did concede six at Bournemouth, where the evergreen Ron Eyre scored a hat-trick and Percy Cherrett, at Crystal Palace for the high-scoring game in March 1927, added one. Rovers also conceded five at Palace and four on five other occasions. In April, Rovers were a goal down in the opening seconds at Somerton Park, Jimmy Gittins scoring for Newport County. Harry Morris scored a hat-trick at Eastville in December, as Swindon Town won 4-1. This game, Cliff Britton's first League appearance for Rovers, featured three penalties missed in quick succession. In Barton's absence, Albert Rotherham missed one for Rovers. The visiting full-back Walter Dickinson then found his kick saved by Whatley, though he successfully converted the rebound. Jack Phillips missed Rovers' second penalty. Rotherham never did score a League goal for Rovers, this being his final home appearance, but he did convert a penalty against Wellingborough in the FA Cup, after Rovers had trailed to a 10th-minute goal.

Apart from the Swindon game, December witnessed some unusual matches. Rovers had acquired the services of David Murray, a 26-year-old South African International, who had played for Bristol City and arrived at Eastville as player-coach. At home to Norwich City, his early goal was a prelude to one from John Paterson and Rovers found themselves 2-0 ahead after only six minutes. They won 2-0. The next home game revived memories of the game with Northampton Town in January 1925. The Cobblers won 2-1 at an increasingly foggy Eastville, their winning goal coming from a bizarre mix-up. Mick Cosgrove passed gently back to his goalkeeper but, in the fog, Whatley

FOOTBALL LEAGUE DIVISION THREE (SOUTH)

SEASON 1928/29

Date	Opponents	Venue	Score	Att	G	2	3	4	5	6	7	8	9	10	11	Goalscorers
21/08/28	SWINDON TOWN	A	1-2	8000	WHATLEY	BARTON	BENNETT	COSGROVE	PIRIE	FALCONER	HOMER	PATERSON	DANDO	TURNER	COMPTON	BARTON pen
28/08/28	WALSALL	A	3-1	6300	WHATLEY	BARTON	ROTHERHAM	COSGROVE	PIRIE	FALCONER	HOMER	PATERSON	ORMSTON	TURNER	COMPTON	COMPTON, COSGROVE, TURNER
01/09/28	TORQUAY UNITED	A	2-1	5000	WHATLEY	BARTON	ROTHERHAM	COSGROVE	PIRIE	FALCONER	HOMER	PATERSON	ORMSTON	TURNER	COMPTON	BARTON pen, PHILLIPS
08/09/28	GILLINGHAM	H	0-1	5000	WHATLEY	BARTON	ROTHERHAM	COSGROVE	PIRIE	FALCONER	HOMER	PATERSON	TURNER	PATERSON	COMPTON	
12/09/28	WALSALL	H	4-1	7000	WHATLEY	BARTON	ROTHERHAM	McCAIG	PERRY	FALCONER	HOMER	PATERSON	TURNER	ROBERTS	COMPTON	COMPTON, PATERSON, ROBERTS, TURNER
15/09/28	PLYMOUTH ARGYLE	H	0-1	12000	WHATLEY	BENNETT	BARTON	COSGROVE	PERRY	FALCONER	HOMER	PATERSON	DANDO	ROBERTS	COMPTON	
22/09/28	FULHAM	H	1-6	10000	WHATLEY	BENNETT	BARTON	COSGROVE	PERRY	FALCONER	HOMER	COSGROVE	DANDO	ROBERTS	COMPTON	COMPTON
29/09/28	QUEENS PARK RANGERS	H	1-1	9000	WHATLEY	BENNETT	BARTON	McCAIG	PERRY	FALCONER	REAY	COSGROVE	DANDO	WHITE	COMPTON	DANDO
06/10/28	LUTON TOWN	A	2-4	10000	WHATLEY	BENNETT	BARTON	COSGROVE	PERRY	ROBERTS	REAY	COSGROVE	PHILLIPS	WHITE	COMPTON	COSGROVE, PHILLIPS
13/10/28	WATFORD	H	0-1	9593	WHATLEY	BENNETT	BARTON	COSGROVE	PIRIE	ROBERTS	REAY	COSGROVE	PHILLIPS	PATERSON	COMPTON	
20/10/28	BRENTFORD	A	2-0	11000	WHATLEY	BENNETT	ROTHERHAM	COSGROVE	PERRY	ROBERTS	REAY	COSGROVE	PHILLIPS	PATERSON	COMPTON	PHILLIPS 2
27/10/28	BOURNEMOUTH	A	2-6	5000	WHATLEY	BENNETT	ROTHERHAM	COSGROVE	PERRY	ROBERTS	REAY	COSGROVE	PHILLIPS	PATERSON	COMPTON	COSGROVE, PHILLIPS
03/11/28	MERTHYR TOWN	H	3-0	9000	WHATLEY	ROTHERHAM	HAYDON	COSGROVE	PERRY	ROBERTS	REAY	COSGROVE	PHILLIPS	MURRAY	KING	KING, MURRAY, PHILLIPS
10/11/28	SOUTHEND UNITED	A	0-1	5764	WHATLEY	BARTON	ROTHERHAM	COSGROVE	PERRY	ROBERTS	REAY	COSGROVE	PHILLIPS	MURRAY	KING	
17/11/28	EXETER CITY	H	1-1	7000	WHATLEY	BARTON	ROTHERHAM	COSGROVE	SMITH	SMITH	REAY	DIX	PHILLIPS	WHITE	COMPTON	PATERSON
01/12/28	NORWICH CITY	H	2-0	7000	WHATLEY	BENNETT	ROTHERHAM	McCAIG	SMITH	ROBERTS	REAY	PATERSON	PHILLIPS	TURNER	COMPTON	PATERSON, PHILLIPS
15/12/28	NORTHAMPTON TOWN	H	1-2	6000	WHATLEY	BENNETT	ROTHERHAM	COSGROVE	SMITH	ROBERTS	HOMER	PATERSON	PHILLIPS	WHITE	COMPTON	PHILLIPS
22/12/28	COVENTRY CITY	A	0-2	14000	WHATLEY	BENNETT	ROTHERHAM	COSGROVE	PERRY	ROBERTS	REAY	PATERSON	PHILLIPS	TURNER	COMPTON	
25/12/28	CRYSTAL PALACE	A	1-1	12106	WHATLEY	BARTON	ROTHERHAM	COSGROVE	PERRY	FALCONER	REAY	PATERSON	PHILLIPS	PATERSON	COMPTON	KING
26/12/28	CRYSTAL PALACE	H	2-5	9083	WHATLEY	BARTON	ROTHERHAM	ROTHERHAM	PERRY	FALCONER	REAY	PATERSON	BENNETT	SPENCER	COMPTON	PIRIE, REAY
29/12/28	SWINDON TOWN	H	1-4	2928	WHATLEY	ROTHERHAM	HAYDON	COSGROVE	PERRY	ROBERTS	HOMER	WALTER	BENNETT	WALTER	COMPTON	BENNETT
05/01/29	TORQUAY UNITED	H	1-0	4837	WHATLEY	BENNETT	ROTHERHAM	COSGROVE	PIRIE	FALCONER	REAY	WALTER	PHILLIPS	PATERSON	KING	ROTHERHAM, WALTER
12/01/29	BRIGHTON & HOVE ALBION	A	0-4	6000	WHATLEY	BENNETT	ROTHERHAM	BRITTON	PERRY	FALCONER	REAY	WALTER	PHILLIPS	MURRAY	KING	
19/01/29	GILLINGHAM	A	2-4	2928	WHATLEY	BARTON	HAYDON	BRITTON	MURRAY	ROBERTS	REAY	COSGROVE	DANDO	MURRAY	KING	KING, MURRAY, PHILLIPS
02/02/29	FULHAM	A	5-3	8000	WHATLEY	BENNETT	BARTON	BRITTON	PERRY	ROBERTS	REAY	COSGROVE	PHILLIPS	PATERSON	KING	REAY 2, COSGROVE, KING, PATERSON
09/02/29	QUEENS PARK RANGERS	H	3-0	10000	WHATLEY	BENNETT	BARTON	BRITTON	PERRY	ROBERTS	REAY	COSGROVE	PHILLIPS	PATERSON	KING	KING 2, PHILLIPS
16/02/29	LUTON TOWN	H	1-1	5000	WHATLEY	BENNETT	ROTHERHAM	COSGROVE	PERRY	ROBERTS	REAY	COSGROVE	PHILLIPS	PATERSON	KING	COSGROVE
23/02/29	WATFORD	A	1-1	6000	WHATLEY	BENNETT	ROTHERHAM	BRITTON	PERRY	ROBERTS	REAY	COSGROVE	PHILLIPS	PATERSON	KING	REAY
02/03/29	BRENTFORD	H	0-2	8000	WHATLEY	BENNETT	ROTHERHAM	BRITTON	PERRY	ROBERTS	REAY	COSGROVE	PHILLIPS	PATERSON	COMPTON	
09/03/29	BOURNEMOUTH	H	1-2	6000	WHATLEY	BENNETT	HAYDON	BRITTON	PERRY	ROBERTS	REAY	COSGROVE	PHILLIPS	PATERSON	COMPTON	SMITH og, LANGFORD og
14/03/29	CHARLTON ATHLETIC	H	2-1	10000	WHATLEY	BENNETT	HAYDON	BRITTON	PERRY	ROBERTS	REAY	COSGROVE	WHITE	PHILLIPS	COMPTON	DANDO 2, COSGROVE, KING
16/03/29	MERTHYR TOWN	A	0-4	3000	WHATLEY	BENNETT	HAYDON	McCAIG	PERRY	FALCONER	REAY	COSGROVE	PHILLIPS	PHILLIPS	COMPTON	
23/03/29	SOUTHEND UNITED	H	4-1	6000	WHATLEY	BENNETT	BENNETT	BRITTON	PERRY	ROBERTS	HOMER	COSGROVE	DANDO	PHILLIPS	COMPTON	DANDO 2, COSGROVE, KING
29/03/29	NEWPORT COUNTY	H	0-3	11000	WHATLEY	DENSLEY	HAYDON	BRITTON	PERRY	ROBERTS	REAY	COSGROVE	DANDO	PHILLIPS	KING	
30/03/29	NEWPORT COUNTY	A	2-2	6000	WHATLEY	BENNETT	HAYDON	BRITTON	PERRY	ROBERTS	REAY	COSGROVE	DANDO	PHILLIPS	KING	DANDO 2
01/04/29	EXETER CITY	A	0-2	6000	WHATLEY	BENNETT	HAYDON	BRITTON	PERRY	ROBERTS	HOMER	COSGROVE	DANDO	PHILLIPS	KING	
06/04/29	BRIGHTON & HOVE ALBION	H	3-0	4849	WHATLEY	BENNETT	HAYDON	BRITTON	MURRAY	ROBERTS	HOMER	COSGROVE	DANDO	PHILLIPS	KING	DANDO 2, COSGROVE
13/04/29	NORWICH CITY	A	1-2	5000	WHATLEY	BENNETT	HAYDON	BRITTON	PERRY	ROBERTS	HOMER	PHILLIPS	DANDO	PHILLIPS	COMPTON	PHILLIPS
20/04/29	CHARLTON ATHLETIC	A	0-4	5000	WHATLEY	BENNETT	HAYDON	BRITTON	PIRIE	ROBERTS	REAY	COSGROVE	DANDO	PHILLIPS	KING	
27/04/29	NORTHAMPTON TOWN	A	1-3	9566	WHATLEY	BARTON	BARTON	BRITTON	MURRAY	FALCONER	HOMER	COSGROVE	MURRAY	MURRAY	COMPTON	MURRAY
01/05/29	PLYMOUTH ARGYLE	H	0-2	7422	WHATLEY	BARTON	BARTON	BRITTON	PIRIE	FALCONER	REAY	COSGROVE	DANDO	PATERSON	COMPTON	
04/05/29	COVENTRY CITY	H	1-1	5000	WHATLEY	BENNETT	HAYDON	COSGROVE	MURRAY	ROBERTS	REAY	COSGROVE	DANDO	PATERSON	COMPTON	COMPTON

FA CUP

Date	Opponents	Venue	Score	Att	G	2	3	4	5	6	7	8	9	10	11	Goalscorers
24/11/28	WELLINGBOROUGH	A	2-1	5556	WHATLEY	BARTON	ROTHERHAM	COSGROVE	PIRIE	SMITH	REAY	PIRIE	PHILLIPS	ROBERTS	COMPTON	ROTHERHAM pen, MURRAY
08/12/28	CRYSTAL PALACE	A	1-3	13500	WHATLEY	BENNETT	PIRIE	COSGROVE	PIRIE	ROBERTS	REAY	COSGROVE	PHILLIPS	MURRAY	COMPTON	PHILLIPS

GLOUCESTERSHIRE CUP FINAL

Date	Opponents	Venue	Score	Att	G	2	3	4	5	6	7	8	9	10	11	Goalscorers
19/09/28	BRISTOL CITY	A	0-2	6923	WHATLEY	BARTON	HAYDON	McCAIG	PERRY	SMITH	HOMER	COSGROVE	DIX	WHITE	COMPTON	

PLAYERS	APPS	GLS
BARTON G	24	5
BENNETT F	31	1
BRITTON C	18	
COMPTON W	22	4
COSGROVE M	37	6
DANDO M	10	5
DENSLEY H	1	
DIX R	1	
FALCONER F	11	
HAYDON J	19	
HOMER S	13	1
KING A	20	7
McCAIG D	9	
ORMSTON A	3	
PATERSON J	26	4
PERRY I	18	
PHILLIPS J	27	13
PIRIE T	12	
REAY G	29	4
ROBERTS T	14	
ROTHERHAM A	28	2
SMITH L	8	
SPENCER S	2	
TURNER H	9	2
WALTER J	7	1
WHATLEY J	41	
WHITE W	8	
OWN GOALS		2

could not see the ball and Rovers had conceded one of the most farcical of goals. In the following home fixture, it was the celebrated Ernie Toseland who gave high-flying Coventry City the lead *en route* to a 2-0 victory.

Another own goal conceded by Rovers led to one of the largest wins of the season. Fair-haired David McCaig, the former Raith Rovers right-half, put through his own net but four Rovers players got on the scoresheet at the right end, as Walsall were beaten 4-1 in September. Southend United were defeated by the same score, while Brighton, Charlton Athletic, Queen's Park Rangers and Merthyr Town were all beaten 3-0. A 2-0 win over Brentford in October proved to be the first of the Bees' club record nine consecutive League defeats. On Easter Saturday, Rovers drew 2-2 with Exeter City at St James' Park. The Grecians' first goal was scored by Harold Houghton, later a Rovers player and the second by the future England International Cliff Bastin, whose shot deflected in off Murray.

Peter Holland of Watford and Norwich City's Wilf Greenwell both missed penalties against Rovers, but Newport County's Sammy Richardson was more fortunate. Having missed his penalty, he was pleased to see the referee order a retake, from which he duly scored. Southend United's Tom Brophy, who had spent 40 minutes as an emergency goalkeeper against Rovers in December 1925, broke his arm during his side's single goal victory over Rovers in November, following a collision with his team-mate Jimmy Frew. The reserve game against Plymouth Argyle reserves in October proved eventful. The visiting centre-half Bill Pullen was sent off the field and, refusing to go, twice punched referee A J Attwood.

Rovers lost in the Gloucestershire Cup final 2-0 to Bristol City, Tom Williams returning to haunt his former side with the second goal. An FA Cup win over Wellingborough, during which game Len Smith broke his leg, simply led to defeat at Crystal Palace, whose third goal was scored by Henry Havelock, a brother of Jack Havelock who joined Rovers from Folkestone in 1933. Young Cliff Britton, whose 18 League games marked the start of a glorious career, was a rare glimmer of hope in a larger more depressing picture. Britton was 'never the most robust of men, but a football stylist' (Archie Ledbrooke and Edgar Turner, *Soccer from the Press Box*). Joe Palmer resigned as manager at the season's end and was replaced by David McLean. The new Rovers manager had enjoyed a hugely successful playing career with Sheffield Wednesday and Scotland. McLean had also appeared for a number of other clubs, including three spells with Forfar Athletic, his home-town club, and a place in the 1925 Scottish Cup final with Dundee. Latterly manager of East Fife, McLean accepted a weekly wage of £10 and became the fifth full-time manager of Bristol Rovers.

1929/30

The new manager had made significant changes to his side. Billy Compton and the veteran Joe Walter joined Bath City, while Bert Turner moved to Brierley Hill Athletic. Len Smith and Albert Rotherham, the latter attracting a £100 fee, moved to League opposition, Merthyr Town and Coventry City respectively. Rovers signed one

Jack Phillips was top goalscorer for two seasons with 13 and 24 goals in seasons 1928/29 and 1929/30

Jimmy Haydon: his last season in 1930 completed a career total of 290 League games for Rovers

Scot – Jock Hamilton from Penicuik – and two from the north-east, Bob Plenderleith, a £150 buy from Sunderland, and the experienced Wally Gillespie for £300 from Newcastle United. Gilbert Shaw had League experience with Grimsby Town. The veteran left-half Tom Wolfe arrived from Charlton Athletic.

For all these transactions, it was a local 19-year-old, Cecil Thomas who, on his debut, scored the only goal as Rovers beat Brighton. This result offered false hope. Rovers were to win only two of the opening 15 League matches. Somehow the side was able to snatch mediocrity from the jaws of success. Merthyr Town, for instance, in their final League season, won 21 points and conceded 135 goals in 42 games. Rovers drew both matches with the South Walian club. Gillingham were gifted two very late goals to snatch a 3-3 draw. Rovers lost 23 games in the League, conceded a then club record of 93 goals, equalling the figure for 1927/28, and finished 20th in Division Three (South), the worst final placing to date.

Perhaps the most entertaining afternoon was when Rovers played the leaders Brentford at Griffin Park in September. The team's charabanc hit an electric standard on its way to the ground and, although no one was injured, three windows were smashed and delays were inevitable. Jack Phillips put Rovers ahead and, after Brentford's former Bristol City forward Cyril Blakemore had missed a penalty, Rovers led 1-0 with 10 minutes remaining. However, Bill Lane equalised and Jackie Foster, another who had previously been at the Ashton Gate club, scored direct from a corner. Rovers lost 2-1 and Brentford went on to win all 21 home League games that season.

SEASON 1929/30

FOOTBALL LEAGUE DIVISION THREE (SOUTH)

Date	Opposition	H/A	G	ATT	G(1)	2	3	4	5	6	7	8	9	10	11	GOALSCORERS
31/08/29	BRIGHTON & HOVE ALBION	H	1-0	10333	WHATLEY	BARTON	HAYDON	C BRITTON	PLENDERLEITH	WOLFE	REAY	COSGROVE	THOMAS	SHAW	ROBERTS	THOMAS
02/09/29	COVENTRY CITY	H	1-3	6000	WHATLEY	BARTON	HAYDON	C BRITTON	PLENDERLEITH	WOLFE	REAY	COSGROVE	THOMAS	SHAW	ROBERTS	SHAW
07/09/29	SWINDON TOWN	A	2-2	5000	WHATLEY	BARTON	HAYDON	C BRITTON	MURRAY	HAMILTON	REAY	PATERSON	PHILLIPS	SHAW	KING	PHILLIPS 2
09/09/29	COVENTRY CITY	A	0-1	13750	WHATLEY	BENNETT	HAYDON	C BRITTON	MURRAY	HAMILTON	REAY	PATERSON	PHILLIPS	SHAW	KING	
14/09/29	PLYMOUTH ARGYLE	H	2-3	11787	WHATLEY	BENNETT	HAYDON	C BRITTON	MURRAY	HAMILTON	REAY	PATERSON	PHILLIPS	SHAW	KING	PHILLIPS, PATERSON
21/09/29	MERTHYR TOWN	A	1-1	4000	DENSLEY	BARTON	HAYDON	C BRITTON	MURRAY	HAMILTON	REAY	COSGROVE	PHILLIPS	PATERSON	KING	PHILLIPS
25/09/29	BRENTFORD	H	1-2	12500	DENSLEY	BARTON	HAYDON	C BRITTON	MURRAY	HAMILTON	REAY	COSGROVE	PHILLIPS	PATERSON	KING	PHILLIPS
28/09/29	TORQUAY UNITED	A	2-0	6175	DENSLEY	BARTON	HAYDON	C BRITTON	MURRAY	McCAIG	REAY	PATERSON	PHILLIPS	COSGROVE	KING	PHILLIPS 2
05/10/29	NEWPORT COUNTY	A	2-2	4000	DENSLEY	BARTON	HAYDON	C BRITTON	PLENDERLEITH	McCAIG	REAY	PATERSON	PHILLIPS	COSGROVE	KING	KING, PHILLIPS
12/10/29	WATFORD	H	1-2	7000	DENSLEY	BARTON	BENNETT	C BRITTON	PLENDERLEITH	McCAIG	REAY	PATERSON	PHILLIPS	DIX	ROBERTS	PHILLIPS
19/10/29	NORWICH CITY	A	2-4	10000	DENSLEY	BARTON	HAYDON	C BRITTON	PLENDERLEITH	McCAIG	REAY	HOMER	PHILLIPS	MURRAY	KING	MURRAY, REAY
26/10/29	CRYSTAL PALACE	H	2-3	6498	WHATLEY	BENNETT	HAYDON	C BRITTON	PLENDERLEITH	HAMILTON	REAY	MURRAY	PHILLIPS	SHAW	KING	MURRAY 2
02/11/29	GILLINGHAM	H	3-3	7000	WHATLEY	BARTON	HAYDON	C BRITTON	PLENDERLEITH	HAMILTON	REAY	MURRAY	PHILLIPS	SHAW	KING	KING, MURRAY, SHAW
09/11/29	NORTHAMPTON TOWN	A	2-3	7000	DENSLEY	BARTON	HAYDON	C BRITTON	PLENDERLEITH	HAMILTON	REAY	MURRAY	PHILLIPS	SHAW	KING	PHILLIPS pen, SHAW
16/11/29	EXETER CITY	A	2-5	6000	DENSLEY	BARTON	HAYDON	C BRITTON	PLENDERLEITH	HAMILTON	REAY	FORBES	PHILLIPS	MURRAY	KING	FORBES, PHILLIPS
23/11/29	SOUTHEND UNITED	H	4-2	6000	WHATLEY	BARTON	HAYDON	C BRITTON	COSGROVE	HAMILTON	REAY	FORBES	PHILLIPS	MURRAY	SHAW	MURRAY 2, REAY, SHAW
21/12/29	QUEENS PARK RANGERS	H	4-1	6117	WHATLEY	BARTON	HAYDON	C BRITTON	PLENDERLEITH	HAMILTON	REAY	FORBES	PHILLIPS	MURRAY	SHAW	PHILLIPS 3, MURRAY
25/12/29	FULHAM	A	2-6	16000	WHATLEY	BARTON	HAYDON	C BRITTON	PLENDERLEITH	HAMILTON	REAY	FORBES	PHILLIPS	MURRAY	KING	FORBES, KING
26/12/29	FULHAM	H	4-1	15000	WHATLEY	BENNETT	HAYDON	C BRITTON	COSGROVE	HAMILTON	REAY	FORBES	PHILLIPS	MURRAY	KING	PHILLIPS 2, HAYDON, MURRAY
28/12/29	BRIGHTON & HOVE ALBION	A	0-1	6494	WHATLEY	BENNETT	HAYDON	C BRITTON	COSGROVE	HAMILTON	REAY	FORBES	PHILLIPS	DIX	KING	
04/01/30	SWINDON TOWN	H	3-2	9000	WHATLEY	BENNETT	HAYDON	C BRITTON	COSGROVE	HAMILTON	REAY	FORBES	PHILLIPS	MURRAY	DIX	DIX, PHILLIPS, REAY
18/01/30	PLYMOUTH ARGYLE	A	0-3	11610	WHATLEY	BENNETT	HAYDON	C BRITTON	COSGROVE	HAMILTON	PATERSON	FORBES	PHILLIPS	MURRAY	DIX	
25/01/30	MERTHYR TOWN	H	2-2	8000	WHATLEY	BENNETT	GILLESPIE	C BRITTON	COSGROVE	HAMILTON	REAY	FORBES	PHILLIPS	MURRAY	DIX	PHILLIPS, REAY
08/02/30	NEWPORT COUNTY	A	2-3	5000	WHATLEY	BENNETT	HAYDON	C BRITTON	PLENDERLEITH	HAMILTON	REAY	FORBES	PHILLIPS	MURRAY	DIX	HAMILTON, PHILLIPS
15/02/30	WATFORD	A	3-4	6158	DENSLEY	GILLESPIE	HAYDON	C BRITTON	COSGROVE	HAMILTON	REAY	FORBES	PHILLIPS	ROBERTS	DIX	DIX, PHILLIPS, DAVISON og
22/02/30	NORWICH CITY	H	0-0	6000	DENSLEY	BARTON	HAYDON	C BRITTON	COSGROVE	HAMILTON	REAY	FORBES	PHILLIPS	DIX	KING	
01/03/30	CRYSTAL PALACE	A	0-3	13018	DENSLEY	BARTON	HAYDON	McCAIG	MURRAY	HAMILTON	REAY	COSGROVE	PHILLIPS	SHAW	FORBES	
08/03/30	GILLINGHAM	H	3-0	6000	DENSLEY	BARTON	HAYDON	FINDLAY	COSGROVE	HAMILTON	REAY	FORBES	PHILLIPS	MURRAY	SHAW	HAYDON pen, MURRAY, SHAW
15/03/30	NORTHAMPTON TOWN	A	1-6	5402	DENSLEY	BARTON	HAYDON	FINDLAY	COSGROVE	HAMILTON	REAY	FORBES	PHILLIPS	MURRAY	SHAW	SHAW
22/03/30	EXETER CITY	H	1-0	6000	WHATLEY	BENNETT	HAYDON	FINDLAY	COSGROVE	HAMILTON	REAY	FORBES	PHILLIPS	MURRAY	SHAW	PHILLIPS
24/03/30	LUTON TOWN	A	0-3	4000	DENSLEY	BARTON	HAYDON	FINDLAY	COSGROVE	HAMILTON	REAY	FORBES	PHILLIPS	MURRAY	SHAW	
29/03/30	SOUTHEND UNITED	A	0-6	5903	DENSLEY	BARTON	BENNETT	FINDLAY	COSGROVE	HAMILTON	REAY	FORBES	PHILLIPS	MURRAY	SHAW	
03/04/30	TORQUAY UNITED	H	1-2	3267	WHATLEY	BENNETT	HAYDON	McCAIG	PLENDERLEITH	ROBERTS	REAY	FORBES	PHILLIPS	DIX	SHAW	REAY
05/04/30	LUTON TOWN	H	5-0	5000	WHATLEY	BENNETT	HAYDON	McCAIG	COSGROVE	HAMILTON	REAY	FORBES	PHILLIPS	DIX	ROBERTS	HAYDON pen, ROBERTS
09/04/30	BOURNEMOUTH	A	2-1	1936	WHATLEY	BENNETT	HAYDON	McCAIG	PLENDERLEITH	HAMILTON	REAY	FORBES	PHILLIPS	DIX	ROBERTS	DIX, FORBES
12/04/30	BOURNEMOUTH	H	1-3	4000	WHATLEY	LITTLEWOOD	HAYDON	FINDLAY	PLENDERLEITH	HAMILTON	REAY	C BRITTON	BENNETT	DIX	ROBERTS	C BRITTON
18/04/30	CLAPTON ORIENT	A	0-0	10195	WHATLEY	BARTON	BENNETT	C BRITTON	PLENDERLEITH	HAMILTON	REAY	FORBES	PHILLIPS	DIX	ROBERTS	
19/04/30	WALSALL	H	3-1	5000	WHATLEY	BENNETT	HAYDON	C BRITTON	PLENDERLEITH	HAMILTON	REAY	FORBES	PHILLIPS	DIX	ROBERTS	DIX, FORBES, PHILLIPS
21/04/30	CLAPTON ORIENT	H	0-3	10195	WHATLEY	BENNETT	HAYDON	C BRITTON	PLENDERLEITH	HAMILTON	REAY	WINNELL	FORBES	DIX	ROBERTS	
26/04/30	QUEENS PARK RANGERS	A	1-2	8000	WHATLEY	BENNETT	HAYDON	C BRITTON	PLENDERLEITH	HAMILTON	THOMAS	WINNELL	PHILLIPS	DIX	SHAW	WINNELL
30/04/30	WALSALL	A	0-0	4000	DENSLEY	BENNETT	HAYDON	C BRITTON	PLENDERLEITH	HAMILTON	THOMAS	WINNELL	PHILLIPS	DIX	SHAW	
03/05/30	BRENTFORD	H	4-1	6500	WHATLEY	BENNETT	BARTON	C BRITTON	PLENDERLEITH	HAMILTON	F BRITTON	WINNELL	PHILLIPS	DIX	SHAW	PHILLIPS 2, DIX, SHAW

FA CUP

Date	Opposition	H/A	G	ATT	G(1)	2	3	4	5	6	7	8	9	10	11	GOALSCORERS
30/11/29	NUNHEAD	A	2-0	3000	WHATLEY	BARTON	HAYDON	C BRITTON	COSGROVE	HAMILTON	REAY	FORBES	PHILLIPS	MURRAY	KING	C BRITTON, PHILLIPS
14/12/29	ACCRINGTON STANLEY	H	4-1	7000	WHATLEY	BARTON	HAYDON	C BRITTON	COSGROVE	HAMILTON	REAY	FORBES	PHILLIPS	MURRAY	KING	REAY 2, FORBES, PHILLIPS
11/01/30	CLAPTON ORIENT	A	0-1	15000	WHATLEY	BENNETT	HAYDON	C BRITTON	COSGROVE	HAMILTON	REAY	FORBES	DANDO	MURRAY	DIX	

GLOUCESTERSHIRE CUP FINAL

Date	Opposition	H/A	G	ATT	G(1)	2	3	4	5	6	7	8	9	10	11	GOALSCORERS
30/09/29	BRISTOL CITY	A	0-0	3000	DENSLEY	BARTON	HAYDON	C BRITTON	PLENDERLEITH	McCAIG	REAY	PATERSON	PHILLIPS	COSGROVE	KING	
22/04/30	BRISTOL CITY	H	1-4	3500	WHATLEY	BARTON	BENNETT	C BRITTON	PLENDERLEITH	HAMILTON	REAY	FORBES	PHILLIPS	DIX	SHAW	PHILLIPS

PLAYERS	APPS	GLS
BARTON G	27	
BENNETT F	18	
BRITTON C	32	1
BRITTON F	1	
COSGROVE M	20	
DENSLEY H	16	
DIX R	18	5
FORBES F	24	4
GILLESPIE W	2	
HAMILTON J	35	1
HAYDON J	37	3
HOMER S	1	
KING A	16	3
LITTLEWOOD C	1	
McCAIG D	7	
MURRAY D	25	9
PATERSON J	9	1
PHILLIPS J	38	24
PLENDERLEITH R	22	
REAY G	38	5
ROBERTS T	11	1
SHAW G	20	7
THOMAS C	4	1
WHATLEY J	26	1
WINNELL W	4	1
WOLFE T	2	
OWN GOAL		1

Yet, Rovers' struggle can be traced directly to the fact that, for the second time in three years, 93 Division Three (South) goals were conceded. It was an uncharacteristic end to Jesse Whatley's decade in the Rovers goal. Shortly before Easter, Ted Bowen's hat-trick, which included a penalty, eased Northampton Town to a 6-1 victory over Rovers. He was to repeat this feat in 1930/31. Two weeks after the trip to Northampton, Rovers crashed 6-0 to Southend United, for whom Fred Baron scored twice in the opening 13 minutes, a first-half hat-trick and four times in all. Bill Haley scored a Christmas Day hat-trick as Fulham, 4-1 up by half-time, also put six goals past Rovers. Tom Wells scored three times at Eastville in November, Northampton Town forwards thus scoring hat-tricks in both League fixtures against Rovers. Exeter City scored four goals in the opening 12 minutes, the first by the future Rovers inside-forward Harry Houghton. George Guyan and Cyril Hemingway scored twice each as The Grecians won 5-2 at St James' Park.

There were some far better performances, of course. Twenty-four hours after the heavy defeat at Craven Cottage, Rovers defeated Fulham 4-1. It was the third consecutive home game in which Rovers had scored four times, Rovers scoring 23 goals and conceding 28 in a run of nine League games. Jack Phillips, the first Rovers player to top 20 League goals since Bill Culley, scored a fine hat-trick in a 4-1 victory over Queen's Park Rangers. In the final game of the season, with safety assured, Rovers ran up an identical scoreline against Brentford with Ronnie Dix, after a two-year gap following his celebrated goal, back on the scoresheet in these and three other games early in 1930.

Rovers, though, had an abysmal away record. They were the only club in the four divisions of the Football League not to win away from home all season. A poor start, including a four-goal defeat at Norwich City led to that 3-3 draw at Gillingham in November, a match of six goalscorers. Thereafter, Rovers lost a club record 13 consecutive away League fixtures. This run ended only in a goalless draw at Walsall in the final away game, before a club-record-equalling lowest League crowd at a Rovers game of only 1,000. During this run, Densley conceded six at Northampton and Southend, five at Exeter, four at Watford and three at Luton Town and Crystal Palace, where Rovers played the final hour with ten men after an injury to Fred Bennett. Whatley conceded six at Fulham and three at Plymouth, Newport, Bournemouth and Orient. These were dismal days for Bristol Rovers.

Watford's 4-3 victory in February was against a Rovers side who played out 65 minutes with only 10 men after Cliff Britton's early injury. The veteran wing-half Neil McBain scored one of the goals and was to become, in March 1947, the oldest player in the history of the Football League when he appeared, at the age of 51, as an emergency goalkeeper for New Brighton against Hartlepool United. Nor surprisingly, McBain was the only 19th-century-born player to appear in League football after World War Two. The previous week, Jock Hamilton had scored for both sides in the 3-2 defeat at home to Newport County.

One rare home victory, in April, was achieved over Bournemouth despite a missed penalty from the normally dependable Jimmy Haydon. Rovers' regular left-back was, with Reay and Phillips, one of three players who missed only four games each all season. Twenty-seven players were used, as Rovers struggled to find a regular combination and battled to combat their lack of success away from home. Whatley's 26 League appearances for Rovers brought his career total to 386 by the time of his retirement at the end of the season. He had been a wonderful servant of the Eastville club throughout the first decade of League action.

Rovers lost the Gloucestershire Cup final to Bristol City in a replay. Sid Homer, later a Rovers outside-right, scored one of the goals and was to score again in this fixture in 1930/31 and 1932/33. In the FA Cup, Rovers survived the potential banana-skin of taking their dubious away record to non-League minnows, Nunhead, destined for the Isthmian League Championship that season. Two George Reay goals helped Rovers to a comfortable 4-1 home victory over Third Division (North) Accrington Stanley. The Peel Park side replied with a goal from inside-right Danny Ferguson. The third-round game at Clapton Orient was a dull affair that hinged on two penalties. Ronnie Dix, Rovers' teenage inside-forward missed from his kick, while Orient's Albert Lyons, seeing Whatley save his penalty, scored from the rebound for the only goal of the game. Arsenal were FA Cup winners, including in their side the future Rovers goalkeeper Charles Preedy and left-back Eddie Hapgood who, rejected by Rovers as a youngster, enjoyed a long and successful career with Arsenal and England and appeared in three FA Cup finals.

Over the summer of 1930, the Stapleton Road end of the pitch was reseeded and Rovers' officials set about rebuilding the side into one that could do justice to its potential in the Football League. Rovers once again fielded a cricket side to meet a Mr A Humphries XI at Downend cricket ground. Wing-half Cliff Britton moved in June to Everton, where he was to become one of the leading lights of his generation, winning domestic honours and England caps before embarking on a successful managerial career. He was generally accepted as the pioneer of the slide-rule pass and helped to revolutionize football tactics in much the same way as Don Revie was to do some 20 years later. Reliable full-back Fred Bennett was also allowed to leave the club after 129 League appearances, joining Third Division (North) side Chester, although he subsequently returned to live and work in Bristol. The biggest loss to Rovers, however, was the retirement of the veteran goalkeeper Jesse Whatley after 372 League appearances in a decade of reliable service. He was to be an active member of the club's former players' association for many years and, right up to his death in March 1982, kept in close contact with Bristol Rovers.

1930/31

Following Rovers' lowest final League position in a decade of Division Three football, the pressure was on manager David McLean's side to perform more consistently in the season ahead. Wholesale changes to the side gave the promise of better things to come. Indeed, only left-back Jimmy Haydon, who retired in the summer of 1931, and left-half Jock Hamilton, of the previous season's players, were to appear in the opening game of the season. Rovers also played for this season in unfamiliar blue shirts and white shorts.

Rovers, with their nine debutants, crashed to a 4-1 defeat in blazing sunshine at home to Northampton in that first game. Centre-forward Joe Pointon, highly experienced at this level with several clubs, scored Rovers' goal from the penalty spot, but it proved to

Manager Captain Albert Prince-Cox brought many
innovative ideas to the club in his six-year spell

be his only goal for the club. He was to miss a penalty in the game against Gillingham. On the other hand, three goals for Northampton's Ted Bowen were Rovers' undoing. It was a second League hat-trick against Rovers in five months for the 27-year-old forward, who spent two successful seasons with Bristol City between 1932 and 1934. Even by the standards set in 1929/30, Rovers' defensive frailties were becoming clearly apparent.

Nine opponents registered League hat-tricks against Rovers during the season, a club record. Coventry City's Billy Lake, who had hit the post but not scored against Rovers the previous season, scored four times in a 5-1 victory in March. Southend United's Jimmy Shankly, brother of the future Liverpool manager, scored twice in the first 16 minutes and completed his hat-trick at Eastville with an 85th minute penalty. Bill Lane not only scored three goals but also struck a late penalty against the crossbar during Brentford's crushing 5-2 victory at Eastville in January. Had Les Berry not saved Alex Stevenson's penalty at Griffin Park, Rovers would have conceded five goals in both League fixtures against the Bees.

Rovers also conceded five goals at home to both Watford, where George James scored three times, and Bournemouth, as well as six at Fulham. The Bournemouth defeat was indeed a remarkable game. Ron Eyre, a thorn in Rovers' side for many years, scored a hat-trick and the former Rovers inside-forward Jack Russell scored twice. Arthur Attwood contributed two goals for Rovers, who were left with only 10 men after an injury to Norman Dinsdale. Three goals were disallowed and Rovers' George Russell missed a penalty. At Fulham, Rovers had held the home side 2-2, before goalkeeper Les Berry conceded four goals in the final 15 minutes. Fred Avey scored three goals in that game, but only five all season for Fulham. This was the third consecutive season in which Rovers had conceded six goals in the League game at Craven Cottage.

Several of the new signings enjoyed a successful season, despite the club's propensity to suffer heavy defeats. It was always going to be tough stepping into Jesse Whatley's boots but goalkeeper Berry, despite conceding 80 goals in 34 League matches, was instrumental in preventing many whitewashes. He was primarily a cricketer of great renown who captained his county and scored more than 30,000 runs between 1924 and 1951. Immediately prior to his arrival at Eastville, he had scored a career-best 232 for Leicestershire against Sussex in the close season of 1930. In October at Somerton Park, he played against the celebrated Worcestershire batsman Bill Fox, Newport County's left-back. Dinsdale was an efficient centre-half and Bert Young a consistent performer

FOOTBALL LEAGUE DIVISION THREE (SOUTH)

Date	Opposition	Venue	Result	Att	G	2	3	4	5	6	7	8	9	10	11	Goalscorers
30/08/30	NORTHAMPTON TOWN	H	1-4	8000	BERRY	PRICE	HAYDON	RICHARDSON	DINSDALE	HAMILTON	ATTWOOD	BALL	POINTON	SCOTT	YOUNG	POINTON pen
03/09/30	GILLINGHAM	A	1-1	5000	BERRY	PRICE	HAYDON	RICHARDSON	DINSDALE	HAMILTON	POINTON	BALL	ATTWOOD	SCOTT	YOUNG	ATTWOOD
06/09/30	BRENTFORD	A	0-4	15000	BERRY	PRICE	DENNIS	RICHARDSON	DINSDALE	HAMILTON	POINTON	BALL	ATTWOOD	SCOTT	YOUNG	
08/09/30	EXETER CITY	H	1-1	5000	BERRY	PRICE	HAYDON	COOPER	DINSDALE	HAMILTON	POINTON	FORBES	ATTWOOD	DIX	TURNBULL	ATTWOOD
13/09/30	CRYSTAL PALACE	H	2-1	5799	BERRY	PRICE	BARTON	FINDLAY	DINSDALE	HAMILTON	FORBES	BALL	ATTWOOD	DIX	YOUNG	FORBES, YOUNG
17/09/30	EXETER CITY	A	3-0	3000	BERRY	DENNIS	PRICE	FINDLAY	DINSDALE	HAMILTON	FORBES	BALL	ATTWOOD	DIX	YOUNG	DIX 2, HAMILTON
20/09/30	SOUTHEND UNITED	A	0-4	6442	BERRY	PRICE	DENNIS	FINDLAY	DINSDALE	HAMILTON	FORBES	BALL	ATTWOOD	DIX	YOUNG	
24/09/30	TORQUAY UNITED	A	3-3	5057	BERRY	PRICE	DENNIS	FINDLAY	DINSDALE	HAMILTON	FORBES	BALL	ATTWOOD	DIX	YOUNG	DIX 2, FINDLAY
27/09/30	LUTON TOWN	H	5-1	8000	BERRY	PRICE	DENNIS	FINDLAY	DINSDALE	HAMILTON	FORBES	BALL	ATTWOOD	DIX	YOUNG	DENNIS pen, DIX 2, FORBES, YOUNG
04/10/30	NOTTS COUNTY	A	0-3	11929	BERRY	PRICE	DENNIS	SCOTT	DINSDALE	HAMILTON	FORBES	BALL	ATTWOOD	DIX	YOUNG	
11/10/30	NEWPORT COUNTY	H	1-1	5000	BERRY	PRICE	DENNIS	COOPER	DINSDALE	HAMILTON	FORBES	BALL	ATTWOOD	DIX	YOUNG	DIX
18/10/30	WATFORD	A	1-5	10000	BERRY	PRICE	DENNIS	FINDLAY	DINSDALE	HAMILTON	FORBES	BALL	ATTWOOD	DIX	YOUNG	ATTWOOD
25/10/30	BOURNEMOUTH	A	0-4	8000	BERRY	BARTON	DENNIS	BLACK	DINSDALE	HAMILTON	ATTWOOD	FORBES	POINTON	DIX	YOUNG	
01/11/30	SWINDON TOWN	H	4-1	8000	BERRY	BARTON	DENNIS	BLACK	DINSDALE	HAMILTON	ATTWOOD	FORBES	POINTON	DIX	YOUNG	ATTWOOD, DIX, DENNIS pen, FORBES
08/11/30	FULHAM	A	2-6	15000	BERRY	BARTON	DENNIS	BLACK	RICHARDSON	HAMILTON	FORBES	BALL	ATTWOOD	DIX	YOUNG	ATTWOOD 2
15/11/30	COVENTRY CITY	H	1-0	6000	BERRY	BARTON	DENNIS	BLACK	DINSDALE	SCOTT	FORBES	BALL	ATTWOOD	DIX	YOUNG	YOUNG
22/11/30	WALSALL	A	2-4	5000	BERRY	BARTON	DENNIS	BLACK	DINSDALE	HAMILTON	FORBES	BALL	ATTWOOD	DIX	YOUNG	YOUNG 2
06/12/30	NORWICH CITY	A	3-1	8000	BERRY	BARTON	RUSSELL	BLACK	DINSDALE	HAMILTON	FORBES	FINDLAY	ATTWOOD	DIX	YOUNG	FORBES 2, DIX
17/12/30	THAMES ASSOCIATION	H	4-0	2948	BERRY	BARTON	RUSSELL	BLACK	DINSDALE	HAMILTON	FORBES	SCOTT	ATTWOOD	DIX	YOUNG	FORBES, DINSDALE, SCOTT, DIX
20/12/30	CLAPTON ORIENT	A	1-3	5625	BERRY	BARTON	RUSSELL	BLACK	DINSDALE	HAMILTON	FORBES	FINDLAY	ATTWOOD	DIX	YOUNG	FINDLAY
25/12/30	BRIGHTON & HOVE ALBION	H	3-3	13229	BERRY	BARTON	HAYDON	BLACK	DINSDALE	HAMILTON	FORBES	RICHARDSON	ATTWOOD	DIX	YOUNG	DINSDALE, DIX, YOUNG
26/12/30	BRIGHTON & HOVE ALBION	A	0-4	9139	BERRY	BARTON	HAYDON	BLACK	DINSDALE	HAMILTON	FORBES	RICHARDSON	ATTWOOD	DIX	YOUNG	
27/12/30	NORTHAMPTON TOWN	A	1-1	10863	BERRY	BARTON	HAYDON	BLACK	DINSDALE	HAMILTON	FORBES	RICHARDSON	ATTWOOD	DIX	YOUNG	ATTWOOD
03/01/31	BRENTFORD	H	2-5	9000	BERRY	BARTON	HAYDON	BLACK	DINSDALE	HAMILTON	FORBES	RICHARDSON	ATTWOOD	DIX	YOUNG	ATTWOOD 2
14/01/31	QUEENS PARK RANGERS	H	3-0	3314	BERRY	BARTON	DENNIS	BLACK	DINSDALE	HAMILTON	FORBES	POINTON	ATTWOOD	DIX	YOUNG	DIX 2, DENNIS pen
17/01/31	CRYSTAL PALACE	A	2-0	14849	BERRY	RUSSELL	HAYDON	BLACK	DINSDALE	COOPER	FORBES	POINTON	ATTWOOD	DIX	YOUNG	DIX, CRILLY og
28/01/31	SOUTHEND UNITED	A	2-3	4000	BERRY	RUSSELL	HAYDON	BLACK	DINSDALE	COOPER	FORBES	FINDLAY	ATTWOOD	DIX	YOUNG	ATTWOOD, DINSDALE
31/01/31	LUTON TOWN	H	1-4	7000	BERRY	BARTON	DENNIS	BLACK	DINSDALE	COOPER	FORBES	FINDLAY	ATTWOOD	DIX	YOUNG	DENNIS pen
07/02/31	NOTTS COUNTY	A	2-2	11000	BERRY	RUSSELL	HAYDON	BLACK	DINSDALE	HAMILTON	FORBES	FINDLAY	ATTWOOD	DIX	YOUNG	YOUNG, FINDLAY
14/02/31	NEWPORT COUNTY	H	2-0	8000	BERRY	BARTON	HAYDON	BLACK	DINSDALE	HAMILTON	FORBES	FINDLAY	ATTWOOD	DIX	YOUNG	FINDLAY, ATTWOOD
21/02/31	WATFORD	A	2-2	6185	BERRY	PRICE	DENNIS	BRYANT	DINSDALE	HAMILTON	FORBES	FINDLAY	ATTWOOD	DIX	YOUNG	ATTWOOD 2
28/02/31	BOURNEMOUTH	H	2-5	8000	BERRY	RUSSELL	DENNIS	BLACK	DINSDALE	HAMILTON	FORBES	FINDLAY	ATTWOOD	DIX	YOUNG	ATTWOOD 2
07/03/31	SWINDON TOWN	A	1-3	4000	BERRY	RUSSELL	DENNIS	BLACK	COOPER	HAMILTON	FORBES	ARMSTRONG	ATTWOOD	DIX	YOUNG	YOUNG
14/03/31	FULHAM	H	2-1	9000	BERRY	RUSSELL	DENNIS	FINDLAY	COOPER	MUIR	HACKETT	FORBES	ATTWOOD	DIX	YOUNG	ATTWOOD 2
28/03/31	WALSALL	H	1-2	6000	BOYCE	RUSSELL	DENNIS	FINDLAY	COOPER	MUIR	FORBES	BALL	ATTWOOD	ARMSTRONG	YOUNG	ATTWOOD
31/03/31	COVENTRY CITY	A	1-5	7632	BOYCE	RUSSELL	DENNIS	BLACK	COOPER	MUIR	FORBES	ARMSTRONG	ATTWOOD	DIX	YOUNG	DIX
04/04/31	QUEENS PARK RANGERS	A	0-2	7000	BOYCE	RUSSELL	DENNIS	BLACK	COOPER	MUIR	FORBES	ARMSTRONG	ATTWOOD	DIX	YOUNG	
06/04/31	TORQUAY UNITED	H	3-1	6000	BOYCE	RUSSELL	DENNIS	BLACK	COOPER	MUIR	FORBES	ARMSTRONG	ATTWOOD	FINDLAY	YOUNG	ATTWOOD, DIX, MUIR
11/04/31	NORWICH CITY	A	3-0	5000	BOYCE	RUSSELL	DENNIS	BLACK	COOPER	MUIR	FORBES	ARMSTRONG	ATTWOOD	DIX	YOUNG	YOUNG, DIX 2
18/04/31	THAMES ASSOCIATION	A	2-1	1713	BOYCE	RUSSELL	DENNIS	FINDLAY	COOPER	MUIR	FORBES	ARMSTRONG	ATTWOOD	DIX	YOUNG	ATTWOOD 2
25/04/31	CLAPTON ORIENT	H	4-1	5000	BOYCE	RUSSELL	PRICE	FINDLAY	COOPER	BLACK	FORBES	ARMSTRONG	ATTWOOD	DIX	YOUNG	ARMSTRONG 2, DIX, ATTWOOD
02/05/31	GILLINGHAM	H	1-0	4302	BOYCE	RUSSELL	DENNIS	BLACK	COOPER	MUIR	FORBES	ARMSTRONG	ATTWOOD	DIX	YOUNG	FINDLAY

FA CUP

Date	Opposition	Venue	Result	Att	G	2	3	4	5	6	7	8	9	10	11	Goalscorers
29/11/30	MERTHYR T	H	4-1	6912	BOYCE	BARTON	DENNIS	RUSSELL	DINSDALE	HAMILTON	FORBES	BALL	ATTWOOD	DIX	YOUNG	ATTWOOD, DIX, FORBES, HAMILTON
13/12/30	STOCKPORT C	H	4-2	17072	BOYCE	BARTON	DENNIS	RUSSELL	DINSDALE	HAMILTON	FORBES	BALL	ATTWOOD	DIX	YOUNG	FORBES 2, BALL, DIX
10/01/31	QUEENS PARK RANGERS	H	3-1	24000	BOYCE	BARTON	DENNIS	RUSSELL	DINSDALE	HAMILTON	POINTON	FORBES	ATTWOOD	DIX	YOUNG	DENNIS 2 pens, ATTWOOD
24/01/31	BLACKBURN ROVERS	A	1-5	25070	BOYCE	BARTON	DENNIS	RUSSELL	DINSDALE	HAMILTON	POINTON	FORBES	ATTWOOD	DIX	YOUNG	DIX

GLOUCESTERSHIRE CUP FINAL

Date	Opposition	Venue	Result	Att	G	2	3	4	5	6	7	8	9	10	11	Goalscorers
01/10/30	BRISTOL CITY	A	1-3	5026	BOYCE	PRICE	DENNIS	FINDLAY	DINSDALE	HAMILTON	FORBES	BALL	ATTWOOD	DIX	YOUNG	DENNIS pen

PLAYERS	APPS	GLS
ARMSTRONG J	9	2
ATTWOOD A	42	24
BALL C	15	
BARTON G	16	
BERRY L	34	
BLACK J	26	
BOYCE T	8	
BRYANT C	1	
COOPER J	15	
DENNIS G	26	4
DINSDALE N	31	4
DIX R	37	19
FINDLAY A	19	5
FORBES F	39	6
HACKETT C	1	
HAMILTON J	28	1
HAYDON J	11	
MUIR J	8	1
POINTON J	9	1
PRICE W	14	
RICHARDSON J	8	
RUSSELL G	17	
SCOTT J	6	
TURNBULL T	1	
YOUNG H	41	7
OWN GOAL		1

at outside-left – he missed only 1 game and scored 7 goals. However, Arthur Attwood's arrival was the key to the fact that Rovers finished the season as high as 15th in Division Three (South). The former Everton forward scored 24 League goals, only two short of Bill Culley's club record and a seasonal total not equalled by a Rovers player until 1951/52. Attwood was also the club's only ever-present and held together a much-changing forward line.

Rovers used 18 different players in the opening five League games and early heavy defeats led to manager McLean's resignation on 17 September, six days after ill health had forced chairman Mark Hasell to resign. McLean was later manager at East Fife and Hearts. His replacement was the charismatic Captain Albert Prince-Cox. A former footballer and boxer, 40-year-old Prince-Cox had refereed a number of Rovers matches in the 1920s. By 1935 he had refereed 32 International matches in 15 countries. He had also at one time reported daily to Buckingham Palace as a Fellow of the Royal Meteorological Society, to present the King with the weather forecast. He arrived at Eastville on 23 October 1930 in a red open-topped sports car with white wheels, bringing with him an air of change. Within a week of his appointment, he had arranged a tour of the Netherlands.

Just 24 hours after a tough League fixture and following an overnight North Sea crossing, Rovers defeated the Dutch national side 3-2 on Sunday 16 November 1930. This historic result was one that, it has to be said, Rovers were a touch fortunate to achieve. The intrinsic skills of the Dutch side and notably 22-year-old outside-right Adje Gerritse were remarkable and centre-forward Gerrit Hulsman scored twice, though the second was apparently from an offside position. Nonetheless, two goals from Ronnie Dix and one from the ever-reliable Attwood earned Rovers a notable victory. A couple of days later, Rovers defeated the top Dutch side Swallows 4-2 in a game played under floodlights.

Indeed, this victory over Holland is but one successful aspect of the season. The 75 League goals scored represented the second highest total since the club's Southern League days. For the first time since 1920/21, the first season in the Football League, Rovers scored in every home game. Indeed, in the penultimate home game, Rovers scored four times in a 20-minute burst against Clapton Orient, avenging December's defeat at Brisbane Road, which had been due to three goals from Karachi-born Reg Tricker. Attwood was ably supported by young Ronnie Dix, whose first regular run in the side brought 19 League goals.

Prince-Cox attempted to instil greater order into his squad. One example of this was the treatment of outside-left Thomas Turnbull. A summer signing from Gainsborough Trinity, Turnbull had played in one league game in September and appeared regularly in the reserves. In January, Prince-Cox suspended him and reported him to the Football League for 'breaking the club's regulations, having not returned to Bristol after one month's absence.' Subsequently, Turnbull found his registration cancelled in February 1933. Prince-Cox was not one to tolerate professional indiscipline.

Over Christmas Rovers suffered their customary heavy defeat at the Goldstone Ground, after John Carruthers had opened the scoring in the first minute. The Brighton forward went on to complete a hat-trick. The first visit of Thames to Eastville saw the visitors include in their side Fred Le May, at 5ft exactly, the shortest player ever to participate in League football. The return fixture in April was not played at Wembley, as some erroneous reports have hinted, but rather in an eerily empty West Ham Greyhound Stadium, the League newcomers' regular home venue. In January, Rovers' home victory over Crystal Palace was sealed with an own goal from Tom Crilly. Bizarrely, Crilly had also scored an own goal for Bristol City while playing for Derby County in September 1923. Not surprisingly, he is the only player to have scored own goals for both Bristol clubs.

Rovers were awarded three penalties against Queen's Park Rangers in five days in January. All three were conceded by Baden Herod and all converted successfully by the reliable left-back George Dennis. Two came in Rovers' FA Cup third round win, where Rovers found themselves 3-0 up inside 20 minutes, and the third in a 3-0 League victory. George Dennis scored a total of 6 League and cup penalties, including one in each League game against Luton Town. Later in the season, new goalkeeper Tom Boyce saved Bill Sheppard's penalty when Rovers met Queen's Park Rangers at Loftus Road on Easter Saturday. Boyce's debut was in a 2-1 home defeat against Walsall, where the winning goal was scored after 75 minutes by the former Rovers forward, Gilbert Shaw, his only League goal for the Saddlers. Ironically, in Rovers' other League fixture against Walsall, the future Pirate Jack Eyres scored for the opposition.

A final run of five consecutive league wins pushed Rovers up towards a respectable mid-table position. In the FA Cup, three comfortable home wins earned Rovers a fourth-round tie at Ewood Park in front of a crowd exceeding 25,000. Ronnie Dix, later a Blackburn player, scored for Rovers, but the home side won 5-1, one of their goals coming from Syd Puddefoot, an FA Cup winner in 1928. Puddefoot had scored a hat-trick for West Ham United against Rovers in a Southern League game in January 1914. Bristol City inflicted a third consecutive Gloucestershire Cup final defeat on Rovers, Syd Homer and Frank Townrow, both Rovers players at some point in their career, grabbing a goal apiece.

1931/32

The Lilywhites changed their colours in 1931, and Rovers opened the new season wearing the now familiar blue-and-white quartered shirts. Manager Albert Prince-Cox reasoned that such a design would make his players appear larger on the field. However, the quartered shirts quickly became established as a key element in the image of Bristol Rovers. Over the summer, terracing had replaced the earth banking at the Muller Road End of Eastville Stadium, as would be the case at the popular Tote End in 1935. This building work had created the familiar oval-shaped terracing – complete with banana-shaped flowerbeds behind the goal – and brought the crowd capacity at this end of the ground to 16,900. Rovers were to finish the season in 18th place and conceded 92 League goals for the second consecutive season, including five to Watford and Crystal Palace, six against Northampton Town and Norwich City and eight at Torquay United.

Joe Riley scored a hat-trick on his League debut for Rovers against Bournemouth in January 1932

For the new season, the previous season's three top scorers Attwood, Dix and Young started in the forward line. However, the manager's policy of bringing experienced, seasoned campaigners to Eastville meant there were a number of new faces in the side. Goalkeeper Joe Calvert, the club's only ever-present in 1931/32, had enjoyed a number of years in senior non-League football and was to play for Watford, post-war, beyond his 41st birthday. Fair-haired left-back Bill Pickering, half-backs Bill Stoddart and John Muir and outside-right Eric Oakton all boasted impressive pedigrees with other League sides. Stoddart was noted for his exceptionally long and accurate throw-ins. Bill Routledge, an accomplished athlete, was excused pre-season training to compete in the prestigious Powderhall Sprint. Bert Young was the first goalscorer in quarters, while Rovers' other scorer in the opening day draw at Bournemouth was Ronnie Dix, the only Bristol-born player in the side. Dix left at the season's end to play Division One football for many years with three clubs. He earned an England cap against Norway in November 1938, scoring once in a 4-0 win.

The second home game of the season was a morale-boosting 6-1 victory over Crystal Palace, who had themselves scored 10 goals in their first 2 League games. Dix, Attwood and Muir scored twice each. This remains one of only two occasions that three Rovers players have scored as many as two goals each in the same League game. However, Attwood scored just one more goal after this win. Then, just 24 hours before the home game with Gillingham, the centre-forward joined Brighton. As can so often be the case, he returned to haunt his former club, as both he and Jack Eyres scored for Brighton in their 4-0 win at Eastville in February.

Attwood's place in the side was taken by veteran Tommy Cook who, in line with Prince-Cox's masterplan, was enjoying one final fling in League football before retirement. Cook's 114 League goals for Brighton between 1922 and 1929 remain a record at that club and he had earned an England cap against Wales in 1925. He was to score 18 goals in only 31 League games for Rovers in 1931/32 to finish as the club's top scorer for the season. Eric Oakton, the second highest goalscorer, achieved only half that figure.

Cook's second game for Rovers was a 4-2 defeat at Brentford in October. The Bees had won 6 of their last 7 games and took the lead in the opening minute when England amateur International Jackie Burns shot past Joe Calvert. Regaining the initiative for his side, Cook scored twice and Rovers appeared to be taking a lead into the half-time

SEASON 1931/32

FOOTBALL LEAGUE DIVISION THREE (SOUTH)

Date	Opponent		Score	ATT	G	2	3	4	5	6	7	8	9	10	11	GOALSCORERS
29/08/31	BOURNEMOUTH	A	2-2	8000	CALVERT	PICKERING	RUSSELL	ROUTLEDGE	STODDART	MUIR	OAKTON	DIX	ATTWOOD	TOWNROW	YOUNG	YOUNG, DIX
31/08/31	QUEENS PARK RANGERS	H	1-1	15000	CALVERT	PICKERING	RUSSELL	ROUTLEDGE	STODDART	MUIR	OAKTON	DIX	ATTWOOD	TOWNROW	YOUNG	TOWNROW
05/09/31	CRYSTAL PALACE	H	6-1	12979	CALVERT	PICKERING	RUSSELL	ROUTLEDGE	STODDART	MUIR	OAKTON	DIX	ATTWOOD	TOWNROW	YOUNG	MUIR 2, ATTWOOD 2, DIX 2
07/09/31	CLAPTON ORIENT	A	0-1	5701	CALVERT	PICKERING	RUSSELL	ROUTLEDGE	STODDART	MUIR	OAKTON	DIX	ATTWOOD	TOWNROW	STORER	
12/09/31	WATFORD	A	2-5	4797	CALVERT	PICKERING	RUSSELL	ROUTLEDGE	STODDART	MUIR	OAKTON	DIX	ATTWOOD	FINDLAY	YOUNG	FINDLAY, BROWN og
16/09/31	CLAPTON ORIENT	H	2-1	10000	CALVERT	PICKERING	RUSSELL	BLACK	STODDART	MUIR	OAKTON	DIX	ATTWOOD	TOWNROW	YOUNG	ATTWOOD, OAKTON
19/09/31	MANSFIELD TOWN	H	1-1	10770	CALVERT	PICKERING	RUSSELL	ROUTLEDGE	STODDART	MUIR	OAKTON	DIX	ATTWOOD	TOWNROW	YOUNG	ROUTLEDGE
26/09/31	BRIGHTON & HOVE ALBION	A	0-2	8197	CALVERT	PICKERING	RUSSELL	ROUTLEDGE	STODDART	MUIR	OAKTON	DIX	ATTWOOD	TOWNROW	YOUNG	
03/10/31	NORWICH CITY	H	0-1	7000	CALVERT	PICKERING	RUSSELL	ROUTLEDGE	STODDART	MUIR	OAKTON	DIX	ATTWOOD	TOWNROW	YOUNG	
10/10/31	SWINDON TOWN	A	1-2	5500	CALVERT	PICKERING	RUSSELL	ROUTLEDGE	COOPER	MUIR	OAKTON	TOWNROW	COOK	DIX	YOUNG	TOWNROW
17/10/31	BRENTFORD	A	2-4	14000	CALVERT	PICKERING	HILL	ROUTLEDGE	STODDART	COOPER	OAKTON	DANDO	COOK	DIX	YOUNG	COOK 2
24/10/31	EXETER CITY	H	2-4	8000	CALVERT	PICKERING	HILL	ROUTLEDGE	STODDART	COOPER	OAKTON	DANDO	COOK	DIX	YOUNG	OAKTON, YOUNG
31/10/31	COVENTRY CITY	A	1-1	15017	CALVERT	PICKERING	HILL	ROUTLEDGE	RUSSELL	COOPER	OAKTON	TOWNROW	COOK	DIX	YOUNG	COOK
07/11/31	GILLINGHAM	H	5-2	7000	CALVERT	RUSSELL	HILL	ROUTLEDGE	PICKERING	COOPER	OAKTON	DIX	COOK	TOWNROW	YOUNG	OAKTON, TOWNROW 2, COOK, YOUNG
14/11/31	LUTON TOWN	A	0-3	7000	CALVERT	RUSSELL	HILL	ROUTLEDGE	PICKERING	COOPER	OAKTON	DIX	COOK	TOWNROW	YOUNG	
21/11/31	CARDIFF CITY	A	2-2	9000	CALVERT	RUSSELL	HILL	ROUTLEDGE	PICKERING	BLAKE	OAKTON	DIX	COOK	MUIR	YOUNG	DIX, COOK
05/12/31	READING	H	2-0	6000	CALVERT	RUSSELL	HILL	ROUTLEDGE	PICKERING	BLACK	OAKTON	DIX	COOK	TOWNROW	YOUNG	OAKTON, TOWNROW
19/12/31	FULHAM	H	2-2	5000	CALVERT	RUSSELL	HILL	ROUTLEDGE	PICKERING	BLACK	OAKTON	DIX	COOK	TOWNROW	YOUNG	COOK 2
25/12/31	THAMES ASSOCIATION	A	2-0	3000	CALVERT	RUSSELL	HILL	ROUTLEDGE	FINDLAY	BLACK	OAKTON	DIX	COOK	TOWNROW	YOUNG	COOK, OAKTON
26/12/31	THAMES ASSOCIATION	H	4-1	18000	CALVERT	RUSSELL	HILL	ROUTLEDGE	FINDLAY	BLACK	OAKTON	DIX	COOK	TOWNROW	YOUNG	COOK, BLACK, FINDLAY 2
28/12/31	NORTHAMPTON TOWN	A	0-6	6087	CALVERT	RUSSELL	HILL	ROUTLEDGE	FINDLAY	BLACK	OAKTON	DIX	COOK	TOWNROW	COOMBS	
02/01/32	BOURNEMOUTH	H	4-1	5000	CALVERT	RUSSELL	SMITH	BLACK	PICKERING	TOWNROW	ROUTLEDGE	COOK	RILEY	DIX	YOUNG	RILEY 3, COOK
09/01/32	SOUTHEND UNITED	A	1-4	6220	CALVERT	RUSSELL	HILL	BLACK	PICKERING	TOWNROW	ROUTLEDGE	COOK	RILEY	DIX	YOUNG	DIX
16/01/32	CRYSTAL PALACE	A	0-5	10691	CALVERT	RUSSELL	HILL	BLACK	PICKERING	TOWNROW	OAKTON	ROUTLEDGE	COOK	DIX	YOUNG	
27/01/32	WATFORD	H	3-2	4000	CALVERT	RUSSELL	SMITH	BLACK	PICKERING	TOWNROW	OAKTON	ROUTLEDGE	COOK	DIX	YOUNG	COOK 2, OAKTON
30/01/32	MANSFIELD TOWN	H	3-0	7118	CALVERT	RUSSELL	SMITH	BLACK	PICKERING	TOWNROW	OAKTON	ROUTLEDGE	COOK	DIX	YOUNG	ROUTLEDGE, COOK, DIX
06/02/32	BRIGHTON & HOVE ALBION	A	0-4	8711	CALVERT	RUSSELL	SMITH	BLACK	STODDART	TOWNROW	OAKTON	ROUTLEDGE	COOK	DIX	COOMBS	
13/02/32	NORWICH CITY	A	0-6	7500	CALVERT	PICKERING	RUSSELL	BLACK	PICKERING	MUIR	OAKTON	DANDO	RILEY	MUIR	DIX	
20/02/32	SWINDON TOWN	H	0-2	6000	CALVERT	SMITH	TOWNROW	BLACK	PICKERING	MUIR	OAKTON	COOK	RILEY	DIX	COOPER	
27/02/32	BRENTFORD	H	2-0	12000	CALVERT	RUSSELL	SMITH	BLACK	STODDART	TOWNROW	OAKTON	ROUTLEDGE	COOK	DIX	YOUNG	COOK, ROUTLEDGE
05/03/32	EXETER CITY	A	0-1	7000	CALVERT	RUSSELL	SMITH	BLACK	STODDART	TOWNROW	OAKTON	ROUTLEDGE	COOK	DIX	YOUNG	
12/03/32	COVENTRY CITY	H	3-1	7000	CALVERT	RUSSELL	SMITH	BLACK	STODDART	TOWNROW	OAKTON	ROUTLEDGE	COOK	DIX	YOUNG	OAKTON, ROUTLEDGE, DIX
19/03/32	GILLINGHAM	A	0-1	4000	CALVERT	RUSSELL	SMITH	BLACK	STODDART	TOWNROW	OAKTON	ROUTLEDGE	COOK	DIX	FINDLAY	
25/03/32	TORQUAY UNITED	H	1-1	10000	CALVERT	RUSSELL	FINDLAY	BLACK	STODDART	TOWNROW	OAKTON	ROUTLEDGE	COOK	DIX	YOUNG	COOK
26/03/32	LUTON TOWN	H	3-1	5000	CALVERT	RUSSELL	FINDLAY	BLACK	STODDART	TOWNROW	OAKTON	ROUTLEDGE	COOK	DIX	YOUNG	OAKTON 2, FINDLAY
28/03/32	TORQUAY UNITED	A	1-8	2830	CALVERT	RUSSELL	FINDLAY	BLACK	STODDART	TOWNROW	OAKTON	ROUTLEDGE	COOK	DIX	YOUNG	YOUNG
02/04/32	CARDIFF CITY	A	1-3	8000	CALVERT	STODDART	PICKERING	ROUTLEDGE	ROUTLEDGE	TOWNROW	OAKTON	DANDO	COOK	FINDLAY	YOUNG	BLACK pen
09/04/32	NORTHAMPTON TOWN	H	3-2	5000	CALVERT	RUSSELL	PICKERING	ROUTLEDGE	STODDART	TOWNROW	OAKTON	DANDO	COOK	FINDLAY	YOUNG	COOK, DIX, RUSSELL
16/04/32	READING	A	0-3	3443	CALVERT	RUSSELL	PICKERING	ROUTLEDGE	STODDART	TOWNROW	OAKTON	DANDO	COOK	FINDLAY	YOUNG	
23/04/32	SOUTHEND UNITED	H	0-0	8000	CALVERT	PICKERING	PICKERING	STODDART	BLAKE	TOWNROW	ROUTLEDGE	ROUTLEDGE	COOK	DIX	YOUNG	
30/04/32	FULHAM	A	2-3	21000	CALVERT	RUSSELL	PICKERING	STODDART	BLAKE	TOWNROW	ROUTLEDGE	DIX	COOK	HILL	OAKTON	COOK, PICKERING
07/05/32	QUEENS PARK RANGERS	A	1-2	7141	CALVERT	STODDART	RUSSELL	BLACK	BLAKE	TOWNROW	OAKTON	DANDO	COOK	DIX	OAKTON	BLACK

FA CUP

Date	Opponent		Score	ATT	G	2	3	4	5	6	7	8	9	10	11	GOALSCORERS
28/11/31	GILLINGHAM	H	5-1	7000	CALVERT	HILL	RUSSELL	ROUTLEDGE	PICKERING	BLACK	OAKTON	DIX	COOK	TOWNROW	YOUNG	DIX, TOWNROW, OAKTON, COOK, RUSSELL
12/12/31	TRANMERE ROVERS	A	0-2	13200	CALVERT	RUSSELL	HILL	ROUTLEDGE	PICKERING	BLACK	OAKTON	DIX	COOK	TOWNROW	YOUNG	

GLOUCESTERSHIRE CUP FINAL

Date	Opponent		Score	ATT	G	2	3	4	5	6	7	8	9	10	11	GOALSCORERS
09/09/31	BRISTOL CITY	H	0-1	10862	CALVERT	PICKERING	RUSSELL	ROUTLEDGE	STODDART	MUIR	OAKTON	DIX	ATTWOOD	FINDLAY	YOUNG	

PLAYERS	APPS	GLS
ATTWOOD A	9	0
BLACK J	23	3
BLAKE H	4	
CALVERT J	42	
COOK T	31	17
COOMBS E	1	
COOPER J	7	
DANDO M	7	
DIX R	40	8
FINDLAY A	10	4
HILL F	16	
MUIR J	13	2
OAKTON E	40	9
PICKERING W	31	1
RILEY J	5	3
ROUTLEDGE W	39	4
RUSSELL G	38	1
SMITH E	8	
STODDART W	25	
STORER J	1	
TOWNROW F	38	5
YOUNG H	34	4
OWN GOAL		1

Bristol Rovers 1931/32. Back row: B Williams (Asst Trainer), Storer, Routledge, Calvert, Berry, Stoddart, Oakton, H Lake (Trainer). Second row: Findlay, Hill, Cooper, Hudson, Bryant, Carter, Townrow, Smart, Riley. Front row: Russell, Bennett, Dix, Attwood, M Menzies (Asst Secretary), Capt. Albert Prince-Cox (Secretary-Manager), Pickering, Young, Black, Muir

interval. Shortly before the break, however, Brentford won a penalty, converted by George Robson and, within seconds of the start of the second-half, Bill Berry put the home side in front. Five minutes from time a second penalty secured victory for the Bees. Robson was only taking penalties in the absence of Bill Lane – and he added another at Torquay seven days later – but he became the second of six opponents to score two penalties against Rovers in a League match.

Occasions when Rovers have scored five goals before half-time are rare. In November, though, five goals in 21 first-half minutes saw Rovers lead Gillingham 5-0, before conceding two goals in the second-half, one scored by Les Ames, the England cricketer and subsequent Test selector. The same opposition suffered a similar fate in the first round of the FA Cup as five Rovers players got on the scoresheet in a 5-1 win. Another comfortable victory was the 4-1 home win over Bournemouth in January. Yorkshireman Joe Riley was given a League debut in this game at centre-forward and he responded with three goals. Only Jimmy McCambridge and Bobby Gould have since equalled this feat of a debut hat-trick for Rovers. Riley himself was sold to Bournemouth in 1935 and was to score a League hat-trick against Rovers for his new club.

However, heavy defeats continued to loom large in Rovers' season. Shortly after Christmas, Northampton were 5-0 ahead by half-time and their 6-0 victory featured two goals each from Harry Lovatt, Tommy Wells and the perennial Ted Bowen. Fred Dawes, who played in this game for Northampton, appeared against Rovers on a number of occasions over 18 years, his final match against the Pirates being Palace's 1-0 victory in

September 1949. Six weeks later, another 6-0 defeat, this time at Carrow Road, saw three opponents again scoring twice – Oliver Brown, Sam Bell and Cyril Blakemore. Indeed Blakemore, a former Bristol City player, had earlier scored against Rovers for both Portsmouth and Crystal Palace, the latter in the extraordinary 7-4 defeat in March 1927. He had also missed a penalty in the controversial game at Brentford in September 1929. Only on three further occasions since 1932 have three opponents scored two or more goals each in a League game against Rovers.

Just when the defence was beginning to act as a unit, the Plainmoor debacle on Easter Monday led Rovers to rethink the structure of the team. The 8-1 defeat equalled the club's heaviest ever loss at that time in League football. Rovers were four goals down by half-time against a supposedly struggling Torquay side. Although outside-left Bert Young pulled a goal back, Rovers were heavily beaten. The final whistle could not come soon enough as Bill Clayson, leading the forward line, scored three times in the final four minutes to take his personal tally for the afternoon to four. Rovers were to finish the season above Torquay in the League table, but the psychological damage inflicted at Plainmoor would take a while to recede.

In October, there was crowd trouble at Eastville. After a second-half penalty appeal had been turned down, with Rovers heading for a 1-0 home defeat against Norwich City, referee Stanley Rous, later president of the Football Association, was assaulted by a drunken spectator.

In January, dense fog meant the Rovers side arrived at The Kursaal only 15 minutes before kick-off in the League game with Southend United. Rovers held the home side 1-1 at half-time, but fell apart in the second-half with Jimmy Shankly scoring twice in a 4-1 defeat. Against Cardiff City, goals were conceded to erstwhile Rovers Jimmy McCambridge, scoring in one fixture, and Harry O'Neill in the other. As the season drew to a close, Rovers visited Fulham and shocked the home side by leading at half-time, Cook having scored following a corner. Nonetheless, with the wind behind them, Fulham produced three second-half goals to secure the Championship, despite Pickering's low drive late in the game. Rovers drew 1-1 at Eastville in March in a benefit game with Bristol City for the amateur Jack Pearce, which raised a total of £9, a significant amount in 1932. Joe Riley had given Rovers the lead in the first minute.

One future Rovers player, Jack Allen, enjoyed huge FA Cup final success. He scored both Newcastle's goals in their 2-1 victory over Arsenal at Wembley. Arsenal, featuring in their side Rovers reject and winner of 30 England caps, Eddie Hapgood, had taken a 13th-minute lead through Bob John before Allen's double strike. The equaliser was heavily disputed, as the ball appeared to have crossed the goal-line before Jimmy Richardson was able to centre.

Rovers fell to Tranmere in the FA Cup and a solitary second-half Sid Elliott goal gave Bristol City a fourth consecutive Gloucestershire Cup victory. One sad postscript to the season was the death of Bill Callender, the Crystal Palace goalkeeper who had conceded those six goals at Eastville in September. In July 1932 following the death of his fiancée, he hanged himself at the Selhurst Park ground.

Over the summer of 1932, greyhound racing first took place at Eastville. The Bristol Greyhound Racing Association was incorporated as a Public Limited Liability Company on 4 March 1932 with 250,000 shares initially sold for two shillings each. On 21 March the club had granted a lease to the Bristol Greyhound Racing Association for £5,000 and an annual £600 rent and the first race was on 16 July. Alarmingly, the greyhound company was given first refusal should Rovers ever choose to sell the ground, and even promised the price would not exceed £13,000. Wartime needs were to lead to such a situation and Rovers' departure from Eastville in 1986 can be traced back to this sequence of events.

1932/33

Rovers' charismatic manager, Albert Prince-Cox, led the club through an exciting season as the side finished ninth in Division Three (South). This performance equalled the club's highest final League position to date. With five former Internationals on their books, Rovers played some exciting football. The manager's response was to take the club on various overseas trips, to Rotterdam in September, to Paris and Amsterdam in the New Year and back to France once the season had finished.

To some it appeared that the manager was simply an eccentric. He arranged for a private aircraft to fly the experienced amateur centre-forward, Vivian Gibbins, from Romford Aerodrome to Filton in time for the 6.15 p.m. kick-off in the September game with Southend United. However, Gibbins responded with a goal in Rovers' 3-1 victory and scored two hat-tricks the following month, in a 5-3 win over Brighton and a 3-0 win at Clapton Orient. The Orient game was apparently ended five minutes early. Not that Rovers would have been too concerned, for the side had lost League games at Brisbane Road in the previous three seasons. Gibbins, 'one of the last great amateurs imbued with the Corinthian spirit', as a journalist for *Athletic News* described him, was Rovers' top scorer with 14 League goals, the only amateur to achieve this feat in Rovers' League history. For this season his tally was closely followed by that of Billy Jackson, whose 11 goals came in the first 16 League matches.

The new season saw the usual influx of players. Left-back Alec Donald, a Scotsman signed from Chelsea, formed a successful full-back partnership with the dependable club captain Bill Pickering. George McNestry was to prove an influential figure at outside-right, while Jackson and Jack Eyres showed promise as a left-wing pairing. There were three goalkeepers employed, yet stability was clear in the fact that, in strong contrast to previous seasons, Rovers conceded four goals in a League game on only two occasions. Season ticket prices remained unchanged at 50 shillings for the most expensive seats, while under-14s could buy a season ticket on the terraces for as little as 10 shillings. Ronnie Dix joined Blackburn Rovers for £3,000 and was to play subsequently for Aston Villa, Derby County, Tottenham Hotspur and Reading. He won an England cap in November 1938, scoring in a 4-0 victory over Norway.

The ability to field as many as five former Internationals was quite some achievement for a Third Division side. Sam Irving, born in Belfast of Scottish parentage, spent one year in the side at right-half. He had won 18 caps for Northern Ireland and, because of the intrusions of war and of playing football in Scotland and the United States during

166

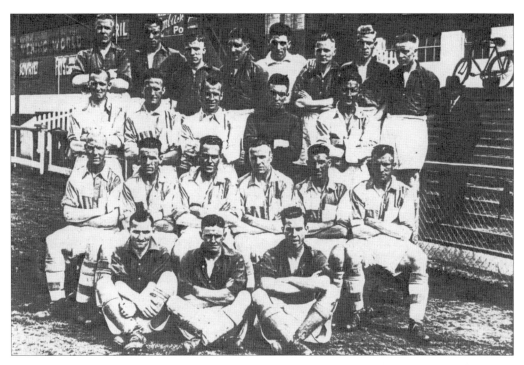

Bristol Rovers 1932/33. Rovers signed the vastly experienced Samuel Irving (third row, third from left) from Chelsea as player-coach. He had won 18 caps for Northern Ireland and won the FA Cup in 1927 with Cardiff City

his 20-year professional career, could lay claim to a number of quirky facts. For instance, he did not score a League goal between October 1914 and March 1927. He also won an FA Cup winners' medal with Cardiff City, but both played in and managed sides in losing Scottish Cup finals, before becoming a director of Dundee United. Irving's only goal for Rovers came at Eastville in December, when Brentford replied with three goals in seven minutes to win 4-2. Alongside Bobby McKay, who had won a Scottish cap in 1927, Rovers fielded three former England Internationals in Vivian Gibbins, Tommy Cook and Jack Townrow, who joined his brother Frank in the half-back line.

The veteran forward Tommy Cook, Rovers' top scorer the previous season, scored only 3 League goals this time before a broken collar-bone, sustained in a collision with Cardiff City's former Rovers full-back George Russell, was to end his career. As one highly experienced player retired, another long and distinguished footballing career was just getting underway. Wally McArthur, who was to appear in 261 League games for Rovers before retiring in 1949, made his debut in April in a goalless draw with Brentford. The Bees were already divisional champions and should have won, but the veteran prolific marksman David Halliday missed a penalty. Rovers also drew at Southend United who, in the process set a club record as yet unsurpassed by the Shrimpers, of 16 consecutive League matches unbeaten.

An exciting victory over Northampton at Eastville in October, 4-3 in Rovers' favour, featured an own goal from the Cobblers' goalkeeper Len Hammond in his 295th League game for the visitors as well as two good goals from Jackson. The return game in early

FOOTBALL LEAGUE DIVISION THREE (SOUTH) — SEASON 1932/33

Date	Opponent	Venue	Score	Att	1 (G)	2	3	4	5	6	7	8	9	10	11	Goalscorers
27/08/32	CRYSTAL PALACE	H	2-3	13588	HARVEY	PICKERING	HOUGH	BLAKE	J TOWNROW	DONALD	McNESTRY	ROUTLEDGE	GIBBINS	EYRES	JACKSON	JACKSON 2
29/08/32	SOUTHEND UNITED	A	2-2	8677	WINDSOR	PICKERING	DONALD	IRVING	J TOWNROW	F TOWNROW	McNESTRY	ROUTLEDGE	GIBBINS	EYRES	JACKSON	GIBBINS, ROUTLEDGE
03/09/32	GILLINGHAM	A	0-2	3085	WINDSOR	PICKERING	DONALD	IRVING	J TOWNROW	F TOWNROW	McNESTRY	COOK	GIBBINS	EYRES	JACKSON	
07/09/32	SOUTHEND UNITED	H	3-1	7000	WINDSOR	PICKERING	DONALD	IRVING	BLAKE	F TOWNROW	McNESTRY	COOK	GIBBINS	EYRES	JACKSON	COOK, GIBBINS, TOWNROW
10/09/32	WATFORD	A	2-0	8000	WINDSOR	PICKERING	DONALD	IRVING	BLAKE	F TOWNROW	McNESTRY	COOK	GIBBINS	EYRES	JACKSON	DANDO, EYRES
17/09/32	CARDIFF CITY	A	3-4	6000	WINDSOR	PICKERING	DONALD	IRVING	BLAKE	F TOWNROW	McNESTRY	COOK	GIBBINS	EYRES	JACKSON	JACKSON 2, EYRES
24/09/32	READING	H	1-0	14000	WINDSOR	PICKERING	DONALD	STODDART	BLAKE	F TOWNROW	McNESTRY	COOK, GIBBINS	GIBBINS	EYRES	JACKSON	McNESTRY
01/10/32	NORWICH CITY	A	1-1	6000	WINDSOR	PICKERING	DONALD	STODDART	BLAKE	F TOWNROW	McNESTRY	COOK	GIBBINS	EYRES	JACKSON	EYRES
08/10/32	BRIGHTON & HOVE ALBION	H	5-3	8869	WINDSOR	PICKERING	DONALD	STODDART	BLAKE	F TOWNROW	McNESTRY	McKAY	GIBBINS	EYRES	JACKSON	GIBBINS 3, EYRES, JACKSON
15/10/32	BRISTOL CITY	A	1-3	25501	WINDSOR	PICKERING	DONALD	STODDART	BLAKE	F TOWNROW	McNESTRY	McKAY	GIBBINS	EYRES	JACKSON	EYRES
22/10/32	NORTHAMPTON TOWN	H	4-3	9000	WINDSOR	PICKERING	DONALD	STODDART	BLAKE	F TOWNROW	McNESTRY	McKAY	GIBBINS	EYRES	JACKSON	GIBBINS 3, JACKSON 2
29/10/32	CLAPTON ORIENT	A	3-0	7083	WINDSOR	PICKERING	DONALD	STODDART	BLAKE	F TOWNROW	McNESTRY	McKAY	GIBBINS	EYRES	JACKSON	GIBBINS 2, JACKSON 2
05/11/32	SWINDON TOWN	H	1-0	11000	WINDSOR	PICKERING	DONALD	BLAKE	LEWIS	F TOWNROW	McNESTRY	McKAY	GIBBINS	EYRES	JACKSON	TAYLOR og
12/11/32	BOURNEMOUTH	A	2-2	5000	WINDSOR	PICKERING	DONALD	BLAKE	LEWIS	F TOWNROW	McNESTRY	McKAY	GIBBINS	EYRES	JACKSON	McNESTRY
19/11/32	NEWPORT COUNTY	H	2-2	8910	WINDSOR	BANN	DONALD	BLAKE	LEWIS	F TOWNROW	McNESTRY	McKAY	GIBBINS	EYRES	JACKSON	GIBBINS 3
03/12/32	EXETER CITY	A	1-0	11000	WINDSOR	PICKERING	DONALD	J TOWNROW	BLAKE	LEWIS	McNESTRY	McKAY	GIBBINS	EYRES	JACKSON	LEWIS
17/12/32	BRENTFORD	H	2-4	17000	WINDSOR	PICKERING	DONALD	BLAKE	BLAKE	F TOWNROW	McNESTRY	McKAY	GIBBINS	EYRES	JACKSON	JACKSON, EYRES
24/12/32	COVENTRY CITY	A	0-2	9000	WINDSOR	PICKERING	DONALD	BLAKE	BLAKE	F TOWNROW	McNESTRY	McKAY	GIBBINS	EYRES	JACKSON	GIBBINS, JACKSON
26/12/32	ALDERSHOT	H	0-1	6360	BEBY	PICKERING	DONALD	IRVING	STODDART	F TOWNROW	McNESTRY	McKAY	GIBBINS	EYRES	JACKSON	GIBBINS, IRVING pen
27/12/32	ALDERSHOT	A	4-1	20064	BEBY	PICKERING	DONALD	IRVING	BLAKE	F TOWNROW	McNESTRY	McKAY	GIBBINS	EYRES	GREEN	McNESTRY 2, COOK 2
31/12/32	CRYSTAL PALACE	A	0-2	10636	BEBY	PICKERING	DONALD	IRVING	BLAKE	GREEN	McNESTRY	COOK	COOK	JACKSON	GREEN	COOK
07/01/33	GILLINGHAM	H	1-0	8000	BEBY	PICKERING	DONALD	IRVING	BLAKE	F TOWNROW	McNESTRY	COOK	COOK	JACKSON	GREEN	DANDO
21/01/33	WATFORD	H	1-3	4202	BEBY	PICKERING	DONALD	IRVING	BLAKE	F TOWNROW	McNESTRY	COOK	DANDO	GIBBINS	GREEN	GREEN
28/01/33	CARDIFF CITY	H	0-0	8000	BEBY	PICKERING	DONALD	IRVING	BLAKE	GREEN	McNESTRY	COOK	COOK	GIBBINS	WYPER	EYRES
11/02/33	READING	A	1-3	7000	BEBY	PICKERING	DONALD	BLAKE	F TOWNROW	F TOWNROW	WYPER	GIBBINS	GIBBINS	JACKSON	GREEN	LEWIS
04/02/33	NORWICH CITY	H	4-0	8000	BEBY	PICKERING	DONALD	IRVING	ROUTLEDGE	DONALD	WYPER	GIBBINS	GIBBINS	JACKSON	GREEN	LEWIS 2, McKAY
11/02/33	BRIGHTON & HOVE ALBION	A	1-1	8000	BEBY	PICKERING	DONALD	IRVING	ROUTLEDGE	F TOWNROW	WYPER	GIBBINS	GIBBINS	JACKSON	GREEN	STEVENSON, GREEN
03/03/33	NORTHAMPTON TOWN	A	2-0	5919	BEBY	PICKERING	DONALD	BLAKE	ROUTLEDGE	F TOWNROW	McKAY	GIBBINS	GIBBINS	STEVENSON	GREEN	GIBBINS
04/03/33	CLAPTON ORIENT	H	1-1	9000	BEBY	PICKERING	DONALD	STODDART	ROUTLEDGE	F TOWNROW	McKAY	GIBBINS	GIBBINS	STEVENSON	GREEN	LEWIS
11/03/33	LUTON TOWN	A	1-1	2000	BEBY	PICKERING	DONALD	IRVING	ROUTLEDGE	F TOWNROW	McKAY	GIBBINS	GIBBINS	STEVENSON	LEWIS	LEWIS 2, McKAY
13/03/33	LUTON TOWN	H	1-0	4000	BEBY	PICKERING	HOUGH	IRVING	ROUTLEDGE	IRVING	McKAY	GIBBINS	GIBBINS	STEVENSON	GREEN	EYRES
18/03/33	SWINDON TOWN	A	1-1	8000	BEBY	PICKERING	DONALD	IRVING	ROUTLEDGE	F TOWNROW	McKAY	GIBBINS	GIBBINS	STEVENSON	GREEN	McNESTRY
25/03/33	BOURNEMOUTH	H	1-3	23475	BEBY	PICKERING	DONALD	IRVING	ROUTLEDGE	F TOWNROW	McKAY	STEVENSON	McKAY	GREEN	GREEN	GIBBINS
29/03/33	BRISTOL CITY	H	0-0	3588	BEBY	PICKERING	DONALD	IRVING	ROUTLEDGE	F TOWNROW	McKAY	GIBBINS	GIBBINS	GIBBINS	JACKSON	
01/04/33	NEWPORT COUNTY	A	1-1	6000	BEBY	PICKERING	DONALD	IRVING	ROUTLEDGE	McNESTRY	McKAY	LEWIS	McNESTRY	McKAY	JACKSON	McNESTRY
08/04/33	QUEENS PARK RANGERS	H	0-0	6000	BEBY	PICKERING	DONALD	IRVING	ROUTLEDGE	McNESTRY	McKAY	GIBBINS	McNESTRY	GIBBINS	GREEN	GIBBINS
14/04/33	QUEENS PARK RANGERS	A	1-1	6646	BEBY	PICKERING	DONALD	IRVING	ROUTLEDGE	BLAKE	McNESTRY	BLAKE	McNESTRY	GIBBINS	GREEN	BLAKE
15/04/33	EXETER CITY	H	4-1	8000	BEBY	PICKERING	DONALD	IRVING	GIBBINS	F TOWNROW	McKAY	LEWIS	RILEY	EYRES	GREEN	GIBBINS 2, RILEY, McNESTRY
17/04/33	TORQUAY UNITED	A	0-2	8000	BEBY	PICKERING	DONALD	IRVING	BLAKE	IRVING	McKAY	LEWIS	RILEY	EYRES	LEWIS	
22/04/33	TORQUAY UNITED	H	1-1	6000	BEBY	PICKERING	DONALD	STODDART	ROUTLEDGE	F TOWNROW	McKAY	WYPER	RILEY	EYRES	WYPER	WYPER
26/04/33	BRENTFORD	A	0-1	2462	BEBY	PICKERING	DONALD	IRVING	McARTHUR	EYRES	McNESTRY	McNESTRY	RILEY	McKAY	JACKSON	
29/04/33	BRENTFORD	H	0-0	9000	BEBY	PICKERING	DONALD	STODDART	McARTHUR	EYRES	WYPER	McNESTRY	McKAY	McKAY	JACKSON	
06/05/33	COVENTRY CITY	A	1-0	4000	BEBY	PICKERING	DONALD	STODDART	ROUTLEDGE	EYRES	McNESTRY	McNESTRY	LEWIS	McKAY	JACKSON	

FA CUP

Date	Opponent	Venue	Score	Att	1	2	3	4	5	6	7	8	9	10	11	Goalscorers
26/11/32	CARDIFF CITY	A	1-1	11000	WINDSOR	PICKERING	DONALD	IRVING	BLAKE	F TOWNROW	McNESTRY	McKAY	GIBBINS	EYRES	JACKSON	JACKSON
30/11/32	CARDIFF CITY	H	4-1	6000	WINDSOR	PICKERING	DONALD	IRVING	BLAKE	F TOWNROW	McNESTRY	McKAY	GIBBINS	EYRES	JACKSON	GIBBINS 2, RILEY, McNESTRY
10/12/32	GILLINGHAM	H	1-1	11000	WINDSOR	PICKERING	DONALD	IRVING	BLAKE	F TOWNROW	McNESTRY	McKAY	GIBBINS	EYRES	LEWIS	EYRES, McNESTRY, JACKSON, F TOWNROW
11/12/32	GILLINGHAM	A	3-1	6511	WINDSOR	PICKERING	DONALD	IRVING	BLAKE	F TOWNROW	McNESTRY	McKAY	GIBBINS	EYRES	JACKSON	EYRES, McNESTRY, JACKSON, F TOWNROW
14/01/33	ALDERSHOT	A	0-1	12000	WINDSOR	PICKERING	DONALD	IRVING	BLAKE	EYRES	McNESTRY	McKAY	GIBBINS	EYRES	JACKSON	

GLOUCESTERSHIRE CUP FINAL

Date	Opponent	Venue	Score	Att	1	2	3	4	5	6	7	8	9	10	11	Goalscorers
14/09/32	BRISTOL CITY	A	3-3	6929	WINDSOR	BANN	BANN	STODDART	McARTHUR	BLAKE	McNESTRY	IRVING	ROUTLEDGE	McKAY	GREEN	IRVING, EYRES, JACKSON
24/04/33	BRISTOL CITY	H	3-4	5809	WINDSOR	PICKERING	HOUGH	IRVING	J TOWNROW	DONALD	WYPER	McNESTRY	RILEY	BLAKE	JACKSON	STODDART, WYPER, McNESTRY

WELSH CUP

Date	Opponent	Venue	Score	Att	1	2	3	4	5	6	7	8	9	10	11	Goalscorers
08/02/33	SWANSEA TOWN	A	0-3	3500	HARVEY	PICKERING	HOUGH	BLAKE	J TOWNROW	DONALD	McNESTRY	BRIGGS	LEWIS	McKAY	GREEN	

PLAYERS

PLAYERS	APPS	GLS
BANN W	1	
BEBY J	24	
BLAKE H	27	2
COOK T	11	3
DANDO M	1	
DONALD A	39	
EYRES J	36	7
GIBBINS V	37	15
GREEN R	22	
HARVEY J	1	
HOUGH E	1	
IRVING S	21	1
JACKSON W	20	11
LEWIS D	23	4
McARTHUR W	1	
McKAY R	27	2
McNESTRY G	35	7
PICKERING W	42	
RILEY J	4	1
ROUTLEDGE W	17	1
STEVENSON J	7	2
TOWNROW J	10	1
WINDSOR F	17	
WYPER W	2	1
OWN GOAL		1

George McNestry scores against Bristol City in March 1933

March saw the first of two League goals from local schoolmaster Bert Blake, a highly dependable centre-half and the nephew of a Spurs goalkeeper. This 1-1 draw proved to be one of seven in the second half of the season. Cardiff City converted one of two penalties awarded in their favour at Ninian Park in November. The 3-1 defeat at Reading saw a sole League appearance for Rovers of Ted Hough, a full-back who had earlier in his career joined Southampton for a fee of 52 pints of beer.

Rovers had four ultimately unsuccessful matches against Bristol City. The League fixture at Ashton Gate ended in a 3-1 defeat, with City's Billy Knox scoring direct from a free-kick taken from just inside his own half, while a George McNestry goal earned a 1-1 draw at Eastville in the spring. City won the Gloucestershire Cup final 4-3 after a 3-3 draw. Rovers had six different goalscorers in these two matches, while the former Rovers outside-right Sid Homer scored two of City's goals in the drawn match.

At the end of September, immediately after the home win over Reading, Prince-Cox took his team to Rotterdam, where they beat a Dutch Representative XI 7-4, with Joe Riley and George McNestry scoring twice each. Rovers also beat The Hague 1-0 and lost 3-0 to Nice, before returning for the game with Norwich City at Carrow Road. On 26 January, just two days before the home game with Cardiff City, Rovers were taken to Paris. Despite a goal from outside-left Tom Wyper, Rovers lost 3-1 to a French Select XI. With a week off in late February, Rovers played East Holland in Amsterdam, losing 3-2 despite goals from Doug Lewis and Jack Eyres.

Modern talk of fixture pile-ups appears trivial when you consider that, into a season of 42 League and 8 senior cup games, Rovers undertook three mid-season tours. The club also hosted the touring Czech side Nachod in April, winning 4-2 through three George Tepper goals and one from Joe Riley. A strong team also represented the club on Good Friday in a testimonial for full-back Ernie Sambidge; Bath City were leading

Rovers 4-2 when the match was abandoned with 20 minutes remaining, Riley having scored twice for Rovers.

To cap the extravagance, Prince-Cox took the Rovers team on an end-of-season tour of Southern France. On 14 May 1933, Rovers played AC Milan at the Stade St Maurice in Nice. Milan won this game 3-1, with a McNestry penalty early in the second-half all Rovers' reward before Romani added the Italian side's third. Four days later, McNestry was again on the scoresheet as Rovers lost 3-1 to a French XI. Nonetheless, having beaten Holland in November 1930 and lost only narrowly in these two prestigious games, Prince-Cox's side was gaining experience to a degree rarely seen at a Division Three side between the wars.

The eight cup games, referred to above, comprise five FA Cup games, the two Gloucestershire Cup matches and a first excursion into the Welsh Cup. A promising FA Cup run, which started with Rovers wearing red at Cardiff City, ended with defeat at Aldershot in the third round, where Rovers went down to a solitary goal from veteran outside-left Jack Lane. That Rovers reached the third round at all was due to Sam Irving's late penalty after Rovers had trailed for 83 minutes at home to Gillingham. The fact that Rovers entered the Welsh Cup is explained by the eagerness of the authorities to open up this tournament. Bristol City, for instance, were to win the Welsh Cup in 1934, with two former Rovers players Joe Riley and Sid Homer in their side. Rovers' first foray ended in a 3-0 defeat at Swansea Town. The Rovers side wore black armbands following the recent death of club director Tommy Walker, a member of the board since 1922 and chairman of the Supporters' Club in 1927, and the referee, a Mr Thorneycroft, was the son of a Newport County director. Rovers also won the Allan Palmer Cup, which they had previously won in 1927, when holders Nottingham Forest were beaten 2-0 before a crowd of 3,200. The goals both came from first-half headers, first from Doug Lewis, converting a Ron Green cross after 22 minutes and then from McNestry, set up by McKay on the stroke of half-time.

The club's director reported a profit for season 1932/33 of £3,577. Bill Pickering, the club's only ever-present in the League, was to repeat this achievement in 1933/34 and 1935/36. He, Donald, McNestry and Eyres, all of whom had played in at least 35 League games, all remained with the club, offering fresh optimism for the season ahead.

1933/34

With the backbone of the previous season's side intact, Rovers needed a goalkeeper and a goalscorer. Manager Prince-Cox made two astute summer signings, Charles Preedy in goal from Arsenal and the Northern Ireland International centre-forward Jimmy McCambridge. The opening fixture of the new season was a local derby at Ashton Gate and would be a good test of how the new team could shape up.

It is difficult to imagine, from the point of view of a Rovers supporter, a more satisfying opening-day result. New signing McCambridge compiled a debut hat-trick of headers as Bristol City were beaten 3-0 before a crowd of 25,500. He thus equalled Joe

SEASON 1933/34

FOOTBALL LEAGUE DIVISION THREE (SOUTH)

Date	Opponent			ATT	G	2	3	4	5	6	7	8	9	10	11	GOALSCORERS
26/08/33	BRISTOL CITY	A	3-0	25521	PREEDY	PICKERING	DONALD	McLEAN	ROUTLEDGE	MOLLOY	JACKSON	McKAY	SMITH	McCAMBRIDGE	TAYLOR	McCAMBRIDGE 3
30/08/33	CRYSTAL PALACE	H	0-1	17657	PREEDY	PICKERING	DONALD	McLEAN	ROUTLEDGE	MOLLOY	McNESTRY	McKAY	SMITH	McCAMBRIDGE	JACKSON	
02/09/33	SOUTHEND UNITED	H	3-1	14000	PREEDY	PICKERING	DONALD	McLEAN	McARTHUR	EYRES	WATSON	McKAY	SMITH	McCAMBRIDGE	TAYLOR	McKAY, NICHOLAS og
06/09/33	CRYSTAL PALACE	A	3-5	15843	PREEDY	PICKERING	DONALD	McLEAN	ROUTLEDGE	MOLLOY	JACKSON	McKAY	McCAMBRIDGE	EYRES	TAYLOR	McCAMBRIDGE, McKAY 2
09/09/33	COVENTRY CITY	H	1-0	14000	PREEDY	PICKERING	DONALD	McLEAN	ROUTLEDGE	EYRES	JACKSON	McKAY	TAYLOR	McCAMBRIDGE	WATSON	McCAMBRIDGE
16/09/33	READING	A	0-0	10000	PREEDY	PICKERING	DONALD	McLEAN	ROUTLEDGE	EYRES	McNESTRY	McKAY	TAYLOR	McCAMBRIDGE	WATSON	
23/09/33	WATFORD	A	0-0	6725	PREEDY	PICKERING	DONALD	McLEAN	ROUTLEDGE	EYRES	McNESTRY	McKAY	TAYLOR	McCAMBRIDGE	WATSON	
30/09/33	CHARLTON ATHLETIC	H	2-5	12000	PREEDY	PICKERING	DONALD	LEWIS	ROUTLEDGE	EYRES	McNESTRY	McKAY	SMITH	TAYLOR	JACKSON	SMITH 2
07/10/33	BOURNEMOUTH	A	0-2	7000	PREEDY	PICKERING	DONALD	WALLINGTON	McLEAN	MOLLOY	McNESTRY	McKAY	SMITH	McCAMBRIDGE	TAYLOR	
14/10/33	CARDIFF CITY	H	3-1	10000	PREEDY	PICKERING	DONALD	WALLINGTON	McLEAN	MOLLOY	McNESTRY	McKAY	SMITH	McCAMBRIDGE	TAYLOR	McKAY 3
21/10/33	CLAPTON ORIENT	H	0-0	8163	PREEDY	PICKERING	DONALD	WALLINGTON	McLEAN	MOLLOY	McNESTRY	McKAY	SMITH	McCAMBRIDGE	TAYLOR	
28/10/33	SWINDON TOWN	H	3-0	10000	PREEDY	PICKERING	DONALD	WALLINGTON	McLEAN	EYRES	McNESTRY	McKAY	SMITH	McCAMBRIDGE	TAYLOR	McKAY 2, McCAMBRIDGE
04/11/33	BRIGHTON & HOVE ALBION	A	2-0	6653	PREEDY	PICKERING	DONALD	WALLINGTON	McLEAN	EYRES	McNESTRY	McKAY	JACKSON	McCAMBRIDGE	TAYLOR	JACKSON, McNESTRY
11/11/33	ALDERSHOT	H	4-1	14000	PREEDY	PICKERING	DONALD	WALLINGTON	McLEAN	EYRES	McNESTRY	McKAY	JACKSON	McCAMBRIDGE	TAYLOR	McCAMBRIDGE 2, McNESTRY 2-1pen
18/11/33	LUTON TOWN	A	2-2	6700	PREEDY	PICKERING	DONALD	WALLINGTON	McLEAN	EYRES	McNESTRY	McKAY	JACKSON	McCAMBRIDGE	TAYLOR	McNESTRY pen, KINGHAM og
02/12/33	TORQUAY UNITED	A	1-2	2124	PREEDY	PICKERING	DONALD	WALLINGTON	McLEAN	EYRES	McNESTRY	McKAY	McCAMBRIDGE	JACKSON	TAYLOR	McNESTRY
16/12/33	NEWPORT COUNTY	A	0-1	4000	WINDSOR	PICKERING	DONALD	WALLINGTON	McLEAN	EYRES	McNESTRY	McKAY	HAVELOCK	McCAMBRIDGE	TAYLOR	
23/12/33	NORWICH CITY	H	3-0	10000	WINDSOR	PICKERING	DONALD	WALLINGTON	McLEAN	MURRAY	McNESTRY	McKAY	HAVELOCK	McCAMBRIDGE	TAYLOR	HAVELOCK 2, McCAMBRIDGE
25/12/33	GILLINGHAM	H	4-2	18000	WINDSOR	PICKERING	DONALD	WALLINGTON	McLEAN	MURRAY	McNESTRY	McKAY	HAVELOCK	McCAMBRIDGE	WATSON	HAVELOCK 2, McNESTRY, McCAMBRIDGE
26/12/33	GILLINGHAM	A	2-3	4516	PREEDY	PICKERING	DONALD	WALLINGTON	McLEAN	MURRAY	McNESTRY	McKAY	HAVELOCK	McCAMBRIDGE	WATSON	McCAMBRIDGE 2
30/12/33	BRISTOL CITY	H	5-1	23907	PREEDY	PICKERING	DONALD	WALLINGTON	McLEAN	MURRAY	McNESTRY	WATSON	HAVELOCK	EYRES	McCAMBRIDGE	EYRES, McCAMBRIDGE 2, McLEAN, McNESTRY, WATSON
06/01/34	SOUTHEND UNITED	A	2-2	5960	PREEDY	PICKERING	DONALD	WALLINGTON	McLEAN	MURRAY	McNESTRY	McKAY	McCAMBRIDGE	EYRES	WATSON	McKAY, McCAMBRIDGE
20/01/34	COVENTRY CITY	A	4-1	13000	PREEDY	PICKERING	DONALD	WALLINGTON	McLEAN	MURRAY	McNESTRY	McKAY	McCAMBRIDGE	EYRES	WATSON	McCAMBRIDGE, McNESTRY, WATSON, EYRES
27/01/34	READING	A	2-2	10000	PREEDY	PICKERING	DONALD	WALLINGTON	McLEAN	MURRAY	McNESTRY	LEWIS	McCAMBRIDGE	EYRES	WATSON	McNESTRY, EYRES
03/02/34	WATFORD	H	1-0	11000	PREEDY	PICKERING	DONALD	WALLINGTON	McLEAN	MURRAY	McNESTRY	McKAY	McCAMBRIDGE	EYRES	WATSON	EYRES
10/02/34	CHARLTON ATHLETIC	A	1-2	12000	PREEDY	PICKERING	DONALD	WALLINGTON	McLEAN	MURRAY	McNESTRY	McKAY	McCAMBRIDGE	HAVELOCK	JACKSON	JACKSON
17/02/34	BOURNEMOUTH	H	3-0	10000	PREEDY	PICKERING	DONALD	WALLINGTON	McLEAN	MURRAY	McNESTRY	McKAY	HAVELOCK	McCAMBRIDGE	JACKSON	HAVELOCK, McNESTRY 2-1pen
24/02/34	CARDIFF CITY	A	5-1	8000	PREEDY	PICKERING	DONALD	WALLINGTON	McLEAN	LEWIS	McNESTRY	McKAY	HAVELOCK	McCAMBRIDGE	JACKSON	McCAMBRIDGE, McNESTRY, HAVELOCK 2, JACKSON
28/02/34	NORTHAMPTON TOWN	H	1-1	5000	PREEDY	PICKERING	DONALD	WALLINGTON	McLEAN	EYRES	McNESTRY	McKAY	HAVELOCK	McCAMBRIDGE	JACKSON	EYRES
03/03/34	CLAPTON ORIENT	A	2-2	11000	PREEDY	PICKERING	TERRY	WALLINGTON	McLEAN	EYRES	McNESTRY	McKAY	HAVELOCK	McCAMBRIDGE	JACKSON	HAVELOCK 2
10/03/34	SWINDON TOWN	A	0-1	7792	PREEDY	PICKERING	DONALD	WALLINGTON	McLEAN	MURRAY	McNESTRY	McKAY	McCAMBRIDGE	EYRES	SMITH	McNESTRY
17/03/34	BRIGHTON & HOVE ALBION	H	1-1	5000	PREEDY	PICKERING	DONALD	WALLINGTON	McLEAN	LEWIS	McNESTRY	McCAMBRIDGE	HAVELOCK	SMITH	WATSON	HAVELOCK
24/03/34	ALDERSHOT	A	1-0	5000	PREEDY	PICKERING	DONALD	WALLINGTON	McLEAN	MURRAY	McNESTRY	McKAY	HAVELOCK	McCAMBRIDGE	JACKSON	McKAY
30/03/34	EXETER CITY	H	1-1	13500	PREEDY	PICKERING	DONALD	WALLINGTON	McLEAN	MURRAY	McNESTRY	McKAY	HAVELOCK	EYRES	JACKSON	
31/03/34	LUTON TOWN	H	0-1	8000	PREEDY	PICKERING	DONALD	WALLINGTON	McLEAN	MURRAY	McNESTRY	McKAY	HAVELOCK	McCAMBRIDGE	TAYLOR	
02/04/34	EXETER CITY	A	0-0	4894	PREEDY	PICKERING	DONALD	WALLINGTON	McLEAN	LEWIS	McNESTRY	McKAY	HAVELOCK	McCAMBRIDGE	TAYLOR	
07/04/34	NORTHAMPTON TOWN	A	2-1	6000	PREEDY	PICKERING	TERRY	WALLINGTON	McLEAN	MURRAY	McNESTRY	McKAY	SMITH	EYRES	TAYLOR	SMITH, McKAY
14/04/34	TORQUAY UNITED	H	4-1	6000	PREEDY	PICKERING	TERRY	WALLINGTON	McLEAN	MURRAY	McNESTRY	McKAY	SMITH	McKAY	TAYLOR	SMITH 3, McNESTRY pen
18/04/34	QUEENS PARK RANGERS	A	0-1	5000	PREEDY	PICKERING	TERRY	WALLINGTON	McLEAN	MURRAY	McNESTRY	McKAY	SMITH	McKAY	TAYLOR	
21/04/34	QUEENS PARK RANGERS	H	2-0	6000	PREEDY	PICKERING	DONALD	WALLINGTON	McLEAN	MURRAY	McNESTRY	McKAY	SMITH	McKAY	McCAMBRIDGE	McKAY, TAYLOR
28/04/34	NEWPORT COUNTY	H	2-0	5000	PREEDY	PICKERING	DONALD	WALLINGTON	McLEAN	MURRAY	TADMAN	McNESTRY	SMITH	McCAMBRIDGE	WATSON	TADMAN, McNESTRY
05/05/34	NORWICH CITY	A	0-0	14000	PREEDY	PICKERING	DONALD	WALLINGTON	McLEAN	MURRAY	TADMAN	McNESTRY	SMITH	McKAY	TAYLOR	

FA CUP

Date	Opponent			ATT	G	2	3	4	5	6	7	8	9	10	11	GOALSCORERS
25/11/33	FOLKESTONE	A	0-0	5000	PREEDY	PICKERING	DONALD	WALLINGTON	McLEAN	EYRES	McNESTRY	McKAY	JACKSON	McCAMBRIDGE	TAYLOR	
29/11/33	FOLKESTONE	H	3-1	9000	PREEDY	PICKERING	DONALD	WALLINGTON	McLEAN	EYRES	McNESTRY	McKAY	HAVELOCK	McCAMBRIDGE	TAYLOR	TAYLOR, McNESTRY, McKAY
09/12/33	ACCRINGTON STANLEY	H	0-1	7000	PREEDY	PICKERING	DONALD	WALLINGTON	McLEAN	MOLLOY	McNESTRY	McKAY	HAVELOCK	McCAMBRIDGE	ROUTLEDGE	

GLOUCESTERSHIRE CUP FINAL

Date	Opponent			ATT	G	2	3	4	5	6	7	8	9	10	11	GOALSCORERS
13/09/33	BRISTOL CITY	H	0-0	8361	PREEDY	PICKERING	DONALD	WALLINGTON	McLEAN	ROUTLEDGE	JACKSON	McKAY	HAVELOCK	TAYLOR	McCAMBRIDGE	
04/04/34	BRISTOL CITY	A	1-2	6278	PREEDY	PICKERING	DONALD	WALLINGTON	McLEAN	MURRAY	McNESTRY	McKAY	HAVELOCK	McCAMBRIDGE	TAYLOR	HAVELOCK

DIVISION THREE (SOUTH) CUP

Date	Opponent			ATT	G	2	3	4	5	6	7	8	9	10	11	GOALSCORERS
13/01/34	COVENTRY CITY	A	2-2	3000	PREEDY	PICKERING	DONALD	WALLINGTON	McLEAN	MURRAY	McNESTRY	McKAY	SMITH	LEWIS	EDWARDS	SMITH, LEWIS
01/02/34	COVENTRY CITY	A	1-2	3000	PREEDY	TERRY	DONALD	WALLINGTON	McLEAN	LEWIS	McNESTRY	ROUTLEDGE	McCAMBRIDGE	COWAN	WATSON	McCAMBRIDGE

PLAYERS	APPS	GLS
DONALD A	38	
EYRES J	27	5
HAVELOCK J	14	10
LEWIS D	4	
JACKSON W	17	3
McARTHUR W	1	
McCAMBRIDGE J	37	17
McKAY R	39	14
McLEAN J	42	1
McNESTRY G	38	15
MOLLOY P	6	
MURRAY W	21	
PICKERING W	42	
PREEDY C	39	
ROUTLEDGE W	8	
SMITH J	12	6
TADMAN G	2	1
TAYLOR A	22	1
TERRY J	4	
WATSON J	14	2
WINDSOR F	3	
OWN GOALS		2

Riley's club record of scoring three goals on his first League appearance for the club. Two more goals in the return game at Eastville in late December were to equal Bill Culley's club record haul of five goals in one season against an individual club. The manner of Rovers' victory gave cause for great optimism.

Of course, a 1-0 home defeat four days later brought Rovers down to earth, especially with George McNestry having to leave the field after only 10 minutes with a broken bone in his hand. However, Rovers were to enjoy a successful season. The final League placing of seventh constituted the highest inter-war League position. Seventy-seven League goals were scored, only one fewer than in 1926/27, while Rovers won 20 League games, an achievement not equalled until 1950/51. Only 11 games were lost. Apart from a 5-3 defeat at Coventry City in September and a 3-2 Boxing Day defeat at Gillingham, no more than two goals were conceded in any game.

One further addition to Rovers' side was centre-half Jock McLean. Signed from Division One Blackburn Rovers, McLean was captain and ever-present in his first two seasons at Eastville. It was surely no coincidence that the only goal of his Rovers career was one of five by which Rovers beat Bristol City in December. Wing-halves Sid Wallington and Bill Murray came into the side as the season progressed and added support for McLean, in what developed into a fine half-back line. In front of them was Jack Havelock, a £330 signing from Folkestone Town. He scored against Rovers in the FA Cup in November, and was the son of Harold Havelock, England's right-side flanker against Wales at a foggy Ashton Gate in January 1908, in the first rugby union International ever played in Bristol.

Clearly a characteristic of the season was the reliability of the defence, where Pickering and McLean were ever-presents and Donald and Preedy barely missed a game. Preedy's enormous contribution to Rovers' cause was epitomized by the game at Brighton in November, where his first-half penalty save from Albion's Robert Farrell laid the foundations for a 2-0 win. Yet, the forward line began to work to great effect. When Prince-Cox arranged to transport supporters by plane to an away game at Cardiff, with participants flying for eight shillings each from Whitchurch Airport, and paying two shillings and sixpence for a stand ticket at Ninian Park, his bizarre entrepreneurial concept was rewarded with a 5-1 victory. Havelock scored twice on this occasion. Bobby McKay scored a hat-trick in the return game with Cardiff. Jimmy Smith, who had scored a British seasonal record 66 goals in 38 Scottish League matches for Ayr United in 1927/28 to inscribe his name in the *Guinness Book of Records*, enjoyed a high point in his brief Rovers stay with a hat-trick in Rovers' 4-1 victory over Queen's Park Rangers. In this game, after McNestry's 12th-minute penalty, Smith scored after 28, 55 and 86 minutes, twice converting rebounds after Albert Taylor had hit the crossbar, to claim the glory despite an injury-time consolation goal in semi-darkness.

Consequently, it appears wholly out of character that Rovers should have found themselves 4-0 down at half-time against Coventry City at Highfield Road. Coventry were riding high in the table, but the dominance of City's Harry Lake and Jock Lauderdale, who scored twice each, was unexpected. The return fixture saw Rovers win 4-1, with young outside-left Jimmy Watson scoring the fourth. Coventry's consolation goal came from Arthur Bacon, an enigmatic forward who had once scored six goals in a League game for Reading against Stoke City. In fact, in the four weeks prior to Rovers' victory, he had scored five times against Gillingham and four goals against Crystal Palace.

On 2 December, Rovers' game at Plainmoor attracted an attendance of just 2,128. Rovers succumbed to the predictable defeat, despite George McNestry's 62nd-minute penalty following a foul on Jack Eyres. Since Torquay's elevation to Division Three (South) in 1927, Rovers have only won seven League games at Plainmoor.

Much of Rovers' success was based on the side's propensity for turning close games into wins. Single-goal victories at Crystal Palace, Aldershot and Northampton Town bore witness to this, while the 47 goals conceded was the club's lowest in the League since 1923/24. Rovers were thus able to win 20 League games for the only time in the inter-war years. Indeed, only in 1955/56 has the club been able to equal this achievement in a 42-match season. One of these wins, in the game at Brighton in November, followed an excellent solo goal by Jackson, who beat three defenders to score one of the greatest goals in the Bristol Rovers story. There was a run of three consecutive victories around early November and another in April, while Rovers only once had to endure as many as four consecutive League matches without a win. Likewise, a seasonal tally of 11 League defeats was the club's lowest since the Southern League Championship season of 1904/05 and was not improved upon until 1952/53, in which season Rovers were Division Three (South) champions.

As the season drew to a close, the former Rovers goalkeeper James Harvey was in the news. Harvey, a Yorkshireman by birth, had played in just one League game for Rovers in 1932 and was spending the 1933/34 season on the books of Frickley Colliery. In April he was charged in court with obtaining £60 by false pretences from two girls he employed at his University Novelty Pool in Barnsley. He was to join Gillingham in the summer and was in the side that lost 4-3 at Eastville in December 1934.

A successful season saw McCambridge as the club's top scorer with 17 League goals, McNestry, McKay and Havelock all also reaching double figures. In the FA Cup, Rovers played out a goalless draw at Folkestone in a blizzard before defeating their Southern League opposition in a replay, but then fell to a goal from Accrington Stanley's top scorer Jackie Cheetham. For the sixth consecutive season, the Gloucestershire Cup final was lost, Bristol City winning 2-1 in a replay, with Joe Riley scoring against his former Rovers team-mates. Rovers also entered the inaugural Division Three (South) Cup tournament but, after a 2-2 draw with Coventry City, were eliminated by the same opposition.

Rovers appeared in the Welsh Cup for the second and final time in the club's history. A Jimmy Hamilton own goal after 33 minutes and Jackson's finish three minutes from time proved sufficient to defeat Wrexham at Eastville. This was followed by a free-scoring draw with Port Vale, where Rovers, an early goal down, scored twice in the 17th minute. McCambridge, Lewis and McNestry from the penalty spot earned Rovers a 3-3 draw. In the replay at Vale Park, Joe Havelock's goal took the game into extra-time before a heavily disputed goal put paid to Rovers' ambitions, the ball being allegedly 'a foot over the line' before it was crossed.

One alarming development during the season was the agreement signed by football and greyhound directors to amend the lease of 21 March 1932. The modification of lease document, agreed on 23 January 1934, saw Rovers essentially lose the club's advantage in the struggle for ownership of Eastville Stadium. The Bristol Greyhound Racing

Association was given the right to inform Rovers at any point if they wished to purchase the ground. Rather than remaining tenants, the greyhound company was now in a position to buy up Eastville Stadium at any stage with only two months' written notice and at a guaranteed price within the range of a maximum £13,000 and minimum £8,000 value. By the onset of war, as financial conditions dictated, Rovers were forced to sell and thereby set up the enforced exile from Bristol that took place in the late 1980s.

Rovers' reserves were involved indirectly in the Taunton Carnival in September 1933, with Madge Coles, the Carnival Queen, symbolically kicking off the fixture at Taunton Town. The reserves, 3-0 ahead after 15 minutes, won 7-3 with Phil Taylor, Jimmy Watson and George Tadman scoring twice each. Jimmy Smith scored five times in the return fixture, when Taunton Town were defeated 7-0 at Eastville in January 1934. In the same calendar month, Smith scored four and Tadman three as the reserves beat Cheltenham Town 12-1.

1934/35

After years of underachievement, Rovers enjoyed a second consecutive season of relative success. Manager Albert Prince-Cox was beginning to see his apparently optimistic plans for the club come to fruition. It was another entertaining season. Rovers finished eighth in Division Three (South), scoring 73 League goals in the process. Several large crowds were attracted to Eastville, including more than 20,000 for the visit of Manchester United in the FA Cup and 25,000 for the home League game with Bristol City. Best of all, though, was the winning of Rovers' first major trophy since the 1904/05 Southern League title.

The only inter-war trophy won by Rovers on a national scale was the 1934/35 Division Three (South) Cup. This tournament ran for a number of years up to World War Two and was, in many respects, a forerunner of the Leyland Daf Trophy that was to offer Rovers a first opportunity to play at Wembley in 1990. George Berry's winner saw off Reading in the first round and Rovers needed a replay with Torquay in the second, two Jimmy Smith goals ensuring victory. Rovers were drawn at home to Exeter City in the semi-final at the end of March. The two sides had drawn in the League four days earlier, but goals from Stan Prout and top scorer George McNestry earned Rovers a 2-1 victory. Harry Poulter scored for the Grecians, who fielded the future Rovers centre-half Harold Webb.

The final was played at Millwall on 15 April before a poor crowd of 2,000. The Den had been selected as a neutral venue after Rovers and Watford had refused to toss a coin to decide home advantage. On a very wet surface Rovers, visibly buoyed by a 4-1 victory over Bournemouth 48 hours earlier, were a goal ahead at half-time, through Bobby McKay's 20th-minute shot. Shortly after half-time, McNestry crossed for Charlie Wipfler to put Rovers 2-0 ahead. With captain Jock McLean leading from the back, Rovers looked in control. Even when Bill Lane pulled a goal back with eight minutes remaining, Irvine Harwood put Rovers 3-1 ahead. In the dying seconds, Vic O'Brien

Bristol Rovers 1934/35. Back row: Pickering, Ellis, Jack Smith. Second row: McNestry, Havelock, Wallington, McLean, Murray, Donald. Front row: Capt. A Prince-Cox (Secretary-Manager), Hope, Wipfler, McKay, Jim Smith, Prout

added a second goal for Watford, but despite this Rovers had won their first major honour in 30 years.

In the League, captain Jock McLean was the only ever-present, although goalkeeper Jack Ellis and defenders Bill Pickering, Alec Donald and Sid Wallington missed very few games. McNestry, who scored 19 League goals from outside-right, played in all but two matches in the League. Stan Prout and Albert Taylor both figured prominently but, of the new signings, Ellis was the one to offer most valuable and consistent service. A tall, confident goalkeeper, he was to appear for Rovers in four consecutive League seasons. Jack Allen was to make few appearances in the Rovers side, but he had been top scorer in two consecutive seasons as Sheffield Wednesday won the League Championship in 1928/29 and 1929/30. Rovers also signed 21-year-old Samuel Edward Jones from Lovells Athletic, the winner of three Welsh amateur caps, but a player who was unable to break into the League side.

The season got off to an unusual start, with the 3-1 defeat at Brighton kicking off at 6.30 p.m. as Sussex were playing the Australian cricket tourists, also at Hove. Rovers conceded five at Southend in only the fifth game, with Harry Lane and Harry Johnson scoring two apiece, the first time since the equivalent weekend 12 months earlier that Rovers had conceded more than three goals in a game. Yet, after failing to win in the opening eight League matches, Rovers clicked into gear. Four consecutive wins set the season on its way and goals were to follow: seven against Northampton and five against Exeter, Crystal Palace and Newport. This first win of the season, 2-0 at home to Queen's Park Rangers, had seen the visitors field Jackie Crawford, an outside-left who had played

Rovers' Sidney Wallington played in the 1935 Division Three (South Cup) final victory over Watford

for England against Scotland in 1931 and who, at 5ft 2 in in height, was shorter than any other opponent in Rovers' League history except the diminutive Fred Le May, who had played for Thames in 1930.

Rovers drew an extraordinary home game with Exeter 5-5, thanks to a hat-trick from Jimmy Smith. Rovers had led 3-0 after half an hour and 5-2 with eight minutes remaining but allowed their opponents to snatch a draw. From the penalty spot the future Rovers centre-back Harold Webb scored the first of the Grecians' five goals. Two highly entertaining 5-3 victories soon followed. In February, Rovers led Crystal Palace 3-1 after only 12 minutes and 4-1 by half-time but eventually held out for a 5-3 win after being reduced to ten men following an injury to Albert Taylor. Five weeks later it was Taylor's turn to shine as his sole League hat-trick contributed to a 5-3 win. His first goal came after only two minutes and all three before half-time as he became, after Sid Leigh in 1921 and Ernie Whatmore six years later, the third Rovers player to complete a first-half League hat-trick.

Rovers' largest League win between the wars was the 7-1 hammering of Northampton Town in January. Goalkeeper Ellis was missing from the side and Rovers, with four changes following defeat at Luton, gave League debuts to the Somerset cricketer Newman Bunce in goal and James Durkan at right-back. Undeterred, Rovers scored seven times, McNestry and Taylor notching two each. Northampton's Dick Brown put a penalty wide of Bunce's goal. This match, however, was watched by a crowd of only 1,500, the lowest ever at a League game played at Eastville. The Cobblers subsequently dropped seven of their side, including goalscorer Tommy Ball, for their next game.

There were also some heavy defeats. Luton's third goal of the six they put past Rovers in January, was the 1000th Rovers had conceded in League football. This goal was in fact an own goal, sliced in after 33 minutes by McLean as Rovers, conceding four goals in 25 first-half minutes, crashed 6-2. Ball completed his hat-trick after 87 minutes, but Rovers maintained that his first strike, following a goalmouth scramble after a quarter of an hour, had not actually crossed the line. Southend United, Reading and Clapton Orient all put five goals past Jack Ellis before Christmas, David Halliday scoring a hat-trick for the O's. Over Easter, Rovers conceded nine goals in a four-day spell, and the side wore unconventional red shirts for the 3-0 defeat at Watford. Billy Baldwin, who scored twice in Gillingham's high-scoring victory at Eastville in the run-up to Christmas, was to win the 1965 All-England Bowls Cup.

On 13 April, for a 4-1 home victory over Bournemouth, Rovers fielded five Macs in their side. This was, in effect, the culmination of a distinct policy between the wars to

SEASON 1934/35

FOOTBALL LEAGUE DIVISION THREE (SOUTH)

Date	Opponent		Score	Att	G	2	3	4	5	6	7	8	9	10	11	Goalscorers
25/08/34	BRIGHTON & HOVE ALBION	A	1-3	11128	ELLIS	PICKERING	DONALD	WALLINGTON	McLEAN	MURRAY	McNESTRY	McKAY	J SMITH	HARWOOD	PROUT	SMITH
29/08/34	SWINDON TOWN	H	2-2	13000	ELLIS	PICKERING	DONALD	WALLINGTON	McLEAN	MURRAY	McNESTRY	McKAY	J SMITH	HARWOOD	PROUT	McKAY, SMITH
01/09/34	LUTON TOWN	H	1-0	12500	ELLIS	PICKERING	DONALD	WALLINGTON	McLEAN	MURRAY	McNESTRY	McKAY	J SMITH	HARWOOD	McCAMBRIDGE	SMITH
05/09/34	SWINDON TOWN	A	0-1	11000	ELLIS	PICKERING	AJ SMITH	WALLINGTON	McLEAN	MURRAY	McNESTRY	HARWOOD	McCAMBRIDGE	McKAY	TAYLOR	
08/09/34	SOUTHEND UNITED	A	1-5	8878	ELLIS	PICKERING	DONALD	WALLINGTON	McLEAN	MURRAY	McNESTRY	HARWOOD	McCAMBRIDGE	McKAY	TAYLOR	HARWOOD
15/09/34	BRISTOL CITY	H	2-2	25000	ELLIS	PICKERING	DONALD	WALLINGTON	McLEAN	MURRAY	PROUT	McKAY	BERRY	McCAMBRIDGE	TAYLOR	McCAMBRIDGE, CLIPSON og
22/09/34	CHARLTON ATHLETIC	A	0-0	7500	ELLIS	PICKERING	DONALD	McLEAN	McARTHUR	MURRAY	McNESTRY	McKAY	McCAMBRIDGE	J SMITH	WIPFLER	
29/09/34	CRYSTAL PALACE	A	2-2	15536	ELLIS	PICKERING	DONALD	WALLINGTON	McLEAN	MURRAY	McNESTRY	McKAY	HAVELOCK	J SMITH	WIPFLER	GOODIER og, McNESTRY
06/10/34	QUEENS PARK RANGERS	H	2-0	6000	ELLIS	PICKERING	DONALD	WALLINGTON	McLEAN	MURRAY	McNESTRY	McKAY	HAVELOCK	J SMITH	WIPFLER	WIPFLER, McNESTRY
13/10/34	TORQUAY UNITED	A	2-1	4487	ELLIS	PICKERING	DONALD	WALLINGTON	McLEAN	MURRAY	McNESTRY	McKAY	HAVELOCK	J SMITH	WIPFLER	HAVELOCK, WIPFLER
20/10/34	MILLWALL	H	2-0	15000	ELLIS	PICKERING	DONALD	WALLINGTON	McLEAN	MURRAY	McNESTRY	McKAY	HAVELOCK	J SMITH	WIPFLER	McNESTRY 2
27/10/34	COVENTRY CITY	A	2-1	9000	ELLIS	PICKERING	DONALD	WALLINGTON	McLEAN	MURRAY	McNESTRY	McKAY	J SMITH	J SMITH	TAYLOR	McNESTRY
03/11/34	NEWPORT COUNTY	H	1-1	8000	ELLIS	PICKERING	DONALD	WALLINGTON	McLEAN	MURRAY	McNESTRY	McKAY	ALLEN	J SMITH	PROUT	SMITH 3, TADMAN, ALLEN
10/11/34	EXETER CITY	A	5-5	10000	ELLIS	PICKERING	DONALD	WALLINGTON	McLEAN	MURRAY	McNESTRY	McKAY	ALLEN	J SMITH	PROUT	SMITH
17/11/34	READING	H	0-3	7000	ELLIS	PICKERING	DONALD	WALLINGTON	McLEAN	MURRAY	McNESTRY	McKAY	J SMITH	HOPE	PROUT	
01/12/34	BOURNEMOUTH	A	0-3	5000	ELLIS	PICKERING	AJ SMITH	WALLINGTON	McLEAN	MURRAY	TADMAN	McKAY	J SMITH	HARWOOD	PROUT	WIPFLER 2
15/12/34	CLAPTON ORIENT	A	2-5	3783	ELLIS	PICKERING	DONALD	WALLINGTON	McLEAN	AJ SMITH	TADMAN	McKAY	J SMITH	HARWOOD	WIPFLER	HARWOOD, TAYLOR 2,
22/12/34	GILLINGHAM	H	4-3	7500	ELLIS	PICKERING	DONALD	WALLINGTON	McLEAN	MURRAY	McNESTRY	POSTIN	J SMITH	HARWOOD	WIPFLER	McNESTRY pen
25/12/34	ALDERSHOT	A	2-1	5000	BUNCE	PICKERING	DONALD	WILDSMITH	McLEAN	McARTHUR	McNESTRY	McCAMBRIDGE	TAYLOR	HARWOOD	WIPFLER	TAYLOR 2
26/12/34	ALDERSHOT	H	1-0	17000	ELLIS	PICKERING	DONALD	WILDSMITH	McLEAN	McARTHUR	McNESTRY	McCAMBRIDGE	TAYLOR	McKAY	WIPFLER	McCAMBRIDGE
29/12/34	BRIGHTON & HOVE ALBION	H	2-6	10987	ELLIS	PICKERING	DONALD	WALLINGTON	McARTHUR	MURRAY	McNESTRY	HARWOOD	ALLEN	HARWOOD	WIPFLER	ALLEN, TAYLOR
05/01/35	LUTON TOWN	A	0-4	9000	ELLIS	McLEAN	DONALD	WALLINGTON	McLEAN	McARTHUR	McNESTRY	McCAMBRIDGE	TAYLOR	HARWOOD	WIPFLER	TAYLOR 2, McNESTRY 2, 1pen,
16/01/35	NORTHAMPTON TOWN	H	7-1	1500	BUNCE	DURKAN	DONALD	WALLINGTON	McLEAN	McARTHUR	McNESTRY	McCAMBRIDGE	TAYLOR	HARWOOD	PROUT	HARWOOD, McCAMBRIDGE
19/01/35	SOUTHEND UNITED	H	2-1	7000	ELLIS	DURKAN	DONALD	WILDSMITH	McLEAN	McARTHUR	McNESTRY	McCAMBRIDGE	TAYLOR	HARWOOD	PROUT	McNESTRY, PROUT
02/02/35	CHARLTON ATHLETIC	A	1-0	12000	ELLIS	PICKERING	DONALD	WILDSMITH	McLEAN	McARTHUR	McNESTRY	TADMAN	TAYLOR	HARWOOD	WIPFLER	McNESTRY
06/02/35	BRISTOL CITY	A	1-1	7911	ADAMS	PICKERING	DONALD	WILSON	McLEAN	McARTHUR	McNESTRY	McCAMBRIDGE	TAYLOR	HARWOOD	PROUT	McNESTRY
09/02/35	CRYSTAL PALACE	H	5-3	7028	ELLIS	PICKERING	COLLEDGE	WILSON	McLEAN	McARTHUR	McNESTRY	McCAMBRIDGE	TAYLOR	HARWOOD	PROUT	OWENS og, McNESTRY, PROUT, HARWOOD, McCAMBRIDGE
16/02/35	QUEENS PARK RANGERS	A	0-2	6000	ELLIS	PICKERING	DONALD	WALLINGTON	McLEAN	McARTHUR	McNESTRY	McCAMBRIDGE	ALLEN	HARWOOD	PROUT	
23/02/35	MILLWALL	A	2-0	7000	ELLIS	PICKERING	DONALD	WALLINGTON	McLEAN	McARTHUR	McNESTRY	McCAMBRIDGE	TAYLOR	HARWOOD	PROUT	McCAMBRIDGE, McNESTRY
02/03/35	COVENTRY CITY	A	0-5	10000	ELLIS	PICKERING	AJ SMITH	WILSON	McLEAN	McARTHUR	POSTIN	McKAY	ALLEN	HARWOOD	PROUT	
09/03/35	NEWPORT COUNTY	A	5-3	6000	ELLIS	PICKERING	DONALD	WILSON	McLEAN	McARTHUR	McNESTRY	McCAMBRIDGE	TAYLOR	HARWOOD	WIPFLER	TAYLOR 3, PROUT, McNESTRY
16/03/35	EXETER CITY	H	2-2	4000	ELLIS	PICKERING	DONALD	WALLINGTON	McLEAN	McARTHUR	McNESTRY	McKAY	TAYLOR	HARWOOD	WIPFLER	McARTHUR, McNESTRY
23/03/35	READING	A	0-1	9000	ELLIS	PICKERING	DONALD	WALLINGTON	McLEAN	McARTHUR	McNESTRY	McKAY	TAYLOR	HARWOOD	WIPFLER	
30/03/35	NORTHAMPTON TOWN	A	0-1	4946	ELLIS	PICKERING	DONALD	WALLINGTON	McLEAN	McARTHUR	McNESTRY	McKAY	TAYLOR	HARWOOD	WIPFLER	
06/04/35	BOURNEMOUTH	H	4-1	5000	ELLIS	PICKERING	DONALD	WALLINGTON	McLEAN	McARTHUR	McNESTRY	McKAY	TAYLOR	HARWOOD	WIPFLER	TAYLOR, WIPFLER, McNESTRY pen
13/04/35	CARDIFF CITY	A	1-4	24500	ELLIS	PICKERING	DONALD	WALLINGTON	McLEAN	McARTHUR	McNESTRY	McKAY	TAYLOR	HARWOOD	WIPFLER	McNESTRY, TAYLOR 2, HARWOOD
19/04/35	WATFORD	H	0-3	4260	ELLIS	PICKERING	DONALD	WALLINGTON	McLEAN	McARTHUR	McNESTRY	McKAY	TAYLOR	HARWOOD	WIPFLER	McARTHUR
20/04/35	CARDIFF CITY	H	3-2	12000	ELLIS	PICKERING	DONALD	WALLINGTON	McLEAN	McARTHUR	McNESTRY	McKAY	TAYLOR	HARWOOD	WIPFLER	TAYLOR, McNESTRY 2, 1pen
22/04/35	WATFORD	A	2-1	7000	ELLIS	PICKERING	DONALD	WALLINGTON	McLEAN	McARTHUR	McNESTRY	McKAY	HARRIS	HARWOOD	TAYLOR	HARRIS 2
27/04/35	CLAPTON ORIENT	H	1-2	5000	ELLIS	PICKERING	DONALD	WALLINGTON	McLEAN	McARTHUR	McNESTRY	McKAY	McCAMBRIDGE	HARWOOD	TAYLOR	TAYLOR
04/05/35	GILLINGHAM	A	1-1	3000	ADAMS	PICKERING	DONALD	WALLINGTON	McLEAN	McARTHUR	McNESTRY	WILDSMITH	TAYLOR	HARWOOD	POSTIN	McNESTRY pen

FA CUP

Date	Opponent		Score	Att	G	2	3	4	5	6	7	8	9	10	11	Goalscorers
24/11/34	HARWICH	H	3-0	8074	ELLIS	PICKERING	DONALD	WALLINGTON	McLEAN	MURRAY	McNESTRY	McKAY	HAVELOCK	J SMITH	PROUT	J SMITH, McNESTRY pen, PROUT
08/12/34	DARTFORD	H	1-0	8000	ELLIS	PICKERING	DONALD	WALLINGTON	McLEAN	MURRAY	McNESTRY	McKAY	HAVELOCK	J SMITH	WIPFLER	McNESTRY pen
12/01/35	MANCHESTER UNITED	H	1-3	20400	ADAMS	ADAMS	DONALD	WALLINGTON	McLEAN	MURRAY	McNESTRY	McKAY	TAYLOR	J SMITH	WIPFLER	McNESTRY

DIVISION THREE (SOUTH) CUP

Date	Opponent		Score	Att	G	2	3	4	5	6	7	8	9	10	11	Goalscorers
19/09/34	READING	H	2-1	3000	ELLIS	PICKERING	DONALD	WALLINGTON	McLEAN	MURRAY	McNESTRY	McKAY	BERRY	McKAY	WIPFLER	HARWOOD, BERRY
31/10/34	TORQUAY UNITED	H	1-1	3000	ELLIS	PICKERING	DONALD	WILDSMITH	McLEAN	MURRAY	TADMAN	McKAY	McCAMBRIDGE	HARWOOD	PROUT	MURRAY
07/11/34	TORQUAY UNITED	A	2-0	2000	ELLIS	PICKERING	AJ SMITH	WALLINGTON	McLEAN	WILDSMITH	TADMAN	McCAMBRIDGE	J SMITH	HARWOOD	PROUT	SMITH 2
21/02/35	NORTHAMPTON TOWN	A	2-0	1060	ELLIS	PICKERING	DONALD	WALLINGTON	McLEAN	McARTHUR	McNESTRY	McKAY	ALLEN	HARWOOD	PROUT	McNESTRY 2
27/03/35	EXETER CITY	A	1-0	2000	ELLIS	PICKERING	WILSON	WILSON	McLEAN	McARTHUR	McNESTRY	McKAY	TAYLOR	HARWOOD	PROUT	PROUT, McNESTRY
13/04/35	WATFORD	A	3-2	2000	ELLIS	PICKERING	DONALD	WALLINGTON	McLEAN	WILSON	McNESTRY	McKAY	TAYLOR	HARWOOD	WIPFLER	McKAY, WIPFLER, HARWOOD

GLOUCESTERSHIRE CUP FINAL

Date	Opponent		Score	Att	G	2	3	4	5	6	7	8	9	10	11	Goalscorers
26/09/34	BRISTOL CITY	A	2-1	5216	ELLIS	PICKERING	DONALD	WALLINGTON	McLEAN	MURRAY	TAYLOR	McNESTRY	J SMITH	McKAY	WIPFLER	McNESTRY pen, SMITH

Appearances & Goals

PLAYERS	APPS	GLS
ADAMS R	2	
ALLEN J	6	2
BERRY G	1	
BUNCE N	2	
DONALD A	38	
DURKAN J	2	
ELLIS J	38	
GOLLEDGE L	1	
HARRIS T	1	
HARWOOD I	28	5
HAVELOCK J	6	1
HOPE H	1	
McARTHUR W	24	3
McCAMBRIDGE J	19	6
McKAY R	25	1
McLEAN J	42	
McNESTRY G	40	19
MURRAY W	19	
PICKERING W	39	
POSTIN E	3	
PROUT S	17	3
SMITH A J	14	
SMITH J	26	7
TADMAN G	4	1
TAYLOR A	26	15
WALLINGTON S	33	
WILDSMITH T	6	
WILSON W	4	
WIPFLER C	18	5
OWN GOALS		3

cultivate scouting links in Scotland and, in some respects, reflected the cosmopolitan make-up of the side. Wing-half McArthur was a Yorkshireman, McNestry came from County Durham and McCambridge from Northern Ireland, while both McKay and McLean were born north of the border.

In the final game of the season Rovers drew 1-1 at Gillingham in an incident-packed afternoon. McNestry scored his 19th goal of the season, a penalty, but the home side missed two spot-kicks through Dick Doncaster, a former Welsh Schoolboy International, and Joe Wiggins. This was the second of five League matches featuring Rovers in which three penalties have been awarded. Elsewhere, Charlton Athletic played through this season with three future Rovers managers in their squad. Fred Ford and Bert Tann could not break into the side, but Bill Dodgin's 25 League appearances included one in a 2-0 victory over Rovers at The Valley in February. Dodgin was to join Rovers as a player in 1936 and as manager in 1969. Charlton were Division Three (South) champions, finishing eight points clear of runners-up Reading.

In the FA Cup, victories over non-League sides Harwich and Dartford without conceding a goal earned Rovers a plum third round tie with Division Two Manchester United. Harwich had held out for 28 minutes, but, after Smith scored, McNestry netted the rebound from his own saved penalty on the stroke of half-time and Prout added a third after the break. A successfully converted McNestry penalty saw off a spirited Dartford performance. Rovers had conceded six at Luton in the run-up to the Manchester United game, losing goalkeeper Jack Ellis in the process with a broken collar-bone. Incredibly, a low McNestry drive after 20 minutes gave Rovers a half-time lead, before three second-half goals in the space of 17 minutes, two from Tommy Bamford and one from George Mutch, brought United a comfortable victory. Rovers beat Bristol City 2-1 in the Gloucestershire Cup final, with Jimmy Smith scoring the winning goal, to win the trophy for the first time since 1928. For the second consecutive season, City's Joe Riley scored against his former club.

Rovers retained the Allan Palmer Cup, which the club had won in 1927 and 1933, but which had not been contested in 1934. As holders, Rovers were invited to play Southampton and found themselves two goals ahead inside 20 minutes through McNestry and Taylor. Southampton pulled level through goals from Fred Tully and Johnny McAlwane, but Rovers ran out 5-2 winners, with Irvine Harwood scoring twice and Taylor adding his second of the game. Two Ted Buckley goals enabled Rovers to defeat Thornbury Town 4-3 in April in a match to raise money for the Berkeley and Almondsbury Hospitals Fund.

1935/36

Prince-Cox had brought relative prosperity to the club but, by the 1935/36 season, the effect of his undoubted charisma was beginning to wane. Rovers avoided having to seek re-election, but an erratic season contributed in part to his ultimate decision to leave the Eastville club in October 1936. Rovers conceded six goals at Aldershot and at

Rovers' Harold Houghton opens the scoring against Arsenal in the 5-1 FA Cup defeat at Eastville

Notts County and, infamously, twelve at Luton Town. A club seasonal record of 95 goals conceded left Rovers 17th in Division Three (South).

Yet the season both started and finished well, in front of the newly-constructed Tote End, whose name derived from the betting totalizer clocks for greyhound racing. There was a covered section to this spectator area in the south-western corner, though the majority was not roofed until 1961. In its heyday, the Tote End was to house a crowd capacity of 12,250. Opening with three straight clean sheets, including a 2-0 win against Bristol City at Ashton Gate, Rovers lost only one of their opening eight League games. Barely 24 hours after the Luton debacle, Rovers defeated Torquay 3-0 at Eastville, while five different players got their names on the scoresheet as Rovers beat Exeter City 6-1 in the final home game of the season. Jack Woodman, who scored twice in both games, was the club's top scorer with 15 League goals.

Two new faces appeared in the goalless draw with Notts County that opened Rovers' 16th league campaign. Outside-right Hugh Adcock was a former England International and the cousin of another England forward, Joe Bradford, while Archie Young could play at left-half or inside-left. Both joined from Leicester City. As the season progressed, Rovers further strengthened the forward line. Harry Barley, a signing from Scunthorpe United, had once scored for New Brighton against Darlington with a shot so hard it had burst the net and apparently floored a ball boy 25 yards behind the goal. George Crisp had made his League debut at Eastville in the Coventry City side beaten 4-1 by Rovers in January 1934, and now joined Rovers with Woodman, the experienced Harry Houghton and former Wolves left-back Jack Preece.

Rovers fielded an experienced side. Jack Ellis, behind a beleaguered defence, found himself with much to do. Right-back Bill Pickering, forming a useful partnership with

Bristol Rovers 1935/36. Back row: Robertson, Ellis. Second row: B Williams (Asst Trainer), P Taylor, Harris, Frater, Young, Murray, H Lake (Trainer). Third row: Barley, Harwood, Rose, Hill, Preece, Wildsmith, Woodman, Adcock, Crisp. Front row: McArthur, Prout, McCambridge, McLean, Capt. A Prince-Cox (Manager), S Hawkins (Secretary), Pickering, Donald, A Taylor, Wallington

Donald and later Preece, was the only ever-present. Behind Woodman, the veteran inside-forwards Harry Houghton and Irvine Harwood weighed in with nine League goals apiece. Yet two youngsters with great futures ahead of them made their League debuts for Rovers as the season progressed. Local-born centre-half Phil Taylor played against Gillingham on his 18th birthday and scored an impressive FA Cup hat-trick against Oldham. He was sold to Liverpool in March in a deal worth £1,000 plus Bill Hartill and subsequently captained his side in an FA Cup final as well as winning 3 England caps. Ray Warren, a 17-year-old Bristolian, played in the home defeat against Queen's Park Rangers and was later to captain Rovers to the Third Division (South) Championship in 1952/53 before retiring in 1956.

When Rovers visited Northampton in September, they trailed 3-0 before scoring three times in the final 20 minutes to earn a draw. The first of these goals came from Eli Postin in his only League appearance of the season. Woodman, who scored the equaliser, missed a number of games over the winter, Tom Harris being one to take full advantage, scoring after only two minutes against Notts County on his recall to the side and going on to complete a hat-trick. Woodman's return to the side in late January saw him score in seven consecutive League games, a club record beaten only by Dai Ward in 1956. Rovers also won 2-1 away to Watford, despite having captain Jock McLean out injured for the remainder of the season.

The defeat at Exeter in December was marked by the late appearance of referee B Ames. A linesman refereed the opening 20 minutes of a game Rovers lost 3-1. Prior to the draw at Southend in January there was a one-minute silence in memory of King

George V who had died five days earlier. Playing Watford in October, Syd Wallington was knocked out before half-time but returned for the second-half with his head in plaster. The 2-2 draw with Aldershot on Easter Saturday saw the visitors field a 41-year-old goalkeeper Billy Robb, at this time the second oldest opponent, behind Norwich City's Albert Sturgess in 1924, that Rovers had faced in the Football League.

Perhaps above all else, this season is best remembered for a string of heavy defeats. In February, Rovers conceded three goals in the opening eight minutes against Crystal Palace, yet lost only 5-3, despite losing goalkeeper Ellis injured, with Pickering going in goal. Albert Dawes scored twice for Crystal Palace in both League meetings with Rovers. Both Notts County and Aldershot put six goals past Rovers. In the latter case, the story goes that Aldershot's chairman, a magistrate, rejected a prisoner's application for bail 'so that I can go and see the Rovers beat Aldershot'. Centre-forward Bertie Lutterloch scored a hat-trick as the Shots recorded a 6-1 victory, their highest League win at the time.

The epitome of Rovers' inter-war struggle was, perhaps, the disastrous visit to Kenilworth Road on Easter Monday. There was little hint of what was to come, for Rovers had drawn their other two Easter games, including one at home to Luton Town. Rovers were unchanged, but Luton selected a reserve wing-half, Joe Payne, as an emergency striker. The experiment paid off, as Payne completed a first-half hat-trick, then added seven more in atrocious weather after half-time. 12-0 remains, by a wide margin, the worst defeat in the history of Bristol Rovers. Luton Town's achievement was the only occasion that a club scored 12 goals in any Third Division (South) fixture. Moreover, Joe Payne, who scored his final nine goals in 46 minutes, eclipsed Tranmere Rovers' Bunny Bell's feat of nine goals in a match and his ten goals in this game stand as a Football League record to this day. Payne was to represent England as a centre-forward and enjoy a distinguished career with Chelsea. He opened the scoring with a low shot after 23 minutes and, after Fred Roberts had scored a second, added two tap-ins in the run-up to half-time. After the interval, the centre-forward could do no wrong and, by the 86th minute, had increased his impressive goal tally to three headers and seven shots. A minute from time, inside-right George Martin, who had initially been falsely credited with the sixth goal, added the 12th.

If Rovers were to pick up the pieces, they could have done far worse than win three of the remaining four League fixtures. That they did reflects admirably on Prince-Cox and his team. Large home victories over two Devon sides and a hard-earned 2-1 victory at Gillingham brought a positive finish to a potentially disastrous season. The opening goal against Exeter City, the only one of inside-right Les Golledge's brief Rovers career, was the 1000th goal Rovers had scored in League football.

In the FA Cup, Rovers defeated Northampton Town 3-1 in a replay, a score which could have been greater but for two second-half penalty misses by Tom Wildsmith. Phil Taylor's hat-trick at home to Oldham Athletic set up a tie with mighty Arsenal at Eastville in the third round. Arsenal were arguably the most powerful football club in the world at this time and boasted a number of household names. However, in the first half, Ted Drake was subdued, Ellis saved a penalty from Cliff Bastin and, sensationally, three minutes before half-time, Houghton shot from the edge of the penalty area and Rovers were ahead. Leading the Gunners at half-time was a huge achievement, but the visitors scored five second-half goals, Bastin and Drake claiming two apiece and went

FOOTBALL LEAGUE DIVISION THREE (SOUTH)

SEASON 1935/36

Date	Opponent	H/A	Score	Att	1	2	3	4	5	6	7	8	9	10	11	Goalscorers
31/08/35	NOTTS COUNTY	A	0-0	15197	ELLIS	PICKERING	DONALD	WALLINGTON	McLEAN	ADCOCK	BARLEY	McCAMBRIDGE	A TAYLOR	YOUNG	PROUT	
02/09/35	CARDIFF CITY	A	0-0	18000	ROBERTSON	PICKERING	DONALD	WALLINGTON	McLEAN	YOUNG	ADCOCK	A TAYLOR	WOODMAN	HARWOOD	PROUT	
07/09/35	BRISTOL CITY	A	2-0	23991	ROBERTSON	PICKERING	DONALD	WILDSMITH	McLEAN	YOUNG	BARLEY	A TAYLOR	WOODMAN	HARWOOD	CRISP	CRISP, WOODMAN
11/09/35	CARDIFF CITY	H	1-1	11000	ROBERTSON	PICKERING	DONALD	WILDSMITH	McLEAN	YOUNG	BARLEY	A TAYLOR	WOODMAN	HARWOOD	CRISP	CRISP
14/09/35	CLAPTON ORIENT	A	0-2	9856	ROBERTSON	PICKERING	DONALD	WALLINGTON	McLEAN	BARLEY	ADCOCK	P TAYLOR	WOODMAN	HARWOOD	CRISP	
18/09/35	GILLINGHAM	H	4-3	7000	ROBERTSON	PICKERING	DONALD	WALLINGTON	McLEAN	WILDSMITH	ADCOCK	P TAYLOR	WOODMAN	HARWOOD	CRISP	WILDSMITH, BUCKLEY, ADCOCK, CRISP
21/09/35	SOUTHEND UNITED	H	3-2	9000	ELLIS	PICKERING	DONALD	P TAYLOR	McLEAN	McARTHUR	BARLEY	HARWOOD	BUCKLEY	HOUGHTON	PROUT	McARTHUR, HARWOOD 2
28/09/35	NORTHAMPTON TOWN	A	3-3	7102	ELLIS	PICKERING	DONALD	P TAYLOR	McLEAN	McARTHUR	POSTIN	HARWOOD	BUCKLEY	HOUGHTON	CRISP	POSTIN, HARWOOD, WOODMAN
05/10/35	CRYSTAL PALACE	H	2-4	10568	ELLIS	PICKERING	DONALD	WILDSMITH	McLEAN	YOUNG	BARLEY	WOODMAN	FRATER	HARWOOD	CRISP	FRATER, CRISP
12/10/35	READING	A	2-3	14000	ELLIS	PICKERING	DONALD	WILDSMITH	McLEAN	YOUNG	BARLEY	WOODMAN	HARWOOD	HOUGHTON	CRISP	HARWOOD, WALLINGTON
19/10/35	WATFORD	H	0-1	6000	ELLIS	PICKERING	DONALD	WILDSMITH	McLEAN	YOUNG	WALLINGTON	WOODMAN	HARWOOD	HOUGHTON	CRISP	
26/10/35	QUEENS PARK RANGERS	A	0-4	9000	ROBERTSON	PICKERING	DONALD	WILDSMITH	McLEAN	YOUNG	ADCOCK	P TAYLOR	BUCKLEY	HOUGHTON	PROUT	
02/11/35	BRIGHTON & HOVE ALBION	H	5-2	7997	ROBERTSON	PICKERING	DONALD	P TAYLOR	McLEAN	YOUNG	BARLEY	HARRIS	HOUGHTON	HARWOOD	PROUT	HARRIS 3, HARWOOD, HOUGHTON
09/11/35	MILLWALL	H	1-2	8000	ELLIS	PICKERING	DONALD	WILDSMITH	McLEAN	YOUNG	BARLEY	HARRIS	HOUGHTON	HARWOOD	CRISP	BARLEY
16/11/35	NEWPORT COUNTY	A	3-0	8000	ELLIS	PICKERING	DONALD	WILDSMITH	McLEAN	WILDSMITH	BARLEY	HARWOOD	FRATER	HOUGHTON	CRISP	HARWOOD, BARLEY 2
23/11/35	COVENTRY CITY	A	1-3	15644	ELLIS	PICKERING	DONALD	WALLINGTON	McLEAN	YOUNG	ADCOCK	HARWOOD	HARRIS	HARWOOD	CRISP	HARRIS
07/12/35	ALDERSHOT	H	1-6	2000	ELLIS	PICKERING	DONALD	WILDSMITH	McLEAN	McARTHUR	BARLEY	P TAYLOR	HARWOOD	HOUGHTON	PROUT	POSTIN E
21/12/35	EXETER CITY	A	1-3	4000	ELLIS	PICKERING	DONALD	WILDSMITH	McLEAN	YOUNG	BARLEY	P TAYLOR	HARRIS	HOUGHTON	PROUT	PREECE J
25/12/35	BOURNEMOUTH	H	2-1	11231	ELLIS	PICKERING	DONALD	WALLINGTON	McLEAN	YOUNG	BARLEY	P TAYLOR	HARRIS	HOUGHTON	PROUT	HARRIS, HOUGHTON
26/12/35	BOURNEMOUTH	A	1-2	12000	ELLIS	PICKERING	DONALD	WALLINGTON	McLEAN	WILDSMITH	ADCOCK	HARWOOD	HARRIS	HOUGHTON	CRISP	P TAYLOR, HOUGHTON
28/12/35	NOTTS COUNTY	H	0-6	8669	ELLIS	PICKERING	DONALD	WALLINGTON	McLEAN	WILDSMITH	BARLEY	HARWOOD	HARRIS	HOUGHTON	CRISP	
04/01/36	BRISTOL CITY	H	1-1	18459	ELLIS	PICKERING	DONALD	WALLINGTON	McLEAN	WILDSMITH	BARLEY	P TAYLOR	HARWOOD	HOUGHTON	CRISP	HOUGHTON
11/01/36	SWINDON TOWN	A	2-1	2418	ELLIS	PICKERING	PREECE	WALLINGTON	McLEAN	WILDSMITH	BARLEY	P TAYLOR	HARWOOD	HOUGHTON	CRISP	P TAYLOR, HOUGHTON
18/01/36	CLAPTON ORIENT	H	1-1	4500	ROBERTSON	PICKERING	PREECE	WALLINGTON	McLEAN	YOUNG	BARLEY	P TAYLOR	HARWOOD	HOUGHTON	CRISP	HOUGHTON
25/01/36	SOUTHEND UNITED	A	1-1	6005	ROBERTSON	PICKERING	PREECE	WALLINGTON	McLEAN	WOODMAN	BARLEY	WOODMAN	WOODMAN	HOUGHTON	CRISP	WOODMAN
01/02/36	NORTHAMPTON TOWN	H	5-2	5359	ROBERTSON	PICKERING	PREECE	MURRAY	McLEAN	WOODMAN	CRISP	P TAYLOR	WOODMAN	HOUGHTON	PROUT	CRISP, HOUGHTON 2, WOODMAN, McARTHUR
08/02/36	CRYSTAL PALACE	A	3-5	11050	ELLIS	PICKERING	PREECE	WALLINGTON	MURRAY	CRISP	WOODMAN	P TAYLOR	WOODMAN	HOUGHTON	PROUT	HOUGHTON, WOODMAN, CRISP
15/02/36	READING	H	1-4	8000	ROBERTSON	PICKERING	PREECE	WALLINGTON	McLEAN	YOUNG	CRISP	P TAYLOR	WOODMAN	HOUGHTON	WOODMAN	HOUGHTON
22/02/36	WATFORD	A	2-1	6000	ELLIS	PICKERING	PREECE	WALLINGTON	McLEAN	MURRAY	ADCOCK	P TAYLOR	HARWOOD	HOUGHTON	PROUT	WOODMAN
29/02/36	MILLWALL	A	2-0	7777	ELLIS	PICKERING	PREECE	WALLINGTON	McLEAN	MURRAY	ADCOCK	P TAYLOR	WOODMAN	HOUGHTON	PROUT	PROUT, WOODMAN
07/03/36	TORQUAY UNITED	H	0-2	2128	ELLIS	PICKERING	PREECE	WALLINGTON	McLEAN	MURRAY	GOLLEDGE	P TAYLOR	WOODMAN	HOUGHTON	PROUT	
14/03/36	QUEENS PARK RANGERS	H	0-1	7106	ELLIS	PICKERING	PREECE	WALLINGTON	MURRAY	YOUNG	WOODMAN	WARREN	WOODMAN	HOUGHTON	PROUT	
21/03/36	NEWPORT COUNTY	A	0-1	6000	ELLIS	PICKERING	PREECE	WALLINGTON	YOUNG	WILDSMITH	ADCOCK	WILDSMITH	WOODMAN	HOUGHTON	PROUT	
28/03/36	COVENTRY CITY	H	3-2	8456	ELLIS	PICKERING	PREECE	WALLINGTON	YOUNG	McARTHUR	WOODMAN	HARTILL	WOODMAN	HOUGHTON	PROUT	HARTILL 2, WOODMAN
04/04/36	SWINDON TOWN	A	0-3	6000	ELLIS	PICKERING	PREECE	WALLINGTON	YOUNG	McARTHUR	ADCOCK	HARTILL	WOODMAN	HOUGHTON	PROUT	
10/04/36	LUTON TOWN	H	2-2	15481	ELLIS	PICKERING	PREECE	WALLINGTON	McLEAN	McARTHUR	BARLEY	COLLEDGE	WOODMAN	HOUGHTON	PROUT	COLLEDGE, WOODMAN 2, McARTHUR
11/04/36	ALDERSHOT	A	2-2	5000	ELLIS	PICKERING	PREECE	WALLINGTON	McLEAN	McARTHUR	BARLEY	HARTILL	WOODMAN	HARWOOD	PROUT	WOODMAN 2, HARWOOD
13/04/36	LUTON TOWN	A	0-12	13962	ELLIS	PICKERING	PREECE	WALLINGTON	McLEAN	YOUNG	BARLEY	HARTILL	WOODMAN	HOUGHTON	PROUT	
14/04/36	TORQUAY UNITED	A	3-0	4000	ELLIS	PICKERING	PREECE	WALLINGTON	McLEAN	WILDSMITH	BARLEY	BUCKLEY	WOODMAN	HOUGHTON	HARWOOD	CRISP, BARLEY
18/04/36	BRIGHTON & HOVE ALBION	H	1-4	5646	ELLIS	PICKERING	PREECE	WALLINGTON	McLEAN	YOUNG	BARLEY	BUCKLEY	WOODMAN	HOUGHTON	HARWOOD	BARLEY, HOUGHTON
25/04/36	EXETER CITY	H	6-1	3000	ELLIS	PICKERING	PREECE	WALLINGTON	McLEAN	WILDSMITH	BARLEY	COLLEDGE	WOODMAN	WOODMAN	CRISP	WILDSMITH pen, WILSON W R 2
01/05/36	GILLINGHAM	A	2-1	3469	ELLIS	PICKERING	PREECE	WALLINGTON	McLEAN	McARTHUR	CRISP	HARTILL	HARTILL	HOUGHTON	CRISP	HARTILL 2

FA CUP

Date	Opponent	H/A	Score	Att	1	2	3	4	5	6	7	8	9	10	11	Goalscorers
30/11/35	NORTHAMPTON TOWN	A	0-0	9093	ELLIS	PICKERING	DONALD	WALLINGTON	McLEAN	BARLEY	ADCOCK	P TAYLOR	HARWOOD	HARWOOD	PROUT	
03/12/35	NORTHAMPTON TOWN	H	3-1	8000	ELLIS	PICKERING	DONALD	WALLINGTON	McLEAN	BARLEY	ADCOCK	P TAYLOR	HARRIS	HARWOOD	PROUT	PROUT 2, P TAYLOR
14/12/35	OLDHAM ATHLETIC	A	1-1	4000	ELLIS	PICKERING	DONALD	WALLINGTON	McLEAN	WILDSMITH	BARLEY	P TAYLOR	HARRIS	HOUGHTON	PROUT	HOUGHTON
18/12/35	OLDHAM ATHLETIC	H	4-1	9550	ELLIS	PICKERING	DONALD	WALLINGTON	McLEAN	WILDSMITH	BARLEY	P TAYLOR	HARWOOD	HOUGHTON	CRISP	P TAYLOR 3, HOUGHTON
11/01/36	ARSENAL	H	1-5	24234	ELLIS	PICKERING	DONALD	WALLINGTON	McLEAN	YOUNG	ADCOCK	P TAYLOR	BUCKLEY	HOUGHTON	CRISP	HOUGHTON

DIVISION THREE (SOUTH) CUP

Date	Opponent	H/A	Score	Att	1	2	3	4	5	6	7	8	9	10	11	Goalscorers
02/10/35	BRISTOL CITY	A	2-4	2000	ROBERTSON	PREECE	DONALD	WALLINGTON	McLEAN	BARLEY	ADCOCK	POSTIN	BUCKLEY	HARWOOD	CRISP	CRISP 2

GLOUCESTERSHIRE CUP FINAL

Date	Opponent	H/A	Score	Att	1	2	3	4	5	6	7	8	9	10	11	Goalscorers
25/09/35	BRISTOL CITY	H	3-1	6293	ELLIS	PICKERING	DONALD	WALLINGTON	McLEAN	McARTHUR	BARLEY	WILDSMITH	BUCKLEY	HARWOOD	CRISP	PICKERING, WILDSMITH pen, HARWOOD

PLAYERS

PLAYERS	APPS	GLS
ADCOCK H	13	1
BARLEY H	17	5
BUCKLEY E	8	2
CRISP G	22	6
DONALD A	21	
ELLIS J	34	
FRATER D	1	1
COLLEDGE L	7	1
HARRIS T	6	1
HARTILL W	8	3
HARWOOD I	26	9
HOUGHTON H	29	9
McARTHUR W	14	2
McCAMBRIDGE J	1	
McLEAN J	27	
MURRAY A	13	
PICKERING T	42	
POSTIN E	1	1
PREECE J	21	
PROUT S	22	2
ROBERTSON A	8	
TAYLOR A	5	1
TAYLOR P	21	2
WALLINGTON S	27	1
WARREN R	1	
WILDSMITH T	18	2
WILSON W R	2	
WOODMAN J	25	8
YOUNG A	24	
		15

on to defeat Sheffield United in the Wembley final at the end of the season. The Arsenal tie drew a crowd of 24,234 and produced takings of £3,552, the most expensive grandstand seats costing 10 shillings each and the cheapest terrace prices being two shillings. Prince-Cox had called for 6,000 tiered chairs to be installed around the ground that, if sold at four shillings each, would have realized a £1,000 profit. But the directors had erected tubular steel-stands, with seats costing a shilling each and, as a result of its unwillingness to back the manager's plans, the club lost almost £700 on the scheme.

Rovers, the holders, were knocked unceremoniously out of the Division Three (South) Cup. The future Rovers inside-forward Willie White scored twice as Bristol City won 4-2. Revenge was sweet as Rovers won 3-1 in the Gloucestershire Cup final. Incidentally, George McNestry, a member of Rovers' victorious 1935 side, was in the Coventry City side that defeated Swindon Town 5-2 on aggregate to win the Division Three (South) Cup. He was the only player ever to win two winner's medals in this short-lived competition. Extra-time goals from Harry Houghton and Ted Buckley gave Rovers victory in the Allan Palmer Cup final when, as holders, Rovers beat challengers Bournemouth 2-1. Rovers' reserves won the Bristol Charity League for a record 12th and final time, while Rovers also competed for the Bristol Hospital Cup in May, clawing back a 4-2 half-time deficit to earn a 5-5 draw with guest opponents Liverpool.

1936/37

The false dawn of an opening day win at The Den gave scant indication of Rovers' prospects for the season ahead. Five players were new to the side that day, from goalkeeper Joe Nicholls, a former Grenadier Guard who stood 6 ft 4 in tall, to outside-left Oliver Tidman. The experienced Bert Watson played at left-half, while Scotsman David Bruce and the former Welsh International Tommy Mills formed a strong right-wing partnership. These players were coached by Walter Moyle, a former manager of the French side Nîmes, appointed on 30 June to replace the veteran Harry Lake, the personal masseur to the nine-time Olympic gold medallist Paavo Nurmi.

Jack Woodman and Harry Houghton scored the goals that beat Millwall. Four consecutive home League games followed and Rovers won the first three of them. Woodman was on form, continuing his rich vein of scoring from the end of 1935/36 by scoring five times in these four straight wins from the start of the season. His fifth, Rovers' second in the 2-0 victory over Northampton Town, was said by many to be one of the finest ever seen at Eastville.

However, although hopes were high, the rot soon set in. Woodman was to score just once more all season, in the heavy New Year defeat at Ashton Gate and was sold to Preston North End once the season was over. Jimmy Cookson scored a hat-trick as Swindon Town humbled Rovers in September. Rovers lost all five League games in October, using 20 different players in the process. More of a blow, perhaps, was manager Albert Prince-Cox's decision to leave Rovers after six years. He had, for a time, successfully turned the club from perennial underachievers into one with the potential to

Bristol Rovers 1936/37. Back row: Raven, O'Mahoney, Pickering, Nicholls, Preece, Harris, Moyle (Trainer) Watson. Front row: Bruce, Mills, Woodman, Houghton, Tidman, McLean

achieve, but the Luton defeat in April 1936 and a string of poor results had taken their toll and he left to promote boxing as successfully in Plymouth as he had already in Bristol.

In November, Rovers appointed Percy Smith as manager. A former Blackburn Rovers and Preston North End player, Smith had also managed Nelson, Bury and Tottenham Hotspur. His Rovers side performed creditably and a final League position of 15th was a satisfactory start, but he was to last only 12 months in the post.

New players were staking claims to regular places. George Tweed and Les Sullivan, both summer signings, broke into the side during the poor run of results. So too did 21-year-old former Manchester United centre-forward Bill Pendergast, who was to score in 12 consecutive League games for Chester in the final season before World War Two. Smith's first move in the transfer market was to return to Preston for Albert Butterworth. He proved to be a shrewd acquisition and played at outside right in each of Rovers' 28 remaining League matches. Smith also brought Syd Wallington back to Eastville, the wing-half first reappearing in the reserves' 12-2 victory over a Monmouthshire Senior League XI in January.

Under Smith's management Rovers achieved some creditable results. Tom Harris scored twice in each of the large wins at home to Cardiff City and Exeter City, while Bournemouth were comprehensively defeated 4-0 at Eastville. However, the turning-point in fortunes was clearly the impressive 3-2 win at Southend in February. In Rovers' previous three away games four goals had been conceded at Bristol City and Northampton Town, as well as five at Brighton on a day when there were no away wins in 35 Football League and FA Cup matches. However, Sullivan was the hero of the day at Southend, creating all three of Rovers' goals. Smith's protégé Butterworth, the ever-reliable Houghton and re-called centre-forward Bill Hartill were the recipients. Smith had successfully resurrected two careers and built his side around them. At Southend, for the first time, he was able to play both Matt O'Mahoney at centre-half and Bill Hartill as centre-forward. The former was to prove a constant in Rovers' side until the war, winning 6 caps for Eire and one for Northern Ireland while on Rovers' books. The latter, recapturing past glories when he had become the top goalscorer in Wolverhampton Wanderers' League history – his 162 goals being a club record until bettered by Steve Bull in March 1991 – was to finish as Rovers' top scorer for the season with 13 goals in only 16 League matches.

Bill Pickering, a long-serving defender who completed three seasons as an ever-present and a spell of 105 consecutive matches

Following victory at Southend, Rovers enjoyed several good wins. Hartill scored a hat-trick in a 5-1 defeat of Torquay and twice in each of 4-0 wins over Orient and Luton Town. This final result was of particular note since the Hatters were divisional champions that season and this victory went some way towards repairing the damage inflicted twelve months earlier at Kenilworth Road. Prior to the comprehensive victory over Luton Town, which attracted a crowd of 15,000, the highest since Boxing Day, Rovers' Supporters' Club opened its new clubhouse, boasting billiards and skittles along with other facilities. Hartill scored 10 goals in a run of seven League games leading up to the Easter period. Yet, heavy defeats at Walsall and, on Good Friday, at Aldershot gave an indication that there was still work to be done. Rovers also lost 4-3 to Notts County at Meadow Lane, where the legendary Scottish forward Hughie Gallacher scored a hat-trick. Gallacher scored twice in the opening nine minutes and Rovers recovered well from 3-0 down before the forward scored his third goal with a 71st-minute run and shot. This was to be the last hat-trick conceded by Rovers in League football until January 1947.

On Easter Saturday, Rovers lost an unusual game 3-1 to Cardiff City at Ninian Park. Rovers fielded the 11 players who had appeared in the previous five games, winning both home matches 4-0 but conceding 13 goals in the three away fixtures. There were three

FOOTBALL LEAGUE DIVISION THREE (SOUTH)

SEASON 1936/37

Date	Opponent		Score	Att	1	2	3	4	5	6	7	8	9	10	11	Goalscorers
29/08/36	MILLWALL	H	2-1	29000	NICHOLS	PICKERING	PREECE	DODGIN	McLEAN	McARTHUR	BUTTERWORTH	MILLS	HARRIS	HOUGHTON	SULLIVAN	WOODMAN, HOUGHTON
02/09/36	SWINDON TOWN	H	2-1	14222	NICHOLS	PICKERING	PREECE	DODGIN	McLEAN	McARTHUR	BUTTERWORTH	MILLS	HARRIS	HOUGHTON	SULLIVAN	BUTTERWORTH, BRUCE
05/09/36	BRISTOL CITY	A	3-1	25638	NICHOLS	PICKERING	PREECE	DODGIN	McLEAN	McARTHUR	BUTTERWORTH	MILLS	HARRIS	HOUGHTON	SULLIVAN	HOUGHTON pen, WOODMAN 2
12/09/36	NORTHAMPTON TOWN	A	2-0	9000	NICHOLS	PICKERING	PREECE	RAVEN	McLEAN	McARTHUR	BUTTERWORTH	MILLS	HARRIS	HOUGHTON	SULLIVAN	MILLS, WOODMAN
16/09/36	NEWPORT COUNTY	H	1-1	10823	NICHOLS	PICKERING	PREECE	DODGIN	McLEAN	WATSON	BRUCE	MILLS	HARTILL	HOUGHTON	SULLIVAN	BRUCE
19/09/36	SWINDON TOWN	A	0-3	13528	NICHOLS	PICKERING	PREECE	RAVEN	McLEAN	McARTHUR	BUTTERWORTH	MILLS	HARTILL	HOUGHTON	SULLIVAN	
23/09/36	BOURNEMOUTH	H	1-1	10435	NICHOLS	PICKERING	PREECE	DODGIN	McLEAN	McARTHUR	WOODMAN	MILLS	HARTILL	HOUGHTON	SULLIVAN	DUCKWORTH og
26/09/36	BRIGHTON & HOVE ALBION	H	1-4	8851	NICHOLS	McLEAN	PREECE	DODGIN	O'MAHONEY	McARTHUR	BRUCE	MILLS	HARTILL	HOUGHTON	SULLIVAN	HARTILL W
03/10/36	WATFORD	A	0-3	10435	NICHOLS	PICKERING	PREECE	DODGIN	McLEAN	McARTHUR	BUTTERWORTH	WARREN	HARTILL	HOUGHTON	SULLIVAN	
10/10/36	SOUTHEND UNITED	H	0-3	9000	NICHOLS	PICKERING	PREECE	DODGIN	McLEAN	McARTHUR	BUTTERWORTH	WARREN	HARTILL	HOUGHTON	SULLIVAN	
17/10/36	TORQUAY UNITED	A	1-2	10031	NICHOLS	PICKERING	PREECE	DODGIN	McLEAN	WATSON	BRUCE	GOLLEDGE	HARTILL	HOUGHTON	SULLIVAN	McLEAN J
24/10/36	NOTTS COUNTY	H	2-3	6398	NICHOLS	PICKERING	PREECE	DODGIN	McLEAN	WATSON	BRUCE	WARREN	O'MAHONEY	HOUGHTON	SULLIVAN	NICHOLS, MILLS
31/10/36	CLAPTON ORIENT	A	1-2	13500	NICHOLS	PICKERING	PREECE	DODGIN	McLEAN	McARTHUR	BUTTERWORTH	MILLS	HARTILL	HOUGHTON	SULLIVAN	O'MAHONEY M
07/11/36	WALSALL	H	3-0	5523	NICHOLS	PICKERING	PREECE	DODGIN	McLEAN	McARTHUR	BRUCE	MILLS	HARRIS	HOUGHTON	SULLIVAN	HOUGHTON, MILLS
14/11/36	LUTON TOWN	A	0-2	6500	NICHOLS	PICKERING	PREECE	RAVEN	McLEAN	McARTHUR	BUTTERWORTH	WARREN	HARRIS	PENDERGAST	SULLIVAN	PICKERING W
21/11/36	CARDIFF CITY	H	5-1	12000	NICHOLS	PICKERING	PREECE	DODGIN	McLEAN	McARTHUR	BUTTERWORTH	MILLS	HARRIS	HOUGHTON	SULLIVAN	HOUGHTON, BUTTERWORTH, SULLIVAN, HARRIS
05/12/36	EXETER CITY	H	4-2	12211	ELLIS	TWEED	PREECE	DODGIN	McLEAN	McARTHUR	BUTTERWORTH	WARREN	HARRIS	HOUGHTON	SULLIVAN	HOUGHTON, SULLIVAN, BUTTERWORTH, HARRIS
19/12/36	QUEENS PARK RANGERS	H	1-1	7905	ELLIS	TWEED	PREECE	DODGIN	McLEAN	McARTHUR	BUTTERWORTH	MILLS	HARRIS	HOUGHTON	SULLIVAN	HARRIS
25/12/36	GILLINGHAM	H	0-1	8000	ELLIS	TWEED	PREECE	DODGIN	McLEAN	McARTHUR	BUTTERWORTH	MILLS	HARRIS	HOUGHTON	SULLIVAN	
26/12/36	GILLINGHAM	A	2-1	9440	ELLIS	TWEED	PREECE	DODGIN	McLEAN	McARTHUR	BUTTERWORTH	MILLS	HARRIS	HOUGHTON	SULLIVAN	HOUGHTON, SULLIVAN, HARRIS
28/12/36	MILLWALL	A	0-3	15000	ELLIS	TWEED	PREECE	DODGIN	McLEAN	McARTHUR	BUTTERWORTH	MILLS	HARRIS	HOUGHTON	SULLIVAN	
02/01/37	BRISTOL CITY	H	1-4	15000	ELLIS	TWEED	PREECE	DODGIN	McLEAN	McARTHUR	BUTTERWORTH	MILLS	HARRIS	HOUGHTON	SULLIVAN	SULLIVAN, HARRIS 2
09/01/37	NORTHAMPTON TOWN	H	1-4	13030	ELLIS	TWEED	PREECE	DODGIN	McLEAN	RAVEN	BUTTERWORTH	MILLS	HARRIS	HOUGHTON	SULLIVAN	HARRIS 2, DODGIN, MILLS
23/01/37	BOURNEMOUTH	A	0-2	8926	ELLIS	TWEED	PREECE	DODGIN	McLEAN	McARTHUR	RAVEN	WOODMAN	HARRIS	HOUGHTON	SULLIVAN	HARRIS
30/01/37	BRIGHTON & HOVE ALBION	A	2-5	3769	ELLIS	TWEED	PREECE	WATSON	O'MAHONEY	McARTHUR	WATSON	MILLS	WOODMAN	PENDERGAST	SULLIVAN	RAVEN J
06/02/37	WATFORD	H	0-1	5000	NICHOLS	TWEED	PREECE	WATSON	McLEAN	McARTHUR	BUTTERWORTH	WARREN	HARRIS	HOUGHTON	SULLIVAN	
13/02/37	SOUTHEND UNITED	A	3-2	5000	NICHOLS	TWEED	PREECE	RAVEN	McLEAN	McARTHUR	BUTTERWORTH	WARREN	HARRIS	HOUGHTON	SULLIVAN	TIDMAN, BUTTERWORTH
20/02/37	TORQUAY UNITED	H	5-1	6443	NICHOLS	TWEED	PREECE	DODGIN	McLEAN	McARTHUR	BUTTERWORTH	MILLS	HARRIS	HOUGHTON	SULLIVAN	HOUGHTON, BUTTERWORTH, HARTILL
24/02/37	READING	A	0-2	6664	NICHOLS	TWEED	PREECE	DODGIN	McLEAN	McARTHUR	BUTTERWORTH	MILLS	HARTILL	HOUGHTON	SULLIVAN	HARTILL 3, HOUGHTON, MILLS
27/02/37	NOTTS COUNTY	A	3-4	6398	NICHOLS	TWEED	PREECE	DODGIN	McLEAN	McARTHUR	BUTTERWORTH	MILLS	HARTILL	HOUGHTON	SULLIVAN	HARTILL, HOUGHTON, BLYTH og
06/03/37	CLAPTON ORIENT	H	4-0	2318	NICHOLS	TWEED	PREECE	DODGIN	McLEAN	McARTHUR	BUTTERWORTH	MILLS	HARTILL	HOUGHTON	SULLIVAN	HARTILL 2, MILLS, HOUGHTON
13/03/37	WALSALL	A	2-5	12549	NICHOLS	TWEED	PREECE	DODGIN	McLEAN	McARTHUR	BUTTERWORTH	MILLS	HARTILL	HOUGHTON	SULLIVAN	HARTILL 2
20/03/37	LUTON TOWN	H	4-0	6000	NICHOLS	TWEED	PREECE	DODGIN	McLEAN	McARTHUR	BUTTERWORTH	MILLS	HARTILL	HOUGHTON	SULLIVAN	SULLIVAN, HARTILL 2, BUTTERWORTH
26/03/37	ALDERSHOT	A	0-4	4000	NICHOLS	TWEED	PREECE	DODGIN	McLEAN	McARTHUR	BUTTERWORTH	MILLS	HARTILL	HOUGHTON	SULLIVAN	
27/03/37	CARDIFF CITY	A	0-3	3000	NICHOLS	TWEED	PREECE	DODGIN	McLEAN	McARTHUR	WOODMAN	MILLS	HARTILL	WALLINGTON	SULLIVAN	
29/03/37	ALDERSHOT	H	1-0	15000	NICHOLS	TWEED	PREECE	DODGIN	McLEAN	McARTHUR	BUTTERWORTH	HOUGHTON	HARTILL	MILLS	SULLIVAN	HOUGHTON pen
03/04/37	CRYSTAL PALACE	A	1-3	5000	NICHOLS	TWEED	PREECE	DODGIN	McLEAN	McARTHUR	BUTTERWORTH	HOUGHTON	WOODMAN	MILLS	SULLIVAN	HOUGHTON
10/04/37	EXETER CITY	A	1-0	9400	NICHOLS	TWEED	PREECE	WALLINGTON	McLEAN	McARTHUR	BUTTERWORTH	HOUGHTON	HARRIS	MILLS	SULLIVAN	McARTHUR, SULLIVAN
17/04/37	READING	H	1-0	9000	NICHOLS	TWEED	PREECE	WALLINGTON	McLEAN	WATSON	BUTTERWORTH	MILLS	HARTILL	HOUGHTON	SULLIVAN	HOUGHTON
24/04/37	QUEENS PARK RANGERS	A	2-3	6282	NICHOLS	TWEED	PREECE	WALLINGTON	McLEAN	McARTHUR	MILLS	HOUGHTON	HARTILL	MILLS	SULLIVAN	HARTILL 2, MILLS, HOUGHTON
01/05/37	NEWPORT COUNTY	H	2-2	7000	NICHOLS	TWEED	PREECE	WATSON	McLEAN	McARTHUR	WARREN	WARREN	O'MAHONEY	PENDERGAST	PENDERGAST	PENDERGAST 2

FA CUP

Date	Opponent		Score	Att	1	2	3	4	5	6	7	8	9	10	11	Goalscorers
09/12/33	LEICESTER CITY	A	2-5	25156	ELLIS	PICKERING	PREECE	DODGIN	O'MAHONEY	McARTHUR	BUTTERWORTH	MILLS	HARRIS	HOUGHTON	SULLIVAN	BUTTERWORTH, McARTHUR
29/11/33	SOUTHPORT	H	2-1	13200	NICHOLS	TWEED	PREECE	DODGIN	McLEAN	WATSON	BUTTERWORTH	MILLS	HARRIS	WOODMAN	TIDMAN	HARRIS, HARTILL
25/11/33	CORINTHIANS	A	2-0	2204	ELLIS	ELLIS	PREECE	DODGIN	McLEAN	McARTHUR	BUTTERWORTH	MILLS	HARRIS	HOUGHTON	SULLIVAN	HARRIS, McARTHUR

DIVISION THREE (SOUTH) CUP

Date	Opponent		Score	Att	1	2	3	4	5	6	7	8	9	10	11	Goalscorers
13/01/34	SWINDON TOWN	A	3-0	1800	NICHOLS	TWEED	PREECE	DODGIN	McLEAN	WATSON	BRUCE	HARTILL	WOODMAN	HOUGHTON	TIDMAN	MILLS 2, BRUCE
01/02/34	WATFORD	A	2-2	1000	NICHOLS	PICKERING	PREECE	DODGIN	McLEAN	BRUCE	BRUCE	HARTILL	WOODMAN	PENDERGAST	TIDMAN	WOODMAN, PENDERGAST

GLOUCESTERSHIRE CUP FINAL

Date	Opponent		Score	Att	1	2	3	4	5	6	7	8	9	10	11	Goalscorers
13/09/33	BRISTOL CITY	A	0-1	5100	NICHOLS	ELLIS	PREECE	RAVEN	O'MAHONEY	McARTHUR	MILLS	MILLS	WOODMAN	PENDERGAST	SULLIVAN	

PLAYERS	APP	GLS
BRUCE D	12	2
BUTTERWORTH A	28	6
DODGIN W	30	1
ELLIS J	13	
GOLLEDGE L	1	
HARRIS T	13	8
HARTILL W	16	13
HOUGHTON H	37	14
McARTHUR W	26	5
McLEAN J	23	
MILLS T	35	8
NICHOLS J	29	
O'MAHONEY M	21	4
PENDERGAST W	4	2
PICKERING W	19	
PREECE J	42	
RAVEN J	5	
SULLIVAN L	26	5
TIDMAN O	16	1
TWEED G	22	
WALLINGTON S	7	
WARREN R	7	1
WATSON H	19	
WOODMAN J	14	6
OWN GOALS		2

penalties awarded in quick succession at Cardiff and, while Arthur Granville scored for the Bluebirds, Harry Houghton converted one of his two for Rovers. This equalled the three penalties awarded in the matches with Swindon Town in 1928 and Gillingham in 1935 and subsequently repeated against Newport County in 1948 and at York City in 1971.

Potential disaster was averted at Eastville on Thursday 22 April by the prompt actions of an alert watchman called Tom Berry. He spotted a fire in a storeroom beneath a stand at 11 p.m. and, though kit was lost, two fire engines had the blaze out within five hours. It was generally recognized that Berry had single-handedly prevented Rovers from suffering the fate which was to befall the club in 1980. After this drama, Rovers were left with two away games to complete a creditable total of 71 League goals scored, with Harris and Mills contributing 8 each behind Hartill. There was also a testimonial for popular full-back Bill Pickering, who scored a penalty as Rovers lost 4-2 to Bristol City. It was the end of a long association with the club, for Pickering moved to Accrington Stanley over the summer. His full-back partner, Jack Preece, had been the only ever-present for the season.

In the FA Cup, a Harris goal in each half defeated prominent amateur side Corinthians at a sparsely populated Crystal Palace. A terrific fire just days later destroyed the site of the Great Exhibition. The opposition fielded, at inside-left, Bill Webster, an England amateur footballer and Middlesex cricketer who was to be president of the MCC in 1976/77. Then victory over Southport brought Division Two Leicester City to Eastville where, quite unlike in 1986, Rovers fell to a crushing defeat. Leicester, who were to be champions of Division Two that season, convincingly defeated Rovers 5-2. There were two goals for Jack Bowers, the former England International who scored 45 League goals in 1936/37 for Derby County and Leicester City. After a 3-0 win at Swindon Town, Rovers were knocked out of the Division Three (South) Cup by Watford. While Bristol City won the Gloucestershire Cup final, Rovers gained revenge by beating the old rivals at cricket. This morale-boosting 15-run victory owed much to the opening partnership of club cricketer Allan Murray and Somerset batsman Newman Bunce.

Rovers' long association with the Allan Palmer Cup, which stretched back to Joe Clennell's goal in 1927, finally closed with defeat at the hands of Bournemouth. The Cherries gained revenge for their loss 12 months earlier by beating holders Rovers 3-1. The former Rovers forward Joe Riley scored a well-taken hat-trick, with a 50th-minute penalty and goals after 53 and 88 minutes, and Hartill pulled a goal back 14 minutes from time. It was the second hat-trick Riley had scored against Rovers that season, for he had contributed all Bournemouth's goals in their 3-0 victory at Dean Court in September. The irony of the situation was not lost on Rovers, since it had been against Bournemouth themselves that Riley had scored three goals on his Rovers debut in January 1932.

The former Rovers manager Alf Homer, who had run the side through the Southern League years between 1899 and 1920 and continued as secretary until 1928, died on 6 January 1937, aged 66.

1937/38

By the summer of 1937, Bristol Rovers were in freefall, heading towards the need to apply for re-election on the eve of World War Two. In some respects, hostilities in Europe helped save the club's bacon. The Prince-Cox years were now but a memory and the quality players who were introduced then were not being replaced. For the new season, a season ticket on the terraces cost £1, one for the wing-stand 40s and for the centre stands 50s.

The only summer signing to make Percy Smith's line-up for the visit to Watford on the opening day of the season was the former Dundee United inside-left Bobby Gardiner. Though standing just 5ft 4in, he was a formidable figure, but quality support was lacking. Rovers crashed 4-0 at Watford, with

Goalkeeper Joe Nicholls conceded eight goals in the FA Cup defeat by Queen's Park Rangers

Jack Preece putting the opening goal of the season past his own goalkeeper, and failed to score in the opening four League games. When Gardiner scored the club's first League goal of the season in the fifth, it was a mere consolation in a 4-1 defeat at Torquay United.

As results went against the club, Jack Howshall was introduced at right-half and Smith signed Ernie Parker and the experienced Harry Roberts. The latter, known as 'The Rock of Gibraltar', was a highly dependable full-back whose career encompassed more than 400 League matches. He was to give Rovers valuable service, as was Albert Iles, whose successful move from Southern League football at last set Rovers scoring goals. Iles was, by far, the club's top scorer with 14 goals in his 31 League games. In September, the former Bristol City stalwart Archie Annan became a Rovers scout, a path later followed by Ashton Gate favourites Wally Jennings and Bob Hewison.

As it happened, the course of the season swung on the FA Cup-tie against Queen's Park Rangers at Eastville in November. The sides had drawn 1-1 only a month earlier and, though Rovers went into the match with only three League wins to their name, a home tie should have given the club every chance of progressing to the second round. As it was, Rangers won 8-1, before a crowd of 8,869 producing gate receipts of £520. Tom Cheetham and Alf Fitzgerald scored three goals each, the only game in Rovers' FA Cup history when two opponents have scored hat-tricks, and Wilf Bott scored twice. Incredibly, the first goal had not arrived until the 27th minute, but Rangers scored five times in 17 minutes to lead 5-0 at the break, with Fitzgerald completing his hat-trick before half-time. Pendergast pulled a consolation goal back after 55 minutes but this result remains to this day the club's heaviest home defeat in first-class competitions.

Bristol Rovers 1937/38 pre-season photo-call. Manager Percy Smith (middle row, third from left) was sacked in November after the 8-1 FA Cup defeat by QPR

Rovers were not so much outplayed as overwhelmed. As with the 12-goal defeat at Luton and 8-goal hammerings at Torquay and Swansea in the inter-war years, the size of the defeat was unexpected and demoralizing.

The immediate fall-out after this sharp Cup exit was the departure of manager Percy Smith after 12 months at the club. Rovers were managerless until January, in which period four players made their first appearances for the team. Out-of-favour Tom Harris joined Southampton in an exchange deal for Tosh Withers, who made his debut in the draw with Notts County. So too did Danny Tolland, a talented but frustrating Irish forward, bought for £550 from Northampton Town, where he had been one of the few inter-war players sent off in a League game. More controversially, the third debutant was full-back Alec Millar, a £150 signing from Margate who had previously spent two years with East Fife. His registration had been bought in July by director Fred Ashmead, while Percy Smith was on holiday yet the defender had never figured in the manager's plans. Once Smith had left, Millar went on to stake a regular place at left-back for more than a season.

During the interregnum, Rovers' form improved. Despite the absence of Iles, Rovers recorded a 5-2 victory over Walsall on Christmas Day, their largest win of the season. Les Sullivan and Tommy Mills scored two each and Tolland notched his first goal for the club. As so often happened in the days of double fixtures, Walsall beat Rovers by the same score 24 hours later, thanks largely to the outstanding form of their 17-year-old goalkeeper, Bert Williams, a post-war England International. Rovers responded with a much-needed single-goal victory over Bristol City, Withers' second-half goal in a keenly fought local derby proving the zenith of his brief League career.

FOOTBALL LEAGUE DIVISION THREE (SOUTH)

SEASON 1937/38

Date	Opponent	H/A	Score	Att	1	2	3	4	5	6	7	8	9	10	11	Goalscorers
28/08/37	WATFORD	H	0-4	11544	NICHOLLS	TWEED	PREECE	WARREN	O'MAHONEY	BUTTERWORTH	HARTILL	WITHERS	ILES	GARDINER	SULLIVAN	
31/08/37	NORTHAMPTON TOWN	H	0-0	7188	NICHOLLS	TWEED	PREECE	WARREN	O'MAHONEY	BUTTERWORTH	MILLS	WITHERS	ILES	GARDINER	SULLIVAN	
04/09/37	MANSFIELD TOWN	H	0-0	8096	NICHOLLS	TWEED	PREECE	WARREN	O'MAHONEY	McARTHUR	MILLS	WITHERS	ILES	GARDINER	SULLIVAN	
06/09/37	NORTHAMPTON TOWN	A	0-2	5590	NICHOLLS	ROBERTS	PREECE	WARREN	O'MAHONEY	McARTHUR	BUTTERWORTH	MILLS	ILES	GARDINER	SULLIVAN	
11/09/37	TORQUAY UNITED	A	1-4	5093	NICHOLLS	ROBERTS	TWEED	WARREN	O'MAHONEY	McARTHUR	BUTTERWORTH	MILLS	HARTILL	GARDINER	SULLIVAN	GARDINER
14/09/37	BOURNEMOUTH	H	2-1	4553	NICHOLLS	ROBERTS	PREECE	WARREN	O'MAHONEY	McARTHUR	BUTTERWORTH	MILLS	HARRIS	PARKER	GARDINER	PARKER, McARTHUR
18/09/37	CLAPTON ORIENT	H	3-2	9000	NICHOLLS	ROBERTS	PREECE	WARREN	O'MAHONEY	McARTHUR	BUTTERWORTH	MILLS	HARRIS	HARTILL	PARKER	BUTTERWORTH, HARTILL, MILLS
25/09/37	SOUTHEND UNITED	A	1-1	7035	NICHOLLS	ROBERTS	PREECE	WARREN	O'MAHONEY	McARTHUR	BUTTERWORTH	MILLS	ILES	HARTILL	PARKER	ILES A
02/10/37	QUEENS PARK RANGERS	H	1-1	12000	NICHOLLS	ROBERTS	PREECE	WARREN	O'MAHONEY	McARTHUR	BUTTERWORTH	MILLS	ILES	HARTILL	PARKER	HOWSHALL J
09/10/37	BRIGHTON & H ALBION	A	0-3	9229	NICHOLLS	ROBERTS	PREECE	WARREN	O'MAHONEY	McARTHUR	RICHARDS	BUTTERWORTH	ILES	McARTHUR	PARKER	
16/10/37	GILLINGHAM	A	1-0	6499	NICHOLLS	ROBERTS	PREECE	HOWSHALL	O'MAHONEY	McARTHUR	RICHARDS	BUTTERWORTH	ILES	GARDINER	PARKER	McARTHUR
23/10/37	EXETER CITY	H	1-1	6448	NICHOLLS	ROBERTS	PREECE	WARREN	O'MAHONEY	McARTHUR	BUTTERWORTH	MILLS	ILES	GARDINER	PARKER	MILLAR A
30/10/37	SWINDON TOWN	A	1-2	10000	NICHOLLS	ROBERTS	PREECE	WARREN	O'MAHONEY	McARTHUR	BUTTERWORTH	WITHERS	ILES	GARDINER	PARKER	O'MAHONEY
06/11/37	ALDERSHOT	H	0-1	7000	NICHOLLS	ROBERTS	PREECE	WARREN	O'MAHONEY	McARTHUR	BUTTERWORTH	HARTILL	ILES	GARDINER	PARKER	
13/11/37	MILLWALL	A	1-2	24000	NICHOLLS	ELLIS	PREECE	WARREN	O'MAHONEY	McARTHUR	MILLS	WITHERS	ILES	GARDINER	SULLIVAN	NICHOLLS!
20/11/37	READING	H	2-2	7977	NICHOLLS	ROBERTS	PREECE	WARREN	O'MAHONEY	McARTHUR	HARRIS	WARREN	ILES	GARDINER	SULLIVAN	RICHARDS W
27/11/37	NOTTS COUNTY	A	1-1	4000	NICHOLLS	ROBERTS	PREECE	WARREN	O'MAHONEY	McARTHUR	RICHARDS	HARTILL	ILES	TOLLAND	GARDINER	PENDERGAST W
04/12/37	WALSALL	H	5-2	10000	NICHOLLS	ROBERTS	MILLAR	WARREN	O'MAHONEY	McARTHUR	RICHARDS	WARREN	ILES	TOLLAND	GARDINER	MILLS 2, SULLIVAN 2, TOLLAND
25/12/37	WALSALL	A	5-2	8000	NICHOLLS	ROBERTS	MILLAR	HOWSHALL	O'MAHONEY	McARTHUR	RICHARDS	WITHERS	ILES	TOLLAND	SULLIVAN	SMITH W
27/12/37	BRISTOL CITY	H	1-0	25000	NICHOLLS	ROBERTS	MILLAR	WARREN	O'MAHONEY	McARTHUR	MILLS	WITHERS	ILES	TOLLAND	GARDINER	MILLS 2, SULLIVAN 2, TOLLAND
28/12/37	BRISTOL CITY	A	0-2	10000	NICHOLLS	ROBERTS	MILLAR	WARREN	O'MAHONEY	McARTHUR	MILLS	WITHERS	ILES	TOLLAND	GARDINER	WITHERS
01/01/38	WATFORD	A	0-2	10000	NICHOLLS	ROBERTS	MILLAR	WARREN	O'MAHONEY	McARTHUR	MILLS	HARTILL	ILES	TOLLAND	GARDINER	TOLLAND D
15/01/38	MANSFIELD TOWN	A	0-1	3222	NICHOLLS	ROBERTS	MILLAR	WARREN	O'MAHONEY	McARTHUR	MILLS	WITHERS	HARTILL	TOLLAND	SULLIVAN	
19/01/38	CRYSTAL PALACE	H	2-3	5492	NICHOLLS	ROBERTS	MILLAR	WARREN	O'MAHONEY	McARTHUR	WARREN	HARTILL	ILES	TOLLAND	GARDINER	MILLS, TOLLAND
22/01/38	TORQUAY UNITED	H	2-0	6095	NICHOLLS	ROBERTS	MILLAR	WARREN	O'MAHONEY	McARTHUR	MILLS	HARTILL	ILES	TOLLAND	GARDINER	ILES 2
29/01/38	CLAPTON ORIENT	A	0-1	4443	NICHOLLS	ROBERTS	MILLAR	WARREN	O'MAHONEY	McARTHUR	MILLS	HARTILL	ILES	TOLLAND	GARDINER	
05/02/38	SOUTHEND UNITED	H	2-1	7500	NICHOLLS	ROBERTS	SMITH	WARREN	O'MAHONEY	McARTHUR	MILLS	WITHERS	ILES	TOLLAND	SULLIVAN	WITHERS, ILES
12/02/38	QUEENS PARK RANGERS	A	0-4	11000	NICHOLLS	ROBERTS	SMITH	WARREN	O'MAHONEY	HOWSHALL	MILLS	WITHERS	ILES	TOLLAND	SULLIVAN	
19/02/38	BRIGHTON & H ALBION	H	0-0	7140	NICHOLLS	ROBERTS	SMITH	WARREN	O'MAHONEY	HOWSHALL	MILLS	WITHERS	ILES	TOLLAND	GARDINER	
26/02/38	GILLINGHAM	A	2-1	4000	NICHOLLS	ROBERTS	SMITH	WARREN	O'MAHONEY	McARTHUR	MILLS	WITHERS	ILES	TOLLAND	GARDINER	ILES, GARDINER
05/03/38	EXETER CITY	H	0-0	6000	NICHOLLS	ROBERTS	SMITH	WARREN	O'MAHONEY	McARTHUR	WARREN	WITHERS	ILES	TOLLAND	GARDINER	
12/03/38	SWINDON TOWN	H	1-2	8000	NICHOLLS	ROBERTS	SMITH	WARREN	O'MAHONEY	McARTHUR	MILLS	MILLS	ILES	TOLLAND	SULLIVAN	ILES 2
19/03/38	ALDERSHOT	A	2-0	5000	NICHOLLS	ROBERTS	SMITH	WARREN	O'MAHONEY	McARTHUR	MILLS	WITHERS	ILES	TOLLAND	GARDINER	ILES, GARDINER
26/03/38	MILLWALL	H	0-2	8300	NICHOLLS	ROBERTS	SMITH	WARREN	O'MAHONEY	McARTHUR	BUTTERWORTH	MILLS	ILES	TOLLAND	GARDINER	
02/04/38	READING	A	0-4	4005	NICHOLLS	ROBERTS	SMITH	WARREN	O'MAHONEY	HOWSHALL	BUTTERWORTH	MILLS	ILES	McARTHUR	GARDINER	
09/04/38	CRYSTAL PALACE	A	1-0	5316	NICHOLLS	ROBERTS	SMITH	WARREN	O'MAHONEY	McARTHUR	BUTTERWORTH	MILLS	ILES	MILLS	GARDINER	ILES
15/04/38	CARDIFF CITY	H	1-1	10000	NICHOLLS	ROBERTS	SMITH	WARREN	O'MAHONEY	McARTHUR	BUTTERWORTH	TOLLAND	ILES	MILLS	GARDINER	BUTTERWORTH
16/04/38	NOTTS COUNTY	H	2-1	3671	NICHOLLS	ROBERTS	SMITH	WARREN	O'MAHONEY	McARTHUR	BUTTERWORTH	TOLLAND	ILES	MILLS	GARDINER	MILLS, ROBERTS pen
18/04/38	CARDIFF CITY	A	1-1	10000	NICHOLLS	ROBERTS	SMITH	WARREN	O'MAHONEY	McARTHUR	BUTTERWORTH	WITHERS	ILES	MILLS	GARDINER	WITHERS, ILES
23/04/38	NEWPORT COUNTY	H	2-0	5000	NICHOLLS	ROBERTS	SMITH	WARREN	O'MAHONEY	McARTHUR	MILLS	WITHERS	ILES	MILLS	GARDINER	MILLS 2, SULLIVAN 2, TOLLAND
30/04/38	BRISTOL CITY	A	0-0	23424	NICHOLLS	ROBERTS	MILLAR	WARREN	O'MAHONEY	McARTHUR	MILLS	WITHERS	ILES	HARTILL	GARDINER	
05/05/38	NEWPORT COUNTY	A	2-2	3500	NICHOLLS	ROBERTS	MILLAR	WARREN	O'MAHONEY	McARTHUR	MILLS	WITHERS	ILES	HARTILL	GARDINER	HARTILL, GARDINER
07/05/38	BOURNEMOUTH	A	3-1	4000	NICHOLLS	MILLAR	MILLAR	HOWSHALL	O'MAHONEY	McARTHUR	MILLS	BUTTERWORTH	HARTILL	McARTHUR	GARDINER	WITHERS, ILES, HARTILL

FA CUP

Date	Opponent	H/A	Score	Att	1	2	3	4	5	6	7	8	9	10	11	Goalscorers
27/11/37	QUEENS PARK RANGERS	H	1-8	8869	NICHOLLS	ROBERTS	PREECE	MCLEAN	O'MAHONEY	MILLS	WARREN	MILLS	HARTILL	PENDERGAST	SULLIVAN	PENDERGAST

GLOUCESTERSHIRE CUP FINAL

Date	Opponent	H/A	Score	Att	1	2	3	4	5	6	7	8	9	10	11	Goalscorers
27/09/37	BRISTOL CITY	H	2-1	3648	NICHOLLS	ROBERTS	MILLAR	HOWSHALL	O'MAHONEY	McARTHUR	MILLS	MILLS	ILES	GARDINER	PARKER	McARTHUR, ILES

PLAYERS	APP	GLS
BUTTERWORTH A	28	2
ELLIS J	1	
GARDINER R	33	5
HARTILL T	5	3
HOWSHALL J	12	3
ILES A	31	14
McARTHUR W	40	2
MILLAR A	12	
MILLS T	30	5
NICHOLLS J	41	
O'MAHONEY M	42	1
PARKER E	9	1
PENDERGAST W	3	1
PREECE J	16	
RICHARDS W	4	
ROBERTS H	37	1
SMITH W	16	
SULLIVAN L	13	5
TOLLAND D	19	2
TWEED G	3	
WARREN R	29	
WITHERS P	4	

On 18 January 1938, Rovers appointed a new manager to succeed Percy Smith. Brough Fletcher, chosen ahead of the veteran Crystal Palace defender Bob Collyer, who had once scored two own goals in a Southern League game against Exeter City in September 1910, had enjoyed a long career with Barnsley as player and manager and had also played for Sheffield Wednesday. His was the task of steadying the ship. In the post-war era, Fletcher might well have been sacrificed following the club's poor showing in 1938/39, but he in fact remained with Rovers a further decade, rebuilding the side after the war and laying the foundations for the future. He it was who discovered young talent such as Geoff Bradford, Harry Bamford and George Petherbridge, in so doing paving the way for the halcyon days of the 1950s.

One player given a late run in the side was Wilf Smith, a full-back signed in the summer from Clevedon Town but never given a game by the former manager. Smith was a regular in the side late in the season, when Rovers' form began to revive. Although he appeared only once the following year, he stayed with the club and became one of the select handful of players to appear for Rovers in League football both sides of World War Two.

There were 4-0 defeats at both Queen's Park Rangers and Reading. In the former Wilf Bott claimed a brace of goals to match his FA Cup achievement, while in the latter four different opponents got on the scoresheet in a one-sided game. However, following defeat at Elm Park, Rovers were unbeaten in their final eight League games of the season, Hartill and Withers both scoring at Dean Court, where Rovers recovered from a goal down to score three times in 20 minutes, in their final matches for the club.

Centre-half Matt O'Mahoney, the only ever-present, contrived to score own goals in consecutive League games in the autumn. He scored past goalkeeper Nicholls in the home draws with Reading and Notts County. Somewhat bizarrely, O'Mahoney was to score again for Reading in February 1939, when he contributed to Rovers' 2-0 defeat at Elm Park. This unintentional feat is worth comparing with Norman Sykes, who scored own goals in both League games with Sunderland in 1961/62, and Phil Bater's own goals in both legs of a League Cup-tie with Walsall in August 1977.

On a positive note, Rovers completed a League double over both Gillingham, for whom the England Test cricketer Laurence Fishlock appeared at outside-left at Eastville in February, and Bournemouth and also won

Centre-half Matt O'Mahoney was a double International while with Rovers, winning 6 caps for Eire in 1938 and 1939 and 1 cap for Northern Ireland in 1939

the Gloucestershire Cup final. Goals from Wally McArthur and Albert Iles gave the club a 2-1 victory over Bristol City at Eastville. Just fewer than 4,000 watched this game, as compared to 25,000 for the equivalent League fixture. When Rovers next won the trophy, 10 years later, McArthur again played a key role.

In July 1938, news reached the club of the death of Harry Horsey, a founder member of the Black Arabs and latterly a chairman of Bristol Rovers. Seldom has one man spent as long as 55 years from a club's formation with his only club, nor have many contributed in as many ways as Horsey. As a player, financial figurehead and member of the board, he epitomized the spirit of the club in its early days and his death closed a chapter in Rovers' history.

1938/39

Being forced to apply for re-election remains the nadir of Bristol Rovers' League history. Rovers had struggled all season and the prospect of finishing in last place in Division Three (South) loomed large. After a heavy defeat at Brighton on the final day of the season, Rovers found themselves stranded below Walsall on goal average, while Orient leapfrogged them with a convincing 5-0 victory over Swindon Town the same afternoon. Rovers were consigned, for what was the only time in the club's history, to seek re-election to the League. This they were to gain comfortably, but the future would surely offer little hope. As it was, the arrival of war meant that Rovers could re-establish themselves in Division Three (South) in the late 1940s.

Yet, the season had begun with a convincing 3-0 victory over Mansfield Town at Eastville. Manager Brough Fletcher had stuck with his inherited side and there were no new faces in the Rovers side, the previous season's top scorer Albert Iles scoring twice. Transfer activity had, however, been brisk and nine new summer signings were to break into the League side, Frank Curran in particular making a big impression. The first change to the side saw Dick Spivey in place of Albert Butterworth for the visit of Southend United. The former Hull City outside-right had scored against the Shrimpers on his Torquay United debut and he repeated this feat for Rovers, his two goals leading the way to a 4-1 win.

However, following the Southend game Rovers endured a run of 13 consecutive League matches without a win. This autumnal spell was a major factor in the club's end-of-season struggle. In one of these games, a 2-1 defeat at Ashton Gate, many records debit both Rovers' Ray Warren and Bristol City's Jim Pearce with own goals. During this run, Rovers briefly recalled Wilf Smith, while nine other players made League debuts, eight of the summer signings and Albert Turner, a free signing in December from Cardiff City. He had previously enjoyed a glut of goals in his four years with Doncaster Rovers. One player who never made the League side was Charlie Hurst, a regular reserve player in 1938/39, whose son Geoff scored a hat-trick in the 1966 World Cup final.

Two factors involved in Rovers' third win of the season should come as no surprise. When this long-awaited event finally did occur, it was against struggling Mansfield

Bristol Rovers 1938/39. Back row: Hartley, Nicholls, Roberts, Millar, Smith, McArthur, Wilson, Warren. Second row: B Fletcher (Manager), Hawkins (Secretary), Bissicks (Director), Webb, Millington, Warhurst, Curran, Kitchen, Whitfield, Baldwin. Front row: Ashmead (Chairman), Humphreys (Director), Hurst, Butterworth, Iles, O'Mahoney, Gardiner, Mills, Kavanagh, Spivey, Hovell and Cool (both Directors)

Town at Field Mill and it came as a result of second-half goals from both Turner and Curran, as well as an angled drive after 20 minutes from the ever-consistent Albert Butterworth. Frank Curran had waited patiently for three months, following his transfer from Accrington Stanley, but he wasted no time in making the centre-forward position his own. 21 goals in only 27 League games included 10 in a five-match spell in the run-up to Easter. He scored Rovers' final pre-war League goal and also the first after the war, when Rovers drew 2-2 with Reading in August 1946.

Curran scored twice in an astonishing game at home to Ipswich Town in February. As they had done against Northampton Town in September 1935, Rovers recovered a three-goal deficit to draw 3-3. On this occasion Curran's goals and one from Tommy Mills, all in the last half hour, earned Rovers a point. Curran also scored four goals when Rovers defeated Swindon Town 5-0 in March. Three of these goals came before half-time, making him the fourth player to complete a first-half hat-trick for Rovers in League football. His personal haul equalled the club individual scoring record for one game, a figure often paralleled but never surpassed.

In some respects, Rovers could consider themselves a touch unfortunate to finish the season in bottom place. Champions Newport County were held to a draw, Rovers did not lose to clubs such as Ipswich Town, Walsall and Queen's Park Rangers and the away wins at Cardiff City and Mansfield Town showed great promise. No opponent scored a League hat-trick against Rovers in 1937/38 or 1938/39. There were none of the black days, such as Luton in 1936, nor Swansea in 1922 nor Torquay in 1932. The club had not finished bottom when the goals dried up in 1922/23, nor after losing 13 consecutive away fixtures in 1929/30. Yet, when the pressure was on, Fletcher's side appeared unable to raise their standards.

Johnny Hancocks, who missed a penalty for Walsall against Rovers at Fellows Park in April, was to enjoy a productive post-war career with Wolverhampton Wanderers

FOOTBALL LEAGUE DIVISION THREE (SOUTH)

SEASON 1938/39

Date	Opponent		Score	ATT	1 (G)	2	3	4	5	6	7	8	9	10	11	GOALSCORERS
27/08/38	MANSFIELD TOWN	H	3-0	10000	NICHOLLS	ROBERTS	MILLAR	WARREN	O'MAHONEY	McARTHUR	BUTTERWORTH	MILLS	ILES	TOLAND	GARDINER	ILES 2, McARTHUR
30/08/38	BRIGHTON & HOVE ALBION	H	1-1	10436	NICHOLLS	ROBERTS	MILLAR	WARREN	O'MAHONEY	McARTHUR	BUTTERWORTH	MILLS	ILES	TOLAND	CURRAN	CURRAN
03/09/38	QUEENS PARK RANGERS	A	1-1	16093	NICHOLLS	ROBERTS	MILLAR	WARREN	O'MAHONEY	McARTHUR	BUTTERWORTH	MILLS	ILES	TOLAND	CURRAN	ILES
07/09/38	ALDERSHOT	A	0-1	6000	NICHOLLS	ROBERTS	MILLAR	WARREN	O'MAHONEY	McARTHUR	BUTTERWORTH	MILLS	ILES	TOLAND	CURRAN	
10/09/38	SOUTHEND UNITED	H	4-1	8969	NICHOLLS	ROBERTS	MILLAR	WARREN	O'MAHONEY	McARTHUR	BUTTERWORTH	MILLS	ILES	TOLAND	CURRAN	CURRAN, BUTTERWORTH
12/09/38	ALDERSHOT	H	5-1	5934	NICHOLLS	ROBERTS	MILLAR	WARREN	O'MAHONEY	McARTHUR	BUTTERWORTH	SPIVEY	ILES A	TOLAND	SPIVEY	TOLAND, SPIVEY 2, ILES
17/09/38	EXETER CITY	A	1-2	8000	NICHOLLS	ROBERTS	MILLAR	WARREN	O'MAHONEY	McARTHUR	BUTTERWORTH	MILLS	ILES	TOLAND	SPIVEY	ILES
24/09/38	CARDIFF CITY	H	1-1	10000	NICHOLLS	ROBERTS	SMITH	WARREN	O'MAHONEY	McARTHUR	BUTTERWORTH	MILLS	ILES	TOLAND	GARDINER	KAVANAGH
01/10/38	IPSWICH TOWN	H	0-0	12784	NICHOLLS	ROBERTS	WEBB	WARREN	O'MAHONEY	McARTHUR	BUTTERWORTH	MILLS	ILES	SPIVEY	SPIVEY	
08/10/38	READING	A	2-4	6000	NICHOLLS	ROBERTS	MILLAR	MILLINGTON	O'MAHONEY	McARTHUR	BUTTERWORTH	MILLS	ILES	GARDINER	GARDINER	McARTHUR W, KITCHEN N
15/10/38	NOTTS COUNTY	H	0-0	7000	NICHOLLS	ROBERTS	MILLAR	WARREN	O'MAHONEY	McARTHUR	BUTTERWORTH	MILLS	ILES	GARDINER	BUTTERWORTH	
22/10/38	BRISTOL CITY	A	1-2	15825	NICHOLLS	ROBERTS	MILLAR	WARHURST	WARHURST	McARTHUR	BUTTERWORTH	MILLS	KAVANAGH	MILLS	MILLS	MILLS
29/10/38	NEWPORT COUNTY	H	0-0	11675	NICHOLLS	ROBERTS	MILLAR	WARHURST	WARHURST	McARTHUR	BUTTERWORTH	GARDINER	KAVANAGH	MILLS	SPIVEY	
05/11/38	CLAPTON ORIENT	A	1-2	4933	NICHOLLS	ROBERTS	MILLAR	WARHURST	WARHURST	McARTHUR	KITCHEN	GARDINER	KAVANAGH	MILLS	GARDINER	GARDINER
12/11/38	TORQUAY UNITED	H	0-1	9243	NICHOLLS	ROBERTS	MILLAR	WARREN	WHITFIELD	McARTHUR	KITCHEN	WARREN	CURRAN	MILLS	GARDINER	
19/11/38	SWINDON TOWN	A	1-2	6603	NICHOLLS	ROBERTS	MILLAR	WARREN	O'MAHONEY	WHITFIELD	BUTTERWORTH	MILLS	CURRAN	GARDINER	O'MAHONEY pen	O'MAHONEY pen
03/12/38	WATFORD	H	1-4	5305	NICHOLLS	ROBERTS	MILLAR	WHITFIELD	O'MAHONEY	McARTHUR	BUTTERWORTH	CURRAN	HARTLEY	TOLAND	TURNER	WARREN
17/12/38	NORTHAMPTON TOWN	A	1-2	3343	NICHOLLS	ROBERTS	MILLAR	McARTHUR	O'MAHONEY	McARTHUR	BUTTERWORTH	CURRAN	HARTLEY	TOLAND	HARTLEY	HARTLEY
24/12/38	MANSFIELD TOWN	A	3-1	7598	NICHOLLS	ROBERTS	MILLAR	WARREN	O'MAHONEY	McARTHUR	BUTTERWORTH	CURRAN	HARTLEY	TOLAND	TURNER	BUTTERWORTH, CURRAN, TURNER
27/12/38	BOURNEMOUTH	H	1-0	9046	NICHOLLS	ROBERTS	MILLAR	WARREN	O'MAHONEY	McARTHUR	BUTTERWORTH	CURRAN	ILES	TOLAND	TURNER	TURNER
31/12/38	QUEENS PARK RANGERS	H	0-0	4000	NICHOLLS	ROBERTS	MILLAR	WARREN	O'MAHONEY	McARTHUR	BUTTERWORTH	CURRAN	CURRAN	ILES	CURRAN	
07/01/39	PORT VALE	A	0-1	5610	NICHOLLS	ROBERTS	MILLAR	WARREN	O'MAHONEY	McARTHUR	BUTTERWORTH	MILLS	GARDINER	TOLAND	TURNER	
14/01/39	SOUTHEND UNITED	A	2-3	5000	NICHOLLS	ROBERTS	MILLAR	WARREN	O'MAHONEY	McARTHUR	BUTTERWORTH	MILLS	CURRAN	GARDINER	CURRAN	MILLS, CURRAN 2
21/01/39	EXETER CITY	H	4-1	5000	NICHOLLS	ROBERTS	MILLAR	WARREN	O'MAHONEY	McARTHUR	BUTTERWORTH	MILLS	CURRAN	GARDINER	CURRAN, CURRAN	CURRAN 2
28/01/39	CLAPTON ORIENT	H	2-0	12000	NICHOLLS	ROBERTS	MILLAR	WARREN	O'MAHONEY	McARTHUR	BUTTERWORTH	MILLS	CURRAN	GARDINER	CURRAN 2	CURRAN 2
04/02/39	IPSWICH TOWN	A	3-3	7209	NICHOLLS	ROBERTS	MILLAR	WARREN	O'MAHONEY	McARTHUR	BUTTERWORTH	MILLS	CURRAN	GARDINER	CURRAN 4, GARDINER	CURRAN, GARDINER
11/02/39	READING	H	0-2	6816	NICHOLLS	ROBERTS	MILLAR	WARREN	O'MAHONEY	McARTHUR	BUTTERWORTH	MILLS	CURRAN	TOLAND	CURRAN	
18/02/39	NOTTS COUNTY	A	1-3	10229	NICHOLLS	ROBERTS	MILLAR	WARREN	O'MAHONEY	WHITFIELD	BUTTERWORTH	MILLS	CURRAN	TOLAND	TURNER	CURRAN
25/02/39	BRISTOL CITY	H	1-1	14824	NICHOLLS	ROBERTS	MILLAR	WARREN	O'MAHONEY	McARTHUR	BUTTERWORTH	MILLS	CURRAN	TOLAND	CURRAN	CURRAN
04/03/39	NEWPORT COUNTY	A	0-2	8000	NICHOLLS	ROBERTS	MILLAR	WARREN	O'MAHONEY	McARTHUR	BUTTERWORTH	MILLS	CURRAN	TOLAND	CURRAN	
11/03/39	CLAPTON ORIENT	H	1-0	3423	NICHOLLS	ROBERTS	MILLAR	WARREN	O'MAHONEY	McARTHUR	BUTTERWORTH	MILLS	CURRAN	TOLAND	CURRAN	CURRAN
18/03/39	EXETER CITY	A	2-2	3631	NICHOLLS	ROBERTS	MILLAR	WARREN	O'MAHONEY	McARTHUR	BUTTERWORTH	MILLS	CURRAN	TOLAND	TURNER	CURRAN 2
25/03/39	TORQUAY UNITED	H	5-0	5000	NICHOLLS	ROBERTS	MILLAR	WARREN	O'MAHONEY	McARTHUR	BUTTERWORTH	MILLS	CURRAN	GARDINER	MILLS, CURRAN 2	MILLS, CURRAN 2
29/03/39	SWINDON TOWN	A	2-5	3000	NICHOLLS	ROBERTS	MILLAR	WARREN	O'MAHONEY	McARTHUR	BUTTERWORTH	MILLS	CURRAN	GARDINER	TURNER	CURRAN 2
01/04/39	BOURNEMOUTH	H	1-2	5634	NICHOLLS	ROBERTS	MILLAR	WHITFIELD	O'MAHONEY	McARTHUR	BUTTERWORTH	MILLS	CURRAN	GARDINER	CURRAN	CURRAN 4, GARDINER
07/04/39	PORT VALE	A	1-2	9549	NICHOLLS	ROBERTS	MILLAR	WHITFIELD	O'MAHONEY	McARTHUR	BUTTERWORTH	MILLS	CURRAN	GARDINER	CURRAN 2	CURRAN, BUTTERWORTH
07/04/39	WALSALL	H	2-0	7753	NICHOLLS	ROBERTS	MILLAR	WARREN	O'MAHONEY	McARTHUR	BUTTERWORTH	MILLS	CURRAN	GARDINER	TURNER	MILLS, GARDINER
08/04/39	WATFORD	A	1-1	7349	NICHOLLS	ROBERTS	MILLAR	WARREN	O'MAHONEY	McARTHUR	BUTTERWORTH	MILLS	CURRAN	GARDINER	CURRAN 2, TURNER, O'MAHONEY	CURRAN 2, TURNER, O'MAHONEY
10/04/39	WALSALL	A	2-2	11714	NICHOLLS	ROBERTS	WHITFIELD	WARREN	O'MAHONEY	McARTHUR	BUTTERWORTH	MILLS	CURRAN	GARDINER	CURRAN, O'MAHONEY	O'MAHONEY pen
15/04/39	CRYSTAL PALACE	H	0-0	4610	NICHOLLS	ROBERTS	MILLAR	WARREN	O'MAHONEY	McARTHUR	BUTTERWORTH	MILLS	CURRAN	GARDINER	SPIVEY	
17/04/39	CRYSTAL PALACE	H	1-1	4620	NICHOLLS	CARTE	MILLAR	WARREN	O'MAHONEY	McARTHUR	BUTTERWORTH	CURRAN	CURRAN	GARDINER	WHITFIELD	WHITFIELD
22/04/39	NORTHAMPTON TOWN	A	1-0	2806	NICHOLLS	CARTE	MILLAR	WHITFIELD	O'MAHONEY	WHITFIELD	BUTTERWORTH	CURRAN	CURRAN	GARDINER	SPIVEY	WHITFIELD
29/04/39	BRIGHTON & HOVE ALBION	A	3-6	2465	NICHOLLS	ROBERTS	MILLAR	WARREN	O'MAHONEY	McARTHUR	BUTTERWORTH	SPIVEY	CURRAN	TOLAND	GARDINER	TOLAND 2, CURRAN, SPIVEY

FA CUP

Date	Opponent		Score	ATT	1 (G)	2	3	4	5	6	7	8	9	10	11	GOALSCORERS
26/11/38	PETERBOROUGH UNITED	H	4-1	7342	NICHOLLS	ROBERTS	MILLAR	WARREN	O'MAHONEY	McARTHUR	BUTTERWORTH	CURRAN	ILES	TOLAND	SPIVEY	TOLAND 2, CURRAN, SPIVEY
10/12/38	BOURNEMOUTH	H	0-3	8000	NICHOLLS	ROBERTS	MILLAR	WARREN	O'MAHONEY	McARTHUR	MILLS	CURRAN	ILES	TOLAND	GARDINER	

GLOUCESTERSHIRE CUP FINAL

Date	Opponent		Score	ATT	1 (G)	2	3	4	5	6	7	8	9	10	11	GOALSCORERS
21/09/38	BRISTOL CITY	A	0-3	2465	NICHOLLS	ROBERTS	WEBB	WARREN	O'MAHONEY	McARTHUR	BUTTERWORTH	SPIVEY	ILES	TOLAND	GARDINER	

PLAYERS	APP	GLS
BUTTERWORTH A	39	4
CARTE R	2	
CURRAN F	27	21
GARDINER R	34	4
HARTLEY S	4	1
ILES A	15	5
KAVANAGH W	6	2
KITCHEN N	2	
McARTHUR W	42	1
MILLAR A	42	
MILLINGTON G	3	
MILLS T	34	4
NICHOLLS J	42	
O'MAHONEY	38	4
ROBERTS H	38	
SMITH W	1	
SPIVEY R	10	4
TOLAND D	15	4
TURNER A	21	4
WARREN R	32	
WARHURST F	4	
WEBB H	1	
WHITFIELD W	10	1

and England. George Raynor played for Aldershot in both their League fixtures with Rovers, before embarking after the war on a long and successful coaching career. Among other achievements, he led Sweden to gold in the 1948 London Olympics and to the 1958 World Cup Final, which was lost to Brazil. Arthur Jepson, Port Vale's goalkeeper in both League fixtures against Rovers in 1938/39, was to play cricket for Nottinghamshire between 1938 and 1959 and was later a Test match umpire. Forty-one-year-old Jim McLaren, who played in Watford's 4-1 victory over Rovers in December, was the second-oldest player to have appeared in a League game involving Rovers between the wars and the last player born in the 19th century to appear in a Rovers League match.

The two heaviest defeats both left stories to relate. At Bournemouth, Rovers led through Curran's 42nd minute goal at half-time, but were forced to take to the field again without the influential Ray Warren. The ten men conceded five second-half goals to lose 5-2. At Brighton needing a point to move away from bottom place, Rovers conceded three goals in each half. Curran scored twice, but so too did Herbert Goffey, Herbert Stephens and Robert Farrell for Albion. Following the achievement of Norwich City and Northampton Town forwards, both in 1931/32, this was the third occasion that three opponents had scored twice each against Rovers in a League game. This feat has since been accomplished only twice post-war – both times inside a month over New Year 1957.

Matt O'Mahoney, who scored an own goal for Reading for a second consecutive season, won six caps for Eire while on Rovers' books and played for Northern Ireland against Scotland in October. This International appearance, made possible by a loophole allowing players born in Eire to participate in the Home Championship competition, made O'Mahoney one of a select band to have represented two different countries. He missed only 4 League matches all season, with Millar, Roberts and Butterworth also regular team members. Goalkeeper Nicholls and left-half McArthur were the club's only ever-presents.

Three-goal margins were the order of the day in Rovers' Cup campaigns, beating Peterborough United and losing at home to Bournemouth, where all three goals came in the final 20 minutes, in the FA Cup and losing the Gloucestershire Cup final to Bristol City. It took just one goal at Newport County to eliminate Rovers from the Third Division (South) Cup. After the reserves' fixture against Tunbridge Wells Rangers in February 1939, inside-right Donal Tolland was admitted to Bristol Homoeopathic Hospital for a blood transfusion.

Through the early months of 1939, the board of directors met regularly to discuss what was considered a serious financial situation for the football club. On 5 May 1939, secretary Sid Hawkins reported that he had informed the greyhound company, in a letter dated 26 April 1939, sanctioned by chairman Fred Ashmead, that Rovers were now prepared to sell Eastville Stadium. Isidore Kerman, chairman of the greyhound company, offered £20,000 for the freehold. There had clearly been little or no consultation with other members of the board, for other directors had simultaneously been engaged in consultations regarding the renewal of rent payments. At the same time, the directors loaned the club £200 to pay the players' wages, with Ashmead personally providing £130 of this amount.

Both Walsall and Bristol Rovers had to suffer the ignominy of applying for re-election to the Football League. Only 12 months earlier, Gillingham, fellow founder members of the Third Division (South), had lost their League status in similar circumstances. As other clubs had shown – Merthyr Town, Aberdare Athletic, Thames Association – falling through the trap door into Southern League football could be to set out on the road of no return. Rovers had a good deal to be concerned about. As it was, Rovers (45 votes) and Walsall (36 votes) comfortably survived the non-League challenge of Gillingham (15 votes), and Chelmsford City and Colchester United with one vote each. Nonetheless, the lesson had been learned and Brough Fletcher and his successors were keen to ensure that such a situation would not repeat itself, once football had re-established itself following World War Two.

1939-46

As war clouds gathered across the continent, Rovers returned to pre-season training for the 1939/40 season. The tireless and effective Matt O'Mahoney, Rovers' most-capped player at the time, joined League newcomers Ipswich Town for £600 in July 1939, after the board had turned down a £750 bid from Bristol City. There were four new faces and a welcome return for Jimmy Watson, but the whole country was in the surreal position of waiting for war. Watson scored twice to give Rovers an unexpected 4-0 victory over Bristol City in a Football League Jubilee Match a week before the new season and give Rovers renewed optimism. As it was, crowds were well down around the country, only 10,000 at Eastville witnessing a 2-2 draw with Reading on the opening day of the season. Watson scored for Rovers just seconds after half-time from a header, his first goal for the club since January 1934, after Ray Warren's 30-yard free-kick had equalised for Rovers. Defeats followed at Ipswich Town and Crystal Palace, the latter with Albert Iles recalled to lead the line. However, only 7,033 were at Selhurst Park, for the evacuation of children was underway and Londoners' minds were understandably elsewhere. Within hours, war had been declared on Germany.

A Football League meeting on 6 September effectively aborted the 1939/40 season and Rovers continued to play a series of friendlies, one of which was an exciting 5-5 draw with Bristol City in October. By the end of that month, a temporary regional league was in place, the South West League, in which Rovers were to finish third, six points behind Torquay United. Crowds, quite naturally, were poor and only 704 saw the final game of a series of four 'home' matches played at Ashton Gate, when Rovers drew 2-2 with the Gulls. The return game in February at Plainmoor attracted only 800 spectators and Rovers trailed after 40 seconds, were 3-0 down after nine minutes and finally lost 5-1, with Torquay United's veteran Albert Hutchinson putting through his own net after an hour.

Rovers fielded a largely weakened but Bristol-based side. Iles was a potent force at centre forward, scoring four times in a 7-0 win over Cardiff City in January. Wilf Whitfield, who scored a hat-trick against Swindon Town, George Tadman, Wally

SEASON 1939/40

FOOTBALL LEAGUE DIVISION THREE (SOUTH)

				ATT	GOALSCORERS	PLAYERS	APPS	GLS
26/08/39	READING	H	2-2	10000	WARREN, WATSON	ANGUS J	1	
30/08/39	IPSWICH TOWN	A	0-2	8884		BARBER A W	3	3
02/09/39	CRYSTAL PALACE	A	0-3	7033		BOOTH L	1	
						BRITTON C	3	
						BUTTEREY A	3	1
						BUTTERWORTH A	3	

REGIONAL LEAGUE SOUTH WEST DIVISION

						CALDWELL R	21	3
21/10/39	SWANSEA TOWN	A	0-0	3000		CRACK F	4	3
28/10/39	NEWPORT COUNTY*	H	2-3	1186	WOODWARD, BARBER	CURRAN F	1	2
04/11/39	TORQUAY UNITED	A	1-2	2500	BARBER	FEEBERY A	3	
11/11/39	BRISTOL CITY	A	3-0	2817	ILES, WOODWARD, BARBER	FLETCHER A	3	1
18/11/39	CARDIFF CITY	A	0-0	2000		FORSTER W	3	
25/11/39	PLYMOUTH ARGYLE*	H	1-2	1311	CALDWELL	GARDINER R	3	
02/12/39	SWINDON TOWN	A	3-3	3512	CALDWELL, ILES, WOODWARD	GILES A	7	
09/12/39	SWANSEA TOWN*	H	1-3	773	ILES	ILES A	29	14
16/12/39	NEWPORT COUNTY	A	1-0	1500	O'MAHONEY	KIRBY J	20	1
23/12/39	TORQUAY UNITED*	H	2-2	704	CRACK, TALBOT	MAGGS P	2	
25/12/39	SWINDON TOWN	H	3-4	2494	CRACK 2, ILES	McARTHUR W	27	1
26/12/39	SWINDON TOWN	A	1-1	5673	WHITFIELD	McNEIL J	1	
30/12/39	BRISTOL CITY*	A	4-2	1966	CURRAN 2, ILES, TALBOT	MITCHINSON F	1	
09/01/40	CARDIFF CITY*	H	7-0	1012	ILES 4, WHITFIELD 2, WOODWARD	MORGAN C	1	
13/01/40	PLYMOUTH ARGYLE	A	0-2	2187		NICHOLLS J	3	
20/01/40	SWINDON TOWN*	H	5-2	1000	WHITFIELD 3, O'MAHONEY KIRBY	O'MAHONEY M	24	5
						SMITH H	10	
10/02/40	TORQUAY UNITED	A	1-5	800	HUTCHINSON og	SMITH W	24	
24/02/40	CARDIFF CITY	A	1-1	3000	ILES	TADMAN G	6	8
02/03/40	PLYMOUTH ARGYLE**	H	1-1	1700	TALBOT	TALBOT F L	19	10
09/03/40	BRISTOL CITY**	H	4-4	2153	ILES, TADMAN, CALDWELL O'MAHONEY	TAYLOR P	5	1
						TURNER A	1	
16/03/40	SWANSEA TOWN*	H	6-2	1116	TALBOT 3, TADMAN 2, O'MAHONEY	WARREN R	10	3
						WATSON J	2	3
22/03/40	NEWPORT COUNTY*	H	3-5	3500	ILES 2, CALDWELL	WATTS R	2	
25/03/40	NEWPORT COUNTY	A	2-0	4179	TADMAN 2	WHITFIELD W	27	7
30/03/40	TORQUAY UNITED**	H	3-2	1749	TALBOT, TADMAN, McARTHUR	WOODWARD W	18	4
06/04/40	BRISTOL CITY	A	1-0	3358	TADMAN	OWN GOAL		1
13/05/40	PLYMOUTH ARGYLE	A	1-4	1000	SMALL, ILES			
01/06/40	CARDIFF CITY**	H	3-3	878	TADMAN 2, TALBOT			

* Home matches played at Ashton Gate
** Home matches played at Aero Engine Ground, Kingswood

DIVISION THREE (SOUTH) CUP

13/04/40	ALDERSHOT	H	2-0	4602	TALBOT, WOODWARD
20/04/40	SOUTHAMPTON	A	1-1	6627	ILES
27/04/40	SOUTHAMPTON	H	3-1	6602	ILES, WHITFIELD 2
04/05/40	SWANSEA TOWN	H	6-0	8000	WHITFIELD, TALBOT, WOODWARD 3 O'MAHONEY
11/05/40	SWANSEA TOWN	A	0-3	5000	
18/05/40	NEWCASTLE UNITED	A	0-1	12000	

FOOTBALL LEAGUE JUBILEE MATCH

19/08/39	BRISTOL CITY	H	4-0	5395	WATSON 2, FLETCHER, BUTTERY

McArthur and Matt O'Mahoney were among the players who had represented the club in League football. However, the system of guest players, which allowed far greater flexibility in player movement, was one that left Rovers' meagre resources depleted still further. Other clubs' players did come to Eastville. Les Talbot and Bill Woodward, for instance, both scored hat-tricks in different games against Swansea Town.

Rovers' squad in training during the late 1930s

Programme team page for the last home game before the Second World War

Bristol Rovers 1945/46. Back row: Neads, H Smith, Davis, Gardiner, Allen, Baldie, Long, Jennings, Topping, Butterworth, Mann (Instructor). Second row: J Bissicks (Director), E Giles, Meacham, Watkins, O'Brian, Weare, Studley, Frowde, Bridge, Williams (Trainer), Cooper (Trainer). Front row: L Champney, Parkinson, Bamford, Peacock, W Smith, C Ferrari (Secretary), Warren (Capt.), B Fletcher (Manager), Lambden, Morgan, Petherbridge, Whitfield, J Hare (Vice-Chairman). Ballboys: K Baker, T Spicer

Eastville Stadium became the setting for other wartime activities. The future president of the USA, Dwight Eisenhower, visited a wartime greyhound meeting, while the bandleader Glenn Miller and a high wire act, The Great Blondini, also appeared at Eastville. There was also an American Football final played before large numbers of servicemen and watched apparently, for wartime restrictions prevent the modern researcher from discovering the true identity, by a member of the British Royal Family. Many contemporary celebrities appeared at the stadium in a bid to boost flagging spirits in the face of continued warfare, among them the famous Joe Davis who, on the evening of 23 April 1945, gave an exhibition of pool and snooker skills.

A number of Rovers players resurfaced at the more glamorous setting of Ashton Gate. Ronnie Dix, along with the veteran Clarrie Bourton, scored for City when Rovers won the derby game after Christmas 4-2. Frank Curran, who had scored twice for Rovers then, added two goals for City in an exciting 4-4 draw at Eastville in March. By the time George Tadman's goal brought victory at Ashton Gate the following month, both Albert Butterworth and Jack Preece were in City's line-up. Also of note is Jack Dugnolle, who scored Plymouth Argyle's opening goal against Rovers in November 1939 and was to score an own goal in April 1946, Rovers' third in a 3-1 victory at Brighton. Len Rich, who had played in Luton's infamous 12-0 win in 1936, scored a hat-trick for Plymouth Argyle when they defeated Rovers 4-1 in May 1940.

Unable to maintain a side, Rovers were obliged to suspend their playing commitments. Like a number of other clubs, they played no matches between the end of the 1939/40 season and the start of 1945/46. One side effect of this inaction was to prove crucial. The club had no revenue and, although at first the board had strongly opposed chairman Fred Ashmead's unilateral decision to sell Eastville to the Bristol

SEASON 1944/45

FRIENDLIES			ATT	GOALSCORERS
RAF XI	H	3-5	2023	LAMBDEN 3
PATCHWAY SPORTS	H	6-2		LAMBDEN 3, FUDGE, OWEN, WILLIAMS
B.A.C	H	5-1	1000	CLARK 3, LAMBDEN, EAGER
EDEN GROVE	H	5-2		LAMBDEN 3, SMART 2
RAF MELKSHAM	H	5-5	1600	LAMBDEN 3, OWEN, PETHERBRIDGE
PAPWORTH ATHLETIC	H	1-0	750	SMITH W
GEORGE ADLAM & SON	H	untraced		
SOUTH BRISTOL CENTRAL	H	4-2		LAMBDEN 2, PETHERBRIDGE, OWEN
RAF MELKSHAM	H	2-5	1450	untraced

GLOUCESTERSHIRE CUP FINAL

BRISTOL CITY	H	0-5	9048	

Rovers formed an amateur team in preparation for the return of professional football the following season. The matches were all played at Eastville Stadium.

Greyhound Racing Association, the sale eventually went through on 3 March 1940. Although the greyhound company had offered more, Eastville had been sold for £12,000. Rovers were granted a lease on 8 March 1940 at £400 per year to continue playing on the ground for a further 21 years.

During the war, Rovers might well have folded had it not been for the support offered by the greyhound company. In the summer of 1942, the company had suggested to Rovers' directors that the club should begin playing matches again and had offered to meet all financial obligations for 1942/43. On 19 September 1944, the company's managing director Constantine Augustus Lucy Stevens and secretary John Patrick Hare were voted on to the board, bringing with them a £3,000 cash injection. 1,500 new shares worth £1 each were created and sold through a loan from the greyhound company for a shilling per share to Con Stevens, who purchased 1,000, and Hare, who bought the remainder. As the matchless 1944/45 season progressed, Rovers' debts mounted. £600 was still owed to the bank, £700 to creditors and £4,700 on outstanding loans. The season's inaction had cost a further £1,000. On 15 June 1945, therefore, Stevens and Hare became chairman and vice-chairman respectively and Charles Ferrari was appointed secretary on 20 August 1945. Effectively, from 29 November 1944, for four years, Rovers became an undisclosed subsidiary of the greyhound company. On 21 September 1945 Lew Champeny, an employee of the greyhound company and a key figure in the events of 1950, was elected to the Rovers board. Various wellwishers waived more than £2,000 of the unpaid loans and it was with a greater sense of optimism and purpose that Rovers pieced together a scratch side in the following weeks.

A number of Rovers players had made names for themselves in wartime football. Above all others, Roy Bentley, rejected by Rovers as a schoolboy, was building a career that led to 12 England caps, a hat-trick against Wales in 1954, and captaining Chelsea to the League Championship in 1955. Ronnie Dix helped Blackpool win the League Cup in 1943. Alec Miller, now with Hearts, played for Scotland in 1943 although, outfoxed by Stanley Matthews, his country lost 8-0 to England. Bobby Gardiner, still officially a Rovers player, 'guested' for Dundee United in the 1940 Scottish Cup final. Fred Chadwick scored six goals for Norwich City, who ran up 10 first-half goals in their extraordinary 18-0 win against Brighton on Christmas Day 1940. David Steele turned

SEASON 1945/46

FOOTBALL LEAGUE DIVISION THREE SOUTH (SOUTH)

Date	Opponent	H/A	Score	ATT	GOALSCORERS
25/08/45	BRISTOL CITY	H	0-3	14906	
29/08/45	TORQUAY UNITED	A	3-0	5000	LAMBDEN, LONG, TALBOT
01/09/45	BRISTOL CITY	A	0-3	10583	
08/09/45	BRIGHTON & HOVE ALBION	A	4-3	6257	HIBBS, R CLARK 2, LONG
10/09/45	ALDERSHOT	H	4-5	5000	HIBBS, R CLARK 3
15/09/45	BRIGHTON & HOVE ALBION	H	2-4	8605	R CLARK, LONG
17/09/45	TORQUAY UNITED	H	3-0	5000	LAMBDEN 2, LONG
22/09/45	EXETER CITY	H	2-1	9200	BUTTERWORTH, TALBOT
29/09/45	EXETER CITY	A	2-2	9000	MILLS, R CLARK
20/10/45	SWINDON TOWN	H	2-0	11500	TALBOT, R CLARK
27/10/45	SWINDON TOWN	A	3-2	12000	BUTTERWORTH, WARREN, R CLARK
03/11/45	READING	A	2-2	7000	LAMBDEN , R CLARK
10/11/45	READING	H	3-3	10000	LAMBDEN 3
01/12/45	CRYSTAL PALACE	H	1-1	13000	R CLARK
19/12/45	CRYSTAL PALACE	A	0-1	4000	
22/12/45	BOURNEMOUTH	H	2-2	7000	WARREN, McGAHIE
24/12/45	CARDIFF CITY	H	2-2	12000	WHITFIELD, R CLARK
26/12/45	CARDIFF CITY	A	2-4	18000	LAMBDEN 2
29/12/45	ALDERSHOT	A	2-3	4000	LAMBDEN 2
05/01/46	BOURNEMOUTH	A	5-3	5000	LAMBDEN 2, DAVIES, BAMFORD, PETHERBRIDGE

FOOTBALL LEAGUE DIVISION THREE SOUTH (SOUTH) CUP

Date	Opponent	H/A	Score	ATT	GOALSCORERS
12/01/46	EXETER CITY	H	2-1	7000	LAMBDEN, PETHERBRIDGE
19/01/46	EXETER CITY	A	1-0	5166	BAMFORD
26/01/46	TORQUAY UNITED	A	0-1	4000	
02/02/46	TORQUAY UNITED	H	2-1	4124	PETHERBRIDGE, BAMFORD
09/02/46	PORT VALE	H	4-2	9500	BUTTERWORTH, GARDINER, BAMFORD, R CLARK
16/02/46	PORT VALE	A	0-1	5000	
23/02/46	CARDIFF CITY	H	1-0	10000	LAMBDEN
02/03/46	CARDIFF CITY	A	0-3	18500	
09/03/46	BOURNEMOUTH	A	3-3	11000	GILES, R CLARK, PETHERBRIDGE
16/03/46	BOURNEMOUTH	H	1-2	9000	WARREN
23/03/46	BRISTOL CITY	H	0-0	25598	
30/03/46	BRISTOL CITY	A	2-1	18099	LAMBDEN, WHITFIELD
06/04/46	SWINDON TOWN	H	0-0	9029	
13/04/46	SWINDON TOWN	A	1-2	11000	LAMBDEN
19/04/46	TORQUAY UNITED	H	3-1	9500	LAMBDEN 2, RUSSELL
20/04/46	BRIGHTON & HOVE ALBION	H	6-1	9347	LAMBDEN 2, MORGAN 2, WARREN, BALDIE
22/04/46	BRIGHTON & HOVE ALBION	A	3-1	7000	PETHERBRIDGE, BALDIE, DUGNOLLE og
27/04/46	WALSALL +	H	1-3	14673	PETHERBRIDGE

+ Semi Final

FA CUP

Date	Opponent	H/A	Score	ATT	GOALSCORERS
17/11/45	SWINDON TOWN	A	0-1	11181	
24/11/45	SWINDON TOWN	H	4-1	11500	BUTTERWORTH 2, MILLS, R CLARK
08/12/45	BRISTOL CITY	A	2-4	19295	MILLS, WHITFIELD
15/12/45	BRISTOL CITY	H	0-2	21045	

FA CUP competition played on a home and away basis.

GLOUCESTERSHIRE CUP FINAL

Date	Opponent	H/A	Score	ATT	GOALSCORERS
24/09/45	BRISTOL CITY	A	1-3	7962	LAMBDEN

PLAYERS

PLAYERS	APPS	GLS
BALDIE Douglas	4	2
BAMFORD Harold	19	4
BINHAM Colin	1	
BURGESS R J	1	
BUTTERWORTH Albert	26	5
CLARK C	3	
CLARK Robert	22	15
DAVIS Robert	10	1
DIXON Walter	1	
FIRTH J W	3	
GARDINER Robert	3	1
GILES Albert	5	1
GINGELL C	3	
HARGETT H	2	
HIBBS Leslie	5	2
LAMBDEN Victor	34	21
LONG C	7	4
McCOURT Francis	3	
McGAHIE J	12	1
MILLS Thomas	10	3
MORGAN James	3	2
PETHERBRIDGE George	18	6
ROBBINS D	1	
RUSSELL John	5	1
SKINNER George	2	
SMITH Harold	13	
SMITH Wilfred V	7	
STUDLEY Eric	5	
TALBOT Francis	10	3
TOPPING Harold	28	
WARREN Raymond	32	4
WATKINS Barry	33	
WEARE A Jack	28	
WHITFIELD Wilfred	36	3
WILLIAMS Vivian	1	
OWN GOAL		1

* Goalscorers include all Div 3 (South) South League and cup matches. Appearances are all matches except Glos Cup Final
All appearances information from *Soccer at War* (Jack Rollin)

out for Bradford Park Avenue in 1942 at the age of 49, scoring in a 3-3 draw with Sheffield Wednesday. Tadman and O'Mahoney played regularly for unfashionable Aberaman. The future Rovers manager Malcolm Allison, under the pseudonym Herbert Schmidt, played for Klagenfurt and Rapid Vienna in 1945.

More unusually, the former Rovers full-back Jack Smith's career ended after his foot was run over by a bus during a blackout in Wolverhampton. Still, Rovers were very fortunate to suffer no World War Two fatalities. Gordon Addy, for instance, whose penalty for Norwich City had been saved by Jesse Whatley in 1921, was among those killed. John Lee, an accomplished opening batsman with Somerset, who had been in the Aldershot side that visited Eastville in 1933/34 and 1934/35, was killed in action on 20 June 1944 near Bazenville, Normandy. Sandy Torrance, who played for Bristol City in the first League derby in 1922 and scored in the 1924 Gloucestershire Cup final, died in the air raid on Bristol on 14 April 1941. Also killed were several other players who had played a number of times against Rovers, including Peter Monaghan who had scored for Bournemouth in the March 1939 fixture, Alan Fowler who had claimed one of Swindon Town's goals three years earlier and the Luton Town pairing of Joseph Coen, a goalkeeper briefly on Rovers' books in 1934, and Charlie Clark. Andrew Wilson, Rovers' manager between 1921 and 1926, died on 13 March 1945 at the age of 64. Locally, several children had died when two bombs fell in Eastville Park on 25 November 1940 and an unexploded German wartime bomb was discovered in 1984 during the construction of the Tesco supermarket next to the stadium. The air raids of 16 and 17 March 1941 affected much of the Eastville and Easton area, including Stapleton Road gasworks and railway station and, while there were 1,299 civilian deaths in Bristol during the Blitz, some 140 people were killed in the district in three air raids between September 1940 and March of the following year.

And so it was that Rovers emerged from the war to participate in the unofficial Division Three (South) in 1945/46. Eastville was unscathed, unlike Ashton Gate, where a stand had been bombed on two consecutive nights in January 1941. Plymouth Argyle and Millwall had suffered fires, Exeter City and Swindon Town had seen their grounds turned into military camps, Newport County's Somerton Park had been commissioned by the Civil Defence and Reading's club offices had been bombed. Further afield there had been similar stories to that of Hartlepool United, where two German bombs from a Zeppelin struck the Victoria Ground on 27 November 1916 and destroyed the wooden grandstand, and Sheffield United, whose Bramall Lane ground was struck by no fewer than ten bombs in December 1940.

On the pitch, young players such as Vic Lambden, George Petherbridge and Harry Bamford were offered first-team football alongside older and more experienced heads such as Albert Butterworth and Tommy Mills. Rovers played Bristol City on Boxing Day 1944 and formed an amateur side in the spring of 1945 in preparation for the new season, Lambden scoring hat-tricks in a 6-2 victory over Patchway Sports, a 5-2 win against Eden Grove and in a defeat and a draw, after Rovers had held a 3-1 half-time lead, against army sides. Three goals from Bert 'Nobby' Clark helped defeat BAC 5-1. Rovers reappointed manager Brough Fletcher on 1 July 1945 and, on 20 August, Charles Ferrari became club secretary to replace Sid Hawkins, who had joined Charlton Athletic. Lambden scored a hat-trick against Reading in November 1945, while 'Nobby'

Clark scored three times against Aldershot in a match Rovers lost 5-4 with the veteran Bill Hullett, whose goals knocked Rovers out of the 1946/47 FA Cup, scoring twice for the visitors. Butterworth, on the other hand, also appeared against Rovers for a Bristol City side that included Jack Preece. Jack Weare saved a 20th-minute Terry Wood penalty at Ninian Park after Lambden had put Rovers ahead, but Cardiff City recovered to win 4-2, Ken Hollyman scoring once in each half. Rovers arrived at Plainmoor in August 1945 with their red-and-white quartered shirts by mistake, which clashed with Torquay United's kit. Lent a set of shirts, Rovers played in all white and won 3-0. There were also some extraordinary Western League results, as Welton Rovers were defeated 14-0 and Soundwell 11-3.

Seven victories and six defeats saw Rovers finish mid-table, in fifth place in their abbreviated division. Rovers also reached the semi-finals of the Division Three (South) Cup where, despite a Vic Lambden goal, Walsall ran out 3-1 winners. In the FA Cup, victory over Swindon Town through four goals in nine first-half minutes was followed by an aggregate defeat against the old rivals from Ashton Gate. Don Clark, who had scored twice when the clubs met in September, grabbed a goal in each leg of this tie. He also scored four times as City won the first post-war Gloucestershire Cup final 5-0 at Eastville. He was to continue to prove a handful for Rovers' defence in the immediate post-war years. More encouragingly, the goalless local derby at Eastville in March had attracted a crowd of over 25,000, lending optimism to the belief that the rebirth of the Football League in 1946 could lead to a golden era for football in Bristol.

1946/47

The anticipated post-war struggle facing Bristol Rovers following several years of inaction was a very real problem in 1946, but New Year 1947 heralded a turn in fortunes for the Eastville club. A run of 10 defeats in 11 League games in the autumn included soul-destroying reversals at Cardiff City and Notts County. However, victory over Crystal Palace on 4 January was the first of 13 in an 18-match run and Rovers were able to finish the first post-war season in 14th place. Bland statistics indicate a clear picture of a season of two halves.

When professional football returned in its recognized format, the general public, starved of full-time sport for so long, were quick to support the new season. Attendances were high – more than 30,000 at Eastville for the visit of Cardiff City, bringing gate receipts of £2,218, and 25,000 for Bristol City. Manager Brough Fletcher, retained by Rovers and nurturing young Bristol-born players, worked to build together a side worthy of the enthusiastic support the side was shown. The club's wage bill to players and officials for 1946/47 came to £9,483. The match programme rose in cost from 2d to 3d. Football had returned in earnest.

Frank Curran, the scorer of Rovers' final goal of the 1938/39 season, scored the first of 1946/47 with a well-placed drive after 20 minutes. The opening day draw at home to Reading also featured a debut goal for Vic Lambden, from Lance Carr's cross 10 minutes

Bristol Rovers 1946/47. Back row: (Players only) Jack Pitt, Jack Weare, Harry Bamford, Wally McArthur, Ray Warren, Barry Watkins. Front row: Ken Wookey, Len Hodges, Fred Leamon, Jimmy Morgan, Lance Carr

after half-time. This was the first of 117 League goals the Bristol-born forward was to score for Rovers in a decade. The first components were being put in place for the all-conquering side of 1952/53. Harry Bamford, Jackie Pitt and George Petherbridge, mainstays of the Rovers side through the halycon days of the 1950s, were given League debuts early in the season. Ray Warren, the captain of that Championship-winning side, was one of three ever-presents in a highly changeable Rovers team. Minute One of the Directors' meeting on 11 November 1946 introduced the infamous 'no buy, no sell' policy although, notably, Con Stevens had already left the meeting, while John Hare and Lew Champeny both voted against.

Curran and Warren were just two of five players to play League football for Rovers both sides of the war. Wilf Smith, Wally Whitfield and Wally McArthur all returned to first-team action. Other players, such as Carr, an ever-present in his only season with the club, and the veteran Harry Smith had enjoyed long and successful careers with other clubs before the war. These were understandably years of great change and it is no surprise that as many as 29 players appeared in the Rovers line-up before the end of December. Indeed, the side that drew with Brighton in December showed six changes to the 11 beaten 3-0 by Northampton Town at Eastville. This constitutes the largest number of changes to any post-war Rovers League side. It is, however, no great surprise to learn that, at this stage, an own goal was Rovers' only score in seven League matches. Continuity was indeed well-nigh impossible to maintain.

One new face in the side, albeit briefly, was reserve player-coach Harry Smith, a former Nottingham Forest and Darlington full-back who became, at 38 years and 43 days, Rovers' oldest League debutant when he appeared in the Northampton Town defeat. Another was Fred Leamon, a former Royal Marine from Jersey. Leamon became the club's top scorer in 1946/47 with 13 League goals. He later represented Wales at bowls and worked as a security guard for BBC television. He died in 1981 after suffering a heart attack at St Paul's Cathedral while working at the wedding of Prince Charles and Lady Diana Spencer. Rovers' third ever-present, besides Carr and Warren, was full-back Barry Watkins, embarking on a run of 52 consecutive League appearances.

Heavy defeats were prominent at home and away early in the season. Teenager Jackie Sewell, a future England International, scored two of six goals Jack Weare conceded at Notts County. He scored twice in a minute, just past the hour mark, twice converting sweeping County moves, against a Rovers defence that had already found itself 3-0 down after 26 minutes. Weare left the field injured at Cardiff City after only seven minutes, with Rovers already trailing to a third-minute Stan Richards goal. Ray Warren played 83 minutes in goal and 10-man Rovers, in unconventional red and white quartered shirts, crashed to a 4-0 defeat. It was the second in Cardiff City's club record run of nine consecutive League victories. Watford scored four times at Eastville in September, where Rovers, 3-0 down after 48 minutes, pulled two goals back before being defeated by a spectacular right-foot drive on the hour by debutant Johnny Usher, whose hat-trick seven days earlier had helped defeat Rovers reserves. There were six goals in a 17-minute spell midway through this 4-3 defeat. The Bristol City side that won 3-0 at Eastville featured a 42-year-old goalkeeper in Alex Ferguson, still the fourth oldest man to appear against Rovers in League football and a club record 21 years after his first League match against Rovers, which had been for Gillingham in September 1925. Mansfield Town, Southend United and Exeter City all scored three times against Rovers in games before Christmas. Southend achieved this feat with full-back Bob Jackson in goal, a secret kept hidden from Rovers after regular goalkeeper Albert Hankey had been injured earlier in the day.

After New Year, as Rovers strung together some good results, heavy defeats recurred less frequently. However, there were demoralizing 3-0 reversals at both Torquay United, for whom Joe Conley scored all the goals, and Leyton Orient. The 4-0 defeat at Ashton Gate in February, with Wilson Thomas and Don Clark scoring twice each, remains Rovers' heaviest loss in league action on that ground. Ironically, though, the side that played that day remained unchanged for a club record of 12 consecutive League games. This in itself symbolizes the rebirth Rovers experienced in the latter stages of this first post-war League season.

A run of five straight wins in February and March first set the club on the right path. Rovers scored three goals in each of the first four victories, several of these emanating from Leamon, who scored twice at Bournemouth. Outside-left Carr scored the only goal of the game, a rising left-foot drive at the Thirteen Arches End after 27 minutes, to defeat Cardiff City at snowy Eastville and he scored Rovers' second at Carrow Road seven days later. This exciting 3-3 draw marked the only League game in the career of Norwich City's goalkeeper Antonio Gallego, a Spanish Civil War refugee. One familiar face in the Aldershot side Rovers defeated in January was Alf Fitzgerald, who had scored an FA Cup hat-trick at Eastville for Queen's Park Rangers in November 1937. Victory at home to Mansfield Town proved to be the third in the Stags' club record run of seven consecutive League defeats.

FOOTBALL LEAGUE DIVISION THREE (SOUTH)

SEASON 1946/47

Date	Opponent	H/A		ATT	G (1)	2	3	4	5	6	7	8	9	10	11	GOALSCORERS
31/08/46	READING	H	2-2	11000	WEARE	W SMITH	WATKINS	PITT	WARREN	WHITFIELD	LEWIS	BAMFORD	LAMBDEN	CURRAN	CARR	LAMBDEN, CURRAN
04/09/46	IPSWICH TOWN	A	2-0	12012	WEARE	W SMITH	WATKINS	PITT	WARREN	WHITFIELD	LEWIS	BAMFORD	LAMBDEN	CURRAN	CARR	LAMBDEN 2
07/09/46	CRYSTAL PALACE	A	1-2	18141	WEARE	W SMITH	WATKINS	PITT	WARREN	WHITFIELD	LEWIS	BALDIE	LAMBDEN	CURRAN	CARR	BALDIE
09/09/46	WATFORD	H	3-4	11838	WEARE	W SMITH	WATKINS	PITT	WARREN	WHITFIELD	LEWIS	BAMFORD	CURRAN	LAMBDEN	CARR	BAMFORD 2, CURRAN
14/09/46	TORQUAY UNITED	H	3-0	14076	WEARE	W SMITH	WATKINS	PITT	WARREN	WHITFIELD	LEWIS	BAMFORD	CURRAN	LAMBDEN	CARR	CURRAN, BAMFORD, LEWIS
18/09/46	WATFORD	A	0-1	4858	WEARE	W SMITH	WATKINS	PITT	WARREN	WHITFIELD	LEWIS	HODGES	CURRAN	LAMBDEN	CARR	
21/09/46	MANSFIELD TOWN	A	1-3	9183	WEARE	W SMITH	WATKINS	PITT	WARREN	WHITFIELD	LEWIS	BAMFORD	CURRAN	LAMBDEN	CARR	CARR L
28/09/46	BRISTOL CITY	A	0-3	25900	WEARE	PEACOCK	WATKINS	PITT	WARREN	WHITFIELD	LEWIS	BAMFORD	CURRAN	LAMBDEN	CARR	
05/10/46	SOUTHEND UNITED	H	1-3	9812	WEARE	PEACOCK	WATKINS	PITT	WARREN	WHITFIELD	LEWIS	PITT	LAMBDEN	CURRAN	CARR	CURRAN
12/10/46	QUEENS PARK RANGERS	A	2-0	20300	WEARE	W SMITH	WATKINS	PITT	WARREN	WHITFIELD	LEWIS	PITT	LAMBDEN	CARR	CARR	LAMBDEN 2
19/10/46	SWINDON TOWN	A	0-1	16015	LILEY	W SMITH	WATKINS	PITT	WINTERS	WHITFIELD	LEWIS	BAMFORD	LAMBDEN	CARR	PETHERBRIDGE	
26/10/46	BOURNEMOUTH	H	0-2	11500	WEARE	WARREN	WATKINS	PITT	WINTERS	WHITFIELD	LEWIS	BAMFORD	LAMBDEN	CARR	PETHERBRIDGE	
02/11/46	CARDIFF CITY	A	0-4	35000	WEARE	WARREN	WATKINS	BAMFORD	WINTERS	WHITFIELD	LEWIS	HAYWARD	CURRAN	CARR	PETHERBRIDGE	
09/11/46	NORWICH CITY	H	1-2	8963	WEARE	WARREN	WATKINS	BAMFORD	WINTERS	WHITFIELD	PITT	PITT	LAMBDEN	CARR	PETHERBRIDGE	HAYWARD
16/11/46	NOTTS COUNTY	A	0-6	7886	LILEY	WARREN	WATKINS	GILES	WINTERS	WHITFIELD	W MORGAN	WOOKEY	BAMFORD	LAMBDEN	CARR	
23/11/46	NORTHAMPTON TOWN	H	0-3	7896	WEARE	WARREN	WATKINS	WARREN	WINTERS	PITT	PETHERBRIDGE	BAMFORD	LAMBDEN	CARR	LEWIS	
07/12/46	BRIGHTON & HOVE ALBION	H	0-0	6097	WEARE	W SMITH	WATKINS	GILES	WARREN	WHITFIELD	PETHERBRIDGE	LAMBDEN	ALLAWAY	CARR	PETHERBRIDGE	
14/12/46	EXETER CITY	A	2-3	7528	WEARE	W SMITH	WATKINS	PITT	WARREN	MCARTHUR	PETHERBRIDGE	LAMBDEN	BAMFORD	CARR	CARR	LEAMON, CARR
21/12/46	PORT VALE	H	0-0	5734	LILEY	PEACOCK	WATKINS	PITT	WARREN	MCARTHUR	WINDLE	WOOKEY	CURRAN	LAMBDEN	CARR	
25/12/46	WALSALL	A	2-2	6624	WEARE	PEACOCK	WATKINS	PITT	WARREN	MCARTHUR	WINDLE	COOK	LAMBDEN	CARR	CARR	WINDLE, LEAMON
26/12/46	WALSALL	H	0-2	14564	WEARE	PEACOCK	WATKINS	PITT	WARREN	MCARTHUR	WINDLE	COOK	LAMBDEN	BAKER	CARR	
28/12/46	READING	A	1-1	14128	WEARE	PEACOCK	H SMITH	PITT	WARREN	MCARTHUR	WINDLE	LAMBDEN	BAMFORD	BAKER	CARR	FLACK og
04/01/47	CRYSTAL PALACE	H	2-1	13341	WEARE	PEACOCK	WATKINS	PITT	WARREN	MCARTHUR	WINDLE	WOOKEY	BAMFORD	BAKER	PETHERBRIDGE	PETHERBRIDGE, WARREN pen
11/01/47	ALDERSHOT	A	2-0	4000	WEARE	BAMFORD	WATKINS	PITT	WARREN	MCARTHUR	WINDLE	WOOKEY	CARR	BAKER	PETHERBRIDGE	LEAMON, CARR
18/01/47	TORQUAY UNITED	A	0-3	6386	WEARE	BAMFORD	WATKINS	PITT	WARREN	MCARTHUR	PEACOCK	WOOKEY	BAKER	CARR	CARR	
25/01/47	MANSFIELD TOWN	H	1-0	9448	WEARE	BAMFORD	WATKINS	PITT	WARREN	MCARTHUR	PEACOCK	WOOKEY	BAKER	CARR	CARR	LEAMON
01/02/47	BRISTOL CITY	H	0-4	17119	WEARE	BAMFORD	WATKINS	PITT	WARREN	MCARTHUR	WOOKEY	HODGES	BAKER	J MORGAN	CARR	
08/02/47	SOUTHEND UNITED	A	3-2	5986	WEARE	BAMFORD	WATKINS	PITT	WARREN	MCARTHUR	WOOKEY	HODGES	LEAMON	J MORGAN	CARR	LEAMON, WARREN pen, CARR
15/02/47	QUEENS PARK RANGERS	H	3-1	18781	WEARE	BAMFORD	WATKINS	PITT	WARREN	MCARTHUR	WOOKEY	HODGES	LEAMON	J MORGAN	CARR	WINTERS, HODGES, CARR
22/02/47	SWINDON TOWN	H	3-0	9000	WEARE	BAMFORD	WATKINS	PITT	WARREN	MCARTHUR	WOOKEY	HODGES	LEAMON	J MORGAN	CARR	LEAMON, LEAMON, MORGAN
01/03/47	BOURNEMOUTH	A	3-1	11000	WEARE	BAMFORD	WATKINS	PITT	WARREN	MCARTHUR	WOOKEY	HODGES	LEAMON	J MORGAN	CARR	LEAMON 2, MORGAN
08/03/47	CARDIFF CITY	H	1-0	30417	WEARE	BAMFORD	WATKINS	PITT	WARREN	MCARTHUR	WOOKEY	HODGES	LEAMON	J MORGAN	CARR	MORGAN, LEAMON
15/03/47	NOTTS COUNTY	H	3-3	18051	WEARE	BAMFORD	WATKINS	PITT	WARREN	MCARTHUR	WOOKEY	HODGES	LEAMON	J MORGAN	CARR	WOOKEY, HODGES, CARR
22/03/47	NORWICH CITY	A	4-1	12087	WEARE	BAMFORD	WATKINS	PITT	WARREN	MCARTHUR	WOOKEY	HODGES	LEAMON	J MORGAN	CARR	LEAMON 2, WOOKEY, WARREN pen
29/03/47	NORTHAMPTON TOWN	H	2-1	6846	WEARE	BAMFORD	WATKINS	PITT	WARREN	MCARTHUR	WOOKEY	HODGES	LEAMON	J MORGAN	CARR	MORGAN, LEAMON
04/04/47	LEYTON ORIENT	A	0-3	13602	WEARE	BAMFORD	WATKINS	PITT	WARREN	MCARTHUR	WOOKEY	HODGES	LEAMON	J MORGAN	CARR	
05/04/47	ALDERSHOT	H	0-0	13777	WEARE	BAMFORD	WATKINS	PITT	WARREN	MCARTHUR	WOOKEY	HODGES	LEAMON	J MORGAN	CARR	
07/04/47	LEYTON ORIENT	H	6-1	14045	WEARE	BAMFORD	WATKINS	PITT	WARREN	MCARTHUR	WOOKEY	HODGES	LEAMON	J MORGAN	CARR	HODGES 2, J MORGAN 2, CARR, PITT pen
12/04/47	BRIGHTON & HOVE ALBION	A	2-1	7685	WEARE	BAMFORD	WATKINS	PITT	WARREN	MCARTHUR	WOOKEY	BALDIE	LEAMON	BALDIE	CARR	BALDIE 2
19/04/47	EXETER CITY	H	1-0	13275	WEARE	BAMFORD	WATKINS	PITT	WARREN	MCARTHUR	WOOKEY	HODGES	LEAMON	J MORGAN	CARR	J MORGAN
26/04/47	PORT VALE	A	1-2	8323	WEARE	BAMFORD	WATKINS	PITT	WARREN	MCARTHUR	WOOKEY	HODGES	BALDIE	CARR	CARR	J MORGAN, CARR
10/05/47	IPSWICH TOWN	H	1-1	10459	WEARE	BAMFORD	WATKINS	PITT	WARREN	MCARTHUR	WOOKEY	HODGES	LEAMON	J MORGAN	CARR	LEAMON

FA CUP

Date	Opponent	H/A		ATT	G (1)	2	3	4	5	6	7	8	9	10	11	GOALSCORERS
30/11/46	MERTHYR TOWN	A	1-3	14000	LILEY	W SMITH	H SMITH	PITT	WARREN	MCARTHUR	PETHERBRIDGE	COOK	LAMBDEN	J MORGAN	CARR	LAMBDEN

GLOUCESTERSHIRE CUP FINAL

Date	Opponent	H/A		ATT	G (1)	2	3	4	5	6	7	8	9	10	11	GOALSCORERS
26/05/47	BRISTOL CITY	A	2-2	17151	WEARE	BAMFORD	WATKINS	PITT	WARREN	MCARTHUR	WOOKEY	HODGES	LEAMON	J MORGAN	CARR	LEAMON, HODGES
07/06/47	BRISTOL CITY	H	0-2	11434	WEARE	BAMFORD	WATKINS	PITT	WARREN	MCARTHUR	WOOKEY	HODGES	LEAMON	J MORGAN	CARR	

PLAYERS	APP	GLS
ALLAWAY J	4	
BAKER C	5	2
BALDIE D	3	1
BAMFORD H	32	8
CARR L	42	8
COOK J	2	
CURRAN F	10	3
GILES A	1	
HAYWARD D	1	
HODGES L	19	5
LAMBDEN V	26	13
LEAMON F	26	13
LEWIS I	13	2
LILEY H		
MCARTHUR W	26	
MORGAN J	15	6
MORGAN W	2	
PEACOCK G	7	
PETHERBRIDGE G	8	1
PITT J	38	1
SMITH H	4	
SMITH W V	9	
WARREN B	42	3
WATKINS B	42	
WEARE J	40	
WHITFIELD W	16	
WINDLE C	7	1
WINTERS H	7	
WOOKEY K	21	3
OWN GOALS		2

Once the goals were flowing, Rovers were to lose just once in a run of 13 League matches to move to mid-table respectability and banish the ghost of pre-war re-election. Notts County, so dominant when they had beaten Rovers at Meadow Lane in November, were humbled 4-1 at Eastville, Leamon again scoring twice. Just three days after a comfortable victory over Rovers at Brisbane Road, Leyton Orient conceded six goals on their visit to Eastville, with Len Hodges and Jimmy Morgan both scoring in each half and Ken Wookey created three goals as Rovers raced to a 6-0 lead on the hour mark. The stage was set for some bigger victories in the years to come.

Ray Warren scored penalties in both League games with Queen's Park Rangers, his first, Rovers' second goal at Loftus Road in October, being the centre-half's first League goal since November 1936, a club record gap of almost 10 years. Wing-half Wally McArthur's goal in the defeat at Port Vale in April was his first since the opening day of the 1938/39 season. Rovers completed their season with a home game with Ipswich Town, whom they were to meet in more dramatic circumstances 12 months later. This match kicked off at 3 p.m., with Bristol City's remaining home game with Queen's Park Rangers starting at 6.30 p.m. Both matches were to result in a 1-1 draw.

The FA Cup brought Rovers no joy as, for the first time since elevation to the Football League in 1920, the club was knocked out by a non-League side. Rovers visited Penydarren Park, where a crowd of 14,000 saw Merthyr Town defeat their opponents 3-1. Rovers had led at half-time through Lambden, but Bill Hullett, the home captain, scored twice. The other goalscorer, George Crisp, had played in 22 League matches for Rovers during the 1935/36 season. The Gloucestershire Cup Final was again lost, Bristol City winning in a replay.

1947/48

However remarkably well Rovers survived having to apply for re-election, ultimate success could not entirely hide the side's shortcomings. Rovers had been a point adrift at the foot of the Division Three (South) with only two games to play. There had been one run of six consecutive defeats and 11 home defeats in total. Manager Brough Fletcher was gradually piecing together the side Bert Tann would lead to great success, but the early steps on the path were faltering ones.

The arrival of the former Fulham outside-left Harold Cranfield, a mere youth at 29, saw 37-year-old Lance Carr move to Merthyr Tydfil on a free transfer. This apart, Rovers opened the new season with a recognizable side. Only 12 players were used in the first 10 League games as Rovers sought greater on-field consistency. As the season progressed, Geoff Fox and Bryan Bush made their first appearances in the side Tann was to inherit. Josser Watling made his League bow on the left, while Fred Chadwick, a prolific wartime goalscorer, played in half a dozen games at inside-forward.

Jackie Pitt, the only ever-present, was level with Fred Leamon as the club's second-highest goalscorer behind young Vic Lambden, who contributed 11 League goals on his return to the side following a ten-month absence. The full-back pairing of Harry

Bamford and Barry Watkins continued to develop, while Ken Wookey's 6 goals from outside-right came at crucial moments in the season. Ralph Jones, later a successful singer who performed at Glyndebourne and at the Edinburgh Festival, was given a run in the side at full-back, but was injured in the 4-0 defeat at Exeter City and was out of football for two years.

Secretary Charles Ferrari resigned on 23 October 1947 and the greyhound company assumed responsibility for the management of Rovers' accounts, with John Gummow appointed secretary on 8 December. Gummow was to serve in this role for a year before the appointment of Ron Moules who continued as club secretary up to his sudden death in 1967.

The Rovers director John Hare had called a meeting on 26 August 1947 to set up a Supporters' Club. The purpose was to back the club financially and vocally, giving a mouthpiece to the paying spectators. As football emerged from the repression of wartime, this appeared a natural step. The first chairman selected was a local solicitor, Herbert John Hampden Alpass. As a cricketer, Hampden Alpass had played in 7 first-class games for Gloucestershire, where he had been a colleague of the former Rovers player Wally Hammond. At the age of 40, he now had considerable energy to put into Bristol Rovers and he was to support the club in a number of ways for many years. For two years he ran the Supporters' Club before resigning in 1949, whereupon Eric Godfrey ran the organization through the glory years of the 1950s. One early committee

Bristol Rovers 1947/48. Back row: Jack Pitt, Ray Warren, Jack Weare, Harry Bamford, Barry Watkins, Wally McArthur. Front row: Ken Wookey, Len Hodges, Vic Lambden, Jimmy Morgan, George Petherbridge

member was Ray Bywater, who remained on the board until January 1966. Other early volunteers included Joan Bruton, Tom Spiller, Bill Creed and Harry Stansfield, whose father had played in goal in Rovers' first Football League match. At its peak, the club was to have a membership of more than 2,000.

On the field, the tally of 11 home League defeats, a club record equalled only in the relegation season of 1992/93, goes some way toward explaining why this was a season of struggle. Don Clark was again one of Bristol City's scorers as they won at Eastville, Doug Lishman scored twice for Walsall in their away victory and a Watkins own goal proved to be Southend United's winner when they visited. The most extraordinary home defeat, however, was clearly Newport County's 3-2 victory on Easter Saturday. Rovers had not scored for four games, but Jackie Pitt successfully converted two early penalties, after just five and six minutes, to equal Jonah Wilcox's achievement on Boxing Day 1925. It was a game of three first-half penalties with County's Len Emmanuel scoring one after 33 minutes in his side's success. Emmanuel, once on Rovers' books and the uncle of a future Rovers midfielder, had himself scored two penalties in the side's 2-2 draw at Somerton Park in November. Rovers conceded four penalties in three League games at this stage. Emmanuel thus became the only opponent to convert three penalties against Rovers in a League season.

To counter this argument, Rovers scored four goals at home to Brighton, as well as at Leyton Orient and Ipswich Town. In November, two goals apiece from Leamon and Len Hodges earned the side a convincing 5-1 victory at Norwich City. The largest victory, however, came at Eastville on Easter Monday. Vic Lambden scored a hat-trick inside nine first-half minutes and a fourth after half-time as Rovers beat Aldershot 7-1 to equal the club's largest League victory at that time. Pitt scored twice, for the second consecutive game as Rovers defeated opponents who had beaten Rovers 2-0 only three days earlier.

After a promising start, Rovers' season began to fall away in the New Year. The Aldershot victory ended a run of six consecutive League defeats, only one short of the club record seven straight losses that started the 1961/62 relegation season. Queen's Park Rangers, with Danny Boxshall scoring twice, and Bristol City both put five goals past Rovers. Don Clark, tormenting Rovers' defence as usual, became on Valentine's Day the only City player to score a League hat-trick in a local derby at Ashton Gate. Rovers trailed 3-0 by half-time to Norwich City, with Les Eyre scoring twice and Driver Allenby once, before Rovers rallied and almost claimed a point. Bamford's 35th-minute own goal was Exeter City's second in Rovers' heavy defeat at St James' Park in March, Dennis Hutchings scoring once in each half.

There had been high-scoring games, both sides for instance scoring at least twice in four consecutive League matches in the autumn. However, with two matches to play, Rovers were fighting for survival. On the morning of Wednesday 28 April, Rovers were bottom of the table with 30 points and two games to play, both against Ipswich Town. Above them stood Norwich City on 31 points, Swindon Town on 32 and Brighton on 33. Incredibly, Rovers followed up a 2-0 home victory over Ipswich Town with a resounding 4-0 victory at Portman Road against opponents who had until very recently harboured genuine Championship hopes. Rovers had clutched a final position of 20th from the jaws of re-election.

FOOTBALL LEAGUE DIVISION THREE (SOUTH)

Date	Opponent	H/A	Score	ATT	G	2	3	4	5	6	7	8	9	10	11	GOALSCORERS
23/08/47	PORT VALE	A	1-1	15714	WEARE	BAMFORD	WATKINS	PITT	WARREN	McARTHUR	WOOKEY	HODGES	LEAMON	MORGAN	CRANFIELD	CRANFIELD
25/08/47	SWINDON TOWN	H	3-1	19372	WEARE	BAMFORD	WATKINS	PITT	WARREN	McARTHUR	WOOKEY	HODGES	LEAMON	MORGAN	CRANFIELD	PITT 2, LEAMON
30/08/47	QUEENS PARK RANGERS	A	0-1	19632	WEARE	BAMFORD	WATKINS	PITT	WARREN	McARTHUR	WOOKEY	HODGES	LEAMON	MORGAN	CRANFIELD	
03/09/47	SWINDON TOWN	A	1-1	18000	WEARE	BAMFORD	WATKINS	PITT	WARREN	McARTHUR	WOOKEY	HODGES	LEAMON	MORGAN	CRANFIELD	WOOKEY
06/09/47	WATFORD	A	2-3	10315	WEARE	BAMFORD	WATKINS	PITT	WARREN	McARTHUR	WOOKEY	HODGES	LEAMON	MORGAN	CRANFIELD	LEAMON, WOOKEY
08/09/47	CRYSTAL PALACE	H	1-1	12430	WEARE	BAMFORD	WATKINS	PITT	WARREN	McARTHUR	WOOKEY	HODGES	LEAMON	MORGAN	CRANFIELD	WARREN pen
13/09/47	BRIGHTON & HOVE ALBION	H	4-1	13833	WEARE	BAMFORD	WATKINS	PITT	WARREN	McARTHUR	WOOKEY	HODGES	LEAMON	CHADWICK	CRANFIELD	LEAMON 2, WOOKEY, CHADWICK
17/09/47	CRYSTAL PALACE	A	0-0	12172	WEARE	BAMFORD	WATKINS	PITT	WARREN	McARTHUR	WOOKEY	HODGES	LEAMON	CHADWICK	CRANFIELD	
20/09/47	NORWICH CITY	H	5-1	15209	WEARE	BAMFORD	WATKINS	PITT	WARREN	McARTHUR	WOOKEY	HODGES	LEAMON	CHADWICK	CRANFIELD	LEAMON 2, HODGES 2, WOOKEY
22/09/47	SWANSEA TOWN	A	2-2	15281	WEARE	BAMFORD	WATKINS	PITT	WARREN	McARTHUR	WOOKEY	HODGES	LEAMON	CHADWICK	CRANFIELD	LEAMON, McARTHUR
27/09/47	BRISTOL CITY	H	0-1	34188	WEARE	BAMFORD	McARTHUR	PITT	WARREN	FOX	WOOKEY	HODGES	LEAMON	CHADWICK	CRANFIELD	
04/10/47	NORTHAMPTON TOWN	A	1-2	15098	WEARE	BAMFORD	WATKINS	PITT	WINTERS	McARTHUR	WOOKEY	HODGES	LEAMON	MORGAN	CRANFIELD	McARTHUR
11/10/47	READING	H	0-0	13000	WEARE	BAMFORD	WATKINS	PITT	WARREN	McARTHUR	WOOKEY	HODGES	LEAMON	MORGAN	CRANFIELD	
18/10/47	WALSALL	A	2-3	17573	WEARE	BAMFORD	WATKINS	PITT	WARREN	McARTHUR	WOOKEY	HODGES	LEAMON	BALDIE	CRANFIELD	PETHERBRIDGE, HODGES
25/10/47	LEYTON ORIENT	H	4-2	11164	WEARE	BAMFORD	WATKINS	PITT	WARREN	McARTHUR	WOOKEY	HODGES	LEAMON	MORGAN	CRANFIELD	WOOKEY, LAMBDEN, PITT pen
01/11/47	EXETER CITY	A	2-2	14399	WEARE	BAMFORD	WATKINS	PITT	WARREN	McARTHUR	WOOKEY	HODGES	LEAMON	MORGAN	CRANFIELD	WOOKEY, MORGAN
08/11/47	NEWPORT COUNTY	H	2-2	12000	WEARE	BAMFORD	WATKINS	PITT	WARREN	McARTHUR	WOOKEY	HODGES	LAMBDEN	MORGAN	CRANFIELD	MORGAN, WOOKEY
15/11/47	SOUTHEND UNITED	A	1-2	12613	WEARE	BAMFORD	WATKINS	PITT	WARREN	McARTHUR	WOOKEY	BALDIE	LAMBDEN	MORGAN	CRANFIELD	BALDIE
22/11/47	NOTTS COUNTY	H	2-4	29437	WEARE	BAMFORD	WATKINS	PITT	WARREN	McARTHUR	WOOKEY	HODGES	LAMBDEN	MORGAN	CRANFIELD	LAMBDEN 2
06/12/47	BOURNEMOUTH	A	0-3	13000	WEARE	BAMFORD	WATKINS	PITT	WINTERS	McARTHUR	WOOKEY	HODGES	LAMBDEN	MORGAN	CRANFIELD	
20/12/47	PORT VALE	H	2-1	11651	WEARE	JONES	WATKINS	PITT	WINTERS	McARTHUR	WOOKEY	HODGES	LAMBDEN	MORGAN	CRANFIELD	LEAMON, McGARRY og
26/12/47	TORQUAY UNITED	A	1-2	16554	WEARE	BAMFORD	WATKINS	PITT	WINTERS	McARTHUR	WOOKEY	HODGES	LAMBDEN	MORGAN	CRANFIELD	CRANFIELD
27/12/47	TORQUAY UNITED	H	2-1	7148	WEARE	BAMFORD	FOX	PITT	WINTERS	McARTHUR	PETHERBRIDGE	HODGES	LAMBDEN	MORGAN	CRANFIELD	MORGAN, PETHERBRIDGE
03/01/48	QUEENS PARK RANGERS	H	2-5	22000	WEARE	BAMFORD	WATKINS	PITT	WINTERS	McARTHUR	PETHERBRIDGE	HODGES	LAMBDEN	MORGAN	CRANFIELD	PITT 2, 2pens
17/01/48	WATFORD	H	3-0	12864	WEARE	BAMFORD	WATKINS	FOX	WARREN	McARTHUR	WOOKEY	HODGES	LAMBDEN	MORGAN	PETHERBRIDGE	MORGAN, PETHERBRIDGE, LAMBDEN
31/01/48	BRIGHTON & HOVE ALBION	A	1-3	14081	WEARE	BAMFORD	WATKINS	PITT	WARREN	McARTHUR	WOOKEY	HODGES	LAMBDEN	MORGAN	PETHERBRIDGE	PETHERBRIDGE
07/02/48	NORWICH CITY	A	2-3	11226	WEARE	BAMFORD	WATKINS	PITT	WARREN	McARTHUR	WOOKEY	WOOKEY	LAMBDEN	WATKINS	PETHERBRIDGE	MORGAN, PETHERBRIDGE
14/02/48	BRISTOL CITY	A	2-5	25908	WEARE	BAMFORD	WATKINS	PITT	WARREN	McARTHUR	WOOKEY	HODGES	LAMBDEN	WATKINS	PETHERBRIDGE	McARTHUR, WATKINS, LAMBDEN
21/02/48	NORTHAMPTON TOWN	H	3-1	5149	WEARE	BAMFORD	WATKINS	PITT	WARREN	McARTHUR	WOOKEY	HODGES	LAMBDEN	WATKINS	PETHERBRIDGE	PETHERBRIDGE, WATKINS, LAMBDEN
28/02/48	READING	A	2-3	14356	WEARE	BAMFORD	WATKINS	PITT	WARREN	McARTHUR	WOOKEY	HODGES	LAMBDEN	MORGAN	PETHERBRIDGE	MORGAN, PETHERBRIDGE
06/03/48	WALSALL	H	2-3	13442	WEARE	BAMFORD	WATKINS	PITT	WARREN	McARTHUR	WOOKEY	HODGES	LAMBDEN	MORGAN	PETHERBRIDGE	MORGAN, PETHERBRIDGE
13/03/48	LEYTON ORIENT	A	0-2	11987	WEARE	BAMFORD	WATKINS	PITT	WARREN	McARTHUR	BUSH	WOOKEY	LEAMON	MORGAN	PETHERBRIDGE	
20/03/48	EXETER CITY	H	0-4	8000	WEARE	WARREN	WATKINS	PITT	BAMFORD	McARTHUR	BUSH	HODGES	LAMBDEN	MORGAN	WATLING	
26/03/48	ALDERSHOT	A	0-2	6980	WEARE	JONES	JONES	PITT	WARREN	McARTHUR	PETHERBRIDGE	HODGES	LAMBDEN	MORGAN	WATLING	
27/03/48	NEWPORT COUNTY	A	2-3	13292	LILEY	JONES	JONES	PITT	WARREN	McARTHUR	PETHERBRIDGE	HODGES	LAMBDEN	MORGAN	WATLING	LAMBDEN, PETHERBRIDGE
29/03/48	ALDERSHOT	H	7-1	10996	LILEY	JONES	JONES	PITT	WARREN	McARTHUR	PETHERBRIDGE	HODGES	LAMBDEN	HODGES	WATLING	LAMBDEN 4, PITT 2, WATKINS
03/04/48	SOUTHEND UNITED	H	0-1	8410	LILEY	BAMFORD	FOX	PITT	WARREN	McARTHUR	PETHERBRIDGE	HODGES	LEAMON	MORGAN	WATLING	
10/04/48	NOTTS COUNTY	A	2-0	12094	LILEY	BAMFORD	FOX	PITT	WARREN	McARTHUR	PETHERBRIDGE	LAMBDEN	LEAMON	HODGES	WATLING	WATKINS, PITT
17/04/48	SWANSEA TOWN	H	1-0	15320	WEARE	BAMFORD	FOX	PITT	WARREN	McARTHUR	PETHERBRIDGE	HODGES	LAMBDEN	WATKINS	WATLING	WARREN
24/04/48	BOURNEMOUTH	H	1-2	14827	WEARE	BAMFORD	FOX	PITT	WARREN	McARTHUR	PETHERBRIDGE	HODGES	LAMBDEN	WATKINS	WATLING	WATKINS
28/04/48	IPSWICH TOWN	A	2-0	8722	WEARE	BAMFORD	WATKINS	PITT	WARREN	McARTHUR	BUSH	WATKINS	LAMBDEN	MORGAN	WATLING	WATKINS, GREEN og
01/05/48	IPSWICH TOWN	H	4-0	10605	WEARE	BAMFORD	FOX	PITT	WARREN	McARTHUR	WOOKEY	WATKINS	LAMBDEN	MORGAN	WATLING	PETHERBRIDGE 2, BUSH, MORGAN

FA CUP

Date	Opponent	H/A	Score	ATT	G	2	3	4	5	6	7	8	9	10	11	GOALSCORERS
29/11/47	LEYTONSTONE	A	2-1	16000	WEARE	BAMFORD	WATKINS	PITT	WARREN	McARTHUR	WOOKEY	HODGES	LAMBDEN	MORGAN	CRANFIELD	BALDIE, LAMBDEN, MORGAN
13/12/47	NEW BRIGHTON	H	4-0	10732	WEARE	BAMFORD	WATKINS	PITT	WARREN	McARTHUR	WOOKEY	HODGES	LAMBDEN	MORGAN	CRANFIELD	MORGAN 2, McARTHUR, LAMBDEN
10/01/48	SWANSEA TOWN	H	3-0	23396	WEARE	BAMFORD	WATKINS	PITT	WARREN	McARTHUR	WOOKEY	HODGES	LAMBDEN	MORGAN	CRANFIELD	WOOKEY, LAMBDEN, MORGAN
24/01/48	FULHAM	A	2-5	20000	WEARE	BAMFORD	WATKINS	PITT	WARREN	McARTHUR	WOOKEY	HODGES	LAMBDEN	MORGAN	CRANFIELD	McARTHUR, PETHERBRIDGE

GLOUCESTERSHIRE CUP FINAL

Date	Opponent	H/A	Score	ATT	G	2	3	4	5	6	7	8	9	10	11	GOALSCORERS
08/05/48	BRISTOL CITY	A	2-1	16000	LILEY	BAMFORD	FOX	PITT	WARREN	McARTHUR	HODGES	WATKINS	LAMBDEN	MORGAN	PETHERBRIDGE	MORGAN, WATKINS

PLAYERS	APP	GLS
BALDIE D	5	1
BAMFORD H	40	
BUSH B	2	
CHADWICK F	6	1
CRANFIELD H	24	2
FOX G	12	
HODGES L	37	5
JONES R	7	
LAMBDEN V	26	11
LEAMON F	17	8
LILEY H	10	
McARTHUR W	41	4
MORGAN J	27	7
PETHERBRIDGE G	15	7
PITT J	42	8
WARREN R	36	3
WATKINS B	34	5
WATLING J	11	
WEARE J	32	
WINTERS H	6	
WOOKEY K	32	6
OWN GOALS		2

As Rovers completed a run of five wins in seven League games, they moved above both Norwich and Brighton on goal average. Both Rovers and Norwich won final-day games away to top-four sides to leave Brighton bottom of the table in the wake of their goalless draw at Swansea. It was, indeed a narrow escape for Rovers and, given the need to apply for re-election in 1938/39 and the club's desperate start to the first post-war season, failure to win at Ipswich Town would have left the club's League future in a perilous state. Indeed Gillingham, who returned to Division Three (South) in 1950, headed a plethora of viable alternatives to a struggling side like Bristol Rovers.

Nonetheless, survival had been achieved and with it were sown the first seeds of a bright future. Bert Tann, who was to succeed Fletcher as manager in January 1950, arrived at Eastville in February and persuaded three of Rovers' staff to attend a Football Association Trainers and Coaches course in May 1948. Trainer Bert Williams, his assistant Wally McArthur and assistant coach Harry Smith were the first Rovers employees to attend such a course and this set a benchmark for the years to follow. There was considerable hope that the future would bring success.

A free-scoring FA Cup run earned Rovers a lucrative fourth-round tie against Division Two Fulham at Craven Cottage. In fact Rovers had only defeated unfancied Leytonstone through Morgan's headed winner, while a pre-war Rovers player, Bill Pendergast, was New Brighton's centre-forward in their 4-0 defeat at Eastville. Lambden and Morgan had both scored in all Rovers' three previous ties and, in their new-found enthusiasm, the Supporters' Club took 1,000 spectators to the Fulham game. Rovers put up a brave show before a 20,000 crowd but lost 5-2, despite goals from McArthur and young George Petherbridge. Arthur Stevens, who was to score twice in Rovers' FA Cup quarter-final on the same ground 10 years later, scored a hat-trick for Fulham. In April, Rovers entertained a touring side, Racing Club Haarlem, winning by a single Lambden goal after 10 minutes and laying the foundations for a close-season tour of the Netherlands. Once survival had been achieved, a 2-1 win at Ashton Gate secured the Gloucestershire Cup, Morgan and Watkins both scoring with low shots inside the opening 18 minutes. Barry Watkins had not scored in his first 62 League games for Rovers, but six league and Cup goals late in the season proved his versatility.

1948/49

Rovers' oft-discussed 'no buy, no sell' policy had its origin in the immediate post-war years. The directors decreed that the club could develop local talent and keep it at Eastville. To this end, only free transfers, generally of peripheral players, were likely to occur. Over the summer of 1948, Fred Chadwick moved to Street and Harold Cranfield to King's Lynn, while Peter Sampson and Bill Roost arrived from local football. Fred Laing from Middlesborough and Newport County's Harry Haddon also arrived on free transfers. When Ken Wookey was sold to Swansea Town in November, the £1,000 transfer fee was put into the players' benefit fund.

Manager Brough Fletcher was continuing to build the side that his successor Bert Tann was to lead into Division Two. Fifth place in Division Three (South) was a good

FOOTBALL LEAGUE DIVISION THREE (SOUTH)

Date	Opponents		Score	Att	G	2	3	4	5	6	7	8	9	10	11	Goalscorers
21/08/48	IPSWICH TOWN	H	1-6	16314	LILEY	BAMFORD	FOX	SAMPSON	WARREN	McARTHUR	WOOKEY	HODGES	LAMBDEN	MORGAN	BUSH	LAMBDEN
26/08/48	BOURNEMOUTH	A	0-1	16067	WEARE	BAMFORD	FOX	PITT	WARREN	McARTHUR	PETHERBRIDGE	HODGES	LAMBDEN	MORGAN	BUSH	
28/08/48	NOTTS COUNTY	A	1-4	33747	WEARE	BAMFORD	FOX	PITT	WARREN	McARTHUR	PETHERBRIDGE	HODGES	LAMBDEN	MORGAN	BUSH	WARREN pen, BUSH, FOULKES og
30/08/48	BOURNEMOUTH	H	4-0	14121	WEARE	BAMFORD	FOX	PITT	WARREN	McARTHUR	PETHERBRIDGE	HODGES	LAMBDEN	MORGAN	BUSH	PETHERBRIDGE, MORGAN 2, HODGES
04/09/48	WALSALL	H	3-0	17244	WEARE	BAMFORD	FOX	PITT	WARREN	McARTHUR	PETHERBRIDGE	HODGES	LAMBDEN	MORGAN	BUSH	LAMBDEN, BUSH
08/09/48	CRYSTAL PALACE	A	0-1	10827	WEARE	BAMFORD	FOX	PITT	WARREN	McARTHUR	PETHERBRIDGE	HODGES	LAMBDEN	MORGAN	BUSH	
11/09/48	TORQUAY UNITED	A	2-0	8360	WEARE	BAMFORD	FOX	PITT	WARREN	McARTHUR	PETHERBRIDGE	HODGES	LAMBDEN	MORGAN	BUSH	LAMBDEN, BUSH
13/09/48	CRYSTAL PALACE	H	1-0	14509	WEARE	BAMFORD	FOX	PITT	WARREN	McARTHUR	PETHERBRIDGE	HODGES	LAMBDEN	MORGAN	BUSH	HODGES
18/09/48	BRISTOL CITY	A	3-1	29740	WEARE	BAMFORD	FOX	PITT	WARREN	McARTHUR	PETHERBRIDGE	HODGES	LAMBDEN	MORGAN	BUSH	PETHERBRIDGE, LAMBDEN, BUSH
20/09/48	MILLWALL	H	2-0	16260	WEARE	BAMFORD	FOX	PITT	WARREN	McARTHUR	PETHERBRIDGE	HODGES	LAMBDEN	MORGAN	WATLING	HODGES, MORGAN, WATLING
25/09/48	NEWPORT COUNTY	H	3-1	21542	WEARE	BAMFORD	FOX	PITT	WARREN	McARTHUR	PETHERBRIDGE	HODGES	LAMBDEN	MORGAN	WATLING	PETHERBRIDGE, MORTON og
02/10/48	SWANSEA TOWN	A	0-5	28350	WEARE	BAMFORD	FOX	PITT	WARREN	McARTHUR	PETHERBRIDGE	HODGES	LAMBDEN	MORGAN	WATLING	
09/10/48	SWINDON TOWN	H	1-1	20720	WEARE	BAMFORD	FOX	PITT	WARREN	McARTHUR	PETHERBRIDGE	HODGES	LAMBDEN	MORGAN	WATLING	LAMBDEN
16/10/48	LEYTON ORIENT	A	2-3	13719	WEARE	BAMFORD	FOX	PITT	WARREN	McARTHUR	PETHERBRIDGE	HODGES	LAMBDEN	MORGAN	WATLING	LAMBDEN 2
23/10/48	SOUTHEND UNITED	H	1-0	13211	WEARE	BAMFORD	FOX	PITT	WARREN	McARTHUR	PETHERBRIDGE	HODGES	LAMBDEN	MORGAN	WATLING	LAMBDEN
30/10/48	NORTHAMPTON TOWN	A	1-0	14641	WEARE	BAMFORD	FOX	PITT	WARREN	McARTHUR	PETHERBRIDGE	HODGES	LAMBDEN	MORGAN	WATLING	MORGAN
06/11/48	ALDERSHOT	H	5-1	9000	WEARE	BAMFORD	FOX	PITT	WARREN	McARTHUR	PETHERBRIDGE	HODGES	LAMBDEN	MORGAN	WATLING	PETHERBRIDGE 2, LAMBDEN, MORGAN, WARREN
13/11/48	BRIGHTON & HOVE ALBION	H	0-0	21879	WEARE	BAMFORD	FOX	PITT	WARREN	McARTHUR	PETHERBRIDGE	HODGES	LAMBDEN	MORGAN	WATLING	
20/11/48	PORT VALE	A	0-2	10342	WEARE	BAMFORD	FOX	PITT	WARREN	McARTHUR	PETHERBRIDGE	HODGES	LAMBDEN	MORGAN	WATLING	
04/12/48	NORWICH CITY	H	0-3	20246	WEARE	BAMFORD	FOX	PITT	WARREN	McARTHUR	PETHERBRIDGE	HODGES	LAMBDEN	MORGAN	WATLING	
18/12/48	IPSWICH TOWN	A	1-0	8751	WEARE	BAMFORD	FOX	PITT	WARREN	McARTHUR	PETHERBRIDGE	LAING	LAMBDEN	MORGAN	WATLING	WARREN pen
25/12/48	WATFORD	H	3-1	13853	WEARE	BAMFORD	FOX	PITT	WARREN	McARTHUR	PETHERBRIDGE	HODGES	LAMBDEN	MORGAN	WATLING	WARREN 2, MORGAN
27/12/48	WATFORD	A	0-0	11949	WEARE	BAMFORD	FOX	PITT	WARREN	McARTHUR	PETHERBRIDGE	HODGES	LAMBDEN	MORGAN	WATLING	
01/01/49	NOTTS COUNTY	H	3-2	11981	WEARE	BAMFORD	FOX	PITT	WARREN	McARTHUR	PETHERBRIDGE	HODGES	LAMBDEN	MORGAN	WATLING	WARREN 2, MORGAN
15/01/49	WALSALL	A	1-0	13000	WEARE	BAMFORD	FOX	PITT	WARREN	McARTHUR	PETHERBRIDGE	HODGES	LAMBDEN	MORGAN	WATLING	LAMBDEN
22/01/49	TORQUAY UNITED	H	1-0	18489	WEARE	BAMFORD	FOX	PITT	WARREN	McARTHUR	PETHERBRIDGE	HODGES	LAMBDEN	MORGAN	WATLING	MORGAN
05/02/49	BRISTOL CITY	H	1-1	27006	WEARE	BAMFORD	FOX	PITT	WARREN	McARTHUR	PETHERBRIDGE	HODGES	LAMBDEN	MORGAN	WATLING	WARREN pen
12/02/49	EXETER CITY	A	3-1	16802	WEARE	BAMFORD	FOX	PITT	WARREN	McARTHUR	PETHERBRIDGE	HODGES	LAMBDEN	ROOST	WATLING	WATLING, PETHERBRIDGE, ROOST 2
19/02/49	NEWPORT COUNTY	A	1-2	21000	WEARE	BAMFORD	FOX	PITT	WARREN	McARTHUR	PETHERBRIDGE	HODGES	LAMBDEN	MORGAN	WATLING	WARREN
26/02/49	SWANSEA TOWN	H	0-0	30216	WEARE	BAMFORD	FOX	PITT	WARREN	McARTHUR	PETHERBRIDGE	HODGES	LAMBDEN	MORGAN	WATLING	
05/03/49	SWINDON TOWN	A	1-1	12688	WEARE	BAMFORD	FOX	PITT	WARREN	McARTHUR	PETHERBRIDGE	HODGES	LAMBDEN	MORGAN	WATLING	HODGES
12/03/49	LEYTON ORIENT	H	1-1	10154	WEARE	BAMFORD	FOX	PITT	WARREN	McARTHUR	PETHERBRIDGE	HODGES	LAMBDEN	MORGAN	WATLING	PETHERBRIDGE
19/03/49	SOUTHEND UNITED	A	0-0	12500	WEARE	BAMFORD	FOX	PITT	WARREN	McARTHUR	BUSH	HODGES	LAMBDEN	HADDON	PETHERBRIDGE	
26/03/49	NORTHAMPTON TOWN	H	1-0	7425	WEARE	BAMFORD	FOX	PITT	WARREN	McARTHUR	PETHERBRIDGE	HODGES	LAMBDEN	HADDON	WATLING	LAMBDEN
02/04/49	ALDERSHOT	A	0-2	11147	WEARE	BAMFORD	FOX	PITT	WARREN	McARTHUR	PETHERBRIDGE	HODGES	LAMBDEN	MORGAN	WATLING	
09/04/49	BRIGHTON & HOVE ALBION	A	1-2	14828	WEARE	BAMFORD	FOX	PITT	WARREN	McARTHUR	PETHERBRIDGE	HODGES	LAMBDEN	MORGAN	WATLING	MORGAN
15/04/49	READING	A	4-1	20836	WEARE	BAMFORD	FOX	PITT	WARREN	McARTHUR	PETHERBRIDGE	WATKINS	ROOST	MORGAN	WATLING	WATKINS, ROOST, WARREN pen
16/04/49	PORT VALE	H	0-1	15268	WEARE	BAMFORD	FOX	PITT	WARREN	McARTHUR	PETHERBRIDGE	HODGES	ROOST	MORGAN	WATLING	
18/04/49	READING	H	1-2	18975	WEARE	BAMFORD	FOX	PITT	WARREN	McARTHUR	PETHERBRIDGE	HODGES	ROOST	MORGAN	WATLING	WARREN pen
23/04/49	MILLWALL	A	1-1	20648	WEARE	BAMFORD	FOX	PITT	WARREN	McARTHUR	PETHERBRIDGE	HODGES	ROOST	MORGAN	WATLING	LAMBDEN
30/04/49	NORWICH CITY	H	2-2	12755	WEARE	BAMFORD	FOX	PITT	WARREN	McARTHUR	PETHERBRIDGE	HODGES	LAMBDEN	MORGAN	WATLING	PETHERBRIDGE 2, LAMBDEN
07/05/49	EXETER CITY	A	1-2	7000	WEARE	BAMFORD	FOX	PITT	WARREN	McARTHUR	PETHERBRIDGE	HODGES	ROOST	MORGAN	WATLING	WARREN pen

FA CUP

Date	Opponents		Score	Att	G	2	3	4	5	6	7	8	9	10	11	Goalscorers
27/11/48	WALSALL	A	1-2	16000	WEARE	BAMFORD	FOX	PITT	WARREN	McARTHUR	PETHERBRIDGE	LAING	LAMBDEN	MORGAN	WATLING	LAMBDEN

GLOUCESTERSHIRE CUP FINAL

Date	Opponents		Score	Att	G	2	3	4	5	6	7	8	9	10	11	Goalscorers
14/05/49	BRISTOL CITY		2-0	15111	LILEY	BAMFORD	FOX	PITT	WARREN	McARTHUR	WATKINS	HODGES	LAMBDEN	LAING	MORGAN	LAMBDEN, MORGAN

PLAYERS	APP	GLS
BAMFORD H	42	
BUSH B	9	3
FOX G	42	
HADDON H	2	
HODGES H	39	5
LAING F	2	
LAMBDEN V	41	13
LILEY H	1	
McARTHUR W	42	
MORGAN J	38	8
PETHERBRIDGE G	39	11
PITT J	41	
ROOST W	6	3
SAMPSON P	1	
WARREN R	42	11
WATKINS B	1	
WATLING J	28	4
WEARE J	41	
WOOKEY K	1	
OWN GOALS		2

indication that the raising of standards was under way at Eastville. Fletcher's side was becoming more consistent both in appearance and in results. Defensive players Harry Bamford, Geoff Fox, Wally McArthur and Ray Warren were all ever-presents, while a further four players missed just one League game each. The side still, however, lacked a prolific goalscorer to partner the ever-improving Vic Lambden. The imminent arrival on the scene of Geoff Bradford was to have a profound effect on Rovers' on-field success.

Preparation for the new season included a two-match visit to the Netherlands. Rovers lost 1-0 to NEC Nijmegen and beat Racing Club Haarlem 4-2, thanks to two goals from Lambden and one apiece from Barry Watkins and Maurice Lockier. However well-prepared the side may have appeared, there was a heavy defeat on the opening day of the season, as Ipswich Town crushed Rovers 6-1 at Eastville. Strangely, this was a third

Harry Bamford, a stalwart full-back, represented the English FA on a tour of Australia in 1951. A talented and popular player, Harry's career total of 486 League appearances for Rovers spanned 13 seasons until his tragic death in 1958

consecutive League fixture against the Suffolk club, yet memories of the four-goal win at Portman Road in May were cast aside as Rovers collapsed to a then-club-record home League defeat. Sampson, making his club debut and on his way to 340 League matches for the Eastville side, and goalkeeper Harry Liley did not play again in the League that season, while Ken Wookey was playing his final game for Rovers. Bill Jennings and John Dempsey scored twice each for Ipswich, who scored 16 goals in their first three League games but finished the season below Rovers in the Division Three (South) table.

After the opening four games, Rovers were to suffer only one heavy defeat, a 5-0 mauling at Swansea Town where the future Welsh International Frank Scrine scored a hat-trick and 28-year-old Roy Paul, later the winner of 33 Welsh caps, also found his name on the scoresheet. Indeed, when Noel Kinsey scored twice and Ron Ashman once for Norwich City on 4 December, it was the final time that season that Rovers conceded three goals in a game. By then, Rovers had also crashed 4-1 at Notts County, whose £20,000 signing of Tommy Lawton had caused great concern over spiralling transfer prices. Lawton scored four times as County beat Ipswich Town 9-2 only 12 days later, but the bubble soon burst and Rovers completed the season six places above the Meadow Lane club.

Thereafter, Rovers enjoyed a relatively trouble-free season. Only 16 players were used in the final 41 League games of the 42-match season. The largest victory was 5-1 at Aldershot. George Petherbridge scored twice, while Warren and the home side's Tom Sinclair both scored from the penalty spot. Jimmy Morgan scored twice in a 4-0 victory over Bournemouth at Eastville. Bill Roost scored a couple of goals on his debut, as

Reading were beaten 4-1 at Eastville on Good Friday and again 24 hours later, as Port Vale lost by the same score, with Josser Watling adding a brace of goals. Three points were taken off Bristol City, a 3-1 win at Eastville being the fourth of sixth straight home victories after the disastrous opening game.

The 1-1 draw with Swindon Town in October, where Lambden scored after 56 minutes for Rovers and Jimmy Bain from Maurice Owen's pass 14 minutes later for the Robins, ended a remarkable run, unparalleled in the club's history, of 37 consecutive League matches without a draw. As is the nature of such records, Rovers proceeded to draw 10 League games in the season, including four in succession in the spring. Three of these 10 draws were secured through Ray Warren penalty kicks. He scored from the penalty spot in both of the last two games, the latter past his future Rovers team-mate Bert Hoyle at Exeter City, to end the season with a club record of seven successful penalties in a season. This match at Exeter was watched by a crowd of 7,000, the lowest at a Rovers game all season.

The lowest attendance at a game played at Eastville was the 11,147 who saw the 2-0 defeat by Aldershot in April. Bearing in mind that Rovers did not attract a five-figure home crowd at all during the relatively successful years between April 1985 and December 1999, much can be made of the club's loyal support in the post-war period. For the third year in succession, the size of crowds had risen, heralding the golden years of the 1950s. In 1948/49 the average attendance for a League game at Eastville was 17,539, the sixth highest in the division, a figure that would increase to the club's seasonal best of 24,662 in 1953/54.

Two prolific goalscorers embellished the fact that only 51 League goals were conceded, the fewest since 1933/34. Guido Roffi, Ynysbwl-born of Italian descent, scored for Newport County against Rovers at Somerton Park in the first of two consecutive seasons. For the third year in succession, Bristol City's Don Clark scored in both League fixtures against Rovers. Although he scored in each of the first six post-war derby matches and remains the only player to score a league hat-trick for the Robins in these games, his total of 9 goals against Rovers still lags behind the figure of 12 goals in local League derbies scored by the prolific John Atyeo.

Rovers did, however, beat Bristol City in September, their first League victory over the old rivals since Christmas 1937. A huge crowd at Eastville saw Jackie Pitt and McArthur in fine form for Rovers. After 25 minutes, feeding off Petherbridge, Lambden beat the veteran Dennis Roberts and drove past George Marks. Five minutes later, Rovers were two goals ahead when Watling volleyed home from 15 yards. Just six minutes after half-time, Lambden's through ball sent Petherbridge through to secure a victory that was straightforward, despite Clark's headed reply from a John Davies cross five minutes from time.

Ipswich Town, having inflicted a heavy defeat on Rovers, featured prominently in the season. Rovers, in white shirts and blue shorts, won 1-0 at Portman Road in December, Jimmy Morgan scoring after 65 minutes from a Petherbridge cross. Ipswich fielded in this game a 40-year-old in the shape of Ossie Parry, who had first played against Rovers in League action as long ago as August 1932, while on Crystal Palace's books. Only seven older players have ever appeared in the League against Rovers. Also in the Ipswich side was the former Rovers centre-half Matt O'Mahoney. In September he had scored an

Bristol Rovers 1949/50. Back row: Frank McCourt, Geoff Fox, Jack Weare, Ray Warren, Harry Bamford, Jack Pitt. Front row: Bryan Bush, Len Hodges, Vic Lambden, Tony James, John Watling

own goal for Notts County, a bizarre companion for the own goal he had conceded while playing in Rovers' colours against Notts County in December 1937.

There was a sharp exit from the FA Cup at Walsall, where home forwards Arthur Aldred and Phil Chapman scored as Rovers lost 2-1. This enabled Rovers to arrange a friendly with Newcastle United on fourth-round day in January, a precursor to the epic FA Cup tie two seasons later. Sadly for the crowd of 25,855, this game was abandoned because of fog just seven minutes after half-time with the score 1-1, Petherbridge having scored for the Pirates. Goals from Lambden, the club's top scorer in the League with 13, and Morgan enabled Rovers to retain the Gloucestershire Cup.

1949/50

One of the major turning points in the history of Bristol Rovers was the appointment of Bertram James Tann as manager early in January 1950. The new manager arrived on the personal recommendation of Sir Stanley Rous and also of Cliff Lloyd, later the secretary of the Professional Footballers' Association and once a Rovers reserves player. Tann, a charismatic 45-year-old Londoner, who had played professional

Captain Ray Warren leads out the team on 11 March 1950 with mascot Tony Spiller.

football with Charlton Athletic, breathed new life into Brough Fletcher's side. He forged close working links with the local community through schools and organizations and established pre-season training camps at Uphill, Weston-super-Mare. His innovative approach even led to an appearance on the quiz show, *The £1,000 Word*, on the first day −14 January 1958 − that the channel destined to become ITV was on the air. His 18 years as manager were to see Rovers reach two FA Cup quarter-finals as well as the distant dreamland of Division Two. In addition, his revival of Rovers' fortunes helped distract some of the attention away from mounting dilemmas off the field.

Over the summer of 1949, Fletcher was once again unable to break away from the board's 'no buy, no sell' policy. This was a restriction that would both restrict Tann but also enable him to build a Rovers side capable of achieving success. Of six new arrivals, only Frank McCourt could claim to be a regular in Rovers' side, although Tony James, a former Brighton inside-left, contributed 5 League goals. Unable to sell, Rovers lost just two players in the close season, both to Trowbridge Town. Harry Haddon was to score more than 200 goals and spend seven years as manager at the Western League club, while Fred Laing left after one season to work at Butlins Holiday Camp in Ayr.

The oft-seen photograph of Bill Roost standing up to the Ipswich Town goal-keeper, Tom Brown, epitomizes in many respects the Rovers of the later Fletcher era. His two goals in that game and two more against Leyton Orient in December brought rare convincing wins, but early season form was largely disappointing. Eight victories and 12 defeats prior to New Year did not inspire confidence. Some young talent had been blooded, most notably Geoff Bradford, who played in depressing defeats at Crystal Palace and at home to Watford. Generally, however, the club was waiting for the major input Tann was to contribute.

By the turn of the year, Rovers were out of the FA Cup, falling to a 19th-minute Maurice Owen goal at Swindon Town. The heaviest defeat had been 4-0 at Carrow Road, where Les Eyre scored twice for Norwich City. Rovers also conceded three goals in a game on four occasions in an early-season fortnight. Trips to Ipswich Town and Southend United both ended in 3-1 defeats, while both Notts County and Bristol City scored three times at Eastville. County's scorers were the England International Tommy Lawton, who scored twice, and outside-left Tom Johnston, while City's victory was a demoralizing blow for which Rovers were to seek ample revenge in January.

Rovers were due to meet Port Vale at Eastville on 10 December, a game that was put back seven days as Vale were obliged to fulfil an FA Cup-tie on that day. Only 9,890 were present on the final Saturday before Christmas Eve as goals from George Petherbridge and Josser Watling earned Rovers a 2-1 victory. For the blank Saturday, a friendly was hastily arranged, with Millwall the visitors to Eastville. Rovers were a goal up through Jimmy Morgan after only five minutes, before succumbing to defeat before a crowd of 4,613. The final game of the Fletcher era was a tepid 1-1 draw at home to Southend United. Bill Roost, Rovers' seasonal top scorer with 13 League goals, was the home side's scorer, following a ninth-minute run and cross from Watling, with Albert Wakefield – who had scored the Shrimpers' second of three first-half goals against Rovers in September – again getting his name on the scoresheet, this time 10 minutes after half-time.

On 2 January, Fletcher was dismissed and his assistant trainer Dick Mann, with the club since November 1945, followed on 31 January. Although the decision had been a unanimous one, it provoked a rift between directors that was to plague Rovers for months. Fletcher himself was to spend just one brief spell in football after leaving Eastville, joining Walsall as manager in 1952; he settled in Bristol, where he died in 1972. Tann's task, as his replacement, was to convert a team of local players and free-transfer signings into a side capable of holding its own in Division Three (South) and subsequently in Division Two. His first game in charge saw Rovers gain ample revenge for September's defeat by beating Bristol City 2-1 before a crowd of 33,697 at Ashton Gate. The combination of the big occasion and the feel-good factor as the new decade opened helped Tann's period as manager to start in the most positive manner possible.

Tann certainly inherited very settled defensive and half-back lines. Harry Bamford and Geoff Fox continued to be models of reliability at full-back, with Fox and centre-half Ray Warren ever-presents and right-half Jackie Pitt missing only 2 games. However, no forward appeared in more games than Roost, whose 28 appearances in 42 League matches made him stand out in attack. There was obviously work to be done in this regard and Geoff Bradford was recalled in February, scoring the opening goal in a 2-0 victory at Watford, the first of a club record 242 in the League. Eleven wins in the first 19 League games under Bert Tann enabled Rovers to finish in ninth place, a respectable finish to the League season. The largest win, 5-1 at home to Norwich City in April, was achieved through five separate goalscorers and Rovers bizarrely completed the season without drawing any away games.

FOOTBALL LEAGUE DIVISION THREE (SOUTH)

SEASON 1949/50

Date	Opposition	H/A	Score	ATT	G	2	3	4	5	6	7	8	9	10	11	GOALSCORERS
20/08/49	PORT VALE	A	0-1	15097	WEARE	BAMFORD	FOX	PITT	WARREN	McARTHUR	PETHERBRIDGE	HODGES	ROOST	MORGAN	WATLING	
22/08/49	IPSWICH TOWN	H	2-0	17508	WEARE	BAMFORD	FOX	PITT	WARREN	McARTHUR	PETHERBRIDGE	HODGES	ROOST	MORGAN	WATLING	ROOST 2
27/08/49	NOTTS COUNTY	A	0-3	24794	WEARE	BAMFORD	FOX	PITT	WARREN	McARTHUR	BUSH	HODGES	ROOST	MORGAN	WATLING	
30/08/49	IPSWICH TOWN	A	1-3	12708	WEARE	BAMFORD	FOX	PITT	WARREN	McARTHUR	BUSH	PETHERBRIDGE	ROOST	MORGAN	WATLING	WATLING
03/09/49	SOUTHEND UNITED	A	1-3	13000	WEARE	BAMFORD	FOX	PITT	WARREN	McARTHUR	BUSH	PETHERBRIDGE	ROOST	MORGAN	WATLING	WATLING
05/09/49	READING	H	2-1	12969	WEARE	BAMFORD	FOX	PITT	WARREN	McARTHUR	PETHERBRIDGE	HODGES	ROOST	JAMES	WATLING	JAMES, WATLING
10/09/49	BRISTOL CITY	H	2-1	34463	WEARE	BAMFORD	FOX	PITT	WARREN	McARTHUR	BUSH	HODGES	ROOST	JAMES	WATLING	ROOST, HODGES
17/09/49	BOURNEMOUTH	A	2-3	18548	WEARE	BAMFORD	FOX	PITT	WARREN	McCOURT	BUSH	HODGES	ROOST	JAMES	WATLING	JAMES, BUSH
24/09/49	CRYSTAL PALACE	H	0-0	15466	LILEY	BAMFORD	FOX	PITT	WARREN	McCOURT	BUSH	BRADFORD	LAMBDEN	JAMES	WATLING	
01/10/49	WATFORD	A	0-2	14996	LILEY	BAMFORD	FOX	PITT	WARREN	McCOURT	BUSH	BRADFORD	LAMBDEN	JAMES	WATLING	
08/10/49	BRIGHTON & HOVE ALBION	H	2-1	16031	WEARE	BAMFORD	FOX	PITT	WARREN	JONES	BUSH	BRADFORD	ROOST	JAMES	WATLING	JAMES
15/10/49	WALSALL	H	1-1	14185	WEARE	BAMFORD	FOX	PITT	WARREN	JONES	BUSH	HODGES	ROOST	JAMES	WATLING	WATLING
22/10/49	SWINDON TOWN	A	1-0	19066	WEARE	BAMFORD	FOX	PITT	WARREN	JONES	BUSH	HODGES	LAMBDEN	JAMES	WATLING	LAMBDEN, JAMES
29/10/49	TORQUAY UNITED	H	2-0	11761	WEARE	BAMFORD	FOX	PITT	WARREN	JONES	BUSH	HODGES	LAMBDEN	JAMES	WATLING	PETHERBRIDGE, HODGES
05/11/49	ALDERSHOT	A	0-1	7567	WEARE	BAMFORD	FOX	PITT	WARREN	McCOURT	BUSH	HODGES	LAMBDEN	MORGAN	WATLING	
12/11/49	SOUTHEND UNITED	H	2-1	12800	WEARE	BAMFORD	FOX	PITT	WARREN	McCOURT	BUSH	HODGES	LAMBDEN	MORGAN	WATLING	PETHERBRIDGE, WATLING
19/11/49	NOTTINGHAM FOREST	A	1-1	15406	WEARE	BAMFORD	FOX	PITT	WARREN	McCOURT	PETHERBRIDGE	HODGES	LAMBDEN	MORGAN	WATLING	HODGES, ROOST 2
03/12/49	NORWICH CITY	A	1-1	15566	WEARE	BAMFORD	FOX	PITT	WARREN	McCOURT	PETHERBRIDGE	HODGES	ROOST	MORGAN	WATLING	ROOST 2
17/12/49	PORT VALE	H	0-2	9890	WEARE	BAMFORD	FOX	PITT	WARREN	McCOURT	PETHERBRIDGE	LAMBDEN	ROOST	MORGAN	WATLING	ROOST, JAMES
24/12/49	NOTTS COUNTY	H	0-4	9207	WEARE	BAMFORD	FOX	PITT	WARREN	McCOURT	PETHERBRIDGE	LAMBDEN	ROOST	MORGAN	WATLING	MORGAN, WATLING
26/12/49	LEYTON ORIENT	A	0-2	31995	WEARE	BAMFORD	FOX	PITT	WARREN	McCOURT	BUSH	LAMBDEN	ROOST	MORGAN	WATLING	BRADFORD, LAMBDEN
27/12/49	LEYTON ORIENT	H	2-1	22540	WEARE	BAMFORD	FOX	PITT	WARREN	McCOURT	BUSH	LAMBDEN	ROOST	MORGAN	WATLING	McCOURT, LAMBDEN 2
31/12/49	SOUTHEND UNITED	A	1-1	33697	WEARE	BAMFORD	FOX	PITT	WARREN	McCOURT	PETHERBRIDGE	HODGES	ROOST	JAMES	WATLING	LAMBDEN, ROOST, WARREN pen
14/01/50	BRISTOL CITY	A	0-2	12211	WEARE	BAMFORD	FOX	PITT	WARREN	McCOURT	PETHERBRIDGE	JAMES	ROOST	MORGAN	WATLING	BRADFORD, LAMBDEN
21/01/50	BOURNEMOUTH	H	2-1	17259	WEARE	BAMFORD	FOX	PITT	WARREN	McCOURT	PETHERBRIDGE	JAMES	ROOST	MORGAN	WATLING	ROOST, JAMES
04/02/50	CRYSTAL PALACE	A	0-0	14591	WEARE	BAMFORD	FOX	PITT	WARREN	McCOURT	BUSH	HODGES	ROOST	WATLING	BUSH	
18/02/50	WATFORD	H	2-0	13149	WEARE	BAMFORD	FOX	PITT	WARREN	McCOURT	BUSH	LAMBDEN	ROOST	WATLING	BUSH	BRADFORD
25/02/50	BRIGHTON & HOVE ALBION	A	3-0	9179	WEARE	BAMFORD	FOX	PITT	WARREN	McCOURT	BUSH	LAMBDEN	ROOST	WATLING	BUSH	BRADFORD, LAMBDEN
04/03/50	WALSALL	A	1-3	14719	WEARE	BAMFORD	FOX	PITT	WARREN	McCOURT	BUSH	LAMBDEN	ROOST	MORGAN	BUSH	LAMBDEN, ROOST, WARREN pen
11/03/50	MILLWALL	H	3-1	11955	WEARE	BAMFORD	FOX	SAMPSON	WARREN	McCOURT	BUSH	BRADFORD	LAMBDEN	JONES	BUSH	McCOURT, LAMBDEN 2
18/03/50	MILLWALL	A	0-1	7806	WEARE	BAMFORD	FOX	SAMPSON	WARREN	JONES	BUSH	BRADFORD	LAMBDEN	JONES	BUSH	
25/03/50	SWINDON TOWN	H	3-1	12121	WEARE	WATKINS	FOX	SAMPSON	WARREN	JONES	BUSH	BRADFORD	LAMBDEN	JONES	BUSH	PETHERBRIDGE, BRADFORD, ROOST, WATKINS, TIPPETT
01/04/50	TORQUAY UNITED	A	2-0	16732	WEARE	WATKINS	FOX	SAMPSON	WARREN	PITT	PETHERBRIDGE	PITT	BRADFORD	ROOST	PETHERBRIDGE	HODGES 2, PARSONS
07/04/50	ALDERSHOT	H	0-3	9698	WEARE	WATKINS	FOX	SAMPSON	WARREN	JONES	HODGES	BRADFORD	LAMBDEN	ROOST	BUSH	ROOST 2, TIPPETT
08/04/50	EXETER CITY	A	0-2	9622	WEARE	WATKINS	FOX	SAMPSON	WARREN	JONES	HODGES	BRADFORD	PARSONS	JAMES	PETHERBRIDGE	PETHERBRIDGE, WATLING
10/04/50	NOTTINGHAM FOREST	H	1-0	12631	WEARE	WATKINS	FOX	PITT	WARREN	JONES	TIPPETT	BRADFORD	ROOST	JAMES	BUSH	PETHERBRIDGE, HODGES
17/04/50	EXETER CITY	H	0-2	10631	WEARE	WATKINS	FOX	PITT	WARREN	JONES	PETHERBRIDGE	BRADFORD	PARSONS	WATKINS	PETHERBRIDGE	
22/04/50	NORTHAMPTON TOWN	A	5-1	8173	WEARE	WATKINS	FOX	PITT	WARREN	McCOURT	PETHERBRIDGE	BRADFORD	ROOST	HODGES	LOCKIER	HODGES 2, PARSONS
24/04/50	NORWICH CITY	H	3-0	11780	WEARE	BAMFORD	FOX	PITT	WARREN	McCOURT	HODGES	BRADFORD	PARSONS	HODGES	LOCKIER	
29/04/50	NEWPORT COUNTY	A	3-2	9252	WEARE	BAMFORD	FOX	PITT	WARREN	McCOURT	HODGES	BRADFORD	PARSONS	ROOST	BUSH	
01/05/50	NORTHAMPTON TOWN	H	1-0	—	WEARE	BAMFORD	FOX	PITT	WARREN	McARTHUR	PETHERBRIDGE	BRADFORD	PARSONS	HODGES	BUSH	
06/05/50	READING	A	0-2	—	WEARE	BAMFORD	FOX	PITT	WARREN	McARTHUR	PETHERBRIDGE	HODGES	PARSONS	WATKINS	WATLING	

FA CUP

Date	Opposition	H/A	Score	ATT	G	2	3	4	5	6	7	8	9	10	11	GOALSCORERS
26/11/49	SWINDON TOWN	A	0-1	19640	WEARE	BAMFORD	FOX	PITT	WARREN	McARTHUR	PETHERBRIDGE	HODGES	LAMBDEN	JAMES	WATLING	LAMBDEN

GLOUCESTERSHIRE CUP FINAL

Date	Opposition	H/A	Score	ATT	G	2	3	4	5	6	7	8	9	10	11	GOALSCORERS
13/05/50	BRISTOL CITY	A	0-2	16560	LILEY	BAMFORD	FOX	PITT	WARREN	McARTHUR	TIPPETT	HODGES	LAMBDEN	JAMES	WATLING	PARSONS

Appearances

PLAYERS	APP	GLS
BAMFORD H	39	
BRADFORD G	18	3
BUSH B	22	1
FOX G	42	
HODGES L	23	5
JAMES A	16	5
JONES R	5	1
LAMBDEN V	20	6
LILEY H	2	
LOCKIER M	2	
McARTHUR W		
McCOURT F	32	
MORGAN J	12	1
PARSONS E	5	2
PETHERBRIDGE G	26	4
PITT J	40	
ROOST W	28	13
SAMPSON P	4	
TIPPETT M	2	2
WARREN R	42	1
WATKINS B	7	1
WATLING J	26	5
WEARE J	28	

However, developments off the field were drawing attention away from the club's performances. Five directors, Bert Hoare, Jim Bissicks, Eric Lloyd, George Humphreys junior and Ernest Smith were distancing themselves from the three with interests in the greyhound company, Con Stevens, John Hare and Lew Champeny. A number of disagreements, notably the role of Rovers at Eastville and the knock-on effects of the 'no buy, no sell' policy, dropped on 1 February, had been fuelled by poor on-field performances. The appointment of a new manager had brought these points to a head. Although Tann's side was now achieving more positive results, the situation with the board of directors continued to deteriorate.

The spring of 1950 witnessed two key developments in the saga. The chairman and vice-chairman, Stevens and Hare, in line with their interests regarding the Bristol Greyhound Racing Association, were relieved of their positions on 21 March. The greyhound company had hitherto handled Rovers' accounts and this task was now taken on by club secretary John Gummow. On 22 March Lloyd became chairman with Hoare as his deputy. In a separate development, an FA Commission met in Bristol on the final day of the month and subsequently fined Rovers £250 after examining the club's books. The greyhound company was instructed to dispose of its controlling interest in the football club and the former secretary, Charles Ferrari, was banned from football management.

As the season drew to a close, the situation appeared to be resolved. In order to lose its controlling interest, the greyhound company sold 400 shares of £1 each, which Mr Hare held as their representative in his capacity as a private individual. In anticipation that the 'non-greyhound' directors were likely to be removed from office, the directors secured the appointment of three new board members. Hampden Alpass, a figure already well-respected in football and cricket circles, Syd Gamlin and Dr Matt Nicholson, gave no promises or undertakings and were duly elected on 18 May, with Alpass as chairman. Sure enough, Jim Bissicks disposed of enough shares to disqualify him from the board, while Hoare, Lloyd, Humphreys and Smith were removed through a poll vote at a shareholders' meeting eight days later. Normal boardroom relations gradually returned, but the question of Rovers' relationship with the greyhound company continued unabated until the club's departure from Eastville in 1986.

There was Rovers interest in the FA Cup final, for a former Eastville favourite, Phil Taylor, was in the Liverpool side beaten 2-0 by Arsenal. Rovers' season was completed by defeat in the Gloucestershire Cup final to a couple of first-half goals from Bristol City's Sid Williams. The attendance of 16,560 brought gate receipts of £1,150 and represents the highest crowd ever to watch a Gloucestershire Cup tie at Ashton Gate. Blackburn Rovers attracted a crowd of 13,349 to Eastville for a January friendly in which Tony James and George Petherbridge scored twice apiece. On 31 July 1950 Rovers reported an annual profit of £2,574.

1950/51

While Rovers' financial affairs continued to come under scrutiny, the side's performances on the field under manager Bert Tann still impressed. Sixth place in Division Three (South) was a fine end-of-season position and a first-ever FA Cup quarter-final, through a cup run that earned the club £5,754, was a major achievement. Rovers' exploits fired the imagination of the success-starved Bristol sporting public. During the summer of 1950, the board had waived its 'no buy, no sell' doctrine to allow two transfers to take place. Goalkeeper Bert Hoyle was signed from Exeter City for £350, while Frank McCourt was sold for £2,000 to Manchester City, where he won 6 Northern Ireland caps. Len Hodges moved on a free transfer to Swansea Town, while veteran wing-half Wally McArthur retired to become assistant trainer.

This season is, of course, primarily remembered for the scintillating FA Cup run that took the club further in the competition than ever before. It was slow in starting, for Rovers required three games to dispose of obdurate non-League Llanelli in the first round. Rovers and Llanelli each played in 11 FA Cup matches in 1950/51, more than any other competing club. The Welsh side boasted Jock Stein, later an influential International manager with Scotland, at centre-half, while their right-half Len Emanuel was well known to the Eastville crowd. Once Rovers had won the second replay 3-1 at

Bristol Rovers 1950/51. Back row: Jack Pitt, Les Edwards, Harry Bamford, Bert Hoyle, Geoff Fox, Peter Sampson, Bert Williams (Trainer). Front row: Bryan Bush, Geoff Bradford, Vic Lambden, Ray Warren, Jimmy Morgan, Josser Watling

100,000 people besiege Stapleton Road in search of tickets for Rovers' historic FA Cup quarter-final replay with Newcastle United

Ninian Park, they still required three more games before disposing of Gillingham 2-1 in appalling weather at White Hart Lane with Ray Warren converting a penalty five minutes from time. The Gills were enjoying their first season back in the Football League after failing to be re-elected in 1938.

Over 13,000 saw the third-round clash with Aldershot. Once Vic Lambden had given Rovers the lead after only eight seconds, it was plain sailing and the 5-1 victory incorporated a Lambden hat-trick. More than 26,000 saw Rovers win at Division Two Luton Town in the next round, George Petherbridge scoring the winning goal. Cup fever gripped Bristol and a new ground record of 31,660, producing receipts of £2,600, gathered at Eastville for the visit of Hull City. The Division Two visitors fielded the veteran former England International Raich Carter and the future England manager Don Revie as their inside-forwards, but two goals from Josser Watling helped give Rovers a convincing 3-0 victory and a place in the quarter-finals for the first time in the club's history. Watling's first followed a goalmouth scramble after 26 minutes and his second, 10 minutes after half-time, crashed in off the crossbar. A quarter of an hour from time, victory was sealed when Roost set up Lambden for the third.

On 24 February 1951 Rovers ground out a goalless draw with Newcastle United in the FA Cup quarter-final at St James' Park. The attendance at this game, 62,787, which produced £7,561 in gate receipts remains the largest ever at a football match involving Bristol Rovers. Around 5,000 Rovers supporters had witnessed this momentous game, but some 100,000 queued at Eastville two days later for tickets for the Wednesday afternoon replay. A line of policemen was deployed to keep about 50,000 people out of Eastville car park as soon as it became evident how over-subscribed the game had become, while His Majesty's Cinema was turned into a medical treatment station. As it was, a number of

Date	Opponent	H/A	Res	ATT	1 GC	2	3	4	5	6	7	8	9	10	11	GOALSCORERS
19/08/50	SWINDON TOWN	H	1-0	19057	HOYLE	BAMFORD	FOX	PITT	WARREN	SAMPSON	PETHERBRIDGE	JAMES	LAMBDEN	ROOST	BUSH	BILLINGTON og
23/08/50	ALDERSHOT	A	1-1	8812	HOYLE	BAMFORD	FOX	PITT	WARREN	SAMPSON	PETHERBRIDGE	JAMES	LAMBDEN	ROOST	BUSH	BRADFORD
26/08/50	COLCHESTER UNITED	A	0-0	13687	HOYLE	BAMFORD	FOX	PITT	WARREN	SAMPSON	PETHERBRIDGE	BRADFORD	LAMBDEN	ROOST	BUSH	
30/08/50	ALDERSHOT	H	3-0	10282	HOYLE	BAMFORD	FOX	PITT	WARREN	SAMPSON	PETHERBRIDGE	BRADFORD	LAMBDEN	ROOST	BUSH	BRADFORD, ROOST, BRADFORD
02/09/50	BRISTOL CITY	A	0-1	28168	HOYLE	BAMFORD	FOX	PITT	WARREN	SAMPSON	PETHERBRIDGE	BRADFORD	LAMBDEN	ROOST	BUSH	
09/09/50	GILLINGHAM	H	3-0	14414	HOYLE	BAMFORD	FOX	PITT	WARREN	SAMPSON	PETHERBRIDGE	BRADFORD	LAMBDEN	ROOST	BUSH	BRADFORD, LAMBDEN, ROOST
09/09/50	CRYSTAL PALACE	A	3-0	16904	HOYLE	BAMFORD	FOX	PITT	WARREN	SAMPSON	PETHERBRIDGE	BRADFORD	LAMBDEN	ROOST	BUSH	HOYLE
13/09/50	GILLINGHAM	A	0-1	12293	HOYLE	BAMFORD	FOX	PITT	WARREN	SAMPSON	PETHERBRIDGE	BRADFORD	LAMBDEN	ROOST	BUSH	
16/09/50	CRYSTAL PALACE	H	2-2	11716	HOYLE	BAMFORD	FOX	PITT	WARREN	SAMPSON	PETHERBRIDGE	BRADFORD	LAMBDEN	ROOST	MURPHY	LAMBDEN 2
23/09/50	BRIGHTON & HOVE ALBION	A	1-0	9518	HOYLE	BAMFORD	FOX	PITT	WARREN	SAMPSON	PETHERBRIDGE	BRADFORD	LAMBDEN	ROOST	MURPHY	LAMBDEN
30/09/50	NEWPORT COUNTY	H	0-2	22944	HOYLE	BAMFORD	FOX	PITT	WARREN	SAMPSON	PETHERBRIDGE	BRADFORD	LAMBDEN	ROOST	MURPHY	
07/10/50	NORWICH CITY	A	2-0	18074	HOYLE	BAMFORD	FOX	PITT	WARREN	SAMPSON	PETHERBRIDGE	BRADFORD	LAMBDEN	ROOST	BUSH	MEYER, LAMBDEN
14/10/50	BOURNEMOUTH	H	2-0	11000	HOYLE	BAMFORD	FOX	PITT	WARREN	SAMPSON	PETHERBRIDGE	MEYER	LAMBDEN	ROOST	BUSH	ROOST W
21/10/50	EXETER CITY	A	4-1	19614	HOYLE	BAMFORD	FOX	PITT	WARREN	SAMPSON	PETHERBRIDGE	MEYER	LAMBDEN	ROOST	BUSH	LAMBDEN, ROOST
28/10/50	SOUTHEND UNITED	H	2-0	16092	HOYLE	BAMFORD	FOX	PITT	WARREN	SAMPSON	PETHERBRIDGE	BRADFORD	LAMBDEN	ROOST	BUSH	PETHERBRIDGE, LAMBDEN, ROOST 2
04/11/50	READING	A	3-1	29654	HOYLE	BAMFORD	FOX	PITT	WARREN	SAMPSON	PETHERBRIDGE	BRADFORD	LAMBDEN	ROOST	BUSH	PETHERBRIDGE, BRADFORD
11/11/50	PLYMOUTH ARGYLE	H	3-2	15000	HOYLE	BAMFORD	FOX	PITT	WARREN	SAMPSON	PETHERBRIDGE	BRADFORD	LAMBDEN	ROOST	BUSH	PETHERBRIDGE 2, BRADFORD
18/11/50	IPSWICH TOWN	A	2-1	15003	HOYLE	BAMFORD	FOX	PITT	WARREN	SAMPSON	PETHERBRIDGE	BRADFORD	LAMBDEN	ROOST	WATLING	PETHERBRIDGE, BRADFORD
16/12/50	LEYTON ORIENT	H	2-1	7030	HOYLE	BAMFORD	FOX	PITT	WARREN	SAMPSON	PETHERBRIDGE	LAMBDEN	ROOST	MORGAN	WATLING	MORGAN, PITT
23/12/50	SWINDON TOWN	A	2-1	17721	HOYLE	BAMFORD	FOX	PITT	WARREN	SAMPSON	PETHERBRIDGE	JAMES	LAMBDEN	ROOST	WATLING	PETHERBRIDGE
25/12/50	COLCHESTER UNITED	H	0-0	10662	HOYLE	BAMFORD	FOX	PITT	WARREN	SAMPSON	PETHERBRIDGE	JAMES	LAMBDEN	ROOST	WATLING	
26/12/50	PORT VALE	A	2-0	13250	HOYLE	BAMFORD	FOX	PITT	WARREN	SAMPSON	LAMBDEN	BRADFORD	ROOST	MORGAN	BUSH	BRADFORD, ROOST
30/12/50	PORT VALE	H	2-0	22409	HOYLE	BAMFORD	FOX	PITT	WARREN	SAMPSON	PETHERBRIDGE	BRADFORD	LAMBDEN	ROOST	WATLING	BRADFORD, LAMBDEN
13/01/51	BRISTOL CITY	H	0-1	31518	HOYLE	BAMFORD	FOX	PITT	WARREN	SAMPSON	PETHERBRIDGE	BRADFORD	LAMBDEN	ROOST	WATLING	
17/01/51	TORQUAY UNITED	A	2-1	10632	HOYLE	BAMFORD	FOX	PITT	WARREN	SAMPSON	PETHERBRIDGE	LAMBDEN	ROOST	MORGAN	WATLING	ROOST, McGUINNESS og
20/01/51	BRIGHTON & HOVE ALBION	H	3-2	3918	HOYLE	BAMFORD	FOX	PITT	WARREN	SAMPSON	PETHERBRIDGE	LAMBDEN	MORGAN	WATLING		LAMBDEN, WATLING, WARREN
31/01/51	TORQUAY UNITED	H	1-1	12000	HOYLE	BAMFORD	FOX	PITT	WARREN	SAMPSON	PETHERBRIDGE	BRADFORD	LAMBDEN	ROOST	WATLING	BRADFORD
03/02/51	NEWPORT COUNTY	A	1-2	4000	HOYLE	BAMFORD	FOX	EDWARDS	WARREN	SAMPSON	LAMBDEN	BRADFORD	ROOST	WATLING		BAMFORD
17/02/51	WALSALL	H	2-1	25294	HOYLE	BAMFORD	FOX	PITT	WARREN	SAMPSON	PETHERBRIDGE	BRADFORD	LAMBDEN	MORGAN	WATLING	MORGAN, BRADFORD
03/03/51	EXETER CITY	H	3-1	8000	HOYLE	BAMFORD	FOX	PITT	WARREN	SAMPSON	PETHERBRIDGE	BRADFORD	LAMBDEN	ROOST	WATLING	BRADFORD, LAMBDEN, WARREN pen
10/03/51	SOUTHEND UNITED	A	2-1	10485	HOYLE	BAMFORD	FOX	PITT	WARREN	SAMPSON	PETHERBRIDGE	BRADFORD	LAMBDEN	ROOST	WATLING	BRADFORD, LAMBDEN
14/03/51	BOURNEMOUTH	A	0-2	13806	HOYLE	BAMFORD	FOX	PITT	WARREN	SAMPSON	PETHERBRIDGE	BRADFORD	LAMBDEN	ROOST	WATLING	
17/03/51	READING	H	4-0	6796	HOYLE	BAMFORD	FOX	PITT	WARREN	SAMPSON	PETHERBRIDGE	BRADFORD	LAMBDEN	ROOST	WATLING	BUSH, BRADFORD, LAMBDEN 2
24/03/51	PLYMOUTH ARGYLE	A	0-2	20003	HOYLE	BAMFORD	FOX	PITT	WARREN	SAMPSON	PETHERBRIDGE	BRADFORD	LAMBDEN	ROOST	WATLING	
26/03/51	NOTTINGHAM FOREST	H	1-2	9177	HOYLE	BAMFORD	FOX	PITT	WARREN	SAMPSON	BUSH	BRADFORD	LAMBDEN	ROOST	WATLING	BRADFORD
31/03/51	IPSWICH TOWN	H	0-1	21066	HOYLE	BAMFORD	FOX	PITT	WARREN	SAMPSON	BUSH	BRADFORD	LAMBDEN	ROOST	WATLING	
07/04/51	LEYTON ORIENT	A	0-1	27157	HOYLE	BAMFORD	FOX	PITT	WARREN	SAMPSON	BUSH	BRADFORD	LAMBDEN	ROOST	WATLING	
11/04/51	WALSALL	A	1-1	16085	HOYLE	BAMFORD	FOX	PITT	WARREN	SAMPSON	BUSH	SAMPSON	LAMBDEN	ROOST	WATLING	SAMPSON
14/04/51	NORTHAMPTON TOWN	H	3-1	8000	HOYLE	BAMFORD	FOX	PITT	WARREN	SAMPSON	PETHERBRIDGE	BRADFORD	LAMBDEN	ROOST	WATLING	BRADFORD 2, WARREN
19/04/51	WATFORD	H	0-1	10085	HOYLE	BAMFORD	FOX	PITT	WARREN	SAMPSON	PETHERBRIDGE	WATLING	LAMBDEN	ROOST	WATLING	WATLING
21/04/51	MILLWALL	A	1-1	13806	HOYLE	BAMFORD	WATKINS	PITT	WARREN	SAMPSON	PETHERBRIDGE	WATLING	LAMBDEN	ROOST	WATLING	WATLING
23/04/51	MILLWALL	H	3-0	11782	HOYLE	BAMFORD	WATKINS	PITT	WARREN	SAMPSON	BRADFORD	LAMBDEN	ROOST	WATLING		WARREN pen, LAMBDEN, BRADFORD
28/04/51	NORWICH CITY	H	3-3	12957	HOYLE	BAMFORD	FOX	EDWARDS	WARREN	SAMPSON	PETHERBRIDGE	BRADFORD	LAMBDEN	ROOST	PETHERBRIDGE	PETHERBRIDGE, BRADFORD
30/04/51	NOTTINGHAM FOREST	A	0-2	28355	HOYLE	BAMFORD	FOX	PITT	WARREN	SAMPSON	PETHERBRIDGE	BRADFORD	LAMBDEN	ROOST	WATLING	
05/05/51	NORTHAMPTON TOWN	A	0-1	10832	HOYLE	WATKINS	FOX	PITT	WARREN	WATKINS	BUSH	PITT	LAMBDEN	ROOST	WATLING	

FA CUP

Date	Opponent	H/A	Res	ATT	1	2	3	4	5	6	7	8	9	10	11	GOALSCORERS
25/11/50	LLANELLY	H	1-1	16594	HOYLE	BAMFORD	FOX	PITT	WARREN	SAMPSON	PETHERBRIDGE	BRADFORD	LAMBDEN	ROOST	BUSH	PETHERBRIDGE
28/11/50	LLANELLY	A	3-1	12943	HOYLE	BAMFORD	FOX	PITT	WARREN	SAMPSON	PETHERBRIDGE	BRADFORD	LAMBDEN	ROOST	BUSH	BUSH
09/12/50	GILLINGHAM	N	2-2	9044	HOYLE	BAMFORD	FOX	PITT	WARREN	SAMPSON	PETHERBRIDGE	BRADFORD	LAMBDEN	ROOST	BUSH	PITT, PETHERBRIDGE, BRADFORD
13/12/50	GILLINGHAM	N	1-1	14420	HOYLE	BAMFORD	FOX	PITT	WARREN	SAMPSON	PETHERBRIDGE	BRADFORD	LAMBDEN	ROOST	BUSH	BUSH, LAMBDEN
18/12/50	GILLINGHAM	N	2-1	10642	HOYLE	BAMFORD	FOX	PITT	WARREN	SAMPSON	PETHERBRIDGE	BRADFORD	LAMBDEN	GOUGH	BUSH	GOUGH
10/01/51	ALDERSHOT	H	5-1	3924	HOYLE	BAMFORD	FOX	PITT	WARREN	SAMPSON	PETHERBRIDGE	BRADFORD	LAMBDEN	ROOST	BUSH	BRADFORD, WARREN pen
27/01/51	LUTON TOWN	A	2-1	13429	HOYLE	BAMFORD	FOX	PITT	WARREN	SAMPSON	PETHERBRIDGE	BRADFORD	LAMBDEN	ROOST	WATLING	LAMBDEN 3, ROOST, PETHERBRIDGE
10/02/51	HULL CITY	H	3-0	26386	HOYLE	BAMFORD	FOX	PITT	WARREN	SAMPSON	PETHERBRIDGE	BRADFORD	LAMBDEN	ROOST	WATLING	LAMBDEN, PETHERBRIDGE
24/02/51	NEWCASTLE UNITED	H	0-0	31660	HOYLE	BAMFORD	FOX	PITT	WARREN	SAMPSON	PETHERBRIDGE	BRADFORD	LAMBDEN	ROOST	WATLING	WARREN pen, LAMBDEN, BRADFORD
28/02/51	NEWCASTLE UNITED	A	1-3	62787	HOYLE	BAMFORD	FOX	PITT	WARREN	SAMPSON	PETHERBRIDGE	BRADFORD	LAMBDEN	ROOST	WATLING	BRADFORD

GLOUCESTERSHIRE CUP FINAL

Date	Opponent	H/A	Res	ATT	1	2	3	4	5	6	7	8	9	10	11	GOALSCORERS
12/05/51	BRISTOL CITY	H	1-1	30074	HOYLE	BAMFORD	FOX	PITT	WARREN	SAMPSON	PETHERBRIDGE	BRADFORD	LAMBDEN	ROOST	BUSH	LAMBDEN

PLAYERS	APP	GLS
BAMFORD H	45	
BRADFORD G	37	15
BUSH B	28	1
EDWARDS L	3	
FOX G	40	
HOYLE H	46	
JAMES A	5	
LAMBDEN V	46	20
MEYER B	2	1
MORGAN J	4	2
MURPHY W	3	
PETHERBRIDGE G	36	6
PITT J	44	1
ROOST W	43	7
SAMPSON P	46	
WARREN E	46	4
WATKINS B	7	
WATLING J	25	3
OWN GOALS		2

The cup replay at Eastville. Geoff Fox diverts a shot from Newcastle's Taylor past a despairing Hoyle for the equalizer. United went on to win 3-1 and eventually lifted the cup at Wembley

businesses shut, supporters tuned in to live wireless commentary and 30,074 crammed into Eastville for the game itself. Fifteen minutes in, amid scenes of incredulous delight, Geoff Bradford scored a fine opportunist goal to give Rovers a surprise lead, prompting strains of the crowd's favourite song 'Goodnight Irene' to echo around the ground. By half-time, however, goals from Ernie Taylor, whose shot deflected in off Geoff Fox, Charlie Crowe and the legendary Jackie Milburn gave the Magpies victory, despite a spirited second-half Rovers revival. Newcastle United went on to win the Cup, the same 11 players who had faced Rovers twice in four days defeating Blackpool at Wembley.

Off the field, Rovers were subjected to a lengthy Board of Trade enquiry under Section 164 of the Companies Act of 1948 into the club's affairs since 1932, published as a report in 1951. This document gives evidence of investigation into serious allegations regarding the relationship between the football club and greyhound companies. In particular, the modification of the 1932 lease in January 1934 and the subsequent hasty sale of Eastville to the greyhound company came in for close scrutiny. Inspectors interviewed Sir Stanley Rous, the Secretary of the Football Association and Isidore Kerman, the chairman of the British Greyhound Racing Association, in London on 14 September 1950. There was also criticism concerning a written report by Hampden Alpass and John Hare, submitted at a board meeting on 17 August 1950, into Rovers' rights as tenants at Eastville. It was clear that no such report had been requested and Syd Gamlin expressed astonishment that this had taken place secretly. Gamlin wished for it to be put on record that 'he considered it improper for this to have taken place without a definite resolution by the Board' (Board of Trade report, 1951, P20, Section IV ii). As previously in 1940, rash decisions by individual directors had serious repercussions for the club. The Board of Trade enquiry found sufficient irregularities for the football and greyhound companies to be separated and Gamlin was removed from the board on 25 April 1951. Rovers claimed the greyhound company owed them £844, but the auditors declared that, of a total of £2,675 payable on work to the stadium, including turnstiles, plumbing and levelling of the car park, Rovers should pay £2,111.

Throughout the 1950/51 season, one key to Rovers' success was their ability to retain a consistent side. Apart from six players who appeared in no more than seven games each, Rovers relied on just 12 regulars. Goalkeeper Bert Hoyle, half-backs Ray Warren and Peter Sampson and top scorer Vic Lambden, the first post-war Rovers player to reach 20 League goals for the season, played in all 58 League, FA Cup and Gloucestershire Cup games. A settled defence was completed by full-backs Harry Bamford and Geoff Fox and right-half Jackie Pitt, who between them, missed just 9 League games all season. In the forward line, Geoff Bradford and Bill Roost ably supported Lambden, with Petherbridge, Watling and Roost competing for the remaining places. Jack Weare, once a fixture in the Rovers goal, could not break into the side and was allowed to join Swansea Town in March 1951.

In completing the season in sixth place, Rovers fell back on an excellent autumnal run of nine wins and three draws. Following defeat at Norwich City in September, the side was unbeaten until going down to the veteran Fred Kurz's 15-yard drive after half an hour at Crystal Palace in January. One November victory was over Orient, for whom the future Rovers left-half 'Chick' Cairney was making his first League appearance. Eastville was developing into a stronghold, where Rovers won 13 and drew three of their first 16 home League matches. Indeed, it was the penultimate League game before Rovers' proud unbeaten home record finally fell to runaway champions Nottingham Forest. Between November 1949 and April 1953 only five home League games out of 81 were lost. There were five-figure crowds at every home match in 1950/51 at an average of 17,763, with the highest at a League game being the 31,518 that saw Lambden's double strike defeat Bristol City in December.

With Colchester United newly elected to the Football League, Rovers had the honour of being the first visitors to Layer Road, where they fought out a goalless draw. It was the same result on Christmas Day, when Rovers and Port Vale met in a League fixture played at Stoke City's Victoria Ground. Swindon Town were beaten 2-1 after Jimmy Bain's goal had put the Robins in front. The home game with Norwich City in February was abandoned after an hour with the pitch waterlogged, after a Lambden brace had put Rovers 2-1 ahead. When it was replayed in April, Rovers overcame a half-time deficit to claim a point in an exciting 3-3 draw, thanks to second-half goals from Lambden and Bradford. Rovers' final five games were all at home, Nottingham Forest, through first-half headers from Johnny Love and Tom Johnson, being the only away side to win.

For the home draw with Ipswich Town in March, when Peter Sampson scored his first goal for the club, Rovers faced their oldest opponent in League history. As goalkeeper, the visitors fielded Mick Burns who, at 42 years 239 days, set a record in games featuring Rovers that remains unsurpassed. A familiar face came back to haunt Rovers in January, for the scorer of Torquay United's 20th-minute goal at Eastville in a 1-1 draw was Wilf Whitfield, who had made his Rovers debut in November 1938 and had last scored on that ground in League football almost 12 years earlier.

On 4 November, Plymouth Argyle arrived at Eastville with an accordion player, who performed contemporary songs around the edge of the pitch prior to the start of the match. One of these songs was Huddie William 'Lead Belly' Ledbetter's 'Goodnight Irene', an old mixed-race song emanating from 1880s Cincinnati, Ohio and first recorded in July 1933. It was sung by Argyle supporters because The Weavers, featuring Pete Seeger, had in 1951 released their own version. As Argyle took a first-half lead, their supporters used the song to taunt home fans. Three Rovers goals in eight second-half minutes provoked a rendition of 'Goodnight Argyle' and the song soon caught on. When Rovers played at Newcastle in the FA Cup quarter-final, the Magpies bowed to pressure and played the Jo Stafford rendition of the song during the pre-match build-up. Lead Belly, born on a plantation near Mooringsport in Louisiana on 20 January 1888, had died in New York on 6 December 1949, so his fame as the self-professed 'king of all 12-string guitar players' was almost entirely posthumous. 'The murderous old minstrel Lead Belly' (*Time* magazine, 14.08.1950), who had spent time in jail for homicide, claimed to have learned 'Goodnight Irene' in 1918 from his uncle Terrell Ledbetter, who had encouraged his early musical interest. As Rovers' FA Cup run gained momentum, 'Goodnight Irene' had been swiftly adopted as a club anthem, sung by generations of Rovers supporters ever since.

All in all, 1950/51 was a season to offer encouragement to Bristol Rovers. A consistent and efficient team was riding high in Division Three (South) and had reached the FA Cup quarter-finals. Manager Bert Tann had successfully taken on the task of maintaining Rovers' post-war promotion push. Despite the traumas of the Board of Trade enquiry, financial irregularities appeared to be a thing of the past as the club sailed into less choppy waters. The considerable support at Eastville was looking forward to many enjoyable years ahead. They were not to be disappointed.

1951/52

On the back of FA Cup success, Rovers built a side that would fulfil its potential in the spring of 1953. The advantage of hindsight is, of course, the wisdom to see what a springboard the 1951/52 season gave to the Championship-winning side. Harry Liley, the veteran goalkeeper, had joined Bath City, while Howard Radford and Andy Micklewright were the only signings to make a sizeable impact on Rovers' promotion push. Radford was initially Bert Hoyle's understudy, but became a key ingredient in Rovers' Division Two side, playing in the League team until 1962. Micklewright played sporadically in this and the promotion season, scoring from inside-right in the large win over Walsall in April 1952. Harry Bamford retained his place in the side following his powerful defensive play during the summer Football Association tour of Australia, in the course of which he had scored 3 goals. Following an inspection by a team from St Ives Research Centre, Bingley, on 6 February 1951, the pitch at Eastville was treated with nitro-chalk at the rate of half an ounce per square yard to counteract the acidity of the turf and allow for an improved playing surface in 1951/52.

Football was on the up in Bristol, with Bristol City also building a side that would reach Division Two. In addition to defeating Division One Preston North End in the FA

Bristol Rovers 1951/52. Back row: Jack Pitt, Harry Bamford, Ray Warren, Bert Hoyle, Geoff Fox, Peter Sampson, George Petherbridge. Front row: Bryan Bush, Geoff Bradford, Vic Lambden, Bill Roost, Josser Watling

Cup, Rovers scored an unprecedented and still unequalled 60 goals at home in League matches this season. Only three times in the club's history has a Rovers team scored five goals in two consecutive League games and two of these instances took place in 1951/52. Rovers scored a club record 22 League goals in April, more even than the 20 of October 1982. With both professional clubs performing well in an era of high attendances, it is little surprise that the derby at Eastville in January drew the highest crowd at any Division Three (South) game that season. The 34,612 constituted a new ground record, since bettered only once and saw goals from Geoff Bradford and George Petherbridge give Rovers a 2-0 victory.

The season began slowly for Rovers. Single-goal defeats at Walsall, to a Hugh Evans header after just 26 minutes, and at home to Watford were interspersed with draws. When Shrewsbury Town visited Eastville in August, Harold Robbins became the first opponent for more than 20 years to score a League hat-trick on that ground, but Rovers still scrambled a 3-3 draw. Tommy Docherty, a namesake of the highly successful manager, scored Norwich City's goal at Eastville to earn a draw, the second of three consecutive seasons he scored against Rovers. Although Rovers had, in 48 hours in September, beaten Aldershot 5-1 and Crystal Palace 4-0, Vic Lambden scoring twice in each game, there was little sign of the success to come. A draw at Millwall on 10 November was the seventh consecutive League game without a win and left Rovers with just five victories in their opening 17 matches.

Manager Bert Tann was not one to panic and it is no coincidence that Rovers fielded an unchanged side for the following game. The side had not won at home for more than two months, but consecutive five-goal victories were to turn the season on its head. With a predominantly Bristol-born and Rovers-bred line-up, the club was to enjoy a hugely successful 18 months that took the club to previously unattained heights.

In front of the hugely popular Bert Hoyle, whom fans showered with oranges after he rashly admitted his fondness for them, was the ever-reliable pairing of Harry Bamford and Geoff Fox. It is unlikely that Rovers will ever again find such a dependable full-back partnership. Captain Ray Warren, at centre-half, was flanked by Jackie Pitt and Peter Sampson. Crucially, Fox, Pitt and Sampson were ever-presents in 1951/52 and the entire back five appeared in every game in the championship season. Also an ever-present was George Petherbridge, whose dazzling right-wing skills were switched to the left the following year. Inside forwards Bill Roost and Barrie Meyer made significant contributions to the side in both seasons. Josser Watling played well but did not score and his replacement, John McIlvenny, was to be the only major change.

Undeniably, the fact that Rovers could boast two hugely prolific goalscorers was a key factor in the side's success. Lambden had proved his pedigree, but continued in fine style. His four goals against Colchester United made him the only player to have scored so many times twice in the League for Rovers. His club-record 29 League goals in 1951/52 were followed by 24 more the following year when, as an ever-present, he helped Rovers towards great success. Bradford, on the other hand, was just beginning to prove his worth and his 26 League goals, including 10 in the final 8 games, served as a prelude to his 33 in 1952/53.

Indeed, goalscoring was not generally a problem to Rovers, who scored 89 in finishing seventh in Division Three (South). The visit of Brighton on 17 November saw Lambden and Bradford on the scoresheet in a 5-0 win. In the very next game, Petherbridge scored four times and became the sixth Rovers player to achieve this feat in the League, as Rovers defeated Torquay United by the same scoreline. He opened the scoring after four minutes and scored with a header and three right-footed shots. Rovers also beat Port Vale 4-1 and scored three times at both Aldershot and Watford, both Lambden and Bradford scoring in all these games, before again hitting a purple patch over Easter. Roost scored twice on Easter Saturday, and Lambden, Bradford and Petherbridge once each, as Gillingham were beaten 5-0. Two days later, Colchester United, who had that week beaten Rovers at Layer Road, were taken apart by a rampant Rovers forward line. Lambden opened the scoring in the first minute, completed his hat-trick after 15 minutes and grabbed a fourth after half-time, with Bradford adding two more in a highly convincing 6-0 victory.

That Rovers did not achieve greater success in 1951/52 must be put down to a lack of consistency. The autumnal run of seven matches without a win was followed by a run of three points in six games around February and two straight defeats after the Colchester game. After November, Rovers still lost at home to the top two sides, Plymouth Argyle and Reading. In February, the side even went two games without scoring. Despite scoring five or more goals in six home matches, Rovers finished 14 points behind eventual champions Plymouth Argyle. There were some clear lessons to be learned and Tann would ensure that all that was required would be done.

FOOTBALL LEAGUE DIVISION THREE (SOUTH)

SEASON 1951/52

DATE	OPPONENT		SCORE	ATT	G 1	2	3	4	5	6	7	8	9	10	11	GOALSCORERS
18/08/51	WALSALL	A	0-1	10798	HOYLE	BAMFORD	FOX	PITT	WARREN	SAMPSON	PETHERBRIDGE	BRADFORD	LAMBDEN	MEYER	WATLING	
20/08/51	SWINDON TOWN	H	1-0	24275	HOYLE	BAMFORD	FOX	PITT	WARREN	SAMPSON	PETHERBRIDGE	BRADFORD	LAMBDEN	MEYER	WATLING	LAMBDEN
25/08/51	SHREWSBURY TOWN	H	3-3	20691	HOYLE	BAMFORD	FOX	PITT	WARREN	SAMPSON	PETHERBRIDGE	BRADFORD	PICKARD	MORGAN	BUSH	PICKARD, WARREN, LAMBDEN
29/08/51	SWINDON TOWN	A	0-0	20540	HOYLE	WATKINS	FOX	PITT	WARREN	SAMPSON	PETHERBRIDGE	BRADFORD	LAMBDEN	PICKARD	WATLING	
01/09/51	ALDERSHOT	H	5-1	17510	HOYLE	WATKINS	FOX	PITT	WARREN	SAMPSON	PETHERBRIDGE	BRADFORD	LAMBDEN	ROOST	BUSH	LAMBDEN 2, ROOST 2, BRADFORD
03/09/51	CRYSTAL PALACE	H	4-0	14467	HOYLE	WATKINS	FOX	PITT	WARREN	SAMPSON	PETHERBRIDGE	BRADFORD	LAMBDEN	MEYER	BUSH	LAMBDEN 2, MEYER, BUSH
08/09/51	WATFORD	A	0-1	20540	HOYLE	WATKINS	FOX	PITT	WARREN	SAMPSON	PETHERBRIDGE	BRADFORD	LAMBDEN	MEYER	BUSH	
12/09/51	CRYSTAL PALACE	A	1-0	10289	HOYLE	BAMFORD	FOX	PITT	WARREN	SAMPSON	PETHERBRIDGE	BRADFORD	LAMBDEN	MEYER	WATLING	PETHERBRIDGE
15/09/51	BRISTOL CITY	H	1-1	29782	HOYLE	BAMFORD	FOX	PITT	WARREN	SAMPSON	PETHERBRIDGE	BRADFORD	LAMBDEN	MEYER	BUSH	MEYER
22/09/51	PLYMOUTH ARGYLE	A	2-1	25893	HOYLE	BAMFORD	FOX	PITT	WARREN	SAMPSON	PETHERBRIDGE	BRADFORD	LAMBDEN	ROOST	WATLING	LAMBDEN, WARREN
29/09/51	NORWICH CITY	H	1-1	26022	HOYLE	BAMFORD	FOX	PITT	WARREN	SAMPSON	PETHERBRIDGE	BRADFORD	LAMBDEN	ROOST	WATLING	BRADFORD
06/10/51	NORTHAMPTON TOWN	A	2-2	20905	HOYLE	BAMFORD	FOX	PITT	WARREN	SAMPSON	PETHERBRIDGE	ROOST	LAMBDEN	MORGAN	WATLING	LAMBDEN, WARREN
13/10/51	READING	H	2-4	15175	HOYLE	BAMFORD	FOX	PITT	WARREN	SAMPSON	PETHERBRIDGE	ROOST	LAMBDEN	BRADFORD	WATLING	PETHERBRIDGE 2
20/10/51	NEWPORT COUNTY	A	1-1	17493	HOYLE	BAMFORD	FOX	PITT	WARREN	SAMPSON	PETHERBRIDGE	BRADFORD	LAMBDEN	ROOST	WATLING	PICKARD
27/10/51	SOUTHEND UNITED	H	1-2	12000	HOYLE	BAMFORD	FOX	PITT	WARREN	SAMPSON	TIPPETT	BRADFORD	LAMBDEN	ROOST	BUSH	PETHERBRIDGE, LAMBDEN
03/11/51	BOURNEMOUTH	A	1-2	17241	RADFORD	BAMFORD	FOX	PITT	WARREN	SAMPSON	PETHERBRIDGE	ROOST	LAMBDEN	BRADFORD	WATLING	ROOST
10/11/51	MILLWALL	H	1-1	23988	HOYLE	WATKINS	FOX	PITT	WARREN	SAMPSON	PETHERBRIDGE	ROOST	LAMBDEN	BRADFORD	WATLING	LAMBDEN
17/11/51	BRIGHTON & HOVE ALBION	H	5-0	18002	HOYLE	BAMFORD	FOX	PITT	WARREN	SAMPSON	PETHERBRIDGE	ROOST	LAMBDEN	BRADFORD	WATLING	LAMBDEN 2, PETHERBRIDGE,
01/12/51	TORQUAY UNITED	H	5-0	19338	HOYLE	BAMFORD	FOX	PITT	WARREN	SAMPSON	PETHERBRIDGE	ROOST	LAMBDEN	BRADFORD	WATLING	WARREN pen, ROOST
08/12/51	IPSWICH TOWN	A	2-1	9546	HOYLE	BAMFORD	FOX	PITT	WARREN	SAMPSON	PETHERBRIDGE	ROOST	LAMBDEN	BRADFORD	WATLING	PETHERBRIDGE 4, LAMBDEN
22/12/51	SHREWSBURY TOWN	A	1-2	7408	HOYLE	BAMFORD	FOX	PITT	WARREN	SAMPSON	PETHERBRIDGE	ROOST	LAMBDEN	BRADFORD	WATLING	PETHERBRIDGE, ROOST
25/12/51	PORT VALE	H	4-1	16691	HOYLE	BAMFORD	FOX	PITT	WARREN	SAMPSON	PETHERBRIDGE	ROOST	LAMBDEN	BRADFORD	WATLING	LAMBDEN 2, BRADFORD,
26/12/51	PORT VALE	A	1-1	16734	HOYLE	BAMFORD	FOX	PITT	WARREN	SAMPSON	PETHERBRIDGE	ROOST	LAMBDEN	BRADFORD	WATLING	LAMBDEN 2, PETHERBRIDGE,
29/12/51	ALDERSHOT	A	3-1	6019	HOYLE	BAMFORD	FOX	PITT	WARREN	SAMPSON	PETHERBRIDGE	BRADFORD	LAMBDEN	MORGAN	BUSH	BRADFORD
05/01/52	WATFORD	H	3-0	10664	HOYLE	BAMFORD	FOX	PITT	WARREN	SAMPSON	PETHERBRIDGE	ROOST	MORGAN	BRADFORD	WATLING	MORGAN
16/01/52	EXETER CITY	A	1-0	7088	HOYLE	BAMFORD	FOX	PITT	WARREN	SAMPSON	PETHERBRIDGE	ROOST	MORGAN	BRADFORD	BUSH	MORGAN
19/01/52	BRISTOL CITY	A	2-0	34612	HOYLE	BAMFORD	FOX	PITT	WARREN	SAMPSON	PETHERBRIDGE	ROOST	LAMBDEN	BRADFORD	WATLING	PITT, BRADFORD, LAMBDEN
26/01/52	PLYMOUTH ARGYLE	H	1-2	28937	HOYLE	BAMFORD	FOX	PITT	WARREN	SAMPSON	PETHERBRIDGE	ROOST	LAMBDEN	BRADFORD	WATLING	SAMPSON
02/02/52	LEYTON ORIENT	H	3-3	10000	RADFORD	BAMFORD	FOX	PITT	WARREN	SAMPSON	PETHERBRIDGE	WATKINS	PICKARD	MORGAN	WATLING	LAMBDEN, BRADFORD, MORGAN
07/02/52	NORWICH CITY	A	0-1	16420	HOYLE	BAMFORD	FOX	PITT	WARREN	SAMPSON	PETHERBRIDGE	ROOST	LAMBDEN	BRADFORD	WATLING	
16/02/52	NORTHAMPTON TOWN	H	0-2	11704	HOYLE	BAMFORD	FOX	PITT	WARREN	SAMPSON	PETHERBRIDGE	ROOST	LAMBDEN	BRADFORD	WATLING	
27/02/52	LEYTON ORIENT	A	1-0	7663	RADFORD	BAMFORD	FOX	PITT	WARREN	SAMPSON	PETHERBRIDGE	ROOST	LAMBDEN	BRADFORD	WATLING	BRADFORD
01/03/52	READING	A	1-2	21915	RADFORD	BAMFORD	FOX	PITT	WARREN	SAMPSON	PETHERBRIDGE	ROOST	LAMBDEN	BRADFORD	WATLING	PETHERBRIDGE, LAMBDEN
08/03/52	NEWPORT COUNTY	H	2-2	18000	RADFORD	BAMFORD	FOX	PITT	WARREN	SAMPSON	PETHERBRIDGE	MICKLEWRIGHT	LAMBDEN	BRADFORD	WATLING	WATLING, PETHERBRIDGE
15/03/52	SOUTHEND UNITED	A	2-0	14496	RADFORD	BAMFORD	FOX	PITT	WARREN	SAMPSON	PETHERBRIDGE	MICKLEWRIGHT	LAMBDEN	BRADFORD	WATLING	PETHERBRIDGE, LAMBDEN
22/03/52	BOURNEMOUTH	H	0-1	10239	RADFORD	BAMFORD	FOX	PITT	WARREN	SAMPSON	PETHERBRIDGE	ROOST	LAMBDEN	BRADFORD	WATLING	
29/03/52	MILLWALL	A	2-1	4666	RADFORD	BAMFORD	FOX	PITT	WARREN	SAMPSON	PETHERBRIDGE	ROOST	LAMBDEN	BRADFORD	TAYLOR	BRADFORD, PETHERBRIDGE
05/04/52	BRIGHTON & HOVE ALBION	A	1-1	14268	RADFORD	BAMFORD	FOX	PITT	WARREN	SAMPSON	PETHERBRIDGE	ROOST	LAMBDEN	BRADFORD	TAYLOR	BRADFORD
11/04/52	COLCHESTER UNITED	H	1-2	12440	RADFORD	BAMFORD	FOX	PITT	POWELL	SAMPSON	PETHERBRIDGE	ROOST	LAMBDEN	MORGAN	WATLING	MORGAN
12/04/52	GILLINGHAM	H	5-0	12877	RADFORD	BAMFORD	FOX	PITT	POWELL	SAMPSON	PETHERBRIDGE	ROOST	LAMBDEN	BRADFORD	WATLING	PITT, BRADFORD, LAMBDEN, BRADFORD, ROOST 2
14/04/52	COLCHESTER UNITED	A	6-0	10594	RADFORD	BAMFORD	FOX	PITT	POWELL	SAMPSON	PETHERBRIDGE	ROOST	LAMBDEN	BRADFORD	WATLING	BRADFORD, LAMBDEN, BRADFORD, MORGAN
19/04/52	TORQUAY UNITED	A	2-4	8259	RADFORD	BAMFORD	FOX	PITT	GREEN	SAMPSON	PETHERBRIDGE	ROOST	LAMBDEN	BRADFORD	WATLING	PETHERBRIDGE, LAMBDEN
23/04/52	GILLINGHAM	A	1-0	9000	RADFORD	BAMFORD	FOX	PITT	POWELL	SAMPSON	PETHERBRIDGE	ROOST	LAMBDEN	BRADFORD	WATLING	SAMPSON
26/04/52	IPSWICH TOWN	H	1-2	9213	RADFORD	BAMFORD	FOX	PITT	WARREN	SAMPSON	PETHERBRIDGE	ROOST	LAMBDEN	BRADFORD	WATLING	BRADFORD 2
28/04/52	WALSALL	H	5-1	12089	RADFORD	WATKINS	FOX	PITT	WARREN	SAMPSON	PETHERBRIDGE	MICKLEWRIGHT	LAMBDEN	BRADFORD	WATLING	BRADFORD 2, PETHERBRIDGE, MICKLEWRIGHT, LAMBDEN
01/05/52	EXETER CITY	H	2-2	9023	RADFORD	WATKINS	FOX	PITT	WARREN	SAMPSON	PETHERBRIDGE	MICKLEWRIGHT	LAMBDEN	BRADFORD	WATLING	LAMBDEN, BRADFORD

FA CUP

DATE	OPPONENT		SCORE	ATT	G 1	2	3	4	5	6	7	8	9	10	11	GOALSCORERS
24/11/51	KETTERING TOWN	H	3-1	18062	HOYLE	BAMFORD	FOX	PITT	WARREN	SAMPSON	PETHERBRIDGE	ROOST	LAMBDEN	BRADFORD	WATLING	LAMBDEN 2, BRADFORD
15/12/51	WEYMOUTH	H	2-0	27808	HOYLE	BAMFORD	FOX	PITT	WARREN	SAMPSON	PETHERBRIDGE	ROOST	LAMBDEN	BRADFORD	WATLING	LAMBDEN, BRADFORD
12/01/52	PRESTON NORTH END	H	2-0	30681	HOYLE	BAMFORD	FOX	PITT	WARREN	SAMPSON	PETHERBRIDGE	ROOST	LAMBDEN	BRADFORD	BUSH	LAMBDEN, PETHERBRIDGE
02/02/52	SOUTHEND UNITED	A	1-2	22424	RADFORD	BAMFORD	FOX	PITT	WARREN	SAMPSON	PETHERBRIDGE	ROOST	LAMBDEN	BRADFORD	WATLING	BRADFORD

GLOUCESTERSHIRE CUP FINAL

DATE	OPPONENT		SCORE	ATT	G 1	2	3	4	5	6	7	8	9	10	11	GOALSCORERS
10/05/51	BRISTOL CITY	A	1-2	16214	RADFORD	WATKINS	FOX	PITT	WARREN	SAMPSON	PETHERBRIDGE	ROOST	LAMBDEN	BRADFORD	WATLING	PETHERBRIDGE

PLAYERS	APP	GLS
BAMFORD H	36	
BRADFORD G	45	26
BUSH B	10	1
FOX G	46	
GREEN S	1	
HOYLE H	29	
LAMBDEN V	44	29
MEYER B	5	1
MICKLEWRIGHT A	6	1
MORGAN J	8	2
PETHERBRIDGE G	46	14
PICKARD L	4	1
PITT G	46	1
POWELL K	4	
RADFORD H	17	
ROOST W	27	7
SAMPSON P	46	1
TAYLOR C	3	
TIPPETT M	1	
WARREN R	41	3
WATKINS B	11	
WATLING J	30	1
OWN GOAL		1

Prior to the game at Brisbane Road on 6 February, Rovers and Leyton Orient observed a one-minute silence in memory of King George VI, who had died at Buckingham Palace the previous day. The match itself was very exciting with Geoff Bradford scoring twice for Rovers and Orient's left half Jackie Deverall contributing an own goal as the sides shared six goals. Another player to share his goals was the ubiquitous Vic Lambden who, not content with the hatful he contributed, contrived to score for both sides in the 1-1 draw at Brighton in April. Only Jock Hamilton had managed previously to score at both ends and, of Rovers' players, only Tim Parkin and Geoff Twentyman have repeated this feat since in League action.

Lambden also scored in both games as Rovers saw off non-League FA Cup opposition in Kettering Town and Weymouth. The visit of the Dorset side attracted a crowd of 27,808, encouraged by the fact that the two previous League games at Eastville had finished 5-0 to Rovers. In the third round, Rovers drew the mighty Preston North End at home. Not only were the Lilywhites founder members of the League, but they were also able to field players of the calibre of Tommy Docherty and Charlie Wayman. On paper at least, Rovers should not have been able to beat their illustrious opponents. Preston were to finish the season seventh in Division One, above FA Cup winners Newcastle United, but Rovers defeated them 2-0 with an efficient display. Before 30,681, Bradford, with an angled first-half drive, and Lambden 13 minutes from time, grabbed their customary goal apiece for a famous victory. In round four, Rovers stumbled at Southend United, losing 2-1, and the Gloucestershire Cup final was lost to Bristol City in May by the same scoreline.

1952/53

Comparisons between Rovers' promotion seasons are perhaps an inevitability. In both 1952/53 and 1973/74, Rovers enjoyed a 27-match unbeaten run before suffering a very shaky patch. Whereas Don Megson's side had a nine-point lead in 1974 and still did not win the Championship, Bert Tann's team almost let slip a 10-point margin over their nearest rivals. In April 1953, Rovers won only two points in a potentially disastrous run of six matches. The goal averages, 1.97 in 1973/74 and 2.02 in 1952/53 are also incredibly similar. Like the 1989/90 Championship side, Rovers won 26 League games in 1952/53, which was then a club record.

This was, however, the first time since elevation to the Football League in 1920 that Rovers had gained promotion and the first Championship since the Southern League in 1904/05. One by one, many of Rovers' fellow Division Three (South) founder members had sampled life in Division Two and now it was to be Rovers' turn. Success was achieved through an ever-present back five and the firepower of Geoff Bradford and Vic Lambden. Bradford's 33 League goals, amazingly 24 of which were scored at Eastville, constituted a club record and went some way towards creating the legendary aura associated with his name to this day. It was typical of his season that he should score a hat-trick on the day promotion was finally secured.

The one significant change in personnel was the addition of John McIlvenny from Cheltenham Town. Although he scored just twice, McIlvenny at outside-right, like

Bristol Rovers 1952/53. Back row: Micklewright, Allcock, Lambden, Green, Hoyle, Dunlop, Cooper, Steeds, Jones.
Middle row: Williams (Trainer), Petherbridge, Edwards, Pickard, Meyer, Powell, Hale, Presley, Bamford, Watling,
Sampson, McIlvenny, Bradford, Watkins, McArthur (Trainer). Front row: Bush, L Champney (Director), Fox,
H J Hampden Alpass (Chairman), Warren (Capt.), B Tann (Manager), Pitt, Leonard, J Gummow (Secretary)

George Petherbridge on the left, was instrumental in creating many of Rovers' club record 92 League goals. Rovers began the season well with a run of four convincing victories early in September. Bradford and Lambden both scored in a 5-3 win at Walsall and a 3-1 home victory over Gillingham, whose scorer Jimmy Scarth was credited with a hat-trick in only two minutes in November, when the Gills defeated Leyton Orient 3-2. Bradford scored a hat-trick of right-foot shots in a 3-0 victory over Torquay United and Rovers won by the same score at Colchester United. After defeat at Millwall, Rovers embarked on a club record 27-match unbeaten run, after which the Championship appeared won.

This incredible run began with a 3-1 victory over Colchester United, where familiar goalscorers Lambden, Bradford and Petherbridge helped complete the double over the Essex club. It was to run from mid-September to the end of March. In October, Rovers had trailed 2-0 at Northampton Town before injury-time goals from Bradford and Bryan Bush had reclaimed an unlikely point. This was the spur for Rovers to set off on a run of 12 consecutive League wins, from 18 October to 17 January. Not only is this run easily a club record, but it was also achieved in spectacular fashion. Rovers conceded just five goals in this run, yet scored seven against Brighton, to record the club's largest League win at the time, five at Ipswich Town and four each past Gillingham and Reading. In every one of these 12 games, Bradford, Lambden or Bush got on the scoresheet. It was an awesome display of the capabilities of Tann's side and one that no Rovers team is likely to repeat.

In two separate matches in November, Rovers scored four goals in 18 minutes. At home to Reading, McIlvenny's 15th-minute goal was followed by further strikes from

Bradford two minutes later and Lambden after 25 minutes. Warren's penalty, incredibly his final goal for the club, preceded a goalless second-half. Two home games later, Rovers repeated the feat against Brighton. After Petherbridge's 18th-minute opener, Rovers scored six second-half goals, a tally equalled only in the game at Reading in January 1999. Roost scored twice, either side of the predictable goals from Lambden and Bradford. Petherbridge claimed his second goal with a quarter of an hour remaining, before the luckless Reg Fox put through his own goal two minutes from time.

Thereafter, Lambden and Bradford scored twice each in a 4-1 victory over Aldershot and again when Coventry City were defeated 5-2. Rovers were involved in a six-goal draw at Brisbane Road for a second consecutive season and beat Ipswich Town 3-0 at Eastville in March in the 27th successive League game without defeat. After Reading, with goals from Ron Blackman and Tom Ritchie, had put paid to this proud record, Rovers proceeded to beat Bournemouth and Swindon Town. The former game, which followed a one-minute silence, as Queen Mary, the widow of King George V, had died four days earlier, featured goals from Bryan Bush and Bournemouth's Jack Cross, both of whom had also scored in the game at Dean Court in November.

It seems implausible, but Rovers won just one of their final nine League games. One of these matches, a draw with Newport County, was remarkably the ninth consecutive visit to Somerton Park in which Rovers had conceded exactly two goals. County included the former Rovers forward, Doug Hayward, in their side and Bill Stroud, later father-in-law to Tony Pulis, scored one of their goals. The sole victory, however, was the

3-1 win at home to County, which secured promotion to Division Two. With impeccable timing, Geoff Bradford, having established a new club seasonal record at Somerton Park, scored a majestic hat-trick to send Rovers up to the heady heights of Division Two. His first-minute sidefoot was followed by headers after 40 and 70 minutes, while beleaguered County, who had at one stage equalised through George Beattie's shot off the underside of the crossbar, lost goalkeeper Harry Fearnley with a broken collar-bone.

After the victory over Newport County, club chairman Hampden Alpass addressed the ecstatic crowd of 29,451 from a microphone in the directors' box: 'My first feeling is one of gratitude to players, manager and staff. Being on top of the table since the middle of September has meant that every club has been out to beat us and every match has been like a cup tie. The strain on the players has been terrific. Secondly, I have a feeling of pride that, after

Rovers' Bert Tann, popular manager who lead the club to its first ever promotion in 1953

THESE GOALS MEANT PROMOTION. *1. Geoff Bradford taps the ball into the Newport net in the first minute. 2. Bradford heads Rovers into a 2-1 lead five minutes before half-time. 3. Bradford completes his hat-trick after 70 mins, heading in for his 33rd goal of the season – a club record that has never been beaten*

all these years, the club has succeeded in reaching the Second Division.' Alpass received the Championship Shield and 13 medals at a Football League meeting held at the Café Royal in London on 13 June. The players split a £275 bonus between them for their achievements. No small part, of course, had been played by Bert Tann, whose dynamic approach to management had inspired Rovers. Supporters, thrilled by the 1950/51 Cup run and now promotion, viewed him with an awed reverence. Never before or since has one individual held such a magnetic sway over Bristol's sporting public.

This final success was achieved without the services of goalkeeper Bert Hoyle. Rovers contrived two goalless draws each with Bristol City and Exeter City and the Ashton Gate encounter drew a crowd of 35,372, the highest at any Division Three (South) ground that season. That evening, in Devon, Hoyle suffered serious injuries in a motor accident and his career with Rovers was sadly and abruptly ended. Howard Radford gamely took over in goal but, as the promotion push began to falter, Tann persuaded the directors to breach their 'no buy, no sell' policy. Bob Anderson, signed from Crystal Palace, played in the final 7 games and went on to appear in Bristol City's Division Three (South) Championship side of 1954/55. No other player has won two Championships from the same division with two clubs from the same city.

A first-minute goal from Roost proved decisive in an FA Cup first round replay against Leyton Orient, after Warren had missed a penalty in the original tie, and

SEASON 1952/53

FOOTBALL LEAGUE DIVISION THREE (SOUTH)

Date	Opposition		Result	ATT	G	2	3	4	5	6	7	8	9	10	11	GOALSCORERS
23/08/52	SHREWSBURY TOWN	H	2-1	24139	HOYLE	BAMFORD	FOX	PITT	WARREN	SAMPSON	JONES	LEONARD	LAMBDEN	BRADFORD	PETHERBRIDGE	LAMBDEN, WARREN
27/08/52	TORQUAY UNITED	A	0-1	10179	HOYLE	BAMFORD	FOX	PITT	WARREN	SAMPSON	JONES	MICKLEWRIGHT	LAMBDEN	BRADFORD	PETHERBRIDGE	
30/08/52	WALSALL	A	5-3	8023	HOYLE	BAMFORD	FOX	PITT	WARREN	SAMPSON	JONES	BUSH	LAMBDEN	BRADFORD	PETHERBRIDGE	BRADFORD, LAMBDEN 2, BUSH 2
01/09/52	TORQUAY UNITED	H	3-0	19248	HOYLE	BAMFORD	FOX	PITT	WARREN	SAMPSON	JONES	BUSH	LAMBDEN	BRADFORD	PETHERBRIDGE	BRADFORD 3
06/09/52	GILLINGHAM	H	3-1	20254	HOYLE	BAMFORD	FOX	PITT	WARREN	SAMPSON	JONES	BUSH	LAMBDEN	BRADFORD	PETHERBRIDGE	BRADFORD, PETHERBRIDGE, LAMBDEN
11/09/52	COLCHESTER UNITED	A	3-0	8960	HOYLE	BAMFORD	FOX	PITT	WARREN	SAMPSON	JONES	BUSH	LAMBDEN	BRADFORD	PETHERBRIDGE	BUSH, LAMBDEN, PETHERBRIDGE
13/09/52	MILLWALL	A	0-3	22622	HOYLE	BAMFORD	FOX	PITT	WARREN	SAMPSON	McILVENNY	BUSH	LAMBDEN	BRADFORD	PETHERBRIDGE	
15/09/52	COLCHESTER UNITED	H	3-1	17536	HOYLE	BAMFORD	FOX	PITT	WARREN	SAMPSON	McILVENNY	BUSH	LAMBDEN	BRADFORD	PETHERBRIDGE	LAMBDEN, PETHERBRIDGE, BRADFORD
20/09/52	BRISTOL CITY	H	0-0	29880	HOYLE	BAMFORD	FOX	PITT	WARREN	SAMPSON	McILVENNY	BUSH	LAMBDEN	BRADFORD	PETHERBRIDGE	
25/09/52	WATFORD	H	3-2	13178	HOYLE	BAMFORD	FOX	PITT	WARREN	SAMPSON	McILVENNY	BUSH	LAMBDEN	BRADFORD	PETHERBRIDGE	LAMBDEN, BUSH, PETHERBRIDGE
27/09/52	EXETER CITY	H	0-0	23373	HOYLE	BAMFORD	FOX	PITT	WARREN	SAMPSON	McILVENNY	BUSH	LAMBDEN	BRADFORD	PETHERBRIDGE	
29/09/52	NORWICH CITY	H	3-1	22847	HOYLE	BAMFORD	FOX	PITT	WARREN	SAMPSON	McILVENNY	LEONARD	LAMBDEN	BRADFORD	PETHERBRIDGE	LAMBDEN, BRADFORD 2
04/10/52	COVENTRY CITY	A	1-1	19052	HOYLE	BAMFORD	FOX	PITT	WARREN	SAMPSON	McILVENNY	BUSH	LAMBDEN	BRADFORD	PETHERBRIDGE	BUSH
11/10/52	NORTHAMPTON TOWN	A	2-2	19043	HOYLE	BAMFORD	FOX	PITT	WARREN	SAMPSON	McILVENNY	BUSH	LAMBDEN	BRADFORD	PETHERBRIDGE	BUSH, BRADFORD
18/10/52	LEYTON ORIENT	H	2-1	24194	HOYLE	BAMFORD	FOX	PITT	WARREN	SAMPSON	McILVENNY	BUSH	LAMBDEN	BRADFORD	PETHERBRIDGE	McILVENNY, LAMBDEN
25/10/52	IPSWICH TOWN	A	5-1	14839	HOYLE	BAMFORD	FOX	PITT	WARREN	SAMPSON	McILVENNY	BUSH	LAMBDEN	BRADFORD	PETHERBRIDGE	BUSH, LAMBDEN, BRADFORD 2, PETHERBRIDGE
01/11/52	READING	H	4-0	26658	HOYLE	BAMFORD	FOX	PITT	WARREN	SAMPSON	McILVENNY	BUSH	LAMBDEN	BRADFORD	PETHERBRIDGE	McILVENNY, PETHERBRIDGE, LAMBDEN, WARREN
08/11/52	BOURNEMOUTH	A	2-1	18632	HOYLE	BAMFORD	FOX	PITT	WARREN	SAMPSON	McILVENNY	BUSH	LAMBDEN	BRADFORD	PETHERBRIDGE	PETHERBRIDGE, BUSH
15/11/52	SOUTHEND UNITED	A	2-1	20227	HOYLE	BAMFORD	FOX	PITT	WARREN	SAMPSON	McILVENNY	BUSH	LAMBDEN	BRADFORD	PETHERBRIDGE	LAMBDEN, BRADFORD
29/11/52	BRIGHTON & HOVE ALBION	H	7-0	11647	HOYLE	BAMFORD	FOX	PITT	WARREN	SAMPSON	McILVENNY	ROOST	LAMBDEN	BRADFORD	PETHERBRIDGE	PETHERBRIDGE 2, ROOST 2, LAMBDEN, BRADFORD, FOX og
13/12/52	CRYSTAL PALACE	H	2-0	20042	HOYLE	BAMFORD	FOX	PITT	WARREN	SAMPSON	McILVENNY	ROOST	LAMBDEN	BRADFORD	PETHERBRIDGE	BRADFORD, LAMBDEN
20/12/52	SHREWSBURY TOWN	H	1-0	8810	HOYLE	BAMFORD	FOX	PITT	WARREN	SAMPSON	McILVENNY	BUSH	LAMBDEN	BRADFORD	PETHERBRIDGE	BUSH
26/12/52	QUEENS PARK RANGERS	H	1-0	13866	HOYLE	BAMFORD	FOX	PITT	WARREN	SAMPSON	McILVENNY	BUSH	LAMBDEN	BRADFORD	ROOST	BRADFORD
27/12/52	QUEENS PARK RANGERS	A	2-1	30995	HOYLE	BAMFORD	FOX	PITT	WARREN	SAMPSON	McILVENNY	BUSH	LAMBDEN	BRADFORD	ROOST	LAMBDEN 2
03/01/53	WALSALL	H	2-0	24171	HOYLE	BAMFORD	FOX	PITT	WARREN	SAMPSON	McILVENNY	BUSH	LAMBDEN	BRADFORD	PETHERBRIDGE	BRADFORD, BUSH
17/01/53	GILLINGHAM	A	4-0	16600	HOYLE	BAMFORD	FOX	PITT	WARREN	SAMPSON	McILVENNY	BUSH	LAMBDEN	BRADFORD	PETHERBRIDGE	BRADFORD, BUSH, FOX, LEWIN og
24/01/53	MILLWALL	H	1-1	31035	HOYLE	BAMFORD	FOX	PITT	WARREN	SAMPSON	McILVENNY	BUSH	LAMBDEN	BRADFORD	PETHERBRIDGE	BRADFORD
31/01/53	ALDERSHOT	H	4-1	18263	HOYLE	BAMFORD	FOX	PITT	WARREN	SAMPSON	McILVENNY	ROOST	LAMBDEN	BRADFORD	PETHERBRIDGE	LAMBDEN 2, BRADFORD 2
07/02/53	BRISTOL CITY	A	0-0	35372	HOYLE	BAMFORD	FOX	PITT	WARREN	SAMPSON	McILVENNY	BUSH	LAMBDEN	BRADFORD	PETHERBRIDGE	
14/02/53	EXETER CITY	A	0-0	13113	RADFORD	BAMFORD	FOX	PITT	WARREN	SAMPSON	McILVENNY	ROOST	LAMBDEN	BRADFORD	PETHERBRIDGE	
21/02/53	COVENTRY CITY	H	5-2	28614	RADFORD	BAMFORD	FOX	PITT	WARREN	SAMPSON	McILVENNY	ROOST	LAMBDEN	BRADFORD	PETHERBRIDGE	LAMBDEN 2, PETHERBRIDGE, BRADFORD 2
28/02/53	NORTHAMPTON TOWN	H	1-1	31115	RADFORD	BAMFORD	FOX	PITT	WARREN	SAMPSON	McILVENNY	BUSH	LAMBDEN	BRADFORD	PETHERBRIDGE	BRADFORD
07/03/53	LEYTON ORIENT	A	3-3	16136	RADFORD	BAMFORD	FOX	PITT	WARREN	SAMPSON	McILVENNY	LEONARD	LAMBDEN	BRADFORD	PETHERBRIDGE	McILVENNY, LAMBDEN 2
14/03/53	IPSWICH TOWN	A	3-0	21244	RADFORD	BAMFORD	FOX	PITT	WARREN	SAMPSON	McILVENNY	BUSH	LAMBDEN	BRADFORD	PETHERBRIDGE	PETHERBRIDGE, BRADFORD, BAMFORD
21/03/53	READING	A	0-2	17789	RADFORD	BAMFORD	FOX	PITT	WARREN	SAMPSON	McILVENNY	BUSH	LAMBDEN	BRADFORD	PETHERBRIDGE	
28/03/53	BOURNEMOUTH	H	2-1	16065	RADFORD	BAMFORD	FOX	PITT	WARREN	SAMPSON	McILVENNY	BUSH	LAMBDEN	BRADFORD	PETHERBRIDGE	LAMBDEN, BUSH
03/04/53	BRIGHTON & HOVE ALBION	A	3-1	24559	RADFORD	BAMFORD	FOX	PITT	WARREN	SAMPSON	PETHERBRIDGE	LEONARD	LAMBDEN	BRADFORD	WATLING	BATCHELOR og, BRADFORD 2
04/04/53	SOUTHEND UNITED	H	1-2	16010	RADFORD	BAMFORD	FOX	PITT	WARREN	SAMPSON	McILVENNY	ROOST	LAMBDEN	BRADFORD	PETHERBRIDGE	BRADFORD
06/04/53	SWINDON TOWN	H	1-2	24406	RADFORD	BAMFORD	FOX	PITT	WARREN	SAMPSON	McILVENNY	ROOST	LAMBDEN	BRADFORD	PETHERBRIDGE	BRADFORD
11/04/53	WATFORD	A	0-3	22614	ANDERSON	BAMFORD	FOX	PITT	WARREN	SAMPSON	McILVENNY	BUSH	LAMBDEN	BRADFORD	PETHERBRIDGE	
13/04/53	NEWPORT COUNTY	H	2-2	16007	ANDERSON	BAMFORD	FOX	PITT	WARREN	SAMPSON	McILVENNY	ROOST	LAMBDEN	BRADFORD	PETHERBRIDGE	LAMBDEN, BRADFORD
18/04/53	BRIGHTON & HOVE ALBION	A	1-2	22800	ANDERSON	BAMFORD	FOX	PITT	WARREN	SAMPSON	PETHERBRIDGE	LEONARD	LAMBDEN	BRADFORD	WATLING	LEONARD
22/04/53	NORWICH CITY	A	0-0	30548	ANDERSON	BAMFORD	FOX	PITT	WARREN	SAMPSON	PETHERBRIDGE	ROOST	LAMBDEN	BRADFORD	WATLING	
25/04/53	NEWPORT COUNTY	A	3-1	29451	ANDERSON	BAMFORD	FOX	PITT	WARREN	SAMPSON	PETHERBRIDGE	LEONARD	LAMBDEN	BRADFORD	WATLING	BRADFORD 3
29/04/53	ALDERSHOT	A	0-0	7593	ANDERSON	BAMFORD	FOX	PITT	WARREN	SAMPSON	PETHERBRIDGE	ROOST	LAMBDEN	BRADFORD	WATLING	
01/05/53	CRYSTAL PALACE	A	0-1	5712	ANDERSON	BAMFORD	FOX	PITT	WARREN	SAMPSON	McILVENNY	BUSH	LAMBDEN	ROOST	PETHERBRIDGE	

FA CUP

Date	Opposition		Result	ATT	G	2	3	4	5	6	7	8	9	10	11	GOALSCORERS
22/11/52	LEYTON ORIENT	A	1-1	10700	HOYLE	BAMFORD	FOX	PITT	WARREN	SAMPSON	McILVENNY	BUSH	LAMBDEN	BRADFORD	WATLING	BRADFORD
24/11/52	LEYTON ORIENT	H	1-0	15032	HOYLE	BAMFORD	FOX	PITT	WARREN	SAMPSON	McILVENNY	ROOST	LAMBDEN	BRADFORD	WATLING	ROOST
06/12/52	PETERBOROUGH UNITED	A	1-0	15280	HOYLE	BAMFORD	FOX	PITT	WARREN	SAMPSON	McILVENNY	ROOST	LAMBDEN	BRADFORD	PETHERBRIDGE	LAMBDEN
10/01/53	HUDDERSFIELD TOWN	H	0-2	34967	HOYLE	BAMFORD	FOX	PITT	WARREN	SAMPSON	PETHERBRIDGE	BUSH	LAMBDEN	BRADFORD	WATLING	

GLOUCESTERSHIRE CUP FINAL

Date	Opposition		Result	ATT	G	2	3	4	5	6	7	8	9	10	11	GOALSCORERS
08/05/53	BRISTOL CITY	H	0-2	19214	RADFORD	ALLCOCK	FOX	PITT	WARREN	SAMPSON	BUSH	LEONARD	LAMBDEN	ROOST	WATLING	

PLAYERS	APP	GLS
ANDERSON R	7	
BAMFORD H	46	1
BRADFORD G	45	33
BUSH B	35	12
FOX G	46	1
HOYLE H	29	
JONES D	6	
LAMBDEN V	46	24
LEONARD P	6	1
McILVENNY J	35	3
MICKLEWRIGHT A	1	
PETHERBRIDGE G	38	10
PITT J	46	
RADFORD H	10	
ROOST W	13	2
SAMPSON P	46	
WARREN R	46	2
WATLING J	5	
OWN GOALS		2

Lambden's goal earned victory over Peterborough United at London Road. The previous two seasons' FA Cup campaigns had earned Rovers plum draws and this was no exception. Rovers faced a third round tie at Huddersfield Town, who were promoted to Division One at the end of the season, and the task was made still tougher when goalkeeper Hoyle left the field injured and the versatile Lambden finished the game in goal. Ten-man Rovers lost respectably 2-0, to goals from Jim Watson and Jim Glazzard. In the Gloucestershire Cup final, first-half goals from John Atyeo and Alec Eisentrager gave Bristol City a 2-0 win, while Rovers drew a cricket game in September, scoring 75-5 in response to a Duke of Beaufort XI's 164 all out. A March crowd of 6,694 at Eastville saw Rovers defeat Trinidad 4-1, Lyons and Bush both scoring twice.

Tann's projection of the club had much to do with the on-field success of 1952/53. The average attendance of 23,411 was the highest in the division and reflects the close affinity felt between the team and its supporters. A largely Bristol-raised side of local men, led by an eloquent and enthusiastic Londoner, had brought long-awaited success to a delighted public. Now the team of local heroes was to face the new and welcome challenge of Division Two football.

1953/54

The promised land had been reached. The fears of those who felt Bert Tann's home-grown side would struggle in their inaugural season in Division Two were proved unfounded, as Rovers finished in ninth place, just 12 points behind the two promoted sides, Leicester City and Everton. Tann had nurtured the team spirit and commitment that had driven the club so far and was now developing it to create a high-quality side. The golden years in the Bristol Rovers story were the days when this largely Bristol-born team came so close to that still elusive place in the top division.

Rovers' arrival in Division Two was announced with a hugely entertaining 4-4 draw with Fulham at Craven Cottage. In predictable fashion, Geoff Bradford opened the scoring after 13 minutes and marked the occasion with a hat-trick while Geoff Fox, four minutes after half-time, scored only his second goal in more than 200 appearances. Bobby Robson, later manager of England, scored the first two of Fulham's three equalisers. Arthur Stevens, whose hat-trick put Rovers out of the FA Cup in 1948, and the future England forward Johnny Haynes, with only the second goal of his League career, scored once each before Bradford pulled Rovers level 15 minutes from time. A crowd of 28,173 saw the first home game, when Doncaster Rovers spoiled the celebrations by winning through a solitary Eddie McMorran goal from Len Graham's defence-splitting pass, although Rovers won 17 corners to Doncaster's three. Rovers began the season with a side composed entirely of players who had helped the club to the Division Three (South) Championship.

The star attraction, once again, was the phenomenal goalscorer Geoff Bradford. He followed up his club record 33 League goals in 1952/53 with 21 goals in only 18 League appearances. Quite what Rovers might have achieved if he had remained injury-free

Bristol Rovers 1953/54. Back row: Gummow (Secretary), Williams (Trainer), Lambden, Pitt, Anderson, Fox, Hoyle, Bamford, Sampson, Duke of Beaufort. Front row: Bradford, Petherbridge, Warren, Roost, Watling. Inset: Hampden-Alpass (Chairman), Tann (Manager)

remains a moot point, for a career-threatening leg injury, suffered after he had scored the opening goal at Plymouth Argyle in November, was to rule him out for almost six months. In true heroic fashion, he made a dramatic comeback in the final match of the season, his knee heavily strapped, and scored a hat-trick as Rovers defeated Stoke City 3-2 at Eastville, his fifth hat-trick of the season. After Rovers had trailed 2-1, two dramatic Bradford headers inside 60 seconds brought an unlikely victory. Although Rovers as a team scored five hat-tricks in 1926/27, Bradford's feat is a clear club record.

Bradford's injury, coupled with the winding-down of Vic Lambden's long career – he scored just twice this season – meant Rovers had to search for adequate free-transfer replacements. Three of the players given first-team opportunities were to play a significant role over the next few years. Peter Hooper was to enthral Rovers supporters for a decade with his close control and powerful shot. Remarkably, he had played for Kenya against Uganda in 1951 while on National Service, but it was at Eastville, with his 35-yard drives and more than 100 League goals, that the young Devonian was to make his mark. Frank Allcock appeared in 59 League games for Rovers before a knee injury ended his career. The player who made the biggest immediate impact, however, was Paddy Hale, who was in effect Bradford's deputy.

Hale's goalscoring record for Rovers is certainly unorthodox. In 19 League appearances in 1953/54, he scored twelve times, never more than one per game, to finish as the club's second-highest scorer. Thereafter, he appeared predominantly as centre-half and never scored again in more than 100 further League matches, before joining Bath City in 1959. On his debut, Hale, the recalled John McIlvenny and Gloucestershire cricketer Barrie Meyer all scored as Rovers defeated eventual champions Leicester City 3-0 at Eastville, in one of the highlights of this first season in Division Two.

Rovers recorded a number of comfortable wins early in the season. Bradford scored all the goals as Rovers won 3-0 at Brentford, while Derby County were defeated by the same score. Bill Roost, Josser Watling and Bradford all scored in consecutive games, as Rovers won 5-1 at Notts County and 4-2 at home to Hull City. Bradford's hat-trick at Meadow Lane was the start of a personal run of 11 goals in seven games prior to his injury. After November, Rovers were to score three times in a match only in the home games with Plymouth Argyle – when Alfie Biggs, a name for Rovers' future, scored his first goal for the club – and Stoke City.

October was a month for draws, with Rovers registering three 3-3 draws in four weeks. First, Rovers went to Elland Road to face a Leeds United side deprived of the League's top scorer, John Charles. Bob Forrest scored a hat-trick, but two Bradford goals earned Rovers a draw. The roles were reversed three weeks later, when Bradford scored an Eastville hat-trick against Luton Town, but did not finish on the winning side. The third six-goal draw was the one in which the club's top scorer was injured on 7 November. Rovers also drew 1-1 at home to Birmingham City in October, Bradford scoring past International goalkeeper Gil Merrick, while Ted Purdon scored against his future club. The attendance broke the ground record and remains, at 35,614, the largest ever at a home League game. It was also the highest at any Rovers game all season, home or away, marginally ahead of the 34,015 at the goalless draw with Everton three days after Christmas. For six consecutive years, 1952/53 to 1957/58, the club's average home crowd topped 20,000 and, in a mood of optimism and enthusiasm, the seasonal average of 24,662 in 1953/54 remains the highest in Rovers' League history.

Urged on by large crowds at home, Rovers produced several notable victories. Away from home, there were not many bad defeats, though Everton were 4-0 winners on Christmas Day, with David Hickson scoring twice before a 27,484 crowd in Rovers' only visit in League football to Goodison Park. A first-ever league visit to Boothferry Park saw Rovers lose 4-1 to Hull City in April, with Sid Gerrie scoring three times and Viggo Jensen, the holder of 15 full Danish caps, converting a penalty. What is remarkable about a Rovers side deprived of their key goalscorer, is the number of low-scoring results through the winter and spring. In a run of 12 League games between December and early April, five were 1-1 draws and two goalless, while four others featured just one goal each. It was a series of mid-table results, but the lack of a consistent goalscorer was abundantly clear.

Promotion to a higher division not only brought a host of new opponents, particularly northern clubs, but also meant Rovers faced a number of high-profile players. Four well-known future managers were in the West Ham United side that drew 2-2 at Eastville in September. Dave Sexton, a goalscorer, Frank O'Farrell and Noel Cantwell were joined in the Hammers' line-up by Malcolm Allison, for the first of 8 League appearances against the side he was to manage in 1992/93. In April, a Jack Froggatt header 15 minutes from time earned the points for a Leicester City side that also included Stan Milburn, Derek Hines and the Football League's all-time top goalscorer, Arthur Rowley. Mel Charles, the experienced Welsh International, scored against Rovers in both meetings with Swansea Town, who also fielded both Len and Ivor Allchurch in the game at the Vetch Field on Easter Saturday. These new experiences were invaluable to the East Bristol boys as their team established itself in Division Two.

SEASON 1953/54

FOOTBALL LEAGUE DIVISION TWO

Date	Opponent		Score	Att	G	2	3	4	5	6	7	8	9	10	11	Goalscorers
20/08/53	FULHAM	A	4-4	25000	ANDERSON	BAMFORD	FOX	PITT	WARREN	SAMPSON	PETHERBRIDGE	BRADFORD	LAMBDEN	MEYER	WATLING	BRADFORD 3, FOX
22/08/53	BLACKBURN ROVERS	A	1-1	26145	RADFORD	BAMFORD	FOX	PITT	WARREN	SAMPSON	PETHERBRIDGE	BRADFORD	LAMBDEN	MEYER	WATLING	MEYER
24/08/53	DONCASTER ROVERS	A	0-1	28173	RADFORD	BAMFORD	FOX	PITT	WARREN	SAMPSON	PETHERBRIDGE	BRADFORD	LAMBDEN	MEYER	WATLING	
29/08/53	DERBY COUNTY	H	3-0	20046	RADFORD	BAMFORD	FOX	PITT	WARREN	SAMPSON	PETHERBRIDGE	BRADFORD	LAMBDEN	MEYER	WATLING	PETHERBRIDGE, LAMBDEN, MEYER
02/09/53	DONCASTER ROVERS	H	0-1	20734	RADFORD	BAMFORD	FOX	PITT	WARREN	CAIRNEY	PETHERBRIDGE	BRADFORD	LAMBDEN	MEYER	WATLING	
05/09/53	BRENTFORD	A	3-0	21600	RADFORD	BAMFORD	FOX	PITT	WARREN	CAIRNEY	PETHERBRIDGE	BRADFORD	LAMBDEN	MEYER	WATLING	BRADFORD 3
07/09/53	BURY	H	2-0	29002	RADFORD	BAMFORD	FOX	PITT	WARREN	CAIRNEY	PETHERBRIDGE	BRADFORD	LAMBDEN	MEYER	WATLING	PETHERBRIDGE, MASSEY og
12/09/53	WEST HAM UNITED	A	2-2	28736	RADFORD	BAMFORD	FOX	PITT	WARREN	CAIRNEY	PETHERBRIDGE	BRADFORD	LAMBDEN	MEYER	WATLING	CAIRNEY, MEYER
16/09/53	BURY	H	1-3	11462	RADFORD	BAMFORD	FOX	PITT	WARREN	SAMPSON	PETHERBRIDGE	BRADFORD	LAMBDEN	MEYER	WATLING	BRADFORD
19/09/53	LINCOLN CITY	A	0-1	24650	RADFORD	BAMFORD	FOX	PITT	WARREN	SAMPSON	PETHERBRIDGE	BRADFORD	LAMBDEN	MEYER	WATLING	
26/09/53	NOTTS COUNTY	H	5-1	16318	RADFORD	BAMFORD	FOX	PITT	WARREN	SAMPSON	PETHERBRIDGE	ROOST	BRADFORD	BUSH	WATLING	BRADFORD 3, ROOST, WATLING
03/10/53	HULL CITY	A	4-2	25224	RADFORD	BAMFORD	FOX	PITT	WARREN	SAMPSON	PETHERBRIDGE	ROOST	BRADFORD	BUSH	WATLING	ROOST 2, BRADFORD, WATLING
10/10/53	LEEDS UNITED	H	3-3	19900	RADFORD	BAMFORD	FOX	PITT	WARREN	SAMPSON	PETHERBRIDGE	LEONARD	BRADFORD	BUSH	WATLING	BRADFORD 2, ROOST
17/10/53	BIRMINGHAM CITY	H	1-3	35614	RADFORD	BAMFORD	FOX	PITT	WARREN	SAMPSON	PETHERBRIDGE	LEONARD	BRADFORD	BUSH	WATLING	BRADFORD
24/10/53	NOTTINGHAM FOREST	A	1-3	22987	RADFORD	BAMFORD	FOX	PITT	WARREN	SAMPSON	PETHERBRIDGE	LEONARD	BRADFORD	BUSH	WATLING	BUSH pen
31/10/53	LUTON TOWN	H	3-3	20002	ANDERSON	BAMFORD	FOX	PITT	WARREN	SAMPSON	PETHERBRIDGE	LEONARD	BRADFORD	BUSH	WATLING	BRADFORD 3
07/11/53	PLYMOUTH ARGYLE	A	0-3	23784	RADFORD	BAMFORD	WATKINS	PITT	WARREN	SAMPSON	PETHERBRIDGE	ROOST	LYONS	MEYER	WATLING	
14/11/53	SWANSEA TOWN	H	0-1	25692	RADFORD	BAMFORD	WATKINS	PITT	WARREN	SAMPSON	PETHERBRIDGE	ROOST	LYONS	MEYER	WATLING	
21/11/53	ROTHERHAM UNITED	A	1-1	13210	RADFORD	BAMFORD	FOX	PITT	WARREN	SAMPSON	PETHERBRIDGE	ROOST	LYONS	MEYER	WATLING	MEYER
28/11/53	LEICESTER CITY	H	3-0	26250	RADFORD	BAMFORD	FOX	PITT	WARREN	SAMPSON	PETHERBRIDGE	BRADFORD	LYONS	MEYER	WATLING	PETHERBRIDGE, BRADFORD, MEYER
05/12/53	STOKE CITY	A	0-3	13177	RADFORD	BAMFORD	FOX	PITT	WARREN	SAMPSON	McILVENNY	ROOST	LYONS	MEYER	WATLING	
12/12/53	FULHAM	H	1-2	22885	RADFORD	BAMFORD	FOX	PITT	WARREN	SAMPSON	McILVENNY	ROOST	LYONS	MEYER	WATLING	MEYER
19/12/53	BLACKBURN ROVERS	A	3-0	22398	RADFORD	BAMFORD	FOX	PITT	WARREN	SAMPSON	McILVENNY	HALE	LYONS	MEYER	WATLING	McILVENNY, HALE, MEYER
25/12/53	EVERTON	A	2-0	27484	RADFORD	BAMFORD	FOX	PITT	WARREN	SAMPSON	McILVENNY	CAIRNEY	LYONS	MEYER	WATLING	McILVENNY, MEYER
28/12/53	EVERTON	H	2-0	34015	ANDERSON	BAMFORD	FOX	PITT	WARREN	SAMPSON	McILVENNY	CAIRNEY	LYONS	MEYER	WATLING	HALE, PITT pen
02/01/54	DERBY COUNTY	H	1-0	16506	RADFORD	BAMFORD	FOX	PITT	WARREN	SAMPSON	McILVENNY	MEYER	LYONS	ROOST	WATLING	PITT
16/01/54	BRENTFORD	H	0-0	20500	RADFORD	BAMFORD	FOX	PITT	WARREN	SAMPSON	McILVENNY	ROOST	HALE	ROOST	WATLING	
23/01/54	WEST HAM UNITED	A	1-1	22250	RADFORD	BAMFORD	FOX	PITT	WARREN	SAMPSON	McILVENNY	BIGGS	HALE	MEYER	WATLING	HALE
06/02/54	LINCOLN CITY	H	2-0	11914	RADFORD	BAMFORD	FOX	CAIRNEY	WARREN	SAMPSON	McILVENNY	HALE	LAMBDEN	MEYER	WATLING	HALE, LAMBDEN
13/02/54	NOTTS COUNTY	A	1-0	20767	RADFORD	BAMFORD	FOX	PITT	WARREN	SAMPSON	McILVENNY	BIGGS	LAMBDEN	HALE	WATLING	HALE
27/02/54	LEEDS UNITED	A	1-1	26772	RADFORD	BAMFORD	FOX	PITT	WARREN	SAMPSON	WILSHIRE	BIGGS	HALE	HALE	WATLING	HALE
06/03/54	BIRMINGHAM CITY	H	1-0	25300	RADFORD	BAMFORD	FOX	PITT	WARREN	SAMPSON	McILVENNY	BIGGS	HALE	LEONARD	HOOPER	LEONARD
13/03/54	NOTTINGHAM FOREST	A	0-0	21753	RADFORD	BAMFORD	FOX	PITT	WARREN	SAMPSON	McILVENNY	BIGGS	HALE	LEONARD	PETHERBRIDGE	
20/03/54	LUTON TOWN	A	1-1	12915	RADFORD	BAMFORD	FOX	PITT	WARREN	SAMPSON	McILVENNY	BIGGS	HALE	LEONARD	WATLING	PITT pen
27/03/54	ROTHERHAM UNITED	H	1-0	19668	RADFORD	BAMFORD	FOX	PITT	WARREN	SAMPSON	McILVENNY	ROOST	HALE	MEYER	PETHERBRIDGE	HALE
03/04/54	LEICESTER CITY	A	3-1	27368	RADFORD	BAMFORD	FOX	PITT	WARREN	SAMPSON	McILVENNY	BIGGS	LAMBDEN	HALE	PETHERBRIDGE	BIGGS, HALE, MEYER
10/04/54	PLYMOUTH ARGYLE	H	1-4	23799	RADFORD	BAMFORD	FOX	PITT	WARREN	SAMPSON	PETHERBRIDGE	BIGGS	HALE	MEYER	HOOPER	HALE
12/04/54	HULL CITY	A	1-4	11541	RADFORD	BAMFORD	FOX	CAIRNEY	MUIR	SAMPSON	PETHERBRIDGE	BIGGS	HALE	MEYER	HOOPER	PETHERBRIDGE
16/04/54	OLDHAM ATHLETIC	H	1-0	21139	CHANDLER	BAMFORD	FOX	PITT	WARREN	SAMPSON	PETHERBRIDGE	BIGGS	HALE	MEYER	HOOPER	HALE
17/04/54	SWANSEA TOWN	A	1-3	21753	CHANDLER	BAMFORD	FOX	PITT	WARREN	SAMPSON	PETHERBRIDGE	MEYER	HALE	CAIRNEY	PETHERBRIDGE	
19/04/54	OLDHAM ATHLETIC	A	0-1	11961	CHANDLER	ALLCOCK	FOX	PITT	WARREN	SAMPSON	BIGGS	MEYER	LAMBDEN	MEYER	PETHERBRIDGE	
24/04/54	STOKE CITY	H	3-2	22687	CHANDLER	ALLCOCK	FOX	PITT	WARREN	SAMPSON	PETHERBRIDGE	BRADFORD	LAMBDEN	MEYER	HOOPER	BRADFORD 3

FA CUP

Date	Opponent		Score	Att	G	2	3	4	5	6	7	8	9	10	11	Goalscorers
09/01/54	BLACKBURN ROVERS	H	0-1	25017	RADFORD	BAMFORD	FOX	PITT	WARREN	SAMPSON	PETHERBRIDGE	CAIRNEY	HALE	STEEDS	WATLING	

GLOUCESTERSHIRE CUP FINAL

Date	Opponent		Score	Att	G	2	3	4	5	6	7	8	9	10	11	Goalscorers
03/05/54	BRISTOL CITY	A	2-2	13668	ANDERSON	ALLCOCK	FOX	CAIRNEY	WARREN	SAMPSON	McILVENNY	MEYER	HALE	ROOST	PETHERBRIDGE	WARREN, MEYER

Appearances and Goals

PLAYERS	APP	GLS
ALLCOCK F	2	
ANDERSON R	3	
BAMFORD H	40	
BIGGS A	12	1
BRADFORD G	18	21
BUSH B	6	1
CAIRNEY C	9	1
CHANDLER R	4	
FOX G	40	1
HALE D	19	12
HOOPER P	4	
LAMBDEN V	15	2
LEONARD P	8	1
LYONS M	10	
McILVENNY J	10	2
MEYER B	27	8
MUIR I	1	
PETHERBRIDGE G	35	4
PETHERBRIDGE G	35	
PITT J	40	3
RADFORD H	35	
ROOST W	15	4
SAMPSON P	38	
WARREN R	41	
WATKINS B	2	
WATLING J	35	2
WILSHIRE P	1	
OWN GOAL		1

Ultimately, the demise of the Bradford-Lambden partnership and lack of adequate replacements hindered Rovers' chances of progressing above mid-table. However, ninth place in this new division was a major achievement upon which to build. While the stability of the side remained relatively intact, it is worth noting that no individual player was an ever-present. The back five, each one a permanent fixture in front of the goalkeeper in the championship season, all missed sporadic games for a variety of reasons. There was no success in the FA Cup where, for the second time inside a month, Blackburn Rovers won at Eastville. Eddie Quigley, once Britain's most expensive footballer, scored the only goal with a low, hard drive after 15 minutes. The Gloucestershire Cup Final was drawn 2-2 with Bristol City, Rovers being indebted, in Bradford's absence, to the veteran club captain Ray Warren's only goal of the season.

1954/55

The bubble was certainly not about to burst. Rovers had spent 26 seasons trying to get into Division Two and were now proving they could stay there. Manager Bert Tann had instilled a confidence and sense of belonging into this homely club and on-field performances indicated the side was capable of holding its own. Even an uncharacteristic late-season lean spell from the prolific Geoff Bradford and humiliating defeats at Rotherham United and Blackburn Rovers, could not dent the infectious enthusiasm at the club. Those who feared a decline was setting in and Rovers were heading back to Division Three (South) were to be proved wrong as season 1955/56 found the club just four points away from promotion to Division One.

Consistency on the field was mirrored in the large crowds that flocked to Eastville every matchday. With an average home crowd of 23,116, Rovers were the third-best supported Division Two side, behind Liverpool and Blackburn Rovers. For a third consecutive season, the average was not only above 20,000, but also higher than that at Bristol City, who were Division Three (South) champions. A new ground record of 35,921 in January saw Rovers defeat Division One Portsmouth 2-1 in the FA Cup third round, with Bradford and Bill Roost scoring past the Northern Ireland International goalkeeper Norman Uprichard to record a famous victory. This ground record did not even see out the month. In round four, Chelsea, League Champions that season for the only time in that club's history, drew a crowd of 35,972 to Eastville. With the former Rovers schoolboy, Roy Bentley, in fine form, Chelsea were able to win 3-1. Even the Gloucestershire Cup final was watched by its highest ever crowd, home or away. 20,097 saw Rovers win 2-1 at Eastville, with Bristol City's Ernie Peacock deflecting the winner into his own net from Biggs' right-wing cross seven minutes after half-time.

Rovers continued to boast a strong defence, with Howard Radford in goal. Right-back Harry Bamford was supported initially by Geoff Fox, who played his 274th and final League game for Rovers in April, and from November by Frank Allcock. Pitt, Warren and Sampson remained the usual half-back line, though Jimmy Anderson, a signing from army football, enjoyed an extended run in the side at left half. Of the forwards, only

Bristol Rovers 1954/55. Back row: Pitt, Bamford, Radford, Warren, Edwards, Anderson. Front row: Petherbridge, Hale, Bradford, Roost, Hooper

Bradford, Roost and Petherbridge enjoyed any consistency in a side again lacking an ever-present. Young Peter Hooper offered glimpses of his potential. Barrie Meyer, Alfie Biggs, Paddy Hale, John McIlvenny and Josser Watling appeared in the forward line.

Vic Lambden, given one final run in the side, contributed 7 goals late in the season. He scored the only goal of the game after 65 minutes at Plymouth Argyle on Easter Monday, from Geoff Bradford's through pass, in what proved to be his final appearance for the side. In almost a decade, he had scored 117 times in 268 League matches and remains the fourth highest goalscorer in Rovers' Football League history. He subsequently joined Trowbridge Town, where he scored more than 150 goals in six highly successful seasons in the Western League. As one long career ended, so too did that of Bryan Bush, whose final appearance in a Rovers shirt came in the debacle at Blackburn Rovers. One new face, though, was Dai Ward, who played at inside left against Nottingham Forest in April, and was to give Rovers many years of valuable service. Over the summer of 1954, William Cowlin and son had erected new gates and railings at a cost of £203 and a stand season ticket for 1954/55 cost six guineas.

The season started in a frenzy of goalscoring from Geoff Bradford. He scored the only goal against Port Vale and was to score 19 goals in 14 League games by 23 October. Ultimately, he was easily the club's top scorer with 26 Division Two goals. In the first week of September, he scored two hat-tricks in 48 hours, first in a 4-1 home victory over Derby County and secondly as Liverpool were defeated 3-0 at Eastville. The goals against Derby came in a frantic 18-minute spell in the opening half hour, with Peter Hooper adding the first of his many Rovers goals, while the Liverpool game was the seventh in succession in which Bradford had scored, a new club record that was to last just 18 months. At this stage, in fact, he had scored in each of his last 9 League appearances, if his final games before injury in November 1953 are taken into consideration.

Rovers also recorded a 5-1 home victory over Leeds United, a fourth consecutive game in which Bradford had scored twice, and a 4-0 win at home to Ipswich Town, thanks to a brace of goals from George Petherbridge. The largest victory, though, was when Swansea Town visited Eastville in the first week of October. Mel Charles, having scored in both fixtures against Rovers the previous season, put through his own net after only six minutes and Bradford doubled Rovers' lead nine minutes later. After half-time, Bradford scored again after 55 minutes, Hooper scored on the hour mark, Ron Burgess contributed an own goal 12 minutes later and Roost added a sixth with a quarter of an hour left. Hooper's second goal, in the last minute, meant Rovers had equalled the club record 7-0 League victory. It was also the second of only three occasions that the opposition has contributed two own goals in a League match.

On 12 September 1954, Jack Lewis, Rovers' inside right in the 1904/05 Southern League Championship season and the winner of a Welsh cap while on Rovers' books, died at the age of 72. Around this time, Rovers' defensive frailties were being exposed. In two consecutive games, as again in December 1957 and November 1992, Rovers conceded five. All the West Ham United forwards, including the future Manchester United manager Dave Sexton, got on the scoresheet in a game played in torrential rain and a thunderstorm. Four days later, Rovers scored three times at Anfield, only for John Evans to score all Liverpool's goals in their 5-3 win. It was a devastating show of goalscoring from an underrated forward and his achievement remains a Liverpool record equalled only by Andy McGuigan and Ian Rush.

The Upton Park game was the first time since October 1948 that Rovers had conceded five goals in a League game, yet Rovers proceeded to lose 6-2 at Rotherham United and let in four at home to Notts County and West Ham United. John Dick scored three of the Hammers' goals at Eastville. Seventy goals were conceded in the League, the club's worst defensive record since 1947/48. The heaviest defeat came at Blackburn Rovers in a match that Rovers had led 3-2 at half-time. Roost had put Rovers ahead after only six minutes and Lambden twice restored the lead after Eddie Crossan and Tommy Briggs had equalised. However, in a one-man second-half, Briggs scored six more for a personal tally of seven and to consign Rovers to an 8-3 defeat.

Briggs was a powerful and strong centre-forward, exactly the type of player Rovers struggled to contain. His first goal had come from a low drive 12 minutes before half-time and his second, Blackburn's third equaliser, was a header from Crossan's free-kick after 48 minutes. Fourteen minutes later he converted Bobby Langton's cross to put the home side ahead. With 12 minutes remaining, Rovers trailed 4-3, but Briggs was to score four times with his right foot in those final minutes, the last as a reluctant penalty-taker to establish a club record. He also hit a post, but Briggs had scored seven goals in 56 minutes to inflict on Rovers their heaviest League defeat since April 1936.

Seven days later, Rovers responded with their largest win of the second half of the season. Fulham, appearing in the snow in red and white quarters, as opposed to Rovers' blue and white quarters, were beaten 4-1 at Eastville, with the future England forward Johnny Haynes scoring their goal. A series of low-scoring games saw Rovers' second season in Division Two end with the club in ninth place in the table. On the long trip to Elland Road, where Rovers lost 2-0 to Leeds United, Bob Forrest's opening goal after

SEASON 1954/55

FOOTBALL LEAGUE DIVISION TWO

Date	Opponent	H	G	ATT	G	2	3	4	5	6	7	8	9	10	11	GOALSCORERS
21/08/54	PORT VALE	H	1-0	32367	RADFORD	BAMFORD	FOX	PITT	WARREN	SAMPSON	PETHERBRIDGE	BIGGS	BRADFORD	MEYER	HOOPER	BRADFORD
25/08/54	BIRMINGHAM CITY	A	1-2	26000	RADFORD	BAMFORD	FOX	PITT	WARREN	SAMPSON	PETHERBRIDGE	HALE	BRADFORD	MEYER	HOOPER	BRADFORD
28/08/54	DONCASTER ROVERS	A	2-2	16399	RADFORD	BAMFORD	FOX	PITT	WARREN	SAMPSON	PETHERBRIDGE	BRADFORD	ROOST	MEYER	HOOPER	BRADFORD, PITT
30/08/54	BIRMINGHAM CITY	H	1-1	26191	RADFORD	BAMFORD	FOX	PITT	WARREN	SAMPSON	PETHERBRIDGE	BRADFORD	ROOST	HALE	HOOPER	BRADFORD
04/09/54	DERBY COUNTY	H	4-1	23500	RADFORD	BAMFORD	EDWARDS	PITT	WARREN	SAMPSON	PETHERBRIDGE	HALE	BRADFORD	ROOST	HOOPER	BRADFORD 3, HOOPER
06/09/54	LIVERPOOL	H	3-0	25574	RADFORD	BAMFORD	EDWARDS	PITT	WARREN	SAMPSON	PETHERBRIDGE	HALE	BRADFORD	ROOST	HOOPER	BRADFORD 3
11/09/54	WEST HAM UNITED	A	2-5	22500	RADFORD	BAMFORD	EDWARDS	PITT	WARREN	SAMPSON	PETHERBRIDGE	HALE	BRADFORD	ROOST	HOOPER	ROOST 2
15/09/54	LIVERPOOL	A	3-5	31100	RADFORD	BAMFORD	EDWARDS	PITT	WARREN	ANDERSON	PETHERBRIDGE	HALE	BRADFORD	ROOST	HOOPER	HOOPER 2, BAMFORD
18/09/54	BLACKBURN ROVERS	H	2-1	26690	RADFORD	BAMFORD	EDWARDS	PITT	MUIR	ANDERSON	PETHERBRIDGE	HALE	BRADFORD	ROOST	HOOPER	ROOST 2
25/09/54	FULHAM	A	3-2	31648	RADFORD	BAMFORD	WATKINS	PITT	MUIR	ANDERSON	PETHERBRIDGE	MEYER	BRADFORD	ROOST	HOOPER	MEYER 2, BRADFORD
02/10/54	SWANSEA TOWN	H	7-0	28731	RADFORD	BAMFORD	WATKINS	PITT	MUIR	ANDERSON	PETHERBRIDGE	BRADFORD	MEYER	ROOST	HOOPER	BRADFORD 2, HOOPER 2, ROOST, CHARLES og, BURGESS og
09/10/54	LUTON TOWN	H	3-2	30654	RADFORD	BAMFORD	WATKINS	PITT	WARREN	ANDERSON	PETHERBRIDGE	BRADFORD	MEYER	ROOST	HOOPER	BRADFORD 2, MEYER
16/10/54	ROTHERHAM UNITED	A	2-6	17478	RADFORD	BAMFORD	WATKINS	PITT	WARREN	ANDERSON	PETHERBRIDGE	BRADFORD	MEYER	ROOST	HOOPER	BRADFORD 2
23/10/54	LEEDS UNITED	A	5-1	24568	RADFORD	BAMFORD	WATKINS	PITT	WARREN	ANDERSON	PETHERBRIDGE	BRADFORD	MEYER	ROOST	HOOPER	MEYER 2, BRADFORD 2, HOOPER
30/10/54	BURY	H	1-3	15373	RADFORD	BAMFORD	WATKINS	PITT	WARREN	ANDERSON	PETHERBRIDGE	BRADFORD	MEYER	ROOST	HOOPER	MEYER
06/11/54	LINCOLN CITY	A	2-2	22102	RADFORD	BAMFORD	WATKINS	PITT	WARREN	CAIRNEY	PETHERBRIDGE	BRADFORD	HALE	ROOST	WATLING	HOOPER, PETHERBRIDGE
13/11/54	HULL CITY	H	1-0	19023	RADFORD	BAMFORD	ALLCOCK	PITT	WARREN	CAIRNEY	PETHERBRIDGE	BRADFORD	MEYER	ROOST	WATLING	BRADFORD
20/11/54	IPSWICH TOWN	A	4-0	20012	RADFORD	BAMFORD	ALLCOCK	PITT	WARREN	ANDERSON	PETHERBRIDGE	BRADFORD	MEYER	ROOST	WATLING	PETHERBRIDGE 2, BRADFORD, MEYER
27/11/54	NOTTINGHAM FOREST	A	0-1	13623	RADFORD	BAMFORD	ALLCOCK	PITT	WARREN	ANDERSON	PETHERBRIDGE	BRADFORD	HALE	ROOST	HOOPER	
04/12/54	STOKE CITY	H	1-1	21240	RADFORD	BAMFORD	ALLCOCK	PITT	WARREN	ANDERSON	PETHERBRIDGE	BIGGS	MEYER	BRADFORD	HOOPER	BIGGS
11/12/54	MIDDLESBROUGH	H	1-1	21051	RADFORD	BAMFORD	ALLCOCK	PITT	WARREN	ANDERSON	McILVENNY	ROOST	LAMBDEN	BRADFORD	PETHERBRIDGE	
18/12/54	PORT VALE	A	0-1	16434	RADFORD	BAMFORD	ALLCOCK	PITT	WARREN	MUIR	McILVENNY	ROOST	LAMBDEN	BRADFORD	WATLING	
25/12/54	NOTTS COUNTY	A	0-2	19647	RADFORD	BAMFORD	ALLCOCK	PITT	MUIR	ANDERSON	McILVENNY	ROOST	MEYER	BRADFORD	WATLING	
27/12/54	NOTTS COUNTY	H	1-4	28855	RADFORD	BAMFORD	FOX	PITT	MUIR	ANDERSON	PETHERBRIDGE	ROOST	LAMBDEN	BRADFORD	HOOPER	LAMBDEN
01/01/55	DONCASTER ROVERS	H	1-0	19153	RADFORD	BAMFORD	FOX	PITT	WARREN	CAIRNEY	PETHERBRIDGE	BUSH	LAMBDEN	BRADFORD	HOOPER	BRADFORD
22/01/55	WEST HAM UNITED	A	2-4	27552	RADFORD	BAMFORD	ALLCOCK	PITT	WARREN	CAIRNEY	PETHERBRIDGE	BRADFORD	LAMBDEN	ROOST	HOOPER	LAMBDEN, BRADFORD
05/02/55	BLACKBURN ROVERS	H	3-8	24600	RADFORD	ALLCOCK	FOX	PITT	WARREN	CAIRNEY	PETHERBRIDGE	BRADFORD	LAMBDEN	ROOST	WATLING	LAMBDEN 2, ROOST, PETHERBRIDGE
12/02/55	FULHAM	H	4-1	19311	RADFORD	BAMFORD	ALLCOCK	PITT	WARREN	SAMPSON	PETHERBRIDGE	BRADFORD	LAMBDEN	ROOST	WATLING	LAMBDEN 2, ROOST
19/02/55	DERBY COUNTY	H	1-1	11000	RADFORD	BAMFORD	ALLCOCK	PITT	WARREN	SAMPSON	PETHERBRIDGE	BRADFORD	LAMBDEN	ROOST	HOOPER	PETHERBRIDGE
05/03/55	ROTHERHAM UNITED	A	1-0	19739	RADFORD	BAMFORD	ALLCOCK	PITT	WARREN	SAMPSON	McILVENNY	BRADFORD	LAMBDEN	ROOST	HOOPER	HOOPER
12/03/55	LEEDS UNITED	H	0-2	16922	RADFORD	BAMFORD	ALLCOCK	PITT	WARREN	SAMPSON	McILVENNY	BRADFORD	MEYER	ROOST	HOOPER	
19/03/55	BURY	A	2-1	17675	RADFORD	BAMFORD	ALLCOCK	PITT	WARREN	SAMPSON	McILVENNY	BIGGS	BRADFORD	ROOST	BIGGS	BRADFORD, MEYER
26/03/55	LINCOLN CITY	H	2-1	6456	RADFORD	BAMFORD	FOX	PITT	MUIR	SAMPSON	PETHERBRIDGE	BIGGS	BRADFORD	ROOST	PETHERBRIDGE	BAMFORD, BRADFORD
31/03/55	SWANSEA TOWN	H	2-0	17804	RADFORD	BAMFORD	ALLCOCK	PITT	WARREN	SAMPSON	PETHERBRIDGE	BIGGS	BRADFORD	ROOST	WATLING	WATLING
02/04/55	HULL CITY	H	1-1	17168	CHANDLER	BAMFORD	ALLCOCK	PITT	MUIR	SAMPSON	PETHERBRIDGE	BIGGS	LAMBDEN	MEYER	WATLING	WATLING
08/04/55	PLYMOUTH ARGYLE	H	1-0	26010	CHANDLER	BAMFORD	ALLCOCK	PITT	WARREN	SAMPSON	PETHERBRIDGE	BIGGS	LAMBDEN	MEYER	WATLING	BIGGS 2, BRADFORD
09/04/55	IPSWICH TOWN	A	3-1	16186	CHANDLER	BAMFORD	ALLCOCK	PITT	WARREN	SAMPSON	PETHERBRIDGE	BIGGS	LAMBDEN	BRADFORD	WATLING	LAMBDEN
11/04/55	PLYMOUTH ARGYLE	A	1-0	26134	CHANDLER	BAMFORD	ALLCOCK	PITT	WARREN	SAMPSON	PETHERBRIDGE	BIGGS	MEYER	WARD	WATLING	BIGGS, MEYER
16/04/55	NOTTINGHAM FOREST	H	2-1	26174	CHANDLER	ALLCOCK	FOX	PITT	MUIR	SAMPSON	PETHERBRIDGE	BIGGS	BRADFORD	MEYER	HOOPER	
23/04/55	STOKE CITY	A	0-2	16694	CHANDLER	BAMFORD	ALLCOCK	PITT	WARREN	SAMPSON	PETHERBRIDGE	BIGGS	ROOST	MEYER	WATLING	MEYER, HOOPER
27/04/55	LUTON TOWN	A	0-2	20097	CHANDLER	BAMFORD	ALLCOCK	PITT	WARREN	SAMPSON	PETHERBRIDGE	BIGGS	BRADFORD	MEYER	WATLING	
30/04/55	MIDDLESBROUGH	H	2-2	14707	CHANDLER	BAMFORD	ALLCOCK	PITT	WARREN	SAMPSON	BIGGS	ROOST	BRADFORD	MEYER	HOOPER	

FA CUP

Date	Opponent	H	G	ATT	G	2	3	4	5	6	7	8	9	10	11	GOALSCORERS
08/01/55	PORTSMOUTH	H	2-1	35921	RADFORD	BAMFORD	FOX	PITT	WARREN	CAIRNEY	PETHERBRIDGE	ROOST	LAMBDEN	BRADFORD	WATLING	BRADFORD, ROOST
29/01/55	CHELSEA	H	1-3	35972	RADFORD	BAMFORD	FOX	PITT	WARREN	CAIRNEY	PETHERBRIDGE	ROOST	LAMBDEN	BRADFORD	WATLING	PITT pen

GLOUCESTERSHIRE CUP FINAL

Date	Opponent	H	G	ATT	G	2	3	4	5	6	7	8	9	10	11	GOALSCORERS
02/05/55	BRISTOL CITY	H	2-1	20097	RADFORD	BAMFORD	FOX	PITT	WARREN	SAMPSON	PETHERBRIDGE	BIGGS	BRADFORD	ROOST	WATLING	WARREN, PEACOCK og

PLAYERS	APP	GLS
ALLCOCK F	24	
ANDERSON J	14	
BAMFORD	40	
BIGGS A	13	4
BRADFORD G	39	26
BUSH B	1	
CAIRNEY C	5	
CHANDLER R	8	
EDWARDS L	5	
FOX G	8	
HALE D	10	
HOOPER P	25	9
LAMBDEN V	12	7
McILVENNY J	6	
MEYER B	20	10
MUIR I	9	
PETHERBRIDGE G	37	
PITT J	42	1
RADFORD H	34	
ROOST W	32	7
SAMPSON P	22	
WARD D	1	
WARREN R	34	
WATKINS B	7	
WATLING J	14	2
OWN GOALS		2

11 seconds constitutes the fastest goal scored in a League match involving Rovers. It had been a long season and many lessons had been learned. Rovers set off for Devon, where the season was rounded off by an extraordinary friendly, won 10-6 at Dawlish, with Bradford contributing four of the goals.

1955/56

In the history of any football club there is a key moment where fate can determine success or otherwise. In the case of Bristol Rovers, bereft of their injured talisman, Geoff Bradford, two late defeats meant missing out narrowly on promotion to Division One. The club has still never attained the dizzy heights of the top division. Neither too, of course, had Coventry City, in many respects a Division Three equal of Rovers, who when finally promoted in 1968, grabbed the opportunity with both hands and enjoyed more than 30 years in the top flight. Rovers missed out by four points, the thin line between success and mediocrity.

With Geoff Fox, Vic Lambden and Bryan Bush gone, the Championship side of 1952/53 was finally breaking up. Ray Warren, after 20 years with the club, played in his 450th and final League game in December, while Bill Roost, John McIlvenny and Josser Watling were being used less frequently in the side. With Howard Radford a pivotal figure in goal, Harry Bamford was now accompanied at full-back by the promising talent of Frank Allcock. Bamford, the only ever-present, again did not score, though he was debited with an own goal against Bury in November. Peter Sampson, George Petherbridge, Barrie Meyer and newly-appointed club captain Jackie Pitt remained of the old guard, with Paddy Hale now assuming the mantle of centre-half and the talented Peter Hooper at outside-left. Alfie Biggs, who scored twice in victories over Nottingham Forest and Sheffield Wednesday, was fast emerging as Bradford's new sidekick. Fred Ford, the new coach, was to share in five excellent seasons, and later returned to Eastville in 1968 as manager.

The role of Geoff Bradford in the Rovers story cannot be underestimated. He scored in all but four of his first 17 matches of the season, seven times scoring twice in a game. Potentially key games at Stoke City and Hull City were both won 2-1, Bradford scoring the goals on both occasions. On 2 October 1955 he became the only player to appear for England while on Rovers' books. The Supporters' Club chartered an aeroplane to take 34 Rovers fans to the game in Copenhagen, including in their number Mrs Bradford as a guest of the club. For the majority of the travellers, this was the first time that they had been in an aeroplane, but their memories of the occasion were to prove priceless. Characteristically, in a 5-1 victory over Denmark, Geoff Bradford scored England's fifth goal, with a low right-foot shot eight minutes from time from Jackie Milburn's flighted cross pass. It was to be his only England cap. Then, having scored a hat-trick in the return fixture with Hull City, Bradford was seriously injured in an FA Cup game at Doncaster Rovers in January. With their star player out for the rest of the season, Rovers' promotion push foundered on the rocks of inadequacy.

October 1955. Geoff Bradford (white shirt) scores England's fifth goal in the 5-1 victory in Denmark

Bristol Rovers 1955/56. Back row: Anderson, Sampson, Nicholls, Bamford, Hale, Muir. Front row: Petherbridge, Biggs, Meyer, Ward, Hooper

FOOTBALL LEAGUE DIVISION TWO

Date	Opponent		Result	Att	G	2	3	4	5	6	7	8	9	10	11	Goalscorers
20/08/55	PORT VALE	A	1-1	21270	RADFORD	BAMFORD	ALLCOCK	PITT	WARREN	SAMPSON	PETHERBRIDGE	BIGGS	MEYER	BRADFORD	WATLING	MEYER
22/08/55	STOKE CITY	H	4-2	21103	RADFORD	BAMFORD	ALLCOCK	PITT	WARREN	SAMPSON	PETHERBRIDGE	BIGGS	MEYER	BRADFORD	WATLING	PITT, MEYER, PETHERBRIDGE, ANDERSON J
27/08/55	DONCASTER ROVERS	H	4-2	23000	RADFORD	BAMFORD	ALLCOCK	PITT	WARREN	SAMPSON	PETHERBRIDGE	BIGGS	MEYER	BRADFORD	WATLING	BAMFORD, MEYER, BRADFORD 2,
29/08/55	STOKE CITY	A	2-1	18875	RADFORD	BAMFORD	ALLCOCK	PITT	WARREN	SAMPSON	PETHERBRIDGE	BIGGS	MEYER	BRADFORD	WATLING	MEYER, BRADFORD 2,
03/09/55	SHEFFIELD WEDNESDAY	A	2-4	30526	RADFORD	BAMFORD	ALLCOCK	PITT	WARREN	SAMPSON	PETHERBRIDGE	BIGGS	MEYER	BRADFORD	WATLING	BRADFORD 2
07/09/55	LIVERPOOL	A	2-0	38320	RADFORD	BAMFORD	ALLCOCK	PITT	MUIR	SAMPSON	PETHERBRIDGE	BIGGS	MEYER	BRADFORD	WATLING	BRADFORD, WATLING
10/09/55	NOTTINGHAM FOREST	H	4-1	25875	RADFORD	BAMFORD	ALLCOCK	PITT	MUIR	SAMPSON	PETHERBRIDGE	BIGGS	MEYER	BRADFORD	WATLING	BIGGS 2, BRADFORD 2
17/09/55	HULL CITY	A	2-1	14014	RADFORD	BAMFORD	ALLCOCK	PITT	MUIR	SAMPSON	PETHERBRIDGE	BIGGS	MEYER	BRADFORD	WATLING	BRADFORD 2
24/09/55	BLACKBURN ROVERS	H	1-0	25489	RADFORD	BAMFORD	ALLCOCK	PITT	WARREN	SAMPSON	PETHERBRIDGE	BIGGS	MEYER	BRADFORD	WATLING	BRADFORD 2
01/10/55	LINCOLN CITY	H	0-2	15076	RADFORD	BAMFORD	ALLCOCK	PITT	WARREN	SAMPSON	PETHERBRIDGE	BIGGS	MEYER	BRADFORD	WATLING	SAMPSON
08/10/55	ROTHERHAM UNITED	A	0-1	12221	RADFORD	BAMFORD	ALLCOCK	PITT	WARREN	SAMPSON	PETHERBRIDGE	BIGGS	MEYER	BRADFORD	WATLING	BRADFORD
15/10/55	SWANSEA TOWN	H	1-2	30122	RADFORD	BAMFORD	ALLCOCK	PITT	WARREN	SAMPSON	PETHERBRIDGE	BIGGS	MEYER	BRADFORD	WATLING	PETHERBRIDGE
22/10/55	BRISTOL CITY	A	1-1	25574	RADFORD	BAMFORD	ALLCOCK	PITT	WARREN	SAMPSON	PETHERBRIDGE	BIGGS	MEYER	BRADFORD	WATLING	RADFORD H
29/10/55	LEEDS UNITED	H	4-1	29574	RADFORD	BAMFORD	ALLCOCK	PITT	WARREN	SAMPSON	PETHERBRIDGE	BIGGS	MEYER	BRADFORD	HOOPER	PITT J
05/11/55	FULHAM	A	5-3	23145	RADFORD	BAMFORD	ALLCOCK	PITT	WARREN	SAMPSON	PETHERBRIDGE	BIGGS	MEYER	BRADFORD	HOOPER	PETHERBRIDGE, BIGGS 2, MEYER, HOOPER
12/11/55	BURY	H	4-2	11625	RADFORD	BAMFORD	ALLCOCK	PITT	WARREN	SAMPSON	PETHERBRIDGE	BIGGS	MEYER	BRADFORD	HOOPER	MEYER 2, BRADFORD, WARD
19/11/55	BARNSLEY	A	3-4	11625	RADFORD	BAMFORD	ALLCOCK	PITT	WARREN	SAMPSON	PETHERBRIDGE	BIGGS	MEYER	BRADFORD	HOOPER	BRADFORD, MEYER
26/11/55	MIDDLESBROUGH	H	7-2	23728	RADFORD	BAMFORD	ALLCOCK	PITT	WARREN	SAMPSON	PETHERBRIDGE	BIGGS	MEYER	BRADFORD	HOOPER	BIGGS 2, MEYER, BRADFORD 2, WATLING
03/12/55	NOTTS COUNTY	A	2-5	15525	RADFORD	BAMFORD	ALLCOCK	PITT	WARREN	SAMPSON	PETHERBRIDGE	BIGGS	MEYER	BRADFORD	HOOPER	HOOPER pen, PETHERBRIDGE
10/12/55	WEST HAM UNITED	H	1-1	20708	RADFORD	BAMFORD	ALLCOCK	PITT	WARREN	SAMPSON	PETHERBRIDGE	BIGGS	MEYER	BRADFORD	HOOPER	HOOPER pen, WARD
17/12/55	PORT VALE	A	1-2	19129	RADFORD	BAMFORD	ALLCOCK	PITT	WARREN	SAMPSON	PETHERBRIDGE	WARD	BRADFORD	MEYER	HOOPER	WARD
24/12/55	DONCASTER ROVERS	H	1-2	12083	RADFORD	BAMFORD	ALLCOCK	PITT	HALE	SAMPSON	PETHERBRIDGE	BIGGS	BRADFORD	MEYER	HOOPER	BRADFORD
26/12/55	LEICESTER CITY	A	2-4	21652	RADFORD	BAMFORD	ALLCOCK	PITT	HALE	SAMPSON	McILVENNY	BIGGS	MEYER	BRADFORD	WATLING	BRADFORD, MEYER
27/12/55	LEICESTER CITY	H	2-1	35000	RADFORD	BAMFORD	ALLCOCK	PITT	HALE	SAMPSON	PETHERBRIDGE	BIGGS	MEYER	BRADFORD	WATLING	MEYER 2
31/12/55	SHEFFIELD WEDNESDAY	H	4-2	30807	RADFORD	BAMFORD	ALLCOCK	PITT	HALE	SAMPSON	PETHERBRIDGE	BIGGS	MEYER	BRADFORD	WATLING	MEYER 2, BRADFORD, WARD
14/01/56	NOTTINGHAM FOREST	A	1-1	12291	RADFORD	BAMFORD	ALLCOCK	ANDERSON	HALE	SAMPSON	PETHERBRIDGE	WARD	MEYER	BRADFORD	WATLING	BRADFORD, MEYER
21/01/56	HULL CITY	H	4-2	23854	RADFORD	BAMFORD	ALLCOCK	PITT	HALE	SAMPSON	PETHERBRIDGE	BIGGS	MEYER	BRADFORD	WATLING	BIGGS 2, MEYER, BRADFORD
04/02/56	BLACKBURN ROVERS	A	0-2	19099	RADFORD	BAMFORD	ALLCOCK	PITT	HALE	SAMPSON	PETHERBRIDGE	BIGGS	MEYER	BRADFORD	WATLING	
11/02/56	LINCOLN CITY	H	4-2	23854	RADFORD	BAMFORD	ALLCOCK	PITT	HALE	SAMPSON	PETHERBRIDGE	BIGGS	BRADFORD	MEYER	WATLING	BIGGS 2, MEYER, BRADFORD 2
18/02/56	BARNSLEY	A	3-0	17649	RADFORD	BAMFORD	ALLCOCK	PITT	HALE	SAMPSON	PETHERBRIDGE	WARD	SEATHERTON	MEYER	WATLING	SEATHERTON, MEYER, HOOPER pen
25/02/56	SWANSEA TOWN	H	1-1	20995	RADFORD	BAMFORD	ALLCOCK	PITT	HALE	SAMPSON	PETHERBRIDGE	WARD	SEATHERTON	MEYER	HOOPER	SEATHERTON
03/03/56	BRISTOL CITY	A	2-1	23528	RADFORD	BAMFORD	ALLCOCK	PITT	HALE	SAMPSON	PETHERBRIDGE	WARD	ROOST	MEYER	HOOPER	ROOST, MEYER
10/03/56	WEST HAM UNITED	A	0-3	35324	RADFORD	BAMFORD	ALLCOCK	PITT	HALE	SAMPSON	PETHERBRIDGE	WARD	ROOST	MEYER	HOOPER	
17/03/56	FULHAM	H	1-2	20000	RADFORD	BAMFORD	ALLCOCK	MUIR	HALE	SAMPSON	PETHERBRIDGE	WARD	MEYER	BRADFORD	HOOPER	MEYER
24/03/56	BURY	A	1-0	21836	NICHOLLS	BAMFORD	EDWARDS	PITT	HALE	SAMPSON	PETHERBRIDGE	WARD	MEYER	BRADFORD	HOOPER	HOOPER
30/03/56	PLYMOUTH ARGYLE	A	2-2	11569	NICHOLLS	BAMFORD	EDWARDS	SAMPSON	HALE	ANDERSON	PETHERBRIDGE	BIGGS	MEYER	WARD	HOOPER	WARD, HOOPER
31/03/56	ROTHERHAM UNITED	H	1-0	27814	NICHOLLS	BAMFORD	EDWARDS	SAMPSON	HALE	ANDERSON	PETHERBRIDGE	BIGGS	MEYER	WARD	WATLING	BIGGS
02/04/56	PLYMOUTH ARGYLE	H	2-1	23367	NICHOLLS	BAMFORD	EDWARDS	SAMPSON	HALE	ANDERSON	PETHERBRIDGE	BIGGS	MEYER	WARD	HOOPER	MEYER, WARD
07/04/56	MIDDLESBROUGH	A	1-4	19181	NICHOLLS	BAMFORD	EDWARDS	MUIR	HALE	ANDERSON	PETHERBRIDGE	BIGGS	BRADFORD	WARD	HOOPER	BIGGS, MEYER
14/04/56	NOTTS COUNTY	A	1-0	12536	NICHOLLS	BAMFORD	EDWARDS	MUIR	HALE	ANDERSON	PETHERBRIDGE	BIGGS	MEYER	WARD	HOOPER	MEYER
21/04/56	LEEDS UNITED	A	2-0	15505	NICHOLLS	BAMFORD	EDWARDS	MUIR	HALE	ANDERSON	PETHERBRIDGE	BIGGS	MEYER	WARD	WATLING	BAMFORD, MEYER, PETHERBRIDGE,
28/04/56	LIVERPOOL	H	1-2	49274	NICHOLLS	BAMFORD	EDWARDS	MUIR	HALE	SAMPSON	PETHERBRIDGE	BIGGS	ROOST	BRADFORD	HOOPER	BRADFORD

FA CUP

Date	Opponent		Result	Att	G	2	3	4	5	6	7	8	9	10	11	Goalscorers
07/01/56	MANCHESTER UNITED	H	4-0	35872	RADFORD	BAMFORD	ALLCOCK	PITT	HALE	SAMPSON	PETHERBRIDGE	BIGGS	MEYER	BRADFORD	WATLING	MEYER 2, BRADFORD, PETHERBRIDGE
28/01/56	DONCASTER ROVERS	H	1-1	35420	RADFORD	BAMFORD	ALLCOCK	PITT	HALE	SAMPSON	PETHERBRIDGE	BIGGS	MEYER	BRADFORD	WATLING	HOOPER 2, MEYER, BRADFORD pen
31/01/56	DONCASTER ROVERS	A	0-1	22093	NICHOLLS	BAMFORD	ALLCOCK	PITT	HALE	SAMPSON	PETHERBRIDGE	BIGGS	ROOST	BRADFORD	WATLING	

GLOUCESTERSHIRE CUP FINAL

Date	Opponent		Result	Att	G	2	3	4	5	6	7	8	9	10	11	Goalscorers
30/04/56	BRISTOL CITY	A	1-0	11952	RADFORD	BAMFORD	ALLCOCK	SYKES	HALE	SAMPSON	PETHERBRIDGE	BIGGS	ROOST	MEYER	HOOPER	MEYER

PLAYERS	APP	GLS
ALLCOCK F	33	
ANDERSON J	9	
BAMFORD H	42	
BIGGS A	26	9
BRADFORD G	27	8
EDWARDS L	9	
HALE D	21	
HOOPER P	25	6
McILVENNY J	1	
MEYER B	40	20
MUIR I	14	
NICHOLLS R	8	
PETHERBRIDGE G	41	4
PITT J	34	1
RADFORD H	34	
ROOST W	4	
SAMPSON P	39	1
SEATHERTON R	2	2
WARD D	27	2
WARREN R	11	
WATLING J	15	1

The Hull game was the ninth and final time Rovers had scored four or more goals at Eastville in League and FA Cup football in 1955/56. Bradford had scored at least once on all nine occasions. The Hull City side included the veteran Stan Mortensen, scorer of a hat-trick in the 1953 'Matthews' FA Cup final and the holder of 25 England caps, but it was Bradford who stole the show with three goals. Promotion rivals Leeds United had been defeated 4-1 at Eastville in October, Bradford claiming a pair of goals on that occasion. The largest victory, however, was a 7-2 mauling of Middlesbrough in November.

Rovers went into the home game with Middlesbrough having scored 16 goals and conceded 10 in their previous four League matches. The crowd of 23,728 anticipated a feast of goals and was duly rewarded. This remains one of only two post-war league fixtures where three Rovers players have scored two or more times each. Bradford opened the scoring after 13 minutes and two Ward goals meant Rovers led 3-0 with only 18 minutes played. Charlie Wayman pulled a goal back just before half-time, Bradford and Hooper put Rovers 5-1 ahead and Lindy Delapenha scored the visitors' second. Hooper's second goal, after 78 minutes, and one from Petherbridge six minutes later left Rovers in the ascendancy.

The euphoria of this 7-2 victory lasted just a week. The following Saturday, at Notts County, Rovers crashed to a 5-2 defeat, their heaviest of the season. Ron Wylie, later manager of West Bromwich Albion, was to score only 5 goals all season, but claimed a hat-trick for County. Bradford-less Rovers later crashed 4-1 at home to Rotherham United with Ian Wilson, the scorer of one of the six at Millmoor in October 1954, weighing in with three goals. Tommy Briggs, after his seven goals the previous season, scored just the once at Ewood Park in February, while Johnny Haynes scored at Eastville for a second consecutive year, playing for a Fulham side which included Jimmy Hill at outside left.

The first all-ticket game ever to be staged at Eastville was the local derby with Bristol City in March. The sides had drawn 1-1 at Ashton Gate in the autumn before a then-record Ashton Gate crowd of 39,583 and the first Division Two clash of these sides in East Bristol was expected to attract a large turnout. Rovers had, prior to this fixture, scored in 43 consecutive home League games, but faced a proven goalscorer in John Atyeo. The attendance of 35,324, though not a ground record, remains in perpetuity as the highest ever at a League game at Eastville. These were the days when thousands flocked into the Tote End, which boasted a maximum capacity at one point of 12,250, and the Muller Road End, where up to 16,900 spectators gathered behind the trademark flowerbeds that formed a colourful if unorthodox backdrop to the goalnet at that end of the pitch. However, despite the massive support in the cauldron of one of Britain's most keenly fought local derbies, Rovers were to lose 3-0, with Atyeo scoring twice.

A new goalkeeper, Ron Nicholls, played his first few games in the winter months. Like Meyer, he was a county cricketer, the fourth-highest-scoring batsman in the history of Gloucestershire and, although potential training clashes between the sports lay ahead, both players contributed well to Rovers' on-field success. Meyer scored a hat-trick at Fulham, as Rovers recorded their largest away win of the season. He was also instrumental in Rovers defeating Liverpool 2-0 at Anfield through Bradford's header three minutes before half-time from Meyer's cross and a low shot from Biggs cutting in from the right after 59 minutes, on the ground which was to see such undiluted success in the years to come.

Geoff Bradford watches as Alfie Biggs' shot beats Manchester United goalkeeper Wood in the sensational 4-0 FA Cup victory at Eastville

The fixture at Elland Road on 21 April 1956 was one of the more crucial League matches in Rovers' history. With Sheffield Wednesday virtual champions, Rovers lay second with 48 points and two games remaining. Leeds United, with three games left, had 46 points, one more than Blackburn Rovers and Nottingham Forest. Victory for Rovers would leave the Eastville side requiring a point at home to Liverpool for promotion to Division One and, in eager anticipation, the Supporters' Club once again chartered an aeroplane for the trip. Dai Ward had scored crucial goals in recent weeks and his goal at Elland Road set a club record, as it was the eighth consecutive League game in which he had scored, eclipsing Bradford's seven in succession earlier in the season which had equalled his own record. Dramatically, from a Petherbridge cross, Ward headed Rovers ahead after only two minutes. Before half-time, though, John Charles had headed home a George Meek cross and set up Jack Overfield for what proved to be Leeds United's winning goal. The Elland Road crowd, 49,274, remains the largest League crowd in front of which Rovers have played. Once the bubble had burst, Rovers also lost to Liverpool. Wednesday were champions with 55 points, Leeds United promoted with 52, while Liverpool, Blackburn Rovers and Leicester City all inched above Rovers on goal average. So close to their target, Rovers were left to wonder what might have happened had 25-goal top scorer Bradford not been injured and wonder why no adequate replacement was found. A final placing of sixth in Division Two remains the highest in Bristol Rovers' history.

The FA Cup brought, as the *Bristol Evening Post* described it, 'Rovers' finest hour'. Matt Busby's Manchester United played at Eastville before a crowd of 35,872 and were defeated 4-0. Although Duncan Edwards was injured, the United side was packed with household names, five of whom were to perish in the Munich air crash in 1958. An opportunist goal from Biggs put Rovers ahead after only ten minutes and Meyer, at the second attempt, doubled the advantage before half-time. Creative and surprisingly confident against such talented opponents, Rovers scored again through Biggs and a late penalty from Bradford, after England left-back Roger Byrne had handled. Rovers were the '£110 team with the million-dollar touch of class', according to Desmond Hackett in the *Daily Express*. It seemed hardly just that Rovers should exit in the fourth round, falling to an angled drive 10 minutes before half-time from inside-right Bert Tindill in a replay at a snowy Doncaster Rovers that was overshadowed by Bradford's horrific injury. Meyer's first-half goal at Ashton Gate enabled Rovers to retain the Gloucestershire Cup.

1956/57

Bert Tann's home-grown side had come close to an unlikely promotion to Division One and had produced an England International in Geoff Bradford, but reality lay around the corner. The 1956/57 season saw some large victories and heavy defeats as the side had to settle for ninth place in Division Two. It was largely an unchanged Rovers side that opened the season with a home victory over Grimsby Town thanks to a Dai Ward 56th-minute reaction shot. With Frank Allcock's enforced retirement casting a shadow over the previous season's success, Les Edwards partnered the evergreen Harry Bamford at full-back, Ron Nicholls appeared regularly in goal and young wing-half Norman Sykes made the first of numerous League appearances.

Rovers scored in each of the first 14 League games of the new season to complete a run of 24 consecutive matches dating back to March 1956. Two more games would have equalled a club record established in 1927, but Rotherham United held Rovers to a goalless draw at Millmoor. The early-season run included a 4-2 win at Doncaster Rovers, Bradford scoring twice, and a 4-0 home win over Stoke City, as Rovers remained unbeaten in their opening five League fixtures. There were equally convincing 4-0 victories at home to Huddersfield Town, which included a blitz of three goals in five

Geoff Bradford starts pre-season training in July 1956.

minutes, and against a Fulham side boasting the England International and former Rovers schoolboy, Roy Bentley, as well as Elton John's uncle Roy Dwight. In March, two Bill Roost goals contributed to a 4-2 home win over Rotherham United.

The two largest wins, however, came in consecutive home fixtures over Christmas. On 22 December, Rovers defeated Doncaster Rovers 6-1 at Eastville. Dai Ward, who scored after 77, 78 and 80 minutes, recorded the fastest League hat-trick by a Rovers player and Barrie Meyer, for the second consecutive Saturday, scored twice. This was the first time Rovers had accumulated 10 League goals against any opposition in a season. The anomalies of post-war football left Rovers to be crushed 7-2 by Bury at Gigg Lane on Christmas Day before beating the same opposition 6-1 on Boxing Day. Peter Hooper, the eighth player to score three times before half-time for Rovers in a League game, scored a hat-trick against Bury, with Meyer again weighing in with two goals. Hooper gave Rovers a sixth-minute lead and completed a 30-minute first-half hat-trick when he scored from the rebound after his 36th-minute penalty had been saved.

Such a convincing home victory stands in direct contrast with Rovers' heaviest defeat for almost two years. Bury had led 3-1 after 79 minutes before five goals in 11 minutes, four of them to the Lancashire side, distorted the scoreline beyond recognition. Stan Pearson, now almost 37 and a member of Manchester United's 1948 FA Cup-winning side, scored a hat-trick while Tom Neill and Eddie Robertson added two goals apiece. Outside-left Norman Lockhart's missed penalty saved Rovers from further embarrassment. Incredibly, within weeks, Rovers had lost by the same 7-2 scoreline at Leicester City where again, for the fifth and most recent time in Rovers' League history, three opponents had scored twice each. One of these, Arthur Rowley, who had also scored at Eastville in September, remains to this day the record aggregate goalscorer in Football League history.

While these two defeats stand out, an extraordinary 5-3 defeat at Ashton Gate in September similarly exposed Rovers' defensive frailties. John Atyeo and Cyril Williams scored twice each for Bristol City, Dai Ward twice for Rovers. Middlesbrough and three Ls – Leicester City, Lincoln City and Liverpool – all won at Eastville but, to counter this, Rovers won six away games, including victories over Notts County at Meadow Lane and West Ham United at Upton Park. At Vale Park, Rovers led 2-0 after 86 minutes but, after a frenetic final four minutes, were left clinging on for a 3-2 win, afforded by two Geoff Bradford goals. This was Port Vale's seventh consecutive League defeat *en route* to a club record nine in succession.

That there was no shortage of goalmouth excitement at Rovers games is illustrated amply by the fact that the local derby with Bristol City at Eastville in February was only the club's second goalless draw since April 1954. Yet, this game provided an incident that, in many respects, epitomized the spirit of Bristol football in those glorious days of the 1950s. Local derbies never have been for the faint-hearted and two tenacious battlers, Rovers' Jackie Pitt and City's Ernie Peacock, were sent off for their misdeeds in a robust game. As they left the field together, the players linked arms, a symbol that rivalry does not necessarily mean enmity and a sign of what football meant to those at the chalkface in the immediate post-war era.

Four minutes from the end of the 2-1 home defeat against Leicester City in September, Hooper's penalty was struck with such ferocity that, rebounding off a post,

Bristol Rovers 1956/57. Back row: R Moules (Asst Secretary), Ovington, Hooper, Meyer, Seatherton, Pyle, Muir, Anderson, Roost, Clare, B Williams (Trainer). Middle row: W McArthur (Trainer), J Gummow (Secretary), Mabbutt, Lawrence, Sykes, Bamford, Radford, Hale, Sampson, Edwards, Watling, B Tann (Manager), F Ford (Coach). Front row: Jones, Pitt, McIlvenny, Warren, Bradford, Ward, Petherbridge, Steeds, Biggs

it set the opposition on the attack. With Rovers players pushed forward for the penalty, Ian McNeil sent Tommy McDonald through to score past an unprepared defence. Three weeks later, Sheffield United took a first-minute lead at Eastville through John Wilkinson, only for Rovers to recover to win 3-1. Similarly, an apparently convincing 3-0 home victory over Notts County in February conceals the fact that County's Gordon Wills missed a penalty. In December, Tommy Briggs revisited the Rovers defence, scoring both Blackburn Rovers' goals in a 2-0 win. He had now scored a total of 10 goals in Rovers' 3 most recent visits to Ewood Park.

All of which hides a surfeit of 3-2 results, which threatened at times to reach epidemic proportions. Rovers won by this score against Leyton Orient, Swansea Town, Nottingham Forest and Port Vale and lost 3-2 at Middlesbrough, Grimsby Town and Fulham. Three consecutive games in the run-up to Easter finished this way. What with 7-2 defeats and 6-1 victories, the team from East Bristol was due a run of unusual results and so it was to prove in 1957/58. This would have to be achieved without left-back Les Edwards, whose place was taken by a rejuvenated Josser Watling, and forward Bill Roost, whose goal at home to Swansea Town in March marked his final game in a nine-year association with the club.

In the FA Cup, Rovers were 3-0 up at Hull City after only nine minutes and held on to win 4-3. Shades of 1981 at Preston, perhaps, and sure enough, victory at Boothferry Park attracted North End and a 32,000 crowd to Eastville. Preston were to finish the season third in Division One and boasted two future Manchester United managers at wing-half – Tommy Docherty and Frank O'Farrell. Rovers had just lost 7-2 at Leicester City, while Preston were to beat Portsmouth 7-1 in Division One only a week later. Although Hooper scored from the penalty-spot after just five minutes, the form book

Date	Opponent	H/A	G	Att	1	2	3	4	5	6	7	8	9	10	11	Goalscorers
18/08/56	GRIMSBY TOWN	H	1-0	27818	RADFORD	BAMFORD	EDWARDS	PITT	HALE	SAMPSON	PETHERBRIDGE	BIGGS	BRADFORD	WARD	HOOPER	WARD
20/08/56	LEYTON ORIENT	A	1-0	20173	RADFORD	BAMFORD	EDWARDS	PITT	HALE	SAMPSON	PETHERBRIDGE	BIGGS	BRADFORD	WARD	HOOPER	BAMFORD
25/08/56	DONCASTER ROVERS	A	4-2	9314	RADFORD	BAMFORD	EDWARDS	PITT	HALE	SAMPSON	PETHERBRIDGE	BIGGS	BRADFORD	WARD	HOOPER	BRADFORD 2, HOOPER, WARD
27/08/56	LEYTON ORIENT	H	3-2	24776	RADFORD	BAMFORD	EDWARDS	PITT	HALE	SAMPSON	PETHERBRIDGE	BIGGS	BRADFORD	WARD	HOOPER	WARD, BIGGS, BRADFORD
01/09/56	STOKE CITY	H	4-0	25430	RADFORD	BAMFORD	EDWARDS	PITT	HALE	SAMPSON	PETHERBRIDGE	BIGGS	BRADFORD	WARD	HOOPER	BRADFORD 2, HOOPER, WARD
03/09/56	HUDDERSFIELD TOWN	A	1-2	14560	RADFORD	BAMFORD	EDWARDS	PITT	HALE	SAMPSON	PETHERBRIDGE	BIGGS	BRADFORD	WARD	HOOPER	HALE
08/09/56	MIDDLESBROUGH	A	2-3	19149	RADFORD	BAMFORD	EDWARDS	PITT	HALE	SAMPSON	PETHERBRIDGE	BIGGS	BRADFORD	WARD	HOOPER	HOOPER, WARD
10/09/56	HUDDERSFIELD TOWN	H	4-0	27533	RADFORD	BAMFORD	EDWARDS	PITT	HALE	SAMPSON	PETHERBRIDGE	BIGGS	BRADFORD	WARD	HOOPER	WARD 2, BIGGS, HOOPER
15/09/56	LEICESTER CITY	A	2-8	26500	RADFORD	BAMFORD	LAWRENCE	PITT	HALE	SAMPSON	PETHERBRIDGE	BIGGS	MEYER	WARD	HOOPER	WARD 2
22/09/56	BRISTOL CITY	H	3-5	36951	RADFORD	BAMFORD	LAWRENCE	PITT	HALE	SAMPSON	PETHERBRIDGE	BIGGS	MEYER	WARD	HOOPER	WARD 2, BIGGS
29/09/56	NOTTS COUNTY	A	2-0	12720	RADFORD	BAMFORD	LAWRENCE	PITT	HALE	SAMPSON	PETHERBRIDGE	BIGGS	ROOST	WARD	HOOPER	BIGGS, HOOPER
06/10/56	SHEFFIELD UNITED	H	3-1	28393	RADFORD	BAMFORD	EDWARDS	PITT	HALE	SAMPSON	PETHERBRIDGE	BIGGS	MEYER	WARD	HOOPER	BRADFORD 2, BIGGS
13/10/56	BARNSLEY	A	1-0	15052	RADFORD	BAMFORD	WATLING	PITT	HALE	SAMPSON	McILVENNY	BIGGS	MEYER	WARD	HOOPER	HOOPER
20/10/56	WEST HAM UNITED	H	1-1	24402	RADFORD	BAMFORD	WATLING	PITT	HALE	SAMPSON	PETHERBRIDGE	BIGGS	ROOST	MEYER	HOOPER	WARD
27/10/56	ROTHERHAM UNITED	A	0-0	11824	RADFORD	BAMFORD	EDWARDS	PITT	HALE	SAMPSON	PETHERBRIDGE	BIGGS	ROOST	MEYER	HOOPER	
03/11/56	LINCOLN CITY	H	0-1	23322	RADFORD	BAMFORD	WATLING	PITT	HALE	SAMPSON	McILVENNY	BIGGS	MEYER	WARD	HOOPER	
10/11/56	SWANSEA TOWN	A	3-2	16833	RADFORD	BAMFORD	EDWARDS	PITT	HALE	SAMPSON	PETHERBRIDGE	BIGGS	BRADFORD	MEYER	HOOPER	ROOST 2, HOOPER
17/11/56	FULHAM	H	4-0	24658	RADFORD	BAMFORD	EDWARDS	PITT	HALE	SAMPSON	PETHERBRIDGE	BIGGS	MEYER	MEYER	HOOPER	BIGGS, ROOST, MEYER, HOOPER
24/11/56	NOTTINGHAM FOREST	A	1-1	17996	NICHOLLS	BAMFORD	EDWARDS	PITT	HALE	SAMPSON	PETHERBRIDGE	BIGGS	MEYER	MEYER	HOOPER	ROOST
01/12/56	PORT VALE	H	2-1	21308	NICHOLLS	BAMFORD	EDWARDS	PITT	HALE	SAMPSON	PETHERBRIDGE	BIGGS	ROOST	MEYER	HOOPER	SAMPSON, HOOPER
08/12/56	BLACKBURN ROVERS	A	0-2	20400	NICHOLLS	BAMFORD	STEEDS	PITT	HALE	SAMPSON	PETHERBRIDGE	BIGGS	ROOST	MEYER	HOOPER	
15/12/56	GRIMSBY TOWN	A	2-3	10460	NICHOLLS	BAMFORD	EDWARDS	PITT	HALE	SAMPSON	PETHERBRIDGE	BIGGS	MEYER	MEYER	HOOPER	ROOST 2
22/12/56	DONCASTER ROVERS	H	6-1	12186	NICHOLLS	BAMFORD	MUIR	PITT	HALE	SAMPSON	PETHERBRIDGE	BIGGS	MEYER	BRADFORD	PETHERBRIDGE	MEYER 2, WARD 3, BRADFORD
25/12/56	BURY	A	2-7	8962	NICHOLLS	BAMFORD	EDWARDS	PITT	BRADFORD	SYKES	PETHERBRIDGE	BIGGS	BRADFORD	PETHERBRIDGE	HOOPER	MEYER, WARD
26/12/56	BURY	H	6-1	19672	NICHOLLS	BAMFORD	EDWARDS	PITT	HALE	SAMPSON	PETHERBRIDGE	WARD	MEYER	BRADFORD	HOOPER	BIGGS 3 (1 pen), MEYER 2, HOOPER
29/12/56	STOKE CITY	A	0-2	31000	NICHOLLS	BAMFORD	EDWARDS	PITT	HALE	SYKES	PETHERBRIDGE	BIGGS	MEYER	SYKES	HOOPER	
12/01/57	MIDDLESBROUGH	H	0-2	24069	NICHOLLS	BAMFORD	EDWARDS	PITT	HALE	ANDERSON	McILVENNY	BIGGS	BRADFORD	SYKES	HOOPER	
19/01/57	LEICESTER CITY	A	2-7	32288	NICHOLLS	BAMFORD	EDWARDS	SYKES	HALE	SAMPSON	McILVENNY	BIGGS	ROOST	SYKES	HOOPER	SAMPSON, HOOPER
02/02/57	BRISTOL CITY	A	0-0	32055	STEEDS	BAMFORD	EDWARDS	PITT	HALE	SAMPSON	McILVENNY	BIGGS	ROOST	WARD	HOOPER	
09/02/57	NOTTS COUNTY	H	3-0	17737	NICHOLLS	BAMFORD	EDWARDS	PITT	HALE	SAMPSON	McILVENNY	WARD	BIGGS	WARD	HOOPER	HOOPER, WARD, SYKES
16/02/57	SHEFFIELD UNITED	A	0-0	18019	MUIR	BAMFORD	EDWARDS	PITT	HALE	SAMPSON	McILVENNY	WARD	MEYER	WARD	HOOPER	
23/02/57	BARNSLEY	H	1-1	14404	NICHOLLS	BAMFORD	EDWARDS	PITT	HALE	SAMPSON	PETHERBRIDGE	BIGGS	SYKES	MEYER	HOOPER	MEYER
02/03/57	WEST HAM UNITED	A	2-1	22500	NICHOLLS	BAMFORD	EDWARDS	PITT	HALE	SAMPSON	McILVENNY	BIGGS	SYKES	MEYER	HOOPER	HOOPER, WARD
09/03/57	ROTHERHAM UNITED	H	4-2	22500	NICHOLLS	BAMFORD	EDWARDS	RICKETTS	HALE	SAMPSON	PETHERBRIDGE	BIGGS	BIGGS	WARD	HOOPER	BRADFORD 2, WARD, BIGGS
16/03/57	LINCOLN CITY	A	0-1	15011	NICHOLLS	BAMFORD	BRADFORD	RICKETTS	PYLE	BRADFORD	McILVENNY	BIGGS	ROOST	BRADFORD	HOOPER	
23/03/57	SWANSEA TOWN	H	0-1	8907	NICHOLLS	BAMFORD	EDWARDS	PITT	HALE	PYLE	McILVENNY	BIGGS	ROOST	WARD	HOOPER	
30/03/57	FULHAM	A	2-3	21270	NICHOLLS	BAMFORD	WATLING	PITT	HALE	SYKES	PETHERBRIDGE	BIGGS	BRADFORD	ROOST	HOOPER	HOOPER 2
06/04/57	NOTTINGHAM FOREST	H	3-2	21087	NICHOLLS	BAMFORD	WATLING	PITT	HALE	SYKES	PETHERBRIDGE	BIGGS	BRADFORD	MEYER	HOOPER	BIGGS, ROOST, MEYER
13/04/57	PORT VALE	A	3-2	9006	NICHOLLS	BAMFORD	EDWARDS	PITT	HALE	SYKES	PETHERBRIDGE	BIGGS	BRADFORD	WARD	HOOPER	BIGGS, WARD, HOOPER
19/04/57	LIVERPOOL	A	1-4	40776	NICHOLLS	BAMFORD	LAWRENCE	PITT	HALE	SYKES	PETHERBRIDGE	BIGGS	BRADFORD	WARD	HOOPER	BRADFORD
20/04/57	BLACKBURN ROVERS	H	0-1	20794	NICHOLLS	BAMFORD	LAWRENCE	PITT	HALE	SYKES	PETHERBRIDGE	BIGGS	BRADFORD	MEYER	HOOPER	
22/04/57	LIVERPOOL	H	0-0	14794	NICHOLLS	BAMFORD	EDWARDS	PITT	HALE	SYKES	PETHERBRIDGE	BIGGS	MEYER	MEYER	HOOPER	

FA CUP

Date	Opponent	H/A	G	Att	1	2	3	4	5	6	7	8	9	10	11	Goalscorers
05/01/57	HULL CITY	H	1-2	22752	NICHOLLS	BAMFORD	EDWARDS	PITT	HALE	SAMPSON	PETHERBRIDGE	BIGGS	MEYER	WARD	HOOPER	HOOPER
26/01/57	PRESTON NORTH END	A	1-4	32000	NICHOLLS	BAMFORD	EDWARDS	PITT	HALE	SAMPSON	PETHERBRIDGE	BIGGS	ROOST	WARD	HOOPER	HOOPER pen

GLOUCESTERSHIRE CUP FINAL

Date	Opponent	H/A	G	Att	1	2	3	4	5	6	7	8	9	10	11	Goalscorers
29/04/57	BRISTOL CITY	H	1-2	14608	RADFORD	BAMFORD	EDWARDS	PITT	HALE	SYKES	PETHERBRIDGE	BIGGS	BRADFORD	MEYER	HOOPER	BRADFORD

PLAYERS	APP	GLS
ANDERSON J	1	
BAMFORD H	39	
BIGGS A	42	11
BRADFORD G	25	11
EDWARDS L	30	
HALE D	39	1
HOOPER P	40	16
LAWRENCE D	5	
McILVENNY J	10	
MEYER B	21	5
MUIR I	2	
NICHOLLS R	28	
PETHERBRIDGE G	32	1
PITT J	39	
PYLE D	1	
RADFORD H	14	
RICKETTS G	2	
ROOST W	10	5
SAMPSON P	33	1
STEEDS C	1	
SYKES N	16	1
WARD D	19	
WATLING J	5	

was not rewritten as North End ran out 4-1 winners. Tom Finney, now 34 and already the holder of 60 of his career total 76 England caps, scored twice and shot wide from a 65th-minute penalty after Paddy Hale had fouled England International Tommy Thompson. The Gloucestershire Cup final was also lost, 2-1 at home to Bristol City.

The Boxing Day fixture marked the retirement, at the age of 69, of Billy Pinnell, Sports Editor of the *Bristol Evening Post*. Affectionately known as 'The Traveller', he had reported on more than 1,500 Rovers and City games, some 600 of which had been matches outside Bristol. An acknowledged authority on the local professional football scene, Pinnell had worked as a reporter on the *Bristol Times* and *Mirror* from 1919 and had been Sports Editor of the *Post* for almost 25 years. Pinnell died, at the age of 89, in January 1977.

1957/58

The FA Cup is a tournament filled with excitement and expectation, although in Rovers' case early disappointment is all too frequent an occurrence. In 1957/58, for the second and most recent time in the club's history, however, Rovers reached the quarter-finals. Unlike 1950/51, they only had to progress from the third round, by dint of Division Two status, but like the previous quarter-final appearance, the run was to end in a 3-1 defeat.

The FA Cup journey began with a convincing 5-0 victory over Division Three (North) side Mansfield Town, four Rovers forwards getting on the scoresheet. The reward for this was a home tie with high-riding Burnley and a crowd of 34,229 was attracted to Eastville. Burnley, finalists four years later, were to finish sixth in Division One and boasted famous names such as England captain and centre-half Jimmy Adamson and Jimmy McIlroy, an inside-forward who won 55 caps for Northern Ireland. Yet, for the second time in three years, Rovers were to defeat top-division opponents. Rovers led through Paddy Hale after 25 minutes until a flurry of mid-second-half goals left the tie all-square. A 2-2 draw meant a potentially tough replay at Turf Moor, but Rovers emerged 3-2 victors, Norman Sykes scoring his first goal for a year and Dai Ward adding a couple. This was a staggering achievement for Rovers. It remains the one occasion that the club has won any fixture before a crowd of over 40,000 and was, until January 2002, the only time Rovers had won away to a top-division club in the FA Cup.

Football supporters in Bristol could not believe their luck as Rovers and City were drawn together in the fifth round. An attendance of 39,126 at Ashton Gate brought gate receipts of £5,439 and witnessed arguably the most exciting of all Bristol derby matches, with seven goals, a missed penalty and a highly controversial Geoff Bradford winner seven minutes from time. Rovers should have taken a first-minute lead, but it was Barry Watkins who scored against his former club three minutes later to give City an early lead. By half-time Sykes, Ward and Barrie Meyer had scored, Ron Nicholls had saved a penalty from Watkins and Rovers led 3-1. However, City recovered to level at 3-3 and, with a quarter-final place up for grabs, Ward's through ball to Bradford, looking suspiciously offside, brought Rovers a 4-3 victory.

Geoff Bradford scoring Rovers' fourth goal in the exciting 4-3 fifth round FA Cup victory over Bristol City at Ashton Gate

The second quarter-final in Rovers' FA Cup history was an all-Division Two affair. However, despite a Bradford goal to parallel the one he had scored in February 1951, Fulham ran out clear winners. George Cohen, an England World Cup winner in 1966, played alongside the old guard of Roy Bentley, Roy Dwight and Johnny Haynes. Jimmy Hill put Fulham ahead from a rebound after his ninth-minute shot had been blocked, and Arthur Stevens, whose goals had knocked Rovers out of the FA Cup in 1948, added close-range goals after 12 and 35 minutes. At the kick-off, a Rovers supporter had run onto the pitch, dribbled the ball and scored, but all Rovers had to cheer was a classic Bradford header from Sykes' 68th minute free-kick.

Rovers approached season 1957/58 with no new personnel, but with converted forwards Josser Watling and Paddy Hale filling the troublesome left-back and centre-half positions respectively. This was to be the final season goalkeeper Ron Nicholls and forward Barrie Meyer were to spend at Eastville, while half-back Jackie Pitt retired at the season's close after 466 League appearances, a figure only bettered by Stuart Taylor and Harry Bamford. Full-back Bamford, who turned 38 in February, was the club's only ever-present, while Geoff Bradford was top-scorer with 20 goals in 33 League matches. In another high-scoring season, Rovers scored 85 and conceded 80 in finishing 10th in Division Two, goalless draws at Huddersfield Town and Notts County sticking out from among a glut of goals.

If FA Cup attendances were high, then so too were those in the League, where the golden years of post-war football coupled with Rovers' years of relative success combined to boost crowd figures. For a sixth consecutive season, the average attendance at Eastville topped 20,000 yet, at 20,604, this was also the final such season in the 20th century. The opposite side of the equation is that the crowd of 5,687 which watched Rovers' 2-0 victory over Cardiff City at Ninian Park in March was the lowest gathering all season for any Division Two fixture.

In a season of unusual results, one of the most remarkable was a 6-4 defeat at Swansea Town in Rovers' final Christmas Day fixture. Despite being bottom of the table, the Swans were two goals ahead after half an hour through Mel Charles and a Cliff Jones penalty and 3-1 up through Ivor Allchurch after 38 minutes. Peter Sampson's first goal for over two years and Dai Ward's seventh goal of the season left the score 3-2 at half-time. Alfie Biggs equalised two minutes after the break and Meyer made the score 4-4 with 20 minutes remaining, after Jones had scored his second. However, Charles scored his second of the game and, with 12 minutes remaining, Jones completed his hat-trick to give Swansea Town a 6-4 win they were acknowledged as having fully deserved. Twenty-four hours later, with George Petherbridge scoring twice, Rovers made a mockery of this result by defeating the Swans 3-0 at Eastville.

As was also the case in September 1954 and November 1992, Rovers contrived to concede five or more goals twice in the space of four days. In this case, following six at the Vetch Field, it was six more at Upton Park. John Smith scored three times as West Ham United won 6-1, just as his team-mate Billy Dare had scored a hat-trick in the Hammers' 3-2 win at Eastville in August. Alan Peacock scored three goals in Middlesbrough's 4-3 victory over Rovers at Ayresome Park in March, the other goal claimed by Brian Clough who scored in both League fixtures against Rovers in 1956/57, 1958/59 and 1959/60.

Bristol Rovers 1957/58. Back row: Sheffield, McCormack, Pyle, Drake, Foster, Jarrold, Baker. Middle row: Mann, McArthur (Trainer), McIlvenny, Sampson, Ricketts, Ward, Biggs, Radford, May, Sykes, Bamford, Hale, Doyle, Pitt. Front row: Edwards, Mabbutt, Smith, Watling, Jones, Bradford, Hillard, Petherbridge, Meyer, Steeds, Hooper

FOOTBALL LEAGUE DIVISION TWO

SEASON 1957/58

Date	Opponent		Score	Att	1	2	3	4	5	6	7	8	9	10	11	Goalscorers
24/08/57	BARNSLEY	A	2-2	12673	RADFORD	BAMFORD	WATLING	PITT	HALE	SAMPSON	PETHERBRIDGE	BIGGS	MEYER	WARD	HOOPER	WARD, BRADFORD
26/08/57	DERBY COUNTY	H	5-2	25371	RADFORD	BAMFORD	WATLING	PITT	HALE	SAMPSON	PETHERBRIDGE	BRADFORD	MEYER	WARD	HOOPER	MEYER 3, HOOPER, BIGGS
31/08/57	WEST HAM UNITED	A	2-3	25910	RADFORD	BAMFORD	WATLING	PITT	HALE	SAMPSON	MABBUTT	BRADFORD	MEYER	WARD	HOOPER	BRADFORD, HOOPER
04/09/57	DERBY COUNTY	A	1-2	20529	RADFORD	BAMFORD	WATLING	PITT	HALE	SAMPSON	PETHERBRIDGE	BRADFORD	MEYER	WARD	HOOPER	WARD 2
07/09/57	SHEFFIELD UNITED	H	0-2	15796	RADFORD	BAMFORD	WATLING	SYKES	HALE	SAMPSON	MABBUTT	BRADFORD	MEYER	WARD	HOOPER	
09/09/57	STOKE CITY	A	5-3	23090	NICHOLS	BAMFORD	WATLING	RICKETTS	HALE	SAMPSON	PETHERBRIDGE	BIGGS	BRADFORD	WARD	HOOPER	BIGGS 3, BRADFORD, WARD
14/09/57	BLACKBURN ROVERS	H	4-0	22822	NICHOLS	BAMFORD	WATLING	PITT	HALE	SAMPSON	PETHERBRIDGE	BIGGS	BRADFORD	WARD	HOOPER	BRADFORD 2, BIGGS, MABBUTT
16/09/57	STOKE CITY	H	4-0	20022	NICHOLS	BAMFORD	WATLING	PITT	HALE	SAMPSON	PETHERBRIDGE	BIGGS	BRADFORD	WARD	HOOPER	BRADFORD 2, PETHERBRIDGE 2
21/09/57	IPSWICH TOWN	A	2-3	20433	NICHOLS	BAMFORD	WATLING	PITT	HALE	SAMPSON	PETHERBRIDGE	BIGGS	BRADFORD	WARD	HOOPER	BIGGS, BRADFORD
28/09/57	NOTTS COUNTY	H	5-2	20388	NICHOLS	BAMFORD	WATLING	PITT	PYLE	SAMPSON	PETHERBRIDGE	BIGGS	BRADFORD	PETHERBRIDGE	HOOPER	PETHERBRIDGE, HOOPER
05/10/57	LINCOLN CITY	A	1-0	9147	NICHOLS	BAMFORD	WATLING	PYLE	HALE	SAMPSON	PETHERBRIDGE	JONES	BRADFORD	WARD	HOOPER	WILLIAMS og
12/10/57	BRISTOL CITY	H	2-3	33465	NICHOLS	BAMFORD	WATLING	RICKETTS	BIGGS	SAMPSON	MEYER	JONES	BRADFORD	WARD	HOOPER	
19/10/57	CARDIFF CITY	A	0-2	23292	NICHOLS	BAMFORD	WATLING	PITT	HALE	SAMPSON	MABBUTT	BIGGS	BRADFORD	WARD	HOOPER	
26/10/57	LIVERPOOL	H	0-2	22640	NICHOLS	BAMFORD	HALE	PITT	HALE	SAMPSON	PETHERBRIDGE	BIGGS	MEYER	WARD	HOOPER	
02/11/57	MIDDLESBROUGH	A	5-0	36686	NICHOLS	BAMFORD	WATLING	SYKES	HALE	SAMPSON	PETHERBRIDGE	JONES	BRADFORD	WARD	HOOPER	JONES 2, PETHERBRIDGE 2, BRADFORD
09/11/57	LEYTON ORIENT	H	3-1	20153	NICHOLS	BAMFORD	WATLING	SYKES	PYLE	SAMPSON	PETHERBRIDGE	JONES	BRADFORD	WARD	HOOPER	BRADFORD 2, PETHERBRIDGE
16/11/57	CHARLTON ATHLETIC	A	3-1	14826	NICHOLS	BAMFORD	WATLING	SYKES	PYLE	SAMPSON	PETHERBRIDGE	JONES	BRADFORD	WARD	HOOPER	MEYER
23/11/57	DONCASTER ROVERS	H	2-3	24217	NICHOLS	BAMFORD	WATLING	SYKES	PYLE	SAMPSON	McILVENNY	MEYER	BRADFORD	WARD	HOOPER	HOOPER, BRADFORD, McILVENNY
30/11/57	ROTHERHAM UNITED	A	1-3	9158	NICHOLS	BAMFORD	WATLING	SYKES	PYLE	SAMPSON	McILVENNY	MEYER	BRADFORD	WARD	HOOPER	MEYER, BRADFORD
07/12/57	HUDDERSFIELD TOWN	H	1-3	17606	NICHOLS	BAMFORD	WATLING	SYKES	PYLE	SAMPSON	PETHERBRIDGE	JONES	BRADFORD	WARD	HOOPER	HOOPER, BRADFORD, McILVENNY
14/12/57	GRIMSBY TOWN	H	0-7	11028	NICHOLS	BAMFORD	WATLING	PITT	HALE	SAMPSON	PETHERBRIDGE	JONES	BRADFORD	WARD	HOOPER	
21/12/57	BARNSLEY	H	1-1	14577	NICHOLS	BAMFORD	WATLING	SYKES	HALE	SAMPSON	PETHERBRIDGE	BIGGS	SYKES	BIGGS	HOOPER	CRUICKSHANK og, BRADFORD 2, HOOPER, SAMPSON
25/12/57	SWANSEA TOWN	A	4-6	13355	NICHOLS	BAMFORD	WATLING	SYKES	HALE	SAMPSON	PETHERBRIDGE	BIGGS	BRADFORD	WARD	HOOPER	BIGGS, BRADFORD
26/12/57	SWANSEA TOWN	H	3-0	11340	NICHOLS	BAMFORD	WATLING	SYKES	HALE	SAMPSON	PETHERBRIDGE	MEYER	BRADFORD	WARD	HOOPER	HOOPER, WARD, BRADFORD
28/12/57	WEST HAM UNITED	H	1-6	28000	NICHOLS	BAMFORD	WATLING	SYKES	HALE	SAMPSON	PETHERBRIDGE	MEYER	BRADFORD	WARD	HOOPER	WARD 2
11/01/58	SHEFFIELD UNITED	A	2-2	19892	NICHOLS	BAMFORD	WATLING	SYKES	PYLE	SAMPSON	PETHERBRIDGE	MEYER	BRADFORD	WARD	HOOPER	WARD 2, McILVENNY, HOOPER
18/01/58	BLACKBURN ROVERS	A	0-2	16000	NICHOLS	BAMFORD	WATLING	SYKES	PYLE	SAMPSON	PETHERBRIDGE	MEYER	BRADFORD	WARD	HOOPER	
01/02/58	IPSWICH TOWN	H	2-1	21554	NICHOLS	BAMFORD	WATLING	SYKES	PYLE	SAMPSON	PETHERBRIDGE	SYKES	BRADFORD	WARD	HOOPER	HOOPER 2, BRADFORD
19/02/58	LINCOLN CITY	H	3-0	13305	NICHOLS	BAMFORD	WATLING	SYKES	PYLE	SAMPSON	PETHERBRIDGE	SYKES	BRADFORD	WARD	HOOPER	WARD, HOOPER 2
22/02/58	DONCASTER ROVERS	A	2-1	17821	NICHOLS	BAMFORD	WATLING	SYKES	PYLE	SAMPSON	PETHERBRIDGE	MEYER	BRADFORD	WARD	HOOPER	WARD 2
08/03/58	LIVERPOOL	A	3-1	19299	NICHOLS	BAMFORD	WATLING	SYKES	PYLE	SAMPSON	PETHERBRIDGE	BIGGS	BRADFORD	WARD	HOOPER	HOOPER, MEYER
15/03/58	MIDDLESBROUGH	H	3-4	20000	NICHOLS	BAMFORD	WATLING	SYKES	PYLE	SAMPSON	McILVENNY	BIGGS	BRADFORD	WARD	HOOPER	RADFORD og, WARD, HOOPER
22/03/58	LEYTON ORIENT	A	4-0	15533	NICHOLS	BAMFORD	WATLING	SYKES	PYLE	SAMPSON	McILVENNY	MEYER	BRADFORD	WARD	HOOPER	WARD 2, BRADFORD
26/03/58	CARDIFF CITY	H	2-0	5687	NICHOLS	BAMFORD	DOYLE	SYKES	PYLE	SAMPSON	McILVENNY	BIGGS	BRADFORD	WARD	HOOPER	BRADFORD, HOOPER
29/03/58	CHARLTON ATHLETIC	H	2-2	20064	NICHOLS	BAMFORD	DOYLE	SYKES	PYLE	SAMPSON	McILVENNY	MEYER	BRADFORD	WARD	HOOPER	HOOPER 2, BIGGS, WARD, PETHERBRIDGE
04/04/58	FULHAM	A	3-3	31109	NICHOLS	BAMFORD	DOYLE	SYKES	PYLE	SAMPSON	McILVENNY	MEYER	BRADFORD	WARD	HOOPER	MEYER, HOOPER
05/04/58	BRISTOL CITY	A	0-3	24782	RADFORD	BAMFORD	DOYLE	SYKES	PYLE	SAMPSON	McILVENNY	HALE	BRADFORD	WARD	HOOPER	
07/04/58	FULHAM	H	1-0	31300	RADFORD	BAMFORD	DOYLE	SYKES	PYLE	SAMPSON	McILVENNY	SYKES	BRADFORD	WARD	HOOPER	HOOPER
12/04/58	ROTHERHAM UNITED	H	0-2	6942	NICHOLS	BAMFORD	DOYLE	PITT	PYLE	SAMPSON	McILVENNY	MEYER	BRADFORD	WARD	HOOPER	
19/04/58	HUDDERSFIELD TOWN	A	1-1	16185	NICHOLS	BAMFORD	DOYLE	PITT	PYLE	SAMPSON	PETHERBRIDGE	BIGGS	BRADFORD	WARD	HOOPER	BIGGS
23/04/58	NOTTS COUNTY	A	0-0	13467	NICHOLS	BAMFORD	WATLING	SYKES	PYLE	SAMPSON	MABBUTT	BIGGS	BRADFORD	PETHERBRIDGE	HOOPER	
26/04/58	GRIMSBY TOWN	A	2-3	10030	NICHOLS	BAMFORD	WATLING	PITT	BRADFORD	SAMPSON	MABBUTT	BIGGS	MEYER	WARD	HOOPER	HALE, SHANNON og

FA CUP

Date	Opponent		Score	Att	1	2	3	4	5	6	7	8	9	10	11	Goalscorers
04/01/58	MANSFIELD TOWN	H	5-0	20446	NICHOLS	BAMFORD	WATLING	SYKES	PYLE	SAMPSON	PETHERBRIDGE	HALE	BRADFORD	WARD	HOOPER	HOOPER, BIGGS, WARD, PETHERBRIDGE
25/01/58	BURNLEY	A	2-2	34229	NICHOLS	BAMFORD	WATLING	SYKES	PYLE	SAMPSON	PETHERBRIDGE	BIGGS	BRADFORD	WARD	HOOPER	MEYER, BRADFORD
28/01/58	BURNLEY	H	3-2	40813	NICHOLS	BAMFORD	WATLING	PITT	PYLE	SAMPSON	PETHERBRIDGE	BIGGS	BRADFORD	WARD	HOOPER	HOOPER, BRADFORD
15/02/58	BRISTOL CITY	A	4-3	39126	NICHOLS	BAMFORD	WATLING	SYKES	PYLE	SAMPSON	PETHERBRIDGE	SYKES	BRADFORD	WARD	HOOPER	MEYER, SYKES, WARD, BRADFORD
01/03/58	FULHAM	A	1-3	42000	NICHOLS	BAMFORD	WATLING	SYKES	PYLE	SAMPSON	PETHERBRIDGE	MEYER	BRADFORD	WARD	HOOPER	BRADFORD

GLOUCESTERSHIRE CUP FINAL

Date	Opponent		Score	Att	1	2	3	4	5	6	7	8	9	10	11	Goalscorers
29/04/58	BRISTOL CITY	A	1-4	10590	RADFORD	BAMFORD	WATLING	SYKES	PITT	SAMPSON	MABBUTT	BIGGS	MEYER	WARD	HOOPER	BRADFORD

PLAYERS	APP	GLS
BAMFORD H	42	
BIGGS A	27	9
BRADFORD G	33	20
DOYLE B	9	
HALE B	24	
HOOPER P	39	14
JONES R	6	3
MABBUTT R	11	2
McILVENNY J	10	3
MEYER B	24	9
NICHOLS R	35	
PETHERBRIDGE G	22	6
PITT J	14	
PYLE D	18	
RADFORD H	7	
RICKETTS G	6	
SAMPSON Pr	37	1
SYKES N	31	
WARD D	36	14
WATLING J	31	
OWN GOALS		4

Yet, the heaviest defeat of the season was at Eastville in December when, in Jackie Pitt's penultimate game for Rovers, Grimsby Town won 7-0 to inflict Rovers' heaviest ever home League defeat. At one stage, the Mariners scored four goals and missed a penalty in the space of 18 second-half minutes. In fact, Hooper, unmarked in front of goal, and Biggs had both spurned opportunities to put Rovers ahead before Ron Stockin, after six minutes, and Gerry Priestley, two minutes later, put the visitors 2-0 up when goalkeeper Nicholls had twice lost control of the ball. Priestley's cross was converted at the second attempt by Johnny Scott a minute before half-time, before Grimsby's four late goals. After seventy minutes, Ron Rafferty scored from the penalty-spot after Sampson had fouled Priestley. Seven minutes later, Jimmy Fell's solo goal made him the fifth Grimsby forward on the scoresheet and his next run led to a second penalty, blasted over the bar by Rafferty. Late goals for Scott and Stockin, their second each of a bizarre game, meant Rovers had lost a League game by seven clear goals for the first time since April 1936. On the other hand, in addition to a successful FA Cup run, Rovers enjoyed some memorable victories of their own. In November, 19-year-old Bobby Jones was given a League debut against Middlesbrough, opened the scoring after just two minutes and later added a second in a 5-0 win. Two Bradford goals helped defeat Blackburn Rovers 4-0, while Leyton Orient were defeated by the same score in a match where Rovers' Hooper and the visitors' Johnny Hartburn both missed penalties. Barrie Meyer's second hat-trick for Rovers enabled Rovers to defeat Derby County 5-2 in August and, a fortnight later, the first hat-trick of Alfie Biggs' blossoming career earned Rovers a 5-3 victory at Stoke City. More bizarrely, in beating Notts County 5-2 at Eastville, Rovers were indebted to own goals from Frank Cruickshank and John McGrath.

The season drew to a close with high-scoring home draws. On Good Friday, Fulham earned a 2-2 draw at Eastville through goals from Roy Dwight, an FA Cup winner in 1959, and the celebrated Jimmy Hill. Twenty-four hours later, another Bradford double eased Rovers towards a 3-3 draw with Bristol City, where all six goals were scored in an extraordinary first-half. The sides met again in the Gloucestershire Cup final, where City won 4-1, as well as hitting the woodwork twice, after Bradford had put Rovers in front from a Biggs pass after only six minutes. The four meetings of the sides had produced a total of 23 goals. The season over, focus was switched to the World Cup in Sweden, where the host nation, coached by George Raynor – a member of the Aldershot side that played Rovers in 1938/39 – reached the final before losing to Brazil.

1958/59

Towards the end of his long and successful career as a full-back with his only League club, Harry Bamford had begun to give back to the community that had supported him for so long. The 3-2 defeat at Derby County in September was his 486th game for Rovers, a club record at the time and since bettered only by Stuart Taylor. In the meantime, he coached schoolboys at Clifton College and it was on his way home from a training session that his motorcycle was involved in a collision with a car. For

Bristol Rovers 1958/59. Back row: Sykes, Sampson, Pyle, Radford, Watling, Doyle. Front row: Petherbridge, Biggs, Bradford, Ward, Hooper

three days, his life hung in the balance before he died of his injuries on 31 October 1958. At a memorial service in St Mary Redcliffe Church, manager Bert Tann said that 'a part of Bristol Rovers died with him'.

Not only had Rovers lost a gifted player, but a pivotal figure in the club's history had died at a point where his career was still not quite over. His influence on the spirit of Rovers in the 1950s was instrumental in the club's success. An annual memorial trophy for sportsmanship among local footballers was set up, awarded on four occasions to Rovers players and won in 1967/68 by Alfie Biggs' brother Bert. On 8 May 1959, a combined Bristol XI featuring six Rovers players defeated Arsenal 5-4 in a testimonial fixture, Geoff Bradford scoring twice, before an Eastville crowd of 28,347 that contributed to the Harry Bamford Memorial Fund. A total of just over £3,709 was raised. It is no coincidence that the days of FA Cup quarter-finals and promotion challenges were over. Following Bamford's death, Rovers fell into a decline that climaxed with relegation in 1961/62 and the scary proximity of Division Four 12 months later.

Over the summer of 1958, Divisions Three and Four were created out of the old geographical leagues. As early as 30 November 1944, the Rovers secretary Sid Hawkins had written to the Football League to say the club directors 'strongly deprecate the suggestion that the Division Three clubs should be divided into Third and Fourth Divisions.' Within the Rovers camp, trouble was brewing as the two county cricketers, Ron Nicholls and Barrie Meyer, unable to make pre-season training because of commitments with Gloucestershire, put in transfer requests amid disputes within the camp. On the eve of the new season, the goalkeeper joined Cardiff City in an exchange deal involving John Frowen. He later played for Bristol City and was to appear in 534 matches for Gloucestershire between 1951 and 1975. Meyer, after 139 League games for Rovers in almost a decade, joined Plymouth Argyle in a deal worth £4,500 plus the services of John Timmins. Another player who later resurfaced at Bristol City, Meyer played 406 times for Gloucestershire and also served as a Test umpire.

Eastville had a 3,000 capacity North Stand constructed through the close season at a cost of £76,000, of which the Supporters' Club, then numbering 6,931 members, paid £10,000. This new stand was officially opened in August, prior to the first home game of the season. Following an away win, this first of five in the League being completed when Orient's George Wright conceded an own goal on his club debut, Rovers defeated Scunthorpe United 4-0 in this fixture, with four forwards getting their names on the scoresheet. By the time the sides met at The Old Show Ground in January, the Iron had scored in 21 consecutive League games but Rovers were able to hold them to a goalless draw. Ken Jones, who made his Scunthorpe United debut that day, was to play in 168 League games for that club.

It was a mixed season for Rovers, for they neither won three League matches in succession nor lost three consecutive League fixtures all season. Rovers scored four at home to Scunthorpe United, Rotherham United and Swansea Town as well as at Cardiff City and, in November, seven times at home to Grimsby Town. The heaviest defeat came in the final away game of the season, 5-2 at Sheffield United. In addition, Rovers lost an exciting game at Charlton Athletic 4-3 and by 4-1 at Lincoln City, where David Pyle contributed an own goal and one of the Imps' three further goalscorers was Roy Chapman – later the father of the striker Lee Chapman – who was himself a scorer for Mansfield Town against Rovers in November 1963 and December 1964.

The greatest personal performance, however, came against Rotherham United at Eastville in March. Geoff Bradford had scored 11 League hat-tricks for Rovers, but never before four times in one match. He had also missed the 3-3 draw at Millmoor in October and, returning after injury only a week before this return fixture, had in fact not scored since Boxing Day. However, a first-minute goal set him on his way and he contributed all his side's goals as Rovers recorded a 4-1 victory. The first Rovers player to score four times in a match in this division, he was also the first to achieve this feat since Vic Lambden on Easter Monday 1952. Not only did this equal a club record as yet unsurpassed, but Bradford also remains the most recent Rovers player to score four League goals in a home fixture, Robin Stubbs, Alan Warboys and Jamie Cureton all having done so since away from home.

The team performance of the season was against Grimsby Town at Eastville in the middle week of October. A masterful 7-3 victory, the only occasion Rovers have won by this scoreline in League football, made light of the fact that Rovers had lost their two previous home games. After a quiet start, the match exploded into life just before half-time, as Dai Ward, after 28 minutes, and Peter Hooper, 11 minutes later, gave Rovers a 2-0 lead, only for Tommy Briggs, whose seven goals for Blackburn Rovers had sunk the Eastville side in February 1955, to pull one back a minute before half-time. Ward extended Rovers' lead and Mike Cullen replied for Grimsby before two Hooper goals in four minutes completed his hat-trick and left Rovers 5-2 ahead. Undeterred, Ron Rafferty, scoring against Rovers in both fixtures for the second consecutive season,

FOOTBALL LEAGUE DIVISION TWO

SEASON 1958/59

Date	Opponent		Score	Att	G (1)	2	3	4	5	6	7	8	9	10	11	Goalscorers
23/08/58	LEYTON ORIENT	A	3-1	17304	RADFORD	BAMFORD	WATLING	SYKES	PYLE	SAMPSON	PETHERBRIDGE	BIGGS	BRADFORD	WARD	HOOPER	PETHERBRIDGE, WARD, WRIGHT og.
30/08/58	SCUNTHORPE UNITED	H	4-0	24273	RADFORD	BAMFORD	WATLING	SYKES	PYLE	SAMPSON	PETHERBRIDGE	BIGGS	BRADFORD	WARD	HOOPER	BRADFORD
03/09/58	DERBY COUNTY	A	2-3	20130	SINCLAIR	BAMFORD	WATLING	SYKES	PYLE	SAMPSON	PETHERBRIDGE	BIGGS	BRADFORD	WARD	HOOPER	BRADFORD, HOOPER, HOOPER pen, WARD
06/09/58	SHEFFIELD WEDNESDAY	A	1-3	28968	RADFORD	BAMFORD	WATLING	SYKES	PYLE	SAMPSON	PETHERBRIDGE	BIGGS	BRADFORD	WARD	HOOPER	WARD, BRADFORD
08/09/58	CARDIFF CITY	H	2-0	20604	RADFORD	BAMFORD	WATLING	SYKES	PYLE	SAMPSON	PETHERBRIDGE	BIGGS	BRADFORD	WARD	HOOPER	WARD, BRADFORD
13/09/58	CARDIFF CITY	A	0-0	30076	RADFORD	BAMFORD	WATLING	SYKES	PYLE	SAMPSON	PETHERBRIDGE	BIGGS	BRADFORD	WARD	HOOPER	
17/09/58	FULHAM	A	4-2	15000	RADFORD	BAMFORD	WATLING	SYKES	PYLE	SAMPSON	PETHERBRIDGE	BIGGS	BRADFORD	WARD	HOOPER	HOOPER pen, WARD, BIGGS,
20/09/58	LINCOLN CITY	A	1-4	9223	RADFORD	BAMFORD	WATLING	SYKES	PYLE	SAMPSON	McILVENNY	BIGGS	BRADFORD	WARD	HOOPER	BRADFORD
22/09/58	DERBY COUNTY	H	2-1	14317	RADFORD	BAMFORD	WATLING	SYKES	PYLE	SAMPSON	McILVENNY	BIGGS	BRADFORD	WARD	HOOPER	WARD 2, BRADFORD
27/09/58	SUNDERLAND	H	2-1	24602	RADFORD	BAMFORD	WATLING	SYKES	PYLE	SAMPSON	McILVENNY	BIGGS	BRADFORD	WARD	HOOPER	McILVENNY, WARD
04/10/58	STOKE CITY	A	2-2	19763	RADFORD	BAMFORD	WATLING	SYKES	PYLE	SAMPSON	McILVENNY	BIGGS	BRADFORD	WARD	HOOPER	McILVENNY, WARD
11/10/58	HUDDERSFIELD TOWN	H	2-1	16773	RADFORD	BAMFORD	WATLING	RICKETTS	PYLE	SAMPSON	McILVENNY	BIGGS	BRADFORD	WARD	HOOPER	McILVENNY, WARD
18/10/58	BARNSLEY	A	0-2	20249	RADFORD	BAMFORD	WATLING	SYKES	PYLE	SAMPSON	PETHERBRIDGE	JONES	BIGGS	WARD	HOOPER	
25/10/58	ROTHERHAM UNITED	H	3-3	7928	RADFORD	BAMFORD	WATLING	SYKES	PYLE	SAMPSON	McILVENNY	JONES	BIGGS	WARD	HOOPER	McILVENNY, BIGGS 2
01/11/58	BRISTOL CITY	H	1-2	32104	RADFORD	BAMFORD	WATLING	RICKETTS	PYLE	SAMPSON	PETHERBRIDGE	JONES	BIGGS	SYKES	HOOPER	SYKES
08/11/58	BRIGHTON & H ALBION	A	1-1	22155	RADFORD	BAMFORD	WATLING	SYKES	PYLE	SAMPSON	PETHERBRIDGE	JONES	BRADFORD	WARD	HOOPER	BRADFORD
15/11/58	GRIMSBY TOWN	H	7-3	15733	RADFORD	BAMFORD	WATLING	SYKES	PYLE	SAMPSON	PETHERBRIDGE	JONES	BRADFORD	WARD	HOOPER	HOOPER 3, WARD 2, BRADFORD 2
22/11/58	LIVERPOOL	A	1-2	39365	RADFORD	BAMFORD	WATLING	SYKES	PYLE	RICKETTS	PETHERBRIDGE	JONES	BRADFORD	WARD	HOOPER	WARD 2
29/11/58	MIDDLESBROUGH	H	3-1	15803	RADFORD	BAMFORD	WATLING	SYKES	PYLE	RICKETTS	PETHERBRIDGE	JONES	BRADFORD	WARD	HOOPER	HOOPER 2
06/12/58	CHARLTON ATHLETIC	A	3-4	13879	NORMAN	BAMFORD	WATLING	SYKES	PYLE	RICKETTS	PETHERBRIDGE	HAMILTON	BRADFORD	WARD	HOOPER	JONES R
13/12/58	SHEFFIELD UNITED	H	1-1	16136	NORMAN	BAMFORD	WATLING	SYKES	PYLE	RICKETTS	PETHERBRIDGE	JONES	BRADFORD	WARD	HOOPER	McILVENNY, WARD
20/12/58	LEYTON ORIENT	H	1-3	10004	NORMAN	BAMFORD	WATLING	SYKES	PYLE	RICKETTS	HAMILTON	JONES	BRADFORD	WARD	HOOPER	WARD, JONES
26/12/58	IPSWICH TOWN	A	2-0	15806	NORMAN	BAMFORD	WATLING	SYKES	PYLE	RICKETTS	PETHERBRIDGE	JONES	BRADFORD	WARD	HOOPER	McILVENNY, WARD
27/12/58	IPSWICH TOWN	H	1-1	20615	NORMAN	BAMFORD	WATLING	SYKES	HILLARD	RICKETTS	PETHERBRIDGE	JONES	BRADFORD	WARD	HOOPER	BRADFORD
03/01/59	SCUNTHORPE UNITED	A	0-0	11130	NORMAN	BAMFORD	WATLING	SYKES	HALE	SAMPSON	PETHERBRIDGE	JONES	BRADFORD	WARD	HOOPER	
31/01/59	FULHAM	A	0-1	23203	NORMAN	BAMFORD	WATLING	SYKES	HALE	MABBUTT	PETHERBRIDGE	JONES	BRADFORD	WARD	HOOPER	
07/02/59	LINCOLN CITY	H	3-0	15279	NORMAN	BAMFORD	WATLING	SYKES	PYLE	MABBUTT	PETHERBRIDGE	BIGGS	BRADFORD	WARD	HOOPER	BIGGS 2, WARD
14/02/59	SUNDERLAND	A	1-3	24188	NORMAN	BAMFORD	WATLING	SYKES	PYLE	MABBUTT	SMITH	BIGGS	BRADFORD	WARD	HOOPER	WARD
21/02/59	STOKE CITY	H	1-0	16341	NORMAN	BAMFORD	WATLING	SYKES	PYLE	MABBUTT	SMITH	BIGGS	WARD	DRAKE	HOOPER	SMITH, WARD
28/02/59	BRIGHTON & H ALBION	H	2-0	15785	NORMAN	BAMFORD	WATLING	SYKES	FROWEN	MABBUTT	DRAKE	BIGGS	BRADFORD	WARD	HOOPER	BRADFORD 4
07/03/59	ROTHERHAM UNITED	A	0-0	5503	NORMAN	BAMFORD	WATLING	SYKES	FROWEN	MABBUTT	DRAKE	BIGGS	BRADFORD	WARD	HOOPER	DRAKE, BRADFORD
14/03/59	BARNSLEY	H	4-1	10810	NORMAN	BAMFORD	WATLING	SYKES	FROWEN	SAMPSON	SMITH	BIGGS	BRADFORD	WARD	HOOPER	WARD, STONEHOUSE og
21/03/59	BRISTOL CITY	A	1-1	26868	NORMAN	BAMFORD	WATLING	SYKES	PYLE	MABBUTT	SMITH	BIGGS	BRADFORD	WARD	HOOPER	HOOPER 2, 1pen, WARD
27/03/59	SWANSEA TOWN	A	1-2	14921	NORMAN	BAMFORD	WATLING	SYKES	PYLE	MABBUTT	SMITH	BIGGS	BRADFORD	WARD	HOOPER	WARD, SMITH
28/03/59	SWANSEA TOWN	H	1-1	16029	NORMAN	BAMFORD	TIMMINS	SYKES	PYLE	MABBUTT	SMITH	BIGGS	BRADFORD	WARD	HOOPER	WARD 2, HOOPER, BRADFORD
30/03/59	HUDDERSFIELD TOWN	A	4-4	15151	NORMAN	BAMFORD	TIMMINS	SYKES	PYLE	MABBUTT	SMITH	BIGGS	BRADFORD	WARD	HOOPER	BRADFORD
04/04/59	GRIMSBY TOWN	H	2-1	9200	NORMAN	BAMFORD	WATLING	SYKES	PYLE	MABBUTT	SMITH	JONES	BRADFORD	WARD	HOOPER	BIGGS
11/04/59	LIVERPOOL	H	3-0	14810	NORMAN	BAMFORD	WATLING	SYKES	PYLE	MABBUTT	FROWEN	JONES	BRADFORD	WARD	HOOPER	BRADFORD
18/04/59	MIDDLESBROUGH	A	2-2	17262	NORMAN	BAMFORD	WATLING	SYKES	PYLE	MABBUTT	SMITH	JONES	BRADFORD	WARD	HOOPER	WARD
20/04/59	SHEFFIELD UNITED	A	2-5	11310	NORMAN	BAMFORD	WATLING	SYKES	PYLE	MABBUTT	SMITH	DRAKE	BRADFORD	WARD	HOOPER	DRAKE, BRADFORD
25/04/59	CHARLTON ATHLETIC	H	2-1	11166	NORMAN	BAMFORD	WATLING	RICKETTS	PYLE	MABBUTT	SMITH	DRAKE	BRADFORD	SYKES	HOOPER	BRADFORD, TOWNSEND og
30/04/59	SHEFFIELD WEDNESDAY	H	2-1	16653	NORMAN	BAMFORD	WATLING	SYKES	PYLE	MABBUTT	SMITH	BIGGS	BRADFORD	GOUGH	HOOPER	BRADFORD, BIGGS

FA CUP

Date	Opponent		Score	Att	G (1)	2	3	4	5	6	7	8	9	10	11	Goalscorers
10/01/59	CHARLTON ATHLETIC	A	0-4	23203	NORMAN	DOYLE	WATLING	SYKES	HALE	SAMPSON	PETHERBRIDGE	JONES	BRADFORD	WARD	HOOPER	

GLOUCESTERSHIRE CUP FINAL

Date	Opponent		Score	Att	G (1)	2	3	4	5	6	7	8	9	10	11	Goalscorers
04/05/59	BRISTOL CITY	H	1-1	11022	HILLARD	DOYLE	WATLING	SYKES	PYLE	MABBUTT	SMITH	WARD	BRADFORD	BIGGS	HOOPER	WARD

PLAYERS	APP	GLS
BAMFORD H	29	3
BIGGS A	33	20
BRADFORD G	29	
DOYLE B	7	1
DRAKE L	5	
FROWEN I	5	
GOUGH A	1	
HALE D	7	
HAMILTON I	1	
HILLARD D	10	
HOOPER P	42	11
JONES R	17	1
MABBUTT R	17	
McILVENNY J	8	
NORMAN M	21	
PETHERBRIDGE G	18	4
PYLE David	31	
RADFORD H	18	
RICKETTS G	9	
SAMPSON P	18	
SINCLAIR H	1	
SMITH G	15	2
SYKES N	41	1
TIMMINS J	3	
WARD J	37	26
WATLING J	39	
OWN GOALS		3

Young Rovers fans cheer on the team at Bristol City in 1959

scored 14 minutes from time. Geoff Bradford, however, scored twice in five minutes, three Rovers players had registered doubles, as against Middlesbrough in November 1955 and Rovers had avenged the 7-0 drubbing of 11 months earlier.

On Easter Monday, Rovers and Swansea Town served up a goal feast at Eastville. Rovers led 3-2 at the interval and, though Bradford had restored the two-goal cushion just after the hour, the home side was forced to settle for a 4-4 draw. The Pirates had taken a fourth-minute lead through Ward, Hooper had added a second 10 minutes later and, though Welsh International Len Allchurch had reduced the deficit after 18 minutes, it had taken Hooper just seven more minutes to put Rovers 3-1 ahead. Once the Swans had scored twice in four minutes midway through the second-half, Rovers were resigned to a second consecutive home draw.

In November goals from Geoff Twentyman – whose son was to be a doyen of the Rovers side – and Brighton & Hove Albion's 1983 FA Cup final manager, Jimmy Melia, gave a Liverpool side featuring their future manager, Ronnie Moran, a tight victory at Anfield. Although Huddersfield Town took just one point off Rovers, their forward Kevin McHale scored in both fixtures, as did the ubiquitous John Atyeo of Bristol City. In January, Bert Tann fielded virtually a first team for a Football Combination game against Portsmouth reserves, Rovers winning 9-1. In that month, Rovers gave a League debut to Ray Mabbutt, a local wing-half who, like his son after him, was to give sterling service to the club for many years. Outside-right Granville Smith also impressed, as did Graham Ricketts at half-back, full-back Doug Hillard and goalkeeper Malcolm Norman. As the old guard began to move on, so a number of players with sizeable contributions to make to the club's story began to seize the moment.

In finishing sixth in Division Two, there were indeed grounds for optimism. Rovers won their final three home games, each time defeating sides with larger reputations and greater spending power and that had beaten Rovers earlier in the season. Two goals from Hooper, the only ever-present, and one from Ward earned a 3-0 victory over Liverpool before Rovers ended the campaign with 2-1 home wins over Charlton Athletic and Sheffield Wednesday. In the latter, Rovers fielded Tony Gough, whose second League appearance was to be for Swindon Town a remarkable 11 years later. He did not play at all in the League during the 1960s. Latterly the captain of Hereford United in their epic FA Cup victory over Newcastle United in 1972, Gough holds the appearance record at Bath City. Wednesday were defeated by a Bradford goal, struck venomously from Doug Hillard's through ball after 11 minutes, the 200th goal of his Rovers career and his 20th of the season to leave him as the club's second highest scorer, behind 26-goal Ward. Also at this time, on 18 April 1959, the former Rovers manager Percy Smith died in Watford, aged 78.

Despite the FA Cup glory of the previous season, Rovers found themselves a goal down within 19 seconds and lost 4-0 at home to Charlton Athletic in the third round. This very early goal, the first of two by South African International Sam Lawrie, was followed by goals from John Summers, who famously scored five times when the Addicks recovered from 5-1 down to beat Huddersfield Town 7-6 in Division Two in December 1957, and Ron White. Rovers took a sensational lead in the Gloucestershire Cup final with the fastest goal in the club's history. From the kick-off, Ward scored after only seven seconds, but Bert Tindill's second-half equaliser for Bristol City left the score all square.

1959/60

W ith the benefit of hindsight, the end of the 1950s can be seen to have drawn to a close the golden years in the Bristol Rovers story. 1959/60 opened with a six-match unbeaten run, but entailed several heavy defeats. Four or more goals were conceded on six occasions as Rovers finished the season in ninth place in Division Two. Relegation in 1961/62 and a long struggle, ultimately successful, the following season to avoid the unprecedented drop into Division Four, lay just around the corner.

It is still difficult for any Rovers supporter to admit this, but Geoff Bradford was no longer the prolific, potent goalscorer he had once been. The five hat-tricks in 1953/54, the two goals in each of four consecutive games in October 1954 and the England cap were a thing of the past. He scored 12 League goals, two against Stoke City in February being his only brace of the season. While Alfie Biggs had recovered from his poor goal return in 1958/59, and was top scorer with 22 League goals, Bobby Jones did not score at all this year. Granville Smith did not pose the threat at outside-right that his early performances had promised. The veteran Peter Sampson's appearance in the opening day draw with Leyton Orient was his only game of the season.

On the other hand, Bert Tann was beginning to weave together a team of young, predominantly Bristolian footballers. A lack of funds hampered his progress, but his task was to glean every nugget from the local football scene. Ray Mabbutt, a prime example

Bristol Rovers 1959/60. Back row: Mabbutt, Sykes, Norman, Pyle, Hillard, Watling. Front row: Smith, Biggs, Bradford, Ward, Hooper

of this policy, was the club's only ever-present in 1959/60. Doug Hillard, David Pyle and Graham Ricketts continued to establish themselves in the side, while local teenage inside-forward Ian Hamilton scored his first goals for the club. Victory over Swansea Town on Boxing Day marked the League debut of 20-year-old Harold Jarman at outside-right, a Rovers player until 1973, a county cricketer with Gloucestershire and an essential ingredient in the long-running recipe of football in Bristol.

Having drawn three of their opening four games, Rovers' first home win came against Ipswich Town in September. The new floodlights at Eastville were used for the first time in this Monday evening game, artificial lighting allowing for greater flexibility over kick-off times. Four 134-ft pylons had been installed at a cost of £16,000 and paid for by the Rovers Supporters' Club, whose chairman Eric Godfrey had been one of the committee that first proposed the concept in April 1959. Prior to the game, Rovers' chairman, Hampden Alpass, expressed his gratitude and added that 'our supporters' club is second to none in the country in its support of the parent club.' Although the home side lost Doug Hillard with a dislocated shoulder just seven minutes after half-time of the first fixture under floodlights, two goals from Peter Hooper gave Rovers victory, while Ted Phillips scored for Ipswich Town in both League fixtures against Rovers. For the following game, at Sunderland, Brian Doyle was given a first appearance of the season and responded with the only goal of his Rovers career.

6 September 1959 marked the opening of floodlights at Eastville Stadium for the visit of Ipswich Town

Rovers lost just three home League games, 2-0 defeats to both Liverpool and Middlesbrough and an astonishing 5-4 against Brighton in October. Prior to the game at Colchester United in January 2000, this was the only occasion Rovers had lost in the League by this score. Alfie Biggs was in the middle of a goalscoring run, in which he had scored Rovers' first in five consecutive fixtures. His 18th-minute goal cancelled out Tommy Dixon's opener. Peter Hooper then twice gave Rovers the lead, with Adrian Thorne, who was to score four times against the Pirates in August 1960, levelling the score at 2-2 on the stroke of half-time. Hooper's second, seven minutes after the break, should have left Rovers in control but, within 12 minutes, two quick fire goals from Bill Curry put Brighton 4-3 ahead. George Petherbridge scored Rovers' second equaliser after 72 minutes, only for half-back Jack Bertolini to pop up with the winning goal 13 minutes from time.

Five-goal defeats were also the order of the day at Middlesbrough and Plymouth Argyle in consecutive away matches before Christmas. At Ayresome Park Brian Clough, later such a successful figurehead at Nottingham Forest, scored a hat-trick in a 5-1 result. He scored again in April when Middlesbrough completed a comfortable double over Rovers. Colin Grainger, the talented musician playing outside left for Sunderland, Eddie Brown of Leyton Orient and Rotherham United's Brian Sawyer all scored in both League fixtures against Tann's side. So too did Graham Moore, as Cardiff City, fielding future Rovers players in Brian Jenkins, for the Ninian Park tie, and John Watkins, drew both games. Rovers lost 4-1 at Villa Park and 4-0 at Anfield, where the future England International Ian Callaghan was making the first of his club record 640 League appearances for Liverpool. Roger Hunt, a World Cup winner in 1966, scored one of the goals.

Portsmouth were defeated 2-0 at Eastville in September, while Swansea Town, Sunderland, Stoke City and Rotherham United all lost 3-1. Rovers scored three times in a glorious 12-minute spell in the opening half-hour to defeat a strong Sunderland side. Towards the end of April, Huddersfield Town and Plymouth Argyle both suffered two-goal defeats at Eastville. Away from home, Rovers won five League games, all by a single

SEASON 1959/60

FOOTBALL LEAGUE DIVISION TWO

Date	Opponent	H/A	Score	ATT	G	2	3	4	5	6	7	8	9	10	11	Goalscorers
22/08/59	LEYTON ORIENT	H	2-2	20003	NORMAN	HILLARD	WATLING	SAMPSON	PYLE	MABBUTT	SMITH	BIGGS	BRADFORD	WARD	HOOPER	HOOPER, BRADFORD
26/08/59	CHARLTON ATHLETIC	A	2-2	13828	NORMAN	HILLARD	WATLING	SYKES	PYLE	MABBUTT	DRAKE	BIGGS	BRADFORD	WARD	HOOPER	WARD , HOOPER pen
29/08/59	LINCOLN CITY	A	1-0	9284	NORMAN	HILLARD	WATLING	SYKES	PYLE	MABBUTT	JONES	BIGGS	BRADFORD	WARD	HOOPER	BRADFORD
05/09/59	ASTON VILLA	H	1-1	26162	NORMAN	HILLARD	WATLING	SYKES	PYLE	MABBUTT	SMITH	BIGGS	BRADFORD	WARD	HOOPER	WARD
07/09/59	IPSWICH TOWN	H	2-1	24093	NORMAN	HILLARD	WATLING	SYKES	PYLE	MABBUTT	SMITH	BIGGS	BRADFORD	WARD	HOOPER	HOOPER 2
12/09/59	IPSWICH TOWN	A	2-2	29968	NORMAN	HILLARD	WATLING	SYKES	PYLE	MABBUTT	DOYLE	BIGGS	BRADFORD	WARD	HOOPER	DOYLE, BRADFORD
16/09/59	SUNDERLAND	A	0-3	10868	NORMAN	HILLARD	WATLING	SYKES	PYLE	MABBUTT	DOYLE	BIGGS	RICKETTS	WARD	TIMMINS	
19/09/59	PORTSMOUTH	H	2-0	20634	NORMAN	HILLARD	WATLING	SYKES	PYLE	MABBUTT	PETH'RBRIDGE	BIGGS	RICKETTS	WARD	HOOPER	BIGGS, WARD
21/09/59	CHARLTON ATHLETIC	H	2-2	24345	NORMAN	HILLARD	DOYLE	SYKES	PYLE	MABBUTT	PETHERBRIDGE	BIGGS	RICKETTS	WARD	HOOPER	BIGGS, HOOPER
26/09/59	STOKE CITY	A	1-0	17990	NORMAN	HILLARD	DOYLE	SYKES	PYLE	MABBUTT	PETHERBRIDGE	BIGGS	RICKETTS	HAMILTON	HOOPER	BIGGS
03/10/59	BRIGHTON & H ALBION	H	4-5	20058	NORMAN	HILLARD	DOYLE	SYKES	PYLE	MABBUTT	PETHERBRIDGE	BIGGS	BRADFORD	WARD	HOOPER	BIGGS, HOOPER 2, PETHERBRIDGE
10/10/59	BRISTOL CITY	A	1-2	27548	NORMAN	HILLARD	WATLING	SYKES	PYLE	MABBUTT	SMITH	BIGGS	BRADFORD	JONES	HOOPER	BIGGS
17/10/59	SCUNTHORPE UNITED	H	1-1	15314	NORMAN	HILLARD	WATLING	SYKES	PYLE	MABBUTT	SMITH	BIGGS	BRADFORD	JONES	HOOPER	HILLARD
24/10/59	ROTHERHAM UNITED	A	0-3	10150	NORMAN	HILLARD	WATLING	SYKES	PYLE	MABBUTT	SMITH	BIGGS	BRADFORD	WARD	HOOPER	
31/10/59	CARDIFF CITY	H	1-1	27549	NORMAN	HILLARD	WATLING	SYKES	PYLE	MABBUTT	BRADFORD	BIGGS	EDGE	WARD	HOOPER	BIGGS
07/11/59	HULL CITY	A	1-3	16972	NORMAN	HILLARD	WATLING	SYKES	PYLE	MABBUTT	BRADFORD	JONES	EDGE	WARD	HOOPER	EDGE
14/11/59	SHEFFIELD UNITED	H	3-2	14649	NORMAN	HILLARD	WATLING	RICKETTS	PYLE	MABBUTT	PETHERBRIDGE	BIGGS	EDGE	WARD	HOOPER	BIGGS, WARD, EDGE
21/11/59	MIDDLESBROUGH	A	1-5	24116	NORMAN	HILLARD	WATLING	RICKETTS	PYLE	MABBUTT	PETHERBRIDGE	BIGGS	EDGE	WARD	HOOPER	BIGGS
28/11/59	DERBY COUNTY	H	2-1	15018	NORMAN	HILLARD	WATLING	RICKETTS	PYLE	MABBUTT	PETHERBRIDGE	SYKES	EDGE	BIGGS	HOOPER	EDGE, HOOPER
05/12/59	PLYMOUTH ARGYLE	A	3-5	16675	NORMAN	HILLARD	WATLING	SYKES	PYLE	MABBUTT	PETHERBRIDGE	BIGGS	EDGE	WARD	HOOPER	WARD, HOOPER pen, BIGGS
12/12/59	LIVERPOOL	H	0-2	15615	NORMAN	HILLARD	WATLING	SYKES	PYLE	MABBUTT	PETHERBRIDGE	BIGGS	EDGE	WARD	HOOPER	
19/12/59	LEYTON ORIENT	A	2-1	6914	NORMAN	HILLARD	WATLING	SYKES	PYLE	MABBUTT	PETHERBRIDGE	BIGGS	BRADFORD	WARD	HOOPER	BIGGS, PETHERBRIDGE
26/12/59	SWANSEA TOWN	H	3-1	16501	NORMAN	HILLARD	WATLING	SYKES	PYLE	MABBUTT	JARMAN	BIGGS	BRADFORD	WARD	HOOPER	BRADFORD, BIGGS 2
28/12/59	SWANSEA TOWN	A	0-3	15270	NORMAN	HILLARD	WATLING	SYKES	FROWEN	MABBUTT	JARMAN	BIGGS	EDGE	JONES	HOOPER	
02/01/60	LINCOLN CITY	H	3-3	14148	NORMAN	HILLARD	WATLING	SYKES	FROWEN	MABBUTT	PETHERBRIDGE	BIGGS	BRADFORD	JONES	HOOPER	BIGGS 2, BRADFORD
16/01/60	ASTON VILLA	A	1-4	29726	NORMAN	HILLARD	WATLING	SYKES	FROWEN	MABBUTT	PETHERBRIDGE	BIGGS	BRADFORD	WARD	HOOPER	BRADFORD
23/01/60	SUNDERLAND	H	3-1	17883	NORMAN	HILLARD	WATLING	SYKES	PYLE	MABBUTT	PETHERBRIDGE	BIGGS	BRADFORD	WARD	HOOPER	BRADFORD, BIGGS, WARD
06/02/60	PORTSMOUTH	A	5-4	14136	RADFORD	HILLARD	WATLING	SYKES	PYLE	MABBUTT	PETHERBRIDGE	BIGGS	BRADFORD	WARD	HOOPER	HOWELLS og, WARD 2, HOOPER 2
13/02/60	STOKE CITY	H	3-1	11421	RADFORD	HILLARD	WATLING	SYKES	PYLE	MABBUTT	PETHERBRIDGE	BIGGS	BRADFORD	WARD	HOOPER	WARD, BRADFORD 2
27/02/60	BRISTOL CITY	A	2-1	27048	RADFORD	HILLARD	WATLING	SYKES	PYLE	MABBUTT	PETHERBRIDGE	BIGGS	BRADFORD	WARD	HOOPER	HOOPER, BIGGS
02/03/60	BRIGHTON & H ALBION	A	2-2	10451	RADFORD	HILLARD	WATLING	SYKES	PYLE	MABBUTT	PETHERBRIDGE	BIGGS	BRADFORD	HAMILTON	HOOPER	BIGGS, BRADFORD
05/03/60	SCUNTHORPE UNITED	A	4-3	9227	RADFORD	HILLARD	WATLING	SYKES	PYLE	MABBUTT	PETHERBRIDGE	BIGGS	BRADFORD	HAMILTON	HOOPER	BRADFORD, MABBUTT, HAMILTON 2
12/03/60	ROTHERHAM UNITED	H	3-1	15126	RADFORD	HILLARD	WATLING	SYKES	PYLE	MABBUTT	PETHERBRIDGE	BIGGS	BRADFORD	HAMILTON	HOOPER	HAMILTON 2, BIGGS
19/03/60	DERBY COUNTY	A	0-1	13539	RADFORD	HILLARD	WATLING	RICKETTS	PYLE	MABBUTT	JARMAN	BIGGS	WARD	HAMILTON	HOOPER	
26/03/60	HULL CITY	H	1-0	12268	RADFORD	HILLARD	WATLING	SYKES	PYLE	MABBUTT	PETHERBRIDGE	BIGGS	BRADFORD	WARD	HOOPER	BIGGS
02/04/60	SHEFFIELD UNITED	A	1-1	14521	RADFORD	HILLARD	WATLING	SYKES	PYLE	MABBUTT	PETHERBRIDGE	BIGGS	BRADFORD	WARD	HOOPER	WARD
09/04/60	MIDDLESBROUGH	H	0-2	15837	RADFORD	HILLARD	WATLING	SYKES	PYLE	MABBUTT	PETHERBRIDGE	BIGGS	EDGE	WARD	HOOPER	
15/04/60	HUDDERSFIELD TOWN	H	2-0	16069	RADFORD	HILLARD	WATLING	SYKES	PYLE	MABBUTT	PETHERBRIDGE	BIGGS	BRADFORD	WARD	HOOPER	BRADFORD, BIGGS
16/04/60	LIVERPOOL	A	0-4	27317	RADFORD	HILLARD	WATLING	FROWEN	PYLE	MABBUTT	PETHERBRIDGE	BIGGS	BRADFORD	WARD	HOOPER	
18/04/60	HUDDERSFIELD TOWN	A	1-0	13820	RADFORD	HILLARD	WATLING	SYKES	PYLE	MABBUTT	PETHERBRIDGE	BIGGS	BRADFORD	WARD	HOOPER	HOOPER
23/04/60	PLYMOUTH ARGYLE	H	2-0	17073	RADFORD	FROWEN	WATLING	SYKES	PYLE	MABBUTT	PETHERBRIDGE	BIGGS	BRADFORD	WARD	HOOPER	BIGGS 2
30/04/60	CARDIFF CITY	A	2-2	25000	RADFORD	FROWEN	WATLING	SYKES	PYLE	MABBUTT	PETHERBRIDGE	BIGGS	BRADFORD	WARD	HOOPER	WARD 2

FA CUP

Date	Opponent	H/A	Score	ATT	G	2	3	4	5	6	7	8	9	10	11	Goalscorers
09/01/60	DONCASTER ROVERS	H	0-0	15522	NORMAN	HILLARD	WATLING	SYKES	FROWEN	MABBUTT	PETHERBRIDGE	BIGGS	JONES	WARD	HOOPER	
12/01/60	DONCASTER ROVERS	A	2-1	15217	NORMAN	HILLARD	WATLING	SYKES	FROWEN	MABBUTT	PETHERBRIDGE	BIGGS	JONES	WARD	HOOPER	BIGGS, WARD
30/01/60	PRESTON NORTH END	H	3-3	38472	NORMAN	HILLARD	WATLING	SYKES	FROWEN	MABBUTT	PETHERBRIDGE	BIGGS	JONES	WARD	HOOPER	BIGGS 2, SMITH og
02/02/60	PRESTON NORTH END	A	1-5	33164	NORMAN	HILLARD	WATLING	SYKES	FROWEN	MABBUTT	PETHERBRIDGE	BIGGS	JONES	WARD	HOOPER	HOOPER

GLOUCESTERSHIRE CUP FINAL

Date	Opponent	H/A	Score	ATT	G	2	3	4	5	6	7	8	9	10	11	Goalscorers
02/05/60	BRISTOL CITY	A	2-3	7195	RADFORD	HILLARD	WATLING	SYKES	FROWEN	MABBUTT	PETHERBRIDGE	BIGGS	BRADFORD	WARD	HOOPER	BIGGS 2

PLAYERS	APP	GLS
BIGGS A	41	22
BRADFORD G	30	12
DOYLE B	5	1
DRAKE L	1	
EDGE A	9	3
FROWEN J	7	
HAMILTON I	5	4
HILLARD D	40	1
HOOPER P	41	13
JARMAN P	3	
JONES R	5	
MABBUTT R	42	1
NORMAN M	28	
PETHERBRIDGE G	27	2
PYLE D	38	
RADFORD H	14	
RICKETTS Gr	10	
SAMPSON P	1	
SMITH G	6	
SYKES N	35	
TIMMINS J	1	
WARD D	34	12
WATLING J	39	
OWN GOAL		1

goal. Victory at Scunthorpe United, in an extraordinary game that finished 4-3, was largely due to Hamilton's first two goals for the club. Rovers had gone ahead after only 18 minutes when Bradford scored following a neat interchange of passes with Hooper, but conceded a goal either side of half-time before Mabbutt equalised. Hamilton's brace, either side of Barrie Thomas' second goal of the game, were both confidently taken, the first from a 15-yard strike on the hour and the winning goal, nine minutes from time, after goalkeeper Ken Jones had only parried a rasping drive from Hooper.

The most remarkably victory, though, was a 5-4 win at Fratton Park. Portsmouth conceded a second-minute own goal through Ron Howells, only for Ron Saunders, later a highly successful manager, to equalise 15 minutes later. Dai Ward's 23rd-minute goal gave Rovers a 2-1 interval lead and, when he scored again two minutes after the break Rovers appeared to have some breathing space. Not so, for Saunders grabbed a second within a minute and, although Hooper put Rovers further ahead, Derek Harris reduced the margin to 4-3 with 17 minutes remaining. Eight minutes from time, Biggs handballed and Reg Cutler drove home the equaliser from the penalty spot. With all to play for, Rovers swept forward and, on 88 minutes, Hooper claimed his second goal of the game to give Rovers a memorable victory.

In the FA Cup, held to a goalless draw at home by Doncaster Rovers, the Eastville side won 2-1 in the replay at Belle Vue. Both Biggs and Ward found their customary way on to the scoresheet, with Albert Broadbent replying for the home side. The reward for this victory was that, for the second time in three years, mighty Preston North End were drawn to play Rovers at Eastville. This fixture against one of the most powerful sides in the country drew a record crowd of 38,472 to Eastville. This figure stood the test of time and now remains in perpetuity the largest attendance ever to assemble at the old stadium. The huge gathering was not to be disappointed, either, as the sides served up a six-goal thriller. Biggs scored twice for Rovers, while the legendary Tom Finney was one of North End's scorers. Gordon Milne, later a very successful manager, was in the Preston side while Jim Smith, who was to play for Stockport County in both League fixtures against Rovers in 1969/70, conceded an own goal. The replay at Deepdale drew a crowd of 33,164, Preston running out 5-1 winners with Finney and Sam Taylor, scorers of a goal apiece in the first game, now claiming two each.

The Gloucestershire Cup final was lost. Bristol City had finished last in Division Two and been relegated but, despite trailing at half-time, defeated Rovers 3-2 to win the trophy, the evergreen John Atyeo scoring twice. Rovers also played Bristol Rugby Club on 4 May in an experimental game of Socby. After a goalless first-half, Bradford scored twice and Hooper once to give Rovers a 3-1 win, with the rugby club's captain John Blake scoring a consolation goal. Coach Fred Ford, a pivotal figure in five excellent seasons, left Rovers to become manager at Ashton Gate.

Dai Ward was rewarded for his talent at club level by representing Wales in their 1-1 draw with England at Cardiff on 17 October 1959. He was, after Jack Lewis in 1906, the second player to play for the full Welsh side while on Rovers' books and he was to win a second cap as a Cardiff City player three years later.

It is all too often the case with a relatively small club that the threat of relegation is never too far away. While Rovers had finished in the top 10 in Division Two for seven consecutive seasons, there was now no money for purchasing replacements for older players. As a younger generation of Bristolians came through the ranks, the club slipped to a final League placing of 17th and two long, trying years lay ahead. Twenty League defeats was the club's worst record since 1947/48 and 92 goals conceded the most since 1935/36. Rovers finished the season just four points above relegated Portsmouth.

Once the season had opened with an unexpected defeat at home to Middlesbrough, in which Rovers twice equalised before falling to Alan Peacock's 79th-minute winning goal, it was clear that a troublesome year lay ahead. Within weeks, Rovers had lost 6-1 at Brighton, where Adrian Thorne became the sixth player to score four goals against Rovers in a League game, and 4-0 at Rotherham United. Rovers were to concede four goals at each of Luton Town, Southampton and Huddersfield Town and five in both encounters with Plymouth Argyle. At home, in addition to Argyle's visit, Rovers were to concede four to Leeds United and three on a total of three occasions in the League.

Bristol Rovers 1960/61. Back row: Sampson, Hillard, Pyle, Radford, Frowen, Mabbutt. Front row: Petherbridge, Biggs, Purdon, Ward, Hooper

George Petherbridge scores Rovers' first goal in a remarkable comeback match on 29 August 1960 after they trailed 4-0 before drawing 4-4

With the familiar names of George Petherbridge, Alfie Biggs, Geoff Bradford, Dai Ward and Peter Hooper, the sole ever-present, in the forward line, it was a very recognizable Rovers forward line that began the season. With the retirement of Brian Doyle, John Frowen became the regular left-back, working behind Ray Mabbutt and in partnership with the solid Doug Hillard. However, a lack of early-season success prompted two departures. Dai Ward left to pursue his career with Cardiff City, where he was to win a second Welsh cap. The deal, worth £10,000, also brought John Watkins to Eastville and the prospect of him and the emerging talent of Harold Jarman on opposing wings certainly filled supporters with optimism. At the season's end, after missing the last 15 games with a fractured leg, Biggs joined Preston North End for £18,000, though he was to return in 15 months.

A final 9 League matches brought to a conclusion the long and reliable career of wing-half Peter Sampson, leaving just Bradford and Petherbridge of the Championship-winning side. After 340 League games for Rovers, Sampson spent two further seasons as captain of Trowbridge Town. However, young Bobby Jones continued to progress and two players for the future, Joe Davis and Terry Oldfield, broke into the side for the first time. The side's only ever-present Hooper, was top scorer with 20 League goals. Another departure was secretary John Gummow who, ill from July 1960, retired five days before Christmas and was replaced by Ron Moules.

The second home game of the season featured the greatest comeback in Rovers' history. Four goals behind at the interval, Rovers staged an exceptional second-half recovery to draw 4-4 with Leeds United at Eastville. Don Revie, later an England manager, had been in the Leeds side that drew 1-1 with Rovers at Elland Road five days earlier, but this Monday fixture still found Rovers facing strong opposition, including centre-half Jack Charlton, a 1966 World Cup winner. The referee, Jack Taylor, was to be in charge of the 1974 World Cup final, where he awarded a controversial first-minute penalty. Leeds were 4-0 up inside 41 minutes. Colin Grainger, a thorn in Rovers' side while with Sunderland in 1959/60, scored after 10 minutes, John Hawksby scored twice, the second after Noel Payton had hit a post and John McCole snapped up a rebound off goalkeeper Malcolm Norman. Rovers, however, approached the second-half with renewed vigour and scored three times in 12 minutes, through Petherbridge, after an interchange of passes with Hillard, Hamilton from a Mabbutt free-kick and Hooper. A very tense half-hour passed until Hooper hit a dramatic equaliser from a Biggs cross with two minutes remaining. Even then, Graham Ricketts had an opportunity to score, but an entertaining game finished with honours even.

Despite the heavy defeats, Rovers were to achieve some very creditable results. The first win of the season, against Rotherham United in the eighth game, was the first of four in six games and there were three straight victories just before Christmas and four in five games in March. Leyton Orient, Swansea Town and Southampton were all beaten 4-2 at Eastville, Hooper scoring on each occasion. Swansea's case was not helped by Mel Nurse, the winner of 12 Welsh International caps, conceding an own goal. Hooper scored again in a 4-1 victory over Luton Town and also in an extraordinary 4-3 home win over Liverpool, where Bobby Jones scored twice for the first of two consecutive League matches. Liverpool's Kevin Lewis scored three times, one from a penalty, in so doing becoming the first of four opponents to score a League hat-trick against Rovers and yet end up on the losing side.

Indeed, Rovers won their last seven home games of the season. Portsmouth, ultimately relegated, were beaten 2-0 in a key fixture in March, with Hooper and Bradford scoring. Sheffield United, already promoted and having reached the FA Cup semi-finals with Len Allchurch in majestic form, were seen off 3-1 in the final home match to complete an improbable League double. From New Year onwards, Rovers were unbeaten at Eastville and recorded a second away win, two Hooper goals defeating Lincoln City at Sincil Bank. A potential win at Swansea Town in February was thwarted by an early injury to goalkeeper Howard Radford, which ended his season and saw Mabbutt play the final 72 minutes in goal. A flurry of goals in January was epitomized by the 3-3 draw with Scunthorpe United, for whom Barrie Thomas scored twice in each of the League meetings with Rovers.

Yet, while the club's home record was good, Rovers contrived to lose 10 of the last 11 away games. As the season drew to a close, these defeats became steadily heavier. Rovers lost 3-0 at Liverpool and Portsmouth, fighting for their survival, and 5-0 at Plymouth Argyle, George Kirby and Wilf Carter scoring twice each. Ominously for 1961/62, these results left Rovers scrapping for points to ensure the retention of Division Two football. This achieved, Rovers crashed 4-0 to Huddersfield Town at Leeds Road on the final day of the season, the home side requiring at least a point to guarantee survival. As it was, Derek Stokes scored twice, as he did in October 1961 on the next occasion the clubs met and as he had at Eastville, before Hamilton struck a consolation goal six minutes from time.

The signs for 1961/62 were bleak. With minimal funds for player recruitment, Bert Tann was able to sign just Brian Carter and John Hills in the summer of 1961. Rovers lost every game in which either of these players appeared. Eighteen players were used in the opening four games, but Rovers lost the first seven, the Huddersfield game at the end of 1960/61 creating a club record eight in succession. Ward and Biggs had left, but

Eastville was underwater yet again in December 1960

young talent in the form of Mabbutt, Jarman and Jones was coming to the fore. Over the close season, though, Bobby Campbell, later Rovers' manager between 1977 and 1979, joined Rovers as trainer. In July 1961, Tann brought Bill Dodgin to Eastville as chief scout. A wing-half with Rovers in 1936/37, he had played alongside Tann and Fred Ford at Charlton Athletic. Dodgin was to be Rovers' manager between August 1969 and July 1972 and his return to Eastville at this point must be viewed as a highly positive move. Mention must also be made of the Social Club, which put together a busy first full working year for its 2,000 members. Tombola, often run by the son of former goalkeeper Harry Stansfield, and dancing evenings proved highly popular, while there was a darts night every Monday and whist on Tuesdays. Sunday evenings were Show night, where Bill McMullen presented a variety of acts, including a fire eater, an Indian fakir and a troupe of performing cats. Brian Jones hosted an increasingly successful Rock 'n' Roll evening every Wednesday.

Rovers made history in September by hosting and winning the first game ever played in the newly-created League Cup. Due to a 7.15 p.m. kick-off, 15 minutes earlier than other ties, Fulham's Maurice Cook is credited with the tournament's first goal and Rovers, with Jarman scoring for the club for the first time, with the opening victory. Hamilton scored twice as Rovers ran up a 5-3 victory at Reading before succumbing to Rotherham United. It was the first match ever played under floodlights at Millmoor and the home side won through goals from Alan Kirkman and Ken Houghton. In the FA Cup, Division One Aston Villa were held to a draw at Eastville but won the replay

SEASON 1960/61

FOOTBALL LEAGUE DIVISION TWO

Date	Opposition		Result	Att	G	2	3	4	5	6	7	8	9	10	11	GOALSCORERS
20/08/60	MIDDLESBROUGH	H	2-3	20302	RADFORD	HILLARD	WATLING	SYKES	PYLE	MABBUTT	PETHERBRIDGE	BIGGS	BRADFORD	WARD	HOOPER	HOOPER, HILLARD
24/08/60	LEEDS UNITED	A	1-1	11330	RADFORD	HILLARD	WATLING	RICKETTS	PYLE	MABBUTT	PETHERBRIDGE	BIGGS	BRADFORD	WARD	HOOPER	HOOPER
27/08/60	BRIGHTON & H ALBION	A	1-6	15437	RADFORD	HILLARD	WATLING	RICKETTS	PYLE	MABBUTT	PETHERBRIDGE	BIGGS	BRADFORD	WARD	HOOPER	BRADFORD
29/08/60	LEEDS UNITED	H	4-4	19028	NORMAN	HILLARD	WATLING	RICKETTS	PYLE	MABBUTT	PETHERBRIDGE	BIGGS	EDGE	HAMILTON	HOOPER	PETHERBRIDGE, HAMILTON, HOOPER 2
03/09/60	IPSWICH TOWN	H	1-1	15467	NORMAN	HILLARD	WATLING	RICKETTS	FROWEN	MABBUTT	PETHERBRIDGE	BIGGS	EDGE	HAMILTON	HOOPER	BIGGS
07/09/60	ROTHERHAM UNITED	A	0-4	8219	NORMAN	HILLARD	WATLING	RICKETTS	PYLE	MABBUTT	PETHERBRIDGE	SYKES	BRADFORD	BIGGS	HOOPER	
10/09/60	SCUNTHORPE UNITED	A	2-1	10262	NORMAN	HILLARD	WATLING	RICKETTS	PYLE	MABBUTT	COGGINS	BIGGS	EDGE	WARD	HOOPER	BIGGS
12/09/60	ROTHERHAM UNITED	H	2-1	13088	NORMAN	HILLARD	WATLING	RICKETTS	PYLE	MABBUTT	COGGINS	JONES	EDGE	WARD	HOOPER	HOOPER pen, WARD
17/09/60	LEYTON ORIENT	H	4-2	15337	BEARPARK	HILLARD	WATLING	SAMPSON	PYLE	MABBUTT	COGGINS	BIGGS	EDGE	JONES	HOOPER	BIGGS 2, HOOPER, EDGE
24/09/60	DERBY COUNTY	A	1-1	12826	BEARPARK	HILLARD	WATLING	SAMPSON	PYLE	MABBUTT	COGGINS	BIGGS	BRADFORD	JONES	HOOPER	HOOPER pen
01/10/60	SWANSEA TOWN	H	4-2	15177	RADFORD	HILLARD	WATLING	SAMPSON	PYLE	MABBUTT	JARMAN	BIGGS	BRADFORD	PURDON	HOOPER	BRADFORD, NURSE og, HILLARD, HOOPER
08/10/60	LUTON TOWN	A	2-4	9373	RADFORD	HILLARD	WATLING	SYKES	PYLE	SAMPSON	JARMAN	MABBUTT	BRADFORD	PURDON	HOOPER	PURDON, BRADFORD
15/10/60	LINCOLN CITY	H	3-1	16853	RADFORD	HILLARD	RIDEOUT	SYKES	PYLE	MABBUTT	JARMAN	BIGGS	COLLINS	HAMILTON	HOOPER	JARMAN, COLLINS, HAMILTON
29/10/60	HUDDERSFIELD TOWN	H	1-2	15381	RADFORD	WATLING	FROWEN	SAMPSON	PYLE	MABBUTT	JARMAN	BRADFORD	COLLINS	HAMILTON	HOOPER	HAMILTON
05/11/60	SUNDERLAND	A	0-2	17942	RADFORD	HILLARD	FROWEN	SYKES	PYLE	MABBUTT	PETHERBRIDGE	BIGGS	OLDFIELD	PURDON	HOOPER	
12/11/60	PLYMOUTH ARGYLE	H	2-5	17005	RADFORD	HILLARD	WATLING	SYKES	PYLE	MABBUTT	PETHERBRIDGE	BIGGS	OLDFIELD	WARD	HOOPER	PETHERBRIDGE, HOOPER
19/11/60	NORWICH CITY	A	1-2	22581	RADFORD	HILLARD	WATLING	SYKES	PYLE	MABBUTT	PETHERBRIDGE	BIGGS	BRADFORD	WARD	HOOPER	BRADFORD
26/11/60	CHARLTON ATHLETIC	H	3-1	10186	RADFORD	HILLARD	FROWEN	SYKES	PYLE	MABBUTT	JARMAN	BIGGS	BRADFORD	WARD	HOOPER	WARD, BRADFORD, BIGGS
03/12/60	SHEFFIELD UNITED	A	3-2	12877	RADFORD	HILLARD	FROWEN	SYKES	PYLE	MABBUTT	JARMAN	BIGGS	BRADFORD	WARD	HOOPER	WARD, BIGGS, HOOPER
10/12/60	STOKE CITY	H	1-1	13407	RADFORD	HILLARD	FROWEN	SYKES	PYLE	MABBUTT	JARMAN	BIGGS	BRADFORD	WARD	HOOPER	BRADFORD
17/12/60	MIDDLESBROUGH	A	1-1	11594	RADFORD	HILLARD	FROWEN	SYKES	PYLE	MABBUTT	JARMAN	BIGGS	BRADFORD	WARD	HOOPER	HOOPER
26/12/60	SOUTHAMPTON	H	2-4	21901	RADFORD	HILLARD	FROWEN	SYKES	PYLE	MABBUTT	JARMAN	JONES	BRADFORD	WARD	HOOPER	JONES, JARMAN
31/12/60	BRIGHTON & H ALBION	H	2-3	12823	RADFORD	HILLARD	FROWEN	SYKES	PYLE	MABBUTT	JARMAN	BIGGS	BRADFORD	WARD	HOOPER	BIGGS 2
14/01/61	IPSWICH TOWN	A	2-3	11939	RADFORD	HILLARD	FROWEN	SYKES	PYLE	MABBUTT	JARMAN	BIGGS	BRADFORD	HOOPER	PETHERBRIDGE	
21/01/61	SCUNTHORPE UNITED	H	3-3	11316	RADFORD	HILLARD	FROWEN	SYKES	PYLE	MABBUTT	JARMAN	BIGGS	BRADFORD	HOOPER	PETHERBRIDGE	SYKES, HORSTEAD og, PETHERBRIDGE
04/02/61	LEYTON ORIENT	A	2-3	12334	RADFORD	HILLARD	FROWEN	SYKES	PYLE	MABBUTT	PETHERBRIDGE	JONES	BRADFORD	HOOPER	WATKINS	BRADFORD, JONES
11/02/61	DERBY COUNTY	H	1-1	11164	RADFORD	HILLARD	FROWEN	SYKES	PYLE	MABBUTT	PETHERBRIDGE	JONES	BRADFORD	HOOPER	WATKINS	PETHERBRIDGE
25/02/61	LUTON TOWN	H	4-1	13102	RADFORD	HILLARD	FROWEN	SYKES	DAVIS	MABBUTT	PETHERBRIDGE	JONES	BRADFORD	HOOPER	WATKINS	BRADFORD 2, PETHERBRIDGE, HOOPER
28/02/61	SWANSEA TOWN	A	1-2	12562	RADFORD	HILLARD	FROWEN	SYKES	DAVIS	MABBUTT	PETHERBRIDGE	JONES	BRADFORD	HOOPER	WATKINS	HOOPER
04/03/61	LINCOLN CITY	A	2-1	15006	RADFORD	HILLARD	FROWEN	SYKES	DAVIS	MABBUTT	JARMAN	JONES	PURDON	HOOPER	WATKINS	HOOPER 2
11/03/61	PORTSMOUTH	H	2-0	5623	NORMAN	HILLARD	FROWEN	SYKES	DAVIS	MABBUTT	JARMAN	JONES	BRADFORD	HOOPER	WATKINS	HOOPER, BRADFORD
18/03/61	STOKE CITY	A	0-2	7826	NORMAN	HILLARD	FROWEN	SYKES	DAVIS	MABBUTT	JARMAN	JONES	BRADFORD	HOOPER	WATKINS	
20/03/61	SOUTHAMPTON	A	4-2	15699	NORMAN	HILLARD	FROWEN	SYKES	DAVIS	MABBUTT	JARMAN	JONES	BRADFORD	HOOPER	WATKINS	BRADFORD, JONES, HILLARD, HOOPER
25/03/61	SUNDERLAND	H	1-0	15261	NORMAN	HILLARD	FROWEN	SYKES	DAVIS	MABBUTT	JARMAN	JONES	BRADFORD	HOOPER	WATKINS	HOOPER
31/03/61	LIVERPOOL	A	0-3	36538	NORMAN	HILLARD	FROWEN	SYKES	DAVIS	MABBUTT	JARMAN	JONES	BRADFORD	HOOPER	WATKINS	
01/04/61	CHARLTON ATHLETIC	H	3-0	9139	NORMAN	HILLARD	FROWEN	SYKES	DAVIS	MABBUTT	JARMAN	JONES	BRADFORD	HOOPER	WATKINS	JONES
04/04/61	LIVERPOOL	H	4-3	16522	NORMAN	HILLARD	FROWEN	SYKES	DAVIS	MABBUTT	JARMAN	JONES	BRADFORD	HOOPER	WATKINS	JONES 2, JARMAN, HOOPER
08/04/61	NORWICH CITY	H	3-1	18234	NORMAN	HILLARD	FROWEN	SYKES	DAVIS	MABBUTT	JARMAN	JONES	JAMES	HOOPER	WATKINS	JONES 2, HOOPER
15/04/61	PLYMOUTH ARGYLE	A	0-5	14026	NORMAN	HILLARD	FROWEN	SYKES	DAVIS	MABBUTT	JARMAN	JONES	BRADFORD	HOOPER	WATKINS	
19/04/61	PORTSMOUTH	A	0-3	10793	NORMAN	HALL	FROWEN	SYKES	DAVIS	BRADFORD	JARMAN	JONES	PURDON	WARD	HOOPER	
22/04/61	SHEFFIELD UNITED	H	3-1	13052	NORMAN	HILLARD	FROWEN	SYKES	DAVIS	MABBUTT	JARMAN	JONES	BRADFORD	WARD	HOOPER	BRADFORD, JARMAN, JONES
29/04/61	HUDDERSFIELD TOWN	A	0-4	10322	NORMAN	HILLARD	FROWEN	SYKES	DAVIS	MABBUTT	JARMAN	JONES	BRADFORD	HAMILTON	HOOPER	

FA CUP

Date	Opposition		Result	Att	G	2	3	4	5	6	7	8	9	10	11	GOALSCORERS
07/01/61	ASTON VILLA	H	1-1	34061	NORMAN	HILLARD	WATLING	SYKES	PYLE	MABBUTT	PETHERBRIDGE	BIGGS	BRADFORD	WARD	HOOPER	BIGGS
09/01/61	ASTON VILLA	A	0-4	26998	NORMAN	HILLARD	FROWEN	SYKES	PYLE	MABBUTT	PETHERBRIDGE	BIGGS	PURDON	WARD	HOOPER	

LEAGUE CUP

Date	Opposition		Result	Att	G	2	3	4	5	6	7	8	9	10	11	GOALSCORERS
26/09/60	FULHAM	H	2-1	20022	RADFORD	HILLARD	WATLING	SAMPSON	PYLE	MABBUTT	JARMAN	BIGGS	BRADFORD	PURDON	HOOPER	ARMAN, BRADFORD
12/10/60	READING	A	5-3	8323	RADFORD	HILLARD	RIDEOUT	SYKES	PYLE	MABBUTT	JARMAN	BIGGS	COLLINS	HAMILTON	HOOPER	AMILTON 2, SYKES, JARMAN
23/11/60	ROTHERHAM UNITED	A	1-3	10912	RADFORD	HILLARD	WATLING	SYKES	PYLE	MABBUTT	PETHERBRIDGE	BIGGS	BRADFORD	WARD	HOOPER	

GLOUCESTERSHIRE CUP FINAL

Date	Opposition		Result	Att	G	2	3	4	5	6	7	8	9	10	11	GOALSCORERS
01/05/61	BRISTOL CITY	H	1-3	12109	NORMAN	HILLARD	FROWEN	STONE	DAVIS	MABBUTT	JARMAN	JONES	BRADFORD	HOOPER	WATKINS	ARMAN

PLAYERS	APP	GLS
BEARPARK I	2	
BIGGS A	23	8
BRADFORD G	32	12
COGGINS P	4	
COLLINS G	2	1
DAVIS J	15	
EDGE A	4	1
FROWEN J	27	
HALL A	1	
HAMILTON I	5	3
HILLARD D	40	3
HOOPER P	42	20
JAMES R	1	
JARMAN H	21	4
JONES E	22	9
MABBUTT R	40	
NORMAN M	17	
OLDFIELD T	2	
PETHERBRIDGE G	19	5
PURDON E	4	1
PYLE D	26	
RADFORD H	23	
RICKETTS G	5	
RIDEOUT B	1	
SAMPSON P	9	
SYKES N	32	1
WARD D	13	3
WATKINS J	14	1
WATLING J	16	
OWN GOALS		2

convincingly, with two goals apiece from Bobby Thompson and England International Gerry Hitchens. Dai Ward was accused by many of lacking interest in this game and, indeed, never appeared in a Rovers shirt again. Two Biggs goals helped defeat Chelsea 3-1 in a friendly in January before an Eastville crowd of 5,245. Rovers gave a debut to David Stone in the Gloucestershire Cup final but, after a goalless first-half, lost 3-1 at home to Bristol City. John Atyeo, who had scored a hat-trick against Brentford 48 hours earlier in the final League game of the season, scored two of the goals.

1961/62

After nine seasons in Division Two, Rovers were relegated to Division Three. It was the end of arguably the most glorious chapter in the club's history. The first seven games of the season were lost and there were 22 League defeats in total, the most since 1936/37. A tally of 13 League victories was, at the time, the lowest since 1947/48. Rovers scored 53 League goals, the lowest figure in the Division Two years, where the club had reached 80 in four consecutive seasons.

In truth, the minimal funds at Bert Tann's disposal, meant it was inevitable the club would struggle. John Hills and Brian Carter, the latter having played for Portsmouth in the nine-goal thriller in February 1960, arrived on free transfers and Micky Slocombe was the only local player to break into the side in the early part of the season. Geoff Bradford began the season at centre-forward, but by Christmas was playing at right-back with the ever-reliable Ray Mabbutt leading the line. Although a tireless worker and key figure in the side, Mabbutt was to score just twice all season. The only ever-present was left-back John Frowen, who completed a run of 66 consecutive League appearances, while Bobby Jones, with one more than Bradford and Peter Hooper, was top scorer on 13 League goals.

It is not just that Rovers lost their opening games, though, but the manner of these defeats that set the stage for the season ahead. A bumper crowd of 19,438 at Eastville on the opening day of the season earned the players a £6 bonus each, but Liverpool, destined to be runaway champions, took the points. This was the first fixture before the newly-roofed Tote End, where the greyhound totalizer clocks, installed in 1935, had now been placed prominently on the roof facia. Bury completed a League double and Rovers crashed 4-0 at Rotherham United even before Rovers' first goals of the season. Bradford scored twice at home to Sunderland, but Rovers still lost and did so again at Scunthorpe United and Stoke City, in Josser Watling's final game for the club. Doug Hillard's broken leg at Scunthorpe ruled him out of football for seven months. Seven straight defeats, or eight if the final game of 1960/61 is included, constitute an unwanted club record and left Rovers adrift at the foot of Division Two.

Through the middle of September, the revival got underway. Consecutive 2-1 victories were followed by a decisive 4-0 win against Leeds United, Hooper scoring twice against a side who were, in fact, to finish just three points above Rovers. A draw at Norwich City followed, but this encouraging run was ended by none other than Alfie

Bristol Rovers 1961/62. Back row: Sykes, Hills, Pyle, Norman, Radford, Frowen, Davis, Hillard. Second row: Petherbridge, Jones, Bradford, Hooper, Watkins, Hamilton. Front row: Mabbutt, Carter

Biggs, who scored the only goal of the game from six yards out two minutes from time as Preston North End defeated his home-town club. Whereas in the relegation season of 1980/81 only 5 League matches were won, this Rovers side certainly proved it could win key games on occasions. A Jones hat-trick contributed to a 4-1 win over Swansea Town, a fifth consecutive home victory and the third of four occasions that Rovers scored as many as four times in a home match. Astonishingly, Rovers completed League doubles over Leyton Orient, who were promoted to Division One, and over sixth-placed Southampton.

On the other hand, though conceding fewer goals than the previous season, Rovers suffered a number of heavy defeats. Their situation is best summarized through the experiences of Keith Havenhand, who only ever scored 14 goals for Derby County but became the only player to register two League hat-tricks in a season against Rovers. Derby won both matches 4-1. Len White also scored three times, with Len Allchurch claiming one of the others, as Newcastle United defeated Rovers 5-2. Although Jarman gave Rovers a fourth-minute lead at Roker Park, Rovers trailed by half-time and conceded three goals in the final quarter of an hour to lose 6-1. Roger Hunt and Ian St John were Liverpool's scorers, as Rovers lost 2-0 at Anfield to a side featuring Ron Yeats, Ian Callaghan, Jimmy Melia and Gordon Milne and that was to win the League Championship in 1963/64. Future Rovers players John Williams and John Brown both scored for Plymouth Argyle at Eastville, though Rovers won 4-3, and Alfie Biggs scored in both League meetings for Preston North End.

However, own goals proved to be something of a problem. John Hills scored an own goal on his debut, a feat paralleled by Sonny Parker in December 2002. When Rovers lost at Brighton in December in the final League appearance of George Petherbridge, who had played in 457 League matches and scored in the first 16 consecutive post-war seasons, it was to a David Pyle own goal after 29 minutes, from Bobby Laverick's low cross. Norman Sykes somehow contrived to concede own goals home and away to Sunderland, a feat paralleled in August 1977 when Phil Bater scored against his own side in both legs of a League cup-tie with Walsall. However, Pyle and Sykes both scored

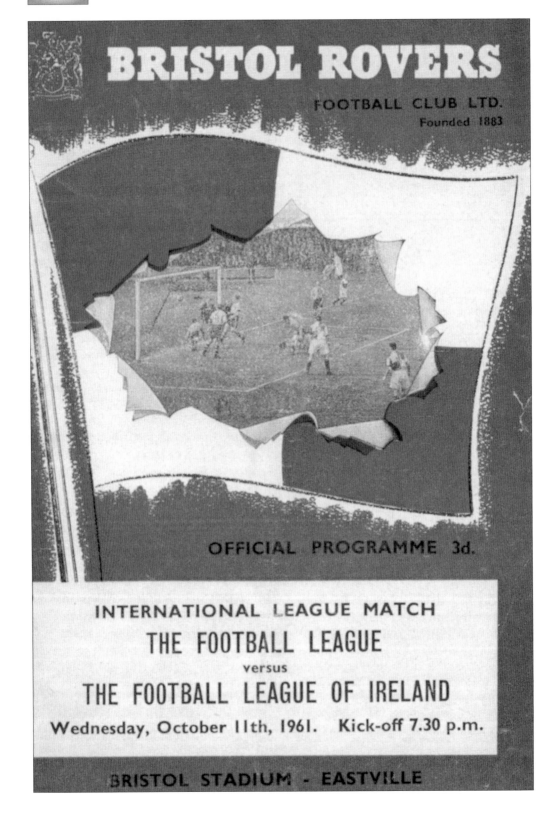

BRISTOL ROVERS

FOOTBALL CLUB LTD.
Founded 1883

OFFICIAL PROGRAMME 3d.

INTERNATIONAL LEAGUE MATCH

THE FOOTBALL LEAGUE
versus
THE FOOTBALL LEAGUE OF IRELAND

Wednesday, October 11th, 1961.   Kick-off 7.30 p.m.

BRISTOL STADIUM - EASTVILLE

own goals in a bizarre 2-0 home defeat to Stoke City in January. Dennis Viollet, who had scored for England against Luxembourg just four months earlier, made his Stoke debut but Rovers contributed both goals by deflecting harmless-looking crosses from Don Ratcliffe into their own net, Pyle six minutes before half-time and Sykes after 66 minutes. In Sykes' case, it was just seven days after his own goal at Roker Park. At half-time in the Stoke game, referee R H Mann of Worcester, who took charge of that season's League Cup final second leg, had to retire after pulling a leg muscle and was replaced by J W Tucker of Loughrane.

On 22 October, the day after a crushing 4-1 defeat at Huddersfield Town, a former Rovers stalwart, Ben Appleby, the club's fourth highest appearance maker in the Southern League days, died at the age of 84. The defeat at Leeds Road was soon followed by heavy defeats against Derby County and Newcastle United. The upshot was that the home game with Middlesbrough at the end of November was watched by the first home crowd under 10,000 for many years. Esmond Million, later a Rovers goalkeeper, was injured in this game but the visitors still inflicted on Rovers one of their seven League defeats at Eastville. Seven days later at Walsall, the first goalless Rovers League match was played since the game at Barnsley in March 1959, a club record run of 114 League fixtures.

Rovers went to Middlesbrough on 14 April out of the relegation zone with five matches to play. Brighton were apparently virtually relegated and the race to avoid the second position saw Leeds United on 30 points, Rovers and Boro on 31 and Swansea Town, with just four games left, on 32. It had not been Rovers' season in the north-east, what with a 5-2 defeat at Newcastle United and a 6-1 hammering at Sunderland, but the 5-0 loss at Ayresome Park left Rovers with much to do. On Good Friday, Rovers drew with a Charlton Athletic side forced to play inside forward John Hewie in goal. Twenty-four hours later, Bradford's two goals earned a draw with Walsall and left Rovers and Leeds United, with two matches remaining, on 33 points above Swansea Town, now with a game in hand, on 32 and a rejuvenated Brighton on 31.

On Easter Monday, as Rovers and Brighton lost, Swansea picked up a point. Twenty-four hours later Leeds United drew with Bury and the Swans beat Plymouth Argyle 5-0. Brighton were relegated and Swansea safe while, with one game left, the remaining relegation place was to be taken by Leeds, on 34 points, or Rovers, a point below them. As Leeds faced the daunting task of visiting Newcastle United, Rovers had to beat Luton Town, a side they had earlier defeated at Eastville. At Kenilworth Road, however, Gordon Turner put the Hatters ahead after three minutes, following a poor goal-kick by Howard Radford, and Alec Ashworth's shot 12 minutes later was deflected in off Dave Bumpstead so that Rovers, in losing 2-0, were relegated with Brighton to Division Three, three points adrift of Leeds United who had unaccountably won 3-0 at St James' Park. Above Leeds and Swansea Town were an incredible eight clubs all on 39 points. Crucially, Rovers had won only twice in the 16 fixtures against these sides.

League performances were reflected in Cup results. Oldham Athletic, a Division Four side, held Rovers in the FA Cup before winning a replay through two John Colquhoun goals at Boundary Park. Rovers beat Hartlepool United 2-1 in the League Cup and held Blackburn Rovers to a draw before the Division One side recorded a straightforward replay victory, Eddie Thomas scoring all four of their goals. Roy McCrohan, later a Rovers player, was a member of the Norwich City side that defeated unfashionable

FOOTBALL LEAGUE DIVISION TWO

SEASON 1961/62

Date	Opponent	H/A		ATT	G	2	3	4	5	6	7	8	9	10	11	GOALSCORERS
19/08/61	LIVERPOOL	H	0-2	19438	NORMAN	HILLS	FROWEN	MABBUTT	DAVIS	CARTER	JARMAN	JONES	BRADFORD	HAMILTON	HOOPER	
22/08/61	BURY	A	0-2	12785	NORMAN	HILLS	FROWEN	MABBUTT	DAVIS	CARTER	JARMAN	JONES	BRADFORD	WATKINS	HOOPER	
26/08/61	ROTHERHAM UNITED	A	0-4	7921	NORMAN	HILLS	FROWEN	MABBUTT	PYLE	CARTER	JARMAN	JONES	BRADFORD	WATKINS	HOOPER	
28/08/61	BURY	H	2-3	13943	RADFORD	HILLARD	FROWEN	MABBUTT	DAVIS	CARTER	HOOPER	HILLARD	OLDFIELD	WATLING	WATKINS	BRADFORD 2
02/09/61	SUNDERLAND	A	1-2	12209	RADFORD	HILLARD	FROWEN	MABBUTT	DAVIS	SLOCOMBE	JARMAN	OLDFIELD	BRADFORD	WATLING	WATKINS	JONES
05/09/61	SCUNTHORPE UNITED	H	1-2	9558	RADFORD	HILLS	FROWEN	MABBUTT	DAVIS	SLOCOMBE	JARMAN	HOOPER	BRADFORD	HAMILTON	A HALL	BRADFORD
09/09/61	STOKE CITY	A	1-2	9075	RADFORD	HILLS	FROWEN	MABBUTT	PYLE	SLOCOMBE	JARMAN	A HALL	JONES	HILLARD	WATLING	HALL A
16/09/61	LEYTON ORIENT	H	2-1	11824	RADFORD	HILLS	FROWEN	MABBUTT	PYLE	SLOCOMBE	PETHERBRIDGE	JONES	BRADFORD	HAMILTON	HOOPER	WATLING
18/09/61	SCUNTHORPE UNITED	H	2-1	14100	RADFORD	HILLS	FROWEN	MABBUTT	PYLE	SLOCOMBE	PETHERBRIDGE	JONES	BRADFORD	HAMILTON	HOOPER	HAMILTON
23/09/61	LEEDS UNITED	A	0-0	13363	RADFORD	HILLS	FROWEN	MABBUTT	PYLE	SLOCOMBE	PETHERBRIDGE	JONES	BRADFORD	HAMILTON	HOOPER	
30/09/61	NORWICH CITY	H	2-2	18869	RADFORD	DAVIS	FROWEN	MABBUTT	PYLE	SLOCOMBE	PETHERBRIDGE	SYKES	BRADFORD	HAMILTON	HOOPER	HAMILTON 2, JONES, HOOPER
07/10/61	PRESTON NORTH END	A	0-1	11331	RADFORD	DAVIS	FROWEN	MABBUTT	PYLE	SLOCOMBE	PETHERBRIDGE	SYKES	BRADFORD	HAMILTON	HOOPER	
14/10/61	PLYMOUTH ARGYLE	H	4-1	12768	RADFORD	DAVIS	FROWEN	MABBUTT	PYLE	SLOCOMBE	PETHERBRIDGE	SYKES	BRADFORD	HOOPER	HOOPER	JONES 3, BRADFORD
21/10/61	HUDDERSFIELD TOWN	A	1-4	11845	RADFORD	DAVIS	FROWEN	MABBUTT	PYLE	SLOCOMBE	PETHERBRIDGE	CARTER	BRADFORD	HAMILTON	HOOPER	BRADFORD 2
28/10/61	SWANSEA TOWN	H	0-1	10622	RADFORD	DAVIS	FROWEN	MABBUTT	PYLE	SLOCOMBE	PETHERBRIDGE	SYKES	BRADFORD	HAMILTON	HOOPER	
04/11/61	SOUTHAMPTON	A	2-0	14840	RADFORD	DAVIS	FROWEN	SYKES	PYLE	SYKES	CARTER	SYKES	BRADFORD	HOOPER	HOOPER	BRADFORD 2
11/11/61	DERBY COUNTY	H	4-1	23180	RADFORD	DAVIS	FROWEN	MABBUTT	PYLE	SYKES	JARMAN	HAMILTON	HOOPER	HAMILTON	PETHERBRIDGE	JONES 2, BRADFORD, HOOPER
18/11/61	NEWCASTLE UNITED	A	1-0	9504	RADFORD	DAVIS	FROWEN	MABBUTT	PYLE	CARTER	JARMAN	HAMILTON	HOOPER	HOOPER	PETHERBRIDGE	HOOPER pen, JONES
25/11/61	WALSALL	H	2-5	9429	RADFORD	DAVIS	FROWEN	MABBUTT	PYLE	SYKES	JARMAN	HAMILTON	PETHERBRIDGE	HOOPER	PETHERBRIDGE	BRADFORD 2
02/12/61	MIDDLESBROUGH	A	0-0	9688	RADFORD	HILLS	FROWEN	MABBUTT	PYLE	SYKES	JARMAN	HAMILTON	PETHERBRIDGE	HOOPER	PETHERBRIDGE	
09/12/61	LEYTON ORIENT	A	0-2	9688	RADFORD	HILLS	FROWEN	MABBUTT	PYLE	SYKES	JARMAN	WILLIAMS	PETHERBRIDGE	HOOPER	PETHERBRIDGE	
16/12/61	LIVERPOOL	H	1-0	29957	RADFORD	DAVIS	FROWEN	BUMPSTEAD	PYLE	MABBUTT	JARMAN	WILLIAMS	JARMAN	HOOPER	PETHERBRIDGE	CARTER
22/12/61	LUTON TOWN	H	0-2	8076	RADFORD	DAVIS	FROWEN	BUMPSTEAD	PYLE	MABBUTT	JARMAN	WILLIAMS	HOOPER	HOOPER	HOOPER	
26/12/61	ROTHERHAM UNITED	A	4-2	13102	RADFORD	DAVIS	FROWEN	SYKES	SYKES	BUMPSTEAD	JARMAN	WILLIAMS	BRADFORD	HOOPER	HOOPER	HAMILTON 2, JONES, HOOPER
30/12/61	BRIGHTON & HOVE ALBION	A	0-1	8951	RADFORD	BRADFORD	FROWEN	SYKES	DAVIS	MABBUTT	JARMAN	WILLIAMS	BRADFORD	HOOPER	HOOPER	
13/01/62	SUNDERLAND	H	1-6	3650	RADFORD	BRADFORD	FROWEN	BUMPSTEAD	PYLE	BUMPSTEAD	JARMAN	BRADFORD	JONES	HOOPER	HOOPER	JARMAN
20/01/62	STOKE CITY	H	3-2	8852	RADFORD	BRADFORD	FROWEN	BUMPSTEAD	PYLE	SYKES	JARMAN	WILLIAMS	JONES	HOOPER	HOOPER	WILLIAMS, MABBUTT, JARMAN
03/02/62	LEYTON ORIENT	H	0-0	14737	RADFORD	BRADFORD	FROWEN	BUMPSTEAD	PYLE	SYKES	JARMAN	WILLIAMS	BRADFORD	HOOPER	HOOPER	
10/02/62	LEEDS UNITED	A	2-1	9108	RADFORD	BRADFORD	FROWEN	BUMPSTEAD	PYLE	SYKES	JARMAN	WILLIAMS	MABBUTT	JONES	HOOPER	HOOPER, JONES
24/02/62	PRESTON NORTH END	H	2-1	10601	RADFORD	BRADFORD	FROWEN	BUMPSTEAD	PYLE	SLOCOMBE	JARMAN	WILLIAMS	MABBUTT	JONES	HOOPER	MABBUTT, JARMAN
27/02/62	NORWICH CITY	A	1-3	9209	RADFORD	BRADFORD	FROWEN	BUMPSTEAD	PYLE	SLOCOMBE	HAMILTON	WILLIAMS	MABBUTT	JONES	HOOPER	HOOPER
03/03/62	PLYMOUTH ARGYLE	H	2-1	10712	RADFORD	BRADFORD	FROWEN	BUMPSTEAD	PYLE	SLOCOMBE	JARMAN	WILLIAMS	MABBUTT	JONES	HOOPER	MABBUTT, JONES
10/03/62	HUDDERSFIELD TOWN	A	1-1	15350	RADFORD	BRADFORD	FROWEN	BUMPSTEAD	PYLE	SLOCOMBE	JARMAN	WILLIAMS	MABBUTT	JONES	HOOPER	JONES
17/03/62	SWANSEA TOWN	H	1-3	5000	RADFORD	BRADFORD	FROWEN	BUMPSTEAD	PYLE	SLOCOMBE	HAMILTON	WILLIAMS	MABBUTT	JONES	HOOPER	HAMILTON
24/03/62	SOUTHAMPTON	H	1-0	12336	RADFORD	BRADFORD	FROWEN	BUMPSTEAD	PYLE	SLOCOMBE	HAMILTON	JONES	BRADFORD	HOOPER	HOOPER	BRADFORD
31/03/62	DERBY COUNTY	A	1-1	8269	RADFORD	BRADFORD	FROWEN	BUMPSTEAD	DAVIS	SLOCOMBE	WATKINS	JONES	BRADFORD	HAMILTON	HOOPER	HAMILTON
07/04/62	NEWCASTLE UNITED	H	2-1	10770	RADFORD	BRADFORD	FROWEN	BUMPSTEAD	DAVIS	SLOCOMBE	HAMILTON	MABBUTT, JONES	BRADFORD	HAMILTON	HOOPER	HOOPER, HAMILTON
14/04/62	MIDDLESBROUGH	A	0-5	10416	RADFORD	BRADFORD	FROWEN	BUMPSTEAD	DAVIS	SLOCOMBE	PETHERBRIDGE	JONES	BRADFORD	HAMILTON	HOOPER	
20/04/62	CHARLTON ATHLETIC	H	1-0	17606	RADFORD	HILLARD	FROWEN	BUMPSTEAD	DAVIS	SLOCOMBE	JARMAN	JONES	OLDFIELD	JONES	HOOPER	JONES
21/04/62	WALSALL	A	2-2	10455	RADFORD	HILLARD	FROWEN	BUMPSTEAD	DAVIS	SLOCOMBE	JARMAN	WILLIAMS	BRADFORD	JONES	HOOPER	HOOPER, BRADFORD
23/04/62	CHARLTON ATHLETIC	H	1-2	16639	B HALL	HILLARD	FROWEN	BUMPSTEAD	DAVIS	MABBUTT	JARMAN	SYKES	BRADFORD	JONES	HOOPER	BRADFORD 2
28/04/62	LUTON TOWN	A	0-2	6555	B HALL	HILLARD	HILLARD	DAVIS	PYLE	MABBUTT	JARMAN	SYKES	BRADFORD	JONES	HOOPER	SYKES

FA CUP

Date	Opponent	H/A		ATT	G	2	3	4	5	6	7	8	9	10	11	GOALSCORERS
08/01/62	OLDHAM ATHLETIC	H	1-1	14610	RADFORD	DAVIS	FROWEN	BUMPSTEAD	PYLE	MABBUTT	BUMPSTEAD	SYKES	BRADFORD	HAMILTON	HOOPER	SYKES
10/01/62	OLDHAM ATHLETIC	A	0-2	27045	RADFORD	DAVIS	FROWEN	BUMPSTEAD	PYLE	SYKES	JARMAN	JONES	BRADFORD	HAMILTON	HOOPER	

LEAGUE CUP

Date	Opponent	H/A		ATT	G	2	3	4	5	6	7	8	9	10	11	GOALSCORERS
11/09/61	HARTLEPOOL UNITED	H	2-1	8469	RADFORD	HILLS	FROWEN	MABBUTT	PYLE	MABBUTT	JARMAN	JONES	BRADFORD	HAMILTON	HOOPER	HOOPER, BRADFORD
02/10/61	BLACKBURN ROVERS	H	1-1	15711	RADFORD	DAVIS	FROWEN	MABBUTT	PYLE	SLOCOMBE	JARMAN	SYKES	BRADFORD	HAMILTON	HOOPER	HOOPER, BRADFORD
16/10/61	BLACKBURN ROVERS	A	0-4	5157	RADFORD	DAVIS	FROWEN	MABBUTT	PYLE	SLOCOMBE	JARMAN	SYKES	BRADFORD	HAMILTON	HOOPER	

GLOUCESTERSHIRE CUP FINAL

Date	Opponent	H/A		ATT	G	2	3	4	5	6	7	8	9	10	11	GOALSCORERS
01/05/62	BRISTOL CITY	A	1-3	9201	B HALL	BRADFORD	HILLARD	SYKES	FROWEN	BUMPSTEAD	JARMAN	HAMILTON	WILLIAMS	JONES	HOOPER	WILLIAMS

PLAYERS	APP	GLS
BRADFORD G	39	12
BUMPSTEAD D	22	
CARTER B	4	
DAVIS J	31	
FROWEN J	42	
HALL A	1	
HALL B	2	
HAMILTON I	10	4
HILLARD D	7	
HILLS J	3	
HOOPER P	38	
JARMAN H	32	6
JONES R	38	13
NORMAN M	3	
MABBUTT R	31	2
OLDFIELD T	3	
PETHERBRIDGE G	17	
PYLE D	25	
RADFORD H	37	
SLOCOMBE M	24	
SYKES N	25	
WATKINS J	9	
WATLING J	2	
WILLIAMS K	13	1

Rochdale 4-0 on aggregate in the League Cup final. Rovers had latterly strengthened their side with the signings of Dave Bumpstead from Millwall and Keith Williams in a £6,500 move from Plymouth Argyle, and it was the latter who scored Rovers' goal in a demoralizing 3-1 defeat in the Gloucestershire Cup final at Ashton Gate. Rovers led at half-time, but Brian Clark's splendid second-half hat-trick won the trophy for Bristol City. The Football League defeated the League of Ireland 5-2 in a representative game at Eastville in October before a crowd of 31,959, with Bryan Douglas of Blackburn Rovers scoring two of their goals.

Tragedy struck in November, when Ian Hamilton's brother John, a promising young player on Rovers' books, died with his wife and daughter in a bungalow fire at Olveston.

1962/63

Although the 3-0 defeat at Hull City in August 1962 was officially Rovers' first game in Division Three, the realigning of the divisions in 1958 had led to a distortion of statistics. The reality was that Rovers were back in the division they had occupied between 1920 and 1953 and in which they have spent the bulk of their League existence. The reality was also that, devoid of financial support, the club was to struggle and, indeed came within minutes of a disastrous second consecutive relegation into the uncharted waters of Division Four.

Manager Bert Tann made strenuous efforts to avoid such a calamity. He had appointed Bill Dodgin in 1961 as chief scout and now, in July 1962, he promoted Bobby Campbell to the post of coach. A fast raiding winger with Chelsea and Reading, Campbell had won two Scottish caps and was manager at Dumbarton before joining Rovers. Both Dodgin and Campbell were to manage Rovers in their own right but, for now, their role was to rebuild the club from the ashes of relegation. There was clearly insufficient talent on Rovers' books and no money to purchase replacements, so their task was to work with the many mediocre local footballers, searching for the rare glimpse of raw skill or character that would enable a young player to break into League football. Long, dark winter evenings were spent carefully building up the skills of numerous players under the dim floodlights of the Muller Road car park ash practice pitches.

The departure of George Petherbridge to Salisbury City left Geoff Bradford as the sole survivor of the Division Three (South) days. Doug Hillard, Norman Sykes, Ray Mabbutt, Harold Jarman and Bobby Jones were all by now experienced Rovers players. The new goalkeeper, with Howard Radford retired, was Esmond Million, signed for £5,000 from Middlesbrough. The same fee bought the accomplished left-back Gwyn Jones from Wolverhampton Wanderers, an excellent musician and alert defender who, in missing only 2 League games in 1962/63, played more times than any other Rovers player. These two players were purchased with the money raised by the sale, after 297 League games and 101 goals, of Peter Hooper to Cardiff City. John Watkins joined Chippenham Town. Rovers also eschewed their quartered shirts in favour of a short-lived white top with blue pin-stripes.

11 May 1963. Rovers' defence repels a Wrexham attack at Eastville

Rovers were able to benefit from the experience of the previous season's signings, Keith Williams, top scorer with 17 League goals, and Dave Bumpstead. This complemented the slow influx of local talent such as Micky Slocombe, Joe Davis, Tom Baker and David Hurford. All 8 of Graham Muxworthy's League appearances, including defeat at Ashton Gate where Rovers trailed 3-0 by half-time and Bobby Williams scored the fourth against his future club, were in April. Glaswegian Alex Munro arrived, initially on trial, and Jimmy Humes joined from Preston North End on the recommendation of Alfie Biggs. Finally, Biggs himself returned in October for £12,000, after 15 months away.

Prior to the new season, a Bristol Combined XI lost 2-1 at Ashton Gate against Arsenal in a match to raise funds for the St Mary Redcliffe Restoration Appeal. Williams scored, while Million, Bradford, Jones and Sykes also played. Life in Division Three soon proved uncomfortable, as a string of poor results testify. An early season 5-2 defeat at Wrexham, where Williams missed a penalty, was followed by a catastrophic October. Rovers lost 3-0 at Swindon Town and equalled an unwanted club record, set in April 1922, by conceding three hat-tricks in a calendar month. In losing 7-2 at Shrewsbury Town, Rovers suffered their heaviest defeat since December 1957. Frank Clarke and Jim McLaughlin scored three times each, the second of three occasions on which two opponents have each scored hat-tricks against Rovers in the League. Arthur Rowley, the League's all-time top scorer, hit the third goal from 25 yards and later hit the crossbar with a free-kick, while the Shrews also fielded Ted Hemsley, who was to play a key role in Rovers' Watney Cup Final triumph in 1972. Two goals down inside ten minutes, after Million twice spilled long-distance shots, Jarman pulled a goal back, Biggs headed against the bar, Hamilton missed an open goal and Williams saw a good shot saved before Rovers conceded two more goals to trail 4-1 at half-time. A fortnight after defeat at Shrewsbury, Rovers lost 3-2 at Southend United, for whom John McKinven scored the first of his two hat-tricks against Rovers.

The season, however, got no easier. Eddie O'Hara scored three times as Rovers lost 4-0 to Barnsley at Oakwell, four Carlisle United players got on the scoresheet at Brunton Park and five Hull City players at Eastville. Bristol City completed a League double over Rovers and Coventry City won 5-0, with Willie Humphries and Ron Rees scoring twice each. On the other hand, two Terry Oldfield goals steered Rovers to a 5-2 victory at home to Halifax Town and the resurgent Biggs scored twice in a 4-1 home win over Brighton. Rovers also won at home to Barnsley who fielded their youngest-ever player in League football, in goalkeeper Alan Ogley at 16 years 226 days. On Good Friday, Rovers recorded a 5-3 win at Queen's Park Rangers, with Williams and Jones scoring twice each. Rovers had led twice but responded to Mark Lazarus giving Rangers a 3-2 lead after 76 minutes with three goals in nine minutes for a well-earned victory. Another encouraging sign was the emerging talent of inside-forward, Ian 'Chico' Hamilton, whose 10 League goals made him joint second highest scorer alongside Jones.

The winter weather of 1962/63 was some of the worst in the 20th century, with snow lying for weeks. The game at Reading on Boxing Day was abandoned after an hour because the pitch was frostbound, with Rovers a goal down. As a result, Rovers did not play between 15 December – two days after the former Scottish International Jimmy Howie, an exceptional Rovers player in the 1902/03 season, had passed away at the Central Middlesex Hospital – and 9 February, when the side began a run of three consecutive victories. Great goalscorers of the 1960s, such as Notts County's Tony Hateley and Jeff Astle, both on the threshold of long and successful careers, scored against Rovers in 1962/63. So too did Dai Ward at Eastville, for a Watford side boasting Bobby Brown, who had represented Great Britain at football in the 1960 Olympics. Another former Rovers forward, Barrie Meyer, celebrated his final game in professional football with a hat-trick in Bristol City's 6-3 victory over Southend United in March. Bobby 'Shadow' Williams, a future Rovers player, scored City's other three goals that day.

In April 1963, the *People* newspaper alleged that goalkeeper Million had accepted a £300 bribe to enable Bradford Park Avenue to beat Rovers. He had allowed a back pass to slip past him and let a cross go, leaving the innocent Kevin Hector, later the winner of two League Championship medals with Derby County, to score twice. Hector was to score against Rovers in the FA Cup in 1975. The match had been drawn 2-2, so Million and his accomplice Williams had received none of the money. Suddenly Rovers were making national headlines for all the wrong reasons. The press uncovered details of how they had unsuccessfully tried to persuade full-back Jones to join them. The Mansfield Town defender, Brian Phillips, a former team-mate of Million's at Middlesbrough, was named as the 'fixer', working on behalf of a syndicate of professional gamblers and was later sentenced at Nottingham Assizes to 15 months' imprisonment.

Rovers had invested £11,500 in transfer fees for Million and Williams and the battle against relegation had not yet been won. However, the club wasted no time in suspending

Bristol Rovers 1962/63. Back row: Ryden, Gardiner, Stone, Hendy, Hillard, Baker. Second row: Bradford, Bumpstead, Sykes, Million, Hall, Humes, Frowen, G Jones. Front row: Slocombe, Oldfield, K Jones, Mabbutt, Hamilton, Williams, Jarman, R Jones, Davis

both players. They and Phillips were fined £50 each at Doncaster Magistrates Court in July 1963 and banned from football for life by the Football Association. Williams was to resurface in South African football, which, at that time lay outside the remit of FIFA, the world governing body. The image of professional football had been tarnished, but Rovers' immediate response to the crisis and the way the club had responded and helped bring the culprits to justice came in for high praise. Rovers were left to survive the relegation dogfight without two key players, but with a clear conscience that the club was working hard to stamp out all that is unsavoury in the game.

By dint of the atrocious winter weather, Rovers extraordinarily played 9 League games in April and five in May. Bradford and Biggs had scored to beat Colchester United, leaving Rovers requiring victory over Halifax Town at The Shay to avoid relegation, prior to the final game, which was lost 2-0 at Port Vale. A narrow 3-2 win at Halifax avoided the prospect of double relegation and Rovers never did appear in Division Four. Yet, it was a close call. A miserly crowd of 2,126, albeit boosted by some 500 enthusiastic Rovers supporters, saw Rovers a goal ahead after two minutes through Jones' shot and 2-0 up ten minutes later when Hamilton headed home Bradford's cross. However, already-relegated Halifax recovered after half-time and equalised through shots from Paddy Stanley and Dennis Fidler. With just 14 minutes remaining, Rovers won a corner and Jones' kick found Hamilton's head to ensure Division Three survival.

FA Cup defeat at Port Vale contrasted with victory over the same opposition in the League Cup. However, after brushing aside Cardiff City, Rovers lost 3-1 in the third

FOOTBALL LEAGUE DIVISION THREE

SEASON 1962/63

Date	Opponent	V	Res	ATT	1	2	3	4	5	6	7	8	9	10	11	GOALSCORERS
18/08/62	HULL CITY	A	0-3	8261	MILLION	HILLARD	G JONES	SLOCOMBE	SYKES	MABBUTT	JARMAN	WILLIAMS	BRADFORD	HAMILTON	R JONES	
21/08/62	NORTHAMPTON TOWN	H	2-2	11649	MILLION	HILLARD	G JONES	MABBUTT	SYKES	DAVIS	JARMAN	WILLIAMS	BRADFORD	OLDFIELD	R JONES	OLDFIELD, WILLIAMS
25/08/62	CRYSTAL PALACE	A	2-0	10889	MILLION	HILLARD	G JONES	WOOD	SYKES	MABBUTT	JARMAN	WILLIAMS	OLDFIELD	RYDEN	R JONES	JARMAN, WILLIAMS
28/08/62	NORTHAMPTON TOWN	A	0-2	15661	MILLION	BRADFORD	G JONES	STONE	SYKES	MABBUTT	JARMAN	WILLIAMS	OLDFIELD	BAKER	R JONES	
01/09/62	WREXHAM	A	2-5	11519	MILLION	BRADFORD	G JONES	STONE	SYKES	MABBUTT	JARMAN	WILLIAMS	OLDFIELD	HAMILTON	R JONES	R JONES, OLDFIELD
04/09/62	PETERBOROUGH UNITED	H	3-1	11860	MILLION	BRADFORD	G JONES	STONE	SYKES	MABBUTT	JARMAN	WILLIAMS	OLDFIELD	HAMILTON	R JONES	WILLIAMS, HAMILTON, R JONES pen
08/09/62	HALIFAX TOWN	H	5-2	9578	MILLION	BRADFORD	G JONES	STONE	SYKES	MABBUTT	JARMAN	WILLIAMS	OLDFIELD	HAMILTON	R JONES	OLDFIELD 2, JARMAN, HAMILTON, SOUTH og
10/09/62	PETERBOROUGH UNITED	A	0-1	13180	MILLION	BRADFORD	G JONES	STONE	SYKES	MABBUTT	JARMAN	WILLIAMS	OLDFIELD	HAMILTON	R JONES	
15/09/62	BRISTOL CITY	H	1-2	20708	MILLION	BRADFORD	G JONES	STONE	SYKES	MABBUTT	JARMAN	WILLIAMS	OLDFIELD	HAMILTON	R JONES	WILLIAMS
18/09/62	BARNSLEY	H	3-2	10256	MILLION	BRADFORD	G JONES	STONE	SYKES	MABBUTT	JARMAN	WILLIAMS	OLDFIELD	HAMILTON	R JONES	JARMAN, HAMILTON, LEIGHTON og
22/09/62	BRIGHTON & H ALBION	A	1-1	7943	MILLION	BRADFORD	G JONES	STONE	SYKES	MABBUTT	HUMES	WILLIAMS	JARMAN	HAMILTON	R JONES	WILLIAMS
29/09/62	CARLISLE UNITED	H	1-1	9104	MILLION	BRADFORD	G JONES	SLOCOMBE	SYKES	MABBUTT	HUMES	WILLIAMS	BIGGS	HAMILTON	R JONES	R JONES
02/10/62	SWINDON TOWN	A	0-3	15028	MILLION	BRADFORD	G JONES	BUMPSTEAD	SYKES	MABBUTT	JARMAN	WILLIAMS	BIGGS	HAMILTON	R JONES	
06/10/62	PORT VALE	H	1-1	12416	MILLION	BRADFORD	G JONES	BUMPSTEAD	SYKES	SLOCOMBE	JARMAN	WILLIAMS	BIGGS	HAMILTON	R JONES	BIGGS
09/10/62	SWINDON TOWN	H	2-0	17702	MILLION	BRADFORD	G JONES	BUMPSTEAD	SYKES	MABBUTT	JARMAN	WILLIAMS	BIGGS	HAMILTON	R JONES	BIGGS, WILLIAMS
13/10/62	SHREWSBURY TOWN	A	2-7	6291	MILLION	BRADFORD	G JONES	BUMPSTEAD	SYKES	MABBUTT	JARMAN	WILLIAMS	BIGGS	HAMILTON	R JONES	JARMAN, WILLIAMS
20/10/62	MILLWALL	A	1-1	11000	MILLION	BRADFORD	G JONES	SLOCOMBE	SYKES	MABBUTT	JARMAN	WILLIAMS	BIGGS	HAMILTON	R JONES	MABBUTT, R JONES pen
27/10/62	SOUTHEND UNITED	A	2-3	9180	MILLION	BRADFORD	G JONES	BUMPSTEAD	SYKES	MABBUTT	JARMAN	BIGGS	OLDFIELD	HAMILTON	R JONES	BRADFORD pen, HAMILTON
10/11/62	NOTTS COUNTY	A	3-1	5950	MILLION	HILLARD	G JONES	BUMPSTEAD	SYKES	MABBUTT	JARMAN	WILLIAMS	OLDFIELD	HAMILTON	R JONES	OLDFIELD, WILLIAMS, JARMAN
17/11/62	BOURNEMOUTH	H	1-2	8025	MILLION	FROWEN	G JONES	BUMPSTEAD	SYKES	MUNRO	JARMAN	BIGGS	OLDFIELD	WILLIAMS	HAMILTON	OLDFIELD
27/11/62	BARNSLEY	A	0-4	8667	MILLION	FROWEN	G JONES	SLOCOMBE	SYKES	MUNRO	JARMAN	WILLIAMS	BIGGS	HAMILTON	MABBUTT	
01/12/62	BRADFORD	H	3-3	6593	MILLION	FROWEN	G JONES	SLOCOMBE	SYKES	MABBUTT	JARMAN	WILLIAMS	BIGGS	HAMILTON	R JONES	MABBUTT, WILLIAMS, HAMILTON
08/12/62	WATFORD	A	1-0	7955	MILLION	HILLARD	G JONES	OLDFIELD	SYKES	MUNRO	JARMAN	WILLIAMS	BIGGS	HAMILTON	R JONES	WILLIAMS
15/12/62	HULL CITY	H	2-5	6059	MILLION	HILLARD	G JONES	OLDFIELD	SYKES	MABBUTT	JARMAN	WILLIAMS	BIGGS	HAMILTON	R JONES	BIGGS, WILLIAMS
02/02/63	BRIGHTON & H ALBION	H	4-1	7816	MILLION	HILLARD	G JONES	OLDFIELD	SYKES	MABBUTT	JARMAN	WILLIAMS	BIGGS	HAMILTON	R JONES	BIGGS 2, WILLIAMS, R JONES
26/02/63	READING	A	1-0	6456	MILLION	HILLARD	G JONES	OLDFIELD	SYKES	MABBUTT	JARMAN	WILLIAMS	BIGGS	HAMILTON	R JONES	WILLIAMS
02/03/63	SHREWSBURY TOWN	H	2-0	7575	MILLION	HILLARD	G JONES	OLDFIELD	SYKES	MABBUTT	JARMAN	WILLIAMS	BIGGS	HAMILTON	R JONES	BIGGS, OLDFIELD
09/03/63	MILLWALL	H	1-2	5260	HALL	HILLARD	G JONES	OLDFIELD	SYKES	MABBUTT	JARMAN	WILLIAMS	BIGGS	HAMILTON	R JONES	HAMILTON
16/03/63	SOUTHEND UNITED	H	1-2	7215	MILLION	HILLARD	G JONES	OLDFIELD	STONE	MUNRO	JARMAN	BIGGS	RYDEN	WILLIAMS	R JONES	RYDEN
20/03/63	CRYSTAL PALACE	H	1-2	15451	MILLION	HILLARD	G JONES	OLDFIELD	STONE	MUNRO	JARMAN	BIGGS	RYDEN	HAMILTON	R JONES	HAMILTON
22/03/63	COLCHESTER UNITED	A	0-1	4560	MILLION	HILLARD	G JONES	BUMPSTEAD	SYKES	MABBUTT	JARMAN	WILLIAMS	BIGGS	HAMILTON	R JONES	
30/03/63	NOTTS COUNTY	H	1-1	5960	MILLION	HILLARD	G JONES	BUMPSTEAD	STONE	SYKES	JARMAN	OLDFIELD	RYDEN	HAMILTON	MABBUTT	HAMILTON
02/04/63	CARLISLE UNITED	A	0-4	5354	MILLION	HILLARD	G JONES	BUMPSTEAD	DAVIS	OLDFIELD	JARMAN	WILLIAMS	BIGGS	HAMILTON	MUXWORTHY	
06/04/63	BOURNEMOUTH	A	1-1	9087	MILLION	HILLARD	G JONES	MABBUTT	DAVIS	OLDFIELD	JARMAN	WILLIAMS	BIGGS	R JONES	MUXWORTHY	BIGGS
12/04/63	QUEENS PARK RANGERS	H	5-3	10165	MILLION	HILLARD	G JONES	MABBUTT	DAVIS	OLDFIELD	JARMAN	WILLIAMS	BIGGS	R JONES	MUXWORTHY	WILLIAMS 2, R JONES 2, BIGGS
13/04/63	COVENTRY CITY	A	2-2	13145	MILLION	HILLARD	G JONES	MABBUTT	DAVIS	OLDFIELD	JARMAN	WILLIAMS	BIGGS	R JONES	MUXWORTHY	WILLIAMS, R JONES
15/04/63	QUEENS PARK RANGERS*	A	0-0	11028	MILLION	HILLARD	G JONES	SLOCOMBE	DAVIS	OLDFIELD	JARMAN	WILLIAMS	RYDEN	R JONES	MUXWORTHY	
20/04/63	BRADFORD	A	2-2	6794	MILLION	HILLARD	G JONES	STONE	DAVIS	OLDFIELD	JARMAN	BIGGS	RYDEN	R JONES	MUXWORTHY	RYDEN, R JONES
23/04/63	BRISTOL CITY	H	1-4	22739	MILLION	HILLARD	G JONES	OLDFIELD	SYKES	MABBUTT	JARMAN	WILLIAMS	RYDEN	R JONES	MUXWORTHY	WILLIAMS
27/04/63	WATFORD	H	3-1	7800	HALL	HILLARD	G JONES	OLDFIELD	SYKES	MABBUTT	JARMAN	R JONES	RYDEN	HAMILTON	MUXWORTHY	RYDEN 2, HILLARD
29/04/63	COVENTRY CITY	H	0-5	20412	HALL	HILLARD	G JONES	OLDFIELD	DAVIS	STONE	JARMAN	BIGGS	RYDEN	HAMILTON	MABBUTT	
08/05/63	READING	H	0-1	7878	HALL	HILLARD	G JONES	OLDFIELD	DAVIS	MABBUTT	JARMAN	R JONES	BIGGS	HAMILTON	BRADFORD	
11/05/63	WREXHAM	H	1-1	7889	HALL	HILLARD	G JONES	BUMPSTEAD	SYKES	MABBUTT	JARMAN	R JONES	BIGGS	HAMILTON	BRADFORD	JARMAN
14/05/63	COLCHESTER UNITED	H	2-0	9004	HALL	HILLARD	G JONES	SLOCOMBE	SYKES	MABBUTT	JARMAN	R JONES	BIGGS	HAMILTON	BRADFORD	BRADFORD, BIGGS pen
18/05/63	HALIFAX TOWN	A	3-2	2126	HALL	HILLARD	G JONES	BUMPSTEAD	SYKES	MABBUTT	JARMAN	R JONES	BIGGS	HAMILTON	BRADFORD	R JONES, BIGGS, HAMILTON 2
20/05/63	PORT VALE	A	0-2	5015	HALL	HILLARD	G JONES	BUMPSTEAD	DAVIS	STONE	JARMAN	BIGGS	OLDFIELD	R JONES	MABBUTT	

* at White City

FA CUP

Date	Opponent	V	Res	ATT	1	2	3	4	5	6	7	8	9	10	11	GOALSCORERS
03/11/62	PORT VALE	H	0-2	8180	MILLION	HILLARD	BRADFORD	SYKES	DAVIS	MABBUTT	JARMAN	WILLIAMS	BIGGS	HAMILTON	R JONES	

LEAGUE CUP

Date	Opponent	V	Res	ATT	1	2	3	4	5	6	7	8	9	10	11	GOALSCORERS
27/09/62	PORT VALE	H	2-0	6126	MILLION	BRADFORD	G JONES	SLOCOMBE	SYKES	MABBUTT	JARMAN	WILLIAMS	OLDFIELD	HAMILTON	R JONES	WILLIAMS, R JONES
23/10/62	CARDIFF CITY	A	2-0	12142	MILLION	BRADFORD	G JONES	BUMPSTEAD	SYKES	MABBUTT	JARMAN	WILLIAMS	OLDFIELD	HAMILTON	R JONES	WILLIAMS, JARMAN
13/11/62	BURY	H	1-3	7194	MILLION	HILLARD	G JONES	BUMPSTEAD	SYKES	MABBUTT	JARMAN	R JONES	OLDFIELD	WILLIAMS	HAMILTON	ROBERTSON og

GLOUCESTERSHIRE CUP FINAL

Date	Opponent	V	Res	ATT	1	2	3	4	5	6	7	8	9	10	11	GOALSCORERS
23/05/63	BRISTOL CITY	H	2-1	8018	HALL	HILLARD	G JONES	OLDFIELD	DAVIS	MABBUTT	JARMAN	WILLIAMS	BIGGS	HAMILTON	BRADFORD	HAMILTON, R JONES

PLAYERS	APP	GLS
BAKER T	1	
BIGGS A	32	9
BRADFORD G	21	2
BUMPSTEAD D	15	
DAVIS J	13	
FROWEN J	3	
HALL B	8	
HAMILTON I	31	10
HILLARD D	29	1
HUMES J	5	
HURFORD D	40	6
JARMAN H	44	
JONES G	44	
JONES R	41	10
MABBUTT R	37	2
MILLION E	38	
MUNRO A	5	
MUXWORTHY G	8	
OLDFIELD T	35	7
RYDEN H	8	4
SLOCOMBE M	8	
STONE D	14	
SYKES N	31	
WILLIAMS K	36	17
WOOD A	1	
OWN GOALS		2

round at Division Two Bury, who fielded at centre-half Bob Stokoe, later a hugely successful manager. Goals from Hamilton and Jones earned Rovers a 2-1 victory over Bristol City at Eastville in the Gloucestershire Cup final.

1963/64

In comparison with the relegation dogfight of 1962/63, the second season in Division Three gave cause for great optimism. Identical tallies of wins and defeats left Rovers in 12th place in the table and seven of the next 10 seasons were to see top-six finishes. While 79 League goals were conceded, the 91 scored has only ever been bettered in the 1952/53 Championship season. Alfie Biggs became the first Rovers player since then to score 30 League goals. The total of 170 goals by both sides in Rovers' 46 League matches constitutes a club seasonal record.

One crucial element in this relative success was the benefit of a settled side. After two seasons as a reserve goalkeeper, Bernard Hall was an ever-present and his full-backs, Doug Hillard and Gwyn Jones, missed just one League game between them. In the forward line, Biggs and Harold Jarman were ever-presents, Bobby Jones, Ian Hamilton and John Brown, a free signing from Plymouth Argyle, all regulars. Brian Jenkins, recruited from Exeter City, and the veteran Geoff Bradford also appeared. With a settled half-back line, Rovers could continue to experiment with youth, Roger Frude and Lindsay Parsons both making League debuts in April. The pin-striped shirt had not been a success and Rovers took to the field in 1963/64 in blue and white striped shirts.

John Frowen, after 84 League games, had returned to Wales to sign for Newport County. After sporadic appearances, several other players had moved on, including Allen Wood to Merthyr Tydfil, Hugh Ryden to Stockport County, Jimmy Humes to Chester, Tom Baker to Dover and Graham Muxworthy to Bridgwater Town. After appearing in the first three winless games of the new season, Dave Bumpstead announced his retirement from football to work in industry, though he later returned to manage Brentwood and Chelmsford City. As Bert Tann cultivated a side fit to survive in Division Three, there was no scope for sentiment and Bradford and Norman Sykes were both dropped. A new-look side was beginning to emerge, with goalkeeper Hall embarking on a run of 115 consecutive League games and Brown, Jarman and Hamilton supporting free-scoring Biggs.

In winning 19 League matches, Rovers scored seven times at home to Shrewsbury Town, five at Brentford and four on five other occasions. In December, a sixth occasion Rovers scored four times proved insufficient for victory. Two first-half Hamilton goals were mirrored by a brace each from Tony Richards and Jack Mudie, as Port Vale drew 4-4 at Eastville. Richards had put the visitors ahead after only 13 minutes, but Rovers three times threw away the lead, with five goals being scored in the space of 16 minutes midway through the second-half. A Hamilton hat-trick earned a 5-2 win at Griffin Park, while Hull City, Bristol City and Notts County all lost 4-0 at Eastville. The win against Bristol City, which started with a Mike Gibson own goal, was rounded off with Geoff

280

Autographed line-up of Bristol Rovers 1963/64. Back row: Bradford, Hillard, Hall, G Jones, Mabbutt. Middle row: Tann (Manager) McArthur, Bumpstead, Oldfield, Sykes, Davis, Stone, Campbell (Trainer). Front row: Jarman, R Jones, Biggs, Hamilton, Jenkins

Bradford's final goal for Rovers. The crowd of 19,451 was bettered only by Rovers' visits to Ashton Gate and to champions Coventry City.

Rovers also recorded 4-3 victories after being 3-1 down away to Southend United and to bottom club Notts County. At Roots Hall, Rovers were a goal down after four minutes, 2-1 down inside 10 minutes and were 3-1 behind following a 65th-minute defensive mix-up. Biggs reduced the deficit 10 minutes later, Hamilton equalised with three minutes remaining and a great comeback was completed when Peter Watson, under pressure from Biggs, steered the ball into his own net to give Rovers victory. At Meadow Lane, 16-year-old Bob Woolley claimed the second goal and Keith Fry scored twice, once from a penalty awarded for handball against Stone, as Rovers trailed 2-1 by half-time and 3-1 seven minutes after the break. The stage was set for Biggs, whose goals after 62, 69 and 80 minutes, the winner from a volley, completed his second hat-trick for the club and earned Rovers a once unlikely victory. Notts County must have dreaded the sight of Biggs for, following his hat-trick at Meadow Lane, he scored twice in a 4-0 win at Eastville to take his seasonal tally to the magical 30 mark. Rovers scored a club record 39 away League goals in 1963/64 and, in January and February, won five consecutive matches away from home to equal a club record set in the 1952/53 Championship year.

The biggest win of all, though, was a seven-goal demolition of Shrewsbury Town at Eastville in March. Four forwards scored, with Jones and Jarman striking twice each and Biggs, from a penalty and Brown once. Centre-half Dave Stone, a former chorister at St Mary Redcliffe who was just establishing himself in the side, scored his first goal for the club. Five goals ahead by half-time for only the second time in the club's history, Rovers equalled their largest ever League win with comparative ease. Seven days later, though, they were brought down to earth when John O'Rourke's hat-trick gave Luton Town a 4-2 victory. O'Rourke was to score 5 of the 6 League goals the Hatters scored against Rovers that season.

There was another 4-2 defeat at Coventry City, though revenge was gained in the FA Cup, while John Atyeo's final League goal against Rovers and one from the former Eastville favourite, Peter Hooper, gave Bristol City an opening day 3-0 win. With the England manager Alf Ramsey in the stand, apparently running the rule over Jarman, Denis Coughlin scored Bournemouth's winner after half an hour at Dean Court and, four days later, Coughlin added two more goals at Eastville as Rovers followed up their 7-0 win with four straight defeats. Similarly, high-flying Crystal Palace were indebted to Peter Burridge, who scored the winner at Selhurst Park and twice at Eastville as his side, en route to promotion, completed a League double over Rovers. The season was completed with heavy defeats at Reading and at Crewe Alexandra. Rovers played their final game at Gresty Road on 25 April, at which point in 1962/63 seven matches had been remaining, against a Crewe side that had to win to avoid relegation. Their 4-1 victory condemned Wrexham, 5-0 losers before a paltry crowd of 4,497 at Port Vale, to the drop.

Although only nine League games were drawn, four of these finished 2-2. Both matches with Peterborough United were four-goal draws, the winner of 43 Northern Ireland caps, Derek Dougan, scoring on both occasions. Joe Haverty, a Rovers player the following season, scored for Millwall in their 2-2 draw at Eastville. When Rovers visited Boundary Park, goals from Hamilton and Jarman were not enough, as Bobby Johnstone became the fourth opponent to score two penalties in a league game. The Gloucestershire Cup Final, too, was a 2-2 draw, with Alex Munro scoring his first goal for the club and the future Rovers forward Bobby Williams scoring Bristol City's second goal.

At the close of the season, Rovers were informed of the death, at the age of 69, of David Steele, who had played in Rovers' first League game. He had won League Championship medals with Huddersfield Town and, as a scout, had been credited with the discovery of Len Shackleton. There was a loss on the field, too, with the retirement of Geoff Bradford, the last survivor of the 1952/53 Championship-winning side. In 462 League appearances, he had scored a club record 242 goals, including 12 hat-tricks. After leaving Rovers, he worked as a tanker driver in Avonmouth and continued to take an interest in the club's progress. In his testimonial game in April, a Bristol United XI lost 4-1 to an International XI. Recalled for the final home game of the season, however, Bradford had been overshadowed by Reading's Dennis Allen who scored a hat-trick as his side, with Peter Shreeves at inside-left, won 5-2. In the previous game, Bert Tann had given a debut to Lindsay Parsons and, thus, a member of the 1973/74 promotion side was in the team prior to the final game of the longest survivor of 1952/53.

Hamilton, perhaps harshly labelled 'the inside forward who never seems to score goals', claimed the first four at home to Shrewsbury Town in the League Cup, with two first-half headers and two shots after the interval. The visitors, managed by Arthur

Eastville Stadium from the air

Rowley, scored twice in 90 seconds to pull the score back, the second when Gwyn Jones' clearance ricocheted into the net off George Boardman, before Biggs added a couple of goals in the last seven minutes. Rovers' League Cup ended in a replay at Gillingham, where Ron Newman scored twice. In the FA Cup, Rovers won at Bournemouth, after Hall had saved Stan Bolton's penalty, and Coventry City, before defeating Division Two Norwich City at Eastville. Round four saw Rovers at Old Trafford, before a crowd of more than 55,000, facing Bobby Charlton and George Best in a very strong Manchester United team. Rovers lost 4-1, with Denis Law's hat-trick including two second-half headers and David Herd scoring once and creating two others. Scottish international Paddy Crerand headed the ball into his own net for Rovers' 71st-minute consolation. While Bristol Rovers, despite visiting this prestigious ground, reported an annual loss of £41,000, the Supporters' Club reported a £100,000 profit.

Meanwhile, plans were afoot to demolish much of the heart of Easton, where 5,000 of the 14,000 population were to be rehoused. The shelving of these plans in later years was to lead to the enforced cheap sale of considerable numbers of homes. Thus, 1,000 inhabitants were forced to move away and 61per cent of the population was rehoused in high-rise tower blocks. This newly constructed accommodation proved a magnet for immigrants from former British colonies, who arrived at this time to fill vacancies in many industries. Their arrival was met with a certain degree of hostility in a land that as yet had no race-discrimination legislation. In 1963, the Bristol Omnibus Company

FOOTBALL LEAGUE DIVISION THREE

SEASON 1963/64

Date	Opponent	H/A	Score	Att	1	2	3	4	5	6	7	8	9	10	11	Goalscorers
24/08/63	BRISTOL CITY	A	0-3	20697	HALL	HILLARD	G JONES	BUMPSTEAD	DAVIS	SYKES	JARMAN	R JONES	BIGGS	HAMILTON	JENKINS	BIGGS A
27/08/63	WREXHAM	H	1-1	9129	HALL	HILLARD	G JONES	BUMPSTEAD	DAVIS	SYKES	JARMAN	R JONES	BIGGS	HAMILTON	JENKINS	BRADFORD G
31/08/63	OLDHAM ATHLETIC	A	0-1	8787	HALL	HILLARD	G JONES	BUMPSTEAD	DAVIS	SYKES	JARMAN	R JONES	BIGGS	HAMILTON	JENKINS	BROWN J
07/09/63	PETERBOROUGH UNITED	H	2-2	12256	HALL	HILLARD	G JONES	OLDFIELD	DAVIS	MABBUTT	JARMAN	BROWN	BIGGS	HAMILTON	BRADFORD	BROWN 2
11/09/63	WREXHAM	A	2-1	6780	HALL	HILLARD	G JONES	OLDFIELD	DAVIS	MABBUTT	JARMAN	BROWN	BIGGS	HAMILTON	BRADFORD	BIGGS 2, JARMAN
14/09/63	SOUTHEND UNITED	H	3-1	8603	HALL	HILLARD	G JONES	OLDFIELD	DAVIS	MABBUTT	JARMAN	BROWN	BIGGS	HAMILTON	BRADFORD	HILLARD 2, BIGGS, BROWN
17/09/63	QUEENS PARK RANGERS	A	0-0	12299	HALL	HILLARD	G JONES	OLDFIELD	DAVIS	MABBUTT	JARMAN	BROWN	BIGGS	HAMILTON	BRADFORD	
21/09/63	WATFORD	H	2-3	9782	HALL	HILLARD	G JONES	OLDFIELD	DAVIS	MABBUTT	JARMAN	BROWN	BIGGS	HAMILTON	BRADFORD	JARMAN, R JONES, BIGGS
28/09/63	COLCHESTER UNITED	A	3-1	10724	HALL	HILLARD	G JONES	OLDFIELD	DAVIS	MABBUTT	JARMAN	BROWN	BIGGS	HAMILTON	BRADFORD	HILLARD, BIGGS, BROWN, BRADFORD
30/09/63	QUEENS PARK RANGERS	H	0-1	8713	HALL	HILLARD	G JONES	OLDFIELD	DAVIS	MABBUTT	JARMAN	BROWN	BIGGS	HAMILTON	BRADFORD	HILLARD D
05/10/63	MILLWALL	A	1-0	6319	HALL	HILLARD	G JONES	OLDFIELD	DAVIS	MABBUTT	JARMAN	BROWN	BIGGS	HAMILTON	BRADFORD	HAMILTON I
08/10/63	HULL CITY	H	4-0	10681	HALL	HILLARD	G JONES	OLDFIELD	DAVIS	MABBUTT	JARMAN	BROWN	BIGGS	HAMILTON	BRADFORD	JARMAN 2, BIGGS, BRADFORD
12/10/63	BRENTFORD	A	1-2	13409	HALL	HILLARD	G JONES	OLDFIELD	DAVIS	MABBUTT	JARMAN	BROWN	BIGGS	HAMILTON	BRADFORD	JONES R
19/10/63	CREWE ALEXANDRA	H	5-2	12854	HALL	HILLARD	G JONES	OLDFIELD	DAVIS	MABBUTT	JARMAN	BROWN	BIGGS	HAMILTON	BRADFORD	HAMILTON 3, BIGGS, BROWN
22/10/63	BARNSLEY	A	1-1	13579	HALL	HILLARD	G JONES	OLDFIELD	DAVIS	MABBUTT	JARMAN	BROWN	BIGGS	HAMILTON	BRADFORD	JONES R
26/10/63	BARNSLEY	H	0-1	18389	HALL	HILLARD	G JONES	OLDFIELD	DAVIS	MABBUTT	JARMAN	BROWN	BIGGS	HAMILTON	BRADFORD	JENKINS B
29/10/63	CRYSTAL PALACE	A	2-1	6338	HALL	HILLARD	G JONES	OLDFIELD	DAVIS	MABBUTT	JARMAN	FRUDE	BIGGS	BROWN	R JONES	HALL B
02/11/63	WALSALL	H	3-0	10840	HALL	HILLARD	G JONES	OLDFIELD	STONE	MABBUTT	JARMAN	FRUDE	BIGGS	HAMILTON	R JONES	FRUDE R
09/11/63	READING	A	1-3	7976	HALL	HILLARD	G JONES	OLDFIELD	STONE	MABBUTT	JARMAN	FRUDE	BIGGS	HAMILTON	R JONES	MABBUTT R
23/11/63	COVENTRY CITY	H	2-2	9104	HALL	HILLARD	G JONES	STONE	DAVIS	MABBUTT	JARMAN	BROWN	BIGGS	HAMILTON	R JONES	GIBSON og, JARMAN, BIGGS, BRADFORD
30/11/63	MANSFIELD TOWN	A	4-4	21901	HALL	HILLARD	G JONES	OLDFIELD	DAVIS	MABBUTT	JARMAN	BROWN	BIGGS	HAMILTON	BRADFORD	HILLARD, BIGGS, BROWN, BRADFORD
07/12/63	BRISTOL CITY	H	2-2	11009	HALL	HILLARD	G JONES	OLDFIELD	DAVIS	MABBUTT	JARMAN	BROWN	BIGGS	HAMILTON	BRADFORD	MABBUTT, BROWN
14/12/63	OLDHAM ATHLETIC	H	3-2	12945	HALL	HILLARD	G JONES	OLDFIELD	DAVIS	MABBUTT	JARMAN	BROWN	BIGGS	HAMILTON	BRADFORD	JARMAN, BROWN, BRADFORD
21/12/63	PORT VALE	A	4-0	11442	HALL	HILLARD	G JONES	OLDFIELD	DAVIS	MABBUTT	JARMAN	BROWN	BIGGS	HAMILTON	R JONES	BIGGS 2, R JONES 2
26/12/63	PORT VALE	H	2-2	12945	HALL	HILLARD	G JONES	OLDFIELD	DAVIS	MABBUTT	JARMAN	BROWN	BIGGS	HAMILTON	R JONES	JARMAN, BIGGS
28/12/63	PETERBOROUGH UNITED	A	0-1	11442	HALL	HILLARD	G JONES	OLDFIELD	DAVIS	MABBUTT	JARMAN	BROWN	BIGGS	HAMILTON	R JONES	
11/01/64	SOUTHEND UNITED	A	2-2	10596	HALL	HILLARD	G JONES	OLDFIELD	DAVIS	MABBUTT	JARMAN	R JONES	BIGGS	HAMILTON	R JONES	BIGGS, R JONES
18/01/64	WATFORD	A	7-0	6061	HALL	HILLARD	G JONES	OLDFIELD	STONE	MABBUTT	JARMAN	R JONES	BIGGS	HAMILTON	R JONES	BIGGS 2, R JONES 2, BIGGS pen, BROWN, STONE
01/02/64	COLCHESTER UNITED	H	3-2	3907	HALL	HILLARD	G JONES	OLDFIELD	STONE	MABBUTT	JARMAN	R JONES	BIGGS	HAMILTON	R JONES	BIGGS 2, HAMILTON
08/02/64	MILLWALL	H	1-0	8703	HALL	HILLARD	G JONES	OLDFIELD	STONE	MABBUTT	JARMAN	R JONES	BIGGS	HAMILTON	R JONES	R JONES
15/02/64	BRENTFORD	H	2-2	9486	HALL	HILLARD	G JONES	OLDFIELD	STONE	MABBUTT	JARMAN	BROWN	BIGGS	HAMILTON	R JONES	HAMILTON
22/02/64	HULL CITY	A	3-1	4747	HALL	HILLARD	G JONES	OLDFIELD	STONE	MABBUTT	JARMAN	BROWN	BIGGS	HAMILTON	R JONES	JARMAN, BIGGS 2, 1pen
29/02/64	SHREWSBURY TOWN	A	2-0	10698	HALL	HILLARD	G JONES	STONE	DAVIS	MABBUTT	JARMAN	BROWN	BIGGS	HAMILTON	R JONES	HAMILTON, BROWN
07/03/64	SHREWSBURY TOWN	H	1-3	6774	HALL	HILLARD	G JONES	OLDFIELD	DAVIS	MABBUTT	JARMAN	BROWN	BIGGS	HAMILTON	R JONES	HAMILTON
14/03/64	WALSALL	A	3-2	12945	HALL	HILLARD	G JONES	OLDFIELD	DAVIS	MABBUTT	JARMAN	BROWN	BIGGS	HAMILTON	R JONES	JARMAN, HAMILTON, BROWN
21/03/64	CRYSTAL PALACE	H	1-4	8902	HALL	HILLARD	G JONES	OLDFIELD	DAVIS	DAVIS	JARMAN	BROWN	BIGGS	HAMILTON	R JONES	BROWN
27/03/64	BOURNEMOUTH	H	3-1	17162	HALL	HILLARD	G JONES	OLDFIELD	DAVIS	MABBUTT	JARMAN	BROWN	BIGGS	HAMILTON	R JONES	BIGGS, HAMILTON, BROWN, WATSON og
28/03/64	BOURNEMOUTH	A	0-1	6612	HALL	HILLARD	G JONES	OLDFIELD	DAVIS	MABBUTT	JARMAN	BROWN	BIGGS	BROWN	R JONES	
31/03/64	LUTON TOWN	A	2-4	12939	HALL	HILLARD	G JONES	STONE	DAVIS	MABBUTT	JARMAN	BROWN	BIGGS	BROWN	R JONES	JARMAN, BIGGS 2, 1pen
04/04/64	NOTTS COUNTY	H	0-1	12006	HALL	HILLARD	G JONES	MABBUTT	DAVIS	MUNRO	JARMAN	BROWN	BIGGS	BROWN	R JONES	
09/04/64	COVENTRY CITY	A	4-3	3883	HALL	HILLARD	G JONES	OLDFIELD	DAVIS	MABBUTT	JARMAN	FRUDE	BIGGS	BROWN	R JONES	R JONES, BIGGS 3
11/04/64	MANSFIELD TOWN	H	0-2	8317	HALL	HILLARD	G JONES	OLDFIELD	DAVIS	MABBUTT	JARMAN	BROWN	BIGGS	HAMILTON	R JONES	
13/04/64	LUTON TOWN	H	0-1	8254	HALL	HILLARD	G JONES	OLDFIELD	DAVIS	MABBUTT	JARMAN	BROWN	BIGGS	HAMILTON	R JONES	
18/04/64	NOTTS COUNTY	A	4-0	7002	HALL	HILLARD	G JONES	OLDFIELD	DAVIS	MABBUTT	JARMAN	BROWN	BIGGS	HAMILTON	R JONES	BIGGS 2, BROWN, OLDFIELD
21/04/64	READING	H	2-5	8002	HALL	HILLARD	G JONES	OLDFIELD	DAVIS	MABBUTT	JARMAN	BROWN	BIGGS	HAMILTON	R JONES	MABBUTT, R JONES
25/04/64	CREWE ALEXANDRA	H	1-4	2086	HALL	HILLARD	G JONES	OLDFIELD	DAVIS	MABBUTT	JARMAN	BROWN	BIGGS	HAMILTON	R JONES	BARNES og

FA CUP

Date	Opponent	H/A	Score	Att	1	2	3	4	5	6	7	8	9	10	11	Goalscorers
16/11/63	BOURNEMOUTH	A	3-1	12402	HALL	HILLARD	G JONES	OLDFIELD	DAVIS	MABBUTT	JARMAN	BROWN	BIGGS	HAMILTON	R JONES	BIGGS, R JONES
07/12/63	COVENTRY CITY	H	2-1	26248	HALL	HILLARD	G JONES	OLDFIELD	DAVIS	MABBUTT	JARMAN	BROWN	BIGGS	HAMILTON	R JONES	BIGGS 2, R JONES
04/01/64	NORWICH CITY	A	2-1	17779	HALL	HILLARD	G JONES	OLDFIELD	DAVIS	MABBUTT	JARMAN	BROWN	BIGGS	HAMILTON	R JONES	JARMAN, BRADFORD
25/01/64	MANCHESTER UNITED	A	1-4	55722	HALL	HILLARD	G JONES	OLDFIELD	DAVIS	MABBUTT	JARMAN	BROWN	BIGGS	HAMILTON	R JONES	CRERAND og

LEAGUE CUP

Date	Opponent	H/A	Score	Att	1	2	3	4	5	6	7	8	9	10	11	Goalscorers
04/09/63	SHREWSBURY TOWN	A	1-1	6950	HALL	HILLARD	G JONES	OLDFIELD	DAVIS	MABBUTT	JARMAN	BROWN	BIGGS	HAMILTON	BRADFORD	BIGGS
23/09/63	SHREWSBURY TOWN	H	6-2	7142	HALL	HILLARD	G JONES	OLDFIELD	DAVIS	MABBUTT	JARMAN	BROWN	BIGGS	HAMILTON	BRADFORD	HAMILTON 4, BIGGS 2
25/09/63	CRYSTAL PALACE	A	2-1	12142	HALL	HILLARD	G JONES	OLDFIELD	DAVIS	MABBUTT	JARMAN	BROWN	BIGGS	HAMILTON	BRADFORD	JARMAN, BIGGS
04/11/63	GILLINGHAM	H	1-1	10149	HALL	HILLARD	G JONES	OLDFIELD	DAVIS	MABBUTT	JARMAN	BROWN	BIGGS	HAMILTON	BRADFORD	BIGGS pen
06/11/63	GILLINGHAM	A	1-3	10771	HALL	HILLARD	G JONES	OLDFIELD	DAVIS	MABBUTT	JARMAN	BROWN	BIGGS	HAMILTON	BRADFORD	BIGGS

GLOUCESTERSHIRE CUP FINAL

Date	Opponent	H/A	Score	Att	1	2	3	4	5	6	7	8	9	10	11	Goalscorers
28/04/64	BRISTOL CITY	A	2-2	7693	HALL	HILLARD	DAVIS	OLDFIELD	STONE	MABBUTT	JARMAN	BROWN	BIGGS	HAMILTON	MUNRO	MUNRO, BROWN

PLAYERS	APP	GLS
BIGGS A	46	30
BRADFORD G	21	4
BROWN J	39	13
BUMPSTEAD D	3	
DAVIS J	34	
FRUDE R	3	
HALL B	46	
HAMILTON I	46	13
HILLARD D	40	2
JARMAN H	46	13
JONES G	45	
JONES R	28	8
MABBUTT R	42	2
MUNRO A	2	
OLDFIELD T	38	1
PARSONS L	1	
STONE D	16	1
SYKES N	3	
OWN GOALS		3

had refused to employ black workers and a boycott of buses, arranged by Paul Stephenson, was endorsed by many public figures, among them the Bishop of Bristol, the Rt Rev. Oliver Tomkins. The Company's decision was to be overturned in the aftermath of a May Day rally in Eastville Park, supported by the Labour Member of Parliament for Bristol South-East, Tony Benn. In August 1963, Raghbir Singh from Clifton was appointed as the first 'non-white' bus conductor in the Bristol area and the process of integration was thus given some scope to develop further.

1964/65

In retaining the shape of the previous season's side, Bert Tann introduced just one close-season signing. Roy McCrohan had played in 385 League games for Norwich City and joined Rovers in a £400 deal from Colchester United. Unable initially to break into a well-drilled side, he appeared in 10 League matches for Rovers, scoring in the draw at Brentford, before working as Bobby Robson's assistant at Ipswich Town. Otherwise, it was a consistent Rovers line-up for the 1964/65 season. Although goalkeeper Bernard Hall was the only ever-present, six other players appeared in more than 40 League matches. Alfie Biggs scored 18 League goals, with Ian Hamilton top-scoring on 21.

The mid-table position obtained 12 months earlier had raised the level of optimism and Rovers, with 82 League goals and more points than in any season since 1952/53, finished in sixth place. Rovers completed the season with consecutive away wins to end up with 20 League victories. This final flourish took the club within four points of promoted rivals, Bristol City. Although City finished with three straight victories to pip Mansfield Town on goal average, the reality was that Rovers were outsiders in the race. A desperate seven-match winless run in February had cost the club dearly, during which time Rovers lost three games in succession to potential promotion rivals, Hull City, Brentford and Bristol City. Defeat at Hull City was preceded by a one-minute's silence in memory of Sir Winston Churchill, the former Prime Minister, who had died six days earlier at the age of 90.

Rovers had, in fact, begun the season in sparkling form. The first four home games were all won, with 18 goals scored. Only one point was dropped in the opening five League fixtures. Alfie Biggs scored the second hat-trick of his Rovers career as Peterborough United were defeated 4-0 at Eastville in September, and 15 goals in the first 14 matches. However, his season was curtailed by injury and, with Ian Hamilton also sidelined with a troublesome knee, Rovers' goal flow could not be maintained. As it was, Harold Jarman and Bobby Jones both contributed significant goals later in the season.

On the opening day of the season, Biggs, Hamilton, Jarman and the impressive John Brown all scored against a strong Mansfield Town side that was ultimately only denied promotion on goal average. In the next two home games, in the space of a few days, Rovers put five goals past both Grimsby Town and champions-to-be Carlisle United. The

Bristol Rovers 1964-65. Back row: Terry Oldfield, Doug Hillard, Bernard Hall, Gwyn Jones, Dave Stone. Front row: Harold Jarman, John Brown, Bobby Jones, Joe Davis, Ian Hamilton, Alex Munro

former game finished 5-3, Rovers leading 3-0 after 32 minutes and 5-1 with 15 minutes to play. Seven separate players got on the scoresheet and the future England manager Graham Taylor played at left-half for the Mariners. Carlisle had led after 18 minutes, only for Rovers again to lead 5-1 with a quarter of an hour left. This was the third and most recent occasion, after two such runs during the 1950/51 season, that Rovers have scored five times in consecutive League fixtures. Rovers were to beat Bournemouth 4-2 in October and record 4-0 victories at home to Workington and Port Vale.

Unusually, Rovers could also claim to have completed a League double over the champions Carlisle United, Jarman and Hamilton both scoring in the 5-2 victory in September and in the 2-1 victory at Brunton Park at New Year. Rovers also led at Ashton Gate, when Joe Davis' second-half penalty, his only goal of the season, threatened to derail Bristol City's promotion push. City recovered to win 2-1. Promotion rivals Gillingham were comprehensively beaten twice, with Jarman scoring one of Rovers' three goals on each occasion. On the other hand, relegated Colchester United claimed two draws with Rovers, lowly Walsall won at Eastville and struggling Exeter City and Southend United both drew on their travels. In addition to the champions, Rovers also completed League doubles over Luton Town, Gillingham and Barnsley.

In October, the local derby at Eastville attracted a crowd of 25,370, the highest at any Rovers League or cup game all season. Later in the campaign, only 2,300 were to see Rovers lose to a 25-yard Dixie Hale volley and an 83rd-minute Jimmy Morgan winner at Workington. However, later in October, there was an astonishing match at Roots Hall where Southend United defeated Rovers 6-3. Hamilton's third-minute opener could not prevent Rovers from trailing 4-1 by half-time, Jimmy McKinven having scored twice. Hamilton scored again after 58 minutes, but the home side led 5-2 with 11 minutes to play. Moments after McKinven had completed his hat-trick, so too did Hamilton for Rovers. It was Hamilton's second hat-trick for the club and the only occasion a Rovers player had scored three goals and ended up on the losing side in a League match. McKinven had previously scored three times when Southend United had beaten Rovers 3-2 in October 1962. This remains one of only two League games featuring Rovers when both sides have included a hat-trick scorer.

As the season progressed, Tann looked to strengthen his squad. The December signing of Irishman Joe Haverty from Millwall went some way towards achieving this aim. At 5ft 3½in the second shortest player to appear for Rovers, Haverty was a highly skilful acquisition and he was to score in the large win against Port Vale. He also played for Eire against Spain while on Rovers' books. Another player to break into the League side was local inside-forward David Hudd, who picked up a career-threatening ankle injury at Barnsley and never reappeared in a Rovers shirt. In Biggs' enforced absence, it was Hamilton who was to lead the way with seven goals in four games over Christmas, including his second hat-trick of the season as Luton Town were beaten 3-2 at Eastville. However, a team that had started so confidently in front of goal now scored just 11 goals in a run of 12 League games between the end of January and Good Friday.

It was, with the benefit of hindsight, probably just as well that Rovers did not gain those four extra points and promotion to Division Two. In the absence of Biggs, the side was no match even for average Division Three sides. The most successful Rovers sides could boast a string of well-known local characters and, although Biggs, Mabbutt and Jarman were household names by 1965, this particular side still lacked depth. The patient work of Tann and his sidekicks continued, work that would ultimately lead to success under Don Megson in 1973/74. One key member of that side, Lindsay Parsons, once again made a few League appearances, while another, the giant Stuart Taylor, was waiting in the wings.

The FA Cup offered Rovers a tantalizing glimpse of glory. Victory at Walsall, where David Stone scored his only goal of the season, drew Southern League Weymouth at Eastville. Eschewing a repeat of the 15-1 victory in November 1900 or even the five-goal win 12 months later, Rovers were perfectly satisfied with a 4-1 scoreline. There then followed a tie that features largely in any perusal of the annals of Stockport County. They fielded a side featuring outside-left Peter Phoenix, who had scored in an FA Cup tie at Eastville in January 1962. However, the Cheshire club was now languishing in the bottom position in Division Four, where they were destined to end the season and, though outplayed, left Eastville with a goalless draw.

By the time of the replay, both sides knew that an away tie at Division One leaders Liverpool awaited the winners. An expectant crowd of 19,624 at Edgeley Park saw County take the lead after half an hour through Derek Hodgkinson, with Frank Beaumont adding a second within a minute. Stung into action, Rovers responded with goals from Mabbutt and Jones in a six-minute second-half spell. With just four minutes remaining, to the delirious delight of the home faithful, Ean Cuthbert's free-kick was

SEASON 1964/65

Date	Opponent	H/A	Res	Att	1	2	3	4	5	6	7	8	9	10	11	Goalscorers
22/08/64	MANSFIELD TOWN	H	4-1	10621	HALL	HILLARD	G JONES	OLDFIELD	DAVIS	MABBUTT	JARMAN	BROWN	BIGGS	HAMILTON	MUNRO	JARMAN, BROWN, BIGGS, HAMILTON
25/08/64	GRIMSBY TOWN	A	1-1	10350	HALL	HILLARD	G JONES	OLDFIELD	DAVIS	MABBUTT	JARMAN	BROWN	BIGGS	HAMILTON	R JONES	BIGGS
29/08/64	LUTON TOWN	A	2-0	9985	HALL	HILLARD	G JONES	OLDFIELD	DAVIS	MABBUTT	JARMAN	BROWN	BIGGS	HAMILTON	R JONES	BROWN, R JONES
01/09/64	GRIMSBY TOWN	H	5-3	15542	HALL	HILLARD	G JONES	OLDFIELD	DAVIS	MABBUTT	JARMAN	BROWN	BIGGS	HAMILTON	R JONES	JARMAN 2, BIGGS, BROWN, R JONES
05/09/64	CARLISLE UNITED	H	5-2	12580	HALL	HILLARD	G JONES	OLDFIELD	DAVIS	MABBUTT	JARMAN	BROWN	BIGGS	HAMILTON	R JONES	JARMAN 2, BIGGS, BROWN, CALDWELL og
09/09/64	PETERBOROUGH UNITED	A	1-3	14420	HALL	HILLARD	G JONES	OLDFIELD	DAVIS	MABBUTT	JARMAN	BROWN	BIGGS	HAMILTON	R JONES	HAMILTON
12/09/64	PORT VALE	A	1-1	7571	HALL	HILLARD	G JONES	STONE	DAVIS	MABBUTT	JARMAN	BROWN	BIGGS	HAMILTON	HAVERTY	HAVERTY
15/09/64	PETERBOROUGH UNITED	H	4-0	17415	HALL	HILLARD	G JONES	OLDFIELD	DAVIS	MABBUTT	JARMAN	BROWN	BIGGS	HAMILTON	HAVERTY	BIGGS 3, 1pen, R JONES
19/09/64	COLCHESTER UNITED	A	2-2	13211	HALL	HILLARD	McCROHAN	OLDFIELD	DAVIS	STONE	JARMAN	BROWN	BIGGS	HAMILTON	R JONES	HAMILTON, BIGGS
26/09/64	BRENTFORD	H	1-1	14150	HALL	HILLARD	McCROHAN	OLDFIELD	DAVIS	STONE	JARMAN	BROWN	McCROHAN	HAMILTON	R JONES	McCROHAN
30/09/64	BOURNEMOUTH	A	1-1	11487	HALL	HILLARD	G JONES	OLDFIELD	DAVIS	STONE	HURFORD	BROWN	BIGGS	HAMILTON	R JONES	HURFORD
03/10/64	BRISTOL CITY	H	2-1	23720	HALL	HILLARD	G JONES	OLDFIELD	DAVIS	STONE	JARMAN	BROWN	BIGGS	HAMILTON	R JONES	HAMILTON, BIGGS
06/10/64	BOURNEMOUTH	H	4-2	14003	HALL	STONE	G JONES	OLDFIELD	DAVIS	MABBUTT	JARMAN	BROWN	BIGGS	HAMILTON	R JONES	BIGGS 2, BROWN, NELSON og
10/10/64	SHREWSBURY TOWN	A	1-2	7345	HALL	STONE	G JONES	OLDFIELD	DAVIS	MABBUTT	JARMAN	BROWN	BIGGS	HAMILTON	R JONES	HAMILTON
14/10/64	OLDHAM ATHLETIC	A	2-1	7777	HALL	HILLARD	G JONES	OLDFIELD	DAVIS	MABBUTT	JARMAN	BROWN	OLDFIELD	HAMILTON	R JONES	HAMILTON 2
17/10/64	READING	H	1-0	12758	HALL	HILLARD	G JONES	OLDFIELD	DAVIS	MABBUTT	JARMAN	BROWN	BIGGS	HAMILTON	R JONES	HAMILTON
20/10/64	OLDHAM ATHLETIC	H	0-0	13210	HALL	HILLARD	G JONES	OLDFIELD	DAVIS	MABBUTT	JARMAN	BROWN	BIGGS	HAMILTON	R JONES	
24/10/64	SOUTHEND UNITED	A	3-6	6335	HALL	HILLARD	G JONES	OLDFIELD	DAVIS	MABBUTT	JARMAN	BROWN	BIGGS	HAMILTON	R JONES	HAMILTON 3
27/10/64	GILLINGHAM	H	3-0	12383	HALL	HILLARD	G JONES	MABBUTT	DAVIS	STONE	JARMAN	BROWN	BIGGS	HAMILTON	R JONES	MABBUTT, BROWN, JARMAN
31/10/64	BARNSLEY	A	1-0	11773	HALL	HILLARD	G JONES	MABBUTT	DAVIS	STONE	JARMAN	BROWN	BIGGS	HAMILTON	R JONES	HAMILTON
07/11/64	SCUNTHORPE UNITED	H	3-0	4056	HALL	HILLARD	G JONES	MABBUTT	DAVIS	STONE	JARMAN	BROWN	BIGGS	HAMILTON	MUNRO	MUNRO, BROWN, JARMAN, R JONES
21/11/64	WATFORD	A	1-1	9130	HALL	HILLARD	G JONES	MUNRO	DAVIS	STONE	JARMAN	BROWN	McCROHAN	HAMILTON	MUNRO	HAMILTON
28/11/64	WORKINGTON	H	4-0	12029	HALL	HILLARD	McCROHAN	OLDFIELD	DAVIS	STONE	JARMAN	BROWN	BIGGS	HAMILTON	MUNRO	HAMILTON 2, BROWN
12/12/64	MANSFIELD TOWN	A	0-3	4784	HALL	HILLARD	G JONES	OLDFIELD	DAVIS	MABBUTT	JARMAN	BROWN	BIGGS	HAMILTON	MUNRO	
19/12/64	LUTON TOWN	H	3-2	10624	HALL	STONE	G JONES	OLDFIELD	DAVIS	MABBUTT	JARMAN	BROWN	BIGGS	HAMILTON	MUNRO	HAMILTON 2, BROWN
26/12/64	QUEENS PARK RANGERS	A	3-1	17698	HALL	STONE	G JONES	OLDFIELD	DAVIS	MABBUTT	JARMAN	BIGGS	R JONES	HAMILTON	MUNRO	HAMILTON, R JONES
28/12/64	QUEENS PARK RANGERS	H	1-3	5220	HALL	STONE	G JONES	OLDFIELD	DAVIS	MABBUTT	JARMAN	BIGGS	R JONES	HAMILTON	MUNRO	BIGGS
02/01/65	CARLISLE UNITED	A	2-1	11233	HALL	STONE	G JONES	MABBUTT	DAVIS	STONE	JARMAN	BROWN	R JONES	HAMILTON	MUNRO	R JONES 2
16/01/65	PORT VALE	H	4-0	10011	HALL	HILLARD	G JONES	MABBUTT	DAVIS	STONE	JARMAN	HUDD	R JONES	HAMILTON	HAVERTY	R JONES 2, HAVERTY, HUDD
23/01/65	COLCHESTER UNITED	H	1-1	4851	HALL	HILLARD	STONE	OLDFIELD	DAVIS	MUNRO	JARMAN	HUDD	R JONES	HAMILTON	HAMILTON	HAMILTON
30/01/65	HULL CITY	A	2-3	28399	HALL	HILLARD	G JONES	OLDFIELD	DAVIS	MABBUTT	JARMAN	BROWN	R JONES	HAMILTON	R JONES	R JONES 2
06/02/65	BRENTFORD	A	1-2	14575	HALL	HILLARD	G JONES	OLDFIELD	DAVIS	BROWN	JARMAN	HUDD	R JONES	HAMILTON	HAVERTY	JARMAN
13/02/65	BRISTOL CITY	A	1-2	23052	HALL	HILLARD	G JONES	OLDFIELD	STONE	MABBUTT	JARMAN	HUDD	BIGGS	HAMILTON	R JONES	DAVIS pen
23/02/65	SHREWSBURY TOWN	H	0-0	13143	HALL	HILLARD	G JONES	OLDFIELD	DAVIS	MUNRO	JARMAN	BROWN	BIGGS	HAMILTON	MUNRO	
27/02/65	READING	A	1-1	7399	HALL	HILLARD	G JONES	OLDFIELD	DAVIS	MABBUTT	JARMAN	BROWN	R JONES	BROWN	MUNRO	BROWN
06/03/65	HULL CITY	H	1-1	19899	HALL	HILLARD	G JONES	OLDFIELD	DAVIS	MABBUTT	JARMAN	HUDD	BIGGS	BROWN	MUNRO	JARMAN
13/03/65	BARNSLEY	H	2-0	3026	HALL	HILLARD	G JONES	OLDFIELD	DAVIS	MABBUTT	JARMAN	BROWN	BIGGS	FRUDE	MUNRO	BIGGS, R JONES
20/03/65	SCUNTHORPE UNITED	A	0-1	13717	HALL	HILLARD	G JONES	OLDFIELD	DAVIS	MABBUTT	JARMAN	BROWN	BIGGS	FRUDE	R JONES	
27/03/65	WALSALL	A	2-0	6650	HALL	HILLARD	G JONES	OLDFIELD	DAVIS	MABBUTT	JARMAN	BROWN	BIGGS	FRUDE	MUNRO	BROWN, R JONES
03/04/65	WATFORD	H	1-0	7509	HALL	HILLARD	G JONES	OLDFIELD	DAVIS	MUNRO	JARMAN	BROWN	R JONES	FRUDE	MUNRO	HAMILTON
09/04/65	WORKINGTON	A	1-2	2300	HALL	HILLARD	G JONES	MABBUTT	DAVIS	MUNRO	JARMAN	BROWN	R JONES	FRUDE	MUNRO	JARMAN
16/04/65	EXETER CITY	H	1-1	12194	HALL	HILLARD	G JONES	MABBUTT	DAVIS	MUNRO	JARMAN	BROWN	R JONES	HAMILTON	HAVERTY	JARMAN
17/04/65	SOUTHEND UNITED	H	2-2	5578	HALL	HILLARD	G JONES	MABBUTT	DAVIS	MUNRO	JARMAN	BROWN	R JONES	HAMILTON	HAVERTY	JARMAN, BIGGS
19/04/65	EXETER CITY	A	1-0	8165	HALL	McCROHAN	G JONES	OLDFIELD	DAVIS	MABBUTT	JARMAN	BROWN	BIGGS	HAMILTON	HAVERTY	JARMAN
24/04/65	GILLINGHAM	A	3-1	11167	HALL	McCROHAN	G JONES	MABBUTT	DAVIS	MABBUTT	JARMAN	BROWN	R JONES	MUNRO	HAVERTY	JARMAN, R JONES, WESTON og

LEAGUE CUP

Date	Opponent	H/A	Res	Att	1	2	3	4	5	6	7	8	9	10	11	Goalscorers
22/09/64	CHESTERFIELD	H	0-2	7815	HALL	HILLARD	G JONES	McCROHAN	DAVIS	MABBUTT	JARMAN	BROWN	R JONES	HAMILTON	R JONES	

FA CUP

Date	Opponent	H/A	Res	Att	1	2	3	4	5	6	7	8	9	10	11	Goalscorers
14/11/64	WALSALL	A	2-0	10576	HALL	HILLARD	G JONES	OLDFIELD	DAVIS	STONE	JARMAN	BROWN	BIGGS	HAMILTON	MUNRO	STONE, R JONES
05/12/64	WEYMOUTH	A	4-1	12468	HALL	HILLARD	G JONES	OLDFIELD	DAVIS	STONE	JARMAN	BROWN	BIGGS	HAMILTON	MUNRO	JARMAN 2, MUNRO, HAMILTON
09/01/65	STOCKPORT COUNTY	H	0-0	12164	HALL	HILLARD	G JONES	MABBUTT	DAVIS	STONE	JARMAN	BROWN	BIGGS	HAMILTON	MUNRO	
11/01/65	STOCKPORT COUNTY	A	2-3	19624	HALL	HILLARD	G JONES	MABBUTT	DAVIS	STONE	JARMAN	BROWN	R JONES	HAMILTON	MUNRO	R JONES, MABBUTT

GLOUCESTERSHIRE CUP FINAL

Date	Opponent	H/A	Res	Att	1	2	3	4	5	6	7	8	9	10	11	Goalscorers
26/04/65	BRISTOL CITY	H	3-2	8907	HALL	HILLARD	G JONES	OLDFIELD	DAVIS	MABBUTT	JARMAN	BROWN	BIGGS	HAMILTON	MUNRO	PARR og, R JONES, HAMILTON

PLAYERS	APP	GLS
BIGGS A	24	18
BROWN J	44	8
DAVIS J	45	1
FRUDE R	6	
HALL B	46	
HAMILTON I	33	20
HAVERTY J	13	1
HILLARD D	29	
HUDD D	5	1
HURFORD H	1	
JARMAN C	44	14
JONES G	43	
JONES R	41	11
MABBUTT R	10	1
McCROHAN R	21	
MUNRO A	32	
OLDFIELD T	32	
PARSONS L	7	
STONE D	22	
OWN GOALS		3

knocked home by Ian Sandiford and Rovers' cup dreams were over. County, though, were to take the lead in front of a 51,000 crowd at Anfield and hold out for a respectable draw before losing in a replay. The key to this opportunity, victory over Rovers on a Monday night at Edgeley Park, is still viewed by many Stockport County supporters as a defining moment in their club's history.

Luck was not on Rovers' side in the League Cup, where goals from Ralph Hunt and Peter Stringfellow gave Division Four Chesterfield a 2-0 victory over Rovers at Eastville. On the other hand, after a goal apiece before half-time, Rovers beat Bristol City 3-2 in the Gloucestershire Cup final at Eastville, Hamilton scoring the winning goal. Arnold Rodgers scored three times for a Bristol City Old Players side that defeated their Rovers counterparts 6-3 at Eastville, with Geoff Fox, George Petherbridge and Geoff Bradford scoring. Further afield, Bath City lost 4-2 to Arsenal in December in a match to mark the official opening of the floodlights at Twerton Park, a ground destined to become Rovers' home in 1986.

E ver the shrewd tactician, manager Bert Tann was slowly moulding a side that was to reap further success in the early 1970s. With the help of men such as Bill Dodgin and Bobby Campbell, a group of players was being honed at minimal expense. Season 1965/66 saw a team of experienced local players, such as Alfie Biggs, Harold Jarman and Doug Hillard, combined with younger Bristolians, such as Dave Stone, Ray Graydon and Stuart Taylor. The cornerstones for the years to come were being put in place.

The 1965/66 season was one of great change nationally. The introduction of substitutes brought a new dimension to the game. Rovers' first nominated substitute, Roy McCrohan, remained unused and was never to appear for the club again. The first time a substitute was used by Rovers was the appearance of Joe Davis in a 3-0 home victory over Walsall in October. This was also the season in which England hosted the World Cup and won the Wembley final. Geoff Hurst, whose father Charlie Hurst had played for Rovers reserves in 1938/39, scored a hat-trick in the final, while Alan Ball, a Rovers player himself in 1982/83, ran the engine-room in midfield.

Despite having finished sixth in 1964/65 Rovers finished the new season in 16th place in Division Three. The total of 64 goals scored in League football was, with the exception of the 1961/62 relegation year, the lowest seasonal total by the club since 1949/50. The absence of goalkeeper Bernard Hall from 3 League matches and an FA Cup defeat in November not only ended a run of 115 League appearances, but also left Hillard as the club's only ever-present. Six players played in more than 40 League matches, but 23 were used in all, Harold Jarman being the top scorer with 13 League goals, three more than Alfie Biggs and Bobby Jones.

What above all transformed Rovers' season into one of mediocrity was a demoralising club record run of 14 consecutive League games without a win. This depressing statistic was to be repeated in the relegation season of 1980/81 and in the club's first season in

Bristol Rovers 1965/66. From left to right: Parsons, Stone, Hillard, G Jones, Munro, Oldfield, Davis, Mabbutt, Brown, McCrohan, Frude, Hall, R Jones, Hamilton, Petts, Weller, Jarman

the basement division, 2001/02. Following victory over Oldham Athletic in the middle of October, Rovers were not to win again until the defeat of Grimsby Town at the end of January sparked a revival of sorts, as Rovers won six out of 10 games. Yet, this previous run of 14 games had included seven draws, two of these against Millwall, who were promoted to Division Two at the season's end. There were also three 1-0 defeats and a 2-0 loss at struggling Oldham Athletic, whose goals came from Albert Quixall, a scorer for Sheffield Wednesday at Eastville as long ago as New Year's Eve 1955, who this time converted a penalty, and Jim Frizzell. Oddly, the only heavy defeat of this dreadful run was a 6-1 mauling at the hands of the Tigers, champions-elect Hull City at Boothferry Park in December, when five opponents found the net.

When heavy defeats arrived, they came just as Rovers were playing well. After a positive run of results, Rovers lost 4-1 at third-placed Queen's Park Rangers on Good Friday, with the future England International Rodney Marsh one of the goalscorers. Revenge victory over Rangers was followed by a 5-2 capitulation at Peterborough United, for whom the former England centre-forward Derek Kevan was a goalscorer. Two big wins in September preceded a 3-0 defeat at Swansea Town and Rovers lost by the same score at Scunthorpe United, as well as losing 4-3 both at Swindon Town and at Brighton. On a Tuesday night in October, Rovers led 2-0 after only 24 minutes at Swindon Town, Jones and Jarman having scored. Eric Weaver and Roger Smart drew the home side level by half-time but, just four minutes after the break, Rovers again gained control with Jarman's second of the game. However, two goals in four minutes, scored by Dennis Brown and Keith Morgan, consigned Rovers to defeat.

Defeat at Brighton came as a result of what the *Bristol Evening Post* described as 'an abysmal display by Rovers' defence.' Charlie Livesey scored Albion's opening goal after 13 minutes and he was to equalise after Brown and Jarman had scored for Rovers shortly after half-time. Livesey then turned provider, creating a goal for Brian Tawse 20 minutes from the end. Oldfield pulled the scores level after 80 minutes but, with only five minutes remaining, Hall misjudged Bob Baxter's free-kick, leaving Wally Gould with a simple tap-in and his goal left Rovers smarting from another high-scoring defeat.

SEASON 1965/66

FOOTBALL LEAGUE DIVISION THREE

Date	Opponent	V	Score	Att	G	2	3	4	5	6	7	8	9	10	11	Substitutes	Goalscorers
21/08/65	GRIMSBY TOWN	A	1-1	5402	HALL	HILLARD	PARSONS	OLDFIELD	DAVIS	MABBUTT	JARMAN	BROWN	BIGGS	HAMILTON	R JONES		R JONES
24/08/65	SHREWSBURY TOWN	H	3-2	10173	HALL	HILLARD	PARSONS	OLDFIELD	DAVIS	MABBUTT	JARMAN	BROWN	BIGGS	HAMILTON	R JONES		BROWN, HAMILTON, WRIGHT og
28/08/65	BRENTFORD	H	1-1	12160	HALL	HILLARD	G JONES	OLDFIELD	DAVIS	MABBUTT	JARMAN	BROWN	BIGGS	HAMILTON	R JONES		BROWN
04/09/65	MANSFIELD TOWN	A	0-2	9560	HALL	HILLARD	G JONES	OLDFIELD	DAVIS	MABBUTT	JARMAN	BROWN	BIGGS	PETTS	R JONES		
07/09/65	SWINDON TOWN	A	0-1	15855	HALL	HILLARD	G JONES	OLDFIELD	DAVIS	MABBUTT	JARMAN	BROWN	BIGGS	HAMILTON	R JONES		
09/09/65	YORK CITY	H	5-1	8500	HALL	HILLARD	G JONES	OLDFIELD	DAVIS	MABBUTT	JARMAN	BROWN	BIGGS	HAMILTON	MUNRO		JARMAN 2, BIGGS, OLDFIELD, MUNRO
18/09/65	OXFORD UNITED	H	3-1	9707	HALL	HILLARD	G JONES	OLDFIELD	DAVIS	MABBUTT	JARMAN	BROWN	BIGGS	R JONES	MUNRO		R JONES 3
25/09/65	SWANSEA TOWN	H	0-3	9500	HALL	HILLARD	G JONES	PETTS	DAVIS	MABBUTT	GRAYDON	BROWN	BIGGS	R JONES	MUNRO	DAVIS 6	
02/10/65	WALSALL	H	3-0	9357	HALL	HILLARD	G JONES	PETTS	STONE	MABBUTT	JARMAN	BROWN	BIGGS	R JONES	MUNRO		R JONES 2, JARMAN
05/10/65	SWINDON TOWN	A	3-4	18065	HALL	HILLARD	G JONES	PETTS	STONE	MABBUTT	GRAYDON	BROWN	BIGGS	R JONES	JARMAN		JARMAN 2, R JONES
09/10/65	BRIGHTON & HOVE ALBION	H	0-0	10418	HALL	HILLARD	G JONES	PETTS	STONE	MABBUTT	GRAYDON	BROWN	PLUMB	HAMILTON	JARMAN		
16/10/65	SCUNTHORPE UNITED	A	0-3	4074	HALL	HILLARD	G JONES	PETTS	DAVIS	MABBUTT	JARMAN	BROWN	PLUMB	HAMILTON	R JONES		
19/10/65	OLDHAM ATHLETIC	H	4-0	8568	HALL	HILLARD	G JONES	OLDFIELD	DAVIS	MABBUTT	JARMAN	BIGGS	PLUMB	HAMILTON	R JONES		PLUMB 2, HAMILTON, JARMAN
23/10/65	WATFORD	H	0-0	8826	HALL	HILLARD	G JONES	OLDFIELD	DAVIS	MABBUTT	JARMAN	BROWN	BIGGS	HAMILTON	R JONES	MUNRO 4	R JONES
25/10/65	MILLWALL	A	3-3	16151	HALL	HILLARD	G JONES	PETTS	DAVIS	MABBUTT	JARMAN	BROWN	BIGGS	MUNRO	R JONES		BIGGS, HILLARD, JARMAN
30/10/65	OLDHAM ATHLETIC	A	0-2	3746	HALL	HILLARD	PARSONS	PETTS	DAVIS	MABBUTT	JARMAN	BROWN	BIGGS	MUNRO	R JONES	FRUDE 8	
06/11/65	SHREWSBURY TOWN	H	0-0	4007	BRIGGS	HILLARD	PARSONS	PETTS	DAVIS	MABBUTT	GRAYDON	WELLER	PLUMB	BROWN	MUNRO	MUNRO 11	
09/11/65	WORKINGTON	H	2-2	7756	BRIGGS	HILLARD	PARSONS	PETTS	DAVIS	MUNRO	JARMAN	FRUDE	PLUMB	BROWN	R JONES		PLUMB, JARMAN
20/11/65	PETERBOROUGH UNITED	A	0-0	6330	HALL	HILLARD	G JONES	OLDFIELD	DAVIS	MABBUTT	JARMAN	BROWN	PLUMB	RONALDSON	R JONES	WELLER 10	MABBUTT
27/11/65	EXETER CITY	A	0-1	5964	HALL	HILLARD	G JONES	OLDFIELD	DAVIS	MABBUTT	JARMAN	BROWN	FRUDE	RONALDSON	R JONES	MUNRO 11	FRUDE
11/12/65	HULL CITY	A	1-6	16349	HALL	HILLARD	G JONES	OLDFIELD	DAVIS	MABBUTT	GRAYDON	PETTS	BIGGS	HAMILTON	JARMAN	MUNRO 4	
27/12/65	BOURNEMOUTH	H	0-0	10031	HALL	HILLARD	G JONES	MUNRO	DAVIS	MABBUTT	JARMAN	R JONES	BIGGS	HAMILTON	WATKINS		
28/12/65	BOURNEMOUTH	A	0-1	6153	HALL	HILLARD	G JONES	OLDFIELD	STONE	MABBUTT	JARMAN	BROWN	BIGGS	HAMILTON	R JONES		
01/01/66	BRIGHTON & HOVE ALBION	H	3-4	14408	HALL	HILLARD	DAVIS	OLDFIELD	STONE	MABBUTT	JARMAN	BROWN	BIGGS	RONALDSON	R JONES		BROWN, JARMAN, OLDFIELD
08/01/66	MILLWALL	H	0-2	9365	HALL	HILLARD	DAVIS	OLDFIELD	STONE	MABBUTT	JARMAN	BROWN	PLUMB	RONALDSON	R JONES		BIGGS
15/01/66	WATFORD	A	0-2	4681	HALL	HILLARD	DAVIS	OLDFIELD	STONE	MABBUTT	JARMAN	FRUDE	BIGGS	BROWN	R JONES		FRUDE 2
29/01/66	GRIMSBY TOWN	H	2-1	8303	HALL	HILLARD	DAVIS	PETTS	STONE	MABBUTT	JARMAN	FRUDE	BIGGS	BROWN	R JONES		BIGGS 3, SCOTT og, JARMAN
05/02/66	BRENTFORD	A	5-0	6240	HALL	HILLARD	DAVIS	PETTS	STONE	MABBUTT	JARMAN	FRUDE	BIGGS	BROWN	R JONES		BIGGS 2, BROWN, R JONES, PETTS, FRUDE
12/02/66	SOUTHEND UNITED	H	5-1	5649	HALL	HILLARD	DAVIS	PETTS	STONE	MABBUTT	JARMAN	BROWN	BIGGS	FRUDE	R JONES		JARMAN, STONE, BROWN
19/02/66	MANSFIELD TOWN	H	6-0	7477	HALL	HILLARD	G JONES	PETTS	STONE	MABBUTT	JARMAN	BROWN	BIGGS	FRUDE	R JONES		FRUDE, R JONES
26/02/66	YORK CITY	A	0-0	8946	HALL	HILLARD	DAVIS	PETTS	STONE	MABBUTT	JARMAN	BROWN	BIGGS	HAMILTON	R JONES		STONE pen
05/03/66	SOUTHEND UNITED	A	3-1	7844	HALL	HILLARD	DAVIS	PETTS	STONE	MABBUTT	JARMAN	BROWN	BIGGS	HAMILTON	R JONES		BIGGS, BURKINSHAW og
12/03/66	OXFORD UNITED	A	0-1	6814	HALL	HILLARD	PARSONS	PETTS	TAYLOR	MABBUTT	JARMAN	BROWN	BIGGS	RONALDSON	MUNRO		MABBUTT
19/03/66	SWANSEA TOWN	H	2-1	7491	HALL	HILLARD	DAVIS	PETTS	TAYLOR	MABBUTT	GRAYDON	BROWN	BIGGS	R JONES	MUNRO	RONALDSON 9	BROWN
26/03/66	WALSALL	H	1-1	8485	HALL	HILLARD	PARSONS	OLDFIELD	DAVIS	MABBUTT	JARMAN	BROWN	BIGGS	R JONES	MUNRO		JARMAN, BIGGS
29/03/66	SCUNTHORPE UNITED	H	2-0	7376	HALL	HILLARD	DAVIS	PETTS	STONE	MABBUTT	JARMAN	BROWN	BIGGS	RONALDSON	R JONES	RONALDSON 5	BROWN, RONALDSON
02/04/66	GILLINGHAM	A	0-2	5344	HALL	HILLARD	DAVIS	OLDFIELD	STONE	MABBUTT	GRAYDON	FRUDE	BIGGS	R JONES	BROWN		
09/04/66	QUEENS PARK RANGERS	A	1-4	13365	HALL	HILLARD	PARSONS	PETTS	DAVIS	MABBUTT	JARMAN	BROWN	BIGGS	RONALDSON	R JONES		MABBUTT
12/04/66	READING	H	1-0	7316	HALL	HILLARD	DAVIS	OLDFIELD	STONE	MABBUTT	GRAYDON	BROWN	BIGGS	R JONES	R JONES		BROWN
16/04/66	QUEENS PARK RANGERS	H	0-0	9203	HALL	HILLARD	DAVIS	PETTS	STONE	MABBUTT	JARMAN	BROWN	BIGGS	RONALDSON	MUNRO	RONALDSON 9	JARMAN, BIGGS
23/04/66	PETERBOROUGH UNITED	A	2-5	4926	HALL	MABBUTT	PARSONS	OLDFIELD	DAVIS	MUNRO	GRAYDON	RONALDSON	BIGGS	R JONES	R JONES	RONALDSON 5	BROWN, RONALDSON
26/04/66	EXETER CITY	H	2-0	6803	HALL	HILLARD	MABBUTT	PETTS	TAYLOR	MABBUTT	JARMAN	FRUDE	BIGGS	BROWN	R JONES	MUNRO 8	JARMAN
29/04/66	WORKINGTON	A	0-0	2557	HALL	HILLARD	DAVIS	PETTS	STONE	MABBUTT	JARMAN	RONALDSON	BIGGS	RONALDSON	R JONES		RONALDSON
06/05/66	READING	A	1-0	7314	HALL	HILLARD	DAVIS	PETTS	STONE	MABBUTT	JARMAN	BROWN	BIGGS	BROWN	R JONES	MUNRO 6	JARMAN
	HULL CITY	H	1-2	9234	HALL	HILLARD	DAVIS	PETTS	TAYLOR	MABBUTT	JARMAN	BROWN	FRUDE	RONALDSON	R JONES		

FA CUP

Date	Opponent	V	Score	Att	G	2	3	4	5	6	7	8	9	10	11	Substitutes	Goalscorers
13/11/65	READING	A	2-3	8873	BRIGGS	HILLARD	G JONES	PETTS	DAVIS	MABBUTT	JARMAN	WELLER	BIGGS	R JONES	MUNRO		HILLARD, R JONES

LEAGUE CUP

Date	Opponent	V	Score	Att	G	2	3	4	5	6	7	8	9	10	11	Substitutes	Goalscorers
21/09/65	WEST HAM UNITED	H	3-3	18354	HALL	HILLARD	G JONES	PETTS	DAVIS	MABBUTT	JARMAN	BROWN	BIGGS	R JONES	MUNRO		BROWN, PETTS, JARMAN
29/09/65	WEST HAM UNITED	A	2-3	13160	HALL	HILLARD	G JONES	PETTS	STONE	MABBUTT	JARMAN	BROWN	BIGGS	R JONES	MUNRO		PETTS, R JONES

GLOUCESTERSHIRE CUP FINAL

Date	Opponent	V	Score	Att	G	2	3	4	5	6	7	8	9	10	11	Substitutes	Goalscorers
12/05/66	BRISTOL CITY	A	1-0	9431	HALL	HILLARD	DAVIS	PETTS	TAYLOR	MABBUTT	JARMAN	FRUDE	BIGGS	RONALDSON	R JONES		JARMAN

Appearances

PLAYERS	APPS	SUBS	GLS
BIGGS A	36		10
BRIGGS R	3		
BROWN J	37		7
DAVIS J	41	1	5
FRUDE R	14	1	5
GRAYDON R	8		
HALL B	43		
HAMILTON I	12		2
HILLARD D	46		1
JARMAN H	42		13
JONES G	20		
JONES R	45		10
MABBUTT R	45		2
MUNRO A	15	6	1
OLDFIELD T	21	1	2
PARSONS L	9		
PETTS J	27		1
PLUMB R	9		3
RONALDSON K	9	2	2
STONE D	18		2
TAYLOR S	3		
WATKINS R	1		
WELLER C	2	1	
OWN GOALS			3

As the season progressed, a number of new signings were able to contribute to Rovers' later success. John Petts, a former England International at Schoolboy level, became a regular choice at right-half and scored in the large victory over struggling Mansfield Town. Chris Weller and Dick Plumb were both tried in the forward line, the latter scoring twice in a 4-0 victory over lowly Oldham Athletic, while Scottish inside-forward Ken Ronaldson scored 2 League goals as the season drew to a close. Rovers scored three or more goals on 11 occasions in the League. Bottom of the table York City lost their goalkeeper Tommy Forgan injured and, with right-back Alan Baker in goal for 75 minutes, lost 5-1 to Rovers. It was the club's largest away win since an identical scoreline at Notts County in September 1953. A week later, Rovers met Oxford United for the first time in League action. A Jones hat-trick past goalkeeper Harry Fearnley, who apparently smoked his pipe whenever his side was attacking, gave Rovers a comfortable 3-1 victory.

The two biggest wins, though, came in February. Having beaten Grimsby Town to end their 14-game spell without a victory, Rovers' goalscoring went berserk as they recorded a 5-0 win at Brentford, Alfie Biggs scoring a hat-trick. It was the first time Rovers had ever won an away League game by such a margin. A fortnight later, the goal machine went one better, as Mansfield Town were defeated 6-0. Biggs, with two more goals, was one of five Rovers scorers, with Roger Frude contributing a rare goal and Jones scoring for the first time in four months before Petts completed the scoring three minutes from time. It was to be September 1971 before Rovers next won a League match by six clear goals. As would befit Rovers' season, though, York City, at the foot of Division Three, visited Eastville seven days later and fought out a goalless draw.

Don Rogers, whose goals were to win a sensational League Cup final for Swindon Town in 1969, scored the only goal of the game at Eastville in September with a terrific 25-yard drive. Keith Burkinshaw, later an FA Cup-winning manager at Tottenham Hotspur, conceded an own goal at Eastville at the end of March, as his Scunthorpe United side was defeated 2-0. The goalless draw at Workington in April marked the first of a club record 546 League appearances made by Stuart Taylor between 1965 and 1980. At 6ft 5in, Taylor is the tallest player to represent Rovers in League action. The inclusion of the Bristol-born central defender as well as Lindsay Parsons in defence marked the first stage in the construction of the side Don Megson would lead to promotion in 1973/74.

While the FA Cup brought Rovers no joy, Megson and the future Rovers full-back Wilf Smith were in the Sheffield Wednesday side that led 2-0 in the FA Cup final at Wembley, only to lose to three Everton goals. Rovers did not progress beyond the first round in the League Cup either, but West Ham United were in fairness more glamorous opponents than Reading and there were two epic matches. The Hammers, FA Cup winners in 1964, were to reach the League Cup final this year before losing over two legs to West Bromwich Albion, and fielded three players, Geoff Hurst, Martin Peters and Bobby Moore who were to win World Cup winners' medals in the summer. A large Eastville crowd saw Hurst open the scoring after only two minutes and, though Brown equalised with a long-range left foot drive, the England striker Johnny Byrne set up another Hurst goal and then scored off the far upright to put West Ham 3-1 ahead after half an hour. Before the interval, Petts reduced the arrears when his low shot arrowed in off a post and he started the move from which Jarman equalised after 58 minutes.

Although Peters later fired against his own post, the Hammers survived. In the replay, Byrne and Hurst gave them a 2-0 half-time lead. Again there was a spirited Rovers revival, Petts volleying home after 54 minutes after Jarman had created an opportunity and Jones equalizing two minutes later when Eddie Bovington slipped. Then, 10 minutes from time, Petts lost control, Hurst fed Byrne and he grabbed the decisive goal.

In the Gloucestershire Cup final, a first-half Jarman goal gave Rovers victory over Bristol City at Ashton Gate. On 29 November 1965, Stapleton Road station closed to goods traffic after more than 100 years of business, leaving the local railway station to Eastville Stadium dealing solely with human transport.

1966/67

O n paper, finishing fifth in Division Three represents the highest final position achieved by Rovers since their return from Division Two five years earlier. In reality, however, missing out on promotion was a bitter blow. Bert Tann's side suffered four straight defeats in the run-up to Christmas, yet still harboured genuine promotion hopes after a run of seven wins in nine games. Entering March, leaders Queen's Park Rangers and Rovers still boasted a six-point gap over the chasing pack. Yet Rovers then endured a run of nine matches without a win to finish, after a final-day defeat, just two points behind promoted Middlesbrough.

Rovers rejected stripes and turned out in 1966/67 in an all blue strip. In contrast, it was not a Rovers side that showed many changes from the previous season. Gwyn Jones, having lost his left-back berth to Joe Davis, had joined Porthmadog and a familiar

Bristol Rovers 1966/67. Back Row: Petts, Munro, Parsons, Hillard, Briggs, Hall, Taylor, Ronaldson, Stone, Mabbutt. Front Row: Jarman, Frude, Brown, Davis, Biggs, Hamilton, R Jones

BRISTOL STADIUM - BRISTOL

BRISTOL
ROVERS
Football Club Ltd.
(1883)

F.A. CUP - 3rd Round

SATURDAY, JANUARY 28th, 1967.   Kick-off 3.0 p.m.

BRISTOL
ROVERS
v
ARSENAL

Souvenir
Programme 1/-   № 8159

A crowd of 35,420 was attracted to watch Arsenal defeat Rovers 3-0 in a third round FA Cup-tie at Eastville

line-up drew 3-3 with Swansea Town on the opening day, with young Stuart Taylor at centre-half. The season kicked off in a wave of optimism, for England were world champions. Alan Ball, who joined Rovers in January 1983, had become the first six-figure transfer in British football by joining cup-holders Everton from Blackpool in August for £110,000. The optimism sweeping Eastville emanated from the successful youth policy, whereby Rovers were able to field Bristol-born players such as Ray Graydon, Alfie Biggs, Doug Hillard and the side's only ever-present Harold Jarman. Laurie Taylor, Wayne Jones and Vic Barney, all products of the youth scheme, broke into the League side as the season progressed, while Larry Lloyd played his first game in the Gloucestershire Cup final.

Success was based around a strong home record. Of the top eight sides, only Watford avoided defeat against Rovers. In fact, their decisive 3-0 victory at Eastville in December was only Rovers' second home League defeat in 15 months. The other home defeat came, bizarrely, at the hands of bottom-club Workington, whose second away win of the season was assured through a Brian Tinnion shot after 28 minutes. This home success was gained through the prolific goalscoring of Biggs, with 23 goals, and 19-goal Jarman. Although no other player contributed more than 5 League goals, a total of 15 Rovers players, the most since 1949/50, made the scoresheet. Rovers completed a League double over five clubs and won away against Reading and Middlesbrough, both of whom finished above them in the table.

Rovers dropped just one point in their opening four League games. Despite defeat at Colchester United, the first five-figure home attendance of the calendar year saw a convincing 3-0 victory over Swindon Town, with Hillard, Jarman and Ian Hamilton scoring. It was the first in another run of three consecutive victories. After five straight home wins, the last being another 3-0 win, this time against Darlington, Mansfield Town were the visitors at Eastville in mid-October. This was a highly entertaining eight-goal draw. The visitors were 2-0 ahead after 35 minutes, only for Ken Ronaldson to reduce the margin three minutes before half-time. John Rowland's second goal put Mansfield 3-1 up after 65 minutes and this sparked a Rovers recovery. Biggs, after 70 minutes and Jarman after 75 and 85 minutes, contributed three goals in a quarter of an hour and Rovers were dramatically in front. As the seconds ticked away, Stuart Brace equalised for the Stags and Rovers had to settle for a 4-4 draw.

Three days later, Rovers again scored four times at Eastville, Jarman again scoring twice in a 4-1 victory over Gillingham, for whom Brian Yeo scored in both League meetings with Rovers. Walsall, Colchester United and Doncaster Rovers, the latter fielding the former Rovers wing-half Norman Sykes, all conceded four goals at Eastville. Rovers also beat Shrewsbury Town 4-3 in a dramatic game at Gay Meadow in November. Rovers already led 2-0, through Biggs and Jarman, when the home side was awarded a 36th-minute penalty against Ray Mabbutt for handball. Bernard Hall saved Trevor Meredith's kick. Seconds after half-time John Manning reduced the arrears only for John Brown, on 49 minutes, and Jarman again, just 19 minutes from the end, to give Rovers a 4-1 lead. Two goals in three minutes set up a tight finish, but Rovers held out to complete a League double over the Shropshire club.

As Christmas approached, and seeing his side lose its way with four consecutive League defeats, Tann splashed out £6,500 to bring the highly experienced right-half

FOOTBALL LEAGUE DIVISION THREE

SEASON 1966/67

Date	Opponent	Venue	Score	ATT	G	2	3	4	5	6	7	8	9	10	11	SUBSTITUTES	GOALSCORERS
20/08/66	SWANSEA TOWN	H	3-3	7688	HALL	HILLARD	DAVIS	PETTS	S TAYLOR	MABBUTT	JARMAN	BROWN	BIGGS	RONALDSON	R JONES		DAVIS pen, JARMAN, BIGGS
27/08/66	MIDDLESBROUGH	A	2-1	10658	HALL	PARSONS	DAVIS	PETTS	S TAYLOR	MABBUTT	JARMAN	BROWN	BIGGS	MUNRO	R JONES		JARMAN, PLUMB
07/09/66	SHREWSBURY TOWN	H	1-0	7145	HALL	HILLARD	DAVIS	STONE	S TAYLOR	MABBUTT	JARMAN	BROWN	BIGGS	PLUMB	MUNRO		STONE
10/09/66	READING	A	2-1	7724	HALL	HILLARD	PARSONS	STONE	S TAYLOR	MABBUTT	JARMAN	R JONES	PLUMB	HAMILTON	MUNRO		PLUMB, MUNRO
17/09/66	COLCHESTER UNITED	A	1-3	4736	HALL	HILLARD	PARSONS	STONE	DAVIS	MABBUTT	JARMAN	R JONES	PLUMB	HAMILTON	MUNRO		BROWN
24/09/66	SWINDON TOWN	H	3-0	10907	HALL	PARSONS	DAVIS	STONE	DAVIS	MABBUTT	JARMAN	BROWN	PLUMB	HAMILTON	MUNRO		HILLARD, JARMAN, HAMILTON
27/09/66	OXFORD UNITED	H	3-0	8745	HALL	HILLARD	DAVIS	STONE	S TAYLOR	MABBUTT	JARMAN	BROWN	BIGGS	HAMILTON	MUNRO		DAVIS pen, BIGGS
01/10/66	READING	H	2-1	10394	BRIGGS	HILLARD	DAVIS	FRUDE	S TAYLOR	MABBUTT	JARMAN	BROWN	BIGGS	HAMILTON	MUNRO	HILLARD 11	HILLARD, HAMILTON
04/10/66	OLDHAM ATHLETIC	A	0-3	14000	BRIGGS	HILLARD	DAVIS	FRUDE	S TAYLOR	MABBUTT	JARMAN	BROWN	BIGGS	RONALDSON	MUNRO		
07/10/66	DARLINGTON	A	3-0	7649	BRIGGS	HILLARD	DAVIS	FRUDE	S TAYLOR	MABBUTT	JARMAN	RONALDSON	BIGGS	BROWN	MUNRO		RONALDSON, BIGGS 2
15/10/66	DONCASTER ROVERS	A	2-3	11614	BRIGGS	HILLARD	DAVIS	FRUDE	S TAYLOR	MABBUTT	JARMAN	RONALDSON	BIGGS	BROWN	MUNRO		FRUDE, BIGGS
18/10/66	MANSFIELD TOWN	H	4-4	7599	BRIGGS	HILLARD	DAVIS	FRUDE	S TAYLOR	MABBUTT	JARMAN	RONALDSON	BIGGS	BROWN	MUNRO		STONE, JARMAN, RONALDSON, BIGGS
22/10/66	GILLINGHAM	H	4-1	9113	BRIGGS	HILLARD	DAVIS	STONE	S TAYLOR	MABBUTT	JARMAN	BROWN	BIGGS	RONALDSON	MUNRO		BIGGS 2, JARMAN, BROWN
29/10/66	GRIMSBY TOWN	A	0-1	7341	HALL	HILLARD	DAVIS	STONE	S TAYLOR	MABBUTT	JARMAN	BROWN	BIGGS	RONALDSON	MUNRO		
02/11/66	SCUNTHORPE UNITED	H	4-2	5768	HALL	HILLARD	PARSONS	STONE	S TAYLOR	MABBUTT	JARMAN	BROWN	BIGGS	RONALDSON	MUNRO		JARMAN 2, BROWN, BIGGS
05/11/66	GILLINGHAM	H	4-3	8963	HALL	HILLARD	PARSONS	STONE	S TAYLOR	MABBUTT	JARMAN	BROWN	BIGGS	RONALDSON	MUNRO		JARMAN 2, RONALDSON, BIGGS
12/11/66	SHREWSBURY TOWN	A	1-1	7226	HALL	HILLARD	PARSONS	STONE	S TAYLOR	MABBUTT	JARMAN	BROWN	BIGGS	RONALDSON	MUNRO		STONE
16/11/66	PETERBOROUGH UNITED	H	1-0	10902	HALL	HILLARD	PARSONS	FRUDE	S TAYLOR	MABBUTT	JARMAN	BROWN	BIGGS	RONALDSON	MUNRO		BIGGS
19/11/66	TORQUAY UNITED	H	0-1	6767	HALL	HILLARD	DAVIS	FRUDE	DAVIS	MABBUTT	JARMAN	FRUDE	PLUMB	FRUDE	PLUMB	FRUDE 10	
03/12/66	COLCHESTER UNITED	A	2-3	11542	HALL	HILLARD	PARSONS	STONE	S TAYLOR	MABBUTT	JARMAN	BROWN	BIGGS	FRUDE	MUNRO		JARMAN 2, BIGGS
10/12/66	BRIGHTON & H ALBION	A	0-3	13312	HALL	HILLARD	PARSONS	STONE	S TAYLOR	MABBUTT	JARMAN	BROWN	BIGGS	BROWN	MUNRO		
17/12/66	GILLINGHAM	H	1-1	8227	HALL	DAVIS	PARSONS	MUNRO	S TAYLOR	MABBUTT	JARMAN	BROWN	PLUMB	BROWN	RONALDSON		JARMAN
26/12/66	QUEENS PARK RANGERS	A	2-2	6041	HALL	DAVIS	PARSONS	STONE	S TAYLOR	MABBUTT	JARMAN	PLUMB	BIGGS	BROWN	MUNRO		JARMAN, MUNRO
27/12/66	WATFORD	A	2-0	6400	HALL	HILLARD	PARSONS	STONE	S TAYLOR	MABBUTT	JARMAN	PLUMB	BIGGS	BROWN	MUNRO		FRUDE, BIGGS
31/12/66	SWANSEA TOWN	A	1-0	15329	HALL	HILLARD	PARSONS	STONE	S TAYLOR	MABBUTT	JARMAN	BROWN	BIGGS	PLUMB	MUNRO		PLUMB, BIGGS
14/01/67	LEYTON ORIENT	H	2-2	10645	HALL	HILLARD	PARSONS	STONE	DAVIS	MABBUTT	JARMAN	BROWN	BIGGS	PLUMB	MUNRO		BIGGS, PLUMB
21/01/67	SWINDON TOWN	A	4-1	15415	HALL	HILLARD	PARSONS	DAVIS	DAVIS	MABBUTT	JARMAN	BROWN	BIGGS	RONALDSON	GRAYDON		RONALDSON, BIGGS 2, PLUMB
04/02/67	COLCHESTER UNITED	H	1-0	15473	HALL	HILLARD	DAVIS	S TAYLOR	DAVIS	MABBUTT	JARMAN	BROWN	BIGGS	PLUMB	W JONES		W JONES
11/02/67	OLDHAM ATHLETIC	A	1-4	7489	DAVIS	HILLARD	DAVIS	S TAYLOR	S TAYLOR	MABBUTT	JARMAN	FRUDE	BIGGS	FRUDE	W JONES		BROWN
18/02/67	WORKINGTON	H	2-1	9482	HILLARD	MABBUTT	MUNRO	S TAYLOR	S TAYLOR	PETTS	JARMAN	BROWN	FRUDE	HAMILTON	RONALDSON	HILLARD 8	FRUDE, PLUMB
25/02/67	DONCASTER ROVERS	A	4-2	2348	HALL	MABBUTT	DAVIS	FRUDE	S TAYLOR	PETTS	JARMAN	W JONES	BIGGS	BROWN	MUNRO	MABBUTT 11	HILLARD, DAVIS pen, PLUMB
04/03/67	MANSFIELD TOWN	H	2-0	9012	HALL	MABBUTT	MUNRO	FRUDE	S TAYLOR	PETTS	JARMAN	BROWN	BIGGS	PLUMB	GRAYDON		FRUDE 2, BIGGS, JARMAN
11/03/67	MIDDLESBROUGH	A	2-1	12815	HALL	MABBUTT	MUNRO	STONE	STONE	PETTS	JARMAN	BROWN	BIGGS	RONALDSON	GRAYDON		BIGGS
18/03/67	WORKINGTON	A	1-1	8619	HALL	MABBUTT	HILLARD	STONE	STONE	PETTS	JARMAN	BROWN	BIGGS	PLUMB	RONALDSON	J WILLIAMS 11	JARMAN, BIGGS
24/03/67	GRIMSBY TOWN	H	0-0	9474	HALL	MABBUTT	HILLARD	STONE	STONE	PETTS	JARMAN	BROWN	BIGGS	R WILLIAMS	W JONES		
25/03/67	BOURNEMOUTH	A	1-1	13924	HALL	MABBUTT	MUNRO	STONE	STONE	PETTS	JARMAN	BROWN	BIGGS	R WILLIAMS	W JONES		J WILLIAMS, JARMAN
27/03/67	WALSALL	H	1-1	7408	HALL	MABBUTT	HILLARD	STONE	S TAYLOR	PETTS	JARMAN	FRUDE	BIGGS	R WILLIAMS	MUNRO	MABBUTT	BIGGS, HAMILTON
01/04/67	BOURNEMOUTH	A	0-0	7350	HALL	MABBUTT	HILLARD	STONE	S TAYLOR	PETTS	JARMAN	BROWN	BIGGS	RONALDSON	MUNRO	JARMAN	
08/04/67	PETERBOROUGH UNITED	H	1-1	9202	HALL	MABBUTT	HILLARD	STONE	S TAYLOR	PETTS	JARMAN	BIGGS	PLUMB	BROWN	MUNRO		MABBUTT
15/04/67	TORQUAY UNITED	A	1-2	14171	HALL	MABBUTT	HILLARD	STONE	S TAYLOR	PETTS	JARMAN	BIGGS	FRUDE	BROWN	MUNRO		JARMAN
22/04/67	BRIGHTON & H ALBION	H	2-2	9042	HALL	MABBUTT	HILLARD	STONE	S TAYLOR	PETTS	JARMAN	BROWN	BIGGS	R WILLIAMS	W JONES		BIGGS 2
24/04/67	DARLINGTON	H	3-0	5104	HALL	MABBUTT	HILLARD	STONE	S TAYLOR	PETTS	JARMAN	BROWN	BIGGS	R WILLIAMS	MUNRO		BIGGS 3, RONALDSON
29/04/67	SCUNTHORPE UNITED	A	1-3	4080	HALL	MABBUTT	HILLARD	STONE	S TAYLOR	PETTS	JARMAN	BROWN	BIGGS	FRUDE	MABBUTT		BIGGS
29/04/67	QUEENS PARK RANGERS	H	2-1	17721	HALL	MABBUTT	HILLARD	J WILLIAMS	S TAYLOR	PETTS	JARMAN	BROWN	BIGGS	W JONES	MABBUTT		BIGGS 2
06/05/67	WATFORD	A	1-3	17530	HALL	HILLARD	HILLARD	J WILLIAMS	STONE	STONE	JARMAN	BROWN	BIGGS	W JONES	MUNRO		W JONES

FA CUP

Date	Opponent	Venue	Score	ATT	G	2	3	4	5	6	7	8	9	10	11	SUBSTITUTES	GOALSCORERS
26/11/66	OXFORD CITY	A	2-2	5100	HALL	HILLARD	PARSONS	STONE	STONE	MABBUTT	JARMAN	BIGGS	BIGGS	RONALDSON	MUNRO		BIGGS, BIGGS
29/11/66	OXFORD CITY	H	4-0	9465	HALL	HILLARD	PARSONS	STONE	STONE	MABBUTT	JARMAN	BIGGS	BIGGS	R WILLIAMS	MUNRO		R WILLIAMS
07/01/67	LUTON TOWN	H	3-2	8408	HALL	HILLARD	PARSONS	STONE	DAVIS	STONE	JARMAN	W JONES	BIGGS	BROWN	MABBUTT		JARMAN, BIGGS
28/01/67	ARSENAL	H	0-3	35420	HILLARD	HILLARD	DAVIS	J WILLIAMS	STONE	MABBUTT	JARMAN	BROWN	BIGGS	PLUMB	MUNRO		J WILLIAMS, JARMAN, DAVIS

LEAGUE CUP

Date	Opponent	Venue	Score	ATT	2	3	4	5	6	7	8	9	10	11	SUBSTITUTES	GOALSCORERS
24/08/66	CARDIFF CITY	A	0-1	5574	HALL	HILLARD	DAVIS	PETTS	STONE	MABBUTT	JARMAN	BROWN	RONALDSON	PLUMB	MUNRO	JARMAN	

GLOUCESTERSHIRE CUP FINAL

Date	Opponent	Venue	Score	ATT	2	3	4	5	6	7	8	9	10	11	SUBSTITUTES	GOALSCORERS
09/05/67	BRISTOL CITY	H	0-3	17433	L TAYLOR	MABBUTT	PARSONS	LLOYD	STONE	MUNRO	GRAYDON	BROWN	FRUDE	BIGGS	W JONES		

APPEARANCES

PLAYERS	APP	SUB	GLS
BARNEY V	0	1	
BIGGS A	41		23
BRIGGS R	9		
BROWN J	34	5	
DAVIS J	31	1	
FRUDE R	14	3	
GRAYDON R	3	3	
HALL B	18		
HAMILTON I	11	3	
HILLARD D	29	4	
JARMAN H	46		19
JONES R	5	1	
MABBUTT R	43	2	1
MUNRO A	40	2	2
PARSONS L	7	1	
PETTS J	17		
PLUMB R	16	5	
RONALDSON K	23	3	
STONE D	42	3	3
TAYLOR L	19		
TAYLOR S	21	1	1
WILLIAMS J	16	1	
WILLIAMS R	4	1	

Johnny Williams to Eastville. A veteran of more than 400 League appearances with Plymouth Argyle, Williams was Bristol-born and the son of a journalist with the *Bristol Evening World*. He was to play in the final 21 League games, scoring the opening goal at home to Oldham Athletic. His namesake Bobby Williams, well known in Bristol circles after many years at Ashton Gate, arrived in a £16,000 move from Rotherham United in March to act as understudy to Ronaldson and the emerging talent of 18-year-old Wayne Jones.

Rovers suffered three 3-0 defeats and lost 4-1 at Oxford United, their heaviest defeat at the Manor Ground. A young Ron Atkinson orchestrated this defeat, with his brother Graham grabbing two of the goals. What cost the side dearly, though, was a club-record run, since equalled in 1975/76, of five consecutive League draws over Easter. Three of these came in home matches, just at a time when Rovers required victory to push for promotion, while there were two drawn games with Bournemouth in the space of three days. In addition, Rovers lost several games they should have won. They went down 3-2 at Doncaster Rovers, who were destined for relegation and for whom the former Pirate Graham Ricketts played. The former Rovers apprentice Laurie Sheffield scored twice. Rovers also lost at Torquay United, whose second goal in front of the highest attendance all season at Plainmoor, was scored after 56 minutes by Robin Stubbs, a Rovers player in 1969. Stubbs had hit the crossbar in the opening seconds of the second-half, with Ron Barnes equalising Bobby Williams' 13th-minute opening goal from the subsequent rebound.

On New Year's Eve at Eastville, during the 2-2 draw with Middlesbrough, Johnny Williams' back pass stuck in the mud and goalkeeper Bernard Hall and Boro's John O'Rourke, who had scored a hat-trick against Rovers in March 1964, collided sickeningly. Hall was rushed unconscious to Frenchay Hospital, with Ray Mabbutt continuing in goal. The injury was more serious than many believed, however, and Hall spent 16 days unconscious. Ultimately, with the best wishes of all football supporters across the country, he was able to return to normal life but not to football. After 163 League games, he was forced to retire on medical grounds and was granted a testimonial game in October 1967 against West Ham United.

Ultimately, though some matches were comfortably won, Rovers were obliged to miss out once again on promotion. At Workington in February, Biggs scored in first-half injury-time with Hamilton adding a second eight minutes from the end. In the final home game, two Biggs goals defeated runaway champions Queen's Park Rangers. Defeat at Watford meant Rovers, having finished their fixtures, still lay in the second promotion place, but could only watch helplessly as other clubs overtook them. Reading won at Workington to go above Rovers on goal average, Watford drew both their games in hand to finish a point higher and Middlesbrough, in defeating both Peterborough United and Oxford United, overtook all three to gain promotion. Back in fifth place, Rovers were left to rue wasted opportunities.

The extent of Rovers' participation in the League Cup was a single-goal defeat at Cardiff City, though a future Rovers goalkeeper, Dick Sheppard, played in the final for West Bromwich Albion, beaten 3-2 by Queen's Park Rangers. The Gloucestershire Cup final was lost 3-0 at home to Bristol City, for whom Tony Ford, later a Rovers full-back, converted a second-half penalty. Another future Rovers player, Terry Cooper, the club's manager between April 1980 and October 1981, was a member of the Leeds United side that lost the 1967 Fairs Cup final 2-0 on aggregate to Dynamo Zagreb.

In the FA Cup, Rovers had to rely on a Joe Davis penalty and an own goal from left-half John Lamb to earn a draw with Isthmian League Oxford City. Defeat avoided, four goals in the replay, three from the talismanic Biggs, brought Rovers a comfortable victory. Division Four Luton Town, conquerors over Exeter City, were no walkover but Rovers won through the odd goal in five to set up a third-round tie at home to Arsenal. A crowd of more than 35,000, the highest at Eastville for seven years, saw Rovers take on an Arsenal side that boasted Frank McLintock, captain of their 1970/71 double-winning side. Rovers were easily beaten 3-0, one of three goalscorers being George Graham, later a successful manager with Arsenal, Leeds United and Tottenham Hotspur.

1967/68

Despite having ended up so close to promotion in 1966/67, Rovers finished the following season in 16th place, albeit a comfortable six points clear of the relegation zone. Long-serving secretary Ron Moules had died suddenly in May 1967, having served the club in this capacity since September 1949. Bert Tann's final summer as Rovers manager saw few changes in playing personnel. Joe Davis had joined Swansea Town for £1,000 at the tail end of the previous season, so Doug Hillard and Alex Munro were full-backs behind goalkeepers Laurie Taylor and Ronnie Briggs, who played in 23 League matches each. Johnny Williams, Stuart Taylor and Dave Stone formed the half-back line.

The forward line included top scorer Alfie Biggs – who scored 11 times before joining Walsall in March – Wayne Jones, Harold Jarman and Ken Ronaldson. The veteran Ray Mabbutt, an occasional utility player, weighed in with 10 goals, one more than Johnny Williams and the returning Bobby Jones. His signing, just days after an opening-day defeat at Bournemouth, could have inspired the club to a successful season. There were no ever-presents and five players wore the number nine shirt. Ian Hamilton's recurring injury problems restricted him to one final game for the team. In League football, only the visits of Peterborough United in November, Reading on Boxing Day and Torquay United on Good Friday drew five-figure crowds at Eastville. In comparison with the preceding years, these were not the best of times and reshuffling in April was Rovers' method of dealing with the situation.

While changes within the club were imminent, alterations in the neighbourhood were taking place in 1967. Plans were already afoot for the M32 motorway, which was to open two years later ominously close to the old stadium. A Sunday market, the brainchild of Ron Moules, had first opened in 1967 in the stadium car park and was extended in 1972 to cover Fridays too. Investigations into the flooding problem, which had plagued the Eastville district for so long, were continuing and flood-relief work, aimed at stemming the flow of the river Frome into land around the South Stand, resolved the problem in the summer of 1968, following a particularly bad winter, in which five million gallons of water had been pumped off the pitch.

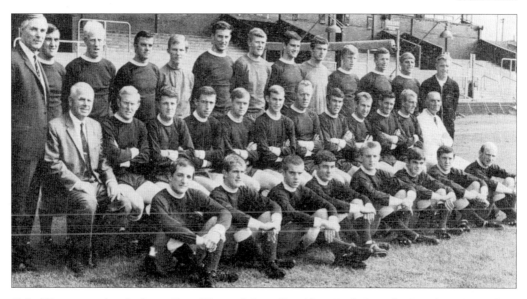

Bristol Rovers 1967/68. Back row: Tann (Manager), Stone, Ronaldson, Frude, L Taylor, S Taylor, Briggs, Lloyd, W Brown, Plumb, J Williams, Hillard, Campbell (Trainer-Coach). Second row: Dodgin (Chief Scout) Petts, R Williams, Jarman, Jones, Barney, Biggs, Bannister, Hamilton, Mabbutt, Graydon, Williams (Asst Trainer). Front row: Parsons, R Brown, Prince, Laycock, Roberts, Higgins, Lowrie, Munro

On the field, in a season of great inconsistency, Rovers never won more than two League games in succession. The best runs were one of three wins in four games in the autumn and a similar spell in December, when two Johnny Williams goals in the final five minutes contributed to a 4-1 victory over Shrewsbury Town. The noted Worcestershire middle-order batsman Ted Hemsley, who had appeared in the 7-2 victory over Rovers in October 1962, now conceded an own goal, by deflecting Bobby Jones' low 32nd-minute cross into his own net for Rovers' equaliser. He was later to miss the crucial penalty when Rovers won the 1972 Watney Cup Final. In contrast, the worst run was one of three consecutive defeats around January.

Rovers scored five times at both Northampton Town and Oldham Athletic and four times each at home to Oldham Athletic, Shrewsbury Town and bottom-of-the-table Scunthorpe United. The Pirates also contrived to beat both sides promoted at the end of the season, Oxford United and Bury. Indeed, the first victory of the season was 2-0 away to eventual champions, Oxford United. Even in losing 3-1 at home to Southport, there was a goal from Ronaldson after only 28 seconds. However, just three days after his final Rovers appearance, ironically against Walsall, top-scorer Biggs moved to join the Saddlers in a £10,000 transfer. Rovers had been stripped of a proven goalscorer.

The most remarkable victory came at Northampton Town in October. A 1-0 win over Barrow gave little indication of what was to come against a side that had won five of its previous six matches, especially as Mabbutt was drafted in as an emergency inside-forward for his first game in two months. As it was, Mabbutt scored a hat-trick, there were six first-half goals, a hat-trick scorer for each club for the second and most recent time in Rovers' club history, and an astonishing 5-4 win for Rovers. In the first half the Cobblers led twice and Rovers once, with home centre-forward Frank Large scoring

Alfie Biggs, veteran centre-forward left Rovers for a second time in March 1968 after 178 goals in 424 League appearances

twice and winning the penalty converted by John Mackin. Mabbutt had scored when Johnny Williams had his shot parried, while Bobby Jones, against his former club, and Williams had also found the net. Level 3-3 at half-time, Rovers took the lead again through Mabbutt and, after Large scored his third of the game, so too did Mabbutt to record the only hat-trick of his career and give Rovers a 5-4 win. Amazingly, Mabbutt was to score twice more as Rovers drew 3-3 at Tranmere Rovers in the next fixture.

Rovers were also involved in two high-scoring wins over Oldham Athletic. In February, after falling behind to an Ian Towers goal after 15 minutes, Rovers took control and Johnny Williams' penalty, his second goal of the game, put Rovers 3-1 up with only 11 minutes to play. However, Towers scored again and, five minutes from time, the former Rovers trainee Laurie Sheffield equalised. In the final seconds, from a Williams free-kick, Biggs headed his second goal of the match to give Rovers a dramatic victory. Yet, the return game in May was even more unlikely, as Rovers recorded their first away win since victory over Northampton more than six months earlier.

In winning 5-3 at Oldham Athletic on the final day of the season, Rovers completed only a second League double. Wayne Jones, after 11 minutes, and Bobby Jones, 15 minutes later, had given Rovers a comfortable half-time lead, only for Ian Wood, after 53 and 58 minutes, to pull the Latics level. Within seconds, Taylor had put Rovers ahead again, before Wood completed his hat-trick 12 minutes from the end. Once again, Rovers replied instantly, Bobby Jones scoring his second goal of a fluctuating game, with Jarman adding the visitors' fifth three minutes later. By scoring what were in fact his only 3 League goals of the season, Wood became the third opponent to score a League hat-trick against Rovers and end up on the losing side.

On five occasions – at Peterborough United, Watford, Northampton Town, Bury and Swindon Town – Rovers conceded four League goals, the heaviest defeat being 4-0 at Vicarage Road, where Watford's star-in-the-making Tony Currie scored twice. The only hat-trick in Rovers matches during 1967/68 was scored by Stockport County's Jim Fryatt in April, when Rovers lost 3-1 at Edgeley Park. Fryatt, who had scored for Southend United at Eastville in March 1963, is also credited with one of the fastest goals in League history, his strike for Bradford Park Avenue against Tranmere Rovers in April 1964 being recorded as four seconds after the kick-off, though current thinking

FOOTBALL LEAGUE DIVISION THREE

Date	Opponent	Res	ATT	G	2	3	4	5	6	7	8	9	10	11	Substitutes	Goalscorers
19/08/67	BOURNEMOUTH	A 1-3	6813	L TAYLOR	MABBUTT	HILLARD	J WILLIAMS	S TAYLOR	MUNRO	GRAYDON	BIGGS	PLUMB	BROWN	JARMAN	FRUDE 9	BIGGS
26/08/67	COLCHESTER UNITED	H 1-3	8260	BRIGGS	MABBUTT	HILLARD	J WILLIAMS	S TAYLOR	MUNRO	JARMAN	BROWN	BIGGS	W JONES	R JONES		MUNRO pen
02/09/67	PETERBOROUGH UNITED	A 1-4	6649	BRIGGS	HILLARD	PARSONS	J WILLIAMS	S TAYLOR	MUNRO	JARMAN	RONALDSON	BIGGS	W JONES	R JONES		JARMAN
06/09/67	OXFORD UNITED	A 2-0	6803	BRIGGS	HILLARD	PARSONS	J WILLIAMS	S TAYLOR	MUNRO	JARMAN	RONALDSON	BIGGS	W JONES	R JONES		SHUKER og, JARMAN
09/09/67	MANSFIELD TOWN	H 2-0	7317	L TAYLOR	HILLARD	PARSONS	J WILLIAMS	S TAYLOR	MUNRO	JARMAN	RONALDSON	BIGGS	W JONES	R JONES		RONALDSON, BIGGS
16/09/67	WATFORD	A 0-4	7500	BRIGGS	HILLARD	PARSONS	BARNEY	STONE	MUNRO	JARMAN	RONALDSON	BIGGS	W JONES	R JONES		
23/09/67	SOUTHPORT	H 1-1	7553	BRIGGS	HILLARD	PARSONS	J WILLIAMS	S TAYLOR	BARNEY	JARMAN	RONALDSON	R JONES	W JONES	MUNRO		RONALDSON
26/09/67	OXFORD UNITED	H 1-1	6938	BRIGGS	HILLARD	PARSONS	J WILLIAMS	S TAYLOR	BARNEY	R JONES	RONALDSON	BIGGS	W JONES	MUNRO		RONALDSON
30/09/67	SCUNTHORPE UNITED	A 1-1	3750	BRIGGS	HILLARD	PARSONS	J WILLIAMS	S TAYLOR	BARNEY	R JONES	RONALDSON	BIGGS	W JONES	MUNRO	JARMAN 8	MUNRO
02/10/67	BARROW	A 1-1	6360	BRIGGS	HILLARD	MUNRO	J WILLIAMS	S TAYLOR	BARNEY	JARMAN	RONALDSON	BIGGS	W JONES	R JONES	STONE 2	
07/10/67	GRIMSBY TOWN	H 3-0	6626	BRIGGS	PARSONS	MUNRO	J WILLIAMS	S TAYLOR	BARNEY	JARMAN	RONALDSON	BIGGS	W JONES	R JONES		J WILLIAMS, RONALDSON, W JONES
14/10/67	GILLINGHAM	A 0-0	6138	BRIGGS	HILLARD	MUNRO	J WILLIAMS	S TAYLOR	BARNEY	JARMAN	RONALDSON	BIGGS	W JONES	R JONES		
21/10/67	WALSALL	H 3-2	7912	BRIGGS	HILLARD	MUNRO	J WILLIAMS	S TAYLOR	BARNEY	JARMAN	RONALDSON	BIGGS	W JONES	R JONES	STONE 6	BIGGS, W JONES
24/10/67	BARROW	H 1-0	7802	BRIGGS	HILLARD	MUNRO	J WILLIAMS	S TAYLOR	BARNEY	JARMAN	RONALDSON	BIGGS	W JONES	R JONES		GRAYDON
28/10/67	NORTHAMPTON TOWN	A 5-4	9126	BRIGGS	HILLARD	MUNRO	J WILLIAMS	S TAYLOR	BARNEY	GRAYDON	R WILLIAMS	BIGGS	W JONES	R JONES	STONE 8	J WILLIAMS, MABBUTT 3, R JONES
04/11/67	TRANMERE ROVERS	A 3-3	6636	BRIGGS	HILLARD	STONE	J WILLIAMS	S TAYLOR	MUNRO	GRAYDON	MABBUTT	BIGGS	W JONES	R JONES	MUNRO 6	MABBUTT 2, R JONES
11/11/67	PETERBOROUGH UNITED	H 2-1	10742	BRIGGS	HILLARD	STONE	J WILLIAMS	S TAYLOR	MUNRO	JARMAN	MABBUTT	BIGGS	W JONES	R JONES		HILLARD, MABBUTT
18/11/67	STOCKPORT COUNTY	A 0-2	9539	BRIGGS	HILLARD	STONE	J WILLIAMS	S TAYLOR	MUNRO	JARMAN	MABBUTT	BIGGS	W JONES	R JONES		
25/11/67	BRIGHTON & H ALBION	H 1-0	10373	BRIGGS	HILLARD	MUNRO	J WILLIAMS	S TAYLOR	STONE	GRAYDON	MABBUTT	PLUMB	W JONES	R JONES		BIGGS
02/12/67	SHREWSBURY TOWN	A 4-1	7454	BRIGGS	HILLARD	MUNRO	J WILLIAMS	S TAYLOR	STONE	JARMAN	R WILLIAMS	BIGGS	W JONES	R JONES		WILLIAMS 2-1pen, R JONES, HEMSLEY og
16/12/67	BOURNEMOUTH	H 2-0	7080	BRIGGS	HILLARD	MUNRO	J WILLIAMS	S TAYLOR	STONE	JARMAN	R WILLIAMS	BIGGS	W JONES	R JONES	PETTS 7	BIGGS, MABBUTT
23/12/67	COLCHESTER UNITED	A 0-2	4324	BRIGGS	HILLARD	MUNRO	J WILLIAMS	S TAYLOR	STONE	MABBUTT	R WILLIAMS	BIGGS	W JONES	R JONES		
26/12/67	READING	H 1-2	13374	BRIGGS	HILLARD	MUNRO	J WILLIAMS	S TAYLOR	STONE	MABBUTT	RONALDSON	BIGGS	W JONES	R JONES		J WILLIAMS pen
30/12/67	READING	A 1-2	7459	L TAYLOR	HILLARD	MUNRO	J WILLIAMS	S TAYLOR	STONE	MABBUTT	RONALDSON	BIGGS	W JONES	R JONES	PETTS 11	RONALDSON
20/01/68	WATFORD	H 0-2	7702	L TAYLOR	HILLARD	MUNRO	J WILLIAMS	S TAYLOR	STONE	MABBUTT	RONALDSON	BIGGS	W JONES	R JONES		
03/02/68	SOUTHPORT	A 1-2	5282	L TAYLOR	PARSONS	MUNRO	J WILLIAMS	S TAYLOR	STONE	GRAYDON	MABBUTT	BIGGS	RONALDSON	R JONES		MABBUTT
10/02/68	SCUNTHORPE UNITED	H 4-0	5666	L TAYLOR	PARSONS	MUNRO	PETTS	S TAYLOR	STONE	RONALDSON	MABBUTT	BIGGS	W JONES	R JONES		RONALDSON, BIGGS, MABBUTT, R JONES
17/02/68	OLDHAM ATHLETIC	A 4-3	6864	L TAYLOR	PARSONS	MUNRO	PETTS	S TAYLOR	STONE	RONALDSON	MABBUTT	BIGGS	W JONES	R JONES		BIGGS 2, J WILLIAMS 2-1pen
24/02/68	GRIMSBY TOWN	A 2-3	3512	L TAYLOR	HILLARD	MUNRO	PETTS	S TAYLOR	STONE	JARMAN	MABBUTT	BIGGS	W JONES	R JONES		S TAYLOR, BIGGS
27/02/68	BURY	A 2-4	9403	L TAYLOR	HILLARD	MUNRO	PETTS	S TAYLOR	STONE	JARMAN	MABBUTT	BIGGS	W JONES	R JONES	JARMAN 7	JARMAN, MABBUTT
02/03/68	GILLINGHAM	H 1-1	5478	L TAYLOR	HILLARD	MUNRO	PETTS	S TAYLOR	STONE	RONALDSON	MABBUTT	BIGGS	W JONES	R JONES		J WILLIAMS pen
09/03/68	BURY	H 3-1	7154	L TAYLOR	HILLARD	MUNRO	PETTS	S TAYLOR	STONE	RONALDSON	MABBUTT	BIGGS	W JONES	R JONES		BIGGS, J WILLIAMS pen, R JONES
11/03/68	MANSFIELD TOWN	A 0-3	6377	L TAYLOR	HILLARD	MUNRO	J WILLIAMS	S TAYLOR	STONE	JARMAN	W JONES	BIGGS	R JONES	RONALDSON	R WILLIAMS 4	
16/03/68	WALSALL	A 1-2	7314	L TAYLOR	PARSONS	MUNRO	PETTS	S TAYLOR	STONE	RONALDSON	W JONES	BIGGS	R JONES	PETTS	PETTS 11	JONES og
23/03/68	NORTHAMPTON TOWN	H 2-2	5413	L TAYLOR	HILLARD	MUNRO	PETTS	S TAYLOR	STONE	JARMAN	J WILLIAMS	BIGGS	R WILLIAMS	JARMAN		S TAYLOR 2
30/03/68	LEYTON ORIENT	A 2-2	4261	L TAYLOR	HILLARD	MUNRO	PETTS	S TAYLOR	STONE	JARMAN	J WILLIAMS	W JONES	R WILLIAMS	R JONES		JARMAN, R WILLIAMS
06/04/68	TRANMERE ROVERS	H 3-1	6602	L TAYLOR	HILLARD	MUNRO	PETTS	S TAYLOR	STONE	RONALDSON	HAMILTON	W JONES	R WILLIAMS	R JONES		W JONES, R JONES 2
12/04/68	TORQUAY UNITED	H 1-0	19470	L TAYLOR	HILLARD	MUNRO	PETTS	S TAYLOR	STONE	JARMAN	W JONES	MABBUTT	R WILLIAMS	R JONES	PARSONS 7	S TAYLOR
13/04/68	STOCKPORT COUNTY	A 1-3	5158	L TAYLOR	PARSONS	MUNRO	PETTS	S TAYLOR	STONE	JARMAN	MABBUTT	PLUMB	R WILLIAMS	R JONES	HILLARD 7	RONALDSON
15/04/68	TORQUAY UNITED	A 2-3	11401	L TAYLOR	HILLARD	MUNRO	PETTS	S TAYLOR	STONE	JARMAN	W JONES	MABBUTT	R WILLIAMS	R JONES	MUNRO 3	S TAYLOR, PLUMB, R WILLIAMS
20/04/68	BRIGHTON & H ALBION	A 3-1	6846	L TAYLOR	HILLARD	MUNRO	J WILLIAMS	S TAYLOR	STONE	GRAYDON	MABBUTT	PLUMB	R WILLIAMS	R JONES	R WILLIAMS 11	PETTS
23/04/68	SWINDON TOWN	H 1-4	11438	L TAYLOR	HILLARD	MUNRO	J WILLIAMS	S TAYLOR	MABBUTT	GRAYDON	W JONES	PLUMB	R WILLIAMS	R JONES		
27/04/68	SHREWSBURY TOWN	H 1-1	11401	L TAYLOR	HILLARD	STONE	J WILLIAMS	S TAYLOR	MABBUTT	GRAYDON	W JONES	PLUMB	R WILLIAMS	R JONES	JARMAN 10	S TAYLOR
30/04/68	LEYTON ORIENT	H 0-2	5749	L TAYLOR	HILLARD	STONE	J WILLIAMS	S TAYLOR	MABBUTT	GRAYDON	W JONES	PLUMB	RONALDSON	JARMAN		
04/05/68	SWINDON TOWN	A 1-2	8928	L TAYLOR	HILLARD	STONE	J WILLIAMS	S TAYLOR	PRINCE	GRAYDON	R JONES	W JONES	RONALDSON	JARMAN	MABBUTT 7	R JONES
11/05/68	OLDHAM ATHLETIC	A 5-3	2089	L TAYLOR	PARSONS	MUNRO	MABBUTT	S TAYLOR	PRINCE	JARMAN	R WILLIAMS	PLUMB	W JONES	R JONES		R JONES 2, W JONES, JARMAN, S TAYLOR

FA CUP

Date	Opponent	Res	ATT	G	2	3	4	5	6	7	8	9	10	11	Substitutes	Goalscorers
09/12/67	ARNOLD	A 3-0	3390	BRIGGS	HILLARD	MUNRO	J WILLIAMS	S TAYLOR	STONE	JARMAN	MABBUTT	BIGGS	W JONES	R JONES	PETTS 3	R JONES, JARMAN, SMITH og
06/01/68	WIMBLEDON	H 4-0	9536	L TAYLOR	HILLARD	MUNRO	J WILLIAMS	S TAYLOR	STONE	MABBUTT	W JONES	BIGGS	RONALDSON	R JONES		BIGGS 2, W JONES, RONALDSON
27/01/68	BRISTOL CITY	A 0-0	37237	L TAYLOR	HILLARD	MUNRO	J WILLIAMS	S TAYLOR	STONE	JARMAN	W JONES	BIGGS	W JONES	R JONES	RONALDSON 7	
30/01/68	BRISTOL CITY	H 1-2	30157	L TAYLOR	HILLARD	MUNRO	J WILLIAMS	S TAYLOR	STONE	JARMAN	W JONES	MABBUTT	W JONES	R JONES		S TAYLOR

LEAGUE CUP

Date	Opponent	Res	ATT	G	2	3	4	5	6	7	8	9	10	11	Substitutes	Goalscorers
23/08/67	READING	A 0-3	7821	L TAYLOR	MABBUTT	PARSONS	J WILLIAMS	S TAYLOR	PRINCE	JARMAN	BROWN	BIGGS	FRUDE	JARMAN	STONE 5	

GLOUCESTERSHIRE CUP FINAL

Date	Opponent	Res	ATT	G	2	3	4	5	6	7	8	9	10	11	Substitutes	Goalscorers
14/05/68	BRISTOL CITY	A 1-1	11375	L TAYLOR	PARSONS	MUNRO	J WILLIAMS	S TAYLOR	PRINCE	JARMAN	W JONES	BIGGS	W JONES	R JONES		MABBUTT

PLAYERS	APP	SUB	GLS
BARNEY V	10		
BIGGS A	31		10
BRIGGS R	23		
BROWN J	2		
FRUDE R	1	1	
GRAYDON R	12		1
HAMILTON I	1		
HILLARD D	37		1
JARMAN H	25	3	5
JONES R	43		10
JONES W	42		3
MABBUTT R	24	1	10
MUNRO A	38	2	2
PARSONS L	19	1	
PETTS J	11	3	1
PLUMB R	9		
PRINCE F	2		
RONALDSON K	23	3	7
STONE D	33	3	
TAYLOR L	23		
TAYLOR S	44		
WILLIAMS J	38		7
WILLIAMS R	15	1	9
OWN GOALS			3

would time it nearer 12 seconds. The future England manager, Graham Taylor, scored in Grimsby Town's 3-2 victory over Rovers in February, while Dennis Rofe, later a Rovers manager, was a teenage goalscoring substitute when Leyton Orient won at Eastville in April. Graham Clapham, whose son Jamie later played for Rovers, appeared in the Shrewsbury Town side against Rovers as the season drew to a close.

In the final weeks of the season, Bert Tann was elevated to the post of general manager and secretary. On 1 April 1968 the directors appointed 52-year-old Fred Ford as the new Rovers manager. A former team-mate at Charlton Athletic of fellow Rovers managers Bill Dodgin and Bert Tann, Ford had also played for Tottenham Hotspur, Millwall and Carlisle United before coaching Rovers between 1955 and 1960. Thereafter, as manager, he had led Bristol City back into Division Two in 1965 before taking over a coaching job at Swindon Town. His son Peter had represented the England rugby side as a flanker in four International fixtures in the spring of 1964. At Eastville, Fred Ford attempted to cobble together a young side, starting with the introduction of Frankie Prince in April.

Rovers' 1967/68 FA Cup run began in Nottinghamshire, where Midland League Arnold were defeated 3-0. Even after their merging with Arnold Kingswell in 1988, this first of two appearances by Arnold in round one of the FA Cup is preserved in the record books for having attracted a ground record attendance of 3,390 to the King George V Playing Fields. After a 4-0 win at Southern League Wimbledon, Rovers were drawn to play Bristol City at Ashton Gate. A well-earned goalless draw before a crowd of 37,237 was followed by the disappointment of defeat at home in the replay. The future Rovers midfielder Alan Ball was in the Everton side defeated 1-0 by West Bromwich Albion in the FA Cup final. Rovers were defeated 3-0 at Reading in the League Cup, which was won by Leeds United, the future Rovers player-manager Terry Cooper scoring the only goal against Arsenal in the final. He also won a Fairs Cup winner's medal after Leeds defeated the Hungarian side Ferencváros 1-0 on aggregate in the final.

On 26 May 1968, the famous Thirteen Arches railway bridge, which had commanded the local skyline, was demolished. 3,200 holes were drilled and when site supervisor John Turner pulled the plunger at the delayed time of 4.20 p.m., 6,000 spectators saw the viaduct collapse in 10 seconds. It took 40 lorries to clear up 4,500 tons of masonry and brickwork. In fact, only 11 arches fell at the first attempt and one shortly afterwards. The stubborn 13th pier was blown up at 7.00 a.m. on 13 June 1968.

1968/69

While the club's youth policy had been the starting point for much of Rovers' post-war development, new manager Fred Ford appreciated that it represented the best hope for the future. With the backing of Douglas Mearns Milne, the new chairman after five years on the board, Ford added new vigour to the development of young local talent. Rovers fielded a particularly young side in 1968/69, yet reached an FA Cup fifth round tie at Everton. Although there were many knocks along the way, the production of the 1973/74 promotion-season side was under way.

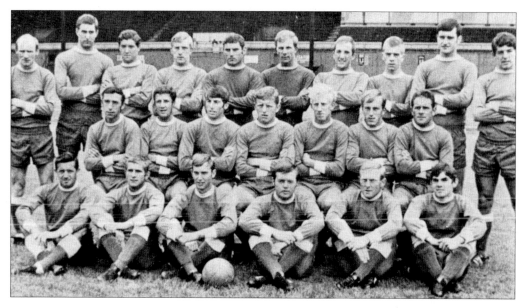

Bristol Rovers 1968/69. Back row: Munro, S Taylor, Lowrie, Roberts, White, L Taylor, Parsons, Prince, Lloyd, Stanton. Second row: Jarman, R Williams, Gadston, Plumb, Ronaldson, Graydon, R Jones. Front row: Mabbutt, Brown, Barney, W Jones, Petts, Higgins

Ford encouraged his younger players to play a pivotal role in the club's fortunes. Nineteen-year-old Larry Lloyd made his League debut on the opening day against Watford and, regardless of results, played in the first 43 League matches of the season. He and a youthful Stuart Taylor, tall and dominating in defence, were fondly known as the 'Twin Towers'. Taylor's 2 League goals included an excellent headed winner after 51 minutes against Oldham Athletic in October. Other players who came through the ranks broke into the side: 18-year-old left-winger Peter Higgins; Bobby Brown, a forward who was a year older; and goalkeeper Laurie Taylor. Glaswegian Tom Stanton, a signing from Mansfield Town, was just 20, a year younger than the former Millwall utility player Trevor Rhodes, once a Wimbledon tennis junior finalist. Rovers lost the experience of Dave Stone and Ronnie Briggs, who both moved to Southend United, and Doug Hillard, who joined Taunton Town, while John Brown's contract was reluctantly terminated as the talented inside forward was increasingly required to work extra shifts on the family farm in Cornwall. At a meeting on 29 August 1968, the Supporters' Club committee, including Eric Godfrey, chairman for 20 years, resigned *en masse* as a protest against the continued losses of the social club.

There was a new twist too, to the continuing development of Eastville Stadium. After much consultation work involving Freeman, Fox and Partners, the M32 motorway was to be constructed to link the city centre with the conveniently close interchange of the north-south M5 with the M4 to London and South Wales. This new 105-ft-wide 'Parkway' superhighway, announced at a cost of £15 million by city engineer James Bennett on 3 April 1964, had led to the demolition of 200 houses. The Minister of Transport Barbara Castle had allowed work to start on 17 May 1968 on a 2-mile stretch from Muller Road to Hambrook at a cost of some £3,263,000. On 14 March 1969 a

Fred Ford was appointed manager in 1968. He left on the eve of the 1969/70 season

£7.5 million second phase was agreed, which would overlook Eastville Stadium. This development finally obliterated the remains of the Baptist Mills Brass Works, a major feature of the area following its inception in 1702 by the Quakers on the site of an old grist mill. A Stapleton merchant, Nehemiah Champion, had been a founder. Abandoned in 1814, all traces now lie forever hidden beneath Junction 3 of the M32. The final buildings and a pear tree appertaining to the Baptist Mills Pottery, a source of great employment in 19th-century Eastville, also vanished for eternity beneath the new construction. There were also more direct implications as far as Eastville Stadium was concerned. An elevated section of the motorway was to cut across the corner between the South Stand and the Muller Road terraces and the hard-shoulder was to attract a steady supply of cars with mysterious ailments on match-days. 'Follow the Rovers,' the folk band The Bollards would sing years later, 'under the shade of the M32.' Eastville's dubious distinction of being the closest League ground to a motorway meant that the noise level became increasingly intrusive.

The highlight of the League season was a large home victory over Mansfield Town in March. Rovers had defeated Gillingham 5-1, with the indefatigable Ray Mabbutt scoring twice, and recorded 4-2 home wins against both Barrow and Barnsley. However, Mansfield's visit to Eastville culminated in the first 6-2 win in Rovers' League history. There was a four-goal flurry in six minutes midway through the first-half, starting with Ken Ronaldson's 18th-minute opener. No sooner had Malcolm Partridge equalised than Harold Jarman and Larry Lloyd, with the only goal of his Rovers career, gave the home side a 3-1 half-time lead. Bobby Brown added a fourth goal after 54 minutes and when Johnny Petts also scored, eight minutes later, victory was sealed. Although Jim Goodfellow pulled a goal back after 70 minutes, Jarman added his second of the game 10 minutes from the end to complete a comprehensive victory.

By means of contrast, the heaviest defeat of the season was a 6-1 defeat at the hands of unfashionable Crewe Alexandra at Gresty Road. Gordon Wallace, a former Liverpool inside left, put the home side ahead after half an hour and Keith Stott doubled the lead moments before half-time, only for Wayne Jones to fire an instant reply. As the second half started, Kevin McHale added a third and the home side provided three more goals before the end. John Regan's goal 22 minutes from the end was followed by two in the final six minutes – an own goal from the unfortunate Lindsay Parsons and a second goal from Regan. Crewe were relegated at the end of the season and Rovers' next visit to Gresty Road was to be in the 1989/90 Division Three Championship season.

While Rovers lost on their travels to each of the bottom three clubs in the division, they also defeated Swindon Town, destined for promotion to Division Two at the season's end. Rovers never won three consecutive League games, but lost four in succession in the spring, including a 4-2 defeat at Barnsley. Only the visits of Swindon Town and Orient drew five-figure crowds to Eastville, where the season's average attendance was 7,118. Of 23 players used, Taylor and Jarman missed just one League game each, with the latter top-scoring with 14 League goals, four more than Bobby Jones. Ray Mabbutt's appearance as centre-forward at Oldham Athletic on Boxing Day, in which he scored Rovers' goal in defeat, was the final one of almost 400 in which this highly dependable player had figured.

In November, towards the end of the convincing 4-2 home victory over Barrow, Ronaldson became the first Rovers substitute to score in League football. Just five days later, Kit Napier's hat-trick, the only one conceded all season by Rovers, earned Brighton a 3-1 victory at the Goldstone Ground. Rovers swiftly got into the habit of losing at regular intervals and by narrow margins. At no point in the season did the club put together a run of more than four consecutive matches without defeat, yet all but nine of the 19 League defeats were by a single goal. This record was tarnished somewhat by the fact that, once clear of relegation worries, Rovers lost both their last two matches 3-0 away to sides destined to lose their League status within a decade.

Towards the end of the season, two former Rovers trainees who had never made the first-team at Eastville, returned to haunt their former club. John Tedesco scored for Plymouth Argyle, who drew 1-1 at Eastville, while Laurie Sheffield claimed one of three goals Luton Town put past Rovers at Kenilworth Road. When the Bedfordshire club visited Eastville 12 days later, Rovers had Alex Munro sent off but held out for a goalless draw. In a late flurry of matches, Rovers won twice in a week against Stockport County and drew with promoted Swindon Town before a crowd of over 20,000 at the County Ground, before crashing to a heavy defeat at Holker Street, Tony Morrin scoring twice for Barrow.

A Swansea Town side inspired by the veteran Mel Nurse won 2-0 at Eastville to knock Rovers out of the League Cup where, in the final, Swindon Town shocked the footballing nation by defeating Arsenal, whose consolation goal was scored by the future Rovers player and manager, Bobby Gould. The Gloucestershire Cup final was disastrous from a Rovers point of view, with five Bristol City players scoring a second-half goal apiece at Eastville to inflict the club's heaviest defeat in the tournament since a 7-1 thrashing at Warmley in February 1892. All this was forgotten, though, as Rovers enjoyed a run of seven FA Cup games, losing only to a solitary goal at Everton in the fifth round.

As is often the way, a stuttering cup run slowly gathered momentum as it progressed. Peterborough United were beaten 3-1 at Eastville and Rovers held out for a goalless draw at Bournemouth, before scraping through in a replay through a solitary Graydon goal. The same player saved Rovers with the club's equalising goal in round three as

FOOTBALL LEAGUE DIVISION THREE

SEASON 1968/69

Date	H/A	Opponents	Score	ATT	G	2	3	4	5	6	7	8	9	10	11	SUBSTITUTES	GOALSCORERS
10/08/68	H	WATFORD	1-1	8077	L TAYLOR	PARSONS	STANTON	S TAYLOR	LLOYD	PRINCE	GRAYDON	R JONES	PLUMB	R JONES	JARMAN		PRINCE
17/08/68	A	WALSALL	2-2	7593	L TAYLOR	PARSONS	STANTON	S TAYLOR	LLOYD	PRINCE	GRAYDON	R JONES	PLUMB	R JONES	JARMAN	BARNEY V	BROWN R
24/08/68	A	BOURNEMOUTH	3-2	6671	L TAYLOR	PARSONS	STANTON	S TAYLOR	LLOYD	PRINCE	GRAYDON	R JONES	W JONES	R JONES	JARMAN	GRAYDON 9	R JONES, JARMAN
27/08/68	H	SHREWSBURY TOWN	3-2	7817	L TAYLOR	PARSONS	STANTON	S TAYLOR	LLOYD	PRINCE	GRAYDON	R JONES	W JONES	R JONES	JARMAN		GADSTON 2, W JONES
31/08/68	A	CREWE ALEXANDRA	1-6	6835	L TAYLOR	PARSONS	STANTON	S TAYLOR	LLOYD	PRINCE	GRAYDON	R JONES	W JONES	R JONES	JARMAN		W JONES
06/09/68	H	HARTLEPOOL UNITED	2-1	7284	L TAYLOR	PARSONS	STANTON	S TAYLOR	LLOYD	PRINCE	GRAYDON	J WILLIAMS	MABBUTT	BROWN	JARMAN		GADSTON 2, W JONES
14/09/68	A	PLYMOUTH ARGYLE	1-3	9333	L TAYLOR	PARSONS	STANTON	S TAYLOR	LLOYD	PRINCE	GRAYDON	J WILLIAMS	MABBUTT	W JONES	JARMAN		JARMAN H
21/09/68	H	NORTHAMPTON TOWN	2-2	8002	L TAYLOR	PARSONS	MABBUTT	S TAYLOR	LLOYD	PRINCE	JARMAN	BARNEY	W JONES	RONALDSON	JARMAN	J WILLIAMS 8	RONALDSON, S TAYLOR
27/09/68	A	SWINDON TOWN	1-3	10364	WHITE	MABBUTT	STANTON	S TAYLOR	LLOYD	PRINCE	JARMAN	W JONES	W JONES	RONALDSON	HIGGINS		JARMAN
05/10/68	H	READING	1-0	10218	WHITE	MABBUTT	STANTON	S TAYLOR	LLOYD	PRINCE	RONALDSON	W JONES	W JONES	W JONES	HIGGINS		
09/10/68	H	OLDHAM ATHLETIC	2-1	6225	L TAYLOR	MABBUTT	STANTON	S TAYLOR	LLOYD	PRINCE	RONALDSON	W JONES	W JONES	W JONES	HIGGINS		R JONES 2+1pen, JARMAN
12/10/68	A	SHREWSBURY TOWN	1-2	6209	L TAYLOR	MABBUTT	STANTON	S TAYLOR	LLOYD	PRINCE	GRAYDON	BARNEY	W JONES	W JONES	JARMAN		RONALDSON
19/10/68	H	ROTHERHAM UNITED	0-1	9693	L TAYLOR	MABBUTT	STANTON	S TAYLOR	LLOYD	PRINCE	GRAYDON	BARNEY	W JONES	W JONES	JARMAN		
26/10/68	A	GILLINGHAM	5-1	5551	L TAYLOR	MABBUTT	STANTON	S TAYLOR	LLOYD	PRINCE	GRAYDON	R JONES	MABBUTT	W JONES	JARMAN		MABBUTT 2, R WILLIAMS, JARMAN, GRAYDON
26/10/68	H	MANSFIELD TOWN	0-0	5608	L TAYLOR	PARSONS	STANTON	S TAYLOR	LLOYD	PETTS	GRAYDON	R WILLIAMS	RHODES	W JONES	JARMAN	R WILLIAMS, JARMAN	
02/11/68	A	TRANMERE ROVERS	0-2	6250	L TAYLOR	PARSONS	STANTON	S TAYLOR	LLOYD	PETTS	GRAYDON	R WILLIAMS	PLUMB	W JONES	JARMAN	PLUMB R	GRAYDON, BROWN
04/11/68	H	BARROW	4-2	4937	L TAYLOR	PARSONS	STANTON	S TAYLOR	LLOYD	PETTS	GRAYDON	R JONES	MABBUTT	W JONES	JARMAN	MABBUTT 2, R WILLIAMS, JARMAN, GRAYDON	JARMAN 2, BARNEY, GRAYDON
09/11/68	A	BRIGHTON & H ALBION	1-3	6395	L TAYLOR	PARSONS	STANTON	S TAYLOR	LLOYD	PETTS	W JONES	R JONES	MABBUTT	RONALDSON	JARMAN	RONALDSON 10	R JONES 2+1pen, JARMAN
23/11/68	A	LEYTON ORIENT	2-1	3442	L TAYLOR	PARSONS	STANTON	S TAYLOR	LLOYD	PETTS	W JONES	R JONES	MABBUTT	RONALDSON	JARMAN	RONALDSON	
30/11/68	H	SOUTHPORT	2-1	4768	L TAYLOR	PARSONS	STANTON	S TAYLOR	LLOYD	PETTS	W JONES	R JONES	MABBUTT	W JONES	JARMAN	MABBUTT	W JONES, GRAYDON
13/12/68	A	ROTHERHAM UNITED	1-1	5611	L TAYLOR	PARSONS	STANTON	S TAYLOR	LLOYD	PETTS	GRAYDON	R JONES	MABBUTT	W JONES	JARMAN	R JONES	
21/12/68	H	GILLINGHAM	2-0	4289	L TAYLOR	PARSONS	STANTON	S TAYLOR	LLOYD	PETTS	GRAYDON	R JONES	W JONES	W JONES	JARMAN		R JONES 2+1pen
26/12/68	A	OLDHAM ATHLETIC	1-2	6796	L TAYLOR	PARSONS	STANTON	S TAYLOR	LLOYD	PETTS	GRAYDON	R JONES	W JONES	W JONES	JARMAN		
18/01/69	H	TRANMERE ROVERS	2-1	5604	L TAYLOR	PARSONS	STANTON	S TAYLOR	LLOYD	PETTS	GRAYDON	R JONES	W JONES	W JONES	JARMAN		
01/02/69	H	BRIGHTON & H ALBION	2-1	8002	L TAYLOR	PARSONS	STANTON	S TAYLOR	LLOYD	PETTS	GRAYDON	R JONES	MABBUTT	W JONES	JARMAN		
18/02/69	A	TORQUAY UNITED	1-0	7373	L TAYLOR	PARSONS	STANTON	S TAYLOR	LLOYD	PETTS	GRAYDON	BARNEY	W JONES	BROWN	JARMAN		
24/02/69	A	BARNSLEY	1-0	6781	L TAYLOR	PARSONS	STANTON	S TAYLOR	LLOYD	PETTS	GRAYDON	BARNEY	W JONES	BROWN	JARMAN		
01/03/69	H	LEYTON ORIENT	4-2	10211	L TAYLOR	PARSONS	STANTON	S TAYLOR	LLOYD	PETTS	GRAYDON	BARNEY	W JONES	BROWN	JARMAN		
04/03/69	A	WATFORD	0-1	13554	L TAYLOR	PARSONS	STANTON	S TAYLOR	LLOYD	PETTS	GRAYDON	BARNEY	W JONES	BROWN	JARMAN		
08/03/69	H	BARNSLEY	2-4	7760	L TAYLOR	PARSONS	STANTON	S TAYLOR	LLOYD	PETTS	GRAYDON	BARNEY	W JONES	BROWN	JARMAN		
11/03/69	H	TORQUAY UNITED	0-1	7199	L TAYLOR	PARSONS	STANTON	S TAYLOR	LLOYD	PETTS	GRAYDON	BARNEY	W JONES	BROWN	JARMAN	GRAYDON, BROWN	
15/03/69	A	BOURNEMOUTH	1-1	7433	L TAYLOR	PARSONS	STANTON	S TAYLOR	LLOYD	PETTS	GRAYDON	BARNEY	W JONES	BROWN	JARMAN		
19/03/69	A	LUTON TOWN	0-3	6989	L TAYLOR	PARSONS	PARSONS	S TAYLOR	LLOYD	PETTS	RONALDSON	BARNEY	W JONES	BROWN	JARMAN		
21/03/69	H	CREWE ALEXANDRA	1-0	14506	L TAYLOR	PARSONS	STANTON	S TAYLOR	LLOYD	PETTS	GRAYDON	BARNEY	W JONES	BROWN	HIGGINS		
25/03/69	H	MANSFIELD TOWN	1-0	5795	L TAYLOR	PARSONS	STANTON	S TAYLOR	LLOYD	PETTS	GRAYDON	BARNEY	MABBUTT	BROWN	JARMAN		
28/03/69	A	HARTLEPOOL UNITED	6-2	5482	L TAYLOR	PARSONS	STANTON	S TAYLOR	LLOYD	PETTS	JARMAN	RONALDSON	W JONES	W JONES	R JONES	JARMAN	RONALDSON, JARMAN 2, LLOYD, BROWN, PETTS
31/03/69	A	LUTON TOWN	0-1	3447	L TAYLOR	PARSONS	STANTON	S TAYLOR	LLOYD	PETTS	JARMAN	RONALDSON	W JONES	W JONES	R JONES		
04/04/69	H	READING	1-0	8112	L TAYLOR	PARSONS	STANTON	S TAYLOR	LLOYD	PETTS	JARMAN	RONALDSON	W JONES	W JONES	R JONES		
05/04/69	H	NORTHAMPTON TOWN	1-3	9424	L TAYLOR	PARSONS	STANTON	S TAYLOR	LLOYD	PETTS	GRAYDON	BARNEY	MABBUTT	BROWN	R JONES		
07/04/69	H	STOCKPORT COUNTY	1-3	6704	L TAYLOR	PARSONS	STANTON	S TAYLOR	LLOYD	PETTS	GRAYDON	BROWN	W JONES	BROWN	R JONES		
12/04/69	A	SWINDON TOWN	1-3	5486	L TAYLOR	PARSONS	STANTON	S TAYLOR	LLOYD	PETTS	JARMAN	RONALDSON	W JONES	GADSTON	MUNRO		
15/04/69	A	STOCKPORT COUNTY	2-2	20401	L TAYLOR	PARSONS	STANTON	S TAYLOR	LLOYD	PETTS	JARMAN	RONALDSON	W JONES	GADSTON	R WILLIAMS		
19/04/69	A	PLYMOUTH ARGYLE	2-0	6053	L TAYLOR	PARSONS	STANTON	S TAYLOR	LLOYD	PETTS	JARMAN	RONALDSON	W JONES	GADSTON	R WILLIAMS		
21/04/69	H	BARROW	1-1	8699	L TAYLOR	PARSONS	STANTON	S TAYLOR	LLOYD	PETTS	JARMAN	RONALDSON	W JONES	GADSTON	R WILLIAMS		
23/04/69	A	SOUTHPORT	0-3	3178	L TAYLOR	LLOYD	STANTON	S TAYLOR	S TAYLOR	PETTS	JARMAN	BROWN	W JONES	GADSTON	R WILLIAMS		
28/04/69	A	SOUTHPORT	0-3	3506	L TAYLOR	S TAYLOR	PARSONS	R JONES	S TAYLOR	PETTS	BROWN	BARNEY	W JONES	GADSTON	R WILLIAMS		

FA CUP

Date	H/A	Opponents	Score	ATT	G	2	3	4	5	6	7	8	9	10	11	SUBSTITUTES	GOALSCORERS
16/11/68	H	PETERBOROUGH UNITED	3-1	7108	L TAYLOR	PARSONS	STANTON	S TAYLOR	LLOYD	PETTS	GRAYDON	R JONES	MABBUTT	RONALDSON	JARMAN		STANTON, MABBUTT, GRAYDON
07/12/68	A	BOURNEMOUTH	0-0	10914	L TAYLOR	PARSONS	STANTON	S TAYLOR	LLOYD	PETTS	GRAYDON	R JONES	MABBUTT	W JONES	JARMAN	BARNEY, JARMAN	
10/12/68	H	BOURNEMOUTH	1-0	11898	L TAYLOR	PARSONS	STANTON	S TAYLOR	LLOYD	PETTS	GRAYDON	R JONES	MABBUTT	W JONES	JARMAN	BROWN	BROWN
04/01/69	H	KETTERING TOWN	1-1	12230	L TAYLOR	PARSONS	STANTON	S TAYLOR	LLOYD	PETTS	GRAYDON	R JONES	MABBUTT	W JONES	JARMAN	GADSTON, W JONES	GADSTON
07/01/69	A	KETTERING TOWN	2-1	9650	L TAYLOR	PARSONS	STANTON	S TAYLOR	LLOYD	PETTS	GRAYDON	R JONES	MABBUTT	W JONES	JARMAN	GADSTON, W JONES	GADSTON, W JONES
25/01/69	H	BOLTON WANDERERS	2-1	16707	L TAYLOR	PARSONS	STANTON	S TAYLOR	LLOYD	PETTS	GRAYDON	R JONES	MABBUTT	W JONES	JARMAN	W JONES	S TAYLOR, GAMMON og
12/02/69	A	EVERTON	0-1	55294	L TAYLOR	PARSONS	STANTON	S TAYLOR	LLOYD	PETTS	GRAYDON	R JONES	MABBUTT	W JONES	JARMAN		

LEAGUE CUP

Date	H/A	Opponents	Score	ATT	G	2	3	4	5	6	7	8	9	10	11	SUBSTITUTES	GOALSCORERS
13/08/68	H	SWANSEA TOWN	0-2	5015	L TAYLOR	PARSONS	MABBUTT	S TAYLOR	LLOYD	PRINCE	GRAYDON	R JONES	PLUMB	R JONES	JARMAN	GADSTON 9	

GLOUCESTERSHIRE CUP FINAL

Date	H/A	Opponents	Score	ATT	G	2	3	4	5	6	7	8	9	10	11	SUBSTITUTES	GOALSCORERS
28/04/69	H	BRISTOL CITY	0-5	14735	L TAYLOR	PARSONS	STANTON	R JONES	LLOYD	PETTS	GRAYDON	BARNEY	PLUMB	BROWN	JARMAN	W JONES 9	

PLAYERS	APP	SUB	GLS
BARNEY V	19		3
BROWN R	20		5
GADSTON J	10		1
GRAYDON R	26	2	6
HIGGINS P	2		
JARMAN H	45		14
JONES R	41		10
JONES W	42		6
LLOYD L	43		4
MABBUTT R	19		4
MUNRO A	1		
PARSONS L	32	1	
PETTS J	32		2
PLUMB R	5		
PRINCE F	11		
RHODES T	2		
RONALDSON K	17	2	3
STANTON T	43		1
TAYLOR L	43		
TAYLOR S	45		2
WHITE K	3		
WILLIAMS J	7	2	
WILLIAMS R	9	2	
OWN GOALS			1

non-League Kettering Town held on to a 1-1 draw at Eastville. It was with some trepidation that Rovers went to Rockingham Road, where League sides had struggled before, but despite going a goal down and relying on Laurie Taylor to save a 65th-minute penalty, victory was secured when Kettering player-manager Steve Gammon conceded a very late own goal. Rovers were drawn away to Division Two Bolton Wanderers, and fell behind to Gareth Williams before two goals from substitute Wayne Jones brought an unexpected win and a snow-delayed fifth round tie before a crowd of 55,294 at Goodison Park. Everton, beaten finalists in 1967/68, fielded Alan Ball, later a Rovers player, and Ray Wilson, both World Cup winners with England in 1966, and won through a Joe Royle goal after 33 minutes, set up by Ball's astute through pass.

One side-effect of the long FA Cup run was national attention on a number of players in the young Rovers side. The Liverpool manager Bill Shankly watched the Everton Cup tie and was to pay Rovers a club-record fee of £55,000 for Larry Lloyd before the season was out. Although Lloyd had appeared in only 51 League and cup games, Shankly had no hesitation in putting his faith in the centre-half's potential. Lloyd was to share in much of the success experienced on Merseyside in the 1970s, winning European Cup winner's medals with Liverpool and Nottingham Forest as well as playing for England. The profit from his sale was swallowed up by the club's overdraft.

1969/70

On the eve of the new season, manager Fred Ford left Rovers after 18 months to accept the vacant post of manager at Swindon Town. This was a blow to Rovers, whose youth policy, inspired by their former coach, was developing further. Ford was to coach at Torquay United and Oxford United, continuing to instil his football experience in his young protégés up to his death in October 1981. In a surprising yet highly effective move, the Rovers directors appointed Bill Dodgin from within. The 58-year-old former Rovers wing-half had managed Southampton, Fulham and Brentford, though he had not held a full-time job as manager for 12 years. His appointment, temporary at first, was made permanent on 19 December 1969 and he stayed in the job until July 1972.

Rovers' supporters were in for some exciting years, for Dodgin's football philosophy was attack-minded and Rovers managed top-six finishes in each of his years in charge. Rovers started the new season with three new faces – Bristol-born goalkeeper Dick Sheppard, a free transfer from West Bromwich Albion; wing-half Gordon Marsland, who arrived in a £6,000 deal from Carlisle United; and the £10,000 centre-forward Robin Stubbs, a legendary figure for many years at Torquay United. Stubbs was top scorer for two seasons, scoring 15 League goals in 1969/70, though Ray Graydon, Harold Jarman and Carl Gilbert all reached double figures. Another new name was Phil Roberts, a 19-year-old former Rovers apprentice, who was to win four Welsh caps after his high-profile move to Portsmouth in 1973.

Some more familiar faces had left, with Ray Mabbutt joining Newport County, Joe Gadston Exeter City and Trevor Rhodes Bath City. Dick Plumb was to become the

Bristol Rovers 1969/70. Back row: S Taylor, Sheppard, Munro, Stanton, L Taylor, Stubbs. Middle row: Campbell (Trainer), R Jones, Ronaldson, Parsons, Petts, B Jones, Marsland, Dodgin (Manager). Front row: Graydon, Brown, Prince, Jarman, Gadston, W Jones

second-highest goalscorer in Yeovil Town's history. After Rovers had lost 1-0 to Gilbert's 50th-minute goal at Gillingham in September, the 21-year-old striker moved to Eastville in an exchange deal that saw Ken Ronaldson make the opposite journey. At this stage, Rovers also found £4,000 to attract the experienced Bristol City full-back Tony Ford to move across the city.

Rovers adopted white shorts from the summer of 1969 to their otherwise all-blue kit. At the start of the season, Rovers hosted the American touring side Dallas Tornado, coached by the former Portsmouth centre-forward Ron Newman. A crowd of 4,313 saw Stubbs and Bobby Jones score in the five minutes prior to half-time and a further burst of goals, from Harold Jarman and Stuart Taylor after 65 and 68 minutes respectively, earned Rovers a comfortable 4-0 win. This form was carried over into League action, where Rovers opened with a goalless draw at Southport, where they had suffered a heavy defeat in their previous game. Rovers dropped just two points in their opening five League matches and suffered only three defeats in the first 16. By the end of October, the club was riding high in Division Three and promotion looked a realistic proposition.

In the opening 14 league fixtures, Rovers scored at least three goals on eight occasions. Stubbs scored twice in a 3-0 win against Tranmere Rovers, when Bryn Jones was given a League debut, and there were identical wins against Brighton and at home to Rotherham United. Rovers drew with Mansfield Town, who lost Jim Goodfellow with a fractured jaw after a collision with Lindsay Parsons. There was also an astonishing 3-3 draw at Eastville in the first-ever League meeting with Rochdale, Tony

Buck scoring a hat-trick for the visitors and still not ending up on the winning side. Rochdale followed up this result with eight consecutive League victories, still a club record run, yet drew their first four meetings with Rovers. However, Rovers' largest win of the season came at Reading where, in a forerunner to the fixture in January 1999, they won 5-1. Rovers led 3-0 after eight minutes, through Ray Graydon, a Colin Meldrum own goal and Bobby Jones, with Graydon adding his second of the game two minutes before half-time. Stubbs put Rovers 5-0 ahead after 48 minutes with Les Chappell, who also scored at Eastville in the return fixture, adding a consolation goal 18 minutes from time.

The good run could not last, however, and Rovers won just the once in their final nine League games of 1969. In each of the last eight League matches of the calendar year, bizarrely, Rovers scored exactly one goal. This run was finished by a convincing 4-1 home win against Mansfield Town, Frankie Prince, a product of the youth scheme, opening the scoring after

Harold Jarman, one of the most talented and popular footballers to play for Rovers. He enjoyed a long career scoring 127 goals in 452 League appearances for the club. He was briefly manager of the club in 1979/80 Jarman has contributed much to the history of Rovers

10 minutes from Bryn Jones' pass and Jarman adding a solo second a minute later. The third goal was an own goal attributed to Sandy Pate, who also put through his own goal at Eastville in March 1972, thus becoming the only opponent to score twice in the League for Rovers. Thereafter, Rovers were able to record 4-2 and 5-2 wins over Bradford City and Bournemouth respectively to finish the season with 80 League goals to their name, the highest total for five years.

After Christmas, Rovers drew four consecutive away matches. One of these was a goalless draw at Millmoor, whereby Rotherham United set a club record as it was their 18th game undefeated since they had lost at Eastville in October, the first six matches in this run having resulted in draws. At the same time, Rovers embarked on a run of six consecutive home League victories, which propelled the side towards the top of the division. The first of these was a 3-0 win against Luton Town, in which both Rovers' full-backs, Ford and Alex Munro, scored penalties, the only occasion that two Rovers players have done so in a League game. This match acted as a form of revenge as Luton Town, promoted at the end of the season, had exacted a 4-0 defeat in September, with the future England centre-forward Malcolm MacDonald scoring one of their goals.

Going into the final few games, Rovers had not conceded three goals in a League game since mid-December. Back-to-back 2-1 wins over Barrow – for whom Jim Mulvaney scored in both meetings with Rovers and Torquay United, for whom Alan Welsh did likewise, as did Stubbs, against his former club – left Rovers in a strong

SEASON 1969/70

Football League Division Three

Date		Opponent	Res	Att	1	2	3	4	5	6	7	8	9	10	11	Substitutes	Goalscorers
09/08/69	A	SOUTHPORT	0-0	3262	SHEPPARD	STANTON	MUNRO	PETTS	S TAYLOR	MARSLAND	GRAYDON	W JONES	STUBBS	R JONES	JARMAN		
16/08/69	H	BARNSLEY	3-3	7348	SHEPPARD	PARSONS	MUNRO	BARNEY	S TAYLOR	MARSLAND	GRAYDON	W JONES	STUBBS	R JONES	JARMAN	B JONES 4	GRAYDON, STUBBS, R JONES
23/08/69	H	READING	5-1	8105	SHEPPARD	PARSONS	MUNRO	ROBERTS	S TAYLOR	MARSLAND	GRAYDON	W JONES	STUBBS	R JONES	JARMAN		GRAYDON 2, MELDRUM og, R JONES, STUBBS
27/08/69	A	PLYMOUTH ARGYLE	1-1	11562	SHEPPARD	PARSONS	MUNRO	ROBERTS	S TAYLOR	MARSLAND	GRAYDON	W JONES	STUBBS	R JONES	JARMAN		MARSLAND, R JONES, STUBBS
30/08/69	H	HALIFAX TOWN	2-0	15198	SHEPPARD	PARSONS	MUNRO	ROBERTS	S TAYLOR	MARSLAND	GRAYDON	W JONES	STUBBS	R JONES	JARMAN	JARMAN 2+1pen	
06/09/69	H	LUTON TOWN	0-4	11768	SHEPPARD	PARSONS	MUNRO	ROBERTS	S TAYLOR	MARSLAND	GRAYDON	W JONES	STUBBS	R JONES	JARMAN		
13/09/69	H	FULHAM	3-2	10633	SHEPPARD	PARSONS	MUNRO	ROBERTS	S TAYLOR	MUNRO	GRAYDON	W JONES	STUBBS	R JONES	JARMAN		JARMAN pen, STUBBS, GRAYDON
17/09/69	H	GILLINGHAM	1-1	5397	SHEPPARD	ROBERTS	PARSONS	MARSLAND	S TAYLOR	MUNRO	GRAYDON	W JONES	STUBBS	R JONES	JARMAN	HIGGINS P	HIGGINS P
20/09/69	A	MANSFIELD TOWN	1-1	6742	SHEPPARD	ROBERTS	PARSONS	MARSLAND	S TAYLOR	MUNRO	GRAYDON	W JONES	STUBBS	R JONES	JARMAN		GRAYDON R
27/09/69	A	ROCHDALE	0-0	8652	SHEPPARD	ROBERTS	PARSONS	MARSLAND	S TAYLOR	MUNRO	GRAYDON	W JONES	STUBBS	R JONES	JARMAN		
30/09/69	H	TRANMERE ROVERS	3-0	9152	SHEPPARD	ROBERTS	STANTON	MARSLAND	S TAYLOR	MUNRO	GRAYDON	W JONES	STUBBS	R JONES	JARMAN	MARSLAND	W JONES, GRAYDON, JARMAN
04/10/69	A	BRIGHTON & H ALBION	3-0	11417	SHEPPARD	ROBERTS	STANTON	MARSLAND	S TAYLOR	MUNRO	GRAYDON	W JONES	STUBBS	R JONES	JARMAN		GRAYDON 2
07/10/69	H	BARNSLEY	0-0	10008	SHEPPARD	ROBERTS	MARSLAND	PRINCE	S TAYLOR	MUNRO	GRAYDON	W JONES	STUBBS	R JONES	JARMAN		
11/10/69	H	ROTHERHAM UNITED	3-0	8807	SHEPPARD	ROBERTS	STANTON	MARSLAND	S TAYLOR	PRINCE	GRAYDON	B JONES	STUBBS	R JONES	JARMAN		STUBBS 2, JARMAN
18/10/69	H	BURY	2-1	10002	SHEPPARD	ROBERTS	STANTON	MARSLAND	S TAYLOR	PRINCE	GRAYDON	B JONES	STUBBS	R JONES	JARMAN		STUBBS, GRAYDON, R JONES
25/10/69	A	BOURNEMOUTH	2-2	6873	SHEPPARD	ROBERTS	STANTON	MARSLAND	S TAYLOR	PRINCE	GRAYDON	B JONES	STUBBS	R JONES	JARMAN		MARSLAND G
01/11/69	H	SHREWSBURY TOWN	1-3	10065	SHEPPARD	ROBERTS	STANTON	MARSLAND	S TAYLOR	PRINCE	GRAYDON	B JONES	STUBBS	R JONES	JARMAN		MUNRO A
08/11/69	A	DONCASTER ROVERS	1-1	8986	SHEPPARD	ROBERTS	STANTON	MARSLAND	S TAYLOR	PRINCE	GRAYDON	B JONES	STUBBS	R JONES	JARMAN		PARSONS L
22/11/69	A	BRADFORD CITY	1-0	2941	SHEPPARD	ROBERTS	PARSONS	MARSLAND	S TAYLOR	PRINCE	GRAYDON	B JONES	STUBBS	R JONES	JARMAN		W JONES, STUBBS
24/11/69	H	STOCKPORT COUNTY	1-0	3080	SHEPPARD	ROBERTS	PARSONS	MARSLAND	S TAYLOR	MUNRO	GRAYDON	B JONES	STUBBS	R JONES	JARMAN		R JONES
29/11/69	A	BARROW	1-1	6675	SHEPPARD	PARSONS	MUNRO	ROBERTS	S TAYLOR	MARSLAND	GRAYDON	B JONES	STUBBS	R JONES	JARMAN		R JONES
13/12/69	H	FULHAM	1-3	12035	L TAYLOR	PARSONS	MUNRO	ROBERTS	S TAYLOR	MARSLAND	GRAYDON	B JONES	STUBBS	R JONES	JARMAN		W JONES
26/12/69	A	READING	1-1	5388	SHEPPARD	PARSONS	MUNRO	ROBERTS	S TAYLOR	MARSLAND	GRAYDON	B JONES	STUBBS	R JONES	JARMAN	S TAYLOR	JARMAN
27/12/69	A	HALIFAX TOWN	4-1	5986	SHEPPARD	PARSONS	MUNRO	ROBERTS	S TAYLOR	PRINCE	GRAYDON	B JONES	STUBBS	R JONES	JARMAN		JARMAN, STUBBS, R JONES
10/01/70	A	MANSFIELD TOWN	1-1	6701	SHEPPARD	PARSONS	MUNRO	ROBERTS	S TAYLOR	PRINCE	GRAYDON	B JONES	STUBBS	R JONES	JARMAN	GILBERT	GRAYDON 2
17/01/70	H	ROCHDALE	4-1	11356	SHEPPARD	PARSONS	MUNRO	ROBERTS	S TAYLOR	PRINCE	GRAYDON	B JONES	STUBBS	R JONES	JARMAN	R JONES 9	GRAYDON, JARMAN, PATE og, GILBERT
24/01/70	A	TORQUAY UNITED	3-1	11820	SHEPPARD	PARSONS	MUNRO	ROBERTS	S TAYLOR	PRINCE	GRAYDON	B JONES	R JONES	GILBERT	JARMAN	R JONES 7	PRINCE, JARMAN, PATE og, GILBERT
31/01/70	H	BRIGHTON & H ALBION	0-2	10095	SHEPPARD	PARSONS	MUNRO	ROBERTS	S TAYLOR	STANTON	GRAYDON	B JONES	R JONES	GILBERT	JARMAN	S TAYLOR	
07/02/70	H	ROTHERHAM UNITED	3-1	11668	SHEPPARD	ROBERTS	MUNRO	STANTON	S TAYLOR	PRINCE	GRAYDON	W JONES	R JONES	GILBERT	JARMAN	GILBERT	GILBERT, JARMAN, STUBBS
10/02/70	H	LUTON TOWN	3-0	13297	SHEPPARD	ROBERTS	MUNRO	STANTON	S TAYLOR	PRINCE	GRAYDON	W JONES	R JONES	GILBERT	HIGGINS		GRAYDON, MUNRO, FORD pen
14/02/70	A	BOURNEMOUTH	0-0	10834	SHEPPARD	ROBERTS	MUNRO	STANTON	S TAYLOR	PRINCE	GRAYDON	W JONES	R JONES	GILBERT	HIGGINS	STUBBS 11	
21/02/70	H	BURY	5-2	10095	SHEPPARD	ROBERTS	MUNRO	STANTON	S TAYLOR	PRINCE	GRAYDON	W JONES	STUBBS	GILBERT	HIGGINS	JARMAN 7	STUBBS 2, GILBERT, W JONES, B JONES
28/02/70	H	WALSALL	2-2	3634	SHEPPARD	ROBERTS	MUNRO	MECSON	S TAYLOR	PRINCE	GRAYDON	W JONES	STUBBS	GILBERT	JARMAN		ATTHEY og, STUBBS, MUNRO pen
03/03/70	A	BRADFORD CITY	3-2	9230	SHEPPARD	ROBERTS	MUNRO	MECSON	S TAYLOR	PRINCE	GRAYDON	W JONES	STUBBS	GILBERT	JARMAN		STUBBS, HIGGINS
07/03/70	A	LEYTON ORIENT	4-2	14334	SHEPPARD	ROBERTS	MUNRO	MECSON	S TAYLOR	PRINCE	GRAYDON	W JONES	STUBBS	GILBERT	JARMAN	JARMAN 7	GRAYDON 2, GILBERT, W JONES, B JONES
14/03/70	A	SOUTHPORT	3-1	11527	SHEPPARD	ROBERTS	MUNRO	MECSON	S TAYLOR	PRINCE	GRAYDON	W JONES	STUBBS	GILBERT	JARMAN	STUBBS 11	STUBBS, GILBERT, MUNRO pen
18/03/70	H	TORQUAY UNITED	2-1	8092	SHEPPARD	ROBERTS	MUNRO	MECSON	S TAYLOR	PRINCE	GRAYDON	W JONES	STUBBS	GILBERT	JARMAN	STUBBS, GILBERT	STUBBS, GILBERT
21/03/70	A	WALSALL	1-2	4442	SHEPPARD	ROBERTS	MUNRO	MECSON	S TAYLOR	PRINCE	GRAYDON	W JONES	STUBBS	GILBERT	HIGGINS	GILBERT, MUNRO pen	GILBERT, MUNRO pen
28/03/70	H	SHREWSBURY TOWN	1-2	22005	SHEPPARD	ROBERTS	MUNRO	MECSON	S TAYLOR	PRINCE	GRAYDON	W JONES	STUBBS	GILBERT	ALLAN	ALLAN 8	HIGGINS
30/03/70	A	LEYTON ORIENT	2-1	6178	SHEPPARD	ROBERTS	MUNRO	MECSON	S TAYLOR	ALLAN	GRAYDON	W JONES	STUBBS	GILBERT	HIGGINS		GILBERT, HIGGINS
31/03/70	H	DONCASTER ROVERS	0-0	19040	SHEPPARD	ROBERTS	MUNRO	MECSON	S TAYLOR	HIGGINS	GRAYDON	W JONES	STUBBS	GILBERT	ALLAN	ALLAN 2	BRANFOOT og
04/04/70	H	PLYMOUTH ARGYLE	3-0	11142	L TAYLOR	ROBERTS	MUNRO	MECSON	S TAYLOR	HIGGINS	GRAYDON	W JONES	STUBBS	GILBERT	ALLAN	ALLAN	ALLAN 2
07/04/70	A	STOCKPORT COUNTY	2-2	17559	SHEPPARD	ROBERTS	MUNRO	MECSON	S TAYLOR	HIGGINS	JARMAN	W JONES	STUBBS	ALLAN	GILBERT	GILBERT 10	ALLAN
14/04/70	H	GILLINGHAM	1-0	18978	SHEPPARD	ROBERTS	MUNRO	MECSON	S TAYLOR	HIGGINS	JARMAN	W JONES	STUBBS	ALLAN	GILBERT	GILBERT	ALLAN
17/04/70	H	TRANMERE ROVERS	2-5	5682	SHEPPARD	STANTON	MUNRO	MECSON	S TAYLOR	PARSONS	JARMAN	W JONES	GILBERT	ALLAN	R JONES	GILBERT 2	GILBERT 2

FA CUP

Date		Opponent	Res	Att	1	2	3	4	5	6	7	8	9	10	11	Substitutes	Goalscorers
15/11/69	H	TELFORD UNITED	3-0	4595	L TAYLOR	STANTON	MUNRO	ROBERTS	S TAYLOR	PRINCE	GRAYDON	W JONES	STUBBS	R JONES	JARMAN	PETTS	STUBBS, R JONES, GRAYDON
06/12/69	A	ALDERSHOT	1-3	9030	L TAYLOR	STANTON	MUNRO	ROBERTS	S TAYLOR	PRINCE	GRAYDON	W JONES	STUBBS	R JONES	JARMAN	STANTON	STUBBS

LEAGUE CUP

Date		Opponent	Res	Att	1	2	3	4	5	6	7	8	9	10	11	Substitutes	Goalscorers
13/08/69	A	BOURNEMOUTH	0-3	7478	SHEPPARD	STANTON	MUNRO	PETTS	S TAYLOR	MARSLAND	GRAYDON	W JONES	STUBBS	R JONES	JARMAN	STANTON	

GLOUCESTERSHIRE CUP FINAL

Date		Opponent	Res	Att	1	2	3	4	5	6	7	8	9	10	11	Substitutes	Goalscorers
22/04/70	A	BRISTOL CITY	1-2	12004	L TAYLOR	STANTON	PARSONS	ROBERTS	S TAYLOR	PARSONS	GRAYDON	W JONES	GILBERT	ALLAN	R JONES	W JONES	W JONES

Appearances & Goals

PLAYERS	APP	SUB	GLS
ALLAN A	6		4
BARNEY V	1		
BROWN R	1		2
FORD A	25		1
GILBERT C	21	2	12
GRAYDON R	40		13
HIGGINS P	16		2
JARMAN H	29		10
JONES B	26	1	2
JONES R	31	3	8
JONES W	39	1	4
MARSLAND G	7		
MECSON D	7		
MUNRO A	33	1	3
PARSONS L	15	2	
PETTS J	1	1	
PRINCE F	19		1
ROBERTS P	38		
SHEPPARD P	41		
STANTON T	12	1	
STUBBS R	38	1	15
TAYLOR L	5		
TAYLOR S	46		1
OWN GOALS			4

promotion position. The situation was further enhanced by two astute signings in March. Dodgin bought as player-coach Don Megson, the veteran Sheffield Wednesday captain, who rapidly emerged as the man being groomed to succeed as manager, and Sandy Allan, a proven goalscorer in European football with Cardiff City.

Promotion was now a realistic target and a crowd of 22,005, the highest at Eastville, local derbies with Bristol City apart, since October 1959, saw a first-minute Gilbert goal earn Rovers victory over the leaders Orient. This was followed by three straight draws, but another huge crowd saw Allan's 24th-minute goal defeat already relegated Stockport County 1-0 and leave Rovers still in the promotion frame. With two games to go, Rovers had 56 points, sitting two points behind Orient and one ahead of Luton Town, both of whom had three matches left including home fixtures with Southport, who desperately needed the points themselves in their battle against relegation. Two victories would, in all likelihood, earn promotion to Division Two.

As it was, a frustrated crowd of 18,978 saw Rovers attack with huge spirit but lose 2-1 at home to Gillingham. A 5-2 defeat at Tranmere Rovers, where Frank Gill, who had previously scored only once all season, scored a hat-trick, represented a hugely disappointing end to a season of great promise. Both their rivals beat Southport, who were relegated by one point and Rovers, with only themselves to blame, finished in third place on 56 points, behind Luton Town on 60 and Orient with 62. Nonetheless, the enthusiasm with which Dodgin's attack-minded side had pushed for promotion gave enormous hope for the years to come. Young Stuart Taylor, the only ever-present, was developing into a pivotal figure at the heart of a side with vast potential.

In the FA Cup, a convincing win at Telford United was followed by defeat at Aldershot, who fielded the veteran Jimmy Melia and for whom Jack Howarth scored twice. The future Rovers player-manager Terry Cooper was in the Leeds United side that lost the 1970 FA Cup final to Chelsea in an epic replay. Participation in the League Cup was even more short-lived. Ted McDougall, later a Manchester United striker, scored twice as Rovers lost 3-0 at Bournemouth. He also scored twice when Rovers drew 2-2 at Dean Court in October and once when Rovers recorded a 5-2 win at Eastville in February, though the Dorset club was relegated to Division Four. For a fourth consecutive year, Rovers were unable to win the Gloucestershire Cup.

1970/71

Heartened by the previous season's success, Bristol Rovers approached 1970/71 with vigour and enthusiasm. Bill Dodgin's side harboured real belief in its capabilities and, perhaps, sixth place, nine points away from promotion, represents a disappointing return. The first-team squad had barely changed. Gordon Marsland spent time on loan at Crewe Alexandra and Oldham Athletic before joining Bath City at the end of the season. Tony Ford was forced to retire after rupturing his spleen in the game at Preston North End in August. While Rovers received £4,000 insurance compensation, Ford carved out a career in coaching at Plymouth Argyle and Hereford

Bristol Rovers 1970/71. Back row: Jarman, W Jones, L Taylor, Tedesco, R Jones. Middle row: Gilbert, Prince, Ford, Sheppard, S Taylor, Parsons, Munro. Front row: Campbell (Trainer) Roberts, Graydon, Stubbs, Allan, B Jones, Higgins, Megson (Player-Coach)

United. Slowly but surely, a team worthy of promotion to Division Two was being constructed. Stuart Taylor, once again an ever-present, Lindsay Parsons, Frankie Prince and Bryn Jones would all star in the 1973/74 side. They were joined by two free-transfer recruits, Walsall's Kenny Stephens and midfielder Gordon Fearnley, previously a team-mate of player-coach Don Megson at Sheffield Wednesday. In the meantime, the side was built around the goalkeeper and centre-backs, the only three to play in every match. Seven players missed fewer than 7 League games each and only 21 players were used in total.

By the season's end, Dick Sheppard had played in goal in the previous 82 competitive matches. In front of him, Phil Roberts, Megson, Taylor and Parsons were a sturdy defence, with Prince joined by at least one Jones – Bobby, Bryn or Wayne. Ray Graydon, scorer of 13 goals from the right, and Harold Jarman, who contributed 12 from the left, provided the crosses for 17-goal top scorer Robin Stubbs. Sandy Allan had a poor season by his standards, scoring only twice, while Carl Gilbert joined Rotherham United in mid-season. Once again, relative success brought good crowds to Eastville, the second highest being 18,875 for the visit of Fulham in February, while 25,836 watched the January visit of Aston Villa, the highest ever crowd for a Division Three game at Eastville. Bruce Rioch, on the threshold of a successful career that won him many Scotland caps, scored the winning goal in this, the fourth meeting of these two clubs this season and, astonishingly, the one watched by the lowest attendance of the four fixtures.

Off the field, Eastville Stadium was undergoing further change. Increasingly hemmed in by developments, it now had the M32 'Parkway' motorway crossing the corner of the ground between the Muller Road End and the South Stand. With the £7,500,000 second stage now operating past the ground, the superhighway was officially opened by John Peyton, the Conservative MP for Yeovil and Minister of Transport, on 18 July

1970. Progressively, as traffic levels increased, the incidence of apparent breakdowns on the eastbound hard-shoulder during home matches grew dramatically and Rovers' games were played to a background din of traffic.

Rovers scored four times in a league game on five occasions. Four second-half goals at Oakwell over New Year, where Stubbs opened the scoring before Stephens, Graydon and Wayne Jones all scored in the final 14 minutes, helped defeat Barnsley 4-0. Reading and Bradford City were beaten 4-0 and 4-2 in consecutive games in November. Four different scorers saw off the Royals, while Jarman scored his first hat-trick in a decade with Rovers to see off Bradford City, for whom Bruce Bannister, later such a pivotal figure at Eastville, scored twice to accompany his goal in the return fixture. There were also two 4-1 away victories – at Shrewsbury Town, where Stubbs scored twice in the final three minutes after Graydon had twice put Rovers in front, and at Gillingham, where Stubbs scored all Rovers' goals, the first occasion that a Rovers player had scored four goals in an away League match. In fact, Jarman was Rovers' star man, as the Pirates overcame a half-time deficit following Kenny Pound's excellent 35th-minute goal after a one-two with Andy Smillie. Stubbs scored four second-half goals with his right foot, after 46, 58, 78 and 82 minutes, set up on each occasion by Jarman. Gilbert, a summer signing from Gillingham, replaced Graydon as a substitute against his former club, who were relegated.

In fact, Rovers were to complete a League double over three of the four relegated clubs. On the other hand, relegated Bury beat Rovers 1-0 at Eastville, with the former England winger John Connelly scoring two minutes before half-time, and 3-0 at Gigg Lane. Connelly scored in both games and Terry McDermott, later a key name at Newcastle United and Liverpool, also scored in the away fixture. Rotherham United's Neil Hague scored both his side's goals in their 2-0 win at Eastville in February and a 35th-minute opener when the sides drew at Millmoor. Rovers claimed a point off champions Preston North End before the BBC *Match of the Day* cameras, but lost both fixtures with Fulham and ultimately finished well in arrears of both clubs.

Despite starting the season with an impressive 14-match run where the only defeat had been at the hands of Preston at Deepdale, Rovers never seriously challenged for a place in the top two. The decisive blow came in the form of an eight-match winless run in the New Year, which included the 3-0 defeat at Bury and a 4-1 deficit at Mansfield Town, where Parsons conceded an own goal. Finishing the season with straight defeats, Dodgin's side

Full-back Phil Roberts was an ever-present for two seasons from 1970 to 1972. Following his transfer to Portsmouth in 1973 he won four Welsh caps

313

FOOTBALL LEAGUE DIVISION THREE

SEASON 1970/71

Date	Opponent	H/A	Score	ATT	1 (G)	2	3	4	5	6	7	8	9	10	11	Substitutes	Goalscorers
15/08/70	ROCHDALE	A	1-1	4496	SHEPPARD	FORD	PARSONS	PRINCE	TAYLOR	ALLAN	GRAYDON	W JONES	STUBBS	GILBERT	JARMAN	GILBERT 10	ALLAN
22/08/70	SHREWSBURY TOWN	A	2-2	8994	SHEPPARD	MUNRO	PARSONS	PRINCE	TAYLOR	B JONES	GRAYDON	W JONES	STUBBS	GILBERT	JARMAN	PARSONS 3	BROWN R
29/08/70	PRESTON NORTH END	A	2-3	7957	SHEPPARD	MUNRO	MUNRO	ROBERTS	TAYLOR	B JONES	GRAYDON	W JONES	STUBBS	GILBERT	JARMAN	STUBBS, GILBERT	
01/09/70	PORT VALE	H	3-0	7931	SHEPPARD	MUNRO	PARSONS	B JONES	TAYLOR	ROBERTS	GRAYDON	W JONES	STUBBS	GILBERT	JARMAN	GRAYDON, ROBERTS	FORD A
05/09/70	WREXHAM	H	3-2	7699	SHEPPARD	ROBERTS	PARSONS	PRINCE	TAYLOR	MEGSON	GRAYDON	W JONES	STUBBS	GILBERT	JARMAN	JARMAN, STUBBS, ROBERTS	GILBERT C
12/09/70	PLYMOUTH ARGYLE	A	0-0	11268	SHEPPARD	ROBERTS	PARSONS	PRINCE	TAYLOR	MEGSON	GRAYDON	W JONES	STUBBS	GILBERT	JARMAN	R JONES, STUBBS, JARMAN	GRAYDON R
19/09/70	WALSALL	H	3-0	8545	SHEPPARD	FORD	PARSONS	PRINCE	TAYLOR	MEGSON	GRAYDON	W JONES	STUBBS	GILBERT	JARMAN	GILBERT	HIGGINS P
22/09/70	DONCASTER ROVERS	H	2-0	11048	SHEPPARD	ROBERTS	PARSONS	PRINCE	TAYLOR	MEGSON	GRAYDON	W JONES	STUBBS	GILBERT	JARMAN		JARMAN H
30/09/70	BRIGHTON & H ALBION	A	0-0	10018	SHEPPARD	ROBERTS	PARSONS	PRINCE	TAYLOR	MEGSON	GRAYDON	W JONES	STUBBS	GILBERT	JARMAN		JONES B
03/10/70	ASTON VILLA	H	1-1	32082	SHEPPARD	ROBERTS	PARSONS	PRINCE	TAYLOR	MEGSON	GRAYDON	W JONES	STUBBS	GILBERT	JARMAN	ALLAN 11	JONES R
10/10/70	CHESTERFIELD	A	3-2	10669	SHEPPARD	ROBERTS	PARSONS	PRINCE	TAYLOR	MEGSON	GRAYDON	W JONES	STUBBS	GILBERT	HIGGINS	MEGSON D	JONES W
17/10/70	GILLINGHAM	H	4-1	4348	SHEPPARD	ROBERTS	PARSONS	PRINCE	TAYLOR	ROBERTS	GRAYDON	STUBBS	GILBERT	W JONES	JARMAN	GRAYDON, W JONES, PHELAN og	MEGSON D
24/10/70	ROCHDALE	H	2-2	11712	SHEPPARD	ROBERTS	PARSONS	PRINCE	TAYLOR	MEGSON	GRAYDON	W JONES	GILBERT	STUBBS	JARMAN	STUBBS 4	MUNRO A
31/10/70	MANSFIELD TOWN	A	2-0	12220	SHEPPARD	ROBERTS	PARSONS	PRINCE	TAYLOR	MEGSON	GRAYDON	W JONES	GILBERT	STUBBS	JARMAN	STUBBS, R JONES	PARSONS L
07/11/70	BURY	H	0-1	10928	SHEPPARD	ROBERTS	PARSONS	PRINCE	TAYLOR	W JONES	GRAYDON	R JONES	GILBERT	B JONES	JARMAN	W JONES	PRINCE F
21/11/70	ROTHERHAM UNITED	H	1-0	7478	SHEPPARD	ROBERTS	PARSONS	PRINCE	TAYLOR	MEGSON	GRAYDON	R JONES	GILBERT	B JONES	JARMAN		ROBERTS P
28/11/70	READING	H	4-0	4546	SHEPPARD	ROBERTS	PARSONS	PRINCE	TAYLOR	MEGSON	GRAYDON	R JONES	STUBBS	B JONES	JARMAN	B JONES, STUBBS 2	SHEPPARD R
05/12/70	BRADFORD CITY	A	4-2	15146	SHEPPARD	ROBERTS	PARSONS	PRINCE	TAYLOR	MEGSON	GRAYDON	R JONES	STUBBS	B JONES	JARMAN		STANTON T
12/12/70	TRANMERE ROVERS	H	2-0	8527	SHEPPARD	ROBERTS	PARSONS	PRINCE	TAYLOR	MEGSON	GRAYDON	R JONES	STUBBS	B JONES	JARMAN		STEPHENS K
18/12/70	TORQUAY UNITED	A	1-1	25836	SHEPPARD	ROBERTS	PARSONS	PRINCE	TAYLOR	W JONES	GRAYDON	R JONES	STUBBS	B JONES	ALLAN	ALLAN 8	STUBBS R
26/12/70	FULHAM	A	0-1	6357	SHEPPARD	ROBERTS	PARSONS	PRINCE	TAYLOR	PRINCE	GRAYDON	R JONES	STUBBS	B JONES	ALLAN		TAYLOR S
02/01/71	BRADFORD CITY	H	0-0	7716	SHEPPARD	ROBERTS	PARSONS	PRINCE	TAYLOR	MEGSON	GRAYDON	B JONES	GILBERT	W JONES	JARMAN	STUBBS, STEPHENS, GRAYDON, W JONES	OWN GOALS
09/01/71	ROTHERHAM UNITED	A	0-2	18075	SHEPPARD	ROBERTS	PARSONS	PRINCE	TAYLOR	MEGSON	STEPHENS	B JONES	GILBERT	W JONES	JARMAN	STUBBS, STEPHENS, GRAYDON, W JONES	
16/01/71	FULHAM	A	1-2	6073	SHEPPARD	ROBERTS	PARSONS	PRINCE	TAYLOR	BROWN	STEPHENS	B JONES	GILBERT	STUBBS	JARMAN	GILBERT	
30/01/71	BURY	A	0-1	11092	SHEPPARD	ROBERTS	PARSONS	PRINCE	TAYLOR	BROWN	STEPHENS	B JONES	GILBERT	ALLAN	R JONES	R JONES 10	
06/02/71	SHREWSBURY TOWN	H	1-0	13971	SHEPPARD	ROBERTS	PARSONS	PRINCE	TAYLOR	B JONES	GRAYDON	R JONES	GILBERT	ALLAN	STEPHENS	R JONES 6	
13/02/71	SWANSEA CITY	H	4-1	3457	SHEPPARD	ROBERTS	PARSONS	PRINCE	TAYLOR	STANTON	GRAYDON	B JONES	GILBERT	ALLAN	STEPHENS	STANTON 9	PRINCE
17/04/71	BARNSLEY	A	0-0	4000	SHEPPARD	ROBERTS	PARSONS	PRINCE	TAYLOR	STANTON	GRAYDON	B JONES	GILBERT	ALLAN	FEARNLEY	STUBBS, TAYLOR	
13/04/71	DONCASTER ROVERS	H	4-0	9249	SHEPPARD	ROBERTS	PARSONS	PRINCE	TAYLOR	W JONES	GRAYDON	B JONES	GILBERT	FEARNLEY	R JONES	GRAYDON, STUBBS	ALLAN, STUBBS, W JONES
10/04/71	TRANMERE ROVERS	A	0-1	6632	SHEPPARD	ROBERTS	PARSONS	PRINCE	TAYLOR	STANTON	GRAYDON	B JONES	GILBERT	FEARNLEY	R JONES	GRAYDON, JARMAN 2	
03/04/71	BARNSLEY	H	1-0	5415	SHEPPARD	ROBERTS	PARSONS	PRINCE	TAYLOR	MEGSON	GRAYDON	B JONES	STUBBS	FEARNLEY	JARMAN	JARMAN, W JONES	
27/03/71	READING	H	3-0	11476	SHEPPARD	ROBERTS	PARSONS	PRINCE	TAYLOR	MEGSON	GRAYDON	B JONES	STUBBS	FEARNLEY	JARMAN	SLEEUWENHOEK og	
23/03/71	TORQUAY UNITED	H	2-0	6182	SHEPPARD	ROBERTS	PARSONS	W JONES	TAYLOR	MEGSON	GRAYDON	B JONES	STUBBS	GILBERT	JARMAN	W JONES	
20/03/71	WREXHAM	A	1-1	10802	SHEPPARD	ROBERTS	PARSONS	PRINCE	TAYLOR	MEGSON	GRAYDON	B JONES	STUBBS	GILBERT	JARMAN	BROWN 11	
16/03/71	PRESTON NORTH END	H	0-1	9008	SHEPPARD	ROBERTS	PARSONS	PRINCE	TAYLOR	MEGSON	GRAYDON	B JONES	STUBBS	GILBERT	GRAYDON	GILBERT 6	
13/03/71	SWANSEA CITY	A	3-1	8435	SHEPPARD	ROBERTS	PARSONS	PRINCE	TAYLOR	MEGSON	STEPHENS	B JONES	STUBBS	ALLAN	STEPHENS	STANTON 9	GRAYDON
06/03/71	PLYMOUTH ARGYLE	A	1-3	8392	SHEPPARD	ROBERTS	PARSONS	W JONES	TAYLOR	STANTON	STEPHENS	BROWN	GILBERT	ALLAN	STEPHENS		
02/03/71	GILLINGHAM	A	1-3	5260	SHEPPARD	ROBERTS	PARSONS	W JONES	TAYLOR	W JONES	GRAYDON	B JONES	STUBBS	FEARNLEY	STEPHENS	GILBERT 7	
17/04/71	WALSALL	H	2-0	3916	SHEPPARD	ROBERTS	PARSONS	PRINCE	TAYLOR	MEGSON	GRAYDON	R JONES	STUBBS	ALLAN	STEPHENS	TAYLOR, GRAYDON	
24/04/71	PORT VALE	A	0-2	4525	SHEPPARD	ROBERTS	PARSONS	PRINCE	TAYLOR	MEGSON	GRAYDON	R JONES	STUBBS	ALLAN	STEPHENS	JARMAN	
01/05/71	BRIGHTON & H ALBION	H	1-3	5530	SHEPPARD	PARSONS	PARSONS	PRINCE	TAYLOR	STANTON	GRAYDON	STEPHENS	STUBBS	STUBBS	JARMAN	STUBBS	

FA CUP

Date	Opponent	H/A	Score	ATT	Substitutes	Goalscorers
21/11/70	FULHAM	A	2-1	12912	R JONES 11	STEPHENS
12/12/70	ALDERSHOT	A	1-1	7748	JARMAN	
15/12/70	ALDERSHOT	H	1-3	10743	STUBBS	

LEAGUE CUP

Date	Opponent	H/A	Score	ATT	Substitutes	Goalscorers
18/08/70	BRIGHTON & H ALBION	H	1-0	7276	ROBERTS	GRAYDON
08/09/70	NEWCASTLE UNITED	H	2-1	16824	B JONES	R JONES 2
07/10/70	NORWICH CITY	A	1-1	11518		
13/10/70	NORWICH CITY	H	3-1	19122	JARMAN 9	TAYLOR, MEGSON, ROBERTS
27/10/70	BIRMINGHAM CITY	A	3-0	21426		HIND og, GILBERT, STUBBS
17/11/70	ASTON VILLA	A	1-1	28720		TAYLOR
25/11/70	ASTON VILLA	H	0-1	36482		

GLOUCESTERSHIRE CUP FINAL

Date	Opponent	H/A	Score	ATT	Substitutes	Goalscorers
04/05/71	BRISTOL CITY	H	1-1	12256	HIGGINS	STEPHENS

PLAYERS	APP	SUB	GLS
ALLAN A	12	3	2
BROWN R	5	1	
FEARNLEY G	5		
FORD A	17	5	3
GILBERT C	42		13
GRAYDON R	46		
HIGGINS P	1	7	
JARMAN H	31	2	12
JONES B	30	1	
JONES R	24	5	3
JONES W	29	5	5
MEGSON D	24		1
MUNRO A	4	1	
PARSONS L	43		1
PRINCE F	39	1	
ROBERTS P	46		
SHEPPARD R	46		
STANTON T	1	4	
STEPHENS K	15	1	
STUBBS R	40		17
TAYLOR S	46		1
OWN GOALS			2

had not achieved its pre-season aspirations in terms of League football, but the League Cup was to provide enormous excitement, as Rovers reached the fifth round for the first time in the club's history.

Rovers had been knocked out of the League Cup in the first round in consecutive seasons, so there was considerable satisfaction when Graydon's 56th-minute goal helped defeat Brighton 1-0 in the opening round. A home-tie followed with Newcastle United, evoking the vivid memories of Rovers' epic 1951 FA Cup matches. The attraction of a major Division One side, boasting household names in Frank Clark, Bobby Moncur and Pop Robson, drew a crowd of 16,824 to Eastville. The many Rovers supporters were not disappointed, as the veteran Bobby Jones scored twice and the Magpies were defeated 2-1. Jones scored again in the next round, as Rovers drew at Carrow Road against Division Two Norwich City. The Canaries held Rovers in the Eastville replay until extra-time, when Rovers opened up a 3-1 lead.

In addition to one First Division side, Rovers knocked three Division Two sides out of the 1970/71 League Cup. The third was Birmingham City when a total of 21,426 spectators gathered at Eastville as Cup fever gripped the Rovers camp. There was every possibility that Rovers could make real progress in the competition and a dominant display in the fourth round left many believing in Rovers' potential. Following an own goal from centre-half Roger Hynd, Gilbert and Stubbs both scored to give Rovers an apparently comfortable 3-0 lead and send them into the quarter-finals for the first time in this tournament.

It was, of course, ironic that, having progressed so far, Rovers would be locked in an all-Division Three clash with Aston Villa. However, the weather dictated much of the play at Eastville, where a draw was a fair result and brought about a replay at Villa Park. If a crowd of 28,780 at Eastville had been considerable Rovers, who were by now in a run which would see them lose only three times in 30 games in all competitions, now held Villa for 89 minutes before 36,482 spectators, as both sides played very well in a spectacular game. Then, in the final seconds, Pat McMahon, who had scored in the first meeting, claimed the decisive winning goal to end Rovers' dreams. With Brian Godfrey, a Rovers midfielder from the end of the season, captaining the side, Villa reached the final before losing to Tottenham Hotspur, who had defeated Bristol City in the semi-finals.

In the FA Cup, high-flying Fulham were beaten by two Gilbert goals, manager Dodgin masterminding victory over the side controlled by his son, Bill junior. But, having drawn at Aldershot, Rovers were brought down to earth in the replay, Jimmy Melia among the goalscorers. Larry Lloyd, a former Rovers centre-half, played for Liverpool in the FA Cup final, his side losing to Arsenal despite taking the lead early in extra-time. Two future Rovers players were winners, Kenny Hibbitt in the short-lived Texaco Cup, where Wolverhampton Wanderers defeated Heart of Midlothian 3-2 on aggregate in the final and, on a more International scale, Terry Cooper, a member of the Leeds United side that won the Fairs Cup final, defeating the Italian side Juventus on the away-goals rule. A Stephens goal from Graydon's pass after 67 minutes and a drawn Gloucestershire Cup final ended Rovers' losing streak in that tournament, while in May goals from Ian Hamilton and Alfie Biggs enabled Rovers Old Players to defeat City Old Players 2-0. In May 1971, Rovers' Wayne Jones earned a full International cap for Wales in a 1-0 European Championship victory over Finland in Helsinki.

1971/72

A very similar Rovers line-up experienced a feeling of déjà vu for, as in 1970/71, Rovers reached a quarter-final and finished sixth in Division Three. The main absentee was Ray Graydon, whose move to Aston Villa set him on the way to three League Cup final appearances and ultimately a successful career in management. Alex Munro, who had appeared in nine consecutive seasons, emigrated to South Africa in the summer of 1971, while Don Megson retired as a player to concentrate on his full-time role as coach. Graydon's place was taken, through an exchange deal with Villa, by the highly experienced former Welsh International midfielder Brian Godfrey, while Mike Green, Rovers' captain in the 1973/74 promotion season, appeared in the side following his summer move from Gillingham.

A number of other players appeared in occasional games for Rovers. Three young goalkeepers, Malcolm Dalrymple, Richard Crabtree and loan signing Allen Clarke, as well as 22-year-old forward Malcolm John each made a League debut. Another product of the South Wales nursery organised by Stan Montgomery, 17-year-old Peter Aitken, made his way into the squad as an unused substitute. As the season progressed, manager Dodgin improved his hand with the signing of two strikers who were to see Rovers into Division Two. Bruce Bannister had built up an excellent reputation at Bradford City as a brave, busy forward and it took a club record £23,000 fee to bring him to Eastville in November. Three months later, in exchange for Robin Stubbs, who had not scored all season, Rovers signed the vastly experienced John Rudge from Torquay United.

Once again, it was the League Cup that sparked Rovers' season into life. A relatively straightforward three-goal victory at Exeter City was followed, for the second consecutive season, by three wins against Division Two opposition. Sandy Allan and Billy Hughes exchanged penalties in two second-half minutes as Rovers defeated a strong Sunderland side, FA Cup winners in 1973, 3-1 at Eastville. Then Stuart Taylor and Harold Jarman scored to put out Charlton Athletic. When Jarman scored again to earn a draw at Queen's Park Rangers, for whom Rodney Marsh scored and both Terry Venables and Gerry Francis played, a crowd of 24,373 was attracted to Eastville to see a Sandy Allan goal, driven home after a three-man move 12 minutes from time, earn Rovers a second consecutive League Cup quarter-final. These remain the only two seasons that Rovers have progressed so far in this tournament.

The quarter-final tie drew a crowd of 33,624 to Eastville, Rovers' highest ever for a home League Cup tie. Rightly so, for Stoke City brought a star-studded side, the Division One club including most notably Gordon Banks, a World Cup winner in 1966 and believed by many to be the best goalkeeper in the world. Banks was kept busy early in the game, but once the veteran George Eastham stamped his authority on the game, Stoke began to dominate. The visitors ran up a four-goal lead, with Jimmy Greenhoff, an FA Cup winner with Manchester United in 1977, and the future Bristol City manager Denis Smith among the four goalscorers. With the job done, the visitors relaxed and both Stubbs and Godfrey, the latter from a penalty, were able to score past Banks. Once more, though, Rovers had shown their qualities as cup fighters.

Bristol Rovers 1971/72. Back row: Brown, W Jones, Stephens, Prince, Higgins, Jarman. Middle row: Campbell (Trainer), R Jones, Roberts, Allan, Sheppard, Parsons, Stanton, Godfrey, Megson (Asst Manager). Front row: Impey, Green, Fearnley, Dodgin (Manager), Stubbs, Taylor, B Jones

Rovers prepared for the new season with the usual flurry of friendlies. One game prior to the 1971/72 season was Rovers' 1-1 draw with Hereford United at Edgar Street on 2 August, Green scoring for Rovers five minutes before half-time and Billy Meadows equalising nine minutes from the end. This game marked the Hereford United debut of David Icke, who saved well from Wayne Jones and Allan; he was a competent goalkeeper and national television sports anchorman who courted national fame in March 1991 by declaring himself to be the son of a 'Godhead'. A spokesman for the Green Party at the time of their relative success in the 1989 European Parliament elections, he has since written a number of books about the meaningfulness of man's existence.

It did not take Rovers long to post warning of their goalscoring potential. After victory over Tranmere Rovers, Bradford City were the second League visitors to Eastville, fielding in their side Terry Owen, whose son Michael was to achieve huge success in later years with Liverpool and England. Rovers were a goal up in the first minute, five ahead inside 25 minutes and scored seven in total for only the eighth occasion in the Pirates' league history. Godfrey opened the scoring early on and his hat-trick in the opening 25 minutes included two stunning long-range volleys. Although the visitors scored before the break, a 5-1 half-time lead was a healthy return and the 7-1 victory was Rovers' largest since March 1964. Bruce Bannister, in the Bantams' attack, was to finish the season as Rovers' top scorer. Yet, just a week later, two Jim Fryatt goals condemned Rovers to defeat at Oldham Athletic.

There was a flurry of penalties at Eastville. Both Allan, against Tranmere Rovers, and Bannister, when Rovers beat Blackburn Rovers 3-0, joined a select band of six Rovers players to have scored two penalties in a League game. When York City visited in October, John Mackin became only the fifth visitor to convert two penalties in a League

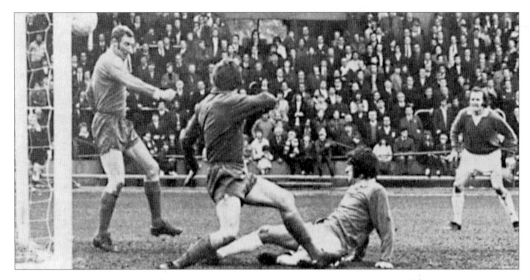

Rovers score against Oldham Athletic in a narrow 1-0 victory on 25 March 1972 with Bill Cranston putting through his own goal

fixture with Rovers. A crowd of 6,876 witnessed an extraordinary game that featured six goals before half-time. Kenny Stephens and Jarman put Rovers 2-0 up in nine minutes and Jarman's second left Rovers 3-1 ahead, but Mackin's first penalty, awarded on the stroke of half-time for a foul by Lindsay Parsons, left the scores level at the break. Stephens put Rovers ahead again after 57 minutes and, four minutes later, Jarman completed the second hat-trick of his Rovers career to put the Pirates 5-3 ahead. Rovers held on for victory, despite a second Mackin penalty 18 minutes from time after handball against Bobby Brown, in his penultimate start before a transfer to Weymouth.

After a few initial concerns, Rovers put together some good runs of results. Between November and February, there was a nine-match unbeaten run, while Rovers also ran up convincing victories over Barnsley, Allan scoring twice in a 3-0 win, and Rochdale, where a 5-2 win included a brace from Bannister. Crucially, there were just four away wins, enabling Rovers to do the double over Tranmere Rovers, Blackburn Rovers and Chesterfield. Aston Villa, for whom Willie Anderson's goal at Eastville sent his side to the top of Division Three, and Bournemouth completed doubles over Rovers, Phil Boyer, an FA Cup winner with Southampton in 1976, scoring in both games for the latter. Kevin Randall, having scored in both the first-ever meetings between Rovers and Chesterfield, also scored in the third as Rovers won 3-1 at Saltergate.

Defensively, Rovers gave little away. From October on, there was no League game in which three or more goals were conceded. Roberts, Taylor, Lindsay Parsons and Frankie Prince were ever-presents, while Bannister's two final-day goals made him the club's top goalscorer. Roberts scored an own goal for Notts County in September to match one he was to score for them on Portsmouth's books in February 1974. Five straight wins in March, with only two goals conceded, hinted at a late challenge for promotion. The key fixture was the Easter Monday trip to leaders Aston Villa, where Rovers selected, in an injury crisis, apprentice goalkeeper Crabtree just a few weeks after his 17th birthday.

SEASON 1971/72

FOOTBALL LEAGUE DIVISION THREE

Date	Opponent		Score	ATT	G	2	3	4	5	6	7	8	9	10	11	SUBSTITUTES	GOALSCORERS
14/08/71	YORK CITY	A	0-0	6360	SHEPPARD	ROBERTS	PARSONS	GODFREY	TAYLOR	PRINCE	STEPHENS	W JONES	ALLAN	STUBBS	B JONES	GREEN 11	
21/08/71	TRANMERE ROVERS	H	2-1	10258	SHEPPARD	ROBERTS	PARSONS	GODFREY	TAYLOR	PRINCE	STEPHENS	W JONES	ALLAN	STUBBS	JARMAN		ALLAN 2, 2pens
28/08/71	TORQUAY UNITED	A	1-0	8635	SHEPPARD	ROBERTS	PARSONS	GODFREY	TAYLOR	PRINCE	STEPHENS	W JONES	ALLAN	STUBBS	JARMAN		W JONES
31/08/71	SWANSEA CITY	A	0-2	6801	SHEPPARD	ROBERTS	PARSONS	GODFREY	TAYLOR	PRINCE	STEPHENS	W JONES	ALLAN	R JONES	JARMAN	BROWN 10	
04/09/71	BRADFORD CITY	H	7-1	8463	SHEPPARD	ROBERTS	PARSONS	GODFREY	TAYLOR	PRINCE	STEPHENS	W JONES	ALLAN	R JONES	JARMAN		GODFREY 3, JARMAN 2, R JONES 2
11/09/71	OLDHAM ATHLETIC	A	2-3	9457	SHEPPARD	ROBERTS	PARSONS	GODFREY	TAYLOR	PRINCE	STEPHENS	W JONES	ALLAN	R JONES	JARMAN	STUBBS 11	ALLAN, GODFREY
18/09/71	BARNSLEY	H	3-0	9278	SHEPPARD	ROBERTS	PARSONS	GODFREY	TAYLOR	PRINCE	STEPHENS	W JONES	ALLAN	R JONES	JARMAN		ALLAN 2, GODFREY
25/09/71	NOTTS COUNTY	A	3-2	13101	CLARKE	ROBERTS	PARSONS	GODFREY	TAYLOR	PRINCE	STEPHENS	W JONES	ALLAN	R JONES	B JONES		R JONES 2, ALLAN
29/09/71	BRIGHTON & H ALBION	A	1-3	12649	SHEPPARD	ROBERTS	PARSONS	GODFREY	TAYLOR	PRINCE	STEPHENS	W JONES	ALLAN	R JONES	B JONES	BROWN 11	R JONES
02/10/71	ASTON VILLA	H	0-1	20428	SHEPPARD	ROBERTS	PARSONS	GODFREY	TAYLOR	PRINCE	STEPHENS	W JONES	ALLAN	R JONES	JARMAN	GREEN	
09/10/71	MANSFIELD TOWN	H	5-4	3830	SHEPPARD	ROBERTS	PARSONS	GODFREY	TAYLOR	PRINCE	STEPHENS	W JONES	ALLAN	R JONES	JARMAN	BROWN 2	JARMAN 3, 1pen, STEPHENS 2
16/10/71	YORK CITY	H	1-0	6876	SHEPPARD	ROBERTS	PARSONS	GODFREY	TAYLOR	PRINCE	STEPHENS	W JONES	ALLAN	R JONES	JARMAN	STANTON 3	STEPHENS
23/10/71	ROCHDALE	A	0-3	4753	SHEPPARD	ROBERTS	PARSONS	GODFREY	TAYLOR	PRINCE	STEPHENS	W JONES	R JONES	R JONES	JARMAN	STANTON 3	
30/10/71	BOLTON WANDERERS	H	2-0	11532	SHEPPARD	ROBERTS	PARSONS	GODFREY	TAYLOR	PRINCE	STEPHENS	W JONES	ALLAN	R JONES	JARMAN	STANTON 7	GODFREY, ROBERTS
06/11/71	WALSALL	A	0-0	3978	SHEPPARD	ROBERTS	PARSONS	GODFREY	TAYLOR	FEARNLEY	STEPHENS	W JONES	ALLAN	R JONES	JARMAN	ALLAN 7	
09/11/71	ROTHERHAM UNITED	H	1-2	13081	SHEPPARD	ROBERTS	PARSONS	GODFREY	TAYLOR	PRINCE	STEPHENS	W JONES	STUBBS	BANNISTER	JARMAN	STANTON 3	JARMAN
13/11/71	SHREWSBURY TOWN	H	3-1	8849	SHEPPARD	ROBERTS	PARSONS	GODFREY	TAYLOR	PRINCE	STEPHENS	W JONES	STUBBS	BANNISTER	JARMAN	STANTON 7	R JONES 2, FELLOWS og
27/11/71	PLYMOUTH ARGYLE	H	2-2	9568	SHEPPARD	ROBERTS	PARSONS	PRINCE	TAYLOR	GODFREY	FEARNLEY	W JONES	STUBBS	BANNISTER	GODFREY	STUBBS 4	W JONES, JARMAN
04/12/71	WREXHAM	A	1-1	6333	SHEPPARD	ROBERTS	PARSONS	PRINCE	TAYLOR	GODFREY	STEPHENS	W JONES	STUBBS	BANNISTER	GODFREY	R JONES 11	GODFREY
18/12/71	BRADFORD CITY	A	0-1	5423	SHEPPARD	ROBERTS	PARSONS	PRINCE	TAYLOR	GREEN	STEPHENS	W JONES	STUBBS	BANNISTER	STEPHENS	R JONES 8	
27/12/71	PORT VALE	H	2-1	12073	SHEPPARD	ROBERTS	PARSONS	PRINCE	TAYLOR	PRINCE	JARMAN	W JONES	ALLAN	BANNISTER	STEPHENS	R JONES 9	BANNISTER pen, PRINCE
01/01/72	BARNSLEY	A	0-0	4499	SHEPPARD	ROBERTS	PARSONS	PRINCE	TAYLOR	GODFREY	STEPHENS	W JONES	STUBBS	BANNISTER	HIGGINS	JARMAN 11	
08/01/72	TORQUAY UNITED	H	2-2	8344	SHEPPARD	ROBERTS	PARSONS	PRINCE	TAYLOR	GODFREY	STEPHENS	W JONES	STUBBS	BANNISTER	HIGGINS		STEPHENS
22/01/72	BRIGHTON & H ALBION	H	2-2	9744	SHEPPARD	ROBERTS	PARSONS	PRINCE	TAYLOR	GODFREY	STEPHENS	W JONES	STUBBS	BANNISTER	HIGGINS	JARMAN 11	HARRISON og, PRINCE
29/01/72	ROTHERHAM UNITED	A	0-0	17728	SHEPPARD	ROBERTS	PARSONS	PRINCE	TAYLOR	GODFREY	STEPHENS	W JONES	RUDGE	BANNISTER	HIGGINS		HIGGINS, STEPHENS
05/02/72	HALIFAX TOWN	A	1-2	2021	SHEPPARD	ROBERTS	PARSONS	PRINCE	TAYLOR	GREEN	STEPHENS	W JONES	RUDGE	BANNISTER	HIGGINS		BANNISTER
12/02/72	ROCHDALE	H	5-2	7042	SHEPPARD	ROBERTS	PARSONS	PRINCE	TAYLOR	GREEN	STEPHENS	W JONES	ALLAN	BANNISTER	HIGGINS	RUDGE 9	STEPHENS, BANNISTER 2, W JONES, PRINCE
19/02/72	BOLTON WANDERERS	A	0-0	8665	SHEPPARD	ROBERTS	PARSONS	PRINCE	TAYLOR	GREEN	STEPHENS	B JONES	RUDGE	BANNISTER	HIGGINS	GODFREY 7	
26/02/72	WALSALL	H	2-1	3001	CRABTREE	ROBERTS	PARSONS	PRINCE	TAYLOR	GREEN	STEPHENS	W JONES	ALLAN	BANNISTER	HIGGINS	STEPHENS 7	STEPHENS, GODFREY
04/03/72	SHREWSBURY TOWN	A	0-2	9151	CRABTREE	ROBERTS	PARSONS	PRINCE	TAYLOR	GREEN	STEPHENS	W JONES	RUDGE	BANNISTER	HIGGINS		ALLAN 2
08/03/72	BOURNEMOUTH	H	2-1	5574	CRABTREE	ROBERTS	PARSONS	PRINCE	TAYLOR	GREEN	JARMAN	R JONES	RUDGE	BANNISTER	HIGGINS	GREEN 3	BANNISTER, PATE og
11/03/72	MANSFIELD TOWN	A	1-0	7290	CRABTREE	ROBERTS	PARSONS	PRINCE	TAYLOR	GREEN	STEPHENS	W JONES	RUDGE	BANNISTER	GODFREY	RUDGE 9	BANNISTER 2, 2pens, RUDGE
14/03/72	BLACKBURN ROVERS	H	1-0	4294	SHEPPARD	ROBERTS	PARSONS	PRINCE	TAYLOR	GREEN	JARMAN	W JONES	RUDGE	BANNISTER	GODFREY	GODFREY 7	BANNISTER
17/03/72	TRANMERE ROVERS	A	1-0	7613	DALRYMPLE	ROBERTS	PARSONS	PRINCE	TAYLOR	GREEN	STEPHENS	W JONES	RUDGE	BANNISTER	GODFREY	STEPHENS 7	CRANSTON og
25/03/72	OLDHAM ATHLETIC	H	2-1	5740	DALRYMPLE	ROBERTS	PARSONS	PRINCE	TAYLOR	GREEN	STEPHENS	W JONES	RUDGE	BANNISTER	GODFREY	STANTON 7	W JONES, B JONES
27/03/72	BLACKBURN ROVERS	A	0-0	3823	CRABTREE	ROBERTS	PARSONS	PRINCE	TAYLOR	GREEN	B JONES	W JONES	ALLAN	BANNISTER	GODFREY	STANTON 7	STANTON
01/04/72	PORT VALE	A	0-0	45158	CRABTREE	ROBERTS	PARSONS	PRINCE	TAYLOR	GREEN	STANTON	W JONES	R JONES	BANNISTER	GODFREY	STANTON 9	
03/04/72	ASTON VILLA	H	1-2	11988	CRABTREE	ROBERTS	PARSONS	PRINCE	TAYLOR	GREEN	W JONES	W JONES	R JONES	JOHN	STEPHENS	JARMAN 11	JOHN
04/04/72	NOTTS COUNTY	H	0-2	5642	CRABTREE	ROBERTS	PARSONS	PRINCE	TAYLOR	GREEN	STEPHENS	W JONES	RUDGE	BANNISTER	GODFREY		
08/04/72	HALIFAX TOWN	H	1-2	8938	SHEPPARD	ROBERTS	PARSONS	JOHN	TAYLOR	PRINCE	JOHN	W JONES	RUDGE	B JONES	JOHN	GODFREY 11	RUDGE
15/04/72	PLYMOUTH ARGYLE	A	1-2	11372	SHEPPARD	ROBERTS	PARSONS	GODFREY	TAYLOR	PRINCE	STEPHENS	W JONES	RUDGE	BANNISTER	B JONES	GODFREY 11	RUDGE
18/04/72	BOURNEMOUTH	A	3-1	5427	SHEPPARD	ROBERTS	PARSONS	GODFREY	TAYLOR	PRINCE	STEPHENS	W JONES	ALLAN	BANNISTER	GODFREY		ALLAN, BANNISTER, STEPHENS
22/04/72	WREXHAM	H	3-1	6881	SHEPPARD	ROBERTS	PARSONS	GODFREY	TAYLOR	PRINCE	STEPHENS	W JONES	ALLAN	STUBBS	GODFREY	RUDGE 10	W JONES, BANNISTER
25/04/72	SWANSEA CITY	H	2-1	4542	SHEPPARD	ROBERTS	PARSONS	GODFREY	TAYLOR	GREEN	STEPHENS	W JONES	STUBBS	FEARNLEY	GODFREY		HIGGINS, TAYLOR, ALLAN
29/04/72	CHESTERFIELD	A	3-1	8006	SHEPPARD	ROBERTS	PARSONS	GODFREY	TAYLOR	PRINCE	STEPHENS	W JONES	ALLAN	STUBBS	HIGGINS		ALLAN, BANNISTER 2
02/05/72	CHESTERFIELD	H	2-4	33624	SHEPPARD	ROBERTS	PARSONS	GODFREY	TAYLOR	PRINCE	STEPHENS	W JONES	ALLAN	RUDGE	HIGGINS		

FA CUP

Date	Opponent		Score	ATT	G	2	3	4	5	6	7	8	9	10	11	SUBSTITUTES	GOALSCORERS
20/11/71	TELFORD UNITED	H	3-0	8762	SHEPPARD	ROBERTS	PARSONS	GODFREY	TAYLOR	PRINCE	STEPHENS	W JONES	ALLAN	BANNISTER	HIGGINS	STUBBS 7	BANNISTER 2, GODFREY
11/12/71	CAMBRIDGE UNITED	H	3-0	8768	SHEPPARD	ROBERTS	PARSONS	GODFREY	TAYLOR	GREEN	STEPHENS	W JONES	STUBBS	BANNISTER	HIGGINS	PRINCE 6	TAYLOR, BANNISTER, GODFREY
15/01/72	LEEDS UNITED	A	1-4	33565	SHEPPARD	ROBERTS	PARSONS	PRINCE	TAYLOR	GODFREY	STEPHENS	W JONES	ALLAN	BANNISTER	HIGGINS	STANTON 9	ALLAN

LEAGUE CUP

Date	Opponent		Score	ATT	G	2	3	4	5	6	7	8	9	10	11	SUBSTITUTES	GOALSCORERS
18/08/71	EXETER CITY	A	3-0	6418	SHEPPARD	ROBERTS	PARSONS	GODFREY	TAYLOR	PRINCE	STEPHENS	W JONES	ALLAN	STUBBS	JARMAN		PRINCE, GILES og, STUBBS
07/09/71	SUNDERLAND	H	3-1	15262	SHEPPARD	ROBERTS	PARSONS	GODFREY	TAYLOR	PRINCE	STEPHENS	W JONES	ALLAN	R JONES	JARMAN		JARMAN, W JONES, ALLAN pen
05/10/71	CHARLTON ATHLETIC	H	2-1	14649	SHEPPARD	ROBERTS	PARSONS	GODFREY	TAYLOR	PRINCE	JARMAN	W JONES	ALLAN	R JONES	FEARNLEY		TAYLOR, JARMAN
26/10/71	QUEENS PARK RANGERS	H	1-1	17045	SHEPPARD	ROBERTS	PARSONS	GODFREY	TAYLOR	PRINCE	STEPHENS	W JONES	FEARNLEY	R JONES	JARMAN		JARMAN
02/11/71	QUEENS PARK RANGERS	A	1-1	24373	DALRYMPLE	ROBERTS	PARSONS	GODFREY	TAYLOR	PRINCE	STEPHENS	W JONES	ALLAN	FEARNLEY	JARMAN		ALLAN
23/11/71	STOKE CITY	H	2-4	33624	SHEPPARD	ROBERTS	PARSONS	GODFREY	TAYLOR	PRINCE	STEPHENS	W JONES	ALLAN	STUBBS	HIGGINS	B JONES 7	STUBBS, GODFREY pen

GLOUCESTERSHIRE CUP FINAL

Date	Opponent		Score	ATT	G	2	3	4	5	6	7	8	9	10	11	SUBSTITUTES	GOALSCORERS
09/05/72	BRISTOL CITY	A	1-1	13137	SHEPPARD	ROBERTS	PARSONS	PRINCE	TAYLOR	GREEN	STEPHENS	W JONES	ALLAN	RUDGE	HIGGINS	B JONES 7	ALLAN

PLAYERS	APP	SUB	GLS
ALLAN A	22	2	11
BANNISTER B	29		12
BROWN R		4	
CLARKE A	1		
CRABTREE R	7		
DALRYMPLE M	3		
FEARNLEY G	3		
GODFREY B	38	2	8
GREEN M	17	3	2
HIGGINS P	12		1
JARMAN H	18	4	7
JOHN M	2		1
JONES B	9	1	1
JONES R	17	3	7
JONES W	45		5
PARSONS L	46		
PRINCE F	46		3
ROBERTS B	46		3
RUDGE J	8	2	3
SHEPPARD R	36		
STANTON T	1	4	1
STEPHENS K	41	1	8
STUBBS R	12	2	1
TAYLOR S	46	2	4
OWN GOALS			4

The crowd at Villa Park was 45,158, the second highest for a League game including Rovers but, despite an inspired performance from the young goalkeeper, Rovers lost 2-1. Even winning the final four matches, Rovers finished well adrift of second-placed Brighton.

After convincing 3-0 wins at home to Telford United and Cambridge United, Rovers played an FA Cup third round tie at Elland Road. Before a crowd of 33,565, Leeds United scored three times in 17 first-half minutes and defeated Rovers 4-1, with Peter Lorimer scoring twice and creating two goals for Johnny Giles. Household names such as Terry Cooper, Billy Bremner, Joe Jordan and Norman Hunter also played. Cooper, a future Rovers player-manager, won an FA Cup winner's medal as Leeds United beat Alan Ball's Arsenal in the Wembley final. With Stoke City winning the League Cup, Rovers had thus been knocked out of both major cup competitions by the eventual victors. The Gloucestershire Cup final was drawn. Kenny Hibbitt, later a Rovers midfielder, was in the Wolverhampton Wanderers side that lost to Tottenham Hotspur on aggregate in an all-English UEFA Cup Final.

The new M32 motorway overhanging the corner of Eastville Stadium was closed for a week after a fire on 14 April on the Eastville slip-road. Of more immediate concern to Rovers was that, in July, manager Bill Dodgin handed over the reins to his coach Don Megson. While Rovers had not achieved immediate success, the bricks were in place for future Rovers triumphs. Progress in League and League Cup football had given time for the younger players to mature. Dodgin remained as chief scout until 1983, keeping a watchful eye on tomorrow's stars through the twilight years of his career, and retained a healthy interest in Rovers' fortunes up to his death, at the age of 90, in October 1999.

The former Rovers manager Brough Fletcher, who had discovered young talent such as Harry Bamford and Geoff Bradford in his time in charge of the club either side of World War Two, died in Bristol on 12 May 1972, aged 79.

1972/73

In July 1972, with Bill Dodgin reverting to his post as chief scout, Rovers appointed from within to make Don Megson the new manager. A relative youngster at 36, the former Sheffield Wednesday full-back had displayed considerable talent as a player and it was hoped he could translate his expertise into good management. Rovers were not to be disappointed. After Andrew Wilson, Brough Fletcher and David McLean, he was the fourth Wednesday player to become manager at Eastville. Megson brought a touch of class to Rovers. He would gather the team for a pre-match lunch at a motel outside Bristol prior to every home game to generate a greater feeling of team spirit. Unlike his predecessor, Megson believed in solid defending and quick counter-attacking, believing in the merit of 1-0 victories, and despite his critics, he succeeded in overseeing the return to Division Two in 1974 and establishing Rovers in this higher division.

Yet, while new hope arose at Eastville, there was considerable mourning for Bert Tann, who died in Bristol on 7 July 1972. Tann had managed Rovers between 1950 and

Bristol Rovers 1972/73. Back row: Jarman, R Jones, Sheppard, Dalrymple, Prince, B Jones. Middle row: Campbell (Trainer), W Jones, D John, Aitken, Stanton, Parsons, Fearnley, Godfrey, Dobson (Player-Coach). Front row: Roberts, Stephens, Taylor, Allan, Megson (Manager), Bannister, Rudge, Green, Higgins

1968, during which time he gained widespread recognition for his shrewd tactical awareness. In 1971, the Football Association had awarded him a medal to commemorate 21 consecutive years with Rovers, in which period he had masterminded the club's first spell in Division Two. A key figure in the history of the club was gone.

Megson had an early opportunity to test his managerial ability in the pre-season Watney Cup. Ironically for a tournament designed to reward the top-scoring non-promoted sides from the previous season, there were just four goals in Rovers' three matches. Rovers strolled to apparently easy 2-0 victories at home to Division One Wolverhampton Wanderers and away to Burnley who, with the future Rovers manager Martin Dobson controlling midfield, were destined to be Division Two champions that season. Bruce Bannister scored in both games. A crowd of 19,768 gathered at Eastville in sweltering heat for the final between Rovers and Division One Sheffield United. The visitors fielded teenage goalkeeper Tom McAlister, later a Rovers player himself, and his fine display kept the final scoreless, though many felt Rovers had deserved to win. The match went to a penalty shoot-out. The first 13 penalties were scored and, with Dick Sheppard saving a crucial spot-kick from the veteran Ted Hemsley, a survivor of Shrewsbury Town's 7-2 win over Rovers a decade earlier, Rovers recorded a 7-6 win. In only his third game in charge, Megson had led the club to its first major cup competition win since 1935.

On the back of this pre-season success, Rovers embarked on a third successive giant-killing run in the League Cup. Two Division Two clubs were beaten, Cardiff City in a replay after Rovers had grabbed a 2-2 draw at Ninian Park, and Brighton. This second-round 4-0 win, in which four different players scored, gave Rovers ample revenge, for it was only four months since the Sussex club had beaten Rovers to the second promotion

New Rovers manager Don Megson and Phil Roberts hold aloft the Watney Cup after the dramatic penalty shoot-out victory over Sheffield United

place. More immediately, victory earned Rovers a prestigious home tie against Manchester United. The attraction of high-profile names such as George Best and Bobby Charlton drew a crowd of 33,597, the highest ever for a League Cup tie at Eastville. John Rudge's goal after an hour earned a 1-1 draw and the opportunity of a replay at Old Trafford, secured only by United through Willie Morgan's equaliser three minutes from time.

Rovers faced a team including nine full Internationals in the Old Trafford replay and the veteran winger Bobby Jones was recalled to add experience to the Division Three side. After Sheppard had saved well from Bobby Charlton, Rudge put Rovers ahead after 30 minutes, when he headed home a corner taken by Lindsay Parsons. Midway through the second-half the home side was awarded a controversial penalty, when Ian Storey-Moore fell under a challenge from Frankie Prince, but Sheppard saved George Best's kick. Good fortune could not last forever, though, and substitute Sammy McIlroy headed an equaliser from a Morgan corner with ten minutes left. Sensationally, four minutes later, a third header from a corner, Bannister's goal created by Kenny Stephens gave Rovers one of the greatest victories in the club's history.

With the impossible achieved, Rovers did not reach the League Cup quarter-finals for a third consecutive season. The 4-0 defeat at Molineux was as comprehensive as the result suggests. Jim McCalliog, an FA Cup winner in 1976 with Southampton, scored twice as Wolverhampton Wanderers, orchestrated by the future Rovers player-coach Kenny Hibbitt, exacted revenge for their earlier Watney Cup humiliation. Nor was there any place to hide for Rovers in the FA Cup. Just five weeks after victory at Manchester United, Rovers suffered the indignity of losing at Isthmian League Hayes. The Middlesex side fully deserved the victory obtained through Bobby Hatt's goal nine minutes into the second-half and the infamous maverick Robin Friday, then a 20-year-old on the verge of a highly entertaining career, stood out as a player to watch. While a Rovers player-to-be, Terry Cooper, was in the Leeds United side unexpectedly defeated by Sunderland in the FA Cup final, a former Rovers centre-half Larry Lloyd, won a UEFA Cup winner's medal, as Liverpool defeated Borussia Moenchengladbach to secure their first European trophy.

It was the unlikely figure of Danish-born midfielder Preben Arentoft who set Rovers on their way in 1972/73, his own goal sealing Blackburn Rovers' 3-0 opening-day defeat at Eastville. While many of the leading sides lost when they visited Bristol, where only unfancied Southend United and York City recorded victories, Rovers' away form was poor. Ultimately, Rovers finished only four points behind promoted Notts County, but the side had lost away to many of the challenging group. Indeed, a paltry figure of 3 League wins away from home, which did not even hint at promotion potential, enabled just two League doubles, over two relegated clubs, Scunthorpe United and Swansea City. The defeat at Grimsby Town featured four disallowed goals, two for Alan Gauden and one for Stuart Brace for the Mariners, as well as one for Bannister for Rovers. Strangely, the former Pirate Carl Gilbert scored twice and conceded three as an emergency goalkeeper, as Rotherham United lost 7-2 to Bournemouth.

However, Rovers were able to score freely at home. Bannister scored twice in a 5-1 win against Shrewsbury Town and Stuart Taylor twice as Scunthorpe United were beaten by the same score. Rovers also defeated Halifax Town and Port Vale 4-1 and recorded two 3-0 wins. Bannister scored from the penalty spot in both fixtures against Rotherham United. While Rovers through the winter recorded eight straight home wins, five away fixtures ended in goalless draws. Both matches with Rochdale were goalless – Stuart Taylor being sent off on Rovers' visit to Spotland – as was Southend United's 1,000th home league fixture, when Rovers played at Roots Hall on a Friday night in November. Dick Sheppard's 35th-minute own goal gave Brentford victory in September while Stewart Houston, on the verge of a long and successful career, scored the Bees' consolation goal in the return fixture.

This match at home to Brentford in November, marked the end of Wayne Jones' promising career. A knee injury was revealed to be a rare bone condition that forced the Wales Under-23 International midfielder to retire from playing the game. Just two months later, goalkeeper Sheppard's career was effectively ended when he suffered a depressed fracture of the skull, diving at the feet of Tranmere Rovers' Eddie Loyden, with Tom Stanton finishing that particular game in goal. Megson made just one major signing, procuring his former Sheffield Wednesday colleague, the erstwhile England Under-23 winger Colin Dobson on a free transfer as player-coach. Now he was forced to strengthen Rovers' squad and the two highly astute purchases he made ensured Rovers would be serious promotion contenders in 1973/74. Goalkeeper Jim Eadie and striker Alan Warboys, who had experienced European football together at Cardiff City, were to be essential ingredients in Megson's successful cocktail. Warboys, a former team-mate of Rovers' manager at Wednesday, became the club's record signing as his move from Sheffield United cost a reputed £35,000.

Suddenly, Rovers' promotion aspirations once again flickered into life. Eadie did not concede a goal in his first five games. All realistic hope disappeared, however, in the space of three days in mid-March as Rovers crashed 4-2 at Shrewsbury Town and 4-3 at Walsall. In the latter game, Rovers trailed to a ninth-minute Bobby Shinton goal at half-time but, after Bannister and Warboys, with his first goal for the club, had put Rovers ahead, a second Warboys goal appeared to seal a 3-2 victory. Referee Jim Whalley of Southport, though, added on seven minutes of injury time. Chris Jones, scored his second goal of the night after 92 minutes, while Barnie Wright's header five

FOOTBALL LEAGUE DIVISION THREE
SEASON 1972/73

Date	Opponent	H/A	Score	Att	1 (G)	2	3	4	5	6	7	8	9	10	11	Substitutes	Goalscorers
12/08/72	BLACKBURN ROVERS	A	3-0	10744	SHEPPARD	ROBERTS	PARSONS	GREEN	TAYLOR	STANTON	STEPHENS	W JONES	ALLAN	BANNISTER	GODFREY	AITKEN P	BANNISTER, GODFREY, ARENTOFT og
19/08/72	HALIFAX TOWN	A	0-3	2812	SHEPPARD	ROBERTS	PARSONS	GREEN	TAYLOR	STANTON	STEPHENS	W JONES	ALLAN	BANNISTER	GODFREY	B JONES 7	
26/08/72	GRIMSBY TOWN	H	2-1	9158	SHEPPARD	ROBERTS	PARSONS	GREEN	TAYLOR	STANTON	STEPHENS	W JONES	ALLAN	BANNISTER	GODFREY	FEARNLEY 4	GODFREY, FEARNLEY
29/08/72	CHESTERFIELD	H	2-2	9409	SHEPPARD	ROBERTS	PARSONS	AITKEN	TAYLOR	STANTON	STEPHENS	W JONES	ALLAN	BANNISTER	GODFREY		STEPHENS, BANNISTER
02/09/72	PORT VALE	H	1-2	3468	SHEPPARD	ROBERTS	PARSONS	GREEN	TAYLOR	STANTON	STEPHENS	W JONES	ALLAN	BANNISTER	GODFREY		FEARNLEY
09/09/72	WREXHAM	H	2-0	8207	SHEPPARD	ROBERTS	PARSONS	GREEN	TAYLOR	STANTON	STEPHENS	W JONES	ALLAN	BANNISTER	GODFREY		GREEN, BANNISTER
16/09/72	OLDHAM ATHLETIC	A	2-0	5827	SHEPPARD	ROBERTS	PARSONS	GREEN	TAYLOR	STANTON	STEPHENS	W JONES	ALLAN	BANNISTER	GODFREY		GODFREY
19/09/72	PLYMOUTH ARGYLE	H	0-3	9572	SHEPPARD	ROBERTS	PARSONS	GREEN	TAYLOR	STANTON	STEPHENS	W JONES	ALLAN	BANNISTER	GODFREY	FEARNLEY 9	
23/09/72	BRENTFORD	H	1-1	8458	SHEPPARD	ROBERTS	PARSONS	GREEN	TAYLOR	STANTON	STEPHENS	W JONES	ALLAN	BANNISTER	GODFREY	DALRYMPLE 1	GODFREY
30/09/72	SWANSEA CITY	H	2-0	9710	SHEPPARD	ROBERTS	PARSONS	GREEN	TAYLOR	STANTON	STEPHENS	W JONES	ALLAN	BANNISTER	GODFREY		STEPHENS, BANNISTER
07/10/72	YORK CITY	A	1-2	3711	SHEPPARD	ROBERTS	PARSONS	GREEN	TAYLOR	GODFREY	STEPHENS	W JONES	RUDGE	BANNISTER	HIGGINS	FEARNLEY	FEARNLEY
14/10/72	ROTHERHAM UNITED	H	1-2	7601	SHEPPARD	ROBERTS	PARSONS	AITKEN	TAYLOR	PRINCE	STEPHENS	W JONES	RUDGE	BANNISTER	GODFREY		FEARNLEY
21/10/72	SHREWSBURY TOWN	H	5-1	4463	SHEPPARD	ROBERTS	PARSONS	AITKEN	TAYLOR	PRINCE	STEPHENS	W JONES	RUDGE	BANNISTER	GODFREY		RUDGE, GODFREY, BANNISTER 2, FEARNLEY
28/10/72	TRANMERE ROVERS	A	1-2	6800	SHEPPARD	ROBERTS	PARSONS	AITKEN	TAYLOR	GODFREY	STEPHENS	W JONES	RUDGE	BANNISTER	GODFREY	FEARNLEY 8	W JONES
04/11/72	WATFORD	H	0-0	3474	SHEPPARD	ROBERTS	PARSONS	AITKEN	TAYLOR	PRINCE	STEPHENS	W JONES	ALLAN	BANNISTER	GODFREY		
07/11/72	BRENTFORD	A	3-1	8351	SHEPPARD	ROBERTS	PARSONS	AITKEN	TAYLOR	PRINCE	STEPHENS	W JONES	RUDGE	BANNISTER	R JONES	FEARNLEY 9	RUDGE, GODFREY, BANNISTER 2, FEARNLEY
11/11/72	NOTTS COUNTY	H	1-0	7907	SHEPPARD	ROBERTS	PARSONS	AITKEN	TAYLOR	PRINCE	STEPHENS	GODFREY	ALLAN	BANNISTER	R JONES	WJONES	RUDGE
24/11/72	BOLTON WANDERERS	A	0-2	6678	SHEPPARD	ROBERTS	PARSONS	AITKEN	TAYLOR	PRINCE	STEPHENS	BANNISTER	RUDGE	BANNISTER	R JONES	GODFREY	
02/12/72	SOUTHEND UNITED	H	0-2	8419	DALRYMPLE	ROBERTS	PARSONS	GREEN	AITKEN	STANTON	JARMAN	BANNISTER	RUDGE	BANNISTER	GODFREY	STANTON 11	
09/12/72	SCUNTHORPE UNITED	H	0-0	8512	DALRYMPLE	ROBERTS	PARSONS	AITKEN	TAYLOR	PRINCE	JARMAN	FEARNLEY	RUDGE	BANNISTER	GODFREY	COOMBES 9	
16/12/72	BOURNEMOUTH	H	5-1	10399	DALRYMPLE	ROBERTS	PARSONS	AITKEN	TAYLOR	PRINCE	JARMAN	FEARNLEY	RUDGE	BANNISTER	DOBSON		RUDGE, GODFREY, BANNISTER 2, 1pen
26/12/72	CHARLTON ATHLETIC	H	1-0	11767	DALRYMPLE	ROBERTS	PARSONS	AITKEN	TAYLOR	PRINCE	JARMAN	RUDGE	RUDGE	BANNISTER	DOBSON		RUDGE
30/12/72	PLYMOUTH ARGYLE	A	0-0	1791	DALRYMPLE	ROBERTS	PARSONS	GREEN	AITKEN	STANTON	STANTON	ALLAN	RUDGE	BANNISTER	DOBSON	STANTON 1	
06/01/73	GRIMSBY TOWN	A	4-1	8468	SHEPPARD	ROBERTS	PARSONS	AITKEN	TAYLOR	STANTON	JARMAN	ALLAN	ALLAN	DOBSON	DOBSON	DOBSON 2	STANTON, JARMAN
13/01/73	TRANMERE ROVERS	H	2-3	8975	SHEPPARD	ROBERTS	PARSONS	AITKEN	TAYLOR	STANTON	JARMAN	GODFREY	JARMAN	DOBSON	JARMAN	STANTON 5	TAYLOR, STANTON, JARMAN
27/01/73	WREXHAM	A	2-0	8909	SHEPPARD	ROBERTS	PARSONS	AITKEN	TAYLOR	STANTON	JARMAN	GODFREY	JARMAN	DOBSON	JARMAN	STANTON 11	DOBSON 2
30/01/73	PORT VALE	A	0-0	3138	SHEPPARD	ROBERTS	PARSONS	AITKEN	GREEN	STANTON	STEPHENS	B JONES	RUDGE	BANNISTER	RUDGE		
03/02/73	NOTTS COUNTY	A	4-1	10019	SHEPPARD	ROBERTS	PARSONS	GREEN	TAYLOR	STANTON	STEPHENS	PRINCE	RUDGE	BANNISTER	DOBSON	FEARNLEY 11	JARMAN, TAYLOR, BANNISTER, PRINCE
10/02/73	OLDHAM ATHLETIC	H	0-2	11938	SHEPPARD	ROBERTS	PARSONS	PRINCE	TAYLOR	STANTON	STEPHENS	B JONES	RUDGE	BANNISTER	DOBSON	FEARNLEY 4	
17/02/73	BLACKBURN ROVERS	H	2-2	9932	SHEPPARD	ROBERTS	PARSONS	PRINCE	TAYLOR	STANTON	STEPHENS	B JONES	RUDGE	BANNISTER	DOBSON	FEARNLEY 11	BANNISTER, RUDGE
24/02/73	BOURNEMOUTH	A	3-3	12378	SHEPPARD	ROBERTS	PARSONS	PRINCE	TAYLOR	STANTON	STEPHENS	B JONES	RUDGE	BANNISTER	DOBSON		WARBOYS, BANNISTER
03/03/73	ROCHDALE	A	2-0	18344	SHEPPARD	ROBERTS	PARSONS	PRINCE	TAYLOR	STANTON	STEPHENS	B JONES	RUDGE	BANNISTER	DOBSON	TAYLOR, STANTON	WARBOYS, BANNISTER 2
10/03/73	ROTHERHAM UNITED	A	0-0	4202	SHEPPARD	ROBERTS	PARSONS	GREEN	TAYLOR	STANTON	STEPHENS	B JONES	RUDGE	BANNISTER	GODFREY	RUDGE, GODFREY, BANNISTER 2, 1pen	
17/03/73	YORK CITY	H	0-0	11176	SHEPPARD	ROBERTS	PARSONS	GREEN	TAYLOR	STANTON	STEPHENS	B JONES	RUDGE	BANNISTER	GODFREY	DOBSON 2	
19/03/73	ROCHDALE	H	3-0	9469	SHEPPARD	ROBERTS	PARSONS	GREEN	TAYLOR	STANTON	STEPHENS	STANTON	WARBOYS	BANNISTER	GODFREY	JARMAN, TAYLOR, BANNISTER, PRINCE	TAYLOR, BANNISTER 2
24/03/73	SHREWSBURY TOWN	H	2-4	3593	EADIE	ROBERTS	PARSONS	GREEN	TAYLOR	STANTON	STEPHENS	W JONES	WARBOYS	BANNISTER	GODFREY	BANNISTER, RUDGE	WARBOYS, BANNISTER, TUMBRIDGE og
31/03/73	WALSALL	H	3-0	4595	EADIE	STANTON	PARSONS	GREEN	TAYLOR	STANTON	STEPHENS	W JONES	WARBOYS	BANNISTER	GODFREY	WARBOYS, BANNISTER	B JONES, HIGGINS, BANNISTER
07/04/73	WATFORD	A	2-0	6798	EADIE	STANTON	PARSONS	PRINCE	TAYLOR	GODFREY	STEPHENS	W JONES	WARBOYS	BANNISTER	HIGGINS	TAYLOR, BANNISTER 2	BANNISTER, RUDGE
14/04/73	SOUTHEND UNITED	A	3-1	6374	EADIE	ROBERTS	PARSONS	PRINCE	TAYLOR	GODFREY	STEPHENS	W JONES	WARBOYS	BANNISTER	HIGGINS	WARBOYS, BANNISTER, TUMBRIDGE og	HIGGINS, BANNISTER pen
20/04/73	SCUNTHORPE UNITED	H	2-0	1784	EADIE	ROBERTS	PARSONS	PRINCE	TAYLOR	GODFREY	STEPHENS	B JONES	WARBOYS	BANNISTER	GODFREY	JARMAN 8	W JONES
24/04/73	SWANSEA CITY	A	3-1	6285	EADIE	ROBERTS	PARSONS	PRINCE	TAYLOR	GODFREY	STEPHENS	STANTON	WARBOYS	BANNISTER	RUDGE		W JONES, GODFREY
28/04/73	CHARLTON ATHLETIC	H	3-3	8348	EADIE	ROBERTS	PARSONS	PRINCE	TAYLOR	GODFREY	STEPHENS	STANTON	ALLAN	GODFREY	RUDGE	WARBOYS, BANNISTER 2	W JONES, BANNISTER pen
01/05/73*	CHESTERFIELD	H	1-0	3849	EADIE	ROBERTS	PARSONS	PRINCE	TAYLOR	PRINCE	COOMBES	COOMBES	ALLAN	GODFREY	RUDGE		GODFREY, BANNISTER, W JONES

FA CUP

Date	Opponent	H/A	Score	Att	1	2	3	4	5	6	7	8	9	10	11	Substitutes	Goalscorers
18/11/72	HAYES	A	0-1	6000	DALRYMPLE	ROBERTS	PARSONS	GREEN	TAYLOR	PRINCE	STEPHENS	STANTON	ALLAN	BANNISTER	HIGGINS	RUDGE 9	

LEAGUE CUP

Date	Opponent	H/A	Score	Att	1	2	3	4	5	6	7	8	9	10	11	Substitutes	Goalscorers
15/08/72	CARDIFF CITY	A	2-2	14541	SHEPPARD	ROBERTS	PARSONS	GREEN	TAYLOR	STANTON	STEPHENS	W JONES	ALLAN	BANNISTER	GODFREY	FEARNLEY 11	WARBOYS, BANNISTER
22/08/72	CARDIFF CITY	H	3-1	14550	SHEPPARD	ROBERTS	PARSONS	GREEN	TAYLOR	STANTON	STEPHENS	W JONES	ALLAN	BANNISTER	GODFREY	FEARNLEY 4	TAYLOR, STANTON, JARMAN
05/09/72	BRIGHTON & H	A	4-0	9530	SHEPPARD	ROBERTS	PARSONS	GREEN	TAYLOR	STANTON	STEPHENS	W JONES	ALLAN	BANNISTER	GODFREY	W JONES, GODFREY	W JONES, GODFREY, BANNISTER, pen
03/10/72	WALSALL	H	3-1	29349	SHEPPARD	ROBERTS	PARSONS	AITKEN	TAYLOR	PRINCE	STEPHENS	W JONES	RUDGE	BANNISTER	GODFREY	W JONES, FEARNLEY, ALLAN, STANTON	W JONES, FEARNLEY, ALLAN, STANTON
11/10/72	MANCHESTER UNITED	H	1-1	33597	SHEPPARD	ROBERTS	PARSONS	AITKEN	TAYLOR	PRINCE	STEPHENS	W JONES	RUDGE	BANNISTER	GODFREY		JARMAN 2
31/10/72	MANCHESTER UNITED	A	0-4	20272	SHEPPARD	ROBERTS	PARSONS	AITKEN	TAYLOR	PRINCE	STEPHENS	W JONES	RUDGE	BANNISTER	GODFREY	ALLAN 11	BANNISTER 2

WATNEY CUP

Date	Opponent	H/A	Score	Att	1	2	3	4	5	6	7	8	9	10	11	Substitutes	Goalscorers
29/07/72	WOLVERHAMPTON W	H	2-0	12489	SHEPPARD	ROBERTS	PARSONS	GREEN	TAYLOR	PRINCE	STEPHENS	W JONES	ALLAN	BANNISTER	GODFREY		BANNISTER, WARBOYS
02/08/72	BURNLEY	H	2-0	10689	SHEPPARD	ROBERTS	PARSONS	PRINCE	TAYLOR	PRINCE	STEPHENS	W JONES	ALLAN	BANNISTER	GODFREY		PRINCE, STEPHENS
05/08/72	SHEFFIELD UNITED *	H	2-0	19768	SHEPPARD	ROBERTS	PARSONS	GREEN	TAYLOR	PRINCE	STEPHENS	W JONES	ALLAN	BANNISTER	GODFREY		BANNISTER pen, STEPHENS

*Final: AET. Rovers won 7-6 on pens

GLOUCESTERSHIRE CUP FINAL

Date	Opponent	H/A	Score	Att	1	2	3	4	5	6	7	8	9	10	11	Substitutes	Goalscorers
01/05/73	BRISTOL CITY	H	2-2	12350	EADIE	ROBERTS	PARSONS	PRINCE	TAYLOR	PRINCE	STEPHENS	COOMBES	WARBOYS	BANNISTER	RUDGE		BANNISTER, WARBOYS

PLAYERS	APP	SUB	GLS
AITKEN P	27		1
ALLAN A	44	1	25
BANNISTER B	5		
COOMBES J	2		1
DALRYMPLE M	5		
DOBSON C	14		1
EADIE I	14		
FEARNLEY B	8	12	
GODFREY B	41		8
GREEN M	13		
HIGGINS P	5		1
JARMAN H	18		4
JONES B	9	1	2
JONES R	4		1
JONES W	14		3
PARSONS L	46		1
PRINCE F	27	1	
ROBERTS P	44		2
RUDGE J	26	4	10
SHEPPARD R	28		
STANTON T	41	2	1
STEPHENS K	42	4	6
TAYLOR S	32	1	5
WARBOYS A	11		5
OWN GOALS			2

minutes later condemned Rovers to a further season in Division Three. However, four wins in the last five games left Rovers in a morale-boosting fifth position. Parsons, the only ever-present, had now appeared in 135 consecutive League matches, while Bannister's 25 League goals was the most by a Rovers player since Alfie Biggs in 1963/64. A late flurry of goals, Warboys and Bannister both scoring in four League games and the Gloucestershire Cup final, which was lost to Bristol City on a penalty shoot-out, ensured qualification again for the Watney Cup. Rovers' prospects for 1973/74 looked highly encouraging.

The final home game also marked the farewell appearance of the North Enclosure's favourite son, the winger Harold Jarman, who had appeared in more than 400 League matches for Rovers since his debut in 1959, and had attained cult status in his later years at Eastville. Jarman was rewarded with a testimonial game against Liverpool and he joined Newport County along with Brian Godfrey. As he left, so too did Phil Roberts, a club record £55,000 sale to Portsmouth, where he won 4 full caps for Wales, and Sandy Allan, who emigrated to South Africa. Bobby Jones, who had also surpassed 400 League games for Rovers, retired in May 1973 and was justly rewarded for his long and loyal service with a testimonial game against West Ham United.

1973/74

O n the evening of Friday 19 April 1974, Rovers drew 0-0 at Southend United to regain Division Two status. More than 1,000 Rovers supporters had made the journey to Roots Hall for this game and the resultant pitch invasion reflected the sense of relief and pride at the club's achievement. Don Megson, building on the groundwork of Bert Tann, Bill Dodgin and Bobby Campbell, had generated a team spirit that would guide the club back out of Division Three. Rovers had also reverted to blue-and-white quartered shirts in 1973 and these old, trusted tops restored the golden years to Eastville with instant effect.

Much of the success was due to the stability of Megson's side. Ever-present goalkeeper Jim Eadie improved on his feat of the previous season by playing a club record 707 minutes in the autumn without conceding a goal. In fact, Rovers conceded only 5 goals in the opening 16 League matches. Dependable left-back Lindsay Parsons, whose missed games in March ended a run of 167 consecutive League appearances, was partnered by Phil Roberts' replacement, the tough-tackling former Bristol City right-back Trevor Jacobs. Ever-present Stuart Taylor and captain Mike Green were dominant centre-halves, while Frankie Prince and another ever-present, Tom Stanton, were forceful figures in midfield. On the wings, Kenny Stephens and Colin Dobson created the opportunities on which forwards Alan Warboys and Bruce Bannister thrived. Beyond these 11 players, only John Rudge and Gordon Fearnley enjoyed extended runs in the side.

Megson's influence on the side was primarily to tighten Rovers' defence. Only 33 goals were conceded in 46 League matches, fewer than any other Division Three club

Bristol Rovers 1973/74. Back row: Bater, Guscott, Moore, Crabtree, Aitken, Powell, Stephens. Middle row: B Jones, Stanton, Green, Taylor, Lewis, Sheppard, Eadie, Warboys, Rudge, Prince, Parsons. Front row: Campbell (Trainer-Coach), Jacobs, M John, Fearnley, Megson (Manager), Bannister, D John, Britten, Dobson (Player-Coach)

and overtaking the club record 36 in 42 League games in 1922/23. With a strong defence, Rovers could embark on a long unbeaten run. In attack, player-of-the-year Warboys, top scorer with 22 League goals, was muscular and strong, while Bannister was quick, the pair becoming known nationally as 'Smash and Grab'. Indeed, when Warboys was sidelined in the spring with a hamstring injury, Rovers began losing games, though it would be wholly unjust to blame his highly competent replacements, Rudge and David Staniforth, a £20,000 March signing from Sheffield United.

The new season opened with a Watney Cup tie against West Ham United, when Rovers outplayed their First Division opponents, yet had to rely on victory in a penalty shoot-out after a 1-1 draw. Disappointingly, Hull City then won by a single goal in the Eastville semi-final, while a solitary Harry Redknapp goal at Bournemouth knocked Rovers out of the League Cup. Kenny Hibbitt, later a Rovers player, scored in the final for Wolverhampton Wanderers, who beat Manchester City 2-1. Division Three, though, presented an entirely different proposition, as Rovers swept all before them, remaining unbeaten for the first 27 games of the season. This achievement equalled a record for the division, set ironically by Rovers in winning the championship in 1952/53. However Rovers set a new record in remaining undefeated for 32 matches between 31 March 1973 and 2 February 1974.

On the opening day of the season, Rovers played away to Bournemouth, whom many believed would be promotion candidates. A morale-boosting 3-0 victory, with Warboys and Bannister both on the scoresheet, set Rovers on track for the success that was to follow. Although Hereford United, Port Vale, York City and Grimsby Town held out for draws at Eastville, Rovers looked increasingly awesome. There were three consecutive 2-0 victories in September, Tom Stanton scoring twice against Halifax Town. Two

Warboys goals helped Rovers towards an impressive 4-2 win over Plymouth Argyle on Boxing Day. The machine kept rolling as Rovers, into the New Year, held out for draws at Charlton Athletic and Halifax Town. They ran off another 3-0 victory over Bournemouth, with Bannister and Warboys both scoring again, and won 3-2 at Aldershot in the first Sunday Football League game in which Rovers participated.

Rovers hit a purple patch just before Christmas. Warboys scored a hat-trick to beat Southport 3-1 in mid-November, the first of three hat-tricks he claimed in four weeks. The Pirates then arrived at Brighton for a 2 p.m. kick-off on 1 December, an hour earlier than usual to save electricity during the Miners' Strike. Rovers had a poor track record at the Goldstone Ground, but the League

Captain Mike Green led Rovers to promotion in 1974. He moved to Plymouth and did the same for them the following season

leaders were facing a side knocked out of the FA Cup only three days earlier by Walton & Hersham. However, few could have predicted an 8-2 win for Rovers, a club record victory and the only occasion two Rovers players had scored three times or more in the same League fixture. Seven days later Warboys scored three more goals and Jacobs his first for the club as Rovers demolished Southend United – for whom the future Rovers assistant manager Dennis Booth played in midfield – 4-0 at Eastville.

The Brighton win, broadcast on national television, was a demoralizing blow to their young manager, Brian Clough. Bannister put Rovers ahead after four minutes, following an excellent move involving Parsons, Dobson and Warboys. Fearnley put Rovers 2-0 up eight minutes later and, though the Welsh International Peter O'Sullivan pulled a goal back, Rovers were 5-1 ahead by the break and Bannister had already completed what was to be the only hat-trick of his Rovers career. After half-time, Warboys took over, adding three more to his first-half goal to become only the second Rovers player to score four goals in an away League game. He could have had more, too, had he not been forced to leave the field at one stage to have stitches inserted in a cut above his eye. Ronnie Howell's 87th-minute consolation goal could not deprive Rovers of a record League win, on the day the reserves won 6-1 against Bristol City reserves. No other Division Three fixture has ever finished in an 8-2 win for the away side.

Once February arrived, Rovers' dreams of going undefeated for an entire season were shattered. Indeed, the Aldershot game in January – a club-record 17th consecutive unbeaten away League game, which left Rovers seven points clear at the top – marked the last time until August 1976 that Warboys and Bannister had both scored in the same League fixture. A single-goal defeat at Wrexham, to Arfon Griffiths' strike a minute after half-time, was followed by a 3-1 loss at Port Vale, when Green ended the match in

Date	Opposition	Venue	Score	Att	C	2	3	4	5	6	7	8	9	10	11	Substitutes	Goalscorers
25/08/73	AFC BOURNEMOUTH	A	3-0	11379	EADIE	JACOBS	PARSONS	GREEN	TAYLOR	STANTON	STEPHENS	JONES	WARBOYS	BANNISTER	DOBSON	FEARNLEY 7	WARBOYS 2, BANNISTER
01/09/73	CHARLTON ATHLETIC	H	1-1	7323	EADIE	JACOBS	PARSONS	GREEN	TAYLOR	PRINCE	JONES	STANTON	WARBOYS	BANNISTER	DOBSON	WARBOYS 2, BANNISTER	WARBOYS, BANNISTER
08/09/73	GRIMSBY TOWN	A	1-1	7640	EADIE	JACOBS	PARSONS	GREEN	TAYLOR	PRINCE	JONES	STANTON	WARBOYS	BANNISTER	DOBSON	COOMBES 1	WARBOYS, BANNISTER
11/09/73	HEREFORD UNITED	H	1-1	12620	EADIE	JACOBS	PARSONS	GREEN	TAYLOR	PRINCE	STEPHENS	STANTON	WARBOYS	BANNISTER	DOBSON	DOBSON C	PRINCE, KING og
15/09/73	HALIFAX TOWN	H	2-0	7485	EADIE	JACOBS	PARSONS	GREEN	TAYLOR	PRINCE	STEPHENS	STANTON	WARBOYS	BANNISTER	DOBSON	EADIE J	BANNISTER, WARBOYS
18/09/73	SHREWSBURY TOWN	A	2-0	3016	EADIE	JACOBS	PARSONS	GREEN	TAYLOR	PRINCE	STEPHENS	STANTON	WARBOYS	BANNISTER	DOBSON	FEARNLEY 7	DOBSON, WARBOYS
22/09/73	BLACKBURN ROVERS	H	2-0	8424	EADIE	JACOBS	PARSONS	GREEN	TAYLOR	PRINCE	STEPHENS	STANTON	WARBOYS	BANNISTER	DOBSON	PRINCE, KING og	WARBOYS
29/09/73	CAMBRIDGE UNITED	A	2-0	8919	EADIE	JACOBS	PARSONS	GREEN	TAYLOR	PRINCE	STEPHENS	STANTON	WARBOYS	BANNISTER	DOBSON	BANNISTER, WARBOYS	FEARNLEY
02/10/73	SHREWSBURY TOWN	H	1-0	11455	EADIE	JACOBS	PARSONS	GREEN	TAYLOR	PRINCE	FEARNLEY	STANTON	WARBOYS	BANNISTER	DOBSON	FEARNLEY 7	BANNISTER
06/10/73	WATFORD	A	0-0	10202	EADIE	JACOBS	PARSONS	GREEN	TAYLOR	PRINCE	STEPHENS	STANTON	WARBOYS	BANNISTER	DOBSON	WARBOYS	
13/10/73	SHREWSBURY TOWN	H	1-0	11455	EADIE	JACOBS	PARSONS	GREEN	TAYLOR	PRINCE	STEPHENS	STANTON	WARBOYS	BANNISTER	DOBSON	BANNISTER	WARBOYS 3
20/10/73	YORK CITY	A	0-0	8776	EADIE	JACOBS	PARSONS	GREEN	TAYLOR	PRINCE	STEPHENS	STANTON	WARBOYS	BANNISTER	DOBSON		
24/10/73	PORT VALE	H	0-0	12501	EADIE	JACOBS	PARSONS	GREEN	TAYLOR	PRINCE	STEPHENS	STANTON	WARBOYS	BANNISTER	DOBSON		WARBOYS
27/10/73	HEREFORD UNITED	H	2-1	9532	EADIE	JACOBS	PARSONS	GREEN	TAYLOR	PRINCE	FEARNLEY	STANTON	WARBOYS	BANNISTER	DOBSON	FEARNLEY 7	TAYLOR
03/11/73	CHESTERFIELD	A	1-0	10198	EADIE	JACOBS	PARSONS	GREEN	TAYLOR	PRINCE	STEPHENS	STANTON	WARBOYS	BANNISTER	DOBSON	JOHN 11	
10/11/73	HUDDERSFIELD TOWN	H	3-1	6058	EADIE	JACOBS	PARSONS	GREEN	TAYLOR	PRINCE	STEPHENS	STANTON	WARBOYS	BANNISTER	DOBSON	WARBOYS 3	WARBOYS 3
17/11/73	WALSALL	A	1-1	10472	EADIE	JACOBS	PARSONS	GREEN	TAYLOR	PRINCE	FEARNLEY	STANTON	WARBOYS	BANNISTER	DOBSON	FEARNLEY	GREEN
01/12/73	SOUTHPORT	H	8-2	11018	EADIE	JACOBS	PARSONS	GREEN	TAYLOR	PRINCE	STEPHENS	STANTON	WARBOYS	BANNISTER	DOBSON	RUDGE 3	FEARNLEY, BANNISTER 3, 1 pen, WARBOYS 4
08/12/73	OLDHAM ATHLETIC	A	4-0	10762	EADIE	JACOBS	PARSONS	GREEN	TAYLOR	PRINCE	STEPHENS	STANTON	WARBOYS	BANNISTER	DOBSON		WARBOYS 3, JACOBS
22/12/73	BRIGHTON & H ALBION	H	2-2	11770	EADIE	JACOBS	PARSONS	GREEN	TAYLOR	PRINCE	STEPHENS	STANTON	WARBOYS	BANNISTER	DOBSON	FEARNLEY 7	STANTON, WARBOYS
26/12/73	SOUTHEND UNITED	A	4-2	4491	EADIE	JACOBS	PARSONS	GREEN	TAYLOR	PRINCE	STEPHENS	STANTON	WARBOYS	BANNISTER	DOBSON		TAYLOR, WARBOYS 2, BANNISTER
29/12/73	CAMBRIDGE UNITED	H	2-2	22353	EADIE	JACOBS	PARSONS	GREEN	TAYLOR	PRINCE	STEPHENS	STANTON	WARBOYS	BANNISTER	DOBSON		STANTON, WARBOYS 2, BANNISTER
01/01/74	PLYMOUTH ARGYLE	A	1-1	14317	EADIE	JACOBS	PARSONS	GREEN	TAYLOR	PRINCE	STEPHENS	STANTON	WARBOYS	BANNISTER	DOBSON	RUDGE 9	WIGGINGTON og
12/01/74	GRIMSBY TOWN	H	4-1	11195	EADIE	JACOBS	AITKEN	GREEN	TAYLOR	PRINCE	STEPHENS	STANTON	RUDGE	BANNISTER	DOBSON		RUDGE
19/01/74	CHARLTON ATHLETIC	A	0-0	11414	EADIE	JACOBS	AITKEN	GREEN	TAYLOR	PRINCE	STEPHENS	STANTON	RUDGE	BANNISTER	DOBSON		
02/02/74	HALIFAX TOWN	A	1-3	4507	EADIE	JACOBS	PARSONS	GREEN	TAYLOR	PRINCE	STEPHENS	STANTON	WARBOYS	BANNISTER	DOBSON	RUDGE 11	WARBOYS, RUDGE, BANNISTER pen
09/02/74	AFC BOURNEMOUTH	H	2-1	21186	EADIE	JACOBS	PARSONS	GREEN	TAYLOR	PRINCE	STEPHENS	STANTON	WARBOYS	BANNISTER	DOBSON	RUDGE 11	BANNISTER 2, WARBOYS
23/02/74	WREXHAM	A	0-1	13196	EADIE	JACOBS	PARSONS	GREEN	TAYLOR	PRINCE	FEARNLEY	STANTON	WARBOYS	BANNISTER	DOBSON	FEARNLEY 7	
02/03/74	PORT VALE	H	1-3	9883	EADIE	JACOBS	PARSONS	GREEN	TAYLOR	PRINCE	RUDGE	STANTON	WARBOYS	BANNISTER	DOBSON	FEARNLEY 1	RUDGE
05/03/74	WATFORD	A	0-1	8505	EADIE	JACOBS	PARSONS	GREEN	TAYLOR	PRINCE	RUDGE	STANTON	WARBOYS	BANNISTER	DOBSON	RUDGE	WARBOYS
09/03/74	ALDERSHOT	H	1-0	14069	EADIE	JACOBS	PARSONS	GREEN	TAYLOR	COOMBES	FEARNLEY	STANTON	WARBOYS	BANNISTER	DOBSON		
12/03/74	ROCHDALE	A	0-1	11374	EADIE	JACOBS	PARSONS	GREEN	TAYLOR	PRINCE	STEPHENS	STANTON	STANIFORTH	BANNISTER	DOBSON	STANIFORTH 10	STANIFORTH
16/03/74	PLYMOUTH ARGYLE	H	2-1	14510	EADIE	JACOBS	PARSONS	GREEN	TAYLOR	PRINCE	STEPHENS	STANTON	STANIFORTH	BANNISTER	DOBSON	STANIFORTH 7	STANIFORTH
19/03/74	HUDDERSFIELD TOWN	A	3-0	10330	EADIE	JACOBS	PARSONS	GREEN	TAYLOR	PRINCE	STANIFORTH	STANTON	FEARNLEY	BANNISTER	DOBSON	STANIFORTH	STANIFORTH
23/03/74	BLACKBURN ROVERS	H	0-0	6290	EADIE	JACOBS	PARSONS	GREEN	TAYLOR	PRINCE	STEPHENS	STANTON	WARBOYS	BANNISTER	RUDGE	BANNISTER 11	BANNISTER
25/03/74	YORK CITY	H	1-1	1856	EADIE	JACOBS	PARSONS	GREEN	TAYLOR	PRINCE	STEPHENS	STANTON	WARBOYS	BANNISTER	O'BRIEN	WARBOYS 7	STANIFORTH, RUDGE
30/03/74	WREXHAM	H	0-0	11559	EADIE	JACOBS	PARSONS	GREEN	TAYLOR	PRINCE	STEPHENS	STANTON	WARBOYS	BANNISTER	O'BRIEN	BANNISTER	BANNISTER
02/04/74	WALSALL	A	2-1	1499	EADIE	JACOBS	PARSONS	GREEN	TAYLOR	PRINCE	STEPHENS	STANTON	WARBOYS	BANNISTER	O'BRIEN	BANNISTER	BANNISTER
05/04/74	ROCHDALE	H	1-0	11370	EADIE	JACOBS	PARSONS	GREEN	TAYLOR	PRINCE	STEPHENS	STANTON	WARBOYS	STANIFORTH	DOBSON	STANIFORTH	STEPHENS
12/04/74	CHESTERFIELD	H	0-0	18692	EADIE	JACOBS	PARSONS	GREEN	TAYLOR	PRINCE	STEPHENS	STANTON	RUDGE	BANNISTER	DOBSON	RUDGE 7	JACOBS 2, BANNISTER
13/04/74	ALDERSHOT	A	1-2	16090	EADIE	JACOBS	PARSONS	GREEN	TAYLOR	PRINCE	STEPHENS	STANTON	RUDGE	BANNISTER	DOBSON	RUDGE 4	STEPHENS
16/04/74	SOUTHPORT	A	1-0	8323	EADIE	JACOBS	PARSONS	GREEN	TAYLOR	PRINCE	STEPHENS	STANTON	WARBOYS	BANNISTER	RUDGE	BANNISTER	BANNISTER
19/04/74	TRANMERE ROVERS	H	1-0	16090	EADIE	JACOBS	PARSONS	GREEN	TAYLOR	PRINCE	STEPHENS	STANTON	WARBOYS	BANNISTER	RUDGE	BANNISTER	BANNISTER
27/04/74	BRIGHTON & H ALBION	H	1-1	19137	EADIE	JACOBS	PARSONS	GREEN	TAYLOR	PRINCE	STEPHENS	STANTON	WARBOYS	BANNISTER	RUDGE	STANIFORTH 11	BANNISTER pen

FA CUP

Date	Opposition	Venue	Score	Att	C	2	3	4	5	6	7	8	9	10	11	Substitutes	Goalscorers
24/11/73	BIDEFORD	A	2-0	4800	EADIE	JACOBS	PARSONS	GREEN	TAYLOR	PRINCE	STEPHENS	STANTON	WARBOYS	BANNISTER	DOBSON	STANIFORTH 10	STANIFORTH, RUDGE
15/12/73	NORTHAMPTON TOWN	A	2-1	6181	EADIE	JACOBS	PARSONS	GREEN	TAYLOR	PRINCE	STEPHENS	STANTON	WARBOYS	BANNISTER	DOBSON	JOHN 7	WARBOYS, BANNISTER
06/01/74	NOTTINGHAM FOREST	A	4-3	23456	EADIE	JACOBS	PARSONS	GREEN	TAYLOR	PRINCE	GREEN	STANTON	WARBOYS	BANNISTER	DOBSON	JONES 11	PRINCE, DOBSON, RUDGE

LEAGUE CUP

Date	Opposition	Venue	Score	Att	C	2	3	4	5	6	7	8	9	10	11	Substitutes	Goalscorers
29/08/73	AFC BOURNEMOUTH	A	0-1	7520	EADIE	JACOBS	PARSONS	GREEN	TAYLOR	PRINCE	JONES	STANTON	WARBOYS	BANNISTER	DOBSON	DOBSON	

GLOUCESTERSHIRE CUP FINAL

Date	Opposition	Venue	Score	Att	C	2	3	4	5	6	7	8	9	10	11	Substitutes	Goalscorers
29/04/74	BRISTOL CITY	A	2-0	15986	EADIE	JACOBS	PARSONS	AITKEN	TAYLOR	PRINCE	FEARNLEY	JONES	WARBOYS	RUDGE	STANIFORTH	DOBSON	STANIFORTH, RUDGE

PLAYERS	APP	SUB	GLS
AITKEN P	6	1	
BANNISTER B	44	1	18
COOMBES J	1		
DOBSON C	39		1
EADIE J	46		
FEARNLEY G	10	6	3
GREEN M	44		3
JACOBS T	46		
JOHN M	2		1
JONES B	4		1
O'BRIEN G	3		
PARSONS L	42		
PRINCE F	43		1
RUDGE J	13	6	4
STANIFORTH D	8	3	2
STANTON T	46		3
STEPHENS K	31	2	3
TAYLOR S	46		2
WARBOYS A	32	1	22
OWN GOALS			2

The fans salute their heroes at Eastville following promotion to Division Two in 1974

goal after Eadie had been stretchered off with concussion. Although two Jacobs goals helped defeat Blackburn Rovers 3-0, the defeats continued, the first at home coming at the hands of Walsall. Stephens and Walsall's Doug Fraser had both been sent off when Rovers visited Fellows Park in November and now in March two Alan Buckley goals inflicted a first loss at Eastville since March 1973.

Rovers played at second-placed York City on 16 March in blustery conditions. Chris Jones had put York ahead seven minutes after half-time and, when Bannister was sent off nine minutes from time, overreacting to a Chris Topping foul, it looked all over for Rovers. Remarkably, four minutes later, Stephens equalised with a low left-wing cross shot, but he was then also sent off for disputing the penalty five minutes into injury time with which Ian Holmes gave the home side victory. Referee Jim Whalley had also allowed seven minutes of injury time at Walsall 12 months earlier, while York's first goalscorer, Chris Jones, had ironically scored twice in the Walsall game. The upshot was that York now stood just three points behind Rovers with a game in hand, and the pressure was back on Rovers.

The worst setback of all, however, was a 2-1 defeat on Easter Saturday at home to promotion rivals Oldham Athletic. Rovers' healthy seven-point lead had been whittled away as the Latics had won 10 consecutive League games. Oldham had beaten Southport 6-0 just 24 hours prior to their game at Eastville. Then a long-range shot from George McVitie and an opportunist goal from top scorer Colin Garwood earned a crucial victory over Rovers. Oldham Athletic, promoted when they beat Huddersfield Town 6-0 a week later, were champions with 62 points, just one point ahead of second-placed

Alan Warboys, part of the 'Smash-and-Grab' duo with Bruce Bannister, scored a magnificent 22 goals during Rovers' promotion season

Rovers and York City, both promoted under the new 'three-up' rule. The point gained at Southend not only ensured promotion, but enabled Rovers to claim a club record, equalled only in 1989/90, as only 5 away games had been lost. A happy crowd of 19,137 at Eastville in the final match saw Rovers recover from Lammie Robertson's 19th-minute goal to draw with Brighton, Bannister converting a penalty five minutes from time after Prince had been fouled by Ron Welch.

'Megson's Marvels' had held out, despite growing pressures, and Rovers were to return to Division Two after an absence of more than a decade. It had been a season of hard work and of numerous club records, most notably the 32-match unbeaten League run. Moreover, many early-season points had been ground out week by week to form a platform for success. It was also a season of milestones, for the draw with Port Vale in October had been Rovers' 1,000th home League game and the draw against York City seven days later Rovers' 2,000th match in the Football League. Yet, what many observers regarded as one of the best performances came in the FA Cup. Rovers had won confidently at Bideford, who fielded only two players with League experience, namely the Exeter City pair of Steve Morris and Graham Moxham, and subsequently at Northampton Town, while their 4-3 defeat at Nottingham Forest, for whom Neil Martin scored twice and the future Rovers player Miah Dennehy played a key role, showed the club could compete with higher division sides. There was much of a positive nature to gain from season 1973/74 and Megson's next challenge would be to maintain the club's newly regained Division Two status.

By the turn of the century, many clubs greeted promotion by splashing into the transfer market and forking out millions of pounds on strengthening their squad. The return to Division Two after 12 seasons away saw no such reaction from Don Megson's Rovers. Despite the sale of captain Mike Green to Plymouth Argyle, where he repeated his success by helping the Pilgrims up from Division Three in his first season, the Rovers manager stuck with his successful side. Perhaps this attitude was reflected in Rovers' season-long struggle to avoid relegation, a situation repeated almost annually until the relegation season of 1980/81.

The previous season's success was rewarded with a summer tour of Australia, New Zealand and Thailand. It was a largely familiar-looking Rovers side that took a point off Notts County before what was to be the largest opening-day crowd for a home game until 1999. There was a brief honeymoon period, Rovers remaining unbeaten for three games with Gordon Fearnley scoring against his former club at Hillsborough and also in the home win over Hull City. Reality soon struck, however, as Rovers faced the long trip to Roker Park, where a rampant Sunderland scored five times. A hat-trick in that game from Billy Hughes was the first conceded in the League by Rovers for more than four years. Rovers responded with a fine home victory over a strong Aston Villa side. Phil Bater, a debutant at full-back, subdued the former Eastville favourite, Ray Graydon, and two first-time shots from Alan Warboys, set up by Peter Aitken on 54 minutes and by Gordon Fearnley five minutes from time, brought about a memorable victory.

There followed sufficient heavy defeats for Rovers to spend the remainder of the season looking anxiously over their shoulders at the relegation zone. Bolton also scored five times, with John Byrom only denied a hat-trick when his manager Ian Greaves credited his third goal to Stuart Lee, and Rovers lost 3-0 to York City, Southampton and Portsmouth. In the game at The Dell, all the goals were scored by England International forward Mick Channon, who was to play for Rovers briefly during 1982/83. He and Joe Riley remain the only two players to have appeared in League football for Rovers and scored a League hat-trick against them. Southampton also won at Eastville, when Eadie pulled a misdirected Channon lob back into his own net 16 minutes from time.

A tough season is always made harder by marginal decisions. Single-goal defeats at home to Southampton and in four tough away games, notably at Villa Park, reflected the fact that results were not going Rovers' way. When Fulham won 2-1 at Eastville in March, Colin Dobson, in his first home League appearance of the season, missed a penalty. Rovers won a right-wing corner in the dying seconds of the goalless draw at home to Orient in November, but the final whistle was blown before substitute John Rudge's flying header hit the net.

The long-awaited local derby at Eastville proved to be a disaster from Rovers' point of view. Having lost three consecutive games in the run-up to the match, Rovers were also deprived of the services of the ever-reliable goalkeeper Jim Eadie. His absence through injury after 84 consecutive League games enabled a one-match recall for Dick

Bristol Rovers 1974/75. Back row: Prince, Stephens, Aitken, Jacobs, Rudge. Middle row: Stanton, Taylor, Eadie, Staniforth, Sheppard, Warboys, Parsons. Front row: Campbell (Trainer-Coach), Fearnley, Bannister, Megson (Manager), B Jones, M John, Dobson (Player-Coach)

Sheppard, who had not played for almost two years since his sickening injury against Tranmere Rovers. Rovers, in fact, led at half-time through Fearnley, before being buried by an avalanche of City goals past the beleaguered Sheppard at the Muller Road end.

Relegation was avoided due to several well-earned victories. After considerable pressure, it took a last-minute header from the dependable Stuart Taylor, following a corner in front of the Tote End, to beat Oxford United in February. Nottingham Forest, European Cup winners within five years, were beaten 4-2 at Eastville, while two Alan Warboys goals defeated Sunderland, FA Cup winners in 1973. Rovers also completed a memorable double over old rivals Oldham Athletic. In a remarkable game at Boundary Park, not dissimilar in excitement level to the match there in 1997, Rovers won 4-3 after a goalless first-half and a bizarre final 45 minutes. Jeff Coombes gave Rovers a 46th-minute lead and, within 20 minutes, the visitors were 3-0 ahead. Once Ian Robins and Maurice Whittle, from a penalty, had cut their lead, Rovers were grateful for Gordon Fearnley's second goal of the game, five minutes from time, which gave them a cushion that Robins promptly halved. Rovers have appeared in other League games featuring seven or more second-half goals, but never after a scoreless first half. Five weeks later, goals from Warboys and Taylor brought victory in the return game.

The introduction of two new faces in March, in young Bristol-born centre-back Graham Day, filling in for the injured Taylor, and experienced midfielder Wilf Smith, brought a string of more positive results. Dobson and the ever-combative Frankie Prince both scored in consecutive fixtures in April. Rovers drew four of their final five away League matches, including the local derby at Ashton Gate courtesy of a 33rd-minute own goal when Dobson's high cross deflected in off Gary Collier's shoulder. Manchester

SEASON 1974/75

FOOTBALL LEAGUE DIVISION TWO

Date	Opponent	Ven	Score	Att	G	2	3	4	5	6	7	8	9	10	11	Substitutes	Goalscorers
17/08/74	NOTTS COUNTY	H	0-0	14365	EADIE	JACOBS	PARSONS	AITKEN	TAYLOR	STANTON	JONES	STANIFORTH	WARBOYS	BANNISTER	RUDGE	STANIFORTH, 11	FEARNLEY
28/08/74	SHEFFIELD WEDNESDAY	H	1-1	14343	EADIE	JACOBS	PARSONS	AITKEN	TAYLOR	PRINCE	JONES	STANTON	WARBOYS	BANNISTER	FEARNLEY		BANNISTER pen, FEARNLEY
31/08/74	HULL CITY	H	2-0	11191	EADIE	JACOBS	PARSONS	AITKEN	TAYLOR	PRINCE	JONES	STANTON	WARBOYS	BANNISTER	FEARNLEY		WARBOYS
07/09/74	SUNDERLAND	A	1-5	24010	EADIE	JACOBS	BATER	AITKEN	TAYLOR	PRINCE	JONES	STANTON	WARBOYS	BANNISTER	FEARNLEY	RUDGE 3	WARBOYS 2
14/09/74	ASTON VILLA	H	1-1	12330	EADIE	JACOBS	PARSONS	AITKEN	TAYLOR	PRINCE	STEPHENS	STANTON	WARBOYS	BANNISTER	FEARNLEY	RUDGE 11	BANNISTER
17/09/74	SHEFFIELD WEDNESDAY	A	1-1	42948	EADIE	JACOBS	PARSONS	AITKEN	TAYLOR	PRINCE	STEPHENS	STANTON	WARBOYS	BANNISTER	FEARNLEY	RUDGE 7	
21/09/74	MANCHESTER UNITED	A	0-2	8706	EADIE	JACOBS	PARSONS	AITKEN	TAYLOR	PRINCE	STEPHENS	STANTON	WARBOYS	BANNISTER	FEARNLEY	RUDGE 2	
25/09/74	FULHAM	A	0-0	10967	EADIE	JACOBS	PARSONS	AITKEN	TAYLOR	PRINCE	STEPHENS	STANTON	WARBOYS	BANNISTER	FEARNLEY	RUDGE 2	
28/09/74	BLACKPOOL	H	1-3	10310	EADIE	JACOBS	PARSONS	AITKEN	TAYLOR	PRINCE	STEPHENS	STANTON	WARBOYS	BANNISTER	FEARNLEY	RUDGE 2	BANNISTER pen
05/10/74	CARDIFF CITY	A	0-3	5800	EADIE	JACOBS	PARSONS	AITKEN	TAYLOR	PRINCE	STEPHENS	STANTON	WARBOYS	BANNISTER	FEARNLEY	RUDGE 11	WARBOYS
12/10/74	YORK CITY	A	0-3	9173	EADIE	JACOBS	PARSONS	AITKEN	TAYLOR	PRINCE	STEPHENS	STANTON	WARBOYS	BANNISTER	FEARNLEY		
19/10/74	MILLWALL	H	2-0	12101	EADIE	BATER	PARSONS	AITKEN	TAYLOR	PRINCE	STEPHENS	STANTON	WARBOYS	BANNISTER	FEARNLEY		BANNISTER pen, STANTON
22/10/74	WEST BROM ALBION	H	0-1	11495	EADIE	BATER	PARSONS	AITKEN	TAYLOR	PRINCE	STEPHENS	STANTON	WARBOYS	BANNISTER	FEARNLEY		BANNISTER, STANTON
26/10/74	NOTTINGHAM FOREST	A	0-1	15182	EADIE	BATER	PARSONS	AITKEN	TAYLOR	PRINCE	STEPHENS	STANTON	WARBOYS	BANNISTER	FEARNLEY		
02/11/74	SOUTHAMPTON	H	0-1	8704	EADIE	BATER	PARSONS	AITKEN	TAYLOR	BATER	STEPHENS	STANTON	WARBOYS	BANNISTER	FEARNLEY	RUDGE 3	
06/11/74	WEST BROM ALBION	A	1-0	21172	EADIE	BATER	BATER	AITKEN	TAYLOR	PRINCE	STEPHENS	STANTON	WARBOYS	BANNISTER	FEARNLEY		WARBOYS, PRINCE
09/11/74	NORWICH CITY	A	1-0	10526	EADIE	BATER	BATER	AITKEN	TAYLOR	PRINCE	STEPHENS	STANTON	WARBOYS	BANNISTER	FEARNLEY	RUDGE 3	BANNISTER
16/11/74	LEYTON ORIENT	H	0-0	7513	EADIE	JACOBS	PARSONS	AITKEN	TAYLOR	PRINCE	STEPHENS	STANTON	WARBOYS	BANNISTER	FEARNLEY	RUDGE 7	
23/11/74	OXFORD UNITED	A	1-0	9329	EADIE	BATER	PARSONS	AITKEN	TAYLOR	PRINCE	RUDGE	STANTON	WARBOYS	BANNISTER	FEARNLEY	STEPHENS 2	PRINCE
30/11/74	BOLTON WANDERERS	H	4-3	9759	EADIE	BATER	PARSONS	AITKEN	TAYLOR	PRINCE	STEPHENS	STANTON	WARBOYS	BANNISTER	BRITTEN		WARBOYS
07/12/74	OLDHAM ATHLETIC	A	0-1	7473	EADIE	BATER	PARSONS	AITKEN	TAYLOR	PRINCE	COOMBES	STANTON	WARBOYS	BANNISTER	FEARNLEY	STANIFORTH 8	COOMBES, WARBOYS, FEARNLEY 2
14/12/74	NOTTS COUNTY	A	0-1	9262	EADIE	BATER	PARSONS	AITKEN	TAYLOR	JONES	COOMBES	COOMBES	WARBOYS	BANNISTER	FEARNLEY	STANIFORTH 8	PRINCE, FEARNLEY
21/12/74	PORTSMOUTH	H	0-1	21556	EADIE	BATER	PARSONS	AITKEN	TAYLOR	STANTON	BRITTEN	COOMBES	WARBOYS	BANNISTER	BRITTEN	JONES 7	
26/12/74	ASTON VILLA	H	1-4	20933	EADIE	BATER	PARSONS	AITKEN	TAYLOR	PRINCE	STANTON	COOMBES	WARBOYS	BANNISTER	FEARNLEY	JONES 10	FEARNLEY
28/12/74	BRISTOL CITY	A	2-1	9456	SHEPPARD	BATER	PARSONS	AITKEN	TAYLOR	PRINCE	FEARNLEY	COOMBES	WARBOYS	STANIFORTH	FEARNLEY		WARBOYS, TAYLOR
11/01/75	OLDHAM ATHLETIC	H	1-5	11432	EADIE	BATER	BATER	AITKEN	TAYLOR	PRINCE	BRITTEN	BANNISTER	WARBOYS	STANIFORTH	FEARNLEY	STEPHENS 11	BANNISTER
18/01/75	BOLTON WANDERERS	A	0-2	12730	EADIE	BATER	PARSONS	AITKEN	TAYLOR	PRINCE	STANIFORTH	STANTON	WARBOYS	BANNISTER	FEARNLEY	STANIFORTH 9	
01/02/75	NORWICH CITY	A	0-3	17490	EADIE	JACOBS	PARSONS	AITKEN	DAY	PRINCE	STANIFORTH	STANTON	WARBOYS	BANNISTER	FEARNLEY		
08/02/75	SOUTHAMPTON	A	1-0	9667	EADIE	JACOBS	BATER	AITKEN	DAY	BATER	STANTON	JONES	WARBOYS	BANNISTER	FEARNLEY	STANIFORTH 7	
15/02/75	OXFORD UNITED	H	0-1	6503	EADIE	JACOBS	BATER	AITKEN	DAY	JONES	STEPHENS	JONES	WARBOYS	BANNISTER	FEARNLEY	STANIFORTH 5	TAYLOR
22/02/75	LEYTON ORIENT	A	0-2	6223	EADIE	JACOBS	BATER	AITKEN	DAY	PRINCE	RUDGE	SMITH	WARBOYS	STANIFORTH	FEARNLEY	FEARNLEY 11	
01/03/75	HULL CITY	H	1-2	11765	EADIE	JACOBS	BATER	AITKEN	DAY	PRINCE	JONES	SMITH	WARBOYS	STANIFORTH	FEARNLEY		PRINCE
11/03/75	FULHAM	H	2-1	8019	EADIE	JACOBS	BATER	AITKEN	DAY	PRINCE	STEPHENS	SMITH	WARBOYS	STANIFORTH	FEARNLEY		WARBOYS 2-1pen
15/03/75	BLACKPOOL	A	0-2	13270	EADIE	JACOBS	BATER	AITKEN	DAY	PRINCE	STANTON	SMITH	WARBOYS	STANIFORTH	FEARNLEY	BANNISTER 7	BANNISTER
22/03/75	SUNDERLAND	A	2-1	19000	EADIE	JACOBS	BATER	AITKEN	DAY	PRINCE	STEPHENS	SMITH	WARBOYS	STANIFORTH	FEARNLEY	BANNISTER 11	
28/03/75	MANCHESTER UNITED	A	0-3	12261	EADIE	JACOBS	BATER	AITKEN	DAY	PRINCE	STANTON	SMITH	WARBOYS	STANIFORTH	DOBSON	STANIFORTH 10	
29/03/75	PORTSMOUTH	A	1-1	28953	EADIE	JACOBS	PARSONS	AITKEN	TAYLOR	PRINCE	STEPHENS	SMITH	WARBOYS	STANIFORTH	DOBSON	STANTON 4	COLLIER og
01/04/75	BRISTOL CITY	H	1-1	9684	EADIE	JACOBS	PARSONS	AITKEN	TAYLOR	PRINCE	STEPHENS	SMITH	WARBOYS	BANNISTER	DOBSON		WARBOYS, PRINCE, DOBSON, STANIFORTH
05/04/75	NOTTINGHAM FOREST	H	4-2	13928	EADIE	JACOBS	PARSONS	AITKEN	TAYLOR	PRINCE	STEPHENS	SMITH	WARBOYS	BANNISTER	DOBSON		DOBSON, PRINCE
12/04/75	CARDIFF CITY	A	2-2	11841	EADIE	JACOBS	PARSONS	AITKEN	TAYLOR	PRINCE	STEPHENS	SMITH	WARBOYS	STANIFORTH	DOBSON	FEARNLEY 3	STANIFORTH
19/04/75	YORK CITY	H	1-3	6243	EADIE	JACOBS	PARSONS	AITKEN	TAYLOR	PRINCE	STEPHENS	SMITH	WARBOYS	STANIFORTH	DOBSON		WARBOYS
26/04/75	MILLWALL	A	1-1		EADIE	JACOBS	PARSONS	AITKEN	TAYLOR	PRINCE	STEPHENS	COOMBES	WARBOYS	BANNISTER	FEARNLEY		

FA CUP

Date	Opponent	Ven	Score	Att	G	2	3	4	5	6	7	8	9	10	11	Substitutes	Goalscorers
04/01/75	BLACKBURN ROVERS	A	2-1	12876	EADIE	BATER	PARSONS	AITKEN	TAYLOR	PRINCE	STANIFORTH	COOMBES	WARBOYS	BANNISTER	FEARNLEY	STANIFORTH 3	FEARNLEY, BANNISTER
27/01/75	DERBY COUNTY	A	0-2	27980	EADIE	BATER	PARSONS	AITKEN	TAYLOR	PRINCE	STANTON	COOMBES	WARBOYS	BANNISTER	FEARNLEY		

LEAGUE CUP

Date	Opponent	Ven	Score	Att	G	2	3	4	5	6	7	8	9	10	11	Substitutes	Goalscorers
20/08/74	PLYMOUTH ARGYLE	H	0-0	8974	EADIE	PARSONS	BATER	AITKEN	TAYLOR	STANTON	JONES	STANIFORTH	WARBOYS	BANNISTER	RUDGE		
27/08/74	PLYMOUTH ARGYLE	A	1-0	11213	EADIE	JACOBS	PARSONS	AITKEN	TAYLOR	PRINCE	JONES	STANTON	WARBOYS	BANNISTER	FEARNLEY	RUDGE 3	WARBOYS
11/09/74	LUTON TOWN	A	1-0	10073	EADIE	JACOBS	PARSONS	AITKEN	TAYLOR	PRINCE	STEPHENS	STANTON	WARBOYS	BANNISTER	FEARNLEY		

GLOUCESTERSHIRE CUP FINAL

Date	Opponent	Ven	Score	Att	G	2	3	4	5	6	7	8	9	10	11	Substitutes	Goalscorers
29/04/75	BRISTOL CITY	H	2-1	11408	EADIE	AITKEN	WILLIAMS	DAY	TAYLOR	PRINCE	STEPHENS	SMITH	WARBOYS	FEARNLEY	BRITTEN		PRINCE, WARBOYS

Appearances

PLAYERS	APP	SUB	GLS
AITKEN P	42		
BANNISTER B	31	2	8
BATER P	30		
BRITTEN M	3		
COOMBES J	7		1
DAY G	9		
DOBSON C	7		2
EADIE J	41		
FEARNLEY G	33	2	6
JACOBS T	27		
JONES B	6	2	
PARSONS L	28		
PRINCE F	39		6
RUDGE J	3	10	
SHEPPARD R	1		
SMITH W S	10	7	2
STANIFORTH D	15	1	2
STANTON T	29	2	
STEPHENS K	26		2
TAYLOR S	33		
WARBOYS A	42		12
OWN GOAL			1

United visited Eastville at Easter, having suffered the ignominy of relegation from Division One 12 months earlier. Rovers, having lost 2-0 at Old Trafford in September, gained a point through substitute Bruce Bannister's last-minute close-range equaliser.

Although able to field a side predominantly unchanged from 1973/74 and largely stable through the season, Rovers undeniably struggled on their much-awaited return to Division Two. Warboys, top scorer for the club with 12 League goals, and the versatile Peter Aitken both played in every League fixture. Yet, Warboys and Bannister never both scored in the same game. For an attacking partnership that had yielded so many goals – both players had scored in seven different League matches the previous season, both bagging hat-tricks at Brighton – this year was a great disappointment. The following season brought little further joy and it was August 1976 before both scored in the same match again.

Rovers players past and future featured, at least nominally, in both major domestic cup finals. Bobby Gould, a Rovers player by 1977, was an unused substitute for West Ham, who beat Fulham 2-0 in the FA Cup final. The only goal in the League Cup final was scored by the former Rovers outside-right Ray Graydon as Aston Villa defeated Norwich City. Graydon had also scored the winning goal after an hour on Boxing Day, capitalising on Taylor's misdirected back pass, as Rovers lost narrowly at Villa Park.

In contrast to these players' achievements, Rovers were not able to feature largely in cup competitions. A solitary Warboys drive four minutes from time disposed of Plymouth Argyle on aggregate in the League Cup, before Luton Town defeated Rovers at Kenilworth Road. Division Two status meant Rovers did not enter the FA Cup until the third round and victory at Blackburn gave Rovers a first appearance for six years in the fourth round. Division Three champions-elect Blackburn Rovers had proved easy prey, but reigning League Champions Derby County beat Rovers comfortably through a goal from Kevin Hector and a Bruce Rioch penalty. The crowd of almost 28,000 at the Baseball Ground was only bettered all season by the 30,000 who saw the local derby at Ashton Gate and the remarkable 42,948 that witnessed Rovers' first League visit to Old Trafford. Rovers retained the Gloucestershire Cup by defeating Bristol City 2-1 with goals from Prince and Warboys.

On 25 February, an Eastville crowd of 3,000 saw England Youth draw 1-1 with Spain Youth in a Youth International qualifying match. The English side contained three future full Internationals in Bryan Robson of West Bromwich Albion, Ray Wilkins of Chelsea and Peter Barnes of Manchester City.

1975/76

Division Two football was proving tough for Don Megson's side. A difficult season in 1974/75 was followed by another of struggle and ultimate success in avoiding relegation. Once again, with limited funds available, the only new names were those nurtured carefully in the club's rapidly growing South Wales nursery. John Rudge's departure was offset by the emergence of David Staniforth, who scored 5 League goals.

Bristol Rovers 1975/76. Back row: Williams, Taylor, Eadie, Lewis, Parsons, Powell. Middle row: Aitken, Britten, Bater, Staniforth, Megson (Manager), Smith, Prince, Stephens, Pulis. Front row: Campbell (Trainer), Jacobs, Fearnley, Warboys, Bannister, Stanton, Dobson (Coach). Sitting: Evans, Guscott, Paul

The average home crowd, despite dropping to 10,022, was nonetheless the final five-figure average attendance at Rovers' home matches in the 20th century.

Defeat at Oldham Athletic on the opening day, when Peter Aitken scored an own goal, marked the League debuts of two of the new influx of young Welsh players. One was David Williams, initially a left-back, later an accomplished midfield general and ultimately player-manager and the holder of a belated Welsh cap. The other was Andrew Evans, who showed immense promise on the left-wing before an exciting career was cruelly cut short by injury in 1977. Tony Pulis, Wayne Powell and Paul Lewis were not far behind. Pulis made his League debut in the cauldron of a local derby at Ashton Gate, where he was later manager. Powell became the first Rovers player to score as a substitute on his League debut, as Rovers recorded a second consecutive 4-2 win over Nottingham Forest, while Lewis deputised for Jim Eadie in the final match of the season.

Eric McMordie's 57th-minute own goal earned victory over York City and, after two creditable draws, Alan Warboys scored both Rovers' goals in a 2-0 victory over Fulham at Craven Cottage, a first away League win since December 1974. Rovers were to record a League double over the previous season's beaten FA Cup finalists. After a promising start, a relegation dogfight was not high on the club's list of expectations. Most surprising of all was that, after his goals at Fulham, Warboys was not to score again in the League until the final game, his tally of three being a highly disappointing return from such a proven goalscorer.

In November, Rovers drew five consecutive League games, thus equalling a club record set in 1966/67, starting with a 1-1 draw with Blackburn Rovers, who thus established their own club record of five consecutive League draws. The most remarkable of these draws was at Roker Park, where Rovers belied their poor record at Sunderland and earned a point through David Williams' first goal for the club. The crowd of 31,356 was the largest at a Rovers game all season. At this stage, after a 12-match unbeaten run, Rovers had in fact only lost two of their opening 18 League matches. Ten of these games, however, had been drawn and the loss of points through the club's inability to turn good performances into victories was to prove a major factor as the season progressed.

In the spring, four consecutive away games were lost 3-0 as Rovers looked over their shoulder at the trap door back to Division Three. Rovers failed to score in five consecutive League games away from Eastville prior to the now customary victory at Blackburn Rovers. Mick Channon, later a Rovers player, and Bobby Stokes, scorer of the winning goal in that season's FA Cup final, were among Southampton's scorers at The Dell. Derek Hales scored twice for Charlton Athletic, while one of three scorers for Plymouth Argyle, led by the former Rovers captain Mike Green, was Paul Mariner, later an England International striker. The Plymouth game marked the final appearance in a Rovers shirt of Colin Dobson, who became youth coach at Coventry City prior to working in footballing circles in the Middle East.

Three consecutive wins in October, against Sunderland and at Portsmouth and Blackpool, proved the highlight of the season. Bruce Bannister scored in all three and the fine 4-1 win at Bloomfield Park also saw Fearnley's first two goals for almost a year and Smith's first League goal for the club. Thereafter, it was to be December 1976 before Rovers next won two consecutive League games. From November to the end of the 1975/76 season only five further League games were won and only two of those by two clear goals. Martyn Britten's 18th-minute goal, his first for the club, paved the way for a 2-0 victory over Portsmouth, while Southampton were defeated at Eastville by two Frankie Prince goals. Ultimately, Rovers' final four away games of the season resulted in heavy defeats.

What made Rovers' continuing struggle all the more galling was the success experienced across the city at Ashton Gate. Excitement levels rose as the season progressed and a lone goal from Clive Whitehead in April was enough to defeat Portsmouth and propel Bristol City, with West Bromwich Albion and Sunderland, into Division One. Top-flight football had returned to Bristol after an absence of 65 years. Yet, this merely emphasized the gulf between the haves and the have-nots. Before, during and after season 1975/76 Don Megson was unable to delve into the transfer market to strengthen Rovers' squad. Another summer's inaction was to be followed by the mid-season sale during 1976/77 of both Warboys and Bannister, the very names that had brought the club to where they were. They were to be replaced, ultimately, not by new signings, but by home-grown talent in the form of Paul Randall and Steve White.

Three future Rovers players were appearing on larger stages as the season drew to a close. Mick Channon won an FA Cup winners' medal as unfancied Southampton, beaten at Eastville three weeks earlier, defeated Manchester United in the final. Stewart Barrowclough's Newcastle United side lost to Manchester City in the League Cup final.

SEASON 1975/76

FOOTBALL LEAGUE DIVISION TWO

Date	Opponent	H/A	Score	Att	G	2	3	4	5	6	7	8	9	10	11	Substitutes	Goalscorers
16/08/75	OLDHAM ATHLETIC	A	0-2	6993	EADIE	SMITH	WILLIAMS	AITKEN	TAYLOR	PRINCE	STEPHENS	STANTON	WARBOYS	BANNISTER	EVANS	FEARNLEY 7	
23/08/75	YORK CITY	H	2-1	8142	EADIE	SMITH	WILLIAMS	AITKEN	TAYLOR	PRINCE	STEPHENS	STANTON	WARBOYS	BANNISTER	EVANS	FEARNLEY 10	BANNISTER, McMORDIE og
30/08/75	BRISTOL CITY	A	1-1	17918	EADIE	SMITH	WILLIAMS	AITKEN	TAYLOR	PRINCE	STEPHENS	PULIS	WARBOYS	BANNISTER	EVANS	FEARNLEY 7	BANNISTER
06/09/75	CHARLTON ATHLETIC	H	0-1	7718	EADIE	SMITH	WILLIAMS	DAY	TAYLOR	AITKEN	STEPHENS	PULIS	WARBOYS	BANNISTER	EVANS	FEARNLEY 7	
13/09/75	FULHAM	A	2-0	11516	EADIE	SMITH	WILLIAMS	DAY	TAYLOR	AITKEN	STEPHENS	PRINCE	WARBOYS	BANNISTER	EVANS	FEARNLEY 3	WARBOYS 2
20/09/75	CARLISLE UNITED	H	0-1	8223	EADIE	SMITH	WILLIAMS	DAY	TAYLOR	BATER	STEPHENS	PRINCE	WARBOYS	BANNISTER	EVANS	FEARNLEY 11	
23/09/75	BOLTON WANDERERS	H	2-2	7992	EADIE	SMITH	WILLIAMS	DAY	TAYLOR	AITKEN	STEPHENS	PRINCE	WARBOYS	BANNISTER	DOBSON		BANNISTER, PRINCE
26/09/75	LEYTON ORIENT	A	0-0	4978	EADIE	SMITH	WILLIAMS	DAY	TAYLOR	AITKEN	STEPHENS	PRINCE	STANIFORTH	BANNISTER	BRITTEN		
04/10/75	NOTTINGHAM FOREST	H	4-2	7689	EADIE	PARSONS	WILLIAMS	DAY	TAYLOR	SMITH	STEPHENS	PRINCE	WARBOYS	BANNISTER	BRITTEN	POWELL 6	PRINCE 2, POWELL, BANNISTER
11/10/75	HULL CITY	H	0-0	5642	EADIE	PARSONS	WILLIAMS	DAY	TAYLOR	SMITH	STEPHENS	PRINCE	STANIFORTH	BANNISTER	DOBSON	POWELL 11	
18/10/75	SUNDERLAND	H	1-0	13577	EADIE	PARSONS	WILLIAMS	DAY	TAYLOR	SMITH	FEARNLEY	PRINCE	STANIFORTH	BANNISTER	DOBSON	STANIFORTH 7	BANNISTER
21/10/75	PORTSMOUTH	H	4-1	9078	EADIE	PARSONS	WILLIAMS	DAY	TAYLOR	SMITH	FEARNLEY	PRINCE	WARBOYS	BANNISTER	DOBSON		STANIFORTH, BANNISTER
25/10/75	BLACKPOOL	A	1-1	9019	EADIE	PARSONS	WILLIAMS	DAY	TAYLOR	SMITH	FEARNLEY	PRINCE	STANIFORTH	BANNISTER	DOBSON		SMITH, FEARNLEY 2, BANNISTER pen
01/11/75	BLACKBURN ROVERS	H	1-1	10534	EADIE	PARSONS	WILLIAMS	DAY	TAYLOR	SMITH	FEARNLEY	PRINCE	WARBOYS	BANNISTER	STANIFORTH	BRITTEN 11	STANIFORTH,
04/11/75	WEST BROM ALBION	H	1-1	13105	EADIE	PARSONS	WILLIAMS	DAY	TAYLOR	SMITH	FEARNLEY	PRINCE	WARBOYS	BANNISTER	FEARNLEY	BRITTEN 9	FEARNLEY
08/11/75	NOTTS COUNTY	A	1-1	10930	EADIE	JACOBS	WILLIAMS	DAY	TAYLOR	SMITH	STANTON	PRINCE	STANIFORTH	BANNISTER	FEARNLEY	STEPHENS 4	STANIFORTH
15/11/75	PLYMOUTH ARGYLE	H	0-0	14121	EADIE	JACOBS	WILLIAMS	DAY	TAYLOR	SMITH	STANTON	FEARNLEY	WARBOYS	BANNISTER	PRINCE	STEPHENS 9	
22/11/75	SUNDERLAND	A	1-3	31356	EADIE	BATER	WILLIAMS	DAY	TAYLOR	SMITH	STANTON	FEARNLEY	STANIFORTH	BANNISTER	PRINCE	BATER 7	WILLIAMS
27/11/75	CHELSEA	H	1-2	16277	EADIE	BATER	WILLIAMS	DAY	TAYLOR	SMITH	STANTON	FEARNLEY	WARBOYS	BANNISTER	PRINCE		WILLIAMS
06/12/75	OXFORD UNITED	H	2-0	6532	EADIE	BATER	PARSONS	DAY	TAYLOR	SMITH	FEARNLEY	STANIFORTH	STANIFORTH	BANNISTER	PRINCE		BANNISTER
13/12/75	YORK CITY	A	0-0	3112	EADIE	BATER	PARSONS	BATER	TAYLOR	SMITH	FEARNLEY	STANTON	WARBOYS	BANNISTER	WILLIAMS		
20/12/75	OLDHAM ATHLETIC	H	1-0	7389	EADIE	BATER	PARSONS	DAY	TAYLOR	PRINCE	SMITH	STANTON	WARBOYS	BANNISTER	PRINCE		BANNISTER
26/12/75	SOUTHAMPTON	A	0-1	19556	EADIE	JACOBS	PARSONS	DAY	DAY	WILLIAMS	STANTON	SMITH	WARBOYS	FEARNLEY	EVANS	BANNISTER 10	
27/12/75	LUTON TOWN	H	0-1	11044	EADIE	JACOBS	PARSONS	DAY	AITKEN	SMITH	STEPHENS	WILLIAMS	STANIFORTH	BANNISTER	DOBSON	POWELL 9	
10/01/76	FULHAM	H	1-0	7863	EADIE	BATER	PARSONS	DAY	TAYLOR	AITKEN	STEPHENS	FEARNLEY	WARBOYS	BANNISTER	DOBSON		BANNISTER
17/01/76	CHARLTON ATHLETIC	A	2-0	8598	EADIE	BATER	PARSONS	WILLIAMS	TAYLOR	PRINCE	STEPHENS	STANTON	WARBOYS	BANNISTER	BRITTEN	STANIFORTH 11	BRITTEN, BANNISTER
31/01/76	PORTSMOUTH	A	0-3	6133	EADIE	JACOBS	PARSONS	DAY	TAYLOR	PRINCE	STEPHENS	WILLIAMS	WARBOYS	POWELL	BRITTEN		
07/02/76	WEST BROM ALBION	A	0-3	17201	EADIE	JACOBS	PARSONS	DAY	TAYLOR	SMITH	STEPHENS	SMITH	STANIFORTH	BANNISTER	DOBSON	STANIFORTH 6	
14/02/76	NOTTS COUNTY	H	0-0	7754	EADIE	JACOBS	WILLIAMS	DAY	TAYLOR	SMITH	STANIFORTH	SMITH	STANIFORTH	BANNISTER	EVANS		
21/02/76	PLYMOUTH ARGYLE	A	0-3	11183	EADIE	JACOBS	WILLIAMS	DAY	TAYLOR	SMITH	STEPHENS	SMITH	WARBOYS	BANNISTER	EVANS		
28/02/76	BLACKPOOL	H	1-1	6686	EADIE	JACOBS	PARSONS	DAY	TAYLOR	SMITH	STEPHENS	SMITH	WARBOYS	BANNISTER	WILLIAMS	WARBOYS 2	TAYLOR
06/03/76	BLACKBURN ROVERS	A	2-1	6765	EADIE	WILLIAMS	PARSONS	DAY	TAYLOR	SMITH	STEPHENS	WILLIAMS	STANIFORTH	BANNISTER	BRITTEN	EVANS 6	STANIFORTH, BANNISTER
13/03/76	HULL CITY	A	0-0	6236	EADIE	WILLIAMS	BATER	DAY	TAYLOR	SMITH	STEPHENS	STANIFORTH	WARBOYS	STANIFORTH	EVANS	POWELL 4	
20/03/76	CHELSEA	A	0-0	16132	EADIE	WILLIAMS	WILLIAMS	AITKEN	TAYLOR	SMITH	BRITTEN	WILLIAMS	STANIFORTH	BANNISTER	EVANS	WARBOYS 7	
27/03/76	OXFORD UNITED	A	1-1	6952	EADIE	WILLIAMS	PARSONS	WILLIAMS	TAYLOR	SMITH	STEPHENS	SMITH	WARBOYS	BATER	BRITTEN	STEPHENS 11	BANNISTER pen
03/04/76	LEYTON ORIENT	H	1-1	5182	EADIE	WILLIAMS	PARSONS	DAY	TAYLOR	SMITH	BRITTEN	BANNISTER	WARBOYS	FEARNLEY	EVANS		SMITH, STANIFORTH
10/04/76	CARLISLE UNITED	A	2-4	5928	EADIE	PARSONS	PARSONS	DAY	TAYLOR	SMITH	STEPHENS	SMITH	STANIFORTH	STANIFORTH	EVANS	STEPHENS 10	PRINCE 2, 1pen
16/04/76	BRISTOL CITY	H	0-2	26430	EADIE	WILLIAMS	WILLIAMS	DAY	TAYLOR	SMITH	STEPHENS	WILLIAMS	WARBOYS	BANNISTER	EVANS	STEPHENS 8	
17/04/76	SOUTHAMPTON	H	2-0	11834	EADIE	PARSONS	PARSONS	DAY	TAYLOR	SMITH	STEPHENS	SMITH	STANIFORTH	BANNISTER	BRITTEN	DAY 11	BRITTEN
19/04/76	LUTON TOWN	A	1-3	7646	LEWIS	WILLIAMS	PARSONS	AITKEN	TAYLOR	SMITH	STEPHENS	STANIFORTH	WARBOYS	STANIFORTH	BRITTEN	STEPHENS 11	
24/04/76	NOTTINGHAM FOREST	A	0-3	12127	EADIE	LEWIS	PARSONS	BATER	TAYLOR	PULIS	STEPHENS	PRINCE	WARBOYS	BRITTEN	AITKEN		
28/04/76	BOLTON WANDERERS	A	1-3	12815	EADIE	BATER	PARSONS	AITKEN	TAYLOR	PRINCE	SMITH	FEARNLEY	WARBOYS	BANNISTER	EVANS		WARBOYS

FA CUP

Date	Opponent	H/A	Score	Att	G	2	3	4	5	6	7	8	9	10	11	Substitutes	Goalscorers
01/01/76	CHELSEA	A	1-1	35226	EADIE	BATER	PARSONS	DAY	WILLIAMS	SMITH	STEPHENS	FEARNLEY	WARBOYS	BANNISTER	STANTON	STANIFORTH 6	WARBOYS
03/01/76	CHELSEA	H	0-1	13939	EADIE	BATER	PARSONS	AITKEN	TAYLOR	WILLIAMS	STEPHENS	FEARNLEY	WARBOYS	BANNISTER	STANTON	STANIFORTH 9	

LEAGUE CUP

Date	Opponent	H/A	Score	Att	G	2	3	4	5	6	7	8	9	10	11	Substitutes	Goalscorers
20/08/75	CARDIFF CITY	A	2-1	6688	EADIE	SMITH	WILLIAMS	DAY	TAYLOR	PRINCE	STEPHENS	STANTON	WARBOYS	BANNISTER	EVANS		WARBOYS, BANNISTER
26/08/75	CARDIFF CITY	H	1-1	7220	EADIE	SMITH	WILLIAMS	AITKEN	TAYLOR	PRINCE	STEPHENS	STANTON	WARBOYS	BANNISTER	EVANS	FEARNLEY 11	STEPHENS
09/09/75	SOUTHAMPTON	A	1-0	10357	EADIE	SMITH	WILLIAMS	DAY	TAYLOR	AITKEN	STEPHENS	PRINCE	WARBOYS	BANNISTER	EVANS	FEARNLEY 11	FEARNLEY
07/10/75	NEWCASTLE UNITED	H	1-1	17141	EADIE	PARSONS	WILLIAMS	DAY	TAYLOR	SMITH	STEPHENS	PRINCE	WARBOYS	BANNISTER	BRITTEN	FEARNLEY 7	STANIFORTH
15/10/75	NEWCASTLE UNITED	A	0-2	25835	EADIE	WILLIAMS	PARSONS	DAY	TAYLOR	SMITH	STEPHENS	PRINCE	WARBOYS	BANNISTER	EVANS		

GLOUCESTERSHIRE CUP FINAL

Date	Opponent	H/A	Score	Att	G	2	3	4	5	6	7	8	9	10	11	Substitutes	Goalscorers
04/05/76	BRISTOL CITY	A	2-3	10278	EADIE	BATER	PARSONS	WILLIAMS	TAYLOR	PRINCE	SMITH	STANTON	STEPHENS	BANNISTER	AITKEN		WILLIAMS, TAYLOR

Appearances

PLAYERS	APP	SUB	GLS
AITKEN P	14		
BANNISTER B	36	1	13
BATER P	16	1	
BRITTEN M	12	2	2
DAY G	32	1	
DOBSON C	8		
EADIE J	41		
EVANS A	15	1	
FEARNLEY G	13	5	3
JACOBS T	9		
LEWIS P	1		
PARSONS L	27		
POWELL W	1	4	1
PRINCE F	31		5
PULIS A	4		
SMITH W S	39		2
STANIFORTH D	20	3	5
STANTON T	8		
STEPHENS K	25	6	
TAYLOR S	39		1
WARBOYS A	30	2	3
WILLIAMS D	41		2
OWN GOAL			1

Even the Anglo-Scottish Cup final, where Middlesbrough beat Fulham 1-0 on aggregate, saw Rovers representation, with Boro's Terry Cooper adding to his already impressive list of domestic and European honours.

A crowd of more than 35,000 saw Rovers earn a highly creditable 1-1 draw in the third round of the FA Cup at Stamford Bridge. Peter Bonetti, Charlie Cooke, Ray Wilkins and Ron Harris were among Chelsea's star names and it took a Bill Garner equaliser from Wilkins' 34th minute free-kick to earn a replay after Warboys' 18th-minute header from a Williams cross had given Rovers an unlikely lead. Forty-eight hours later, a solitary Kenny Swain goal handed Chelsea a 1-0 replay victory.

There was more success in the League Cup. Cardiff City were disposed of in the first round, with Warboys and Bannister, free from the shackles of Division Two expectation, both for once getting on the scoresheet in the away leg. Substitute Gordon Fearnley's 83rd-minute goal at The Dell, after Mick Channon had shot wide from a penalty, brought a third round tie at home to Newcastle United. Rovers had chances to win, but were taken to a replay that was lost in front of a crowd of more than 25,000 at St James' Park to the eventual finalists. Irving Nattrass and Tommy Craig, from a penalty, scored the replay goals, with considerable help from the instrumental Stewart Barrowclough, later a Rovers player. An exciting Gloucestershire Cup final was lost 3-2 at Ashton Gate, despite goals for Rovers from David Williams and Stuart Taylor.

The implications of the 1975 Safety of Sports Grounds Act led to £70,000 being invested in Eastville Stadium. However, this served simply as a reminder to Rovers that their lease of the ground was due to expire in 1979. With hindsight, it is easy to see what steps could have been taken at this stage concerning the club's future in Bristol.

1976/77

As Bristol City embarked on their much-heralded return to top-flight football, Bristol Rovers attempted to steady the ship and attain at least mid-table status in Division Two. Yet, it was difficult to see how this could be achieved. With the exception of emerging young Welsh talent, a struggling team was now ageing. Without the arrival of new faces, it was clearly going to be another long, hard season.

The players who appeared in the Rovers side on the opening day of the season constituted, broadly speaking, the side that had won only 5 of its final 29 League matches in 1975/76. Blackpool were the visitors to Eastville and, with Bob Hatton scoring twice, they ran out comfortable 4-1 winners, Warboys scoring his first goal at home in sixteen months. However, Megson had few options in team selection. Money was still not available for buying new players and all he could attempt was a reshuffle. Wilf Smith, David Williams and Peter Aitken were all tried in defence and midfield and young full-back Phil Bater was recalled on the right and later on the left.

In comparison with certain seasons earlier in Rovers' League history, there were no disastrous results. It was just as well, for goal average had replaced goal difference, as a means to calculate League tables. By their own standards, though, Rovers were dealt

Bristol Rovers 1976/77. Back row: Day, Paul, V Jones, Eadie, Taylor, G Jones, Warboys, Prince, Parsons. Middle row: Aitken, Smith, Bater, Powell, Thomas, O'Donnell, Pulis, Guscott, Stephens, Campbell (Trainer). Front row: W Jones (Trainer), Evans, Williams, Britten, Megson (Manager), Bannister, Staniforth, Foreman, Dobson (Coach)

several crushing blows. Blackpool scored four times when Rovers visited Bloomfield Road and another 4-0 defeat, this time at Oldham Athletic, featured a hat-trick from Vic Halom. In addition to the FA Cup defeat, Rovers were also crushed by Wolves at Eastville over Christmas. The Wolves side, heading for the Division Two Championship, was certainly a strong one, but to go five goals behind before David Williams' last-minute consolation goal indicated the extent of work required on the team.

On a positive note, Rovers won their first away game, with both Alan Warboys and Bruce Bannister scoring at Cardiff. For 'Smash' and 'Grab', a partnership that had terrorised defences at will during the early part of 1973/74, this represented the first time since January 1974, more than two-and-a-half years previously, that both had scored in the same League match. A huge win over Notts County in September, where both David Staniforth and the recalled Gordon Fearnley scored pairs, their first goals of the season, was the biggest victory at Eastville since October 1972. A significantly comfortable 3-0 win against Hull City in November featured a first Rovers goal for the highly promising Andrew Evans, after six minutes, and Alan Warboys' 100th League goal just two minutes before half-time.

The home fixture with Hereford United in November summed up, in many ways, the intense frustration of the season. Both Warboys and Bannister were able to score early on, with Rovers leading 2-0 inside 10 minutes. It was the first-ever League meeting of the clubs and newly-promoted Hereford seized their opportunities to lead 3-2 after just 18 minutes, with Steve Davey scoring twice, even affording the luxury of a missed penalty from Dixie McNeil, whose shot four minutes from time, following a foul by Taylor, went wide of the post. Although a Wayne Powell goal, after David Staniforth's shot 17 minutes from time had been blocked, earned a draw at Edgar Street, Rovers never gained the opportunity for revenge, as Hereford were relegated that season and

Popular forward Bruce Bannister contributed 80 goals in 206 league appearances in six seasons

never returned to Division Two. Bannister's goal proved to be his last for the club, as the old guard from 1973/74 was dismantled.

Two mid-season sales were to alter the make-up of Rovers' side radically. Bruce Bannister had scored only 4 goals in 18 games and was sold to Plymouth Argyle in December in a deal that brought Jimmy Hamilton to Eastville. Hamilton was to score just once in his Rovers career. Alan Warboys left for Fulham, his sixth League club, in a deal worth £30,000. The pair met up again later at Hull City before both embarked on successful business careers, Bannister's sports-shoe manufacturing company in Bradford proving particularly lucrative. By the season's end, when Jim Eadie joined Bath City and Kenny Stephens moved to Hereford, only the ever-reliable Stuart Taylor was left from the promotion season. These players were not replaced by experienced footballers, but by teenage stars in the making and, at least in the meantime, Rovers were destined to continue to struggle in Division Two.

There was, though, some hope. Seventeen-year-olds Martin Thomas, who replaced Eadie in goal for January's game at Charlton Athletic, and Vaughan Jones, who was to captain Rovers in the 1989/90 Championship season, both made their first League appearances. Rovers regularly fielded five young Welsh-born players in the side, products of the club's nursery system. On the other hand, they were not ready to deal

FOOTBALL LEAGUE DIVISION TWO

Date	Opponent	H/A	Result	ATT	G	2	3	4	5	6	7	8	9	10	11	SUBSTITUTES	GOALSCORERS
21/08/76	BLACKPOOL	H	1-4	5845	EADIE	SMITH	AITKEN	DAY	TAYLOR	WILLIAMS	STEPHENS	STANIFORTH	WARBOYS	BANNISTER	EVANS		WARBOYS
25/08/76	CARDIFF CITY	A	2-1	12680	EADIE	BATER	WILLIAMS	DAY	TAYLOR	AITKEN	STEPHENS	SMITH	WARBOYS	BANNISTER	EVANS		WARBOYS, BANNISTER
28/08/76	OLDHAM ATHLETIC	H	0-0	6345	EADIE	BATER	PARSONS	DAY	TAYLOR	AITKEN	STEPHENS	SMITH	WARBOYS	BANNISTER	EVANS		
04/09/76	FULHAM	A	0-1	21127	EADIE	BATER	PARSONS	WILLIAMS	TAYLOR	AITKEN	STANIFORTH	SMITH	WARBOYS	BANNISTER	PRINCE	STEPHENS 6	
11/09/76	LEYTON ORIENT	H	1-0	5494	EADIE	AITKEN	BATER	DAY	TAYLOR	PRINCE	STEPHENS	FEARNLEY	WARBOYS	BANNISTER	BRITTEN	STANIFORTH 3	WARBOYS
18/09/76	BLACKBURN ROVERS	A	0-0	7751	EADIE	AITKEN	PARSONS	DAY	TAYLOR	PRINCE	STEPHENS	FEARNLEY	WARBOYS	BANNISTER	STANIFORTH	BRITTEN 3	
25/09/76	NOTTS COUNTY	H	5-1	6238	EADIE	AITKEN	WILLIAMS	DAY	TAYLOR	PRINCE	STEPHENS	FEARNLEY	WARBOYS	BANNISTER	STANIFORTH		FEARNLEY 2, STANIFORTH 2, WARBOYS
02/10/76	MILLWALL	A	0-2	8205	EADIE	AITKEN	WILLIAMS	DAY	TAYLOR	PRINCE	STEPHENS	FEARNLEY	WARBOYS	BANNISTER	STANIFORTH		
05/10/76	CHELSEA	H	2-1	13199	EADIE	AITKEN	WILLIAMS	DAY	TAYLOR	PRINCE	STEPHENS	FEARNLEY	WARBOYS	BANNISTER	STANIFORTH		BANNISTER, STANIFORTH
16/10/76	BOLTON WANDERERS	A	0-1	12771	EADIE	AITKEN	WILLIAMS	AITKEN	TAYLOR	PRINCE	STEPHENS	FEARNLEY	WARBOYS	BANNISTER	STANIFORTH		
23/10/76	PLYMOUTH ARGYLE	H	1-1	10258	EADIE	DAY	WILLIAMS	AITKEN	TAYLOR	PRINCE	STEPHENS	FEARNLEY	WARBOYS	BANNISTER	POWELL		PRINCE
30/10/76	CHARLTON ATHLETIC	H	1-1	8183	EADIE	DAY	WILLIAMS	AITKEN	TAYLOR	PRINCE	STEPHENS	FEARNLEY	WARBOYS	BANNISTER	POWELL		FEARNLEY
06/11/76	LUTON TOWN	A	2-4	7066	EADIE	DAY	PARSONS	AITKEN	TAYLOR	PRINCE	STEPHENS	FEARNLEY	WARBOYS	BANNISTER	POWELL	EVANS 8	BANNISTER, WARBOYS
13/11/76	HEREFORD UNITED	A	2-3	8485	EADIE	DAY	PARSONS	WILLIAMS	TAYLOR	PRINCE	STEPHENS	FEARNLEY	WARBOYS	BANNISTER	POWELL		WARBOYS, BANNISTER
20/11/76	BURNLEY	H	1-1	10271	EADIE	BATER	PARSONS	PRINCE	TAYLOR	WILLIAMS	STEPHENS	EVANS	WARBOYS	BANNISTER	STANIFORTH		WILLIAMS
27/11/76	HULL CITY	A	3-0	6424	EADIE	BATER	PARSONS	PRINCE	TAYLOR	WILLIAMS	STEPHENS	FEARNLEY	WARBOYS	BANNISTER	STANIFORTH	AITKEN 8	STANIFORTH, WARBOYS, EVANS
04/12/76	NOTTINGHAM FOREST	A	2-4	16302	EADIE	BATER	PARSONS	AITKEN	TAYLOR	WILLIAMS	STEPHENS	FEARNLEY	WARBOYS	BANNISTER	STANIFORTH	EVANS 9	WILLIAMS, FEARNLEY
11/12/76	CARLISLE UNITED	H	2-1	5496	EADIE	BATER	PARSONS	PRINCE	TAYLOR	WILLIAMS	STEPHENS	FEARNLEY	WARBOYS	BANNISTER	STANIFORTH		STANIFORTH, FEARNLEY
18/12/76	SHEFFIELD UNITED	A	1-3	15201	EADIE	BATER	PARSONS	PRINCE	TAYLOR	WILLIAMS	STEPHENS	FEARNLEY	WARBOYS	HAMILTON	STANIFORTH		WILLIAMS
27/12/76	WOLVES	H	1-5	20660	EADIE	BATER	PARSONS	DAY	TAYLOR	WILLIAMS	STEPHENS	FEARNLEY	WARBOYS	HAMILTON	STANIFORTH	EVANS 4	WARBOYS
29/12/76	SOUTHAMPTON	A	1-2	19790	THOMAS	BATER	PARSONS	AITKEN	TAYLOR	WILLIAMS	STEPHENS	FEARNLEY	WARBOYS	GUSCOTT	HAMILTON		AITKEN
01/01/77	LUTON TOWN	H	0-0	7185	EADIE	BATER	PARSONS	DAY	TAYLOR	AITKEN	STEPHENS	FEARNLEY	WARBOYS	STANIFORTH	HAMILTON		
03/01/77	CHARLTON ATHLETIC	A	3-4	9742	THOMAS	EADIE	PARSONS	AITKEN	TAYLOR	WILLIAMS	STEPHENS	FEARNLEY	WARBOYS	STANIFORTH	EVANS	EVANS 3	WILLIAMS 2, STANIFORTH
15/01/77	CARDIFF CITY	H	1-1	9272	EADIE	BATER	PARSONS	AITKEN	TAYLOR	DAY	STEPHENS	WILLIAMS	WARBOYS	STANIFORTH	HAMILTON		WARBOYS pen
22/01/77	BLACKPOOL	A	0-4	9288	EADIE	BATER	PULIS	DAY	TAYLOR	AITKEN	STEPHENS	WILLIAMS	WARBOYS	STANIFORTH	HAMILTON	POWELL 3	
05/02/77	OLDHAM ATHLETIC	A	0-4	9529	EADIE	BATER	PULIS	DAY	TAYLOR	AITKEN	STEPHENS	WILLIAMS	WARBOYS	STANIFORTH	HAMILTON	FEARNLEY 10	
12/02/77	FULHAM	H	2-1	11140	EADIE	BATER	PARSONS	DAY	TAYLOR	PRINCE	STEPHENS	WILLIAMS	STANIFORTH	HAMILTON	EVANS	AITKEN 6	DAY, WILLIAMS
19/02/77	LEYTON ORIENT	A	1-2	4062	EADIE	BATER	PULIS	DAY	TAYLOR	AITKEN	STEPHENS	FEARNLEY	STANIFORTH	HAMILTON	HAMILTON	EVANS 3	EVANS
05/03/77	NOTTS COUNTY	A	1-2	10058	EADIE	BATER	PULIS	DAY	TAYLOR	PRINCE	WILLIAMS	POWELL	STANIFORTH	POWELL	EVANS	EVANS 3	
08/03/77	BLACKBURN ROVERS	H	0-0	5628	EADIE	BATER	PARSONS	DAY	TAYLOR	AITKEN	STEPHENS	FEARNLEY	STANIFORTH	AITKEN	EVANS	FOREMAN 6	
12/03/77	MILLWALL	H	0-0	6242	EADIE	WILLIAMS	PARSONS	DAY	TAYLOR	PULIS	WILLIAMS	FEARNLEY	STANIFORTH	HAMILTON	EVANS		
19/03/77	CHELSEA	A	0-2	26916	EADIE	WILLIAMS	PARSONS	PRINCE	JONES	AITKEN	STEPHENS	FEARNLEY	STANIFORTH	HAMILTON	EVANS		
02/04/77	PLYMOUTH ARGYLE	A	1-1	10307	EADIE	BATER	PARSONS	DAY	TAYLOR	PRINCE	WILLIAMS	FEARNLEY	DAY	STANIFORTH	BRITTEN	HAMILTON 9	WILLIAMS
05/04/77	WOLVES	H	2-4	19149	EADIE	BATER	AITKEN	DAY	TAYLOR	PRINCE	WILLIAMS	AITKEN	POWELL	STANIFORTH	WILLIAMS	HAMILTON 10	STANIFORTH, WILLIAMS pen
09/04/77	SOUTHAMPTON	H	2-3	11479	EADIE	BATER	PULIS	DAY	TAYLOR	PRINCE	STEPHENS	AITKEN	POWELL	STANIFORTH	WILLIAMS	HAMILTON 5	POWELL
11/04/77	HEREFORD UNITED	A	1-1	7195	EADIE	BATER	PULIS	DAY	TAYLOR	PRINCE	WILLIAMS	AITKEN	POWELL	STANIFORTH	WILLIAMS		POWELL
16/04/77	BURNLEY	A	1-1	6373	EADIE	BATER	PULIS	DAY	TAYLOR	PRINCE	WILLIAMS	AITKEN	POWELL	STANIFORTH	WILLIAMS		HAIGH og
23/04/77	HULL CITY	H	1-0	4599	EADIE	BATER	PARSONS	DAY	TAYLOR	PRINCE	STEPHENS	AITKEN	POWELL	STANIFORTH	WILLIAMS	EVANS 6	BATER
30/04/77	NOTTINGHAM FOREST	H	3-2	8893	EADIE	BATER	PARSONS	DAY	TAYLOR	AITKEN	STEPHENS	WILLIAMS	POWELL	STANIFORTH	HAMILTON	HAMILTON 8	STANIFORTH, POWELL, HAMILTON
07/05/77	CARLISLE UNITED	A	3-2	7396	EADIE	BATER	PARSONS	DAY	TAYLOR	AITKEN	STEPHENS	WILLIAMS	POWELL	STANIFORTH	HAMILTON		POWELL 3
14/05/77	SHEFFIELD UNITED	H	3-1	7304	EADIE	BATER	PARSONS	PULIS	TAYLOR	JONES	STEPHENS	WILLIAMS	POWELL	HAMILTON	HAMILTON		WILLIAMS 2
17/05/77	BOLTON WANDERERS	H	2-2	6991	EADIE	BATER	PARSONS	PULIS	TAYLOR	PRINCE	STEPHENS	WILLIAMS	POWELL	STANIFORTH	HAMILTON		

FA CUP

Date	Opponent	H/A	Result	ATT	G	2	3	4	5	6	7	8	9	10	11	SUBSTITUTES	GOALSCORERS
08/01/77	NOTTINGHAM FOREST	A	1-1	17700	EADIE	BATER	PARSONS	AITKEN	TAYLOR	DAY	STEPHENS	WILLIAMS	WARBOYS	EVANS	HAMILTON	BANNISTER 11	WILLIAMS
11/01/77	NOTTINGHAM FOREST	H	1-1	12348	EADIE	BATER	PARSONS	AITKEN	TAYLOR	DAY	STEPHENS	WILLIAMS	WARBOYS	STANIFORTH	HAMILTON	BANNISTER 4	WARBOYS
18/01/77	NOTTINGHAM FOREST	H	0-6	5736	EADIE	BATER	PARSONS	AITKEN	TAYLOR	DAY	STEPHENS	WILLIAMS	WARBOYS	STANIFORTH	HAMILTON		

LEAGUE CUP

Date	Opponent	H/A	Result	ATT	G	2	3	4	5	6	7	8	9	10	11	SUBSTITUTES	GOALSCORERS
14/08/76	CARDIFF CITY	A	1-2	8496	EADIE	SMITH	AITKEN	DAY	TAYLOR	PRINCE	STEPHENS	WILLIAMS	WARBOYS	BANNISTER	STANIFORTH		WARBOYS pen
17/08/76	CARDIFF CITY	H	4-4	5592	EADIE	SMITH	PARSONS	DAY	TAYLOR	PRINCE	STEPHENS	WILLIAMS	WARBOYS	BANNISTER	EVANS	JONES 9	WILLIAMS, BANNISTER 2, 1 pen, PRINCE

GLOUCESTERSHIRE CUP FINAL

Date	Opponent	H/A	Result	ATT	G	2	3	4	5	6	7	8	9	10	11	SUBSTITUTES	GOALSCORERS
24/05/77	BRISTOL CITY	H	0-1	10432	EADIE	BATER	PARSONS	PULIS	JONES	PRINCE	WILLIAMS	STANIFORTH	POWELL	AITKEN	HAMILTON		

PLAYERS	APP	SUB	GLS
AITKEN P	33	2	1
BANNISTER B	18		4
BATER P	30		1
BRITTEN M	2	1	
DAY G	30		1
EADIE J	41		
EVANS A	10	6	2
FEARNLEY G	22	1	5
FOREMAN W	0	1	
GUSCOTT R	1		
HAMILTON J	14	4	1
JONES V	14		
PARSONS L	26		
POWELL W	13	1	6
PRINCE F	29		1
PULIS A	9		
SMITH W S	5		
STANIFORTH D	34	1	9
STEPHENS K	38	1	
TAYLOR S	40		
THOMAS M	1		
WARBOYS A	26		11
WILLIAMS D	39		10
OWN GOAL			1

with some of the more experienced names in football. Chelsea, Nottingham Forest and Southampton all brought big-name players to Eastville. The legendary maverick Robin Friday was in the Cardiff City side that drew 1-1 at Eastville in January, while George Best scored the only goal of the game, with a first-minute miss-hit shot, when Fulham defeated Rovers at Craven Cottage in September.

At least the season finished on a high note, with Rovers reaching 15th place in the table following a late seven-match unbeaten run. Young Wayne Powell, belatedly recalled to the side, scored 6 goals in this run. His 85th-minute far-post header at home to Sheffield United completed a memorable hat-trick, the first in the League by a Rovers player since December 1973. He had been given just one League start in 1975/76 and this spell in the spring of 1977 represented the high-point of his Rovers career. With Rovers safe from relegation, there was a final 2-2 draw with Bolton Wanderers, who were reduced to 10 men by the sending-off of Paul Jones. Special mention should also be made of late wins at Hull City and Carlisle United, the latter through substitute Hamilton's sole League goal for the club after Rovers had earlier trailed 2-0.

There were many changes through the season. No player appeared in every game. Top-scorer Warboys and his sidekick Bannister had left the club. However, Rovers did, for a third consecutive season, survive relegation, achieving League doubles over Hull City, Sheffield United and Carlisle United along the way. Elsewhere, former Rovers player Larry Lloyd, in the Anglo-Scottish Cup final, and Ray Graydon, in the League Cup final, were achieving greater success. Rovers' scouts were busy monitoring the progress of young Paul Randall, whose mid-season transfer from Glastonbury to Frome Town had brought him goalscoring success. On his shoulders much of Rovers' immediate future was to rest.

Once again, cup competitions brought little joy for Rovers. Larry Lloyd's Nottingham Forest were held to two 1-1 draws but Rovers capitulated in the second replay at Villa Park. Forest scored six times without reply, with England International Tony Woodcock scoring twice. Four other household names, Viv Anderson, Ian Bowyer, John O'Hare and Peter Withe also featured on a decidedly one-sided scoresheet. At this point, Rovers conceded 14 goals in a run of three League and cup matches. In the League Cup, Warboys and Bannister both scored penalties against Cardiff City, one in each leg, but Rovers were eliminated 6-5 on aggregate after Tony Evans had scored all the visitors' goals in an exciting 4-4 draw at Eastville. Rovers had led 4-2 on the night and 5-4 on aggregate with just over 20 minutes remaining, before Evans headed past Eadie to complete his hat-trick. His fourth goal, eight minutes from time, sealed the visitors' overall victory. Bristol City won the Gloucestershire Cup final with a single-goal victory at Eastville.

1977/78

It was the form of teenage striker Paul Randall that stood out in 1977/78. The summer signing from Frome Town scored 20 goals in 28 (plus 3 as sub) League matches. He was the first Rovers player since Alan Warboys in 1973/74 to break the magical seasonal tally of 20 League goals. Yet it was not simply the goalscoring that marked Randall out, but his all-round contribution to the team. With him in the side, despite some heavy defeats, Rovers were to finish the season in 18th place in Division Two.

Promoted Cardiff City were Rovers' opening day opponents. Rovers fielded just one new face in Randall, though Martin Thomas, Eadie's long-term successor in goal, had only one League match under his belt. Randall's debut goal at Ninian Park was one of four in his opening five games. After drawing the first three games, Rovers were not to win until the ninth, when David Williams scored twice against a Mansfield Town side that featured Colin Foster, whose son Steve was to play such an integral part in the Rovers side a quarter of a century later. Randall's absence from that match meant that he was not on the winning side in a League fixture until Guy Fawkes' Day.

As the new season unfolded, Don Megson entered the transfer market in search of big-name players to bolster his side. With Bristol City temporarily on top of Division One, it was clearly time to build up Rovers' stature. The experienced former Crystal Palace full-back Tony Taylor arrived on trial and quickly gained a regular place in the side. Mike Barry joined Rovers from Carlisle United in an exchange deal that took Jimmy Hamilton to Brunton Park, while the former Birmingham City footballer Paul Hendrie arrived on a free transfer. The biggest-name signing, however, was the highly experienced forward Bobby Gould, who joined Rovers, his seventh League club, for £10,000 the day before Rovers were due to meet Blackburn Rovers at Eastville.

Bristol Rovers 1977/78. Back row: Parsons, Bater, G Jones, Thomas, Hamilton, V Jones. Second row: Campbell (Coach), Aitken, White, Taylor, Harding, Pulis, Britten, W Jones (Physio). Third row: Megson (Manager), Foreman, Staniforth, Prince, Stephens, Evans, Powell, Dobson (Coach). Front row: Griffiths, Shaw, Palmer, Mabbutt, Mabbutt, Clarke, England

Paul Randall scored two memorable goals to knock Division Two Southampton out of the FA Cup in January 1978

It was very much a new-look Rovers side that faced Blackburn on 15 October. Eighteen-year-old Glyn Jones was in goal, Taylor, Barry and Hendrie all played and, in the absence of Randall, Gould made his club debut. It was an opening game to remember; Gould scored a first-half hat-trick and David Staniforth added another midway through the second-half as Rovers ran up a convincing 4-1 win. Only Joe Riley and Jimmy McCambridge, in Rovers' long Football League history, can match Gould's achievement of three goals on his debut. Rovers, it was said, had turned the corner and the tough away fixture at White Hart Lane seven days later was anticipated with relish.

Tottenham Hotspur's relegation to Division Two meant a first-ever League meeting with Rovers and television cameras were there to record the game. It turned into a living nightmare for Rovers, who crashed to their heaviest post-war defeat. For all the pre-match optimism, Rovers were three goals behind by half-time, with the former Bristol City striker Colin Lee opening the scoring after five minutes, conceded four goals in a nine-minute spell and ended up beaten 9-0. Lee scored four goals and Ian Moores three in 26 second-half minutes, only the third occasion that two opponents had scored hat-tricks in a League game against Rovers. Future England International managers scored in the last minute of each half, Peter Taylor on the stroke of half-time and Glenn Hoddle the soul-destroying ninth in the dying seconds. One player who was singled out for praise was goalkeeper Jones. He was largely credited with keeping the score down to single figures. He played again on the same pitch only nine days later, this time helping the reserves to a 1-1 draw.

It took Rovers just seven days to recover sufficiently to manage a goalless draw at home to a strong Southampton side and to return to winning ways, once Randall was back against Millwall. The Southampton game, though, marked the end of winger Andrew Evans' career. Just days after his 20th birthday, Evans broke his right ankle in this game and a career of great promise was brought to a sad and premature end. Nor were Rovers able to shake the Spurs defeat wholly from their systems. Sunderland put five goals past the recalled Martin Thomas, Steve Taylor scored a hat-trick in Oldham Athletic's 4-1 win and three goals from Malcolm Poskett led Rovers to an embarrassing 4-0 home defeat at the hands of Brighton. For the first time in 15 years and the last time in the 20th century, Rovers had conceded four League hat-tricks in a season. The 77 League goals conceded in finishing 18th in Division Two also constituted the club's worst defensive record for a decade.

The major after-effect of these results was the departure in November of manager Don Megson, who took over at Portland Timbers in the North American Soccer League. Rovers promoted from within, with the former Scottish International Bobby Campbell, the club's trainer since May 1961, being swiftly appointed manager, a post he held for two years. He was the third Scottish International footballer to manage the club. Under his leadership results improved to a certain degree. There was a morale-boosting 3-2 home win over Sunderland, featuring Stuart Taylor's first goal in almost two years and Rovers put three goals without reply past Crystal Palace. Late-season 4-1 wins over Sheffield United and Stoke City, for whom Garth Crooks scored in both meetings with Rovers, saw Randall and his fellow teenager Steve White score three times between them in each game. White weighed in with 4 goals in his first 8 League appearances.

Randall, however, was not to be outdone. A rich vein of goalscoring through the spring saw him score in eight consecutive League games in which he played. From late December until early April, he was to score in 13 out of 14 League appearances. This included a goal in an exciting 2-2 draw with Charlton Athletic, when Bobby Gould converted an 87th-minute penalty and the visitors had Phil Warman sent off. Randall also scored in a 3-1 victory over Millwall in a match played at Fratton Park as The Den had been closed following crowd trouble. It was significant that Randall should score the only goal of the final game of the season in a victory at Hull City to give an element of hope for Rovers' prospects in the forthcoming season.

Short-lived participation in the League Cup was compounded by the fact that Phil Bater contrived to score own goals for Walsall in both legs of a 3-1 aggregate defeat. The former Rovers centre-half Larry Lloyd was in the Nottingham Forest side that won this trophy for the first of two consecutive seasons.

There was an attendance of more than 20,000 at every one of Rovers' four FA Cup-ties. Rovers were drawn to play Sunderland at Roker Park, only weeks after their 5-1 defeat there. Despite missing David Williams, Bobby Gould's 21st-minute lobbed goal after Staniforth had flicked on Day's free-kick earned an outstanding 1-0 win. Southampton were the visitors to Eastville in the fourth round and a memorable pair of goals from Paul Randall brought a comprehensive victory. When Ipswich Town visited snowy Eastville in February, two David Williams goals seemed to be leading Rovers to a third FA Cup

FOOTBALL LEAGUE DIVISION TWO

SEASON 1977/78

Date	Opposition	Venue	Score	Att	G	2	3	4	5	6	7	8	9	10	11	Substitutes	Goalscorers
20/08/77	CARDIFF CITY	A	1-1	7000	THOMAS	AITKEN	BATER	DAY	S TAYLOR	PRINCE	STEPHENS	WILLIAMS	RANDALL	HAMILTON	EVANS	STANIFORTH 9	RANDALL
23/08/77	NOTTS COUNTY	H	2-2	5208	THOMAS	AITKEN	BATER	DAY	S TAYLOR	PRINCE	STEPHENS	WILLIAMS	RANDALL	HAMILTON	EVANS	STANIFORTH 9	WILLIAMS, RANDALL
27/08/77	FULHAM	H	0-0	6426	THOMAS	AITKEN	BATER	DAY	S TAYLOR	PRINCE	STEPHENS	WILLIAMS	POWELL	STANIFORTH	EVANS	WILLIAMS	
03/09/77	BLACKPOOL	A	1-3	8219	THOMAS	AITKEN	BATER	DAY	S TAYLOR	PRINCE	STEPHENS	WILLIAMS	RANDALL	STANIFORTH	EVANS	PULIS 9	STANIFORTH
10/09/77	LUTON TOWN	H	1-2	5940	THOMAS	AITKEN	BATER	DAY	S TAYLOR	PRINCE	STANIFORTH/BARRY	WILLIAMS	RANDALL	STANIFORTH	EVANS	HENDRIE 8	STANIFORTH
17/09/77	LEYTON ORIENT	A	1-2	5104	THOMAS	AITKEN	BATER	DAY	S TAYLOR	PRINCE	HENDRIE	STANIFORTH	RANDALL	WHITE	EVANS	HENDRIE 8	STANIFORTH, GOULD
24/09/77	OLDHAM ATHLETIC	H	0-0	4550	THOMAS	AITKEN	BATER	DAY	S TAYLOR	PRINCE	STANIFORTH/BARRY	WILLIAMS	GOULD	STANIFORTH	EVANS		HARDING
30/09/77	CHARLTON ATHLETIC	A	1-2	8412	THOMAS	AITKEN	BATER	DAY	S TAYLOR	PRINCE	STANIFORTH/BARRY	WILLIAMS	GOULD	STANIFORTH	EVANS		STANIFORTH, GOULD
04/10/77	MANSFIELD TOWN	H	0-0	4980	THOMAS	AITKEN	A TAYLOR	PULIS	S TAYLOR	PRINCE	WILLIAMS	GOULD	STANIFORTH	BARRY		WILLIAMS, S TAYLOR, STANIFORTH
15/10/77	BURNLEY	H	3-1	7207	THOMAS	AITKEN	A TAYLOR	DAY	S TAYLOR	PRINCE	WILLIAMS	GOULD	STANIFORTH	RANDALL		POWELL
22/10/77	BLACKBURN ROVERS	H	3-1	6431	THOMAS	AITKEN	A TAYLOR	DAY	S TAYLOR	PRINCE	HENDRIE	GOULD	STANIFORTH	EVANS		GOULD, BARRY, RANDALL
29/10/77	TOTTENHAM HOTSPUR	A	1-3	26311	THOMAS	AITKEN	A TAYLOR	DAY	S TAYLOR	PRINCE	BARRY	PULIS	GOULD	STANIFORTH	RANDALL		RANDALL 2
05/11/77	SOUTHAMPTON	A	0-9	6205	THOMAS	AITKEN	A TAYLOR	DAY	S TAYLOR	PRINCE	BARRY	WILLIAMS	GOULD	STANIFORTH	BARRY	RANDALL 11	STANIFORTH 2, RANDALL
12/11/77	MILLWALL	H	1-1	24633	THOMAS	AITKEN	A TAYLOR	DAY	S TAYLOR	AITKEN	WILLIAMS	PULIS	GOULD	STANIFORTH	RANDALL	HENDRIE 6	RANDALL
19/11/77	SUNDERLAND	H	1-5	7878	THOMAS	WILLIAMS	A TAYLOR	DAY	S TAYLOR	PRINCE	WILLIAMS	PULIS	GOULD	STANIFORTH	RANDALL	RANDALL 11	GOULD, RANDALL
26/11/77	BOLTON WANDERERS	A	2-0	13177	THOMAS	AITKEN	BATER	DAY	S TAYLOR	PULIS	AITKEN	HENDRIE	GOULD	STANIFORTH	RANDALL	BARRY	RANDALL
03/12/77	SHEFFIELD UNITED	A	1-1	5351	THOMAS	AITKEN	BATER	DAY	S TAYLOR	PRINCE	BARRY	PULIS	GOULD	STANIFORTH	RANDALL		GOULD, RANDALL
17/12/77	HULL CITY	H	2-3	10613	THOMAS	AITKEN	BATER	DAY	S TAYLOR	PRINCE	BARRY	PULIS	GOULD	STANIFORTH	POWELL		HARDING
26/12/77	STOKE CITY	H	3-2	6516	THOMAS	AITKEN	BATER	DAY	S TAYLOR	PRINCE	BARRY	PULIS	GOULD	STANIFORTH	RANDALL		GOULD, HOADLEY og
27/12/77	SUNDERLAND	H	3-0	25509	THOMAS	AITKEN	BATER	DAY	S TAYLOR	PRINCE	BARRY	PULIS	GOULD	STANIFORTH	RANDALL	RANDALL 11	RANDALL, WHITE, GOULD pen
31/12/77	BRIGHTON & H ALBION	A	3-0	11688	G JONES	AITKEN	BATER	DAY	S TAYLOR	PRINCE	BARRY	PULIS	GOULD	STANIFORTH	RANDALL	PULIS 8	GOULD pen, RANDALL
02/01/78	CRYSTAL PALACE	A	2-3	8471	G JONES	AITKEN	BATER	HARDING	S TAYLOR	PRINCE	BARRY	WILLIAMS	GOULD	STANIFORTH	RANDALL		GOULD, S TAYLOR
14/01/78	NOTTS COUNTY	H	2-3	11945	G JONES	AITKEN	BATER	HARDING	S TAYLOR	PRINCE	BARRY	PULIS	GOULD	STANIFORTH	RANDALL	STANIFORTH 2, RANDALL	POWELL
21/01/78	CARDIFF CITY	A	3-2	8424	THOMAS	AITKEN	BATER	WILLIAMS	S TAYLOR	PRINCE	BARRY	PULIS	POWELL	STANIFORTH	RANDALL		
	FULHAM	H	1-1	7304	THOMAS	AITKEN	BATER	HARDING	S TAYLOR	PRINCE	BARRY	PULIS	POWELL	WILLIAMS	RANDALL		RANDALL
08/02/78	BLACKPOOL	A	2-1	5913	THOMAS	AITKEN	BATER	DAY	S TAYLOR	PRINCE	BARRY	PULIS	GOULD	WHITE	RANDALL		WILLIAMS, GOULD
11/02/78	LUTON TOWN	A	2-1	9416	THOMAS	AITKEN	BATER	DAY	S TAYLOR	PRINCE	WILLIAMS	PULIS	GOULD	WHITE	RANDALL	POWELL 10	WILLIAMS, S TAYLOR, STANIFORTH
25/02/78	LEYTON ORIENT	H	2-0	7740	THOMAS	AITKEN	BATER	DAY	S TAYLOR	PRINCE	BARRY	PULIS	GOULD	WHITE	RANDALL	POWELL 11	GOULD, S TAYLOR
04/03/78	CHARLTON ATHLETIC	H	2-2	7520	THOMAS	AITKEN	BATER	DAY	S TAYLOR	PRINCE	BARRY	PULIS	GOULD	STANIFORTH	RANDALL	HENDRIE 11	GOULD, S TAYLOR
11/03/78	BURNLEY	H	2-2	11780	THOMAS	WILLIAMS	BATER	DAY	S TAYLOR	HARDING	BARRY	WILLIAMS	POWELL	POWELL	RANDALL		RANDALL, DAINES og
18/03/78	BLACKBURN ROVERS	A	3-2	17708	THOMAS	AITKEN	BATER	DAY	S TAYLOR	PRINCE	WILLIAMS	WILLIAMS	GOULD	STANIFORTH	WILLIAMS	WILLIAMS	WILLIAMS, RANDALL
25/03/78	TOTTENHAM HOTSPUR	A	2-3	13428	THOMAS	AITKEN	BATER	DAY	S TAYLOR	PRINCE	BARRY	PULIS	GOULD	WHITE	RANDALL	STANIFORTH 2, POWELL	STANIFORTH
27/03/78	CRYSTAL PALACE	H	1-3	24826	THOMAS	AITKEN	BATER	DAY	S TAYLOR	PRINCE	BARRY	PULIS	GOULD	WHITE	RANDALL	HENDRIE 10	GOULD 3 STANIFORTH
01/04/78	SOUTHAMPTON	A	3-1	3322	THOMAS	AITKEN	BATER	DAY	S TAYLOR	PRINCE	WILLIAMS	PULIS	GOULD	WHITE	RANDALL	HENDRIE 7	BARRY 7
04/04/78	MILLWALL*	A	4-1	7192	THOMAS	AITKEN	BATER	DAY	S TAYLOR	WILLIAMS	BARRY	PULIS	GOULD	WHITE	RANDALL	FOREMAN 4	FOREMAN 4
08/04/78	SHEFFIELD UNITED	H	0-3	7659	THOMAS	AITKEN	BATER	DAY	S TAYLOR	PRINCE	BARRY	PULIS	GOULD	STANIFORTH	RANDALL		
15/04/78	OLDHAM ATHLETIC	H	4-1	20393	THOMAS	AITKEN	BATER	DAY	S TAYLOR	WILLIAMS	BARRY	PULIS	GOULD	WILLIAMS	RANDALL	WILLIAMS 10	GOULD, RANDALL, WHITE 2
22/04/78	BOLTON WANDERERS	A	0-4	9789	THOMAS	AITKEN	BATER	DAY	HARDING	PRINCE	BARRY	PULIS	GOULD	WILLIAMS	RANDALL		
24/04/78	BRIGHTON & H ALBION	H	4-1	3182	THOMAS	AITKEN	BATER	PULIS	HARDING	WILLIAMS	BARRY	PULIS	GOULD	PULIS	RANDALL	HAMILTON	WILLIAMS, RANDALL 2, WHITE
22/04/78	STOKE CITY	H	4-1	6121	THOMAS	AITKEN	BATER	DAY	S TAYLOR	PRINCE	BARRY	PULIS	POWELL	HAMILTON	EVANS	FOREMAN 2, V JONES 9	WILLIAMS, RANDALL 2
24/04/78	MANSFIELD TOWN	A	0-3		THOMAS	AITKEN	BATER	DAY	S TAYLOR	PRINCE	STEPHENS	WILLIAMS	POWELL	HAMILTON	RANDALL		
29/04/78	HULL CITY	A	1-0	3645	THOMAS	AITKEN	BATER	DAY	S TAYLOR	PRINCE	BARRY	WILLIAMS	PULIS	HAMILTON	RANDALL		RANDALL

* played at Fratton Park, Portsmouth

LEAGUE CUP

Date	Opposition	Venue	Score	Att												Substitutes	Goalscorers
13/08/77	WALSALL	H	1-2	3467	THOMAS	AITKEN	BATER	DAY	S TAYLOR	PRINCE	STEPHENS	WILLIAMS	POWELL	HAMILTON	EVANS	FOREMAN	WILLIAMS pen
16/08/77	WALSALL	A	0-1	5445	THOMAS	BATER	AITKEN	DAY	S TAYLOR	PRINCE	STEPHENS	WILLIAMS	POWELL	HAMILTON	EVANS	PRINCE	

FA CUP

Date	Opposition	Venue	Score	Att												Substitutes	Goalscorers
07/01/78	SUNDERLAND	H	1-0	26214	THOMAS	AITKEN	BATER	DAY	S TAYLOR	PRINCE	BARRY	PULIS	GOULD	STANIFORTH	RANDALL	HENDRIE 11	
28/01/78	SOUTHAMPTON	A	2-0	26525	THOMAS	AITKEN	BATER	DAY	S TAYLOR	PRINCE	STEPHENS	PULIS	GOULD	HAMILTON	EVANS		FOREMAN
18/02/78	IPSWICH TOWN	H	2-0	23456	THOMAS	AITKEN	BATER	DAY	S TAYLOR	PRINCE	BARRY	PULIS	GOULD	WILLIAMS	RANDALL	WILLIAMS 2	
28/02/78	IPSWICH TOWN	A	0-3	29532	THOMAS	AITKEN	BATER	DAY	S TAYLOR	PRINCE	BARRY	PULIS	GOULD	STANIFORTH	RANDALL	WILLIAMS 10	

GLOUCESTERSHIRE CUP FINAL

Date	Opposition	Venue	Score	Att												Substitutes	Goalscorers
02/05/78	BRISTOL CITY	A	0-3	10178	THOMAS	AITKEN	BATER	DAY	S TAYLOR	PRINCE	BARRY	WILLIAMS	GOULD	POWELL	RANDALL	HENDRIE, WHITE	

PLAYERS	APP	SUB	GLS
AITKEN P	36		
BARRY M	34	1	2
BATER P	41		
DAY G	34		
EVANS A	9	1	
FOREMAN W	1		
GOULD R	32		10
HAMILTON J	2		
HARDING S	6	1	
HENDRIE P	4	8	1
JONES G	5		
POWELL W	37		2
PRINCE F	21	2	
PULIS P	28	3	2
RANDALL P	37		8
STANIFORTH D	27	2	8
STEPHENS K	7		
TAYLOR A	12		
TAYLOR S	39		2
THOMAS M	37		
WHITE S	4	4	
WILLIAMS D	32	1	8
OWN GOALS			3

quarter-final appearance. However, deep into injury time, Robin Turner equalised to break Rovers' hearts. Ipswich won the replay at Portman Road with ease and went on to win the Cup that season for what remains the only time in the club's history.

Bristol City retained the Gloucestershire Cup, a crowd of 10,178 at Ashton Gate witnessing their comfortable three-goal victory over Rovers. There was also a 3-1 defeat on the same ground in the Anglo-Scottish Cup, in which competition Rovers also lost to a single goal at home to Plymouth Argyle and drew with Birmingham City to find themselves eliminated at the end of the group stage. A Rovers Old Players side defeated Bristol City Old Players 1-0 on 28 February, thanks to a Geoff Bradford goal. The introduction of speedway to Eastville, where meetings were held between 1977 and 1979, meant the pitch was necessarily reduced to 110 x 70 yards, making it, with those of Halifax Town and Swansea City, the smallest in the Football League.

1978/79

Bobby Campbell's pre-season plans, like those of so many managers before him, were heavily restricted by the absence of spending power. For all the major transfer fees ahead – Barrowclough's fee in 1979 was to remain a club record until Rovers were back in Division Two more than a decade later – Campbell's structuring was slow and quiet. Youngsters such as Vaughan Jones, Gary Clarke, Gary Mabbutt and Paul Petts were allowed to develop and break into the League side. The only significant summer signing was that of the former Eire International winger Miah Dennehy, a £20,000 signing from Walsall at the end of July. He had scored the first-ever hat-trick in an Irish Cup final, when playing for Cork Hibernian against Waterford in 1972, but he did not manage a goal in his first season at Eastville.

Before the season could begin in earnest, Rovers participated for a second consecutive year in the Anglo-Scottish Cup. Dennehy and Clarke both played in a 1-0 home victory over Cardiff City and young striker Alan Hoult replaced goalscorer Paul Randall near the end. Rovers then lost embarrassingly 6-1 at Bristol City – Tom Ritchie scoring a hat-trick – and 2-1 at Fulham and were eliminated. The League Cup followed a similar pattern, with Peter Aitken scoring a rare goal with a 25-yard drive as Rovers led Hereford United, who featured Wayne Powell in their side, 2-0 and missed a penalty in the first round first leg. They then crashed 4-0 at Edgar Street to lose 5-2 on aggregate.

Revenge over Fulham was swift as Rovers, with Dennehy making his League debut and six Welsh-born players in the side, defeated the Cottagers 3-1 at Eastville. The first goal was scored after 15 minutes by Paul Randall who was to enjoy continued early-season success. Bobby Gould scored in the first two League matches before joining Hereford United as player-coach. A run of two early away defeats was arrested by a confidence-boosting 4-2 home win over Cardiff City. A sixth-minute Steve Grapes own goal from Mike Barry's inswinging corner put Rovers on their way, with Paul Randall scoring and David Staniforth adding two close-range finishes. John Buchanan scored a penalty in both fixtures for Cardiff City against Rovers.

Bristol Rovers 1978/79. Back row: Bater, Randall, Malpass, Taylor, Harding, White, Aitken. Second row: W Jones (Physio), England, Brown, Staniforth, G Jones, Dodgin (Manager), Thomas, Pulis, Prince, Palmer, Jarman (Youth Coach). Third row: Hendrie, Evans, V Jones, Campbell (Manager) Barry, Hoult, Williams. Front row: M Shaw, J Shaw, G Williams, Mabbutt, Clarke, Griffiths

The 3-0 defeat at Charlton Athletic in August had marked Stuart Taylor's 487th League appearance for Rovers, surpassing Harry Bamford's club record. His 500th game, a 2-1 home win over Sheffield United, came just seven days after the extraordinary return tie with Charlton. Rovers had won all seven of their home games prior to the London side's visit, including an impressive victory over Blackburn Rovers 4-1, with Randall scoring his first League hat-trick, and over Newcastle United 2-0, when Randall claimed both goals. A winning goal from Staniforth had defeated a strong Orient side featuring, in Tunji Banjo and John Chiedozie, two Nigerian International midfielders. Equally, Charlton boasted an unbeaten away record, but nothing indicated the ten-goal thriller that was to unfold.

After Dick Tydeman had put the visitors ahead on 15 minutes, Randall responded with two quick goals so that Rovers led by the half-hour mark. In the four minutes leading up to half-time though, Keith Peacock created goals for Martyn Robinson and Mick Flanagan and Rovers trailed 3-2 at the break. Flanagan put Charlton two goals ahead after 49 minutes and, though David Williams narrowed the gap, Robinson's second goal, after 63 minutes, restored the visitors' two-goal lead. After Peter Aitken's shot was saved just three minutes later, Randall completed his hat-trick and Williams equalised from the penalty spot after a 68th minute foul on substitute Paul Hendrie. Rovers' second 5-5 draw in League football, the first being against Exeter City in November 1934, had seen 10 goals in a frenetic 53-minute spell in the middle of the match.

December, however, brought a turnaround in fortunes. A 5-0 defeat at Roker Park, where Wayne Entwistle grabbed a hat-trick, was followed by a dramatic end to Rovers' unbeaten home record. Full-backs Brian Chambers and Nick Chatterton both scored penalties as Rovers lost 3-0 at home to Millwall. Rovers were to win only two more home League games all season. It was time for action on the transfer front and Campbell, having earlier secured Norwich City's 18-year-old winger Phil Lythgoe on a month's loan, succeeded in buying the midfielder he required in Gary Emmanuel. The nephew of a former Rovers trialist, Emmanuel commanded a club record fee of £50,000 as he joined Rovers from Birmingham City.

At the end of December, to the major disappointment of Rovers fans, Paul Randall was sold to Stoke City for a club record fee of £180,000. He had scored 33 goals in 49 (plus 3 as sub) League matches over an 18-month period and was not easily replaced. Steve White scored twice at Luton and twice more in the win at Millwall, the latterly by the same 3-0 margin as the Eastville fixture, yet the goals no longer flowed so freely. Prior to the Burnley game, where Vaughan Jones, from the penalty spot after 35 minutes, recorded his first League goal for Rovers, the side had gone four matches without a goal. It was to be a year after Randall's departure before Rovers next scored four times in a League match.

Relegation was staved off. Sixteenth place in Division Two reflected much of the early-season success. The reserves, meanwhile, finished ninth in the Football Combination, their highest final position since 1968/69 and a height never again attained in the 20th century. After three straight defeats, Rovers rested Stuart Taylor for the final game of the season, leaving Martin Thomas and David Williams as the club's only ever-presents. Williams scored the only goal at Wrexham in the final game of the season, with a 20-yard drive from Keith Brown's pass 12 minutes from time, to end as the club's second highest scorer behind Randall. This last match saw Rovers field the youngest side in the club's history. Brown, Martin Shaw, Dave Palmer and Mike England were given first full League appearances; England was to wait over six years for his second League match. Gary Emmanuel, at 25, was the oldest player in a side with an average age of 20.

Larry Lloyd, Alan Ball and Tony Sealy, all Rovers players at some point in their careers, appeared in the League Cup final. Lloyd was also a European Cup winner for the first of two consecutive years, as Nottingham Forest beat Malmö 1-0 in the final. Tim Parkin, a Rovers player in 1981, was in the Malmö squad and went on to play in the World Club Championship match as the Swedish side stood in for Forest, only to lose 3-1 on aggregate to the South American Champions, Olimpia from Paraguay.

The FA Cup saw Rovers record 1-0 wins at Swansea City and at home to Charlton Athletic before losing at Portman Road to Ipswich Town for a second consecutive season. Steve White scored in all three matches. Charlton had defeated Southern League Maidstone United in the third round despite floodlight failure in the replay, after their strikers Mick Flanagan and Derek Hales had been sent off in the initial tie for fighting each other. Rovers' fourth round victory was to be Flanagan's only appearance for Charlton in the second-half of the season. The crowd at the fifth round game, 23,231, was the largest to watch Rovers all season, and spectators saw Rovers overwhelmed by an Ipswich Town side destined to finish sixth in Division One. The Cup holders won

FOOTBALL LEAGUE DIVISION TWO

Date	Opponent		Score	ATT	G	2	3	4	5	6	7	8	9	10	11	SUBSTITUTES	GOALSCORERS
19/08/78	FULHAM	H	3-1	5950	THOMAS	JONES	BATER	PULIS	TAYLOR	PRINCE	DENNEHY	WILLIAMS	GOULD	RANDALL	BARRY	AITKEN 7	RANDALL, GOULD, BARRY
22/08/78	OLDHAM ATHLETIC	A	1-3	6005	THOMAS	AITKEN	BATER	PULIS	TAYLOR	PRINCE	DENNEHY	WILLIAMS	GOULD	RANDALL	BARRY	JONES 7	GOULD
26/08/78	CHARLTON ATHLETIC	A	0-3	7745	THOMAS	AITKEN	BATER	PULIS	TAYLOR	AITKEN	DENNEHY	WILLIAMS	STANIFORTH	RANDALL	BARRY	STANIFORTH 10	
02/09/78	CARDIFF CITY	H	4-2	6855	THOMAS	AITKEN	BATER	DAY	TAYLOR	AITKEN	DENNEHY	WILLIAMS	STANIFORTH	RANDALL	BARRY	GOULD 7	GRAPES og, RANDALL, GOULD, STANIFORTH 2
09/09/78	LUTON TOWN	H	2-0	6508	THOMAS	PULIS	BATER	DAY	TAYLOR	PRINCE	DENNEHY	WILLIAMS	STANIFORTH	RANDALL	BARRY	STANIFORTH 10	STANIFORTH, RANDALL
16/09/78	WEST HAM UNITED	A	0-2	22189	THOMAS	PULIS	BATER	DAY	TAYLOR	PRINCE	DENNEHY	WILLIAMS	STANIFORTH	RANDALL	BARRY		
23/09/78	WREXHAM	H	2-1	7619	THOMAS	PULIS	BATER	DAY	TAYLOR	PRINCE	DENNEHY	WILLIAMS	STANIFORTH	RANDALL	BARRY	AITKEN 2	RANDALL, WILLIAMS
30/09/78	CAMBRIDGE UNITED	A	1-1	5513	THOMAS	BATER	DAY	AITKEN	TAYLOR	PRINCE	DENNEHY	WILLIAMS	STANIFORTH	RANDALL	HENDRIE	HENDRIE 7	WILLIAMS
07/10/78	BLACKBURN ROVERS	H	1-1	7111	THOMAS	BATER	DAY	AITKEN	TAYLOR	PRINCE	DENNEHY	WILLIAMS	STANIFORTH	RANDALL	HENDRIE		
14/10/78	NOTTS COUNTY	A	1-2	8646	THOMAS	BATER	DAY	AITKEN	TAYLOR	PRINCE	DENNEHY	WILLIAMS	WHITE	RANDALL	LYTHGOE	CLARKE 10	WHITE
21/10/78	LEYTON ORIENT	H	2-1	7234	THOMAS	BATER	DAY	AITKEN	TAYLOR	PRINCE	DENNEHY	WILLIAMS	STANIFORTH	RANDALL	LYTHGOE	HENDRIE	PRINCE, STANIFORTH
28/10/78	LEICESTER CITY	A	0-0	12498	THOMAS	BATER	DAY	AITKEN	TAYLOR	HENDRIE	DENNEHY	WILLIAMS	STANIFORTH	RANDALL	HENDRIE	HENDRIE 11	
04/11/78	NEWCASTLE UNITED	H	2-0	10582	THOMAS	BATER	DAY	AITKEN	TAYLOR	HENDRIE	DENNEHY	WILLIAMS	STANIFORTH	RANDALL	HENDRIE	HENDRIE 6	HENDRIE
11/11/78	FULHAM	A	0-3	10296	THOMAS	BATER	DAY	AITKEN	TAYLOR	HENDRIE	DENNEHY	WILLIAMS	WHITE	RANDALL	HENDRIE	WHITE 7	
18/11/78	CHARLTON ATHLETIC	H	5-5	8107	THOMAS	BATER	DAY	AITKEN	TAYLOR	PRINCE	DENNEHY	WILLIAMS	STANIFORTH	RANDALL	WHITE	WHITE 3	RANDALL 3, WILLIAMS 2, 1pen
25/11/78	SHEFFIELD UNITED	A	2-0	8434	THOMAS	JONES	BATER	AITKEN	TAYLOR	PRINCE	DENNEHY	WILLIAMS	STANIFORTH	RANDALL	WHITE	HENDRIE 6	RANDALL 2
02/12/78	SUNDERLAND	H	0-5	18864	THOMAS	JONES	BATER	DAY	TAYLOR	PRINCE	DENNEHY	WILLIAMS	STANIFORTH	EMMANUEL	WHITE	WHITE 7	
09/12/78	MILLWALL	H	0-3	7112	THOMAS	DAY	BATER	DAY	TAYLOR	JONES	DENNEHY	WILLIAMS	STANIFORTH	EMMANUEL	STANIFORTH	MABBUTT 2	
16/12/78	BURNLEY	A	0-3	9119	THOMAS	DAY	BATER	HARDING	TAYLOR	PRINCE	DENNEHY	WILLIAMS	STANIFORTH	EMMANUEL	HENDRIE	WHITE 7	
23/12/78	STOKE CITY	H	0-0	7897	THOMAS	JONES	JONES	DAY	TAYLOR	PRINCE	PETTS	WILLIAMS	STANIFORTH	RANDALL	MABBUTT	MABBUTT	
26/12/78	CRYSTAL PALACE	A	1-0	21605	THOMAS	DAY	HARDING	HARDING	TAYLOR	HENDRIE	PETTS	WILLIAMS	STANIFORTH	RANDALL	MABBUTT	WHITE	WHITE 2
30/12/78	PRESTON NORTH END	H	1-0	12600	THOMAS	DAY	BATER	DAY	TAYLOR	PRINCE	DENNEHY	WILLIAMS	STANIFORTH	RANDALL	MABBUTT	HENDRIE 7	DENNEHY
06/01/79	WEST HAM UNITED	A	2-3	6002	THOMAS	BATER	JONES	EMMANUEL	TAYLOR	HENDRIE	EMMANUEL	WILLIAMS	STANIFORTH	EMMANUEL	WHITE	WHITE 2	WHITE 2, WILLIAMS
20/01/79	LUTON TOWN	H	0-1	12418	THOMAS	BATER	JONES	TAYLOR	TAYLOR	EMMANUEL	HENDRIE	WILLIAMS	WHITE	STANIFORTH	AITKEN	DENNEHY 11	
10/02/79	CAMBRIDGE UNITED	A	0-0	5904	THOMAS	DAY	BATER	HARDING	TAYLOR	HARDING	DENNEHY	WILLIAMS	WHITE	STANIFORTH	HENDRIE	DENNEHY 8	
24/02/79	NOTTS COUNTY	H	2-2	6887	THOMAS	DAY	BATER	HARDING	TAYLOR	PRINCE	DENNEHY	WILLIAMS	WHITE	EMMANUEL	HENDRIE	STANIFORTH 11	PRINCE, WHITE
03/03/79	LEYTON ORIENT	A	1-1	5078	THOMAS	DAY	BATER	AITKEN	TAYLOR	HARDING	DENNEHY	WILLIAMS	WHITE	EMMANUEL	STANIFORTH	WILLIAMS 2	WILLIAMS 2
10/03/79	LEICESTER CITY	H	1-1	6381	THOMAS	DAY	BATER	AITKEN	TAYLOR	CLARKE	DENNEHY	WILLIAMS	WHITE	EMMANUEL	MABBUTT	WILLIAMS	WILLIAMS
17/03/79	BRIGHTON & H ALBION	A	1-2	8290	THOMAS	DAY	BATER	AITKEN	TAYLOR	BARRY	EMMANUEL	WILLIAMS	WHITE	MABBUTT	EMMANUEL	MABBUTT 7	
20/03/79	OLDHAM ATHLETIC	A	0-0	5405	THOMAS	DAY	BATER	AITKEN	TAYLOR	PRINCE	DENNEHY	WILLIAMS	STANIFORTH	BROWN	EMMANUEL	CLARKE 7	
24/03/79	BRIGHTON & H ALBION	H	0-1	1406	THOMAS	DAY	BATER	AITKEN	TAYLOR	EMMANUEL	EMMANUEL	WILLIAMS	STANIFORTH	WHITE	HENDRIE	CLARKE 6	
31/03/79	SHEFFIELD UNITED	A	0-2	8554	THOMAS	DAY	BATER	AITKEN	TAYLOR	EMMANUEL	DENNEHY	WILLIAMS	STANIFORTH	MABBUTT	EMMANUEL	STANIFORTH	
07/04/79	SUNDERLAND	H	0-0	8003	THOMAS	DAY	BATER	AITKEN	TAYLOR	EMMANUEL	DENNEHY	WILLIAMS	STANIFORTH	MABBUTT	EMMANUEL	WILLIAMS	
14/04/79	CRYSTAL PALACE	H	0-1	10986	THOMAS	DAY	BATER	AITKEN	TAYLOR	HENDRIE	DENNEHY	WILLIAMS	WHITE	BROWN	EMMANUEL		
16/04/79	SUNDERLAND	A	0-3	23024	THOMAS	DAY	BATER	AITKEN	TAYLOR	PRINCE	DENNEHY	WILLIAMS	WHITE	SHAW	EMMANUEL	CLARKE 6	
21/04/79	BURNLEY	H	2-0	18679	THOMAS	DAY	BATER	HARDING	TAYLOR	PRINCE	DENNEHY	WILLIAMS	WHITE	PETTS	EMMANUEL	BROWN 9	WHITE, WILLIAMS
28/04/79	STOKE CITY	A	0-2	5947	THOMAS	HARDING	BATER	AITKEN	TAYLOR	PRINCE	DENNEHY	WILLIAMS	MABBUTT	BROWN	EMMANUEL	BROWN 10	
02/05/79	NEWCASTLE UNITED	A	3-0	5266	THOMAS	HARDING	BATER	HARDING	TAYLOR	PRINCE	DENNEHY	WILLIAMS	WHITE	MABBUTT	EMMANUEL	PETTS 6	JONES pen, WHITE, WHITE 2, WILLIAMS
05/05/79	MILLWALL	H	0-3	9625	THOMAS	DAY	BATER	HARDING	TAYLOR	STANIFORTH	PETTS	WILLIAMS	MABBUTT	MABBUTT	EMMANUEL		
07/05/79	PRESTON NORTH END	H	0-1	5814	THOMAS	AITKEN	BATER	AITKEN	TAYLOR	PRINCE	PETTS	EMMANUEL	WHITE	BROWN	WHITE		
10/05/79	WREXHAM	A	1-0	6136	THOMAS	PALMER	BATER	PALMER	TAYLOR	SHAW	PETTS	EMMANUEL	MABBUTT	BROWN	EMMANUEL		WILLIAMS

FA CUP

Date	Opponent		Score	ATT	G	2	3	4	5	6	7	8	9	10	11	SUBSTITUTES	GOALSCORERS
09/01/79	SWANSEA CITY	A	1-0	16052	THOMAS	JONES	BATER	HARDING	TAYLOR	AITKEN	HENDRIE	WILLIAMS	WHITE	MABBUTT	AITKEN	DENNEHY 11	WHITE
05/02/79	CHARLTON ATHLETIC	H	1-0	9623	THOMAS	DAY	BATER	HARDING	TAYLOR	PRINCE	DENNEHY	WILLIAMS	WHITE	RANDALL	HENDRIE	MABBUTT 10	WHITE
26/02/79	IPSWICH TOWN	A	1-6	23231	THOMAS	JONES	BATER	HARDING	TAYLOR	PRINCE	DENNEHY	WILLIAMS	WHITE	EMMANUEL	HENDRIE	STANIFORTH 11	WHITE

LEAGUE CUP

Date	Opponent		Score	ATT	G	2	3	4	5	6	7	8	9	10	11	SUBSTITUTES	GOALSCORERS
12/08/78	HEREFORD	A	2-1	5001	THOMAS	THOMAS	BATER	PULIS	TAYLOR	PRINCE	DENNEHY	WILLIAMS	RANDALL	STANIFORTH	BARRY	CLARKE 9	AITKEN, STANIFORTH
16/08/78	HEREFORD UNITED	H	0-4	5130	THOMAS	AITKEN	BATER	PULIS	TAYLOR	PRINCE	DENNEHY	WILLIAMS	RANDALL	HOUT	BARRY	GOULD 10	

GLOUCESTERSHIRE CUP FINAL

Date	Opponent		Score	ATT	G	2	3	4	5	6	7	8	9	10	11	GOALSCORERS
15/05/79	BRISTOL CITY	H	0-2	6661	THOMAS	PALMER	BATER	AITKEN	TAYLOR	WILLIAMS	EMMANUEL, PETTS	MABBUTT	WHITE	BROWN	BROWN	

PLAYERS	APP	SUB	GLS
AITKEN P	31	1	1
BARRY M	12		1
BATER P	36		
BROWN K	1	2	
CLARKE G	2	4	
DAY G	24		
DENNEHY J	29	3	
EMMANUEL G	21		
ENGLAND M	1		
GOULD R	3	1	
HARDING S	10		
HENDRIE P	13	6	
JONES V	21	1	1
LYTHGOE P	1	1	
MABBUTT G	8	3	
PALMER D	1		
PETTS P	9	1	
PRINCE F	26		
PULIS A	7		
RANDALL P	21		13
SHAW M	1		
STANIFORTH D	31	2	6
TAYLOR S	41		
THOMAS M	42		
WHITE S	23	4	10
WILLIAMS D	42		10
OWN GOAL			1

with two goals from Alan Brazil and one each from Arnold Muhren, Paul Mariner, Mick Mills and substitute David Geddis.

Rovers also hosted testimonial games at Eastville for midfielder Frankie Prince – 0-2 against Bristol City – and goalkeeper Dick Sheppard, which West Bromwich Albion won 3-2. The most unusual match, though, was against the touring Zambian national side on 24 October. A crowd of 4,000 saw Rovers beat Zambia 4-1 at Eastville, with goals from Paul Randall, Phil Lythgoe, Miah Dennehy and David Williams.

1979/80

Two highly experienced players were signed in the summer of 1979 to add strength to the Rovers side. At the end of July, Bobby Campbell paid £100,000 to Birmingham City for the services of Stewart Barrowclough, a former Barnsley and Newcastle United winger who had won 5 England Under-23 caps. This was to be the record fee spent by the club until 1991. Two weeks later, Terry Cooper arrived from Bristol City as player-coach. Cooper had won 20 England caps while on Leeds United's books and was to be Rovers' manager before the season was out.

Within days of Cooper's arrival, Rovers had let an away lead slip, to be knocked out of the League Cup on aggregate by Torquay United. League form, however, appeared more consistent. Two consecutive home wins were followed by a highly creditable draw at Birmingham City. The speedy and dependable Barrowclough scored from the penalty spot in three consecutive League games – a club record later equalled by Ian Holloway in October 1990 – and scored six penalties in all this season, including one in each game with Orient.

All illusions, however, were shattered by a heavy defeat at Cambridge that set Rovers on a run of poor results through the autumn. Floyd Streete gave the home side a first-minute lead and Lindsay Smith and Alan Biley added goals either side of half-time. Although David Williams pulled a goal back after an hour, Cambridge United's 4-1 victory was sealed 19 minutes from time, when Steve Spriggs was left unmarked following Biley's overhead kick. Spriggs stood just 5ft 2in tall, and only Fred Le May in 1930/31, amongst Rovers' League opponents, was shorter. This was the first of nine defeats in 14 games that sent Rovers tumbling down the table and ultimately lost Campbell his job.

While Bobby Campbell stayed in Bristol, working outside professional football, Rovers appointed youth coach Harold Jarman as his temporary successor. Not only was Jarman the first Bristolian to manage the club, but he was also a figure who had gained huge respect in his 14 years as a Rovers player. Within days of his arrival, successive home wins over Oldham Athletic and Swansea City led the side to believe it could pull clear of relegation. Under his guidance, Rovers beat Chelsea 3-0 and secured enough points to avoid Division Three football. It was, therefore, scant reward for Jarman when, with just two matches remaining, his application for the full-time manager's job was turned down and Terry Cooper was appointed.

Bristol Rovers 1979/80. Back row: Penny, V Jones, England, Harding, Palmer, Griffiths, Brown. Middle row: Bater, Hughes, Pulis, Thomas, Kite, Stevens, G Williams, Dean, Mabbutt. Front row: Emmanuel, Gillies, Barrowclough, Cooper (Player-Manager), Bates, Barrett, D Williams

In October, an easily distinguishable character in English football, Brian Kilcline, had appeared at Eastville on his League debut. His first professional club, Notts County, won this particular game 3-2. Kilcline's most famous day was the 1987 FA Cup final, where he and Spurs' Gary Mabbutt, who was in the Rovers side against Notts County, both got on the scoresheet. Three days later, Rovers were undone by Bob Hatton, who scored a first-half hat-trick as Luton Town won 3-1 at Kenilworth Road, Gary Emmanuel's only goal of the season reducing the deficit after half-time. It was Luton who paid £195,000 on Christmas Eve for the signature of Rovers' exciting young forward, Steve White. It was a club-record transfer fee received by Rovers but the two main strikers had now been sold in the space of 12 months.

No sooner had White left, than Rovers ran up their largest win of the season. Swansea City were beaten 4-1 at Eastville with the Welshman Alan Waddle, a cousin of the England International Chris Waddle, scoring for both sides either side of half-time before Miah Dennehy, set up three times by Barrowclough in 34 second-half minutes, scored a memorable hat-trick. They were to be the mercurial winger's last three goals for the club for, after a trial with Cardiff City, he began the 1980/81 season at Trowbridge Town. Frankie Prince, who had won four Welsh Under-23 caps during a long association with the club, played his last game for Rovers in the heavy defeat at bottom-of-the-table Charlton Athletic, while centre-half Stuart Taylor made the last of his club record 546 Football League appearances in the 3-3 draw with Preston North End at Eastville in March. There were six goals in 29 second-half minutes as Rovers, 2-0 up just after the hour mark, dropped a point thanks to Peter Aitken's own goal three minutes from time. Young Tony Pulis, who scored Rovers' third goal against Preston after 82 minutes, also scored in the victory over Chelsea. In a fine team performance, where Aitken was outstanding, Shaun Penny grabbed two goals to give Rovers a convincing win. This victory, however, was marred by the disgraceful behaviour of some spectators at the Chelsea end, who pushed down a wall supporting the Muller Road terraces.

Jarman's approach was to go for experience and 30-year-old Chic Bates arrived at Eastville in March. He played in the final 11 League games of the season and scored in consecutive home draws with Sunderland and Leicester City, two of the promoted clubs. Youth was also given a go, as the season drew to a close, with Paul Petts and Mike Barrett being offered League experience. The former was the son of an Eastville favourite, Johnny Petts and, like his father, was an

Record signing Stewart Barrowclough, whose transfer fee of £100,000 was unbroken for 12 years

England Youth International. The latter was a natural ball-playing wingman, whose close control and ability to beat opponents was to endear him to an adoring Eastville public. New manager Cooper gave debuts to two young Welsh players, Mark Hughes, a cousin of the England defender Emlyn Hughes, and Ashley Griffiths, in the meaningless final game of the season at home to West Ham United. The Hammers treated the game as a warm-up for the FA Cup final seven days later where Trevor Brooking's 13th-minute header proved enough to defeat Arsenal.

Martin Thomas in goal had played a key role in maintaining Rovers' Division Two status. Rovers only conceded four goals in a game twice and Thomas was able to keep five consecutive clean sheets in early spring until finally beaten by a Teddy Maybank goal at Fulham. Thomas was one of a number of Welsh players in the side. Indeed, 11 out of the 25 players used in the League during 1979/80 were born in South Wales. Bristol-born goalkeeper, Phil Kite, was given his club debut in the Gloucestershire Cup final, while the unfortunate Andrew Evans, was granted a testimonial game against Southampton at Eastville. Prior to Geoff Merrick's testimonial game at Ashton Gate on 12 May, Rovers Old Players played out a goalless draw against Bristol City Old Players.

The former Rovers defender Larry Lloyd was in the successful Nottingham Forest side that retained the European Cup when John Robertson's goal defeated SV Hamburg in Madrid and set up a World Club Championship final against Nacional of Uruguay. He missed the League Cup final, where Forest lost 1-0 to a Wolverhampton Wanderers side containing two future Rovers players, Kenny Hibbitt and Paul Bradshaw. Rovers were to experience no joy in any of the Cup tournaments. Goals from Gordon Cowans and

FOOTBALL LEAGUE DIVISION TWO

SEASON 1979/80

Date	Opponent	H/A	Score	Att	G	2	3	4	5	6	7	8	9	10	11	Substitutes	Goalscorers
18/08/79	QPR	A	0-2	12652	THOMAS	PULIS	BATER	AITKEN	HARDING	EMMANUEL	B'CLOUGH	WILLIAMS	WHITE	DENNEHY	COOPER		
21/08/79	LUTON TOWN	A	3-2	5614	THOMAS	PULIS	BATER	AITKEN	HARDING	EMMANUEL	B'CLOUGH	WILLIAMS	WHITE	DENNEHY	CLARKE		DENNEHY, WHITE 2
25/08/79	SHREWSBURY TOWN	H	2-1	5713	THOMAS	PULIS	BATER	AITKEN	HARDING	EMMANUEL	B'CLOUGH	WILLIAMS	WHITE	DENNEHY	CLARKE	MABBUTT 10	B'CLOUGH 2
01/09/79	BIRMINGHAM CITY	A	1-1	15330	THOMAS	BATER	WILLIAMS	AITKEN	HARDING	EMMANUEL	B'CLOUGH	WILLIAMS	WHITE	DENNEHY	COOPER	DENNEHY	B'CLOUGH pen,
08/09/79	WATFORD	H	1-1	7625	THOMAS	BATER	WILLIAMS	AITKEN	HARDING	EMMANUEL	B'CLOUGH	WILLIAMS	WHITE	DENNEHY	COOPER	DENNEHY	BATES P
15/09/79	CAMBRIDGE UNITED	A	1-4	4423	THOMAS	PULIS	BATER	AITKEN	HARDING	MABBUTT	B'CLOUGH	WILLIAMS	WHITE	DENNEHY	COOPER	WILLIAMS	BROWN K
22/09/79	PRESTON NORTH END	A	2-3	7555	THOMAS	TAYLOR	BATER	AITKEN	HARDING	EMMANUEL	B'CLOUGH	WILLIAMS	PENNY	DENNEHY	COOPER	CLARKE 10	COOPER T
29/09/79	CARDIFF CITY	H	2-3	8949	THOMAS	PULIS	BATER	AITKEN	TAYLOR	MABBUTT	B'CLOUGH	WILLIAMS	PENNY	DENNEHY	COOPER	TAYLOR, PENNY	CLARKE 10
06/10/79	NOTTS COUNTY	H	2-3	5372	THOMAS	PULIS	BATER	AITKEN	TAYLOR	MABBUTT	B'CLOUGH	WILLIAMS	PENNY	DENNEHY	COOPER	MABBUTT 4	COOPER T
09/10/79	CHELSEA	A	1-3	8507	THOMAS	MABBUTT	BATER	AITKEN	TAYLOR	EMMANUEL	B'CLOUGH	WILLIAMS	PENNY	DENNEHY	COOPER	EMMANUEL	DENNEHY, B'CLOUGH
13/10/79	LUTON TOWN	H	0-1	18236	THOMAS	MABBUTT	BATER	AITKEN	HARDING	EMMANUEL	B'CLOUGH	WILLIAMS	WHITE	PENNY	COOPER	EMMANUEL	EMMANUEL G
20/10/79	CHARLTON ATHLETIC	A	3-0	5472	THOMAS	MABBUTT	BATER	AITKEN	HARDING	PRINCE	B'CLOUGH	PRINCE	WHITE	PENNY	WILLIAMS	DENNEHY 6	GRIFFITHS A
27/10/79	LEYTON ORIENT	H	1-2	4645	THOMAS	MABBUTT	WILLIAMS	AITKEN	HARDING	EMMANUEL	B'CLOUGH	EMMANUEL	WHITE	PENNY	CLARKE	HARDING, S	HARDING S
03/11/79	QPR	H	1-3	8531	THOMAS	MABBUTT	WILLIAMS	AITKEN	TAYLOR	EMMANUEL	B'CLOUGH	EMMANUEL	PENNY	PENNY	CLARKE	CLARKE	HUGHES M
10/11/79	WREXHAM	A	3-0	9188	THOMAS	BATER	WILLIAMS	AITKEN	TAYLOR	EMMANUEL	B'CLOUGH	EMMANUEL	DENNEHY	PENNY	PENNY	PENNY	JONES G
17/11/79	NEWCASTLE UNITED	H	1-2	7626	THOMAS	BATER	WILLIAMS	AITKEN	TAYLOR	BATER	B'CLOUGH	BATER	WHITE	DENNEHY	PULIS	BATER, WHITE	JONES G
24/11/79	SUNDERLAND	A	2-3	21793	THOMAS	B'CLOUGH	WILLIAMS	AITKEN	TAYLOR	PARKINSON	B'CLOUGH	PARKINSON	WHITE	DENNEHY	PULIS	PARKINSON, WHITE	PARKINSON N
01/12/79	BURNLEY	H	1-1	5273	THOMAS	V JONES	WILLIAMS	PRINCE	TAYLOR	PARKINSON	B'CLOUGH	PARKINSON	WHITE	DENNEHY	PULIS	PENNY 7	PENNY'S
08/12/79	WEST HAM UNITED	A	1-2	17763	THOMAS	BATER	WILLIAMS	MABBUTT	TAYLOR	BATER	B'CLOUGH	EMMANUEL	DENNEHY	PENNY	PULIS	MABBUTT 7	PETTS P
15/12/79	OLDHAM ATHLETIC	H	2-0	9230	THOMAS	BATER	WILLIAMS	MABBUTT	TAYLOR	PRINCE	B'CLOUGH	EMMANUEL	DENNEHY	BATES	PULIS	BARRETT 7	PRINCE F
26/12/79	SWANSEA CITY	A	4-1	4596	THOMAS	BATER	WILLIAMS	MABBUTT	TAYLOR	PRINCE	B'CLOUGH	EMMANUEL	WHITE	BATES	PULIS	PULIS A	PULIS A
29/12/79	SHREWSBURY TOWN	A	1-3	21579	THOMAS	BATER	WILLIAMS	MABBUTT	TAYLOR	PRINCE	B'CLOUGH	WILLIAMS	WHITE	DENNEHY	PULIS	WADDLE og, DENNEHY 3	THOMAS M
01/01/80	LEICESTER CITY	H	0-3	9351	THOMAS	BATER	WILLIAMS	MABBUTT	TAYLOR	AITKEN	B'CLOUGH	EMMANUEL	DENNEHY	BROWN	PULIS	B'CLOUGH 2, 1 pen	PRINCE F
12/01/80	BIRMINGHAM CITY	H	0-0	11020	THOMAS	V JONES	WILLIAMS	MABBUTT	HARDING	AITKEN	B'CLOUGH	EMMANUEL	DENNEHY	BROWN	V JONES	V JONES 10	PENNY
19/01/80	CAMBRIDGE UNITED	H	0-0	5394	THOMAS	V JONES	COOPER	AITKEN	TAYLOR	MABBUTT	B'CLOUGH	WILLIAMS	PENNY	DENNEHY	PULIS		
02/02/80	WATFORD	A	1-0	6810	WILLIAMS	B'CLOUGH	COOPER	MABBUTT	HARDING	AITKEN	WILLIAMS	EMMANUEL	DENNEHY	BROWN	PULIS	V JONES 5	WADDLE og, DENNEHY 3
09/02/80	CARDIFF CITY	A	3-0	14176	THOMAS	V JONES	COOPER	AITKEN	TAYLOR	PRINCE	B'CLOUGH	WILLIAMS	PENNY	MABBUTT	PULIS		PULIS A
16/02/80	FULHAM	H	1-1	4744	THOMAS	V JONES	COOPER	AITKEN	TAYLOR	PRINCE	B'CLOUGH	WILLIAMS	PENNY	MABBUTT	PULIS		TAYLOR S
23/02/80	CHELSEA	H	3-0	14476	THOMAS	V JONES	COOPER	AITKEN	TAYLOR	PRINCE	B'CLOUGH	WILLIAMS	PENNY	MABBUTT	PULIS	EMMANUEL 6	WHITE S
26/02/80	FULHAM	A	1-1	6022	THOMAS	V JONES	COOPER	AITKEN	TAYLOR	MABBUTT	B'CLOUGH	WILLIAMS	PENNY	MABBUTT	PULIS	PENNY 2, PULIS	WILLIAMS D
01/03/80	CHARLTON ATHLETIC	H	3-0	5798	THOMAS	V JONES	COOPER	AITKEN	TAYLOR	AITKEN	B'CLOUGH	WILLIAMS	MABBUTT	MABBUTT	PULIS	WILLIAMS	OWN GOALS
08/03/80	LEYTON ORIENT	A	0-4	4858	THOMAS	V JONES	COOPER	BATER	TAYLOR	MABBUTT	B'CLOUGH	WILLIAMS	MABBUTT	MABBUTT	PULIS	DENNEHY 6	
11/03/80	PRESTON NORTH END	H	3-3	6022	THOMAS	V JONES	COOPER	AITKEN	TAYLOR	AITKEN	B'CLOUGH	WILLIAMS	MABBUTT	BATES	MABBUTT	WILLIAMS, B'CLOUGH, PULIS	
15/03/80	NOTTS COUNTY	A	0-0	5698	THOMAS	V JONES	COOPER	AITKEN	BATER	MABBUTT	B'CLOUGH	WILLIAMS	BATES	BATES	PULIS		
22/03/80	WREXHAM	H	1-0	5440	THOMAS	V JONES	COOPER	AITKEN	BATER	B'CLOUGH	B'CLOUGH	WILLIAMS	BATES	BATES	PULIS	MABBUTT 9	B'CLOUGH pen
29/03/80	NEWCASTLE UNITED	A	1-3	19011	THOMAS	V JONES	EMMANUEL	AITKEN	BATER	B'CLOUGH	PETTS	WILLIAMS	PENNY	BATES	PULIS	MABBUTT 7	BANTON og
04/04/80	FULHAM	A	1-0	7289	THOMAS	V JONES	COOPER	AITKEN	HARDING	PETTS	PETTS	EMMANUEL	PENNY	BATES	BARRETT	BARRETT 7	PENNY
05/04/80	SWANSEA CITY	H	0-2	11730	THOMAS	V JONES	COOPER	AITKEN	BATER	BATER	B'CLOUGH	WILLIAMS	PENNY	BATES	PULIS		BARRETT 7
12/04/80	BURNLEY	A	1-1	5270	THOMAS	V JONES	COOPER	AITKEN	BATER	BATER	PETTS	WILLIAMS	PENNY	BATES	PULIS	V JONES pen	
19/04/80	SUNDERLAND	H	2-2	9757	THOMAS	V JONES	COOPER	AITKEN	HARDING	BATER	B'CLOUGH	WILLIAMS	PENNY	BATES	MABBUTT	B'CLOUGH, BATES	
23/04/80	LEICESTER CITY	A	1-1	8205	THOMAS	V JONES	COOPER	AITKEN	HARDING	AITKEN	B'CLOUGH	WILLIAMS	PENNY	BARRETT	MABBUTT	BATES	PENNY
26/04/80	OLDHAM ATHLETIC	A	1-2	5202	THOMAS	V JONES	COOPER	AITKEN	HARDING	B'CLOUGH	B'CLOUGH	WILLIAMS	BATES	BATER	BATER	BATES	
03/05/80	WEST HAM UNITED	H	0-2	9824	THOMAS	BATER	COOPER	HUGHES	MABBUTT	GRIFFITHS	B'CLOUGH	PULIS	PENNY	BATES	BARRETT	WILLIAMS	

FA CUP

Date	Opponent	H/A	Score	Att	G	2	3	4	5	6	7	8	9	10	11	Substitutes	Goalscorers
04/01/80	ASTON VILLA	H	1-2	16060	THOMAS	PULIS	COOPER	MABBUTT	TAYLOR	WILLIAMS	B'CLOUGH	PRINCE	WHITE	DENNEHY	PULIS	PETTS 11	B'CLOUGH

LEAGUE CUP

Date	Opponent	H/A	Score	Att	G	2	3	4	5	6	7	8	9	10	11	Substitutes	Goalscorers
11/08/79	TORQUAY UNITED	A	2-1	4506	THOMAS	PULIS	BATER	AITKEN	HARDING	WILLIAMS	B'CLOUGH	PRINCE	WHITE	DENNEHY	COOPER	BATER	B'CLOUGH
14/08/79	TORQUAY UNITED	H	1-3	3758	THOMAS	PULIS	BATER	AITKEN	HARDING	WILLIAMS	B'CLOUGH	WILLIAMS	WHITE	DENNEHY	V JONES	V JONES	EMMANUEL

GLOUCESTERSHIRE CUP FINAL

Date	Opponent	H/A	Score	Att	G	2	3	4	5	6	7	8	9	10	11	Substitutes	Goalscorers
06/05/80	BRISTOL CITY	A	0-1	5584	KITE	BATER	COOPER	V JONES	HARDING	AITKEN	B'CLOUGH	PULIS	PENNY	BATES	WILLIAMS		WILLIAMS

PLAYERS	APP	SUB	GLS
AITKEN P	41	1	
BARRETT M	2	1	
BARROWCLOUGH S	38		12
BATER P	34		
BATES P	11		1
BROWN K	2	1	
CLARKE G	4	1	
COOPER T	25		
DENNEHY J	18	2	
EMMANUEL G	19	2	
GRIFFITHS A	1		
HARDING S	21		
HUGHES M	1		
JONES G	4		
JONES V	19	4	
MABBUTT G	27	6	
PARKINSON N	5	1	
PENNY S	32		9
PETTS P	3		
PRINCE F	11		
PULIS A	31	3	
TAYLOR S	38		
THOMAS M	21		
WHITE S	15		6
WILLIAMS D	39	1	4
OWN GOALS			2

Gary Shaw earned FA Cup success at Eastville for a very talented Aston Villa team, while Les Lawrence scored in both legs as a struggling Torquay United side put Rovers out of the League Cup. It was the same story in the Gloucestershire Cup, where Rovers, having lost the first two games under Cooper's management, lost to a second-half goal from Howard Pritchard at Ashton Gate.

A temporary extension to Rovers' tenancy at Eastville enabled the club to remain in east Bristol into the 1980s. However, fears continued to grow for the long-term future and what the club could not afford was to suffer as disastrous a season as the one that now lay ahead. In the meantime, along with all other Division Two venues, the stadium was brought under the specifications of the 1975 Safety of Sports Grounds Act, the brief of which was now extended beyond the top division. This act stated that all

On 11 March 1980 Stuart Taylor made his last League appearance for Rovers. His total of 546 is a club record unlikely ever to beaten

grounds with a capacity exceeding 10,000 were to be 'designated' and therefore hold a safety certificate issued by the local authority. Eastville stadium fell into this bracket and, amid spiralling costs and falling attendances, a late 1970s phenomenon, Rovers were forced to comply with legal requirements. This the club clearly did not, for Rovers were later fined £200 for making unauthorized changes to the layout of the stadium.

1980/81

It was a season of record lows. Only five League wins all season, only four wins at Eastville in any competition, just 34 League goals, including 21 at home. It was Valentine's Day before Rovers had recorded their second win of the season. The previous victory had been the first in 17 matches under Terry Cooper. Overshadowing this was the South Stand fire in August and Rovers' enforced absence from Eastville. Relegation, after seven seasons in Division Two, became inevitable. Rovers finished seven points adrift of Bristol City who were also relegated.

There were huge restrictions imposed on Cooper as he attempted to convert his vast playing experience into managerial success. Funds were being used to develop the Hambrook training ground and there was no money available for the much-needed introduction of new players. Meanwhile, the directors were unable to forge an

Bristol Rovers 1980-81. Back row: Penny, V Jones, S Williams, D Williams, Slatter. Middle row: Bater, McCaffrey, Thomas, Kite, Hughes, Randall. Front row: G Williams, Gillies, B Williams, Cooper (Manager), Holloway, Mabbutt, Barrett, Westaway

agreement with the Bristol Stadium Company over the lease of Eastville. A new licence for the stadium to comply with the Safety of Sports Grounds Act was to reduce the ground capacity from 30,000 to 12,500. Repercussions from the ill-advised sale of Eastville in 1940 were now placing Rovers in the downward spiral that would lead to the move to Twerton Park in 1986. The long-serving club secretary Peter Terry retired on 5 October to be replaced by Marjorie Hall. Self-made businessman Barry Bradshaw joined the board and, over the summer, youth-team development officer Gordon Bennett became Chief Executive, in which role he would make a huge contribution to staving off bankruptcy over the next few years. Bennett had donated his prize of £1,000, after being named Britain's top football fan in 1968, to the club to enable the establishment of a youth side and he had undertaken a series of fundraising events across the years. Now he was able to put into action much of what he believed.

The next major blow to Rovers was not too far away. Overnight, following Rovers' opening-day draw with Orient where David Williams and John Chiedozie had scored in the opening 16 minutes, a mystery fire badly damaged the South Stand at Eastville. The club's administrative offices and changing rooms were destroyed. Eastville was left as a shell, with seating only in the North Stand and the traffic noise from the M32 motorway now increasingly evident. It was a depressing situation. Cooper's young, inexperienced side was forced to play three League games and two League Cup-ties at Ashton Gate and, when they returned to their damaged home in October, were so deeply into their club record run of 20 League games without a win that relegation appeared the only possible outcome.

Exile at Ashton Gate was fraught with problems. The thought of playing on 'enemy territory' put off a number of spectators and only 3,808 saw the game with Oldham Athletic and 3,047 the League Cup game with York City. Even the potentially lucrative visit of fallen giants Newcastle United drew only 5,171 to the borrowed stadium. Rovers drew all three League games there and the only League Cup win was as a result of an own goal. Indeed, own goals accounted for two of Rovers' miserly three goals at Ashton Gate. Kevin Moore of Grimsby Town, who scored in the first game there, was later a Rovers player and his goal against Birmingham City in October 1992 was therefore his second for the club, after a gap of over 12 years.

Cooper signed three experienced players in Aiden McCaffrey, Donnie Gillies, for two seasons of dependable play, and Bob Lee. McCaffrey, a one-time pupil of the Olympic athlete Brendan Foster, had represented England Youth while on Newcastle United's books and, following a £50,000 move from Derby County, was promptly made Rovers captain. Though a centre-back, he was the club's top scorer with five League goals, level with the defensively-minded Gary Mabbutt, who had scored his first goal for the club in the 3-1 defeat at Notts County in October. Mabbutt was one of a vast number of young players who were being blooded in Division Two. Vaughan Jones and Mark Hughes were claiming places in the side on merit and young Geraint Williams became increasingly essential to Rovers' midfield cause as the season progressed. Mike Barrett scored his first League goal for Rovers in an eventful 3-3 draw with Sheffield Wednesday at a subdued Eastville in October. Each side scored in the opening six minutes and Barrett's 75th-minute equaliser followed, two minutes later, by a Chic Bates goal put Rovers ahead, only for David Grant to equalise for Wednesday after 84 minutes. Stewart Barrowclough contributed just two League goals and returned to his home town club Barnsley at the end of February.

On 4 November, Rovers finally ended their club record run of 10 home League games without a victory. This first win of the season, 3-1 over Watford – where Rovers were 2-0 up inside 27 minutes with Mabbutt added a third nine minutes after the interval – brought little respite for it was followed by another run of 14 League matches without a win. Through December, Rovers picked up just one point in eight League games. This was achieved at home to Notts County when, with a 65th-minute equaliser to Iain McCulloch's goal, Steve Williams became, at 17 years and 236 days, Rovers' youngest post-war goalscorer in League football. It was the only goal he ever scored for Rovers. Another of Ronnie Dix's pre-war records was challenged but remained unsurpassed, as Neil Slatter made his debut in the home game with Shrewsbury Town, at the age of 16 years and 216 days.

Amid these runs of poor results, Rovers never quite suffered the humiliating defeats that threatened. West Ham United, Division Two champions, won just 1-0 and 2-0, the latter before a crowd of 23,544 at Upton Park. Only Queen's Park Rangers, Sheffield Wednesday and Luton Town scored four goals in a game. The Hatters won 4-2 after Christmas at Eastville with their South African-born striker Brian Stein scoring the last

17 August 1980. A devastating fire to the South Grandstand at Eastville resulted in the club's temporary move to Ashton Gate for six League and cup matches

hat-trick to be scored on the ground before Steve White in January 1986. His younger brother, Mark Stein, was to play against Rovers for the first time an astonishing 18 years later, when he appeared for Bournemouth in October 1998.

The big news on 29 January was that the crowd's favourite, Paul Randall was returning to Rovers. The out-of-favour Chic Bates had moved to Shrewsbury Town and supporters clubbed together to help raise the £50,000 required to bring Randall back from Stoke City. He returned in time for the local derby with Bristol City, which drew the season's only five-figure crowd to Eastville for a second successive goalless draw with the equally struggling rivals. The Mabbutt brothers, Kevin and Gary, who played in both derby games this season, remain the only pair of brothers to oppose each other in matches between Rovers and City. A collection was made at the next home game, in mid-February against Bolton Wanderers, no doubt boosted when Randall scored a first-minute goal and later added a second in Rovers' second win of the season. He scored again, from Penny's pass a minute before half-time, at Cambridge United, as Rovers ended a run of 23 away League games without a victory, second only to the 29 winless away matches between March 1929 and September 1930, and Rovers also beat Chelsea and Preston North End. Randall's arrival was followed by the departure of winger Stewart Barrowclough, who returned to his first club, Barnsley.

Chelsea was one of the clubs involved in the battle developing above the two Bristol clubs for the third relegation spot. Two sides managed by World Cup winners played against Rovers in 1980/81 and, while Jack Charlton's Sheffield Wednesday scored seven times in two games, Geoff Hurst's Chelsea side was less successful. It had taken

SEASON 1980/81

FOOTBALL LEAGUE DIVISION TWO

Date	Opponent	Ven	G	ATT	2	G	3	4	5	6	7	8	9	10	11	Substitutes	Goalscorers
16/08/80	LEYTON ORIENT	H	1-1	5831	GILLIES	THOMAS	BATER	HUGHES	MABBUTT	COOPER	B'CLOUGH	D WILLIAMS	D WILLIAMS	PENNY	GRIFFITHS	JONES 9	D WILLIAMS
19/08/80	QPR	A	0-4	9731	GILLIES	THOMAS	BATER	MABBUTT	HUGHES	LEE	McCAFFREY	B'CLOUGH	D WILLIAMS	BATES	GRIFFITHS	PULIS 11	
23/08/80	BRISTOL CITY	H	0-0	16937	GILLIES	THOMAS	BATER	MABBUTT	HUGHES	HUGHES	McCAFFREY	B'CLOUGH	D WILLIAMS	BATES	PENNY	PULIS 7	
30/08/80	GRIMSBY TOWN +	H	0-0	4461	JONES	THOMAS	BATER	McCAFFREY	MABBUTT	HUGHES	B'CLOUGH	D WILLIAMS	BATES	PULIS	LEE		
06/09/80	BOLTON WANDERERS	A	0-2	8712	GILLIES	THOMAS	BATER	McCAFFREY	MABBUTT	HUGHES	PULIS	D WILLIAMS	BATES	PENNY	LEE		
13/09/80	OLDHAM ATHLETIC +	H	0-0	3808	GILLIES	THOMAS	BATER	McCAFFREY	MABBUTT	HUGHES	PULIS	D WILLIAMS	B'CLOUGH	PENNY	LEE	JONES 9	
20/09/80	CARDIFF CITY	A	1-2	6122	GILLIES	THOMAS	BATER	McCAFFREY	MABBUTT	HUGHES	BARRETT	D WILLIAMS	B'CLOUGH	PENNY	LEE	BATES 2	McCAFFREY, MOORE og
27/09/80	NEWCASTLE UNITED +	H	0-0	5171	GRIFFITHS	THOMAS	BATER	McCAFFREY	MABBUTT	HUGHES	B'CLOUGH	D WILLIAMS	B'CLOUGH	PENNY	LEE	BATES 9	
04/10/80	CAMBRIDGE UNITED	A	0-2	5231	GILLIES	THOMAS	BATER	McCAFFREY	MABBUTT	HUGHES	B'CLOUGH	D WILLIAMS	B'CLOUGH	PENNY	LEE	JONES 4	
08/10/80	CHELSEA	A	0-2	13108	COOPER	THOMAS	COOPER	MABBUTT	McCAFFREY	HUGHES	LEE	D WILLIAMS	LEE	PENNY	PENNY		
11/10/80	NOTTS COUNTY	H	1-3	7292	COOPER	THOMAS	BATER	McCAFFREY	MABBUTT	HUGHES	GILLIES	D WILLIAMS	BROWN	LEE	BARRETT	LEE 10	LEE
18/10/80	SHEFFIELD WEDNESDAY	H	0-3	4401	BATER	THOMAS	COOPER	McCAFFREY	MABBUTT	HUGHES	B'CLOUGH	D WILLIAMS	B'CLOUGH	BATES	BARRETT	BATES 10	MABBUTT
25/10/80	PRESTON NORTH END	A	0-0	5807	COOPER	THOMAS	BATER	McCAFFREY	MABBUTT	HUGHES	B'CLOUGH	D WILLIAMS	B'CLOUGH	BATES	BARRETT	EMMANUEL 7	
01/11/80	WEST HAM UNITED	H	3-1	6328	GILLIES	THOMAS	BATER	McCAFFREY	HUGHES	COOPER	B'CLOUGH	G WILLIAMS	MABBUTT	BATES	BARRETT		MABBUTT, BARRETT, BATES
04/11/80	WATFORD	H	1-3	5450	GILLIES	THOMAS	BATER	McCAFFREY	HUGHES	COOPER	B'CLOUGH	G WILLIAMS	MABBUTT	BATES	BARRETT		
08/11/80	SHREWSBURY TOWN	A	1-3	4446	GILLIES	THOMAS	BATER	McCAFFREY	HUGHES	COOPER	B'CLOUGH	G WILLIAMS	MABBUTT	BATES	BARRETT		BROWN
11/11/80	WATFORD	H	2-2	6636	GILLIES	THOMAS	BATER	McCAFFREY	HUGHES	COOPER	B'CLOUGH	G WILLIAMS	MABBUTT	BATES	BARRETT	EMMANUEL 7	BATES, McCAFFREY, MABBUTT
15/11/80	LEYTON ORIENT	A	2-2	5100	GILLIES	THOMAS	BATER	McCAFFREY	HUGHES	COOPER	PENNY	G WILLIAMS	MABBUTT	PENNY	BARRETT	EMMANUEL 6	G WILLIAMS
22/11/80	DERBY COUNTY	H	2-2	6258	JONES	THOMAS	BATER	McCAFFREY	HUGHES	COOPER	PENNY	G WILLIAMS	MABBUTT	BATES	BARRETT	EMMANUEL 7	B'CLOUGH pen
29/11/80	BLACKBURN ROVERS	A	0-2	8025	PULIS	THOMAS	BATER	McCAFFREY	HUGHES	COOPER	LEE	G WILLIAMS	MABBUTT	BATES	BARRETT	EMMANUEL 6	
06/12/80	WREXHAM	H	1-1	4562	JONES	THOMAS	BATER	McCAFFREY	LEE	EMMANUEL	S WILLIAMS	G WILLIAMS	MABBUTT	D WILLIAMS	BARRETT		McCAFFREY 2
13/12/80	SHEFFIELD WEDNESDAY	A	1-4	14008	JONES	THOMAS	BATER	McCAFFREY	LEE	EMMANUEL	S WILLIAMS	G WILLIAMS	MABBUTT	D WILLIAMS	BARRETT		McCAFFREY
19/12/80	NOTTS COUNTY	A	1-1	3552	JONES	THOMAS	PULIS	McCAFFREY	LEE	COOPER	S WILLIAMS	B'CLOUGH	LEE	D WILLIAMS	BARRETT		JONES pen
26/12/80	SWANSEA CITY	H	2-4	15135	KITE	THOMAS	BATER	McCAFFREY	MABBUTT	EMMANUEL	S WILLIAMS	B'CLOUGH	LEE	D WILLIAMS	BARRETT	B'CLOUGH 7	S WILLIAMS
27/12/80	LUTON TOWN	A	1-2	7010	KITE	THOMAS	JONES	McCAFFREY	MABBUTT	COOPER	S WILLIAMS	B'CLOUGH	LEE	MABBUTT	BARRETT	GILLIES 5	EMMANUEL
10/01/81	DERBY COUNTY	A	1-2	15018	KITE	THOMAS	BATER	McCAFFREY	HUGHES	EMMANUEL	G WILLIAMS	G WILLIAMS	LEE	MABBUTT	B'CLOUGH	COOPER 11	B'CLOUGH, MABBUTT
17/01/81	GRIMSBY TOWN	H	0-0	9601	KITE	THOMAS	JONES	McCAFFREY	HUGHES	EMMANUEL	B'CLOUGH	G WILLIAMS	MABBUTT	RANDALL	B'CLOUGH	ROUTLEDGE 5	
31/01/81	OLDHAM ATHLETIC	A	0-0	10087	JONES	THOMAS	BATER	McCAFFREY	HUGHES	EMMANUEL	G WILLIAMS	G WILLIAMS	RANDALL	RANDALL	MABBUTT		
07/02/81	CHELSEA	H	2-1	5552	JONES	THOMAS	COOPER	McCAFFREY	HUGHES	EMMANUEL	B'CLOUGH	G WILLIAMS	LEE	RANDALL	MABBUTT	PENNY 9	RANDALL 2
14/02/81	OLDHAM ATHLETIC	H	2-1	5368	JONES	McALISTER	COOPER	McCAFFREY	HUGHES	EMMANUEL	B'CLOUGH	G WILLIAMS	RANDALL	PENNY	S WILLIAMS	LEE 9	
21/02/81	NEWCASTLE UNITED	A	0-0	14180	McALISTER	McALISTER	COOPER	McCAFFREY	HUGHES	EMMANUEL	B'CLOUGH	G WILLIAMS	RANDALL	PENNY	S WILLIAMS	LEE 7	
28/02/81	CARDIFF CITY	A	0-1	7525	McALISTER	McALISTER	COOPER	McCAFFREY	MABBUTT	EMMANUEL	S WILLIAMS	G WILLIAMS	RANDALL	MABBUTT	D WILLIAMS		
07/03/81	CAMBRIDGE UNITED	H	3-1	4050	McALISTER	McALISTER	GILLIES	McCAFFREY	HUGHES	EMMANUEL	PENNY	G WILLIAMS	RANDALL	MABBUTT	MABBUTT		RANDALL, D WILLIAMS, PENNY
14/03/81	CHELSEA	H	1-0	7565	McALISTER	McALISTER	JONES	McCAFFREY	HUGHES	EMMANUEL	G WILLIAMS	D WILLIAMS	RANDALL	PENNY	MABBUTT	GRIFFITHS 9	HUGHES
21/03/81	WATFORD	A	1-3	10162	McALISTER	McALISTER	JONES	McCAFFREY	HUGHES	EMMANUEL	G WILLIAMS	D WILLIAMS	RANDALL	PENNY	MABBUTT	COOPER 3	MABBUTT, PENNY
28/03/81	PRESTON NORTH END	A	0-2	4427	McALISTER	McALISTER	JONES	McCAFFREY	HUGHES	EMMANUEL	G WILLIAMS	D WILLIAMS	RANDALL	PENNY	MABBUTT	COOPER 7	
04/04/81	WEST HAM UNITED	H	0-2	23344	McALISTER	McALISTER	COOPER	McCAFFREY	HUGHES	EMMANUEL	G WILLIAMS	BARRETT	RANDALL	LEE	MABBUTT	SLATTER 10	PENNY
11/04/81	SHREWSBURY TOWN	A	0-1	4151	McALISTER	McALISTER	SLATTER	McCAFFREY	HUGHES	EMMANUEL	G WILLIAMS	BARRETT	RANDALL	PENNY	MABBUTT	D WILLIAMS 8	
18/04/81	LUTON TOWN	A	0-1	9009	McALISTER	McALISTER	SLATTER	McCAFFREY	HUGHES	EMMANUEL	G WILLIAMS	D WILLIAMS	RANDALL	LEE	MABBUTT	D WILLIAMS 2	PENNY
21/04/81	SWANSEA CITY	A	1-3	8250	McALISTER	McALISTER	SLATTER	McCAFFREY	HUGHES	G WILLIAMS	BARRETT	D WILLIAMS	RANDALL	PENNY	MABBUTT	HOLLOWAY 5	BARRETT
25/04/81	WREXHAM	A	1-3	3220	WESTAWAY	McALISTER	BATER	McCAFFREY	HUGHES	G WILLIAMS	BARRETT	D WILLIAMS	RANDALL	PENNY	MABBUTT	G WILLIAMS 10	BARRETT
02/05/81	BLACKBURN ROVERS	A	0-1	9078	GILLIES	McALISTER	BATER	McCAFFREY	HUGHES	D WILLIAMS	EMMANUEL	COOPER	RANDALL	PENNY	MABBUTT		

+ These matches played at Ashton Gate, Bristol

FA CUP

Date	Opponent	Ven	G	ATT	2	G	3	4	5	6	7	8	9	10	11	Substitutes	Goalscorers
03/01/81	PRESTON NORTH END	A	4-3	6348	KITE	THOMAS	JONES	McCAFFREY	HUGHES	EMMANUEL	G WILLIAMS	B'CLOUGH	D WILLIAMS	B'CLOUGH	BARRETT	PENNY 9	MABBUTT, B'CLOUGH, BARRETT, G WILLIAMS
24/01/81	SOUTHAMPTON	A	1-3	23597	JONES	KITE	JONES	McCAFFREY	HUGHES	HUGHES	B'CLOUGH	LEE	MABBUTT	G WILLIAMS	COOPER		G WILLIAMS

LEAGUE CUP

Date	Opponent	Ven	G	ATT	2	G	3	4	5	6	7	8	9	10	11	Substitutes	Goalscorers
09/08/80	EXETER CITY	A	1-1	4702	GILLIES	THOMAS	BATER	MABBUTT	HUGHES	COOPER	B'CLOUGH	D WILLIAMS	S WILLIAMS	BATES	EMMANUEL	JONES 11	BATES
12/08/80	EXETER CITY *	H	1-1	4070	GILLIES	THOMAS	BATER	HUGHES	MABBUTT	COOPER	B'CLOUGH	D WILLIAMS	BATES	EMMANUEL	BARRETT		BATES
27/08/80	YORK CITY	A	1-2	3405	GILLIES	THOMAS	BATER	McCAFFREY	MABBUTT	LEE	B'CLOUGH	D WILLIAMS	BATES	PENNY	HUGHES	JONES 7	McCAFFREY
03/09/80	YORK CITY + **	H	1-0	3047	GILLIES	THOMAS	BATER	McCAFFREY	MABBUTT	HUGHES	B'CLOUGH	D WILLIAMS	B'CLOUGH	LEE	PULIS	BATES 10	FAULKNER og
23/09/80	PORTSMOUTH +	A	0-0	6982	JONES	THOMAS	BATER	McCAFFREY	MABBUTT	HUGHES	PULIS	D WILLIAMS	B'CLOUGH	BATES	PENNY	LEE	
30/09/80	PORTSMOUTH	A	0-2	18965	JONES	THOMAS	BATER	McCAFFREY	MABBUTT	HUGHES	HUGHES	D WILLIAMS	B'CLOUGH	BATES	PENNY		

* Rovers won 7-6 on pens
** AET: Rovers won on away goals rule

GLOUCESTERSHIRE CUP FINAL

Date	Opponent	Ven	G	ATT	2	G	3	4	5	6	7	8	9	10	11	Substitutes	Goalscorers
05/05/81	BRISTOL CITY*	H	0-1	2558	McALISTER	GILLIES	BATER	McCAFFREY	HUGHES	EMMANUEL	D WILLIAMS	SLATTER	RANDALL	G WILLIAMS	MABBUTT	PENNY	

* AET: Score after 90 mins 0-0

PLAYERS	APP	SUB	GLS
BARRETT M	23		3
BARROWCLOUGH S	22	1	2
BATER P	24		
BATES P	15	3	2
BROWN K	1		
COOPER T	23	3	
EMMANUEL G	19	4	1
GILLIES D	30	1	
GRIFFITHS A	5	1	
HOLLOWAY I	0	1	
HUGHES M	38		
JONES V	18	3	1
KITE P	4		
LEE R	19	4	2
MABBUTT G	42		5
McALISTER T	13		
McCAFFREY A	38		5
PENNY S	20	1	3
PULIS A	6	2	
RANDALL P	15	1	3
ROUTLEDGE A	0	1	
SLATTER N	3	1	
THOMAS M	25		
WESTWAY K	1		
WILLIAMS D	24	1	3
WILLIAMS G	26	2	1
WILLIAMS S	8		1
OWN GOAL			1

68 minutes at Stamford Bridge before Chelsea took the lead, when Rovers striker Bob Lee, who scored just twice for the Pirates in an entire season, scored a spectacular 30-yard own goal. A minute later, Clive Walker had secured a 2-0 victory. Chelsea's single-goal defeat at Eastville in March was the first of nine consecutive League games in which the Pensioners had failed to score and, as Chelsea hovered precariously above the relegation drop, wags inevitably pointed out that they were saved only by a pair of drooping Bristols. As it was, Preston North End, albeit on goal average, was the third club to drop into Division Three.

Rovers somehow contrived to play six League Cup ties. Exeter City were beaten on penalties and York City on the away goals rule before Rovers lost in a replay at Portsmouth, Steve Perrin and David Gregory scoring the goals that took Pompey through to the fourth round. Bristol City were Gloucestershire Cup final winners through an extra-time goal from Kevin Mabbutt. In the League, the only ever-present was the ever-improving Gary Mabbutt, with McCaffrey and Hughes also regulars. A late substitute at Wrexham in April was debutant Ian Holloway, beginning a long and fruitful association with the club. He had become Britain's first Associate Schoolboy when he signed for Rovers on his 14th birthday.

The real excitement came in the FA Cup where Rovers, on 3 January, with only one League win all season, found themselves 4-0 up by half-time at Preston. Rovers were two goals ahead inside six minutes through Mabbutt and Stewart Barrowclough, with Barrett adding a third after 38 minutes and Geraint Williams a fourth on the stroke of half-time. Graham Houston and Alex Bruce pulled goals back and, when Dublin-born substitute Paul McGee made the score 4-3, it left debutant 17-year-old goalkeeper Phil Kite and his defence nervously seeing out time. With this remarkable away win behind them Rovers, with 4,000 travelling fans supporting them, lost 3-1 at Southampton in the fourth round.

1981/82

A combination of events had led to Rovers' future at Eastville becoming the major talking point in the summer of 1981. New safety regulations, which had seriously reduced the ground capacity, financial problems within the club and belt-tightening in the aftermath of the devastating South Stand fire were all critical factors. In July 1981, the Stevens family, which had been key shareholders for 40 years, lost control of the club to Martin Flook and Barry Bradshaw, who had been able to benefit from the directors' £75,000 new-share issue.

At the same time, Rovers were taking the decision to go to the High Court regarding compensation for losing their rights as tenants at Eastville. Discussions over a new lease had broken down and Rovers demanded £700,000 from the Stadium Company if they were to accept a move from their established 'home' since 1897. Rovers also wanted a 21-year lease on a sliding scale. The Stadium Company offered £100,000 compensation and a three or five-year lease involving profit-making schemes through gate receipts and

Bristol Rovers 1981/82. Back row: Smith, Sherwood, Curle, Bailey. Middle row: Jones (Physio), Pulis (Player-Coach), Hughes, Parkin, Cashley, Randall, Kite, Barrrett, Stephens, Dolling (Physio). Front row: Waite, Holloway, G Williams, D Williams, McCaffrey, B Williams, Slatter

takings from the bars and car parks. At the High Court in London in November 1981 Rovers were awarded £280,000, a figure that the club's directors reluctantly accepted.

The impending loss of a home base, a departure in fact delayed until 1986, sparked a renewed search for a stadium elsewhere. The Rovers chairman Martin Flook offered Bristol City £450,000 to buy Ashton Gate, an apparently audacious bid that, given City's perilous financial state as the club plummeted towards Division Four, was not as outrageous as it would at first appear. However, the creation of Bristol City (1982) plc on 15 February scuppered Flook's plans. As the season drew to a close, Rovers were investigating a £45,000 ground-sharing scheme at Ashton Gate and were, indeed, offered a similar scheme with Bath City at Twerton Park at an annual rent of £15,000. As it was, Rovers' directors finally worked out a five-year lease for £52,000 with their landlords at Eastville.

Financial problems, however, though minimal in comparison to those experienced at this time at Ashton Gate, would not disappear entirely. Rovers recorded a loss for the year of £335,146, a figure partly attributable to transfer fees and the introduction of several expensive player contracts, while gate receipts continued to fall. The club had also purchased, in March 1982, an artificial pitch for the Hambrook training ground for £125,000, albeit with some aid from Sports Council grants. Rovers approached their centenary year with a great deal of uncertainty hanging over their immediate future.

On the pitch, a largely unchanged side faced the first season back in Division Three. Two new faces were the experienced Brian Williams, once the youngest player to appear for Bury and now signed from Swindon Town, and the Melksham Town striker Archie Stephens, a relatively late entrant to League Football at the age of 27. Another was the former Blackburn Rovers centre-half Tim Parkin, who had played for Malmö in the

World Club Championship final and who, to comply with Swedish transfer regulations at that time, was technically an Almondsbury Greenway player for half-an-hour during his £15,000 move to Eastville. With three Williamses controlling the heart of the team, young Phil Kite commanding in goal and a burgeoning attacking partnership in Stephens and Randall, ably supported by Mike Barrett, Rovers got off to a good start. Stephens scored twice on his full debut at home to Burnley and followed this up with two more at Reading seven days later. There were also wins at Preston and Exeter. Therefore, it came as some surprise when – just days after the death of the former Rovers manager Fred Ford, whose funeral attracted many celebrated names to St Bernadette's Church, Whitchurch – Terry Cooper, was dismissed on 19 October, following a defeat at home to Swindon Town and replaced temporarily by Rovers' Chief Scout, the former Chelsea and Exeter City full-back Ron Gingell. Cooper signed for Doncaster Rovers as a player before, at the season's end, becoming manager of Bristol City.

The new permanent manager was another high-profile former player, Bobby Gould, who had signed for Rovers as a player four years earlier and had latterly been on the books of Aldershot. He retained Cooper's squad and began to work it into the side that would achieve significant on-field success in the autumn of 1982. Yet one major problem was home defeats, six in total in 1981/82 including one in December against Carlisle United, to a goal scored after 11 minutes by the former Rovers striker Bob Lee, playing alongside the future Rover Paul Bannon, in what was to be player-coach Gary Pendrey's only League game for the Pirates. By the end of the season, Rovers had secured a mid-table finish. Randall was the club's top scorer with 12 League goals, Stephens and David Williams contributing 11 each, while Brian Williams was the sole ever-present.

Following Ford's death, three other key figures in the history of Bristol Rovers were to die during the season. Dr Douglas Mearns Milne, who passed away on 14 January at Abbots Leigh, aged 65, was a thoracic surgeon at Frenchay and had served on Rovers' board from 1962 and as chairman from 1968 to 1978. At a meeting of directors on 22 July, his 5,404 shares in the club were devolved to his son Alastair. On 19 March, at the age of 87, goalkeeper Jesse Whatley, who had played in a club record 246 consecutive League games between 1922 and 1928 and in 386 in all, died in Chipping Sodbury. Forty-eight hours later, Bert Williams, Rovers' groundsman in 1918 and long-time trainer from 1920 to 1962, died in Bristol at the age of 80. The board of directors resolved on 25 March to donate £50 in regard to Williams to the Friends of Frenchay Hospital and £50 in Whatley's memory to Dr Barnardo's.

There were some ponderous games – 40 free-kicks were awarded in the first-half as Rovers ground out a 1-0 victory over Chesterfield at Eastville in January, thanks to Randall's goal 10 minutes after half-time, but generally the season was far more positive. Rovers recorded some well-earned victories, most notably the doubles recorded over Exeter City and Huddersfield Town. For the 3-2 home win against the Grecians, Rovers introduced a 17-year-old midfielder Steve Bailey and it was his appearance that led to the club being deducted two League points. An oversight meant that he had not been registered with the League and the loss of these points, though not seriously affecting the club, slightly distorted Rovers' League standing by the end of the season.

March saw a succession of unusual events. At Swindon Town, having earlier lost 4-0 at both Burnley and Plymouth Argyle, Rovers crashed to a 5-2 defeat, the Robins thus

FOOTBALL LEAGUE DIVISION THREE

Date	Opponent	Venue	Score	ATT	G	2	3	4	5	6	7	8	9	10	11	Substitutes	Goalscorers
29/08/81	CHESTER CITY	H	2-2	5554	KITE	GILLIES	SLATTER	McCAFFREY	PARKIN	B WILLIAMS	CURLE	D WILLIAMS	MABBUTT	RANDALL	BARRETT	COOPER 10	CURLE, D WILLIAMS
05/09/81	CHESTERFIELD	A	0-2	3501	KITE	GILLIES	SLATTER	McCAFFREY	PARKIN	B WILLIAMS	CURLE	D WILLIAMS	MABBUTT	STEPHENS	COOPER	STEPHENS 10	
12/09/81	BURNLEY	H	2-1	5083	KITE	GILLIES	SLATTER	McCAFFREY	PARKIN	HUGHES	BARRETT	D WILLIAMS	MABBUTT	STEPHENS	COOPER	CURLE 6	STEPHENS 2
19/09/81	READING	A	3-0	4947	KITE	GILLIES	SLATTER	McCAFFREY	PARKIN	RANDALL	BARRETT	D WILLIAMS	MABBUTT	STEPHENS	COOPER	CURLE 11	RANDALL, STEPHENS 2
23/09/81	EXETER CITY	A	3-1	5510	KITE	GILLIES	SLATTER	McCAFFREY	PARKIN	RANDALL	BARRETT	D WILLIAMS	MABBUTT	STEPHENS	COOPER	CURLE 10	D WILLIAMS, McCAFFREY, RANDALL
26/09/81	LINCOLN CITY	H	0-2	6112	KITE	GILLIES	SLATTER	McCAFFREY	PARKIN	HUGHES	BARRETT	D WILLIAMS	MABBUTT	RANDALL	G WILLIAMS	CURLE 4	
29/09/81	WIMBLEDON	H	2-2	5364	KITE	GILLIES	SLATTER	McCAFFREY	PARKIN	STEPHENS	BARRETT	D WILLIAMS	MABBUTT	RANDALL	G WILLIAMS		MABBUTT 2
03/10/81	PRESTON NORTH END	A	1-0	4964	KITE	GILLIES	SLATTER	McCAFFREY	PARKIN	STEPHENS	BARRETT	D WILLIAMS	MABBUTT	RANDALL	G WILLIAMS	COOPER 3	STEPHENS
09/10/81	SOUTHEND UNITED	H	0-1	4530	KITE	GILLIES	SLATTER	McCAFFREY	PARKIN	B WILLIAMS	STEPHENS	D WILLIAMS	STEPHENS	B WILLIAMS	B WILLIAMS	RANDALL 10	
17/10/81	SWINDON TOWN	H	1-4	8779	KITE	GILLIES	SLATTER	McCAFFREY	PARKIN	B WILLIAMS	STEPHENS	D WILLIAMS	STEPHENS	HUGHES	B WILLIAMS		STEPHENS
21/10/81	OXFORD UNITED	H	1-1	4422	KITE	GILLIES	JONES	McCAFFREY	PARKIN	MABBUTT	G WILLIAMS	D WILLIAMS	MABBUTT	RANDALL	B WILLIAMS	BARRETT 7	RANDALL
24/10/81	HUDDERSFIELD TOWN	H	3-2	5064	THOMAS	JONES	GILLIES	McCAFFREY	HUGHES	HUGHES	SLATTER	D WILLIAMS	STEPHENS	MABBUTT	B WILLIAMS	CURLE 7	RANDALL, STEPHENS, McCAFFREY
31/10/81	DONCASTER ROVERS	A	2-4	6694	KITE	JONES	GILLIES	McCAFFREY	HUGHES	MABBUTT	GILLIES	D WILLIAMS	STEPHENS	RANDALL	RANDALL		MABBUTT, STEPHENS
03/11/81	NEWPORT COUNTY	H	2-0	6464	THOMAS	JONES	JONES	HUGHES	HUGHES	MABBUTT	GILLIES	D WILLIAMS	STEPHENS	STEPHENS	B WILLIAMS		RANDALL, D WILLIAMS
07/11/81	GILLINGHAM	H	2-0	5518	THOMAS	JONES	JONES	HUGHES	MABBUTT	MABBUTT	MABBUTT	GILLIES	STEPHENS	RANDALL	B WILLIAMS		RANDALL, CURLE
14/11/81	MILLWALL	A	0-0	5970	THOMAS	JONES	CURLE	McCAFFREY	HUGHES	MABBUTT	MABBUTT	GILLIES	RANDALL	RANDALL	B WILLIAMS		
28/11/81	WALSALL	H	1-2	4311	THOMAS	JONES	CURLE	McCAFFREY	HUGHES	BARRETT	BARRETT	GILLIES	STEPHENS	STEPHENS	B WILLIAMS	CURLE 10	BARRETT
05/12/81	FULHAM	H	1-2	4489	THOMAS	JONES	B WILLIAMS	McCAFFREY	PENDRY	BARRETT	BARRETT	GILLIES	STEPHENS	RANDALL	B WILLIAMS	PARKIN 11	B WILLIAMS
19/12/81	CARLISLE UNITED	A	0-1	3759	THOMAS	JONES	B WILLIAMS	HUGHES	PARKIN	GILLIES	GILLIES	GILLIES	PENNY	G WILLIAMS	D WILLIAMS	CURLE 7	
26/12/81	PORTSMOUTH	H	0-0	11395	THOMAS	JONES	SLATTER	MABBUTT	PARKIN	MABBUTT	BARRETT	D WILLIAMS	D WILLIAMS	RANDALL	D WILLIAMS	STEPHENS 10	
29/12/81	BRISTOL CITY	A	0-4	12355	THOMAS	JONES	GILLIES	McCAFFREY	PARKIN	MABBUTT	GILLIES	D WILLIAMS	STEPHENS	RANDALL	D WILLIAMS	STEPHENS 7	
02/01/82	PLYMOUTH ARGYLE	H	1-0	7058	THOMAS	JONES	SLATTER	McCAFFREY	PARKIN	JONES	SLATTER	D WILLIAMS	STEPHENS	G WILLIAMS	B WILLIAMS	BARRETT 4	McCAFFREY
19/01/82	CHESTERFIELD	H	1-0	4853	THOMAS	JONES	SLATTER	McCAFFREY	PARKIN	BARRETT	MABBUTT	D WILLIAMS	STEPHENS	RANDALL	B WILLIAMS	CURLE 10	RANDALL
23/01/82	READING	A	1-1	2040	THOMAS	JONES	CURLE	McCAFFREY	PARKIN	MABBUTT	G WILLIAMS	D WILLIAMS	GILLIES	RANDALL	B WILLIAMS	GILLIES 10	RANDALL
30/01/82	READING	H	1-1	5355	THOMAS	JONES	SLATTER	McCAFFREY	PARKIN	MABBUTT	G WILLIAMS	D WILLIAMS	STEPHENS	RANDALL	B WILLIAMS	GILLIES 7	MABBUTT
06/02/82	BURNLEY	A	0-4	5724	THOMAS	JONES	SLATTER	McCAFFREY	PARKIN	MABBUTT	BARRETT	D WILLIAMS	STEPHENS	RANDALL	B WILLIAMS	STEPHENS 4	
09/02/82	EXETER CITY	H	3-2	4987	KITE	JONES	HUGHES	BAILEY	PARKIN	PARKIN	BARRETT	D WILLIAMS	STEPHENS	RANDALL	B WILLIAMS	KELLY 9	PARKIN, RANDALL 2
13/02/82	PRESTON NORTH END	H	2-0	5003	KITE	JONES	HUGHES	BAILEY	PARKIN	MABBUTT	BARRETT	D WILLIAMS	STEPHENS	RANDALL	B WILLIAMS		D WILLIAMS, STEPHENS
20/02/82	WIMBLEDON	A	2-0	2408	KITE	HOLLOWAY	HUGHES	BAILEY	MABBUTT	B WILLIAMS	B WILLIAMS	D WILLIAMS	STEPHENS	RANDALL	KELLY	CURLE 8	BARRETT, D WILLIAMS
27/02/82	SOUTHEND UNITED	H	2-1	4910	KITE	JONES	HUGHES	BAILEY	PARKIN	HUGHES	BARRETT	D WILLIAMS	STEPHENS	RANDALL	B WILLIAMS		PARKIN, STEPHENS
06/03/82	SWINDON TOWN	A	2-5	6689	KITE	JONES	MABBUTT	GILLIES	PARKIN	HUGHES	BARRETT	STEPHENS	RANDALL	RANDALL	B WILLIAMS		B WILLIAMS, VALENTINE og
13/03/82	HUDDERSFIELD TOWN	A	1-1	6156	KITE	JONES	MABBUTT	BAILEY	PARKIN	HUGHES	D WILLIAMS	STEPHENS	RANDALL	RANDALL	B WILLIAMS		B WILLIAMS pen
16/03/82	NEWPORT COUNTY	A	1-1	5312	KITE	JONES	SLATTER	BAILEY	PARKIN	HUGHES	BARRETT	D WILLIAMS	STEPHENS	RANDALL	B WILLIAMS		
20/03/82	DONCASTER ROVERS	H	3-0	4597	KITE	JONES	SLATTER	BAILEY	PARKIN	HUGHES	SLATTER	D WILLIAMS	RANDALL	RANDALL	B WILLIAMS		MABBUTT, RANDALL, D WILLIAMS
22/03/82	BRENTFORD	H	1-2	5843	KITE	JONES	HUGHES	BAILEY	PARKIN	MABBUTT	MABBUTT	D WILLIAMS	STEPHENS	RANDALL	MABBUTT	CURLE 2	
27/03/82	GILLINGHAM	A	0-2	5100	KITE	JONES	SLATTER	BAILEY	PARKIN	HUGHES	BARRETT	D WILLIAMS	STEPHENS	RANDALL	BARRETT	KELLY 4	
03/04/82	MILLWALL	H	1-1	4279	KITE	JONES	GILLIES	BAILEY	PARKIN	HUGHES	BARRETT	D WILLIAMS	STEPHENS	MABBUTT	B WILLIAMS	RANDALL 2	D WILLIAMS
10/04/82	PORTSMOUTH	H	1-1	4833	KITE	JONES	RANDALL	RANDALL	PARKIN	BAILEY	BAILEY	D WILLIAMS	MABBUTT	MABBUTT	B WILLIAMS	PENNY 7	D WILLIAMS, RANDALL
12/04/82	BRISTOL CITY	H	1-2	10791	KITE	JONES	SLATTER	G WILLIAMS	PARKIN	HUGHES	BARRETT	D WILLIAMS	MABBUTT	MABBUTT	B WILLIAMS	McCAFFREY 9	D WILLIAMS pen, SLATTER
17/04/82	FULHAM	A	2-4	6849	KITE	JONES	SLATTER	G WILLIAMS	PARKIN	MABBUTT	BARRETT	D WILLIAMS	MABBUTT	MABBUTT	B WILLIAMS	BAILEY 11	STEPHENS, BAILEY
24/04/82	WALSALL	H	2-1	3677	KITE	JONES	SLATTER	G WILLIAMS	PARKIN	MABBUTT	BAILEY	D WILLIAMS	STEPHENS	RANDALL	B WILLIAMS	SMITH 10	B WILLIAMS pen, D WILLIAMS
01/05/82	LINCOLN CITY	A	0-1	4024	THOMAS	JONES	SLATTER	G WILLIAMS	PARKIN	MABBUTT	BAILEY	D WILLIAMS	STEPHENS	RANDALL	B WILLIAMS		
03/05/82	BRENTFORD	A	1-2	4314	THOMAS	JONES	SLATTER	McCAFFREY	PARKIN	G WILLIAMS	BAILEY	D WILLIAMS	STEPHENS	CURLE	B WILLIAMS	BARRETT 7	
08/05/82	PLYMOUTH ARGYLE	H	2-3	4025	THOMAS	JONES	SLATTER	G WILLIAMS	PARKIN	MABBUTT	CURLE	D WILLIAMS	STEPHENS	PENNY	B WILLIAMS	BARRETT 7	B WILLIAMS pen, D WILLIAMS
11/05/82	OXFORD UNITED	A	1-0	4754	THOMAS	JONES	McCAFFREY	McCAFFREY	HUGHES	MABBUTT	CURLE	D WILLIAMS	MABBUTT	PENNY	B WILLIAMS	RANDALL 7	PENNY
15/05/82	CARLISLE UNITED	A	2-1	6653	THOMAS	McCAFFREY	JONES	G WILLIAMS	PARKIN	MABBUTT	RANDALL	D WILLIAMS	STEPHENS	HUGHES	B WILLIAMS		HUGHES 2

FA CUP

Date	Opponent	Venue	Score	ATT	G	2	3	4	5	6	7	8	9	10	11	Substitutes	Goalscorers
21/11/81	FULHAM	H	1-2	4489	THOMAS	JONES	B WILLIAMS	McCAFFREY	HUGHES	MABBUTT	CURLE	D WILLIAMS	STEPHENS	RANDALL	B WILLIAMS	BARRETT 8	D WILLIAMS pen

LEAGUE CUP

Date	Opponent	Venue	Score	ATT	G	2	3	4	5	6	7	8	9	10	11	Substitutes	Goalscorers
02/09/81	CREWE ALEXANDRA	A	1-1	2137	KITE	GILLIES	SLATTER	McCAFFREY	PARKIN	B WILLIAMS	CURLE	D WILLIAMS	MABBUTT	RANDALL	COOPER	HUGHES 7	MABBUTT
15/09/81	CREWE ALEXANDRA	H	1-0	4050	KITE	GILLIES	SLATTER	HUGHES	PARKIN	McCAFFREY	CURLE	D WILLIAMS	MABBUTT	STEPHENS	BARRETT	COOPER 4	PARKIN
27/08/??	NORTHAMPTON TOWN	H	1-2	4476	KITE	GILLIES	COOPER	McCAFFREY	PARKIN	MABBUTT	BARRETT	D WILLIAMS	STEPHENS	RANDALL	G WILLIAMS	S WILLIAMS 10	STEPHENS
03/09/??	NORTHAMPTON TOWN	A	1-3	3543	KITE	JONES	GILLIES	HUGHES	HUGHES	MABBUTT	RANDALL	D WILLIAMS	STEPHENS	B WILLIAMS	BARRETT	PENNY 2	D WILLIAMS

GLOUCESTERSHIRE CUP FINAL

Date	Opponent	Venue	Score	ATT	G	2	3	4	5	6	7	8	9	10	11	Substitutes	Goalscorers
08/09/81	BRISTOL CITY	A	1-0	4022	KITE	GILLIES	SLATTER	McCAFFREY	PARKIN	HUGHES	BARRETT	D WILLIAMS	MABBUTT	STEPHENS	B WILLIAMS		McCAFFREY

PLAYERS	APP	SUB	GLS
BAILEY S	15	1	1
BARRETT M	29	3	2
COOPER T	5	10	
CURLE K	10	10	2
GILLIES D	26	2	
HOLLOWAY	1		
HUGHES M	22		2
JONES V	34		
KELLY E	3	2	
KITE P	27		
MABBUTT G	45		5
McCAFFREY A	28	1	3
PARKIN T	39	1	2
PENDREY G	1		
PENNY S	5	1	1
RANDALL P	34	3	12
SLATTER N	28	1	1
SMITH D	0	1	
STEPHENS A	35	4	11
THOMAS M	19		
WESTAWAY K	1		
WILLIAMS B	37		4
WILLIAMS D	46		11
WILLIAMS G	16	1	
OWN GOAL			1

totalling 9 League goals in 2 games past Phil Kite. Tim Parkin became the fifth Rovers player to score for both sides in the same game, while the future Rovers midfielder, Roy Carter, from a penalty and Paul Rideout, scorer of Everton's winning goal in the 1995 FA Cup final, added a goal apiece. Three days later referee Tony Glasson of Salisbury abandoned the game with Oxford United on a waterlogged Eastville after 64 minutes, shortly after Keith Cassells had equalised Paul Randall's first-half opener. It was the first home game abandoned since February 1951. Only four days later, despite losing Kite injured, and with Vaughan Jones playing in goal, Rovers defeated Huddersfield Town 2-0, their first win at Leeds Road since April 1960.

Two of Rovers' opponents this season were to feature in England's semi-final defeat against Germany in the 1990 World Cup finals in Italy. Trevor Steven was in the Burnley side defeated by two Stephens goals at Eastville in September, while 20-year-old Peter Beardsley of Carlisle was to reappear against Rovers in the Fulham side in November 1998 after a record gap of almost 17 years between League appearances against Rovers. Bristol City's goalkeeper for the local derby in December was the Swedish International Jan Möller. At the opposite end of the spectrum, David Smith played in the final 10 minutes of the 2-1 win against Walsall in April to record the shortest League career of any Rovers player.

In the League Cup, aggregate victory over Crewe Alexandra was followed by defeat against Northampton Town, who scored five times over the two legs. Tony Mahoney scored his first-ever goal for the Cobblers, while left-back Alex Saxby scored for the first time for more than a year. The FA Cup brought no joy, either, with two goals from Dean Coney earning Fulham victory at Eastville. The future Rovers player Gary Waddock was a losing FA Cup finalist with Queen's Park Rangers. There was, however, a ray of hope from the unlikely source of the Gloucestershire Cup final, where Aiden McCaffrey's far-post goal, after Barrett's 48th-minute centre had been flicked on by Gary Mabbutt, brought what was the first of four consecutive victories over Bristol City in this competition. The season concluded with the high-profile transfer of Martin Thomas to Newcastle United, where the genial goalkeeper was to earn a well-deserved full International cap with Wales.

1982/83

An air of uncertainty hung over Eastville as Rovers approached their centenary year. Amid groundsharing talks with both Bristol City and Bath City, the board of directors made another concerted attempt to buy Eastville back from the Stadium Company. It was an audacious bid, given Rovers' perilous financial state, and one promptly dismissed. The Eastville site was one with huge commercial viability for developers, standing so close to the M32 motorway and thus within easy access of the M4 and M5. The case put forward by Bristol Rovers was deemed relatively insignificant. With hindsight, there was little hope that the club could remain at Eastville beyond the end of the current lease in 1987. Attention was now turned to a green-belt site at Stoke

Bristol Rovers 1982/83. Back row: Bailey, Parkin, Cashley, Withey, Kite, Curle, Smith. Middle row: Gingell (Chief Scout), Balcombe, Stephens, Hughes, Randall, Gould (Manager), McCaffrey, Slatter, Platnauer, Kelly, McDowell (Coach). Front row: Hills (Coach), Hole (Director), Holmes (Chairman), Flook, Cussen, Palmer (All Directors), Pulis (Player-Coach). Sitting: Holloway, B Williams, D Williams, Barrett, G Williams, Sherwood

Gifford, to the north of the city, where Rovers' directors now began seeking planning permission for a £10 million sports complex including a football stadium.

Yet, on the pitch, the tide was turning. In the wake of relegation in 1980/81, new manager Bobby Gould was now building a side that could realistically challenge for a return to Division Two. Extra revenue was generated through a shirt-sponsorship deal, Great Mills DIY becoming the first name emblazoned on Rovers' tops. The team made a successful pre-season Scottish tour, winning at Partick Thistle, Falkirk and Ayr United. Yet the side would have to battle without Gary Mabbutt, a Rovers favourite like his father before him, whose £105,000 move to Tottenham Hotspur preceded 16 England caps during a hugely successful career. Once the season got underway, a series of large wins, incredibly six League and one League Cup victory before Christmas being by four-goal margins, raised the level of excitement around Eastville. Gould contributed to this shrewdly by adding some high-profile names to his close-knit and largely locally based squad.

Arguably, the two biggest footballing names to have, albeit briefly, graced the Rovers side were signed by Gould. In October, the highly experienced forward Mick Channon was signed from Newcastle United. He had won 46 full caps for England, scoring 21 goals and had enjoyed a hugely successful career, largely with Southampton, where he remains the all-time record aggregate goalscorer. His infectious enthusiasm for the game inspired the Rovers side, but his trademark windmill goal celebration was never seen at Eastville for, kept out of the side by Ian Holloway, he departed goalless in December, to join Norwich City. Red-haired Alan Ball, who arrived in January, ended a

Former England World Cup winner Alan Ball enjoyed a good season at Rovers in 1982/83

momentous career with 17 League appearances and two memorable goals for Rovers. The winner of 72 full England caps, he had once attracted a record British transfer fee, when he moved from Everton to Arsenal in December 1971 for £220,000 and was an eminently recognizable figure on the football circuit. 'I'm not a believer in luck,' he is credited as saying, 'but I do believe you need it.' His position in midfield in England's 1966 side meant that he is the only World Cup winner to have played football for Rovers. Ball's tremendous 30-yard goal, following a left-wing throw-in, to defeat Huddersfield Town in April was a wonderful way to end a 21-year professional playing career.

Rovers enjoyed an astonishingly successful first half of the season. Despite a crushing opening day defeat by Brentford at Griffin Park and a potentially demoralizing home defeat against Lincoln City, the string of good results through the autumn gave very real hopes of promotion. Two 4-0 wins in Devon, in the League Cup at Torquay United and the League at Plymouth Argyle, set Rovers scoring seemingly at will. Despite the sending-off of the veteran Roy McFarland at Eastville, Bradford City would not have anticipated a 4-1 defeat, Randall scoring a brace of goals for the second consecutive game. Later the same month, Rovers defeated Wigan Athletic and Millwall 4-0 each and Reading 3-0 as well as winning 5-1 at Orient. It was an awesome display of firepower.

The first-ever visit of Wigan Athletic to Eastville marked the return of the former Rovers centre-back Larry Lloyd. Sadly for him, he and his team-mate Alex Cribley were both sent off, the first time two opponents had been sent off against Rovers in a League game. Graham Withey, a £5,000 summer signing from Bath City, became the first Rovers substitute to score twice in one game, a club record subsequently equalled in May 2001 by Mark Walters. Indeed, Withey proved to be a real thorn in Wigan's side for, recovering from a mid-season ankle injury, he and Paul Randall both scored twice, once each either side of half-time, in February as Rovers won 5-0 at Springfield Park to record what remains the heaviest home defeat in Wigan's League history. Randall and Withey both scored in three minutes midway through the first-half, and the latter's second goal in the final minute sealed a memorable victory. It remained the Latics' worst League defeat of all time until Carl Saunders inspired Rovers to a 6-1 victory at Twerton Park in March 1990.

Perhaps the most encouraging result was the 5-1 home victory over a Portsmouth side heading for the Division Three Championship. In a totally one-sided encounter, five Rovers players, sequentially shirt numbers five to nine, were to score before Billy Rafferty's very late consolation goal. The players wore black armbands to the memory of Jimmy Dickinson, the Portsmouth legend who had died four days earlier. This match highlighted Rovers' potential, even against stronger opposition. The side was also devastatingly ruthless, as illustrated by the three goals in three minutes on the hour that helped defeat Wrexham 4-0 in December. Three players called Williams scored in this game, emulating the feat of three Keetley brothers for Doncaster Rovers against Durham City in Division Three (North) in April 1927.

As Bristol City slipped temporarily to the foot of Division Four, it appeared Rovers were destined for great things. However, inconsistency set in and, ultimately, seventh place in Division Three was an acceptable final League position. At Cardiff City, Brian Williams was sent off and Rovers lost a televised game 3-1, despite a goal from the veteran Les Bradd, still Notts County's all-time record goalscorer, in his sole League appearance on loan from Wigan Athletic. Young Keith Curle, a major discovery, scored against Millwall after only 25 seconds, but was then sent off and Rovers drew 1-1. As a gesture of goodwill by the Rovers Board of Directors, free coach travel was arranged to take Rovers fans to Walsall in April, only for the side to lose 5-0. Rovers also played 85 minutes of the game at Bradford in February with an orange ball, then conceded two very late goals when a flatter, white ball was substituted, to lose 2-0. The defeat at Bramall Lane in May, despite being Sheffield United's ninth consecutive home league victory, was watched by the lowest post-war League crowd at that ground.

Rovers also conceded eight goals in three days after Christmas. The 4-2 defeat at Oxford United was a psychological blow against promotion rivals, while the eight-goal draw with Exeter City at Eastville was quite simply a dropped point. Bristol-born Peter Rogers had twice put the Grecians ahead, but Paul Randall's second equaliser, five minutes before half-time, followed swiftly by a goal from Ian Holloway and a Keith Viney own goal gave Rovers a commanding 4-2 half-time lead. However, Exeter were let off the hook as George Delve, after 51 minutes, and Stan McEwan, 20 minutes from time, earned the visitors a draw. The first-half of this game had featured a mercurial display from Mike Barrett, whose fine run and shot, saved by Len Bond, had rebounded into the net off Viney on the stroke of half-time. The unfortunate defender was himself to play for Rovers in a loan spell in September 1988.

In fact, Rovers won a number of key games in the spring, but the impetus for promotion had been lost. The big win at Wigan was the first of three consecutive victories, Randall scoring a first-minute goal against Orient and Withey scoring five times in this run to end up as second-highest scorer with 10 goals. Top scorer Randall scored his 20th of the season in a storming second-half display as Rovers swept aside Preston North End at Eastville in April. Rovers crushed Chesterfield 3-0, the side's only ever-present Phil Kite keeping a clean sheet. Despite the consistent form of individuals in key positions, Rovers never challenged seriously for promotion and manager Bobby Gould resigned in May 1983 to rejoin one of his other former clubs, Division One Coventry City.

There had been limited success in Cup competitions. Nick Platnauer, a close-season signing from Bradford Town, then managed by Bobby Gould's brother Trevor, had

FOOTBALL LEAGUE DIVISION THREE

SEASON 1982/83

Date	Opposition	Venue	Result	Att	1	2	3	4	5	6	7	8	9	10	11	Substitutes	Goalscorers
28/08/82	BRENTFORD	A	1-5	5542	KITE	STEPHENS	SLATER	G WILLIAMS	HUGHES	McCAFFREY	CURLE	D WILLIAMS	RANDALL	KELLY	BARRETT	WITHEY 5	WITHEY
04/09/82	DONCASTER ROVERS	H	2-0	3617	KITE	SLATER	B WILLIAMS	G WILLIAMS	PARKIN	McCAFFREY	CURLE	D WILLIAMS	RANDALL	KELLY	BARRETT	KELLY 9	BARRETT, KELLY
07/09/82	GILLINGHAM	H	2-1	3668	KITE	SLATER	B WILLIAMS	G WILLIAMS	PARKIN	McCAFFREY	CURLE	D WILLIAMS	RANDALL	KELLY	BARRETT	KELLY 10	BARRETT, CURLE
11/09/82	CHESTERFIELD	H	0-0	1990	KITE	SLATER	B WILLIAMS	G WILLIAMS	PARKIN	McCAFFREY	CURLE	STEPHENS	KELLY	RANDALL	BARRETT	RANDALL 10	
18/09/82	LINCOLN CITY	A	1-2	4177	KITE	B WILLIAMS	G WILLIAMS	PULIS	PARKIN	McCAFFREY	PLATNAUER	D WILLIAMS	STEPHENS	KELLY	BARRETT	STEPHENS 7	RANDALL
25/09/82	PRESTON NORTH END	H	2-2	3880	KITE	SLATER	B WILLIAMS	G WILLIAMS	PARKIN	McCAFFREY	HOLLOWAY	D WILLIAMS	STEPHENS	RANDALL	BARRETT	SHERWOOD 2	STEPHENS, RANDALL
28/09/82	PLYMOUTH ARGYLE	A	4-0	3343	KITE	SLATER	B WILLIAMS	G WILLIAMS	PARKIN	McCAFFREY	HOLLOWAY	CHANNON	STEPHENS	KELLY	BARRETT	BARRETT, G WILLIAMS	RANDALL 2, KELLY, D WILLIAMS
02/10/82	BRADFORD CITY	A	4-1	4451	KITE	SLATER	B WILLIAMS	G WILLIAMS	PARKIN	McCAFFREY	HOLLOWAY	D WILLIAMS	KELLY	RANDALL	BARRETT	HOLLOWAY 1	BARRETT 2, KELLY, D WILLIAMS
09/10/82	NEWPORT COUNTY	H	0-2	5912	KITE	SLATER	B WILLIAMS	G WILLIAMS	PARKIN	McCAFFREY	HOLLOWAY	D WILLIAMS	KELLY	RANDALL	BARRETT	SHERWOOD 9	
16/10/82	WIGAN ATHLETIC	A	4-0	4439	KITE	SLATER	B WILLIAMS	G WILLIAMS	PARKIN	McCAFFREY	HOLLOWAY	D WILLIAMS	STEPHENS	RANDALL	BARRETT	HUGHES 9	RANDALL 2, PARKIN, D WILLIAMS
19/10/82	MILLWALL	H	4-0	7241	KITE	SLATER	B WILLIAMS	G WILLIAMS	PARKIN	McCAFFREY	HOLLOWAY	D WILLIAMS	STEPHENS	KELLY	BARRETT	KITE P	WITHEY 2, RANDALL, McCAFFREY, HOLLOWAY
23/10/82	LEYTON ORIENT	A	5-1	2534	KITE	SLATER	B WILLIAMS	CURLE	PARKIN	McCAFFREY	HOLLOWAY	D WILLIAMS	WITHEY	RANDALL	BARRETT	McCAFFREY A	D WILLIAMS 2, RANDALL, G WILLIAMS pen, WITHEY
30/10/82	READING	H	3-0	7270	KITE	SLATER	B WILLIAMS	G WILLIAMS	PARKIN	McCAFFREY	HOLLOWAY	D WILLIAMS	WITHEY	RANDALL	BARRETT	HOLLOWAY 2, D WILLIAMS, WITHEY	
02/11/82	AFC BOURNEMOUTH	H	0-0	6263	KITE	SLATER	B WILLIAMS	G WILLIAMS	SHERWOOD	McCAFFREY	HOLLOWAY	WITHEY	RANDALL	BARRETT	HOLLOWAY	RANDALL 2, HOLLOWAY, VINEY og	
05/11/82	SOUTHEND UNITED	A	0-1	3480	KITE	SLATER	B WILLIAMS	G WILLIAMS	SHERWOOD	McCAFFREY	HOLLOWAY	WITHEY	RANDALL	PLATNAUER	BARRETT	BRADD	
13/11/82	PORTSMOUTH	H	5-1	9389	KITE	SLATER	B WILLIAMS	G WILLIAMS	PARKIN	McCAFFREY	CHANNON	WITHEY	PLATNAUER HOLLOWAY	RANDALL	BARRETT	STEPHENS, RANDALL	
27/11/82	OXFORD UNITED	A	2-4	9551	KITE	B WILLIAMS	G WILLIAMS	HUGHES	PARKIN	McCAFFREY	PLATNAUER	D WILLIAMS	STEPHENS	RANDALL	BARRETT	PULIS 10	STEPHENS, RANDALL
29/12/82	EXETER CITY	A	4-4	8160	KITE	B WILLIAMS	G WILLIAMS	PULIS	PARKIN	McCAFFREY	HOLLOWAY	D WILLIAMS	STEPHENS	RANDALL	BARRETT	PLATNAUER 9	STEPHENS, RANDALL 2
01/01/83	CARDIFF CITY	H	1-3	11050	KITE	B WILLIAMS	G WILLIAMS	PULIS	PARKIN	McCAFFREY	HOLLOWAY	D WILLIAMS	BRADD	RANDALL	BARRETT	BARRETT 7	BRADD
15/01/83	DONCASTER ROVERS	A	2-0	3234	KITE	SLATER	B WILLIAMS	G WILLIAMS	PARKIN	McCAFFREY	CURLE	CARTER	STEPHENS	RANDALL	BARRETT	STEPHENS, RANDALL	STEPHENS, RANDALL
22/01/83	BRENTFORD	H	1-2	5449	KITE	SLATER	B WILLIAMS	PULIS	SHERWOOD	McCAFFREY	CURLE	CARTER	BRADD	RANDALL	BARRETT	STEPHENS, RANDALL	BRADD
29/01/83	CHESTERFIELD	A	3-0	6066	KITE	SLATER	B WILLIAMS	HOLLOWAY	PARKIN	McCAFFREY	BALL	KELLY	WILLIAMS 10	RANDALL	BARRETT	CARTER, RANDALL	CARTER, RANDALL
05/02/83	PLYMOUTH ARGYLE	H	2-0	6556	KITE	SLATER	B WILLIAMS	G WILLIAMS	PARKIN	McCAFFREY	BALL	D WILLIAMS	PLATNAUER	RANDALL	BARRETT	PLATNAUER 4	PLATNAUER, RANDALL
12/02/83	BRADFORD CITY	A	0-2	4261	KITE	SLATER	B WILLIAMS	G WILLIAMS	PARKIN	McCAFFREY	BALL	D WILLIAMS	PLATNAUER	RANDALL	BARRETT	PLATNAUER, BALL	
19/02/83	NEWPORT COUNTY	H	1-3	6812	KITE	B WILLIAMS	G WILLIAMS	HOLLOWAY	PARKIN	McCAFFREY	BALL	D WILLIAMS	PLATNAUER	RANDALL	BARRETT	STEPHENS 6	PLATNAUER
26/02/83	WIGAN ATHLETIC	A	5-0	3288	KITE	B WILLIAMS	G WILLIAMS	HOLLOWAY	PARKIN	McCAFFREY	BALL	G WILLIAMS	STEPHENS	RANDALL	BARRETT	PLATNAUER 4	RANDALL, WITHEY 2, PLATNAUER
05/03/83	LEYTON ORIENT	H	3-0	5642	KITE	SLATER	B WILLIAMS	HOLLOWAY	PARKIN	McCAFFREY	BALL	D WILLIAMS	STEPHENS	RANDALL	BARRETT	HOLLOWAY 5	B WILLIAMS, B WILLIAMS
12/03/83	READING	A	2-1	4270	KITE	SLATER	B WILLIAMS	PULIS	PARKIN	McCAFFREY	BALL	HOLLOWAY	WITHEY	RANDALL	BARRETT	HOLLOWAY 8	WITHEY 2, RANDALL
19/03/83	SOUTHEND UNITED	H	2-2	6025	KITE	SLATER	B WILLIAMS	PULIS	PARKIN	McCAFFREY	BALL	PULIS	WITHEY	RANDALL	BARRETT	WITHEY 2	RANDALL 2, PLATNAUER
26/03/83	PORTSMOUTH	A	0-1	17828	KITE	B WILLIAMS	G WILLIAMS	PULIS	PARKIN	McCAFFREY	BALL	PULIS	WITHEY	WITHEY	BARRETT	HOLLOWAY 7	
29/03/83	SHEFFIELD UNITED	A	2-1	6595	KITE	B WILLIAMS	G WILLIAMS	PULIS	PARKIN	McCAFFREY	BALL	HOLLOWAY	WITHEY	WITHEY	BARRETT	HOLLOWAY 8	WITHEY, KELLY
02/04/83	EXETER CITY	H	1-0	5741	KITE	SLATER	B WILLIAMS	G WILLIAMS	PARKIN	McCAFFREY	BALL	PULIS	STEPHENS	RANDALL	BARRETT	HOLLOWAY 9	STEPHENS, KELLY
05/04/83	OXFORD UNITED	H	0-1	8190	KITE	SLATER	B WILLIAMS	G WILLIAMS	PARKIN	McCAFFREY	BALL	HOLLOWAY	STEPHENS	RANDALL	BARRETT	CURLE	
09/04/83	READING	H	0-1	4559	KITE	SLATER	B WILLIAMS	G WILLIAMS	PARKIN	McCAFFREY	BALL	HOLLOWAY	STEPHENS	RANDALL	BARRETT	RANDALL 9	
12/04/83	MILLWALL	A	1-1	4873	KITE	SLATER	B WILLIAMS	G WILLIAMS	SLATER	McCAFFREY	BALL	HOLLOWAY	STEPHENS	RANDALL	BARRETT	STEPHENS 7	BARRETT, RANDALL, STEPHENS
16/04/83	PRESTON NORTH END	H	3-2	5189	KITE	SLATER	B WILLIAMS	G WILLIAMS	PARKIN	McCAFFREY	BALL	HOLLOWAY	WITHEY	RANDALL	BARRETT	WITHEY 10	
22/04/83	WREXHAM	A	0-0	2053	KITE	SHERWOOD	B WILLIAMS	G WILLIAMS	PARKIN	McCAFFREY	BALL	HOLLOWAY	WITHEY	RANDALL	BARRETT	BALL	
30/04/83	HUDDERSFIELD TOWN	A	1-0	8919	KITE	SLATER	B WILLIAMS	G WILLIAMS	PARKIN	McCAFFREY	BALL	HOLLOWAY	WITHEY	WITHEY	BARRETT	WITHEY 9	RANDALL 5
02/05/83	HUDDERSFIELD TOWN	H	1-0	7694	KITE	SLATER	B WILLIAMS	G WILLIAMS	PARKIN	McCAFFREY	G WILLIAMS	HOLLOWAY	PLATNAUER	RANDALL	BARRETT	PLATNAUER, BALL	WILLIAMS D
07/05/83	GILLINGHAM	A	0-1	4024	KITE	SLATER	B WILLIAMS	PULIS	PARKIN	McCAFFREY	BALL	HOLLOWAY	PLATNAUER	WITHEY	BARRETT	ADAMS 5	WITHEY
14/05/83	CARDIFF CITY	H	1-1	10731	KITE	SLATER	B WILLIAMS	CURLE	PARKIN	McCAFFREY	BALL	G WILLIAMS	PLATNAUER	STEPHENS	PLATNAUER	PLATNAUER	

LEAGUE CUP

Date	Opposition	Venue	Result	Att												Substitutes	Goalscorers
01/09/82	TORQUAY UNITED	H	2-2	3259	KITE	SLATER	B WILLIAMS	G WILLIAMS	PARKIN	McCAFFREY	D WILLIAMS	CURLE	STEPHENS	RANDALL	BARRETT	KELLY 2	RANDALL, D WILLIAMS
15/09/82	TORQUAY UNITED	A	4-0	3204	KITE	SLATER	B WILLIAMS	G WILLIAMS	PARKIN	McCAFFREY	PLATNAUER	D WILLIAMS	STEPHENS	RANDALL	BARRETT	STEPHENS 7	PLATNAUER, BARRETT, RANDALL, STEPHENS
05/10/82	SWANSEA CITY	H	1-0	9279	KITE	SLATER	B WILLIAMS	G WILLIAMS	PARKIN	McCAFFREY	D WILLIAMS	HOLLOWAY	STEPHENS	RANDALL	BARRETT	STEPHENS 11	PARKIN
26/10/82	SWANSEA CITY	A	0-3	9775	KITE	SLATER	B WILLIAMS	G WILLIAMS	PARKIN	McCAFFREY	HOLLOWAY	D WILLIAMS	STEPHENS	RANDALL	BARRETT	CHANNON 11	

FA CUP

Date	Opposition	Venue	Result	Att												Substitutes	Goalscorers
20/11/82	WYCOMBE WANDERERS	H	1-0	6420	KITE	B WILLIAMS	G WILLIAMS	HUGHES	PARKIN	McCAFFREY	PLATNAUER	D WILLIAMS	RANDALL	WITHEY	BARRETT	STEPHENS	STEPHENS
11/12/82	PLYMOUTH ARGYLE	H	2-2	9018	KITE	B WILLIAMS	G WILLIAMS	HUGHES	PARKIN	McCAFFREY	D WILLIAMS	HOLLOWAY	RANDALL	WITHEY	BARRETT	D WILLIAMS 2	D WILLIAMS 2
20/12/82	PLYMOUTH ARGYLE	A	0-1	9130	KITE	B WILLIAMS	G WILLIAMS	PULIS	PARKIN	McCAFFREY	CHANNON	D WILLIAMS	RANDALL	WITHEY	BARRETT		

GLOUCESTERSHIRE CUP FINAL

Date	Opposition	Venue	Result	Att												Substitutes	Goalscorers
21/09/82	BRISTOL CITY	H	2-1	4369	CASHLEY	SLATER	B WILLIAMS	G WILLIAMS	PULIS	PARKIN	McCAFFREY	HOLLOWAY	D WILLIAMS	STEPHENS	RANDALL	STEPHENS, HOLLOWAY	STEPHENS, HOLLOWAY

GOALKEEPERS / PLAYERS

PLAYERS	APP	SUB	GLS
ADAMS M	0	1	
BALL A	17		2
BARRETT M	32	2	1
BRADD L	1		1
CHANNON M	4	4	
CURLE K	11	1	2
HOLLOWAY I	26	5	7
HUGHES M	9	4	
KITE P	46		
McCAFFREY A	45		3
PARKIN T	21	3	7
PLATNAUER N	41	3	
PULIS A	16	1	
RANDALL P	38		20
SHERWOOD J	36	2	
SLATER H	11	6	2
STEPHENS A	19		6
WILLIAMS B	43		2
WILLIAMS D	24	1	9
WILLIAMS G	35	3	3
WITHEY P	19	3	10
OWN GOAL			1

scored on his debut as Rovers beat Torquay United 4-0 at Plainmoor, before losing a League Cup second-round tie on aggregate to Swansea City. Despite the high-scoring League form, a solitary Archie Stephens goal defeated non-League Wycombe Wanderers in the FA Cup. Rovers then lost in a replay to Plymouth Argyle, over whom they were to complete a League double. Ian Holloway's curling right-wing strike retained the Gloucestershire Cup, while Spurs won 3-2 at Eastville in April's centenary match.

One footnote to 1982/83 is that Rovers used a substitute in 43 League games, an English record for all clubs from 1965 to 1987 when only one replacement per team was allowed each game.

1983/84

A s Rovers' directors continued negotiations regarding the club's long-term home, the centenary year was rounded off by the first months in charge for a new manager. Bobby Gould was succeeded from within by David Williams. In fending off the applications of Alan Ball, who became coach at Portsmouth, and Larry Lloyd, who joined Notts County, Williams became, at 28, the League's youngest manager. He appointed Wayne Jones as his assistant and retained much of the squad that had served Rovers so well in 1982/83.

Graham Withey, Nick Platnauer and Errington Kelly rejoined their former manager at Coventry City, where Bobby Gould's appointment had led to Rovers receiving £30,000 compensation. Jeff Sherwood moved to Bath City on a free transfer. Williams initially brought just one new player to the club although, as the season progressed, the experienced goalkeeper Ray Cashley joined from Bristol City and Carlisle United's Paul Bannon was signed in an £8,000 deal. The 'new' player was an old hand – Steve White, who returned to Eastville from Charlton Athletic in a deal worth £35,000. So it was that a very recognizable Rovers side lost the first game of the new season at Newport County. Archie Stephens, who scored a consolation goal in this match after coming on as a substitute, was initially out of favour but became the club's seasonal top scorer with 13 League goals.

Once again, a successful pre-season tour of Scotland prefaced a promising opening to a new season. Rovers were unbeaten against Airdrieonians, Hamilton Academical and Kilmarnock but lost 2-0 at Morton to goals from Bobby Houston and Mungo MacCallum. As the League season got underway, Rovers won 10 of their opening 16 fixtures and gave promise of a return to the previous season's form. Indeed, although the goals never flowed at the rate seen the previous autumn, Rovers were to finish fifth in Division Three and were in fact to lose only 3 of 46 home League games under Williams' management.

In stark contrast to 1982/83, Rovers scored four goals in a game on only three occasions. Newport County were convincingly defeated 4-0, but Rovers required own goals to beat Scunthorpe United and Walsall. The latter game was notable for the unlikely fact that both sides' player-managers scored, Williams contributing Rovers'

Bristol Rovers 1983/84. Back row: Williams Cashley, Kite, Holloway, Hughes, G Williams, Parkin, Curle, Withey, Jones (Asst Manager), Pulis (Coach). Front row: Adams, Randall, Slatter, Platnauer, McCaffrey, Barrett, Stephens, B Williams, Sherwood

second, with Alan Buckley replying for the Saddlers. On the other hand, Rovers conceded four goals in only two League games, at Lincoln City, where the future England International John Fashanu grabbed a hat-trick and, at the season's end, after a goalless first-half, at promotion-bound Sheffield United.

What bore an uncanny resemblance to the previous season was how Rovers' form crumbled in December. Yet again, it was defeat at Oxford United over Christmas that was a huge psychological blow. In this instance, though, it followed hot on the heels of a first home defeat of the season, in which Hull City could afford the luxury of Brian Marwood's missed penalty and still beat Rovers 3-1. This defeat finally shattered all illusions of Rovers' invulnerability, which had been strengthened earlier by the convincing nature of the side's performance in defeating Burnley and enhancing their growing early-season reputation.

Rovers endured one late-winter run of four League games without a goal, but were nonetheless more consistent across the season. However, while home form was undeniably strong, the team lacked a certain cutting edge in away matches. Six away League wins was no poor record, but equally was not one that suggested a promotion challenge in earnest. These away wins came in pairs. There were 1-0 wins at Orient and Bournemouth at the end of September, the latter after Phil Kite had saved a penalty from the future Rovers striker Trevor Morgan. There were 2-1 wins in January at Southend United, where the veteran former England forward Trevor Whymark was making his debut for the Shrimpers, and Exeter City, where Rovers supporters invaded the pitch, six policeman were injured and there were 24 arrests. Finally, late wins at Gillingham and Bradford City, through Archie Stephens' goals, brought Rovers to a seasonal total of four League doubles.

Rotherham United's Mick Gooding became only the sixth opponent to score two penalties in a League game against Rovers. He had put his side ahead at Millmoor in the second minute, but the game was to finish 2-2 with Rovers' only ever-present and

SEASON 1983/84

FOOTBALL LEAGUE DIVISION THREE

			ATT	G	2	3	4	5	6	7	8	9	10	11	SUBSTITUTES	GOALSCORERS
27/08/83 NEWPORT COUNTY	A	1-2	5015	KITE	SLATTER	B WILLIAMS	G WILLIAMS	PARKIN	McCAFFREY	HOLLOWAY	D WILLIAMS	WHITE	RANDALL	BARRETT	STEPHENS 8	STEPHENS
03/09/83 SOUTHEND UNITED	H	2-1	4410	KITE	SLATTER	B WILLIAMS	G WILLIAMS	PARKIN	McCAFFREY	HOLLOWAY	PULIS	WHITE	RANDALL	BARRETT		HOLLOWAY, RANDALL
06/09/83 BRENTFORD	H	3-1	5148	KITE	SLATTER	B WILLIAMS	G WILLIAMS	PARKIN	McCAFFREY	HOLLOWAY	PULIS	WHITE	RANDALL	BARRETT		WHITE, B WILLIAMS, BARRETT
10/09/83 PORT VALE	A	0-2	4308	KITE	SLATTER	B WILLIAMS	G WILLIAMS	PARKIN	McCAFFREY	HOLLOWAY	PULIS	WHITE	RANDALL	BARRETT	STEPHENS 11	
17/09/83 EXETER CITY	H	2-0	4813	KITE	SLATTER	B WILLIAMS	BATER	PARKIN	McCAFFREY	HOLLOWAY	PULIS	WHITE	STEPHENS	BARRETT	RANDALL 9	PARKIN, STEPHENS
23/09/83 LEYTON ORIENT	A	1-0	4206	KITE	SLATTER	B WILLIAMS	BATER	PARKIN	McCAFFREY	HOLLOWAY	PULIS	WHITE	STEPHENS	BARRETT		PULIS
27/09/83 AFC BOURNEMOUTH	A	1-0	3328	KITE	SLATTER	B WILLIAMS	BATER	PARKIN	McCAFFREY	HOLLOWAY	G WILLIAMS	WHITE	STEPHENS	BARRETT	RANDALL 10	WHITE
01/10/83 BOLTON WANDERERS	H	2-1	5621	KITE	SLATTER	B WILLIAMS	BATER	PARKIN	McCAFFREY	HOLLOWAY	G WILLIAMS	WHITE	RANDALL	BARRETT		BARRETT, RANDALL
08/10/83 WIMBLEDON	A	1-1	3462	KITE	SLATTER	B WILLIAMS	BATER	PARKIN	McCAFFREY	HOLLOWAY	PULIS	WHITE	RANDALL	BARRETT	STEPHENS 9	BARRETT
15/10/83 BRADFORD CITY	H	1-0	3861	KITE	SLATTER	B WILLIAMS	BATER	PARKIN	McCAFFREY	HOLLOWAY	PULIS	STEPHENS	RANDALL	G WILLIAMS	WHITE 11	RANDALL
18/10/83 PLYMOUTH ARGYLE	A	1-1	4896	KITE	SLATTER	B WILLIAMS	BATER	PARKIN	McCAFFREY	HOLLOWAY	PULIS	STEPHENS	RANDALL	G WILLIAMS	WHITE 4	G WILLIAMS
25/10/83 SCUNTHORPE UNITED	H	4-1	5324	KITE	SLATTER	B WILLIAMS	BATER	PARKIN	McCAFFREY	HOLLOWAY	G WILLIAMS	STEPHENS	RANDALL	BARRETT	WHITE 10	B WILLIAMS pen, BARRETT, STEPHENS, GREEN og
29/10/83 WALSALL	A	1-2	4964	KITE	SLATTER	B WILLIAMS	BATER	PARKIN	McCAFFREY	HOLLOWAY	G WILLIAMS	WHITE	RANDALL	BARRETT	STEPHENS 10	STEPHENS
01/11/83 PRESTON NORTH END	H	3-1	5635	KITE	SLATTER	B WILLIAMS	BATER	PARKIN	McCAFFREY	HOLLOWAY	G WILLIAMS	WHITE	STEPHENS	BARRETT	RANDALL 10	G WILLIAMS, BARRETT, RANDALL
05/11/83 ROTHERHAM UNITED	A	2-2	3957	KITE	SLATTER	B WILLIAMS	BATER	PARKIN	McCAFFREY	HOLLOWAY	G WILLIAMS	RANDALL	WHITE	BARRETT		HOLLOWAY, B WILLIAMS pen
12/11/83 BURNLEY	H	2-1	7021	KITE	SLATTER	B WILLIAMS	BATER	PARKIN	McCAFFREY	HOLLOWAY	G WILLIAMS	WHITE	RANDALL	BARRETT		BATER, B WILLIAMS pen
26/11/83 LINCOLN CITY	A	0-4	3709	KITE	SLATTER	B WILLIAMS	BATER	PARKIN	McCAFFREY	HOLLOWAY	G WILLIAMS	WHITE	RANDALL	BARRETT	STEPHENS 9	
03/12/83 SHEFFIELD UNITED	H	1-1	7472	KITE	SLATTER	B WILLIAMS	BATER	PARKIN	McCAFFREY	HOLLOWAY	G WILLIAMS	STEPHENS	RANDALL	BARRETT		B WILLIAMS
17/12/83 HULL CITY	H	1-3	5673	KITE	SLATTER	B WILLIAMS	BATER	PARKIN	McCAFFREY	HOLLOWAY	D WILLIAMS	STEPHENS	RANDALL	BARRETT	WHITE 7	PARKIN
26/12/83 OXFORD UNITED	A	2-3	12748	CASHLEY	SLATTER	B WILLIAMS	BATER	PARKIN	McCAFFREY	D WILLIAMS	G WILLIAMS	STEPHENS	PULIS	WHITE		STEPHENS 2
27/12/83 GILLINGHAM	H	3-0	5996	CASHLEY	SLATTER	B WILLIAMS	BATER	PARKIN	McCAFFREY	D WILLIAMS	G WILLIAMS	STEPHENS	PULIS	WHITE	BARRETT 9	STEPHENS, D WILLIAMS, WHITE
30/12/83 MILLWALL	A	0-1	4885	CASHLEY	SLATTER	B WILLIAMS	BATER	PARKIN	McCAFFREY	D WILLIAMS	G WILLIAMS	STEPHENS	PULIS	WHITE	BARRETT 2	
09/01/84 SOUTHEND UNITED	A	2-1	2564	CASHLEY	SLATTER	B WILLIAMS	BATER	PARKIN	McCAFFREY	BARRETT	G WILLIAMS	STEPHENS	PULIS	WHITE		B WILLIAMS, BARRETT
14/01/84 NEWPORT COUNTY	H	4-0	6041	CASHLEY	SLATTER	B WILLIAMS	PULIS	PARKIN	McCAFFREY	HOLLOWAY	G WILLIAMS	STEPHENS	WHITE	BARRETT	D WILLIAMS 10	STEPHENS 2, G WILLIAMS 2
21/01/84 EXETER CITY	A	2-1	5310	CASHLEY	SLATTER	B WILLIAMS	PULIS	PARKIN	McCAFFREY	HOLLOWAY	G WILLIAMS	STEPHENS	WHITE	BARRETT		WEBSTER og, SLATTER
28/01/84 PORT VALE	H	0-0	6502	CASHLEY	SLATTER	B WILLIAMS	PULIS	PARKIN	McCAFFREY	HOLLOWAY	G WILLIAMS	WHITE	RANDALL	BARRETT	D WILLIAMS 9	
04/02/84 BOLTON WANDERERS	A	0-3	5399	CASHLEY	SLATTER	B WILLIAMS	G WILLIAMS	PARKIN	McCAFFREY	HOLLOWAY	PULIS	WHITE	RANDALL	BARRETT	D WILLIAMS 4	
11/02/84 LEYTON ORIENT	H	0-0	4741	CASHLEY	SLATTER	B WILLIAMS	PULIS	PARKIN	McCAFFREY	D WILLIAMS	G WILLIAMS	STEPHENS	BANNON	BARRETT		
14/02/84 PRESTON NORTH END	A	0-1	3813	CASHLEY	SLATTER	B WILLIAMS	HOLLOWAY	PARKIN	McCAFFREY	D WILLIAMS	PULIS	STEPHENS	BANNON	RANDALL	G WILLIAMS 10	
18/02/84 WALSALL	H	4-2	5643	CASHLEY	SLATTER	B WILLIAMS	PULIS	PARKIN	McCAFFREY	D WILLIAMS	HOLLOWAY	STEPHENS	BANNON	BARRETT	RANDALL 10	BANNON, D WILLIAMS, HART og, RANDALL
25/02/84 SCUNTHORPE UNITED	A	2-2	2737	CASHLEY	SLATTER	B WILLIAMS	PULIS	PARKIN	McCAFFREY	HOLLOWAY	BATER	WHITE	BANNON	BARRETT	RANDALL 10	WHITE 2
03/03/84 PLYMOUTH ARGYLE	H	2-0	5619	CASHLEY	SLATTER	B WILLIAMS	PULIS	PARKIN	McCAFFREY	HOLLOWAY	BATER	WHITE	BANNON	D WILLIAMS	RANDALL 10	BANNON, WHITE
06/03/84 ROTHERHAM UNITED	H	2-0	5264	CASHLEY	SLATTER	B WILLIAMS	PULIS	PARKIN	McCAFFREY	HOLLOWAY	BATER	WHITE	BANNON	D WILLIAMS	RANDALL 6	D WILLIAMS, BANNON
10/03/84 BURNLEY	A	0-0	6296	CASHLEY	BATER	B WILLIAMS	PULIS	PARKIN	HUGHES	HOLLOWAY	D WILLIAMS	WHITE	BANNON	RANDALL	STEPHENS 10	
17/03/84 WIMBLEDON	H	1-1	5383	CASHLEY	HUGHES	BATER	PULIS	PARKIN	McCAFFREY	G WILLIAMS	D WILLIAMS	STEPHENS	WHITE	B WILLIAMS	BARRETT7	WHITE
27/03/84 WIGAN ATHLETIC	H	2-1	7072	CASHLEY	SLATTER	BATER	PULIS	PARKIN	McCAFFREY	RANDALL	D WILLIAMS	WHITE	BANNON	B WILLIAMS	STEPHENS 10	B WILLIAMS, WALSH og
31/03/84 BRENTFORD	A	2-2	4067	CASHLEY	SLATTER	BATER	PULIS	PARKIN	McCAFFREY	RANDALL	D WILLIAMS	BANNON	WHITE	B WILLIAMS	STEPHENS 9	B WILLIAMS, WHITE
07/04/84 AFC BOURNEMOUTH	H	1-3	5032	CASHLEY	SLATTER	BATER	PULIS	PARKIN	McCAFFREY	RANDALL	D WILLIAMS	WHITE	BANNON	B WILLIAMS	STEPHENS 9	PULIS
14/04/84 SHEFFIELD UNITED	A	0-4	12688	CASHLEY	SLATTER	BATER	PULIS	PARKIN	McCAFFREY	G WILLIAMS	BARRETT	WHITE	BANNON	B WILLIAMS	STEPHENS 10	
17/04/84 WIGAN ATHLETIC	A	0-0	2665	CASHLEY	SLATTER	BATER	G WILLIAMS	HUGHES	McCAFFREY	HOLLOWAY	BARRETT	WHITE	STEPHENS	B WILLIAMS		
21/04/84 OXFORD UNITED	H	1-1	6397	CASHLEY	SLATTER	B WILLIAMS	G WILLIAMS	HUGHES	McCAFFREY	HOLLOWAY	D WILLIAMS	STEPHENS	WHITE	BARRETT	RANDALL 7	STEPHENS
23/04/84 GILLINGHAM	A	2-1	3400	CASHLEY	SLATTER	B WILLIAMS	G WILLIAMS	HUGHES	McCAFFREY	HOLLOWAY	D WILLIAMS	STEPHENS	WHITE	BARRETT		STEPHENS 2
28/04/84 LINCOLN CITY	H	3-1	3245	CASHLEY	SLATTER	B WILLIAMS	G WILLIAMS	HUGHES	McCAFFREY	HOLLOWAY	D WILLIAMS	STEPHENS	WHITE	BARRETT		WHITE, BARRETT 2
02/05/84 BRADFORD CITY	A	1-0	3271	CASHLEY	BATER	B WILLIAMS	G WILLIAMS	HUGHES	McCAFFREY	HOLLOWAY	D WILLIAMS	STEPHENS	WHITE	BARRETT		STEPHENS
08/05/84 MILLWALL	H	3-2	5347	CASHLEY	SLATTER	B WILLIAMS	G WILLIAMS	HUGHES	McCAFFREY	HOLLOWAY	D WILLIAMS	WHITE	RANDALL	BARRETT	BATER 5	B WILLIAMS pen, RANDALL, BARRETT
12/05/84 HULL CITY	A	0-0	11657	CASHLEY	SLATTER	B WILLIAMS	G WILLIAMS	HUGHES	McCAFFREY	HOLLOWAY	D WILLIAMS	WHITE	RANDALL	BARRETT	BATER 7	

FA CUP

19/11/83 BARNET	A	0-0	2650	KITE	SLATTER	B WILLIAMS	BATER	PARKIN	McCAFFREY	HOLLOWAY	G WILLIAMS	WHITE	RANDALL	BARRETT	STEPHENS 10	
22/11/83 BARNET	H	3-1	5338	KITE	SLATTER	B WILLIAMS	BATER	PARKIN	McCAFFREY	HOLLOWAY	G WILLIAMS	WHITE	RANDALL	BARRETT		HOLLOWAY, BARRETT, SLATTER
10/12/83 BRISTOL CITY	H	1-2	14396	KITE	SLATTER	B WILLIAMS	BATER	PARKIN	McCAFFREY	HOLLOWAY	G WILLIAMS	STEPHENS	RANDALL	BARRETT	WHITE 10	STEPHENS

LEAGUE CUP

30/08/83 AFC BOURNEMOUTH	A	2-1	3473	KITE	SLATTER	B WILLIAMS	G WILLIAMS	PARKIN	McCAFFREY	HOLLOWAY	PULIS	WHITE	RANDALL	BARRETT		RANDALL, HOLLOWAY
13/09/83 AFC BOURNEMOUTH	H	2-2	4564	KITE	SLATTER	B WILLIAMS	G WILLIAMS	PARKIN	McCAFFREY	HOLLOWAY	PULIS	WHITE	STEPHENS	BARRETT	RANDALL 10	B WILLIAMS pen, STEPHENS
04/10/83 BRIGHTON & H ALB	A	2-4	9417	KITE	SLATTER	B WILLIAMS	PULIS	PARKIN	McCAFFREY	HOLLOWAY	G WILLIAMS	WHITE	RANDALL	BARRETT	STEPHENS 10	BARRETT, SLATTER
25/10/83 BRIGHTON & H ALB*	H	2-1	5324	KITE	SLATTER	B WILLIAMS	G WILLIAMS	PARKIN	McCAFFREY	HOLLOWAY	WHITE	STEPHENS	RANDALL	BARRETT		BARRETT, WHITE

* AET: Score at 90 mins 2-0

ASSOCIATE MEMBERS CUP

28/02/84 NEWPORT COUNTY	A	1-0	2116	CASHLEY	SLATTER	B WILLIAMS	PULIS	PARKIN	McCAFFREY	HOLLOWAY	BATER	WHITE	BANNON	D WILLIAMS		BANNON
13/03/84 PORT VALE	H	2-0	2558	KITE	HUGHES	BATER	G WILLIAMS	PARKIN	McCAFFREY	BARRETT	D WILLIAMS	STEPHENS	VASSALL	B WILLIAMS	WHITE 10, NOBLE 2,	B WILLIAMS, STEPHENS
03/04/84 SOUTHEND UNITED	A	2-1	1480	KITE	SLATTER	B WILLIAMS	G WILLIAMS	HUGHES	McCAFFREY	HOLLOWAY	D WILLIAMS	STEPHENS	ADAMS	BARRETT	METCALFE 6	HUGHES, ADAMS
14/05/84 AFC BOURNEMOUTH	A	0-1	2810	CASHLEY	SLATTER	B WILLIAMS	HOLLOWAY	HUGHES	McCAFFREY	G WILLIAMS	D WILLIAMS	WHITE	RANDALL	BARRETT	BATER 7, STEPHENS 11	

GLOUCESTERSHIRE CUP FINAL

20/09/83 BRISTOL CITY *	A	3-2	6538	KITE	BATER	B WILLIAMS	HOLLOWAY	PARKIN	McCAFFREY	RANDALL	PULIS	WHITE	STEPHENS	BARRETT	CURLE	McCAFFREY, WHITE, CURLE

* AET Score at 90 mins 1-1

PLAYERS	APP	SUB	GLS
BANNON P	11		3
BARRETT M	33	3	9
BATER P	30	2	1
CASHLEY R	27		
HOLLOWAY I	36		2
HUGHES M	9		
KITE P	19		
McCAFFREY A	45		
PARKIN T	39		2
PULIS A	28		2
RANDALL P	24	8	6
SLATTER N	43		1
STEPHENS A	24	10	13
WHITE S	38	4	9
WILLIAMS B	46		9
WILLIAMS D	21	3	3
WILLIAMS G	33	1	4
OWN GOALS			4

Centenary match action. Rovers take on their first ever opponents Wotton in 1983 wearing a special Black Arabs kit for the occasion

unlikely candidate as second-highest scorer, Brian Williams, also scoring from the spot in a match of three penalties. Rovers' winning goal at home to Wigan Athletic in March was a 52nd-minute headed own goal by Steve Walsh, who was to give loyal service into the new millennium to Leicester City, who featured a certain Gary Lineker on the goalscoring list when their reserves defeated Rovers reserves 5-3 in November.

One huge disappointment was Randall's inability to follow up his 20 League goals with a meaningful contribution in 1983/84. He scored just 6 goals in the League, while Steve White was also unable to reach double figures. Stephens was never consistently in Rovers' starting line-up, while the side grew to depend increasingly on Mike Barrett. Not only did Barrett contribute 9 League goals, but his presence was hugely important to those around him and his rare ability to beat even the most dogged defender enthralled the crowd. In the last home game of the season, Millwall had led 2-0 before Barrett had inspired a comeback and scored a sensational last-minute winning-goal himself.

In defence, Rovers possessed a developing star in full-back Neil Slatter. He had earned a first full International cap for Wales against Scotland in Cardiff in May 1983 and was to play on 10 occasions for the full Welsh side while on Rovers' books, and 22 times in all. His full-back partnership with Brian Williams flourished both through the reliability of both players and a good tactical understanding. Rovers conceded just 54 League goals, the fewest since the 1975/76 season.

In the League Cup, Rovers defeated Bournemouth 4-3 on aggregate, despite Brian Williams scoring a penalty and an own goal in the home leg. It is rare indeed for Rovers to win at Dean Court, but this season the feat had been achieved in League and cup before the end of September. Division Two Brighton were stretched in the second round, with the influential Barrett scoring in both legs as Rovers clawed back a 4-2 deficit to take the tie into extra-time. Sadly from Rovers' point of view, the only goal added in this period was scored by the visitors' Terry Connor, later on Rovers' coaching staff. Rovers avoided a potential banana skin in the FA Cup by drawing with non-League Barnet at Underhill, before a comfortable replay victory set up a mouth-watering tie with Bristol City. It was the first meeting of the sides in this competition since 1968, but the Division Four side snatched victory at Eastville through Tom Ritchie's 88th-minute winner.

Rovers also participated in the newly formed Associate Members Cup, winning three times before losing at Bournemouth. The early disinterest in a tournament designed for lower-division clubs is apparent in the attendances. For instance, only 1,480 turned out to see Rovers win at Southend United on a Tuesday night in April, but they witnessed dramatic events, as Aiden McCaffrey swallowed his tongue in an accidental collision with Phil Kite. His life was saved by the prompt action of the club physiotherapist, Roy Dolling. This competition was used as a vehicle for blooding new talent, with Paul Vassall and Wayne Noble playing against Port Vale and Mike Adams, who headed the winning goal six minutes after half-time, and Carl Metcalfe at Southend.

November saw a testimonial at Eastville for the unfortunate Steve Bailey, whose career had been cut short by a knee injury. Bobby Gould's Coventry City supplied the opposition and the former Rovers striker Graham Withey scored the winning goal. The following month Rovers returned to the scene of their first fixture to play a centenary game against Wotton Rovers, which Rovers, in distinctive Black Arabs shirts with a yellow sash, won 4-0, Barrett scoring twice. Two days later, Newcastle United visited Eastville for another centenary match, Randall's hat-trick leading Rovers to a 5-4 victory. Meanwhile, the former Rovers player Gary Mabbutt ended the season with a UEFA Cup winner's medal with Tottenham Hotspur.

1984/85

That player-manager David Williams' side was consistent and settled is abundantly clear from the paucity of close-season transfer deals. Mark Hughes and Tony Pulis joined South Wales sides – the defender on a free transfer to Swansea City and the midfielder moving to Newport County for £8,000. Until events on the eve of the new season sadly rendered it inevitable, the manager did not venture into the transfer market for new players. Off the pitch, the promotion of Gordon Bennett to managing director on 25 June 1984 was a significant advance, as it was he who steered the club into less financially choppy waters towards the end of the decade.

Just days before the new season, however, the club was rocked by tragic news. Mike Barrett was dead. Rovers' inspirational winger had struggled in pre-season training, entered hospital for tests and died of cancer on 14 August, aged only 24. The entire Eastville camp shared the grief felt by his pregnant wife and his funeral six days later was well-attended. Rovers swiftly organized a game against Aston Villa for the benefit of his family, goals from Tim Parkin and David Williams giving Rovers a 2-1 win. From the angle of team selection, the player-manager delved hurriedly but wisely into the transfer market to sign Mark O'Connor from Queen's Park Rangers for £20,000. O'Connor, despite the unenviable task of stepping into Barrett's shoes, played at least a part in every game of the season and contributed 8 League goals.

Rovers started the season as if on a mission to secure promotion at the earliest possible opportunity. Of the opening seven League games, six were won, while Rovers also gained a creditable goalless draw at Burnley. Archie Stephens and Paul Randall, forming a productive forward partnership, appeared to be scoring goals frequently enough for Rovers to mount a serious challenge. An autumnal blip saw Rovers draw three consecutive home matches and lose three in a row away, the worst being 3-0 before a seasonal best League crowd of 18,672 at Ashton Gate, with Glyn Riley scoring twice for Bristol City. However, still unbeaten at home, Rovers hit a golden patch in December.

The Randall-Stephens partnership was flourishing and, once O'Connor started to score too, Rovers won four consecutive games in the League. O'Connor scored in all

Bristol Rovers 1984/85. Back row: Kendall (Kit-Man), Dolling (Physio), White, Bannon, Cashley, Kite, Parkin, McCaffrey, G Williams, Jarman (Youth Manager), Jones (Asst Manager). Front row: Bater, Slatter, B Williams, D. Williams (Manager), Holloway, Stephens, Randall

these games and Randall in all but one. It may have been the first away win since September, but the 4-1 win at Orient was achieved through a masterful team display and was followed by comfortable home victories over Newport County and Swansea City. When Rovers went 3-0 ahead at Brentford on Boxing Day, O'Connor, Randall and Stephens having scored, the side appeared in absolute control, but was about to hit a brick wall. Stephens was involved in an incident with the home side's Steve Wignall and both players were sent off. Bizarrely, this event seemed to set off a chain of events.

Following the victory at Griffin Park, Archie Stephens' final League goal for Rovers could not prevent the side crashing to a 4-1 defeat at Gillingham. Soon out of favour, Stephens moved to Middlesbrough in March for £20,000. Despite the efforts of his replacement, Paul Bannon, there was no return to the pre-Christmas form. Rovers lost four consecutive League games in the New Year and won only one of the final seven matches of the season. While only Bolton Wanderers and Orient, clubs Rovers had beaten on their travels, won at Eastville, Rovers conversely won just one away game after Boxing Day. It was the lack of success away from Eastville that knocked the promotion charge off the rails, with Rovers finishing in sixth place.

This sole away win in the latter half of the season came at Cambridge United, where defenders Tim Parkin and Neil Slatter both scored, watched by the lowest crowd since January 1935 at a League game involving Rovers. It was the second of four consecutive wins, a beacon of hope as the season drew to an end. At this time, goalkeeper Ron Green, on loan from Shrewsbury Town, kept five consecutive clean sheets. Indeed, it was his eighth home game before Orient's Ian Juryeff, after 52 minutes, became the first opponent to score past him at Eastville. Bristol City were beaten in a gale by a 20th-minute Ian Holloway goal in front of the last five-figure crowd ever to watch League football at Eastville. The next time Rovers attracted a crowd of more than 10,000 to a home League game was to be on Boxing Day 1999. Burnley were defeated 4-0 for Rovers' largest League win in 15 months. Brentford conceded two penalties at Eastville, both converted by Brian Williams, only the fifth Rovers player to achieve such a feat in the League, and many observers considered Rovers unfortunate not to be awarded a third penalty late in the game.

Goalkeeper Jon Hallworth and midfielder Paul Raynor, both of whom went on to enjoy long footballing careers elsewhere, appeared briefly on loan. At Newport County in May, where Brian Williams, who later missed a penalty, scored his side's first goal in 315 minutes, Rovers gave a full League debut to Gary Penrice, a home-grown talent who was to serve Rovers well for many years. It was Penrice who scored with a 26th-minute header in the 1-1 draw with York City on the final day of the season and he was to become in due course the only player to score for Rovers on four home grounds. Winger Chris Smith, who had represented the Gloucestershire Youth XI, was granted a solitary League appearance in the York game. David Williams, chaired off the field despite gifting the visitors an injury-time equaliser in that game, moved to Norwich City within weeks for £40,000 where he was to appear in Division One football and won a first full Welsh cap against Saudi Arabia in February 1986.

Rovers had survived a relatively successful season with a largely unchanged side. Cashley and Green had shared goalkeeping responsibilities, Vaughan Jones had returned to his first club from Cardiff City and was to play a momentous role in Rovers'

League Cup action at Highbury. Ian Holloway takes on Arsenal's David O'Leary in a 4-0 first-leg defeat

near-future, and the influential Geraint Williams had joined Derby County for £40,000. A solid defence, with Brian Williams again the club's only ever-present, had conceded only 48 League goals, the lowest since the 1973/74 promotion season. Williams' 100th consecutive League game was Rovers' 2,500th match in the League, a 2-1 win at Walsall in March, where Randall's two goals, prior to a seven-match goal drought, took his seasonal League tally to 18.

In the League Cup, two goals each from Randall and David Williams gave a forceful Rovers side a 5-1 lead from the away leg against Swindon Town, a very safe margin despite an unconvincing and ultimately disappointing second-leg display. This set up a lucrative tie with Arsenal, for whom the legendary Northern Ireland goalkeeper Pat Jennings played in both games. A crowd of more than 28,000 at Highbury saw a first leg in which Rovers' hopes were killed off by three goals in the final quarter of an hour, even though Steve White's goal a minute after half-time earned a draw when the return leg drew more than 10,000 to Eastville. Cashley conceded an unfortunate own goal after 20 minutes when Tommy Caton's header rebounded to him off the crossbar, but redeemed himself by saving a Tony Woodcock penalty after 66 minutes. Mick Channon, on Rovers' books just two seasons earlier, was in the Norwich City side that beat Sunderland 1-0 in the Wembley final.

An apparently straightforward first-round FA Cup-tie with King's Lynn nearly turned disastrous. Four minutes after half-time, the Linnets took a shock lead when Richard Johnston's shot rebounded off the crossbar for Clive Adams to score. It took four minutes for David Williams to equalise, but the winning goal took a long time to materialize. Four minutes from time, Brian Williams' cross was turned into his own net

SEASON 1984/85

FOOTBALL LEAGUE DIVISION THREE

Date	Opponent	Venue	Score	Att	G	2	3	4	5	6	7	8	9	10	11	Substitutes	Goalscorers
25/08/84	BOLTON WANDERERS	A	1-0	4469	CASHLEY	SLATTER	B WILLIAMS	G WILLIAMS	PARKIN	McCAFFREY	HOLLOWAY	D WILLIAMS	STEPHENS	RANDALL	O'CONNOR	BATER 10	STEPHENS
01/09/84	PRESTON NORTH END	H	3-0	5357	CASHLEY	SLATTER	B WILLIAMS	G WILLIAMS	PARKIN	McCAFFREY	HOLLOWAY	D WILLIAMS	STEPHENS	RANDALL	O'CONNOR	BATER 9	STEPHENS 2, RANDALL
08/09/84	BURNLEY	A	0-0	5362	CASHLEY	SLATTER	B WILLIAMS	G WILLIAMS	PARKIN	McCAFFREY	HOLLOWAY	D WILLIAMS	STEPHENS	RANDALL	O'CONNOR	BATER 8	
15/09/84	READING	H	1-0	5197	CASHLEY	SLATTER	B WILLIAMS	G WILLIAMS	PARKIN	McCAFFREY	HOLLOWAY	D WILLIAMS	STEPHENS	RANDALL	O'CONNOR		HOLLOWAY, RANDALL
18/09/84	BRADFORD CITY	H	2-0	5247	CASHLEY	SLATTER	B WILLIAMS	G WILLIAMS	PARKIN	McCAFFREY	HOLLOWAY	BATER	STEPHENS	RANDALL	O'CONNOR	D WILLIAMS 7	RANDALL 2
22/09/84	LINCOLN CITY	A	2-1	2168	CASHLEY	SLATTER	B WILLIAMS	G WILLIAMS	PARKIN	McCAFFREY	HOLLOWAY	BATER	STEPHENS	RANDALL	O'CONNOR		WHITE
29/09/84	AfC BOURNEMOUTH	H	1-0	5216	CASHLEY	SLATTER	B WILLIAMS	G WILLIAMS	PARKIN	McCAFFREY	HOLLOWAY	D WILLIAMS	WHITE	RANDALL	O'CONNOR		
02/10/84	YORK CITY	A	0-1	7197	CASHLEY	SLATTER	B WILLIAMS	G WILLIAMS	PARKIN	McCAFFREY	HOLLOWAY	D WILLIAMS	WHITE	RANDALL	O'CONNOR		
06/10/84	DERBY COUNTY	H	2-1	7862	CASHLEY	SLATTER	B WILLIAMS	G WILLIAMS	PARKIN	McCAFFREY	HOLLOWAY	D WILLIAMS	WHITE	RANDALL	O'CONNOR	BATER 9	RANDALL 2
13/10/84	ROTHERHAM UNITED	A	3-3	5177	CASHLEY	BATER	B WILLIAMS	G WILLIAMS	PARKIN	McCAFFREY	HOLLOWAY	D WILLIAMS	WHITE	RANDALL	O'CONNOR		D WILLIAMS 2, RANDALL
20/10/84	DONCASTER ROVERS	H	1-1	5611	CASHLEY	SLATTER	B WILLIAMS	G WILLIAMS	PARKIN	SLATTER	HOLLOWAY	D WILLIAMS	WHITE	RANDALL	O'CONNOR	BATER 8	D WILLIAMS
23/10/84	WIGAN ATHLETIC	A	0-1	3022	CASHLEY	SLATTER	B WILLIAMS	G WILLIAMS	PARKIN	McCAFFREY	HOLLOWAY	D WILLIAMS	STEPHENS	RANDALL	O'CONNOR		
27/10/84	HULL CITY	H	1-1	5438	CASHLEY	SLATTER	B WILLIAMS	G WILLIAMS	PARKIN	McCAFFREY	HOLLOWAY	D WILLIAMS	STEPHENS	RANDALL	O'CONNOR		STEPHENS
03/11/84	PLYMOUTH ARGYLE	A	0-3	5818	CASHLEY	SLATTER	B WILLIAMS	G WILLIAMS	PARKIN	McCAFFREY	HOLLOWAY	D WILLIAMS	STEPHENS	RANDALL	BATER	O'CONNOR 10	SLATTER, RANDALL
10/11/84	BRISTOL CITY	H	1-1	18672	CASHLEY	SLATTER	B WILLIAMS	G WILLIAMS	PARKIN	McCAFFREY	HOLLOWAY	D WILLIAMS	STEPHENS	RANDALL	O'CONNOR		STEPHENS
24/11/84	MILLWALL	H	1-1	5917	CASHLEY	SLATTER	B WILLIAMS	BATER	PARKIN	McCAFFREY	HOLLOWAY	D WILLIAMS	STEPHENS	RANDALL	O'CONNOR	WHITE 9	O'CONNOR 2, RANDALL, HOLLOWAY
30/11/84	LEYTON ORIENT	A	4-1	2404	CASHLEY	SLATTER	B WILLIAMS	BATER	PARKIN	McCAFFREY	HOLLOWAY	D WILLIAMS	STEPHENS	RANDALL	O'CONNOR	WHITE 10	D WILLIAMS, O'CONNOR
15/12/84	NEWPORT COUNTY	H	2-0	5405	CASHLEY	SLATTER	B WILLIAMS	BATER	PARKIN	McCAFFREY	HOLLOWAY	D WILLIAMS	STEPHENS	RANDALL	O'CONNOR	WHITE 11	STEPHENS, RANDALL, O'CONNOR
22/12/84	SWANSEA CITY	A	4-2	5546	CASHLEY	SLATTER	B WILLIAMS	BATER	PARKIN	McCAFFREY	HOLLOWAY	D WILLIAMS	STEPHENS	RANDALL	O'CONNOR		STEPHENS
26/12/84	BRENTFORD	H	3-0	5254	CASHLEY	SLATTER	B WILLIAMS	BATER	PARKIN	McCAFFREY	HOLLOWAY	D WILLIAMS	STEPHENS	RANDALL	O'CONNOR		HOLLOWAY, D WILLIAMS
29/12/84	GILLINGHAM	A	1-4	6598	CASHLEY	SLATTER	B WILLIAMS	BATER	PARKIN	McCAFFREY	HOLLOWAY	D WILLIAMS	WHITE	RANDALL	O'CONNOR	JONES 9	WHITE, D WILLIAMS
01/01/85	CAMBRIDGE UNITED	H	2-1	6324	CASHLEY	SLATTER	B WILLIAMS	BATER	PARKIN	McCAFFREY	HOLLOWAY	D WILLIAMS	WHITE	RANDALL	O'CONNOR	STEPHENS 9	HOLLOWAY, D WILLIAMS
12/01/85	PRESTON NORTH END	A	2-2	3136	HALLWORTH	SLATTER	B WILLIAMS	BATER	PARKIN	McCAFFREY	HOLLOWAY	D WILLIAMS	WHITE	RANDALL	O'CONNOR	STEPHENS 10	RANDALL
26/01/85	READING	A	2-3	4648	HALLWORTH	SLATTER	B WILLIAMS	BATER	PARKIN	McCAFFREY	HOLLOWAY	D WILLIAMS	WHITE	RANDALL	O'CONNOR	JONES 10	
29/01/85	BOLTON WANDERERS	H	1-2	3982	CASHLEY	SLATTER	B WILLIAMS	BATER	PARKIN	McCAFFREY	HOLLOWAY	D WILLIAMS	WHITE	STEPHENS	O'CONNOR	STEPHENS 10	B WILLIAMS
02/02/85	AfC BOURNEMOUTH	A	0-1	5000	CASHLEY	SLATTER	B WILLIAMS	BATER	PARKIN	McCAFFREY	HOLLOWAY	D WILLIAMS	WHITE	STEPHENS	O'CONNOR	BANNON 11	
13/02/85	BRADFORD CITY	H	2-2	5428	CASHLEY	SLATTER	B WILLIAMS	BATER	PARKIN	B WILLIAMS	HOLLOWAY	D WILLIAMS	WHITE	BANNON	O'CONNOR	HOLLOWAY 2	HOLLOWAY, BANNON
23/02/85	PLYMOUTH ARGYLE	A	0-1	5953	GREEN	SLATTER	B WILLIAMS	JONES	PARKIN	JONES	HOLLOWAY	D WILLIAMS	RANDALL	BANNON	O'CONNOR	D WILLIAMS 2	O'CONNOR, PARKIN
02/03/85	WIGAN ATHLETIC	H	2-0	6380	GREEN	SLATTER	B WILLIAMS	BATER	PARKIN	JONES	HOLLOWAY	D WILLIAMS	RANDALL	BANNON	O'CONNOR		RANDALL
05/03/85	DONCASTER ROVERS	A	0-2	3883	GREEN	SLATTER	B WILLIAMS	BATER	PARKIN	JONES	G WILLIAMS	D WILLIAMS	RANDALL	BANNON	O'CONNOR	HOLLOWAY 2	
08/03/85	ROTHERHAM UNITED	A	2-2	3651	GREEN	SLATTER	B WILLIAMS	BATER	PARKIN	JONES	HOLLOWAY	D WILLIAMS	RANDALL	BANNON	O'CONNOR	D WILLIAMS 2	RANDALL 2
16/03/85	ROTHERHAM UNITED	H	1-0	4083	GREEN	SLATTER	B WILLIAMS	BATER	PARKIN	JONES	HOLLOWAY	G WILLIAMS	RANDALL	BANNON	O'CONNOR		B WILLIAMS 2, 2 pens, BANNON
23/03/85	DERBY COUNTY	A	0-0	10041	GREEN	SLATTER	B WILLIAMS	BATER	PARKIN	JONES	HOLLOWAY	D WILLIAMS	RANDALL	BANNON	O'CONNOR		SLATTER, PARKIN
30/03/85	WALSALL	H	2-1	4829	GREEN	SLATTER	B WILLIAMS	BATER	PARKIN	JONES	HOLLOWAY	D WILLIAMS	RANDALL	BANNON	O'CONNOR	RAYNOR 8	HOLLOWAY
02/04/85	LINCOLN CITY	A	2-1	4159	GREEN	SLATTER	B WILLIAMS	BATER	PARKIN	RAYNOR	HOLLOWAY	D WILLIAMS	RANDALL	BANNON	O'CONNOR	WHITE 8	RANDALL 2, BANNON, PARKIN
06/04/85	BRENTFORD	H	3-0	4519	GREEN	SLATTER	B WILLIAMS	BATER	PARKIN	JONES	HOLLOWAY	RAYNOR	RANDALL	BANNON	O'CONNOR		
08/04/85	CAMBRIDGE UNITED	A	2-0	1711	GREEN	SLATTER	B WILLIAMS	BATER	PARKIN	JONES	HOLLOWAY	RAYNOR	RANDALL	BANNON	O'CONNOR		B WILLIAMS
13/04/85	BRISTOL CITY	H	1-0	12957	GREEN	SLATTER	B WILLIAMS	B WILLIAMS	PARKIN	JONES	HOLLOWAY	RAYNOR	RANDALL	BANNON	O'CONNOR	BANNON 10	O'CONNOR, BANNON, WHITE
16/04/85	BURNLEY	A	4-0	4866	GREEN	SLATTER	B WILLIAMS	BATER	McCAFFREY	JONES	HOLLOWAY	PENRICE	WHITE	BANNON	O'CONNOR		O'CONNOR, BANNON
20/04/85	MILLWALL	H	0-1	7416	GREEN	SLATTER	B WILLIAMS	B WILLIAMS	PARKIN	JONES	HOLLOWAY	WHITE	RANDALL	BANNON	O'CONNOR	PENRICE 7	PENRICE
23/04/85	WALSALL	A	0-0	4040	GREEN	SLATTER	B WILLIAMS	BATER	PARKIN	JONES	WHITE	PENRICE	RANDALL	BANNON	O'CONNOR		
27/04/85	LEYTON ORIENT	A	0-1	2549	GREEN	SLATTER	B WILLIAMS	B WILLIAMS	PARKIN	JONES	PENRICE	WHITE	RANDALL	BANNON	O'CONNOR		
05/05/85	NEWPORT COUNTY	H	3-2	2302	GREEN	SLATTER	B WILLIAMS	B WILLIAMS	PARKIN	JONES	PENRICE	D WILLIAMS	RANDALL	BANNON	O'CONNOR		
11/05/85	GILLINGHAM	A	2-3	2716	GREEN	SLATTER	BATER	B WILLIAMS	PARKIN	JONES	HOLLOWAY	D WILLIAMS	RANDALL	BANNON	O'CONNOR		
14/05/85	YORK CITY	H	1-1	3692	GREEN	SMITH	BATER	B WILLIAMS	SLATTER	JONES	HOLLOWAY	D WILLIAMS	RANDALL	BANNON	O'CONNOR		

FA CUP

Date	Opponent	Venue	Score	Att	G	2	3	4	5	6	7	8	9	10	11	Substitutes	Goalscorers
17/11/84	KINGS LYNN	H	2-1	3841	CASHLEY	SLATTER	B WILLIAMS	BATER	PARKIN	McCAFFREY	HOLLOWAY	D WILLIAMS	STEPHENS	RANDALL	O'CONNOR		D WILLIAMS, ADAMS og
08/12/84	BRISTOL CITY	H	3-1	19367	CASHLEY	SLATTER	B WILLIAMS	BATER	PARKIN	McCAFFREY	HOLLOWAY	D WILLIAMS	STEPHENS	RANDALL	O'CONNOR	G WILLIAMS 2	O'CONNOR, RANDALL 2
05/01/85	IPSWICH TOWN	H	1-2	12257	CASHLEY	G WILLIAMS	B WILLIAMS	BATER	PARKIN	McCAFFREY	HOLLOWAY	D WILLIAMS	STEPHENS	RANDALL	O'CONNOR		HOLLOWAY

LEAGUE CUP

Date	Opponent	Venue	Score	Att	G	2	3	4	5	6	7	8	9	10	11	Substitutes	Goalscorers
27/08/84	SWINDON TOWN	A	5-1	4905	CASHLEY	SLATTER	B WILLIAMS	G WILLIAMS	PARKIN	McCAFFREY	HOLLOWAY	D WILLIAMS	STEPHENS	RANDALL	O'CONNOR	BATER 8	B WILLIAMS pen, RANDALL 2, D WILLIAMS 2
04/09/84	SWINDON TOWN	H	0-1	3862	CASHLEY	SLATTER	B WILLIAMS	G WILLIAMS	PARKIN	McCAFFREY	HOLLOWAY	D WILLIAMS	STEPHENS	RANDALL	O'CONNOR		
25/09/84	ARSENAL	A	0-4	28871	CASHLEY	SLATTER	B WILLIAMS	G WILLIAMS	PARKIN	McCAFFREY	HOLLOWAY	BATER	STEPHENS	RANDALL	O'CONNOR		
09/10/84	ARSENAL	H	1-1	10408	CASHLEY	SLATTER	B WILLIAMS	G WILLIAMS	PARKIN	McCAFFREY	HOLLOWAY	D WILLIAMS	WHITE	RANDALL	O'CONNOR	NOBLE 11	WHITE

FRIEGHT ROVER TROPHY

Date	Opponent	Venue	Score	Att	G	2	3	4	5	6	7	8	9	10	11	Substitutes	Goalscorers
22/01/85	SWANSEA CITY	A	0-2	2648	HALLWORTH	D WILLIAMS	B WILLIAMS	BATER	PARKIN	McCAFFREY	HOLLOWAY	G WILLIAMS	WHITE	RANDALL	O'CONNOR	BRAIN 1, PENRICE 8	
19/03/85	SWANSEA CITY	H	0-0	2223	GREEN	D WILLIAMS	B WILLIAMS	BATER	PARKIN	McCAFFREY	HOLLOWAY	D WILLIAMS	WHITE	RANDALL	O'CONNOR	PENRICE 9, WHITE 3	

GLOUCESTERSHIRE CUP FINAL

Date	Opponent	Venue	Score	Att	G	2	3	4	5	6	7	8	9	10	11	Substitutes	Goalscorers
21/05/85	BRISTOL CITY*	H	3-1	4033	GREEN	SLATTER	BATER	B WILLIAMS	McCAFFREY	JONES	PENRICE	WHITE	RANDALL	BANNON	O'CONNOR	TANNER, SMITH	WHITE, TANNER, BANNON

* AET Score at 90 mins 1-1

PLAYERS	APP	SUB	GLS
BANNON P	16	2	5
BATER P	34	5	
CASHLEY R	26		
GREEN R	18		
HALLWORTH J	2		
HOLLOWAY I	41	1	6
JONES V	18	2	
McCAFFREY A	27		
O'CONNOR M	45	1	8
PARKIN T	43		3
PENRICE G	4	1	
RANDALL P	43		18
RAYNOR P	7	1	
SLATTER N	37		2
SMITH C	1		
STEPHENS A	22	2	10
WHITE S	14	4	3
WILLIAMS B	46		4
WILLIAMS D	34	3	6
WILLIAMS G	28		

by the unfortunate Adams to nullify his earlier goal. This set up a second-round tie before a crowd of 19,367 at Ashton Gate, where Rovers gained ample revenge for the previous season's result by beating Bristol City 3-1. O'Connor scored Rovers' first and Randall added two more before half-time to complete a noteworthy victory. Division One Ipswich Town were the visitors in the third round and, despite a volleyed goal from Ian Holloway, ran out worthy winners.

Participation in the Freight Rover Trophy ended promptly, as a result of Geraint Williams' own goal from a Chris Marustik cross four minutes prior to half-time and substitute Dean Saunders' 53rd-minute penalty for Swansea City. A fourth consecutive Gloucestershire Cup final victory was secured when Rovers scored twice in extra-time. White's goal had put Rovers ahead by half-time, only for Bristol City to equalise through an Alan Walsh penalty. Nineteen-year-old Nicky Tanner, on as a substitute for his club debut, scored an astonishing 30-yard extra-time goal before the revitalized Paul Bannon added a third in his final game for the club.

At the close of the season, just weeks before a £80,000 move to Oxford United, Neil Slatter played in his 10th International for Wales, marking the occasion with an own goal in a 4-2 defeat in Norway, to set a record for International appearances by a player on the books of Bristol Rovers, which was to stand until 2001.

1985/86

The previous two seasons had been successful and, but for an inconsistent away record, Rovers might have found their way back into Division Two. Nonetheless, manager David Williams decided his job was done and moved to Norwich City and later Bournemouth as a player. Away from Eastville, his playing career hit new heights and he was rewarded with five full International appearances for Wales in 1986 and 1987. Williams was replaced by Bobby Gould who, in his two years away from Eastville, had struggled to create a team to his liking at Highfield Road but had nevertheless kept Coventry City in Division One.

Gould's reappointment was the last major decision made by club directors Martin Flook and Barry Bradshaw. Both men had provided Rovers with loans at crucial times since taking control of the club in the summer of 1981, but resigned when pleas to build a new stadium at Stoke Gifford finally collapsed. Discussions about a multi-sports complex on this site had dragged on for two years, but Rovers had faced considerable opposition from residents as well as the local authority planners. The decision not to proceed was to leave Rovers with little option but to leave Eastville and ground-share with Bath City from the end of the season. The Popplewell Report, delivered in January 1986 (Command Paper 9710) in the aftermath of the Bradford fire and Heysel tragedy, ordered that Twerton Park should be incorporated within the stadia covered by the 1975 Safety of Sports Grounds Act. Geoff Dunford and Roy Redman bought up chairman Flook's shareholding in the club and held, at times through 1985/86, three board meetings a week simply to keep the club afloat. The Stadium Company frequently

Bristol Rovers 1985/86. Back row: Weston, O'Connor, Bater, White, Randall, Mehew, Cassidy, Howells, Obi. Middle row: Jarman, Badock, Spring, Parkin, Green, Carter, Tanner, Stevenson, Scales, Kendall (Kit Man). Front row: Penrice, V Jones, Bradshaw (Director), Bennett (Chief Executive), Gould (Manager), Flook (Chairman), Davies, Cockram

placed injunctions on Rovers playing at Eastville and, on one occasion, this was lifted only on the Friday evening prior to a Saturday fixture.

Not only did Rovers approach the new season with new directors and a restored manager but, in order to tackle the ever-increasing losses, many of the more experienced players were released. A squad of considerably younger players reduced the wage bill but led to a tougher season on the pitch. Rovers finished the season sixteenth in Division Three. Fifteen of Rovers' 23 home League games were played before crowds of under 4,000 and these attendance figures fell away as the club recorded just two victories in the final 19 League games of a miserable season.

The season opened with a misleadingly exciting six-goal draw with Darlington at Feethams. Rovers were giving club League debuts to five players, two of whom, Steve Badock and Byron Stevenson from the penalty spot, were able to mark the occasion with a goal. The full-back pairing of Andy Spring and Ian Davies, the latter once Norwich City's youngest-ever player, did not last long. Phil Bater, an own goal scorer against all-conquering Reading, was given a run in the side, as were promising young defenders John Scales and Nicky Tanner. Mike England, back in the side in September, over six years after his only previous game in a Rovers shirt, ended the season at left-back. Tim Parkin completed another successful season before moving to Swindon Town in a deal worth £28,500 in June 1986.

It took Rovers seven League games to record their first win of the season and it was October and the fifth home game before Rovers scored a League goal at Eastville. That

Rovers' Trevor Morgan takes the ball around Leicester City goalkeeper Andrews for Rovers' third goal in the shock 3-1 defeat of the Division One club. It was Rovers' first win over top-division opposition since 1958

first victory, an astonishing 4-3 victory over Wolverhampton Wanderers on a Tuesday night at Molineux, was achieved through two Badock goals, his final ones for the club, after Paul Randall and Steve White had both put their names on the scoresheet against the future England goalkeeper Tim Flowers. Indeed, Rovers also won at Swansea City before recording the elusive first home League victory.

As the season unfolded, Rovers tried and rejected a number of players. John Vaughan came on loan from West Ham United in goal, while Allan Cockram, Tony Obi and Richard Iles made just 1 appearance each in the League. Other players with a role to play in years to come made their League bows. David Mehew and Tim Carter were joined by Gary Smart, Wayne Noble and Darren Carr. Two new signings, however, stood out from the pack. Gerry Francis, the former England captain and the holder of 12 full International caps, joined as a non-contract player in September 1985 and his influence in 28 League appearances undoubtedly helped Rovers retain their Division Three status. Trevor Morgan, a £15,000 buy from Francis' former club, Exeter City, was the architect of Rovers' late autumn revival in fortunes.

It was Morgan's goal, a far-post header from Gary Penrice's 83rd-minute free-kick, that brought about victory at Swansea City in his first full appearance. Thereafter, a purple patch of 7 goals in 3 games endeared Morgan to the Rovers supporters and began to restore some belief in a youthful side's ability. His convincing hat-trick against Rotherham United in mid-October brought the long-awaited first victory at Eastville and this was followed up by two first-half goals at Doncaster Rovers seven days later.

Eastville Stadium sees the supermarket development on what was once the training pitch and greyhound kennels. The football club left the stadium in May 1986

Indeed, on the stroke of half-time at Belle Vue, as Gary Smart, on as an early substitute for his debut, rounded goalkeeper Paul Allen, it appeared Rovers might be about to repeat their prolific goalscoring of the previous week. As it happened, Smart hit the side-netting – the goal for which he would forever remain a hero in Rovers' hearts would not be scored until New Year's Day 1987.

The season was saved by a run of 10 wins in 16 League games between mid-October and February. White's hat-trick against Darlington in January was the first by a Rovers player at Eastville since Boxing Day 1979 and his goal seven minutes before half-time from Mark O'Connor's centre against Doncaster Rovers completed a League double. Severe weather conditions meant Rovers played no away League games between Boxing Day and 4 February, when they won at Bolton Wanderers. Yet this more positive mid-season spell also included a 6-1 defeat at Bournemouth and a 4-0 loss at Wigan Athletic. Rovers were to lose 4-0 at York City and in the FA Cup at Luton Town as well as 6-0 at Walsall. The total of 75 goals conceded in the League was only exceeded once since 1967/68.

Rovers played nine games in March and didn't win any. April opened without Paul Randall, who joined Yeovil Town on a free transfer, but with a full League debut for Phil Purnell, another player set to figure prominently in years to come. Despite his presence and a 57th-minute lead over Wigan Athletic through Stevenson's shot, an instant equaliser from a Graham Barrow header deprived Rovers of a much-needed victory. When Rovers did win, it was at the unlikely setting of Derby County's Baseball Ground,

Morgan and White scoring after Alan Buckley had missed a penalty for the home side. Purnell scored twice at Lincoln City in the penultimate fixture when Morgan, easily top scorer with 16 goals compared to White's 12, ended up in goal after Ron Green had been injured.

White's goal at Chesterfield in November had been expunged when the game was abandoned due to fog with the score 1-1 at half-time. When the game was replayed in April, it drew a crowd of 1,800, the lowest at a Rovers game all season, with Tony Reid and Phil Walker scoring for the home side, who won 2-0. The return game 11 days later was to be the final game ever played at Eastville. A crowd of only 3,576 saw Morgan's goal earn a 1-1 draw, Brian Scrimgeour scoring for Chesterfield. Few of those present suspected that this really was a final farewell to Rovers' home since 1897. A moment of history passed by and events over the summer led Rovers towards a decade of exile from the city of Bristol. The immediate effect of Rovers' departure was that a fourth weekly greyhound meeting could be added to Eastville's schedule, rendering it the busiest greyhound track in the United Kingdom. Twelve acres were sold to a supermarket chain for £2,000,000 plus an annual income of £150,000, leaving a once-glorious stadium a very sorry sight.

The newly sponsored Milk Cup saw Rovers defeat Newport County over two legs, before two Tommy Wright penalties at St Andrew's helped ease Division One Birmingham City through over two legs. Randall scored in three of the four games in this tournament. The former Rovers winger Ray Graydon enjoyed a third success in this competition, this time as assistant manager to the victorious Oxford United side that beat Queen's Park Rangers in the final. An early exit from the Freight Rover Trophy was coupled with defeat in the Gloucestershire Cup final. Bristol City's Steve Johnson did not score in the League all season for his club, but his second-half penalty at Ashton Gate in September enabled the Robins to regain the trophy.

In the FA Cup, Gerry Francis scored his only goal for Rovers to seal a 3-1 victory at Brentford and a win at Swansea City was set up by Morgan's first-minute penalty. The third round brought Division One Leicester City and a 9,392 crowd to Eastville for the last big occasion the old stadium was to host. 44-year-old goalkeeping coach Bob Wilson came within a whisker of being called into the side, but it was a recognizable Rovers side that matched Leicester in an evenly contested first-half. Five minutes after half-time, after Tanner had been fouled by Russell Osman, Stevenson fired in a 30-yard free-kick to put Rovers ahead. Three minutes later, with the crowd still buzzing, Morgan scored a second in off a post and he repeated the feat 16 minutes from time, rounding the goalkeeper after exchanging passes with Mark O'Connor. Despite Gary McAllister's penalty, following a foul by Tim Parkin, Rovers had secured a major FA Cup victory, their first over top division opposition for 28 years. Parkin, who played in more games than any other Rovers player in 1985/86, conceded an own goal as Rovers crashed out of the cup on Luton Town's artificial pitch.

FOOTBALL LEAGUE DIVISION THREE

Date	Opponent	ATT		Score	G	2	3	4	5	6	7	8	9	10	11	SUBSTITUTES	GOALSCORERS
18/08/85	DARLINGTON	4196	A	3-3	GREEN	SPRING	DAVIES	STEVENSON	PARKIN	JONES	BADOCK	O'CONNOR	RANDALL	PENRICE	TANNER	WHITE 11	BADOCK, STEVENSON pen, WHITE
24/08/85	BRENTFORD	4140	H	0-1	GREEN	SPRING	DAVIES	STEVENSON	PARKIN	JONES	BADOCK	O'CONNOR	RANDALL	PENRICE	TANNER	WHITE 2	
26/08/85	READING	3529	A	2-3	GREEN	SPRING	DAVIES	STEVENSON	PARKIN	JONES	BADOCK	O'CONNOR	WHITE	PENRICE	BATER		DAVIES, PENRICE
31/08/85	DERBY COUNTY	4961	H	0-0	GREEN	SPRING	DAVIES	COCKRAM	PARKIN	JONES	BADOCK	O'CONNOR	WHITE	PENRICE	BATER	SCALES 4	
07/09/85	NEWPORT COUNTY	2775	A	0-3	VAUGHAN	SPRING	BATER	OBI	PARKIN	JONES	BADOCK	O'CONNOR	RANDALL	PENRICE	WHITE	TANNER 7	
14/09/85	LINCOLN CITY	3077	H	0-0	VAUGHAN	SCALES	BATER	FRANCIS	PARKIN	JONES	BADOCK	O'CONNOR	RANDALL	PENRICE	WHITE	MORGAN 2	
17/09/85	WOLVES	3244	A	4-3	VAUGHAN	SPRING	BATER	FRANCIS	PARKIN	ENGLAND	BADOCK	WHITE	MORGAN	RANDALL	O'CONNOR	DAVIES 6	RANDALL, BADOCK 2, WHITE
21/09/85	WALSALL	3787	H	0-1	VAUGHAN	DAVIES	BATER	TANNER	PARKIN	ENGLAND	WHITE	MORGAN	RANDALL	PENRICE	O'CONNOR	BADOCK 10	
28/09/85	SWANSEA CITY	4008	H	1-0	VAUGHAN	DAVIES	BATER	STEVENSON	PARKIN	ENGLAND	BADOCK	STEVENSON	MORGAN	RANDALL	O'CONNOR	WHITE 7	MORGAN
01/10/85	NOTTS COUNTY	3549	H	1-1	GREEN	DAVIES	BATER	STEVENSON	PARKIN	ENGLAND	WHITE	SPRING	MORGAN	RANDALL	O'CONNOR	TANNER 10	PENRICE
05/10/85	PLYMOUTH ARGYLE	5662	A	2-4	GREEN	BATER	DAVIES	STEVENSON	PARKIN	ENGLAND	WHITE	FRANCIS	MORGAN	RANDALL	O'CONNOR	SMART 8	MORGAN 2
12/10/85	ROTHERHAM UNITED	3499	H	5-2	GREEN	BATER	DAVIES	STEVENSON	PARKIN	ENGLAND	WHITE	SMART	MORGAN	RANDALL	O'CONNOR	MEHEW 9	WHITE, MORGAN 3, PARKIN
19/10/85	DONCASTER ROVERS	3032	A	0-0	GREEN	TANNER	DAVIES	STEVENSON	PARKIN	ENGLAND	WHITE	SMART	MORGAN	PENRICE	O'CONNOR	RANDALL 4	
22/10/85	BOLTON WANDERERS	4308	H	2-1	GREEN	TANNER	DAVIES	STEVENSON	PARKIN	ENGLAND	WHITE	BATER	MORGAN	PENRICE	O'CONNOR		WHITE, STEVENSON
26/10/85	AFC BOURNEMOUTH	3798	A	1-6	GREEN	TANNER	BATER	STEVENSON	PARKIN	ENGLAND	WHITE	TANNER	MORGAN	PENRICE	O'CONNOR	RANDALL 6	RANDALL
02/11/85	YORK CITY	4174	H	0-1	GREEN	TANNER	BATER	RANDALL	JONES	JONES	PENRICE	TANNER	MORGAN	WHITE	O'CONNOR		
05/11/85	BURY	2959	H	2-1	GREEN	BATER	BATER	STEVENSON	PARKIN	JONES	PENRICE	TANNER	MORGAN	WHITE	O'CONNOR		TANNER, WHITE
09/11/85	BLACKPOOL	4707	H	2-4	GREEN	BATER	DAVIES	FRANCIS	PARKIN	JONES	PENRICE	TANNER	MORGAN	WHITE	O'CONNOR		TANNER, MORGAN
23/11/85	CARDIFF CITY	4563	H	2-1	GREEN	SCALES	BATER	PENRICE	JONES	JONES	FRANCIS	TANNER	MORGAN	WHITE	O'CONNOR		O'CONNOR, PENRICE
14/12/85	GILLINGHAM	4224	H	1-0	GREEN	BATER	BATER	PENRICE	PARKIN	JONES	FRANCIS	TANNER	MORGAN	WHITE	O'CONNOR		MORGAN
22/12/85	BRENTFORD	5742	A	0-1	GREEN	BATER	TANNER	STEVENSON	PARKIN	JONES	FRANCIS	TANNER	MORGAN	WHITE	O'CONNOR		
26/12/85	WIGAN ATHLETIC	3711	A	0-4	GREEN	JONES	TANNER	STEVENSON	PARKIN	JONES	FRANCIS	TANNER	MORGAN	WHITE	O'CONNOR		
28/12/85	READING	7555	H	0-2	CARTER	JONES	TANNER	RANDALL	PARKIN	JONES	FRANCIS	TANNER	RANDALL	WHITE	O'CONNOR		
18/01/86	DARLINGTON	3395	H	3-1	GREEN	SPRING	BATER	STEVENSON	PARKIN	JONES	FRANCIS	PENRICE	MORGAN	WHITE	O'CONNOR	NOBLE 7	WHITE 3
01/02/86	NEWPORT COUNTY	3284	A	2-0	GREEN	SCALES	TANNER	STEVENSON	PARKIN	JONES	FRANCIS	PENRICE	MORGAN	WHITE	O'CONNOR	BATER 5	O'CONNOR, MORGAN
04/02/86	BOLTON WANDERERS	3672	A	2-0	GREEN	SCALES	TANNER	STEVENSON	PARKIN	SPRING	FRANCIS	PENRICE	MORGAN	WHITE	O'CONNOR	NOBLE 9	PARKIN, WHITE
08/02/86	DONCASTER ROVERS	3894	H	2-0	GREEN	SCALES	TANNER	STEVENSON	PARKIN	SPRING	FRANCIS	PENRICE	MORGAN	WHITE	O'CONNOR		WHITE
01/03/86	SWANSEA CITY	3098	A	0-0	GREEN	SPRING	TANNER	STEVENSON	PARKIN	SPRING	FRANCIS	PENRICE	RANDALL	WHITE	O'CONNOR		
04/03/86	NOTTS COUNTY	3183	A	1-2	GREEN	SCALES	TANNER	TANNER	PARKIN	SPRING	FRANCIS	PENRICE	MORGAN	WHITE	O'CONNOR	SPRING 10	MORGAN
08/03/86	PLYMOUTH ARGYLE	4667	H	1-2	GREEN	SCALES	TANNER	TANNER	PARKIN	SPRING	FRANCIS	PENRICE	MORGAN	WHITE	NOBLE	BADOCK 7	
12/03/86	YORK CITY	2857	A	0-4	GREEN	SCALES	TANNER	TANNER	PARKIN	SPRING	NOBLE	PENRICE	MORGAN	WHITE	O'CONNOR		
15/03/86	ROTHERHAM UNITED	2734	A	0-2	GREEN	SCALES	BATER	SPRING	PARKIN	SPRING	FRANCIS	PENRICE	MORGAN	WHITE	O'CONNOR		
18/03/86	WALSALL	3734	H	0-6	GREEN	SCALES	BATER	BATER	PARKIN	JONES	BADOCK	PENRICE	MORGAN	WHITE	STEVENSON	SCALES 6	
22/03/86	AFC BOURNEMOUTH	3928	H	1-1	GREEN	BATER	BATER	TANNER	PARKIN	JONES	WHITE	PENRICE	MORGAN	STEVENSON	O'CONNOR	PURNELL 7	PENRICE, WHITE
25/03/86	WOLVES	3378	A	2-3	GREEN	BATER	BATER	TANNER	PARKIN	JONES	BADOCK	PENRICE	MORGAN	STEVENSON	PURNELL	MEHEW 11	MORGAN pen
29/03/86	BRISTOL CITY	12171	A	0-2	GREEN	SCALES	BATER	TANNER	PARKIN	JONES	FRANCIS	PENRICE	MORGAN	STEVENSON	O'CONNOR		
01/04/86	WIGAN ATHLETIC	3428	H	1-1	GREEN	SCALES	BATER	ENGLAND	PARKIN	JONES	BADOCK	PENRICE	MORGAN	STEVENSON	PURNELL	MEHEW 7	STEVENSON
05/04/86	BURY	1866	A	1-1	GREEN	SCALES	BATER	ENGLAND	PARKIN	ILES	WHITE	PENRICE	FRANCIS	PURNELL	STEVENSON	MEHEW 10	MORGAN
09/04/86	DERBY COUNTY	11033	A	2-0	GREEN	SPRING	BATER	TANNER	PARKIN	JONES	BADOCK	PENRICE	MORGAN	STEVENSON	PURNELL	NOBLE 4	WHITE, MORGAN
12/04/86	BLACKPOOL	3472	H	1-0	GREEN	SPRING	BATER	ENGLAND	PARKIN	JONES	FRANCIS	PENRICE	MORGAN	PURNELL	BADOCK	PURNELL 11	PENRICE
15/04/86	CHESTERFIELD	1800	A	0-2	GREEN	TANNER	BATER	ENGLAND	PARKIN	JONES	FRANCIS	PENRICE	MORGAN	STEVENSON	PURNELL	STEVENSON 5	
19/04/86	CARDIFF CITY	2735	A	1-1	GREEN	SCALES	ENGLAND	TANNER	PARKIN	JONES	FRANCIS	PENRICE	MORGAN	PURNELL	O'CONNOR	PURNELL 2	SCALES
22/04/86	CHESTERFIELD	9926	H	0-1	GREEN	SCALES	ENGLAND	TANNER	PARKIN	JONES	FRANCIS	PENRICE	MORGAN	STEVENSON	PURNELL	BADOCK 11	
26/04/86	LINCOLN CITY	3576	A	2-2	GREEN	SCALES	ENGLAND	NOBLE	PARKIN	JONES	FRANCIS	TANNER	MORGAN	WHITE	O'CONNOR	STEVENSON 5	MORGAN
30/04/86	LINCOLN CITY	2233	H	2-2	GREEN	SCALES	ENGLAND	STEVENSON	STEVENSON	JONES	FRANCIS	PENRICE	MORGAN	WHITE	O'CONNOR	PURNELL 2	
03/05/86	GILLINGHAM	2050	A	0-2	GREEN	SCALES	BATER	STEVENSON	CARR	JONES	FRANCIS	PENRICE	MORGAN	WHITE	O'CONNOR	BADOCK 11	

FA CUP

Date	Opponent	ATT		Score	G	2	3	4	5	6	7	8	9	10	11	SUBSTITUTES	GOALSCORERS
16/11/85	BRENTFORD	4716	A	3-1	GREEN	SCALES	BATER	TANNER	PARKIN	JONES	FRANCIS	PENRICE	MORGAN	WHITE	O'CONNOR	RANDALL 2	PENRICE, WHITE, FRANCIS
07/12/85	SWANSEA CITY	4230	H	2-1	GREEN	SCALES	BATER	TANNER	PARKIN	JONES	PENRICE	TANNER	MORGAN	PENRICE	BATER		MORGAN pen, WHITE
04/01/86	LEICESTER CITY	9392	H	3-1	GREEN	SCALES	ENGLAND	STEVENSON	PARKIN	JONES	PENRICE	TANNER	MORGAN	WHITE	O'CONNOR		STEVENSON, MORGAN 2
25/01/86	LUTON TOWN	12463	A	0-4	GREEN	SCALES	BATER	STEVENSON	PARKIN	JONES	FRANCIS	TANNER	MORGAN	WHITE	O'CONNOR		

LEAGUE CUP

Date	Opponent	ATT		Score	G	2	3	4	5	6	7	8	9	10	11	SUBSTITUTES	GOALSCORERS
20/08/85	NEWPORT COUNTY	2777	H	2-0	GREEN	SPRING	DAVIES	STEVENSON	PARKIN	JONES	BADOCK	O'CONNOR	WHITE	PENRICE	TANNER	RANDALL 2	RANDALL, BADOCK
03/09/85	NEWPORT COUNTY	2012	A	0-1	GREEN	SPRING	TANNER	COCKRAM	PARKIN	JONES	RANDALL	O'CONNOR	WHITE	PENRICE	BATER		
24/09/85	BIRMINGHAM CITY	4332	H	2-3	GREEN	SCALES	BATER	FRANCIS	PARKIN	JONES	PENRICE	STEVENSON	RANDALL	WHITE	O'CONNOR	BADOCK 4	O'CONNOR, RANDALL
08/10/85	BIRMINGHAM CITY	3686	A	1-2	GREEN	TANNER	DAVIES	STEVENSON	PARKIN	JONES	BADOCK	FRANCIS	WHITE	RANDALL	O'CONNOR	ENGLAND 6	RANDALL

FREIGHT ROVER TROPHY

Date	Opponent	ATT		Score	G	2	3	4	5	6	7	8	9	10	11	SUBSTITUTES	GOALSCORERS
15/01/86	HEREFORD UNITED	1770	A	0-2	GREEN	SCALES	PORTCH	STEVENSON	PARKIN	JONES	BADOCK	PENRICE	MORGAN	STEVENSON	O'CONNOR	SMART 7	O'CONNOR, WHITE
21/01/86	SWINDON TOWN	2335	H	2-1	GREEN	SCALES	BATER	FRANCIS	PARKIN	SPRING	TANNER	PENRICE	MORGAN	WHITE	O'CONNOR	RANDALL 7, PORTCH 3	

GLOUCESTERSHIRE CUP FINAL

Date	Opponent	ATT		Score	G	2	3	4	5	6	7	8	9	10	11	SUBSTITUTES	GOALSCORERS
09/09/85	BRISTOL CITY	4894	A	0-1	VAUGHAN	SCALES	TANNER	FRANCIS	PARKIN	JONES	SPRING	O'CONNOR	RANDALL	PENRICE	BATER		

PLAYERS	APP	SUB	GLS
BADOCK S	14	3	3
BATER P	26	1	
CARR D	1		
CARTER T	2		.
COCKRAM A	1		
DAVIES I	13	1	1
ENGLAND M	17		
FRANCIS G	28		
GREEN R	38		
ILES R	1		
JONES V	32		
MEHEW D	0	4	
MORGAN T	35	1	16
NOBLE W	3	3	
OBI A	1		
O'CONNOR M	34		2
PARKIN T	43		5
PENRICE G	39	1	2
PURNELL P	9	2	2
RANDALL P	15	2	2
SCALES J	27	1	1
SMART G	2	1	
SPRING A	18	1	
STEVENSON B	29	1	3
TANNER N	35	2	2
VAUGHAN J	6	3	
WHITE S	37	3	12

1986/87

In May 1986, to save the club an annual cost of £30,000 plus expenses to hire Eastville, Rovers' board of directors took the historic decision to leave the club's spiritual home. A groundsharing scheme was drawn up with Bath City, whereby Rovers paid £65,000 per year to play home matches at Twerton Park. This ground, constructed on recreation land donated in 1909 by Thomas Carr and opened as Innox Park on 26 June of that year, had been the hosts' home since 1932 and was built on the side of a hill on the edge of the city, some 15 miles from the traditional hotbed of Rovers support in east Bristol. Rovers by name, Rovers by nature, it appeared. It was a revolutionary move, in that a League club was sharing with a non-League side in a different city but, in 1986, it was an integral part of Rovers' immediate survival. An emergency meeting of the Western League committee on 23 July 1986 discussed the knock-on effects of the move, with Bath City reserves due to play at Hambrook, Rovers' training ground, though they later began a groundsharing scheme with Radstock Town. Rovers' identity was questioned, support was down 25 per cent on the previous season and financial hardships continued, but the club survived. Ultimately, success, as epitomized by the Championship season of 1989/90, was to lead to the club's return to Bristol after a decade of groundsharing.

Bath, 'that city of medicinal springs and homoeopathic winters,' (Cohen) had enjoyed prosperity in Roman times and had been strategic enough to be selected by Dunstan as the site for King Edgar's coronation in AD 959. 'The resort of the sound rather than the sick,' as Daniel Defoe described it, had risen to prominence in Georgian times, its population rising from some 2,000 in 1700 to 34,000 by 1800. To the west of the city, Twerton parish, previously owned by Queen Edith, the wife of Edward the Confessor, had been under the jurisdiction of the Bishop of Coutances in 1086. A portion of the parish had been added to Bath through the 1868 Boundary Act and the entirety of the parish of St Michael, whose church was rebuilt in 1885/86 though its registers date from 1538, was added by the Bath (Extension) Order of 9 November 1911. The foundation stone of St Peter's, Twerton had been laid on St Peter's day 1876 by Beatrice Buckle, the wife of a former vicar of the parish and the church had been consecrated four years later to the day, on the warm Tuesday morning of 29 June 1880, by Lord Charles Hervey, Bishop of Bath and Wells. The population of the ecclesiastical parish of Twerton in 1911 was 13,807, having been 7,683 in 1893. Twerton, where the novelist Henry Fielding had lived in the 19th century, had been connected to Bath by the electric tramway, which opened on New Year's Day 1904, to replace a previous horse-drawn system, and which offered a fleet of 36 double-deckers, six single-deckers and a water car with snow broom.

Rovers rented Twerton Park from Bath City for an annual fee of £20,000 plus a percentage of gate receipts, while the club's offices remained in Keynsham. Twerton Park was an unlikely setting for League football, with a stand of 780 black and white seats built into the hillside. Cliftonhill, home of Albion Rovers, was the only similar example in British first-class football. 'The views are spectacular and it is well worth

Bristol Rovers 1986/87. Back row: Noble, Weston, Mehew, Portch, Purnell. Middle row: Dolling (Physio), Boyle, Scales, Carr, Carter, Morgan, Tanner, Hibbitt, Kendall (Kit man). Second row: Penrice, Jones, G Dunford (Director), Gould (Manager), D Dunford, R Craig (Directors), Alexander, Smart. Front row: Gould, Eyles, Yates, Carota, Davidson, Howells, Dryden (Apprentices)

the…walk up the steep Lansdown hill.' (Fanny Charles, Blackmore Vale, 12.5.2000, P60.) Towering above was Beckford's Tower, a 154-ft folly built in 1825 for the eccentric William Thomas Beckford by his protégé, Henry Edmund Goodridge, and under which both men are buried. Residents in the aptly named Freeview Road could watch home matches from their upstairs windows. It would take some getting used to.

Bobby Gould's side opened the season with a 3-0 win at Walsall. It was a poor indication of results to follow, as Rovers lost 21 League games, conceded 75 goals for a second consecutive season and finished in 19th place. Even Walsall were to gain revenge by defeating Rovers 3-0 in the return fixture. Four new faces appeared in the side for the opening day. Kenny Hibbitt, who scored the opening goal, and Tarki Micallef added experience to a side boasting many young players developed at Eastville, such as Tanner, Scales, Carter, Penrice and Smart. Other youngsters were given opportunities, Gerry Francis appeared just 5 times in the League and the only really consistent newcomer to emerge was Geoff Twentyman.

Nonetheless, the first bricks for the 1989/90 Championship season were being positioned. Twentyman, an August signing from Preston North End, missed only 3 League games, Gary Penrice only 4, Vaughan Jones, Ian Alexander and Phil Purnell enjoyed protracted spells in the side, while 17-year-old Steve Yates made his League debut on Shrove Tuesday at Darlington. As in the Championship season, David Mehew was Rovers' top scorer, his tally of 10 League goals giving him two more than Trevor Morgan, who joined Bristol City in January.

The start of the new season coincided with news of the death of George Endicott, at the age of 92. He was a well-respected club trainer through many generations of Bristol

Rovers' amateur forward Mark Johns heads Rovers' winning goal after coming from two goals behind to defeat Chesterfield 3-2 at Twerton

Rovers players. The first home League game at Twerton Park, or the 'Azteca Stadium', as Gould termed it, resulted in a 1-0 victory over Bolton Wanderers, despite the sending off of Nicky Tanner, to send Rovers briefly to the top of Division Three. A crowd of 4,092 saw Trevor Morgan, the scorer of the club's final goal at Eastville, register the first League goal on the new ground from a 17th-minute penalty after he had been fouled by Mark Came. However, both the crowd and the result were misleading. Attendances dropped, Rovers lost seven times at Twerton Park in the League alone and survival was not assured until the final game of the season. In a bid to boost funds, the home game with Swindon Town over Easter was held at Ashton Gate and an inflated crowd of over 8,000 saw Rovers lead 3-1 shortly after half-time before losing, with the former Rovers striker Steve White and Dave Bamber, a competitor at the 1979 World Student Games, among the goalscorers.

In moving to Bath, Rovers had lost a considerable proportion of the traditional support. Season 1986/87, amid poor on-field performances and before a new generation of supporters could be found in the new surroundings, marks the lowest point in League attendance in Rovers' history. The seasonal home average of 3,246 remains the lowest the club experienced in the 20th century. On their travels, only 1,206 saw the defeat at Doncaster Rovers in May, the lowest attendance at a post-war League game involving Bristol Rovers. There were also some crushing blows, with Port Vale, Gillingham and Wigan Athletic all emulating Swindon Town's four goals. Rovers lost 5-0 at Mansfield Town in January, with Keith Cassells becoming the eighth opponent to score four goals in a League game, and 6-1 at Blackpool, for whom Paul Stewart, a scorer for Tottenham Hotspur in the 1991 FA Cup final, scored twice.

A 2-2 draw with Newport County in December, Rovers' fourth consecutive home draw in League and cup, marked a new experiment, as it was Rovers' first home League game on a Sunday. The attendance was 2,660 and this well-intentioned plan was soon scrapped. It survived long enough, however, for Rovers to beat York City through a Gary Penrice goal on a Friday night in January and to stage the Swindon Town game at Ashton Gate on a Sunday. The concept was to attract spectators at a time when there was no competition from Bristol City or the rugby clubs of Bristol and Bath. Not only did this imply Rovers were settling for second-best, something the 1989/90 season was to strive to contradict, but it was a scheme to which supporters did not readily respond. Only 2,597 saw the victory over York City and Rovers reverted to losing or drawing home matches on Saturdays.

Rovers were involved in two League fixtures in the north-east within four weeks of each other in the spring. The game at Ayresome Park was won for Middlesbrough by the future England International Stuart Ripley's 60th-minute goal, in a game where Boro's full-back Brian Laws slipped in taking a penalty in first-half injury time, sending the ball shooting away for a throw-in and leaving him in a crumpled heap, out injured for the rest of the season. A 1-1 draw at Darlington on Shrove Tuesday featured two goals in a minute during the second half. Rovers' directors generously rewarded travelling fans with a half-time urn of tea. By the end of the match, the dregs in the plastic cups had frozen in the chill north-eastern wind. The Darlington game was one in which 17-year-old Steve Yates, a name for the future, made his League debut in a side including experienced journeymen David Rushbury and Bob Newton.

One of the most important goals in Rovers' history. Winger Phil Purnell beats Newport County goalkeeper Dillon to secure the points and to ensure that they were not relegated

Undeniably the game of the season was at Ashton Gate in an early kick-off on New Year's Day. Rovers were clearly underdogs and a strong Bristol City side pounded Tim Carter's goal. City had 11 shots on target to Rovers' two and, in addition, Paul Fitzpatrick and Steve Neville both hit the Rovers bar. To make matters worse, an injury to Carter meant David Mehew spent the final 15 minutes of the first-half in goal as ten-man Rovers attempted to stem City's flow. Then, incredibly, three minutes from time, Gary Smart's 20-yard shot dipped under the bar to give Rovers an unlikely victory. It was results such as this and the four wins in the last eight League games that kept Rovers in Division Three. The largest was 4-0 at home to Carlisle United, even though Jeff Meacham, a new signing from Trowbridge Town, who had opened the scoring with his first goal for the club, ended up in goal with the veteran Paul Bradshaw off the field injured. Meacham scored 5 goals to help keep Rovers alive, two of them at home to Chester City, when Rovers clawed back a 2-1 deficit to win after Graham Barrow, scorer of the visitors' second goal had been sent off before half-time for a foul on Rovers' matchwinner John Scales. Ultimately, Rovers required a point at Newport County on the final day to retain their Division Three place, a mission accomplished with Phil Purnell scoring the game's only goal.

For the second year running, Rovers drew Brentford in the FA Cup. This year, after poor weather saw the tie called off several times, Brentford won in a replay, the second of three meetings of the clubs in December, with Ian Weston becoming the first Rovers player ever to be sent off on his club debut, a record matched by Wayne Carlisle in March 2002. A former Rovers player, Gary Mabbutt, scored for Tottenham Hotspur in their 3-2 FA Cup final defeat at the hands of Coventry City as did Clive Allen, whose younger brother Bradley was to join Rovers in November 2002. Reading put six goals past Rovers in a two-legged League Cup tie, with Trevor Senior scoring a hat-trick and substitute Dean Horrix once as Rovers crashed 4-0 at Elm Park. The Gloucestershire Cup final was held over to the following season as fixtures piled up towards the season's close, but Bristol City nonetheless effectively knocked Rovers out of the Freight Rover Trophy. Their 3-0 victory, through goals from David Moyes, Rob Newman and Alan Walsh, remains Rovers' heaviest ever defeat in this competition.

1987/88

Three games into the new season, with Rovers sitting on top of Division Three, the trials and tribulations of 1986/87 seemed a thing of the past. Rovers won their first two home games of 1987/88, at Twerton Park, by convincing margins. By February, Rovers hovered precariously above the relegation zone. However, March saw the side's first back-to-back wins of the season and nine victories in the final 14 League matches saw the team rise from 20th to the heady heights of eighth in the table.

It had been a summer of significant change among the playing staff. In truth, Rovers could not afford the larger wage demands of more experienced professionals and the emphasis was very much on untried youth, especially as two substitutes were now required for every League game. While Kenny Hibbitt remained at the club, it was John

SEASON 1986/87

FOOTBALL LEAGUE DIVISION THREE

Date	Opponent	V	Score	ATT	1	2	3	4	5	6	7	8	9	10	11	SUBSTITUTES	GOALSCORERS
23/08/86	WALSALL	A	3-0	6269	CARTER	TANNER	SCALES	JONES	SMALLEY	HIBBITT	ALEXANDER	PENRICE	MORGAN	MEHEW	MICALLEF	ALEXANDER 10	HIBBITT, MORGAN 2
30/08/86	BOLTON WANDERERS	H	1-0	4092	CARTER	TANNER	SCALES	JONES	SMALLEY	HIBBITT	FRANCIS	PENRICE	MORGAN	MEHEW	PURNELL	SMART 7	MORGAN pen
06/09/86	YORK CITY	A	0-1	3795	CARTER	TANNER	SCALES	HIBBITT	TWENTYMAN	JONES	ALEXANDER	PENRICE	MORGAN	MEHEW	MICALLEF	SMART 4	
13/09/86	MANSFIELD TOWN	H	0-0	2802	CARTER	SMALLEY	SMALLEY	HIBBITT	TWENTYMAN	JONES	ALEXANDER	PENRICE	MORGAN	MICALLEF	MICALLEF	SMART 10	
17/09/86	MIDDLESBROUGH	A	1-2	3768	CARTER	SMALLEY	JONES	FRANCIS	TWENTYMAN	SMALLEY	ALEXANDER	PENRICE	MORGAN	MEHEW	TANNER	SMART 11	MICALLEF
20/09/86	ROTHERHAM UNITED	A	1-0	2702	CARTER	SMALLEY	JONES	FRANCIS	TWENTYMAN	SMALLEY	ALEXANDER	PENRICE	MORGAN	MEHEW	TANNER	SMART 10	TANNER
27/09/86	BLACKPOOL	H	2-2	3417	HAMMOND	SCALES	CARR	SMART	TWENTYMAN	SMALLEY	ALEXANDER	PENRICE	MORGAN	MEHEW	TANNER	SCALES 2	JONES, MEHEW
30/09/86	NOTTS COUNTY	A	0-3	3409	HAMMOND	HAMMOND	DRYDEN	SMART	TWENTYMAN	TWENTYMAN	ALEXANDER	PENRICE	MORGAN	MEHEW	TANNER	NOBLE 7	
04/10/86	CHESTERFIELD	H	3-2	2768	HAMMOND	PURNELL	CARR	NOBLE	SMALLEY	SMALLEY	SCALES	PENRICE	JOHNS	MEHEW	TANNER	SCALES 2	MEHEW, ALEXANDER, JOHNS
11/10/86	WIGAN ATHLETIC	A	3-4	2438	CARTER	CARTER	TANNER	HIBBITT	NOBLE	SMALLEY	SCALES	PENRICE	JOHNS	MEHEW	SCALES	NOBLE 7	MEHEW 2, HIBBITT pen
18/10/86	PORT VALE	H	0-0	3053	CARTER	TANNER	TANNER	HIBBITT	TWENTYMAN	SMALLEY	ALEXANDER	PENRICE	MORGAN	MEHEW	ALEXANDER	CARR 11	
21/10/86	FULHAM	A	2-2	2351	CARTER	TANNER	TANNER	HIBBITT	TWENTYMAN	CARR	CARTER	PENRICE	MORGAN	MEHEW	ALEXANDER	CARR 10	MORGAN, MEHEW
25/10/86	CARLISLE UNITED	A	0-2	2799	CARTER	CARTER	TANNER	MICALLEF	TWENTYMAN	JONES	CARTER	PENRICE	MORGAN	MEHEW	NOBLE	CARR 11	
04/11/86	SWINDON TOWN	A	2-1	9070	CARTER	CARTER	TANNER	HIBBITT	TWENTYMAN	JONES	ALEXANDER	HIBBITT	MORGAN	MEHEW	NOBLE	CARR 10	MORGAN 2
08/11/86	BURY	H	1-1	2947	CARTER	CARTER	TANNER	HIBBITT	TWENTYMAN	JONES	ALEXANDER	PENRICE	MORGAN	MEHEW	MICALLEF		MEHEW
22/11/86	CHESTER CITY	A	1-3	2026	CARTER	CARTER	TANNER	HIBBITT	TWENTYMAN	JONES	ALEXANDER	PENRICE	MORGAN	MEHEW	TANNER	CARR 10	MORGAN
14/12/86	NEWPORT COUNTY	A	1-4	2660	CARTER	CARTER	CARR	HIBBITT	TWENTYMAN	JONES	NOBLE	PENRICE	MORGAN	PURNELL	TANNER	SMART 7	SMART, NOBLE
19/12/86	GILLINGHAM	H	1-4	4488	CARTER	HIBBITT	DRYDEN	SMART	TWENTYMAN	JONES	NOBLE	PENRICE	MORGAN	PURNELL	TANNER	MICALLEF 8	MORGAN
26/12/86	AFC BOURNEMOUTH	H	3-3	3573	CARTER	SCALES	CARR	NOBLE	TWENTYMAN	JONES	ALEXANDER	PENRICE	MORGAN	ALEXANDER	TANNER	PENRICE 7	SMART, MEHEW
28/12/86	BRISTOL CITY	A	2-1	4510	CARTER	SCALES	CARR	SMART	TWENTYMAN	JONES	PENRICE	SMART	MORGAN	PURNELL	TANNER	NOBLE 2	SMART
01/01/87	DARLINGTON	A	1-0	1722	CARTER	SCALES	CARR	SMART	TWENTYMAN	JONES	DRYDEN	SMART	MORGAN	MEHEW	TANNER	PURNELL 3	SMART, PENRICE
17/01/87	BOLTON WANDERERS	A	2-2	4087	CARTER	SCALES	CARR	TWENTYMAN	TWENTYMAN	CARR	DRYDEN	WESTON	TURNER	MICALLEF	TANNER	PURNELL 2	PENRICE
23/01/87	YORK CITY	H	1-0	2597	CARTER	SCALES	CARR	TWENTYMAN	TWENTYMAN	CARR	PENRICE	SMART	TURNER	MICALLEF	TANNER	SMART 9	
31/01/87	MANSFIELD TOWN	A	0-5	2718	CARTER	SCALES	PENRICE	WESTON	TWENTYMAN	CARR	RUSHBURY	SMART	TURNER	MICALLEF	TANNER	HIBBETT 4	
07/02/87	MIDDLESBROUGH	H	0-1	11639	CARTER	SCALES	SCALES	HIBBITT	TWENTYMAN	CARR	RUSHBURY	SMART	TURNER	MICALLEF	MICALLEF	MICALLEF 11	
14/02/87	NEWPORT COUNTY	H	0-2	2467	CARTER	SCALES	DRYDEN	HIBBITT	TWENTYMAN	CARR	PENRICE	PENRICE	MORGAN	ALEXANDER	TANNER	CLEMENT 4	
21/02/87	BLACKPOOL	A	1-6	3434	CARTER	SCALES	TANNER	HIBBITT	TWENTYMAN	CARR	PENRICE	ALEXANDER	TURNER	MEHEW	MICALLEF	PURNELL 9	MEHEW
28/02/87	NOTTS COUNTY	H	0-0	2978	CARTER	SCALES	TANNER	WESTON	TWENTYMAN	CAWLEY	RUSHBURY	PENRICE	NEWTON	MEHEW	NOBLE	ALEXANDER 10	
03/03/87	DARLINGTON	H	1-1	1350	CARTER	SCALES	TANNER	WESTON	TWENTYMAN	YATES	RUSHBURY	PENRICE	NEWTON	MEHEW	NOBLE	JONES 7	PENRICE
11/03/87	WALSALL	H	0-3	2282	CARTER	SCALES	RUSHBURY	WESTON	TWENTYMAN	RUSHBURY	PENRICE	TANNER	NEWTON	MEHEW	NOBLE		
14/03/87	PORT VALE	A	1-4	2758	CARTER	SCALES	TANNER	CARR	TWENTYMAN	TANNER	CLEMENT	PENRICE	NEWTON	PURNELL	HIBBITT	CAWLEY 4	PENRICE
18/03/87	FULHAM	H	0-0	2448	CARTER	SCALES	CARR	HIBBITT	TWENTYMAN	TANNER	CLEMENT	PENRICE	NEWTON	PURNELL	HIBBITT	SCALES 9	
21/03/87	WIGAN ATHLETIC	A	1-0	2635	BRADSHAW	SCALES	RUSHBURY	CARR	TWENTYMAN	TANNER	CLEMENT	TANNER	MEACHAM	TANNER	HIBBITT		PENRICE, TURNER, PURNELL pen
28/03/87	CHESTERFIELD	A	1-1	2157	BRADSHAW	JONES	CARTER	HIBBITT	TWENTYMAN	TANNER	CLEMENT	PENRICE	MEACHAM	MEACHAM	HIBBITT	MICALLEF 1	
04/04/87	BURY	A	0-1	1960	BRADSHAW	BRADSHAW	RUSHBURY	CARR	TWENTYMAN	TANNER	ALEXANDER	PENRICE	TURNER	SCALES	PURNELL	RUSHBURY 11	
11/04/87	SWINDON TOWN *	H	3-4	8196	BRADSHAW	JONES	CARTER	CAWLEY	TWENTYMAN	TANNER	PURNELL	PENRICE	TURNER	MEACHAM	HIBBITT		MEACHAM, PENRICE 2, PURNELL
18/04/87	BRISTOL CITY	A	0-2	4695	CARTER	JONES	CARTER	CAWLEY	TWENTYMAN	TANNER	PURNELL	PENRICE	TURNER	MEACHAM	HIBBITT		
20/04/87	AFC BOURNEMOUTH	A	0-2	10034	CARTER	BRADSHAW	CARTER	CAWLEY	TWENTYMAN	TANNER	ALEXANDER	PENRICE	TURNER	SCALES	PURNELL		
24/04/87	CARLISLE UNITED	H	4-0	2435	CARTER	JONES	CARTER	CAWLEY	TWENTYMAN	TANNER	PURNELL	PENRICE	TURNER	MEACHAM	HIBBITT	MICALLEF 1	MEACHAM 2, SCALES
25/04/87	GILLINGHAM	A	0-2	3166	CARTER	JONES	SCALES	CAWLEY	TWENTYMAN	TANNER	PURNELL	PENRICE	TURNER	MEACHAM	HIBBITT	RUSHBURY 11	
28/04/87	CHESTER CITY	H	3-2	2323	CARTER	JONES	CARTER	CAWLEY	TWENTYMAN	TANNER	SMART	ALEXANDER	TURNER	MEACHAM	MICALLEF	NEWTON 6	MEACHAM, HINCHLEY og
30/04/87	DARLINGTON	A	2-1	2765	CARTER	JONES	CARTER	CAWLEY	TWENTYMAN	TANNER	PURNELL	PENRICE	TURNER	MEACHAM	HIBBITT	RUSHBURY 10	
02/05/87	DONCASTER ROVERS	A	0-2	1206	CARTER	JONES	SCALES	JONES	TWENTYMAN	TANNER	SMART	PENRICE	TURNER	MEACHAM	HIBBITT	MEHEW 2	
04/05/87	BRENTFORD	H	0-3	3513	CARTER	SCALES	JONES	CAWLEY	TWENTYMAN	TANNER	PURNELL	PENRICE	TURNER	MEACHAM	HIBBITT	TURNER 4	MEACHAM, MEHEW
06/05/87	DONCASTER ROVERS	A	2-3	3003	CARTER	SCALES	CARTER	CAWLEY	TWENTYMAN	JONES	PURNELL	PENRICE	WESTON	MEACHAM	HIBBITT		PURNELL
09/05/87	NEWPORT COUNTY	A	1-0	3160	CARTER	JONES	RUSHBURY	CAWLEY	TWENTYMAN	TANNER	PURNELL	PENRICE	TURNER	MEACHAM	HIBBITT		

* played at Ashton Gate

FA CUP

Date	Opponent	V	Score	ATT	1	2	3	4	5	6	7	8	9	10	11	SUBSTITUTES	GOALSCORERS
03/12/86	BRENTFORD	H	0-0	3035	CARTER	SCALES	HIBBITT	HIBBITT	TWENTYMAN	JONES	ALEXANDER	PENRICE	MORGAN	MICALLEF	TANNER	PURNELL 10, NOBLE 7	
06/12/87	BRENTFORD	A	0-2	3848	CARTER	SCALES	CARR	HIBBITT	TWENTYMAN	JONES	WESTON	PENRICE	MORGAN	PURNELL	TANNER	NOBLE 4, BOYLE 7	

LEAGUE CUP

Date	Opponent	V	Score	ATT	1	2	3	4	5	6	7	8	9	10	11	SUBSTITUTES	GOALSCORERS
27/08/86	READING	H	1-2	3790	CARTER	TANNER	SCALES	JONES	CARR	HIBBITT	ALEXANDER	PENRICE	MORGAN	MEHEW	PURNELL	FRANCIS 6, SMART 11	PENRICE
03/09/86	READING	A	0-4	4300	CARTER	TANNER	SCALES	JONES	TWENTYMAN	HIBBITT	ALEXANDER	PENRICE	MORGAN	MEHEW	PURNELL	FRANCIS 7, CARR 11	

FREIGHT ROVER TROPHY

Date	Opponent	V	Score	ATT	1	2	3	4	5	6	7	8	9	10	11	SUBSTITUTES	GOALSCORERS
16/12/86	BRISTOL CITY	A	0-3	6903	CARTER	TANNER	HIBBITT	JONES	CARR	TWENTYMAN	ALEXANDER	PENRICE	MORGAN	PURNELL	NOBLE	SCALES 10, MEHEW 11	
07/12/86	EXETER CITY	H	1-1	1608	HIBBITT	SCALES	CARR	SMART	TWENTYMAN	JONES	DRYDEN	PENRICE	MORGAN	MEHEW	TANNER	MICALLEF 2, TURNER 7	MICALLEF

GLOUCESTERSHIRE CUP FINAL

Held over until next season

Appearances

PLAYERS	APP	SUB	GLS
ALEXANDER I	20	2	1
BRADSHAW P	5		
CARR D	17	3	
CARTER T	38		
CAWLEY T	9	1	
CLEMENT A	5	1	
DRYDEN R	6		
FRANCIS G	5		
HAMMOND N	3		
HIBBITT K	27	1	3
JOHNS M	2		1
JONES V	33		1
MEACHAM J	12		5
MEHEW D	20	1	10
MICALLEF C	15	3	1
MORGAN T	19		8
NEWTON R	7	1	
NOBLE W	13	2	1
PENRICE G	42	1	7
PURNELL P	18	3	3
RUSHBURY D	14	2	
SCALES J	41	2	1
SMALLEY M	10		
SMART G	9	7	4
TANNER N	44	1	1
TURNER G	16	1	
TWENTYMAN G	43		
WESTON I	11		
YATES S	2		
OWN GOAL			1

Bristol Rovers 1987/88. Back row: Purnell, Reece, Alexander, Portch, Martyn, Carter, Weston, Eaton, Penrice. Middle row: Howells, Jones, Boyle, Wiffill, Meacham, Turner, Mehew, Tanner, Carr, Twentyman, Dryden, Kendall (Kit Man). Front row: Stokes (Director), G Dunford (Director), Hibbitt (Asst Manager), D Dunford (Chairman), Francis (Manager), Craig (Director), Twyford (Secretary), Bulpin (Coach), Dolling (Physio)

Scales who left, joining Wimbledon in a £70,000 deal. Bobby Gould left the club for a third time, ending his second two-year spell as manager by moving back to the capital, taking Scales as an integral part of his Wimbledon side that would stun the footballing nation by winning the FA Cup. Gary Smart moved to Cheltenham Town and Wayne Noble, the last player released by Gould, joined Yeovil Town. Two veterans, David Rushbury and Bob Newton, the latter indirectly, transferred to Goole Town.

The replacement for Gould was Gerry Francis, already a well-known face at Bristol Rovers. It was an inspired decision to appoint him, as he was to lead Rovers to continuing success. Under his guidance, there was to be the Division Three championship, a first Wembley appearance and a return of self-belief to the side soon known by elements within the media as 'Ragbag Rovers'. Francis had a 'fascinating style of management' (Roy Dolling) and is quoted as saying with regard to one particularly inept first-half performance, 'what I said to them at half-time would be unprintable on the radio.' He inherited a side boasting the experience of Kenny Hibbitt and already featuring several key figures in the success to come, Vaughan Jones, Ian Alexander, Geoff Twentyman, David Mehew, Gary Penrice and Phil Purnell, to name a few. These were soon joined by midfielder Andy Reece, a smart acquisition from Willenhall.

During August 1987, three masterstrokes from Francis altered the Rovers side considerably and paved the way for future glory years. First, he signed goalkeeper Nigel Martyn on a free transfer from the Cornish side St Blazey. The tall, confident Cornishman proved to be a shrewd acquisition and one of the most popular figures at

Gary Penrice nets the only goal of the match on 12 April 1988 to defeat Bristol City at Twerton Park

the club. His transfer to Crystal Palace in November 1989 was to make him Britain's first £1 million goalkeeper and he went on to play for England. Next, Francis paid just £10,000, initially as a loan from himself to the club, to bring Ian Holloway back from Brentford to his home club, where the influential midfielder was to play a pivotal role in the club's success. Finally, to fill the need for a goalscorer, Devon White arrived, a few days into the season, from Shepshed Charterhouse to make an immediate impression.

White stepped into the breach at the 11th hour, when Robbie Turner missed the train from his Cardiff home, and scored the second goal as Rovers raced to a 3-0 half-time lead over Aldershot. His reputation was made. Even though Mike Ring pulled a goal back, Rovers' second consecutive 3-1 home victory, and Penrice's fourth goal in three games, put the side top of Division Three, above pre-season favourites Sunderland on goal difference. Indeed Rovers had already earned a draw at Roker Park and were to embarrass the eventual divisional champions still further in February. Devon White's powerful, physical presence was to be a major factor in Rovers' success. His goals against Bristol City in May 1990 to seal promotion and at Wembley against Tranmere Rovers were to earn him an undisputed place in Rovers folklore.

Reality soon returned, of course, as Rovers lost 2-1 at Blackpool to be knocked off top perch. All three goals came in a four-minute spell midway through the second-half, the winner coming from a controversial penalty, calmly converted by the veteran Tony Cunningham for his second goal of the game. It was to be the side's away form that produced greatest concern. Rovers managed to draw at Sunderland, Bristol City, Notts

Warm-up time at Twerton Park. The ground developments Rovers introduced transformed the facilities in their 10-year spell in Bath

County and Walsall, all of whom were in the top eight at the time, but lost to a range of lower-table and apparently beatable opposition. It was not until 5 March, when goals from White, Purnell and Mehew earned an emphatic 3-0 win at Chester City, that Rovers recorded their first away win of the season. By then, though, the side was in 20th place in the division and alarm bells were ringing.

Rovers' home form, on the other hand, was reasonably good. Fourteen out of 23 League matches, plus all three League Cup and FA Cup-ties, were won and Rovers remained unbeaten at 'Fortress Twerton' from mid-December. The three sides automatically relegated were all beaten, Doncaster Rovers and Grimsby Town both conceding four goals at Twerton Park with Purnell and White on the scoresheet on both occasions. The leaders Sunderland visited Twerton Park and, in a game that altered the flow of Rovers' season, were crushed 4-0. Manager Francis gave David Mehew a first League start and he scored the third goal. Holloway had rifled Rovers ahead six minutes before half-time and the top two scorers, Penrice and White, both also hit the target. The Rokerites were knocked off top spot and Rovers' season was back on track. This game, however, was marred by a robust challenge from Sunderland's Gordon Armstrong that broke Kenny Hibbitt's leg and effectively ended his 20-year professional career.

FOOTBALL LEAGUE DIVISION THREE

Date	Opponent		Res	ATT	G	2	3	4	5	6	7	8	9	10	11	Substitutes	Goalscorers
15/08/87	ROTHERHAM UNITED	H	3-1	3339	MARTYN	ALEXANDER	DRYDEN	HIBBITT	CARR	JONES	WIFFILL	REECE	TURNER	PENRICE	PURNELL	EATON 7	TURNER, PENRICE 2
22/08/87	SUNDERLAND	A	1-1	13058	MARTYN	ALEXANDER	DRYDEN	HIBBITT	CARR	JONES	HOLLOWAY	REECE	TURNER	PENRICE	PURNELL	MEACHAM 9	PENRICE
29/08/87	ALDERSHOT	A	3-1	3396	MARTYN	ALEXANDER	DRYDEN	HIBBITT	CARR	JONES	MEACHAM	WIFFILL	WHITE	PENRICE	PURNELL	TWENTYMAN 2	MEACHAM, WHITE, PENRICE
31/08/87	BLACKPOOL	H	1-2	3317	MARTYN	ALEXANDER	DRYDEN	HIBBITT	CARR	JONES	MEACHAM	WESTON	WHITE	PENRICE	PURNELL	TURNER 11	WHITE
05/09/87	WIGAN ATHLETIC	A	2-3	3168	MARTYN	ALEXANDER	DRYDEN	HIBBITT	CARR	JONES	HOLLOWAY	REECE	WHITE	PENRICE	PURNELL	TURNER 8, TWENTYMAN 3	PURNELL, WHITE
12/09/87	BRISTOL CITY	A	3-3	14746	CARTER	ALEXANDER	TANNER	HIBBITT	TWENTYMAN	JONES	HOLLOWAY	REECE	WHITE	PENRICE	PURNELL	TURNER 9	JONES, REECE, HOLLOWAY
16/09/87	YORK CITY	H	2-1	3177	CARTER	ALEXANDER	TANNER	HIBBITT	TWENTYMAN	JONES	HOLLOWAY	REECE	WHITE	PENRICE	PURNELL	TURNER 9	JONES, PENRICE
19/09/87	NORTHAMPTON T	A	0-2	3655	CARTER	ALEXANDER	TANNER	HIBBITT	TWENTYMAN	JONES	HOLLOWAY	REECE	WHITE	PENRICE	PURNELL	TURNER 4	
26/09/87	FULHAM	H	1-3	4614	CARTER	ALEXANDER	TANNER	CARR	TWENTYMAN	JONES	HOLLOWAY	REECE	WHITE	PENRICE	PURNELL	MEACHAM 4	WHITE
29/09/87	NOTTS COUNTY	A	1-1	4334	CARTER	ALEXANDER	TANNER	CARR	TWENTYMAN	JONES	HOLLOWAY	REECE	WHITE	PENRICE	PURNELL	TURNER 4	PENRICE
03/10/87	MANSFIELD TOWN	H	2-1	2980	CARTER	ALEXANDER	TANNER	CARR	TWENTYMAN	JONES	HOLLOWAY	REECE	MEACHAM	PENRICE	PURNELL	MEACHAM 4	PENRICE, MEACHAM
10/10/87	GILLINGHAM	A	0-3	4399	CARTER	ALEXANDER	TANNER	CARR	TWENTYMAN	JONES	HOLLOWAY	REECE	WHITE	PENRICE	PURNELL	MEACHAM 5	
17/10/87	CHESTER CITY	H	2-2	3038	CARTER	ALEXANDER	TANNER	CLARK	TWENTYMAN	JONES	HOLLOWAY	REECE	WHITE	PENRICE	PURNELL	MEACHAM 7	WHITE, PENRICE
19/10/87	PORT VALE	H	1-2	3598	MARTYN	ALEXANDER	DRYDEN	CLARK	TURNER	JONES	HOLLOWAY	REECE	WHITE	PENRICE	PURNELL		PENRICE
24/10/87	DONCASTER ROVERS	H	4-0	2817	MARTYN	ALEXANDER	TANNER	CLARK	TURNER	JONES	HOLLOWAY	REECE	WHITE	PENRICE	PURNELL	MEACHAM 11	PURNELL 2-1pen, JONES, WHITE
31/10/87	BRENTFORD	A	1-1	4487	MARTYN	ALEXANDER	TANNER	CLARK	HIBBITT	JONES	HOLLOWAY	REECE	WHITE	PENRICE	PURNELL	MEACHAM 7	PENRICE
04/11/87	PRESTON NORTH END	H	1-2	2804	MARTYN	ALEXANDER	TWENTYMAN	HIBBITT	CLARK	JONES	HOLLOWAY	MEACHAM	WHITE	PENRICE	PURNELL	MEACHAM 11	HIBBITT
07/11/87	CHESTERFIELD	H	2-0	2633	MARTYN	ALEXANDER	TWENTYMAN	HIBBITT	CLARK	JONES	HOLLOWAY	MEACHAM	WHITE	PENRICE	PURNELL	REECE 4	PURNELL pen, MEACHAM
21/11/87	BURY	A	1-4	2356	MARTYN	ALEXANDER	TWENTYMAN	HIBBITT	CLARK	JONES	HOLLOWAY	MEACHAM	WHITE	PENRICE	PURNELL		HIBBITT
28/11/87	GRIMSBY TOWN	H	4-2	2787	MARTYN	ALEXANDER	TANNER	HIBBITT	CLARK	JONES	HOLLOWAY	MEACHAM	WHITE	PENRICE	PURNELL		PENRICE, PURNELL, WHITE, MEACHAM
12/12/87	WALSALL	A	0-0	4234	MARTYN	ALEXANDER	TANNER	HIBBITT	CLARK	JONES	HOLLOWAY	REECE	WHITE	PENRICE	PURNELL	MEACHAM 4	
19/12/87	BRIGHTON & H ALB	H	3-1	3589	MARTYN	ALEXANDER	TANNER	HIBBITT	CLARK	JONES	HOLLOWAY	MEACHAM	WHITE	PENRICE	PURNELL	REECE 8, TWENTYMAN 4	HOLLOWAY
26/12/87	FULHAM	A	3-1	4718	MARTYN	ALEXANDER	TANNER	HIBBITT	TWENTYMAN	JONES	HOLLOWAY	REECE	WHITE	PENRICE	PURNELL	CARR 5	HOLLOWAY, PENRICE, WHITE
28/12/87	SOUTHEND UNITED	A	2-4	4094	MARTYN	ALEXANDER	TANNER	HIBBITT	TWENTYMAN	JONES	HOLLOWAY	FRANCIS	WHITE	PENRICE	PURNELL	EATON 2	WHITE, PURNELL
01/01/88	ALDERSHOT	H	0-3	4593	MARTYN	ALEXANDER	TANNER	HIBBITT	CLARK	JONES	HOLLOWAY	WESTON	JOSEPH	PENRICE	PURNELL	REECE 4	
16/01/88	NORTHAMPTON T	H	1-2	4473	MARTYN	ALEXANDER	TANNER	CLARK	HIBBITT	JONES	HOLLOWAY	REECE	JOSEPH	PENRICE	PURNELL	EATON 2	ALEXANDER
06/02/88	WIGAN ATHLETIC	H	0-1	3827	MARTYN	ALEXANDER	TWENTYMAN	CLARK	HIBBITT	JONES	HOLLOWAY	JOSEPH	WHITE	PENRICE	PURNELL	MEACHAM 2, REECE 8	
13/02/88	SOUTHEND UNITED	H	0-0	3099	MARTYN	ALEXANDER	TWENTYMAN	CLARK	HIBBITT	JONES	HOLLOWAY	REECE	WHITE	PENRICE	PURNELL	MEHEW 8	
20/02/88	ROTHERHAM UNITED	A	4-0	2966	MARTYN	ALEXANDER	TWENTYMAN	CLARK	MEHEW	JONES	HOLLOWAY	REECE	WHITE	PENRICE	PURNELL	REECE 5, WESTON 10	WHITE
24/02/88	SUNDERLAND	A	4-0	4501	MARTYN	ALEXANDER	TWENTYMAN	CLARK	MEHEW	JONES	HOLLOWAY	REECE	WHITE	PENRICE	PURNELL		HOLLOWAY, WHITE, MEHEW, PENRICE
27/02/88	MANSFIELD TOWN	H	0-1	3191	MARTYN	ALEXANDER	TWENTYMAN	CLARK	MEHEW	JONES	HOLLOWAY	REECE	WHITE	PENRICE	PURNELL		
02/03/88	NOTTS COUNTY	A	1-1	4075	MARTYN	ALEXANDER	TWENTYMAN	CLARK	MEHEW	JONES	HOLLOWAY	REECE	McCLEAN	PENRICE	PURNELL	TANNER 9	TWENTYMAN
05/03/88	CHESTER CITY	A	3-0	2067	MARTYN	ALEXANDER	TWENTYMAN	CLARK	MEHEW	JONES	HOLLOWAY	REECE	McCLEAN	PENRICE	PURNELL		WHITE, PURNELL, MEHEW
12/03/88	GILLINGHAM	H	2-0	3846	MARTYN	ALEXANDER	TWENTYMAN	CLARK	MEHEW	JONES	HOLLOWAY	REECE	WHITE	PENRICE	TANNER		PENRICE, PURNELL
19/03/88	BRENTFORD	H	0-0	3380	MARTYN	ALEXANDER	TWENTYMAN	CLARK	MEHEW	JONES	HOLLOWAY	REECE	WHITE	PENRICE	TANNER		
25/03/88	DONCASTER ROVERS	A	1-0	1311	MARTYN	ALEXANDER	TWENTYMAN	CLARK	MEHEW	JONES	HOLLOWAY	REECE	WHITE	PENRICE	TANNER		PENRICE
02/04/88	CHESTERFIELD	A	1-0	2208	MARTYN	ALEXANDER	TWENTYMAN	CLARK	MEHEW	JONES	HOLLOWAY	REECE	WHITE	PENRICE	TANNER	McCLEAN 11	PENRICE
04/04/88	BURY	H	1-0	4264	MARTYN	ALEXANDER	TWENTYMAN	CLARK	MEHEW	JONES	HOLLOWAY	REECE	WHITE	PENRICE	TANNER		MEHEW
08/04/88	PRESTON NORTH END	A	1-3	5336	MARTYN	ALEXANDER	TWENTYMAN	CLARK	MEHEW	JONES	HOLLOWAY	REECE	WHITE	PENRICE	PURNELL	McCLEAN 9, WESTON 7	PENRICE
12/04/88	BRISTOL CITY	H	2-4	5947	MARTYN	ALEXANDER	TWENTYMAN	CLARK	MEHEW	JONES	HOLLOWAY	REECE	WHITE	PENRICE	TANNER	McCLEAN 9, PURNELL 5	MEHEW 3, WHITE
15/04/88	YORK CITY	A	4-0	1834	MARTYN	ALEXANDER	TANNER	CLARK	MEHEW	JONES	HOLLOWAY	REECE	WHITE	PENRICE	PURNELL		PENRICE
23/04/88	PORT VALE	A	1-0	3780	MARTYN	ALEXANDER	TANNER	CLARK	MEHEW	JONES	HOLLOWAY	REECE	WHITE	PENRICE	PURNELL		MEHEW, WHITE
27/04/88	BLACKPOOL	H	2-0	3546	MARTYN	ALEXANDER	TANNER	CLARK	MEHEW	JONES	HOLLOWAY	REECE	WHITE	PENRICE	TANNER		MEHEW, HOLLOWAY, WHITE
30/04/88	GRIMSBY TOWN	A	0-0	2505	MARTYN	ALEXANDER	TANNER	CLARK	MEHEW	JONES	HOLLOWAY	REECE	WHITE	PENRICE	TANNER		
02/05/88	WALSALL	H	3-0	6328	MARTYN	ALEXANDER	TANNER	CLARK	MEHEW	JONES	HOLLOWAY	REECE	WHITE	PENRICE	TANNER	McCLEAN 11, WESTON 10	MEHEW, HOLLOWAY, WHITE
07/05/88	BRIGHTON & H ALB	A	1-2	19800	MARTYN	ALEXANDER	TANNER	CLARK	MEHEW	JONES	HOLLOWAY	REECE	WHITE	PENRICE	PURNELL		CLARK

LEAGUE CUP

Date	Opponent		Res	ATT	G	2	3	4	5	6	7	8	9	10	11	Substitutes	Goalscorers
19/08/87	HEREFORD UNITED	H	1-0	2796	MARTYN	ALEXANDER	DRYDEN	HIBBITT	TWENTYMAN	JONES	WIFFILL	REECE	TURNER	PENRICE	PURNELL	MEACHAM 7, CARR 5	PENRICE
26/08/87	HEREFORD UNITED	A	0-2	2963	MARTYN	ALEXANDER	DRYDEN	HIBBITT	CARR	JONES	WIFFILL	REECE	TURNER	PENRICE	PURNELL	MEACHAM 7	

FA CUP

Date	Opponent		Res	ATT	G	2	3	4	5	6	7	8	9	10	11	Substitutes	Goalscorers
14/11/87	MERTHYR TYDFIL	H	6-0	4635	MARTYN	ALEXANDER	TANNER	HIBBITT	TWENTYMAN	JONES	HOLLOWAY	MEACHAM	WHITE	PENRICE	PURNELL	DRYDEN 2, REECE 10	PENRICE 3, WHITE 2, MEACHAM
05/12/87	V S RUGBY	A	1-1	3168	MARTYN	ALEXANDER	TANNER	HIBBITT	TWENTYMAN	JONES	HOLLOWAY	MEACHAM	WHITE	PENRICE	PURNELL	REECE, 4, DRYDEN 8	MEACHAM
17/12/87	V S RUGBY	H	4-0	2846	MARTYN	ALEXANDER	TANNER	CARR	TWENTYMAN	JONES	HOLLOWAY	MEACHAM	WHITE	PENRICE	PURNELL	EATON 4	PENRICE, ALEXANDER, WHITE, REECE
09/01/88	SHREWSBURY TOWN	A	1-2	6554	MARTYN	ALEXANDER	TANNER	CLARK	TWENTYMAN	JONES	HOLLOWAY	REECE	WHITE	PENRICE	PURNELL		PENRICE

SHERPA VAN TROPHY

Date	Opponent		Res	ATT	G	2	3	4	5	6	7	8	9	10	11	Substitutes	Goalscorers
13/10/87	TORQUAY UNITED	A	0-2	1513	MARTYN	ALEXANDER	TANNER	CARR	TWENTYMAN	JONES	HOLLOWAY	REECE	WHITE	PENRICE	PURNELL	MEACHAM 7	
28/10/87	HEREFORD UNITED	H	0 2	2158	MARTYN	ALEXANDER	TANNER	CLARK	HIBBITT	JONES	HOLLOWAY	REECE	WHITE	PENRICE	PURNELL	MEACHAM 8	

GLOUCESTERSHIRE CUP FINAL

Date	Opponent		Res	ATT	G	2	3	4	5	6	7	8	9	10	11	Substitutes	Goalscorers
02/12/87	BRISTOL CITY *	H	1-2	1376	CARTER	WESTON	YATES	CLARK	TWENTYMAN	EATON	HOWELLS	REECE	TURNER	SUGRUE	DRYDEN	BOYLE 10	REECE
15/03/88	BRISTOL CITY	A	1-3	2278	STEVENS	PATTERSON	YATES	HOWELLS	TANNER	EATON	WESTON	FRANCIS	McCLEAN	BOYLE	DRYDEN	CAROTA 8, MEHEW 11	CAROTA

* Final carried over from 1986-87

Players

PLAYERS	APP	SUB	GLS
ALEXANDER I	45		1
CARR D	8	1	
CARTER T	8		
CLARK W	31		1
DRYDEN R	6		
EATON J	0	3	
FRANCIS G	1		
HIBBITT K	24		2
HOLLOWAY I	43		5
JONES V	46		3
JOSEPH F	3		
MARTYN N	38		
McCLEAN C	2	4	
MEACHAM J	7	7	4
MEHEW D	17	7	8
PENRICE G	46		18
PURNELL P	40	1	8
REECE A	35	5	1
TANNER N	25	1	
TURNER R	3	6	1
TWENTYMAN G	35	3	1
WESTON I	2	3	
WHITE D	39		15
WIFFILL D	2		

Bristol Rovers 1988/89. Back row: Twentyman, Reece, Yates, Weston, Clark, White, Martyn, Meacham, McClean, Dryden, Stapleton, Alexander. Front row: Dolling (Physio), Jones, Penrice, Purnell, Hibbitt (Asst Manager), Francis (Manager), Bulpin (Coach), Smith, Holloway, Mehew, Kendall (Kit Man)

Seven days after the visit of Sunderland, new leaders Notts County were held 1-1 at Twerton Park with Geoff Twentyman bizarrely scoring his only two goals of the season. He thus became only the fourth Rovers player to score for both sides in a League match. Early-season heavy defeats at Gillingham, Southend United, Bury and Aldershot now behind them, Rovers embarked on a glorious run of results to rescue their season. Twice, Nigel Martyn kept six consecutive clean sheets as Rovers conceded goals in only one of 13 League matches between early March and early May. During this run, Rovers were able to complete League doubles over Doncaster Rovers, York City and Chesterfield. The victory at Saltergate was won through a Penrice goal created by debutant Christian McClean. Sadly, though, Chesterfield's Dave Perry fractured his right knee in a collision with Purnell, an injury that was to end his career. Bury were in the middle of a five-match goalless spell when they earned a draw at Twerton Park. A 48th-minute Penrice goal, the penultimate of the 18 that rendered him the club's seasonal top scorer, was enough to beat Bristol City, with whom Rovers had shared six goals at Ashton Gate in mid-September.

Behind Penrice and White, Rovers were competently served by eight goals each from Purnell and Mehew. While Purnell's goals were predominantly early in the season, Mehew started only the final 17 games of the season. His contribution to the run of victories and Rovers' resultant surge up the divisional table should not be underestimated. Three of his goals came in the space of 29 minutes during a highly convincing 4-0 victory at York City, watched by only 1,834, while a mere 1,311 saw the single goal victory at Doncaster, the lowest crowd of the season at a Bristol Rovers League match. By way of contrast, 19,800 were at Brighton on the final day of the season, where Billy Clark's first League goal, toe-poking home an Andy Reece corner after 68 minutes, could not prevent the Seagulls gaining the win they required for promotion to Division Two.

Stewart Phillips scored in successive 2-0 victories for Hereford United, which knocked Rovers out of the Littlewoods Cup and Sherpa Van Trophy. The former Rovers defender Keith Curle won a winner's medal as Reading defeated Luton Town at Wembley in the Simod Cup Final. Another player previously on Rovers' books, Paul Bannon, meanwhile, scored a hat-trick on Valentine's Day as Thessalonikis beat Lavadiakos 4-1 in the Greek Division One. Mark Walters, later a Rovers player, scored Aston Villa's goal against Bournemouth in October 1987 to enable Villa to become the first club to score 6,000 Football League goals. In the FA Cup, Rovers recorded their largest win since 1900, when a Penrice hat-trick helped defeat Merthyr Tydfil 6-0. It took two attempts, but Rovers eventually beat VS Rugby with ease, before losing 2-1 at Division Two Shrewsbury Town, for whom a former Eastville favourite Brian Williams scored a second-half winning goal. It was a major surprise when Bobby Gould, only months after leaving Rovers, led Wimbledon to a 1-0 victory over Liverpool in the FA Cup final, with Scales appearing as a late substitute for Terry Gibson.

Despite a goal from Andy Reece after 68 minutes, Rovers lost the Gloucestershire Cup final, held over from 1986/87, 2-1 at home to Bristol City. Three months later, Rovers lost again, when the 1987/88 final was also won by City. Marco Carota, who never appeared in League action for Rovers, scored a consolation goal 19 minutes from time after City had run up a 3-0 lead before half-time.

1988/89

A position in the Division Three play-off final and missing out on promotion by one goal offered a glimpse of what was to follow the previous season. In many respects, the promotion push had begun in earnest in March 1988 and Rovers' form through 1988/89 reflected that of the latter stages of 1987/88. Gerry Francis stuck largely to this side, which was beginning to gel as a unit capable of great success. Gary Penrice scored 20 League goals and, alongside ever-presents Nigel Martyn and Geoff Twentyman, five other players appeared in at least 42 of Rovers' 46 League fixtures.

Nigel Martyn once again proved what a crucial figure he was to Rovers' success. Promoted sides excepted, no other Division Three side conceded so few League goals and defeat at Bramall Lane in September 1988, when Ian Bryson scored twice for Sheffield United, was the last time until February 1992 that Rovers conceded four goals in a League game. Although Simon Stapleton appeared in the opening game, converted winger Ian Alexander recovered from swallowing his tongue in an FA Cup tie against Fisher Athletic to form a strong full-back partnership with captain Vaughan Jones. First Billy Clark and later the consistent Steve Yates, his wages paid by the Rovers' President's Club in Rovers' perilous financial situation, appeared alongside the dependable Geoff Twentyman in central defence. Mehew, Holloway, Reece and Purnell continued as the midfield quartet, each regularly supplying goals, with Penrice partnering Devon White in attack.

Nigel Martyn was an ever-present in 1988/89. He kept a clean sheet for 645 minutes in the autumn of 1989 before his record £1 million transfer to Crystal Palace

If one cog was missing from the success story to come, it was perhaps Devon White's good luck in front of goal. His 5 League goals were not a fair reflection on his commitment to the side's cause and it was significant that his stand-in, Christian McClean, fared no better at first. White and McClean, both more than 6ft tall, complemented perfectly the style of Penrice and loan signing Dennis Bailey, who scored in 8 of his first 11 League matches for Rovers.

Rovers were trailing at half-time in their first four League matches, yet lost just one of these. Penrice, White, Reece and Purnell scored twice each in home matches as, by mid November, Rovers had won six out of eight home League games and lay fourth in the table. Bizarrely, no Rovers player was to score twice in a game at Twerton Park for the remainder of the season, though only Brentford, Bury and Cardiff City recorded away victories on the ground. The fixture against Bury featured a Reece own goal as well as two goals for the Shakers from their 30-year-old striker, Steve Elliott. This remains the only occasion Bury have won an away League game against Rovers. Reece also scored an own goal early in the home game with Aldershot.

A successful season is perhaps best illustrated by matches played against mid-table Huddersfield Town and divisional champions Wolverhampton Wanderers. Rovers recorded their largest win of the season, 5-1, against the Terriers at the end of October and fought their way to a goalless draw with all-conquering Wolves at Twerton Park on Boxing Day. Once the return fixtures were played, Bailey had arrived on loan from Crystal Palace and he scored twice as Rovers, overturning a half-time deficit, beat Huddersfield 3-2 at Leeds Road. Wolves scored 96 League goals in winning the Championship by an eight-point margin and had scored 16 times in their last four games at Molineux. Yet, when Rovers visited on Easter Monday, Rovers kept at bay Steve Bull and Andy Mutch, with 30 and 18 League goals respectively already to their names, and became the only club to win at Molineux all season. It was a superb turn and shot after 40 minutes from Bailey that earned Rovers perhaps their greatest result of the season.

On-field success, quite naturally, led to an increase in attendances. An average home crowd of 5,259 took note of an attendance of 8,480 on Boxing Day and 8,676 for the local derby, while more than 20,000 watched Rovers' 1-0 victories at Ashton Gate and Molineux. Penrice's goals in both derby games against Bristol City earned four points, as Rovers repeated, though less dramatically, the New Year exploits of two seasons earlier at Ashton Gate. At Twerton Park, City's Rob Newman saw his well-struck penalty saved by Martyn, who continued to prove his worth in Rovers' goal.

In addition to Huddersfield Town, Rovers also completed League doubles over Chester City, Chesterfield and Gillingham. At Priestfield, Rovers trailed at half-time to a Steve Lovell penalty before recovering to beat Gillingham 3-2. A home victory over

Dennis Bailey scores a superb winning goal at Wolverhampton Wanderers, which led to Wolves' only home defeat of the season

Gary Penrice, leading goalscorer with 18 and 20 goals respectively in seasons 1987/88 and 1988/89

Swansea City in April, Rovers' ninth consecutive League game without defeat, was achieved against opposition fielding the former Rovers player Paul Raynor and using, as a substitute, Stewart Phillips, whose goals for Hereford United had knocked Rovers out of two cup competitions the previous season. Rovers also recorded a 2-1 victory away to then high-flying Northampton Town, with Paul Smith, an able and bustling stand-in for David Mehew, from a Keith Viney pass, scoring his only goal of the season. Viney was appearing in his first game for the Pirates on loan from Exeter City, in whose colours, in December 1982, he had scored an own goal in Rovers' favour.

It speaks volumes for Rovers' consistency that a five-match winless run and no goals in the final four League games of the season did not prevent the Pirates from reaching the promotion play-offs. Their rivals in the play-offs, a system into its third season devised to increase late season mid-table interest, would include Fulham and Port Vale, both of whom played Rovers during this last barren run. A second-half Penrice goal was all Rovers had to show from a semi-final first-leg at Twerton Park, but this slender lead over Fulham was ample. At Craven Cottage four days later, four second-half goals earned Rovers a convincing 5-0 aggregate victory. Clark, Holloway, Bailey and Reece all scored against a Fulham side boasting future Rovers midfielders Ronnie Maugé and Justin Skinner.

Rovers were left to face Port Vale over two legs for promotion to Division Two. A record Twerton Park crowd of 9,042 saw Penrice score again, as Rovers led 1-0 at half-time in the first-leg against a side that had finished the season with 10 points more than Rovers. However, Robbie Earle, later the scorer in 1998 of the first World Cup finals goal ever scored by Jamaica, scored a crucial second-half equaliser to leave the Pirates with a mountain to climb. Earle had scored for Vale in both League fixtures against Francis' side and his second-half far-post header before a crowd of 17,353 in the second leg at Vale Park consigned Rovers to a further season in Division Three. Nonetheless, the seeds of hope had been sown and were to come to fruition over the coming 12 months.

Cup competitions brought Rovers little joy in 1988/89. Eliminated early from the Littlewoods Cup, through Trevor Aylott's second-half goal in the first leg at Bournemouth, Rovers also suffered the humiliation of an FA Cup defeat at Kettering Town. A comfortable win over Fisher Athletic, who fielded a young Ken Charlery, set up a tricky away tie that, after a goalless first-half, Rovers lost 2-1 at Rockingham Road. All Rovers had to show for their efforts was an Andy Reece consolation goal after 70 minutes. Kettering featured several experienced players, including Lil Fuccillo and Ernie Moss, and the former Peterborough United and Brentford striker Robbie Cooke scored both their goals. Nonetheless, it was a demoralizing and embarrassing result in front of the BBC *Match of the Day* cameras.

The Sherpa Van Trophy at least gave a hint of Rovers' Cup run of 1989/90. A first-half Reece goal saw off Bristol City, and Cardiff City were also beaten before Rovers fell to Mark Loram's goal for Torquay United in the quarter-finals. The Gulls, with Ian Weston and Paul Smith in their side, were to lose the Wembley Final 4-1 to Bolton Wanderers, for whom the former Rovers striker Trevor Morgan contributed the final goal. Two second-half Mehew goals and a third in the final minute from White brought Rovers a 3-0 victory over Bristol City in the Gloucestershire Cup final, the club's most convincing victory in this tournament since the game against Staple Hill in January 1898.

Date	Opponent	H/A	Score	Att	1	2	3	4	5	6	7	8	9	10	11	Substitutes	Goalscorers
27/08/88	WIGAN ATHLETIC	H	3-2	4080	MARTYN	STAPLETON	TWENTYMAN	CLARK	MEHEW	JONES	HOLLOWAY	REECE	WHITE	PENRICE	PURNELL	ALEXANDER, PENRICE 2, WHITE	PENRICE 2, WHITE
03/09/88	SHEFFIELD UNITED	A	1-4	9586	MARTYN	STAPLETON	TWENTYMAN	CLARK	MEHEW	JONES	HOLLOWAY	REECE	WHITE	PENRICE	PURNELL	BAILEY D	PURNELL, BAILEY
10/09/88	ALDERSHOT	H	2-2	3382	MARTYN	ALEXANDER	TWENTYMAN	CLARK	WHITE	JONES	HOLLOWAY	REECE	WHITE	PENRICE	PURNELL	WHITE 2	PURNELL, MEHEW
17/09/88	BOLTON WANDERERS	A	1-1	4821	MARTYN	ALEXANDER	TWENTYMAN	CLARK	WHITE	JONES	HOLLOWAY	REECE	WHITE	PENRICE	PURNELL	SMITH	PURNELL
21/09/88	BRENTFORD	H	1-1	3836	MARTYN	ALEXANDER	TWENTYMAN	CLARK	SMITH	JONES	HOLLOWAY	REECE	WHITE	PENRICE	PURNELL	VINEY 4	REECE, McCLEAN
24/09/88	NORTHAMPTON T	A	2-1	3886	MARTYN	ALEXANDER	TWENTYMAN	VINEY	SMITH	CLARK	HOLLOWAY	REECE	WHITE	PENRICE	PURNELL	SMITH, PENRICE	PURNELL, MEHEW 2
01/10/88	CARDIFF CITY	H	2-2	5038	MARTYN	ALEXANDER	TWENTYMAN	CLARK	SMITH	JONES	HOLLOWAY	REECE	WHITE	PENRICE	PURNELL	PENRICE, HOLLOWAY	PURNELL, MEHEW
05/10/88	PRESTON NORTH END	H	1-0	3689	MARTYN	ALEXANDER	TWENTYMAN	CLARK	SMITH	JONES	HOLLOWAY	REECE	McCLEAN	PENRICE	PURNELL	STAPLETON 2	McCLEAN
08/10/88	MANSFIELD TOWN	A	1-0	3381	MARTYN	ALEXANDER	TWENTYMAN	YATES	SMITH	JONES	HOLLOWAY	REECE	McCLEAN	PENRICE	PURNELL		PENRICE
15/10/88	NOTTS COUNTY	H	2-0	4183	MARTYN	ALEXANDER	TWENTYMAN	YATES	SMITH	JONES	HOLLOWAY	REECE	McCLEAN	PENRICE	PURNELL		PURNELL, MEHEW 2
22/10/88	CHESTER CITY	A	4-1	3611	MARTYN	ALEXANDER	TWENTYMAN	YATES	SMITH	JONES	HOLLOWAY	REECE	WHITE	PENRICE	PURNELL		PURNELL 2, HOLLOWAY, REECE
26/10/88	READING	H	1-3	7150	MARTYN	ALEXANDER	TWENTYMAN	YATES	MEHEW	JONES	HOLLOWAY	REECE	WHITE	PENRICE	PURNELL		REECE, McCLEAN
29/10/88	HUDDERSFIELD TOWN	H	5-1	4460	MARTYN	ALEXANDER	TWENTYMAN	YATES	MEHEW	JONES	HOLLOWAY	REECE	WHITE	PENRICE	PURNELL		PURNELL, MEHEW 2
05/11/88	CHESTERFIELD	A	3-0	2480	MARTYN	ALEXANDER	TWENTYMAN	YATES	MEHEW	JONES	HOLLOWAY	REECE	WHITE	PENRICE	PURNELL		PURNELL, MEHEW
08/11/88	SOUTHEND UNITED	A	2-0	2453	MARTYN	ALEXANDER	TWENTYMAN	YATES	MEHEW	JONES	HOLLOWAY	REECE	WHITE	PENRICE	PURNELL		REECE, PENRICE
12/11/88	WOLVES	H	2-0	4826	MARTYN	ALEXANDER	TWENTYMAN	YATES	MEHEW	JONES	HOLLOWAY	REECE	WHITE	PENRICE	PURNELL		PENRICE 2
26/11/88	BRISTOL CITY	A	3-1	23191	MARTYN	ALEXANDER	TWENTYMAN	YATES	SMITH	JONES	HOLLOWAY	REECE	WHITE	PENRICE	PURNELL		HOLLOWAY, PENRICE 2
03/12/88	SWANSEA CITY	H	1-0	4803	MARTYN	ALEXANDER	TWENTYMAN	YATES	SMITH	JONES	HOLLOWAY	REECE	WHITE	PENRICE	PURNELL		PENRICE
17/12/88	SHEFFIELD UNITED	H	0-0	6623	MARTYN	ALEXANDER	TWENTYMAN	YATES	SMITH	JONES	HOLLOWAY	REECE	WHITE	PENRICE	PURNELL	McCLEAN 5	
26/12/88	ALDERSHOT	A	1-0	3101	MARTYN	ALEXANDER	TWENTYMAN	YATES	SMITH	JONES	HOLLOWAY	REECE	McCLEAN	PENRICE	PURNELL	CLARK 2	PENRICE
31/12/88	BOLTON WANDERERS	H	3-1	5815	MARTYN	ALEXANDER	TWENTYMAN	YATES	SMITH	JONES	HOLLOWAY	REECE	McCLEAN	PENRICE	PURNELL	McCLEAN 9	PURNELL 5, PENRICE
02/01/89	BURY	A	1-0	5375	MARTYN	ALEXANDER	TWENTYMAN	YATES	SMITH	JONES	HOLLOWAY	REECE	McCLEAN	PENRICE	REECE	McCLEAN 5	NIXON 9
14/01/89	GILLINGHAM	H	1-2	5568	MARTYN	ALEXANDER	TWENTYMAN	YATES	SMITH	JONES	HOLLOWAY	REECE	McCLEAN	PENRICE	REECE	WHITE 5	BAILEY
21/01/89	BURY	H	2-1	4004	MARTYN	ALEXANDER	TWENTYMAN	YATES	MEHEW	JONES	HOLLOWAY	MEHEW	McCLEAN	PENRICE	REECE	McCLEAN 11	REECE, PENRICE
28/01/89	FULHAM	A	2-1	2529	MARTYN	ALEXANDER	TWENTYMAN	YATES	WHITE	JONES	HOLLOWAY	BAILEY	McCLEAN	PENRICE	REECE	WHITE 5	BAILEY
04/02/89	BLACKPOOL	H	0-1	6250	MARTYN	ALEXANDER	TWENTYMAN	YATES	WHITE	JONES	HOLLOWAY	BAILEY	McCLEAN	PENRICE	REECE	McCLEAN 5	PURNELL, BAILEY
11/02/89	PORT VALE	A	1-1	4669	MARTYN	ALEXANDER	TWENTYMAN	YATES	WHITE	JONES	HOLLOWAY	BAILEY	McCLEAN	PENRICE	REECE	WHITE 9	MEHEW
18/02/89	WOLVES	A	0-3	7365	MARTYN	ALEXANDER	TWENTYMAN	YATES	WHITE	JONES	HOLLOWAY	BAILEY	WHITE	PENRICE	PURNELL	WHITE 9	MEHEW, PENRICE
25/02/89	READING	H	0-1	5176	MARTYN	ALEXANDER	TWENTYMAN	YATES	SMITH	JONES	SMITH	BAILEY	WHITE	McCLEAN	McCLEAN	McCLEAN 5	
01/03/89	MANSFIELD TOWN	H	0-0	4573	MARTYN	ALEXANDER	TWENTYMAN	YATES	HAZEL	JONES	HOLLOWAY	BAILEY	WHITE	McCLEAN	McCLEAN	McCLEAN 5	
04/03/89	CHESTER CITY	H	2-0	3082	MARTYN	ALEXANDER	TWENTYMAN	YATES	HAZEL	JONES	HOLLOWAY	BAILEY	WHITE	PENRICE	PURNELL	WHITE 8	WHITE
11/03/89	HUDDERSFIELD TOWN	A	2-1	4684	MARTYN	ALEXANDER	CLARK	YATES	HAZEL	REECE	HOLLOWAY	BAILEY	REECE	PENRICE	PURNELL	HIBBITT 5	BAILEY, PENRICE
14/03/89	CHESTERFIELD	H	3-2	4105	MARTYN	ALEXANDER	TWENTYMAN	YATES	MEHEW	JONES	HOLLOWAY	BAILEY	WHITE	PENRICE	PURNELL	BAILEY 2, JONES pen	BAILEY 2, JONES pen
25/03/89	NOTTS COUNTY	A	1-1	8676	MARTYN	ALEXANDER	TWENTYMAN	YATES	MEHEW	JONES	HOLLOWAY	BAILEY	McCLEAN	PENRICE	PURNELL	BAILEY 10, WHITE 9	REECE, PENRICE
27/03/89	PRESTON NORTH END	A	1-0	20913	MARTYN	ALEXANDER	CLARK	YATES	MEHEW	JONES	HOLLOWAY	BAILEY	McCLEAN	PENRICE	PURNELL	WHITE 11	BAILEY
01/04/89	ALDERSHOT	H	1-0	5355	MARTYN	ALEXANDER	TWENTYMAN	YATES	MEHEW	JONES	HOLLOWAY	BAILEY	WHITE	PENRICE	PURNELL	WHITE 9	BAILEY
05/04/89	BOLTON WANDERERS	A	2-2	6969	MARTYN	ALEXANDER	TWENTYMAN	YATES	WHITE	JONES	HOLLOWAY	MEHEW	McCLEAN	PENRICE	PURNELL	WHITE 9	REECE, PENRICE
08/04/89	CARDIFF CITY	A	1-2	7558	MARTYN	ALEXANDER	TWENTYMAN	YATES	WHITE	JONES	HOLLOWAY	MEHEW	McCLEAN	PENRICE	PURNELL	McCLEAN 11	PENRICE, BAILEY
15/04/89	BRISTOL CITY	H	2-1	9645	MARTYN	ALEXANDER	TWENTYMAN	YATES	WHITE	JONES	HOLLOWAY	REECE	McCLEAN	PENRICE	PURNELL	McCLEAN 5	BAILEY, PENRICE 2
22/04/89	BRENTFORD	A	1-2	7558	MARTYN	ALEXANDER	TWENTYMAN	YATES	WHITE	JONES	HOLLOWAY	REECE	McCLEAN	PENRICE	PURNELL	WHITE 5	BAILEY
28/04/89	NORTHAMPTON T	H	3-2	5568	MARTYN	ALEXANDER	TWENTYMAN	YATES	MEHEW	JONES	HOLLOWAY	REECE	White	PENRICE	PURNELL 5	WHITE 11	MEHEW
01/05/89	GILLINGHAM	A	3-2	6250	MARTYN	ALEXANDER	TWENTYMAN	YATES	WHITE	JONES	HOLLOWAY	REECE	NIXON 9	PENRICE	PURNELL 5		HOLLOWAY, PENRICE 2
03/05/89	SOUTHEND UNITED	H	3-2	4004	MARTYN	ALEXANDER	TWENTYMAN	WHITE	SMITH	JONES	HOLLOWAY	BAILEY	McCLEAN	McCLEAN 10	McCLEAN		
06/05/89	FULHAM	H	0-3	7302	MARTYN	ALEXANDER	TWENTYMAN	WHITE	SMITH	JONES	HOLLOWAY	BAILEY	McCLEAN	PENRICE	McCLEAN	McCLEAN 9	
09/05/89	PORT VALE	H	0-1	6136	MARTYN	ALEXANDER	TWENTYMAN	WHITE	SMITH	JONES	HOLLOWAY	REECE	REECE	PENRICE	PURNELL		
13/05/89	BURY	A	0-0	3073	MARTYN	ALEXANDER	TWENTYMAN	WHITE	SMITH	JONES	HOLLOWAY	REECE	REECE	BAILEY	McCLEAN		

PLAY OFFS

Date	Opponent	H/A	Score	Att	1	2	3	4	5	6	7	8	9	10	11	Substitutes	Goalscorers
21/05/89	FULHAM	H	1-0	9029	MARTYN	ALEXANDER	TWENTYMAN	YATES	HAZEL	JONES	HOLLOWAY	BAILEY	WHITE	PENRICE	PURNELL	MEHEW 8	PENRICE
25/05/89	FULHAM	A	4-0	10668	MARTYN	ALEXANDER	TWENTYMAN	YATES	HAZEL	REECE	HOLLOWAY	BAILEY	REECE	PENRICE	PURNELL	BAILEY 10, McCLEAN 5	CLARK, HOLLOWAY, BAILEY, REECE
31/05/89	PORT VALE	A	1-1	9042	MARTYN	ALEXANDER	CLARK	YATES	WHITE	JONES	HOLLOWAY	BAILEY	McCLEAN	PENRICE	PURNELL	McCLEAN 7	PENRICE
03/06/89	PORT VALE	H	0-1	17353	MARTYN	ALEXANDER	CLARK	YATES	WHITE	JONES	HOLLOWAY	REECE	REECE	PENRICE	PURNELL		

FA CUP

Date	Opponent	H/A	Score	Att	1	2	3	4	5	6	7	8	9	10	11	Substitutes	Goalscorers
20/11/88	FISHER ATHLETIC	H	3-0	5161	MARTYN	ALEXANDER	TWENTYMAN	YATES	WHITE	JONES	HOLLOWAY	REECE	WHITE	PENRICE	PURNELL	SMITH 5, DRYDEN 11	JONES, PENRICE, HOLLOWAY pen
10/12/88	KETTERING TOWN	A	1-2	4950	MARTYN	ALEXANDER	TWENTYMAN	YATES	WHITE	JONES	HOLLOWAY	REECE	WHITE	PENRICE	PURNELL	SMITH 5, McCLEAN 8	PENRICE

LEAGUE CUP

Date	Opponent	H/A	Score	Att	1	2	3	4	5	6	7	8	9	10	11	Substitutes	Goalscorers
30/08/88	AFC BOURNEMOUTH	A	0-1	4601	MARTYN	STAPLETON	TWENTYMAN	CLARK	MEHEW	JONES	HOLLOWAY	REECE	WHITE	PENRICE	PURNELL		
07/09/88	AFC BOURNEMOUTH	H	0-0	4057	MARTYN	STAPLETON	TWENTYMAN	CLARK	MEHEW	JONES	HOLLOWAY	REECE	WHITE	PENRICE	PURNELL		

SHERPA VAN TROPHY

Date	Opponent	H/A	Score	Att	1	2	3	4	5	6	7	8	9	10	11	Substitutes	Goalscorers
23/11/88	BRISTOL CITY	H	1-0	2940	MARTYN	ALEXANDER	TWENTYMAN	YATES	MEHEW	JONES	HOLLOWAY	REECE	WHITE	PENRICE	PURNELL	MEHEW 8	PENRICE
14/12/88	EXETER CITY	A	1-0	1609	MARTYN	ALEXANDER	TWENTYMAN	YATES	MEHEW	JONES	HOLLOWAY	REECE	WHITE	PENRICE	PURNELL		MEHEW
24/01/89	CARDIFF CITY	H	2-1	4029	MARTYN	ALEXANDER	TWENTYMAN	YATES	SMITH	JONES	HOLLOWAY	REECE	McCLEAN	McCLEAN	PURNELL		SMITH, REECE
22/02/89	TORQUAY UNITED	A	0-1	4316	MARTYN	ALEXANDER	TWENTYMAN	YATES	WHITE	JONES	HOLLOWAY	REECE	REECE	McCLEAN	PURNELL		

GLOUCESTERSHIRE CUP FINAL

Date	Opponent	H/A	Score	Att	1	2	3	4	5	6	7	8	9	10	11	Substitutes	Goalscorers
17/08/88	BRISTOL CITY	H	3-0	1664	MARTYN	STAPLETON	TWENTYMAN	CLARK	JONES	JONES	HOLLOWAY	REECE	WHITE	MEHEW	PURNELL	SMITH, MEACHAM	MEHEW 2, WHITE

PLAYERS	APP	SUB	GLS
ALEXANDER I	42		
BAILEY D	17		9
CLARK W	10	1	
DRYDEN R	0	1	
HAZEL I	3		
HIBBITT K	0	1	
HOLLOWAY I	44		6
JONES V	45		2
MARTYN N	46		
McCLEAN D	16	12	2
MEHEW D	31	7	7
NIXON P	0	1	
PENRICE G	43		20
PURNELL P	35	2	7
REECE A	42		7
SMITH P	14	2	1
STAPLETON S	7		
TWENTYMAN G	46		1
VINEY K	4	1	1
WHITE D	31	9	5
YATES S	35		

1989/90

Thirty-seven years after topping Division Three (South), Rovers were crowned Division Three champions in 1989/90 with a club record 93 points. It was a momentous achievement for Gerry Francis' 'Ragbag Rovers' at their temporary home outside Bristol. The elusive promotion was achieved on a glorious if tense Wednesday night when Bristol City were defeated at Twerton Park. Then, with the Championship secured, Rovers could enjoy the icing on the cake provided by the club's first-ever appearance at Wembley Stadium.

The side that earned this success was largely that which had shown such potential already. Francis stuck with the tried and tested formula, bringing in Ian Willmott, New Zealand International Paul Nixon and Tony Sealy to play sporadic but crucial roles. Sealy scored twice in the win at Shrewsbury Town in November that took Rovers back to the top of the table, while Nixon's five goals included the final one as Rovers sealed the Championship at Blackpool in May. It was, however, the experienced hands that held the side together. Twentyman, Mehew, player of the year Holloway and captain Vaughan Jones were all ever-presents, while Alexander, Yates, Reece and White appeared in more than 40 League matches.

In securing the Division Three Championship, Rovers remained unbeaten at home for the only season in the club's history. There were scares, of course, with Sealy's last-minute equaliser earning a November draw with 10-man Blackpool and Rovers trailing to Cardiff City before two injury time goals earned an unlikely 2-1 victory. Rovers lost just five times in 46 games, a Division Three record, and equalled the club's tally of 26 League victories in 1952/53. Yet, it was achieved the hard way. Rovers, in fact, trailed at half-time in three games and only scored more than three goals in one match. The exceptional game was a 6-1 victory over Wigan Athletic in March, where Carl Saunders, a February signing from Stoke City to replace Gary Penrice, scored the first League hat-trick seen at Twerton Park. This was the Latics' record League defeat, eclipsing the 5-0 loss suffered when Rovers visited Springfield Park in February 1983.

An August Gloucestershire Cup final victory over Bristol City set the tone for the season. On a hot August afternoon, David Mehew's 37th minute goal defeated Brentford and Rovers followed this up with a first post-war League victory at Field Mill, the first of a club record 11 away league wins. Three first-half goals against Notts County in a third narrow victory sent Rovers to the top of Division Three. In the next home game, when Preston North End visited Twerton Park, three more first-half goals sealed a comfortable victory, with Twentyman heading the opener against his former club. Bristol City were hovering ominously close and the sides met at the end of September with two points separating them in the League. The highest crowd to see Rovers all season, 17,432, witnessed a goalless draw, as Francis' side held on with 10 men following the dismissal of Alexander 11 minutes before half-time.

Nigel Martyn's impressive goalkeeping displays were beginning to attract the attention of larger clubs. This burgeoning reputation was enhanced still further by a run of 645 minutes without conceding a goal, just short of Jim Eadie's club record

Bristol Rovers 1989/90. Back row: Reece, Nixon, Willmott, Yates, Jones, Alexander, Purnell. Second row: Twentyman, McClean, Cawley, Martyn, White, Clark, Hazel, Browning. Front row: Dolling (Physio), Penrice, Mehew, Bulpin (Coach), Francis (Manager), Hibbitt (Asst Manager), Sealy, Holloway, Kendall (Kit Man)

707 minutes set in 1973/74. The run ended with Mark Kelly's 80th-minute equaliser for Cardiff City at Twerton Park in mid-October, in a match in where Ian Holloway missed a penalty. The following game epitomized the season for, trailing 1-0 at half-time to an ultimately relegated Northampton Town team for whom Steve Brown had scored the first goal of his career, Rovers were 2-1 down with 11 minutes to play. Then Nixon grabbed an equaliser, Holloway converted a penalty and the unfortunate Trevor Quow put through his own net to give Rovers a 4-2 victory.

With Gary Penrice moving to Watford for £500,000, Rovers were further depleted when Nigel Martyn became Britain's first £1 million goalkeeper, his transfer to Crystal Palace smashing Rovers' club record. Before the season was out, he appeared for his new club in the FA Cup final where his near-namesake Lee Martin, himself a Rovers player in 1996, smashed a rising left-foot volley past him in the replay to win the cup for Manchester United. Martyn was to break his own transfer record in a move to Leeds United in July 1996, which led to International recognition with England. In exchange, Palace's reserve goalkeeper Brian Parkin moved to Bristol to appear in the final 30 League games of the season and kick-start a career that saw two Wembley appearances with Rovers even before an unlikely comeback in the 1999/2000 season.

Early promotion rivals, Birmingham City, with Dennis Bailey in attack, were the Boxing Day opposition for the first imposed all-ticket game. Rovers then saw off the threat of Tranmere Rovers, but only after David Fairclough had been stretchered off. Rovers gave a trial to Sunday football, playing three home games on spring Sundays, won at Preston North End, where Mehew's goal after an hour gave the side its only win in four League matches played on artificial pitches and faced, in Swansea City's 42-year-old Tommy Hutchison, the second oldest opponent in the club's League history. The real threat, however, came from Ashton Gate, where Bristol City had put together an impressive run of results and had claimed top spot in the division. Rovers, with a game in hand through the spring, were waiting for City to slip.

Even the calmest of Rovers supporters was put on the emotional treadmill as the side, with the scent of promotion in its nostrils, recorded six consecutive 2-1 victories in the run-up to Easter. Devon White's two goals earned victory at Craven Cottage, even after Fulham had equalised 16 minutes from time, when Clive Walker's shot deflected in off Yates, Jones and a post. In the next five games, Rovers went a goal down each time, but won them all. Cardiff City, eventually relegated by a point, were perhaps the hardest done by, Rovers scraping home, after losing Sealy with a broken right leg, with two goals in 11 nail-biting injury-time minutes. In White's absence, the unorthodox yet distinctive figure of Christian McClean scored decisive goals in each of the next three games. At Brisbane Road, Mehew's goal earned a victory after Rovers had arrived at the ground only 20 minutes prior to kick-off. Rovers also recovered a two-goal deficit, which would have been worse if referee Philip Wright had awarded a penalty at 2-0 for a clear trip by Willmott on Birmingham City's Robert Hopkins. Instead, Rovers rallied to draw 2-2, with the former Eastville favourite Martin Thomas conceding an own goal.

As Bristol City stuttered, the local derby on 2 May assumed gargantuan proportions. If Rovers won to preserve their unbeaten home record, promotion to Division Two would be assured, but defeat would hand the Championship to City. It was certainly not a night for the faint-hearted. A glorious two-goal display from White, one in each half and a late Holloway penalty sealed the promotion push and Rovers were back in Division Two. A night of high drama before a record home crowd for a game at Twerton Park, 9,831, will live long in the memory. Yet, to ensure that Bristol City, also promoted, could not steal the Championship away, victory was essential at already-relegated Blackpool in the final game. More than 5,000 Rovers supporters made the trip to Bloomfield Road, where a second successive 3-0 victory, with Phil Purnell scoring in the final minute of the first-half and substitute Paul Nixon in the final minute of the second-half, saw Rovers secure the Championship in a carnival atmosphere. Vaughan Jones was able to lift the trophy at his own testimonial game a week later.

Early exits from the Littlewoods Cup, at Portsmouth, and FA Cup, to Reading, for whom Trevor Senior scored a 71st-minute winning goal in a first-round second replay, merely highlight the club's success elsewhere. A draw with Torquay United and victories over Exeter City and Gillingham earned Rovers a Leyland Daf Cup quarter-final meeting with Brentford. This was won in a penalty shoot-out, as was a semi-final with Walsall, Brian Parkin saving three kicks each time. Rovers now faced Notts County over two legs for the right to meet Tranmere Rovers in a Wembley final. A 58th-minute header from David Mehew in the first leg and a strong rearguard action at Meadow Lane, as well as County having a last-minute 'goal' controversially disallowed, earned Rovers a first-ever visit to the Twin Towers. Mehew's 18 League and three cup goals had, bizarrely, all come in separate matches.

There were some 32,000 Rovers fans at Wembley in the 53,317 crowd on 20 May and, despite the result, it was a wonderful day of celebration. A veterans' warm-up game saw Rovers and Tranmere draw 1-1, Alan Warboys and Frank Worthington scoring the

Captain Vaughan Jones holds aloft the Championship Trophy at his Testimonial match at Twerton Park

goals in a show that also featured George Best, Bobby Moore OBE, four members of the pop group Spandau Ballet and the England rugby International Wade Dooley and which was refereed by the veteran Jack Taylor. Just 10 minutes from the start of the final, the former Rovers defender Mark Hughes crossed and, from Chris Malkin's flick-on, Ian Muir scored. Six minutes after half-time, substitute Nixon's cross found White who, at the second attempt, shot right-footed high into the net for the equaliser.

SEASON 1989/90

FOOTBALL LEAGUE DIVISION THREE

Date	Opponent	V	Score	Att	G	2	3	4	5	6	7	8	9	10	11	Substitutes	Goalscorers
19/08/89	BRENTFORD	H	1-0	5835	MARTYN	ALEXANDER	TWENTYMAN	YATES	MEHEW	JONES	HOLLOWAY	REECE	WHITE	PENRICE	WILLMOTT	HAZEL 11	MEHEW
26/08/89	MANSFIELD TOWN	A	1-0	3050	MARTYN	ALEXANDER	TWENTYMAN	YATES	MEHEW	JONES	HOLLOWAY	REECE	WHITE	PENRICE	WILLMOTT	NIXON 10	MEHEW
02/09/89	NOTTS COUNTY	H	3-2	4753	MARTYN	ALEXANDER	TWENTYMAN	YATES	MEHEW	JONES	HOLLOWAY	REECE	WHITE	PENRICE	WILLMOTT	NIXON 10	PENRICE, WHITE, JONES
09/09/89	BOLTON WANDERERS	A	0-1	5913	MARTYN	ALEXANDER	TWENTYMAN	YATES	MEHEW	JONES	HOLLOWAY	REECE	WHITE	PENRICE	WILLMOTT	SEALY 8	
16/09/89	PRESTON NORTH END	H	3-0	4350	MARTYN	ALEXANDER	TWENTYMAN	YATES	MEHEW	JONES	HOLLOWAY	REECE	WHITE	PENRICE	WILLMOTT		TWENTYMAN, PENRICE, WHITE
23/09/89	BRISTOL CITY	A	1-0	17432	MARTYN	ALEXANDER	TWENTYMAN	YATES	MEHEW	JONES	HOLLOWAY	REECE	WHITE	PENRICE	WILLMOTT		MEHEW, PENRICE
26/09/89	LEYTON ORIENT	A	0-0	4675	MARTYN	ALEXANDER	TWENTYMAN	YATES	MEHEW	JONES	HOLLOWAY	REECE	WHITE	PENRICE	WILLMOTT		
30/09/89	READING	H	1-0	6120	MARTYN	ALEXANDER	TWENTYMAN	YATES	MEHEW	JONES	HOLLOWAY	REECE	WHITE	PENRICE	WILLMOTT		MEHEW
07/10/89	FULHAM	H	2-0	5811	MARTYN	NIXON	TWENTYMAN	YATES	MEHEW	JONES	HOLLOWAY	REECE	WHITE	PENRICE	WILLMOTT	HAZEL 2	MEHEW
14/10/89	BURY	A	0-0	3969	MARTYN	ALEXANDER	TWENTYMAN	YATES	MEHEW	JONES	HOLLOWAY	REECE	WHITE	PENRICE	WILLMOTT	SEALY 4	
17/10/89	CARDIFF CITY	A	1-1	6372	MARTYN	ALEXANDER	TWENTYMAN	NIXON	MEHEW	JONES	HOLLOWAY	REECE	WHITE	PENRICE	WILLMOTT	SEALY 4	WHITE, NIXON, HOLLOWAY pen,
21/10/89	NORTHAMPTON T	H	4-2	4920	MARTYN	ALEXANDER	TWENTYMAN	NIXON	MEHEW	JONES	HOLLOWAY	REECE	WHITE	PENRICE	WILLMOTT	SEALY 10	QUOW og
28/10/89	CHESTER CITY	H	0-0	2618	MARTYN	ALEXANDER	TWENTYMAN	YATES	MEHEW	JONES	HOLLOWAY	REECE	WHITE	SEALY	NIXON		
01/11/89	HUDDERSFIELD TOWN	A	2-2	6467	MARTYN	ALEXANDER	TWENTYMAN	YATES	MEHEW	JONES	HOLLOWAY	REECE	WHITE	SEALY	NIXON	WILLMOTT 7	NIXON, MEHEW
04/11/89	BLACKPOOL	H	1-1	5520	MARTYN	ALEXANDER	TWENTYMAN	YATES	MEHEW	JONES	HOLLOWAY	REECE	WHITE	SEALY	NIXON		SEALY
11/11/89	SHREWSBURY TOWN	A	3-2	5623	MARTYN	ALEXANDER	TWENTYMAN	YATES	MEHEW	JONES	HOLLOWAY	REECE	McCLEAN	SEALY	NIXON	McCLEAN 10	SEALY 2, HOLLOWAY
25/11/89	SWANSEA CITY	H	2-1	4038	PARKIN	ALEXANDER	TWENTYMAN	YATES	MEHEW	JONES	HOLLOWAY	REECE	WHITE	HAZEL	NIXON	CAWLEY 4	MEHEW, WHITE
02/12/89	WALSALL	A	2-1	3473	PARKIN	CAWLEY	TWENTYMAN	WILLMOTT	MEHEW	JONES	HOLLOWAY	REECE	WHITE	SEALY	NIXON	HAZEL 11	WHITE, MEHEW
15/12/89	CREWE ALEXANDRA	H	0-0	6573	PARKIN	ALEXANDER	TWENTYMAN	YATES	MEHEW	JONES	HOLLOWAY	REECE	WHITE	SEALY	NIXON	CAWLEY 7	
26/12/89	BIRMINGHAM CITY	A	0-1	6821	PARKIN	ALEXANDER	TWENTYMAN	YATES	MEHEW	JONES	HOLLOWAY	REECE	WHITE	SEALY	NIXON	McCLEAN 11	NIXON, VICKERS og
30/12/89	TRANMERE ROVERS	A	2-3	7750	PARKIN	ALEXANDER	TWENTYMAN	YATES	MEHEW	JONES	HOLLOWAY	REECE	WHITE	SEALY	NIXON	McCLEAN 11	MEHEW, HOLLOWAY pen
01/01/90	ROTHERHAM UNITED	H	1-0	5339	PARKIN	ALEXANDER	TWENTYMAN	YATES	MEHEW	JONES	HOLLOWAY	REECE	WHITE	SEALY	NIXON	PURNELL 10,	TWENTYMAN
13/01/90	MANSFIELD TOWN	H	1-0	7414	PARKIN	ALEXANDER	TWENTYMAN	YATES	MEHEW	JONES	HOLLOWAY	REECE	WHITE	SEALY	NIXON	PURNELL 11,	McCLEAN
20/01/90	BRENTFORD	A	1-2	7772	PARKIN	ALEXANDER	TWENTYMAN	YATES	MEHEW	JONES	HOLLOWAY	REECE	WHITE	NIXON	PURNELL	BROWNING 10	REECE
28/01/90	BOLTON WANDERERS	H	2-0	5956	PARKIN	ALEXANDER	TWENTYMAN	YATES	MEHEW	JONES	HOLLOWAY	REECE	WHITE	SAUNDERS	PURNELL	BYRNE 11	MEHEW
10/02/90	PRESTON NORTH END	A	1-0	6223	PARKIN	ALEXANDER	TWENTYMAN	YATES	MEHEW	JONES	HOLLOWAY	REECE	WHITE	SAUNDERS	PURNELL	BYRNE 11	SAUNDERS 2
18/02/90	WALSALL	H	2-0	5664	PARKIN	ALEXANDER	TWENTYMAN	YATES	MEHEW	JONES	HOLLOWAY	REECE	WHITE	SAUNDERS	PURNELL		
24/02/90	SWANSEA CITY	A	3-1	5169	PARKIN	ALEXANDER	TWENTYMAN	YATES	MEHEW	JONES	HOLLOWAY	REECE	WHITE	SEALY	PURNELL	SEALY 10, WILLMOTT 11	MEHEW, SAUNDERS 3, ALEXANDER, HOLLOWAY
03/03/90	WIGAN ATHLETIC	H	6-1	6147	PARKIN	ALEXANDER	TWENTYMAN	YATES	MEHEW	JONES	HOLLOWAY	REECE	WHITE	SAUNDERS	PURNELL		MEHEW
06/03/90	READING	A	0-0	7018	PARKIN	ALEXANDER	TWENTYMAN	YATES	MEHEW	JONES	HOLLOWAY	REECE	WHITE	SAUNDERS	PURNELL	SEALY 10,	
11/03/90	LEYTON ORIENT	H	2-1	5656	PARKIN	ALEXANDER	TWENTYMAN	YATES	MEHEW	JONES	HOLLOWAY	REECE	WHITE	SAUNDERS	PURNELL	SEALY 5, WHITE 2	WHITE, PURNELL
17/03/90	FULHAM	A	2-1	5552	PARKIN	ALEXANDER	TWENTYMAN	YATES	MEHEW	JONES	HOLLOWAY	REECE	WHITE	SAUNDERS	PURNELL	SEALY 10,	NIXON, MEHEW
21/03/90	BURY	H	2-1	4631	PARKIN	ALEXANDER	TWENTYMAN	YATES	MEHEW	JONES	HOLLOWAY	REECE	NIXON	SAUNDERS	PURNELL	SAUNDERS 10, WILLMOTT 2	MEHEW, McCLEAN
24/03/90	CARDIFF CITY	H	2-1	3774	PARKIN	ALEXANDER	TWENTYMAN	YATES	MEHEW	JONES	HOLLOWAY	McCLEAN	WHITE	SAUNDERS	PURNELL	WHITE 9	MEHEW, McCLEAN
31/03/90	NORTHAMPTON T	A	2-1	2352	PARKIN	ALEXANDER	TWENTYMAN	YATES	MEHEW	JONES	HOLLOWAY	McCLEAN	WHITE	SAUNDERS	PURNELL	WHITE 8	REECE
04/04/90	WIGAN ATHLETIC	A	2-1	6589	PARKIN	ALEXANDER	TWENTYMAN	YATES	MEHEW	JONES	HOLLOWAY	REECE	WHITE	SAUNDERS	PURNELL	WHITE 11	
07/04/90	CHESTER CITY	A	1-1	4359	PARKIN	ALEXANDER	TWENTYMAN	YATES	MEHEW	JONES	HOLLOWAY	REECE	WHITE	SAUNDERS	NIXON	PURNELL 11	MEHEW, JONES
10/04/90	HUDDERSFIELD TOWN	H	2-0	6794	PARKIN	ALEXANDER	TWENTYMAN	YATES	MEHEW	JONES	HOLLOWAY	REECE	WHITE	SAUNDERS	NIXON	PURNELL 11	HAZEL 2, WHITE, THOMAS og
14/04/90	ROTHERHAM UNITED	A	1-1	7250	PARKIN	ALEXANDER	TWENTYMAN	YATES	MEHEW	JONES	HOLLOWAY	REECE	WHITE	SAUNDERS	NIXON	PURNELL 11, HAZEL 8	WHITE
16/04/90	BIRMINGHAM CITY	H	2-2	12438	PARKIN	ALEXANDER	TWENTYMAN	YATES	MEHEW	JONES	HOLLOWAY	WHITE	McCLEAN	SAUNDERS	NIXON	McCLEAN 11, HAZEL 10	TWENTYMAN, HOLLOWAY pen
21/04/90	CREWE ALEXANDRA	A	1-1	12723	PARKIN	ALEXANDER	TWENTYMAN	YATES	MEHEW	JONES	HOLLOWAY	McCLEAN	WHITE	SAUNDERS	NIXON	McCLEAN 8	MEHEW
23/04/90	TRANMERE ROVERS	H	1-0	10142	PARKIN	ALEXANDER	TWENTYMAN	YATES	MEHEW	JONES	HOLLOWAY	McCLEAN	WHITE	SAUNDERS	NIXON	McCLEAN 9, NIXON 11	HOLLOWAY pen
26/04/90	NOTTS COUNTY	A	1-3	9831	PARKIN	ALEXANDER	TWENTYMAN	YATES	MEHEW	JONES	HOLLOWAY	McCLEAN	WHITE	SAUNDERS	NIXON	NIXON 11	WHITE 2, HOLLOWAY pen
28/04/90	SHREWSBURY TOWN	H	3-0	9831	PARKIN	ALEXANDER	TWENTYMAN	YATES	MEHEW	JONES	HOLLOWAY	REECE	WHITE	SAUNDERS	PURNELL		MEHEW, PURNELL, NIXON
02/05/90	BRISTOL CITY	H	3-0	9831	PARKIN	ALEXANDER	TWENTYMAN	YATES	MEHEW	JONES	HOLLOWAY	REECE	WHITE	SAUNDERS	PURNELL		
05/05/90	BLACKPOOL	A	3-0	6776	PARKIN	ALEXANDER	TWENTYMAN	YATES	MEHEW	JONES	HOLLOWAY	REECE	WHITE	SAUNDERS	PURNELL		

LEAGUE CUP

Date	Opponent	V	Score	Att	G	2	3	4	5	6	7	8	9	10	11	Substitutes	Goalscorers
23/08/89	PORTSMOUTH	H	1-0	4727	MARTYN	ALEXANDER	TWENTYMAN	YATES	MEHEW	JONES	HOLLOWAY	REECE	WHITE	PENRICE	WILLMOTT	McCLEAN 10	PENRICE
29/08/89	PORTSMOUTH	A	0-2	5287	MARTYN	ALEXANDER	TWENTYMAN	YATES	MEHEW	JONES	HOLLOWAY	REECE	WHITE	PENRICE	WILLMOTT		

FA CUP

Date	Opponent	V	Score	Att	G	2	3	4	5	6	7	8	9	10	11	Substitutes	Goalscorers
17/11/89	READING	H	1-1	6115	PARKIN	ALEXANDER	TWENTYMAN	YATES	MEHEW	JONES	HOLLOWAY	REECE	WHITE	SEALY	NIXON	HAZEL 10,	REECE
21/11/89	READING	A	1-1*	6015	PARKIN	ALEXANDER	TWENTYMAN	YATES	MEHEW	JONES	HOLLOWAY	REECE	WHITE	SEALY	NIXON	McCLEAN 8	MEHEW
27/11/89	READING	H	0-1	6782	PARKIN	ALEXANDER	TWENTYMAN	YATES	MEHEW	JONES	HOLLOWAY	McCLEAN	WHITE	SEALY	NIXON		

* AET Score at 90 mins 0-0

LEYLAND DAF CUP

Date	Opponent	V	Score	Att	G	2	3	4	5	6	7	8	9	10	11	Substitutes	Goalscorers
07/11/89	TORQUAY UNITED	H	1-1	2218	MARTYN	ALEXANDER	TWENTYMAN	YATES	MEHEW	JONES	HOLLOWAY	REECE	WHITE	SEALY	NIXON	BROWNING 11	WHITE
17/01/90	EXETER CITY	H	3-0	3136	PARKIN	ALEXANDER	TWENTYMAN	YATES	MEHEW	JONES	HOLLOWAY	REECE	McCLEAN	SEALY	PURNELL	NIXON 10	HOLLOWAY pen, SEALY, MEHEW
06/02/90	BRENTFORD *	H	2-2	2724	PARKIN	ALEXANDER	TWENTYMAN	YATES	MEHEW	JONES	HOLLOWAY	REECE	WHITE	NIXON	PURNELL	BYRNE 5	NIXON
14/03/90	WALSALL **	A	0-0	4409	PARKIN	WILLMOTT	TWENTYMAN	YATES	MEHEW	JONES	HOLLOWAY	REECE	WHITE	SAUNDERS	PURNELL	BYRNE 5	HOLLOWAY pen, SAUNDERS
28/03/90	NOTTS COUNTY***	H	0-0	6480	MARTYN	ALEXANDER	TWENTYMAN	YATES	MEHEW	JONES	HOLLOWAY	McCLEAN	WHITE	NIXON	PURNELL	McCLEAN 8	MEHEW
02/04/90	NOTTS COUNTY***	A	0-0	10857	MARTYN	ALEXANDER	TWENTYMAN	YATES	MEHEW	JONES	HOLLOWAY	REECE	WHITE	SAUNDERS	PURNELL	McCLEAN 8	WHITE
20/05/90	TRANMERE R****	N	1-2	48402	PARKIN	ALEXANDER	TWENTYMAN	NIXON	MEHEW	JONES	HOLLOWAY	REECE	WHITE	SAUNDERS	PURNELL	NIXON 2, McCLEAN 11	WILLMOTT, PENRICE

* AET Score at 90 mins 1-1 Rovers won 4-3 on pens
** AET won 3-2 on pens
*** Southern Area Final
**** National Final at Wembley Stadium

GLOUCESTERSHIRE CUP FINAL

Date	Opponent	V	Score	Att	G	2	3	4	5	6	7	8	9	10	11	Substitutes	Goalscorers
08/08/89	BRISTOL CITY	A	2-1	6153	PARKIN	ALEXANDER	TWENTYMAN	YATES	MEHEW	JONES	HOLLOWAY	REECE	WHITE	PENRICE	WILLMOTT	CAWLEY, HAZEL	WILLMOTT, PENRICE

Appearances

PLAYERS	APP	SUB	GLS
ALEXANDER I	43		1
BROWNING M	0	1	
BYRNE D	0	2	
CAWLEY P	2	2	
HAZEL I	5	6	8
JONES V	46		2
MARTYN N	16		
McCLEAN C	10	5	4
MEHEW D	46		18
NIXON P	21	6	5
PARKIN B	30		
PENRICE G	12	5	3
PURNELL P	12	7	5
REECE A	43		2
SAUNDERS C	19	1	
SEALY A	12	7	3
TWENTYMAN G	46		3
WHITE D	40	3	12
WILLMOTT I	14	3	
YATES S	42		
OWN GOALS			3

David Mehew heads the winning goal in the first leg of the Southern Area Leyland Daf Final over Notts County at Twerton Park

However, 17 minutes from time, Jim Steel's header consigned Rovers to defeat. Nonetheless, it was a major achievement for a club of the stature of Bristol Rovers to reach a Wembley final. The season had brought much greater success than any realistic Rovers fan could have dreamed of.

1990/91

I t is perhaps typical of Bristol Rovers that the long-awaited return to Division Two should be overshadowed by events off the field. The all-conquering side of 1989/90 understandably found the going considerably harder in the higher division, but a final placing of 13th, the club's highest since 1959/60, was commendable. However, the actions of arsonists and further rebuffs to Rovers' hopes of a move back to Bristol provided many of the overriding memories.

The continued search for a stadium nearer Rovers' fan base in east Bristol was still encountering problems. With the proposal for a move to Stoke Gifford rejected, much emphasis had been placed on a potential move to Mangotsfield. With the huge success of the 1989/90 season, the club now appeared more likely to interest the local authorities, who seemed keen to jump on the bandwagon, given the on-field success and aspirations of both Bristol clubs. Suddenly Bristol was being touted as a sporting city.

Bristol Rovers 1990/91. Back row: Bloomer, Twentyman, Mehew, White, Yates, Clark, Hazel, Reece. Second row: Kendall (Kit Man), Jones, Hewitson, Nixon, Willmott, Kelly, Parkin, Browning, Boothroyd, Pounder, McClean, Dolling (Physio). Front row: Purnell, Alexander, Holloway, Muxworthy (Youth Coach), Francis (Manager), Bulpin (Coach), Saunders, Sealy

Yet, disappointment was to strike on two fronts in September 1990. First, the plans for a stadium at Mangotsfield were rejected and secondly, a week later in the early hours of 16 September, a serious fire damaged the Main Stand at Twerton Park.

There was little doubt as to the perpetrators of the stadium fire. Seven so-called 'supporters' of Bristol City, returning from a 2-1 defeat at West Bromwich Albion, went back to the scene of their side's disappointment in May, attempted to burn down the stand and, in court, were found guilty of arson. Repair costs to the Main Stand were to run to £800,000, although Rovers did receive financial aid from Bath Rugby Football Club as well as a £300 donation from Sheffield Wednesday supporters following their visit in October. Moreover, there was a pre-arranged commitment to a £90,000 family stand, which opened in December. Yet again, precisely at the point when Rovers promised on-field success, politics and finance interfered in the club's affairs.

At the same time, Rovers were obliged to comply with the increasing legal requirements imposed following the tragedies at Bradford, Hillsborough and Heysel. The 1985 Sporting Event (Control of Alcohol) Act had prevented those being suspected of drunkenness gaining access to the ground and the 1986 Public Order Act enabled clubs to impose exclusion orders for 'hooligan-related offences'. This was followed by the 1991 Football Offences Act, which banned obscene and racially offensive chanting and forbade spectators from entering the field of play.

Apart from the departure of stand-in Peter Cawley and the arrival of the exciting Tony Pounder, it was largely the championship-winning side that attained a respectable mid-table finish. Some argued it was a return to the halcyon days of the 1950s, with

Grandstand fire at Twerton Park on 16 September 1990 saw plenty of disruption and loss of revenue for the club

Rovers' paltry financial clout virtually necessitating a return to the 'no buy, no sell' policy that dictated the early post-war years. Others argued that the club stood to suffer almost immediate relegation if, in this era of huge spending, a number of key positions were not filled by expensive signings. As it was, 'Ragbag Rovers' retained their Division Two standing with relative ease.

If life in a higher division was to prove difficult for Rovers, as many claimed, there certainly was little sign of it. A narrow defeat at Leicester City, with Ian Alexander contributing a bizarre own goal and Vaughan Jones scoring the club's first goal back in Division Two, was followed by victory at home to Charlton Athletic, the visitors' eighth in a club record run of 10 consecutive League defeats. Devon White, on 16 minutes, and David Mehew after 49 put Rovers ahead before Robert Lee scored for the Addicks four minutes from time. As early as mid-October Rovers won back-to-back away games at Swindon Town and Middlesbrough. Ian Holloway scored from penalties in both games and coolly converted another after forty-two minutes of a 1-0 home victory over Oxford United. He had equalled Stewart Barrowclough's club record from 1979 of scoring penalties in three consecutive League matches, but Holloway never scored again from the penalty-spot for Rovers.

On a Wednesday night in September, Blackburn Rovers recorded a 2-1 victory at Twerton Park to end Rovers' proud run of 34 home League matches unbeaten. Three days later, Sheffield Wednesday also won at 'Fortress Twerton'. On 6 October, Rovers only avoided dropping into the relegation zone – reorganisation having meant only two

FOOTBALL LEAGUE DIVISION TWO

Date	Opponent		Score	Att	G	2	3	4	5	6	7	8	9	10	11	Substitutes	Goalscorers
25/08/90	LEICESTER CITY	A	2-3	13648	PARKIN	ALEXANDER	TWENTYMAN	YATES	MEHEW	JONES	HOLLOWAY	REECE	WHITE	SAUNDERS	POUNDER	HAZEL 5	WHITE, JONES
01/09/90	CHARLTON ATHLETIC	H	2-1	5357	PARKIN	ALEXANDER	TWENTYMAN	YATES	MEHEW	JONES	HOLLOWAY	REECE	WHITE	SAUNDERS	POUNDER	BLOOMER 5	WHITE, MEHEW
08/09/90	WOLVES	A	1-1	17912	PARKIN	ALEXANDER	TWENTYMAN	YATES	MEHEW	JONES	HOLLOWAY	REECE	WHITE	SAUNDERS	POUNDER	HAZEL 5	HOLLOWAY
15/09/90	HULL CITY	H	1-1	4734	PARKIN	ALEXANDER	TWENTYMAN	YATES	MEHEW	JONES	HOLLOWAY	REECE	WHITE	SAUNDERS	POUNDER		MEHEW
22/09/90	IPSWICH TOWN	H	1-2	11084	PARKIN	ALEXANDER	TWENTYMAN	YATES	MEHEW	JONES	HOLLOWAY	REECE	WHITE	SAUNDERS	POUNDER	NIXON 8	SAUNDERS
29/09/90	NOTTS COUNTY	A	2-3	6563	PARKIN	ALEXANDER	TWENTYMAN	YATES	MEHEW	JONES	HOLLOWAY	REECE	WHITE	SAUNDERS	PURNELL	McCLEAN 10	SAUNDERS, HOLLOWAY pen
03/10/90	BLACKBURN ROVERS	H	1-2	5200	PARKIN	ALEXANDER	TWENTYMAN	YATES	NIXON	JONES	HOLLOWAY	REECE	WHITE	POUNDER	PURNELL	PURNELL 5	WHITE
06/10/90	SHEFFIELD WEDS	H	0-1	6413	PARKIN	BLOOMER	TWENTYMAN	YATES	NIXON	JONES	HOLLOWAY	REECE	WHITE	POUNDER	PURNELL	PURNELL 2, McCLEAN 11	
13/10/90	SWINDON TOWN	A	2-0	11494	PARKIN	BLOOMER	TWENTYMAN	YATES	NIXON	JONES	HOLLOWAY	REECE	WHITE	SAUNDERS	POUNDER	MEHEW 5 ALEXANDER 2	POUNDER, HOLLOWAY pen
20/10/90	MIDDLESBROUGH	A	2-1	18589	PARKIN	BLOOMER	TWENTYMAN	YATES	NIXON	JONES	HOLLOWAY	REECE	WHITE	SAUNDERS	POUNDER	MEHEW 5	WHITE, HOLLOWAY pen
24/10/90	OXFORD UNITED	H	1-0	5526	PARKIN	BLOOMER	TWENTYMAN	YATES	MEHEW	JONES	HOLLOWAY	REECE	WHITE	SAUNDERS	POUNDER	MEHEW 5	HOLLOWAY pen
27/10/90	PORTSMOUTH	H	1-2	6500	PARKIN	BLOOMER	TWENTYMAN	YATES	MEHEW	JONES	HOLLOWAY	REECE	WHITE	SAUNDERS	POUNDER	MEHEW 5, ALEXANDER 2	WHITE
03/11/90	WEST BROM ALBION	A	1-3	10997	PARKIN	ALEXANDER	TWENTYMAN	YATES	MEHEW	JONES	HOLLOWAY	REECE	WHITE	SAUNDERS	NIXON	MEHEW 10	MEHEW, POUNDER
07/11/90	BARNSLEY	H	2-1	4563	PARKIN	ALEXANDER	TWENTYMAN	YATES	MEHEW	JONES	HOLLOWAY	REECE	WHITE	SAUNDERS	NIXON	PURNELL 11, BLOOMER 8	NIXON, MEHEW
10/11/90	PORT VALE	A	2-0	5661	PARKIN	ALEXANDER	TWENTYMAN	YATES	MEHEW	JONES	HOLLOWAY	REECE	WHITE	SAUNDERS	POUNDER	SAUNDERS 11	MEHEW
17/11/90	OLDHAM ATHLETIC	H	1-0	8285	PARKIN	ALEXANDER	TWENTYMAN	YATES	MEHEW	JONES	HOLLOWAY	REECE	WHITE	SAUNDERS	NIXON	SAUNDERS 11	DRYSDALE og
24/11/90	MILLWALL	A	1-1	6936	PARKIN	ALEXANDER	TWENTYMAN	YATES	MEHEW	JONES	HOLLOWAY	REECE	WHITE	SAUNDERS	NIXON	NIXON 11, BLOOMER 8	MEHEW, WHITE
01/12/90	LEICESTER CITY	H	2-0	6542	PARKIN	ALEXANDER	TWENTYMAN	YATES	MEHEW	JONES	HOLLOWAY	REECE	WHITE	SAUNDERS	POUNDER		MEHEW
15/12/90	NEWCASTLE UNITED	A	1-1	9291	PARKIN	ALEXANDER	TWENTYMAN	YATES	MEHEW	JONES	HOLLOWAY	REECE	WHITE	SAUNDERS	POUNDER	NIXON 5	
22/12/90	BRIGHTON & H ALB	A	1-0	5791	PARKIN	ALEXANDER	TWENTYMAN	YATES	MEHEW	JONES	HOLLOWAY	REECE	WHITE	SAUNDERS	POUNDER	NIXON 11	SAUNDERS
26/12/90	PLYMOUTH ARGYLE	H	1-0	6643	PARKIN	ALEXANDER	TWENTYMAN	YATES	MEHEW	JONES	HOLLOWAY	REECE	WHITE	SAUNDERS	POUNDER	NIXON 5	SAUNDERS
29/12/90	WEST HAM UNITED	A	2-2	8469	PARKIN	ALEXANDER	TWENTYMAN	YATES	MEHEW	JONES	HOLLOWAY	REECE	WHITE	SAUNDERS	POUNDER	NIXON 5	SAUNDERS 2
01/01/91	CHARLTON ATHLETIC	H	0-1	7932	PARKIN	ALEXANDER	TWENTYMAN	YATES	MEHEW	JONES	HOLLOWAY	REECE	WHITE	SAUNDERS	POUNDER		
12/01/91	WOLVES	A	2-2	5606	PARKIN	ALEXANDER	TWENTYMAN	YATES	MEHEW	JONES	HOLLOWAY	REECE	WHITE	SAUNDERS	POUNDER	BLOOMER 2, SEALY 5	SAUNDERS, WHITE
19/01/91	BRISTOL CITY	H	1-1	6042	PARKIN	ALEXANDER	TWENTYMAN	YATES	MEHEW	JONES	HOLLOWAY	REECE	WHITE	SAUNDERS	POUNDER	SEALY 5	SAUNDERS
26/01/91	HULL CITY	A	3-2	7054	PARKIN	ALEXANDER	TWENTYMAN	YATES	MEHEW	JONES	HOLLOWAY	REECE	WHITE	SAUNDERS	POUNDER	BLOOMER 2	MEHEW 2, SAUNDERS
02/02/91	WATFORD	A	0-2	5302	PARKIN	ALEXANDER	TWENTYMAN	YATES	MEHEW	JONES	HOLLOWAY	REECE	WHITE	SAUNDERS	POUNDER	SEALY 5 BLOOMER 4	
16/02/91	PORT VALE	H	3-1	5736	PARKIN	ALEXANDER	TWENTYMAN	YATES	MEHEW	JONES	HOLLOWAY	REECE	WHITE	SAUNDERS	POUNDER	SEALY 5	HOLLOWAY, WHITE, SAUNDERS
23/02/91	BARNSLEY	A	2-3	7166	PARKIN	ALEXANDER	TWENTYMAN	YATES	MEHEW	JONES	HOLLOWAY	REECE	WHITE	SAUNDERS	POUNDER	SEALY 5, GORDON 9	ALEXANDER, SAUNDERS
26/02/91	MILLWALL	H	0-1	6197	PARKIN	ALEXANDER	TWENTYMAN	YATES	HAZEL	JONES	HOLLOWAY	REECE	WHITE	SAUNDERS	POUNDER	SEALY 5, GORDON 9	
02/03/91	BRISTOL CITY	A	1-0	5587	PARKIN	BLOOMER	TWENTYMAN	CLARK	SEALY	JONES	HOLLOWAY	REECE	WHITE	SAUNDERS	POUNDER	SEALY 11	SEALY
05/03/91	NEWCASTLE UNITED	H	0-1	22227	PARKIN	ALEXANDER	TWENTYMAN	CLARK	SEALY	WILLMOTT	HOLLOWAY	REECE	WHITE	SAUNDERS	POUNDER	WILLMOTT 2	
09/03/91	OLDHAM ATHLETIC	A	0-2	5969	PARKIN	BOOTHROYD	TWENTYMAN	CLARK	SEALY	WILLMOTT	HOLLOWAY	REECE	WHITE	SAUNDERS	POUNDER	SEALY 11, MEHEW 5	
12/03/91	BLACKBURN ROVERS	A	2-2	12775	PARKIN	ALEXANDER	TWENTYMAN	CLARK	SEALY	JONES	HOLLOWAY	REECE	WHITE	SAUNDERS	POUNDER	SEALY 5, GORDON 8	HOLLOWAY, SAUNDERS
16/03/91	NOTTS COUNTY	H	1-1	4878	PARKIN	ALEXANDER	TWENTYMAN	CLARK	SEALY	JONES	HOLLOWAY	REECE	WHITE	SAUNDERS	BAILEY	MEHEW 11,	CLARK
20/03/91	SWINDON TOWN	A	1-2	6123	PARKIN	ALEXANDER	TWENTYMAN	CLARK	SEALY	JONES	HOLLOWAY	REECE	WHITE	SAUNDERS	BAILEY	MEHEW 11,	SAUNDERS, SEALY
23/03/91	SHEFFIELD WEDS	H	1-3	25074	PARKIN	ALEXANDER	TWENTYMAN	CLARK	SEALY	JONES	HOLLOWAY	REECE	WHITE	SAUNDERS	BAILEY	GORDON 11	SAUNDERS
30/03/91	BRIGHTON & H ALB	H	1-2	6276	PARKIN	ALEXANDER	TWENTYMAN	CLARK	SEALY	JONES	HOLLOWAY	REECE	WHITE	SAUNDERS	BAILEY	POUNDER 11, MEHEW 5	REECE
01/04/91	NEWCASTLE UNITED	A	1-3	17509	PARKIN	ALEXANDER	TWENTYMAN	CLARK	SEALY	JONES	HOLLOWAY	REECE	WHITE	SAUNDERS	BAILEY	POUNDER 11	SEALY, WHITE
06/04/91	PLYMOUTH ARGYLE	H	0-0	5668	PARKIN	ALEXANDER	TWENTYMAN	BOOTHROYD	MEHEW	JONES	HOLLOWAY	REECE	WHITE	SAUNDERS	BAILEY	POUNDER 5, BOOTHROYD 11	
13/04/91	IPSWICH TOWN	H	1-0	4983	PARKIN	ALEXANDER	TWENTYMAN	CLARK	MEHEW	JONES	HOLLOWAY	REECE	WHITE	SAUNDERS	BAILEY	MEHEW 5, POUNDER 11	SEALY
20/04/91	MIDDLESBROUGH	H	2-0	5722	PARKIN	ALEXANDER	TWENTYMAN	CLARK	MEHEW	JONES	HOLLOWAY	REECE	WHITE	SAUNDERS	POUNDER	MEHEW 5,	SAUNDERS pen, BAILEY
27/04/91	OXFORD UNITED	A	1-3	6744	PARKIN	ALEXANDER	TWENTYMAN	CLARK	MEHEW	JONES	HOLLOWAY	REECE	WHITE	SAUNDERS	POUNDER	POUNDER 5	WHITE
04/05/91	PORTSMOUTH	A	1-3	9410	PARKIN	ALEXANDER	TWENTYMAN	CLARK	MEHEW	JONES	HOLLOWAY	REECE	WHITE	SAUNDERS	POUNDER	POUNDER 11, YATES 4	SAUNDERS
08/05/91	WEST HAM UNITED	H	0-1	23054	PARKIN	ALEXANDER	TWENTYMAN	YATES	BOOTHROYD	JONES	HOLLOWAY	REECE	WHITE	SAUNDERS	POUNDER	HAZEL 5	
11/05/91	WEST BROM ALBION	H	1-1	7595	PARKIN	ALEXANDER	TWENTYMAN	YATES	MEHEW	JONES	HOLLOWAY	REECE	WHITE	SAUNDERS	POUNDER	HAZEL 2, CLARK 5	POUNDER

LEAGUE CUP

Date	Opponent		Score	Att	G	2	3	4	5	6	7	8	9	10	11	Substitutes	Goalscorers
29/08/90	TORQUAY UNITED	H	1-2	2461	PARKIN	ALEXANDER	TWENTYMAN	YATES	MEHEW	JONES	HOLLOWAY	REECE	WHITE	SAUNDERS	POUNDER	McCLEAN 5	TWENTYMAN
04/09/90	TORQUAY UNITED	A	1-1	3533	PARKIN	ALEXANDER	TWENTYMAN	YATES	MEHEW	JONES	HOLLOWAY	REECE	WHITE	SAUNDERS	POUNDER		ALEXANDER

FA CUP

Date	Opponent		Score	Att	G	2	3	4	5	6	7	8	9	10	11	Substitutes	Goalscorers
05/01/91	CREWE ALEXANDRA	H	0-2	6143	PARKIN	BLOOMER	TWENTYMAN	YATES	MEHEW	JONES	HOLLOWAY	REECE	GORDON	SAUNDERS	POUNDER	NIXON 1	

ZENITH DATA SYSTEMS CUP

Date	Opponent		Score	Att	G	2	3	4	5	6	7	8	9	10	11	Substitutes	Goalscorers
20/11/90	WATFORD	A	2-1	3076	PARKIN	ALEXANDER	TWENTYMAN	YATES	MEHEW	JONES	HOLLOWAY	REECE	WHITE	SAUNDERS	POUNDER	NIXON 7, PURNELL 11	SAUNDERS, MEHEW
18/12/90	CRYSTAL PALACE	A	1-4	5209	PARKIN	ALEXANDER	TWENTYMAN	YATES	MEHEW	JONES	HOLLOWAY	REECE	WHITE	SAUNDERS	POUNDER		POUNDER

GLOUCESTERSHIRE CUP FINAL

Date	Opponent		Score	Att	G	2	3	4	5	6	7	8	9	10	11	Substitutes	Goalscorers
15/08/90	BRISTOL CITY	H	1-4	4208	PARKIN	PARKIN	TWENTYMAN	YATES	HAZEL	JONES	BLOOMER	REECE	McCLEAN	SAUNDERS	POUNDER	BOOTHROYD	BROWNING, JONES pen

Players	App	Sub	Gls
ALEXANDER I	37	2	1
BAILEY D	6		1
BLOOMER R	7	6	
BOOTHROYD A	2	1	
CLARK W	13	1	1
GORDON C	1	3	
HAZEL I	2	4	
HOLLOWAY I	46		7
JONES V	44		1
KELLY G	0	2	
McCLEAN C	2	11	8
MEHEW D	30	11	8
NIXON P	10	6	1
PARKIN B	39		
POUNDER A	39	6	3
PURNELL P	3	3	
REECE A	46		1
SAUNDERS C	36	2	16
SEALY A	9	9	4
TWENTYMAN G	46		
WHITE D	45		11
WILLMOTT I	2	1	
YATES S	33	1	
OWN GOAL			1

clubs would be relegated – because of the three second-half goals Oxford United conceded at Barnsley. Nonetheless, by the first week in December Rovers lay in ninth place in the table, the highest placing in an encouraging season. At this stage, the club was in the middle of a morale-boosting nine-match unbeaten run, which ended abruptly when Jimmy Quinn scored West Ham United's 68th minute winning goal on New Year's Day. However, enough had been done to satisfy the claim that Rovers were in this division by right.

As the season wore on, Francis recalled Willmott, briefly, and Billy Clark who, after many substitute appearances and missing the entire promotion season through injury, played in his first games since October 1988. Clark first played in March in the cauldron of a local derby and, before the month was out he had contributed an own goal, one of five conceded all season by Rovers defenders, in a 2-1 defeat at Hillsborough. Adrian Boothroyd and Gavin Kelly both broke into the League side and, two years on, Dennis Bailey enjoyed a second if less prolific loan spell with the club.

Over Easter, Rovers' Jekyll and Hyde character came to the fore. Goalkeeper Parkin was sent off in a 3-1 defeat at home to Brighton, with stand-in Ian Alexander saving the subsequent penalty from John Byrne, who missed another penalty against Rovers in September 1992, when on Sunderland's books. Forty-eight hours later, before a crowd of 17,509, second-half goals from Devon White and Tony Sealy earned a notable 2-0 victory at Newcastle United. Rovers then finished the season with demoralizing 3-1 defeats at Oxford United, where Vaughan Jones' second own goal of the season left Rovers three down by half-time, and Portsmouth, for whom John Beresford opened the scoring after only 38 seconds. In depriving West Bromwich Albion of a final day win – Tony Pounder contributing his third goal of the season 19 minutes from time following Jones' near-post corner – Rovers effectively relegated the Hawthorns club.

Osvaldo Ardiles, a World Cup winner with Argentina in 1978, was the manager of Rovers' opponents in three of Rovers' League victories. Pounder's first goal for the club helped Rovers record a 2-0 victory at Swindon Town in October. A 2-1 win against the same opposition completed the first of Rovers' two League doubles, but only after Nestor Lorenzo, a member of the Argentinian side that lost the 1990 World Cup final, had hit a Twerton Park post. Shortly afterwards, Ardiles took over the reins at Newcastle United in time to suffer a third defeat at the hands of Gerry Francis' side.

Once again, relative success was based on a consistently settled side. Twentyman, Holloway and Reece were ever-presents, but in truth the team virtually picked itself for much of the season. Parkin proved himself an adept goalkeeper and an experienced defence was not in the habit of shipping goals regularly. Carl Saunders, after enjoying a mid-season purple patch of 9 goals in 10 League matches, finished the year as the club's top goalscorer with 16 goals in League action. David Mehew's two goals in a 3-2 home victory over Bristol City in January 1991 constituted the first occasion since November 1988 that the talented midfielder, top scorer in 1990/91, had contributed more than one in a League game.

There was disappointment in the FA Cup. Division Three Crewe Alexandra won 2-0 at Twerton Park, with the former Rovers defender Darren Carr scoring one of the goals. Bob Bloomer had been forced into goal once Parkin was carried off the field injured, but this is no excuse for a humiliating experience. Another former Rovers defender, Gary

Mabbutt, now an England International, captained Tottenham Hotspur to victory over Nottingham Forest in the 1991 FA Cup final. There was also an early exit from the Rumbelows Cup where, although full-backs Alexander and Twentyman both scored, Rovers lost on aggregate to Division Three Torquay United.

One benefit of being in Division Two was qualification for the Zenith Data Systems Cup. Rovers played in just two games in this tournament, taking a half-hour lead through Tony Pounder before losing to Crystal Palace who, with the former Rovers goalkeeper Nigel Martyn in their side, went on to win the Wembley final. Bristol City scored twice in each half, Nicky Morgan contributing half their goals, as Rovers were beaten 4-1 in the Gloucestershire Cup final.

1991/92

After the disappointments regarding proposed stadia in Stoke Gifford and Mangotsfield, Rovers at last appeared on the verge of finalising plans for a move nearer its spiritual home in east Bristol. The new site was at Hallen Marsh, a 70-acre site in close proximity to the proposed M49 motorway, which was due to open in 1996. Good road and rail links would, of course, be essential, as Rovers attempted to build on the fact that Bristol boasted two Division Two sides. The new stadium was also seen as a means to attract major national and international sporting events to a West Country arena.

Plans to develop the Hallen Marsh site into a multi-sport complex were drawn up by Severnside Sportsworld, an organisation effectively run by the Rovers directors Denis and Geoff Dunford. Spectator, a leading American facilities management company, was called in to advise and by December 1991 the local authorities appeared to be in favour. Yet, the Bristol Rovers story is not so straightforward. No sooner were plans being tabled than it was revealed that the site was too close to a chemical plant to satisfy safety regulations. The deal was off, the Dunfords had lost an alleged £300,000, already invested into the scheme, and Rovers' increasingly desperate search for a new Bristol home continued.

It was inevitable that Gerry Francis' success at Rovers on a shoestring budget should lead to interest from larger clubs. Sure enough, he left Rovers in the summer of 1991 to become manager at Queen's Park Rangers. While at Loftus Road, he accumulated a number of players who had served him so well at Twerton Park, Ian Holloway, Dennis Bailey, Devon White, Gary Penrice and Steve Yates all rejoining their former manager. On the other hand, a large number of Queen's Park Rangers players were to make the opposite move, untried youngsters such as Graeme Power and Steve Parmenter as well as record signing Andy Tillson. For his part, Francis was later manager at Tottenham Hotspur before returning for a second spell as manager at Loftus Road, the ground where he had made his name as a player.

The new manager was Martin Dobson, an erstwhile classy midfielder with Burnley for many years, Everton and Bury and the winner of 5 full England caps. He had been manager at Northwich Victoria and had spent five years in charge of Bury prior to his arrival at Twerton Park. While Holloway followed Francis to London in a £230,000

Bristol Rovers 1991/92. Back row: Stewart, Hazel, Clark, Willmott, Browning, White, Mehew, Maddison, Yates, Evans. Second row: Rofe (Chief Coach), Dolling (Physio), Reece, Parkin, Bloomer, Kelly, Wilson, Kendall, Dobson (Manager). Front row: Purnell, Boothroyd, Saunders, Twentyman, Pounder, Alexander, Archer, Chenoweth

deal, Rovers also lost Tony Sealy to Finnish football and the distinctive Christian McClean, who joined Swansea City prior to many years as a peripatetic striker in Essex non-League circles. Dobson was able to call upon the services of two experienced signings in Fulham's Justin Skinner and Derby County's Steve Cross. While Richard Evans and the former Manchester United midfielder David Wilson started in the side, it was Lee Maddison and Gareth Taylor who, both selected by Dobson, began careers that would bring success with Rovers and beyond.

In starting the season temporarily without the suspended Carl Saunders, Dobson also unleashed the talents of 18-year-old Marcus Stewart, already the winner of 12 England Schoolboy caps, who had worked his way up through the youth system. After a left-foot volley in a meeting with Ipswich Town, in which Ian Alexander saw his 47th-minute penalty saved by Craig Forrest, Stewart scored twice at Tranmere Rovers in his second game, becoming in the process Rovers' youngest penalty scorer when he converted a last-minute equaliser. Over the coming seasons, Stewart established himself as one of the brightest prospects produced by Rovers in recent years. His excellent first touch and ability to take on opponents soon drew the attention of larger clubs, but Rovers were to retain him long enough for him to score the side's goal at Wembley in the 1995 play-off final.

Yet Dobson's side lost six of its first nine League games and the manager's brief tenure was over. He later returned to football as Youth Development Officer at Division One Bolton Wanderers. The one victory, 2-1 at home to Oxford United, marked the first game of the season for captain Vaughan Jones. His return lasted all of 60 seconds before he suffered a broken leg that ruled him out for a further 14 months. Coach Dennis Rofe was quickly elevated to the post of manager on 10 January 1992. He too enjoyed a long professional career, winning one England Under-23 cap and enjoying almost a decade as Leicester City's left-back after making his League debut as a goalscoring substitute in Orient's 2-0 win at Rovers in April 1968.

FOOTBALL LEAGUE DIVISION TWO

Date	Opponent	V	G	ATT	G	2	3	4	5	6	7	8	9	10	11	SUBSTITUTES	GOALSCORERS
17/08/91	IPSWICH TOWN	H	3-3	6444	PARKIN	ALEXANDER	TWENTYMAN	YATES	MEHEW	BOOTHROYD	EVANS	REECE	WHITE	STEWART	POUNDER	PURNELL 7	STEWART, WHITE 2
23/08/91	TRANMERE ROVERS	A	2-2	10150	PARKIN	BOOTHROYD	CLARK	YATES	MEHEW	WILLMOTT	WILSON	REECE	WHITE	STEWART	POUNDER	PURNELL 5	STEWART 2-1pen
31/08/91	NEWCASTLE UNITED	H	1-2	6334	PARKIN	BOOTHROYD	TWENTYMAN	YATES	MEHEW	WILLMOTT	WILSON	REECE	WHITE	STEWART	POUNDER	SKINNER, PURNELL 7	SKINNER
04/09/91	BRISTOL CITY	A	0-1	20183	PARKIN	BOOTHROYD	TWENTYMAN	YATES	BOOTHROYD	ARCHER	SKINNER	REECE	WHITE	STEWART	PURNELL	SAUNDERS 7	
07/09/91	GRIMSBY TOWN	H	2-3	4641	PARKIN	ALEXANDER	TWENTYMAN	YATES	SKINNER	EVANS	POUNDER	REECE	WHITE	STEWART	ARCHER	ARCHER 11, SAUNDERS 6	WHITE, EVANS
14/09/91	SOUTHEND UNITED	A	0-2	4670	PARKIN	ALEXANDER	TWENTYMAN	YATES	CLARK	CROSS	WILSON	REECE	WHITE	SAUNDERS	STEWART	BOOTHROYD 5, SAUNDERS 7	
17/09/91	SWINDON TOWN	H	1-0	11391	PARKIN	ALEXANDER	TWENTYMAN	YATES	CLARK	JONES	BOOTHROYD	CROSS	WHITE	SAUNDERS	STEWART	ARCHER 6, BROWNING 9	
21/09/91	OXFORD UNITED	A	2-1	4854	PARKIN	ALEXANDER	TWENTYMAN	YATES	CLARK	SKINNER	MEHEW	CROSS	WHITE	SAUNDERS	PURNELL	BROWNING 7	ALEXANDER, CROSS
28/09/91	BRIGHTON & H ALB	H	1-3	6392	PARKIN	ALEXANDER	TWENTYMAN	YATES	CROSS	SKINNER	MEHEW	REECE	WHITE	SAUNDERS	PURNELL	BROWNING 10	SAUNDERS
05/10/91	MIDDLESBROUGH	A	2-1	4936	PARKIN	ALEXANDER	TWENTYMAN	YATES	CROSS	SKINNER	MEHEW	REECE	WHITE	BROWNING	POUNDER	PURNELL 6	ARCHER, BROWNING
12/10/91	CHARLTON ATHLETIC	A	0-1	5685	PARKIN	ALEXANDER	TWENTYMAN	YATES	CROSS	SKINNER	MEHEW	REECE	WHITE	BROWNING	POUNDER	PURNELL 9,	
19/10/91	PLYMOUTH ARGYLE	H	1-1	14746	PARKIN	ALEXANDER	TWENTYMAN	YATES	CROSS	SKINNER	MEHEW	REECE	WHITE	BROWNING	POUNDER	STEWART 10	BROWNING
26/10/91	SUNDERLAND	A	1-1	5049	PARKIN	ALEXANDER	TWENTYMAN	YATES	CROSS	SKINNER	MEHEW	REECE	WHITE	SAUNDERS	POUNDER	PURNELL 7	
02/11/91	PORT VALE	H	3-3	3365	PARKIN	BOOTHROYD	TWENTYMAN	YATES	CROSS	SKINNER	MEHEW	REECE	WHITE	SAUNDERS	POUNDER	PURNELL 7	REECE
09/11/91	BARNSLEY	A	3-2	8536	PARKIN	ALEXANDER	TWENTYMAN	YATES	CROSS	SKINNER	MEHEW	REECE	WHITE	SAUNDERS	POUNDER	STEWART 11	SAUNDERS 2, SKINNER
16/11/91	WATFORD	H	1-1	6688	PARKIN	ALEXANDER	TWENTYMAN	YATES	CROSS	SKINNER	MEHEW	REECE	WHITE	SAUNDERS	POUNDER	STEWART 10	REECE, POUNDER, SAUNDERS
20/11/91	LEICESTER CITY	A	1-1	5064	PARKIN	ALEXANDER	TWENTYMAN	YATES	CROSS	SKINNER	MEHEW	REECE	WHITE	SAUNDERS	POUNDER	STEWART 7, CLARK 11	REECE
23/11/91	DERBY COUNTY	H	2-3	10095	PARKIN	ALEXANDER	TWENTYMAN	YATES	CROSS	SKINNER	MEHEW	REECE	WHITE	SAUNDERS	POUNDER	PURNELL 7	MEHEW
30/11/91	MILLWALL	A	1-0	6513	PARKIN	ALEXANDER	TWENTYMAN	YATES	CROSS	SKINNER	MEHEW	REECE	WHITE	SAUNDERS	POUNDER	CLARK 2	MEHEW
07/12/91	CAMBRIDGE UNITED	H	2-2	7824	PARKIN	KELLY	TWENTYMAN	YATES	CROSS	SKINNER	MEHEW	REECE	WHITE	SAUNDERS	POUNDER	STEWART 11, BOOTHROYD 7	MEHEW, WHITE
14/12/91	BLACKBURN ROVERS	A	0-3	5280	PARKIN	KELLY	TAYLOR G	YATES	CROSS	SKINNER	MEHEW	REECE	WHITE	SAUNDERS	POUNDER	STEWART 11, BOOTHROYD 7	
21/12/91	BRISTOL CITY	H	2-2	12295	PARKIN	ALEXANDER	TWENTYMAN	YATES	CROSS	SKINNER	MEHEW	REECE	WHITE	SAUNDERS	POUNDER	STEWART 5	WHITE, POUNDER, SAUNDERS
26/12/91	PORTSMOUTH	A	0-3	6306	PARKIN	ALEXANDER	TWENTYMAN	YATES	CROSS	SKINNER	MEHEW	REECE	WHITE	SAUNDERS	POUNDER		
28/12/91	NEWCASTLE UNITED	A	1-2	10710	PARKIN	ALEXANDER	TWENTYMAN	YATES	CROSS	SKINNER	MEHEW	REECE	WHITE	SAUNDERS	POUNDER	PURNELL 5 BLOOMER 11	WHITE
01/01/92	LEICESTER CITY	H	1-1	19329	PARKIN	ALEXANDER	MOORE	YATES	MADDISON	SKINNER	CROSS	REECE	WHITE	SAUNDERS	POUNDER	CROSS 6, STEWART 9	SAUNDERS
11/01/92	TRANMERE ROVERS	H	1-1	6673	PARKIN	ALEXANDER	MOORE	YATES	MADDISON	SKINNER	CROSS	REECE	WHITE	SAUNDERS	POUNDER	STEWART 11, BOOTHROYD 7	STEWART
18/01/92	IPSWICH TOWN	A	0-1	7138	PARKIN	ALEXANDER	MOORE	YATES	CLARK	SKINNER	MEHEW	REECE	WHITE	SAUNDERS	POUNDER	STEWART 11	
29/01/92	PORTSMOUTH	H	0-0	10435	PARKIN	ALEXANDER	MOORE	YATES	CLARK	SKINNER	MEHEW	REECE	WHITE	SAUNDERS	POUNDER	STEWART 10	
01/02/92	PLYMOUTH ARGYLE	A	0-0	5330	PARKIN	ALEXANDER	MOORE	YATES	CROSS	SKINNER	MEHEW	REECE	BROWNING	SAUNDERS	STEWART	STEWART 11	
08/02/92	SUNDERLAND	H	2-1	6631	PARKIN	ALEXANDER	TAYLOR G	YATES	CROSS	SKINNER	MEHEW	REECE	WHITE	SAUNDERS	POUNDER	MADDISON 7, STEWART 11	SAUNDERS 2, 1pen
15/02/92	DERBY COUNTY	A	0-1	6318	PARKIN	ALEXANDER	HOPKINS	YATES	CROSS	SKINNER	MEHEW	REECE	WHITE	SAUNDERS	POUNDER	STEWART 11	
22/02/92	MILLWALL	H	3-2	11154	PARKIN	ALEXANDER	HOPKINS	CLARK	CROSS	SKINNER	MEHEW	REECE	WHITE	SAUNDERS	POUNDER	MADDISON 7	WHITE, MEHEW, BARBER og
28/02/92	CAMBRIDGE UNITED	A	1-6	5747	PARKIN	ALEXANDER	HOPKINS	CLARK	MADDISON	SKINNER	MEHEW	REECE	WHITE	SAUNDERS	POUNDER	STEWART 7, BLOOMER 8	HEANEY og
07/03/92	BLACKBURN ROVERS	H	3-0	6164	PARKIN	ALEXANDER	HOPKINS	CLARK	MADDISON	SKINNER	MEHEW	REECE	WHITE	SAUNDERS	POUNDER	BLOOMER 5, STEWART 11	MEHEW 2, WHITE
11/03/92	WOLVES	A	1-1	6313	PARKIN	ALEXANDER	CLARK	YATES	BLOOMER	SKINNER	MEHEW	REECE	BROWNING	STEWART	ARCHER	SAUNDERS 10, HOPKINS 11	WHITE
14/03/92	PORT VALE	H	1-1	6968	PARKIN	ALEXANDER	CLARK	YATES	BLOOMER	SKINNER	MEHEW	REECE	WHITE	SAUNDERS	POUNDER	SAUNDERS 10, HOPKINS 11	SAUNDERS
21/03/92	BARNSLEY	A	0-0	5861	PARKIN	YATES	CLARK	YATES	MADDISON	SKINNER	MEHEW	REECE	WHITE	STEWART	POUNDER	HOPKINS 7, STEWART 11	
28/03/92	WATFORD	H	0-1	5665	PARKIN	ALEXANDER	CLARK	YATES	BLOOMER	SKINNER	PURNELL	CROSS	TAYLOR J	STEWART	POUNDER	BLOOMER 6,	
01/04/92	SOUTHEND UNITED	H	4-1	7496	PARKIN	ALEXANDER	CLARK	YATES	MADDISON	SKINNER	MEHEW	REECE	TAYLOR J	STEWART	POUNDER	STEWART 7, BLOOMER 8	MEHEW, STEWART, TAYLOR 2
04/04/92	GRIMSBY TOWN	A	1-0	5375	PARKIN	ALEXANDER	CLARK	YATES	MADDISON	SKINNER	MEHEW	REECE	TAYLOR J	STEWART	POUNDER	MADDISON 7	TAYLOR
12/04/92	SWINDON TOWN	A	2-2	4859	PARKIN	ALEXANDER	CLARK	YATES	YATES	SKINNER	MEHEW	REECE	TAYLOR J	STEWART	POUNDER	BLOOMER 5, BROWNING 10	CLARK
18/04/92	OXFORD UNITED	H	2-2	6905	PARKIN	ALEXANDER	CLARK	YATES	YATES	SKINNER	MEHEW	REECE	TAYLOR J	STEWART	POUNDER	BLOOMER 5, BROWNING 10	TAYLOR, POUNDER
20/04/92	BRIGHTON & H ALB	A	4-1	6891	PARKIN	ALEXANDER	TWENTYMAN	YATES	CLARK	SKINNER	MEHEW	REECE	TAYLOR J	SAUNDERS	POUNDER	BROWNING 10 BOOTHROYD 11	POUNDER, TAYLOR 3
24/04/92	MIDDLESBROUGH	H	1-2	14057	PARKIN	ALEXANDER	TWENTYMAN	YATES	CROSS	SKINNER	MEHEW	REECE	WHITE	BROWNING	POUNDER		TAYLOR
02/05/92	CHARLTON ATHLETIC	H	1-0	7630	PARKIN	ALEXANDER	TWENTYMAN	YATES	MADDISON	SKINNER	MEHEW	REECE	WHITE	SAUNDERS	POUNDER		MEHEW

PLAYERS	APP	SUB	GLS
ALEXANDER I	41		1
ARCHER L	3	2	
BLOOMER R	4	5	
BOOTHROYD A	8	5	
BROWNING M	3	6	
CLARK W	22	3	1
CROSS S	31	1	2
EVANS R	2	1	1
HOPKINS J	4	2	
JONES V	1		
KELLY G	3		
MADDISON L	8	2	
MEHEW D	37		9
MOORE K	7		
PARKIN B	43		
POUNDER A	38	2	4
PURNELL P	5	7	4
REECE A	42		10
SAUNDERS C	31	5	10
SKINNER J	41	1	2
STEWART M	17	16	5
TAYLOR G	1		
TAYLOR J	8		5
TWENTYMAN G	25		8
WHITE D	35		10
WILLMOTT I	2		
WILSON D	3		
YATES S	39		2
OWN GOALS			2

LEAGUE CUP

Date	Opponent	V	G	ATT	G	2	3	4	5	6	7	8	9	10	11	SUBSTITUTES	GOALSCORERS
25/09/91	BRISTOL CITY	H	1-3	5155	PARKIN	ALEXANDER	TWENTYMAN	YATES	CLARK	ARCHER	BOOTHROYD	CROSS	WHITE	STEWART	ARCHER	BROWNING 10	LLEWELLYN og
08/10/91	BRISTOL CITY *	A	4-2	9880	PARKIN	ALEXANDER	CLARK	YATES	CROSS	SKINNER	MEHEW	REECE	WHITE	BROWNING	POUNDER	CLARK 2, PURNELL 7	WHITE 2, MEHEW 2
30/10/91	NOTT'M FOREST	H	0-2	17529	PARKIN	ALEXANDER	TWENTYMAN	YATES	CROSS	SKINNER	MEHEW	REECE	WHITE	SAUNDERS	POUNDER	PURNELL 7	

* AET Score at 90 mins 3-2. Rovers won on away goals

FA CUP

Date	Opponent	V	G	ATT	G	2	3	4	5	6	7	8	9	10	11	SUBSTITUTES	GOALSCORERS
05/01/92	PLYMOUTH ARGYLE	H	5-0	6767	PARKIN	ALEXANDER	CLARK	YATES	MADDISON	SKINNER	CROSS	REECE	BROWNING	SAUNDERS	POUNDER	POUNDER 3	ALEXANDER, SAUNDERS 4
05/02/92	LIVERPOOL	H	1-1	9484	PARKIN	ALEXANDER	CLARK	YATES	CROSS	SKINNER	MEHEW	REECE	WHITE	SAUNDERS	POUNDER	STEWART 11, BOOTHROYD 5	SAUNDERS
11/02/92	LIVERPOOL	A	1-2	30142	PARKIN	ALEXANDER	CLARK	YATES	CROSS	SKINNER	MEHEW	REECE	WHITE	SAUNDERS	POUNDER	STEWART 9, BROWNING 7	SAUNDERS

ZENITH DATA SYSTEMS CUP

Date	Opponent	V	G	ATT	G	2	3	4	5	6	7	8	9	10	11	SUBSTITUTES	GOALSCORERS
02/10/91	IPSWICH TOWN	A	1-3	1490	PARKIN	ALEXANDER	TWENTYMAN	YATES	CROSS	WILLMOTT	EVANS	REECE	WHITE	STEWART	ARCHER	STEWART 9, BROWNING 7	POUNDER

GLOUCESTERSHIRE CUP FINAL

Date	Opponent	V	G	ATT	G	2	3	4	5	6	7	8	9	10	11	SUBSTITUTES	GOALSCORERS
17/08/91	BRISTOL CITY	A	2-3	6796	PARKIN	ALEXANDER	TWENTYMAN	YATES	HAZEL	SKINNER	PURNELL	REECE	MEHEW	SAUNDERS	POUNDER	BOOTHROYD 5, BROWNING 10	PURNELL, MEHEW

Marcus Stewart, aged 18, scores on his League debut for Rovers against Ipswich Town in a thrilling 3-3 draw

The season had started dramatically with Rovers repeating their feat of February 1939 by recovering a three-goal deficit at home to Ipswich Town. As on the previous occasion, the centre-forward scored twice, Devon White's brace of goals earning an unlikely point after Ipswich had led 3-0 with 26 minutes left. In the next home game, Justin Skinner scored a last-minute consolation after coming on as substitute for his debut. He was a £130,000 club record signing from Fulham, a transfer deal finally exceeding the fee paid for Stewart Barrowclough as long ago as 1979. The Rovers midfield now added the craft of Skinner to the efforts of Mehew, Reece and Pounder.

There were some high-scoring games at Twerton Park, notably a 3-3 draw with Port Vale and a second consecutive 3-2 victory over Bristol City. A similar win at home to Millwall came courtesy of Devon White's last-minute winning goal. Away from home, Rovers lost 1-0 at Portman Road in Ipswich Town's 2,000th League game and 1-0 at Derby County, for whom the most-capped England International, Peter Shilton, played in goal. At 42 years 151 days, he is the third oldest opponent to face Rovers in League football. Amid all the changes, no single Rovers player appeared in every League game.

The heaviest defeat of the season, and Rovers' worst loss since February 1987, came at the Abbey Stadium on a Friday evening in February. Cambridge United, who scored four goals in an 11-minute second-half spell after half-time, went second in the table by beating Rovers 6-1. Earlier, Cambridge had earned a draw at Twerton Park in December, when the future England international Dion Dublin and his fellow striker John Taylor had both scored equalisers. At the Abbey Stadium, five opponents scored against Rovers, Neil Heaney became only the third opponent to score for both sides in a League game and for the first time against Rovers, both the opposition's substitutes scored. One of these substitutes was John Taylor, later Cambridge United's all-time top goalscorer, but at that stage struggling to score regularly. Within weeks, Taylor was a Rovers player and a very astute signing he proved to be, his 8 goals in as many appearances leaving him just behind Saunders and White on 10, with Mehew on 9 goals. Taylor scored twice against Southend United and three times against Brighton as Rovers recorded two 4-1 victories in April. His goals were to prove invaluable the following season, despite Rovers suffering relegation.

Rovers' cup games in 1991/92 were certainly not dull. The season began with a Gloucestershire Cup final defeat at Ashton Gate, where two Rovers defenders, Ian Alexander and Geoff Twentyman, were sent off. All the goals in a 3-2 defeat were scored before half-time. In the League Cup, the sides met again and, having lost the Twerton Park leg 3-1 to Bristol City, Rovers appeared dead and buried. However, at Ashton Gate, a crowd of 9,880 saw Rovers score three times in a strong second-half display as they won 4-2 to defeat the local rivals on the away goals rule. On a night of typically high passions, old heads White and Mehew scored twice each. Despite fears of a rerun of the 1977 FA Cup tie, Rovers lost just 2-0 in the next round to a Nottingham Forest side featuring Stuart Pearce and Teddy Sheringham. Two goals from Ipswich Town's David Lowe sent Rovers out of the Zenith Data Systems Cup at the first hurdle. Former Pirate, Kevin Moore, scored for Southampton as they lost the Wembley final in March.

In the FA Cup, Ian Alexander gave Rovers an early lead in the third round tie with West Country rivals Plymouth Argyle, who featured in their side Rob Turner and Steve Morgan, both Rovers players at some point in their career. Then Carl Saunders took over, scoring two minutes before half-time and adding a second-half hat-trick. His feat of four goals in 27 minutes was the first occasion since Jack Jones in November 1901 that a Rovers player had scored so many in an FA Cup tie and it was Rovers' largest win in this tournament since 1987/88. Rovers thereby earned a plum home game with Liverpool and a then ground record of 9,484 watched a thrilling 1-1 draw, players called Saunders scoring for both clubs. Dean Saunders, however, hit the headlines after receiving a three-match ban for elbowing Alexander, an offence missed by the referee but captured by television cameras. Extraordinarily, Carl Saunders' powerful long-range right-foot volley gave Rovers an interval lead at Anfield but, before a 30,142 crowd, Liverpool won through goals from Steve McManaman and Dean Saunders and progressed to beat Paul Hardyman's Sunderland side in the final.

1992/93

Amid the disappointment of continued rebuffs in their attempts to return to a home ground in Bristol, Rovers lost their position in the newly renamed Division One, relegated with Cambridge United and Brentford. The nomenclature is deceptive. This apparent first season for Rovers in Division One came as a result of a renaming process, stemming from the creation of a Premier Division, first won in 1992/93 by Manchester United. In reality, Rovers continued their slow nomadic bounce between the old Divisions Two and Three.

Rovers began the new season without Adrian Boothroyd, who had joined Heart of Midlothian and Bob Bloomer, now with Cheltenham Town. However, the side bore a

Bristol Rovers 1992/93. Back row: Taylor, Maddison, Mehew, Gurney, Reece, Saunders, Stewart, Boothroyd, Jones, Evans. Second row: Dolling, Clark, Taylor, Kelly, Browning, Yates, Parkin, Twentyman, Skinner, Kendall (Kit Man). Front row: Tovey, Purnell, Chenoweth, Alexander, Cross, Rofe (Manager), Gill (Youth Team Manager), Pounder, Hardyman, Wilson, Archer

strong resemblance to that which had finished mid-table in 1991/92 and attacking options looked exciting, with John Taylor, Carl Saunders and Marcus Stewart all in contention for places. Taylor and Stewart scored fluently early in the season, but Saunders, starting as first choice, only got onto the scoresheet in October, after being relegated to substitute. Goalscoring was not a problem for Rovers. The side relegated in 1980/81 had scored only 34 times in the League, whereas 55 goals were scored this time round, Taylor contributing 14.

The real problem in 1992/93 was the frequency of League defeats. Rovers lost a club record 25 League games in being relegated and the total of 11 home defeats equalled the tally set in 1947/48. In the first home game of the season, having previously been unbeaten in 16 matches at Twerton Park, Rovers conceded four goals for the first time on that ground. Then, on 3 November, Rovers lost 5-1 at home to Barnsley, the heaviest home defeat since December 1976. This was followed by a 5-1 defeat at Wolverhampton Wanderers, Rovers conceding five goals in consecutive games for only the third time in the club's League history. They were staring relegation in the face.

Another worrying feature of the early part of this season was the club's propensity for conceding penalties. There were five penalties given away in the first four League games. During the third match, in which Rovers recorded their only win in the first 13 League fixtures, Brentford were awarded two, Gary Blissett scoring from one seven minutes after half-time before Mickey Bennett squandered the second, 19 minutes from the end. At Watford, Jason Drysdale, whose father Brian had played against Rovers for both Hartlepool United and Bristol City, scored a penalty after only five minutes. Gavin Kelly, replacing Brian Parkin in goal, saved penalties, one from Dean Saunders at Villa Park and one from Ray Houghton at Twerton Park, in each of the FA Cup ties with Aston Villa. John Byrne, who had missed a penalty for Brighton against Rovers 18 months earlier, missed another as Rovers scrambled a 1-1 draw at Sunderland. Bristol-born Julian Dicks

SEASON 1992/93

FOOTBALL LEAGUE DIVISION ONE

Date	Opponent		Score	Att	G	2	3	4	5	6	7	8	9	10	11	Substitutes	Goalscorers
15/08/92	OXFORD UNITED	A	1-2	7333	PARKIN	ALEXANDER	CLARK	YATES	HARDYMAN	SKINNER	MEHEW	REECE	TAYLOR	SAUNDERS	POUNDER	STEWART 7, CROSS 11	TAYLOR
19/08/92	SWINDON TOWN	H	3-4	6150	PARKIN	ALEXANDER	CLARK	YATES	HARDYMAN	SKINNER	MEHEW	REECE	TAYLOR	SAUNDERS	POUNDER	STEWART 11, CROSS 6	MEHEW, STEWART, HARDYMAN
22/08/92	BRENTFORD	H	2-1	5779	PARKIN	ALEXANDER	CLARK	YATES	HARDYMAN	SKINNER	CROSS	REECE	TAYLOR	SAUNDERS	POUNDER	CROSS 7, STEWART 11	REECE
25/08/92	CHARLTON ATHLETIC	A	1-4	4719	PARKIN	ALEXANDER	CLARK	YATES	HARDYMAN	MADDISON	CROSS	REECE	TAYLOR	SAUNDERS	POUNDER	STEWART 11, TWENTYMAN 6	TAYLOR 2
28/08/92	TRANMERE ROVERS	A	1-2	5458	PARKIN	ALEXANDER	TWENTYMAN	YATES	HARDYMAN	MADDISON	CROSS	SKINNER	TAYLOR	STEWART	POUNDER	SAUNDERS 10, CLARK 8	STEWART
05/09/92	NEWCASTLE UNITED	H	1-2	7487	PARKIN	ALEXANDER	TWENTYMAN	YATES	WILSON	CLARK	CROSS	SKINNER	TAYLOR	STEWART	WILSON	SAUNDERS 11	STEWART pen, TAYLOR
12/09/92	SWINDON TOWN	A	2-2	10006	PARKIN	ALEXANDER	TWENTYMAN	YATES	MADDISON	WILSON	POUNDER	SKINNER	TAYLOR	STEWART	HARDYMAN	SAUNDERS 3, POUNDER 11	
19/09/92	GRIMSBY TOWN	H	0-3	5320	PARKIN	ALEXANDER	TWENTYMAN	YATES	MADDISON	WILSON	MEHEW	REECE	TAYLOR	STEWART	HARDYMAN	SAUNDERS 7, CROSS 8	
26/09/92	SWINDON TOWN		1-1	15593	PARKIN	ALEXANDER	TWENTYMAN	YATES	MADDISON	WILSON	CHANNING	REECE	TAYLOR	STEWART	HARDYMAN	REECE 6,	STEWART
03/10/92	NOTTS COUNTY	H	3-3	5031	PARKIN	ALEXANDER	TWENTYMAN	YATES	MADDISON	WILSON	CHANNING	REECE	TAYLOR	STEWART	HARDYMAN	MEHEW 7, SAUNDERS 10	STEWART pen, SAUNDERS
10/10/92	WATFORD	A	2-4	7624	PARKIN	ALEXANDER	CLARK	YATES	HARDYMAN	SKINNER	CHANNING	REECE	TAYLOR	SAUNDERS	CROSS	SAUNDERS 5	
17/10/92	WEST HAM UNITED	H	0-4	6187	KELLY	ALEXANDER	MOORE	YATES	HARDYMAN	WILSON	CHANNING	BROWNING	TAYLOR	SAUNDERS	POUNDER	MEHEW 4, CROSS 6	MOORE
24/10/92	BIRMINGHAM CITY	A	1-2	9874	KELLY	ALEXANDER	MOORE	YATES	HARDYMAN	WILSON	CHANNING	BROWNING	TAYLOR	SAUNDERS	POUNDER	MEHEW 11	SAUNDERS
31/10/92	MILLWALL	H	1-0	5378	KELLY	ALEXANDER	MOORE	CLARK	HARDYMAN	TILLSON	CHANNING	BROWNING	TAYLOR	SAUNDERS	POUNDER	MEHEW 7, ARCHER 11	MEHEW
03/11/92	BARNSLEY		1-5	5019	KELLY	ALEXANDER	CLARK	YATES	HARDYMAN	TILLSON	CHANNING	BROWNING	TAYLOR	SAUNDERS	WADDOCK	MEHEW 4, BROWNING 9	SAUNDERS
07/11/92	WOLVES	H	1-5	12163	KELLY	ALEXANDER	TILLSON	YATES	HARDYMAN	JONES	CHANNING	BROWNING	TAYLOR	SAUNDERS	WADDOCK	MEHEW 5	TAYLOR
14/11/92	DERBY COUNTY	A	1-1	12666	PARKIN	ALEXANDER	TILLSON	YATES	HARDYMAN	JONES	CHANNING	BROWNING	TAYLOR	SAUNDERS	WADDOCK	MEHEW 7	CHANNING
21/11/92	PETERBOROUGH UTD	H	1-1	6120	PARKIN	ALEXANDER	TILLSON	YATES	HARDYMAN	JONES	CHANNING	BROWNING	TAYLOR	SAUNDERS	WADDOCK	MEHEW 2	CHANNING
28/11/92	LEICESTER CITY	A	1-0	12848	PARKIN	ALEXANDER	TILLSON	YATES	HARDYMAN	JONES	CHANNING	STEWART	STEWART	SAUNDERS	WADDOCK		SAUNDERS, CHANNING
05/12/92	LUTON TOWN	H	2-0	6245	PARKIN	ALEXANDER	TILLSON	YATES	HARDYMAN	JONES	CHANNING	STEWART	STEWART	SAUNDERS	WADDOCK		CHANNING, STEWART, SAUNDERS
13/12/92	BRISTOL CITY	A	4-0	7106	PARKIN	ALEXANDER	TILLSON	YATES	HARDYMAN	JONES	CHANNING	STEWART	STEWART	SAUNDERS	WADDOCK		TAYLOR
18/12/92	CAMBRIDGE UNITED	H	1-0	4027	KELLY	ALEXANDER	TILLSON	YATES	HARDYMAN	BROWNING	CHANNING	STEWART	STEWART	SAUNDERS	WADDOCK	EVANS 6	BROWNING
26/12/92	PORTSMOUTH	A	1-4	14268	KELLY	ALEXANDER	TILLSON	YATES	HARDYMAN	JONES	BROWNING	STEWART	STEWART	SAUNDERS	WADDOCK	MEHEW 6	TAYLOR
28/12/92	SOUTHEND UNITED	H	0-2	7707	KELLY	ALEXANDER	TILLSON	YATES	HARDYMAN	CHANNING	BROWNING	STEWART	STEWART	SAUNDERS	WADDOCK	EVANS 9	
09/01/93	GRIMSBY TOWN	A	0-2	4922	KELLY	ALEXANDER	TILLSON	YATES	HARDYMAN	EVANS	BROWNING	CHANNING	TAYLOR	SAUNDERS	WADDOCK		
16/01/93	SUNDERLAND	H	2-2	6140	KELLY	ALEXANDER	TILLSON	YATES	HARDYMAN	JONES	CHANNING	CHANNING	TAYLOR	SAUNDERS	WADDOCK	STEWART 9, EVANS 10	STEWART, HARDYMAN
27/01/93	CHARLTON ATHLETIC	H	3-0	5096	KELLY	CHANNING	CLARK	YATES	HARDYMAN	JONES	EVANS	CHANNING	STEWART	SAUNDERS	WADDOCK	EVANS 7,	STEWART 2, ALEXANDER
30/01/93	BRENTFORD	A	3-0	7527	KELLY	ALEXANDER	CLARK	YATES	HARDYMAN	JONES	BROWNING	CHANNING	STEWART	SAUNDERS	WADDOCK	TAYLOR 6,	SAUNDERS,
06/02/93	OXFORD UNITED	H	0-1	5593	KELLY	ALEXANDER	TILLSON	YATES	HARDYMAN	JONES	BROWNING	CHANNING	TAYLOR	STEWART	WADDOCK	CLARK 8, TAYLOR 10	
20/02/93	TRANMERE ROVERS	H	0-1	5135	KELLY	ALEXANDER	TILLSON	YATES	HARDYMAN	JONES	BROWNING	CHANNING	TAYLOR	SAUNDERS	WADDOCK	CLARK 4	
24/02/93	NEWCASTLE UNITED	A	0-0	29372	KELLY	ALEXANDER	TILLSON	YATES	HARDYMAN	REECE	BROWNING	CHANNING	TAYLOR	SAUNDERS	WADDOCK	BROWNING 8	
27/02/93	WATFORD	H	0-3	5702	KELLY	ALEXANDER	TILLSON	YATES	HARDYMAN	JONES	SKINNER	REECE	TAYLOR	STEWART	WADDOCK	STEWART 7	SAUNDERS pen
06/03/93	NOTTS COUNTY	A	0-3	6445	KELLY	ALEXANDER	TILLSON	YATES	HARDYMAN	JONES	REECE	REECE	TAYLOR	SAUNDERS	WADDOCK	MEHEW 5	MEHEW
10/03/93	DERBY COUNTY	H	1-3	13294	KELLY	ALEXANDER	TILLSON	YATES	HARDYMAN	JONES	MEHEW	BROWNING	STEWART	SAUNDERS	WADDOCK	TAYLOR 9, CLARK 2	TAYLOR
13/03/93	WOLVES	A	1-1	5982	KELLY	ALEXANDER	TILLSON	YATES	HARDYMAN	JONES	MEHEW	BROWNING	STEWART	SAUNDERS	WADDOCK	CLARK 5	POUNDER, SAUNDERS, TAYLOR
20/03/93	LUTON TOWN	A	1-1	7717	PARKIN	ALEXANDER	TILLSON	YATES	MADDISON	POUNDER	MEHEW	REECE	TAYLOR	SAUNDERS	WADDOCK	STEWART 2	REECE
24/03/93	PETERBOROUGH UTD	H	3-1	4855	PARKIN	ALEXANDER	TILLSON	YATES	MADDISON	POUNDER	MEHEW	REECE	STEWART	SAUNDERS	WADDOCK	CHANNING 7, STEWART 10	TAYLOR
27/03/93	BARNSLEY	H	1-5	5220	KELLY	ALEXANDER	TILLSON	YATES	CLARK	POUNDER	MEHEW	REECE	TAYLOR	STEWART	WADDOCK	EVANS 10, CHANNING 7	STEWART
03/04/93	LEICESTER CITY	A	0-0	5270	KELLY	ALEXANDER	TILLSON	YATES	CLARK	POUNDER	CHANNING	SKINNER	TAYLOR	STEWART	WADDOCK	HARDYMAN 2, SAUNDERS 6	
06/04/93	BRISTOL CITY	H	1-2	21854	KELLY	ALEXANDER	TILLSON	YATES	CLARK	POUNDER	CHANNING	EVANS	TAYLOR	STEWART	WADDOCK	SAUNDERS 10	CLARK
10/04/93	PORTSMOUTH	H	0-3	6154	KELLY	ALEXANDER	TILLSON	YATES	CLARK	HARDYMAN	CHANNING	EVANS	TAYLOR	STEWART	WADDOCK	REECE 6, SAUNDERS	
14/04/93	SOUTHEND UNITED	A	0-3	3929	KELLY	ALEXANDER	TILLSON	YATES	CLARK	MEHEW	CHANNING	EVANS	TAYLOR	SAUNDERS	WADDOCK	REECE 6, STEWART 7	
17/04/93	CAMBRIDGE UNITED	A	1-2	16682	KELLY	MADDISON	TILLSON	YATES	CLARK	MEHEW	CHANNING	SKINNER	TAYLOR	STEWART	WADDOCK	REECE 6, STEWART 11	TAYLOR 2, SAUNDERS
24/04/93	WEST HAM UNITED	A	1-2	15821	PARKIN	MADDISON	TILLSON	YATES	CLARK	MEHEW	CHANNING	ARCHER	TAYLOR	SAUNDERS	WADDOCK	DAVIS 10, REECE 6	ARCHER, STEWART, DAVIS
01/05/93	BIRMINGHAM CITY	H	3-3	5150	KELLY	MADDISON	TILLSON	YATES	HARDYMAN	EVANS	BROWNING	STEWART	TAYLOR	SAUNDERS	WADDOCK	MEHEW 8	
08/05/93	MILLWALL	A	3-0	15821	PARKIN	MADDISON	CLARK	YATES	HARDYMAN	EVANS	BROWNING	SAUNDERS	TAYLOR	STEWART	WADDOCK	TWENTYMAN 6	

FA CUP

Date	Opponent		Score	Att	G	2	3	4	5	6	7	8	9	10	11	Substitutes	Goalscorers
02/01/93	ASTON VILLA	A	1-1	27040	KELLY	ALEXANDER	TILLSON	YATES	HARDYMAN	EVANS	BROWNING	STEWART	TAYLOR	SAUNDERS	WADDOCK	MEHEW 8	BROWNING
20/01/93	ASTON VILLA	H	0-3	8880	PARKIN	JONES	CLARK	YATES	HARDYMAN	EVANS	BROWNING	SAUNDERS	TAYLOR	STEWART	WADDOCK	TWENTYMAN 6	

LEAGUE CUP

Date	Opponent		Score	Att	G	2	3	4	5	6	7	8	9	10	11	Substitutes	Goalscorers
23/09/92	MANCHESTER CITY	A	0-0	9967	PARKIN	ALEXANDER	TWENTYMAN	YATES	MADDISON	WILSON	CROSS	SKINNER	TAYLOR	SAUNDERS	HARDYMAN	REECE 6	
07/10/92	MANCHESTER CITY *	H	1-2	7823	PARKIN	ALEXANDER	TWENTYMAN	YATES	MADDISON	WILSON	MEHEW	SKINNER	TAYLOR	STEWART	HARDYMAN	SAUNDERS 5, CROSS 11	REECE

* AET Score at 90 mins 1-1

ANGLO ITALIAN CUP

Date	Opponent		Score	Att	G	2	3	4	5	6	7	8	9	10	11	Substitutes	Goalscorers
02/09/92	WEST HAM UNITED *	A	2-2	4809	PARKIN	ALEXANDER	TWENTYMAN	YATES	HARDYMAN	MADDISON	CROSS	SKINNER	TAYLOR	STEWART	POUNDER	BROWNING 11, CLARK 6	STEWART 2
16/09/92	SOUTHEND UNITED	H	3-0	3007	PARKIN	ALEXANDER	TWENTYMAN	YATES	MADDISON	WILSON	HARDYMAN	SKINNER	TAYLOR	STEWART	POUNDER	SAUNDERS 11	STEWART pen, SAUNDERS, HARDYMAN

* Rovers & West Ham Utd had identical records but Rovers went out of competition after a toss of a coin

GLOUCESTERSHIRE CUP FINAL

Date	Opponent		Score	Att	G	2	3	4	5	6	7	8	9	10	11	Substitutes	Goalscorers
05/08/92	BRISTOL CITY	H	2-1	3722	KELLY	ALEXANDER	TILLSON	YATES	CLARK	HARDYMAN	MEHEW	SKINNER	TAYLOR	SAUNDERS	POUNDER	WILSON	STEWART, MEHEW, STEWART

PLAYERS	APP	SUB	GLS
ALEXANDER L	41		1
ARCHER L	1	1	1
BEASLEY A	1		
BROWNING M	17	2	1
CHANNING J	23	2	3
CLARK W	19	5	1
CROSS S	6	5	
DAVIS M	0	1	1
EVANS R	6	5	
HARDYMAN P	36	1	4
JONES V	12		
KELLY G	19		
MADDISON L	12		
MEHEW D	14	10	3
MOORE K	4		1
PARKIN B	26		
POUNDER A	17	1	1
REECE A	22	4	2
SAUNDERS C	33	8	11
SKINNER J	12		
STEWART M	27	11	11
TAYLOR J	39	3	14
TILLSON A	29		
TWENTYMAN G	7	1	
WADDOCK G	31		
WILSON D	8		
YATES S	44		

Malcolm Allison was appointed Rovers' manager from November 1992 until March 1993

scored penalties for West Ham United in both their League games against Rovers.

Dennis Rofe had suffered a traumatic start to the season as Rovers manager. Rovers conceded 4 goals in 4 of their 12 opening games and also suffered a demoralizing 3-0 home defeat to Grimsby Town. West Ham United's visit to Twerton Park saw hapless Rovers lose 4-0 and Paul Hardyman, a summer signing from Sunderland following a Cup final appearance, was sent off as the first was conceded. Clive Allen, the scorer of Tottenham Hotspur's opening goal in the 1987 FA Cup final, created one goal and scored the fourth five minutes from time, after Mark Robson's shot had rebounded off the crossbar. After only 17 wins in 53 League games, Rofe's tenure came to an end, and he subsequently worked as a coach to Stoke City and Southampton. He was succeeded from within the club by a man initially appointed to work alongside him.

On Tuesday 10 November 1992, as a last throw of the dice, Rovers appointed a larger-than-life figure as the new manager. If Albert Prince-Cox had been the figurehead for the 1930s revival, so too could Malcolm Allison in the 1990s. During a long playing career, he had played on eight occasions against Rovers in League football. Amongst the litany of achievements with the many clubs he had served as manager, the 1967/68 League Championship with Manchester City stood out. He is the only Rovers manager who has led a club to this honour. Allison's side was strengthened by two players signed shortly before his arrival, Gary Waddock and the club's new record signing for £370,000, Andy Tillson. Both players had joined from Queen's Park Rangers just hours before the 5-1 defeat at Molineux, in which they had appeared.

Initially, Allison's arrival instigated a change in Rovers' fortunes, Vaughan Jones returned to the side after an absence of more than a year. A run of four straight victories without conceding a goal offered fresh hope. During the first three of these, recent arrival Justin Channing, a £250,000 signing, scored in the 25th minute of each game, his only three goals of the season. The third was easily the brightest moment of a gloomy season, as Rovers won 4-0 against a Bristol City side boasting the future England striker Andy Cole. City also fielded Danish International central defender Bjørn Kristensen and the 30-year-old Polish International Dariusz Dziekanowski. Three goals in 13 second-half minutes helped Rovers to record their largest victory in a local derby since December 1963. However, this great run ended at Fratton Park, where Portsmouth beat Rovers 4-1, the first of three straight defeats. In scoring all Pompey's goals, Guy Whittingham became only the 12th opponent to score four or more times in a League game against Rovers. It was a record-breaking season for

Whittingham, who set a club seasonal record with his 44th goal of a productive season, scored at Twerton Park in April. Then Stan Collymore inspired Southend United to victory at Twerton Park after Ian Alexander had been sent off.

By then, though, despite a 3-0 win at Brentford and a creditable goalless draw with champions-elect Newcastle United, before a crowd of 29,372 at St James' Park, Malcolm Allison had left, ending a long, largely successful and enigmatic association with Football League management. Coach Steve Cross, who had appeared in his last game as a player in October, took temporary charge for three games, prior to the appointment on 15 March 1993 of John Ward. It was too late to prevent the inevitable relegation, but it was a positive move. A player himself of great experience, Ward had spent 16 months as manager at York City and had served as assistant to Graham Taylor at Watford, Aston Villa and England, and soon proved himself to be a progressive and enthusiastic leader. Over the next three years, under Ward's leadership, Rovers were able to re-establish themselves as a force in Division Two football and return to Wembley in 1995. With relegation apparent, he took the opportunity to blood young talent, with Gareth Taylor, Andy Gurney and Mike Davis among those promoted to the first-team squad before the season was over.

Under Ward, at first, there was little change. A dull goalless draw in driving rain with Leicester City, where the visitors' David Lowe had hit a post before his 35th-minute red card, was followed by derby-day defeat at Ashton Gate, with Ian Alexander sent off again. Despite taking a second-half lead at Upton Park in April through Billy Clark's first goal of the season, defeat against West Ham United saw Rovers relegated for the third time in the club's history. There was frenetic action nine points above Rovers on the final day, with all sorts of relegation permutations possible before Brentford and Cambridge United finally dropped with Rovers. In 1920, Rovers had appeared in the first League game at the Den and now they appeared in the last, spoiling Millwall's final day at their old ground with a 3-0 win. The game was twice held up by pitch invasions before Mike Davis, on as a substitute for his debut, registered Rovers' last Division One goal.

Rovers' only season in the short-lived Anglo-Italian Cup saw only matches in this country against Southend United and West Ham United, with the club being eliminated by virtue of a toss of a coin, conducted over the telephone. The Gloucestershire Cup final, by contrast, was won through Marcus Stewart's last-minute goal, after Andy Cole had given Bristol City a half-time lead. In the League Cup, Rovers held out for a goalless draw at Maine Road but, despite the hilarity of the Manchester City substitute Flitcroft being announced as 'Gary Flipflop', were defeated at Twerton Park by the Division One side, Lee Maddison conceding an own goal. Likewise, in the FA Cup, a well-earned draw at Villa Park, before a crowd of 27,040, earned a lucrative home replay. Rovers, though, collapsed under pressure and Aston Villa could even afford the luxury of a missed penalty in running out 3-0 winners. The future Rovers midfielder Graham Hyde was in the Sheffield Wednesday side beaten by Arsenal in both the FA and League Cup Finals.

1993/94

The return of Division Two – formerly Division Three – football to Twerton Park renewed the call for a new stadium in Bristol. Having lost out, in recent years, on proposed sites at Stoke Gifford, Mangotsfield and Hallen Marsh, the search was becoming increasingly intense. Several other League clubs, Brighton and Chester City being two examples, played home matches in towns other than their own but, as Rovers approached a decade's tenancy at Twerton Park, fears grew that the club would have lost the support of a whole generation in east Bristol.

The clamour for such a move became embodied in the work of the Bristol Party, a political group that formed in October 1993. There had been a precedent, for the Valley Party, which stood for elections in May 1990, had helped hasten Charlton Athletic's long-awaited return to their spiritual home. The Bristol Party, lent support by Tom Pendry, the Labour Party's Shadow Minister for Sport, strove to recreate in Bristol the perceived superior leisure facilities of other cities. Partnership with housing and community organisations was demanded in order to restore a sense of pride in all aspects of Bristol life. In the local elections of May 1994, the Bristol Party polled 4,000 votes and won no seats, although its call for a healthier political attitude to sports as well as Rovers' return had been heard loud and clear.

In December 1993, as the party's work grew, Rovers expressed interest in a fourth potential site for a new stadium. The proposed spot comprised 60 acres within the ICI complex at Pilning, again within easy access of the planned M49 motorway. A stadium

Bristol Rovers 1993/94. Back row: Wright, Clark, Tillson, McLean, Taylor, Browning, White, Maddison. Second row: Dolling (Physio), Alexander, Channing, Waddock, Law, Parkin, Hardyman, Pritchard, Stewart, James (Physio). Third row: Kendall (Kit Man), Booth (Asst Manager), Stokes (Director), D Dunford (Chairman), Ward (Manager), G Dunford (Director), Craig, Roydon (Directors), Cross (Coach), Gill (Youth Team Manager). Front row: Archer, Tovey, Gurney, Davis, Paul, Sterling, Hayfield

here could house 20,000 spectators, as well as offering a greyhound track, that recurring leitmotif through the Rovers story since 1932, an exhibition centre and a School of Excellence. Discussions began to the backdrop of the increasingly politicized demands for Rovers' return to the Bristol area. Such a call from the club's supporters was one that would not go away.

On the field, the season opened with a disappointing single-goal defeat at home to Bournemouth. Unbeknown to the crowd, this was to be the final Rovers appearance for Steve Yates, who rejoined Gerry Francis at Queen's Park Rangers shortly afterwards in a deal worth £750,000. Three other key members of the 1989/90 Championship side, David Mehew, Andy Reece and Geoff Twentyman, had slipped out of League football over the summer. It was also the first time Nationwide League sides had been able to use up to three substitutes. Rovers selected a substitute goalkeeper for every League game and this paid off in the return game at Bournemouth. The home side, very convincing at times, had led by three first-half goals before the highly controversial sending off of Rovers' goalkeeper Brian Parkin. Rovers promptly took off Gary Waddock, replacing him with Martyn Margetson, so that, although a man short, they at least played on with a recognized goalkeeper.

After five games, Rovers had scored four goals, all by John Taylor. He was to score 22 League goals, including goals in a run of four consecutive matches in the autumn. This spell included a first-minute goal that led to victory over Cardiff City at Ninian Park and goals in exciting home victories over Burnley and Bradford City. Burnley found themselves three goals in arrears when Worrell Sterling, an exciting and skilful winger signed in the close season for £140,000 from Peterborough United, created the second before scoring the third with a spectacular 35-yard volley on the stroke of half-time. This game also featured a new centre-back partnership between debutant defender Ian Wright and Ian McLean, a Scottish-born player who scored his first goal for Rovers that day and won his first full cap for Canada in January 1995, while on Rovers' books. Against Bradford City, Rovers trailed 3-2 before two late penalties by Marcus Stewart gave the home side an unlikely victory. He thus became the sixth Rovers player to convert two penalties in a League match.

In September, Rovers lost 3-0 at Hull City, all of whose goals were scored by Dean Windass, only the third League hat-trick conceded by Rovers since 1983. Astonishingly, Brentford players managed to score hat-tricks in both games against Rovers, equalling the achievements of Northampton Town in 1929/30 and Derby County in 1961/62. In January, Denny Mundee scored all Brentford's goals in a game at Griffin Park that Rovers won 4-3. Only three other opponents had previously scored a hat-trick against Rovers in the League and ended up on the losing side. Joe Allon then became the first opponent to score a hat-trick at Twerton Park. Rovers' captain Gary Waddock suffered a broken nose in the build-up to the first goal but the side was easily defeated by a Brentford side that ran up three first-half goals before Allon ran through a ragged defence after half-time to complete his hat-trick.

In November, the former Rovers goalkeeper Tim Carter was in the first Hartlepool United side to meet Rovers since 1968/69. His side almost left Twerton Park with a win, too, denied only by Justin Skinner's last-minute equaliser. In their next League game, Rovers travelled to top-of-the-table Stockport County and left Edgeley Park with

FOOTBALL LEAGUE DIVISION TWO

Date	Opponents	Venue	Score	Att	G	2	3	4	5	6	7	8	9	10	11	Substitutes	Goalscorers
14/08/93	AFC BOURNEMOUTH	H	0-1	7234	PARKIN	ALEXANDER	HARDYMAN	WADDOCK	CLARK	YATES	STERLING	TAYLOR	STEWART	BROWNING	ARCHER	MADDISON 11, DAVIS 10	
21/08/93	LEYTON ORIENT	A	2-1	4155	PARKIN	CHANNING	MADDISON	BROWNING	CLARK	WRIGHT	STERLING	TAYLOR	SKINNER	WADDOCK	ARCHER	TAYLOR 2	TAYLOR 2
28/08/93	FULHAM	H	2-1	5261	PARKIN	CHANNING	MADDISON	WADDOCK	CLARK	WRIGHT	STERLING	TAYLOR	STEWART	BROWNING	ARCHER	ARCHER L	BROWNING, STERLING
01/09/93	BRIGHTON & H ALB	A	2-0	5675	PARKIN	CHANNING	MADDISON	WADDOCK	CLARK	WRIGHT	STERLING	TAYLOR	SAUNDERS	BROWNING	ARCHER	BROWNING 9, ALEXANDER 7	SKINNER, ARCHER, STERLING
04/09/93	HULL CITY	A	0-3	5362	PARKIN	CHANNING	MADDISON	WADDOCK	WRIGHT	CLARK	STERLING	TAYLOR	SAUNDERS	BROWNING	ARCHER	DAVIS 9, ALEXANDER 7, DAVIS 9	
11/09/93	PORT VALE	H	2-0	4908	PARKIN	CHANNING	MADDISON	BROWNING	WRIGHT	McLEAN	STERLING	TAYLOR	POUNDER	WADDOCK	ARCHER	POUNDER 11	TAYLOR, ARCHER
15/09/93	EXETER CITY	H	1-1	5001	PARKIN	CHANNING	MADDISON	BROWNING	WRIGHT	McLEAN	STERLING	TAYLOR	POUNDER	WADDOCK	ARCHER	STEWART 9	TAYLOR
18/09/93	ROTHERHAM UNITED	A	1-1	4000	PARKIN	ALEXANDER	MADDISON	BROWNING	CLARK	McLEAN	STERLING	TAYLOR	SAUNDERS	WADDOCK	ARCHER	GURNEY A	BROWNING
25/09/93	BURNLEY	H	3-1	5732	PARKIN	ALEXANDER	MADDISON	BROWNING	WRIGHT	McLEAN	STERLING	TAYLOR	SKINNER	POUNDER	ARCHER	EVANS R	SKINNER, TAYLOR, STERLING
02/10/93	BARNET	A	2-1	3158	PARKIN	ALEXANDER	MADDISON	BROWNING	WRIGHT	McLEAN	STERLING	TAYLOR	SKINNER	POUNDER	ARCHER	HARDYMAN P	TAYLOR, STERLING
09/10/93	BRADFORD CITY	H	4-3	5323	PARKIN	ALEXANDER	MADDISON	BROWNING	WRIGHT	McLEAN	STERLING	TAYLOR	SKINNER	WADDOCK	ARCHER	DAVIS 8	BROWNING, TAYLOR 2, SKINNER
16/10/93	CARDIFF CITY	H	2-1	5563	PARKIN	ALEXANDER	MADDISON	BROWNING	WRIGHT	McLEAN	STERLING	TAYLOR	SKINNER	WADDOCK	ARCHER	CLARK 5, SKINNER 11	McLEAN, TAYLOR
23/10/93	PLYMOUTH ARGYLE	A	0-0	7558	PARKIN	ALEXANDER	MADDISON	BROWNING	WRIGHT	McLEAN	STERLING	TAYLOR	SKINNER	WADDOCK	ARCHER	DAVIS 10	
30/10/93	HUDDERSFIELD T	H	0-1	5612	PARKIN	ALEXANDER	MADDISON	BROWNING	WRIGHT	McLEAN	STERLING	TAYLOR	SKINNER	WADDOCK	HARDYMAN	SKINNER 9	
02/11/93	YORK CITY	A	1-0	3758	PARKIN	CHANNING	MADDISON	BROWNING	WRIGHT	CLARK	STERLING	TAYLOR	DAVIS	WADDOCK	ARCHER	TAYLOR	SKINNER
06/11/93	HARTLEPOOL UNITED	A	1-1	5308	PARKIN	CHANNING	MADDISON	BROWNING	WRIGHT	McLEAN	STERLING	TAYLOR	SKINNER	WADDOCK	ARCHER		ARCHER
20/11/93	STOCKPORT COUNTY	A	2-0	5250	PARKIN	CHANNING	MADDISON	BROWNING	WRIGHT	McLEAN	STERLING	TAYLOR	SKINNER	WADDOCK	ARCHER	McLEAN 6	SKINNER, TAYLOR
27/11/93	CAMBRIDGE UNITED	H	2-1	4407	PARKIN	CHANNING	MADDISON	BROWNING	WRIGHT	McLEAN	STERLING	TAYLOR	SKINNER	WADDOCK	ARCHER	PAUL 9	BROWNING
11/12/93	LEYTON ORIENT	H	1-1	4604	PARKIN	CHANNING	MADDISON	BROWNING	WRIGHT	McLEAN	STERLING	TAYLOR	SKINNER	WADDOCK	ARCHER	TAYLOR	TAYLOR
18/12/93	AFC BOURNEMOUTH	A	0-3	4811	PARKIN	CHANNING	MADDISON	BROWNING	WRIGHT	McLEAN	STERLING	TAYLOR	STEWART	WADDOCK	ARCHER	BROWNING	
01/01/94	SWANSEA CITY	H	0-0	5127	PARKIN	CHANNING	MADDISON	BROWNING	WRIGHT	McLEAN	STERLING	TAYLOR	STEWART	SKINNER	ARCHER	MARGETSON 10	
05/02/94	HUDDERSFIELD T	A	3-3	13318	PARKIN	CHANNING	MADDISON	CHANNING	WRIGHT	EVANS	STERLING	TAYLOR	STEWART	WADDOCK	ARCHER	CHANNING 7, PAUL 9	STEWART 2, TAYLOR
12/02/94	BRENTFORD	H	1-2	6285	PARKIN	CHANNING	MADDISON	HARDYMAN	WRIGHT	STEWART	STERLING	TAYLOR	SKINNER	WADDOCK	ARCHER	STEWART 10, PAUL 9	TILLSON A
19/02/94	FULHAM	A	1-0	5605	PARKIN	CHANNING	MADDISON	BROWNING	WRIGHT	TILLSON	STERLING	TAYLOR	HARDYMAN	WADDOCK	ARCHER	MARGETSON 10	TAYLOR
26/02/94	HULL CITY	H	4-3	6941	PARKIN	CHANNING	MADDISON	BROWNING	WRIGHT	TILLSON	STERLING	TAYLOR	HARDYMAN	WADDOCK	ARCHER	SKINNER 11	SKINNER, ARCHER, STERLING
15/01/94	CARDIFF CITY	A	3-1	3311	PARKIN	CHANNING	MADDISON	WADDOCK	CLARK	TILLSON	STERLING	TAYLOR	SKINNER	WADDOCK	ARCHER	HARDYMAN 8, McLEAN 6	BROWNING, TAYLOR 2, SKINNER
05/03/94	PORT VALE	H	0-2	9682	KELLY	CHANNING	MADDISON	BROWNING	WRIGHT	McLEAN	STERLING	TAYLOR	HARDYMAN	WADDOCK	ARCHER	HARDYMAN 9	
12/03/94	READING	H	1-1	7494	PARKIN	CHANNING	MADDISON	BROWNING	WRIGHT	McLEAN	STERLING	TAYLOR	HARDYMAN	WADDOCK	ARCHER	HARDYMAN 11	TAYLOR
19/03/94	HUDDERSFIELD T	H	0-0	5127	PARKIN	CHANNING	MADDISON	BROWNING	WRIGHT	McLEAN	STERLING	TAYLOR	HARDYMAN	WADDOCK	ARCHER	McLEAN 9	
15/03/94	EXETER CITY	A	3-3	10651	PARKIN	CHANNING	MADDISON	CHANNING	WRIGHT	McLEAN	STERLING	TAYLOR	WADDOCK	SKINNER	ARCHER	HARDYMAN 8, STEWART 2	SKINNER, ARCHER, STERLING
19/03/94	BRENTFORD	A	0-1	4399	PARKIN	CHANNING	MADDISON	CHANNING	CLARK	McLEAN	STERLING	TAYLOR	WADDOCK	SKINNER	ARCHER	DAVIS 10, McLEAN 11	
22/03/94	WREXHAM	H	1-2	3184	PARKIN	CHANNING	MADDISON	BROWNING	CLARK	McLEAN	EVANS	TAYLOR	HARDYMAN	WADDOCK	POUNDER	EVANS 11, McLEAN 2	ARCHER, STERLING
26/03/94	BARNET	A	2-3	5703	PARKIN	CHANNING	MADDISON	BROWNING	WRIGHT	McLEAN	STERLING	TAYLOR	HARDYMAN	WADDOCK	POUNDER	STEWART 11	TILLSON A
30/03/94	BLACKPOOL	H	2-1	4231	PARKIN	CHANNING	MADDISON	CHANNING	WRIGHT	McLEAN	STERLING	DAVIS	CHANNING	SKINNER	POUNDER	McLEAN 5, CLARK 10	POUNDER 2, STEWART
02/04/94	READING	A	2-2	8035	PARKIN	CHANNING	MADDISON	HARDYMAN	WRIGHT	McLEAN	STERLING	TAYLOR	CHANNING	SKINNER	POUNDER	PAUL 8, McLEAN 11	WRIGHT
04/04/94	WREXHAM	A	0-2	3961	PARKIN	CHANNING	MADDISON	HARDYMAN	WRIGHT	McLEAN	STERLING	TAYLOR	CHANNING	SKINNER	POUNDER	McLEAN 5, TOVEY 2	
09/04/94	SWANSEA CITY	A	0-2	3961	PARKIN	CHANNING	MADDISON	HARDYMAN	WRIGHT	McLEAN	STERLING	TAYLOR	CHANNING	SKINNER	POUNDER	PAUL 8, McLEAN 11	
16/04/94	YORK CITY	H	1-0	5007	PARKIN	CHANNING	MADDISON	HARDYMAN	WRIGHT	McLEAN	STERLING	TAYLOR	CHANNING	SKINNER	POUNDER	McLEAN 5, TOVEY 2	STEWART 10, McLEAN 2
23/04/94	HARTLEPOOL UNITED	H	1-2	1409	PARKIN	PRITCHARD	HARDYMAN	WADDOCK	WRIGHT	McLEAN	STERLING	TAYLOR	CHANNING	SKINNER	ARCHER	STEWART 10, McLEAN 2	STEWART M
30/04/94	STOCKPORT COUNTY	H	1-2	4189	PARKIN	PRITCHARD	HARDYMAN	WADDOCK	WRIGHT	McLEAN	STERLING	TAYLOR	CHANNING	SKINNER	ARCHER	GURNEY 3	TAYLOR
07/05/94	CAMBRIDGE UNITED	H	3-1	4402	PARKIN	GURNEY	GURNEY	WADDOCK	WRIGHT	McLEAN	STERLING	TAYLOR	CHANNING	SKINNER	ARCHER	STEWART 10, McLEAN 2	TAYLOR 2, CHANNING

LEAGUE CUP

Date	Opponents	Venue	Score	Att	G	2	3	4	5	6	7	8	9	10	11	Substitutes	Goalscorers
18/08/93	WEST BROM ALBION	H	1-4	4562	PARKIN	ALEXANDER	MADDISON	CHANNING	CLARK	TILLSON	STERLING	TAYLOR	STEWART	SKINNER	ARCHER	BROWNING 8	STERLING
25/08/93	WEST BROM ALBION	A	0-0	9123	PARKIN	ALEXANDER	MADDISON	CHANNING	CLARK	TILLSON	STERLING	TAYLOR	STEWART	SKINNER	ARCHER		

AUTOGLASS TROPHY

Date	Opponents	Venue	Score	Att	G	2	3	4	5	6	7	8	9	10	11	Substitutes	Goalscorers
28/09/93	TORQUAY UNITED	A	1-0	2445	PARKIN	ALEXANDER	MADDISON	BROWNING	WRIGHT	McLEAN	STERLING	TAYLOR	SKINNER	SKINNER	ARCHER	SAUNDERS 8	McLEAN
20/10/93	CARDIFF CITY	A	3-0	2035	PARKIN	ALEXANDER	MADDISON	BROWNING	WRIGHT	McLEAN	STERLING	TAYLOR	SKINNER	SKINNER	ARCHER	DAVIS 8, CLARK 10	SKINNER, STEWART 2
01/12/93	FULHAM *	H	2-2	2882	PARKIN	CHANNING	MADDISON	BROWNING	WRIGHT	McLEAN	STERLING	TAYLOR	BROWNING	WADDOCK	ARCHER	BROWNING 2	BROWNING, STEWART 2

* AET Score after 90 mins 2-2 Rovers lost 3-4 on pens

FA CUP

Date	Opponents	Venue	Score	Att	G	2	3	4	5	6	7	8	9	10	11	Substitutes	Goalscorers
14/11/93	WYCOMBE WDRS	H	1-2	6421	PARKIN	CHANNING	MADDISON	BROWNING	CLARK	McLEAN	STERLING	TAYLOR	SKINNER	SKINNER	ARCHER	SAUNDERS 9, SKINNER 9	ARCHER

GLOUCESTERSHIRE CUP FINAL

Date	Opponents	Venue	Score	Att	G	2	3	4	5	6	7	8	9	10	11	Substitutes	Goalscorers
05/08/93	BRISTOL CITY *	A	1-1	6698	PARKIN	CHANNING	MADDISON	WADDOCK	CLARK	YATES	WRIGHT	TAYLOR	STEWART	BROWNING	ARCHER	DAVIS 8, MADDISON 11	CLARK

* BRISTOL CITY Rovers won 5-3 on pens

* AET Score after 90 mins 0-0, Rovers won 5-3 on pens

PLAYERS	APP	SUB	GLS
ALEXANDER I	15	3	
ARCHER L	37	5	
BROWNING M	30	1	4
CHANNING J	28	1	5
CLARK W	34	2	1
DAVIS M	2	8	
EVANS R	2	1	
GURNEY A	2	1	
HARDYMAN P	17	8	1
KELLY G	1		
MADDISON L	36	1	
MARGETSON M	2	1	
McLEAN I	17	10	2
PARKIN B	43		
PAUL M	0	4	
POUNDER A	8	2	2
PRITCHARD A	11		
SAUNDERS C	4	3	
SKINNER J	27	2	5
STERLING W	43		5
STEWART M	23	6	5
TAYLOR I	44	1	22
TILLSON A	12	1	
TOVEY P	0	1	
WADDOCK G	39		
WRIGHT I	29		1
YATES S	1		
OWN GOAL			1

a fine 2-0 win. John Taylor and Lee Archer were Rovers' scorers, while Jim Gannon missed a penalty, found the referee ordering it to be retaken following an infringement and promptly missed again. County fielded 6ft 7in striker, Kevin Francis, one of the tallest players ever to appear against Rovers in League action. Rovers drew with Reading in January, thanks to Billy Clark heading in off the crossbar before half-time from Justin Skinner's free-kick, in a match that saw Marcus Browning sent off after 49 minutes and the visitors' Uwe Hartenberger after 67 minutes for violent conduct, just four minutes after his arrival as a substitute.

A series of fine end-of-the-season results eased Rovers into a comfortable final League position of eighth. A run of five straight defeats was halted when relegation-bound Barnet came for their sole League visit and were despatched 5-2. Justin Channing had, until a week earlier, gone 15 months without a goal, but contributed a hat-trick to defeat the Bees. Worrell Sterling's first-minute goal was enough to defeat Blackpool. Tony Pounder's first two goals for more than a year helped defeat Wrexham 3-2, while Taylor's brace against his former club, Cambridge United, gave Rovers a convincing away victory on the final day of the season.

The process of rebuilding the side had begun. Lee Maddison was a consistent performer at left-back and the acquisition of Telford United's right-back David Pritchard offered the prospect of another solid full-back partnership. Justin Skinner and Marcus Browning were developing as reliable midfielders, while Taylor's goals had brought relative success. There were still changes to be made, however. Wright and McLean never started again in the same side while, following Carl Saunders' mid-season move, Taylor joined Bradford City in a £300,000 summer move. Rovers needed a new striking partner for Marcus Stewart. Off the field, Rovers lent weight to the 'Let's kick Racism out of Football' Campaign, run by the Commission for Racial Equality, the Professional Footballers' Association and the Football Trust. Meanwhile, the old Eastville stadium suffered another fire on 13 February 1994, caused by a mouse gnawing through wire, necessitating 100 firefighters and four months of repair work.

Rovers retained the Gloucestershire Cup, 5-3 on penalties after a 1-1 draw, the winning kick being taken by Browning. A goalless 90 minutes had been followed by extra-time, in which Clark, from Stewart's cross, scored for Rovers and Matt Bryant, whose brother Simon later played in the Rovers side, equalised for Bristol City four minutes from the end. Kit man Ray Kendall was also granted a testimonial at the end of the season, when a 1,500 crowd raised £4,000. Rovers, with Pounder and the substitute Sterling scoring, drew 2-2 with Premiership Coventry City, whose goals came from Julian Darby and Peter Atherton.

That success in the major cup competitions was not forthcoming is a major understatement. Home defeats at the hands of West Bromwich Albion and Wycombe Wanderers brought Rovers' interest to a swift conclusion. Albion's convincing 4-1 League Cup first-round first-leg win at Twerton Park, Kevin Donovan scoring two second-half goals, made the second leg meaningless. Division Three Wanderers ended Rovers' FA Cup aspirations with Dave Carroll's second-half winning goal earning them a home tie with Cambridge United. After victories over Torquay United and Cardiff City in the Auto Windscreens Shield, Rovers drew 2-2 at home to Fulham, Lee Maddison conceding an own goal and were eliminated from the tournament after a penalty shoot-out.

1994/95

Ultimately, a season has to be assessed on achievement. Rovers appeared at Wembley Stadium in May 1995, for the second time in the club's 112-year history. Though they were unsuccessful in their attempts to regain the Division One place lost two years earlier, a positive feeling about Rovers' on-field potential was beginning to return. Moreover, by the end of the season, Northavon District Council was showing signs of being in favour of the club's proposed move to Pilning. So, despite the disappointment of final-day defeat against Huddersfield Town in the play-offs, hopes were high in the Rovers camp.

The one major addition to the Rovers squad was Paul Miller, an experienced striker signed from Premiership Wimbledon for £100,000 in August. Miller added a cutting edge to the side, contributing 16 League goals to finish the season as the club's top scorer. The extra-time goal at Crewe Alexandra, which took Rovers to Wembley, was not his best of the season, but was arguably his most crucial. Tom White and goalkeeper Marcus Law came through the youth scheme to make first-team appearances, while Carl Heggs' loan spell included a Tuesday-night consolation goal at Bradford City in February. Andy Collett arrived in a £100,000 move from Middlesbrough on transfer-deadline day in March to act as goalkeeping cover for Brian Parkin.

The relative success of 1994/95 was achieved despite the absence, for long stretches of the season, of the highly influential Marcus Stewart. In one purple patch through the winter, he scored 12 goals in 10 League matches and scored in eight consecutive League and Cup games in which he played between November 1994 and Valentine's Day 1995. It is worth noting that, prior to an 11-match unbeaten run, starting in March, Rovers stood in 11th place in their division. Player-of-the-year Worrell Sterling was the club's only ever-present, and scored his only goal, with a forceful left-foot drive from 20 yards, in a 1-1 draw at Huddersfield Town's new Alfred McAlpine Stadium in February.

Although Rovers were unbeaten for the first eight League matches of the new season, they found themselves in seventh place in Division Two. Five of these games had been drawn, three of them being goalless draws, while Rovers had beaten York City 3-1, Rotherham United – through three first-half goals at Millmoor – and Wrexham. The Welsh side put up a strong fight at Twerton Park before succumbing to a 4-2 defeat. Billy Clark's second-minute header from Justin Skinner's corner and Gareth Taylor's first goal for the club had twice put Rovers ahead, only for Wrexham to equalise both times. However, Karl Connolly's 85th-minute goal served only to spur Rovers on, with another Clark header and Miller's burst through the Robins' defence giving Rovers all the points. Indeed Clark, with 6 League goals in the season, more than doubled his career total with the club.

When the unbeaten record went, in the ninth game – Shrewsbury Town's Ian Stevens, a customary scorer against Rovers, scoring the winning goal before half-time – it was to the first goal conceded away from home all season. Rovers' bubble had burst and, despite recovering a two-goal half-time deficit at home to Crewe Alexandra, Taylor scoring twice, the heaviest defeat of the season was to follow. With Marcus Law an

Bristol Rovers 1994/95. Back row: Clark, Taylor, Parkin, Tillson, Collett, Skinner, White. Second row: McLean, Maddison, Davis, Hayfield, Miller, Tovey, Wright, Browning, Paul. Third row: Connor, Kendall, Cross (Coach), Ward (Manager), Booth (Asst Manager), Gill (Youth Manager), James (Physio), Dolling (Physio). Front row: Hardyman, Sterling, Stewart, Archer, Channing, Pritchard, Gurney

unlucky debutant in goal, Rovers found themselves 2-0 down at Griffin Park after only five minutes, Brentford's Nicky Forster's two early goals leading Rovers to a 3-0 loss. Brentford were to finish second in the division, while Rovers, from this lowest seasonal placing of 15th, slowly climbed the table into a play-off position.

A run of seven wins and a draw between 5 November and 4 February began to propel Rovers back up the table. The first win, 4-0 against Bradford City, showed the potential of a revitalized Rovers side, Marcus Stewart scoring twice in this game and twice again in three of the next four matches. Four straight home matches either side of Christmas were won, Lee Archer scoring twice in a 3-0 victory over Chester City on New Year's Eve. In poor weather, the only League fixture honoured in January was an exciting 3-2 victory over Oxford United, who had led through Mark Druce goals after 12 and 15 minutes. The arrival of Taylor as substitute sparked Rovers into life and his 73rd-minute goal was the first of three in seven minutes, Miller and Stewart helping Rovers snatch an improbable victory from the jaws of defeat.

The sad news in Rovers circles at this time was the death on 30 December 1994 of Geoff Bradford. Although more than 12 players have represented their country while at Bristol Rovers, Bradford remains the only one to have appeared for England. His name became synonymous with the club through the halcyon days of the 1950s, when he scored for Rovers in two FA Cup quarter-finals and helped establish the club in Division Two football. His career total of 242 League goals remains a club record and, in his 462 League appearances for his only club, he scored a Rovers record 12 hat-tricks. It is highly unlikely that, as the image of football continues to develop with the years, any player will quite capture the hearts of Bristol Rovers supporters as Geoff Bradford was able to do.

FOOTBALL LEAGUE DIVISION TWO

				ATT	G	2	3	4	5	6	7	8	9	10	11	SUBSTITUTES	GOALSCORERS
13/08/94	PETERBOROUGH UTD	A	0-0	5695	PARKIN	PRITCHARD	MADDISON	CHANNING	CLARK	TILLSON	STERLING	STEWART	PAUL	SKINNER	ARCHER	TAYLOR 11 BROWNING 8	
20/08/94	YORK CITY	H	3-1	3697	PARKIN	PRITCHARD	GURNEY	CHANNING	CLARK	TILLSON	STERLING	MILLER	STEWART	SKINNER	ARCHER	BROWNING 11	CLARK, MILLER, STEWART
27/08/94	WYCOMBE WDRS	A	0-0	5895	PARKIN	PRITCHARD	GURNEY	CHANNING	CLARK	TILLSON	STERLING	MILLER	STEWART	SKINNER	ARCHER	TAYLOR 9, BROWNING 11	
31/08/94	BLACKPOOL	H	0-0	3762	PARKIN	PRITCHARD	GURNEY	CHANNING	CLARK	TILLSON	STERLING	MILLER	TAYLOR	WADDOCK	ARCHER		
03/09/94	STOCKPORT COUNTY	A	2-2	4263	PARKIN	PRITCHARD	GURNEY	CHANNING	CLARK	TILLSON	STERLING	MILLER	TAYLOR	SKINNER	ARCHER	BROWNING 10	TILLSON, ARCHER
10/09/94	ROTHERHAM UNITED	H	3-0	2596	PARKIN	PRITCHARD	GURNEY	CHANNING	CLARK	TILLSON	STERLING	MILLER	TAYLOR	SKINNER	ARCHER	PAUL 9	MILLER 2, WILDER og
13/09/94	SWANSEA CITY	A	0-0	3226	PARKIN	PRITCHARD	GURNEY	CHANNING	CLARK	TILLSON	STERLING	MILLER	TAYLOR	SKINNER	ARCHER		
17/09/94	WREXHAM	H	4-2	4441	PARKIN	PRITCHARD	GURNEY	CHANNING	CLARK	TILLSON	STERLING	MILLER	TAYLOR	SKINNER	ARCHER		CLARK 2, TAYLOR, MILLER
24/09/94	SHREWSBURY TOWN	A	0-1	4596	PARKIN	PRITCHARD	GURNEY	CHANNING	CLARK	TILLSON	STERLING	MILLER	TAYLOR	SKINNER	ARCHER	BROWNING 10, WRIGHT 4	
01/10/94	CREWE ALEXANDRA	H	2-2	4862	PARKIN	PRITCHARD	GURNEY	CHANNING	CLARK	WRIGHT	STERLING	MILLER	PAUL	SKINNER	ARCHER	BROWNING 10 MADDISON 8	TAYLOR 2
08/10/94	BRENTFORD	A	0-3	5330	LAW	PRITCHARD	GURNEY	CHANNING	CLARK	WRIGHT	STERLING	BROWNING	PAUL	SKINNER	ARCHER	MADDISON 3, DAVIS 9	
15/10/94	CARDIFF CITY	H	2-2	3936	LAW	PRITCHARD	MADDISON	CHANNING	CLARK	TILLSON	STERLING	BROWNING	TAYLOR	SKINNER	ARCHER	GURNEY 10, McLEAN 5	CLARK, CHANNING
22/10/94	BRIGHTON & H ALB	H	3-0	4107	COLLETT	PRITCHARD	GURNEY	CHANNING	CLARK	TILLSON	STERLING	MILLER	STEWART	SKINNER	BROWNING	TAYLOR 8	STEWART, MILLER 2
29/10/94	BIRMINGHAM CITY	A	0-2	15886	COLLETT	PRITCHARD	GURNEY	CHANNING	CLARK	TILLSON	STERLING	MILLER	STEWART	SKINNER	BROWNING	TAYLOR 9, ARCHER 10	
01/11/94	CAMBRIDGE UNITED	A	1-1	2328	COLLETT	PRITCHARD	GURNEY	CHANNING	CLARK	TILLSON	STERLING	MILLER	STEWART	SKINNER	BROWNING		TILLSON
05/11/94	BRADFORD CITY	H	4-0	4247	COLLETT	PRITCHARD	GURNEY	CHANNING	CLARK	TILLSON	STERLING	MILLER	STEWART	SKINNER	BROWNING	TAYLOR 8, ARCHER 4	STEWART 2, OLIVER og, BROWNING
19/11/94	HULL CITY	A	2-0	4450	PARKIN	PRITCHARD	GURNEY	CHANNING	CLARK	TILLSON	STERLING	TAYLOR	STEWART	SKINNER	BROWNING	ARCHER 4, PAUL 10	STEWART 2
26/11/94	HUDDERSFIELD TOWN	H	1-1	5679	PARKIN	PRITCHARD	GURNEY	BROWNING	CLARK	TILLSON	STERLING	MILLER	STEWART	SKINNER	ARCHER	TAYLOR 8	MILLER
10/12/94	YORK CITY	A	3-0	3094	PARKIN	PRITCHARD	GURNEY	BROWNING	CLARK	TILLSON	STERLING	MILLER	STEWART	SKINNER	ARCHER	HARDYMAN 11	SKINNER, STEWART 2
17/12/94	PETERBOROUGH UTD	H	3-1	4635	PARKIN	CHANNING	GURNEY	BROWNING	CLARK	WRIGHT	STERLING	MILLER	STEWART	SKINNER	ARCHER	HARDYMAN 11	STEWART 2, 1pen, GURNEY
26/12/94	AFC BOURNEMOUTH	H	2-1	6913	PARKIN	GURNEY	MADDISON	BROWNING	CLARK	WRIGHT	STERLING	MILLER	STEWART	SKINNER	ARCHER	TAYLOR 6, HARDYMAN 11	MILLER, STEWART
31/12/94	CHESTER CITY	H	3-0	5629	PARKIN	PRITCHARD	GURNEY	BROWNING	CLARK	TILLSON	STERLING	MILLER	STEWART	SKINNER	ARCHER	TAYLOR 10, HARDYMAN 2	ARCHER 2, STEWART
14/01/95	OXFORD UNITED	H	3-2	5875	PARKIN	CHANNING	GURNEY	BROWNING	CLARK	TILLSON	STERLING	MILLER	STEWART	HARDYMAN	ARCHER	TAYLOR 10, PAUL 9	TAYLOR, MILLER, STEWART
04/02/95	HUDDERSFIELD TOWN	A	1-1	10389	PARKIN	PRITCHARD	GURNEY	BROWNING	CLARK	TILLSON	STERLING	MILLER	HEGGS	SKINNER	CHANNING	TAYLOR 9	STERLING
07/02/95	BRADFORD CITY	A	1-2	4243	PARKIN	PRITCHARD	GURNEY	BROWNING	WHITE	TILLSON	STERLING	MILLER	HEGGS	SKINNER	CHANNING	TAYLOR 11	HEGGS
14/02/95	BRIGHTON & H ALB	A	2-1	5316	PARKIN	PRITCHARD	GURNEY	BROWNING	WHITE	TILLSON	STERLING	MILLER	STEWART	CHANNING	ARCHER	HEGGS 8, TAYLOR 9	STEWART, ARCHER
18/02/95	OXFORD UNITED	A	0-0	6349	PARKIN	PRITCHARD	GURNEY	BROWNING	WHITE	TILLSON	STERLING	MILLER	STEWART	CHANNING	ARCHER	TAYLOR 8, HEGGS 9	
25/02/95	CREWE ALEXANDRA	A	1-2	4222	PARKIN	PRITCHARD	GURNEY	BROWNING	WHITE	TILLSON	STERLING	TAYLOR	STEWART	CHANNING	ARCHER	HEGGS 4, MILLER 9	MILLER
01/03/95	HULL CITY	H	0-2	3707	PARKIN	PRITCHARD	GURNEY	BROWNING	CLARK	TILLSON	STERLING	MILLER	STEWART	SKINNER	CHANNING	ARCHER 11	
04/03/95	SHREWSBURY TOWN	H	4-0	4338	PARKIN	PRITCHARD	GURNEY	BROWNING	CLARK	TILLSON	STERLING	MILLER	TAYLOR	SKINNER	ARCHER	DAVIS 9	TAYLOR, ARCHER, BROWNING, MILLER pen
07/03/95	STOCKPORT COUNTY	A	1-2	3580	PARKIN	PRITCHARD	GURNEY	BROWNING	CLARK	TILLSON	STERLING	MILLER	TAYLOR	SKINNER	ARCHER	CHANNING 9	MILLER
11/03/95	WYCOMBE WDRS	H	1-0	5118	PARKIN	PRITCHARD	GURNEY	BROWNING	CLARK	TILLSON	STERLING	MILLER	TAYLOR	SKINNER	ARCHER		TAYLOR
15/03/95	CAMBRIDGE UNITED	H	2-1	3734	PARKIN	PRITCHARD	GURNEY	BROWNING	CLARK	TILLSON	STERLING	MILLER	TAYLOR	SKINNER	ARCHER	CHANNING 11	MILLER, TAYLOR
18/03/95	BLACKPOOL	A	2-0	4484	PARKIN	PRITCHARD	GURNEY	BROWNING	CLARK	TILLSON	STERLING	MILLER	TAYLOR	SKINNER	ARCHER	CHANNING 11	MILLER, SKINNER
22/03/95	ROTHERHAM UNITED	H	2-0	4420	PARKIN	PRITCHARD	MADDISON	BROWNING	CLARK	TILLSON	STERLING	MILLER	TAYLOR	SKINNER	ARCHER	CHANNING 11	TAYLOR, CLARK
25/03/95	WREXHAM	A	1-1	3170	PARKIN	PRITCHARD	MADDISON	BROWNING	CLARK	TILLSON	STERLING	MILLER	TAYLOR	SKINNER	ARCHER	CHANNING 9	ARCHER
29/03/95	BIRMINGHAM CITY	H	1-1	8010	PARKIN	PRITCHARD	MADDISON	CHANNING	CLARK	TILLSON	STERLING	MILLER	STEWART	SKINNER	ARCHER	TAYLOR 9	WHYTE og
01/04/95	SWANSEA CITY	H	1-0	7062	PARKIN	PRITCHARD	MADDISON	CHANNING	CLARK	TILLSON	STERLING	MILLER	STEWART	SKINNER	ARCHER	TAYLOR 10, BROWNING 9	TAYLOR
04/04/95	PLYMOUTH ARGYLE	A	1-1	6743	PARKIN	PRITCHARD	MADDISON	CHANNING	CLARK	TILLSON	STERLING	MILLER	STEWART	BROWNING	ARCHER		MILLER
08/04/95	CHESTER CITY	A	0-0	2241	PARKIN	PRITCHARD	MADDISON	CHANNING	CLARK	TILLSON	STERLING	MILLER	STEWART	BROWNING	ARCHER	TAYLOR 10, GURNEY 11	
11/04/95	LEYTON ORIENT	A	2-1	2338	PARKIN	PRITCHARD	MADDISON	BROWNING	CLARK	TILLSON	STERLING	MILLER	STEWART	CHANNING	TAYLOR	ARCHER 6, GURNEY 12	MILLER, CHANNING
15/04/95	PLYMOUTH ARGYLE	H	2-0	7068	PARKIN	PRITCHARD	MADDISON	CHANNING	CLARK	WRIGHT	STERLING	MILLER	STEWART	SKINNER	TAYLOR	BROWNING 9, ARCHER 10	TAYLOR, WRIGHT
18/04/95	AFC BOURNEMOUTH	A	0-2	7020	PARKIN	PRITCHARD	MADDISON	BROWNING	CLARK	WRIGHT	STERLING	MILLER	TAYLOR	SKINNER	CHANNING	ARCHER 3	
22/04/95	LEYTON ORIENT	H	1-0	4838	PARKIN	PRITCHARD	GURNEY	BROWNING	CLARK	TILLSON	STERLING	MILLER	TAYLOR	SKINNER	CHANNING	STEWART 4, ARCHER 11	CLARK
29/04/95	CARDIFF CITY	A	1-0	5462	PARKIN	PRITCHARD	GURNEY	STEWART	CLARK	TILLSON	STERLING	MILLER	TAYLOR	SKINNER	CHANNING	ARCHER 7, BROWNING 9	STEWART
06/05/95	BRENTFORD	H	2-2	8501	PARKIN	PRITCHARD	GURNEY	STEWART	CLARK	TILLSON	STERLING	MILLER	TAYLOR	SKINNER	CHANNING	BROWNING 4, ARCHER 11	TAYLOR 2

PLAY OFFS

14/05/95	CREWE ALEXANDRA	H	0-0	8538	PARKIN	PRITCHARD	GURNEY	STEWART	CLARK	TILLSON	STERLING	MILLER	TAYLOR	SKINNER	ARCHER	CHANNING 4	
17/05/95	CREWE ALEXANDRA *	A	1-1	6578	PARKIN	PRITCHARD	GURNEY	STEWART	CLARK	TILLSON	STERLING	MILLER	TAYLOR	SKINNER	CHANNING	BROWNING 10, ARCHER 11	MILLER
28/05/95	HUDDERSFIELD TOWN	A	1-2	59175	PARKIN	PRITCHARD	GURNEY	STEWART	CLARK	TILLSON	STERLING	WRIGHT	TAYLOR	SKINNER	CHANNING	BROWNING 9, ARCHER 11	STEWART

* AET Score at 90 mins 0-0. Rovers win on away goals

LEAGUE CUP

17/08/94	PORT VALE	H	1-3	3307	PARKIN	PRITCHARD	MADDISON	CHANNING	CLARK	TILLSON	STERLING	MILLER	STEWART	SKINNER	ARCHER		TILLSON
23/08/94	PORT VALE	A	1-1	4728	PARKIN	PRITCHARD	GURNEY	CHANNING	CLARK	TILLSON	STERLING	MILLER	STEWART	SKINNER	ARCHER	TAYLOR 10, BROWNING 4	STEWART

FA CUP

12/11/94	BATH CITY	A	5-0	6751	PARKIN	PRITCHARD	GURNEY	CHANNING	CLARK	TILLSON	STERLING	MILLER	STEWART	SKINNER	BROWNING	ARCHER 4	STEWART, MILLER 4
03/12/94	LEYTON ORIENT	A	2-0	5071	PARKIN	PRITCHARD	GURNEY	BROWNING	CLARK	TILLSON	STERLING	MILLER	STEWART	SKINNER	ARCHER	HARDYMAN 11	STEWART 2
07/01/95	LUTON TOWN	A	1-1	7571	PARKIN	CHANNING	GURNEY	HARDYMAN	CLARK	TILLSON	STERLING	MILLER	STEWART	SKINNER	ARCHER	TAYLOR 8	STEWART
18/01/95	LUTON TOWN	H	0-1	4218	PARKIN	PRITCHARD	GURNEY	BROWNING	CLARK	TILLSON	STERLING	MILLER	TAYLOR	CHANNING	ARCHER	HARDYMAN 2	

AUTO WINDSCREENS SHIELD

27/09/94	OXFORD UNITED	A	2-2	1518	PARKIN	PRITCHARD	GURNEY	BROWNING	CLARK	WRIGHT	PAUL	MILLER	TAYLOR	SKINNER	ARCHER		SKINNER pen, CLARK
19/10/94	AFC BOURNEMOUTH	H	1-1	1728	COLLETT	PRITCHARD	MADDISON	CHANNING	CLARK	TILLSON	STERLING	PAUL	STEWART	BROWNING	GURNEY	McLEAN 8, SKINNER 6	STEWART pen
29/11/94	CAMBRIDGE UNITED	H	4-2	2373	PARKIN	PRITCHARD	GURNEY	BROWNING	CLARK	TILLSON	STERLING	MILLER	STEWART	SKINNER	ARCHER		SKINNER, STEWART 2 (I pen), MILLER
10/01/95	LEYTON ORIENT *	A	0-0	1381	PARKIN	CHANNING	GURNEY	HARDYMAN	CLARK	TILLSON	STERLING	MILLER	TAYLOR	SKINNER	ARCHER	PAUL 9, MADDISON 10	

* AET Score at 90 mins 0-0 Rovers lost 3-4 on pens

GLOUCESTERSHIRE CUP FINAL

03/08/94	BRISTOL CITY *	H	0-0	3699	PARKIN	PRITCHARD	MADDISON	GURNEY	CLARK	TILLSON	STERLING	STEWART	PAUL	BROWNING	WADDOCK	CHANNING 4, TAYLOR 9	

*AET Rovers won 11-10 on pens

PLAYERS	APP	SUB	GLS
ARCHER L	32	10	6
BROWNING M	31	10	2
CHANNING J	35	5	2
CLARK W	42		6
COLLETT A	4		
DAVIS M	0	2	
GURNEY A	35	3	1
HARDYMAN P	1	4	
HEGGS C	2	3	1
LAW M	2		
MADDISON L	12	2	
McLEAN I	0	1	
MILLER P	41	1	16
PARKIN B	40		
PAUL M	2	3	
PRITCHARD D	43		
SKINNER J	38		2
STERLING W	46		1
STEWART M	26	1	15
TAYLOR G	23	16	12
TILLSON A	40		2
WADDOCK G	1		
WHITE T	4		
WRIGHT I	6	1	1
OWN GOALS			3

After four consecutive home games, all five fixtures in February took place away from home, the only victory coming at Brighton. March brought a second 4-0 home victory, with four different players getting on the scoresheet against Shrewsbury Town. Following defeat at Stockport County, Rovers were to lose just once in the last 15 games of the scheduled season. Among nine victories in this run, Rovers completed League doubles over Rotherham United and Leyton Orient and recorded commendable wins at Blackpool and at Cardiff City. Orient's defeats were part of a series of nine in succession that led to the London side's inevitable relegation; they fielded in their side Kevin Austin, who was to join Rovers from Cambridge United in the summer of 2002. There was almost a victory over a strong Birmingham City side to add to this list, after Rovers led at half-time through an own goal from Chris Whyte, whose gentle backpass had trickled bizarrely past goalkeeper Ian Bennett. Birmingham, who won the only automatic promotion slot as champions, equalised 17 minutes from time when substitute Steve Claridge headed home a cross from Portuguese winger José Dominguez.

With Rovers and Brentford already assured play-off places, the sides played out an exciting 2-2 draw, including a towering headed goal from Taylor, his second of the game, before a seasonal best home crowd in regular League fixtures of 8,501. Even more saw the goalless draw with Crewe Alexandra at Twerton Park in the play-offs and, with the aggregate score remaining goalless, the second leg at Gresty Road went into extra-time. At stake was a game at Wembley against Huddersfield Town, who had beaten Brentford on penalties, with the winners promoted to Division One. Substitute Darren Rowbotham put Crewe ahead in extra-time, but Miller's scrambled equaliser saw Rovers through on the 'away goals' rule.

On 28 May 1995, before a crowd of 59,175, the second highest – after the FA Cup tie at Newcastle in February 1951 – to watch a Rovers game, the club made the second Wembley appearance in its history. Behind to an Andy Booth goal, Marcus Stewart's equaliser just seconds before half-time offered renewed hope. Stewart also hit the bar with a 35-yard shot and Andy Gurney hit his own crossbar while Gareth Taylor missed an open goal, but it was Chris Billy's diving header that brought Huddersfield Town victory. Rovers were to remain in Division Two for the time being, but in an exciting game, they had performed well. Gurney and Pritchard, in particular, had formed a powerful full-back partnership and Lee Maddison's £25,000 transfer to Northampton Town therefore came as little surprise.

Although initially leading through Andy Tillson's goal, an early Coca-Cola Cup exit against Port Vale included a goal in each leg from Lee Glover. Likewise, after draws with Oxford United and Bournemouth and four goals against Cambridge United, Rovers were knocked out of the Auto Windscreens Shield in a penalty shoot-out at Leyton Orient, youngster Martin Paul missing the vital kick. The former Rovers defender John Scales was a Coca-Cola Cup winner with Liverpool, while Devon White scored the winning goal at Wembley as Notts County defeated Ascoli 2-1 in the Anglo-Italian Cup Final. Rovers won the Gloucestershire Cup Final for the final time in the club's history, defeating Bristol City 11-10 on penalties after a goalless draw at Twerton Park.

The FA Cup threw up an intriguing tie, with Rovers drawn to play away to their landlords Bath City. Stewart put Rovers ahead after 18 minutes via a post, after Justin Channing's shot had hit the crossbar. Bath, who fielded former Rovers players Vaughan

Golden Goal. Paul Miller scores the extra-time equalizing goal at Crewe Alexandra to book Rovers' place in the Play Off final at Wembley.

Jones and Gary Smart, had Grantley Dicks sent off for a foul on Pritchard, before Miller scored four goals in 23 second-half minutes, registering with a header and shots with both feet. Miller's goals, emulating those of Carl Saunders three years earlier, gave Rovers a convincing 5-0 victory. Two Stewart goals defeated Leyton Orient and only a John Hartson goal prevented Rovers winning at Division One Luton Town in the third round. The Hatters, with Gary Waddock in midfield against his former club, won the Twerton Park replay through a second-half Dwight Marshall goal.

1995/96

Hopes had been high that Rovers could be successful in 1995/96, but high achievement was not forthcoming. After reaching Wembley through the play-offs, a final League placing of 10th in Division Two was a relative disappointment. A second route to Wembley, the Auto Windscreen Shield, turned abruptly into a cul-de-sac when Rovers, requiring essentially only a draw at home to Shrewsbury Town in order to return to the Twin Towers, inexplicably lost to the Division Three side. More humiliating by far was the FA Cup exit at Hitchin Town, the type of banana skin all League clubs dread. In addition, local government reorganization meant the proposed stadium site at Pilning was now in the administrative district of South Gloucestershire and the new councillors were not in favour. Like numerous schemes before it to bring Rovers back home to Bristol, the plan was reluctantly shelved.

At the end of an exhausting and demoralizing season, John Ward left Rovers after three years as manager. Under his guidance, the club had won 64 out of 149 League matches, re-established itself in Division Two, played in the Southern Final of the Auto Windscreen Shield and reached a play-off final in May 1995. Within a year of leaving Rovers, Ward was to return to management with Bristol City, leading the Robins to promotion to Division

One in 1997/98 and was later assistant manager at Wolverhampton Wanderers. His successor as Rovers manager, in the summer of 1996, was to be a very familiar face and Ian Holloway's return coincided with Rovers' reappearance in Bristol.

Eight players made a Rovers debut in 1995/96, yet only one, Peter Beadle, could claim to be a regular in the side. Josh Low appeared in the team in four consecutive seasons, Jon French and Matt Hayfield in three each, yet none was picked consistently by Ward, nor indeed by Holloway. Three players, of whom Damian Matthew and Steve Morgan had both played top-division football, arrived at Twerton Park on loan. Beadle, a £50,000 signing from Watford, joined Rovers in the aftermath of the Hitchin Town debacle and became the tall target man Rovers had missed since the departures of Devon White and John Taylor. His two goals at Ashton Gate secured a significantly confidence-boosting 2-0 victory over his future club Bristol City in January.

Twice in the opening five home League games, Rovers' opponents found themselves reduced to nine men. Only once before had two members of the opposition been sent off in a League game. However, Rovers could only draw 2-2 with Swansea City after Steve Torpey, later of Bristol City, and the former Rovers striker Carl Heggs had both been sent off. Then, with Martin Paul scoring on his first start of the season, Rovers defeated Brentford 2-0, with the visitors having centre-backs Martin Grainger and Jamie Bates sent off. Rovers also suffered an uncharacteristic 4-1 home defeat at the hands of Swindon Town, for whom Kevin Horlock scored a hat-trick. The only other opponent to score a hat-trick at Twerton Park had been Joe Allon on the previous occasion Rovers had conceded four goals in a League match. The Cameroon International Charlie Ntamark was another recipient of a red card, when Rovers met Walsall in February.

On 29 September 1995, Gareth Taylor, with four goals to his name already, was sold to Crystal Palace for a club record £1.6 million. He was replaced in November by the prolific Beadle, who was to score in four consecutive League matches in the spring. Of greater immediacy was Marcus Stewart's renewed goalscoring form. He scored after only

Bristol Rovers 1995/96. Back row: Wyatt, Clark, Taylor, Higgs, Parkin, Collett, Skinner, McLean, Wright. Second row: Archer, Pritchard, Stewart, Tillson, Browning, Miller, Sterling, Channing. Third row: Dolling (Youth Dev.), Kendall (Kit Man), Gill (Youth Team Manager), Ward (Manager), Cross (Asst manager), Connor (Coach), James (Physio). Front row: Gurney, French, Hayfield, Davis, Paul, Tovey, White, Maddison

26 seconds of the home game with Hull City and added a goal in eight of nine consecutive games in the spring to compile an impressive seasonal total of 21 League goals to end the year as the highest individual goalscorer in Division Two. It was no surprise when, after a career total of 57 goals in 137 (plus 34 as sub) League appearances for Rovers, Stewart joined Huddersfield Town in a £1.2 million deal at the end of the season.

Rovers used their full allocation of substitutes for the first time when they visited Brighton in October. Ian McLean, Martin Paul and Tom White all played their part, but Rovers lost 2-0 after conceding a farcical goal to George Parris after 51 minutes. Goalkeeper Andy Collett, who gradually ousted Brian Parkin from his long-held position, had not seen Parris waiting by the goalpost as he shaped to take a goalkick. The Brighton player waited for Collett to ground the ball, tackled him, rounded him and scored a perfectly justifiable goal. At this stage, following an excellent win at Bradford City, Rovers endured a run of seven matches without a win. This ended when Stewart scored twice in a 2-0 victory over Oxford United, which set Rovers off on a club record 23 consecutive League matches in which the side scored. Although there had been 26 consecutive games between March and December 1927, this spell constituted the longest run within a season.

There were three games of note in a 10-day patch in mid-February. Rovers celebrated the club's 3,000th Football League fixture since election to Division Three (South) in 1920 with a 3-1 win at Hull City, Marcus Browning after 63 minutes joining the ubiquitous Beadle and Stewart on the scoresheet. Seven days later Rovers scraped a single-goal victory at home to Rotherham United, even though the visitors, bereft of injured goalkeeper Matthew Clarke, had played the entire second-half with full-back Gary Bowyer in goal. The following Tuesday, Andy Tillson's first goal for 15 months was not enough as Rovers lost 3-2 at Wrexham. Some records debit Justin Channing with two own goals and he would certainly be the only Rovers player to have achieved this feat. The first, after 25 minutes, resulted from Barry Hunter's header, which pinballed off both Clark and Channing, while the second, 30 minutes later, was a more clearcut diversion of Peter Ward's cross. 'Two were own goals attributed to ... Channing' (Kevin Fahey, 'Rovers' own-goal horror', *Western Daily Press*, 21.2.96); '[Rovers] contributed to their downfall by conceding two own goals' (Mark Currie, 'Battle of Nerves', *Daily Post*, 21.2.96); reported the press. Yet, the national papers, Wrexham FC and the general consensus of opinion awarded the first goal to Hunter.

Despite a late flurry of victories, including six 1-0 wins in the New Year, five in a run of seven home matches, Rovers lacked the consistency to challenge seriously for a play-off place. A 4-2 defeat at home to Bristol City proved particularly demoralizing and four goals were also conceded at Notts County. Ultimately, all play-off hopes were killed off in a 2-0 defeat at Stockport County where John Jeffers, later to score in the first game at the Memorial Ground, created both goals. The final position, 10th, though commendable, was not enough to hold on to Ward or Stewart. However, the summer of 1996, heralded a new era in the history of Bristol Rovers, the return of the prodigal son Ian Holloway on 13 May as manager, a return to an east Bristol home and the prospect of prosperous days ahead.

In the Coca Cola Cup, a first-minute Stewart goal helped Rovers towards a 4-2 second leg and 5-3 aggregate victory over Gillingham. Stewart completed his hat-trick, while the visitors' opening goal was scored by Dennis Bailey against his former club. In the second round, a single first-half John Moncur goal gave West Ham United victory at Twerton Park,

FOOTBALL LEAGUE DIVISION TWO

Date	Opponent	V	Score	ATT	G	2	3	4	5	6	7	8	9	10	11	Substitutes	Goalscorers
12/08/95	CARLISLE UNITED	A	2-1	8003	PARKIN	PRITCHARD	GURNEY	BROWNING	CLARK	TILLSON	STERLING	MILLER	STEWART	SKINNER	TAYLOR		CLARK, STEWART
19/08/95	SWANSEA CITY	H	2-2	6689	PARKIN	PRITCHARD	GURNEY	BROWNING	CLARK	WRIGHT	STERLING	MILLER	STEWART	SKINNER	TAYLOR		TAYLOR 2
26/08/95	WALSALL	A	1-1	4851	PARKIN	PRITCHARD	GURNEY	BROWNING	CLARK	WRIGHT	STERLING	MILLER	STEWART	SKINNER	TAYLOR		TAYLOR
29/08/95	BURNLEY	H	1-2	5646	PARKIN	PRITCHARD	GURNEY	BROWNING	CLARK	WRIGHT	STERLING	MILLER	STEWART	SKINNER	TAYLOR		TAYLOR
02/09/95	WREXHAM	H	1-2	6031	PARKIN	PRITCHARD	GURNEY	WYATT	CLARK	WRIGHT	STERLING	MILLER	STEWART	SKINNER	TAYLOR	HAYFIELD 10	
09/09/95	YORK CITY	A	1-0	4047	PARKIN	PRITCHARD	GURNEY	BROWNING	CLARK	WRIGHT	STERLING	MILLER	STEWART	SKINNER	TAYLOR	CHANNING 11	STEWART
12/09/95	ROTHERHAM UNITED	A	2-2	2739	PARKIN	PRITCHARD	GURNEY	BROWNING	CLARK	WRIGHT	WYATT	MILLER	STEWART	SKINNER	TAYLOR	ARCHER 7, McLEAN 3	MILLER
16/09/95	SWINDON TOWN	H	1-4	7025	PARKIN	PRITCHARD	GURNEY	BROWNING	CLARK	WRIGHT	ARCHER	MILLER	STEWART	SKINNER	TAYLOR		MILLER
23/09/95	BRENTFORD	H	2-0	5131	PARKIN	PRITCHARD	CHANNING	BROWNING	CLARK	TILLSON	PAUL	MILLER	STEWART	SKINNER	WYATT	CLARK 5, HAYFIELD 10	STEWART pen, PAUL
30/09/95	OXFORD UNITED	A	2-1	6091	PARKIN	PRITCHARD	GURNEY	BROWNING	WRIGHT	TILLSON	STERLING	PAUL	STEWART	SKINNER	CHANNING	HAYFIELD 8	BROWNING, STEWART
07/10/95	AFC BOURNEMOUTH	H	0-2	5171	PARKIN	PRITCHARD	GURNEY	BROWNING	WRIGHT	TILLSON	STERLING	PAUL	STEWART	SKINNER	CHANNING	ARCHER 2	
14/10/95	BRADFORD CITY	A	3-2	5817	COLLETT	PRITCHARD	GURNEY	BROWNING	WRIGHT	TILLSON	STERLING	PAUL	STEWART	SKINNER	ARCHER	DAVIS 8	GURNEY, ARCHER, STEWART
21/10/95	NOTTS COUNTY	H	0-3	6078	COLLETT	CHANNING	GURNEY	BROWNING	WRIGHT	TILLSON	STERLING	PAUL	STEWART	SKINNER	ARCHER	DAVIS 8	
28/10/95	BLACKPOOL	A	0-3	5658	COLLETT	CHANNING	GURNEY	BROWNING	McLEAN	TILLSON	STERLING	DAVIS	STEWART	SKINNER	ARCHER	McLEAN 5, PAUL 8	
31/10/95	PETERBOROUGH UTD	H	1-1	3877	COLLETT	CHANNING	GURNEY	BROWNING	CLARK	TILLSON	STERLING	PAUL	STEWART	SKINNER	ARCHER	WYATT 4	WHITE 2
04/11/95	WYCOMBE WDRS	A	1-1	4241	COLLETT	HAYFIELD	GURNEY	BROWNING	CLARK	TILLSON	STERLING	FRENCH	STEWART	SKINNER	BEADLE	DAVIS 4	GURNEY
18/11/95	STOCKPORT COUNTY	H	1-3	4886	PARKIN	WRIGHT	CHANNING	BROWNING	CLARK	TILLSON	CHANNING	MILLER	STEWART	SKINNER	McLEAN	MILLER 8	GURNEY
25/11/95	BRENTFORD	A	1-3	4326	PARKIN	PRITCHARD	CHANNING	BROWNING	CLARK	TILLSON	STERLING	MILLER	STEWART	SKINNER	McLEAN	PAUL 11	MILLER
09/12/95	OXFORD UNITED	H	2-0	5679	PARKIN	HAYFIELD	CHANNING	BROWNING	CLARK	TILLSON	STERLING	TOVEY	STEWART	SKINNER	PAUL	BEADLE 11	
16/12/95	CREWE ALEXANDRA	A	2-0	4051	PARKIN	CHANNING	CHANNING	BROWNING	CLARK	TILLSON	STERLING	PAUL	STEWART	TOVEY	BEADLE	SKINNER 11	STEWART 2
23/12/95	SHREWSBURY TOWN	H	1-2	4944	PARKIN	CHANNING	CHANNING	BROWNING	CLARK	TILLSON	STERLING	MILLER	STEWART	TOVEY	BEADLE	SKINNER 11, ARMSTRONG 10	BROWNING
26/12/95	HULL CITY	A	2-2	4267	COLLETT	CHANNING	CHANNING	BROWNING	CLARK	TILLSON	GURNEY	MILLER	STEWART	MATTHEW	BEADLE		STEWART 2
06/01/96	BRISTOL CITY	A	2-2	20007	PARKIN	CHANNING	CHANNING	BROWNING	CLARK	TILLSON	ARMSTRONG	MILLER	STEWART	MATTHEW	BEADLE		GURNEY, BEADLE
13/01/96	CARLISLE UNITED	H	2-0	5196	PARKIN	CHANNING	CHANNING	BROWNING	CLARK	TILLSON	STERLING	MILLER	STEWART	MATTHEW	BEADLE		BEADLE 2
20/01/96	WALSALL	A	2-1	4948	COLLETT	CHANNING	ARMSTRONG	BROWNING	CLARK	TILLSON	STERLING	MILLER	STEWART	MATTHEW	BEADLE		BEADLE, STEWART pen
03/02/96	HULL CITY	H	3-1	3311	COLLETT	CHANNING	ARMSTRONG	BROWNING	CLARK	TILLSON	STERLING	MILLER	STEWART	MATTHEW	BEADLE		STEWART, BROWNING, BEADLE
10/02/96	ROTHERHAM UNITED	A	1-0	5412	COLLETT	CHANNING	ARMSTRONG	BROWNING	CLARK	TILLSON	STERLING	MILLER	STEWART	MATTHEW	BEADLE		STEWART
17/02/96	WREXHAM	A	2-3	3235	COLLETT	CHANNING	ARMSTRONG	BROWNING	CLARK	TILLSON	STERLING	MILLER	STEWART	MATTHEW	BEADLE	PAUL 7	BEADLE, TILLSON
20/02/96	SWINDON TOWN	A	1-2	11697	COLLETT	CHANNING	GURNEY	BROWNING	CLARK	TILLSON	STERLING	MILLER	STEWART	MATTHEW	PAUL		STEWART
24/02/96	YORK CITY	H	0-0	4013	COLLETT	CHANNING	GURNEY	BROWNING	CLARK	TILLSON	GURNEY	TOVEY	STEWART	MATTHEW	BEADLE		
27/02/96	SHREWSBURY TOWN	A	2-2	5004	COLLETT	CHANNING	ARMSTRONG	BROWNING	CLARK	TILLSON	GURNEY	TOVEY	STEWART	TOVEY	BEADLE	FRENCH 4	GURNEY, STEWART
02/03/96	CREWE ALEXANDRA	H	2-1	4091	COLLETT	GURNEY	ARMSTRONG	BROWNING	CLARK	TILLSON	STERLING	TOVEY	STEWART	TOVEY	BEADLE	STERLING 2, WRIGHT 10	FRENCH, STEWART
09/03/96	BRISTOL CITY	H	2-1	8648	COLLETT	GURNEY	ARMSTRONG	BROWNING	CLARK	WRIGHT	STERLING	CHANNING	STEWART	CHANNING	FRENCH	PAUL 4, WRIGHT 11	GURNEY, CLARK
16/03/96	CHESTERFIELD	A	1-2	4748	COLLETT	GURNEY	ARMSTRONG	BROWNING	CLARK	TILLSON	STERLING	CHANNING	STEWART	CHANNING	BEADLE	FRENCH 10	STEWART
23/03/96	CHESTERFIELD	H	1-0	3513	COLLETT	GURNEY	MORGAN	BROWNING	CLARK	WRIGHT	ARCHER	FRENCH	STEWART	CHANNING	BEADLE	STERLING 8	BEADLE
26/03/96	AFC BOURNEMOUTH	A	1-2	4607	COLLETT	GURNEY	MORGAN	BROWNING	CLARK	TILLSON	ARCHER	MILLER	STEWART	CHANNING	BEADLE	WRIGHT 3, FRENCH 2	MILLER
30/03/96	BRADFORD CITY	H	1-0	4008	COLLETT	GURNEY	GURNEY	BROWNING	CLARK	TILLSON	ARCHER	MILLER	STEWART	CHANNING	BEADLE	FRENCH 7	BEADLE
02/04/96	BRIGHTON & H ALB	A	1-0	5385	COLLETT	GURNEY	ARMSTRONG	BROWNING	CLARK	TILLSON	ARCHER	MILLER	STEWART	CHANNING	BEADLE	SKINNER 11	BEADLE
06/04/96	NOTTS COUNTY	H	2-0	4661	COLLETT	GURNEY	ARMSTRONG	BROWNING	CLARK	WRIGHT	ARCHER	MILLER	STEWART	CHANNING	BEADLE	ARCHER 8	STEWART, BEADLE
09/04/96	BLACKPOOL	A	1-0	5626	COLLETT	GURNEY	GURNEY	BROWNING	CLARK	TILLSON	SKINNER	MILLER	STEWART	CHANNING	BEADLE	ARCHER 2	BEADLE
13/04/96	PETERBOROUGH UTD	H	0-0	4884	COLLETT	GURNEY	ARMSTRONG	BROWNING	CLARK	TILLSON	SKINNER	MILLER	STEWART	CHANNING	BEADLE	FRENCH 11, WHITE 2	
20/04/96	BURNLEY	A	1-0	9368	COLLETT	GURNEY	ARMSTRONG	BROWNING	WRIGHT	TILLSON	SKINNER	MILLER	STEWART	CHANNING	BEADLE	ARCHER 2	STEWART
23/04/96	STOCKPORT COUNTY	H	0-0	6935	COLLETT	GURNEY	ARMSTRONG	BROWNING	WRIGHT	TILLSON	STERLING	MILLER	STEWART	CHANNING	BEADLE		
27/04/96	WYCOMBE WDRS	A	2-1	7050	COLLETT	GURNEY	ARMSTRONG	BROWNING	CLARK	TILLSON	STERLING	MILLER	STEWART	CHANNING	BEADLE	GURNEY 2, FRENCH 11, LOW 10	BROWNING, STEWART

PLAYERS	APP	SUB	GLS
ARCHER L	13	6	1
ARMSTRONG C	13	13	1
BEADLE P	26	1	12
BROWNING M	45		4
CHANNING J	35	1	
CLARK W	38		2
COLLETT A	26		
DAVIS M	1	3	
FRENCH I	3		1
GURNEY A	42	1	6
HAYFIELD M	0	1	
LOW J	0	1	
MATTHEW D	8		
McLEAN I	4	3	
MILLER P	37	1	4
MORGAN S	5		
PARKIN B	20		
PAUL M	9	4	
PRITCHARD D	12		
SKINNER J	23	5	
STERLING W	28	2	
STEWART M	44		21
TAYLOR G	7		4
TILLSON A	38		1
TOVEY P	8		
WHITE T	0	2	
WRIGHT I	15	3	
WYATT M	3	1	

LEAGUE CUP

Date	Opponent	V	Score	ATT	G	2	3	4	5	6	7	8	9	10	11	Substitutes	Goalscorers
15/08/95	GILLINGHAM	A	1-1	3827	PARKIN	PRITCHARD	GURNEY	BROWNING	CLARK	TILLSON	STERLING	MILLER	STEWART	SKINNER	TAYLOR	WRIGHT 6	STEWART, MILLER
23/08/95	GILLINGHAM	H	4-2	3601	PARKIN	PRITCHARD	GURNEY	BROWNING	CLARK	TILLSON	STERLING	MILLER	STEWART	SKINNER	TAYLOR	WYATT 10	STEWART 3, MILLER
20/09/95	WEST HAM UNITED	H	0-1	7103	PARKIN	PRITCHARD	GURNEY	BROWNING	CLARK	TILLSON	STERLING	MILLER	STEWART	SKINNER	TAYLOR	DAVIS 11	
04/10/95	WEST HAM UNITED	A	0-3	15375	PARKIN	PRITCHARD	GURNEY	BROWNING	CLARK	TILLSON	STERLING	MILLER	STEWART	SKINNER	CHANNING		

FA CUP

Date	Opponent	V	Score	ATT	G	2	3	4	5	6	7	8	9	10	11	Substitutes	Goalscorers
11/11/95	HITCHIN TOWN	A	1-2	3001	COLLETT	CHANNING	GURNEY	PRITCHARD	McLEAN	TILLSON	STERLING	WRIGHT	STEWART	SKINNER	ARCHER	CHANNING 4	ARCHER

AUTO WINDSCREENS SHIELD

Date	Opponent	V	Score	ATT	G	2	3	4	5	6	7	8	9	10	11	Substitutes	Goalscorers
17/10/95	BRIGHTON & H ALB	A	2-0	1191	COLLETT	CHANNING	GURNEY	BROWNING	WRIGHT	McLEAN	STERLING	PAUL	STEWART	SKINNER	ARCHER	DAVIS 7, HAYFIELD 9, HOPE 11	DAVIS, ARCHER
07/11/95	CAMBRIDGE UNITED	H	3-0	1805	PARKIN	WRIGHT	GURNEY	FRENCH	McLEAN	TILLSON	STERLING	HAYFIELD	STEWART	SKINNER	ARCHER	WHITE 8, PAUL 11	FRENCH, STEWART 2
28/11/95	AFC BOURNEMOUTH	A	2-1	3479	PARKIN	PRITCHARD	GURNEY	BROWNING	CLARK	TILLSON	STERLING	MILLER	STEWART	TOVEY	PAUL	FRENCH 10	BROWNING, TILLSON
09/01/96	FULHAM *	A	1-0	3761	COLLETT	CHANNING	GURNEY	BROWNING	CLARK	TILLSON	STERLING	MILLER	STEWART	TOVEY	BEADLE	TOVEY 10	STEWART 2
13/02/96	PETERBOROUGH UTD	H	1-0	5212	COLLETT	PARKIN	GURNEY	BROWNING	CLARK	TILLSON	STERLING	MILLER	STEWART	MATTHEW	FRENCH	WRIGHT 11	STEWART pen
05/03/96	SHREWSBURY T **	H	1-1		COLLETT	GURNEY	MORGAN	BROWNING	CLARK	TILLSON	CHANNING	MILLER	STEWART	MATTHEW	BEADLE		MATTHEW
12/03/96	SHREWSBURY T **	A	0-1	7050	COLLETT	GURNEY	MORGAN	BROWNING	CLARK	TILLSON	CHANNING	PAUL	STEWART	TOVEY	BEADLE		

* AET: match won on sudden death

** AET: match won in sudden death

Twerton Park pictured from the air in August 1995

before three second-half goals at Upton Park saw Rovers eliminated 4-0 on aggregate. Exit from the FA Cup was far more nightmarish. As if being drawn away to Hitchin Town was not enough to strike anticipatory fear into the mind of any Rovers supporter, the ICIS Premier Division side took the lead through a Steve Conroy header after only 47 seconds and went further ahead when Lee Burns chipped an outstanding second in the ninth minute. Rovers were able to pull one goal back, through Lee Archer, but it was clearly an afternoon to forget, as Hitchin Town held on for a thoroughly deserved victory.

While the former Rovers player John Rudge led the Port Vale team of which he was manager to the Anglo-Italian Cup final at Wembley and a 5-2 defeat at the hands of Genoa, Rovers were themselves only minutes from a third visit to Wembley. Elsewhere, victory over Brighton, Cambridge United and Bournemouth earned Rovers a tough tie at Fulham. The Auto Windscreen Shield had adopted the Golden Goal rule, whereby the first goal scored in extra-time would be the winner, and Stewart's second goal of the night proved just that. His penalty then defeated Peterborough United and Rovers just had to overcome Shrewsbury Town over two legs to reach Wembley. After Damian Matthew's goal at Gay Meadow, a goalless draw would have taken Rovers through. However, Stewart's 56th-minute penalty was saved by Paul Edwards and, 17 minutes from time, Ian Reed crossed for Ian Stevens, who also scored in both League fixtures against Rovers, to notch the goal which killed off Rovers' hopes.

The history of any football club involves a series of crossroads at which the future direction is determined. One of the crucial moments in the history of Bristol Rovers came in the summer of 1996. The 10-year wait for a return to a home base in north Bristol was at a dramatic end. The prodigal son returned to manage his former club. No fewer than 14 players were to make a Rovers debut in 1996/97, while the prolific Marcus Stewart was sold. It was a moment of great anticipation and hope.

Bristol Rugby Football Club, operating at the Memorial Ground in Horfield, was running into ever-deeper financial waters. In April 1996 it became a Limited Company but only 278 of its 2,000 founder shareholders invested further. In a desperate situation, the rugby club offered Rovers the opportunity to buy half the ground for £2.3 million. It was the moment Rovers' dreams of moving back to Bristol came to fruition. The ground, bought by the rugby club in 1921 for £26,000, had seen some development, though much more would be necessary in order to house League football. The pitch, at 101 x 68 metres, was the smallest in the Football League and there was room for only 740 away supporters on the Centenary Stand Terrace, a figure increased to 1,161 by August 1998. The Centenary Stand, constructed in 1988 and then rebuilt at the constructors' expense following renewed fire safety regulations in the wake of the Bradford fire, represented merely a first step in the redevelopment of the stadium.

John Ward's successor as Rovers manager in May 1996 was a hugely popular choice. Ian Holloway epitomized the spirit of the club. A local player, returning for a third spell with a club with which he had experienced triumph and despair, Holloway now brought his vast resources of enthusiasm and commitment into his first management job. The

Bristol Rovers 1996/97. Back row: Beadle, Clark, Collett, Tillson, Higgs, Miller, Skinner, Martin.
Second row: French, Gurney, Hayfield, Browning, Parmenter, Ramasut, Power, Pritchard, Archer, Bowey, White.
Front row: Dolling, Harte, Gill (Youth Team Coach), Connor (Reserve Team Coach), Holloway (Player-Manager),
Twentyman (Asst Manager), Kite (Physio), Cureton, Kendall (Kit Man), Lockwood

FOOTBALL LEAGUE DIVISION TWO

Date	Opponent	V	Score	ATT	2	3	4	5	6	7	8	9	10	11	SUBSTITUTES	GOALSCORERS
17/08/96	PETERBOROUGH UTD*	H	1-0	6232	COLLETT	LOCKWOOD	BROWNING	CLARK	TILLSON	HOLLOWAY	GURNEY	MILLER	ARCHER	BEADLE	MILLER 9, SKINNER 8	BEADLE
24/08/96	PRESTON NORTH END	H	0-0	9752	COLLETT	LOCKWOOD	BROWNING	CLARK	TILLSON	HOLLOWAY	GURNEY	ARCHER	BEADLE	PARMENTER	SKINNER 7, FRENCH 11	
31/08/96	STOCKPORT COUNTY	H	1-1	6380	COLLETT	LOCKWOOD	BROWNING	CLARK	TILLSON	HOLLOWAY	GURNEY	PARMENTER	BEADLE	BROWNING	CURETON 9	ARCHER
07/09/96	MILLWALL	A	0-2	7881	COLLETT	LOCKWOOD	BROWNING	CLARK	TILLSON	HOLLOWAY	GURNEY	MILLER	BEADLE	PARMENTER	MILLER 11	
10/09/96	AFC BOURNEMOUTH	H	3-2	4170	COLLETT	LOCKWOOD	BROWNING	CLARK	TILLSON	HOLLOWAY	GURNEY	MILLER	BEADLE	PARMENTER	LOCKWOOD 10	TILLSON, PARMENTER, BEADLE
14/09/96	WATFORD	H	0-1	6256	COLLETT	LOCKWOOD	BROWNING	CLARK	TILLSON	HOLLOWAY	GURNEY	MILLER	ARCHER	BEADLE		
17/09/96	WREXHAM	A	0-1	2401	COLLETT	LOCKWOOD	BROWNING	CLARK	TILLSON	HOLLOWAY	GURNEY	PARMENTER	ARCHER	BEADLE		
21/09/96	PLYMOUTH ARGYLE	A	1-0	8379	COLLETT	LOCKWOOD	BROWNING	CLARK	TILLSON	HOLLOWAY	SKINNER	CURETON	ARCHER	BEADLE		BEADLE
28/09/96	CHESTERFIELD	H	2-0	5008	COLLETT	LOCKWOOD	BROWNING	CLARK	POWER	HOLLOWAY	GURNEY	CURETON	ARCHER	BEADLE		CURETON, BROWNING
01/10/96	YORK CITY	A	2-2	3714	COLLETT	LOCKWOOD	BROWNING	CLARK	POWER	HOLLOWAY	GURNEY	CURETON	ARCHER	BEADLE		GURNEY, CURETON
04/10/96	CREWE ALEXANDRA	A	2-0	6211	COLLETT	LOCKWOOD	BROWNING	CLARK	POWER	HOLLOWAY	GURNEY	CURETON	ARCHER	BEADLE		CURETON, BEADLE
12/10/96	NOTTS COUNTY	H	1-1	4558	COLLETT	LOCKWOOD	SKINNER	CLARK	POWER	HOLLOWAY	MILLER	CURETON	LOCKWOOD	CURETON		CURETON
15/10/96	ROTHERHAM UNITED	A	2-0	2490	COLLETT	LOCKWOOD	BROWNING	CLARK	POWER	HOLLOWAY	MILLER	CURETON	LOCKWOOD	CURETON		CURETON, GURNEY
19/10/96	BLACKPOOL	H	0-0	5823	COLLETT	MARTIN	BROWNING	CLARK	TILLSON	HOLLOWAY	MILLER	CURETON	ARCHER	BEADLE		
26/10/96	BURY	A	1-2	4082	COLLETT	MARTIN	BROWNING	CLARK	TILLSON	HOLLOWAY	MILLER	CURETON	MILLER	BEADLE		HARRIS
29/10/96	BRENTFORD	H	2-1	5163	COLLETT	GURNEY	BROWNING	CLARK	TILLSON	HOLLOWAY	MILLER	CURETON	ARCHER	BEADLE		BEADLE, CLARK
02/11/96	GILLINGHAM	A	0-0	5530	COLLETT	WHITE	BROWNING	CLARK	TILLSON	HOLLOWAY	MILLER	CURETON	LOCKWOOD	BEADLE		
12/11/96	SHREWSBURY TOWN	A	0-2	2331	HIGGS	POWER	BROWNING	CLARK	TILLSON	HOLLOWAY	MILLER	RAMASUT	LOCKWOOD	BEADLE		
19/11/96	BURNLEY	H	1-2	4123	COLLETT	LOCKWOOD	BROWNING	CLARK	TILLSON	HOLLOWAY	SKINNER	RAMASUT	BEADLE	BEADLE		MILLER
23/11/96	LUTON TOWN	A	2-3	5315	COLLETT	LOCKWOOD	BROWNING	CLARK	TILLSON	HOLLOWAY	GURNEY	ARCHER	BEADLE	BEADLE		
30/11/96	BURY	H	4-3	4496	COLLETT	LOCKWOOD	BROWNING	CLARK	TILLSON	HOLLOWAY	GURNEY	ARCHER	BEADLE	CURETON		
03/12/96	WALSALL	A	0-1	4084	COLLETT	LOCKWOOD	BROWNING	CLARK	TILLSON	HOLLOWAY	GURNEY	ARCHER	LOCKWOOD	CURETON		
15/12/96	BRISTOL CITY	H	1-2	11674	COLLETT	LOCKWOOD	BROWNING	CLARK	TILLSON	HOLLOWAY	GURNEY	CURETON	LOCKWOOD	BEADLE		
21/12/96	WYCOMBE WDRS	H	3-4	4465	COLLETT	LOCKWOOD	BROWNING	CLARK	TILLSON	HAYFIELD	GURNEY	CURETON	CURETON	BEADLE		CURETON, HARRIS, LOCKWOOD
26/12/96	AFC BOURNEMOUTH	A	0-1	5036	COLLETT	LOCKWOOD	CLARK	GAYLE	TILLSON	SKINNER	HARRIS	CURETON	BEADLE	LOCKWOOD	GURNEY 7	
11/01/97	CHESTERFIELD	A	0-1	3305	COLLETT	MARTIN	BROWNING	GAYLE	TILLSON	SKINNER	MILLER	LOCKWOOD	BEADLE	CURETON, BROWNING	LOCKWOOD 10	
18/01/97	YORK CITY	H	1-1	4470	COLLETT	MARTIN	BROWNING	WHITE	TILLSON	SKINNER	MILLER	CURETON	LOCKWOOD	BEADLE	CURETON 7, ARCHER 3	
21/01/97	BRENTFORD	A	0-1	4191	COLLETT	LOCKWOOD	BROWNING	WHITE	TILLSON	MILLER	SKINNER	CURETON	ARCHER	BEADLE		
01/02/97	SHREWSBURY TOWN	H	2-0	4924	COLLETT	LOCKWOOD	BROWNING	WHITE	TILLSON	MILLER	SKINNER	CURETON	ARCHER	BEADLE		
08/02/97	GILLINGHAM	H	2-0	6900	COLLETT	LOCKWOOD	BROWNING	WHITE	TILLSON	MILLER	SKINNER	CURETON	ARCHER	BEADLE		
15/02/97	LUTON TOWN	H	3-2	5612	COLLETT	LOCKWOOD	BROWNING	WHITE	TILLSON	SKINNER	MILLER	CURETON	ARCHER	BEADLE	HOLLOWAY 10	
22/02/97	BURNLEY	A	2-2	8847	COLLETT	LOCKWOOD	BROWNING	WHITE	TILLSON	SKINNER	MILLER	ARCHER	LOCKWOOD	BEADLE	HAYFIELD 10	
25/02/97	PLYMOUTH ARGYLE	H	2-0	6005	COLLETT	LOCKWOOD	BROWNING	WHITE	TILLSON	SKINNER	MILLER	ARCHER	BEADLE	BEADLE	ALSOP 11, ARCHER 9	
01/03/97	WALSALL	H	2-0	5891	COLLETT	LOCKWOOD	BROWNING	WHITE	TILLSON	SKINNER	MILLER	ARCHER	LOCKWOOD	BEADLE	ALSOP 8, HAYFIELD 10	
08/03/97	WYCOMBE WDRS	A	0-2	5386	COLLETT	MARTIN	BROWNING	WHITE	TILLSON	SKINNER	HAYFIELD	ARCHER	HAYFIELD	BEADLE	ALSOP 11, HAYFIELD 10	
16/03/97	BRISTOL CITY	H	1-2	8078	COLLETT	MARTIN	HAYFIELD	WHITE	TILLSON	SKINNER	MILLER	ARCHER	BEADLE	BENNETT	BENNETT 7, RAMASUT 4	
18/03/97	WATFORD	A	0-1	6139	COLLETT	MARTIN	SKINNER	WHITE	TILLSON	HOLLOWAY	HAYFIELD	BENNETT	ALSOP	BENNETT	ALSOP 11, BEADLE 10, CLARK 8	
23/03/97	PRESTON NORTH END	H	0-1	6405	COLLETT	MARTIN	SKINNER	WHITE	TILLSON	HOLLOWAY	ALSOP	LOCKWOOD	BEADLE	ALSOP	GURNEY 7	
29/03/97	PETERBOROUGH UTD	A	2-1	6132	COLLETT	MARTIN	SKINNER	WHITE	TILLSON	HOLLOWAY	ALSOP	LOCKWOOD	BEADLE	PARMENTER	ALSOP 11, BEADLE 7	
31/03/97	WREXHAM	H	0-0	6225	COLLETT	MARTIN	SKINNER	WHITE	TILLSON	HOLLOWAY	ALSOP	CURETON	BEADLE	PARMENTER		
05/04/97	STOCKPORT COUNTY	A	1-0	5689	COLLETT	MARTIN	SKINNER	WHITE	TILLSON	HOLLOWAY	ALSOP	CURETON	BEADLE	BENNETT		
08/04/97	MILLWALL	H	1-0	5324	COLLETT	MARTIN	SKINNER	WHITE	TILLSON	HOLLOWAY	ALSOP	CURETON	BEADLE	BENNETT		
12/04/97	CREWE ALEXANDRA	A	0-1	4281	COLLETT	MARTIN	SKINNER	WHITE	TILLSON	MILLER	ALSOP	CURETON	BEADLE	BENNETT		
20/04/97	NOTTS COUNTY	A	1-0	6309	COLLETT	HAYFIELD	SKINNER	WHITE	TILLSON	ALSOP	BENNETT	POWER	POWER	BENNETT		MONINGTON og
26/04/97	BLACKPOOL	H	2-3	6673	COLLETT	HAYFIELD	CLAPHAM	GAYLE	WHITE	LOCKWOOD	ALSOP	LOCKWOOD	MORGAN	MORGAN		
03/05/97	ROTHERHAM UNITED	H	1-2	3950	HIGGS	PRITCHARD	HAYFIELD	GAYLE	WHITE	LOCKWOOD	ALSOP	CURETON	BEADLE	BENNETT		

* Played at Twerton Park

LEAGUE CUP

Date	Opponent	V	Score	ATT	2	3	4	5	6	7	8	9	10	11	SUBSTITUTES	GOALSCORERS
20/08/96	LUTON TOWN	A	0-3	2643	COLLETT	MARTIN	LOCKWOOD	BROWNING	CLARK	TILLSON	HOLLOWAY	GURNEY	MILLER	ARCHER	BEADLE · WHITE 6, PARMENTER 9	ARCHER
04/09/96	LUTON TOWN	H	2-1	2320	COLLETT	MARTIN	LOCKWOOD	BROWNING	CLARK	TILLSON	HOLLOWAY	GURNEY	CURETON	ARCHER	PARMENTER · FRENCH 11	GURNEY

FA CUP

Date	Opponent	V	Score	ATT	2	3	4	5	6	7	8	9	10	11	SUBSTITUTES	GOALSCORERS
16/11/96	EXETER CITY	H	1-2	5841	COLLETT	PRITCHARD	POWER	LOCKWOOD	CLARK	TILLSON	HOLLOWAY	MILLER	CURETON	BEADLE	RAMASUT · SKINNER 6, FRENCH 8, LOW 11	PARMENTER

AUTO WINDSCREENS SHIELD

Date	Opponent	V	Score	ATT	2	3	4	5	6	7	8	9	10	11	SUBSTITUTES	GOALSCORERS
10/12/96	BRENTFORD	H	1-2	2752	COLLETT	MARTIN	CLARK	BROWNING	TILLSON	HAYFIELD	GURNEY	CURETON	ARCHER	PARMENTER · LOCKWOOD 3, SKINNER 8, PARMENTER 10	HARRIS

GLOUCESTERSHIRE CUP FINAL

Date	Opponent	V	Score	ATT	2	3	4	5	6	7	8	9	10	11	SUBSTITUTES	GOALSCORERS
17/08/96	BRISTOL CITY	A	0-1	4932	COLLETT	GURNEY	POWER	CLARK	WHITE	TILLSON	LOCKWOOD	LOW	BEADLE	PARMENTER	LOCKWOOD · HARRIS	

Appearances and Goals

PLAYERS	APP	SUB	GLS
ALSOP J	10	3	6
ARCHER I	18	6	3
BEADLE P	36	1	12
BENNETT F	24	2	2
BROWNING M	24	2	1
CLAPHAM J	2		
CLARK W	26	1	1
COLLETT J	44		
CURETON	33	5	11
FRENCH J	3	1	
GAYLE B	7	2	
GURNEY A	21	3	2
HARRIS J	5	1	2
HAYFIELD M	12	5	1
HIGGS S	2		
HOLLOWAY I	29	2	
LOCKWOOD M	36	3	
MARTIN D	25		
MILLER P	22	3	2
MORGAN R	1		
PARMENTER S	10	4	2
POWER G	16		
PRITCHARD D	26		
RAMASUT T	5	6	
SKINNER J	29	5	2
TILLSON A	38		2
WHITE T	18	3	1
ZABEK L	0	1	
OWN GOAL			1

inevitable sale of Marcus Stewart, who joined Huddersfield Town for £1.2 million deal, injected much-needed cash into the club and was to generate a further £260,000 when the player moved on to Ipswich Town in February 2000. Of Holloway's recruits, the greatest impact was made by Jamie Cureton, a Bristol-born striker who arrived from Norwich City and soon acquired the knack of scoring Division Two hat-tricks. Transfer fees apart, Rovers were able to announce a turnover of £1.374 million for 1996/97.

Over the summer, a once prolific Rovers goalscorer, Vic Lambden, died in Bristol. Lambden had served his only League club with distinction, scoring on his debut in the first post-war game in 1946 and remaining an integral part of the side until 1955. Latterly a very successful foil for the indispensable Geoff Bradford, who had died eighteen months earlier, Lambden scored 117 goals in 268 League matches before spending six free-scoring seasons in Western League football with Trowbridge Town. He remains the fourth highest goalscorer in the club's history.

The opening game of the season, billed as the first game back in Bristol, proved instead to be the last one in Bath, with Andy Gurney's 11th-minute strike earning all three points. Peterborough United, in this game, fielded one former Rovers defender in Aidy Boothroyd and a future striker in Giuliano Grazioli, who signed for Ray Graydon's Rovers in the close season of 2002. The long-awaited return took place a fortnight later, when Stockport County were the visitors. Although Lee Archer's goal put Rovers ahead after 12 minutes, an equaliser 17 minutes from time by John Jeffers ensured that, as in the final Eastville game a decade earlier, the match finished 1-1. The first victory in a home match in Bristol since April 1986 was to follow, as Rovers clawed back a half-time deficit to beat Bournemouth 3-2.

With new-signing Cureton scoring twice against Chesterfield on his home debut and following this up with further strikes, Rovers moved slowly up the table. In early October, a 2-0 home victory over second-placed Crewe Alexandra, with long-range second-half goals from Cureton and Gurney, put Rovers into ninth place, which was to be their highest placing of the season. The fact that the side recorded just two wins in the following 17 League games explains why Holloway's first season in charge brought no immediate success. In one of these games, captain Andy Tillson was booked after only 20 seconds for a foul on Richard Cresswell, from which Nigel Pepper put York City ahead from the penalty spot. One of these two victories, however, followed Marcus Browning's goal two minutes after half-time in farcical circumstances, when Brentford goalkeeper Kevin Dearden reacted to a phantom whistler in the crowd, while the other was an extraordinary 4-3 success at home to Bury in November. Peter Beadle scored a nine-minute hat-trick shortly before half-time, only for Bury to pull back two goals in first-half injury-time. Billy Clark's only goal of the season, just seconds after the interval, was the sixth goal inside 16 minutes. Bury were Division Two champions this season, this defeat being the only League game in which the Shakers conceded four goals. Yet, three days later Rovers lost tamely to a Walsall side inspired by Sierra Leone International John Keister. Rovers also squandered a 3-1 lead at home to Wycombe Wanderers. The visitors' players had been told by manager John Gregory before the game that they faced a fine for any shots from outside the penalty area, but three long-range goals steered them to a 4-3 win.

On 19 October 1996, for the first time, Rovers and the rugby club played home matches on the same day. At 3 p.m., Rovers took on Blackpool, with a crowd of 5,823 witnessing a goalless draw. With the posts hastily changed, Bristol RFC were able to kick-off at 7.30 p.m., in a European Conference Group B game which was lost 18-16 to Narbonne, before a crowd of 2,000. In the early days, the longer grass required for the 15-a-side game drew some criticism from opposition managers, but six sides, including relegated Rotherham United, recorded League wins at the Memorial Ground. The new £2 million West Stand, which increased the ground capacity to 9,173, was opened prior to Bristol's game with Auckland Blues in February and reopened 48 hours later before an extraordinary game with Luton Town. Tony Thorpe, later a Bristol City player, was fouled after 10 minutes by Tom White and converted the penalty himself. Midway through the first-half, seconds after Paul Miller's equaliser for Rovers, the Bulgarian International Bontcho Guentchev, who had played as a substitute against Italy in a 1994 World Cup semi-final in New York, was sent off for a foul on David Pritchard. Andy Tillson and Ian Holloway gave Rovers a commanding lead, before Gary Waddock pulled a goal back against his former club 10 minutes from time.

There were some excellent Rovers performances, giving optimism for the task ahead. In particular, Rovers played astonishingly well to hold table-topping Brentford to a goalless draw in a hugely entertaining match at Griffin Park in January. Yet, there were also unsavoury moments, such as the crowd disturbances at the derby match in December, with pictures being broadcast live on Sky Sports. With Rob Edwards sent off, 10-man City appeared to be holding on for a single-goal victory until Beadle's last-minute equaliser sparked a confrontation between rival supporters on the pitch. It was generally appreciated that the action of Rovers fans had been predominantly celebratory, but Bristol City, for the lack of adequate crowd control, were handed a suspended two-point deduction.

If the Ashton Gate crowd of 18,674 was more than double any other attendance all season at a Rovers game, the 8,078 for the return fixture constituted an embryonic football record at the Memorial Ground. Sadly, Rovers were two goals down to Bristol City before Julian Alsop scored with nine minutes remaining, Beadle becoming the first player to miss a penalty in a Bristol League derby and hovered one place above the relegation zone. Consecutive victories over Preston North End, Peterborough United and Wrexham averted the danger and enabled Holloway to look to the future, with Tom White, Frankie Bennett, Josh Low and Lee Zabek making appearances.

In an unsettled side, Holloway himself was the only player to start both the first and last games of a disappointing season. While Beadle and Cureton scored 12 and 11 League goals respectively, the final league placing of 17th owed much to the lack of goalscoring support. After his heroics of 1995/96, Miller scored just twice, as did regular midfielders Skinner, Archer and Marcus Browning. At Luton Town in November, where Rovers lost to a last-minute Tony Thorpe penalty, Jason Harris, on loan from Crystal Palace, became only the fourth Rovers player to score a debut goal as a substitute. He scored past Ian Feuer, Luton's American-born goalkeeper who, at 6ft 7in, emulated Kevin Francis in 1993/94 as the tallest opponent to face Rovers in League Football.

A first-round exit from the Coca-Cola Cup at the hands of Luton Town, for whom David Oldfield scored in both legs, mirrored Rovers' early departure from the Auto Windscreens Shield, beaten at home by Brentford. Likewise, the FA Cup brought scant consolation for Rovers, who lost at home to Division Three strugglers Exeter City, who had scored twice in the second half before the Rovers substitute Steve Parmenter pulled a goal back in the dying seconds. The former Rovers defender Darren Carr was in the Division Two Chesterfield side that led 2-0 before losing in a replay in an FA Cup semi-final against Middlesbrough. Two years after the penultimate game, the 99th and last Gloucestershire Cup final was decided in August in Bristol City's favour by substitute Shaun Goater's second-half goal.

1997/98

Rovers' second season back in Bristol saw the side qualify comfortably for the play-offs, but not regain Division One status. In an eventful year, Rovers scored 70 League goals, a figure the club had not exceeded since the Championship season of 1989/90 and higher than that scored by any other club in the division. Ultimately, the reward of a visit to Wembley for Ian Holloway's side came within reach before disappearing entirely in an uncharacteristic display in the play-off second leg at Northampton Town.

The vastly experienced Billy Clark moved to Exeter City and Paul Miller, after only 2 League goals in a disappointing 1996/97 season, joined Lincoln City, whom he helped to promotion from Division Three. With the enforced retirement of Lee Martin and Lee Archer's belated transfer to Yeovil Town, Holloway needed to strengthen the side prior to the new season. This was achieved primarily on 20 May 1997, when the club spent £150,000 on Woking Town's Steve Foster and £200,000 on Barry Hayles from Stevenage Borough. Rovers had purchased two of the most talented players on the non-League circuit. Hayles' control, strength and powerful running were a key factor in the club's success and he scored 23 goals in his first season. Foster brought a calm authority

Bristol Rovers 1997/98. Back row: Foster, Clark, Beadle, Perry, Collett, Alsop, Higgs, Martin, Low, Ramasut, Tillson. Second row: White, Skinner, Hayfield, Pritchard, Hayles, Parmenter, Bennett, Zabek, French, Power, Lockwood, Gayle. Front row: Penrice, Cureton, Trollope (Centre of Excellence Director), Dolling (Youth Dev.), Holloway (Player-Manager), Bater (First Team Coach), Kite (Physio), Kendall (Kit Man), Brown, Teague

SEASON 1997/98

FOOTBALL LEAGUE DIVISION TWO

Date	Opponent			ATT	G	2	3	4	5	6	7	8	9	10	11	SUBSTITUTES	GOALSCORERS
09/08/97	PLYMOUTH ARGYLE	H	1-1	7386	COLLETT	PERRY	POWER	PARMENTER	GAYLE	TILLSON	HOLLOWAY	PENRICE	ALSOP	CURETON	HAYLES	FOSTER 3, RAMASUT 4, BEADLE 9	HAYLES
16/08/97	YORK CITY	A	1-0	3307	COLLETT	PERRY	WHITE	BENNETT	GAYLE	TILLSON	HOLLOWAY	PENRICE	ALSOP	CURETON	HAYLES	RAMASUT 4	HAYLES
23/08/97	CARLISLE UNITED	H	3-1	6044	COLLETT	PERRY	WHITE	PENRICE	GAYLE	TILLSON	HOLLOWAY	BENNETT	ALSOP	CURETON	HAYLES	BEADLE 10	BENNETT, HAYLES, PENRICE
30/08/97	BURNLEY	A	0-0	9887	COLLETT	PERRY	PRITCHARD	PENRICE	GAYLE	TILLSON	HOLLOWAY	BENNETT	ALSOP	CURETON	HAYLES	RAMASUT 8	
02/09/97	AFC BOURNEMOUTH	A	1-1	5550	COLLETT	PERRY	PRITCHARD	PENRICE	GAYLE	WHITE	HOLLOWAY	BENNETT	ALSOP	CURETON	HAYLES	BEADLE 9, RAMASUT 8	CURETON pen
09/09/97	WALSALL	H	2-0	6225	COLLETT	PERRY	PRITCHARD	PENRICE	GAYLE	TILLSON	HOLLOWAY	RAMASUT	BEADLE	CURETON	HAYLES		RAMASUT, HAYLES
13/09/97	GILLINGHAM	H	1-2	6572	COLLETT	PERRY	PRITCHARD	PENRICE	GAYLE	TILLSON	HOLLOWAY	RAMASUT	BEADLE	CURETON	HAYLES	BENNETT 10, ALSOP 9	HAYLES
20/09/97	CHESTERFIELD	A	0-0	5309	COLLETT	PERRY	PRITCHARD	PENRICE	GAYLE	TILLSON	HOLLOWAY	RAMASUT	BEADLE	CURETON	HAYLES	BENNETT 10	
27/09/97	OLDHAM ATHLETIC	A	4-4	5990	HIGGS	PERRY	PRITCHARD	PENRICE	GAYLE	TILLSON	HOLLOWAY	RAMASUT	BEADLE	CURETON	HAYLES	BENNETT 10, FOSTER 4	BEADLE 2, HAYLES, CURETON pen
04/10/97	WREXHAM	H	1-0	6829	COLLETT	PERRY	FOSTER	PENRICE	GAYLE	TILLSON	HOLLOWAY	RAMASUT	BEADLE	CURETON	HAYLES	BENNETT 9, ZABEK 10	RAMASUT
14/10/97	WATFORD	H	1-2	8110	COLLETT	PERRY	FOSTER	PENRICE	GAYLE	TILLSON	HOLLOWAY	ALSOP	BEADLE	CURETON	HAYLES	LOW 10	PENRICE
18/10/97	WYCOMBE WDRS	A	0-1	5836	COLLETT	PERRY	FOSTER	PENRICE	GAYLE	TILLSON	LOCKWOOD	ALSOP	BEADLE	CURETON	HAYLES	FRENCH 8	
21/10/97	BRENTFORD	A	3-2	3967	COLLETT	PERRY	FOSTER	PENRICE	GAYLE	TILLSON	HOLLOWAY	RAMASUT	BEADLE	LOCKWOOD	HAYLES		HAYLES 2, BEADLE
25/10/97	BLACKPOOL	H	0-3	6183	COLLETT	PERRY	FOSTER	PENRICE	GAYLE	TILLSON	HOLLOWAY	RAMASUT	BEADLE	LOCKWOOD	HAYLES	CURETON 8, LOW 10, ALSOP 5	
01/11/97	NORTHAMPTON T	A	1-1	7264	COLLETT	PRITCHARD	FOSTER	PENRICE	GAYLE	TILLSON	HOLLOWAY	FRENCH	BEADLE	LOCKWOOD	HAYLES	CURETON 3	CURETON
04/11/97	BRISTOL CITY	H	1-2	7552	COLLETT	PRITCHARD	LOCKWOOD	PENRICE	GAYLE	TILLSON	HOLLOWAY	FRENCH	BEADLE	CURETON	HAYLES	WHITE 5, ALSOP 8	TILLSON
08/11/97	FULHAM	H	2-3	6166	COLLETT	PRITCHARD	FOSTER	PENRICE	WHITE	TILLSON	HOLLOWAY	LOCKWOOD	ALSOP	CURETON	HAYLES	RAMASUT 8	PENRICE 2
18/11/97	PRESTON NORTH END	A	2-1	7798	COLLETT	PRITCHARD	FOSTER	PENRICE	WHITE	TILLSON	LOW	HAYFIELD	ALSOP	LOCKWOOD	HAYLES	CURETON 3, PARMENTER 9	PENRICE, ALSOP
22/11/97	SOUTHEND UNITED	A	1-1	3653	COLLETT	PRITCHARD	LOCKWOOD	PENRICE	WHITE	TILLSON	LOW	HAYFIELD	ALSOP	CURETON	HAYLES	PERRY 10, BEADLE 9, PARMENTER 7	BEADLE pen
29/11/97	MILLWALL	H	2-1	5542	COLLETT	PRITCHARD	PERRY	PENRICE	WHITE	TILLSON	LOW	HAYFIELD	BEADLE	LOCKWOOD	HAYLES	ALSOP 4, HOLLOWAY 7	BEADLE, HAYLES
02/12/97	WIGAN ATHLETIC	A	0-3	2738	COLLETT	PRITCHARD	PERRY	PENRICE	WHITE	TILLSON	LOW	HAYFIELD	BEADLE	LOCKWOOD	HAYLES	HOLLOWAY 8, PARMENTER 10, ALSOP 4	
12/12/97	GRIMSBY TOWN	H	0-4	4801	COLLETT	PRITCHARD	BASFORD	PENRICE	WHITE	TILLSON	LOW	HAYFIELD	BEADLE	LOCKWOOD	HAYLES	ALSOP 4, CURETON 8, HOLLOWAY 7	
20/12/97	LUTON TOWN	A	4-2	5266	COLLETT	HAYFIELD	LOCKWOOD	PENRICE	WHITE	FOSTER	HOLLOWAY	RAMASUT	BEADLE	CURETON	HAYLES	BASFORD 8	CURETON, HAYLES 2, BEADLE
26/12/97	WALSALL	A	1-0	6634	COLLETT	PRITCHARD	LOCKWOOD	PENRICE	WHITE	FOSTER	HOLLOWAY	RAMASUT	BEADLE	CURETON	HAYLES	HAYFIELD 10	BEADLE
28/12/97	AFC BOURNEMOUTH	H	5-3	7256	COLLETT	PRITCHARD	LOCKWOOD	PENRICE	WHITE	FOSTER	HOLLOWAY	RAMASUT	BEADLE	CURETON	HAYLES	BASFORD 7, ALSOP 11	BEADLE 3, HAYLES 2
10/01/98	PLYMOUTH ARGYLE	A	2-1	6850	COLLETT	PRITCHARD	LOCKWOOD	PENRICE	WHITE	FOSTER	HOLLOWAY	RAMASUT	BEADLE	CURETON	HAYLES	BENNETT 8, ZABEK 7, TILLSON 10	CURETON, HAYLES
17/01/98	BURNLEY	H	1-0	7208	COLLETT	PERRY	LOCKWOOD	PENRICE	WHITE	FOSTER	HOLLOWAY	BASFORD	BEADLE	CURETON	HAYLES	BENNETT 8, HAYFIELD 11	CURETON
24/01/98	CARLISLE UNITED	A	1-3	5725	COLLETT	PERRY	LOCKWOOD	PENRICE	WHITE	FOSTER	HOLLOWAY	BASFORD	BEADLE	CURETON	HAYLES	BENNETT 8, HAYFIELD 3	CURETON
31/01/98	GILLINGHAM	A	1-1	5593	HIGGS	PERRY	BASFORD	ZABEK	WHITE	FOSTER	HOLLOWAY	HAYFIELD	BEADLE	CURETON	HAYLES	LOCKWOOD 8, BENNETT 11	CURETON pen
07/02/98	CHESTERFIELD	H	3-1	5481	HIGGS	PERRY	BASFORD	ZABEK	WHITE	FOSTER	HOLLOWAY	BENNETT	BEADLE	CURETON	HAYLES	PENRICE 4, PRITCHARD 3 HAYFIELD 9	BENNETT, CURETON 2
14/02/98	WREXHAM	A	0-1	3716	HIGGS	PERRY	PRITCHARD	PENRICE	WHITE	FOSTER	ZABEK	HAYFIELD	BENNETT	CURETON	HAYLES	WHYTE 9, LOCKWOOD 7, POWER 2	
21/02/98	OLDHAM ATHLETIC	H	3-1	5789	HIGGS	PRITCHARD	POWER	PENRICE	WHITE	FOSTER	SKINNER	BENNETT	RAMASUT	CURETON	HAYLES	HAYFIELD 8, ZABEK 4,	HAYLES 2, RAMASUT
24/02/98	WYCOMBE WDRS	H	3-1	5805	HIGGS	PRITCHARD	POWER	PENRICE	WHITE	FOSTER	SKINNER	RAMASUT	BEADLE	CURETON	HAYLES	HOLLOWAY 4, WHYTE 7	HAYLES, BEADLE, RAMASUT
28/02/98	WATFORD	A	2-3	12186	HIGGS	PRITCHARD	POWER	PENRICE	WHITE	FOSTER	SKINNER	RAMASUT	BEADLE	CURETON	HAYLES	WHYTE 8, HOLLOWAY 4	WHITE, CURETON
03/03/98	FULHAM	A	0-1	6843	HIGGS	PRITCHARD	POWER	HOLLOWAY	WHITE	FOSTER	SKINNER	RAMASUT	BEADLE	CURETON	HAYLES	WHYTE 8, LOW 5	
07/03/98	NORTHAMPTON T	H	0-2	6535	JONES	PRITCHARD	POWER	HOLLOWAY	FOSTER	TILLSON	BENNETT	RAMASUT	BEADLE	CURETON	HAYLES	ZABEK 8, LOW 7	
10/03/98	YORK CITY	H	1-2	4289	COLLETT	PERRY	POWER	PENRICE	FOSTER	TILLSON	HOLLOWAY	RAMASUT	BEADLE	CURETON	HAYLES	HAYFIELD 3,	RAMASUT
14/03/98	BRISTOL CITY	A	0-2	17086	COLLETT	PRITCHARD	POWER	PENRICE	FOSTER	TILLSON	HOLLOWAY	RAMASUT	BEADLE	CURETON	LOW	BENNETT 11, HAYFIELD 3	
21/03/98	PRESTON NORTH END	H	2-2	5278	COLLETT	PRITCHARD	POWER	PENRICE	FOSTER	TILLSON	HOLLOWAY	HAYFIELD	BEADLE	CURETON	HAYLES	RAMASUT 8,	CURETON pen, HAYLES
27/03/98	SOUTHEND UNITED	H	2-0	5323	JONES	PERRY	PRITCHARD	PENRICE	FOSTER	TILLSON	HOLLOWAY	RAMASUT	BEADLE	CURETON	HAYLES	HAYFIELD 8, WHITE 10	TILLSON, HAYLES
04/04/98	MILLWALL	A	1-1	5635	JONES	PERRY	PRITCHARD	PENRICE	FOSTER	TILLSON	ZABEK	RAMASUT	BEADLE	CURETON	HAYLES	BENNETT 8	ZABEK
10/04/98	WIGAN ATHLETIC	H	5-0	6038	JONES	PRITCHARD	LOCKWOOD	HOLLOWAY	FOSTER	TILLSON	ZABEK	RAMASUT	BEADLE	CURETON	HAYLES		HAYLES, RAMASUT, BEADLE 3
13/04/98	GRIMSBY TOWN	A	2-1	5484	JONES	PRITCHARD	LOCKWOOD	HOLLOWAY	FOSTER	TILLSON	ZABEK	RAMASUT	BEADLE	CURETON	HAYLES		HAYLES 2
18/04/98	LUTON TOWN	H	2-1	8038	JONES	PRITCHARD	LOCKWOOD	HOLLOWAY	FOSTER	TILLSON	ZABEK	RAMASUT	BEADLE	CURETON	HAYLES		BEADLE, TILLSON
25/04/98	BLACKPOOL	A	0-1	7057	JONES	PRITCHARD	LOCKWOOD	HOLLOWAY	FOSTER	TILLSON	ZABEK	RAMASUT	BEADLE	CURETON	HAYLES	PENRICE 4,	
02/05/98	BRENTFORD	H	2-1	9043	JONES	PRITCHARD	LOCKWOOD	PENRICE	FOSTER	TILLSON	ZABEK	RAMASUT	BEADLE	CURETON	HAYLES	HAYFIELD 8, BENNETT 10	CURETON, HAYLES

PLAY OFFS

Date	Opponent			ATT	G	2	3	4	5	6	7	8	9	10	11	SUBSTITUTES	GOALSCORERS
10/05/98	NORTHAMPTON T	H	3-1	9173	JONES	PRITCHARD	LOCKWOOD	PENRICE	FOSTER	TILLSON	ZABEK	RAMASUT	BEADLE	BENNETT	HAYLES	POWER 8, HAYFIELD 10	BEADLE pen, BENNETT, HAYLES
13/05/98	NORTHAMPTON T	A	0-3	7501	JONES	PRITCHARD	LOCKWOOD	PENRICE	FOSTER	TILLSON	ZABEK	RAMASUT	BEADLE	BENNETT	HAYLES	HAYFIELD 8, POWER 10	

FA CUP

Date	Opponent			ATT	G	2	3	4	5	6	7	8	9	10	11	SUBSTITUTES	GOALSCORERS
14/11/97	GILLINGHAM	H	2-2	4825	COLLETT	PRITCHARD	FOSTER	PENRICE	WHITE	TILLSON	HOLLOWAY	HAYFIELD	ALSOP	LOCKWOOD	HAYLES	LOW 2, FRENCH 9	ALSOP, HOLLOWAY
28/11/97	GILLINGHAM	A	2-0	4459	COLLETT	PRITCHARD	PERRY	PENRICE	WHITE	TILLSON	LOW	HAYFIELD	BEADLE	LOCKWOOD	HAYLES	FRENCH 7	HAYLES, PENRICE
05/12/97	WISBECH TOWN	A	2-0	3593	COLLETT	PRITCHARD	PERRY	PENRICE	WHITE	TILLSON	LOW	HAYFIELD	BEADLE	LOCKWOOD	HAYLES		BEADLE.HAYLES
03/01/98	IPSWICH TOWN	H	1-1	8610	COLLETT	PRITCHARD	LOCKWOOD	PENRICE	WHITE	FOSTER	HOLLOWAY	RAMASUT	BEADLE	CURETON	HAYLES	BENNETT 8	BEADLE
13/01/98	IPSWICH TOWN	A	0-1	11362	COLLETT	PRITCHARD	LOCKWOOD	PENRICE	WHITE	FOSTER	HOLLOWAY	RAMASUT	BEADLE	CURETON	HAYLES	HAYFIELD 8, BENNETT 10, PERRY 2	

LEAGUE CUP

Date	Opponent			ATT	G	2	3	4	5	6	7	8	9	10	11	SUBSTITUTES	GOALSCORERS
11/08/97	BRISTOL CITY	A	0-0	9341	COLLETT	PERRY	FOSTER	BEADLE	GAYLE	TILLSON	HOLLOWAY	PENRICE	ALSOP	CURETON	HAYLES	BENNETT 4	
26/08/97	BRISTOL CITY *	H	1-2	5872	COLLETT	PERRY	PRITCHARD	BENNETT	GAYLE	TILLSON	HOLLOWAY	PENRICE	ALSOP	CURETON	HAYLES	BEADLE 9, LOCKWOOD 10	ALSOP

* AET Score at 90 mins 1-1

AUTO WINDSCREENS SHIELD

Date	Opponent			ATT	G	2	3	4	5	6	7	8	9	10	11	SUBSTITUTES	GOALSCORERS
08/12/97	CAMBRIDGE UNITED	H	1-0	2386	HIGGS	PRITCHARD	BASFORD	HOLLOWAY	PERRY	SMITH	LOW	PARMENTER	BEADLE	ALSOP	CURETON	TILLSON 6, LOCKWOOD 8, HAYLES 10	CURETON
06/01/98	EXETER CITY	A	2-1	1851	COLLETT	SMITH	BASFORD	ZABEK	TILLSON	FOSTER	HAYFIELD	BENNETT	ALSOP	LOCKWOOD	LOW	BEADLE 9, HAYLES 11	BENNETT, TILLSON
28/01/98	WALSALL *	H	0-1	4165	HIGGS	PERRY	LOCKWOOD	PENRICE	WHITE	FOSTER	HOLLOWAY	BASFORD	BEADLE	CURETON	HAYLES	WHYTE 9	

* AET Rovers beaten in sudden death

PLAYERS	APP	SUB	GLS
ALSOP J	10	7	1
BASFORD L	5	2	
BEADLE P	36	4	15
BENNETT F	8	11	2
COLLETT A	30		
CURETON J	39	4	13
FOSTER S	32	2	
FRENCH J	2	1	
GAYLE B	16		
HAYFIELD M	9	9	
HAYLES B	45		23
HIGGS S	8		
HOLLOWAY I	34	5	
JONES L	8		
LOCKWOOD M	22	2	
LOW J	6	4	
PARMENTER S	1	3	
PENRICE G	38	2	5
PERRY J	24	1	
POWER G	9	1	
PRITCHARD D	32	1	
RAMASUT T	25	6	6
SKINNER J	4		
TILLSON A	32	1	3
WHITE T	22	2	1
WHYTE D	0	4	
ZABEK L	9	4	1

to the defence, where he ably replaced Clark alongside club captain Andy Tillson. Holloway also recruited the combative and highly experienced Cardiff City full-back and captain Jason Perry on a free transfer.

On the opening day of the season Graeme Power dislocated his shoulder during the 1-1 draw with Plymouth Argyle at the Memorial Ground, and was out of first-team football for six months. This was the start of a season's toils to fill the troublesome left-back position. Rovers fielded seven different players in the apparently jinxed number three shirt during the season, including Luke Basford, who made his debut in a disastrous 4-0 home defeat against Grimsby Town just weeks before his 17th birthday. In a bizarre way, Power's unfortunate injury reflected that of Jack Stockley, also against Plymouth Argyle on the opening day of the season, who had been out of the game for eight months some 76 years earlier.

Rovers were involved in a number of high-scoring games. In September, they were 3-0 down at Oldham Athletic after 24 minutes, Stuart Barlow scoring twice, before Peter Beadle scored a couple of goals in three minutes and created an equaliser for Barry Hayles on the stroke of half-time. After such an outstanding first-half, Oldham's fourth goal was cancelled out by Jamie Cureton's penalty three minutes from time, after handball by Scott McNiven, for a 4-4 draw. There were also six first-half goals when Rovers won 4-2 at Luton Town in December and, eight days later, Rovers again scored four goals before half-time in winning 5-3 against Bournemouth. Beadle, who completed a first-half hat-trick in this game with a fine 30-yard shot, also scored three goals in 11 minutes when Rovers defeated Wigan Athletic 5-0 in April. Bournemouth's Steve Robinson became only the fourth opponent to score a penalty in both League games against Rovers, one in the 5-3 defeat and one in a 1-1 draw at Dean Court in September preceded by a two-minute silence in memory of Diana, Princess of Wales, who had died in Paris two days earlier.

Sendings-off proved to be a talking-point of the season. Millwall's Brian Law was sent off in both League games against Rovers and the Lions had players dismissed in both fixtures in 1998/99. Luke Basford, at 17 years 87 days became the youngest Rovers player to receive a red card in a League game, late in the 1-1 draw with Gillingham, who had taken the lead through Iffy Onuora after only 38 seconds. However, nothing could prepare Rovers for the five red cards issued on a frosty evening in Wigan in December by referee Kevin Lynch. David Pritchard received a second yellow card only seconds before half-time and was promptly joined by Jason Perry, Andy Tillson and Wigan's Graeme Jones for alleged pushing while the resultant free-kick was about to be taken. These decisions were viewed by many as harsh, as was Josh Low's second-half dismissal for a second booking, in a game generally considered fair and clean. Nonetheless, seven-man Rovers, only the second League club to suffer this fate, after Hereford United in November 1992, made the headlines for all the wrong reasons.

Gary Penrice, back in the side after a popular summer transfer from Watford, became the only Rovers player to have scored a League goal on all four of the club's home grounds. His goal in a 3-1 victory over Carlisle United in August was his first for the club since October 1989, a gap between Rovers goals only exceeded by Ray Warren and Wally McArthur. Among the good wins were some poorer results. Ian Stevens, for instance, whose goal in 1996 had deprived Rovers of a trip to Wembley, scored a hat-trick

Barry Hayles receives the Golden Boot Award from Vice Chairman Geoff Dunford for his 23 League goals, which was the highest tally by one player that year

when Carlisle United gained revenge by beating Rovers 3-1 at Brunton Park in January, while Carl Heggs played well against his former club in March, a foul on him by David Pritchard leading to the second goal in Northampton Town's 2-0 victory. As Rovers moved towards the play-offs, David Whyte arrived on loan and Lee Jones, destined for many games in Rovers' goal, joined as cover for Andy Collett.

In addition to his consistent goalscoring, Hayles missed just one League game, the demoralizing 2-0 local derby defeat at Ashton Gate before the highest crowd, 17,086, to watch Rovers in League action all season. It was a fifth consecutive league defeat for Rovers. No Rovers player appeared in as many games this season as Hayles. Cureton scored in five consecutive League matches early in the New Year and he and Beadle both scored highly respectable seasonal goal totals. Ultimately, Rovers needed to win at home to Brentford on the final day to relegate their opponents and secure a play-off place. These targets were achieved, even though Penrice was sent off early in the match and despite the fact that Cureton broke a leg late on. Amid great tension, the reliable figure of Barry Hayles scored a winning goal six minutes from time in front of a record ground attendance at the Memorial Stadium. Even more spectators, 9,173, who produced record takings of £74,952, saw Beadle and Frankie Bennett give Rovers a two-goal lead inside 37 minutes of the play-off semi-final first leg. When Hayles added a third just seconds after half-time, Wembley beckoned but, crucially, Northampton Town grabbed a late John Gayle goal. In the second leg, Rovers' dreams fell apart as the Cobblers scored three times, the first by Carl Heggs, for a 4-3 aggregate win.

After a goalless draw at Ashton Gate, Rovers crashed out of the Coca Cola Cup to Junior Bent's extra-time winner for Bristol City at the Memorial Stadium. Victories over Cambridge United and Exeter City counted for nothing as Walsall's French striker

Roger Zokou Boli scored a Golden Goal just seconds into extra-time to knock Rovers out of the Auto Windscreens Shield at the quarter-final stage. In the absence of the now defunct Gloucestershire Cup, Rovers fielded a reserve team in the county Senior Challenge Cup, a tournament dating back to 1936, beating Mangotsfield United but losing 6-0 to Bristol City reserves in a semi-final in which Colin Cramb scored all the goals. In the FA Cup, Rovers required an 87th-minute equaliser at home to Gillingham before winning the replay comfortably in Kent. Having to travel to Wisbech Town in round two brought back uncomfortable memories of Hitchin Town in 1995. However, Rovers were better prepared and won professionally through goals from Beadle, seven minutes after half-time, and Hayles, 11 minutes from the end, against a side fielding a 39-year-old in Jackie Gallagher. The third-round draw paired Rovers with Ipswich Town, who fielded the popular former Rovers midfielder, Geraint Williams. Rovers might have beaten their Division One opponents in a gale and hailstorm at the Memorial Stadium, leading from Beadle's 36th-minute goal, but Mick Stockwell grabbed a deserved equaliser 19 minutes from time. David Johnson's low shot three minutes before half-time in the replay at Portman Road ended Rovers' FA Cup aspirations for another year. The National Football Programme Directory voted Rovers' matchday magazine as the best in Division Two.

As an eventful season drew to a close, dramatic developments ended Rovers' 58-year wait for a home of their own. Their hosts at the Memorial Ground, Bristol Rugby Club, had forged a deal early in January 1998 to sell the ground to the parcel carrier firm Amtrak for just over £1 million, a good deal less than the £2.2 million at which it had been valued in 1996. Rovers would continue to pay an annual rent of £90,000. Then, when the buyers withdrew their offer, the rugby club was placed in receivership on 17 April 1998 and Rovers invoked a buyout clause that enabled the 12-acre ground to be bought up for £100,000. A newly formed Memorial Stadium Company made the purchase in the names of both clubs but, since Geoff Dunford was chairman of the new organisation, it was abundantly clear Rovers held the upper hand. While it was obvious that considerable work would be required on improvements to floodlighting and cover, as well as seating at the South End, both clubs were quick to point out their future could lie elsewhere. Plans for a multi-sport stadium near Pilning were rejected at the end of April by landowners ICI, with developers valuing the newly renamed Memorial Stadium at £6 million.

Shortly before these momentous events, Eastville Stadium, Rovers' home between 1897 and 1986, finally closed. The last greyhound meeting on 27 October 1997, where entry fees were sentimentally waived, signalled the end of the road for a ground so integral to the club's history. The arrival on site in March 1999 of furniture giants Ikea did, however, have one saving grace, for the Swedish firm often uses a tall local landmark to advertise its store and a solitary floodlight was left standing as a poignant reminder of the good and bad memories the old stadium would forever hold.

1998/99

A side that promised much, lacked consistency and, after hovering a little lower in the table, finished in 13th place in Division Two. Rovers were without Jason Perry and Graeme Power, who had moved to Lincoln City and Exeter City respectively, and Tom Ramasut, who joined several clubs on trial before signing in November 1998 for Merthyr Tydfil. On the eve of the new season, Peter Beadle made a surprise £300,000 move to John Rudge's Port Vale, while November saw Fulham pay Rovers £2 million, a record fee received, for Barry Hayles. This income helped outweigh an operating loss of £664,791 in the year to June 1999 and leave Rovers with a £1,014,784 profit. Nonetheless, supporters were left to wonder where the side would find sufficient goalpower.

They need not have worried. At one stage over New Year, Rovers scored 12 goals in three games. Jamie Cureton, whose three League hat-tricks were all registered away from home, scored 25 goals in the League and Jason Roberts, a Grenada International who overcame the tag of being a 'replacement' for Hayles, added 16, in addition to a record-breaking seven in the FA Cup. Rovers also made a large number of other summer signings, notably Marcus Andreasson from Swedish football and Cameroon player Gui Ipoua from Spain. Ipoua, whose elder brother Samuel had played for Cameroon in the 1998 World Cup finals, contributed just 3 League goals, plus the only goal when Rovers unveiled Mangotsfield United's Cossham Street floodlights in March. Frenchman Stéphane Léoni, Trevor Challis, Rob Trees, Jamie Shore and Michael Meaker all made significant contributions, as did mid-season signings David Hillier, a League Championship winner with Arsenal, and 17-year-old striker Nathan Ellington, the Surrey county high-jump champion.

After conceding a second-minute goal to Andy Payton in the opening day defeat at Burnley, Rovers overcame Reading 4-1, Meaker scoring against his former club and Cureton converting one of two penalties. Controversy struck at Gillingham, where both sides were reduced to nine men. Goalkeeper Lee Jones was sent off with Challis and the home side's Barry Ashby and Adrian Pennock as referee Matt Messias of York dealt with a 21-man injury-time flare-up. Mark Smith made his debut in that game and, astonishingly, Rovers were reduced to nine men in each of his first three League appearances. Roberts and Trees were sent off as Rovers held on for a 1-0 home victory over Bournemouth in October, followed seven days later by Meaker and Challis in defeat at Northampton Town, for whom Carl Heggs was again on the scoresheet.

By Christmas, Rovers lay 17th in the table, with just five home wins to their name. A first away win should have been forthcoming at Wycombe, where Wanderers brought on a last-minute substitute, Dannie Bulman, for his League debut and the 19-year-old scored an equaliser after being on the field for just 26 seconds. He was to score the goal in May 2001 that consigned Rovers to basement-division football for the first time in the club's history. A single-goal defeat at champions-elect Fulham saw Rovers face the former England International, Peter Beardsley, who had previously faced the Pirates a club record 16 years 323 days earlier, while on the books of Carlisle United. It was not until 28 December that Rovers recorded the first of their five away League victories.

Bristol Rovers 1998/99. Back row: Zabek, Challis, J Shore, Hayles, Smith, Bater, Cureton, Bennett, Trees, Basford. Second row: Brinsford (Secretary), Dolling (Youth Dev.), Foster, Claridge, Beadle, Collett, White, Jones, Andreasson, Tillson, French, Low, Kite (Physio). Front row: Wesson, Gingell, Craig, Holloway, Dunford, Penrice, Bradshaw, Kendall, Bater

Home form could be suspect, too. Three second-half goals saw off struggling Lincoln City, but Macclesfield Town drew 0-0 at the Memorial Stadium in the sides' first ever meeting, yet were to lose nine of their next 10 League matches. David Gregory, who had scored for both sides in a chaotic first-half against Stoke City seven days earlier, earned Colchester United a share of the points with a last-minute penalty. Rovers also threw away a two-goal half-time lead for a 2-2 draw with Preston North End, who were becoming, after Notts County, only the second club to appear in 4,000 League games. Strangely, an identical scoreline in the return game at Deepdale meant Preston were the first League club to draw 1,000 League matches.

Both Walsall and Burnley won 4-3 at the Memorial Stadium. Rovers led Walsall 2-0 after only four minutes through Cureton and Hayles, but were pegged back by half-time, Mark Smith conceding an own goal. Andy Rammell and the Icelandic midfielder Bjarni Larusson both scored in the last ten minutes with Rovers a man short after Trees had been stretchered off. Burnley, on the other hand, took the lead four times, with all three Rovers equalisers arriving before half-time. It was only the 10th time that as many as six goals had been scored in the first half of a League game involving Rovers.

In December, Rovers drew 0-0 at Maine Road before a crowd of 24,976 in the first League meeting with Manchester City. This was followed by the first away victories of the season, a convincing 3-0 win against Colchester United and a powerful 6-0 success at Reading. Rovers also dominated Stoke City to record a memorable 4-1 victory at the Staffordshire side's newly christened Britannia Stadium and came from behind for wins at Blackpool and Macclesfield Town. With Roberts scoring freely in the FA Cup, Cureton, the side's only ever-present, hit a rich vein of goals in the New Year. He hit four second-half goals at Reading and a hat-trick after half-time at Walsall who, under manager Ray Graydon, a former Rovers player, had led 2-0 and were heading for promotion to Division One. On the final day of the season, his third hat-trick of the season brought Rovers a win at Macclesfield Town, where they had trailed 3-1 just two minutes after half-time.

FOOTBALL LEAGUE DIVISION TWO

Date	Opponent	H/A	Score	ATT	G	2	3	4	5	6	7	8	9	10	11	SUBSTITUTES	GOALSCORERS
08/08/98	BURNLEY	A	1-2	11781	JONES	TREES	CHALLIS	ZABEK	FOSTER	ANDREASSON	HOLLOWAY	MEAKER	ROBERTS	CURETON	HAYLES	IPOUA 10	ANDREASSON
15/08/98	READING	H	4-1	7529	JONES	TREES	CHALLIS	ZABEK	FOSTER	ANDREASSON	HOLLOWAY	MEAKER	ROBERTS	CURETON	HAYLES	HAYLES 2, IPOUA	HAYLES, MEAKER, CURETON pen, ROBERTS
22/08/98	GILLINGHAM	A	0-0	4896	JONES	TREES	CHALLIS	TREES	FOSTER	SMITH	HOLLOWAY	MEAKER	IPOUA	CURETON	ROBERTS	IPOUA 8, PENRICE 9	
29/08/98	WIGAN ATHLETIC	H	3-2	6140	JONES	TREES	CHALLIS	TREES	FOSTER	SMITH	HOLLOWAY	MEAKER	IPOUA	CURETON	ROBERTS	COLLETT 3	BENNETT, ROBERTS, CURETON
31/08/98	WYCOMBE WDRS	A	1-1	4318	JONES	TREES	CHALLIS	HOLLOWAY	FOSTER	SMITH	HOLLOWAY	MEAKER	IPOUA	CURETON	ROBERTS	HAYLES 9, SMITH 2	BASFORD
05/09/98	PRESTON NORTH END	H	2-2	6702	JONES	LEONI	CHALLIS	TREES	FOSTER	SMITH	SHORE	MEAKER	PHILLIPS	CURETON	ROBERTS	ELLINGTON 7	FOSTER, PENRICE, CURETON 9, ELLINGTON 10
08/09/98	CHESTERFIELD	A	0-0	5416	COLLETT	LEONI	BASFORD	TREES	FOSTER	SMITH	HOLLOWAY	HILLIER	PENRICE	CURETON	ELLINGTON		
12/09/98	LUTON TOWN	H	0-2	5558	COLLETT	LEONI	BASFORD	TREES	FOSTER	SMITH	HOLLOWAY	HILLIER	ANDREWS	CURETON	ELLINGTON		
19/09/98	LINCOLN CITY	A	3-0	6991	COLLETT	LEONI	BASFORD	TREES	FOSTER	SMITH	HOLLOWAY	HILLIER	ANDREWS	CURETON	ROBERTS	LEONI 3, PENRICE 4, ROBERTS 10	CURETON 2, 1pen
26/09/98	YORK CITY	H	0-1	3305	COLLETT	LEONI	BASFORD	HOLLOWAY	FOSTER	SMITH	HOLLOWAY	HILLIER	HOLLOWAY	CURETON	ROBERTS	HAYLES 9, SMITH 2	
03/10/98	AFC BOURNEMOUTH	A	0-1	7526	COLLETT	LEONI	CHALLIS	PENRICE	FOSTER	SMITH	HOLLOWAY	HILLIER	PENRICE	CURETON	ROBERTS	ROBERTS 9, SMITH 2, SHORE 7	
10/10/98	NORTHAMPTON T	H	1-3	6023	JONES	LEONI	CHALLIS	ZABEK	FOSTER	SMITH	HOLLOWAY	HILLIER	ROBERTS	CURETON	HAYLES	IPOUA 8, ZABEK 10, HOLLOWAY 7	HOLLOWAY
17/10/98	WREXHAM	A	1-0	6072	JONES	LEONI	CHALLIS	ZABEK	FOSTER	SMITH	HOLLOWAY	MEAKER	IPOUA	CURETON	HAYLES	LEONI 8, PENRICE 4, ROBERTS 10	LEONI
20/10/98	STOKE CITY	H	1-0	6752	JONES	LEONI	CHALLIS	ZABEK	FOSTER	THOMSON	HOLLOWAY	MEAKER	IPOUA	CURETON	HAYLES	LOW 10, PENRICE 4	McKEEVER
24/10/98	NOTTS COUNTY	A	1-1	4822	JONES	TREES	CHALLIS	ZABEK	FOSTER	SMITH	HOLLOWAY	MEAKER	IPOUA	CURETON	HAYLES	MEAKER 7, IPOUA 9, HOLLOWAY 4	LOW
31/10/98	WALSALL	H	3-4	5753	JONES	LEONI	CHALLIS	ZABEK	FOSTER	THOMSON	HOLLOWAY	HILLIER	IPOUA	CURETON	HAYLES	HOLLOWAY 2, IPOUA 8, ZABEK 10	IPOUA 2, HOLLOWAY 7
07/11/98	FULHAM	A	0-1	11575	JONES	LEONI	CHALLIS	PENRICE	FOSTER	THOMSON	SHORE	HILLIER	IPOUA	CURETON	HAYLES	TREES 2, PENRICE 9	
10/11/98	BLACKPOOL	H	0-2	5361	JONES	LEONI	CHALLIS	TREES	FOSTER	THOMSON	SHORE	HILLIER	PENRICE	CURETON	HAYLES	TREES 8, SHORE 11, BENNETT 9	
21/11/98	MILLWALL	A	1-1	5755	JONES	LEONI	CHALLIS	HOLLOWAY	FOSTER	THOMSON	HOLLOWAY	HILLIER	PENRICE	CURETON	HAYLES	LEONI 8, SHORE 7, BENNETT 9	TROUGHT
28/11/98	OLDHAM ATHLETIC	H	0-0	2614	JONES	LEONI	CHALLIS	TREES	FOSTER	THOMSON	SHORE	HILLIER	PHILLIPS	CURETON	HAYLES	FOSTER 8, PENRICE 9, ELLINGTON 10	
12/12/98	MANCHESTER CITY	A	0-2	24976	JONES	LEONI	CHALLIS	HOLLOWAY	FOSTER	THOMSON	HOLLOWAY	HILLIER	PENRICE	CURETON	HAYLES	ELLINGTON 9	
18/12/98	COLCHESTER UNITED	H	2-2	5039	JONES	LEONI	ZABEK	TREES	FOSTER	TILLSON	SMITH	MEAKER	PENRICE	CURETON	ROBERTS	CURETON, HAYLES 2	CURETON 2, 1pen
26/12/98	COLCHESTER UNITED	A	0-0	4609	JONES	LEONI	CHALLIS	ZABEK	FOSTER	TILLSON	SHORE	MEAKER	IPOUA	CURETON	ROBERTS	SHORE 7	
28/12/98	WREXHAM	H	3-0	7129	JONES	LEONI	CHALLIS	TREES	FOSTER	TILLSON	HOLLOWAY	MEAKER	ROBERTS	CURETON	HAYLES	CURETON, HAYLES 2	CURETON, HAYLES 2
09/01/99	BURNLEY	H	3-4	13258	JONES	LEONI	CHALLIS	TREES	FOSTER	THOMSON	HOLLOWAY	MEAKER	ROBERTS	CURETON	HAYLES	HAYLES 2	ROBERTS, CURETON, HAYLES 2
16/01/99	READING	A	6-0	6249	JONES	PETHICK	CHALLIS	TREES	FOSTER	THOMSON	HOLLOWAY	McKEEVER	McKEEVER	CURETON	ROBERTS	PENRICE 7	PENRICE, ROBERTS, LEE
30/01/99	COLCHESTER UNITED	H	1-1	12270	JONES	PRITCHARD	CHALLIS	PETHICK	FOSTER	THOMSON	HOLLOWAY	LEE	LEE	CURETON	ROBERTS	PENRICE 8, TROUGHT 2	CURETON, ROBERTS
06/02/99	PRESTON NORTH END	A	2-2	6361	JONES	PRITCHARD	BASFORD	FOSTER	THOMSON	FOSTER	LEE	LEE	McKEEVER	CURETON	ROBERTS	LOW 4, PENRICE 8, LEONI 2	ROBERTS 2
23/02/99	LUTON TOWN	H	0-1	5735	JONES	PRITCHARD	CHALLIS	FOSTER	THOMSON	THOMSON	SHORE	HILLIER	IPOUA	CURETON	HAYLES	BASFORD 8, SHORE 3, ROBERTS 9	
27/02/99	GILLINGHAM	H	0-1	4235	JONES	PRITCHARD	CHALLIS	FOSTER	THOMSON	THOMSON	HOLLOWAY	HILLIER	IPOUA	CURETON	HAYLES	ROBERTS 9, MEAKER 8	
06/03/99	LINCOLN CITY	H	2-0	5749	JONES	PRITCHARD	CHALLIS	FOSTER	THOMSON	THOMSON	HOLLOWAY	HILLIER	IPOUA	CURETON	ROBERTS	LEONI 3, PENRICE 4, ROBERTS 10	ROBERTS, CURETON
09/03/99	YORK CITY	H	0-1	7181	KUIPERS	BASFORD	LEONI	FOSTER	THOMSON	THOMSON	HOLLOWAY	HILLIER	PENRICE	CURETON	ROBERTS	McKEEVER 9, MEAKER 8, PENRICE 9	
12/03/99	AFC BOURNEMOUTH	H	2-3	8011	JONES	PRITCHARD	CHALLIS	FOSTER	TROUGHT	TROUGHT	HOLLOWAY	HILLIER	HOLLOWAY	CURETON	ROBERTS	SMITH 6, McKEEVER 9, PENRICE 11	THOMSON, ROBERTS
20/03/99	WALSALL	A	3-3	4967	JONES	PRITCHARD	CHALLIS	TREES	FOSTER	TILLSON	HOLLOWAY	HILLIER	ANDREWS	CURETON	ROBERTS	TROUGHT 5, ELLINGTON 4	CURETON 3, 1pen
27/03/99	WYCOMBE WDRS	H	0-2	4833	JONES	PRITCHARD	CHALLIS	TREES	FOSTER	TILLSON	SHORE	HILLIER	ANDREWS	CURETON	ELLINGTON	TREES 7, TROUGHT 2	
30/03/99	NOTTS COUNTY	H	1-1	5899	JONES	PRITCHARD	CHALLIS	TREES	FOSTER	FOSTER	LEE	HILLIER	HOLLOWAY	CURETON	ROBERTS	ELLINGTON 6, FOSTER 9, ELLINGTON	ELLINGTON
03/04/99	WIGAN ATHLETIC	A	0-1	3568	JONES	PRITCHARD	CHALLIS	TREES	FOSTER	THOMSON	HOLLOWAY	LEONI	IPOUA	CURETON	ROBERTS	LOW 10, PENRICE 4	
05/04/99	NORTHAMPTON T	H	1-1	3087	JONES	PRITCHARD	CHALLIS	TREES	FOSTER	ANDREASSON	LEE	TROUGHT	FOSTER	CURETON	IPOUA	HOLLOWAY 8, PENRICE 2	IPOUA
10/04/99	STOKE CITY	A	2-1	6580	WILLIAMS	PRITCHARD	CHALLIS	PETHICK	FOSTER	THOMSON	HOLLOWAY	LEE	PENRICE	CURETON	ELLINGTON	PENRICE 8, TROUGHT 2	PENRICE
13/04/99	OLDHAM ATHLETIC	A	1-0	17823	WILLIAMS	PRITCHARD	CHALLIS	FOSTER	THOMSON	THOMSON	HOLLOWAY	LEE	McKEEVER	CURETON	ROBERTS	SHORE 9, ZABEK 8	SHORE
20/04/99	CHESTERFIELD	A	0-0	3913	WILLIAMS	PRITCHARD	CHALLIS	FOSTER	THOMSON	THOMSON	HOLLOWAY	LEE	PENRICE	CURETON	IPOUA	LEONI 8	
24/04/99	BLACKPOOL	A	2-1	2621	WILLIAMS	PRITCHARD	CHALLIS	FOSTER	THOMSON	THOMSON	HOLLOWAY	LEE	IPOUA	CURETON	ROBERTS	PENRICE 8	CURETON 2, ROBERTS
27/04/99	MILLWALL	A	3-0	5033	WILLIAMS	PRITCHARD	CHALLIS	FOSTER	THOMSON	FOSTER	HOLLOWAY	HILLIER	PENRICE	CURETON	ELLINGTON	LEONI 8, PENRICE 4, ROBERTS 8	CURETON 2, 1pen
01/05/99	MANCHESTER CITY	H	2-2	8033	WILLIAMS	TREES	CHALLIS	TREES	FOSTER	FOSTER	HOLLOWAY	HILLIER	PENRICE	CURETON	ROBERTS	PRITCHARD 10	PRITCHARD, CURETON
08/05/99	MACCLESFIELD	A	4-3	3186	JOHNSTON	PETHICK	CHALLIS	TREES	FOSTER	ANDREASSON	SHORE	MEAKER	IPOUA	CURETON	ROBERTS		CURETON 2, LEE, ROBERTS

LEAGUE CUP

Date	Opponent	H/A	Score	ATT												
11/08/98	LEYTON ORIENT *	A	1-1	2663	JONES	TREES	CHALLIS	ZABEK	FOSTER	SMITH	HOLLOWAY	MEAKER	IPOUA	CURETON	HAYLES	CURETON
18/08/98	LEYTON ORIENT **	H	1-2	4235	JONES	TREES	CHALLIS	ZABEK	FOSTER	ANDREASSON	HOLLOWAY	MEAKER	ROBERTS	CURETON	HAYLES	HAYLES

FA CUP

Date	Opponent	H/A	Score	ATT												
14/11/98	WELLING UNITED	H	3-0	5381	JONES	LEONI	CHALLIS	PENRICE	FOSTER	SMITH	HOLLOWAY	MEAKER	PENRICE	CURETON	ROBERTS	PENRICE 4, LEONI 3, IPOUA 7
05/12/98	EXETER CITY	A	2-2	4352	JONES	LEONI	CHALLIS	ZABEK	FOSTER	TROUGHT	HOLLOWAY	MEAKER	PENRICE	CURETON	ROBERTS	PENRICE, CURETON
15/12/98	EXETER CITY	H	5-0	5093	JONES	LEONI	CHALLIS	ZABEK	FOSTER	TROUGHT	LEE	MEAKER	TREES	CURETON	ROBERTS	ZABEK, SHORE 2, CURETON, ROBERTS
02/01/99	ROTHERHAM UNITED	H	1-0	6056	JONES	LEONI	CHALLIS	TREES	FOSTER	TILLSON	HOLLOWAY	MEAKER	ROBERTS	CURETON	HAYLES	ROBERTS
23/01/99	LEYTON ORIENT	A	3-0	9274	JONES	PRITCHARD	CHALLIS	PETHICK	FOSTER	THOMSON	HOLLOWAY	LEE	ROBERTS	CURETON	ROBERTS	ROBERTS 2, LEE
13/02/99	BARNSLEY	A	1-4	17508	JONES	PRITCHARD	CHALLIS	TREES	FOSTER	THOMSON	SHORE	HILLIER	ROBERTS	CURETON	HAYLES	ROBERTS

AUTO WINDSCREENS SHIELD

Date	Opponent	H/A	Score	ATT												
08/12/98	WALSALL **	A	2-2	2210	JONES	LEONI	CHALLIS	ZABEK	FOSTER	TROUGHT	SHORE	MEAKER	IPOUA	CURETON	ROBERTS	CURETON, SHORE

* AET score at 90 min 1-1
** Rovers lost 4-5 on pens

PLAYERS

PLAYERS	APP	SUB	GLS
ANDREASSON M	4	4	1
ANDREWS B	3	3	
BASFORD L	6	1	1
BENNETT F	1	3	1
CHALLIS T	38		
COLLETT A	3		
CURETON	46		25
ELLINGTON N	1	9	1
FOSTER S	41	2	1
HAYLES	17	9	9
HILLIER D	13	4	
HOLLOWAY	33	4	3
IPOUA G	15	9	3
JOHNSTON R	1		
JONES L	32		
KUIPERS M	1		
LEE D	10	1	2
LEONI S	25	5	1
LOW J	5	2	1
McKEEVER M	5	4	1
MEAKER M	17	3	1
PARMENTER S	5	2	
PENRICE G	10	7	2
PETHICK R	9	6	
PHILLIPS M	2		
PRITCHARD D	11	1	1
ROBERTS J	32	5	16
SHORE J	18	6	2
SMITH M	21	2	
THOMSON A	33	1	1
TILLSON A	33	1	
TREES R	8	3	
TROUGHT M	6	3	1
WILLIAMS A	9		
ZABEK L	9	2	1

An aerial view of the Memorial Stadium, taken in July 1998

The most incredible result was, undeniably, the victory over Reading in the new Madejski Stadium. Eighth-placed Reading had just beaten Wrexham 4-0 and gave a debut to the former Rovers player Andy Gurney. A crowd of 13,258 saw a goalless first-half before Rovers scored six times without reply in the space of 41 minutes for their largest away win since December 1973. The irrepressible Cureton scored the first four in 21 minutes, only the 11th occasion that a Rovers player had scored as many in a League match, while Roberts added two goals in the final couple of minutes. Rovers had scored 10 goals in the season against Reading, a figure only previously achieved against Doncaster Rovers in 1956/57, while Cureton's penalty, his second goal, made him the sixth Rovers player since 1920 to score from the penalty spot in both fixtures against the same opposition.

Lior David, a nephew of the celebrated paranormalist Uri Geller, scored twice as a substitute for Swansea City reserves, as they defeated Rovers reserves 4-2 in a South West Trophy game in September. Rovers' reserves gave trials that month to the Nigerian International Ben Iroha, who later joined Watford, and Icelandic Under-21 goalkeeper Ólafur Gunnarsson, though neither made the first team. The reserves also lost to a goal in each half at Forest Green Rovers in the Gloucestershire Senior Challenge Cup. Rovers' matchday programme was nominated the best in the division by *Programme Monthly* magazine and in the League Programme of the Year survey commissioned by the Wirral Programme Club. The former club director Hampden Alpass, a one-time Gloucestershire cricketer, died on 16 March 1999 at the age of 92.

Rovers' FA Cup exploits more than made up for early exits from the Worthington Cup, to an extra-time goal for Division Three Leyton Orient from substitute Mark Warren, and the Auto Windscreens Shield, where Rovers threw away a two-goal lead at Walsall before losing in a penalty shoot-out. The FA Cup was an altogether more successful competition from a Rovers perspective. A second-half Roberts hat-trick saw off the challenge of non-League Welling United and Rovers twice equalised at Exeter City before demolishing the Grecians 5-0 in a one-sided replay. Three goals in 10 second-half minutes, two by Shore, set up a comfortable victory with Roberts scoring the fifth, a goal his supreme performance merited. Léoni's first goal for the club, after a swift interchange of passes with Roberts on the stroke of half-time, brought victory in a potentially awkward third-round tie at Rotherham United.

As the FA Cup campaign gathered pace, so did expectations. Matt Lockwood was in the Leyton Orient side Rovers were expected to brush aside in the fourth round. Revenge was gained for the Worthington Cup defeat, but it was a real struggle before a capacity crowd and it was only after Roberts broke the deadlock with 14 minutes remaining that Rovers visibly relaxed to run out 3-0 victors. Of all the possible fifth-round opponents, Barnsley might have offered Rovers the easiest passage to a third quarter-final, but Craig Hignett scored a sparkling hat-trick and Rovers crashed to a 4-1 defeat. Roberts' consolation goal, seven minutes from time, made him the overall top scorer in the 1998/99 tournament, the first Bristol Rovers player ever to achieve this feat. No Rovers player had scored as many FA Cup goals in a season since Jack Jones in 1901/02. The use of numbers on players' shirts, first adopted in 1939, was extended in June 1999 to encourage clubs to show players' names and squad numbers.

1999/2000

It was a very bitter pill to swallow but, at the close of an eventful, topsy-turvy season, Rovers let a clear opportunity of promotion slip, sank through the play-off places and finished seventh in Division Two. Ultimately, a late run of only six points out of a possible 30 was to undo all the positive early-season form. Yet the side bore great similarity to that of 1998/99. Despite Gui Ipoua joining Scunthorpe United, Ian Holloway retiring from playing to focus on management and Jamie Shore out all season to undergo pioneering knee surgery, Rovers' side retained a familiar appearance.

Four International players were welcome additions to the side, while promising youngsters Bobby Zamora and Simon Bryant, the latter being the club's youngest post-war debutant, broke into the team. The Latvian international captain, Vitalijs Astafjevs, and former England midfielder Mark Walters were to prove inspirational mid-season purchases. Nigel Pierre, a Trinidadian striker, showed promise until his application for a work permit was rejected on the grounds that Jack Warner, who owned his former club, had tried to bribe governmental officials in return for the promise of his vote for England's bid to host the 2006 World Cup. Early in the season, Ronnie Maugé proved to have been an astute signing, but the experienced midfielder broke a leg playing in a

Bristol Rovers 1999/2000. Back row: Pethick, Hillier, Challis, Shore, Meaker, Smith, Mauge, Trees, Bennett, Cureton, White, Leoni, Pritchard. Second row: Watola (Co. Sec), Kite (Physio), Zamora, Trought, Foster, Thomson, Kuipers, Johnston, Jones, Andreasson, Tillson, Roberts, Ellington, Dolling (Youth Dev.), Brinsford (Secretary). Front row: Wesson, Gingell, Stokes, Craig, Thompson (Coach), G Dunford, Holloway (Player-Manager), D Dunford, Penrice (Player-Coach), Bradshaw, Andrews, Kendall, Bater

Gold Cup match for Trinidad and Tobago against Mexico in February and his absence precipitated Rovers' late-season demise.

Early-season success engendered great optimism in north-east Bristol. A pre-season testimonial for Lee Martin drew a ground record of 10,534 to the Memorial Stadium to see Rovers draw 2-2 with European Champions Manchester United, with David Beckham and Paul Scholes in midfield, after falling behind to an Ole Gunnar Solskjaer strike. The best opening-day crowd since 1974, 8,514, watched Rovers' 800th League draw, a match in which Brentford, whose central defender Hermann Hreidarsson was sent off for a professional foul two minutes from time, set a club record of 17 League matches unbeaten. Danny Boxall, Ijah Anderson and Rob Quinn, who were to sign for Rovers in the summer of 2002, was in the Bees' side. On Boxing Day after a lunchtime kick-off, Rovers' sixth consecutive victory was watched by the first five-figure crowd at a home League game for 14 years. The highest of four such attendances was the 11,109 to witness the draw with Wigan Athletic in March. Amid such optimism, a £100,000 roof at the Blackthorn End, formerly the clubhouse terrace, was opened prior to a convincing 3-0 victory over Luton Town in November, after Man of the Match Andy Thomson and Walters, with a glorious free-kick, had put Rovers two goals ahead after only 19 minutes.

There was a player sent off in each of the first six League games to add to one at Macclesfield Town on the final day of 1998/99. Ronnie Maugé's August dismissal after 20 minutes at Priestfield was the third consecutive season a Rovers player was sent off at Gillingham. Trevor Challis was dismissed against Burnley, again in August, but Rovers received no further red cards. By contrast, no fewer than 10 opponents were sent off. Slowly but surely, Rovers climbed the table, with Jason Roberts scoring freely and victory at Notts County left the side top of Division Two through much of October. Surviving a stutter in late autumn, a run of six straight victories, Walters' first six appearances for the club, left Rovers positively placed at the turn of the millennium. The side had kept seven clean sheets in the first 10 away League fixtures.

FOOTBALL LEAGUE DIVISION TWO

SEASON 1999/2000

Date		Opponent	Res	Att	1	2	3	4	5	6	7	8	9	10	11	SUBSTITUTES	GOALSCORERS
07/08/99	H	BRENTFORD	0-0	8514	JONES	PRITCHARD	CHALLIS	FOSTER	THOMSON	TILLSON	MAUGE	HILLIER	CURETON	ROBERTS	PETHICK	BENNETT 11	
14/08/99	A	GILLINGHAM	1-0	6234	JONES	PRITCHARD	CHALLIS	FOSTER	THOMSON	TILLSON	MAUGE	HILLIER	CURETON	ROBERTS	PETHICK	ASTAFJEVS 9, ELLINGTON 10	ROBERTS
21/08/99	A	OXFORD UNITED	1-0	7617	JONES	PRITCHARD	CHALLIS	FOSTER	THOMSON	TILLSON	MAUGE	HILLIER	CURETON	ROBERTS	ELLINGTON	ELLINGTON 2	ROBERTS
28/08/99	A	WREXHAM	2-0	3365	JONES	PRITCHARD	CHALLIS	FOSTER	THOMSON	TILLSON	MAUGE	HILLIER	CURETON	ROBERTS	ELLINGTON	ELLINGTON 7	CURETON, ROBERTS
30/08/99	H	BURNLEY	1-0	7624	JONES	PRITCHARD	CHALLIS	FOSTER	THOMSON	TILLSON	MAUGE	HILLIER	CURETON	ROBERTS	ELLINGTON	ELLINGTON 7	CURETON
04/09/99	A	SCUNTHORPE UNITED	2-0	4496	JONES	ANDREASSON	CHALLIS	FOSTER	THOMSON	TILLSON	MAUGE	HILLIER	CURETON	ROBERTS	PETHICK	PENRICE 7	CURETON 2
11/09/99	A	WIGAN ATHLETIC	1-3	6927	JONES	PRITCHARD	CHALLIS	FOSTER	THOMSON	TILLSON	MAUGE	HILLIER	CURETON	ROBERTS	PETHICK	ROBERTS 2	CURETON
18/09/99	H	OLDHAM ATHLETIC	3-3	6574	JONES	PRITCHARD	CHALLIS	FOSTER	THOMSON	TILLSON	MAUGE	BRYANT	CURETON	PRITCHARD	PETHICK	CURETON 2, BENNETT 9	ELLINGTON, ROBERTS, CURETON
25/09/99	A	NOTTS COUNTY	2-0	6197	JONES	BRYANT	CHALLIS	FOSTER	THOMSON	TILLSON	MAUGE	HILLIER	CURETON	ROBERTS	PETHICK	BENNETT 10	CURETON 2
02/10/99	H	BLACKPOOL	3-1	7715	TAYLOR	PRITCHARD	CHALLIS	FOSTER	THOMSON	TILLSON	MAUGE	HILLIER	CURETON	ROBERTS	PETHICK	LEONI 3, BRYANT 8, ELLINGTON 10	CURETON 2-pen, TILLSON
09/10/99	H	CARDIFF CITY	1-1	7363	TAYLOR	PRITCHARD	CHALLIS	FOSTER	THOMSON	TILLSON	MAUGE	HILLIER	CURETON	ROBERTS	PETHICK	BRYANT 2, ELLINGTON 9, LEONI 3	ELLINGTON
17/10/99	A	BRISTOL CITY	1-0	16011	TAYLOR	PRITCHARD	CHALLIS	FOSTER	THOMSON	TILLSON	MAUGE	HILLIER	CURETON	ROBERTS	PETHICK	ELLINGTON 2, BRYANT 7	CURETON
19/10/99	A	AFC BOURNEMOUTH	1-0	5613	JONES	PRITCHARD	CHALLIS	FOSTER	THOMSON	TILLSON	MAUGE	HILLIER	CURETON	ROBERTS	PETHICK		
23/10/99	H	NOTTS COUNTY	0-1	8188	JONES	PRITCHARD	CHALLIS	FOSTER	THOMSON	TILLSON	MAUGE	HILLIER	CURETON	ROBERTS	PETHICK	CURETON	
26/10/99	A	MILLWALL	0-0	5397	JONES	PRITCHARD	CHALLIS	BRYANT	THOMSON	TILLSON	MAUGE	HILLIER	CURETON	ROBERTS	PETHICK		
06/11/99	H	WYCOMBE WDS	1-1	5167	JONES	PRITCHARD	CHALLIS	FOSTER	THOMSON	TILLSON	MAUGE	HILLIER	CURETON	ELLINGTON	PETHICK	THOMSON	THOMSON
20/11/99	A	CHESTERFIELD	2-0	2875	JONES	PRITCHARD	WALTERS	FOSTER	THOMSON	TILLSON	MAUGE	HILLIER	CURETON	ELLINGTON	PETHICK	BENNETT 11, ZAMORA 9	ELLINGTON
27/11/99	H	LUTON TOWN	3-0	7805	JONES	PRITCHARD	WALTERS	FOSTER	THOMSON	TILLSON	MAUGE	HILLIER	CURETON	ELLINGTON	PETHICK	PETHICK 8	THOMSON, WALTERS
04/12/99	A	BRENTFORD	3-0	6843	JONES	PRITCHARD	CHALLIS	FOSTER	THOMSON	TILLSON	MAUGE	HILLIER	CURETON	ROBERTS	PETHICK	BENNETT 10, WALTERS 7, ELLINGTON 9	CURETON, TROUGHT, THOMSON
11/12/99	H	COLCHESTER UNITED	2-1	7023	JONES	PRITCHARD	WALTERS	FOSTER	THOMSON	TILLSON	MAUGE	HILLIER	CURETON	ROBERTS	PETHICK	BENNETT 3, CHALLIS 11	ROBERTS 2
18/12/99	H	MILLWALL	2-1	10379	JONES	PRITCHARD	WALTERS	FOSTER	THOMSON	TILLSON	MAUGE	HILLIER	CURETON	ROBERTS	PETHICK	ELLINGTON 3, CHALLIS 8	ROBERTS 2, WALTERS
26/12/99	A	PRESTON NORTH END	1-2	16680	JONES	PRITCHARD	CHALLIS	FOSTER	THOMSON	TILLSON	MAUGE	HILLIER	CURETON	ROBERTS	PETHICK	ROBERTS 2, WALTERS	ROBERTS 2
28/12/99	H	CAMBRIDGE UNITED	1-0	9822	JONES	PRITCHARD	CHALLIS	FOSTER	THOMSON	TILLSON	MAUGE	HILLIER	CURETON	ELLINGTON	PETHICK	ZABEK 6, BENNETT 7, TROUGHT 2	WALTERS
03/01/00	A	COLCHESTER UNITED	4-5	4482	JONES	PRITCHARD	WALTERS	FOSTER	THOMSON	TILLSON	BRANT	HILLIER	CURETON	ELLINGTON	WALTERS	BENNETT 2, CHALLIS 11	CURETON 3, PETHICK, WALTERS
08/01/00	A	CAMBRIDGE UNITED	2-1	6943	PARKIN	PRITCHARD	WALTERS	FOSTER	THOMSON	BYRNE	MAUGE	HILLIER	CURETON	ROBERTS	WALTERS	PARKIN 1, ELLINGTON 5, MEAKER 9	CURETON 2, FOSTER
15/01/00	A	GILLINGHAM	2-1	7023	PARKIN	TAYLOR	CHALLIS	FOSTER	THOMSON	TILLSON	MAUGE	HILLIER	CURETON	ELLINGTON	PETHICK	PETHICK 6, ELLINGTON 7	PETHICK, CURETON-pen, WALTERS
22/01/00	A	OXFORD UNITED	5-0	7355	PARKIN	PETHICK	CHALLIS	TROUGHT	THOMSON	WHITE	BYRNE	TREES	CURETON	WALTERS	WALTERS	BYRNE 10, LEONI 7	BYRNE, CURETON 3, PETHICK
29/01/00	H	WREXHAM	3-1	8196	JONES	PRITCHARD	CHALLIS	FOSTER	THOMSON	TILLSON	MAUGE	TREES	CURETON	ROBERTS	ELLINGTON	ASTAFJEVS 2, ELLINGTON 11	ELLINGTON, TREES, ROBERTS
05/02/00	A	BURNLEY	0-1	13526	JONES	ASTAFJEVS	CHALLIS	FOSTER	THOMSON	TILLSON	MAUGE	TREES	CURETON	ROBERTS	ELLINGTON	ELLINGTON 3, ZAMORA 8	
12/02/00	H	SCUNTHORPE UNITED	4-1	8236	JONES	PRITCHARD	CHALLIS	FOSTER	THOMSON	TILLSON	ASTAFJEVS	HILLIER	CURETON	ROBERTS	WALTERS	ELLINGTON 3, ZAMORA 8	CURETON 2, 1 pen, ASTAFJEVS, THOMSON
19/02/00	A	LUTON TOWN	4-1	6520	JONES	PRITCHARD	CHALLIS	FOSTER	THOMSON	TILLSON	ASTAFJEVS	HILLIER	CURETON	ELLINGTON	WALTERS	TREES 7	CURETON 2, 1 pen, ASTAFJEVS, THOMSON
26/02/00	H	OLDHAM ATHLETIC	4-1	5839	JONES	PRITCHARD	CHALLIS	FOSTER	THOMSON	TILLSON	ASTAFJEVS	HILLIER	CURETON	ROBERTS	PETHICK	TREES 10, ELLINGTON 11	CURETON 2, 1 pen, ASTAFJEVS, THOMSON
04/03/00	A	WIGAN ATHLETIC	1-0	11109	JONES	PRITCHARD	CHALLIS	FOSTER	THOMSON	TILLSON	ASTAFJEVS	HILLIER	CURETON	ROBERTS	PETHICK	PIERRE 11	GREEN og
07/03/00	H	READING	3-1	8053	JONES	PRITCHARD	CHALLIS	FOSTER	THOMSON	TILLSON	ZABEK	HILLIER	CURETON	ROBERTS	PETHICK	MEAKER 4, ZAMORA 11, ELLINGTON 3	CURETON 2, 1 pen, ELLINGTON
11/03/00	H	BURY	1-0	8765	JONES	PRITCHARD	CHALLIS	FOSTER	THOMSON	TILLSON	ASTAFJEVS	LEONI	CURETON	ROBERTS	PETHICK	LEONI 6, ZAMORA 11	ELLINGTON
18/03/00	A	WYCOMBE WDRS	3-1	11707	JONES	PRITCHARD	CHALLIS	FOSTER	THOMSON	TILLSON	ASTAFJEVS	PIERRE	CURETON	ROBERTS	ELLINGTON	LEONI 11, ELLINGTON 3	WALTERS, CURETON, ASTAFJEVS
22/03/00	H	CHESTERFIELD	0-3	12858	JONES	PRITCHARD	CHALLIS	FOSTER	THOMSON	TILLSON	ASTAFJEVS	HILLIER	CURETON	ELLINGTON	WALTERS	TREES 7, PIERRE 10, ELLINGTON 11	
25/03/00	A	READING	0-3	9312	JONES	PRITCHARD	CHALLIS	FOSTER	THOMSON	TILLSON	STEWART	HILLIER	ELLINGTON	ROBERTS	WALTERS	PIERRE 11	
01/04/00	H	MILLWALL	3-3	7771	JONES	PETHICK	CHALLIS	FOSTER	THOMSON	TILLSON	ELLINGTON	HILLIER	ROBERTS	ELLINGTON	WALTERS	TREES 7, PIERRE 10, ELLINGTON 11	WALTERS, CURETON, ASTAFJEVS
04/04/00	A	STOKE CITY	0-1	4536	JONES	PETHICK	CHALLIS	ANDREASSON	THOMSON	TILLSON	ASTAFJEVS	HILLIER	ROBERTS	WALTERS	WALTERS	STEWART 3, ELLINGTON 7, LEONI 3	
08/04/00	H	CAMBRIDGE UNITED	1-1	10111	JONES	LEONI	CHALLIS	FOSTER	THOMSON	TILLSON	ASTAFJEVS	HILLIER	ROBERTS	ELLINGTON	WALTERS	WOLLEASTON 2, STEWART 3	ROBERTS
15/04/00	A	PRESTON NORTH END	1-1	10805	JONES	PRITCHARD	CHALLIS	FOSTER	THOMSON	TILLSON	ELLINGTON	HILLIER	ELLINGTON	ROBERTS	WALTERS	WOLLEASTON 7, ELLINGTON 10	ROBERTS, WALTERS
22/04/00	A	BRISTOL CITY	2-0	5635	PARKIN	ANDREASSON	CHALLIS	FOSTER	THOMSON	TILLSON	ELLINGTON	HILLIER	ROBERTS	WALTERS	WALTERS	WOLLEASTON 4, WALTERS 11	ROBERTS, WALTERS
24/04/00	H	BLACKPOOL	2-0	8847	JONES	ANDREASSON	LEONI	FOSTER	ANDREASSON	TILLSON	ELLINGTON	HILLIER	ROBERTS	WALTERS	ELLINGTON	LEONI 6, ZAMORA 8, MEAKER 10	WALTERS, CURETON
29/04/00	A	AFC BOURNEMOUTH	1-2	6655	PARKIN	PETHICK	CHALLIS	FOSTER	THOMSON	TILLSON	MAUGE	HILLIER	PRITCHARD	CURETON	ELLINGTON	TROUGHT 8	WALTERS, CURETON
06/05/00	A	CARDIFF CITY	0-1	6145	PARKIN	PETHICK	CHALLIS	FOSTER	THOMSON	TILLSON	ELLINGTON	HILLIER	ZABEK	CURETON	ROBERTS	PENRICE 7, ELLINGTON 3, MEAKER 10	

FA CUP

Date		Opponent	Res	Att												SUBSTITUTES	GOALSCORERS
31/10/00	A	PRESTON NORTH END	0-1	6145	PARKIN	PETHICK	CHALLIS	FOSTER	THOMSON	TILLSON	MAUGE	HILLIER	CURETON	ROBERTS	CHALLIS	PENRICE 7, ELLINGTON 3, MEAKER 10	

LEAGUE CUP

Date		Opponent	Res	Att												SUBSTITUTES	GOALSCORERS
10/08/99	H	LUTON TOWN	2-0	2984	JONES	PRITCHARD	CHALLIS	FOSTER	THOMSON	TILLSON	MAUGE	HILLIER	CURETON	ROBERTS	PETHICK		ROBERTS 2
25/08/99	A	LUTON TOWN	2-2	4414	JONES	PRITCHARD	CHALLIS	FOSTER	THOMSON	TILLSON	MAUGE	HILLIER	CURETON	ROBERTS	PETHICK	TREES 7	ROBERTS, WALTERS
14/09/99	A	BIRMINGHAM CITY	1-1	17457	JONES	PRITCHARD	ANDREASSON	FOSTER	THOMSON	TILLSON	ASTAFJEVS	HILLIER	CURETON	PRITCHARD	WALTERS	BRYANT 7, ASTAFJEVS 3, TREES 12	ROBERTS
21/09/99	H	BIRMINGHAM CITY	0-1	5456	JONES	PRITCHARD	CHALLIS	FOSTER	ANDREASSON	TILLSON	MAUGE	HILLIER	CURETON	CURETON	WALTERS	BRYANT 9, BENNETT 8	

AUTO WINDSCREENS SHIELD

Date		Opponent	Res	Att												SUBSTITUTES	GOALSCORERS
11/01/00	A	NORTHAMPTON T*	0-0	2443	JONES	PRITCHARD	CHALLIS	FOSTER	THOMSON	TILLSON	MAUGE	HILLIER	PRITCHARD	PRITCHARD	ROBERTS	BRYANT 9, ZAMORA 8, MEAKER 10	
24/01/00	H	READING	1-2	4948	JONES	PARKIN	BYRNE	FOSTER	THOMSON	TILLSON	BYRNE	PRITCHARD	CURETON	CURETON	ROBERTS	ELLINGTON 4, WALTERS 3	CURETON-pen

* AET Rovers won 5-3 on pens

PLAYERS	APP	SUB	GLS
ANDREASSON M.	6	13	2
ASTAFJEVS V.	13	6	
BENNETT F.	0	10	
BRYANT S.	9	6	
BYRNE S.	1		
CHALLIS T.	36	4	
CURETON	46		22
ELLINGTON N.	12	25	4
EVANS R.	1		
FOSTER S.	43	1	
HILLIER D.	39		
JONES L.	36		
LEONI S.	3	6	
MAUGE R.	22		
MEAKER M.	0	2	
PARKIN B.	3		
PENRICE G.	0	3	
PETHICK R.	40	1	2
PIERRE N.	2	1	
PRITCHARD	41		1
ROBERTS J.	41	3	22
STEWART J.	1	3	
TAYLOR S.	3		
THOMSON A.	43		4
TILLSON A.	43		5
TRESS R.	5	5	1
TROUGHT M.	2	2	1
WALTERS M.	28	22	9
WHITE T.	3		
WOLLEASTON R.	0	4	
ZABEK L.	3	4	
ZAMORA R.	0	4	
OWN GOAL			1

After Jamie Cureton had scored the club's first goal of the New Year, Rovers' tightly knit defence with Thomson, Steve Foster and captain Andy Tillson prominent, fell apart in an extraordinary game at Layer Road. A goal up after 11 minutes, when Roberts took five attempts to force the ball over the line, Rovers conceded an equaliser to Colchester United before half-time. When Titus Bramble, on loan from Ipswich Town, fouled David Pritchard, this injury ending the pugnacious full-back's season, Cureton's 57th-minute penalty put Rovers 3-1 up. Seven minutes later, Cureton could have sent Rovers into a 4-2 lead, but missed from a second penalty. Instead, Karl Duguid

Jamie Cureton left Rovers for £200,000 after scoring 72 League goals in three seasons

scored twice in three minutes, only for substitute Nathan Ellington to equalise for Rovers when Robbie Pethick's cross rebounded off the crossbar with four minutes remaining. In the dying moments, home substitute Lomana Trésor Lua-Lua, a Zairian striker who had scored Colchester's consolation goal in Horfield earlier in the season, burst through the Rovers defence for a dramatic winning goal.

In the League, Rovers played just twice away from home during January, but both games produced great excitement. The 5-4 defeat at Layer Road was followed by a 5-0 win at Oxford United as Rovers echoed the Madejski Stadium performance of 12 months earlier. Cureton scored either side of half-time and, after Pethick and Ellington had scored in the space of 60 seconds, he completed another away hat-trick 10 minutes from time. Pethick's first goal for the club matched the achievement of Challis against Wigan Athletic and that of Rob Trees when Rovers defeated Wrexham in January to return to the top of Division Two.

More unexpected was David Pritchard's winning goal at Chesterfield in November, where he became bizarrely the first Rovers midfielder to score all season. The unlikely sight of this first Football League goal from Pritchard led 19-year-old Ben Davies to honour a promise to walk home from Saltergate, being accompanied on his 154-mile walk by Ralph and Sue Ellis, Mike Bullock, Paul Thomas and John Spilsbury. This charity walk, which raised £3255.70 for Macmillan Cancer Research and the Supporters' Club 'Raise the Roof' fund, reached the Memorial Stadium in time for the return fixture in which Chesterfield, with Steve Blatherwick sent off, were comfortably defeated to leave Rovers in late March seven points inside the promotion places and 14 points inside the play-off places.

Rovers were playing devastatingly well. Consecutive 4-1 victories at Luton Town and Oldham Athletic merely illustrated the power of the side, Cureton and Roberts scoring twice each after Luton had scored inside a quarter of an hour. Rovers' first win at Boundary Park since December 1974 was a foregone conclusion once two Cureton goals and one for Astafjevs had put the side 3-0 up after only 11 minutes, although the Latvian was stretchered off before half-time. Later, Rovers were to record a highly committed and hugely impressive first derby win at the Memorial Stadium. This followed a goalless draw in October at Ashton Gate – where Bristol City fielded the Hungarian Vilmos Sebok as substitute – just 24 hours after the death of Bill Dodgin, a pre-war Rovers player and successful club manager from December 1969 to July 1972.

From being so ensconced in the promotion places, Rovers' fall from grace was dramatic. Even the final home programme of the season contained messages of hope that Rovers could avoid the play-offs, by gaining automatic promotion, but few thought they could do so by slipping up so severely. Lowly Reading achieved a League double over Rovers, who also lost at relegated Blackpool and Cardiff City. John Macken's 41st-minute goal, after Paul McKenna had hit a post, enabled Preston to win at the Memorial Stadium. Had Rovers defeated the champions-elect, they would have kept their fate in their own hands with just four games to play. With only already-relegated Cardiff City to play, Rovers still stood in a play-off position, requiring just a victory. A win at Reading on 22 March would have put Rovers top of Division Two. Defeat to Scott Young's 27th-minute header from Mark Bonner's right-wing corner at Ninian Park left them two points adrift of the play-off places. Cureton, the club's only ever-present, had scored 22 League goals, to finish the season as joint top-scorer with Roberts.

While there had been injuries, with Shore out all season and Maugé and Pritchard missing the run-in, Rovers' sharp decline was inexplicable. Half of the 12 League defeats all season came in those fateful final 10 games, in which Rovers won just once, a morale-boosting Easter Saturday victory over a Bristol City side that included the Moldovan International Ivan Testimetanu. Only 11 games were drawn in Division Two all season, the most exciting being the home fixture with Stoke City in April. A goal down after 10 minutes, Rovers twice led only to draw 3-3, with the visitors' Peter Thorne completing a well-taken hat-trick. It was the first hat-trick conceded in the League by Rovers since February 1994 and the sixth occasion an opponent had scored three times and not ended up on the winning side. Sadly, two spectators raced onto the pitch in an

Bristol Rovers 2000/01. Back row: Hillier, Meaker, Scott, Trought, Foran, Culkin, Parkin, Richards, Jones, Evans, Cameron, Smith. Second row: Brown (Kit Man), Mauge, Thomson, Penrice (Asst Manager), Holloway (Manager), Thompson (Reserve Team Manager), Kite (Physio), Foster, Walters, Kendall. Front row: Challis, Ellington, J Shore, Hogg, Ellis, Bignot, Pritchard, Trees, Pethick, Bryant, Wilson

attempt to attack the visiting goalkeeper Gavin Ward and were rightly arrested and subsequently banned by the club. This incident led to an FA enquiry, held on 30 June, at which Rovers were found guilty of failing to control their supporters and given a suspended sentence of one docked League point and a £10,000 fine. This punishment would only be imposed if a similar offence were to occur within 12 months.

After Roberts had seen off Luton Town, Rovers were knocked out of the Worthington Cup by Birmingham City. Likewise a slick Preston North End side put paid to hopes of a repeat of the 1998/99 FA Cup success. On-loan midfielder Shaun Byrne scored the winning penalty, after Brian Parkin, in his first start for almost exactly four years, had saved one in a penalty shoot-out following a goalless draw at Northampton Town in the Auto Windscreens Shield. Rovers went out tamely at home to Reading in the next round. In the Gloucestershire Senior Challenge Cup, a Rovers reserves side lost to Bristol City reserves, Simon Clist scoring 10 minutes from the end of extra-time. The former Rovers goalkeeper Nigel Martyn was in the Leeds United side that reached the UEFA Cup semi-finals. Meanwhile, Rovers' matchday magazine was voted Division Two programme of the year by the *National Programme Directory* for the second time in three years. Despite turnover at the stadium rising from £1.79 million to £2.32 million, Rovers reported an overall loss of £885,531 on the year to 30 June 2000, largely through spiralling operating costs and wages.

The Memorial Stadium hosted an England Under-15 International against Holland in March. Before a crowd of 5,344, Blackburn Rovers' Andy Bell headed the winning goal shortly before half-time for an England side boasting Bristol Rovers' full-back Neil Arndale. In May, Sue Smith of Tranmere Rovers scored 10 minutes after half-time to give England a 1-0 victory over Switzerland at the Memorial Stadium, before a crowd of 2,587, in a qualifying game for the women's Euro 2001 tournament. Twenty-four hours later, on the same ground, 7,775 spectators watched Leicester defeat Bristol 30-23 to secure rugby union's Allied Dunbar League Championship.

2000/01

A season that opened with great optimism ended in tears on a Wednesday night in May, as Rovers slipped into the basement division for the first time. Relegation ended Rovers' record of being the only club never to have played in either the top or the bottom division of the Football League. Requiring at least a point at home to Wycombe Wanderers, Rovers conceded a 73rd-minute deflected shot from Daniel Senda and a spectacular volley from Dannie Bulman five minutes later. A spirited revival, kickstarted by a goal from substitute Kevin Gall, did not produce the late equaliser Rovers needed to keep their hopes alive.

Only six minutes into the season, at a warm, sunny Memorial Stadium, Jamie Cureton was fouled by Bournemouth's Stevland Angus and stroked home the resultant penalty past French goalkeeper Mikael Menetrier to give Rovers an early lead. Rovers were unbeaten in their opening 12 League and cup games and recorded comprehensive victories at Brentford and at second-in-the-table Cambridge United. However, the warning signs

FOOTBALL LEAGUE DIVISION TWO

Date	Opponent	Venue	Result	ATT	G	2	3	4	5	6	7	8	9	10	11	SUBSTITUTES	GOALSCORERS
12/08/00	AFC BOURNEMOUTH	H	1-1	8046	CULKIN	BIGNOT	WILSON	FOSTER	FORAN	JONES	PETHICK	ASTAFJEVS	ELLINGTON	EVANS	WALTERS	CAMERON 7, BRYANT 3, HOGG 9	ALLSOPP pen
20/08/00	PETERBOROUGH UTD	A	2-2	6997	CULKIN	BIGNOT	WILSON	FOSTER	THOMSON	JONES	HOGG	ASTAFJEVS	ELLINGTON	EVANS	BRYANT	CAMERON 9, ELLIS 10, PETHICK 7	CURETON, ELLINGTON
28/08/00	BRENTFORD	A	6-2	5434	CULKIN	BIGNOT	WILSON	FOSTER	THOMSON	JONES	HOGG	ASTAFJEVS	ELLINGTON	EVANS	BRYANT	CAMERON 10, ELLIS 9, WALTERS 11	ASTAFJEVS 2, ELLINGTON, HOGG 2, JONES
09/09/00	NOTTS COUNTY	H	1-1	5511	CULKIN	BIGNOT	WILSON	FOSTER	THOMSON	JONES	HOGG	ASTAFJEVS	ELLINGTON	EVANS	WALTERS	BRYANT 3, WALTERS 11	BIGNOT
12/09/00	WYCOMBE WDRS	A	1-1	4718	CULKIN	BIGNOT	WILSON	FOSTER	THOMSON	JONES	HOGG	ASTAFJEVS	ELLINGTON	EVANS	BRYANT	PARKIN 1, WALTERS 8	BRYANT
16/09/00	WIGAN ATHLETIC	A	0-0	8109	CULKIN	GLENNON	WILSON	FOSTER	THOMSON	JONES	HOGG	ASTAFJEVS	ELLINGTON	EVANS	BRYANT	WALTERS 3, FORAN 7, ELLIS 9	
23/09/00	CAMBRIDGE UNITED	H	3-0	4624	CULKIN	BIGNOT	CHALLIS	FOSTER	ANDREASSON	JONES	PETHICK	ASTAFJEVS	ELLINGTON	EVANS	BRYANT	ELLIS 9, HOGG 7	ELLIS 3, PLUMMER
30/09/00	LUTON TOWN	H	3-3	7901	CULKIN	BIGNOT	WILSON	FOSTER	JONES	HOGG	WALTERS	ASTAFJEVS	ELLINGTON	EVANS	BRYANT	PLUMMER 9, FORAN 10, MEAKER 5	PARRIN 1, FORAN 10, MEAKER 5
06/10/00	BURY	A	0-1	3279	CULKIN	BIGNOT	WILSON	FOSTER	THOMSON	JONES	HOGG	ASTAFJEVS	ELLINGTON	EVANS	CHALLIS	PLUMMER 9	
14/10/00	NORTHAMPTON T	A	0-1	7704	CULKIN	BIGNOT	WILSON	FOSTER	THOMSON	JONES	HOGG	ASTAFJEVS	ELLINGTON	EVANS	WALTERS	CHALLIS 7, WALTERS 6	
17/10/00	ROTHERHAM UNITED	A	1-2	6910	CULKIN	BIGNOT	WILSON	FOSTER	PLUMMER	JONES	WALTERS	ASTAFJEVS	ELLINGTON	EVANS	BRYANT	ELLIS 3, PLUMMER 6	ELLINGTON 2
21/10/00	SWINDON TOWN	H	3-1	8097	CULKIN	BIGNOT	CHALLIS	ANDREASSON	FORAN	JONES	WALTERS	ASTAFJEVS	ALLSOPP	EVANS	BRYANT	HILLIER 7, ELLIS 7, DAGNOGO 10	ALLSOPP 2, WALTERS 3
24/10/00	COLCHESTER UNITED	A	1-2	2951	CULKIN	BIGNOT	WILSON	FOSTER	ANDREASSON	FORAN	HOGG	ASTAFJEVS	ALLSOPP	EVANS	CHALLIS	EVANS pen	ELLIS
28/10/00	OLDHAM ATHLETIC	H	0-2	6110	HOGG	BIGNOT	WILSON	FOSTER	JONES	FORAN	HOGG	ASTAFJEVS	ALLSOPP	EVANS	BRYANT		
04/11/00	OXFORD UNITED	A	1-0	5407	CULKIN	BIGNOT	WILSON	FOSTER	THOMSON	JONES	HOGG	ASTAFJEVS	ELLINGTON	EVANS	BRYANT		FOSTER
11/11/00	WALSALL	H	1-0	7540	CULKIN	PETHICK	JONES	FOSTER	THOMSON	HOGG	MAUGE	HOGG	OWUSU	ELLINGTON	BRYANT		ANDREASSON, M WILLIAMS og.
22/11/00	MILLWALL	A	1-2	5502	CULKIN	BIGNOT	WILSON	FOSTER	JONES	FORAN	WALTERS	ASTAFJEVS	CAMERON	ELLINGTON	BRYANT	CAMERON	EVANS
25/11/00	WREXHAM	A	0-1	2575	CULKIN	PETHICK	CHALLIS	FOSTER	THOMSON	JONES	HOGG	HILLIER	CAMERON	BRYANT	WALTERS	FOSTER	
02/12/00	SWANSEA CITY	H	0-0	5563	CULKIN	BIGNOT	WILSON	FOSTER	THOMSON	JONES	MAUGE	ASTAFJEVS	ELLINGTON	EVANS	ASTAFJEVS	ASTAFJEVS 4, ELLINGTON 11	
16/12/00	STOKE CITY	A	0-3	6838	CULKIN	BIGNOT	WILSON	FOSTER	THOMSON	HOGG	PLUMMER	ASTAFJEVS	ELLINGTON	EVANS	WALTERS	WALTERS 3, BARRETT 5	
22/12/00	BRISTOL CITY	H	2-3	16696	CULKIN	BIGNOT	WILSON	FOSTER	THOMSON	HOGG	MAUGE	PLUMMER	EVANS	RICHARDS	WALTERS	WALTERS 7, LEE 3	ELLINGTON 10, HOGG 2, GALL 11
26/12/00	READING	A	2-2	8029	CULKIN	BIGNOT	CHALLIS	FORAN	THOMSON	HOGG	WILSON	CAMERON	OWUSU	ELLINGTON	WALTERS	FORAN 4, ASTAFJEVS 9, MAUGE 7	ELLINGTON 2
13/01/01	BRENTFORD	H	1-1	6933	CULKIN	PETHICK	WILSON	FOSTER	THOMSON	JONES	WILSON	PETHICK	LEE	ELLINGTON	WALTERS	GALL 10, OWUSU 8	FOSTER, PLUMMER
20/01/01	PETERBOROUGH UTD	H	2-0	11767	CULKIN	BIGNOT	WILSON	FOSTER	MEAKER	BRYANT	MAUGE	HILLIER	ELLINGTON	BRYANT	BRYANT	BIGNOT, CAMERON	ELLINGTON, THOMSON
03/02/01	MILLWALL	H	0-3	10828	CULKIN	BIGNOT	WILSON	FOSTER	THOMSON	JONES	MAUGE	ASTAFJEVS	RICHARDS	WALTERS	WALTERS	ELLIS 11, PETHICK 7	ELLIS
10/02/01	NOTTS COUNTY	A	0-0	6914	CULKIN	WILSON	CHALLIS	FOSTER	THOMSON	HOGG	PLUMMER	ASTAFJEVS	OWUSU	McKEEVER	ELLINGTON	ELLINGTON 10, CAMERON 7	CAMERON
17/02/01	SWINDON TOWN	H	6-2	7271	CULKIN	WILSON	CHALLIS	FOSTER	THOMSON	HOGG	MAUGE	ASTAFJEVS	RICHARDS	OWUSU	McKEEVER	CAMERON 10	
24/02/01	WIGAN ATHLETIC	H	2-1	7079	CULKIN	WILSON	CHALLIS	FOSTER	THOMSON	HOGG	MAUGE	PLUMMER	OWUSU	McKEEVER	WALTERS	JONES 5, BRYANT 8, ELLINGTON 9	ASTAFJEVS, ELLINGTON
27/02/01	CAMBRIDGE UNITED	A	2-1	3466	CULKIN	BIGNOT	CHALLIS	FOSTER	THOMSON	JONES	BRYANT	ASTAFJEVS	OWUSU	EVANS	ELLIS	ELLINGTON 10, HOGG 2, ELLIS 11	FOSTER
03/03/01	LUTON TOWN	A	0-1	7405	CULKIN	BIGNOT	CHALLIS	FOSTER	THOMSON	JONES	WILSON	BRYANT	OWUSU	McKEEVER	ASTAFJEVS	THOMSON 3, RICHARDS 10	
06/03/01	NORTHAMPTON T	H	2-1	4552	CULKIN	BIGNOT	CHALLIS	FOSTER	THOMSON	JONES	WILSON	ASTAFJEVS	EVANS	ELLINGTON	McKEEVER	MAUGE 11, RICHARDS 7	McKEEVER M
10/03/01	BURY	H	2-0	7065	CULKIN	BIGNOT	CHALLIS	FOSTER	THOMSON	JONES	WILSON	ASTAFJEVS	EVANS	ELLINGTON	BRYANT	MAUGE 9, McKEEVER 3, ASTAFJEVS 8	MAUGE R
17/03/01	ROTHERHAM UNITED	H	0-3	7098	CULKIN	BIGNOT	WILSON	FOSTER	THOMSON	JONES	MAUGE	ASTAFJEVS	EVANS	ELLINGTON	BRYANT	McKEEVER 11, CHALLIS 6, ELLIS 7	MEAKER M
24/03/01	SWINDON TOWN	A	1-4	12274	CULKIN	BIGNOT	WILSON	FOSTER	THOMSON	JONES	MAUGE	ASTAFJEVS	OWUSU	EVANS	ASTAFJEVS	McKEEVER 7, CHALLIS 6, ELLIS 7	OWUSU A
31/03/01	STOKE CITY	A	0-0	9361	CULKIN	BIGNOT	WILSON	FOSTER	THOMSON	JONES	WILSON	BRYANT	EVANS	ELLINGTON	ASTAFJEVS	EVANS 9, McKEEVER 8, JONES 11	JONES S
03/04/01	BRISTOL CITY	A	1-1	6505	CULKIN	BIGNOT	WILSON	FOSTER	THOMSON	JONES	MAUGE	PLUMMER	ELLINGTON	EVANS	WALTERS	WALTERS 11, ELLIS 10	ELLINGTON
07/04/01	SWANSEA CITY	H	1-0	3962	CULKIN	PETHICK	CHALLIS	FOSTER	THOMSON	JONES	WILSON	McKEEVER	ELLINGTON	EVANS	WALTERS	EVANS, MEAKER 8, JONES 11	FOSTER
09/04/01	PORT VALE	A	1-2	6540	CULKIN	BIGNOT	JONES	FOSTER	THOMSON	HOGG	WILSON	HOGG	LEE	ELLINGTON	WALTERS	WALTERS 11, ASTAFJEVS 2	
11/04/01	PETERBOROUGH UTD	A	1-2	6540	CULKIN	BIGNOT	JONES	FOSTER	THOMSON	HOGG	PARTRIDGE	HOGG	LEE	CAMERON	BRYANT	WALTERS 5, PLUMMER 8, McKEEVER 11	LEE
14/04/01	COLCHESTER UNITED	H	2-0	6551	CULKIN	BIGNOT	JONES	FOSTER	FORAN	BRYANT	MAUGE	ASTAFJEVS	ELLINGTON	CAMERON	BRYANT	PARTRIDGE 9, MAUGE 2, ASTAFJEVS 8	HOGG
16/04/01	OLDHAM ATHLETIC	A	0-1	6883	CULKIN	WILSON	JONES	FOSTER	THOMSON	BRYANT	PLUMMER	GALL	LEE	CAMERON	ASTAFJEVS	CAMERON 10	
21/04/01	OXFORD UNITED	H	6-2	7554	CULKIN	WILSON	JONES	FOSTER	THOMSON	PLUMMER	MAUGE	GALL	HOGG	LEE	ASTAFJEVS	WALTERS 2, OWUSU 11	LEE, ELLINGTON 2, ASTAFJEVS, WALTERS 2, 1 pen
28/04/01	WALSALL	A	1-2	7130	CULKIN	WILSON	JONES	FOSTER	THOMSON	BRYANT	MAUGE	ASTAFJEVS	HOGG	CAMERON	LEE	CAMERON 10, WALTERS 2, LEE 3	ELLINGTON
30/04/01	PORT VALE	H	0-3	7340	CULKIN	MAUGE	JONES	FOSTER	THOMSON	PLUMMER	PARTRIDGE	ASTAFJEVS	OWUSU	EVANS	PLUMMER	WALTERS 9, PARTRIDGE 6, GALL 11	
02/05/01	WYCOMBE WDRS	H	1-2	8264	CULKIN	BIGNOT	JONES	FOSTER	THOMSON	PLUMMER	PARTRIDGE	HOGG	OWUSU	EVANS	PLUMMER	FORAN 4, ASTAFJEVS 9, MAUGE 7	GALL
05/05/01	WREXHAM	A	4-0	6418	CULKIN	BIGNOT	WILSON	FORAN	JONES	PLUMMER	BRYANT	ASTAFJEVS	ELLINGTON	EVANS	WALTERS	PARTRIDGE, ASTAFJEVS, WALTERS 5	WALTERS 2, 1 pen, PARTRIDGE, ELLINGTON

LEAGUE CUP

Date	Opponent	Venue	Result	ATT	G	2	3	4	5	6	7	8	9	10	11	SUBSTITUTES	GOALSCORERS
23/08/00	PLYMOUTH ARGYLE	H	2-1	3498	CULKIN	BIGNOT	WILSON	FOSTER	THOMSON	JONES	PARTRIDGE	ASTAFJEVS	ELLINGTON	EVANS	BRYANT	WALTERS 10, FORAN 6	ELLINGTON, EVANS
05/09/00	PLYMOUTH ARGYLE	A	1-1	5228	CULKIN	BIGNOT	WILSON	FOSTER	THOMSON	CHALLIS	PARTRIDGE	HOGG	ELLINGTON	EVANS	BRYANT	ELLIS 9, FORAN 6	BIGNOT, CAMERON
20/09/00	EVERTON	H	1-1	25564	CULKIN	BIGNOT	WILSON	FOSTER	THOMSON	JONES	PETHICK	HOGG	OWUSU	EVANS	BRYANT	PLUMMER 9, ELLIS 9, WALTERS 10	HOGG
27/09/00	EVERTON*	A	0-3	7340	CULKIN	BIGNOT	WILSON	FORAN	THOMSON	JONES	PETHICK	MAUGE	OWUSU	ELLINGTON	WALTERS	PLUMMER 8, ELLIS 9, WALTERS 10	BIGNOT
31/10/00	SUNDERLAND	H	1-2	11435	CULKIN	BIGNOT	WILSON	FOSTER	THOMSON	JONES	PETHICK	ASTAFJEVS	ELLINGTON	EVANS	BRYANT	PLUMMER 8, MEAKER 11, HOGG 2	ELLINGTON

*AET Score at 90 mins 1-1, Rovers won 4-2 on pens

FA CUP

Date	Opponent	Venue	Result	ATT	G	2	3	4	5	6	7	8	9	10	11	SUBSTITUTES	GOALSCORERS
19/11/00	CARDIFF CITY	A	1-5	8013	CULKIN	BIGNOT	WILSON	FOSTER	THOMSON	JONES	MAUGE	HOGG	HOGG	JOHANSEN	BRYANT	WALTERS 5, ELLIS 6,	JORDAN og

LD VANS TROPHY

Date	Opponent	Venue	Result	ATT	G	2	3	4	5	6	7	8	9	10	11	SUBSTITUTES	GOALSCORERS
09/12/00	TORQUAY UNITED	A	2-0	1370	BIGNOT	WILSON	FOSTER	THOMSON	JONES	MAUGE	ASTAFJEVS	HOGG	OWUSU	EVANS	BRYANT	HILLIER 8, ELLIS 10, ELLIS 6,	ELLINGTON, EVANS
09/01/01	PLYMOUTH ARGYLE	H	3-0	3781	BIGNOT	WILSON	FOSTER	THOMSON	JONES	MAUGE	HOGG	HOGG	OWUSU	ELLIS	BRYANT	JONES 5, WALTERS 11, RICHARDS 10	ASTAFJEVS 2, EVANS pen
30/01/01	SOUTHEND UNITED	A	0-1	2192	BIGNOT	WILSON	FOSTER	THOMSON	JONES	MAUGE	ASTAFJEVS	MEAKER	ELLINGTON	EVANS	BRYANT	JONES 9, PETHICK 2, WALTERS 11, RICHARDS 10	

GOALSCORERS

PLAYERS	APP	SUB	GLS
ALLSOPP D	4	2	
ANDREASSON M	4	5	
ASTAFJEVS V	34	1	
BARRETT G	1		
BIGNOT M	26		
BRYANT S	27	3	1
CAMERON M	6	8	2
CHALLIS T	19		
CURETON J		1	
DAGNOGO M		2	
ELLINGTON N	36		15
ELLIS C	2	13	4
EVANS M	19	2	4
FORAN M	9	3	
FOSTER S	44		3
GALL K	3	7	2
GLENNON M	1		
HILLIER D		3	
HOGG L	31	3	
JOHANSEN R		2	
JONES S	37	2	4
LEE C	8	5	2
McKEEVER M	5	14	
MAUGE R	14	2	
MEAKER M	2	5	
OWUSU A	11	6	
PARKIN B	2		
PARTRIDGE R	4	2	
PETHICK R	11	7	
PLUMMER D	17	3	
RICHARDS J	2	4	
THOMSON A	31	1	1
WALTERS M	15	4	
WILSON C	36		1
OWN GOAL			1

were already there and Rovers, in particular, had not yet won at home. Jason Roberts had commanded a club record fee of £2 million to move to West Bromwich Albion, but the sales of influential defender Andy Tillson for just £10,000 to early leaders Walsall whom he captained to promotion via the play-offs and, after the opening game, of Cureton to Reading were regarded by supporters with disbelief. Rovers had sold three forwards, in Roberts, Cureton and Bobby Zamora for a profit of just over £2 million. Zamora was to be the top scorer in the League as Brighton were Division Three champions, while Cureton and Roberts scored 30 and 16 times respectively. In their place, Nathan Ellington was top scorer but was never able to count on a reliable attacking partner, Vitalijs Astafjevs' 5 goals rendering him an unlikely second highest scorer for the season. Rovers failed to score in 19 of their 46 League fixtures.

Moreover, new signing Martin Cameron was ruled out for much of the season following an ankle injury sustained in the closing minutes of the large victory at Griffin Park, while new club captain Andy Thomson broke his foot in September. Nick Culkin, a season-long loan signing, one of seven loan players, was an inspirational goalkeeper, his 56th-minute penalty save from Richard Hughes being a pivotal moment in paving the way to a morale-boosting victory at Bournemouth in February, while Player of the Year Steve Foster also missed few games. Beyond these two, however, few players could lay claim to a regular place in the side, although Astafjevs and Ellington often appeared alongside the new generation of Rovers players in Simon Bryant and Lewis Hogg. The club's Young Player of the Year, Hogg made his League debut as an opening day substitute and scored his first two goals at Brentford. New signings Che Wilson and Scott Jones, alongside Marcus Bignot early in the season, were also pivotal figures, but Rovers used a seasonal total of 35 players.

The long unbeaten run ended at second-placed Bury in October, where the home side recorded their 1,500th League win. Bury's goalkeeper Paddy Kenny was booked after hauling down Ellington, as was Jason Jarrett for a foul that forced Culkin to leave the field, but Rovers lost Foster to a red card for retaliation. The substitute goalkeeper was Brian Parkin, who thus set a post-war club appearance record for a goalkeeper. Culkin was also unable to finish the game at Wycombe, following a foul that earned Andy Rammell a sending-off and caused Rovers to be fined £10,000 after alleged comments from the bench were reported by the fourth official, Mike Tingey. There was also controversy at Meadow Lane where, after Ellington had missed a penalty, Notts County equalised in the last minute in bizarre circumstances. With Foster injured, Culkin kicked the ball out of play but, rather than returning the throw to Rovers as is customary, Craig Ramage threw to Richard Liburd whose cross was turned in by Mark Stallard. In the ensuing confusion, Ramage was sent off for threatening Bignot. All in all, eight Rovers players and eight opponents were sent off during the 2000/01 season. Controversial events were also seen at Wigan, after which referee Bill Burns rang Rovers to apologise for not awarding a penalty following a blatant second-half foul on Ansah Owusu by goalkeeper Derek Stillie. The attendance at Wrexham, some 2,575 souls, was the lowest to watch a Rovers League game since the journey to Shrewsbury Town in November 1996.

Early in the season, Rovers could rely on a goals from a variety of sources. Marcus Andreasson fired home from 10 yards for his first goal for the club, one of three goals in 23 first-half minutes at Swindon Town in October, where 2,400 Rovers supporters saw

Mark Walters star against his former club. Bignot scored with his left knee after just 27 seconds on the Friday before Christmas, but Rovers lost to three second-half goals at Ashton Gate, including one headed home by the former Rovers player Peter Beadle, four minutes after coming on as a substitute. Then, following a dramatic Boxing Day draw with Reading, in which Hogg was sent off for a foul on goalscorer Neil Smith and Trevor Challis followed for retaliation, and which also marked the official opening of the Family Enclosure roof, Rovers went an astonishing 576 minutes without a goal in League or cup football. This run, which included defeat to Cureton's right-foot drive three minutes before half-time at Reading, and celebrations that led to repercussions, was to end when Astafjevs scrambled the ball past French goalkeeper Lionel Perez to give Rovers a 33rd-minute lead over Cambridge United. This goal, coupled with substitute Ellington's header a minute after half-time, finally gave Rovers their long-awaited first home League win of the season. They were the last League side to do so and the winless run since Easter Saturday had finally stretched to 13 home League matches.

Ultimately, Rovers' six home League wins equalled the total of away League victories. Success at Dean Court for a second consecutive season was, though, the only victory away from home after the first week in November and Rovers lost their final six away matches. Only on one occasion in the season were consecutive League fixtures won and Rovers recorded ten draws at home and 15 in all, eight of them goalless. Three points from any one of these, for instance the local derby where a seasonal highest home crowd of 9,361 saw Bristol City earn a point when Steve Phillips saved Scott Jones' penalty deep into injury time – one of four penalties Rovers squandered all season – would with hindsight have prevented relegation. A run through the winter of 12 League games without a win cost manager Ian Holloway his job on 29 January. He subsequently succeeded the former Rovers manager Gerry Francis at Queen's Park Rangers, taking Bignot with him, but was unable to prevent the West London side's eventual relegation from Division One. Promotion from within saw Garry Thompson, a former Coventry City striker who had served Rovers in a coaching capacity since 1997, appointed as caretaker manager.

Rovers crashed to a 4-1 defeat at Stoke City, for whom full-back Mikael Hansson scored with two shots in the opening 15 minutes, and suffered three-goal defeats at both promoted sides, Millwall, where Dwayne Plummer and goalscorer Tim Cahill were both sent off, and Rotherham United, as well as at home to both Potteries sides. Stoke City's visit in December featured the first occasion since Bob Hatton in 1979 that Rovers had conceded a first-half hat-trick. Peter Thorne, in scoring after two, 20 and 40 minutes from two sidefoots and a header from Bjarni Gudjohnsen's cross, became only the fifth opponent to have scored hat-tricks against Rovers in two separate League matches and the first to do so twice on Rovers' home ground. Scott Jones and Stoke substitute Ben Petty were both sent off in the second half.

On three occasions, Rovers recorded League victories by four clear goals, a margin never suffered in defeat in the League. A comfortable 6-2 win at Brentford was only the second time the club had won by this score in the Football League, a third such occasion duly arriving when already-relegated Oxford United visited in April. From a goal behind, Rovers scored five second-half goals including three in the final 10 minutes and Mark Walters contributed two in the last four minutes to equal Graham Withey's feat, accomplished in October 1982, of scoring twice as a substitute. Oxford goalkeeper Richard

Knight was sent off 11 minutes from the end, with Phil Wilson saving the resultant Plummer penalty with his first touch in senior football. Wilson was himself booked in conceding a second penalty in the last minute that Walters, who had also set up the third goal for the impressive Astafjevs, successfully converted. It was the first time since Alex Munro and Tony Ford against Luton Town in February 1970 that Rovers had used two penalty-takers in one game and, following Peter Beadle in November 1997, Walters was only the second Rovers substitute to score from the penalty-spot in League football.

A goalless draw with Notts County in February sent Rovers into the relegation zone, from which, as games-in-hand were frittered away, escape was only sporadic. In April defeats came thick and fast, with two Monday evening losses at the hands of a rejuvenated Port Vale side especially damaging. Tony Carss of Oldham Athletic, Port Vale's Marc Bridge-Wilkinson and Wycombe Wanderers' Dannie Bulman all scored spectacular long-range goals to consign Rovers to defeat. Three straight losses led to relegation on 2 May, 11 years to the day since promotion had been achieved from the same division. With hindsight, only a point had been required from consecutive home fixtures and a seventh home League defeat sent Rovers through the trap door, just a point below Swindon Town. Final-day victory over Wrexham, where Walters doubled his seasonal goal tally after two first-half mistakes by Lee Roche against opponents who had Danny Williams and Lee Trundle sent off, left Rovers with a minus-four goal difference. Denis Lawrence in the Wrexham side was, at 6ft 7in, as tall as any opponent the club had faced. The matchday programme once again won the divisional Programme of the Year award.

Once Cameron and Bignot had registered their first goals for the club to see off Plymouth Argyle, Rovers enjoyed a hugely successful Worthington Cup run. A crowd of more than 25,000 at Goodison Park, which included more than 3,000 from Bristol, saw Premier Division Everton, who fielded the veteran England midfielder Paul Gascoigne as a substitute, stunned by Hogg's volleyed equaliser three minutes from time. Then, on an emotional night at the Memorial Stadium, Bignot's 58th-minute goal, after Ellington's initial shot had been saved, took Rovers into a penalty shoot-out where Plummer despatched the decisive kick to give the home side a memorable scalp. Sunderland then attracted a new record attendance of 11,433 to the ground, only for Don Hutchison's second goal of the game, off a post three minutes from time, to earn the Black Cats a 2-1 victory. Rovers lost at Cirencester Town in the Gloucestershire Senior Challenge Cup and, after two victories over Devon opposition, at Southend United in the LDV Vans Trophy. The first round of the FA Cup saw Rovers revisit the theatre of the previous May's end-of-season disappointment. Following a Sunday lunchtime kick-off to suit live coverage on the satellite television channel, Sky TV, Rovers took an eighth-minute lead through an own goal by Cardiff City's debutant defender, Andrew Jordan, a former Bristol City player, before being destroyed by four second-half goals, with the Zambian-born teenage striker Rob Earnshaw scoring a 31-minute hat-trick for the Division Three side.

2001/02

A ny promotion hopes that Rovers supporters may have entertained prior to the club's first ever season in the League's lowest division were dashed as Rovers struggled through an unrewarding and at times difficult campaign. A season that began with great optimism turned into one of the low points of the Pirates' long history. Ultimately a final Division Three placing of 23rd was only achieved thanks to the forlorn struggle of Halifax Town, whose second direct relegation from the Football League was confirmed by Sergio Ommel's late, scrambled winning goal for Rovers against Kidderminster Harriers in April. Nathan Ellington's 15 League goals made him the club's top scorer in the League, despite his March move to Wigan Athletic. Goalkeeper Scott Howie was the only ever-present in the side.

The new manager was unveiled as Gerald Charles James Francis, the very man who had led Rovers to the Division Three Championship in 1989/90 and had rebuilt the side in preparation for the long-awaited return to Bristol. On this occasion, however, he was not able to make many changes in personnel, though the experienced goalkeeper Howie signed on a free transfer. Rovers also acquired three of Francis' former protégés at Queen's Park Rangers in Alvin Bubb, Ross Weare and Rik Lopez. Mark Smith made a welcome return to first-team action at Carlisle United in October, his first start for the side since December 1998. Robbie Pethick moved to Brighton, where he won a Division Two Championship medal alongside former Rovers team-mates Michel Kuipers and Bobby Zamora, while Marcus Andreasson returned to Sweden to join Bryne FK.

The firework display that greeted the Rovers side and its returning manager for the opening day encounter at home to Torquay United proved a false dawn. An enthusiastic and patient crowd of more than 10,000 saw the Gulls' Tony Bedeau hit the post after only two minutes from Eifion Williams' right-wing cross before the first of four consecutive League and cup victories was earned. On the evening of 25 August, Rovers sat proudly on the top of the table. However Gerry Francis, reappointed to much acclaim in the close season, was never able to recapture the glory years of a decade earlier and stood down for personal reasons on Christmas Eve.

The second Francis era was marked by a goal drought of worrying proportions. Martin Cameron's crisp downward header five minutes from the end of a televised defeat at home to runaway League leaders Plymouth Argyle in October — the first Rovers game for over a decade shown live on terrestrial television — was the club's first for 491 minutes since the same player's 14-yard shot a minute before half-time at home to Oxford United. The next goal was 509 minutes away, Cameron's 54th-minute penalty being Rovers' first away goal for 646 minutes, shattering a previous worst run of 580 minutes set in the spring of 1986.

Defeat at Darlington was down partly to a spectacular last-minute save by the former Rovers goalkeeper Andy Collett from substitute Bubb's header. Other former Rovers players were to score decisive goals, Julian Alsop providing Cheltenham Town's 70th-minute winning goal on their first League visit to Bristol and Martin Phillips sweeping the ball home from a second-minute left-wing corner when eventual champions

Bristol Rovers 2001/02. Back row: Astafjevs, Bryant, Richards, Cameron, Foster, Trought, Clarke, Howie, Weare, Thomson, Foran, McKeever, A Shore. Second row: Brown (Kit Man), Bubb, Challis, J Shore, Plummer, Jones, Wilson, Ellington, Mauge, Hillier, Gall, Hogg, Pritchard, Smith, Wesson (Director Youth Education). Front row: Gingell (Fitness coach), Kite (Physio), Andrews, Stokes (Directors), Thompson (Asst Manager), D Dunford (Chairman), Francis (Manager), G Dunford (Vice-Chairman), Penrice (Coach), Craig and Bradshaw (Directors), Bater (Youth Coach), Dolling (Youth Dev.), Brinsford (Secretary)

Plymouth Argyle were the visitors. The Pilgrims scored after only 29 seconds in the return fixture, Marino Keith shooting home right-footed after Steve Adams' shot had rebounded off the post. Scott Partridge, a former Bristol City striker, scored in the first minute of each half of Rovers' first ever League encounter with Rushden and Diamonds, for whom the Jamaican International Onandi Lowe scored in both one-sided meetings. The former Rovers club captain Andy Tillson was outstanding in the Northamptonshire side's decisive 3-0 win at the Memorial Stadium in March. Drewe Broughton scored in both Rovers' first Football League encounters with Kidderminster, for whom midfielder Sam Shilton, whose father had appeared against Rovers as a 42-year-old in 1992, hit the crossbar in the fixture at Aggborough with a lob in the closing stages.

On 6 October, while England and Greece fought out a crucial World Cup qualifier, Rovers played at Brunton Park in the only 3 p.m. kick-off in the Nationwide League. The game was lost to Steve Halliday's 11th-minute goal from Mark Winstanley's left-wing cross before an understandably paltry crowd of 1,849, the lowest at a Rovers game since the fixture at York City in April 1988. There were six red cards accumulated by Rovers players during the season, five of them in Division Three with Mark Walters, dismissed 10 minutes from time at Exeter City in October, becoming the oldest ever Rovers recipient. When Rovers lost after leading at Swansea, both Astafjevs and Mike Trought were sent off in the closing four minutes. Nottingham referee Frazer Stretton dismissed three Kidderminster players at the Memorial Stadium on April Fool's Day. Abdou Sall was sent off after only four minutes for the foul that led to James Quinn's penalty, Rovers' first goal for 301 minutes, and was followed by goalkeeper Gary Montgomery and Ian Foster, with Rovers' substitute Sergio Ommel, who had earlier hit the crossbar, scoring the winning goal two minutes from time. Equally bizarrely, York City's Graham Potter became only the fourth opponent to score for both sides in a League encounter.

FOOTBALL LEAGUE DIVISION THREE

Date	Opponent	H/A	Score	Att	1 (G)	2	3	4	5	6	7	8	9	10	11	Substitutes	Goalscorers
11/08/00	TORQUAY UNITED	H	1-0	10127	HOWIE	WILSON	CHALLIS	FOSTER	THOMSON	TROUGHT	GALL	MAUGE	WEARE	BRYANT	HILLIER	PRITCHARD 8, CAMERON 12	FOSTER
18/08/00	SCUNTHORPE UNITED	A	2-1	3393	HOWIE	WILSON	CHALLIS	FOSTER	THOMSON	TROUGHT	GALL	MAUGE	WEARE	BRYANT	ASTAFIEVS	JONES 3, CAMERON 9	ASTAFIEVS V
25/08/00	LUTON TOWN	H	3-2	9057	HOWIE	WILSON	WILSON	FOSTER	THOMSON	TROUGHT	GALL	MAUGE	CAMERON	ELLINGTON	BRYANT	BUBB 10, LOPEZ 3	ELLINGTON, WEARE
27/08/00	DARLINGTON	A	0-1	4487	HOWIE	WILSON	JONES	FOSTER	THOMSON	FORAN	GALL	HOGG	CAMERON	ELLINGTON	BRYANT	BUBB 10, CAMERON 9	
01/09/00	SHREWSBURY TOWN	A	0-0	6942	HOWIE	WILSON	JONES	FOSTER	THOMSON	FORAN	BRYANT	HOGG	CAMERON	ELLINGTON	HILLIER	BUBB 10, CAMERON 9	
08/09/00	LEYTON ORIENT	H	1-3	5433	HOWIE	WILSON	JONES	FOSTER	THOMSON	FORAN	BRYANT	HOGG	CAMERON	ELLINGTON	HILLIER	CARLISLE M	
15/09/00	LINCOLN CITY	A	1-0	3204	HOWIE	WILSON	LOPEZ	FOSTER	THOMSON	FORAN	GALL	MAUGE	WEARE	ELLINGTON	HILLIER	CARLISLE W	
18/09/00	SOUTHEND UNITED	H	2-1	5743	HOWIE	WILSON	LOPEZ	FOSTER	THOMSON	FORAN	GALL	MAUGE	WEARE	HAMMOND	HILLIER	CARLISLE T	CAMERON, THOMSON
22/09/00	YORK CITY	H	2-2	6933	HOWIE	WILSON	CHALLIS	FOSTER	THOMSON	FORAN	GALL	MAUGE	HAMMOND	ELLINGTON	HILLIER	CAMERON 9	CAMERON, POTTER og
29/09/00	OXFORD UNITED	A	1-1	7678	HOWIE	WILSON	LOPEZ	FOSTER	THOMSON	FORAN	GALL	HOGG	CAMERON	HAMMOND	HILLIER	HAMMOND 9, WALTERS 2, BUBB 7	CAMERON
06/10/00	CARLISLE UNITED	H	0-1	1849	HOWIE	PRITCHARD	WILSON	FOSTER	SMITH	TROUGHT	CALL	TONER	CAMERON	GILROY	GALL	GILROY 9, WALTERS 11	
13/10/00	MACCLESFIELD	A	0-1	6554	HOWIE	WILSON	CHALLIS	FOSTER	THOMSON	CALL	BRYANT	TONER	CAMERON	GILROY	BRYANT	HAMMOND 10, BUBB 8	
20/10/00	HALIFAX TOWN	H	0-0	1898	HOWIE	WILSON	CHALLIS	FOSTER	THOMSON	BRYANT	GALL	TONER	CAMERON	ROSS	WALTERS	ROSS 7, BUBB 9	
28/10/00	EXETER CITY	A	0-1	3899	HOWIE	WILSON	CHALLIS	FOSTER	THOMSON	CARLISLE	GALL	OMMEL	GILROY	ROSS	WALTERS	CAMERON 10, JONES 3, BUBB 11	
04/11/00	PLYMOUTH ARGYLE	H	1-2	6889	SMITH	WILSON	CHALLIS	FOSTER	THOMSON	PLUMMER	HILLIER	OMMEL	BUBB	WALTERS	CHALLIS	ASTAFIEVS 3, ROSS 10	
07/11/00	KIDDERMINSTER HRS	A	0-2	3588	SMITH	WILSON	LOPEZ	THOMSON	FORAN	PLUMMER	HILLIER	HOGG	ROSS	ELLINGTON	CHALLIS	CAMERON 10, ROSS 11	
10/11/00	HALIFAX TOWN	A	2-0	6921	SMITH	WILSON	CHALLIS	THOMSON	FORAN	JONES	HILLIER	HOGG	GALL	ELLINGTON	WALTERS	ASTAFIEVS, ROSS 11	OMMEL, ELLINGTON
06/11/00	CHELTENHAM TOWN	H	0-0	4913	SMITH	WILSON	CHALLIS	THOMSON	FORAN	MAUGE	HILLIER	OMMEL	CAMERON	CHALLIS	BUBB	PLUMMER 2, CAMERON 9	
24/11/00	HULL CITY	H	0-1	9680	SMITH	WILSON	SANCHEZ LOPEZ	FOSTER	THOMSON	JONES	HILLIER	OMMEL	GALL	CHALLIS	ASTAFIEVS	BUBB 8, WALTERS 11	
20/11/00	MANSFIELD TOWN	H	0-0	5043	SMITH	WILSON	SANCHEZ LOPEZ	FOSTER	THOMSON	JONES	HILLIER	OMMEL	GALL	CHALLIS	McKEEVER	OMMEL 8, WALTERS 11	
01/12/00	ROCHDALE	A	1-3	4570	SMITH	WILSON	SANCHEZ LOPEZ	FOSTER	THOMSON	MAUGE	HILLIER	HOGG	WEARE	CAMERON	WALTERS	SMITH 2, PLUMMER 11, CAMERON 9	OMMEL, ELLINGTON
17/12/00	RUSHDEN & DMDS	A	0-0	4557	SMITH	WILSON	WILSON	FOSTER	THOMSON	WILSON	ASTAFIEVS	HOGG	WEARE	CHALLIS	SHORE D	FORAN 5, GALL 2, OMMEL 3	

LEAGUE DIVISION THREE (continued)

Date	Opponent	H/A	Score	Att	1 (G)	2	3	4	5	6	7	8	9	10	11	Substitutes	Goalscorers
29/12/01	RUSHDEN & DMDS	H	0-3	5240	SMITH	WILSON	JONES	FOSTER	THOMSON	FORAN	HILLIER	HOGG	OMMEL	WALTERS	OMMEL	WALTERS 11, JONES 3, LOPEZ 3	
12/01/01	EXETER CITY	H	1-1	6691	SMITH	WILSON	JONES	FOSTER	FORAN	PLUMMER	QUINN	HOGG	OMMEL	ELLINGTON	WALTERS	WALTERS 11, CAMERON 9	
15/01/01	SHREWSBURY TOWN	H	1-0	3475	SMITH	WILSON	CHALLIS	JONES	THOMSON	PLUMMER	QUINN	HOGG	OMMEL	ELLINGTON	GALL	WALTERS 7, MAUGE 3, CAMERON 9	ELLINGTON
19/01/01	TORQUAY UNITED	A	1-2	3493	SMITH	WILSON	CHALLIS	JONES	FORAN	PLUMMER	QUINN	TONER	OMMEL	ELLINGTON	SHORE D	ASTAFIEVS, OMMEL 11	
22/01/01	SWANSEA CITY	A	4-1	725	SMITH	WILSON	CHALLIS	JONES	FORAN	PLUMMER	HILLIER	TONER	OMMEL	ELLINGTON	McKEEVER	HOGG 10, RICHARDS 8, WALTERS 11	QUINN pen, OMMEL
02/02/01	OXFORD UNITED	H	2-0	7467	SMITH	WILSON	CHALLIS	FOSTER	THOMSON	PLUMMER	HILLIER	HOGG	OMMEL	ELLINGTON	McKEEVER	ASTAFIEVS 7, WALTERS 11	OMMEL, ELLINGTON
09/02/01	MACCLESFIELD	H	2-0	6482	SMITH	WILSON	CHALLIS	FOSTER	THOMSON	JONES	HILLIER	HOGG	GALL	CHALLIS	WALTERS	HOGG 10, TROUGHT 4, WALTERS 11	OMMEL
12/02/01	LINCOLN CITY	A	2-1	2149	SMITH	WILSON	CHALLIS	THOMSON	FORAN	JONES	HILLIER	HOGG	BUBB	CHALLIS	WALTERS	McKEEVER 10, OMMEL 8	OMMEL
16/02/02	LUTON TOWN	H	1-2	5651	SMITH	WILSON	CHALLIS	THOMSON	FORAN	JONES	HILLIER	HOGG	GALL	CHALLIS	McKEEVER	SMITH 2, McKEEVER 8	THOMAS
19/02/02	SOUTHEND UNITED	H	1-1	5741	SMITH	WILSON	CHALLIS	THOMSON	FORAN	WILSON	HILLIER	HOGG	WEARE	BUBB	WALTERS	WALTERS 11, McKEEVER 8	ARNDALE 2, CLARKE 1, GILROY 9
23/02/02	LINCOLN CITY	H	2-2	247	SMITH	WILSON	CHALLIS	FOSTER	THOMSON	JONES	QUINN	HOGG	THOMAS	ELLINGTON	GALL	JONES 7, WALTERS 11, GALL 5	
26/02/02	SOUTHEND UNITED	A	1-0	5651	SMITH	SANCHEZ LOPEZ	CHALLIS	FOSTER	THOMSON	CARLISLE	QUINN	TONER	THOMAS	ELLINGTON	SHORE D	SMITH, ASTAFIEVS 3,	
05/03/02	HARTLEPOOL	H	1-1	3699	SMITH	WILSON	CHALLIS	FOSTER	THOMSON	WILSON	HILLIER	HOGG	CAMERON	CHALLIS	SHORE D	CHALLIS 7, WALTERS 11, GALL 10	FORAN
12/03/02	HARTLEPOOL	A	1-3	7458	SMITH	WILSON	TROUGHT	FOSTER	THOMSON	FORAN	HILLIER	HOGG	CAMERON	ELLINGTON	CHALLIS	CHALLIS 7, WALTERS 11, GALL 10	
09/04/01	CARLISLE UNITED	H	5-3	7458	SMITH	WILSON	TROUGHT	FOSTER	THOMSON	ASTAFIEVS	HILLIER	HOGG	OMMEL	ELLINGTON	GALL	FORAN 5, WALTERS 11, JONES 3,	

FA CUP

Date	Opponent	H/A	Score	Att	1 (G)	2	3	4	5	6	7	8	9	10	11	Substitutes	Goalscorers
17/11/01	ALDERSHOT	A	0-0	5059	HOWIE	SMITH	CHALLIS	FOSTER	THOMSON	ASTAFIEVS	HILLIER	MAUGE	CAMERON	CAMERON	HILLIER	TROUGHT 6, BUBB 7	
27/11/01	ALDERSHOT	H	4-1	4848	HOWIE	SMITH	CHALLIS	FOSTER	THOMSON	WEARE	QUINN	MAUGE	CAMERON	WEARE	HILLIER	ASTAFIEVS, WALTERS 11, GALL 10	CAMERON pen
08/12/01	PLYMOUTH ARGYLE	A	3-2	6141	HOWIE	TROUGHT	HOGG	FOSTER	THOMSON	FORAN	CALL	MAUGE	CAMERON	CAMERON	CHALLIS	THOMAS 7, WALTERS 11, CALL 10	WILSON 8, BRYANT 8, GALL 10
18/12/01	PLYMOUTH ARGYLE	H	3-2	5763	HOWIE	FORAN	HOGG	FORAN	WILSON	CARLISLE	QUINN	HOGG	WEARE	GALL	ASTAFIEVS	OMMEL, HOGG, ELLINGTON	
06/01/02	DERBY COUNTY	A	3-1	18549	HOWIE	SMITH	LOPEZ R	FORAN	JONES	CARLISLE	QUINN	HOGG	CAMERON	ELLINGTON	GALL	McKEEVER 8, WALTERS 11,	
05/02/02	GILLINGHAM	A	0-1	9772	HOWIE	WILSON	CHALLIS	WILSON	JONES	CARLISLE	HOGG	HOGG	HAMMOND	ELLINGTON	CHALLIS	ELLINGTON 3	

LEAGUE CUP

Date	Opponent	H/A	Score	Att	1 (G)	2	3	4	5	6	7	8	9	10	11	Substitutes	Goalscorers
21/08/01	WYCOMBE WDRS	A	1-0	3166	HOWIE	WILSON	CHALLIS	FOSTER	THOMSON	TROUGHT	CALL	MAUGE	WEARE	ELLINGTON	HILLIER	CAMERON 9, JONES 3,	HILLIER
11/09/01	BIRMINGHAM CITY	A	0-3	5582	HOWIE	WILSON	CHALLIS	FOSTER	THOMSON	FORAN	CALL	MAUGE	WEARE	ELLINGTON	HILLIER	CAMERON 9, HAMMOND 11	

LD VANS TROPHY

Date	Opponent	H/A	Score	Att	1 (G)	2	3	4	5	6	7	8	9	10	11	Substitutes	Goalscorers
31/10/01	YEOVIL TOWN *	H	4-3	4301	HOWIE	SMITH	CHALLIS	FOSTER	THOMSON	FORAN	GALL	MAUGE	CAMERON	ROSS	PLUMMER	BUBB 7, WALTERS 6, BRYANT 8, GALL 10	CAMERON 9, BUBB 8
05/12/01	DAGENHAM & R'BRG	A	4-1	3028	HOWIE	WILSON	CHALLIS	THOMSON	FORAN	TROUGHT	HOGG	OMMEL	CAMERON	ELLINGTON	PLUMMER	WILSON 8, CAMERON 9, GALL 10	WILSON 9, BUBB 8
09/01/02	BRISTOL CITY	A	0-3	1736	HOWIE	WILSON	CHALLIS	PLUMMER	FORAN	TROUGHT	HOGG	GALL	OMMEL	CHALLIS	CHALLIS	CAMERON 9, WALTERS 11, GALL 10	

*AET Score at 90 mins 1-1. Rovers won 5-4 on pens

PLAYERS	APP	SUB	GLS
ARNDALE N		1	
ASTAFIEVS V	14	5	1
BRYANT S	8	5	
BUBB A	10		
CAMERON M	14	14	4
CARLISLE W		5	
CARLISLE T	28	1	
CHALLIS T	46		
CLARKE R			
ELLINGTON N	27		2
FORAN M	30	1	
FOSTER S	33		15
GALL K	25	5	5
GILROY D	2		4
HAMMOND E	2		3
HILLIER D	27	1	
HOGG L	22	1	
HOWIE S	14		
JONES S	5	2	
LOPEZ R	5	4	
MAUGE R	14	2	
McKEEVER M	5	8	
OMMEL S	18	5	8
PLUMMER D	12	13	
PRITCHARD D	4		
QUINN J	6		
RICHARDS J	1		
ROSS N	2	3	
SANCHEZ LOPEZ C	6		
SHORE D	2	9	
SMITH M	17	2	
THOMAS J	7	3	
THOMSON A	29	2	
TONER C	6	1	
TROUGHT M	37	1	
WALTERS M	7	19	
WEARE R	9	1	
WILSON C	38		
OWN GOAL			1

His quickly taken 74th-minute free-kick from the edge of the penalty area was cancelled out 10 minutes later when he steered Ellington's cross past his own goalkeeper to give Rovers a late lead.

The new manager was Garry Thompson, who had worked as Rovers' coach since 1997 but whose temporary tenure of the post 12 months earlier had seen Rovers relegated. He had enjoyed a long career with many clubs and had won six England Under-21 caps while appearing as centre-forward for Coventry City. Thompson's time as manager opened with an impressive series of performances and some high-scoring and high-profile victories. Responding to a change in leadership, Rovers crushed Leyton Orient in a highly entertaining Boxing Day fixture at the Memorial Stadium. Ellington's first hat-trick for the club, one of three in less than a month, all came from low drives, two in

Gerry Francis returned to Rovers for a second spell but left at Christmas after a run of poor results and performances

three first-half minutes and a third after 73 minutes to register Rovers' 3,000th home League goal. With the former Rovers defender Matt Lockwood on as a half-time substitute, Orient rallied with three second-half goals of their own and Rovers ran out 5-3 winners. After the phenomenal result in the third round of the FA Cup, Ellington also grabbed three goals in a deceptively easy 4-1 victory at home to Swansea City in January, before Rovers endured a dismal run of results through the spring.

After the initial honeymoon period, Rovers lapsed into their losing ways. One particularly poor run in the spring of six consecutive defeats – just one short of the club record set in 1961 – was halted by Ellington's right-footed 64th minute equaliser at Hartlepool United, his final goal for the club. One cause for optimism was the goalscoring form of Dutch-born Ommel, a foil for Ellington signed on a free transfer from Icelandic football, where he had played alongside Moussa Dagnogo at KR Reykjavik, and was to end the season as Rovers' second highest goalscorer. Another overseas-born player was Carlos López Sánchez, who joined Rovers in February from the Madrid side Getafe. Thompson left the club after a run of one win in 13 games and, with Phil Bater temporarily guiding Rovers through the final three defeats, Rovers appointed their former winger Ray Graydon to the post of manager on 26 April 2002.

Away from the pitch, too, there were rumblings of discontent. On the last Friday in October, the club was temporarily put up for sale by the majority shareholders, Ron Craig and Geoff Dunford. The latter succeeded his father as club chairman and there were further additions to the board of directors in the spring. New floodlights to an American design were installed at a cost of £150,000 and first used for the convincing victory over Swansea City in January. The older floodlights were dismantled on 28 June

2002 and transported by a Bridgwater firm to their new home at Aldershot Town's training ground. Yet it was the frozen pitch that caused the abandonment after only 12 minutes of the home game with Hartlepool United in mid-December, the first Rovers home game to be abandoned since March 1982.

The oasis in the desert that was the 2001/02 season, was Rovers' FA Cup run. A hesitant pair of games with Ryman Premier Division side Aldershot Town was decided only when Astafjevs' 84th-minute deflected shot brought a replay victory, with the visitors' Richard Gell later sent off. Visibly growing in confidence, Rovers then earned a deserved draw at high-flying Plymouth Argyle, where Mark Walters' 59th-minute equaliser made him the second oldest scorer in the club's FA Cup history. An enthralling replay saw Rovers' 2-0 lead clawed back by a powerful visiting side, before Ellington struck the winner with a rasping drive three minutes from time to set up a third round tie away to Premiership Derby County.

Since the establishment of the Premiership in 1992, no top division side had lost to one from below Division Two. The achievement of Bristol Rovers in winning away to Derby County ranks alongside the greatest of the club's successes. It was the seventh occasion that Rovers had won an FA Cup tie against top division opponents but, given Rovers' League status, it was a most memorable occasion. Moreover, the only other away victory over a club of this stature had been at Burnley in 1958, when Rovers were in the old Division Two. A ground record of 6,602 away supporters were among the 18,000 crowd at Pride Park on the first Sunday in January to witness the biggest shock of the third round.

Mart Poom, with 77 full International caps for Estonia, played in goal for Derby, with Argentinians Horacio Carbonari and Luciano Zavagno in front of him and two highly experienced Italians in the side in the shape of Fabrizio Ravanelli and Benito Carbone. After just 14 minutes Rovers took the lead when Howie's long kick was headed over the advancing goalkeeper by Ellington. The same player added a second five minutes before half-time with a right-foot shot after a mazy run had taken him past François Grenet and the former Lens defender Youl Mawene. Astonishingly, with a goal that would have graced any occasion, Ellington completed his hat-trick after 62 minutes with a cracking right-foot volley and there was even time for Mark Walters to hit a post late in the game. Even a scrambled consolation goal, two minutes from time from the White Feather himself, Ravanelli, could not mar the occasion for the Rovers players and supporters. Incredibly, it was the first time ever that a Rovers player had scored three goals in an away FA Cup tie. Then, armed with the knowledge that a trip to play the eventual FA Cup winners at Highbury awaited the victors, Rovers were outplayed at Gillingham in the fourth round, losing to a side that included former Rovers players Marcus Browning and Gui Ipoua when Ty Gooden's right-footed free-kick after 32 minutes was headed into his own net by the unfortunate Ronnie Maugé.

Meanwhile, the Worthington Cup brought a degree of revenge for Rovers, in orange shirts and socks after their black and grey quarters were deemed to constitute a colour clash, were able to win at Wycombe Wanderers, the club whose victory in May had condemned Rovers to Division Three. The single goal came from an unlikely source, as experienced midfielder David Hillier struck his first goal for the club after 65 minutes. His second goal came at home to Luton Town four days later. Andy Johnson and

Nathan Ellington enjoyed another good season the highlight being scoring a hat-trick to knock out Premiership side Derby County from the FA Cup. He was later sold to Wigan Athletic on transfer deadline day

Michael Johnson were both on the scoresheet as the 2001 beaten finalists Birmingham City were comfortable winners at the Memorial Stadium in the second round. The LDV Vans Trophy also ended in a 3-0 defeat, this time at Ashton Gate, but only after victories over non-League opposition. Michael McIndoe's cross-shot from the right had given Tom White's Yeovil Town the lead, but he was to miss the decisive kick as Rovers won the penalty shoot-out 5-4 and Ellington's first two goals for over three months paved the way to a comfortable victory over Dagenham & Redbridge.

Kevin Gall represented the Welsh Under-21 side as a substitute against Belarus in October, while Astafjevs won the latest of his impressive tally of Latvian caps in playing against Scotland on the same night. To the summer of 2002, Astafjevs has appeared 94 times for Latvia. Neil Arndale, a final-day debutant for Rovers had represented England in the European Under-17 Championships earlier in the season. Former Rovers players Bobby Zamora and Stuart Taylor were in the England Under-21 squad for the European Championships held in Switzerland in May 2002 and goalkeeper Nigel Martyn travelled to the Far East as part of the England squad for the 2002 World Cup finals. Finally, Rovers hosted the International on Mothering Sunday between England Under-18 and their Lithuanian counterparts, which the home side won by four clear goals.

Denis Dunford, the former chairman of Bristol Rovers, served the club from 1986, and was replaced by his son Geoff

2002/03

With fifteen minutes to go in the penultimate game of the season, Wayne Carlisle curled his right-footed twenty-metre free-kick past Darlington's former Rovers goalkeeper Andy Collett to secure Rovers' third consecutive victory and ensure the Pirates' continued status as a Football League club. Such a nail-biting conclusion to the season had tried the patience of even the most confident supporter and had seemed implausible at the start of the campaign. Newly appointed as manager, the former Rovers outside-right Ray Graydon and his assistant John Still, a former manager at both Barnet and Peterborough United as well as the captain of the Bishop's Stortford side which defeated Ilford 4-1 in the 1974 FA Amateur Cup final at Wembley, had recruited a number of players for the 2002/03 season, which the club approached in a positive frame of mind. Graydon instilled in his players a greater sense of discipline and this certainly had a bearing on their eleventh-hour escape from the clutches of relegation. However, twenty-one debutants were amongst the thirty-three players used as the manager's first season at his home town club proved tougher than he had envisaged.

The Mansfield Town defender Adam Barrett, who had experienced promotion from the basement division in 2001/02, was joined in the centre of defence by the untried former Sheffield Wednesday and West Ham United youngster Anwar Uddin, whilst Brentford's former Eire Under-21 international Danny Boxall accompanied them at full-back. A decade of Football League experience had hinted that Kevin Austin could become a pivotal figure in the Rovers story, though the powerful former Cambridge United defender's Rovers debut was delayed through injury until late

Bristol born, former Rovers winger, Ray Graydon was appointed Rovers manager for season 2002/03

September. Oxford United's Rob Quinn, another former Eire Under-21 international and erstwhile colleague at Crystal Palace of Danny Boxall, joined Wayne Carlisle, now joining Rovers on a permanent basis, in midfield. Two new strikers, in the form of Paul Tait, who had fallen out of favour at Crewe Alexandra, and the influential Swindon Town player Giuliano Grazioli, gave early promise of their goalscoring potential. Grazioli had been given his first break in the professional game by John Still at Peterborough and, once Still had moved to Barnet, had scored five times against his former manager's side when the two clubs met in a Division Three game at Underhill in September 1998, Peterborough winning 9-1.

With six debutants in the side, Rovers took a fifth-minute lead at Plainmoor on the opening day of the 2002/03 season, Grazioli scoring the first goal recorded in the Third Division that season. However, succumbing to a Torquay United comeback, Rovers discovered that further struggles lay ahead. Tait, who had not scored a league goal for two and a half years, missed a 41st-minute penalty at Carlisle and was sent off on the stroke of half time at Darlington in October. Grazioli missed a second-half penalty at home to Exeter City. Rovers were two goals behind at both Scunthorpe, where a point was rescued by Wayne Carlisle's successful last-minute penalty kick, and before the

FOOTBALL LEAGUE DIVISION THREE

SEASON 2002/03

Date	Opponent	V	Score	ATT	G	2	3	4	5	6	7	8	9	10	11	SUBSTITUTES	GOALSCORERS
10/08/02	TORQUAY UNITED	A	1-2	4937	HOWIE	BOXALL	CHALLIS	UDDIN	BARRETT	BRYANT	CARLISLE	QUINN	TAIT	GRAZIOLI	McKEEVER	RICHARDS 6, ASTAFJEVS 11	GRAZIOLI
13/08/02	HULL CITY	H	1-1	7501	HOWIE	BOXALL	CHALLIS	UDDIN	BARRETT	BRYANT	CARLISLE	QUINN	TAIT	GRAZIOLI	McKEEVER	ASTAFJEVS 7, GILROY 9	GRAZIOLI
17/08/02	ROCHDALE	A	1-2	6478	HOWIE	BOXALL	CHALLIS	UDDIN	BARRETT	BRYANT	CARLISLE	QUINN	TAIT	GRAZIOLI	McKEEVER	HOGG 6, RICHARDS 11	BRYANT
24/08/02	CARLISLE UNITED	H	0-0	6475	CLARKE	BOXALL	CHALLIS	UDDIN	BARRETT	HYDE	CARLISLE	QUINN	TAIT	GRAZIOLI	McKEEVER	GALL 10	
27/08/02	SWANSEA CITY	H	3-1	6644	HOWIE	BOXALL	CHALLIS	UDDIN	BARRETT	HOGG	CARLISLE	QUINN	TAIT	GRAZIOLI	ASTAFJEVS	McKEEVER 11, BRYANT 6, RICHARDS 10	GRAZIOLI, TAIT, ASTAFJEVS
31/08/02	SCUNTHORPE UNITED	A	2-2	3778	HOWIE	BOXALL	CHALLIS	UDDIN	BARRETT	BRYANT	CARLISLE	QUINN	TAIT	GRAZIOLI	ASTAFJEVS	WARREN 11, BRYANT 6, RICHARDS 10	QUINN, CARLISLE (pen)
08/09/02	MACCLESFIELD TOWN	A	1-2	1814	HOWIE	BOXALL	CHALLIS	UDDIN	BARRETT	HYDE	CARLISLE	QUINN	TAIT	GRAZIOLI	ASTAFJEVS	RICHARDS 10, HOGG 6	CARLISLE (pen)
14/09/02	EXETER CITY	H	1-1	6498	HOWIE	BOXALL	CHALLIS	UDDIN	BARRETT	LEE	CARLISLE	QUINN	COOTE	GRAZIOLI	ARNDALE	WARREN 11	BOXALL
17/09/02	BURY	H	2-1	5493	HOWIE	BOXALL	CHALLIS	UDDIN	BARRETT	LEE	CARLISLE	QUINN	TAIT	COOTE	HOGG	HOGG 10, GALL 7, McKEEVER 11	BRYANT, CARLISLE
21/09/02	SHREWSBURY TOWN	A	5-2	3510	HOWIE	BOXALL	CHALLIS	UDDIN	BARRETT	BRYANT	CARLISLE	QUINN	TAIT	GRAZIOLI	McKEEVER	McKEEVER 6, AUSTIN 2, HOGG 11	GRAZIOLI 3, CARLISLE, ASTAFJEVS
28/09/02	KIDDERMINSTER HRS	H	1-2	9447	HOWIE	BOXALL	CHALLIS	UDDIN	BARRETT	BRYANT	CARLISLE	QUINN	TAIT	GRAZIOLI	ASTAFJEVS	McKEEVER 6, RICHARDS 10, HOGG 11	CARLISLE
05/10/02	DARLINGTON	A	0-1	2849	HOWIE	BOXALL	BRYANT	UDDIN	BARRETT	AUSTIN	CARLISLE	QUINN	TAIT	GRAZIOLI	ASTAFJEVS	GRAZIOLI 4	
12/10/02	LINCOLN CITY	H	2-0	6135	CLARKE	BOXALL	BRYANT	UDDIN	BARRETT	AUSTIN	CARLISLE	QUINN	TAIT	COOTE	McKEEVER	McKEEVER 11, RICHARDS 6, AUSTIN 10, GALL 11	COOTE, GRAZIOLI (pen)
19/10/02	YORK CITY	H	1-2	3616	HOWIE	BOXALL	CHALLIS	UDDIN	BARRETT	AUSTIN	CARLISLE	QUINN	TAIT	GRAZIOLI	McKEEVER	BOXALL 3, BRYANT 4, RICHARDS 6	McKEEVER
26/10/02	LEYTON ORIENT	H	1-2	6625	HOWIE	BOXALL	CHALLIS	PLUMMER	BARRETT	LEE	CARLISLE	QUINN	TAIT	GRAZIOLI	McKEEVER	GILROY 10, BRYANT 4, RICHARDS 11	GRAZIOLI (pen)
29/10/02	HARTLEPOOL UTD	A	0-1	3889	HOWIE	BOXALL	BRYANT	UDDIN	BARRETT	HYDE	ASTAFJEVS	QUINN	TAIT	GRAZIOLI	HODGES	HODGES 10, ASTAFJEVS 7, CARLISLE 10	
02/11/02	AFC BOURNEMOUTH	A	0-1	6924	HOWIE	BOXALL	CHALLIS	UDDIN	BARRETT	LEE	CARLISLE	QUINN	TAIT	GRAZIOLI	ARNDALE	HOGG 6, GRAZIOLI 4	
09/11/02	SOUTHEND UNITED	H	0-3	5691	HOWIE	BOXALL	CHALLIS	UDDIN	BARRETT	BRYANT	CARLISLE	QUINN	TAIT	GRAZIOLI	McKEEVER	BOXALL 3, BRYANT 6, RICHARDS 6	
23/11/02	WREXHAM	A	1-2	6328	HOWIE	BOXALL	ROSE	UDDIN	BARRETT	AUSTIN	ASTAFJEVS	QUINN	TAIT	STREET	LLEWELLYN	ASTAFJEVS 8, STREET 5	LLEWELLYN
30/11/02	RUSHDEN & DMDS	H	0-3	3960	HOWIE	BOXALL	ROSE	UDDIN	BARRETT	AUSTIN	CARLISLE	QUINN	TAIT	STREET	LLEWELLYN	BRYANT 4, BOXALL 2, STREET 11	
14/12/02	OXFORD UNITED	A	1-2	5864	HOWIE	BOXALL	ROSE	ASTAFJEVS	BARRETT	AUSTIN	CARLISLE	QUINN	TAIT	STREET	HYDE	STREET 11, BOXALL 3, TAIT 9	STREET
21/12/02	CAMBRIDGE UNITED	H	1-0	3370	HOWIE	BOXALL	ROSE	ASTAFJEVS	BARRETT	AUSTIN	CARLISLE	QUINN	TAIT	GILROY	STREET	GRAZIOLI 10, TAIT 9, CARLISLE 11	GILROY
26/12/02	SWANSEA CITY	A	1-3	5079	ROSE	BOXALL	CHALLIS	ASTAFJEVS	BARRETT	AUSTIN	CARLISLE	QUINN	TAIT	GILROY	STREET	GILROY 7, CARLISLE 10	ASTAFJEVS
28/12/02	BOSTON UNITED	H	0-1	8311	ROSE	BOXALL	CHALLIS	STREET	BARRETT	AUSTIN	ASTAFJEVS	QUINN	TAIT	GILROY	HYDE	ASTAFJEVS 7, GALL 11	
04/01/03	HULL CITY	A	0-1	14913	HOWIE	BOXALL	CHALLIS	ASTAFJEVS	BARRETT	AUSTIN	CARLISLE	QUINN	TAIT	ALLEN	HYDE	ALLEN 10, McKEEVER 11	
14/01/03	TORQUAY UNITED	H	1-0	6196	HOWIE	BOXALL	CHALLIS	ASTAFJEVS	BARRETT	AUSTIN	CARLISLE	QUINN	TAIT	ALLEN	STREET	ALLEN 11, HOGG 4	QUINN
18/01/03	BOSTON UNITED	A	2-1	6617	ROSE	BOXALL	CHALLIS	ASTAFJEVS	BARRETT	AUSTIN	CARLISLE	QUINN	TAIT	STREET	LLEWELLYN	ALLEN 10, HOGG 4	ALLEN, HOGG
25/01/03	SCUNTHORPE UNITED	H	0-0	3209	ROSE	BOXALL	CHALLIS	ASTAFJEVS	BARRETT	AUSTIN	STREET	QUINN	TAIT	GILROY	LLEWELLYN	CARLISLE 9, RAMMELL 11	
01/02/03	CARLISLE UNITED	A	1-2	6347	ROSE	BOXALL	CHALLIS	ASTAFJEVS	BARRETT	AUSTIN	STREET	QUINN	TAIT	GILROY	LLEWELLYN	DI PIEDI 11, STREET 9	GILROY 10
08/02/03	SOUTHEND UNITED	A	2-2	7257	HOWIE	BOXALL	HYDE	ASTAFJEVS	BARRETT	AUSTIN	STREET	QUINN	DI PIEDI	GRAZIOLI	LLEWELLYN	DI PIEDI 11, STREET 9	LLEWELLYN 2
15/02/03	AFC BOURNEMOUTH	H	2-2	4708	HOWIE	BOXALL	HYDE	ASTAFJEVS	BARRETT	AUSTIN	STREET	QUINN	DI PIEDI	GRAZIOLI	LLEWELLYN	GRAZIOLI 10, McKEEVER 11	GRAZIOLI 10, TAIT 9
22/02/03	MACCLESFIELD TOWN	H	0-0	6347	HOWIE	BOXALL	ANDERSON	ASTAFJEVS	BARRETT	AUSTIN	CARLISLE	QUINN	TAIT	GRAZIOLI	STREET	PARKER 7, McKEEVER 7	
01/03/03	EXETER CITY	A	0-1	6005	HOWIE	BOXALL	ANDERSON	UDDIN	BARRETT	AUSTIN	CARLISLE	QUINN	TAIT	GRAZIOLI	STREET	CARLISLE 11, ALLEN 9, HOGG 4	
04/03/03	BURY	A	1-0	5759	HOWIE	BOXALL	ANDERSON	HYDE	BARRETT	AUSTIN	CARLISLE	QUINN	TAIT	GRAZIOLI	STREET	TAIT 9, McKEEVER 11	CARLISLE
08/03/03	SHREWSBURY TOWN	H	2-1	2454	HOWIE	BOXALL	ANDERSON	HYDE	BARRETT	AUSTIN	CARLISLE	QUINN	TAIT	GRAZIOLI	STREET	ALLEN 10, McKEEVER 11	CARLISLE, GRAZIOLI (pen)
15/03/03	LEYTON ORIENT	A	2-1	6839	HOWIE	BOXALL	ANDERSON	HYDE	BARRETT	AUSTIN	CARLISLE	QUINN	TAIT	GRAZIOLI	RAMMELL	PARKER 3, ALLEN 10, ASTAFJEVS 11	ASTAFJEVS, CARLISLE
18/03/03	YORK CITY	H	0-1	4081	HOWIE	PARKER	ANDERSON	HYDE	BARRETT	AUSTIN	CARLISLE	QUINN	TAIT	GRAZIOLI	RAMMELL	TAIT 9, GILROY 10, ASTAFJEVS 11	
22/03/03	HARTLEPOOL UTD	H	0-2	8248	HOWIE	PARKER	ANDERSON	HYDE	BARRETT	AUSTIN	ASTAFJEVS	QUINN	RAMMELL	LLEWELLYN	GRAZIOLI	GILROY 10, HOGG 11, GALL 8	
29/03/03	LINCOLN CITY	A	1-2	6557	HOWIE	PARKER	ANDERSON	HYDE	BARRETT	AUSTIN	ASTAFJEVS	QUINN	RAMMELL	GRAZIOLI	LLEWELLYN	ALLEN 10, HOGG 11, CARLISLE 3	HYDE
05/04/03	DARLINGTON	H		3550	HOWIE	PARKER	ANDERSON	HYDE	BARRETT	ASTAFJEVS	CARLISLE	QUINN	TAIT	ALLEN	ASTAFJEVS	HODGES, ASTAFJEVS, BRYANT	HYDE
12/04/03	OXFORD UNITED	H		6736	PARKER	BOXALL	AUSTIN	PLUMMER	BARRETT	ASTAFJEVS	CARLISLE	QUINN	TAIT	GRAZIOLI	BRYANT	RAMMELL, ASTAFJEVS	TAIT
19/04/03	CAMBRIDGE UNITED	A		1658	PARKER	BOXALL	AUSTIN	PLUMMER	BARRETT	PARKER	ASTAFJEVS	QUINN	TAIT	GRAZIOLI	BRYANT	LLEWELLYN, ASTAFJEVS	
21/04/03	WREXHAM	H		3330	PARKER	BOXALL	CHALLIS	AUSTIN	BARRETT	ASTAFJEVS	CARLISLE	QUINN	DI PIEDI	GRAZIOLI	BRYANT	RAMMELL 2, ASTAFJEVS	LLEWELLYN 2
26/04/03	RUSHDEN & DMDS	A		7563	PARKER	BOXALL	CHALLIS	AUSTIN	BARRETT	ASTAFJEVS	CARLISLE	QUINN	RAMMELL	LLEWELLYN	BRYANT	RAMMELL 4, BOXALL 2, STREET 11	BRYANT, CARLISLE
03/05/03	KIDDERMINSTER HRS	H	1-1	3872	PARKER	BOXALL	CHALLIS	AUSTIN	BARRETT	AUSTIN	CARLISLE	QUINN	TAIT	LLEWELLYN	HODGES	STREET 7	

LEAGUE CUP

Date	Opponent	V	Score	ATT	G	2	3	4	5	6	7	8	9	10	11	SUBSTITUTES	GOALSCORERS
20/08/02	BOSTON UNITED	H	0-2	4555	HOWIE	BOXALL	CHALLIS	UDDIN	BARRETT	HOGG	CARLISLE	QUINN	TAIT	GRAZIOLI	McKEEVER	GALL 7, RICHARDS 9	GRAZIOLI

FA CUP

Date	Opponent	V	Score	ATT	G	2	3	4	5	6	7	8	9	10	11	SUBSTITUTES	GOALSCORERS
16/11/02	RUNCORN HALTON	H	0-0	4135	HOWIE	BOXALL	CHALLIS	PLUMMER	BARRETT	ASTAFJEVS	CARLISLE	QUINN	TAIT	ALLEN	BRYANT	AUSTIN 3, BRYANT 11	
26/11/02	RUNCORN HALTON*	A	3-1	2434	HOWIE	BOXALL	CHALLIS	AUSTIN	BARRETT	ASTAFJEVS	CARLISLE	QUINN	TAIT	GILROY	BRYANT	GILROY 10, HOGG 11	GRAZIOLI og, GRAZIOLI (pen)
07/12/02	ROCHDALE	H	1-1	4369	ROSE	BOXALL	AUSTIN	PLUMMER	BARRETT	HYDE	CARLISLE	QUINN	TAIT	GRAZIOLI	ASTAFJEVS	ALLEN 10, CALL 8	UDDIN, ASTAFJEVS
17/12/02	ROCHDALE	A	2-3	2206	HOWIE	BOXALL	BRYANT	AUSTIN	BARRETT	PARKER	CARLISLE	QUINN	TAIT	ALLEN	ASTAFJEVS	HOGG 11, CARLISLE 3	COOTE

LD VANS TROPHY

Date	Opponent	V	Score	ATT	G	2	3	4	5	6	7	8	9	10	11	SUBSTITUTES	GOALSCORERS
22/10/02	EXETER CITY	A	0-1	1613	CLARKE	BOXALL	BRYANT	AUSTIN	BARRETT	PARKER	ASTAFJEVS	QUINN	LEE	COOTE	McKEEVER	GILROY 11, GALL 4	

*AET Score at 90 mins 1-1

PLAYERS	APP	SUB	GLS	SQUAD NO
ALLEN B	5	3	1	31
ANDERSON I	14			18
ARNDALE N		7		23
ASTAFJEVS V	26	7	8	25
AUSTIN K	31	2		6
BARRETT A	45		6	
BOXALL D	35	4		
BRYANT S	14	8	1	15
CARLISLE W	35	6	7	11
CHALLIS T	16			21
CLARKE A	4			1
COOTE A	2	1		28
DI PIEDI M	3	2	1	19
GALL K	8			18
GILROY D	28	6	11	
GRAZIOLI G	1		17	10
HODGES L	7	1		
HOGG C	7	8	1	16
HOWIE S	44			
HYDE G	21	4		12
LEE D		1		3
LLEWELLYN C	14	9	2	27
McKEEVER M	7	9		
PARKER S	13			34
PLUMMER C	2	44		30
QUINN R	44	2	4	22
RAMMELL A		8	8	
RICHARDS J	8	17		
ROSE R	9			33
STREET K	32			32
TAIT P	33	8	1	
UDDIN A	17	1	4	
WARREN C	2			12
OWN GOAL			1	

Bristol Rovers 2002-03. Back row: Giuliano Grazioli, Drew Shore, Anwar Uddin, Rob Scott, Kevin Austin, Scott Howie, Ryan Clarke, Paul Tait, David Gilroy, Rob Quinn, Vitalijs Astafjevs, Mark McKeever. Middle row: Rod Wesson (Youth Education), Stewart Naughton (Centre of Excellence), Danny Boxall, Kevin Gall, Wayne Carlisle, Justin Richards, Adam Barrett, Simon Bryant, Lewis Hogg, Dwayne Plummer, Trevor Challis, Steve Bissix (Physio), Roger Harding (Kit Manager). Front row: Roger Brinsford (Secretary), Steve Burns, Colin Williams, Denis Dunford (all Directors), John Still (Asst Manager), Geoff Dunford (Chairman), Ray Graydon (Team Manager), Ron Craig (Vice Chairman), Phil Bater (Youth Football), Bob Andrews, Barry Bradshaw (Directors), Phil Kite (Physio), Toni Watola (Co. Secretary)

Sky TV cameras at Macclesfield. Rochdale, who arrived without their kit, borrowed Rovers' third choice of black and stone quartered shirts and proceeded to hit the bar twice before half time en route to a victory at the Memorial Stadium which confirmed Rovers' worst start to a season since 1985/86. By this stage, Rovers were also out of the Worthington Cup, defeated at home by Boston United, who were to find themselves four goals behind to Cardiff City by half-time in the next round. By dint of their poor league placing in 2001/02 and the fact that Ipswich Town had been given a bye thanks to their UEFA Cup success, Rovers were obliged to play off for a once-automatic place in the first-round draw. Having staged the first-ever League Cup tie in 1960, Rovers had now also hosted – and lost – the first preliminary round tie in the history of the competition.

Yet, good times lay around the corner. Tait's long-awaited first goal, a 52nd-minute header in the home win over Swansea City, after which he hit the crossbar with an audacious forty-yard lob, proved the break he needed. The former Everton trainee was to score in four consecutive home games in the autumn. His striking partner, Grazioli, scored in each of his first two games in a Rovers shirt and added a hat-trick in the space of thirty minutes at Shrewsbury Town in September, when Rovers hit a purple patch. The 5-2 victory at Gay Meadow, coming as it did on the back of a hard-fought home win over Bury, helped propel Rovers away from the now-customary penultimate position towards mid-table safety. A settled side and the promise of better days to come was bolstered in the autumn with renewed talk of converting the Memorial Stadium into an all-seater complex capable of holding 20,000 spectators. Furthermore, plans for a multi-million-pound sports development project, backed by South Gloucestershire Council, were drawn up to include a 10,000m² purpose-built sports complex, floodlit all-weather pitches, laboratories, a gymnasium, indoor theatres and studios and the promise of vocational and educational courses being on offer.

As Christmas approached, Rovers hit the bottom of Division Three for the first time, after a club record run of eight consecutive league defeats that followed York City's Stephen Blackstone's last-minute equaliser at Bootham Crescent. During this disastrous run, there was a four-game spell in which Rovers failed to score, the worst result coming at home to Wrexham, who managed nineteen shots on target to Rovers' two. The record-breaking eighth defeat in a row was a 3-1 loss at Cambridge in December, in which Sonny Parker conceded a debut own goal after seventeen minutes, to emulate the feat of John Hills who, in August 1961, had scored for Liverpool after 65 minutes of his first appearance for Rovers. Combined with Boston United's emphatic 6-0 win at home to Shrewsbury Town, this result left Rovers at an all-time low.

However, the process of rebuilding had already started. Graydon's ability to search far and wide for extra players began to reap its rewards as seven players arrived on loan. Of these, Adrian Coote and Chris Llewellyn, whose two goals at Wrexham brought Rovers back from 2-0 down only for the side to lose to a Carlos Edwards goal two minutes from time, both offered international experience, while David Lee had played for Hull City against Rovers in November 2001. Six highly experienced players were signed as the season progressed and they had major roles to play as the relegation battle developed. Bradley Allen was a brother of the England international Clive and the son of Les, a league and FA Cup double winner with Spurs in 1960/61; Graham Hyde, sent off at Cambridge, had appeared in FA Cup and League Cup finals whilst on the books of Sheffield Wednesday; Ijah Anderson, Kevin Street and Lee Hodges possessed vast experience of life in the lower divisions; whilst the former Manchester United youngster Andy Rammell had scored Barnsley's opening goal when Rovers were defeated 5-1 at Twerton Park in November 1992 as well as being sent off when Rovers defeated Wycombe Wanderers at Adams Park in September 2000. The loosening of the club's purse strings by chairman Geoff Dunford and his supportive board proved to be highly significant in Rovers' ultimately successful battle against relegation to the Conference.

Nevertheless, Rovers had an intense battle on their hands to retain their 83-year-old Football League status. In three consecutive home games around New Year, Rovers trailed, Wayne Carlisle scored and defeat was averted. Moreover, in the third of these, Rovers' first home win in three months, Scunthorpe actually led 1-0 after 86 minutes. Ben Futcher, at 6ft 7in as tall as any opponent in Rovers' long history, deflected a Mark McKeever shot into his own net after seventeen minutes of the game at home to Lincoln City and then scored his side's winning goal at Sincil Bank. After four straight draws, an unexpected but thoroughly deserved win at Bury, Rovers' first at Gigg Lane since March 1956, was earned when Rob Quinn waltzed through the home side's defence after 65 minutes. A revitalising run of seven games without defeat offered hope but was shattered abruptly by a spectacular long-range goal from York City's Darren Edmondson after the former Rovers trialist Jon Parkin had struck a first-half penalty against a post. Rovers also took early leads against the top two sides in successive home games in the run-up to Easter, Hartlepool United who featured the former Rovers goalkeeper Anthony Williams and Marcus Bignot's latest side, Rushden and Diamonds. Vitalijs Astafjevs

Andy Rammell challenges former Rovers goalkeeper Andy Collett in the penultimate home match when Rovers' defeated Darlington 2-1 to secure their league status

returned to the side to score crucial goals in three consecutive matches in the spring and leave the veteran Latvian international captain as an unlikely second highest scorer at the club, behind 11-goal Grazioli. Beneath Rovers, the maelstrom gathered momentum – for the first time, two clubs would be automatically relegated to the Conference and there was so little to choose between a multitude of sides. Rovers were bottom of the table again after the draw at Southend United in February and were only out of the drop zone on goal difference as late as 19 April. At home to the other struggling sides, Rovers gained few points, losing disappointingly to Carlisle United and drawing with Boston United, Exeter City, Macclesfield Town and Shrewsbury Town.

The final season before the Second World War notwithstanding, Rovers were now in the most perilous position in the club's Football League history. Back in 1939, re-election was secured without any great worries. Between 1931 and 1951 only one club – Gillingham in 1938 – had failed to be re-elected and they swiftly returned to the league after the war. The trap door to Conference football was, by 2003, proving to be something of a chasm. For six consecutive seasons, from 1996/97, the relegated side had never yet returned to league action and the Conference contained eight former league sides in 2002/03. As Bristol Rugby Club teetered on the brink of financial ruin and faced being swallowed up by their arch-rivals Bath, dropping a division, both in footballing and in financial terms, was not a viable option for Rovers. As it was, figures released for the year to June 2002 showed that Rovers had made an overall loss of £608,402, compared with a deficit of £174,000 over the previous twelve months. Yet Rovers could count on considerable support, taking some 2,876 away fans to Oxford, 1,711 to Torquay, 1,582 to Exeter and 1,286 to Bournemouth. On the final day of the season, Kidderminster's highest home crowd of the season was partly explained by the presence of 1,591 away supporters who were able to cheer Tait's 71st-minute header from Llewellyn's right-wing corner on a ground where Rovers have not won since Easter Monday 1898. One notable supporter, Malcolm Norman, had by the summer of 2003 not missed a home league game for thirty-three years. Rovers' average home league attendance for 2002/03 was 6,934, greater than fifteen Division Two clubs and three sides in Division One. Consequently, the directors gave their full backing to December's launch of the Share Issue Scheme, the long-term aim of which was to bring some £3,000,000 to the club. This involved establishing a holding company that would include all shareholders, the largest of which would be the Supporters' Club, whose 700,000 shares effectively gave them the casting vote in any major future decision-making process. Celebrities such as the boxer Jane Couch soon signed up and the club was already assured of over £10,000 per month by the season's end. Moreover, this scheme funded the signing of Andy Rammell, whose four goals in three games over Easter secured Rovers' immediate Football League future.

A distinct lack of success in the LD Vans Trophy and League Cup was barely bettered in the FA Cup. Rovers required extra time in a replay at Runcorn and, after Barrett had conceded an own goal, only won through after the home side's Lee Parle had been sent off for a second bookable offence. Following a home draw with Rochdale, an exciting replay was lost by the odd goal in five at Spotland. Premiership side Leicester City were the visitors in May for a testimonial game for Roy Dolling, whose 38 years with the club in many capacities had ended upon his retirement in 2001.

In July popular full-back David Pritchard who unfortunately had to retire due to injury enjoyed a much deserved testimonial match against his home-town club, Wolverhampton Wanderers. Newly promoted to the Premiership Wolves defeated Rovers by a solitary goal. Over 3,500 fans turned out to honour Pritchard who made a brief second-half appearance.

An all-conquering Rovers women's side, managed by Tony Ricketts, won its first eight Premier League Southern Division games of 2002/03, the seventh being a comprehensive 13-0 victory over Barking, Trudy Williams scoring six times and Stef Curtis five. Williams scored seven times in the Gloucestershire County Cup Final in May in which Rovers, courtesy of a 10-1 victory over Forest Green Rovers, secured the trophy for a fifth consecutive year. The 'Gas Girls' were promoted to the Premier League in the spring and reached the semi-finals of the FA Cup, where they lost 7-2 to a powerful Fulham side which included Rachel McArthur, whose paternal grandfather Wally had served Rovers so loyally either side of the Second World War.

AFTERWORD

Bamford and Barrett steal ghosts on a drizzled field

Ben Gunstone

Rovers' third season in the basement division began in sweltering heat. An opening day victory at Scunthorpe, where Lee Hodges scored the winning goal two minutes from time against his former club, was played out in a temperature of 90° F, as hot as at the home game with Northampton Town in September 1908. Six new faces appeared in this game, four permanent signings and Calum Willock, who joined on loan from Fulham. Goalkeeper Kevin Miller could claim well over 500 appearances in the Football League and had played against Rovers for Watford in 1996/97 and for Exeter City in 2002/03. Christian Edwards, from Nottingham Forest, had won a Welsh cap in the centre of defence, while Oxford United's midfielder Dave Savage, the winner of five caps with Eire, had scored a penalty for Northampton against Rovers in March 2001. The loss of top scorer Giuliano Grazioli to Barnet was part of a swap deal that brought the exciting striker Manuel 'Junior' Agogo to the Memorial Stadium. Ghanaian by birth and fluent in two African dialects, Agogo had enjoyed spells with six separate league clubs as well as two top North American sides.

The new squad also included veteran Andy Rammell, the highly experienced striker who, after scoring four important goals to secure Rovers' status as a league club, had to miss the start of the season due to two knee operations. The popular youth team coach, Phil Bater was promoted from within to the post of first-team coach.

Two first-half goals in five minutes from Wayne Carlisle, appropriately at Carlisle's Brunton Park, and an excellent right-foot winner from Hodges after seventy minutes against Kidderminster brought early season success and Rovers even recovered to draw after trailing 2-0 inside fourteen minutes at home to Macclesfield Town. Despite an early exit from the League Cup, Rovers made a highly promising start on the field to the 2003/04 season. No history of Bristol Rovers could be complete without a further twist to the question of their home ground. In September 2003, South Gloucestershire Arenas proposed a 30,000-seater sports complex on a 220-hectare site near the A49 at Easter Compton, some six miles from the Memorial Stadium, to include a stadium for football, rugby and greyhound racing with provision for 10,000 spectators. By 2008, Geoff Dunford concurred, both Bristol's professional football clubs could be sharing these facilities.

This is the Bristol Rovers story. It is one of triumphs and disasters, of brushes with glory and of eternal years of optimism. The phoenix will rise once again from the ashes. The Pirates have sailed all too often into troubled waters and the choppy seas of the basement division are no exception, but all must hope that calmer straits lie ahead and that the good ship Bristol Rovers can steer an even course through the oceans of time to come.

Bristol Rovers 2003/04. Front row: Stewart Naughton (Centre of Excellence), Paul Tait, Dave Savage, Ryan Clarke, Kevin Miller, Christian Edwards, Andy Rammell, Kevin Austin, Phil Kite (Physio). Second row: Roger Brinsford (Secretary), Roger Harding (Kit Manager), Simon Bryant, Anwar Uddin, Rob Quinn, Sonny Parker, Wayne Carlisle, Rod Wesson (Youth Education), Ian Holtby (Stadium Manager). Third row: Pete Thornell, Colin Williams (Directors), Ijah Anderson, Adam Barrett, Junior Agogo, Danny Boxall, Kevin Street, Kevin Spencer, Steve Burns (Directors). Front row: Barry Bradshaw (Director), John Still (Asst Manager), Graham Hyde, Ron Craig (Vice Chairman), Ray Graydon (Manager), Geoff Dunford (Chairman), Lee Hodges, Phil Bater (Coach), Denis Dunford (Director)

Southampton et Bristol Rovers à Paris

Deux des plus fameuses équipes professionnelles anglaises ont montré pour la première fois aux Français ce que c'était que l'Association

Une passe un peu forte.
Un avant des "Saints" vient de passer à un de ses coéquipiers, mais le coup est un peu fort et la balle est partie trop loin.

Aux prises dans un dribbling.
Le fameux demi-centre de Southampton, Jepp (culotte noire) est aux prises avec Corbett, auquel il vient d'enlever la balle.

Grâce à la sportivité de l'*Auto*, deux des meilleures équipes professionnelles du sud de l'Angleterre, le Southampton Football-Club et les Bristol Rovers, nous ont offert, dimanche, au Parc des Princes, une leçon pratique de football-association. Je crains, malheureusement, que cette leçon n'ait pas été comprise par la majorité des 5.000 spectateurs présents malgré le mauvais temps. En effet, il est évident, — et le nombre des buts, 5, marqués de part et d'autre, le prouve surabondamment — il est évident, dis-je, que les deux équipes anglaises n'ont pas disputé un match. Elles ont cherché à faire du beau jeu et les applaudissements qui saluèrent maints arrêts superbes du merveilleux gardien de but de Bristol, Cartlidge; le jeu splendide du demi de Southampton, Jepp; les esquives, les feintes, les passes à ras de terre, d'une précision superbe des avants de Southampton, prouvèrent que le public, du moins une certaine partie, comprenait les beautés du football joué par de tels virtuoses.

Alors pourquoi regretter l'absence d'une lutte plus âpre, qui nous aurait privés d'un spectacle aussi beau? Outre - Manche, jamais je n'ai vu deux grandes équipes jouer aussi bien que l'ont fait au Parc nos deux hôtes. Et cela se conçoit aisément. Il y a, là-bas, en jeu, de tels intérêts, honorifiques ou pécuniaires, que la brutalité n'est pas toujours exempte de la partie. Rien de cela ne se présenta dimanche et la leçon, pour ceux qui voudront la comprendre, sera profitable.
GEO CAIZAC.

Devant les buts de Southampton.
Lock, le gardien de but (culotte noire) avec ses arrières attend le ballon qui vient d'être lancé en l'air d'un coup de tête d'un de ces dernier, mais il est marqué par trois avants adverses.

Une passe interceptée. .
Hughes, de Southampton (culotte noire) va passer le ballon à Jeffries qui se prépare à partir, mais Roberts, de Bristol (culotte blanche) arrive juste à temps pour intercepter la passe.

On 21 March 1909 Rovers and Southampton played an exhibition match in Paris which ended 5-5. Coverage of this unusual friendly encounter was published in a French sports magazine which included these rare action photographs

BRISTOL ROVERS

CLUB STATISTICS

CLUB RECORDS

Most wins (in a season)	26	1952/53, 1989/90
Most defeats	25	1992/93
Most draws	17	1922/23, 1953/54, 1973/74, 1975/76, 1988/89
Most League points (2 for win)	64	1952/53
Most League points (3 for win)	93	1989/90
Most home wins	17	1952/53, 1971/72, 1972/73
Most home defeats	11	1947/48, 1992/93
Most home draws	11	1988/89
Most away wins	11	1989/90
Most away defeats	18	1936/37
Most away draws	11	1969/70
Consecutive wins	12	08.10.1952–17.01.1953
Consecutive defeats	8	29.04.1961–09.09.1961, 26.10.2002–21.12.2002
Consecutive draws	5	18.03.1967–01.04.1967, 01.11.1975–22.11.1975
Fewest wins (in a season)	5	1980/81
Fewest defeats	5	1989/90
Fewest draws	4	1927/28
Fewest home wins	4	1980/81
Fewest away wins	0	1929/30
Fewest home defeats	0	1989/90
Fewest away defeats	5	1973/74,1989/90
Fewest home draws	2	1971/72
Fewest away draws	0	1949/50
Consecutive home wins	10	16.01.1935–23.04.1935
Consecutive away wins	5	25.10.1952–26.12.1952, 18.01.1964–29.02.1964
Consecutive home defeats	5	28.09.1946–23.11.1946
Consecutive away defeats	13	16.11.1929–26.04.1930
Consecutive home draws	6	23.10.1965–08.01.1966
Consecutive away draws	4	15.04.1938–05.05.1938, 27.12.1969–25.02.1970, 04.12.1971–29.01.1972
Unbeaten home and away	32	07.04.1973–27.01.1974
Unbeaten at home	34	18.02.1989–15.09.1990
Unbeaten away	17	07.04.1973–27.01.1974
Matches without a draw	37	15.11.1947–09.10.1948
Goalless draws in a season	10	1922/23 (no goalless draws in six separate seasons)
Goalless draws in succession	3	26.12.1922–20.01.1923
Consecutive games without a goalless draw	114	07.03.1959-02.12.1961
Unbeaten run within a season	27	15.09.1952–14.03.1953, 25.08.1973–27.01.1974
Games without a win	20	05.04.1980–01.11.1980
within a season	14	23.10.1965–15.01.1966, 16.08.1980–01.11.1980, 29.09.2002–21.12.2001
Games without a home win	13	29.04.2000–24.02.2001
Games without an away win	29	16.03.1929–17.09.1930
Goals scored in a season	92	1952/53
Goals scored at home	60	1951/52
Goals scored away	39	1963/64
Fewest goals scored in season	34	1980/81
Fewest goals scored in home games	21	1980/81
Fewest goals scored in away games	10	1922/23
Most goals conceded in season	95	1935/36
Most goals conceded in home games	42	1992/93
Most goals conceded in away games	64	1935/36
Fewest goals conceded in season	33	1973/73
Fewest goals conceded in home games	13	1924/25,1984/85
Fewest goals conceded in away games	17	1922/23

Goals scored in:

consecutive games	26	26.03.1927–03.12.1927
in home games	43	16.01.1954–03.03.1956
in away games	21	06.03.1990–12.01.1991
from start of season – home	22	1950/51
from start of season – away	13	1988/89
Scored in consecutive games		
within a season – home	22	1950/51
within a season – away	21	1964/65
No goals in consecutive games	6	14.10.1922–18.11.1922
in home games	4	24.08.1985–21.09.1985,
		14.02.1987–18.03.1987
in away games	6	06.10.2001–24.11.2001
Most League goals in a season	33	Geoff Bradford, 1952/53
Most League goals in career	242	Geoff Bradford, 1949–64
Most League appearances	546	Stuart Taylor, 1966–80
Most seasons as ever-present	5	Ray Warren and Jesse Whatley
Shortest Rovers career	10 minutes as substitute	David Smith
Youngest League player	Ronnie Dix	(15 y 173 d), 03.03.1928
Oldest League player	Jack Evans	(39 y 68 d), 09.04.1928
Youngest League opponent	Bob Woolley (Notts Co)	(16 y 101 d), 09.04.1964
Oldest League opponent	Mick Burns (Ipswich T),	(42 y 239 d), 31.03.1951
Youngest League goalscorer	Ronnie Dix	(15 y 180 d), 10.03.1928
Youngest hat-trick scorer	Phil Taylor	(18 y 61 d), 18.12.1935
Youngest player sent off	Luke Basford (17 y 87 d)	31.01.1998
Played in most consecutive games	Jesse Whatley,	246, Aug 1922–Apr 1928
Scored in most consecutive games	Dai Ward	8, 17.03.1956–21.04.1956
Most caps while on club's books	Vitalijs Astsfjevs	22, Latvia
Longest gap between League appearances	7 years 353 days	Wilf Smith (1938–46)
in peacetime	6 years 233 days	Joe Walter (1922–28)
while remaining on Rovers' books	3 years 122 days	Les Edwards (1951–54)
Record transfer fee paid	£2,000,000	Barry Hayles, Nov 1998
	£2,000,000	Jason Roberts, July 2000
Record transfer fee received	£370,000	Andy Tillson, Nov 1992
Largest crowd at a Rovers game	62,787	Newcastle, FA Cup, 24.02.1951
at a home game	38,472	Preston, FA Cup, 30.01.1960
at a League game – home	35,614	Birmingham C, 17.10.1953
at a League game – away	49,274	Leeds U, 21.04.1956
Smallest home crowd – League	1,500	Northampton T, 16.01.1935
Smallest away crowd – League	1,000	Merthyr, 26.12.1927
	1,000	Walsall, 30.04.1930
Highest home seasonal League average	24,662	1953/54
Lowest home seasonal League average	3,246	1986/87
First home game under floodlights	07.09.1959	v. Ipswich T
Tallest player to represent Rovers	Stuart Taylor	6' 5"
Shortest player to represent Rovers	Sid Homer	5'2"
Tallest player to play against Rovers	Kevin Francis	6'7"(for Stockport County)
	Ian Feuer	6'7" (for Luton Town)
	Denis Lawrence	6'7" (for Wrexham)
	Ben Futcher	6'7" (for Lincoln)
Fastest hat-trick by a Rovers player	Dai Ward (3 in 4 mins)	v. Doncaster Rovers, 22.12.1956
Fastest hat-trick from start of match	Vic Lambden (3 in first 15 mins)	v. Colchester U, 14.04.1952
Gap between matches against Rovers	16 years 323 days	Peter Beardsley
		(19.12.1981–07.11.1998)
Longest gap between first and last League	21 years 23 days	Alex Ferguson
appearance against Rovers		(05.09.1925–28.09.1946)
First nominated substitute	Roy McCrohan	21.08.1965
First used substitute	Joe Davis	02.10.1965
First substitute to score	Ken Ronaldson	04.11.1968
First Sunday game	06.01.1974	v. Nottingham Forest, FA Cup
First overseas match	21.03.1909	v. Southampton in Paris
First all-ticket game	03.03.1956	v. Bristol City
First player to be sent off	04.02.1922	Bill Panes v. Luton Town
First player to be sent off (on debut)	30.03.2002	Wayne Carlisle v. Plymouth Argyle

RECORD AGAINST OTHER LEAGUE CLUBS

1920-2003

	P	HOME					AWAY					TOTAL			
		W	D	L	GF	GA	W	D	L	GF	GA	W	D	L	GF	GA
ABERDARE ATHLETIC	12	5	0	1	13	4	1	1	4	3	8	6	1	5	16	12
AFC BOURNEMOUTH	96	27	7	14	95	62	11	10	27	41	80	38	17	41	136	142
ALDERSHOT	34	11	4	2	40	15	8	2	7	24	27	19	6	9	64	42
ASTON VILLA	8	1	1	2	4	4	0	1	3	3	8	1	2	5	7	12
BARNET	2	1	0	0	5	2	1	0	0	2	1	2	0	0	7	3
BARNSLEY	28	6	6	2	24	19	5	3	6	19	20	11	9	8	43	39
BARROW	6	3	0	0	7	3	0	1	2	1	5	3	1	2	8	8
BIRMINGHAM CITY	12	1	5	0	7	6	0	3	3	6	10	1	8	3	13	16
BLACKBURN ROVERS	30	9	2	4	30	10	5	4	6	15	24	14	6	10	45	34
BLACKPOOL	32	6	6	4	17	18	5	2	9	21	31	11	8	13	38	49
BOLTON WANDERERS	26	7	4	2	19	12	2	3	8	8	23	9	7	10	27	35
BOSTON UNITED	2	0	1	0	1	1	0	1	0	0	0	0	2	0	1	1
BRADFORD PARK AVENUE	2	0	1	0	3	3	0	1	0	2	2	0	2	0	5	5
BRADFORD CITY	18	8	1	0	28	8	4	2	3	12	12	12	3	3	40	20
BRENTFORD	70	16	8	11	52	41	13	8	14	58	57	29	16	25	110	98
BRIGHTON & HOVE ALBION	94	21	13	13	86	54	10	8	29	60	107	31	21	42	146	161
BRISTOL CITY	88	16	15	13	62	56	8	15	21	42	70	24	30	34	104	126
BURNLEY	26	8	3	2	23	12	1	6	6	8	19	9	9	8	31	31
BURY	34	11	3	3	33	18	2	5	10	13	33	13	8	13	46	51
CAMBRIDGE UNITED	24	8	3	1	18	9	5	4	3	20	20	13	7	4	38	29
CARDIFF CITY	50	12	10	3	41	27	8	7	10	36	42	20	17	13	77	69
CARLISLE UNITED	20	4	3	3	17	10	4	1	5	12	19	8	4	8	29	29
CHARLTON ATHLETIC	50	14	9	2	51	30	4	6	15	31	54	18	15	17	82	84
CHELSEA	8	3	0	1	7	3	0	1	3	0	5	3	1	4	7	8
CHELTENHAM TOWN	2	0	0	1	1	2	0	1	0	0	0	0	1	1	1	2
CHESTER CITY	12	4	2	0	16	8	2	3	1	7	4	6	5	1	23	12
CHESTERFIELD	30	12	3	0	30	11	5	5	5	11	11	17	8	5	41	22
COLCHESTER UNITED	22	7	4	0	27	9	3	2	6	17	18	10	6	6	44	27
COVENTRY CITY	26	7	3	3	25	17	1	3	9	14	34	8	6	12	39	51
CREWE ALEXANDRA	12	2	2	2	8	7	1	0	5	5	15	3	2	7	13	22
CRYSTAL PALACE	52	14	5	7	50	30	5	2	19	23	52	19	7	26	73	82
DARLINGTON	10	5	0	0	11	3	1	2	2	7	6	6	2	2	18	9
DERBY COUNTY	24	6	3	3	24	17	2	3	7	11	18	8	6	10	35	35
DONCASTER ROVERS	28	10	2	2	33	12	5	2	7	22	25	15	4	9	55	37
EVERTON	2	0	1	0	0	0	0	0	1	0	4	0	1	1	0	4
EXETER CITY	68	14	15	5	66	43	7	10	17	32	50	21	25	22	98	93
FULHAM	52	14	7	5	50	30	6	5	15	37	60	20	12	20	87	90
GILLINGHAM	80	28	4	8	82	40	10	7	23	40	60	38	11	31	122	100
GRIMSBY TOWN	30	8	3	4	31	30	3	5	7	15	23	11	8	11	46	53
HALIFAX TOWN	14	7	0	0	17	3	1	4	2	5	8	8	4	2	22	11
HARTLEPOOL UNITED	8	2	1	1	4	3	0	1	3	2	6	2	2	4	6	9
HEREFORD UNITED	4	0	1	1	3	4	0	2	0	1	1	0	3	1	4	5
HUDDERSFIELD TOWN	26	6	6	1	24	12	5	3	5	15	20	11	9	6	39	32
HULL CITY	40	8	7	5	32	25	7	3	10	17	30	15	10	15	49	56
IPSWICH TOWN	30	8	6	1	29	18	7	1	7	25	20	15	7	8	54	38
KIDDERMINSTER HARRIERS	4	1	0	1	3	3	0	1	1	1	3	1	1	2	4	6
LEEDS UNITED	10	3	2	0	18	7	0	3	2	5	8	3	5	2	23	15
LEICESTER CITY	16	2	5	1	9	6	1	2	5	8	19	3	7	6	17	25
LEYTON ORIENT	84	23	10	9	72	44	13	10	19	59	64	36	20	28	131	108
LINCOLN CITY	32	7	4	5	27	15	7	1	8	16	22	14	5	13	43	37
LIVERPOOL	16	4	1	3	14	10	1	0	7	7	22	5	1	10	21	32

		HOME					AWAY					TOTAL			
	P	W	D	L	GF	GA	W	D	L	GF	GA	W	D	L	GF	GA
LUTON TOWN	76	19	12	7	76	45	5	9	24	38	91	24	21	31	114	136
MACCLESFIELD TOWN	6	0	2	1	1	3	1	0	2	6	7	1	2	3	7	10
MANCHESTER CITY	2	0	1	0	2	2	0	1	0	0	0	0	2	0	2	2
MANCHESTER UNITED	2	0	1	0	1	1	0	0	1	0	2	0	1	1	1	3
MANSFIELD TOWN	38	12	6	1	44	16	3	3	13	11	35	15	9	14	55	51
MERTHYR TOWN	20	6	4	0	16	5	3	4	3	15	17	9	8	3	31	22
MIDDLESBROUGH	24	5	2	5	26	19	3	2	7	15	26	8	4	12	41	45
MILLWALL	72	20	9	7	53	33	9	11	16	33	45	29	20	23	86	78
NEWCASTLE UNITED	14	2	3	2	8	7	1	2	4	6	13	3	5	6	14	20
NEWPORT COUNTY	60	17	7	6	62	34	4	10	16	31	54	21	17	22	93	88
NORTHAMPTON TOWN	70	13	12	10	60	50	8	9	18	39	73	21	21	28	99	123
NORWICH CITY	48	13	6	5	52	29	4	8	12	25	44	17	14	17	77	73
NOTTINGHAM FOREST	18	6	1	2	19	14	0	2	7	6	18	6	3	9	25	32
NOTTS COUNTY	74	12	18	7	57	44	6	9	22	46	84	18	27	29	103	128
OLDHAM ATHLETIC	44	12	7	3	32	18	4	4	14	29	49	16	11	17	61	67
OXFORD UNITED	34	10	3	4	25	15	5	4	8	23	25	15	7	12	48	40
PETERBOROUGH UNITED	22	6	4	1	22	11	1	6	4	12	20	7	10	5	34	31
PLYMOUTH ARGYLE	76	16	11	11	62	48	7	11	20	46	76	23	22	31	108	124
PORT VALE	50	14	8	3	47	24	2	6	17	16	39	16	14	20	63	63
PORTSMOUTH	26	5	3	5	18	12	2	3	8	10	24	7	6	13	28	36
PRESTON NORTH END	32	9	4	3	28	16	3	7	6	18	22	12	11	9	46	38
QUEENS PARK RANGERS	58	15	8	6	53	28	7	3	19	33	62	22	11	25	86	90
READING	80	20	12	8	70	45	10	5	25	46	74	30	17	33	116	119
ROCHDALE	14	1	4	2	12	12	1	4	2	5	7	2	8	4	17	19
ROTHERHAM UNITED	50	16	2	7	47	29	2	12	11	23	45	18	14	18	70	74
RUSHDEN & DIAMONDS	4	0	0	2	1	5	0	0	2	2	5	0	0	4	3	10
SCUNTHORPE UNITED	26	8	5	0	32	11	4	5	4	19	20	12	10	4	51	31
SHEFFIELD UNITED	22	7	4	0	25	13	2	3	6	12	24	9	7	6	37	37
SHEFFIELD WEDNESDAY	10	2	2	1	10	8	0	1	4	6	14	2	3	5	16	22
SHREWSBURY TOWN	44	14	6	2	47	19	8	4	10	32	37	22	10	12	79	56
SOUTHAMPTON	16	3	2	3	10	8	1	0	7	6	20	4	2	10	16	28
SOUTHEND UNITED	84	25	7	10	85	50	5	11	26	44	89	30	18	36	129	139
SOUTHPORT	8	3	0	1	8	5	0	1	3	1	6	3	1	4	9	11
STOCKPORT COUNTY	14	2	3	2	8	9	3	0	4	6	8	5	3	6	14	17
STOKE CITY	28	9	3	2	27	15	5	1	8	23	28	14	4	10	50	43
SUNDERLAND	24	8	3	1	24	13	0	5	7	12	35	8	8	8	36	48
SWANSEA CITY	66	17	11	5	70	35	9	9	15	39	63	26	20	20	109	98
SWINDON TOWN	76	20	5	13	66	48	8	8	22	45	69	28	13	35	111	117
THAMES ASSOCIATION	4	2	0	0	8	1	2	0	0	4	1	4	0	0	12	2
TORQUAY UNITED	54	19	5	3	52	16	7	6	14	29	48	26	11	17	81	64
TOTTENHAM HOTSPUR	2	0	0	1	2	3	0	0	1	0	9	0	0	2	2	12
TRANMERE ROVERS	20	8	0	2	15	5	4	4	2	16	15	12	4	4	31	20
WALSALL	78	23	6	10	83	42	11	10	18	51	73	34	16	28	134	115
WATFORD	84	18	7	17	58	56	6	8	28	40	81	24	15	45	98	137
WEST BROMWICH ALBION	6	1	2	0	4	3	0	1	2	3	8	1	3	2	7	11
WEST HAM UNITED	20	0	3	7	8	20	1	1	8	9	24	1	4	15	17	44
WIGAN ATHLETIC	24	8	3	1	30	11	2	2	8	11	21	10	5	9	41	32
WIMBLEDON	4	0	2	0	3	3	0	1	1	1	2	0	3	1	4	5
WOLVERHAMPTON WANDERERS	12	0	5	1	5	9	3	1	2	10	12	3	6	3	15	21
WORKINGTON	6	1	1	1	6	3	1	1	1	3	2	2	2	2	9	5
WREXHAM	38	13	3	3	36	16	3	4	12	19	31	16	7	15	55	47
WYCOMBE WANDERERS	14	4	0	3	11	10	1	4	2	4	6	5	4	5	15	16
YORK CITY	36	7	5	6	23	21	6	5	7	20	20	13	10	13	43	41
TOTALS	3340	871	445	354	3039	1854	373	407	890	1838	3004	1244	852	1244	4877	4858

Notes:
Rovers have played against 104 different clubs.
The only current league club they have never met is Arsenal.

MANAGERIAL RECORDS

1920-2003

BEN HALL

Born: Ecclesall, nr Sheffield 6 March 1881
Died: 1963
July 1920 – 27 May 1921

	P	W	D	L	F	A	PTS
League	42	18	7	17	68	57	43
FA Cup	2	1	0	1	11	6	
Glos Cup Final	1	0	0	1	0	1	

ANDREW WILSON

Born: Irvine, Scotland 10 December 1880
Died: 13 March 1945
21 June 1921 – 20 April 1926

	P	W	D	L	F	A	PTS
League	210	69	58	83	247	267	196
FA Cup	13	4	4	5	13	14	
Glos Cup Final	7	1	2	4	5	11	

JOE PALMER

Born: Yorkshire c 1890
17 May 1926 – 21 April 1929

	P	W	D	L	F	A	PTS
League	126	43	20	63	205	252	106
FA Cup	9	4	2	3	16	16	
Glos Cup Final	3	1	0	2	1	6	

DAVID McLEAN

Born: Forfar, Scotland 13 December 1887
Died: 1967
29 May 1929 – 17 Sept 1930

	P	W	D	L	F	A	PTS
League	52	14	11	27	83	115	39
FA Cup	3	2	0	1	6	2	
Glos Cup Final	3	0	1	2	2	7	

CAPTAIN ALBERT PRINCE-COX

Born: Southsea 8 August 1890
23 Oct 1930 – 10 Oct 1936

	P	W	D	L	F	A	PTS
League	251	96	57	98	419	448	259
FA Cup	22	11	5	6	43	30	
Glos Cup Final	9	2	2	5	13	16	

CAPTAIN ALBERT PRINCE-COX continued

	P	W	D	L	F	A	PTS
Div 3 South Cup	9	5	2	2	18	14	
Welsh Cup	4	1	1	2	6	8	

PERCY J SMITH

Born: Burbage, Leicester Spring 1880
Died: Watford 18 April 1959
5 Nov 1936 – 27 Nov 1937

	P	W	D	L	F	A	PTS
League	45	14	9	22	68	84	37
FA Cup	4	2	0	2	7	14	
Glos Cup Final	2	1	0	1	2	2	
Div 3 South Cup	1	0	0	1	0	1	

BROUGH FLETCHER

Born: Mealsgate, Co Durham 9 March 1893
Died: Bristol 12 May 1972
18 Jan 1938 – April 1940/Aug 1945 – 2 Jan 1950

	P	W	D	L	F	A	PTS
League	213	74	48	91	291	315	196
FA Cup	9	4	0	5	18	17	
Glos Cup Final	5	2	1	2	6	8	

BERT TANN

Born: Plaistow, London 4 May 1914
Died: Bristol 7 July 1972
3 Jan 1950 – 1 April 1968

	P	W	D	L	F	A	PTS
League	801	331	193	277	1381	1236	855
FA Cup	59	26	15	18	103	88	
League Cup	19	7	4	8	31	34	
Glos Cup Final	18	5	4	9	22	34	

FRED FORD

Born: Dartford 10 February 1916
Died: Oxford 16 October 1981
1 April 1968 – 21 July 1969

	P	W	D	L	F	A	PTS
League	56	20	12	24	78	89	52
FA Cup	11	6	3	2	17	7	
League Cup	1	0	0	1	0	2	
Glos Cup Final	2	0	1	1	1	6	

BILL DODGIN (SENIOR)

Born: Gateshead 17 April 1909
Died: Godalming 16 October 1999
6 Aug 1969 – 1 July 1972

	P	W	D	L	F	A	PTS
League	138	60	41	37	224	165	161
FA Cup	8	4	1	3	15	12	
League Cup	14	8	3	3	23	15	
Glos Cup Final	3	0	2	1	3	4	

DON MEGSON

Born: Sale 12 June 1936
2 July 1972 – 21 Nov 1977

	P	W	D	L	F	A	PTS
League	234	80	75	79	293	304	235
FA Cup	11	3	3	5	12	19	
League Cup	19	6	6	7	24	25	
Glos Cup Final	5	2	1	2	8	7	

BOBBY CAMPBELL

Born: Glasgow 28 June 1922
21 Nov 1977 – 11 Dec 1979

	P	W	D	L	F	A	PTS
League	78	26	18	34	102	125	70
FA Cup	7	4	1	2	8	11	
League Cup	4	2	0	2	5	9	
Glos Cup Final	2	0	0	2	0	5	

HAROLD JARMAN

Born: Bristol 4 May 1939
12 Dec 1979 – 24 April 1980

	P	W	D	L	F	A	PTS
League	23	7	9	7	25	23	30
FA Cup	1	0	0	1	1	2	

TERRY COOPER

Born: Castleford 12 July 1943
24 April 1980 – 19 Oct 1981

	P	W	D	L	F	A	PTS
League	54	9	15	30	49	84	37
FA Cup	2	1	0	1	5	6	
League Cup	9	2	4	3	7	9	
Glos Cup Final	3	1	0	2	1	2	

RON GINGELL (CARETAKER)

Born: Bradord-on-Avon February 1920
Died: Bristol 20 October 1981

	P	W	D	L	F	A	PTS
League	1	0	1	0	1	1	1

BOBBY GOULD

Born: Coventry 12 June 1946
21 Oct 1981 – 14 May 1983
16 May 1985 – 26 June 1987

	P	W	D	L	F	A	PTS
League	81	36	15	30	127	107	123
	92	27	24	41	100	150	105
	173	63	39	71	227	257	228
FA Cup	4	1	1	2	4	3	
	6	3	1	2	8	9	
	10	4	2	4	12	12	
League Cup	5	2	1	2	8	8	
	6	1	0	5	6	12	
	11	3	1	7	14	20	
Glos Cup Final	1	1	0	0	2	1	
	1	0	0	1	0	1	
	2	1	0	1	2	2	

DAVID WILLIAMS

Born: Cardiff 11 March 1955
27 May 1983 – 15 May 1985

	P	W	D	L	F	A	PTS
League	92	43	25	24	134	102	154
FA Cup	6	3	1	2	10	7	
League Cup	8	3	2	3	14	15	
Glos Cup Final	2	2	0	0	6	3	

GERRY FRANCIS

Born: Chiswick, London 6 December 1951
8 July 1987 – 13 May 1991
10 July 2001 – 24 Dec 2001

	P	W	D	L	F	A	PTS
League	184	78	57	49	262	201	291
	22	5	6	11	16	27	21
	206	83	63	60	278	228	313
FA Cup	10	3	3	4	18	10	
	4	2	2	0	5	3	
	14	5	5	4	23	13	
League Cup	8	2	2	4	4	8	
	2	1	0	1	1	3	
Glos Cup Final	5	2	0	3	8	11	
ZDS Cup	2	1	0	1	3	3	

MARTIN DOBSON
Born: Blackburn 14 February 1948
2 July 1991 – 3 Oct 1991

	P	W	D	L	F	A	PTS
League	9	1	2	6	11	18	5
League Cup	1	0	0	1	1	3	
Glos Cup Final	1	0	0	1	2	3	
ZDS Cup	1	0	0	1	1	3	

DENNIS ROFE
Born: Fulham 1 June 1950
5 Oct 1991 – 9 Nov 1992

	P	W	D	L	F	A	PTS
League	53	17	15	21	70	89	66
FA Cup	3	1	1	1	7	3	
League Cup	4	1	1	2	5	6	
AI Cup	2	1	1	0	5	2	
Glos Cup Final	1	1	0	0	2	1	

MALCOLM ALLISON
Born: Dartford 5 September 1927
14 Nov 1992 – 27 Feb 1993

	P	W	D	L	F	A	PTS
League	16	6	3	7	17	19	21
FA Cup	2	0	1	1	1	4	

STEVE CROSS (CARETAKER)
Born: Wolverhampton 22 December 1959
6 – 14 March 1993

	P	W	D	L	F	A	PTS
League	3	0	1	2	2	7	1

JOHN WARD
Born: Lincoln 7 April 1951
20 March 1993 – 31 May 1996

	P	W	D	L	F	A	PTS
League	149	64	40	45	202	176	232
Play Offs	3	1	1	1	2	3	
FA Cup	6	2	1	3	10	6	
League Cup	8	1	3	4	8	15	
AG/AWS Trophy	13	7	4	2	20	9	
Glos Cup Final	2	2	0	0	1	1	

IAN HOLLOWAY

Born: Kingswood, Bristol 12 March 1963
13 June 1996 – 29 Jan 2001

	P	W	D	L	F	A	PTS
League	208	76	59	73	279	244	287
Play Offs	2	1	0	1	3	4	
FA Cup	14	6	3	5	24	18	
League Cup	15	4	5	6	15	20	
AWS Trophy	9	5	0	4	12	8	
Glos Cup Final	1	0	0	1	0	1	

GARRY THOMPSON (CARETAKER)

Born: Birmingham 7 October 1959
30 Jan 2001 – 5 May 2001
24 Dec 2001 – 9 April 2002

	P	W	D	L	F	A	PTS
League	22	7	5	10	25	28	
	21	6	5	10	22	27	
	43	13	10	20	47	55	49
FA Cup	2	1	0	1	3	2	
LDV Trophy	2	0	0	2	0	4	

PHIL BATER (CARETAKER)

Born: Cardiff 26 October 1955
10 – 20 April 2002

	P	W	D	L	F	A	PTS
League	3	0	1	2	2	6	1

RAY GRAYDON

Born: Bristol 21 July 1947
23 April 2002 –

	P	W	D	L	F	A	PTS
League	46	12	15	19	50	57	51
FA Cup	4	1	2	1	6	5	
League Cup	1	0	0	1	0	2	
LDV Trophy	1	0	0	1	0	1	

	Lge Matches
Bert Tann	801
Albert Prince-Cox	251
Don Megson	234
Brough Fletcher	213
Andrew Wilson	210
Ian Holloway	208
Gerry Francis	206
Bobby Gould	173
John Ward	149
Bill Dodgin	138
Joe Palmer	126
David Williams	92
Bobby Campbell	78
Fred Ford	56
Terry Cooper	54
Dennis Rofe	53
David McLean	52
Ray Graydon	46
Percy Smith	45
Garry Thompson	43
Ben Hall	42
Harold Jarman*	23
Malcolm Allison	16
Martin Dobson	9
Phil Bater*	3
Steve Cross*	3
Ron Gingell*	1

* indicates Caretaker-Manager

Above: *John Ward led Rovers to the 1995 play-offs*
Below left: *Bert Tann, Rovers' longest serving manager, who led the club to their first ever promotion in 1953*
Below right: *Terry Cooper, former England International and Rovers' manager in 1980/81*

485

ROVERS FULL INTERNATIONALS

	Position Played	International Career	Full Caps	Rovers Lge Career
ENGLAND				
Hugh Adcock	Winger	1929-30	5	1935-36
Alan Ball	Midfield	1965-75	72	1982-83
Jack Ball	Forward	1928	1	1921-22
Billy Beats	Forward	1901-02	2	1903-06
Geoff Bradford*	Forward	1955	1	1949-64
Cliff Britton	Wing Half	1935-37	9	1928-30
Michael Channon	Forward	1973-78	46	1982-83
Tommy Cook	Forward	1925	1	1931-33
Terry Cooper	Full Back	1969-75	20	1979-81
Keith Curle	Defender	1992	3	1981-83
Ronnie Dix	Forward	1938	1	1927-32
Gerry Francis	Midfield	1975-76	12	1985-88
Vivian Gibbins	Forward	1924-25	2	1932-33
George Kinsey	Defender	1892-96	4	1897-1902
Larry Lloyd	Defender	1971-80	4	1968-69
Gary Mabbutt	Defender	1982-92	16	1978-82
Nigel Martyn	Goalkeeper	1992-02	23	1987-90
John Scales	Defender	1995	3	1985-87
Philip Taylor	Wing Half	1947	3	1935-36
John Townrow	Defender	1925-26	2	1932-33
Mark Walters	Winger	1991	1	1999-2002
NORTHERN IRELAND				
Ronnie Briggs*	Goalkeeper	1962-65	2	1965-68
Harry Buckle	Winger	1903-08	3	1907-08
Adrian Coote	Striker	1999-2000	6	2002-03
Sam Irving	Defender	1923-31	18	1932-33
Matthew O'Mahoney*	Defender	1939	1	1936-39
Jim McCambridge	Forward	1930-32	4	1933-36
Frank McCourt	Wing Half	1952-53	6	1949-50
Jimmy Quinn	Forward	1996-2003	28	2001-02
Ciran Toner	Midfield	2003	2	2001-02
SCOTLAND				
James Howie	Forward	1905-08	3	1902-03
Bobby McKay	Forward	1927	1	1932-35
David Steele	Wing Half	1923	3	1919-22
Tommy Tait	Wing Half	1911	1	1903-06
WALES				
Marcus Browning*	Midfield	1996-97	5	1989-97
Jack Evans	Winger	1912-23	8	1926-28
Brian Godfrey	Midfield	1964-65	3	1971-73
Jeff Hopkins	Defender	1983-90	16	1991-92
Wayne Jones*	Midfield	1971	1	1966-72
Jack Lewis	Forward	1899-1901 & 1904-06	1	1904-06
Chris Llewellyn	Midfield	1998	2	2002-03
Tommy Mills	Forward	1934-35	4	1936-39
Jason Perry	Full Back	1994	1	1997-98
Billy Richards	Winger	1933	1	1937-38
Phillip Roberts	Full Back	1974-75	4	1969-73
Neil Slatter*	Full Back	1983-89	22	1980-85
Byron Stevenson	Midfield	1978-82	15	1985-86
Gareth Taylor	Striker	1995-2003	11	1991-95
Martin Thomas	Goalkeeper	1987	1	1976-82

	Position Played	International Career	Full Caps	Rovers Lge Career
Dai Ward*	Forward	1959-62	2	1954-61
David Williams	Midfield	1986-87	5	1975-85
Geraint Williams	Midfield	1988-96	13	1980-85

CANADA
Ian McLean*	Defender	1995	2	1993-96

EIRE
Graham Barrett	Striker	2002	1	2000-01
Jeremiah Dennehy	Winger	1972-77	11	1978-80
Mickey Evans	Striker	1998	1	2000-01
Joe Haverty*	Winger	1956-67	32	1964-85
Matthew O'Mahoney*	Defender	1938-39	6	1936-39
Gary Waddock	Midfield	1980-90	21	1992-94

GHANA
Ansah Owusu	Striker	2001-02	5	2000-01

GRENADA
Jason Roberts*	Striker	1998-2001	6	1998-2000

JAMAICA
Barry Hayles	Striker	2001-03	7	1997-99

KENYA
Peter Hooper*	Winger	1951	1	1953-62

LATVIA
Vitalijs Astafjevs	Midfield	1982-2003	94	1999-2003

NEW ZEALAND
Joe Kissock	Full Back	1923-25	15	1921-22
Paul Nixon	Forward	1988	6	1988-91

SOUTH AFRICA
David Murray	Forward	1924	21	1928-30

TRINIDAD & TOBAGO
Kevin Austin	Defender	1999	1	2002-03
Ronnie Mauge*	Midfield	2000	8	1999-2002
Nigel Pierre*	Striker	2000-03	35	1999-2000

* Indicates international honour awarded while a Bristol Rovers player

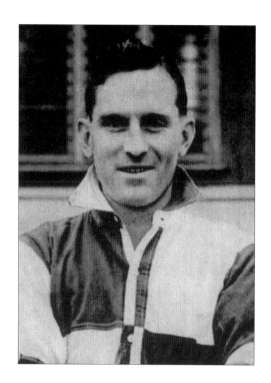 

Bristol Rovers stalwarts, clockwise from top left: Vic Lambden, Jackie Pitt, Peter Hooper and Bobby Jones.

PLAYERS NAME	DATE & PLACE OF BIRTH	DATE & PLACE OF DEATH	APPS	GLS	PREVIOUS CLUB	NEXT CLUB
ALDIN C J			1	0	1910	1911
APPLEBY Arthur Benjamin	1876 Burton on Trent	22.10.1961 Bristol	180	9	1903 West Bromwich Albion	1908 Leighton
BEATS William Edwin	13.11.1871 Wolstanton	6.4.1936 Reading	94	44	5.1906 Wolverhampton Wdrs	5.1906 Port Vale
BECTON Thomas	1878 Preston	8.11.1957 Fulwood	25	3	14.6.1901 Kettering Town	31.10.1902 Kettering Town
BENNETT Harry	1878 Bristol		1	0	1905 Frys Athletic	1906 Fishponds United
BENNETT Hubert Henry	1889/90 Oldbury On Severn	22.7.1968 Bristol	101	0	1.1911 Thornbury G School	1915 Retired
BLUNT William Joseph	Stafford		3	1	6.1912 Wolverhampton Wdrs	1913
BOUCHER Thomas Charles	1874 West Bromwich		27	10	7.5.1900 Bristol	1.8.1901 Bristol City
BOULTON W J	1886 Bristol		3	0	7.5.1901	1902
BOXLEY Harold H	1894 Stockbridge		6	0	2.5.1912 Kidderminster Harriers	1913 Wellington Town
BOYCE Albert			1	0	1900	1901
BOYLE F	1888 Lincoln		1	0	17.9.1910 Gainsborough Trinity	1911
BOYLE Patrick	1885/6		29	1	21.5.1907 Aberdeen	1908 New Brompton
BRADLEY Martin	1887 Goldenhill	1958 South Kirkly	8	1	30.5.1911 Sheffield Wednesday	1912
BRANDON William Thomas	28.5.1892 Blackburn	1.5.1956 Liverpool	26	0	9.1919 West Ham United	6.1920 Hull City
BROGAN James	1890 Burnbank		106	24	1910 Glasgow Football	1915
BROMAGE George	Derby		13	0	1911	1912
BROWN G E			13	0	2.9.1899	1900
BROWN Robert 'Daddy'	Liverpool		24	3	14.5.1898 Southampton	1900 Queens Park Rangers
BROWN Thomas E	Bristol		7	0	1912 Weston Super Mare	1913
BUCKLE Harold Redmond	1882 Belfast		33	10	4.5.1907 Portsmouth	29.6.1908 Coventry City
BULLOCK Walter George	Bristol	Bristol	5	1	1919 Welton Rovers	1920 Douglas
CADDICK Joseph	1889 Birmingham		27	7	1914 Worcester City	1.1915 13th Worcester Regiment
CARTLIDGE Arthur	12.6.1880 Stoke	08.1940 Stoke	258	0	3.5.1901 Stoke	14.4.190 Aston Villa
CHALMERS James	3.12.1877 Old Luce		8	1	13.5.1908 Glasgow Rangers	11.1908 Clyde
CHANNING P			2	0	1910	1911
CHANNON Frederick			1	0	1919	1920 Wolverhampton Wdrs
CLARK David C	1882/83 Sligo	17.3.1937 Bristol	8	0	1.7.1904 Glossop North End	1906 Southend United
CLARK William B	1881 Airdrie	1940	133	35	3.5.1904 Port Glasgow Athletic	4.1908 Sunderland
CLARKE William Gibb	1880 Mauchline		20	3	3.8.1900 East Stirlingshire	9.1901 Aston Villa
CORBETT Frederick	1.1.1881 West Ham	15.4.1924 Brentford			14.12.1901 West Ham United	1903 Bristol City
"					18.4.1904 Bristol City	22.5.1905 Brentford
"					19.6.1908 Brentford	1911 Gillingham
CROMPTON George Ellis	17.7.1886 Ramsbottom	17.5.1953 Barnstaple	139	52	3.5.1913 Exeter City	20.7.1921 Exeter City
CROSSLEY Arthur 'Fred'	17.12.1895 Radcliffe, Lancs	20.3.1965 Burnley	108	26	13.11.1919 Norwich City	1920 Chorley Town
DARGUE J	Scotland		2	3	4.5.1908 Heart of Midlothian	1909 New Brompton
DARKE Thomas William			36	3	1903 Eastville Athletic	4.9.1904 Bristol City
DAVIES William Henry	1874 Blakeley, Lancs		3	0	20.8.1900 Bedminster	1903
DAVIS			49	0	1903	1904
DAVISON George A	1890 Newcastle U Tyne		2	0	1914 Coventry City	1920 West Stanley
DEMMERY William	Kingswood 1877	28.12.1955 Bristol	57	20	25.1.1909 Bristol City	1910 Douglas
DIXON Thomas	Cramlington	1941	7	0	4.1913 Watford	1914 Blyth Spartans
DODSLEY George	Basford		17	3	5.1910 Denaby United	1911
DRAYCOTT William Levi	15.2.1869 Derby	16.6.1963 Luton	6	0	14.7.1900 Bedminster	21.8.1901 Wellingborough
DUNKLEY Albert Edward	1877 Northampton	1949	54	9	15.5.1904 Blackburn Rovers	23.8.1906 Blackpool
DUNN Hugh	1878 Johnstone		155	1	15.5.1901 Preston North End	12.5.1906 Port Vale

PLAYERS NAME	DATE & PLACE OF BIRTH	DATE & PLACE OF DEATH	APPS	GLS	PREVIOUS CLUB	NEXT CLUB
EDWARDS T G			1	0	1914	1915
ELMORE George V	9.1884 Wednesbury	1952	21	5	1903 West Bromwich Albion	9.9.1904 Witton Albion
FARNALL Thomas	1871 Gloucester		20	0	21.5.1901 Watford	1903 Bradford City
FISHER William	1873		12	5	7.5.1898 Burton Swifts	6.1900 Derby County
FLOYD William Bertram	Scunthorpe		34	0	11.5.1908 New Brompton	1909 Gainsborough Trinity
FORTUNE James J	1890 Dublin		5	0	1914 Queens Park Rangers	1915 Dublin
GALLACHER Hugh M	Glasgow	12.1920 Glasgow	8	2	1913	1915
GANGE J	Bristol		2	0	1910 Greenbank	1912
GEDDES Alfred Jasper	4.1871 West Bromwich	4.10.1927 Bristol	7	0	1901 Bristol City	1902 Bristol City
GERRISH William Webber	12.1884 Bristol	1916 during World War One	49	11	1904 Freemantle	14.4.1909 Aston Villa
GLENDENNING John	Bristol		2	0	1909 Staple Hill	1911
GOULD William	Burton on Trent		38	1	10.5.1906 Leicester Fosse	6.5.1907 Glossop North End
GRAHAM John Lang	7.8.1881 Dalry	15.5.1965 Saltcoats	17	4	3.5.1902 Kilmarnock	11.5.1903 Glasgow Celtic
GRAY James A "Bert"	1878 Bristol		32	3	1903 Royal Albert	11.5.1904 Aston Villa
GRAY Richard	1877 Derby		53	0	8.5.1899 Burton Swifts	5.5.1902 Burton United
GRIFFITHS Arthur	16.3.1879 Birmingham		105	1	15.10.1897 Lozells	1.1904 Notts County
GRIFFITHS Hillary	8.1871 Wednesfield		47	14	3.5.1900 Burton Swifts	2.5.1901 Reading
"		16.3.1937 Wednesfield	44	1	3.5.1904 Nottingham Forest	6.10.1905 Millwall
GRIFFITHS Joseph Leonard	1892 Wolverhampton		13	0	2.5.1912 Dudley	5.1920 Bury
GRUBB W Harold	Bristol	2.5.1943 Bristol	13	3	1919 Clifton St Vincents	1920 Bath City
HAGGARD W J			77	2	1911 Barry Town	1913
HALES Walter Harry	Bristol		1	0	6.5.1904 Bristol City	8.5.1908 New Brompton
HALL William John			93	0	12.5.1905 Bolton Wanderers	1906 Manchester City
HANDLEY Frank Bradford	Longbridgehayes		23	0	4.5.1907 Wolverhampton Wdrs	1910 Crewe Alexandra
HARDMAN John A	1889 Miles Platting		2	0	28.10.1914 Derby County	Deceased
HARGETT George H Andrew	Bristol	2.1917 France	2	1	1903 Bristol St George	9.5.1904 Bristol City
HARRIS George			13	1	25.8.1899 Bristol St George	1900
HARRIS Harry	1891/92		1	0	2.5.1912 Kidderminster Harriers	1913 Newport County
HARVEY			219	1	1901	1902
HARVIE David	Saltcoats		20	6	1910 Stevenston Thistle	1920 Retired
HASTIE George	Glasgow		8	3	6.1910 Kilmarnock	1911 Bath City
HAXTON John			1	0	1904 Motherwell	1906 Aberdeen
HENDERSON JamesThomas	Sunderland		27	2	27.9.1919 Glossop North End	1920 Derby County
HIGGINS Martin "Sandy"	1883 Grimsby		7	0	4.5.1908 Grimsby Town	1909 New Brompton
HORSEY Henry James "Harry"	29.8.1867 Eastville, Bristol	7.1938 Bristol	26	10	1883	1900 Retired
HOWES Denis			34	5	1919	1922 Bath City
HOWIE James "Jimmy"	19.3.1878 Galston	23.3.1970 Bristol	3	1	16.5.1902 Kettering Town	5.1903 Newcastle United
HUGHES Archibald Morris	1885 Neilston	13.12.1962 London	5	2	5.2.1911 Exeter City	1912
HUGHES John Harvey	Glasgow		4	0	1911 Cardiff Corinthians	1912 Bath City
HUGHES Clarence Leslie			23	6	1919 Bristol City	1920 Bristol City
HULME Joseph Arthur	18.12.1877 Leek	1916	30	1	4.5.1901 Wellingborough	1902 Brighton
HURLEY Walter Edwin "Ben"	11.10.1892 Bristol		3	0	22.8.1910 Bristol University	1919 Blandford
HUTCHINSON Harold B	1885 Blantyre		14	7	30.5.1906 Greenock Morton	2.7.1908 Norwich City
HUXTABLE Thomas	South Wales				10.4.1905	1906
HYAM James William	Bristol				21.11.1919	5.1920 Aberdare Athletic

PLAYERS NAME	DATE & PLACE OF BIRTH	DATE & PLACE OF DEATH	APPS	GLS	PREVIOUS CLUB	NEXT CLUB
JACK Walter Robert	1875 Grangemouth	1936	11	6	1903 Leith	3.5.1904 West Bromwich Albion
JARVIE Gavin	1879 Newton,Lanarkshire		89	1	3.5.1904 Airdrie	7.1907 Sunderland
JONES Charles T	7.1888 Birmingham		5	0	23.4.1909 Birmingham	1910
JONES James Walter	4.1890 Wellington		39	12	10.2.1911 Aston Villa	1920
JONES John Thomas 'Jack'	1874 West Bromwich	13.9.1903 London	76	36	8.6.1897 Small Heath	5.5.1902 Tottenham Hotspur
KAY Harry	1895/96 Elsecar		1	0	1913 Rotherham County	1914
KIFFORD John 'Jack'	1878 Paisley		28	0	14.7.1900 Derby County	4.6.1901 West Bromwich Albion
KINSEY George	20.6.1866 Burton on Trent	1.1911	5	0	15.6.1897 Notts County	17.9.1902 Burton Early Closing
LAMB Junior			6	0	19.10.1901	1902
LAMONT James	1875 Cowlairs		27	2	19.5.1899 Bedminster	1900
LATHAM Frederick 'Frank'	Bristol		6	2	6.3.1901	1907 Bristol City
LAURIE John	Glasgow		42	3	4.5.1909 Blackburn Rovers	1910
LEE Thomas	1876 Alnwick				21.6.1899 Sunderland	5.1900 Hebburn Argyle
"	"		22	0	29.1.1901 South Shields	12.3.1902 Hebburn Argyle
LEONARD John	Scotland		5	2	8.5.1899 Bedminster	1900
LEWIS John 'Jack'	8.1882 Aberystwyth	12.9.1954 Burton on Trent	81	30	5.9.1899 Kidderminster Harriers	4.5.1900 Portsmouth
LONG Edward 'Ted'	1890 Trowbridge		18	0	3.5.1904 Burton United	14.5.1906 Brighton
LYON William John 'Jimmy'	Clachnuscudden		49	2	10.11.1911 Portsmouth	1912 Westbury United
McCALL John			7	1	3.5.1901 Walsall	2.5.1903 Manchester City
McCOLL Adam	Scotland		32	1	6.6.1902 Edinburgh Hibernians	1903 Notts County
McCUBBIN Alexander C	Greenock		9	2	12.1909 Partick Thistle	1911
McCANN Henry	1888 Falkirk		21	9	7.5.1908 Greenock Morton	1909 Greenock Morton
McDONALD Hugh Lachlan	1884 Kilwinning	27.8.1920	2	0	1914 Exeter City, 7.2.1914 Fulham	1914 Retired
McINNES Thomas	22.3.1870 Glasgow		19	9	9.10.1899	1900 Bedford Q E
McINTYRE R			3	0	15.5.1901	1902
McKENZIE John W	9.1885 Montrose	1943	20	0	15.5.1909 Aston Villa	1910
McLEAN John C 'Jack'	22.5.1872 Port Glasgow		29	1	5.5.1902 Bristol City	4.1903 Millwall Athletic
MAGGS W			1	0	1914	1915
MAINDS Colin	1886 Dundee		23	0	8.1913 Third Lanark	1914
MARRIOTT Walter Wallace	4.1880 Northampton		56	6	2.5.1902 Wellingborough	6.5.1904 Northampton Town
MASON H			6	0	1914	1915
MASON James	Wolverhampton		14	5	5.1909 Wolverhampton Wdrs	1910
MORGAN Frederick Jerry	1892 Bristol		1	0	1919 Caerphilly Town	1925 Brislington Wednesday
MORRIS Samuel Herbert	02.1886 Handsworth, Birmingham		89	6	1911 Birmingham	7.1919 Brentford
MUIR Robert Bruce	23.9.1876 Kilmarnock	1953 Toronto, Canada	46	6	27.6.1901 Kilmarnock	5.1903 Glasgow Celtic
MURPHY Edward J	1882	1922	2	1	21.8.1907 Swindon Town	1908
MURRAY William			10	3	1913	1914
NEILSON John	20.2.1887 Gosforth		49	6	4.5.1900	1902
NEVIN John W 'Jack'			23	0	5.1912 West Bromwich Albion	1914 Dolphin
NICHOLS William			1	0	8.5.1908	1.1910 Merthyr Town
NICHOLLS	Bristol		2	0	4.5.1900	1901 Bristol City
OLLIS Harry	1876 Preston		1	0	1905	1906
ORR J Ronald			2	0	23.12.1905	1906
OVENS Gilbert	1884/85 Bristol	17.3.1963 Bristol	66	0	1904	1910 Chelsea
OWENS Isaac	1881 Darlington	1908	17	6	16.5.1906 Plymouth Argyle	5.1907 Crystal Palace

PLAYERS NAME	DATE & PLACE OF BIRTH	DATE & PLACE OF DEATH	APPS	GLS	PREVIOUS CLUB	NEXT CLUB
PALMER William	11.1887 Barnsley		57	4	1912 Rotherham County	5.1913 Everton
"			18	0	7.1919 Everton	8.1922 Gillingham
PANES William Charles Allen	9.10.1887 Bristol	12.1.1961 Bristol	51	13	1916 Bath City	5.7.1924 Sneyd Park
PAUL John			31	3	6.5.1899 Derby County	1901
PAYNE Charles E	Birmingham		216	42	1914 Worcester City	1915
PEPLOW William Watling	1885 Derby		5	1	4.5.1908 Birmingham	1915 Retired
PHILLIPS George	Bristol		63	2	1908 Rotherham County	1919 Douglas
PHILLIPS Harry	1882	during World War One	12	1	1910 Mexborough	1913
PIERCE John			1	1	14.6.1901 Preston North End	1902
POWELL A W			116	0	1912 Mangotsfield United	1913
PUDAN Albert Ernest 'Dick'	West Ham, London		47	6	12.7.1902 West Ham United	29.6.1907 Newcastle United
RANKIN J (aka BARNES)	Blantyre		24	7	9.1910 Cambuslang Rangers	1912
RAWLINGS Edward	Bristol		28	10	1919	1920 Bridgend Town
RICHARDS George			1	0	1911	1913
RIDDELL Frederick	Newhall		22	0	5.1909 Derby County	1910
RITCHIE Archibald			82	28	5.9.1899 Derby County	3.8.1900 Swindon Town
ROBERTS John			65	3	5.1907 Wolverhampton Wdrs	1910 Wrexham
ROBERTSON William	1873 Pontypool		1	0	11.5.1899 Small Heath	1904
ROBSON David J			28	0	1903 Willington Athletic	1904
RODGERS A	1886		62	12	11.1909 Aston Villa	1911
ROE Harold	Bristol		178	1	1912 Greenbank Rovers	1920
RONEY Peter	15.1.1887 Rutherglen	25.8.1930 Clydebank	5	3	3.5.1909 Norwich City	1915 17th Middlesex Regmt
ROWLANDS William Harold	Bristol		2	0	1902 Clifton United	1903
ROWLEY Arthur	1870 Stoke on Trent		1	1	18.5.1899 Stoke	1900
SAUNDERS John			40	3	1909 Stafford Rangers	9.1910 Coventry City
SAVAGE Arthur	Bristol	20.3.1970 Redditch	4	0	4.10.1906	1909 Merthyr Town
SCOTHERN Albert Edward	12.9.1882 Nottingham		1	0	1907	1909 Retired
SCOTT James Brogan	Edinburgh		1	0	9.1910 Cambuslang Rangers	1911
SHAPCOTT J A	Bristol		103	6	4.9.1906	1907
SHAW William J	1886 Muirkirk		1	0	9.10.1909 Kilmarnock	7.1912 Dumbarton Harp
SHERDLEY			50	16	1906	1907
SHERVEY James Cousins	1883	29.6.1956 Weston-S-Mare	9	0	1909	1914
SILVESTER Bertie Edward	Worcester		32	9	5.1910 Worcester City	1911 Orient
SIMS Stephen	11.12.1895 Bristol	2.1973 Weston-S-Mare	1	0	7.1919 Leicester Fosse	6.7.1922 Burnley
SKUSE Edward O			105	3	1919	1920
SMART John 'Jack'	Kingswood, Bristol		70	35	1905 Bristol East	8.1910 Reading
SMITH Andrew W	1879 Slamannan, Stirling		2	0	5.1903 West Bromwich Albion	23.3.1906 Millwall Athletic
SMITH H			31	10	1912	1913
SMITH John	1882 Wednesfield		3	0	4.5.1907 Birmingham	6.5.1908 Norwich City
SPELVINS E	Witton Park, Durham		57	8	1910 Ilkeston	1911
SQUIRES Arthur	1886 Redbourn, Herts	27.5.1953 West Clandon	57	0	5.1913 Watford	1915 Watford
STANSFIELD Harold Harry	2.1891 Bolton on Dearne	14.3.1940 Bristol	22	1	15.11.1912 Bath City	1921
STEELE David Morton	26.7.1894 Carluke, Lanark	23.5.1964 Stanningley	2	0	21.11.1919 Douglas Water Thistle	8.5.1922 Huddersfield Town
STONE Gilbert Rider			2	0	1905 Chipping Sodbury	1906
STONE William A			2	0	10.7.1899 Aberdare Athletic	1900

PLAYERS NAME	DATE & PLACE OF BIRTH	DATE & PLACE OF DEATH	APPS	GLS	PREVIOUS CLUB	NEXT CLUB
STRANG Thomas Robert			59	1	21.5.1907 Aberdeen	6.1909 New Brompton
SWEET A H			1	0	1906	1907
TAIT Thomas Somerville	13.9.1879 Carluke, Lanark		96	1	1903 Airdrie	30.5.1906 Sunderland
TAYLOR Archibald	1882 Dundee		9	0	10.5.1905 Bolton Wanderers	5.5.1906 Brentford
TAYLOR David W	Shrewsbury		26	0	28.5.1914 Heart of Midlothian	1915 Darlington
TAYLOR R			2	0	1909	1910
THOMAS Albert E	Bristol		12	0	1919	1920
THOMPSON R			10	2	16.1.1914 GooleTown	1914
THOMSON John L	1895 South Bank, Durham		12	4	15.1.1920 Falkirk	1920
TOUT William Edwin Brown	1884 Hereford	19.5.1960 Bath	2	0	1903 Redfield Rovers	5.9.1904 Bristol East
TURNER Samuel Isaiah	8.1882 Oldbury		30	9	4.5.1907 Brierley Hill Alliance	16.6.1908 Coventry City
VAIL Thomas			2	0	6.5.1899 Lochgelly United	18.12.1899 Swindon Town
VAUGHAN William 'Billy'	18.12.1898 Willenhall		3	0	3.4.1920 Willenhall	1921 Shrewsbury Town
VEYSEY Arthur John		5.1976 Walsall	1	0	1902 Winchester OB	1904 Wolverhampton Wdrs
WALKER David 'Davie'	1884 Oakdene,Walsall	30.10.1935 Walsall	78	28	2.5.1905 Wolverhampton Wdrs	4.7.1907 West Bromwich Albion
"			107	12	18.6.1911 Leicester Fosse	1912 Willenhall Swifts
WALKER 'George' Robert	1884 Northallerton		2	0	10.1912 Luton Town	1915 Middlesbrough
WALLACE F			42	8	1909	1910
WALTER Joseph Dorville	16.8.1895 Bristol	24.5.1995 Bristol	13	0	1919 Horfield United	8.5.1922 Huddersfield Town
WASSELL Harold 'Harry'	21.9.1879 Stourbridge	1951	1	0	13.5.1904 Small Heath	13.5.1905 Queens Park Rangers
WEAR A			12	0	1919	1920
WELSH Christopher			18	2	17.7.1899 Hebburn Athletic	4.9.1900 Hebburn Argyle
WESTON William H	Bristol		98	0	1919	1920
WESTWOOD Joseph 'Jack'	1895/96 Jump		14	0	1913 Rotherham Town	1914 Rotherham Town
WESTWOOD John William	Sheffield		29	1	5.1909 Denaby United	1915 Rotherham United
WHATLEY Jesse Winter	20.1.1895 Trowbridge	19.3.1982 Chipping Sodbury	48	18	10.1919 Trowbridge Town	9.1931 Stapleton Institute
WHITTON Percival Albert	14.1.1892 Taunton	11.1974 Bristol	1	0	1918 Taunton Town	7.1920 Aberaman Athletic
WILCOX Frederick Jeremiah	7.7.1880 Bristol	1954	106	1	8.1901 Glendale	20.3.1903 Small Heath
WILLIAMS Albert			1	0	1902	1903
WILLIAMS Louis	1888 Longton, Staffs		16	2	5.1909 Bradford City	6.1912 Port Vale
WILLIAMS S M	Longton, Staffs		35	12	1910	1911
WILLIAMS William 'Bill'			3	1	13.8.1900 Blackburn Rovers	15.8.1901 Newton Heath
WILSON D	1880		19	0	1903 Northampton Town	1905
WOODHALL Frank	Bristol		33	14	9.1910	1911 New Zealand
YOUNG James G	1880/81		12		8.7.1902 Barrow	1.5.1903 Glasgow Celtic
YOUNG John 'Jack'	Hurlford				26.5.1906 Kilmarnock	18.5.1907 Notts County
OWN GOALS SCORED BY OPPONENTS			12			

Notes:

Total appearances and goals records are for Southern League matches only 1899-1920

Total number of players to have represented the club in the Southern League was 211.

PLAYERS NAME	CAREER	DATE & PLACE OF BIRTH	DATE & PLACE OF DEATH	APPS	GLS	PREVIOUS CLUB	NEXT CLUB
ADAMS Michael Alan	1982-83	20.02.1965 Weston-s-Mare		0+1	0	21.02.1983 Banwell	22.05.1984 Bath C
ADAMS Robert James	1934-35	28.02.1917 Coleford	01.09.1970 Blakeney	2	0	31.10.1934 Cardiff C	08.1935 Millwall
ADCOCK Hugh	1935-36	10.04.1903 Coalville	16.10.1975 Coalville	13	1	04.07.1935 Leicester C	11.09.1936 Folkestone
AITKEN Peter Gerald	1972-80	30.06.1954 Penarth		230+4	3	04.07.1972 apprentice	30.11.1980 Bristol C
ALEXANDER Ian	1986-94	26.01.1963 Glasgow		284+7	6	28.08.1986 Pezoporikos,Cy	27.10.1994 Yate T
ALLAN Alexander Begg	1969-73	29.10.1947 Forfar		51+7	18	15.03.1970 Cardiff C	04.05.1973 Cape T
ALLAWAY James	1946-47	23.04.1922 Bristol		4	0	13.01.1946 amateur	09.1947 Bristol C
ALLCOCK Francis Edward	1953-56	07.09.1925 Nottingham		59	9	10.06.1952 Cheltenham T	23.11.1956 Retired
ALLEN Bradley James	2002-03	13.09.1971 Romford		5+3	1	28.11.2002 Peterborough	10.09.2003 Hornchurch
ALLEN John William Alcroft	1934-35	31.01.1903 Newburn	19.11.1957 Burnopfield	6	2	02.11.1934 Newcastle U	28.08.1935 Gateshead
ALSOP Julian Mark	1996-98	28.05.1973 Nuneaton		20+13	4	14.02.1997 Halesowen T	06.03.1998 Swansea C
ALLSOPP Daniel*	2000-01	10.08.1978 Melbourne, Aus		4+2	0	13.10.2000 Manchester C	(loan)
ANDERSON Jjah Massai	2002-03	30.12.1975 Hackney		14	0	07.02.2003 Brentford	
ANDERSON James McFarland	1954-57	25.09.1932 Glasgow		24	0	27.04.1953 RAOC Hilsea	07.06.1957 Chester
ANDERSON John Robert	1952-54	09.11.1924 Durham		10	0	12.03.1953 Crystal P	05.11.1954 Bristol C
ANDREASSON Marcus	1998-00	13.07.1978 Studerande, Swe		5+1	0	15.07.1998 Osters IF, Swe	23.08.1999 Kalmar FF, Swe
"	2000-01			9	1	23.03.2000 Kalmar FF, Swe	22.11.2001 Bryne FK, Norway
ANDREWS Bradley James	1998-99	08.12.1979 Bristol		3	0	18.03.1999 Norwich C	07.1999 Mangotsfield U
ARCHER Lee	1991-97	06.11.1972 Bristol		104+22	13	18.07.1991 YTS	06.10.1997 Yeovil T
ARMITAGE Harold A	1922-26	16.08.1901 Sheffield	02.09.1973 Crewe	122	0	19.05.1922 Sheffield W	11.08.1926 Lincoln C
ARMSTRONG James William	1930-31	06.09.1901 Swalwell-on-Tyne	08.1977 Gateshead	9	2	06.03.1931 Luton T	1931 Walker C
ARMSTRONG Steven Craig*	1995-96	23.05.1975 South Shields		13+1	0	05.01.1996 Nottingham F	(loan)
ARNDALE Neil Darren	2001-03	26.04.1984 Bristol		1+2	0	19.04.2002 YTS	
ASHFORD James William	1926-27	24.05.1897 Barnborough	02.1970 Poole	12	0	19.05.1926 Doncaster R	10.1928 Scunthorpe U
ASHTON Sir Hubert	1924-25	13.02.1898 Calcutta, India	17.06.1979 South Weald	1	0	23.08.1924 Corinthians	21.08.1926 Orient
ASTAFJEVS Vitalijs	1999-03	03.04.1971 Riga, Latvia		88+22	16	22.12.1999 Skonto Riga, Lat	15.07.2003 Admira W Austria
ATTWOOD Arthur Albert	1930-32	01.12.1901 Walsall		51	27	31.05.1930 Everton	06.11.1931 Brighton
AUSTIN Kevin Levi	2002-03	12.02.1973 Hackney		31+2	0	01.07.2002 Cambridge U	
BADOCK Stephen William	1985-86	10.09.1958 Kensington		14+3	3	26.06.1985 Portway-Bristol	07.1986 Gloucester C
BAILEY Dennis Lincoln*	1988-89	13.11.1965 Lambeth		17	9	28.02.1989 Crystal P	(loan)
BAILEY Steven John	1990-91			6	1	27.03.1991 Birmingham C	(loan)
"	1981-82	12.03.1964 Bristol		15+1	1	12.03.1982 apprentice	09.12.1983 Paulton R
BAKER Clifford Henry	1946-47	11.01.1924 Bristol		5	2	12.11.1946 Coalpit Heath	09.08.1948 Bath C
BAKER Thomas Arthur	1962-63	09.08.1939 Charlton		1	0	10.1956 local football	02.03.1963 Dover
BALDIE Douglas Wilson	1946-48	16.04.1921 Scoon		8	4	02.04.1946 Luton T	20.08.1948 Chippenham U
BALL Alan James	1982-83	12.05.1945 Farnworth	10.11.1998 Bristol	17	2	26.01.1983 Eastern U	17.05.1983 Minehead T
BALL Christopher George	1930-31	31.10.1906 Leek, Staffs		15	0	01.07.1930 Colwyn Bay U	04.12.1931 Bristol C
BALL John	1921-22	29.10.1900 Hazel Grove	12.1989 Coventry	22	4	12.05.1921 Sheffield U	1922 Wath Ath
BAMFORD Henry Charles	1946-58	08.10.1920 Bristol	31.10.1958 Bristol	486	5	13.12.1945 St Phillips Marsh	Deceased
BANN William Edward	1932-33	15.08.1902 Broxburn	16.03.1973 Haringey	1	0	04.06.1932 Brentford	09.1933 Aldershot
BANNISTER Bruce Ian	1971-77	14.04.1949 Bradford		202+4	80	05.11.1971 Bradford C	16.12.1976 Plymouth A
BANNON Paul Anthony	1983-85	15.11.1956 Dublin		27+2	8	26.01.1984 Carlisle U	05.07.1985 NAC Breda, Holland
BARLEY Henry Frank	1935-36	02.1905 Grimsby	08.1958 Scunthorpe	17	5	10.05.1935 Scunthorpe U	23.05.1936 Barrow
BARNES Kossuth Seed	1921-22	05.1892 Preston	12.10.1965 Sunderland	17	0	16.11.1921 Durham C	1922 Houghton
BARNEY Victor Roy	1966-70	18.11.1947 Oxford		30+1	3	06.12.1965 Oxford U	1970 Glastonbury
BARRATT Josiah	1926-27	21.02.1895 Bulkington	04.1968 Coventry	21	4	11.08.1926 Lincoln C	1927 Nuneaton T
BARRETT Adam Nicholas	2002-03	29.11.1979 Dagenham		45	1	01.07.2002 Mansfield T	
BARRETT Graham*	2000-01	06.10.1981 Dublin		0+1	0	13.12.2000 Arsenal	(loan)
BARRETT Michael John	1979-84	12.09.1959 Bristol	14.08.1984 Bristol	119+9	18	15.10.1979 Shirehampton	Deceased

PLAYERS NAME	CAREER	DATE & PLACE OF BIRTH	DATE & PLACE OF DEATH	APPS	GLS	PREVIOUS CLUB	NEXT CLUB
BARROWCLOUGH Stewart James	1979-81	29.10.1951 Barnsley		60+1	14	25.07.1979 Birmingham C	26.02.1981 Barnsley
BARRY Michael James	1977-79	22.05.1953 Hull		46+1	3	09.09.1977 Carlisle U	14.04.1979 Columbus, USA
BARTON George McIntosh	1928-31	15.10.1899 Newtongrange	08.1970 Weston-s-Mare	66	5	24.05.1928 Raith R	15.08.1932 Bedminster
BASFORD Luke William	1997-99	06.01.1980 Lambeth		11+5	0	09.07.1998 YTS	31.07.1999 Kingstonian
BATER Philip Thomas	1974-81	26.10.1955 Cardiff		211+1	2	10.1973 apprentice	10.09.1981 Wrexham
"	1983-86			90+8	1	15.09.1983 Wrexham	26.06.1986 Brentford
BATES Philip Desmond	1979-81	28.11.1949 West Bromwich		26+3	4	07.03.1980 Swindon T	16.12.1980 Shrewsbury T
BEADLE Peter Clifford	1995-98	13.05.1972 Lambeth		98+11	39	17.11.1995 Watford	06.08.1998 Port Vale
BEARPARK Ian Harper	1960-61	13.11.1939 Stonehouse	12.1997 Devon	2	0	12.09.1960 Stonehouse	31.12.1960 Exeter C
BEASLEY Andrew*	1992-93	05.02.1964 Sedgley		1	0	25.03.1993 Mansfield T	(loan)
BEBY John Victor	1932-33	23.08.1907 Gillingham	08.04.1976 Rochester	24	0	04.10.1932 Gillingham	07.07.1933 Crystal P
BELL Harold	1920-21	1898 Sheffield		2	0	12.08.1920 Barnsley	07.1921 Castleford T
BENNETT Frank	1996-00	03.01.1969 Birmingham		15+29	4	23.11.1996 Southampton	14.03.2000 Exeter C
BENNETT Frederick	1925-30	02.10.1906 Bristol	20.08.1990 Bristol	129	2	04.12.1925 H J Packers	07.1930 Chester
BERRY George	1933-35	1910 Bristol				04.1933 Bristol C	26.09.1935 Yeovil & P
BERRY George Leslie	1920-21	28.04.1906 Dorking	15.02.1985 Great Glen	34	0	21.05.1920 Barnsley	02.11.1921 Brentford
BETHUNE John	1953-61	19.10.1888 Milngavie	23.01.1955 Sittingbourne	30	0		17.07.1961 Preston NE
BIGGS Alfred George	1953-61	08.02.1936 Bristol		214	77	02.1953 Juniors	17.07.1961 Preston NE
"	1962-68			210	101	05.10.1962 Preston NE	16.03.1968 Walsall
BIGNOT Marcus	2000-01	22.08.1974 Birmingham		26	0	03.09.2000 Crewe A	16.03.2001 QPR
BIRD Walter Smith	1920-21	08.1891 Hugglescote	02.03.1965 Coalville	21	5	12.05.1920 Grimsby T	06.1921 Dundee
BLACK John Ross	1930-32	26.05.1900 Denny	14.12.1993 Scunthorpe	49	3	22.10.1930 Luton T	1932 Normandy Pk
BLAKE Herbert Charles	1931-33	16.03.1908 Bristol	04.1986 Bath	31	2	06.09.1931 Yeovil & P	14.11.1935 Bath C
BLOOMER Robert Stephen	1990-92	21.06.1966 Sheffield		11+11	0	22.03.1990 Chesterfield	15.08.1992 Cheltenham T
BOOTHROYD Adrian Neil	1990-92	08.02.1971 Bradford		10+6	0	20.06.1990 Huddersfield T	18.11.1992 Hearts
BOWERS Alfred George	1925-26	05.1895 Bow		3	0	12.06.1925 Charlton A	1926 QPR
BOXALL Daniel James	2002-03	24.08.1977 Croydon		35+4	0	01.07.2002 Brentford	
BOXLEY Harold H	1920-23	1894 Stourbridge		47	0	08.1920 Derby C	1923 Bournemouth
BOYCE Thomas Dodd	1930-31	02.08.1905 Paisley		8	0	04.07.1930 Clydebank	09.07.1931 Leith Ath
BOYES Kenneth Cecil	1922-23	17.11.1895 Southampton	06.10.1963 Eastleigh	2	0	17.06.1922 Southampton	24.07.1923 Weymouth
BRADD Leslie John*	1982-83	05.11.1947 Buxton		1	1	30.12.1982 Wigan A	(loan)
BRADFORD Geoffrey Reginald	1949-64	18.07.1927 Bristol	30.12.1994 Bristol	462	242	01.08.1949 Soundwell	1964 Retired
BRADSHAW Paul William	1986-87	28.04.1956 Altrincham		5	0	03.1987 Walsall	07.1987 Newport C
BRIGGS William Ronald	1965-68	29.03.1943 Belfast		35	0	25.05.1965 Swansea T	22.07.1968 Frome T
BRITTEN Martyn Edward	1974-77	01.05.1955 Bristol		17+3	2	05.1973 apprentice	06.08.1977 Reading
BRITTON Clifford Samuel	1928-30	29.08.1909 Bristol	01.12.1975 Hull	50	1	1926 Bristol St G	04.06.1930 Everton
BRITTON Francis George	1929-30	03.03.1910 Bristol	02.1979 Worcester	1	0	17.09.1927 Bristol St G	12.06.1930 Blackburn R
BROWN John	1963-68	29.07.1940 Wadebridge		156	32	07.1963 Plymouth A	1968 Wadebridge R
BROWN Keith Timothy	1978-81	28.09.1959 Bristol		4+3	0	10.1977 Bristol St G	12.07.1981 Bath C
BROWN Robert	1968-72	14.05.1949 Bristol		28+7	4	06.1967 apprentice	24.07.1972 Weymouth
BROWNING Marcus Trevor	1989-97	22.04.1971 Bristol		152+22	11	18.07.1989 YTS	14.02.1997 Huddersfield T
BRUCE David	1936-37	23.11.1911 Perth	15.09.1976 Bridge of Earn	12	2	27.04.1936 Leicester C	12.08.1937 St Mirren
BRYANT Clifford Samuel	1930-31	21.05.1913 Kingswood	02.12.1997 Kingswood	1	0	1930 Wesley R	05.1932 Blackburn R
BRYANT Simon Christopher	1999-03	22.11.1982 Bristol		58+17	2	11.01.2000 YTS	
BUBB Alvin Ryan	2001-02	11.10.1982 Paddington		3+10	0	18.06.2001 QPR	17.08.2002 Billericay T
BUCKLEY Edward Colston	1935-36	13.09.1912 Trethomas	08.1971 Trethomas	8	2	22.08.1935 Wolves	05.1937 Tranmere R
BUMPSTEAD David John	1961-64	06.11.1935 Rainham		40	0	28.11.1961 Millwall	10.1963 Retired
BUNCE William Newman	1934-35	17.04.1911 Pill	29.05.1981 Pill	2	0	28.06.1933 Leicester C	01.1936 Bath C
BURNELL Albert Edward	1925-26	12.05.1901 Bristol		9	3	10.1925 Barton Hill S	26.09.1932 Dockland S
BUSH Bryan	1947-55	25.04.1925 Bristol	04.1987 Bristol	113	19	10.1947 Soundwell	04.08.1955 Trowbridge T

495

PLAYERS NAME	CAREER	DATE & PLACE OF BIRTH	DATE & PLACE OF DEATH	APPS	GLS	PREVIOUS CLUB	NEXT CLUB
BUTTERWORTH Albert	1936-39	20.03.1912 Ashton-u-Lyne	01.1991 Ashton-under-Lyne	95	12	13.11.1936 Preston NE	07.1946 Stalybridge C
BYRNE David Stuart*	1989-90	05.03.1961 Hammersmith		0+2	0	01.02.1990 Plymouth A	(loan)
BYRNE Shaun Ryan*	1999-00	21.01.1981 Taplow		1+1	0	07.01.2000 West Ham U	(loan)
CAIRNEY Charles	1953-55	21.09.1926 Blantyre	25.03.1995 Airdrie	14	1	08.07.1953 Barry T	08.1955 Headington U
CALVERT Joseph William	1931-32	03.02.1907 Bullcroft		42	0	08.05.1931 Frickley C	11.05.1932 Leicester C
CAMERON Martin George	2000-03	16.06.1978 Dunfermline		16+23	6	30.06.2000 Alloa A	19.07.2002 St Mirren
CARLISLE Wayne Thomas	2001-03	09.09.1979 Lisburn		39+6	7	28.03.2002 Crystal P	
CARR Darren John	1985-88	04.09.1968 Bristol		26+4	0	20.08.1986 apprentice	28.01.1988 Newport C
CARR Lance Lanyon	1946-47	18.02.1910 Johannesburg, SA	05.1983 Greenwich	42	8	30.07.1946 Newport C	17.07.1947 Merthyr T
CARTE Robert	1938-39	11.10.1913 Doncaster	07.1986 Gainsborough	2	0	16.03.1939 Luton T	06.1939 Gainsborough T
CARTER Brian	1961-62	17.11.1938 Weymouth		4	1	30.06.1961 Portsmouth	10.03.1962 Bath C
CARTER Roy William*	1982-83	19.02.1954 Torpoint		4	1	29.12.1982 Torquay U	(loan)
CARTER Timothy Douglas	1985-88	05.10.1967 Bristol		47	0	08.10.1985 apprentice	24.12.1987 Sunderland
CASHLEY Alec Raymond	1983-85	23.10.1951 Bristol		53	0	16.08.1982 Clevedon T	22.07.1985 Trowbridge T
CAWLEY Peter E*	1986-87	15.09.1965 Walton-on-Thames		9+1	0	26.02.1987 Wimbledon	(loan)
"	1989-90			1+2	0	31.07.1989 Wimbledon	06.07.1990 Southend U
CHADWICK Frederick William	1947-48	08.11.1913 Manchester	08.02.1987 Bristol	6	1	22.07.1947 West Ham U	28.08.1948 Street
CHALLIS Trevor Michael	1998-03	23.10.1975 Paddington		138+8	1	15.07.1998 QPR	02.08.2003 Telford U
CHANCE George Harry	1920-24	25.12.1896 Stourbridge	11.07.1952 Quarry Bank	80	11	05.1920 Brierley HA	06.1924 Gillingham
CHANDLER Raymond EJ	1953-55	14.08.1931 Bath		12	0	26.06.1953 Bristol C	16.06.1956 Swindon T
CHANNING Justin Andrew	1992-96	19.11.1968 Reading		121+9	10	07.01.1993 QPR	05.07.1996 Leyton Orient
CHANNON Michael Roger	1982-83	28.11.1948 Orcheston		4+5	0	17.10.1982 Newcastle U	22.12.1982 Norwich C
CHARLESWORTH George W	1924-26	29.11.1901 Bristol	19.08.1965 Bristol	20	2	03.05.1921 Barton Hill S	20.05.1926 QPR
CLAPHAM James Richard*	1996-97	07.12.1975 Lincoln		4+1	0	27.03.1997 Tottenham H	(loan)
CLARK William Raymond	1987-97	19.05.1967 Christchurch		235+13	12	21.01.1988 Bournemouth	31.10.1997 Exeter C
CLARKE Allen Frederick*	1971-72	02.12.1952 Crayford		1	0	09.09.1971 Charlton A	(loan)
CLARKE Gary	1978-80	06.11.1960 Boston		6+5	0	06.11.1978 Bristol C	1980 Bath C
CLARKE Ryan James	2001-03	30.04.1982 Bristol		2+1	0	26.04.2002 YTS	
CLEMENT Andrew David*	1986-87	12.11.1967 Cardiff		5+1	0	05.03.1987 Wimbledon	(loan)
CLENNELL Joseph	1926-27	19.02.1889 New Silksworth	28.02.1965 Blackpool	19	5	24.09.1926 Stoke	10.1927 Rochdale
COCKRAM Allan Charles	1985-86	08.10.1963 Kensington		1	0	08.08.1985 Tottenham H	12.1985 Farnborough T
COGGINS Philip Raymond	1960-61	10.07.1940 Bristol		4	0	07.1960 Bristol C	04.07.1961 Wellington T
COLLETT Andrew Alfred	1994-99	28.10.1973 Stockton		107	0	23.03.1995 Middlesbrough	01.03.1999 Rushden & D
COLLINS George Cornelius	1960-61	06.08.1935 Barry		2	1	09.06.1960 Ton Pentre	08.1961 Hereford U
COMPTON William Alfred	1928-29	05.04.1896 Bristol	29.02.1976 Bournemouth	21	3	24.05.1928 Exeter C	08.1929 Bath C
COOK John Albert	1946-47	27.06.1929 Bristol		2	0	14.09.1946 Coalpit Heath	12.08.1952 Bridgwater T
COOK Thomas Edwin Reed	1931-33	05.01.1901 Cuckfield	15.01.1950 Brighton	42	20	06.11.1931 Northfleet	1933 Retired
COOMBES Jeffrey	1972-75	01.04.1954 Rhondda		10+1	1	08.04.1972 apprentice	1975 Ton Pentre
COOMBS Ernest Horace	1931-32	01.05.1908 Frome	16.05.1971 Frome	1	0	11.09.1931 Coleford A	10.05.1932 Bristol C
COOPER John Henry	1930-32	22.04.1904 Smethwick	04.1980 Dudley	22	0	05.07.1930 Walsall	07.1931 Torquay U
COOPER Terence	1979-82	12.07.1944 Brotherton		53+6	2	07.08.1979 Bristol C	11.11.1981 Doncaster R
COOTE Adrian*	2002-03	30.09.1978 Great Yarmouth		4+1	1	24.10.2002 Colchester U	(loan)
COSGROVE Michael Docherty	1928-30	1901 Dundee		58	6	10.05.1928 Aberdeen	1930 Retired
CRABTREE Richard Edward	1971-72	06.02.1955 Exeter		7	0	02.09.1970 apprentice	08.08.1975 Dawlish T
CRANFIELD Harold Richard	1947-48	25.12.1917 Chesterton	12.1990 King's Lynn	7	2	27.06.1947 Fulham	1948 King's Lynn
CRICHTON Alexander	1925-26	12.06.1899 Bellshill		7	0	11.06.1925 Bradford PA	1926 Retired
CRISP George Henry	1935-36	30.06.1911 Pontypool	27.03.1982 Penrhiwceiber	22	6	31.07.1935 Coventry C	06.1936 Newport C
CROMPTON George Ellis	1920-21	17.07.1886 Ramsbottom	17.05.1953 Barnstaple	41	10	03.05.1913 Exeter C	20.02.1921 Exeter C
CROSS Stephen Charles	1991-93	22.12.1959 Wolverhampton		37+6	2	12.09.1991 Derby C	10.06.1996 Mangotsfield U

PLAYERS NAME	CAREER	DATE & PLACE OF BIRTH	DATE & PLACE OF DEATH	APPS	GLS	PREVIOUS CLUB	NEXT CLUB
CUFF William Peter	1923-24	03.03.1901 Bristol	11.1969 Bristol	2	0	25.08.1921 Victoria A	05.09.1932 Co-op WS
CULKIN Nicholas James*	2000-01	06.07.1978 York		45	0	01.07.2000 Manchester U	(loan)
CULLEY William Neill	1925-28	26.08.1892 Kilwinning	09.11.1955 Irvine	57	45	21.01.1926 Weymouth	07.1928 Swindon T
CURETON Jamie	1996-01	28.08.1975 Bristol		165+9	72	20.09.1996 Norwich C	23.08.2000 Reading
CURLE Keith	1981-83	14.11.1963 Bristol		21+11	4	20.11.1981 apprentice	10.11.1983 Torquay U
CURRAN Frank	1938-47	31.05.1917 Ryton-on-Tyne		37	24	14.06.1938 Accrington S	16.05.1947 Shrewsbury T
CURRIE Walter Robertson	1922-23	05.10.1895 Auchterderran	24.09.1998 Southport	42	0	11.05.1922 Leicester C	1923 Lochgelly U
DAGNOGO Moussa Moustapha	2000-01	30.01.1972 Paris		0+2	0	29.09.2000 U Madeira	10.01.2001 Ayr U
DALRYMPLE Malcolm Owen	1971-73	08.10.1951 Bedford		7	0	13.10.1971 Luton T	03.1973 Margate T
DANDO Maurice	1928-33	07.1905 Bristol	25.09.1949 Plymouth	18	5	30.08.1928 Bath C	13.07.1933 York C
DAVIES Ian Claude	1985-86	29.03.1957 Bristol		13+1	1	08.08.1985 Diss T	25.11.1985 Swansea C
DAVIES Royston	1927-28	19.10.1903 Merthyr Tydfil	15.10.1944 Gloucester	2	0	12.05.1927 Merthyr T	1928 Ebbw Vale
DAVIS Joseph T	1960-67	24.08.1938 Bristol		210+1	4	03.1956 Soundwell	10.03.1967 Swansea T
DAVIS Michael Vernon	1992-96	19.10.1974 Bristol		3+14	1	26.04.1993 Yate T	30.07.1996 Bath C
DAWS James	1924-25	27.05.1898 Mansfield	06.1985 Birmingham	29	0	15.05.1924 Birmingham	31.07.1925 Mansfield W
DAY Graham George	1974-79	22.11.1953 Bristol		129+1	1	05.1973 Bristol St G	26.03.1979 Portland T
DENNEHY Jeremiah	1978-80	29.03.1950 Cork		47+5	6	22.07.1978 Walsall	09.09.1980 Trowbridge T
DENNIS George Thomas	1930-31	12.09.1897 Moira	13.10.1969 Burton-upon-Trent	26	4	05.05.1930 Norwich C	1932 Burton T
DENSLEY Arthur Herbert	1927-30	11.05.1903 Bristol	05.1982 Bristol	23	0	1923 YMCA	11.08.1931 Bath C
DICK Andrew	1925-26	1900 Aberdeen		19	0	11.06.1925 Aberdeen	1927 Motherwell
DINSDALE Norman	1930-31	20.06.1898 Hounslet	10.1970 Nottingham	31	3	13.06.1930 Coventry C	1932 Kidderminster H
DI PIEDI Michele*	2002-03	04.12.1980 Palmero, Italy		3+2	0	22.02.2003 Sheffield W	(loan)
DIX Ronald William	1927-32	05.09.1912 Bristol	02.04.1998 Bristol	100	33	25.02.1928 South St	09.05.1932 Blackburn R
DOBSON Colin	1972-76	09.05.1940 Eston		63	4	03.06.1972 Huddersfield T	05.1976 Coventry C
DODGIN William	1936-37	17.04.1909 Gateshead	16.10.1999 Godalming	30	1	04.05.1936 Charlton Ath	07.1937 Orient
DONALD Alexander	1932-36	29.05.1900 Kirkintilloch		136	0	06.05.1932 Chelsea	07.1936 Dunfermline A
DOUGLAS George Harold	1926-28	18.08.1893 Stepney	24.01.1979 Southborough	45	5	07.08.1926 Oldham A	05.07.1928 Tunbridge Wells
DOYLE Joseph Brian	1957-60	15.07.1930 Manchester	22.12.1992 Blackpool	43	1	26.06.1957 Exeter C	1960 Retired
DRAKE Leonard	1958-60	26.07.1937 Dorchester		8	1	25.05.1957 Dorchester T	1962 Weymouth
DRYDEN Richard Andrew	1986-89	14.06.1969 Stroud		12+1	0	14.07.1987 YTS	08.03.1989 Exeter C
DUCKERS Samuel Edward	1925-26	28.11.1903 Stafford	02.1972 Stafford	1	0	07.05.1925 Stafford R	1926 Stafford R
DUNCAN Thomas Grossett	1926-27	01.09.1897 Lochgelly	09.02.1940 Leicester	13	2	18.05.1926 Halifax T	1927 Kettering T
DURKAN James	1934-35	14.07.1915 Bannockburn		2	0	27.07.1934 Cardiff C	08.1935 King's Park
EADIE James	1972-77	04.02.1947 Kirkintilloch		183	6	15.02.1973 Cardiff C	12.09.1977 Bath C
EATON Jason Cord	1987-88	29.01.1969 Bristol		0+3	0	06.1987 Olveston U	1988 Clevedon T
EDGE Anthony	1959-61	14.03.1937 Wirral		13	4	08.1959 Devizes T	28.11.1960 Bath C
EDWARDS Leslie Raymond	1950-57	12.04.1924 Guildford		47	0	06.05.1948 Nailsea U	05.08.1958 Trowbridge T
EDWARDS Samuel	1924-25	05.1898 Dudley Port		33	5	07.08.1924 Kidderminster H	1925 Stourbridge
ELLINGTON Nathan Levi Fontaine	1998-02	02.07.1981 Bradford		76+40	35	18.02.1999 Walton & H	28.03.2002 Wigan A
ELLIS Clinton	2000-01	07.07.1977 Brent		2+13	1	01.06.2000 Chelsea	14.07.2001 released
ELLIS John	1934-38	25.01.1908 Tyldesley	01.1994 Tyldesley	86	0	27.07.1934 Wolves	27.05.1938 Hull C
EMMANUEL John Gareth	1978-81	01.02.1954 Swansea		59+6	2	29.01.1979 Birmingham C	22.07.1981 Swindon T
ENGLAND Michael "	1978-79	04.01.1961 Kingswood		1	0	11.07.1977 Frampton R	1979 Bath C
	1985-86			17	0	09.1985 Forest Gn R	11.08.1986 Bath C
EVANS Andrew David Stanley	1975-78	03.10.1957 Swansea		34+8	2	09.1975 apprentice	12.1977 Retired
EVANS John Hugh	1926-28	31.01.1889 Bala		63	7	03.06.1926 Cardiff C	05.1928 Retired
EVANS Michael James	2000-01	01.01.1973 Plymouth		19+2	4	18.08.2000 West Brom A	23.03.2001 Plymouth A
EVANS Rhys Karl*	1999-00	27.01.1982 Swindon		4	0	25.02.2000 Chelsea	(loan)

PLAYERS NAME	CAREER	DATE & PLACE OF BIRTH	DATE & PLACE OF DEATH	APPS	GLS	PREVIOUS CLUB	NEXT CLUB
EVANS Richard William	1991-94	12.04.1968 Ebbw Vale		9+6	1	08.08.1991 Weymouth	06.08.1994 Yeovil T
EYRES John	1932-34	20.03.1899 Northwich	02.10.1975 Gainsborough	63	12	23.05.1932 Brighton	07.1934 York C
FALCONER Fleming	1927-29	24.05.1899 Hutchesontown		20	0	09.03.1928 Bo'ness	1931 Linlithgow Rose
FEARNLEY Gordon	1970-77	25.01.1950 Bradford		94+26	21	03.07.1970 Sheffield W	05.1977 Toronto Metros, Can
FINDLAY Alexander	1929-32	26.12.1902 Wishaw		37	9	12.02.1930 Musselburgh	23.07.1932 Wrexham
FORAN Mark James	2000-02	30.10.1973 Aldershot	10.1985 Bristol	39+4	2	11.08.2000 Crewe A	05.08.2002 Telford U
FORBES Frederick James	1929-31	05.08.1894 Edinburgh		63	10	14.11.1929 Plymouth A	09.07.1931 Leith Ath
FORBES James	1926-28	14.03.1896 Walker-on-Tyne	29.03.1939 Walker-on-Tyne	59	5	01.07.1926 Bolton W	07.1928 Workington
FORD Anthony Michael	1969-71	26.11.1944 Thornbury		28	1	04.12.1969 Bristol C	30.03.1971 Retired
FOREMAN William Ernest	1976-78	03.02.1958 Havant		0+2	0	19.05.1976 Bournemouth	1978 Australia
FOSTER Jabez	1925-26	15.09.1902 Darlaston	08.1971 Walsall	3	1	14.05.1925 Kettering T	25.08.1926 Gillingham
FOSTER Stephen	1997-02	03.12.1974 Mansfield		193+4	7	20.05.1997 Woking	12.08.2002 Doncaster R
FOX Geoffrey Roy	1947-55	19.01.1925 Bristol	01.01.1994 Worcester	276	2	22.06.1947 Ipswich T	01.10.1955 Swindon T
FRANCIS Gerald Charles	1985-88	06.12.1951 Chiswick		33+1	1	07.09.1985 Wimbledon	1986 Wimbledon
FRATER David Thomas	1935-36	08.02.1911 Pontypridd	12.1986 Pontypridd	1	1	09.04.1935 Swindon T	1936 Retired
FRENCH Jonathan Charles	1995-97	25.09.1976 Keynsham		8+9	1	15.07.1995 YTS	28.07.1998 Hull C
FROWEN John	1958-63	11.10.1931 Trelewis		84	0	11.08.1958 Cardiff C	14.03.1963 Newport C
FRUDE Roger Gordon	1963-68	19.11.1946 Plymouth	14.06.1996 Plymouth	38+3	8	19.11.1963 apprentice	29.09.1967 Mansfield T
FURNISS Samuel	1921-24	09.03.1895 Sheffield	11.03.1977 Sheffield	90	2	12.05.1921 Sheffield U	08.12.1924 Swindon T
GADSTON Joseph Edward	1968-69	13.09.1945 Hanwell		10+1	5	05.1968 Cheltenham T	05.11.1969 Exeter C
GALL Kevin Alexander	2000-03	04.02.1982 Merthyr		28+20	5	22.03.2001 Newcastle U	01.02.2003 Yeovil Town
CANE George B Herbert	1920-21	02.1886 Kingswood	19.06.1967 Bristol	1	0	12.10.1920 Douglas	1921 Bradford C
GARDINER Robert	1937-39	02.09.1912 Dundee	04.1993 Dundee	66	10	14.07.1937 Dartford	1939 Dundee U
GARDNER James R	1925-26	29.07.1902 Peckham		32	4	05.08.1925 Yeovil & P	06.1926 Orient
GAYLE Brian Wilbert	1996-98	06.03.1965 Kingston-u-Thames		23	0	03.07.1997 Rotherham U	19.12.1997 Shrewsbury T
GIBBINS William Vivian	1932-33	10.08.1901 Forest Gate	21.11.1979 Herne Bay	37	15	08.06.1932 Brentford	24.08.1933 Southampton
GIBBS Arthur	1924-25	1898 Stafford		19	0	08.05.1924 Brierley HA	11.07.1925 Weymouth
GILBERT Carl Graham	1969-71	20.03.1948 Folkestone		38+7	15	22.11.1969 Gillingham	11.03.1971 Rotherham U
GILES Albert Edgar	1946-47	04.05.1924 Swansea		1	0	18.10.1945 RAF service	12.08.1947 Glastonbury
GILLESPIE William Blyth	1929-30	29.10.1903 Fife		2	0	28.06.1929 Newcastle U	07.1930 St Mirren
GILLIES Donald George	1980-82	20.06.1951 Glencoe		56+3	9	23.05.1980 Bristol C	26.10.1983 Paulton R
GILROY David Miles	2001-03	13.12.1982 Yeovil		5+10	0	01.08.2001 YTS	
GLENNON Matthew William*	2000-01	08.10.1978 Stockport		1	0	15.09.2000 Bolton W	(loan)
GODFREY Brian Cameron	1971-73	01.05.1940 Flint		79+2	16	26.05.1971 Aston Villa	09.06.1973 Newport C
COLLEDGE Leslie Howard	1934-37	03.08.1911 Chipping Sodbury	19.07.1989 Bristol	9	1	09.02.1935 Bristol C	1937 Lincoln C
GOUGH Colin Kenneth*	1990-91	17.01.1963 Stourbridge		1+3	0	23.01.1991 Birmingham C	(loan)
GOUGH Anthony Michael	1958-59	18.03.1940 Bath		1	0	05.1958 Bath C	1959 Swindon T
GOULD Robert Alfred	1977-79	12.06.1946 Coventry		35+1	12	14.10.1977 Wolves	13.09.1978 Hereford U
GRAYDON Raymond Jack	1965-71	21.07.1947 Bristol		131+2	33	22.09.1965 Hambrook	26.05.1971 Aston Villa
GRAZIOLI Giuliano Stefano	2002-03	23.03.1975 Marylebone		28+6	11	01.07.2002 Swindon T	01.08.2003 Barnet
GREEN Michael Clive	1971-74	08.09.1946 Carlisle		74+3	2	05.07.1971 Gillingham	22.07.1974 Plymouth A
GREEN Ronald Clarence George	1932-33	12.03.1912 Bristol	16.10.1979 Bristol	22	2	03.06.1932 Bath C	07.1933 Arsenal
GREEN Ronald Rex	1984-86	03.10.1956 Birmingham		56	0	01.03.1985 Shrewsbury T	21.08.1986 Scunthorpe U
GREEN Stanley	1951-52	06.09.1928 West Bromwich		1	0	04.1952 Accles & P	1953 Midlands football
GRIFFITHS Ashley Russell	1979-81	05.01.1961 Barry		6+1	0	01.1979 apprentice	28.06.1981 Torquay U
GRIFFITHS Lewis Henry	1925-26	07.09.1903 Tonypandy	07.1985 Tonypandy	1	0	04.02.1926 Mid Rhondda U	17.09.1926 Torquay U
GURNEY Andrew Robert	1993-97	25.01.1974 Bristol		100+8	9	10.07.1992 St Valier	07.10.1997 Torquay U
GUSCOTT Raymond Melvin	1976-77	18.11.1957 Newport		1	0	11.1975 Clifton A	09.1977 Minehead
HACKETT Christopher Edward	1930-31	09.02.1903 Mansfield	02.1983 Leicester	1	0	15.03.1930 Scunthorpe U	09.1931 Loughborough C
HADDON Harold Llewellyn	1948-49	08.04.1923 Cardiff		2	0	06.01.1949 Newport C	04.08.1949 Trowbridge T

498

PLAYERS NAME	CAREER	DATE & PLACE OF BIRTH	DATE & PLACE OF DEATH	APPS	GLS	PREVIOUS CLUB	NEXT CLUB
HALE Denzil	1953-59	09.04.1928 Clevedon		120	12	19.02.1952 Clevedon T	29.07.1959 Bath C
HALL Arthur Brian	1960-62	24.03.1937 Eynsham		2	0	23.08.1958 Oxford C	02.1962 King's Lynn
HALL Bernard Raymond	1961-67	08.07.1942 Bath		163	0	02.09.1959 Twerton YC	1967 Retired
HALL Joseph E	1920-22	1890 Boldon		28	0	07.08.1920 Manchester C	1922 Newport C
HALLWORTH Jonathan Geoffrey*	1984-85	26.10.1965 Stockport		2	0	12.01.1985 Ipswich T	(loan)
HAMILTON Ian	1958-68	12.09.1940 Bristol		149	60	01.1958 Thornbury	07.1968 Newport C
HAMILTON James	1976-77	14.06.1955 Uddingston		16+4	2	16.12.1976 Plymouth A	09.09.1977 Carlisle U
HAMILTON John P	1929-31	25.04.1909 Armadale	05.1983 Bristol	63	2	03.06.1929 Penicuik J	1931 Thornbury T
HAMMOND Elvis Zark*	2001-02	06.10.1980 Accra, Ghana		3+4	0	01.08.2001 Fulham	(loan)
HAMMOND Nicholas David*	1986-87	07.09.1967 Hornchurch		3	0	23.08.1986 Arsenal	(loan)
HAMMOND Walter Reginald	1921-24	19.06.1903 Dover	02.07.1965 Durban	19	2	13.06.1921 Union Jack	1924 Ryde Sports
HARDING Stephen John	1977-80	23.07.1956 Bristol		37+1	1	30.05.1977 Bristol C	22.07.1981 Trowbridge T
HARDYMAN Paul George T	1992-95	11.03.1964 Portsmouth		54+13	5	14.07.1992 Sunderland	04.08.1995 Wycombe W
HARRIS Jason Andre Sebastian*	1996-97	24.11.1976 Sutton		5+1	2	22.11.1996 Crystal P	(loan)
HARRIS Thomas F	1934-38	1915 Plymouth		28	16	23.04.1935 Plymouth K	06.12.1937 Southampton
HARTILL William John	1935-38	18.07.1905 Wolverhampton	07.1980 Walsall	36	19	13.03.1936 Liverpool	1938 Street
HARTLEY Sydney	1938-39	22.01.1914 Gomershall	05.1987 Huddersfield	4	1	27.05.1938 Gillingham	1939 Tunbridge WR
HARVEY Edward Lee	1921-22	08.1892 Birmingham		5	0	12.09.1921 Sheffield W	1922 Retired
HARVEY James Douglas	1932-33	07.08.1911 York	05.1965 Sheffield	1	0	02.08.1932 Frickley C	1933 Frickley C
HARWOOD Irvine	1934-36	05.12.1905 Bradford		51	14	30.03.1934 Wolves	05.1936 Walsall
HAVELOCK John	1933-35	11.05.1904 Hartlepool	06.1973 Walsall	20	11	02.12.1933 Folkestone	01.08.1935 Aylesford PM
HAVERTY Joseph	1964-65	17.02.1936 Dublin	07.1981 Scunthorpe	13	1	04.12.1964 Millwall	1965 Shelbourne
HAYDON James Gilbert	1921-30	04.05.1901 Bristol	21.09.1969 Bristol	290	5	11.11.1921 Newton OB	11.12.1931 Kingswood
HAYFIELD Matthew Anthony	1995-98	08.08.1975 Bristol		24+17	5	13.07.1994 YTS	10.10.1998 Yeovil T
HAYLES Barrington Edward	1997-99	17.04.1972 London		62	32	20.05.1997 Stevenage B	17.11.1998 Fulham
HAYWARD Douglas Stanworth	1946-47	28.03.1920 Wellington		1	0	27.09.1946 Huddersfield T	20.11.1946 Newport C
HAZEL Ian	1988-89	01.12.1967 Merton		3	0	27.02.1989 Wimbledon	(loan)
"	1989-90			4+10	0	10.07.1989 Wimbledon	30.01.1992 Maidstone U
HEGGS Carl Sydney*	1994-95	11.10.1970 Leicester		2+3	1	27.01.1995 West Brom A	(loan)
HEINEMANN Charles Adolph	1925-26	29.02.1904 Stafford	13.05.1974 Hornchurch	3	1	07.05.1925 Stafford R	08.1926 Port Vale
HENDRIE Paul	1977-79	27.03.1954 Glasgow		17+14	1	05.09.1977 Portland T	26.07.1979 Halifax T
HIBBITT Kenneth	1986-89	03.01.1951 Bradford		51+2	5	04.08.1986 Coventry C	15.05.1990 Retired
HIGGINS Peter Clive	1968-73	12.11.1950 Cardiff		36+1	5	02.1969 apprentice	07.1973 Doncaster R
HIGGS Shane Peter	1996-98	13.05.1977 Oxford		10	0	12.07.1995 YTS	10.07.1998 Worcester C
HILL Francis William	1931-32	11.1910 Grimsby		16	0	06.1931 Portsmouth	08.1932 Crewe A
HILLARD Douglas Alfred	1958-68	10.08.1935 Bristol	06.01.1997 Bristol	313+5	12	30.05.1957 Bristol MH	06.1968 Taunton T
HILLIER David	1998-02	19.12.1969 Blackheath		82+1	1	24.02.1999 Portsmouth	14.08.2002 Barnet
HILLS John Raymond	1961-62	24.02.1934 Northfleet		7	0	19.07.1961 Tottenham H	1962 Margate
HODGES Lee Leslie*	2002-03	02.03.1978 Plaistow		7+1	0	21.03.2003 Rochdale	(loan)
HODGES Leonard Herbert	1946-50	17.02.1920 Bristol	05.08.1959 Bristol	118	20	09.08.1946 Soundwell	28.07.1950 Swansea T
HOGG Lewis James	2000-03	13.09.1982 Bristol		53+4	3	01.08.1999 YTS	10.08.2003 Barnet
HOLCROFT Sydney	1924-27	08.1901 Aston	05.1934 Birmingham	33	9	17.05.1924 Stourbridge	1927 Willenhall
HOLLOWAY Ian Scott	1980-85	12.03.1963 Kingswood		104+7	15	18.03.1981 apprentice	19.07.1985 Wimbledon
"	1987-91			179	26	21.08.1987 Brentford	12.08.1991 QPR
"	1996-99			96+11	0	13.05.1996 QPR	26.02.2001 QPR
HOMER Sydney	1927-30	14.01.1903 Bloxwich	22.01.1983 Walsall	38	4	22.06.1927 Wolves	08.11.1929 Bristol C
HOOPER Peter John	1953-62	02.02.1933 Teignmouth		297	101	05.05.1953 Dawlish T	02.07.1962 Cardiff C
HOPE Henry	1934-35	1914 Newcastle-upon-Tyne		1	0	06.05.1934 Chopwell	17.04.1935 Bristol C
HOPKINS Jeffrey	1991-92	14.04.1964 Swansea		4+2	0	05.03.1992 Crystal P	13.07.1992 Reading

PLAYERS NAME	CAREER	DATE & PLACE OF BIRTH	DATE & PLACE OF DEATH	APPS	GLS	PREVIOUS CLUB	NEXT CLUB
HOUGH Edward	1932-33	04.12.1899 Walsall	03.09.1978 Birmingham	1	0	22.12.1932 Portsmouth	1933 Portsmouth Elect
HOUGHTON Harold	1935-37	26.08.1906 Liverpool	03.02.1986 Liverpool	63	23	01.11.1935 Norwich C	24.09.1937 South Liverpool
HOWARTH James Thomas	1922-23	15.04.1890 Bury	20.09.1969 Rochdale	21	4	09.11.1922 Leeds U	07.05.1923 Lovells A
HOWES Denis	1920-22	23.03.1898 Bristol	23.03.1970 Bristol	21	0	1919 local football	1922 Bath C
HOWIE Scott	2001-03	04.01.1972 Glasgow		90	0	31.07.2001 Reading	10.08.2003 Shrewsbury T
HOWSHALL John Henry	1937-38	12.07.1912 Normacott	24.12.1962 Hanley	21	0	26.06.1937 Southport	26.07.1938 Accrington S
HOYLE Herbert	1950-53	22.04.1920 Baildon	06.07.2003 Dawlish	104	0	10.05.1950 Exeter C	08.1953 Exmouth T
HUDD David Clive	1964-65	09.07.1944 Bristol		5	1	22.07.1963 O Georgians	13.08.1966 Cheltenham T
HUGHES Mark	1979-84	03.02.1962 Port Talbot		73+1	3	01.02.1980 apprentice	30.07.1984 Swansea C
HUMES James	1962-63	06.08.1942 Carlisle		2	0	23.06.1962 Preston NE	07.1963 Chester
HURFORD David George	1962-65	17.01.1945 Bristol		6	0	01.1963 Old Sodbury	29.05.1965 Cheltenham T
HYDE Graham	2002-03	10.11.1970 Doncaster		21	1	26.11.2002 Birmingham C	
ILES Albert Kitchener	1937-39	09.10.1914 Tunbridge Wells	30.11.1979 Cambridge	46	19	24.09.1937 Tunbridge WR	07.1939 Street
ILES Richard	1985-86	21.05.1967 Bristol		1	0	03.1986 Longwell GA	07.1986 Mangotsfield U
IPOUA Gui	1998-99	14.01.1976 Douala, Cameroon		15+9	3	07.08.1998 Ath Madrid, Sp	27.08.1999 Scunthorpe U
IRVING Samuel Johnstone	1932-33	28.08.1894 Belfast		21	1	06.05.1932 Chelsea	1933 Retired
JACKSON William	1932-34	05.09.1902 Farnworth	17.01.1969 Dundee	37	14	23.05.1932 Leicester C	05.1934 Cardiff C
JACOBS Trevor Frederick	1973-76	28.11.1946 Bristol	11.1974 Blackpool	82	3	21.05.1973 Bristol C	07.1976 Bideford
JAMES Royston William	1960-61	19.02.1941 Bristol		1	0	07.1960 O Georgians	01.1962 Minehead
JAMES Thomas Anthony	1949-51	16.09.1919 Ynysybwl	07.04.1990 Bristol	21	5	30.06.1949 Brighton	04.08.1951 Bath C
JARMAN Harold James	1959-73	04.05.1939 Bristol		440+12	127	07.08.1959 Victoria A	14.05.1973 Newport C
JENKINS Brian	1963-64	01.08.1935 Treherbert		7	0	07.1963 Exeter C	1964 Merthyr T
JOHANSEN Rune Buer*	2000-01	01.04.1978 Tromso, Norway		0-2	0	10.11.2000 Tromso, Norway	(loan)
JOHN Malcolm	1971-74	09.12.1950 Bridgend		4+1	2	09.1971 Swansea C	05.10.1974 Northampton T
JOHNS Mark S	1986-87	17.05.1959 Bristol		2	1	09.1986 Bristol Manor Farm	1987 Bristol MF
JOHNSTON Raymond Stephen	1998-99	05.05.1981 Bristol		1	0	01.08.1998 YTS	07.2000 Clevedon T
JONES Brynley H	1969-75	08.02.1948 Llandrindod Wells		84+6	6	28.05.1969 Cardiff C	09.07.1975 Yeovil T
JONES Desmond	1952-53	15.03.1930 Rhondda		6	0	27.05.1952 Swansea C	18.06.1954 Workington
JONES Glyn Alan	1977-80	29.03.1959 Newport		9	0	29.03.1977 Aston V	10.07.1980 Shrewsbury T
JONES Glynfor Robert	1962-66	20.03.1935 Llandwrog		153	0	27.07.1962 Wolves	1966 Porthmadog
JONES Lee	1997-00	09.08.1970 Pontypridd		76	0	06.03.1998 Swansea C	12.07.2000 Stockport C
JONES Philip Wayne	1966-73	20.10.1948 Treorchy		218+6	28	10.1966 apprentice	04.11.1972 Retired
JONES Ralph	1947-50	19.05.1921 Maesteg	18.01.1997 Bridgend	12	1	04.12.1947 Newport C	11.08.1951 Bath C
JONES Richard	1925-26	06.06.1900 Ashton-in-Makerfield		8	0	12.06.1925 Exeter C	1926 Colwyn Bay U
JONES Robert Stanley	1957-67	28.10.1938 Bristol		250	64	05.1956 Soundwell	27.09.1966 Northampton T
"	1967-73			160+11	37	25.08.1967 Swindon T	11.08.1973 Minehead
JONES Scott	2000-02	01.05.1975 Sheffield		51+7	3	07.09.2000 Barnsley	05.08.2002 York C
JONES Vaughan	1976-82	02.09.1959 Tonyrefail		93+8	3	12.07.1976 apprentice	07.07.1982 Newport C
"	1984-93			277+3	9	21.03.1985 Cardiff C	26.03.1993 Bath C
JOSEPH Francis*	1987-88	06.03.1960 Kilburn	03.1991 Bristol	3	0	22.01.1988 Reading	(loan)
KAVANAGH Walter	1938-39	27.10.1917 Ireland	09.01.1975 Prestwick	6	0	11.07.1938 Tunbridge WR	1939 Retired
KEDENS James Anderson	1926-27	19.04.1901 Auchinleck		1	0	09.12.1926 Ardeer T	1927 Glenburn R
KELLY Errington Edison	1981-83	08.04.1958 St Vincent, WI		12+6	3	22.09.1981 Ledbury T	31.01.1983 Lincoln C
KELLY Gavin John	1990-94	29.09.1968 Beverley		30	0	01.07.1990 Hull C	07.1994 Scarborough
KENNY David Brown	1920-21	1891 Maybole		11	0	12.05.1920 Grimsby T	1921 Nainamo C, Canada
KING Alfred	1927-30	06.06.1906 Wallyford		45	10	07.03.1928 Wallyford B	1930 Tranmere R
KISSOCK Joseph Gartshore	1921-22	05.06.1893 Coatbridge	01.09.1959 San Francisco	18	0	13.06.1921 Bury	1922 Peebles R
KITCHEN Norman	1938-39	26.07.1911 Sunderland	05.11.1998 Northampton	2	0	06.07.1938 Southport	28.07.1939 Workington
KITE Philip David	1980-84	26.10.1962 Kingswood		96	0	26.10.1980 apprentice	15.08.1984 Southampton
KUIPERS Michels	1998-99	26.06.1974 Amsterdam, Holl		1	0	23.01.1999 SDW Amsterdam	10.06.2000 Brighton

PLAYERS NAME	CAREER	DATE & PLACE OF BIRTH	DATE & PLACE OF DEATH	APPS	GLS	PREVIOUS CLUB	NEXT CLUB
LAING Frederick James	1948-49	25.02.1920 Glasgow		2	0	28.07.1948 Middlesbrough	04.08.1949 Trowbridge T
LAMBDEN Victor David	1946-55	24.10.1925 Bristol	04.07.1996 Bristol	268	117	18.10.1945 Oldland	04.08.1955 Trowbridge T
LAW Marcus William	1994-95	28.09.1975 Coventry		2	0	13.07.1994 YTS	16.03.1995 Stafford R
LAWRENCE David	1956-57	12.05.1933 Poole		5	0	13.06.1955 Poole T	11.06.1957 Reading
LEA Thomas	1922-24	02.09.1890 Shrewsbury	11.1979 Shrewsbury	49	1	03.08.1922 Wolves	07.1924 Shrewsbury T
LEAMON Frederick William	1946-48	11.05.1919 Jersey	27.08.1981 London	43	21	26.11.1946 Newport C	07.1949 Brighton
LEE Christian Earl	2000-01	08.10.1976 Aylesbury		8+1	2	22.03.2001 Gillingham	07.09.2001 Farnborough T
LEE David John	1998-99	26.11.1969 Kingswood		10+1	1	24.12.1998 Chelsea	28.10.1999 Crystal P
LEE David John Francis*	2002-03	28.03.1980 Basildon		5	0	17.10.2002 Brighton	(loan)
LEE Robert Gordon	1980-81	02.02.1953 Melton Mowbray		19+4	2	10.08.1980 Sunderland	30.07.1981 Carlisle U
LEIGH Alfred Sydney	1920-22	08.1893 Shardlow	05.1958 Nottingham	68	36	16.05.1920 Derby C	1922 Retired
LENNON George Ferguson	1925-26	24.05.1899 Kilwinning	09.1984 Kilwinning	4	0	25.07.1925 Weymouth	05.1926 Retired
LEONARD Patrick Desmond	1952-54	25.07.1929 Dublin		14	2	15.07.1952 Bath C	29.06.1954 Colchester U
LEONI Stephane	1998-00	01.09.1976 St Michiel, France		27+11	4	18.08.1998 FC Metz, France	07.09.2000 Dundee U
LEWIS Dudley Reginald James	1932-34	19.11.1909 Kensington	24.04.1987 Bath	27	4	28.07.1932 QPR	05.1934 Exeter C
LEWIS Idris	1946-47	26.08.1915 Tonypandy	03.1996 Swansea	13	2	31.07.1946 Sheffield W	12.11.1946 Newport C
LEWIS Paul Samuel	1975-76	27.09.1956 Rhondda		1	0	10.1974 apprentice	03.1979 Barry T
LIDDELL James Brown	1921-23	10.01.1898 Partick		31	5	11.05.1921 Albion R	01.1924 Preston NE
LILEY Henry John Gerald	1946-50	19.08.1918 Trowbridge		27	0	12.10.1946 Bristol C	08.08.1951 Bath C
LITTLEWOOD George Charles P	1929-30	1903 Tipton	17.09.2001 Weston-s-Mare Badminton	1	0	14.02.1930 Worcester C	29.10.1931 Badminton
LLEWELLYN Christopher Mark*	2002-03	29.08.1979 Merthyr Tydfil		14	3	22.02.03 Norwich C	(loan)
LLOYD Laurence Valentine	1968-69	06.10.1948 Bristol		43	1	06.07.1967 apprentice	23.04.1969 Liverpool
LOCKIER Maurice Reginald	1949-50	27.11.1924 Bristol		2	0	21.07.1947 Chester	02.05.1952 Bath C
LOCKWOOD Matthew Dominic	1996-98	17.10.1976 Rochford		58+5	1	22.07.1996 QPR	10.08.1998 Orient
LOFTHOUSE James	1923-26	24.03.1894 St Helens	08.1954 Windsor	105	15	01.12.1923 Rotherham C	05.1926 QPR
LOPEZ Rik	2001-02	25.12.1979 Northwich Park		5+2	0	09.08.2001 QPR	18.03.2002 released
LOW Joshua David	1995-99	15.02.1979 Bristol		11+11	0	19.08.1996 YTS	27.05.1999 Orient
LUNN Frederick Levi	1922-23	08.11.1895 Marsden	02.1972 Huddersfield	31	10	18.05.1922 Sheffield W	06.1923 Southend U
LYONS Michael Charles	1953-54	31.01.1932 Bristol		2	0	08.07.1953 Bristol C	05.07.1956 Bournemouth
LYTHGOE Philip*	1978-79	18.12.1959 Norwich		6	0	22.09.1978 Norwich C	(loan)
MABBUTT Gary Vincent	1978-82	23.08.1961 Bristol		122+9	10	23.08.1977 apprentice	28.07.1982 Tottenham H
MABBUTT Raymond William	1957-69	13.03.1936 Aylesbury		392+3	27	11.08.1956 Oxford C	09.09.1969 Newport C
McALISTER Thomas Gerald*	1980-81	10.12.1952 Clydebank		13	0	13.02.1981 Swindon T	(loan)
McARTHUR Walter	1932-50	21.03.1912 Denaby	10.09.1980 Bristol	261	14	02.02.1933 Goldthorpe U	1950 Retired
McCAFFREY Aiden	1980-85	30.08.1957 Jarrow		183+1	11	20.08.1980 Derby C	22.06.1985 Exeter C
McCAIG David	1928-30	26.11.1906 Carluke		16	0	14.07.1928 Raith R	1930 Retired
McCAMBRIDGE James Joseph	1933-36	24.09.1905 Larne	15.05.1990 Larne	58	23	22.05.1933 Ballymena U	24.09.1935 Exeter C
McCLEAN Christian Alphonso	1987-91	17.10.1963 Colchester		28+23	3	24.03.1988 Clacton T	07.1991 Swansea C
McCOURT Francis Joseph	1949-50	09.12.1925 Portadown		32	1	20.09.1945 Shamrock R	30.11.50 Manchester C
McCROHAN Roy	1964-65	22.09.1930 Reading		10	1	03.08.1964 Colchester U	07.1966 Crawley T
McILVENNY John Anthony	1952-59	02.03.1930 Hinckley		79	11	18.07.1952 Cheltenham T	06.06.1959 Reading
McKAY Robert	1932-35	02.09.1900 Govan		91	17	11.11.1932 Charlton A	29.06.1935 Newport C
McKEEVER Mark Anthony	1998-99	16.11.1978 Derry		5+2	0	10.12.1998 Sheffield W	(loan)
"	2000-03			20+15	0	09.03.2001 Sheffield W	21.07.03 Weston-Super-Mare
McKENNA John Guthrie	1927-28	28.10.1910 Newcastle-u-Tyne	08.1974 Torquay	10	0	28.07.1927 Walker C	08.1928 Workington
McLEAN Ian	1993-94	13.08.1966 Paisley		21+14	2	15.09.1993 Portland T	09.1994 Cardiff C
McLEAN John Calderwood	1933-37	30.03.1908 Busby, Lanarks.	02.04.1988 Bristol	134	1	30.05.1933 Blackburn R	27.08.1938 Street
McNESTRY George	1932-35	07.01.1908 Chopwell	03.1998 Gateshead	113	42	23.05.1932 Luton T	25.06.1935 Coventry C
MADDISON Lee Robert	1991-95	05.10.1972 Bristol		68+5	0	18.07.1991 YTS	26.10.1995 Northampton T

PLAYERS NAME	CAREER	DATE & PLACE OF BIRTH	DATE & PLACE OF DEATH	APPS	GLS	PREVIOUS CLUB	NEXT CLUB
MARGETSON Martyn Walter*	1993-94	08.09.1971 Neath		2+1	1	07.12.1993 Manchester C	(loan)
MARSLAND Gordon P	1969-70	20.03.1945 Blackpool		16	1	10.06.1969 Carlisle U	30.07.1971 Bath C
MARTIN Lee Andrew	1996-97	05.02.1968 Hyde		25	0	22.07.1996 Glasgow Celtic	01.08.1998 Glossop NE
MARTYN Antony Nigel	1987-90	11.08.1966 St Austell		101	0	06.08.1987 St Blazey	17.11.1989 Crystal P
MATTHEW Damian*	1995-96	23.09.1970 Islington		8	0	12.01.1996 Crystal P	(loan)
MAUGE Ronald Carlton	1999-02	10.03.1969 Islington		50+3	9	05.07.1999 Plymouth A	03.08.2002 St Albans
MEACHAM Jeffrey	1986-88	06.02.1962 Bristol		19+7	9	27.03.1987 Trowbridge T	08.1988 Weymouth
MEAKER Michael John	1998-01	18.08.1971 Greenford		19+8	2	01.08.1998 Reading	16.02.2001 Plymouth A
MEGSON Donald Harry	1969-71	12.06.1936 Sale		31	1	10.03.1970 Sheffield W	05.1971 Retired
MEHEW David Stephen	1985-94	29.10.1967 Camberley		195+27	63	11.07.1985 Leeds U	23.03.1994 Exeter C
MEYER Barrie John	1953-58	21.08.1932 Bournemouth		139	60	21.11.1949 Sneyd Pk	21.08.1958 Plymouth A
MICALLEF Constantinous	1986-87	24.01.1961 Cardiff		15+3	1	12.08.1986 Cardiff C	08.1987 Barry T
MICKLEWRIGHT Andrew Alfred	1951-53	31.01.1931 Birmingham		7	1	27.01.1952 Smethwick	05.05.1953 Bristol C
MILLAR Alexander	1937-39	1905 Coaltown of Balgonie		52	0	12.07.1937 Margate	15.05.1939 Bristol C
MILLER Paul Anthony	1994-97	31.01.1968 Bisley		105+5	20	16.08.1994 Wimbledon	08.08.1997 Lincoln C
MILLINGTON George Edgar	1938-39	01.11.1911 Birmingham	27.10.2000 Telford	3	0	11.07.1938 Runcorn	12.1948 Donnington Wood
MILLION Esmond	1962-63	15.03.1938 Ashington		38	0	27.06.1962 Middlesbrough	26.04.1963 banned for life
MILLS Thomas James	1936-39	28.11.1911 Ton Pentre		99	17	27.04.1936 Leicester C	1939 Chester
MOLLOY Peter	1933-34	20.04.1909 Rossendale		6	0	18.05.1933 Fulham	02.02.1934 Cardiff C
MOORE Kevin Thomas*	1991-92	29.04.1958 Grimsby		7	0	09.01.1992 Southampton	(loan)
"	1992-93			4	1	17.10.1992 Southampton	(loan)
MORGAN Francis Gerald	1920-25	1892 Bristol		115	25	1919 Caerphilly T	1925 Brislington W
MORGAN Ryan Stephen	1996-97	12.07.1978 Bristol		1	0	25.03.1997 YTS	01.10.1997 Eagle Hse YC
MORGAN Stephen Alfonso*	1995-96	19.09.1968 Oldham		5	0	01.03.1996 Coventry C	(loan)
MORGAN Trevor James	1985-87	30.09.1956 Forest Gate		54+1	24	19.09.1985 Exeter C	23.01.1987 Bristol C
MORGAN William James	1946-52	19.06.1922 Bristol		104	24	22.04.1946 Avonmouth	02.05.1952 Stonehouse
MORGAN Wynfrwd	1946-47	07.08.1925 Abergwynfi		2	0	09.08.1946 Coventry C	1947 Retired
MUIR Ian Baker	1953-57	16.02.1929 Motherwell		26	0	27.05.1953 Motherwell	04.06.1957 Oldham A
MUIR John Baker	1930-32	18.11.1903 Hamilton		21	3	06.03.1931 Luton T	11.1932 Arbroath
MUNRO Alexander	1962-71	03.10.1944 Glasgow		159+10	11	01.10.1962 Drumchapel	1971 Durban, SA
MURPHY William Robinson	1950-51	22.03.1928 Barrhead		3	0	07.1950 Exeter C	1951 Retired
MURRAY Allan Ferguson	1935-36	31.05.1907 Heywood	15.01.1995 Rochdale	13	0	09.05.1935 Fulham	07.1936 Crystal P
MURRAY David James	1928-30	1902 Cape Town, SA		39	12	11.11.1928 Bristol C	06.1930 Swindon T
MURRAY William Thomas	1933-35	09.11.1904 Alexandria	17.07.1941 Retford	40	0	20.12.1933 Barrow	08.1935 Folkestone
MUXWORTHY Graham John	1962-63	11.10.1938 Bristol		8	0	25.06.1960 Chippenham T	01.07.1963 Bridgwater T
NEWTON Robert	1986-87	23.11.1956 Chesterfield		7+1	0	23.02.1987 Hartlepool U	07.1987 Shepshed C
NICHOLLS Joseph Henry	1936-39	08.03.1905 Nottingham	20.06.1973 Nottingham	112	0	13.05.1936 Tottenham H	1939 Retired
NICHOLLS Ronald Bernard	1955-58	04.12.1933 Sharpness	23.07.1994 Cheltenham	71	0	02.11.1954 Fulham	11.08.1958 Cardiff C
NIXON Paul	1988-91	23.09.1963 Seaham		31+13	6	26.01.1989 Seaham RS	27.03.1991 Lei Sun, Hong Kong
NOBLE Wayne Ian	1985-87	11.06.1967 Bristol		16+5	1	19.07.1983 apprentice	26.03.1987 Yeovil T
NORMAN Malcolm Allen	1958-62	24.10.1934 Cardiff		69	0	19.05.1958 Cardiff Cor	1962 Kidderminster H
NORTON Joseph Patrick	1920-22	1890 Leicester		36	2	13.05.1920 Leicester C	06.1922 Swindon T
O'BRIEN Gerald*	1973-74	10.11.1949 Glasgow		3	0	15.03.1974 Southampton	(loan)
O'CONNOR Mark Andrew	1984-86	10.03.1963 Southend		79+1	10	13.08.1984 QPR	27.03.1986 Bournemouth
O'MAHONEY Matthew Augustine	1936-39	19.01.1913 Mullinavat	25.01.1992 Norwich	101	6	04.05.1936 Wolves	28.07.1939 Ipswich T
O'NEILL Harold	1922-23	11.1894 Castle Ward		17	0	02.08.1922 Sheffield W	16.08.1923 Swindon T
OAKTON Albert Eric	1931-32	28.12.1906 Kiveton Park	05.08.1981 Sheffield	40	9	12.05.1931 Scunthorpe U	10.05.1932 Chelsea
OBI Anthony Lloyd	1985-86	15.09.1965 Birmingham		1	0	08.08.1985 Aston V	22.10.1985 Oxford U
OLDFIELD Terence James	1960-66	01.04.1939 Bristol		131+1	11	02.1958 Clifton St Vincents	05.07.1966 Wrexham
OMMEL Sergio	2001-02	02.09.1977 Den Haag, Holl		18+5	8	24.11.2001 KR Reykjavik, Ic	26.07.2002 Stormvogels T

PLAYERS NAME	CAREER	DATE & PLACE OF BIRTH	DATE & PLACE OF DEATH	APPS	GLS	PREVIOUS CLUB	NEXT CLUB
ORMSTON Arthur	1927-29	03.06.1900 Amble, Alnwick	13.10.1947 Oldham	27	15	13.06.1927 Bradford C	17.11.1928 Oldham A
OWUSU Ansah Ossei*	2000-01	22.11.1979 Hackney		11+6	0	09.02.2001 Wimbledon	(loan)
PALMER David John	1978-79	10.04.1961 Bristol		1	0	11.07.1977 apprentice	13.09.1980 Bath C
PALMER William	1920-22	11.1887 Barnsley		45	0	1912 Rotherham C	08.1922 Gillingham
PANES William Charles	1920-22	09.10.1887 Bristol	12.01.1961 Bristol	73	10	1916 Bath C	05.07.1924 Sneyd Pk
PARKER Ernest Simmonds	1937-38	18.12.1913 Annerley	02.1983 Brighton	9	1	14.07.1937 Bournemouth	01.1938 Retired
PARKER John	1922-24	1899 Shrewsbury		27	6	12.05.1922 Shrewsbury T	09.1924 Winsford U
PARKER Sonny	2002-03	28.02.1983 Middlesbrough		13+2	0	16.12.2002 Birmingham C	
PARKIN Brian	1989-96	12.10.1965 Birkenhead		241	0	11.11.1989 Crystal P	28.06.1996 Wycombe W
"	1999-01			2+3	0	31.10.1999 Notts C	24.11.2000 Retired
PARKIN Timothy John	1981-86	31.12.1957 Penrith		205+1	12	26.08.1981 Almondsbury T	14.07.1986 Swindon T
PARKINSON Noel David*	1979-80	16.11.1959 Hull		5	1	02.11.1979 Ipswich T	(loan)
PARMENTER Steven James	1996-98	22.01.1977 Chelmsford		11+7	2	12.07.1996 QPR	05.03.1998 Yeovil T
PARSONS Edward John	1949-50	22.03.1928 Bristol	05.01.1996 Bristol	5	2	26.09.1949 Frome T	12.1951 Frome T
PARSONS Lindsay William	1963-77	20.03.1946 Bristol		354+6	0	20.03.1964 apprentice	30.07.1977 Torquay U
PARTRIDGE Richard Joseph*	2000-01	12.09.1980 Dublin		4+2	1	20.03.2001 Liverpool	(loan)
PATERSON John	1927-30	1904 Kirkcaldy		46	5	07.02.1928 Wellesley J	03.1932 St Saviour's, Canada
PATTISON John William	1922-24	10.04.1897 Durham	11.04.1970 Bristol	12	1	18.09.1922 Derby C	06.1924 Leadgate Pk
PAUL Martin	1993-96	02.02.1975 Whalley		11+11	1	18.07.1991 Castle Cary	05.07.1996 Doncaster R
PEACOCK George	1946-47	10.02.1924 Pontypool	02.1984 Wales	7	1	10.05.1946 Pentwyn	1947 Gloucester C
PENDERGAST William James	1936-37	13.04.1915 Pen-y-Groes, Rhyl	05.2001 Pen-y-Groes	7	3	04.05.1936 Wolves	07.12.1937 Colchester U
PENDREY Gary James	1981-82	09.02.1949 Winson Green		1	0	17.12.1981 Torquay U	26.07.1982 Walsall
PENNY Shaun	1979-82	24.09.1957 Bristol		57+3	13	09.07.1979 Bristol C	17.06.1982 Kotkan, Finland
PENRICE Gary Kenneth	1984-90	23.03.1964 Bristol		186+2	54	04.09.1983 Mangotsfield U	14.11.1989 Watford
"	1997-00			48+21	6	22.07.1997 Watford	01.03.2002 Retired
PERRY Ivor Leslie	1927-29	08.1904 Ystrad		35	0	24.05.1927 Torquay U	01.11.1932 Walton-on-Thames
PERRY Jason	1997-98	02.04.1970 Caerphilly		24+1	0	30.06.1997 Cardiff C	13.07.1998 Lincoln C
PETHERBRIDGE George Ernest	1946-62	19.05.1927 Devonport	25.02.1973 Penzance	457	85	18.10.1945 Syston	28.07.1962 Salisbury C
PETHICK Robert John	1998-01	08.09.1970 Tavistock		60+3	2	12.02.1999 Portsmouth	02.07.2001 Brighton
PETTS John William	1965-70	02.10.1938 Edmonton	02.1970 Warley	88+4	3	19.06.1965 Reading	22.06.1970 Bath C
PETTS Paul Andrew	1978-80	27.09.1961 Hackney		12+1	0	1978 apprentice	23.07.1980 Shrewsbury T
PHILLIPS John	1928-30	24.06.1899 Kew	03.01.1966 Tunbridge Wells	65	37	26.09.1928 Brentford	01.07.1930 Coventry C
PHILLIPS Martin John*	1998-99	13.03.1976 Exeter		2	0	26.02.1999 Portsmouth	(loan)
PHILLIPS Wilfred John	1923-25	09.08.1895 Brierley Hill	30.04.1974 London	90	35	17.05.1923 Bilston U	19.11.1925 Millwall
PICKARD Leonard James	1951-52	29.11.1924 Barnstaple		4	1	22.12.1950 Barnstaple T	29.08.1953 Bristol C
PICKERING William Harry	1931-37	01.11.1901 Birmingham		215	1	18.05.1931 Colwyn Bay U	16.06.1937 Accrington S
PIERRE Nigel Nigus	1999-00	02.06.1979 Port of Spain, Trin		1+2	0	17.02.2000 Joe Public, Trin	02.03.2001 Hibernian
PIRIE Thomas Stuart	1928-29	09.12.1896 Glasgow		12	0	05.05.1928 Cardiff C	02.1929 Brighton
PITHER George	1924-25	24.06.1899 Kew		2	0	21.08.1924 Millwall	08.1925 Torquay U
PITT John Harry	1946-58	20.05.1920 Willenhall		466	16	31.07.1946 Aberavon	07.1960 Retired
PLATNAUER Nicholas Robert	1982-83	10.06.1961 Leicester		21+3	7	31.07.1982 Bedford T	05.08.1983 Coventry C
PLENDERLEITH Robert	1929-30	1909 Scotland		22	0	31.08.1929 Sunderland	26.08.1930 Sunderland BP
PLUMB Richard Keith	1965-69	24.09.1946 Swindon		39	8	30.04.1965 Swindon T	16.10.1968 Yeovil T
PLUMMER Christopher Scott*	2002-03	12.10.1976 Isleworth		2	0	05.11.2002 QPR	(loan)
PLUMMER Dwayne Jermaine	2000-02	12.05.1978 Bristol		29+6	1	06.09.2000 Chesham U	01.08.2002 Aylesbury
POINTON Joseph	1930-31	02.1905 Leek	02.1939 Leek	9	1	28.06.1930 Torquay U	08.1931 Walsall
POSTIN Eli	1934-36	03.06.1908 Dudley	08.1991 Dudley	4	1	27.07.1934 Cardiff C	20.11.1935 Wrexham
POUNDER Antony Mark	1990-94	11.03.1966 Yeovil		102+11	10	18.07.1990 Weymouth	26.08.1994 Hereford U
POWELL Kenneth Leigh	1951-52	25.09.1924 Chester		4	0	18.07.1951 Exeter C	1953 Wellington T
POWELL Wayne	1975-78	25.10.1956 Caerphilly		25+7	10	07.1972 apprentice	06.1978 Hereford U

503

PLAYERS NAME	CAREER	DATE & PLACE OF BIRTH	DATE & PLACE OF DEATH	APPS	GLS	PREVIOUS CLUB	NEXT CLUB
POWER Graeme Richard	1996-98	07.03.1977 Northwick Park		25+1	0	06.07.1996 QPR	06.08.1998 Exeter C
PREECE John Causer	1935-38	30.04.1914 Wolverhampton		79	0	03.05.1935 Wolves	07.1938 Bradford C
PREEDY Charles James	1933-34	11.01.1900 Neemuch, India	28.02.1978 Lakenheath	39	0	03.07.1933 Arsenal	23.08.1934 Luton T
PRICE John William	1923-24	09.06.1900 Ibstock	03.11.1984 Coalville	5	0	07.1923 Leicester C	06.1924 Swindon T
PRICE Walter	1930-31	13.08.1896 Aberdare		13	0	06.10.1930 Plymouth A	1931 Retired
PRINCE Francis Anthony	1967-80	01.12.1949 Penarth		360+2	22	12.1967 apprentice	07.1980 Exeter C
PRITCHARD David Michael	1993-02	27.05.1972 Wolverhampton		157+6	1	22.02.1994 Telford U	08.11.2001 Retired
PROUT Stanley Sylvester	1934-36	22.01.1911 Fulham	01.1996 Thanet	39	5	28.06.1934 Chelsea	29.06.1934 Chester
PULIS Anthony Richard	1975-81	16.01.1958 Newport		78+7	3	01.09.1975 apprentice	1981 Happy Valley, Hong Kong
"	1982-84			44+1	2	07.06.1982 Happy Valley	09.07.1984 Newport C
PURDON Edward John	1960-61	01.03.1930 Johannesburg, SA		4	1	19.09.1960 Bath C	05.1961 Toronto Roma, Canada
PURNELL Philip	1985-92	16.09.1964 Bristol		130+23	22	09.1985 Mangotsfield U	28.01.1994 Clevedon T
PYLE Walter David	1956-62	12.12.1936 Trowbridge	08.02.2002 Trowbridge	139	2	05.07.1955 Trowbridge T	13.07.1962 Bristol C
QUINN Robert John	2002-03	08.11.1976 Sidcup		44	2	01.07.2002 Oxford U	(loan)
QUINN Stephen James*	2001-02	15.12.1974 Coventry		6	1	22.03.2002 West Brom A	(loan)
RADFORD William Howard	1951-62	08.09.1930 Abercynon		245	0	08.1951 Penrhiwceiber	1962 Retired
RAMASUT Mahan William Thomas	1996-98	30.08.1977 Cardiff		30+12	6	08.08.1996 Norwich C	24.10.1998 Merthyr T
RAMMELL Andrew Victor	2002-03	10.02.1967 Nuneaton		7	4	26.03.2003 Wycombe W	
RANDALL Paul	1977-79	16.02.1958 Liverpool		49+3	33	12.08.1977 Frome T	28.12.1978 Stoke C
"	1980-86			169+19	61	29.01.1981 Stoke C	07.03.1986 Yeovil T
RAVEN James	1936-37	29.03.1908 Nottingham	02.01.1965 Nottingham	7	0	22.04.1936 Brentford	06.08.1937 Wrexham
RAYNOR Paul James*	1984-85	29.04.1966 Nottingham		7+1	0	28.03.1985 Nottingham F	(loan)
REAY George Turnbull	1928-30	02.1903 East Howdon	15.08.1962 York	67	9	24.05.1928 Raith R	01.07.1930 Coventry C
REECE Andrew John	1987-93	05.09.1962 Shrewsbury		230+9	17	11.08.1987 Dudley T	07.12.1993 Hereford U
RHODES Trevor Charles	1968-69	09.08.1948 Southend		2	0	07.1968 Millwall	18.06.1969 Bath C
RICHARDS Justin	2000-03	16.10.1980 Sandwell		3+13	0	18.01.2001 West Brom A	21.03.2003 Stevenage Borough
RICHARDS William Edward	1937-38	08.1905 Abercanaid		4	0	25.05.1937 Brighton	08.1938 Folkestone T
RICHARDSON John	1930-31	1909 Johannesburg	30.09.1956 Wolverhampton	8	0	23.07.1929 Wallacestone	1931 Falkirk
RICKETTS Graham Anthony	1956-61	30.07.1939 Oxford		32	0	13.07.1954 Oxford Schools	05.07.1961 Stockport C
RIDEOUT Brian James	1960-61	15.09.1940 Bristol		1	0	30.08.1956 Carlton Pk	28.07.1962 Yeovil T
RILEY Joseph	1931-33	1908 Sheffield		9	4	08.05.1931 Goldthorpe U	25.05.1933 Bristol C
ROBERTS Francis	1924-25	1902 Motherwell		2	0	06.1924 Glasgow Rgrs	1926 Ayr Utd
ROBERTS Henry Bromley	1937-38	27.06.1906 Crofton	08.1977 Leeds	77	1	09.09.1937 Plymouth A	12.08.1939 Frickley C
ROBERTS Jason Andre Davis	1998-00	25.01.1978 Park Royal		73+5	38	06.08.1998 Wolves	26.07.2000 West Brom A
ROBERTS Phillip Stanley	1969-73	24.02.1950 Cardiff		174+1	6	11.1968 apprentice	12.05.1973 Portsmouth
ROBERTS Thomas	1925-30	1903 Bristol		120	6	11.03.1925 Trowbridge T	07.1930 Lovells A
ROBERTSON Alfred Joseph	1935-36	02.07.1908 Sunderland	05.1984 Clayton-le-Moors	8	0	08.05.1935 Orient	26.06.1936 Accrington S
RONALDSON Kenneth	1965-69	27.09.1945 Edinburgh		72+4	15	07.07.1965 Aberdeen	22.11.1969 Gillingham
ROOST William Charles	1948-57	22.03.1924 Bristol		178	49	10.09.1948 Stonehouse	17.05.1957 Swindon T
ROSE Harold Bernard	1922-23	05.1900 Reading	05.1990 Reading	14	0	10.05.1921 Reading	1924 Mid Rhondda U
ROSE Richard Alan*	2002-03	08.09.1982 Pembury		9	0	13.12.2002 Gillingham	(loan)
ROSS Neil James*	2001-02	10.08.1982 West Bromwich		2+3	0	23.10.2001 Stockport C	
ROTHERHAM Albert Edward	1925-29	11.1903 Wednesbury	05.1966 Chipping Sodbury	46	0	11.06.1925 Darlaston	13.06.1929 Coventry C
ROUTLEDGE Thomas Alan	1980-81	06.05.1960 Wallsend		0+1	0	08.1980 Bath University	03.1982 football in north-east
ROUTLEDGE William H	1931-34	1911 Haltwhistle		64	5	03.08.1931 Chelsea	21.05.1934 York C
ROWLEY Joseph	1926-28	13.10.1899 Wellington	02.1982 Oswestry	61	17	06.08.1926 Coventry C	10.1928 Oakengates T
RUDGE John Robert	1971-75	21.10.1944 Wolverhampton		50+20	17	17.02.1972 Torquay U	04.03.1975 Bournemouth
RUMNEY John	1926-27	05.1898 Dipton	02.1969 York	8	2	20.05.1926 Merthyr T	07.1927 Consett
RUSHBURY David Graham	1986-87	20.02.1956 Wolverhampton		14+2	2	26.02.1987 Doncaster R	1987 Goole T
RUSSELL Cecil John	1927-28	19.06.1904 Northfield	10.12.1995 Blackwell	22	6	14.06.1927 Birmingham	07.1928 Worcester C

PLAYERS NAME	CAREER	DATE & PLACE OF BIRTH	DATE & PLACE OF DEATH	APPS	GLS	PREVIOUS CLUB	NEXT CLUB
RUSSELL George Henry	1930-32	01.08.1902 Atherstone		55	1	12.01.1931 Northampton	02.12.1932 Cardiff C
RUTHERFORD John	1922-23	1897 Bedlington	09.1930 Morpeth	29	1	18.09.1922 Cardiff C	1923 Mold
RYDEN Hugh Johnston	1962-63	07.04.1943 Dumbarton		8	4	26.05.1962 Leeds U	27.07.1963 Stockport C
SAMBIDGE Ernest Baden	1922-25	07.08.1900 Newcastle-u-Tyne		23	0	31.05.1922 Spennymoor U	1925 Bath C
SAMPSON Peter Stanley	1948-61	09.07.1927 Great Watering	27.11.1979 Bristol	340	4	28.01.1948 Devizes T	05.07.1961 Trowbridge T
SANCHEZ LOPEZ Carlos	2001-02	22.07.1979 Madrid,Sp		6	0	08.02.2002 Getafe CF,Sp	26.04.2002 released
SAUNDERS Carl Stephen	1989-94	26.11.1964 Marston Green		123+19	42	02.02.1990 Stoke C	23.12.1993 Oxford U
SCALES John Robert	1985-87	04.07.1966 Harrogate		68+4	2	11.07.1985 Leeds U	16.07.1987 Wimbledon
SCORER Robert	1923-25	05.10.1898 Felling	13.06.1971 Crewe	37	0	11.1923 Hull C	07.1925 Wigan B
SCOTT John Fisher	1930-31	11.1904 Kiveton Park		6	1	09.1930 Portsmouth	06.01.1931 Kiveton Pk
SEALY Anthony John	1989-91	07.05.1959 Hackney		21+16	7	11.09.1989 Brentford	05.1991 Myllykosken, Finland
SEATHERTON Raymond	1955-56	20.05.1932 Tiverton		2	2	15.02.1955 Minehead	1956 Minehead
SHAW Gilbert Alexander	1929-30	04.04.1906 Pwllheli	08.1980 Birmingham	20	7	24.06.1929 Grimsby T	05.1930 Walsall
SHAW Martin John	1978-79	14.09.1960 Bristol		1+1	0	15.09.1978 apprentice	1980 Bath C
SHEPPARD Richard James	1969-75	14.02.1945 Bristol	18.10.1998 Bristol	151	0	05.06.1969 West Brom A	01.06.1975 Weymouth
SHERWOOD Jeffrey	1982-83	05.10.1959 Bristol		16+2	0	07.06.1982 Bath C	17.09.1983 Bath C
SHORE Andrew J	2001-02	08.04.1982 Bristol		9	0	01.08.2001 YTS	18.12.2002 Bath C
SHORE James Andrew	1998-02	01.09.1977 Bristol		18+6	2	21.07.1998 Norwich C	10.07.2002 Retired
SIMS Stephen	1920-21	11.12.1895 Bedminster	02.1973 Weston-s-Mare	66	8	07.1919 Leicester F	06.07.1922 Burnley
"	1926-27			13	1	04.09.1926 Bristol C	07.1927 Newport C
SINCLAIR Harvey Patrick	1958-59	30.11.1933 Bournemouth		1	0	01.09.1958 Yeovil T	07.1959 Fulham
SKINNER Justin	1991-98	30.01.1969 Hounslow		174+13	11	27.08.1991 Fulham	28.05.1998 Hibernian
SLATER Neil John	1980-85	30.05.1964 Cardiff		147+1	4	01.07.1980 YTS	12.07.1985 Oxford U
SLOCOMBE Michael J	1961-63	03.05.1941 Bristol		32	0	1956 Dings Crusaders	1963 Welton R
SMALLEY Mark Anthony	1986-87	02.01.1965 Newark		10	0	12.08.1986 Nottingham F	05.02.1987 Orient
SMART Gary Michael	1985-87	08.12.1963 Bristol		11+8	4	11.10.1985 Bristol St G	08.1987 Cheltenham T
SMEATON Alexander Richardson	1923-24	29.09.1900 South Shields	26.09.1956 Yatesbury	5	1	07.1923 Hepburn C	06.1925 Halifax T
SMITH Arthur John	1934-35	27.11.1911 Merthyr Tydfil	07.06.1975 Weymouth	4	0	27.07.1934 Wolves	31.03.1935 Swindon T
SMITH Christopher James	1984-85	28.03.1966 Christchurch		1	0	05.1985 Cheltenham T	08.1985 Mangotsfield U
SMITH David J	1981-82	13.10.1964 Frome		0-1	0	01.07.1981 Frome Coll	12.10.1982 Yeovil T
SMITH Edward	1931-32	22.02.1902 Sunderland	05.1972 Luton	8	0	06.1931 Preston NE	05.08.1932 Vauxhall M
SMITH Granville	1958-60	04.02.1937 Penrhiwceiber		21	2	14.05.1957 Juniors	06.06.1960 Newport C
SMITH Henry Stanley	1946-47	11.10.1908 Newburn	13.06.1993 Throckley	3	0	17.08.1939 Darlington	1947 Retired
SMITH James Terence	1933-35	12.03.1902 Old Kilpatrick		26	13	08.05.1933 Tunbridge WR	28.06.1935 Newport C
SMITH Leonard	1926-29	11.1895 Worcester	1975 Bridgepoint, Connecticut	45	0	14.06.1926 Leeds U	06.1929 Merthyr T
SMITH Mark Jonathan	1998-02	13.09.1979 Bristol		28+5	0	09.07.1998 YTS	15.08.2002 Cirencester
SMITH Paul Stuart	1988-89	05.10.1967 Wembley		14+2	1	15.07.1988 Brentford	08.03.1989 Torquay U
SMITH Sidney	1923-25	1900 Gateshead		39	2	17.05.1923 St Peter's A	1925 Retired
SMITH Wilfred Samuel	1974-77	03.09.1946 Neumunster	14.04.1968 Pucklechurch	54	2	04.03.1975 Coventry C	11.1976 Chesterfield
SMITH Wilfred Victor	1937-47	07.04.1918 Pucklechurch	03.01.1987 Wallasey	26	0	06.09.1937 Clevedon T	27.12.1946 Newport C
SPENCER Samuel	1928-29	18.01.1902 Middlesbrough	03.1973 Hull	2	0	01.06.1928 Aberdeen	12.1928 Newry T
SPIVEY Richard	1938-39	18.08.1916 Hull		10	4	04.07.1938 Torquay U	19.07.1939 Southport
SPRING Andrew John	1985-86	17.11.1965 Gateshead		18+1	0	22.06.1985 Coventry C	1986 Hartlepool U
STALLARD Trevor	1925-26	06.03.1905 Cwmparc	02.1999 Southampton	2	0	21.01.1926 Weymouth	16.08.1926 Weymouth
STANIFORTH David Albry	1973-79	06.10.1950 Chesterfield		135+18	32	08.03.1974 Sheffield U	20.06.1979 Bradford C
STANSFIELD Harold H	1920-21	02.1891 Bolton-on-Dearne	14.03.1940 Bristol	3	0	15.11.1912 Bolton C	1922 Retired
STANTON Thomas	1968-76	03.05.1948 Glasgow		160+12	7	22.06.1968 Mansfield T	1976 Weymouth
STAPLETON Simon John	1988-89	10.12.1968 Oxford		4+1	0	08.05.1988 Portsmouth	01.08.1989 Wycombe W
STEEDS Cecil	1956-57	11.01.1929 Bristol		1	0	21.05.1952 Bristol C	14.08.1958 Bath C

PLAYERS NAME	CAREER	DATE & PLACE OF BIRTH	DATE & PLACE OF DEATH	APPS	GLS	PREVIOUS CLUB	NEXT CLUB
STEELE David Morton	1920-22	29.07.1894 Carluke	23.05.1964 Stanningley	67	2	21.11.1919 Douglas WT	08.05.1922 Huddersfield T
STEPHENS Arthur	1981-85	19.05.1954 Liverpool		100+27	40	12.08.1981 Melksham T	20.03.1985 Middlesbrough
STEPHENS Kenneth John	1970-78	14.11.1946 Bristol		212+11	11	19.10.1970 Walsall	21.10.1977 Hereford U
STERLING Worrell Ricardo	1993-96	08.06.1965 Bethnal Green		117+2	6	29.07.1993 Peterborough U	04.07.1996 Lincoln C
STEVENSON John Alexander	1932-33	27.02.1898 Wigan	12.03.1979 Carlisle	7	1	13.02.1933 Chester	1933 Falkirk
STEVENSON William Byron	1985-86	07.09.1956 Llanelli		30+1	3	15.07.1985 Birmingham C	1986 Garforth T
STEWART Jordan Barrington*	1999-00	03.03.1982 Birmingham		1+3	0	23.03.2000 Leicester C	(loan)
STEWART William Marcus Paul	1991-96	07.11.1972 Bristol		137+34	57	18.07.1991 YTS	02.07.1996 Huddersfield T
STOCKLEY George Thomas	1921-22	26.11.1891 Hockley	01.06.1971 Winson Green	5	0	13.06.1921 Brierley Hill A	06.1922 Aberaman A
STODDART William Michael	1931-33	29.10.1907 Leadgate	12.02.1972 Lanchester	40	0	06.07.1931 Southampton	14.07.1933 Accrington S
STONE David Kenneth	1962-68	29.12.1942 Bristol		145+3	6	03.1960 Sneyd Pk	08.06.1968 Southend U
STORER John Arthur	1931-32	03.01.1908 Swinton	01.07.1972 Luton	1	0	21.05.1931 Barnsley	02.02.1932 Mansfield T
STREET Kevin	2002-03	25.11.1977 Crewe		13+7	1	29.11.2002 Northwich Vic	
STUBBS Robin Gregory	1969-72	22.04.1941 Warley		90+3	32	10.07.1969 Torquay U	17.02.1972 Torquay U
SULLIVAN Leslie Gordon	1936-38	06.08.1912 Croydon	01.1996 Stockport	40	10	22.04.1936 Brentford	09.07.1938 Chesterfield
SYKES Norman Albert John	1956-64	16.10.1936 Bristol		214	5	23.05.1952 Juniors	09.1964 Plymouth A
TADMAN George Henry	1933-35	05.05.1914 Rainham	28.09.1994 Bristol	5	2	02.06.1933 Gillingham	06.1935 Gillingham
TAIT Paul	2002-03	24.10.1974 Newcastle		33 + 8	7	05.07.2002 Crewe Alex	
TANNER Nicholas	1985-88	24.05.1965 Kingswood		104+3	3	19.04.1985 Mangotsfield U	08.07.1988 Liverpool
TAYLOR Albert	1933-36	1910 Ashington		53	17	22.05.1933 Chelsea	08.1936 Lincoln C
TAYLOR Anthony	1977-78	06.09.1946 Glasgow		12	0	01.09.1977 Athlone T	03.02.1978 Portsmouth
TAYLOR Gareth Keith	1991-96	25.02.1973 Weston-s-Mare		31+16	16	29.07.1991 Southampton	29.09.1995 Crystal P
TAYLOR Geoffrey Arthur	1951-52	22.01.1923 Henstead		3	0	29.09.1951 Rennes, France	12.1952 SC Bruhl, Switz.
TAYLOR John	1922-23	1900 Newcastle-u-Tyne		5	1	17.05.1922 St Peter's A	06.1924 Leadgate Pk
TAYLOR John Patrick	1991-94	24.10.1964 Norwich		91+4	44	28.03.1992 Cambridge U	13.07.1994 Bradford C
TAYLOR Lawrence Desmond	1966-70	23.11.1947 Exeter		90	0	06.12.1965 apprentice	10.1970 Chelmsford C
TAYLOR Philip Henry	1933-36	18.09.1917 Bristol		21	2	24.11.1933 Bristol St G	13.03.1936 Liverpool
TAYLOR Stuart	1965-80	18.04.1947 Bristol		546	28	30.12.1965 Hanham A	21.05.1980 Bath C
TAYLOR Stuart James*	1999-00	28.11.1980 Romford		4	0	24.09.1999 Arsenal	(loan)
TERRY James Cyril	1933-34	08.1909 Bloxwich		4	0	09.03.1933 Yeovil & P	07.1934 Kidderminster H
THOM John	1927-28	18.05.1899 Hurlford		6	4	16.06.1927 Leeds U	08.1928 Workington
THOMAS Cecil Edward	1929-30	1910 Pill	08.1966 Aldershot	4	1	31.08.1929 Pill A	07.1930 Thames
THOMAS James Alan*	2001-02	16.01.1979 Swansea		7	1	22.03.2002 Blackburn R	(loan)
THOMAS Martin Richard	1976-82	28.11.1959 Senghenydd		162	0	10.09.1977 apprentice	13.07.1983 Newcastle U
THOMSON Andrew John	1998-02	28.03.1974 Swindon		124+3	6	15.01.1999 Portsmouth	28.03.2002 Wycombe W
THOMSON John Youngman	1921-22	05.06.1896 West Greenock		6	0	11.05.1921 Caledonian J	06.1922 Alloa Ath
THOMSON William	1924-26	03.01.1895 Parkhead		21	0	02.10.1924 Leicester C	11.1925 Inverness C
TIDMAN Oliver Eustace	1936-37	16.03.1911 Margate	20.12.2000 Kent	16	1	07.05.1936 Stockport C	07.1937 Orient
TILLSON Andrew	1992-00	30.06.1966 Huntingdon		250+3	11	05.11.1992 QPR	05.08.2000 Walsall
TIMMINS John	1958-60	30.05.1936 Brierley Hill		4	0	21.08.1958 Plymouth A	1960 Wellington T
TIPPETT Michael Frederick	1949-50	11.06.1930 Cadbury Heath		8	2	09.04.1948 Cadbury H	04.08.1955 Chippenham U
TOLLAND Donal	1937-39	19.03.1905 Ireland	1950s Ireland	34	3	03.12.1937 Northampton T	07.1939 football in USA
TONER Ciaran*	2001-02	30.06.1981 Craigavon		6	0	28.03.2002 Tottenham H	(loan)
TOVEY Paul William	1993-96	05.12.1973 Wokingham		8+1	0	24.07.1992 YTS	22.07.1996 Bath C
TOWNROW Francis Albert	1931-33	27.11.1902 West Ham		50	6	06.06.1931 Bristol C	19.08.1933 Taunton T
TOWNROW John Ernest	1932-33	28.03.1901 Stratford	11.04.1969 Knaresborough	10	0	10.05.1932 Chelsea	1933 Fairbairn Hse
TREES Robert Victor	1998-00	18.12.1977 Manchester		38+8	1	13.06.1998 Stalybridge C	07.02.2001 Leigh RMI
TROTMAN Reginald Wilfred	1927-28	08.1906 Bristol	05.01.1970 Bath	3	1	1927 Kingswood	07.1928 Rochdale
TROUGHT Michael John	1998-02	19.10.1980 Bristol		25+8	0	18.03.1999 YTS	15.07.2002 Bath C

PLAYERS NAME	CAREER	DATE & PLACE OF BIRTH	DATE & PLACE OF DEATH	APPS	GLS	PREVIOUS CLUB	NEXT CLUB
TURNBULL Thomas	1930-31	11.1906 Morpeth		1	0	28.06.1930 Gainsborough T	01.1935 Gateshead
TURNER Albert	1938-39	03.09.1907 Sheffield		21	4	14.12.1938 Cardiff C	20.07.1939 Bath C
TURNER Herbert Lewis	1928-29	05.1899 King's Norton		9	2	01.06.1928 Torquay U	04.1929 Brierley HA
TURNER Robert Peter	1986-88	18.09.1966 Littlethorpe		19+7	2	29.01.1987 Cardiff C	17.12.1987 Wimbledon
TWEED George Edward	1936-38	04.12.1910 Newmarket	20.02.1971 Wells	25	0	12.08.1936 Coventry C	20.10.1937 Gillingham
TWENTYMAN Geoffrey	1986-93	10.03.1959 Liverpool		248+4	6	29.08.1986 Preston NE	12.02.1993 Yate T
UDDIN Anwar	2002-03	01.11.1981 Tower Hamlets		17+1	1	01.07.2002 Sheffield W	
VAUGHAN John*	1985-86	26.06.1964 Isleworth		6	0	05.09.1985 West Ham U	(loan)
VAUGHAN William	1920-21	18.12.1898 Willenhall	05.1976 Walsall	6	1	03.04.1920 Willenhall	1922 Merthyr T
VINEY Keith Brian*	1988-89	26.10.1957 Portsmouth		2+1	0	22.09.1988 Exeter C	(loan)
WADDOCK Gary Patrick	1992-95	17.03.1962 Kingsbury		71	1	05.11.1992 QPR	08.12.1994 Luton T
WAINWRIGHT Arthur Henry	1922-24	11.1894 Barnsley	18.01.1968 Barnsley	16	0	17.05.1922 Gresley R	07.1924 Barrow
WALLINGTON Sidney Percival	1933-37	15.10.1908 Small Heath	12.1989 Birmingham	94	1	24.08.1933 Shirley T	05.1937 Worcester C
WALTER Joseph Dorville	1920-22	16.08.1895 Bristol	24.05.1995 Bristol	75	11	02.08.1920 Horfield A	08.05.1922 Huddersfield T
	1928-29			7	1	1928 Blackburn R	08.1929 Bath C
WALTERS Mark Everton	1999-02	02.06.1964 Birmingham		46+36	13	17.11.1999 Swindon T	16.08.2002 Ilkeston T
WALTON James	1923-24	03.12.1904 Sacriston	20.11.1982 Leeds	40	1	05.07.1923 Leeds U	18.11.1924 Brentford
WARBOYS Alan	1972-77	18.04.1949 Goldthorpe		141+3	53	06.03.1973 Sheffield U	17.02.1977 Fulham
WARD David	1954-61	16.07.1934 Barry	12.01.1996 Barry	175	90	24.11.1954 Barry T	21.02.1961 Cardiff C
WARHURST Francis	1938-39	05.1917 Sheffield		4	0	06.07.1938 Bath C	1945 Plymouth A
WARREN Christer Simon	2002-03	10.10.1974 Weymouth		0-2	0	05.09.2002 QPR	08.10.2002 Eastleigh
WARREN Raymond Richard	1936-56	23.06.1918 Bristol	13.03.1988 Bristol	450	28	12.03.1936 Parson St OB	1956 Retired
WATKINS John Victor	1960-62	09.04.1933 Bristol		23	0	21.02.1961 Cardiff C	03.08.1962 Chippenham T
WATKINS Randall Burnell 'Barry'	1946-55	30.11.1921 Bedlinog		115	7	18.10.1945 BAC Patchway	1957 Retired
WATKINS Robert Stephen	1965-66	20.12.1946 Bristol		1	0	13.07.1965 Bristol C	20.07.1966 Glastonbury
WATLING John Daniel	1947-62	11.05.1925 Bristol		323	19	01.1947 St Andrews BC	05.1963 Retired
WATSON Herbert Leonard	1936-37	20.11.1908 Springwell		19	0	22.04.1936 Brentford	1937 Retired
WATSON James Boyd	1933-34	14.08.1910 Govan		14	2	09.05.1933 Tunbridge WR	06.1934 Northampton T
WEARE Arthur John	1946-50	21.09.1912 Newport	13.10.1939 Isleworth	141	0	29.11.1945 West Ham U	03.1951 Barry T
WEARE Ross Michael	2001-02	19.03.1977 Perivale		9+1	1	18.06.2001 QPR	26.04.2002 Retired
WEBB George H	1922-23	1900 Birmingham		2	0	14.10.1922 Derby C	11.1923 Wellington T
WEBB Harold	1938-39	15.05.1901 Fulham		1	0	06.1938 Newport C	1939 Retired
WELLER Christopher William	1965-66	25.12.1939 Reading		2+1	0	16.06.1965 Bournemouth	18.01.1966 Bournemouth
WESTAWAY Kevin David	1980-81	24.11.1962 Bristol		2	0	24.11.1980 apprentice	10.07.1982 Clevedon T
WESTON Ian Paul	1986-88	06.05.1968 Bristol		13+3	0	05.1986 apprentice	08.09.1988 Torquay U
WHATLEY Jesse Winter	1920-30	20.11.1895 Trowbridge	19.03.1982 Westerleigh	372	0	27.10.1919 Trowbridge T	1930 Stapleton Inst
WHATMORE Ernest	1923-28	25.04.1900 Kidderminster	31.07.1991 Kidderminster	134	40	06.1923 Shrewsbury T	06.1928 QPR
WHITE Devon Winston	1987-92	02.03.1964 Nottingham		190+12	52	21.08.1987 Shepshed C	28.03.1992 Cambridge U
WHITE Raymond Sidney	1968-69	14.01.1948 Rochford		3	0	04.07.1968 Southend U	11.07.1969 Brentwood
WHITE Stephen James	1977-80	02.01.1959 Chipping Sodbury		46+4	20	11.07.1977 Mangotsfield U	24.12.1979 Luton T
WHITE Thomas Matthew	1983-86			89+11	24	25.08.1983 Charlton A	08.07.1986 Swindon T
WHITE William T	1994-00	26.01.1976 Bristol		47+7	1	13.07.1994 YTS	02.08.2000 Yeovil T
WHITFIELD Wilfred	1928-29	1907 Kirkcaldy		8	0	19.06.1928 Reading	07.1930 Charlton A
WHYTE David Anthony	1938-47	17.11.1916 Chesterfield	02.1971 Bath	26	1	29.06.1938 Worksop	01.1947 Torquay U
WIFFILL David Phillip	1997-98	20.04.1971 Greenwich		0-4	0	11.02.1998 Ipswich T	16.03.1998 Southend U
WILCOX Jonah Charles	1987-88	19.04.1961 Thornbury		2	0	08.1987 Bath C	31.05.1988 Stroud
WILDSMITH Thomas	1925-26	19.01.1894 Coleford	05.08.1956 Shipham	32	18	07.05.1925 New Brighton	10.05.1926 QPR
WILLIAMS Anthony Simon	1934-36	08.01.1913 Sheffield	28.02.1976 Sheffield	24	2	27.07.1934 Wolves	05.1936 Doncaster R
WILLIAMS Brian	1998-99	20.09.1977 Ogwr		9	0	25.03.1999 Blackburn R	(loan)
	1981-85	05.11.1955 Salford		163	20	22.07.1981 Swindon T	07.1985 Bristol C

507

PLAYERS NAME	CAREER	DATE & PLACE OF BIRTH	DATE & PLACE OF DEATH	APPS	GLS	PREVIOUS CLUB	NEXT CLUB
WILLIAMS David Geraint	1980-85	05.01.1962 Cwmparc		138+3	8	12.01.1980 apprentice	29.03.1985 Derby C
WILLIAMS David Michael	1975-85	11.03.1955 Cardiff		342+10	66	08.1975 Clifton A	13.07.1985 Norwich C
WILLIAMS John Stanley	1966-69	16.08.1935 Bristol		66+3	10	20.12.1966 Plymouth A	06.1969 Plymouth A
WILLIAMS Robert Gordon	1966-69	17.02.1940 Bristol		28+1	5	16.03.1967 Rotherham U	08.1969 Reading
WILLIAMS Ronald Albert Keith	1961-63	14.01.1937 Eastham		49	18	29.01.1962 Plymouth A	26.04.1963 banned for life
WILLIAMS Steven John	1980-81	27.04.1963 Barry	12.12.1999 Barry	8	1	10.07.1979 Cadoxton Imps	01.08.1982 Barry T
WILLIAMS Thomas Hutchinson	1925-28	23.05.1899 Ryhope	14.12.1960 Easington	75	27	21.01.1926 Mid Rhondda	19.06.1928 Bristol C
WILLMOTT Ian Michael	1989-92	10.07.1968 Bristol		18+4	0	08.12.1988 Weston-s-Mare	1992 Clevedon T
WILSHIRE Peter John	1953-54	15.10.1934 Bristol		1	0	1952 Kingswood	06.1955 Bristol C
WILSON Che Christian Aaron	2000-02	17.01.1979 Ely		74+1	0	08.07.2000 Norwich C	10.08.2002 Cambridge C
WILSON David Graham	1991-93	20.03.1969 Todmorden		11	0	29.07.1991 Manchester U	06.1993 FC Haka, Finland
WILSON William	1925-26	1902 New Seaham		24	0	11.06.1925 Worcester C	15.02.1926 Willenhall
WILSON William Raynor	1934-36	11.1910 Rotherham		6	0	27.07.1934 Rotherham U	1936 Bristol C
WINDLE Charles	1946-47	08.01.1917 Barnsley	1975 Yorkshire	7	1	19.12.1946 Exeter C	1947 Retired
WINDSOR Foster	1932-34	09.03.1908 Bristol	19.03.1985 Bristol	20	1	14.08.1931 Wesley R	18.08.1934 Bath C
WINNELL Walter	1929-30	04.02.1908 Sheffield	09.1986 Sheffield	4	1	30.03.1930 Luton T	05.1930 Chesterfield
WINSPER R Thomas	1921-22	05.1895 West Bromwich	05.02.1968 Sutton Coldfield	23	0	12.05.1921 Hednesford T	08.08.1922 Willenhall
WINTERS Herbert Richard	1946-48	14.04.1920 Bristol		13	0	18.07.1946 Westerleigh	1952 Retired
WIPFLER Charles John	1934-35	15.07.1915 Trowbridge	01.06.1983 Petts Wood	18	5	21.08.1934 McCall's	07.1935 Hearts
WITHERS Edward Peter	1937-38	08.09.1915 Ower	07.01.1994 Bear Cross	17	4	03.12.1937 Southampton	1938 Bramtoco
WITHEY Graham Alfred	1982-83	11.06.1960 Bristol		19+3	10	02.08.1982 Bath C	05.08.1983 Coventry C
WOLFE Thomas Henry	1929-30	07.03.1900 Barry Dock	23.03.1954 Edgware	2	0	07.08.1929 Charlton A	04.03.1930 Westerham
WOLLEASTON Robert Ainsley*	1999-00	21.12.1979 Perivale		0+4	0	23.03.2000 Chelsea	(loan)
WOOD Alan Herbert	1962-63	13.01.1941 Newport		1	0	08.1962 Lovells A	01.1963 Merthyr T
WOODHALL William Henry	1923-24	12.1900 Lower Gornal	31.12.1963 Lower Gornal	38	13	17.05.1923 Bilston U	1925 Dudley Bean
WOODMAN John Albert	1935-37	09.07.1914 Bristol	16.01.1984 Bristol	39	21	23.05.1935 Melrose	13.07.1937 Preston NE
WOOKEY Kenneth William	1946-49	11.01.1922 Newport	11.01.2003 Newport	54	9	27.12.1946 Newport C	03.11.1948 Swansea T
WRAGGE Francis	1923-26	09.02.1898 Wolverhampton	11.1973 Shrewsbury	62	1	17.05.1923 Oakengates	07.1926 Stafford R
WRIGHT Ian Matthew	1993-96	10.03.1972 Lichfield		50+4	1	29.10.1993 Stoke C	26.06.1996 Hull C
WYATT Michael James	1995-96	12.09.1974 Bristol		3+1	0	21.07.1995 Bristol C	30.07.1996 Bath C
WYPER Henry Thomas	1932-33	08.10.1900 Coatbridge		11	2	21.01.1933 Chester	19.05.1933 Accrington S
YATES Stephen	1986-94	29.01.1970 Bristol		196+1	0	01.07.1986 Trainee	17.08.1993 QPR
YOUNG Archibald Wishart	1935-36	10.12.1906 Twechar	05.07.1980 Exmouth	24	0	26.07.1935 Leicester C	18.06.1936 Exeter C
YOUNG Herbert	1930-32	04.09.1899 Liverpool	05.1976 Liverpool	75	11	28.07.1930 QPR	1932 Swindon T
ZABEK Lee Kevin	1997-00	13.10.1978 Bristol		21+8	1	28.07.1997 YTS	08.08.2000 Exeter C
ZAMORA Robert Lester	1999-00	16.01.1981 Barking		0+4	0	01.07.1999 YTS	10.08.2000 Brighton
OWN GOALS SCORED BY OPPONENTS					106		

Notes: * Indicates player was on loan

Previous Club – YTS means Youth Training scheme. Juniors means taken on as groundstaff. Apprentice means taken on as an apprentice professional.

Career record excludes any Cup appearances and goals. Also excludes the three matches during the abandoned season 1939/40.

From Rovers' entry into the Football League in the 1920/21 season until the end of the 2002/03 season there were 707 different players used in their 3,340 League matches played.

Modern heroes, clockwise from top left: Andy Tillson, Neil Slatter, David Williams and Vitalijs Astafjevs

Some of the 34,000 Rovers supporters in the Tote End at Eastville pictured on 25 January 1958 before their FA Cup 2-2 draw with Burnley. Rovers caused a giant killing by defeating their First Division opponents 3-2 in the replay

Page 512
Above: *Thousands of Rovers supporters travelled to Craven Cottage, Fulham for the FA Cup quarter-final which the London club won by 3-1. The tie attracted a crowd of 42,000*

Below: *Rovers Cheer Ladies at Eastville Stadium about 1952*

BRISTOL ROVERS LEAGUE MATCHES RECORD

Season	League	Pos	Pld	W	D	L	F	A	Pts	Top League Goalscorer
2002/2003	Nationwide League Division Three	20th	46	12	15	19	50	57	51	Grazioli 11
2001/2002	Nationwide League Division Three	23rd	46	11	12	23	40	60	45	Ellington 15
2000/2001	Nationwide League Division Two	21st	46	12	15	19	53	57	51	Ellington 15
1999/2000	Nationwide League Division Two	7th	46	23	11	12	69	45	80	Cureton 22 Roberts 22
1998/1999	Nationwide League Division Two	13th	46	13	17	16	65	56	56	Cureton 25
1997/1998	Nationwide League Division Two	5th	46	20	10	16	70	64	70	Hayles 23
1996/1997	Nationwide League Division Two	17th	46	15	11	20	47	50	56	Beadle 12
1995/1996	Endsleigh League Division Two	10th	46	20	10	16	57	60	70	Stewart 21
1994/1995	Endsleigh League Division Two	4th	46	22	16	8	70	40	82	Stewart 15
1993/1994	Endsleigh League Division Two	8th	46	20	10	16	60	59	70	Taylor 22
1992/1993	Barclays League Division One	24th	46	10	11	25	55	87	41	Taylor 14
1991/1992	Barclays Second Division	13th	46	16	14	16	60	63	62	Saunders 10 White 10
1990/1991	Barclays Second Division	13th	46	15	13	18	56	59	58	Saunders 16
1989/1990	Barclays Third Division	1st	46	26	15	5	71	35	93	Mehew 18
1988/1989	Barclays Third Division	5th	46	19	17	10	67	51	74	Penrice 20
1987/1988	Barclays Third Division	8th	46	18	12	16	68	56	66	Penrice 18
1986/1987	Today Third Division	19th	46	13	12	21	49	75	51	Mehew 10
1985/1986	Canon Third Division	16th	46	14	12	20	51	75	54	Morgan 16
1984/1985	Canon Third Division	6th	46	21	12	13	66	48	75	Randall 18
1983/1984	Canon Third Division	5th	46	22	13	11	68	54	79	Stephens 13
1982/1983	English Third Division	7th	46	22	9	15	84	58	75	Randall 20
1981/1982	English Third Division	12th	46	18	9	19	58	65	63	Randall 12
1980/1981	English Second Division	22nd	42	5	13	24	34	65	23	Mabbutt 5 McCaffrey 5
1979/1980	English Second Division	19th	42	11	13	18	50	64	35	Barrowclough 12
1978/1979	English Second Division	16th	42	14	10	18	48	60	38	Randall 13
1977/1978	English Second Division	18th	42	13	12	17	61	77	38	Randall 20
1976/1977	English Second Division	15th	42	12	13	17	53	68	37	Warboys 11
1975/1976	English Second Division	18th	42	11	16	15	38	50	38	Bannister 13
1974/1975	English Second Division	19th	42	12	11	19	42	64	35	Warboys 12
1973/1974	English Third Division	2nd	46	22	17	7	65	33	61	Warboys 22
1972/1973	English Third Division	5th	46	20	13	13	77	56	53	Bannister 25
1971/1972	English Third Division	6th	46	21	12	13	75	56	54	Bannister 12
1970/1971	English Third Division	6th	46	19	13	14	69	50	51	Stubbs 17
1969/1970	English Third Division	3rd	46	20	16	10	80	59	56	Stubbs 15
1968/1969	English Third Division	16th	46	16	11	19	63	71	43	Jarman 14
1967/1968	English Third Division	16th	46	17	9	20	72	78	43	Biggs, Jones R, Mabbutt 10
1966/1967	English Third Division	5th	46	20	13	13	76	67	53	Biggs 23
1965/1966	English Third Division	16th	46	14	14	18	64	64	42	Jarman 13
1964/1965	English Third Division	6th	46	20	15	11	82	58	55	Hamilton 20
1963/1964	English Third Division	12th	46	19	8	19	91	79	46	Biggs 30
1962/1963	English Third Division	19th	46	15	11	20	70	88	41	Williams 17
1961/1962	English Second Division	21st	42	13	7	22	53	81	33	Jones R 13
1960/1961	English Second Division	17th	42	15	7	20	73	92	37	Hooper 20
1959/1960	English Second Division	9th	42	18	11	13	72	78	47	Biggs 22
1958/1959	English Second Division	6th	42	18	12	12	80	64	48	Ward 26
1957/1958	English Second Division	10th	42	17	8	17	85	80	42	Bradford 20
1956/1957	English Second Division	9th	42	18	9	15	81	67	45	Ward 19
1955/1956	English Second Division	6th	42	21	6	15	84	70	48	Bradford 25
1954/1955	English Second Division	9th	42	19	7	16	75	70	45	Bradford 26
1953/1954	English Second Division	9th	42	14	16	12	64	58	44	Bradford 21
1952/1953	English Third Division (South)	1st	46	26	12	8	92	46	64	Bradford 33
1951/1952	English Third Division (South)	7th	46	20	12	14	89	53	52	Lambden 29
1950/1951	English Third Division (South)	6th	46	20	15	11	64	42	55	Lambden 20
1949/1950	English Third Division (South)	9th	42	19	5	18	51	51	43	Roost 13
1948/1949	English Third Division (South)	5th	42	19	10	13	61	51	48	Lambden 13
1947/1948	English Third Division (South)	20th	42	13	8	21	71	75	34	Lambden 11
1946/1947	English Third Division (South)	14th	42	16	8	18	59	69	40	Leamon 13
1938/1939	English Third Division (South)	22nd	42	10	13	19	55	61	33	Curran 21
1937/1938	English Third Division (South)	15th	42	13	13	16	46	61	39	Iles 14
1936/1937	English Third Division (South)	15th	42	16	4	22	71	80	36	Houghton 14
1935/1936	English Third Division (South)	17th	42	14	9	19	69	95	37	Woodman 15
1934/1935	English Third Division (South)	8th	42	17	10	15	73	77	44	McNestry 19
1933/1934	English Third Division (South)	7th	42	20	11	11	77	47	51	McCambridge 17
1932/1933	English Third Division (South)	9th	42	15	14	13	61	56	44	Gibbins 15
1931/1932	English Third Division (South)	18th	42	13	8	21	65	92	34	Cook 17
1930/1931	English Third Division (South)	15th	42	16	8	18	75	92	40	Attwood 24
1929/1930	English Third Division (South)	20th	42	11	8	23	67	93	30	Phillips 24
1928/1929	English Third Division (South)	19th	42	13	7	22	60	79	33	Phillips 13
1927/1928	English Third Division (South)	19th	42	14	4	24	67	93	32	Ormston 15
1926/1927	English Third Division (South)	10th	42	16	9	17	78	80	41	Culley 26
1925/1926	English Third Division (South)	19th	42	15	6	21	66	69	36	Wilcox 19
1924/1925	English Third Division (South)	17th	42	12	13	17	42	49	37	Phillips 9 Whatmore 9
1923/1924	English Third Division (South)	9th	42	15	13	14	52	46	43	Phillips 23
1922/1923	English Third Division (South)	13th	42	13	16	13	35	36	42	Lunn 10
1921/1922	English Third Division (South)	14th	42	14	10	18	52	67	38	Leigh 15
1920/1921	English Third Division	10th	42	18	7	17	68	57	43	Leigh 21
1919/1920	Southern League Div 1	17th	42	11	13	18	61	78	35	Sims 9
1914/1915	Southern League Div 1	16th	38	14	3	21	53	75	31	Davison 15
1913/1914	Southern League Div 1	17th	38	10	11	17	46	67	31	Crompton 13
1912/1913	Southern League Div 1	16th	38	12	9	17	55	64	33	Brogan 11
1911/1912	Southern League Div 1	17th	38	9	13	16	41	62	31	Peplow 7 Richards 7
1910/1911	Southern League Div 1	16th	38	10	10	18	42	55	30	Peplow 9
1909/1910	Southern League Div 1	13th	42	16	10	16	37	48	42	Corbett 13
1908/1909	Southern League Div 1	5th	40	17	9	14	60	63	43	Corbett 19
1907/1908	Southern League Div 1	6th	38	16	10	12	55	40	42	Roberts 14
1906/1907	Southern League Div 1	14th	38	12	8	17	55	54	33	Young 14
1905/1906	Southern League Div 1	8th	34	15	5	14	56	56	35	Lewis 13
1904/1905	Southern League Div 1	1st	34	20	8	6	74	36	48	Smith 19
1903/1904	Southern League Div 1	3rd	34	17	8	9	66	42	42	Beats 18
1902/1903	Southern League Div 1	5th	30	13	8	9	46	34	34	Howie 11
1901/1902	Southern League Div 1	9th	28	12	5	13	43	39	29	Jones 14
1900/1901	Southern League Div 1	7th	28	14	4	10	46	35	32	Jones 11
1899/1900	Southern League Div 1	10th	28	11	3	14	46	55	25	Jones 12
1898/1899	Birmingham & District League	4th	34	20	5	9	132	49	46	McCairns 32
1897/1898	Birmingham & District League	3rd	30	20	4	6	84	34	44	McLean 11
1896/1897	Western League Div 1	5th	16	7	2	7	24	23	14	Gallier 6
1895/1896	Western League Div 1	2nd	20	14	1	5	57	22	29	Gallier 15
1894/1895	Bristol & District League Div 1	6th	22	10	4	8	46	40	24	Horsey 17
1893/1894	Bristol & District League Div 1	9th	18	5	2	11	30	39	12	Horsey 8
1892/1893	Bristol & District League	6th	16	6	3	7	36	39	15	Laurie A 7